The Descendants

of

JEAN MONTY

1702(?)-1755

Monty ✛ Monta ✛ Monte
Montee ✛ Montie
Families

Revised Edition

Jeanne R. Monty

HERITAGE BOOKS
2009

HERITAGE BOOKS
AN IMPRINT OF HERITAGE BOOKS, INC.

Books, CDs, and more—Worldwide

For our listing of thousands of titles see our website
at
www.HeritageBooks.com

Published 2009 by
HERITAGE BOOKS, INC.
Publishing Division
100 Railroad Ave. #104
Westminster, Maryland 21157

Other books by the author:
*The Descendants of Jean Monty, 1693(?)-1755:
Monty/Monte/Montee/Montie Familes*

International Standard Book Numbers
Paperbound: 978-0-7884-4933-8
Clothbound: 978-0-7884-8188-8

IN MEMORIAM

Ernest L. Monty

1897-1985

TABLE OF CONTENTS

PREFACE

This is a revised and expanded version of *The Descendants of Jean Monty, 1683(?)-1755* (Bowie, MD: Heritage Books, 1999). Much new information has come to light in the last ten years, and many corrections and additions needed to be made. I have also added an eighth generation to the previous seven. My purpose as ever is to trace Jean Monty's descendants as completely and accurately as possible, to debunk the various myths that have arisen around him and them, and to enable persons who include a female Monty in their ancestry to place her accurately within the family. Descendants in the male line have been followed through the eighth generation, corresponding roughly to persons born in the early or mid 20th century. Children of Monty mothers are listed in their mother's section with their spouses though not their children: they belong to another family's history.

FORMAT

This book is divided by generations, beginning with Jean Monty whose children are assigned a number representing the order of their birth. The Henry System is then used but with a dot separating each discrete number. The first digit in each case refers to one of Jean Monty's children, the second to that person's children, and so on through the generations. For example his fifth child, Gaspard, is assigned the number 5. His own seventh child is 5.7, and in turn this child's tenth child is 5.7.10, and so on down to any one of his descendants in the eighth generation. One can also read back from, say, 5.7.7.1.4.6 to that person's parents (5.7.7.1.4), grandparents (5.7.7.1), etc. The main advantage here is that one can track any line either forward or backward and determine relationships without having to have recourse to any outside point of reference.

Each numbered section follows the same pattern: 1) name of a Monty descendant and spouse(s), if applicable, with dates of birth (b), baptism (bp), marriage(s) (m), death (d) and burial (bur); 2) notes on an individual's life, reasons for approximate or uncertain dates, relationships with other individuals named in this book, additional sources of information, etc.; 3) list of children. Children of Monty mothers are identified as fully as possible. Children of Monty fathers are assigned a Henry number followed by their name(s) and years of birth, marriage(s), and death. All other information will be found in their own individual section in the following generation.

I have tried to be as clear as possible and to always make a distinction between birth and baptism, death and burial, place of death and place of residence of the deceased. Information is repeated as often as is necessary to make each segment self-contained. Women are referred to in the text by their maiden names unless a reference to their husband's surname is needed. "Mrs." will then be used. Similarly, a widowed or divorced woman whose maiden name I do not know is identified by her previous title as Mrs. (Whatever) who later married a Monty descendant.

Names of American states have been abbreviated according to the US Postal Service code. No abbreviations are used for Canadian provinces save for the Province of Quebec (QC). The term refers here to the territory of the province created by the Act of Confederation of 1867, regardless of its actual status as an English or French colony. The same principle applies to American localities: names of present-day states are used rather than those of the former Territories or even foreign jurisdictions (Detroit under French rule, for example) in which certain events took place. I hope to be forgiven these anachronisms in the interest of clarity.

Question marks follow dates derived from secondary or uncertain sources, most often censuses which are notoriously unreliable but also death records which can sometimes be quite imprecise.

SOURCES

I have relied for information mainly on original records attesting to a recent birth, marriage or death. Other primary sources include War Department records, Court records and Naturalization records, World War I and World War II Draft Registration cards, Notarial archives in the Canadian Province of Quebec, and the American Social Security Death Index (SSDI). US and Canadian censuses, though less reliable as to dates and places of birth, have been used extensively to document individuals' and families' places of residence at various times. If two or more sources disagree I rely, in the absence of any other evidence, on the record which is closest in time to the event described.

Genealogical dictionaries and journals, previously published family histories, local histories of towns and counties where the Montys and their children were early settlers, newspaper reports of births, marriages, and deaths, compilations of births or baptisms, marriages, and deaths or burials in several Canadian and American municipalities, counties, and states, cemetery and funeral home records, etc. have served as guides to my own research. I have retained what I could verify but have usually omitted what could not be corroborated. Whenever I have included names or facts otherwise unknown to me, my notes refer to the specific source.

In the United States, my basic sources are the Vital Records kept by various city, county, and state authorities. Most are available on microfilm through the LDS Family History Library in Salt Lake City, UT. A number of states have also made available on the Internet the Indexes to their Vital Records though generally only for a limited number of years. Each state also has its own GenWeb site which may include selected Vital records. The amount and quality of the information provided varies greatly from state to state and, unfortunately, very little exists before 1908. One must often depend on secondary sources of various degrees of reliability.

Early US censuses (1790-1840) are of minimal value: they offer little more than the name of the head of household and the number of persons in that household. From 1850 through 1930 they provide a substantial amount of information about a person's age, state or country of origin, occupation, spouse, and children. Other data collected vary from census to census. The most useful has been the 1900 census which also includes the month and year of birth, place of birth, parents' place of birth, year of entry into the United States and year of naturalization, if applicable, number of years a person has been married, and number of children a woman has borne. Since the information provided has proved to be generally accurate, I have accepted the 1900 census as a basic document when no other source was available. I have also accepted as correct the dates found in the SSDI unless an actual birth or death certificate shows otherwise.

State censuses vary greatly in the quantity and quality of the information provided. Some merely list the heads of household and do little more than fill in the gaps between US censuses. Others are more complete and may include such precise (and occasionally very helpful) information as the town or county where an individual was born, the length of his/her residence in the present locality, or the full names of his/her parents and where they were married.

Catholic Church records are of some help, especially in the areas of Upper New York State, New England, and Michigan where a fairly large number of Montys remained Catholic. Many are available on microfilm through the LDS Family History Library. Some are included in the "Early US French Catholic Church Records" in the Drouin Collection now available on the Internet. When the records themselves are not available, I have used a number of compilations of Catholic baptisms, marriages, and burials in New York and New England. Those published by the *American Canadian Genealogical Society* of Manchester, NH, and the *American-French Genealogical Society* of Woonsocket, RI, have been especially useful, though the information provided is always subject to verification.

Early newspapers are becoming increasingly available on the Internet and can be invaluable in areas of the country where few other contemporary records exist. The "Northern New York Historical Newspapers" on the Northern New York Library Network Web site, in particular, have been used extensively. I consider their reports of births, marriages, and deaths which occurred only a few days before publication to be authoritative. Other Web sites focus on late 20th-century and 21st-century newspaper obituaries. In the absence of a death certificate, they can help ascertain the place of a person's death if other than the place of residence noted in the SSDI (on a trip away from home, for example, or a hospital in a neighboring town or even state). Much information can also be gathered there about a deceased person's family. To the extent that the facts have not been verified, the original newspaper source has been cited.

Other sources which can be found on microfilm from the LDS Family History Library include Army records from the American Revolution to World War II, wills and letters of administration, deeds, court papers, etc. Military and Veterans' records are plentiful on the Internet. The various states' Tombstone Transcription Projects and the *Findagrave* Web site have often been a good substitute for missing death records, especially if photographs are included. While dates on a monument may not always reflect the correct date of birth, one can assume that at least the year of death is accurate.

In Canada, the Vital Records of the Provinces of Alberta, British Columbia, Ontario, and Manitoba contain information on a few Monty descendants. Most resided however in the Province of Quebec where, until very recently, the civil register was composed of copies of church records (baptisms, marriages, and burials – not birth or death) which were furnished annually to the civil authorities by the priests and ministers of the Province's parishes. As a result there are almost always two sets of documents for each locality: the original church records and the copies which are the civil records. The former, from the origins to about 1900, are available on microfilm through the LDS Family History Library; the latter, till about 1940, have recently become available on the Internet as part of the Drouin Collection. I have used the original church records whenever possible to avoid the possibility of copy error. All references are to the Catholic Church records unless otherwise indicated in my notes.

In either case, it is the date and place of baptism and burial that determines the location of the record, not the date and place of birth or death, normally found in the text. One major drawback for persons unfamiliar with the immediate area (and this applies to compilations also, such as the ones from the University of Montreal's *Programme de recherche en démographie historique [PRDH]* for years prior to 1800): localities are defined in terms of parishes rather than municipalities. The two often coincide, but not always. On the other hand, two or more parishes of the same name may exist in two or more different localities. To avoid confusion I use the names of municipalities rather than parishes.

For the years after 1940 I have relied for marriages on the numerous published compilations of Catholic and Protestant marriages in the Province of Quebec (many are now on the Internet as a result of the recent partnership between World Vital Records and Quintin Publications) and for deaths on various Canadian newspaper obituaries.

The Canadian censuses of 1851, 1881, 1891, 1901, and 1911 have been consulted, with mixed results. They can of course attest to the moves made by certain families within Canada and, in a few cases, between Canada and the United States. The 1851 census is also helpful in that it most often lists married women in the Province of Quebec under their maiden names, thus providing a clear identification. The day, month, and year of birth stated in the 1901 census however are so often at variance with the dates indicated in a person's baptismal record or in prior or later censuses that I have no great confidence in its accuracy. The same is true for the 1911 census. I have used these censuses only when no other records were available to me and placed a question mark after a doubtful date of birth.

NAMES AND SURNAMES

In order to facilitate identification, names used are those which a person bore as an adult. It is not unusual for a child, given two or more names at his birth or baptism, to be known later on by only one of them, or even by a variation of one or both. Individuals will then be listed under the name used at their marriage(s), death, births of their children, etc. Their baptismal name will be found in my notes. Quite often an initial Marie/Mary or Joseph given at birth disappears from later records. I then use only the person's second name. When insufficient evidence exists I have kept both, e.g. Marie Louise. No hyphen is used for it may be that the child was later known as Marie, Louise, or Marie-Louise. Hyphens are reserved for those cases when both names are known to have been used on a regular basis, e.g. Jean-Baptiste. Alternative spellings and/or nicknames, which appear in a surprising number of official documents, are separated by a slash e.g. Mary/Polly or Francis/Frank.

Because of the constant emigration from French-speaking Canada to the English-speaking United States, problems of nomenclature often arise. A name given at birth to a French Canadian child may be anglicized in later years. If he emigrated as an adult, there may be a number of documents referring to him under either name. I then use a slash to indicate that fact (e.g. Jean Monty's son François/Francis). If a child arrived in the United States at an early age and was henceforth known under the English version of his name (Henry e.g. rather than Honoré) then that name is used for identification, with a reference in my notes to the baptismal name.

For all this adult signatures are the best evidence. Also significant are army records including World War I and World War II Registration cards, naturalization papers, names on marriage and death records, cemetery records, tombstone inscriptions, and the SSDI.

The same principle applies to surnames. Signatures provide the best proof of a name's spelling. Jean Monty's children always signed Monty, regardless of the spelling of their names in the related texts. That is also true of most of their descendants, with two major exceptions, both in the American Midwest. Montie became the patronymic of some, but not all, of the descendants of François Xavier Monty (3.9.3) and of Basile Monty (13.3.8). Abraham Monty (4.4.7) changed his name to Montee in the second half of the 19th century. There are other isolated instances of voluntary and permanent name changes, to Monta and Monte. A slash (Monty/Montie) indicates that a change occurred during the individual's lifetime. When I have found neither signature nor evidence of constant use of an alternative spelling, I have used Monty — with my apologies to those relatives whose name change I may have overlooked.

Names of spouses and of children of Monty mothers present similar problems, less easily solved since information here is less abundant. For each person I have used the spelling found in the relevant document(s) and noted any prior or subsequent change. Prior changes are usually due in Canada to the French rendering of an English, American, Dutch, Irish, Swiss, Portuguese, etc. surname or in the United States to the Anglicization of a French surname. Subsequent changes are noted mainly in Canada where, for example, Deneau became Daigneault, Binet became Vinet, etc. A slash marks the most common variant spelling.

In Canada the custom of appending a surname to the patronymic (e.g. Catudal dit St. Jean) often leads to confusion. An individual may be identified by either name during his lifetime and his children may in turn adopt either name. I have used both names in such cases, unless the evidence overwhelmingly favored one over the other.

ACKNOWLEDGEMENTS

I have been aided in my work by many genealogists of the past. Three substantial works have been especially useful. Christian Denissen's *French Families of the Detroit River Region, 1701-1936* (revised and expanded, 1987) is invaluable in tracing the Montie family of Michigan. Betty Ramsey's *Monty/Montee History* (1981) contains a wealth of personal information mainly on the descendants of Abraham Montee (4.4.7). In turn, Louise Monty's *Généalogie de la famille Monty* (1993) concentrates on the Canadian Montys.

A special acknowledgement is due the Church of Jesus Christ of Latter-Day Saints which, long before the Internet, had gathered an extraordinary collection of genealogical records and documents and made them available to researchers in their Family History Centers worldwide. Without this help I could not have amassed so much primary documentation on so many far-flung Montys. The Family History Center in Metairie, LA, was my "home away from home" for many years. To the many volunteers I have met there goes my deepest appreciation.

Several relatives had shared with me the results of their own research before 1999. Many more have since written to make corrections or additions or to suggest new paths of inquiry. To all of you who have enabled me to make substantial revisions to this work, a very heartfelt *Thank you*.

One last note. This is an unfinished work. Many mysteries remain; too many dates are still only approximate; some lines have not been followed through to the eighth generation as intended; there are bound to be rectifiable omissions and inaccuracies. I would be happy to hear about any additional information or corrections to be made. I hope that in spite of its limitations my work will provide a solid enough foundation for others to build on in the future.

Jeanne R. Monty
Mandeville, LA

May 2009

THE FIRST GENERATION

JEAN MONTY (Dominge Monty & Jeanne Benoist) b 1702?, Gascony, France; d & bur 11 & 12 Sep 1755, Chambly, QC. He married there 27 Feb 1729 Marie Marthe Poyer (Jacques Poyer dit Lapintade & Marguerite Dubois) b & bp there 21 Aug 1710; m (2) there 17 Jan 1760 Filbert/Philibert Menien/Menient (Nicholas Menien & Marie Vablet); d & bur there 6 & 7 Jun 1796.

Very little is known about Jean Monty's ancestry and early life. A number of Canadian records allow us to follow his career as a marine in Canada fairly closely but I know of only three, in 1726, 1729, and 1755, that shed any light on his past. All are available on the Internet as part of the Drouin Collection.

The earliest document, the *Registre des malades* of the Hôtel-Dieu du Précieux Sang of Quebec, QC, notes for the month of February 1726 that "Jean Monty de Cominge," a 24-year-old soldier in the Company of M. de Péan (Jacques Hughes Péan de Livaudière), was admitted to the hospital on 9th of the month and was released on the 16th. Jean Monty's marriage record of 27 Feb 1729 in Fort St. Louis of Chambly, QC, adds that his parents were "Dominge Monty et Jeanne Benoist ses père et mère de la paroisse de Bernard de levesches de Cominge," while the burial record of Jean Baptiste (sic) Monty notes that he was 62 years old when he died in Chambly on 11 Sep 1755.

This last document may not be too trustworthy as to the name or age of the decedent. I believe the name Jean-Baptiste is wrong. It is the only time he was so named. All other church and civil records in Chambly, Montreal, and Quebec name him simply Jean Monty or Jean Monty dit Gascon. It is probable that the error in the burial record was due to simple carelessness: Father Mercereau, who was substituting at the funeral for Father Carpentier, the long-time pastor of St. Joseph's church, and who may not have known the deceased very well, may have assumed that Jean was the short form of Jean-Baptiste, a name which would become quite common in French Canada. The overwhelming bulk of evidence however shows that the proper name is Jean Monty.

Another disturbing thing about the burial record is the alleged age of the deceased: 62 years old. That is the source for the year of birth, 1693, which most genealogists and compilers have adopted. I have previously indicated my reservations about that date. Among other things, Jean Monty would have been unusually old when he arrived in Canada: French marines were ordinarily recruited when in their late teens or early to mid-twenties and sent to their overseas stations with little or no delay. He would also have been unusually old at his marriage. In this respect, the records of the Hôtel-Dieu of Quebec indicating that he was born in 1701 or 1702 make more sense. They are also more likely to be correct since they are earlier in time.

Several entries on one of the Internet's major genealogy sites show (2008) that Jean Monty was born on 17 Apr 1702. They do not provide documentary evidence though they all repeat the same information obviously taken from a common source. Since this includes a number of absurdities (his father, born in 1667, died in 1693; his mother, born in 1666, died in 1670) I have disregarded all information from that source and from those who mindlessly copied it.

Jean Monty was born in the Comminges area of Gascony, as stated in the records of the Hôtel-Dieu of Quebec of 9 Feb 1726. He was also known as "Jean Monty dit Gascon" when he purchased land on 15 Feb 1732 from his father-in-law Jacques Poyer de la Pintade (Notarial Archives, Montreal, QC, notary Nicolas Augustin Guillet de Chaumont). His marriage record unfortunately does not include the usual formula "natif de ..." to specify the place of his birth but states only that his parents were from the parish (not necessarily the town) of St. Bernard in the diocese of Comminges. He may not have been born there. All the act says is that his parents were living in that parish when he married (or perhaps when he left France, or when he had last heard of them).

No birth or baptismal record has been found in the parishes named for St. Bernard in the old diocese of Comminges and in the adjoining diocese of Toulouse into which it was later incorporated. But this is far from conclusive: I and most other researchers, I believe, were looking until recently for records from the early 1690s. A new search may need to be undertaken in the records for the years around 1702. Many were destroyed in the Toulouse area during the French Revolution, but some survived. We can always hope.

Another point of contention is the name of Jean Monty's father. The original church records in the church at Fort St. Louis state clearly that Jean Monty's father was Dominge Monty. Copies generally have the more usual French name Dominique, which is what is shown in almost all genealogical entries concerning the family. I believe that the first spelling of the name, precisely because it is unusual and would require special attention on the scribe's part, is the most trustworthy. It may hint at a Spanish origin. But given his wife's typically French name it is highly probable that he at least married in France.

Jean Monty arrived in Canada no later than the fall of 1725, was in Quebec in early 1726, and was a private in the *Compagnies Franches de la Marine* at Fort St. Louis in Chambly when he was godfather to one of his comrades' children on 16 Apr 1728. He married Marie Marthe Poyer there on 27 Feb 1729, the witnesses being Capt. Péan de Livaudière, Commandant of the Fort, and Ensign Claude Hertel de Beaulac whose own marriage on the same day is recorded just above Jean Monty's. So far as I know there was no written marriage contract.

By 1740, at the birth of his daughter Marie Joseph, Jean Monty had become a sergeant and was in fact the only sergeant at the fort when the garrison was sharply reduced in the 1740s. He remained a sergeant there for the rest of his life and never took advantage of the inducements, including land grants and monetary awards, offered by the French government to encourage those men who had been recruited in France to settle in Canada after their initial term of service. It may be that he had originally signed up for life (his enlistment papers have not been found) or that he was influenced by his father-in-law who also stayed in the military throughout his life. It may also be that he simply preferred the life of a marine on garrison duty to that of a farmer/settler.

He certainly achieved a certain standing in the community if one goes by the names and quality of his children's godparents. Many came from the military; others were members of the Hertel family, his wife's relatives — though the two often overlap. To name a few from the years 1730 to 1743: Capt. Gaspard Adhémar de Lantagnac, Commandant of Fort St. Louis and his wife; the wife and daughter of Capt. Nicolas-Marie Renaud des Meloises, Commandant of Fort St. Louis; Lt. Claude Pecaudy de Contrecoeur (Commandant of Fort Duquesne in 1754) and his wife; Lt. Clément Sabrevois de Bleury (Commandant of Fort St. Frédéric in 1747); Ensign and later Lt. Claude Hertel, *sieur* de Beaulac, and his wife; Lt. Louis Herbin; Etienne Robert, *sieur* de la Morandière, 2nd engineer; Louis Hertel de Beaulac, *sieur* de Chambly; the wife of Jean-Baptiste Boucher de Niverville, *seigneur* of Chambly. It is indeed a distinguished list of sponsors.

There are other indications of the couple's social standing such as later references, on 18 Sep 1752 and 7 Jun 1754, to the "Sr Jean Monty, demeurant à Chambly, & dame Marthe Poyer" and to the "Sr Monty" (Notarial Archives, Montreal, QC, notary Lalanne). It is significant also that almost all the children, both male and female, received a certain degree of education, perhaps from the resident chaplain at the fort or from the parish priest in Chambly after that parish was established in 1739. With the exception of Gaspard and Antoine they were all literate, or at least could sign their names. This may not have been too unusual in the case of sons, but it was not customary in the case of daughters who seldom received any education at all save in the higher classes of society: Marie Marthe Poyer was herself illiterate.

But all this pertains to Jean Monty's later years. On his arrival in Chambly as a private and single, and later as a sergeant and married man, he lived in the fort with his fellow marines. By all accounts life on garrison duty there was relatively peaceful during the first half of the 18th century. I know of no military action in which Jean Monty was directly involved. The Fort St. Louis which he knew, and which still exists today, was the third of the name to be built on a site overlooking the rapids of Chambly, at the southern end of a basin formed by a widening of the Richelieu River. It was built of stone from 1709 to 1711 to replace an earlier wooden structure which had itself replaced the original fort erected in 1665 and destroyed by fire in 1702. Its configuration is simple. The square building consists of an outer wall, with bastions at the four corners, and an interior wall, with the space between the

2

two subdivided on two stories to make individual rooms or chambers. The interior court thus created became the parade ground.

The builders of the new fort seemingly anticipated that it would play a major role in the colony's defense. Governor Vaudreuil claimed in 1712 that it could accommodate 500 soldiers and that another 500 could be put up in an emergency (Louise Monty, *Généalogie de la famille Monty*, I, 96). This may well be an exaggeration, belied partly by the physical plant as we see it today and partly by the fact that the normal complement of a marine company in Canada as established in 1690 by the *Ministre de la Marine* Pontchartrain never exceeded 100 soldiers and 7 or 8 officers, and was often much less. In 1725, for example, the number of soldiers was set at 30, with a corresponding reduction in the number of officers (Gallup and Shaffer, *La Marine: The French Colonial Soldier in Canada, 1745-1761*, p. 199). But that was an ideal. In fact, the situation in Chambly was often quite different: in 1720 the garrison consisted of 50 men; in 1741, 30 men and 5 officers, including NCOs; in 1742, 6 men, 1 officer, and 1 sergeant; in 1746, 5 men, 1 officer, 1 sergeant (Louise Monty, I, 96). Whether the fort had been built to accommodate 100 or 500 men, there was more than ample room for the needs of a small garrison. I cannot imagine that the duties of a sergeant in charge of 5 or 6 men were very onerous.

Jean Monty had become a landowner in Chambly a few years after his marriage. As "Jean Monty dit Gascon" he purchased on 15 Feb 1732 from his father-in-law a lot of 2 *arpents* on the Richelieu River (the act says "rivière Saurelle" = Sorel, one of several names given over time to the Richelieu) by 30 *arpents* in depth, ad-joining on one side the property of Mathurin Lebeau and on the other that of his brother-in-law Antoine Grisé, husband of Françoise Marguerite Poyer. He paid 600 *livres* cash, assumed all rents and duties due the *seigneur* of Chambly, and renounced for himself and his wife all claims to any future inheritance from his in-laws (Notarial Archives, notary Guillet de Chaumont). This may not have been a very good move, at least financially. For "Le Sr Monty" received only 530 *livres* when he sold that property to François Bertin (Aubertin) and his wife on 7 Jun 1754. The act specifies that there were no buildings on the lot: "sans Batiment construit" (Notarial Archives, notary Lalanne). The family obviously did not live on that land.

The only other piece of property acquired by Jean Monty is a concession granted by Joseph Claude Boucher de Niverville, *seigneur* of Chambly, on 18 Sep 1752 "au Sr Jean Monty demeurant à Chambly & dame Marthe Poyer." It was a small, irregular lot, of little more than 1 acre, located "au Bourg St. Jean de Chambly" (known also as "Faubourg St. Jean-Baptiste de Chambly"), measuring 1 *arpent* on the Richelieu River by 1 *arpent* and 3 rods on one side and 1 *arpent* on the other, and adjoining the property of Pierre Jean-Marie Gilbert (Notarial Archives, notary Lalanne). The family may have lived on the property for the three years preceding Jean Monty's death, though this would argue a long-delayed, and to my mind improbable, conversion to homesteading on his part. He was above all a soldier. He became a landowner; there is no evidence that he ever became a homesteader. At any event there is no mention of a house on his property either then or later.

I am inclined to believe that the fort was the family's home, even after 1752. The military authorities frowned on such arrangements, which is in itself a left-handed confirmation that they existed. Louise Monty (1, 98) has also found specific evidence that women and children did indeed live on occasion at Fort St. Louis on either a temporary or a permanent basis.

The officers and men living at the fort were regularly provided with bedding, furniture, and some basic household goods and utensils. If the Monty family was among them, then several of the rather odd features of the inventory taken on 28 Jan 1774 of the community property held by Jean Monty and his wife at the time of his death can begin to make sense. Their personal property, valued at 103 *livres*, 10 *sols*, 3 *deniers*, included 2 iron buckets, 2 cooking pots, 1 grill, 1 frying pan, 1 roasting spit, 1 cooker, a pair of andirons, 1 iron, 1 funnel, 3 tureens, 1 soup tureen, 1 earthenware dish, 1 oil and vinegar cruet, 1 mustard pot, 1 salt-cellar, 1 pepper-mill, 1 stone jug, 1 tin lantern, 1 teapot, 1 tin coffeepot, 11¾ pounds of tin, 1 earthenware plate, 1 tin cup, 6 iron forks, 7 chairs, 1 wardrobe, 1 very bad mirror, 1 iron candle holder with a pair of snuffers and a snuffer holder, 1 pig, 1 iron shovel, 1 tomahawk, 1 wooden spoon, 60 pounds of lard, and 1 bladder of grease (Notarial Archives, notary Antoine

3

Grisé).

Most of the items listed are household goods or tools, including the tomahawk often used as a hand-ax (Gallup and Shaffer, p. 114). The tin, lard, grease, and even the pig could come under the heading of supplies — though the amount of tin and lard seems overly large and may represent items of trade. What I find most significant, though, are the omissions. It would appear that the couple had acquired in 26 years of marriage seven chairs, a wardrobe, and a mirror but no table, bed, or any other piece of household furniture. The kitchen contained several cooking appliances and serving dishes, special containers for condiments as well as a teapot and a coffeepot but no tableware (plates, knives, spoons, cups, etc.) save for six iron forks, a tin cup, and a wooden spoon — and these last two items would probably have been used to prepare rather than eat meals. It is not merely that the missing items would probably be inexpensive. If even a wooden spoon and a funnel, each valued at 3 *sols* apiece, can be included, so should an aggregate amount for the tableware a family of ten or more must have needed. It could be that the missing items were brought to the marriage by Marie Marthe Poyer and were not part of the community property. Without a marriage contract, it is impossible to tell. It seems to me that the most likely reason for the odd gaps in the inventory is that it includes only the items the couple acquired on their own to supplement those already present in their furnished quarters at the fort. Only then does the inventory make sense: it is not the inventory of a homeowner, however poor he may be; it is the inventory of someone who has the wherewithal to add a few modest extras to the basic household goods and furniture supplied by a landlord, in this case the French marines.

In addition to personal property, the inventory also lists debts and real estate. The community owed 79½ and 70 *livres* to Pierre Jean-Marie Gilbert and Pierre Joubert respectively, and smaller amounts to the parish priest (funeral expenses?) and the notary (preparation of the inventory?) for a total debt of 167 *livres* and 10 *sols*. The real estate almost certainly refers to the 1752 concession though there is a slight discrepancy in the description of the lot: it is said in 1774 to be of 2 *arpents* in depth. I cannot account for this variance unless it is related to one of the debts incurred by the community, either to Pierre Joubert or to Pierre Jean-Marie Gilbert, whose property adjoined the Montys'. Jean Monty may have acquired a small parcel of land from either of them to square off the original irregularly-shaped lot, though I have been unable to find any record of it or of any later acquisition he may have made. It is unlikely that a house was built on that property during Jean Monty's lifetime. The section of the inventory dealing with real estate makes no mention of one. The personal property however is said to be found "dans laditte maison" (the aforesaid house) which is nevertheless neither previously mentioned nor later identified. It could be that a house was built after Jean Monty's death and not part of the community property or, more probably, that the reference is to the house where Marie Marthe Poyer was living with her second husband: the record indicates that she still had in her possession all items of personal property dating from her first marriage.

All assets listed in the inventory were community property. By law the widow would receive half, while the surviving children would share the other half among themselves. By general agreement she kept all the personal property. She also received half of the real estate, i.e. ½ *arpent* on the river by 2 *arpents* in depth. As for the children, most of them had sold their shares to their brother-in-law Jean-Baptiste Clément Racine, husband of Marguerite Monty, even before the formal division was recorded in 1774. Only Marie (Marie Joseph) Monty, widow of Joseph Boileau, and Clément Monty still held their rights to the inherited property. They later sold their lots, each measuring 18 feet on the river by 2 *arpents* in depth, to their neighbor Jean-Marie Gilbert on 20 Aug 1776 (notary Grisé).

Jean Monty died in Chambly on 11 Sep 1755 and was buried the following day in the cemetery of St. Joseph's church in Chambly. The burial record does not mention the cause of death but notes that he had received the last rites of the Catholic Church. Present at the funeral were Capt. Jean-Baptiste Hertel de Rouville, Commandant of the fort of Chambly, and the notary Antoine Grisé de Villefranche, Jean Monty's nephew.

More than two centuries later, Jean Monty was still remembered. In 1989 a street in Chambly was named after him, and in 1993 a Monty family reunion was hosted by some of his descendants who still live in the area.

Marie Marthe Poyer was born and baptized at Fort St. Louis of Chambly on 21 Aug 1710. She was the daughter of Jacques Poyer dit Lapintade (occasionally de la Pintade), a French sergeant in the *Compagnies Franches de la Marine*, and Marguerite Dubois whose maternal ancestors had been prominent in military circles in Canada since the early years of the colony. In fact she and the Hertels, *seigneurs* of Chambly, were step-cousins. Their common grandmother, Marie Marguerie, had married twice. By her first marriage, to Jacques Hertel de la Frenière, she had a son François whose children later shared the seigneury of Chambly. By her second, to Quentin Moral de St. Quentin, she had a daughter Marie Marthe whose daughter Marguerite Dubois became Jean Monty's mother-in-law. Given the small population of Canada during the French colonial period, such interconnections between families were not unusual. I do not know how much Jean Monty's military career and life were influenced by his wife's ties to the most prominent family in Chambly. It remains that Hertel de Saint Louis, Hertel de Beaulac, Hertel de Chambly, Hertel de Rouville, Hertel de Cournoyer, as well as their sister Marguerite Thérèse and her husband Jean-Baptiste Boucher de Niverville were a constant presence in his life.

I know next to nothing about Marie Marthe Poyer's life as a girl or as the wife of Jean Monty. We have no signature. When required, she simply made her mark. She had fourteen children of whom ten, six boys and four girls, survived to maturity. When she was left a widow at age 45, eight of the children, ranging in age from 8 to 21, were still at home. She may have continued to live for a time at the fort of Chambly. She then received on 18 Jul 1758 by private contract ("sous seing privé") from Louis Herbin and *dame* Madeleine Niverville a lot in Chambly of 3 *arpents* on the Richelieu River by 25 *arpents* in depth, adjoining on one side the property of Pierre Boileau and on the other the property of the Bourbonnais heirs. This she sold to her son Clément Monty for 60 *livres* on 15 May 1763 (Notarial Archives, notary Grisé).

She was then living "au faux Bourg St Jean Baptiste du d¹ Chambly" with her second husband, Filbert Menien, whom she had married in Chambly on 17 Jan 1760. According to the marriage record, he was the son of Nicolas Menien and Marie Vablet and was born in Burgundy. He signed Filbert Menien, though the act itself refers to Philibert Menien. In later documents his signature alternates between Filbert Menien and Menient, while many scribes still write in the text Philibert or Philippe Menien or Menient or Meuniau or even Meunier.

It is said that he was originally a soldier who came to Canada before the British conquest of 1763. By 1765 he was a farmer or settler whose household in Chambly included a man, a woman, one female domestic, three cows, and a horse (Canadian census). All of Jean Monty's children save Antoine had married by then. The couple was on its own. Yet they continued to be involved with the family, attending the marriages of Jean Monty's children and the baptisms and marriages of his grandchildren.

Marie Marthe Poyer died in Chambly on 6 Jun 1796 at the age of 86 and was buried there the next day. She was then identified as Marie Marthe Poigné, wife of Filbert Menien. Nevertheless when the town of Chambly named a street after her in 1989, it recognized her as Marie Marthe Poyer.

Children:

1	Amable	1730-1754&1757-1804
2	Marguerite	1733-1750-1799
3	Claude	1734-1759-1799
4	François	1736-1760-1809
5	Gaspard	1737-1760-1819
6	Geneviève	1738-1756-1821
7	Marie Joseph	1740- -1740
8	Clément	1740-1764-1830
9	Marie Angélique	1742-1761&1782-1810
11	Marie Joseph	1744-1763&1779-1832

10	Alexis	1743- -1743
12	Geneviève Amable	1746- -
13	Antoine	1747-1770-1829
14	Marie Françoise	1748- -1748

1   **MONTY, Amable** b & bp 10 & 11 Aug 1730, Chambly, QC; d & bur there 6 & 8 Jun 1804. He married (1) 4 Nov 1754, Laprairie, QC, **Marie Anne Lebert** (Jacques Lebert & Barbe Elisabeth Brosseau) b & bp there 18 Feb 1737; d & bur 3 & 5 Sep 1755, Chambly, QC.

He married (2) 4 Jul 1757, Chambly, QC, **Marie Angélique Létourneau** (Joseph Létourneau & Marie Angélique Bouteiller) b & bp there 5 Mar 1739; d & bur 27 & 29 Apr 1822, Longueuil, QC.

Jean Monty's oldest child was named Jean Amable at his baptism. He seems however never to have used his first name: his signature, beautifully clear and distinctive, is always Amable Monty. He was a farmer in Chambly, QC, and owned land there at various times as well as in the seigneuries of Longueuil and Montarville; the Notary Antoine Grisé recorded real estate transactions in Chambly on 10 May 1767, in Chambly and Longueuil, QC, on 3 Oct 1770, in Montarville on 18 Oct 1772, and in the "faubourg St. Jean-Bte de Chambly" on 24 Sep 1773 (Notarial Archives, Montreal, QC, notary Grisé, #584, #835, #982, #1048). This last, a sale to Jean-Baptiste Racine, husband of Marguerite Monty (2), refers to Amable Monty's share of the property inherited from his father. He also leased to Charles Mouton on 29 Sep 1781 a farm in Chambly which was later sold to Guillaume Bell on 11 Feb 1785 (Notarial Archives, notary Grisé, #2095, #2764).

Amable Monty was much involved in the life of the family, perhaps because he was the oldest son. He was always present not only at his brothers' and sisters' marriages, when he generally signed as a witness, but also at the births, marriages, and deaths of numerous relatives. He and his second wife were godparents to several nieces and nephews as well as to grandchildren both in Chambly and in Longueuil. Yet in spite of this family feeling, and for all his sixteen children, Amable Monty left no direct descendants bearing his name. Of his five sons only one, Amable (1.2), survived childhood, and no trace has been found of any marriage or children (But see my speculations concerning Abraham Monty, spouse of Johanna Monty [4.4.1]). Those Montys who claim descent from the elder Amable do so through his daughter Marguerite (1.16) whose granddaughter Onésime Daignault married her third cousin Prudent Monty (5.7.1.12).

Marie Angélique Létourneau did not remain in Chambly after her husband's death. She had been living in Longueuil when she died, probably in the household of her daughter Marguerite and her first husband who were residents there.

Children of the second marriage:

1.1	Marie Angélique	1758-	-1765
1.2	Amable	1760-	-
1.3	Louise	1762-1779-1806	
1.4	Marie Anne	1764-	-1765
1.5	Geneviève	1766-	-1766
1.6	Marie	1767-	-1770
1.7	Antoine	1768-	-1774
1.8	Honoré	1770-	-1774
1.9	Angélique	1771-1786-1794	
1.10	Marie Desanges	1772?-1791&1831&1840-1851	
1.11	Marie Anne	1773-	-1773
1.12	Marie Anne	1774-	-
1.13	Marie Angélique	1776-	-
1.14	Louis	1777-	-1777
1.15	Joseph	1779-	-1780
1.16	Marguerite	1783-1798&1820&1843&1853-1864	

2   **MONTY, Marguerite** b & bp 22 Mar 1733, Chambly, QC; d & bur there 18 & 19 Apr 1799. She married there 9 Feb 1750 **Jean-Baptiste Clément Racine** (François Clément Racine & Louise Elisabeth Lecompte) b & bp 8 & 9 Jan 1727, Quebec, QC; d & bur

12 & 13 Jan 1805, Chambly, QC.

Jean-Baptiste Racine was a carpenter in Quebec, QC, for a few years after his marriage. His two oldest children were born there though the younger children were born in Chambly, QC, where their father was a master carpenter and house builder. His burial record notes that he was a farmer, although there is little evidence that he ever held land for more than brief periods at a time. Thus when he acquired on 24 Sep 1773 from some of his in-laws their shares of Jean Monty's land in the "faubourg St. Jean-Bte de Chambly," he sold that parcel of land on 28 Jan 1774, the very day the formalities of the succession were completed (Notarial Archives, Montreal, QC, notary Antoine Grisé, #1048, #1073). Sales were also recorded on 20 Sep 1774, 10 Mar 1779, and 27 Sep 1781, and a lease to Charles Truchon of land in the barony of Longueuil on 23 Jul 1783 (Notarial Archives, notary Grisé, #1141, #1456, #2136, #2503). No purchases were found.

Children:

i   **Jean-Baptiste Racine** b & bp 13 & 14 Mar 1752, Quebec, QC; bur 30 Jul 1752, St. Augustin, QC.

ii **Marguerite Racine** b & bp 23 May 1753, Quebec, QC; d & bur 26 & 27 May 1840, Chambly, QC. She married (1) there 7 Nov 1768 **Joseph Bréard/Breillard** (Charles Bréard & Marie Anne Petit) b & bp 21 & 22 Jan 1742, Varennes, QC.

She was a widow when she married (2) 7 Jun 1785, Chambly, QC, **François Hins/Hinse/Hains** (Joseph Hins & Marie Dorothée Gaumond) b & bp 14 & 15 Apr 1762, Montmagny, QC; m (2) 8 Jan 1844, Chambly, QC, Adélaïde Guenet, widow of Pierre Bricot; d & bur there 4 & 6 Jun 1854.

iii **Jean-Baptiste Racine** b & bp 29 Aug 1754, Chambly, QC; d & bur there 29 Aug 1754.

iv **Marie Louise Racine** b & bp 15 Aug 1755, Chambly, QC.

v   **Claude Racine** b & bp 27 Aug 1756, Chambly, QC; d & bur there 19 Sep 1756.

vi **Jean-Baptiste Racine** b & bp 23 & 24 Sep 1758, Chambly, QC; d & bur there 23 Jul 1759.

vii **Marie Geneviève Racine** b & bp 27 Mar 1760, Chambly, QC; d & bur there 15 May 1760.

viii **Marie Angélique Racine** b & bp 6 & 7 Mar 1761, Chambly, QC; d & bur there 25 & 26 Mar 1810. She married before 1794 **Arthur Strachan** b 1764?, Scotland; m (2) 10 Oct 1813, Chambly, QC, Geneviève Laurent (Pierre Laurent & Geneviève Poupart); d & bur 19 & 21 Feb 1840, Iberville, QC, at the age of 76.

ix **Louis Racine** b & bp 1 & 2 Mar 1763, Chambly, QC; d & bur there 11 May 1763.

x   **Radegonde Racine** b & bp 14 & 15 Feb 1764, Chambly, QC; d & bur there 27 & 28 Mar 1765.

xi **Charles Racine** b & bp 24 Apr 1765, Chambly, QC; d & bur there 9 Jun 1765.

xii **Françoise Racine** b & bp 6 May 1766, Chambly, QC; d & bur there 23 & 24 Jun 1766.

xiii **Marie Agathe Racine** b & bp 29 Jun 1767, Chambly, QC; d & bur there 20 & 21 Jul 1767.

xiv **Marie Françoise Racine** b & bp 25 & 26 Feb 1769, Chambly, QC; d & bur there 14 & 15 Aug 1769.

xv **Marie Marthe Racine** b & bp 30 May 1771, Chambly, QC; d & bur there 18 & 19 Oct 1771.

xvi **Angélique Racine** b & bp 11 & 14 Nov 1772, Chambly, QC; d & bur there 9 & 11 Dec 1772.

xvii **Elisabeth/Isabelle Racine** b & bp 6 & 7 Nov 1773, Chambly, QC; d & bur 24 & 26 Jan 1840, St. Jean, QC. She married 19 Oct 1790, Chambly, QC, **Alexandre Vigeant** (Alexandre Vigeant & Geneviève Gaboriau) b & bp there 2 Oct 1763; d & bur there 13 & 14 Sep 1816.

xviii **Jean-Baptiste Racine** b & bp 13 Mar 1775, Chambly, QC; d & bur there 9 & 10 Jun 1775.

xix **Charlotte Racine** b & bp 21 Jul 1776, Chambly, QC; d & bur there 29 & 30 Jul

1776.
xx **Pierre Racine** b & bp 10 & 11 Aug 1777, Chambly, QC; d & bur there 18 & 21 Aug 1777.

3 **MONTY, Claude** b 4 Aug 1734, Chambly, QC; d & bur there 4 & 5 Aug 1799. He married there 28 Nov 1759 **Marie Anne Boyer** (Jean-Baptiste Boyer & Marie Anne Aguenier) b & bp 12 & 13 May 1738, Laprairie, QC; d & bur 21 & 23 Jan 1810, Chambly, QC.

Claude Monty was a farmer in Chambly, QC, and was present there, like his brother Amable, on numerous family occasions. His signature, Claude Montÿ, is notable in that he consistently used a diæresis over the y of his name. His children did not continue the practice.

At the time of the 1765 census his assets consisted of 50 *arpents* of land, of which two were under cultivation, and one cow. He apparently was also a weaver, who hired his services in 1770 to Thomas Boille "en qualité de tisserand" (Notarial Archives, Montreal, QC, notary Antoine Grisé, #840).

Real estate transactions recorded by notary Grisé include a sale of land on 15 Jul 1757 in the "bourg St. Jean Baptiste" (#47); a purchase of 2 *arpents* by 25 "au rapide Ste Thérèse," on the Richelieu river between Chambly and St. Jean, on 3 Aug 1761 (#247 — probably the farm where he was living in 1765); and a sale of land on 19 Jul 1762 in Chambly (#296).

All of his descendants in the male line came to the United States before 1870 and became known under a variety of surnames. His oldest son participated in the American Revolution and lived after the war in small agricultural communities in Northeastern New York and Vermont, where the surname Monta frequently appears. Several grandsons and great-grandsons left Canada in the 1830s and 1840s to settle in Warren Co., NY, where Monty and Montee long coexisted, and in Wayne Co., MI, where Montie became prevalent. The last one to emigrate, in the late 1860s, moved to the industrial towns of Massachusetts and Rhode Island where he and his children were named Monte as often as Monty.

Children:

3.1	Claude/Cloud	1760-1786-1839
3.2	Marie Louise	1761- -1762
3.3	Joseph	1763-1789-1832
3.4	Marie Angélique	1764- -1765
3.5	Pierre	1765-1787-1817
3.6	Marie Françoise	1767- -
3.7	Julie	1768-1787-p1842
3.8	Marie	1770-1787-a1812
3.9	Jean-Baptiste	1774-1794-1825
3.10	Anonymous	1776- -1776
3.11	Antoine	1779- -1779

4 **MONTY, François/Francis** b & bp 20 Feb 1736, Chambly, QC; d 8 Feb 1809, Chazy, NY. He married 21 Jan 1760, Chambly, QC, **Josette/Marie Joseph Bergevin** (François Bergevin dit Langevin & Thérèse Villeneuve) b & bp 1 Mar 1743, Charlesbourg, QC; d 1822?, Clinton Co., NY.

François/Francis Monty was named François Amable at his baptism. There is no evidence that he ever used the second name, reserved for his older brother Jean Amable (1). His signature is François Monty in all Canadian records and in a few American records, although here he was more generally known as Francis Monty. His petition to George Washington of 29 Apr 1780 is signed thus; so are his petitions to Congress in 1794 and 1795 requesting an invalid pension and compensation for services during the Revolution. His army records are also in the name of Francis Monty, though there are several variant spellings of the surname in the Company Muster Rolls and the Field and Staff Muster Rolls: Monty appears 29 times; Montee 7 times, Mounty twice, Montay and Monte once each. After the war, Monty appears in all official records save in some US censuses in New York state, where Montey was a common though not predominant form for a while.

Little is known of François Monty's life in Canada before 1775. Church re-cords in Chambly, QC, reveal little more than the bare facts of his marriage and of the births of his children. His marriage contract of 20 Feb 1860 shows that he settled 300 *livres* on his bride-to-be (Notarial Archives, Montreal, QC, notary Antoine Grisé, #136), a sum considerably less than the settlements of 1,000 *livres* made by his brothers Amable and Gaspard at about the same time. He occasionally attended the weddings of his brothers and sisters, but not always. He was absent for example from his brother Gaspard's marriage, just a few months after his own, though his wife Josette Bergevin was present. Neither did he or his wife become god-parents after their marriage to any of their nieces and nephews. They perhaps had no very close ties to the family — which would also explain at least in part why Francis Monty appar-ently never returned to Canada after the Revolution, even on a temporary basis, as did his own nephew Claude Monty (3.1) and his son-in-law Major Clément Gosselin (4.9) among many others.

François Monty was certainly a landowner in Chambly, although I have found no re-cord of purchases. We know however through the records of notary Grisé that he sold some land in Chambly on 20 Sep 1764 and some more "au rapide Ste Thérè-se," on the Richelieu river between Chambly and St. Jean, on 6 Oct 1772. He also sold to his brother-in-law Jean-Baptiste Clément Racine his share of the property he had inherited from his father in the "faubourg St. Jean-Bte de Chambly" on 24 Sep 1773 (#485, #972, #1048). He was perhaps a farmer like his brothers, but there is no hint of it in the documents I have seen.

François Monty joined the American army in Canada on 25 Nov 1775 as an ensign in Col. James Livingston's First Canadian regiment in which he served, in the companies of Capts. Abraham Livingston, Jean-Baptiste Allin, and James Robichaux, until 1 Jan 1781. He was promoted to 2nd Lt. on 18 Dec 1776 and to 1st Lt. on 20 Nov 1777, in which rank he re-mained until his discharge. The title of Captain which certain family members gave him in the 19th century is incorrect: the automatic promotions authorized by Congress on 30 Sep 1783 applied only to those officers who were on active duty at the end of the war. And in fact he never styled himself, during or after the war, as anything but Lieutenant.

Col. Livingston's regiment participated in the siege of Quebec under Gen. Montgom-ery's command in the fall of 1775 and retreated to Chambly in the spring of 1776 and to New York State a few months later. It was in Crown Point in June, at Fort Ticonderoga in July and August, in Albany in September, and finally in Fishkill, for winter quarters, in November. The following spring Francis Monty was sent to Canada by Maj. Gen. Philip John Schuyler to gather information about the British forces and to deliver letters from Gen. Schuyler and Gen. Horatio Gates to American partisans in the Chambly area. His contact there, Antoine Lavallée, whom he met on 30 May 1777, has not been identified. He returned in July to his regiment in Loudon's Ferry and then in Johnstown, PA, where winter quarters were estab-lished from December 1777 through April 1778. Then on to Peekskill, NY, in May and June, and to Rhode Island where "he ... received a musket wound in his left thigh" at the battle of Quaker Hill on 29 Aug 1778 (War Department Records). The wound may not have healed properly: for the remainder of 1778 and the early part of 1779 the Company Muster Rolls, dated from Bristol, RI, and Freetown, PA, increasingly indicate that he was on furlough, and at times specifically on furlough in Albany, NY. He was "on command at Slades Ferry", NY, in April 1779, in Freetown from June through September, and in a "camp [Windham] near Morristown," NJ, from November 1779 to June 1780 (with a furlough in Albany from 26 No-vember through December 1779).

Camp Windham served not only as winter quarters for the troops in 1779 but also as Gen. Washington's own headquarters from December 1779 to June 1880. It was from there that Francis Monty petitioned George Washington for a reconsideration of two of his sons' enrollments. He also reviewed his own participation in the American army during the years 1775 through 1777. The entire document (Library of Congress microfilm) is worth quoting.

Camp Wendham April 29th 1780

May it please your Excellency
    Conceiving you to be the Father of the Army, and knowing the Justness, that Ever

Reigns, in your Breast, is what Induces me to Apply to your Excellency for Redress in a Cause wherin I Conceive myself much Injured. Your Excellency must know that five years ago I enterd this Service in Canada as a Lieutenant that on our being Repulsed I was obliged to Quit the Country and Happily Brought my Family with me, and having Two Sons thought I could not Employ them Better than Employ them in the Service of a Country whose Cause I had Espoused, accordingly I Engaged them to Serve in the Regiment to which I Belongd as Volunteers or whilst I Continued in the Service they not being of age I made their Inlistment myself, the Country having occasion to send some one into Canada with Letters and to gain Intelligence I was Employed by General Schuyler for occasion went and Fortunately succeeded and on my return was surprised to find my Children were mustered in my Absence for During the Warr, by a Captain with whom they have signed no Inlistment Therefore Humbly beg your Excellency will give me, or order the Col to give me a Certificate to the Contrary, that In Case any Accident should Happen to me my Children may have it in their power to be Free, and Enjoy that Liberty they Have so Gloriously Contended for, and the Favor will be Ever Thankfully acknoledged by your Excellencys

Most Obed[t] Hble Servant

(signed) Francis Monty Lt

I do not know that this letter achieved its goal. His sons Jacques/James (4.3) and Amable/Abraham (4.5), who had joined the same regiment as their father in 1776 and later served in Capt. Olivie's company, Col. Moses Hazen's Second Canadian regiment, did in fact remain in that unit until the end of the war.

Francis Monty was "on command" in Albany from June to October 1880, and "absent by leave" in November and December 1780, prior to his discharge on 1 Jan 1781. Why did he leave the army? Given the fact that all but one of his sons remained in the army (the three youngest, Joseph, Placide, and John had enlisted in Fishkill in the spring of 1780), one must rule out disenchantment with the American cause. His injuries may have been a factor: they were severe enough to assure him an invalid's pension in 1794. He may not have wished to commit himself, at the age of 44, to another five-year tour of duty as an officer. He may also have been a casualty of the reorganization of the army of 1 Jan 1781 which dismantled Col. Livingston's regiment by merging it with Col. Hazen's.

The War Department has no further record of Francis Monty's activities during the Revolution. Yet a "List of Officers and Soldiers in the Regiment Commanded by General Moses Hazen in the Revolutionary War," endorsed by the former regimental adjutant, Lt. Benjamin Mooers, includes Francis Monty S[r] as a "volunteer" in Capt. Clément Gosselin's 7th company (John Andrew Bilow, *French Canadian and Acadian Genealogical Review*, IX, 259). If that is correct, his movements from 1781 to 1783 would correspond to those of Hazen's regiment: Albany, NY, and the Valley of the Mohawk in June 1781 to guard against an attack by the British; West Point, NY, in July 1781; Dobbs Ferry and Northern New Jersey in August 1781 to protect Staten Island; Williamsburg and Yorktown, VA, in September 1781 during the siege of Yorktown; Lancaster, PA, in December 1781 to guard prisoners of war; Pompton, NJ, in December 1782 for winter quarters; and finally Newburgh, NY, in June 1783 when the troops were mustered out (Allan S. Everest, *Moses Hazen and the Canadian Refugees in the American Revolution*, pp. 175-176). It is probably then that he signed the Parchment Roll of the Society of the Cincinnati. His name is fourteenth on a list headed by George Washington, Jean-Baptiste Joseph Laumoy, and Thaddeus Kosciusko. Not bad company indeed!

On 26 Jul 1783, Lt. Benjamin Mooers, his cousin Ensign Zaccheus Peaslee, and Lt. Francis Monty left Poughkeepsie, NY, with nine Canadians to found a settlement on the western shore of Lake Champlain. They arrived at Point au Roche (later Hazenburgh and now Beekmantown, NY) on 10 Aug 1783 and immediately began clearing the land, building a log house, and exploring the area (Everest, p. 143). The Monty family soon followed: a census of

Canadian refugees on Lake Champlain in September 1784 includes not only Francis Monty with a wife and two unnamed children but also his sons Francis (with wife and child), Placid, John, and Julian (Joseph?). The following year, a list of "Canadian Refugees Drawing Provisions — Receiving Certificates from the Contractor's Stores" refers to Francis Monty, his wife Joset (sic), daughter Catherine, and sons Francis and Julian on Lake Champlain, Jack Monty in Albany, and Flavien (?) Monty in N. City, probably Newburgh, NY. A later census of Canadians living on Lake Champlain, dated 11 Aug 1787, includes Lt. Monty with a family of seven, François Monty with a family of four, Jaque (Jacques/ James) Monty with a family of three, and LEnfant Monty (who may be Amable but whose identity I have been unable to establish conclusively) with a family of four (Bilow, pp. 241-254).

By a law of 11 May 1784 the state of New York set aside some bounty land for former soldiers and refugees on Lake Champlain, in Clinton county. At the balloting held on 10 Sep 1787 Lt. Francis Monty, as an officer, was allotted 1,000 acres in the Refugee Patent: lots 88 and 151 of 80 acres each and lots 27 and 242 of 420 acres each. Most of this undeveloped acreage was relatively far from the shores of the lake, where the early colonists had settled while awaiting the long-promised land distribution. Like many others, Francis Monty elected to remain where he was and gave power of attorney for the sale of his lots to Benjamin Mooers at Plattsburgh, NY, on 10 Nov 1789, as he did also when an additional 200 acres was granted to him on 22 Jan 1790 under the 1785 Land Ordinance (Bounty Land Warrant #1393).

The land on which he had settled in the Point au Roche Patent was originally a part of Champlain, NY, before being included in 1804 in the newly established town of Chazy. His real property, according to the first assessment roll for the town of Champlain in 1798, consisted of "50 acres adjoining Monty's Bay & near Dean's Patent on the north, one log house ($25), one log barn 30 x 20 feet, valued $225." In the forty-three items of real property in what is now the town of Chazy, twenty-seven houses are listed. Only one was assessed at more than $50; the others ranged in value from $2 to $50, with a median of $10 (*The Plattsburgh Republican*, September 1798, cited in Neil Jane Barnett Sullivan & David Randall Martin, *A History of the Town of Chazy, Clinton County, NY*, pp. 70-71). Francis Monty's house was then comfortably in the higher range of assessments for the area in which he lived.

By an Act of Congress of 7 June 1794 Francis Monty also received an invalid's pension of $80 per annum. It was hardly a munificent sum considering the inflation that had ravaged the country since 1778 when a lieutenant in Hazen's regiment was paid $26.50 monthly (Everest, p. 62). Another 1794 petition to the Third Congress for "Compensation as a Spy in Revolutionary War" was denied after an adverse committee report of 20 Jan 1796 ("Journal of the 4th Congress" in *List of Private Claims ...*, p. 384).

Francis Monty died intestate in Chazy, NY, on 8 Feb 1809 and was buried, according to tradition, near a large unmarked boulder on his farm (Sullivan & Martin, p. 70). The date of his death is found in the records of the War Department and of the Society of the Cincinnati as well as in two depositions of 15 Aug 1846 in the Clinton Co. Circuit Court in Plattsburgh, NY, sworn to by his son Joseph Monty (4.8) and his grandson Christopher Monty (4.4.3). The date of 15 Feb 1812 given by his granddaughter Mrs. Barbary Morrison (4.4.5) in her 1856 affidavit (Appendix I) cannot be correct: Mrs. Josette Monty was named administrator of her deceased husband's estate on 18 Mar 1811 (Clinton Co. Surrogate's Court, I, 55-56).

Josette Bergevin (occasionally Langevin) was named Marie Josephte at her baptism and Marie Joseph in her marriage contract. On all other occasions such as at her marriage, at the births and deaths of her children, in US censuses, in the 1811 letters appointing her administrator of her husband's estate, her name is simply Joset or Josette. That is the name I have adopted.

According to her husband's statement in his 1780 petition to George Washington, Josette Bergevin left Canada with her husband and children in the spring of 1776. Her whereabouts during the war are uncertain. Two camps were established for the families of Canadian soldiers, the larger one in Albany, and a smaller one near Fishkill. Francis Monty was present at times in each locality. Three of his sons joined the army in Fishkill in the spring of 1780 and two other children, John and Louisa, were baptized "near Fishkill" in 1781. On the other hand, one finds from the Muster Rolls that he was quite often in Albany "on command" or "absent by leave" in 1778, 1779, and the best part of 1880. His daughter Marie Madeleine/Mary (4.7) married there in 1783. The family may have lived in either or both localities.

Josette Bergevin joined her husband on Lake Champlain soon after his arrival there: she was a resident in September 1784. I have been unable to verify the date of her death. Her granddaughter Mrs. Barbary (Monty) Morrison stated in 1856 that she "died about 1822." Since she was certainly wrong in the date of her grandfather's death (see above), it may be that her memory was equally at fault in the case of her grandmother's death.

Many of Francis Monty's descendants have inherited his adventurous spirit. They left their mark in Clinton county, NY, especially around Chazy and Plattsburgh, where they gave their name to Monty's Bay, Monty Road, Monty Street School, etc. A few still remain in the area but many others have left. Some migrated south to Essex and Warren counties, NY, and to urban centers in neighboring New England states. Others journeyed west in search perhaps of more fertile agricultural lands. In the beginning of the 21st century these descendants are found in almost every state of the Union, though the South is somewhat under-represented. Their surname is still usually Monty save mainly for the descendants of his grandson Abraham Monty/ Montee (4.4.7) who became the patriarch of a large Montee family in the Midwest and West (see Betty Ramsey's *Monty-Montee History)*. One also finds a few isolated and sporadic changes to Monta, Monte, or Montey.

The fate of other descendants is still uncertain for there are few primary records relating to the early years of Clinton county. The best guides I have found are two court documents of October and November 1856 in which Mrs. Barbary (Monty) Morrison (4.4.5) and John Monty Jr. (4.11.1) established the lines of descent from their grandfather (Appendix I). I have been able to confirm and at times elaborate on much of what they said. Unfortunately some gaps remain as I was unable to follow through on their information. Their depositions must then stand on their own.

Children:

4.1	Joseph	1760-	-1760
4.2	François	1761-	-
4.3	Jacques/James	1763-	-1809
4.4	François/Francis Jr.	1764-	-1818
4.5	Amable/Abraham	1765?-	-
4.6	Antoine	1766-	-
4.7	Mary/Marie Madeleine	1767-1784-	
4.8	Joseph	1768?-1808-1853	
4.9	Catherine	1769-1790-1840	
4.10	Placide	1770-1807-1847	
4.11	John	1771?-	-1861
4.12	Cunégonde	1772-	-1772
4.13	Pierre	1773-	-
4.14	Charlotte Michel	1775-	-
4.15	Louisa/Lizzy	-	-

5   **MONTY, Gaspard** b & bp 9 Apr 1737, Chambly, QC; d & bur 24 & 26 Jul 1819, St. Mathias, QC. He married 19 May 1760, Chambly, QC, **Marie Thérèse Denoyer/Desnoyers dit Demarest** (Pierre Denoyer dit Demarest & Marie Joseph Létourneau) b & bp there 3 Feb 1740; d & bur 25 & 27 Feb 1808, St. Mathias, QC.

Gaspard Monty (Gaspard Antoine Amable at his baptism) was a farmer in Chambly, QC, until 1769 and then in Pointe Olivier, now St. Mathias, QC, a locality on the Richelieu river almost directly across from Chambly. He had purchased land from Laurent Vigeant dit Taupier on 25 Jul 1763 and from François Lanoix on 18 Nov 1769, and was granted a concession in the seigneury of Ramezay on 12 Nov 1781 (Notarial Archives, Montreal, QC, notary Antoine Grisé, #367, #738, #2180).

The area around the present-day St. Mathias was a center of pro-American sentiment in Canada in the 1770s and indeed became one of the rallying points for the troops invading Canada in 1775. Nothing is known of any overt actions Gaspard Monty might have taken to help the American cause. The *Memoirs* of Lt. Benjamin Mooers, adjutant of Col. Moses Hazen's Second Canadian regiment in the Continental Army, refer to indirect help he gave the Americans after the retreat of 1776. Lt. Mooers had come to the Richelieu valley in August 1779 to gather information concerning the British forces in the area. Among his contacts, he mentions a "Capt. —, of the militia of Chambly, who was a particular friend of Colonel Hazen. From him I secured valuable information, as also from Gaspar (sic) Monty, an old acquaintance of Col. Hazen, and a brother to Lieut. Monty in our service" (cited in Bilow, "Movements of Hazen's Regiment," p. 255). One may assume that when his own brother François/Francis (4) was sent to Canada in May 1777 he had been no less forthcoming with information.

Many of Gaspard Monty's descendants have remained in Canada, mainly in the Richelieu Valley and in Montreal, QC. Those who emigrated did so at a relatively late date and generally settled between 1870 and 1910 in the industrial towns of New England where they still reside for the most part. They kept close ties with Canada and often married Canadian spouses. Some who died in the United States were buried in Canada. Others returned there after having spent many years in the United States. As a result one sees many fractured families: some children went to Canada with their parents while others remained in New England. Language also poses a problem, as names and sometimes surnames change according to a person's place of residence. In both countries however the patronymic has generally remained Monty.

Children:

5.1	Marie Thérèse	1761- -1770
5.2	Louise	1762-1780-1813
5.3	Marie Elisabeth/Isabelle	1764-1787-1841
5.4	Marie Anne	1766- -1770
5.5	Pierre	1767- -
5.6	Félicité	1769- -1770
5.7	Louis	1771-1790-1833
5.8	Joseph	1773- -1776
5.9	Marie	1774-1793&1824-1860
5.10	Joseph	1776-1801-1812
5.11	Claire	1778- -1784
5.12	Marie Amable	1780- -1781
5.13	Marie Amable	1782- -1784
5.14	Charlotte	1784-1817-1849

6   **MONTY, Geneviève** b & bp 22 Aug 1738, Chambly, QC; d & bur 12 & 13 May 1821, St. Mathias, QC. She married 27 Jan 1756, Chambly, QC, **Pierre Binet dit Deslauriers/Vinet** (Jacques Binet & Françoise Fortin) b 1724?, France; d & bur 13 & 15 Jul 1819, St. Mathias, QC, at about 95 years of age.

Pierre Binet dit Deslauriers first came to Canada as a French soldier serving in the company of M. de Languedoc at the fort of Chambly. He remained in Canada after the British conquest of 1763 and moved at some time before 1778 to Pointe Olivier, now St. Mathias, QC, where he was a master mason. There the surname became Vinet, which is the most common modern form of the patronymic.

His burial record is misleading: it refers to his widow as Magdeleine Monty. Yet two of the witnesses, Joseph Hébert and Louis Chedeville, identified in the text as sons-in-law of the deceased, were in fact the husbands of Josette (ix) and Isabelle (xiv) Binet/Vinet, daughters of Pierre Binet and Geneviève Monty.

Children:

i   **Claude François Binet** b & bp 1 Dec 1757, Chambly, QC; d & bur there 1 Apr 1760.

ii   **Marie Louise Binet** b & bp 15 Aug 1759, Chambly, QC; d & bur there 6 Sep 1759.

iii   **Charles Binet/Vinet** b & bp 23 & 24 Sep 1761, Chambly, QC; d & bur 21 & 22

Mar 1805, St. Mathias, QC. He married there 19 Jan 1784 **Marie Barré** (Jean-Baptiste Barré & Agathe Larocque) b & bp 16 Aug 1754, Chambly, QC; m (2) 16 Sep 1805, St. Mathias, QC, Pierre Bérard (Michel Bérard & Cécile Durel), widower of Angélique Patenaude; d & bur there 1 & 3 Nov 1818.

iv   **Geneviève Binet/Vinet** b & bp 19 & 20 May 1763, Chambly, QC; d & bur 17 & 18 Feb 1831, Marieville, QC.

v   **Julie Hippolyte Binet** b & bp 3 Oct 1764, Chambly, QC.

vi   **Pierre Binet** b & bp 28 Jul 1766, Chambly, QC.

vii   **Marie Anne Binet/Vinet** b & bp 7 & 8 Oct 1767, Chambly, QC; d & bur 13 & 14 Nov 1790, St. Mathias, QC. She married there 15 Feb 1790 **François Soutierre** (Jean Soutierre & Marie Agathe Davignon) b & bp 3 May 1756, Chambly, QC; m (1) 17 May 1779, St. Mathias, QC, Josephte Barrière (René Barrière & Agathe Laporte); m there (3) 11 Feb 1793 Marie Josette Fonteneau (Pascal Fonteneau & Marie Anne Desnoyers).

viii   **Marie Joseph Binet/Vinet** bp 25 Apr 1769, Chambly, QC. She married 2 Aug 1784, Chambly, QC, **Jean-Baptiste Ménard/Mainard dit Bellerose** (Jean-Baptiste Ménard & Marguerite Chauvin) b & bp 18 & 19 Nov 1762, Boucherville, QC.

ix   **Marie Josephte/Josette Binet/Vinet** b & bp 28 Feb & 2 Mar 1771, Chambly, QC; d & bur there 23 & 25 Mar 1803. She married 24 Jan 1785, St. Mathias, QC, **Joseph Hébert** (Joseph Hébert & Charlotte Dame) b & bp 28 & 29 Jan 1763, Boucherville, QC; m (2) 13 Feb 1804, Chambly, QC, Marie Judith Surprenant (Jacques Surprenant & Marie Josephte Baudin); d & bur 3 & 5 May 1843, Iberville, QC.

x   **Pierre Binet/Vinet** b & bp 29 Apr 1773, Chambly, QC.

xi   **Marie Louise Binet/Vinet** b 1775?, QC; d & bur 13 & 15 Dec 1793, St. Mathias, QC, at the age of 18. She married there 14 Jan 1793 **Michel Desnoyers** (Michel Desnoyers & Marie Anne Blain) b & bp 17 & 18 Nov 1771, Chambly, QC.

xii   **François Binet/Vinet** b & bp 17 Feb & 2 Mar 1777, Chambly, QC. He married 26 Jun 1797, St. Mathias, QC, **Marie Louise Bessette** (Charles Bessette & Marie Blain) b & bp 3 & 4 Jul 1776, Chambly, QC.

xiii   **Marguerite Binet/Vinet** b & bp 21 Oct 1778, St. Mathias, QC. She married there 15 Feb 1802 **Louis Jarry** (Pierre Jarry & Marie Anne Bonin) b & bp 20 Oct 1776, Verchères, QC.

xiv   **Isabelle/Marie Elisabeth Vinet** b & bp 2 & 3 Feb 1781, Chambly, QC; d & bur 6 & 8 Jul 1850, St. Jean, QC. She married (1) 8 Feb 1796, St. Mathias, QC, **Pierre Bresse** (Pierre Bresse & Madeleine [or Catherine?] Labadie) b & bp 1 & 2 Oct 1762, Montreal, QC; d & bur 8 & 10 May 1802, St. Mathias, QC.

She married (2) 7 Feb 1803, St. Mathias, QC, **Louis Demers dit Chedeville** (Amable Demers & Marie Anne Favreau) b & bp 5 & 6 Jul 1780, Chambly, QC.

7   **MONTY, Marie Joseph** b & bp 10 Mar 1740, Chambly, QC; bur there 14 May 1740.

8   **MONTY, Clément** b & bp 26 Dec 1740 & Jan 1741, Chambly, QC; d & bur 31 Jan & 2 Feb 1830, St. Mathias, QC. He married 27 Feb 1764, Chambly, QC, **Louise Boileau** (René Boileau & Marie Anne Robert) b & bp there 20 Dec 1742 & 15 Mar 1743; d & bur 23 & 25 Jan 1814, St. Mathias, QC.

Clément Monty (Clémens [sic] Marie at his baptism) was originally a farmer in Chambly, QC. According to the 1765 local census, he then had a wife and one son under 15 years of age and owned two cows, one horse, and two pigs. By September 1774 he was a farmer in Pointe Olivier, now St. Mathias, QC, where he remained until his death.

He made a number of real estate transactions: he purchased on 15 May 1763 from his mother Marthe Poyer for 60 *livres* a lot of 3 *arpents* by 25 in the "faubourg St. Jean-Baptiste de Chambly"; made an exchange with Augustin Bombardier on 26 Sep 1770; sold to Jean Marie Gilbert on 20 Aug 1776 his share of the land he had inherited from his father; received two land grants, on 3 Oct 1778 and 26 Oct 1779, from the *sieur* Hertel de Rouville; and again sold land on 1 Aug 1780 to François Godreau and on 4 Nov 1782 to Charles Fréchet (Notarial Archives, Montreal, QC, notary Antoine Grisé, #356, #833, #1209, #1402, #1567, #1747, #2634).

Louise Boileau (Marie Louise at her baptism) was a sister of Joseph Boileau, first husband of Marie Joseph Monty (11).

There are to my knowledge no Monty descendants of Clément left in Canada. His sons remained there but his grandsons and great-grandsons emigrated one by one from the early 1840s through the end of the 19th century. The first to leave settled in the agricultural areas of New Hampshire, New York, and Wisconsin. A later wave of emigrants, in the 1870s and 1880s, settled mainly in the industrial towns of Massachusetts and Connecticut. In both New England and the Midwest the surname gene-rally remained Monty.

Children:

8.1	Clément	1764-1786-1825
8.2	Marie Louise	1766-1783&1790-1834
8.3	Philibert/Philippe	1768-1805-1839
8.4	Bruno	1771- -1772
8.5	Marie Geneviève	1773- -1773
8.6	Félicité	1774- -1776
8.7	Madeleine	1777-1796-1848
8.8	Catherine	1780-1798-
8.9	Marguerite	1782-1811-1831
8.10	Marie Archange	1789- -1790

9   **MONTY, Marie Angélique** b & bp 4 Aug 1742, Chambly, QC; d & bur 26 & 28 Mar 1810, Montreal, QC. She married (1) 23 May 1761, Chambly, QC, **Louis Courtin** (Jean Courtin & Marie Durard) b 1731?, France; m (1) 22 Feb 1756, Quebec, QC, Marie Anne Chaloux (Pierre François Chaloux dit St. Pierre & Marie Boisdoré); d & bur 5 & 6 Mar 1780, Montreal, QC, at the age of 49.

She married (2) 4 Feb 1782, Montreal, QC, **Jean-Baptiste Mauray** (Robert Mauray & Elisabeth Leroux) b 1744?, France; d & bur 9 & 11 Mar 1795, Montreal, QC, at the age of 51.

The marriage contract between Marie Angélique Monty and Louis Courtin was signed before the notary Antoine Grisé on 21 May 1761 in Chambly, QC (Notarial Archives, Montreal, QC, #234). He was the master baker at the French fort there, in charge of all food supplies for the garrison. The couple's first two children were born in Chambly, where Louis Courtin bought some land from Amable Boileau on 5 Apr 1763 in the "faubourg St. Jean Baptiste" (notary Grisé, #354). The family soon moved to Montreal, QC, where two children were born in 1765 and 1766. The following year another child, born en route from Montreal to Detroit, then a French trading post where Louis Courtin had taken employment as a master baker, was baptized in Ste Anne's Church in Detroit. There follows a gap of a few years in the family's history. By 1771 though Louis Courtin was again a master baker in Montreal, where the last four children were born. He was buried in the chapel of St. Amable in Montreal. An inventory of the couple's community property was drawn up on 1 Feb 1782, prior to Marie Angélique Monty's second marriage (notary Grisé, #2227).

Jean-Baptiste Mauray (also Maurais, Moré, Mauret) was a wig-maker in Montreal. The couple's marriage contract was signed in Chambly on 3 Feb 1782 (notary Grisé, #2228).

Children:

i   **Marie Marthe Courtin** b & bp 4 Sep 1762, Chambly, QC. She probably died before a sister of the same name (v) was baptized on 24 Oct 1767.

ii   **Marie Angélique Courtin** b & bp 8 Aug 1763, Chambly, QC; & bur 26 & 28 Aug 1819, St. Laurent, QC. She married 3 Mar 1783, Montreal, QC, **Laurent Verdon** (Pierre Verdon & Marguerite Groux) b & bp 4 Jun 1760, St. Laurent, QC; d & bur there 24 & 26 May 1818.

iii   **Pierre Courtin** b & bp 25 Jul 1765, Montreal, QC; d & bur there 4 & 5 Aug 1765.

iv   **Catherine Courtin** b & bp 5 Sep 1766, Montreal, QC; d & bur there 14 & 15 Sep

1766.

v   **Marie Marthe Courtin** b 15 Oct 1767, in a canoe on the Great Lakes; bp 24 Oct 1767, Detroit; d & bur 22 & 23 Mar 1773, Montreal, QC.

vi   **Charles Courtin** b & bp 11 & 12 Oct 1771, Montreal, QC.

vii   **Jean-Baptiste Courtin** b & bp 18 Jan 1773, Montreal, QC. He married there 25 Feb 1811 **Julie Sarrasin** (Pierre Sarrasin & Marie Imbault Matha) b & bp there 14 Oct 1768; d & bur there 19 & 21 Apr 1849.

viii   **Marie Courtin** b & bp 14 & 15 Nov 1775, Montreal, QC; bur 1 Jul 1776, Longueuil, QC.

ix   **Marie Madeleine Courtin** b & bp 5 Sep 1778, Montreal, QC. She married (1) there 9 May 1796 **Louis Roy** (André Roy & Marie Anne Lebaire) b & bp there 24 & 25 Dec 1769.

She was a widow when she married (2) 23 Jul 1810, Montreal, QC, **Pierre Damour** (François Damour & Louise Robert) b & bp 2 & 4 Sep 1786, Laval, QC.

[The marriage records of Notre Dame church in Montreal, QC (fol. 19) name Louis Roy's bride Marie-Angélique Courtin. The bride's signature however is quite clearly Marie Madeleine Courtin. His widow was also named Marie Madeleine when she remarried in 1810.]

10   **MONTY, Alexis** b & bp 14 Nov 1743, Chambly, QC; d & bur there 15 Nov 1743.

11   **MONTY, Marie Joseph** b 30 Dec 1744, Chambly, QC; d & bur 14 & 16 Apr 1832, Champlain, NY, & Chambly, QC. She married (1) 14 Feb 1763, Chambly, QC, **Joseph Boileau** (René Boileau & Marie Anne Robert) b & bp there 11 Jan 1739; d & bur there 7 & 8 Oct 1772.

She married (2) 25 Jan 1779, Chambly, QC, **Pierre Ayot/Aillot** (Guillaume Aillot & Marie Anne Levasseur) b & bp 6 & 7 Apr 1735, Kamouraska, QC; d Oct 1814, Champlain, NY.

Marie Joseph Monty was never called anything but Marie Monty as an adult: at her marriages, at her children's baptisms, and at her death. Her marriage contract with Joseph Boileau, signed in Chambly, QC, on 14 Feb 1763 before the notary Antoine Grisé, is in the name of Marie Monty (Notarial Archives, Montreal, QC, #338). She received as Marie Monty her share of Jean Monty's land in 1774. She was Marie Monty at the sale of that property to Jean-Marie Gilbert on 20 Aug 1776 as well as at a later sale to Louis Guillot on 10 Nov 1778, prior to her second marriage (notary Grisé, #1209, #1406).

Her first husband, Joseph Boileau, was a brother of Louise Boileau, wife of Clément Monty (8), and also of Lt. Amable Boileau and Pvt. Pierre Boileau of Col. Moses Hazen's Second Canadian regiment, in which several Montys also served during the American Revolution.

Pierre Ayot, Marie Monty's second husband, was a supporter of the American cause from the very beginning of the American invasion of Canada in 1775. As captain of a company of militia he mounted several raids against British partisans on the South shore of the St. Lawrence near Quebec city and, with Clément Gosselin (4.9), generally fomented rebellion in the period before and during the siege of Quebec in 1775. He disappeared for a few years after the American army's retreat from Quebec in early 1776. Some have said that he was a prisoner of the British, others that he was an officer in the Continental Army before settling in New York State in the mid-1780s. I have found no evidence that he was other than a refugee. He certainly did not serve in either of the two Canadian regiments. Indeed Clément Gosselin, by then a Captain in Col. Moses Hazen's Second Canadian regiment, mentioned to his wife in a letter of 28 Oct 1778 that "pierre ayot n'est point a l'armée on ne cest point la ou yl est personne n'en a eu connoissance" (Canadian Archives, Haldimand Papers, B. 1842, vol. I, pt. 2, p. 597). My translation: "Pierre Ayot is not with the army; his whereabouts are unknown; nobody has heard of him." The fact that even Clément Gosselin, a formerly close ally and conspirator, knew nothing of Pierre Ayot's whereabouts in 1778 suggests that he had indeed remained in Canada for few years after 1776. This would explain how, at his marriage to Marie

Monty in January 1779, he could be referred to as being of the parish of Chambly. The fact that she had sold her property there in November 1778 suggests that the couple did not intend to remain in the area after their marriage.

There is no trace of Pierre Ayot in New York State until 1786, when he was living in the Point au Roche Patent in Clinton county. The following year "piere ayot," the head of a two-member family, is included in a list of Canadian officers, soldiers, and refugees residing on Lake Champlain on 11 Aug 1787 (Bilow, "Census of Canadian Refugees in New York State, 1784, 1785, 1787," p. 253). When the balloting for bounty land took place on 10 Sep 1787, he received $333^{1}/_{3}$ acres in the Refugee Patent in Champlain (lot #3) where he remained until his death. One must suppose that he had fulfilled the residency requirement and had lived in the state of New York for at least two years after 1 Nov 1782. He was survived by his widow and a stepdaughter, Mrs. Marie (Boileau) Vincelet (i) of Rouses Point, NY.

Children:
- i **Marie Boileau** b & bp 8 & 9 Oct 1763, Chambly, QC; d & bur there 20 & 23 Feb 1855. She married there 26 Jan 1784 **Pierre Vincelet** (Jacques Vincelet & Marie Louise Barré) b & bp there 4 & 5 Jan 1763; d & bur there 26 & 28 Jan 1845.
- ii **Joseph Boileau** b & bp 12 Dec 1765, Chambly, QC; d & bur there 8 & 9 Jun 1770.
- iii **Isabelle/Elisabeth Boileau** b & bp 7 Sep 1767, Chambly, QC; d & bur there 5 & 6 Jun 1770.
- iv **Radegonde Boileau** b & bp 3 & 4 Sep 1769, Chambly, QC; d & bur there 8 & 9 Jun 1770.
- v **Joseph Boileau** b & bp 28 May 1771, Chambly, QC; d & bur there 12 & 13 Jul 1776.

12   **MONTY, Geneviève Amable** b & bp 28 Jan 1746, Chambly, QC.

No later trace is found of this child. I would surmise that she died in infancy and her burial record was lost.

13   **MONTY, Antoine** b & bp 19 & 20 Mar 1747, Chambly, QC; d & bur there 24 & 26 Jun 1829. He married there 1 Oct 1770 **Catherine Piédalue** (Julien Piédalue & Félicité Bourassa) b & bp there 7 & 11 Sep 1751; d & bur there 4 & 6 Apr 1825.

Antoine Monty was a farmer and blacksmith first in Longueuil, QC, and then, from at least 1774, in Chambly, QC, where most of his children were born. It may be that his departure from Longueuil coincided with the sale of land in the seigneury of Longueuil on 20 Sep 1774. He later received a land grant from the *sieur* Dechambault in Longueuil 28 Dec 1780 and bought from Pierre Fréchette and his wife in Chambly on 13 Jul 1802 two other lots in the area (Notarial Archives, Montreal, QC, notary Antoine Grisé, #1159 and #1816; notary François Leguay, *fils*, #3097).

The stone house which Antoine Monty built in 1786 in Chambly on the Mont Royal river still existed at the end of the 20th century. It passed after his death to his son Joseph (13.9), his grand-daughter Marcelline Monty (13.9.8), and then to her son Adélard Raymond (viii), thus going out of the strictly "Monty" family.

His descendants have remained to a large extent in the Province of Quebec, where they can be found mainly around Montreal, in the Richelieu valley, and in the Eastern Townships. Some are still living in Chambly and hosted a Monty family re-union there in 1993. An early emigrant was his daughter Euphrosine who came to New York state with her husband and children in the 1830s. Several of his grand-children also emigrated, generally in the 1850s, apparently in search of new farm land in Vermont, New Hampshire, and Illinois. Sporadic emigration continued until at least the mid-20th century. The family name remained Monty with only a few exceptions, especially in Illinois, where one finds the surname Montie.

Children:

13.1	Catherine	1772-1792&1814-1837
13.2	Félicité	1774- -1774
13.3	Antoine	1775-1794-1864

13.4	Marie Joseph	1777-1801-1842
13.5	Elisabeth/Isabelle	1780-1800-1822
13.6	Geneviève	1782-1805-1862
13.7	Marie Louise	1783-1809-
13.8	Amable	1785-1805-1847
13.9	Joseph	1788-1810&1861-1862
13.10	Euphrosine	1790-1809-
13.11	Angélique	1792-1814-1814
13.12	Casimir	1794- -1797

14   **MONTY, Marie Françoise** b & bp 16 Sep 1748, Chambly, QC; d & bur there 22 Oct 1748.

1.1 **MONTY, Marie Angélique** b & bp 9 & 10 Jan 1758, Chambly, QC; d & bur there 9 & 10 Mar 1765.

1.2 **MONTY, Amable** b & bp 6 Jan 1760, Chambly, QC.

Apart from his baptismal record, I have found little documentation concerning Amable Monty. He was present in Chambly, QC, though, at the marriages of his sisters Louise (1.3) and Marguerite (1.16) in 1779 and 1798 respectively. In both cases his signature is quite distinct from that of his father Amable Monty.

There is a remote possibility that he was the Amable Monty, a farmer on Lake Champlain, father of an anonymous daughter who was born in New York State on 12 Jan 1802 and was buried later that month in St. Luc, QC. The mother's name was Josette Monty. I do not know if Monty was her maiden name (Canadian usage) or her married name (American usage) and have been unable to identify the couple.

It is also possible that Amable Monty was known in New York State as Abraham Monty, husband of Johanna Monty, daughter of Francis Monty Jr. (4.4). His parents are still unknown, but see my speculations at 4.4.1.

In any event Amable Monty, son of Amable Monty and Marie Angélique Létourneau, should not be confused with his cousin Amable/Abraham Monty (4.5), son of François/Francis Monty and Josette Bergevin, who participated in the American Revolution and settled in Clinton County, NY, after the war. The latter's affiliation is made quite clear in a number of court records in the United States.

1.3 **MONTY, Louise** b & bp 16 Jan 1762, Chambly, QC; d & bur there 24 & 25 Jul 1806. She married there 27 Sep 1779 **François Gélineau** (Nicolas Gélineau & Louise Bourdon) b & bp 8 Nov 1751, Longueuil, QC; d & bur 19 & 23 Oct 1824, St. Luc, QC.

François Gélineau (also Gélinot) was a farmer in Chambly, QC, until at least 1806 and later became an innkeeper in St. Luc, QC. He was a brother of Joseph Gélineau, husband of Angélique Monty (1.9).

Children:
i **François Gelineau** b & bp 18 & 19 Oct 1779, Chambly, QC; d & bur there 18 & 19 Oct 1780.
ii **Marie Louise Gélineau** b & bp 20 & 22 Oct 1780, Chambly, QC.
iii **Angélique Gélineau** b & bp 28 Jun 1782, Chambly, QC. She married there 8 Nov 1802 **Pascal Dubuc** (Michel Dubuc & Josette/Marie Joseph Lepage dit St. Antoine) b & bp 6 & 7 Nov 1767, Longueuil, QC.
iv **Jean-Baptiste Gélineau** b & bp 29 & 30 Apr 1784, Chambly, QC. He married there 15 Feb 1808 **Josephte Noiseux** (Jean Noiseux & Marie Angélique Deschamps) b & bp there 24 Apr 1784.
v **Marie Louise Gélineau** b & bp 15 & 16 Mar 1787, Chambly, QC.
vi **Marie Desanges Gélineau** b & bp 16 Oct 1790, Chambly, QC; d & bur there 25 & 26 Dec 1795.
vii **François Gélineau** b & bp 24 Feb 1794, St. Mathias, QC. He married 14 Sep 1818, Chambly, QC, **Charlotte Cognac** (Pierre Cognac & Marie Denicourt) b & bp there 14 Nov 1791; d & bur 23 & 27 Dec 1892, St. Valentin, QC.
viii **Alexis Gélineau** b & bp 17 & 18 Oct 1795, Chambly, QC; d & bur there 24 & 26 Dec 1795.

1.4 **MONTY, Marie Anne** b & bp 20 & 21 May 1764, Chambly, QC; d & bur there 18 Mar 1765.

1.5 **MONTY, Geneviève** b & bp 20 & 21 Jan 1766, Chambly, QC; d & bur there 3 & 4 Feb 1766.

1.6   **MONTY, Marie** b & bp 26 & 27 Apr 1767, Chambly, QC; bur there 16 May 1770 at the age of 3 under the name of Marie Anne.

1.7   **MONTY, Antoine** b & bp 13 & 14 Aug 1768, Chambly, QC; d & bur there 14 & 16 Sep 1774.

1.8   **MONTY, Honoré** b & bp 5 & 8 Feb 1770, Chambly, QC; d & bur there 5 & 6 Jul 1774.

1.9   **MONTY, Angélique** b & bp 20 & 21 Oct 1771, Chambly, QC; d & bur there 17 & 18 Aug 1794. She married there 7 Nov 1786 **Joseph Gélineau** (Nicolas Gélineau & Marie Louise Bourdon) b & bp 11 & 12 Jan 1760, Longueuil, QC; d & bur 2 & 4 Nov 1829, Marieville, QC.

Joseph Gélineau (also Gélinot) was a brother of François Gélineau, husband of Louise Monty (1.3).

Children:
i   **Joseph Gélineau** b & bp 13 & 14 May 1788, Chambly, QC; d & bur there 22 & 24 Dec 1823. He married there (1) 21 Feb 1814 a first cousin once removed, **Angélique Monty** (Antoine Monty [13] & Catherine Piédalue) b & bp there 25 Sep 1792; d & bur there 23 & 24 Dec 1814.

He married (2) 28 Jul 1817, Chambly, QC, **Charlotte Cognac** (Barthélemy Cognac & Charlotte Denicourt) b & bp there 25 & 26 Jul 1797; d & bur there 15 & 17 Jun 1822.

ii   **Marie Marguerite Gélineau** b & bp 1 & 2 Dec 1789, Chambly, QC. She married 11 Feb 1811, Boucherville, QC, **André Potvin** (Louis Potvin & Marguerite Lague) b & bp 1 & 2 Jun 1786, Longueuil, QC; d & bur 1 & 4 Jan 1866, Farnham, QC.

iii   **Alexis Gélineau** b & bp 7 & 8 Nov 1790, Chambly, QC; d & bur there 11 & 12 Nov 1790.

iv   **Rosalie Gélineau** b & bp 3 & 4 Aug 1792, Chambly, QC; d & bur there 28 & 29 Dec 1795.

1.10   **MONTY, Marie Desanges** b 1772?; d & bur 27 & 29 Oct 1851, St. Valentin, QC, at the age of 79. She married (1) 1 Mar 1791, Chambly, QC, **Alexis Patenaude** (François Patenaude & Charlotte Ménard) b & bp 11 Oct 1770, Chambly, QC; d & bur 4 & 5 Mar 1825, Napierville & L'Acadie, QC.

She married (2) 18 Apr 1831, St. Valentin, QC, **Jean-Baptiste Alexandre** (Jacques Alexandre & Marie Anne Gendron) b & bp 9 Jan 1768, St. François de la Rivière du Sud, QC, m (1) 16 Jul 1787, L'Acadie, QC, Marie Louise Guenet (François Guenet & Marie Pélagie Déjadon); d & bur there 16 &18 Jun 1839.

She married (3) under the name of Marie Montier, widow of Jean-Baptiste Alexandre, 28 Jan 1840, St. Valentin, QC, **Louis Roch/Roque** (Jean-Baptiste Touin dit Roque & Angélique Clément) b 1769?; m (1) 17 Jul 1820, Laprairie, QC, Marie Amable Babeu (André Babeu & Amable Chrétien), widow of Antoine Daigneau; d & bur 14 & 15 Aug 1847, St. Valentin, QC, at the age of 78.

Alexis Patenaude (also Patenode, Patenotre) was originally a farmer in Chambly, QC, where his children were baptized until 1809. He later was a farmer and/or laborer in Lacolle, St. Luc, L'Acadie, and St. Valentin, QC.

Children:
i   **Alexis Patenaude** b & bp 10 & 11 May 1791, Chambly, QC; d & bur there 13 & 14 Aug 1791.

ii   **Anonymous Patenaude** b 13 Jan 1792, Chambly, QC; d & bur there 13 & 14 Jan 1792.

iii   **Marie Desanges Patenaude** b & bp 16 & 17 Jan 1793, Chambly, QC; d & bur 24 & 26 Feb 1825, Napierville, QC. She married 18 Feb 1811, L'Acadie, QC, **Fran-**

çois **Firmin Hébert** (Simon Hébert & Marguerite Richard) b & bp 25 & 28 Sep 1787, Laprairie, QC; m (2) 15 Nov 1825, St. Luc, QC, Esther Hudon (Basile Hudon & Madeleine Dunord); d & bur 25 & 27 Dec 1869, Drummondville, QC.

iv **Marguerite Patenaude** b & bp 2 Jul 1795, Chambly, QC; d & bur there 26 & 27 Aug 1795.

v **Alexis Patenaude** b & bp 2 Jul 1797, Chambly, QC; d & bur 22 & 27 Feb 1854, St. Valentin, QC. He married 9 Nov 1824, St. Luc, QC, **Louise Ménard** (Jean Ménard & Marguerite Courtemanche) b & bp 12 & 15 Jun 1802, L'Acadie, QC; m (2) 16 Nov 1854, Keeseville, NY, her brother-in-law Ignace Martin (François Martin & Marie Houle), widower of Marguerite Patenaude (x).

vi **Marguerite Patenaude** b & bp 24 Feb 1799, Chambly, QC; d & bur there 25 & 26 Feb 1799.

vii **François Patenaude** b & bp 18 Nov 1800, Chambly, QC; d & bur 27 & 29 Jan 1884, St. Valentin, QC. He married 13 Jan 1824, Chambly, QC, **Marguerite Cognac** (Barthélemy Cognac & Charlotte Denicourt) b & bp there 5 Sep 1798; d & bur 19 & 21 Dec 1879, St. Valentin, QC.

viii **Léon Patenaude/Patno** b & bp 16 Sep 1802, Chambly, QC; d 14 Aug 1883, North Hero, VT. He married (1) 30 May 1825, St. Luc, QC, **Marie Henriette Trempe** (François Trempe & Marguerite Germain) b 1810?; d & bur 30 & 31 Oct 1837, St. Valentin, QC, at the age of 27.

He married (2) 1838? **Esther Cameron** (Jean Moïse Cameron/Camerer/Cameraire & Françoise Valois) b & bp 30 Oct & 1 Dec 1819, Berthier-en-Haut, QC; d 3 Apr 1885, VT.

ix **David Patenaude** b & bp 23 & 24 Mar 1805, Chambly, QC; d & bur 7 & 9 Apr 1884, St. Valentin, QC. He married 6 Feb 1826, Napierville, QC, **Marie Olive Côté** (Louis Romain Côté & Marie Tremblay) b & bp 19 Oct 1808, St. Luc, QC; d & bur 6 & 8 Apr 1867, St. Valentin, QC.

x **Marguerite Patenaude** b & bp 7 & 11 Apr 1809, Chambly, QC; d between 1850 and 1855. She married 3 Oct 1826, Napierville, QC, **Ignace Martin** (François Martin & Marie Houle) b & bp 6 Feb 1805, Laprairie, QC; m (2) 16 Nov 1854, Keeseville, NY, his sister-in-law Louise Ménard (Jean Ménard & Marguerite Courtemanche), widow of Alexis Patenaude (v); d & bur 17 & 19 Nov 1871, St. Valentin, QC.

xi **Angélique Patenaude** b & bp 18 Feb & 13 Jun 1811, L'Acadie, QC; d & bur 23 & 25 Sep 1827, Napierville, QC.

xii **Anonymous Patenaude** b 24 Jan 1816, St. Luc, QC; d & bur there 24 & 30 Jan 1816.

xiii **Anonymous Patenaude** b 28 Jul 1817, St. Luc, QC; d & bur there 28 & 30 Jul 1817.

1.11 **MONTY, Marie Anne** b & bp 28 & 29 Jul 1773, Chambly, QC; d & bur there 31 Aug & 1 Sep 1773.

1.12 **MONTY, Marie Anne** b & bp 23 Sep 1774, Chambly, QC.

1.13 **MONTY, Marie Angélique** b & bp 27 & 28 Apr 1776, Chambly, QC.

1.14 **MONTY, Louis** b & bp 28 & 29 Nov 1777, Chambly, QC; d & bur there 16 & 17 Dec 1777.

1.15 **MONTY, Joseph** b & bp 3 & 4 Sep 1779, Chambly, QC; d & bur there 17 & 19 Sep 1780.

1.16 **MONTY, Marguerite** b & bp 5 & 6 Mar 1783, St. Mathias, QC; d & bur 12 & 14 Apr 1864, Beloeil, QC. She married (1) 22 Oct 1798, Chambly, QC, **François Deniau** (Louis Deniau & Angélique Gagnier) b & bp 30 Oct & 1 Nov 1767, Longueuil, QC; d & bur there 4 & 6 Jul 1818.

She married (2) 18 Jan 1820, Longueuil, QC, **Michel Bray dit Labonté** (Joseph Bray dit Labonté & Agathe Picard) b & bp there 22 & 23 Jan 1782; d & bur there 16 &18 Oct 1841.

She married (3) 30 Jan 1843, Longueuil, QC, **Jean-Baptiste Desautels** (Joseph Desautels & Angélique Tétro) b & bp 31 May 1780, St. Charles, QC; m (1) 9 Nov 1812, Longueuil, QC, Charlotte Viau (Joseph Viau & Catherine Vincent), widow of François Charron; d & bur there 19 & 22 Dec 1845.

She married (4) 24 Nov 1853, Beloeil, QC, **Charles Huot** (Marc Antoine Huot & Josette/Josephte Robert dit Lafontaine) b & bp 1 & 2 Apr 1784, Chambly, QC; m (1) 17 Oct 1814, Beloeil, QC, Clémentine Dumont (Jean-Baptiste Dumont & Marie Leblanc); d & bur there 4 & 9 Sep 1871.

François Deniau was a farmer in Longueuil, QC. His son Basile (v) was the father of Onésime Daignault who married Prudent Monty (5.7.1.12), a third cousin, while his daughter Anastasie (x) was the mother of Alfred Patenaude who married Hermine Monty (13.3.1.12), also a third cousin. François Deniau's children were known under several surnames: Deniau, Daignault, Daigneault, or Daigneau. The standard form is now Daigneau.

Michel Bray was a carpenter in Longueuil at his marriage but was described as a farmer at the births of his children. He was a brother of Francoise Bray, wife of his stepson François Xavier Daignault (ii).

Jean-Baptiste Desautels was a farmer in Longueuil. His widow was living with her daughter Marguerite (iv) and her husband in Beloeil, QC, in 1851 (Canadian census).

Charles Huot was a farmer in Chambly, QC, when he married Marguerite Monty but was a resident of Beloeil at his death.

Children:
i   **Angélique Deniau/Daignault** b & bp 12 Sep 1799, Longueuil, QC; d & bur 7 & 11 Apr 1864, Beloeil, QC. She married 18 Nov 1816, Longueuil, QC, **Victor Vandandaigue dit Gadbois** (André Vandandaigue dit Gadbois & Marguerite Adam) b & bp 15 May 1794, Beloeil, QC; d & bur there 15 & 19 Jan 1869.

ii **François Xavier Deniau/Daignault** b & bp 24 Sep 1801, Longueuil, QC; d & bur there 15 & 18 Feb 1846. He married there 5 Feb 1822 his stepfather's sister, **Françoise Bray dit Labonté** (Joseph Bray dit Labonté & Agathe Picard) b & bp there 10 Jun 1793.

iii **Christine Deniau/Daignault** b & bp 20 & 21 Nov 1804, Longueuil, QC; d & bur there 7 & 9 Feb 1836. She married around 1822 **James Reuben Wait** (James Wait & Catherine Hodienne) b & bp 13 & 14 Oct 1788, Chambly, QC; m (2) 15 Apr 1837, Montreal, QC (American Presbyterian Church), Emma Forbes.

iv **Marguerite Deniau/Daignault** b & bp 11 Jul 1806, Longueuil, QC. She married there 11 Oct 1825 **Antoine Provost** (Ambroise Provost & Marie Louise Augé dit Lemieux) b & bp 30 Sep 1798, Longue Pointe, QC.

v   **Basile Deniau/Daignault** b & bp 10 & 11 Mar 1808, Chambly, QC; d & bur 23 & 25 May 1859, Longueuil, QC. He married 9 Feb 1830, Beloeil, QC, **Julienne Vandandaigue dit Gadbois** (André Vandandaigue dit Gadbois & Françoise Fournier) b & bp there 17 & 18 Feb 1809; d & bur 27 & 29 Feb 1908, Montreal, QC.

vi **Narcisse Deniau/Daignault** b & bp 26 & 27 Oct 1809, Longueuil, QC; d & bur there 1 & 2 Jul 1822.

vii **Henriette Deniau/Daignault** b & bp 2 Dec 1811, Longueuil, QC; d & bur 21 & 23 Mar 1895, Chambly, QC. She married 26 Oct 1830, Longueuil, QC, **David Larocque** (Michel Larocque & Marie Agathe Piédalue) b & bp 12 & 13 Mar 1802, Chambly, QC; d & bur there 23 & 25 Jan 1881.

viii **Justine Deniau/Daignault** b & bp 26 & 27 Aug 1813, Longueuil, QC.

ix **Augustin Deniau/Daignault** b & bp 2 & 3 Sep 1815, Longueuil, QC.

x   **Anastasie/Euphrasie Deniau/Daignault** b & bp 26 Feb 1818, Longueuil, QC; d & bur there 12 & 15 May 1848. She married there 5 Oct 1841 **Michel Patenaude** (Michel Patenaude & Louise Lériger) b & bp there 26 & 27 May 1813; m there (2) 31 Jul 1849, Olympe Daignault (François Daignault & Scholastique Pagé); d & bur

4 & 6 Oct 1900, Laprairie, QC.
- xi   **Rosalie Bray dit Labonté** b & bp 29 & 30 Jul 1820, Longueuil, QC.
- xii   **Césarie Bray dit Labonté** b & bp 28 Nov 1821, Longueuil, QC; d & bur there 19 & 20 Jul 1822.
- xiii   **Aglaé Bray dit Labonté** (twin) b & bp 9 & 10 Jun 1823, Longueuil, QC.
- xiv   **Honorée Bray dit Labonté** (twin) b & bp 9 & 10 Jun 1823, Longueuil, QC.

3.1   **MONTY, Claude/Cloud** b & bp 7 Jun 1760, Chambly, QC; d 31 Jul 1839, Colchester, VT. He married 21 Nov 1786, Chambly, QC, **Marie Josette/Josephte Fontaine** (Joseph Fontaine & Marie Reine Labonté) b & bp 28 Jun & 4 Aug 1771, Lake Champlain & Chambly, QC; d between 1830 and 1839, probably in Vermont.

Claude Monty's adult life is fairly well documented through his army records in the American Revolution and the subsequent petitions and affidavits of 1818, 1819 and 1820 in support of his applications for an army pension. They belie many of the myths which later gained currency, that he was born in France, for example, and that he came to America with Lafayette.

He was born and baptized in Chazy, QC, and was 15 years old when he joined the American army in the fall of 1775 as a private in Col. Bedel's New Hampshire regiment, Capt. Antrema's company. Of the eight Montys who eventually served in the Continental Army, he is the only one who did not originally enlist in one of the two Canadian regiments. He served under Gen. Montgomery at the siege of Quebec, participated in the army's retreat in the spring of 1776, and was taken prisoner at the Cedars (Les Cèdres) in May 1776. He rejoined the American army in Albany, NY, after his release and reenlisted on 21 Nov 1776 for the duration of the war in Col. Moses Hazen's Second Canadian regiment, Capt. Olivie's company. He was at the battles of White Plains, Brunswick, Brandywine, Stillwater, Germantown, and Yorktown, and was discharged in June 1783 in New Windsor, NY (War Department records).

Claude Monty returned to Canada and lived there intermittently for a few years after the war. He married there and his first child was born there in 1788. His name does not appear during that time in the lists of Canadian soldiers or refugees living on Lake Champlain. Yet he must have satisfied the minimum residency requirement for bounty land in the state of New York for he was allotted 500 acres of land in the Refugee Patent (lot 100 of 80 acres and lot 115 of 420 acres) on 10 Sep 1787. A further Bounty Land Warrant (#13424) was issued on 4 Feb 1790 as a result of the 1785 US Land Ordinance.

He remained in the United States for a few years at that time: four children were born in New York State and Vermont from 1789 through 1793. He then went back to Chambly where these four children were baptized in July 1796 and where two daughters were born in 1796 and 1798. From then on the family was divided, at least geographically: three daughters married in Marieville, QC, and stayed in Canada; the sons returned to the United States and settled in Vermont.

As for Claude Monty himself, he appears never to have resided in any one place for very long. He was in Champlain, NY, in 1800, although without a family (US census). From 1805 to 1814 the church records in Marieville, QC, indicate that he and his wife were members of that parish, which may or may not mean much: those same records refer in 1805 to "feue" (deceased) Josephte Fontaine, who was nonetheless still alive in Marieville in 1814, in Plattsburgh, NY, in 1820, and in South Hero, VT, in 1830. On 2 Sep 1817, Claude Montee (sic) took the freeman's oath in South Hero (South Hero Town and Vital Records). The following April, however, when he petitioned for a pension under the Act of Congress of 18 Mar 1818, he did so as a resident of Plattsburgh. After some delay resulting from the War Department's uncertainty concerning his identity, a pension of $8 per month payable semi-annually, with arrears from 4 Mar 1818, was granted on 22 Jul 1819 (certificate #12608).

The cause of the War Department's uncertainty will delight any who have struggled to read hastily written early 19th-century notes and documents, to cope with ever-changing spellings of ancestors' names, and to reconcile known facts with the sometimes inaccurate or incomplete memories of the participants. A memo from the War Department, dated 4 Sep 1818, commented on Claude Monty's application in which he claimed to have enlisted in 1775 and to have served until the end of the war in Col. Hazen's regiment: "It appears that a man of the name of Claud Monty is on the roll (28 Jan 1776 without any other remark) but not Cloud Monty there is a <u>Claude Monti p^r enlisted 21 Nov. 76</u> — this requires explanation as to the name & precise time of entering service."

The matter of Claude Monty's two enlistments was in fact addressed in his pension application, in which he clearly stated that "I enlisted in the army of the United States at Chambly in Lower Canada in the Regiment of Col. Bedel in Captain Antrema's company, under the command of General Montgomery on his expedition to Quebec in the fall of 1775, That I afterwards enlisted in the company & Regiment first above mentioned [Col. Hazen's regiment, Capt. Olivie's company] in the Spring of 1776 at Albany for during the war..." Between the enlistments of 1775 and 1776 came a few months when he was a prisoner of war in Canada. His story, taken in its entirety, seems plausible. I would question only the date of his enrollment in Albany as early 1776, for he was then a prisoner of war. But he could well have been on the rolls of the New Hampshire regiment in January 1776 as Claud Monty before enlisting in the fall of that year in Col. Hazen's regiment as Claude Monti.

Lt. Benjamin Mooers, a former adjutant in Hazen's regiment, addressed the question of name(s) in two affidavits recorded in the Court of Common Pleas in Plattsburgh. A first, brief statement of 23 Apr 1818 to the effect that "Cloud Monty belonged to said Regiment more than nine months untill the end of the war" having been deemed insufficient, a second one was sworn to on 3 Jun 1819. In its very detailed recital of the obvious it testifies as much to the old soldier's exasperation at the minutiae pursued by the bureaucracy as to the young man's presence in the army: "Benjamin Mooers of Plattsburgh being sworn says that he knows the within named Cloud Monty to be the same person who was a private in Hazens Regiment in the war of the revolution that he was a Canadian and his name was pronounced Cloud but whether it was spelled Cloud or Claude he does not know as the said Monty could not write his own name & the pronunciation in the French language would be about the same & that the said Monty's father was of the same Christian name but did not belong to the regiment while this deponent was attached to it, and whether the within applicant was on the rolls by the name of Cloud Monty or with a Junior attached to his name this deponent does not recollect — this Deponent has been acquainted with the said Monty ever since this deponent Joined Hazens Regiment in 1778 that he has lived near him a great part of the time and he has for some part of the time lived with deponent as a labourer and has seen him every two or three years ever since the revolution — that when he was in the regiment the said Monty was a young man apparently about twenty years old & further says that there was no other Cloud or Claude Monty in this regiment to the deponents recollection or belief while he belonged to it & further says not."

The veteran's pension was undoubtedly welcome: an affidavit recorded on 4 Oct 1820 in the Court of Common Pleas in Plattsburgh clearly demonstrates need. Claude Monty then owned no real estate. His personal effects, excepting bedding and clothing, include only "1 Hog, 1 Pot, 1 Kettle, 1 tea Kettle" valued at a total of $6, and "3 Cups & saucers, 1 tea pot & 2 Knives & forks" valued at a total of 75½ cents. Added to the list of assets is the statement: "I am by occupation a farmer but from age and infirmity cannot labor much. My family consists of my wife Mary aged seventy six with a broken leg and wholly helpless." No doubt there is some attempt here to emphasize the old soldier's misfortunes: the 1820 affidavits in Plattsburgh all follow the same, almost ritualistic, formulas and all conclude with a reference to old age and infirmity. But then the war had ended 37 years previously. As for Claude Monty's wife, she was 49 in 1820, not 76.

Cloud Monty remained in Plattsburgh until the summer of 1824 when he be-came a resident of South Hero, VT, and had his pension transferred to Grand Isle county, VT, on 4 Sep 1824. He remained there until at least 1830 when he was head of a household which included his wife and his son John's family (US census). Ten years later, according to the list of pensioners of the Revolutionary War included in the 1840 US census, Claud Monty, age 88 (sic), was living on 1 Jun 1840 in his son John Monty's household in Colchester, VT.

And here a problem arises. The Colchester Vital Records as well as the inscription on his tombstone in the Munson Cemetery there indicate that "Cloud Monty died Jul 31 1839 Æ 80." I cannot believe that the Vital Records would have recorded his death while he was still alive. The 1840 census must be wrong. I can only speculate that for some reason Cloud Monty's death was not reported to the federal authorities until the following year when his son John was named administrator of his estate on 5 Sep 1840 (Chittenden Co., VT, Probate Court, #1050).

The baptismal record of Marie Josette Fontaine in Chambly, QC, states that her parents were residents "au lac Champlain." This refers generally to the northwestern shores of the lake around the present-day Plattsburgh and even as far south as Ticonderoga where the French had established a fort during their colonial days. It is impossible to pinpoint the exact location. Her father was a private in Col. James Livingston's First Canadian regiment during the American Revolution and was awarded in September 1787 by the state of New York 500 acres of bounty land in the Refugee Patent (lots 42 and 109).

The date and place of her death are unknown. She was still alive in South Hero in 1830 (US census). She may have predeceased her husband. I have found no record of her death in Colchester.

Children:

3.1.1	Claude	1788- -1788
3.1.2	Catherine	1789?-1805&1833-1878
3.1.3	Jean-Baptiste/John	1790- &1842-1868
3.1.4	Marie Anne	1792?-1814-1881
3.1.5	Joseph	1793?- -1861
3.1.6	Marguerite	1796-1820-1876
3.1.7	Suzanne	1798- -
3.1.8	Benjamin	- -

3.2　　**MONTY, Marie Louise** b & bp 4 Dec 1761, Chambly, QC; d & bur there 20 Aug 1762.

3.3　　**MONTY, Joseph** b & bp 4 & 5 Feb 1763, Chambly, QC; d & bur 5 & 7 Feb 1832, Iberville, QC. He married 17 Nov 1789, Chambly, QC, **Marie Louise Goguet** (Joseph Goguet & Marie Marthe Fontaine) b & bp there 24 Jul 1770.

Joseph Monty was originally a farmer and/or laborer in Chambly, QC, and later in St. Luc, QC. He predeceased his wife. His two surviving sons, Joseph and Jacques/Jacob, emigrated in the late 1830s and early 1840s and lived in New York State where their surname most often became Montee.

Children:

3.3.1	Charlotte	1791-1810-1812
3.3.2	Joseph	1792-1816-1869
3.3.3	Félicité	1793- -1794
3.3.4	Antoine	1795- -1795
3.3.5	Antoine	1796?-1819-1830?
3.3.6	Jacques/Jacob	1797-1822-
3.3.7	Marie Amable	1799- -1800

3.4　　**MONTY, Marie Angélique** b & bp 27 Feb 1764, Chambly, QC; d & bur there 17 May 1765.

3.5　　**MONTY, Pierre** b & bp 15 & 16 May 1765, Chambly, QC; d & bur 10 & 12 Sep 1817, St. Luc, QC. He married 30 Oct 1787, Chambly, QC, **Marguerite Elisabeth Amelotte/Amelot** (Pierre Amelotte & Amable Gendron) b & bp 31 Aug 1765, Châteauguay, QC; d & bur 10 & 12 Jul 1832, Iberville, QC.

Pierre Monty was a farmer in Chambly, QC, and in St. Mathias, QC, until about 1801, and at the Mille Roches near St. Luc, QC, from 1802 on. His only surviving son, Jean-Baptiste (3.5.13) emigrated in the 1830s and was known in Vermont as John Monta.

Children:

3.5.1	Pierre	1788-	-1788
3.5.2	Pierre	1789-	-1789
3.5.3	Marguerite	1791-	-1792
3.5.4	Charlotte	1792-1822	-1836
3.5.5	Jean-Baptiste	1794-	-1794
3.5.6	Louis	1795-	-1795
3.5.7	Jean-Baptiste	1796-	-1796
3.5.8	Antoine	1797-	-1797
3.5.9	Marie Marguerite	1798-	-1798
3.5.10	Marie Madeleine	1799-	-1799
3.5.11	Marie Angélique	1800-	-1800
3.5.12	Marguerite	1802-	-1802
3.5.13	Jean-Baptiste/John	1803-	-
3.5.14	Pierre	1804-	-1804
3.5.15	Louis	1806-	-1806
3.5.16	Pierre	1807-	-1807
3.5.17	Marie Agnès	1809-1830-	

3.6   **MONTY, Marie Françoise** b & bp 8 Mar 1767, Chambly, QC.

3.7   **MONTY, Julie Amable/Julienne** b & bp 23 Dec 1768, Chambly, QC. She married there 19 Jun 1787 **Julien Mainard/Ménard** (Joseph Mainard & Marie Jeanne Aupry) b & bp there 16 & 17 Oct 1761; d before July 1842.

Julie Amable Monty (baptismal name) was generally known as simply Julie Monty. She was named Julienne however at her marriage and Judith at the birth of a daughter Marie Judith (v) whose name may well have been substituted for Julie. More troubling is the appearance of an Angélique Monty, wife of Julien Ménard, on at least two occasions in Chambly, QC: one at the baptism of Marie Joseph (iv) in 1794, and the second at the marriage of Marie Louise (iii) in 1814. I can not find anywhere else any evidence of a Julien Ménard/Angélique Monty couple in Canada and believe the children's mother to be Julie Monty.

Julien Ménard (Mainard at his marriage and occasionally at the births of his children) was a brother of Françoise Ménard, wife of Jean-Baptiste Monty (3.9). He was at various times a laborer and/or farmer in Chambly, where most of his children were born, in Pointe Olivier, the present St. Mathias, QC, and in St. Luc, QC. He was deceased when his daughter Marguerite (xiii) married in 1842.

Children:

i   **Marie Anne Ménard** b & bp 25 & 26 Dec 1787, L'Acadie, QC.

ii   **Julien Amable Ménard** b & bp 11 & 12 Jan 1790, Chambly, QC. He married 21 Feb 1814, St. Luc, QC, **Marie Louise Desgranges** (Jacques Desgranges & Marguerite Deneau) b & bp 3 & 4 Dec 1791, Longueuil, QC.

iii   **Marie Louise Ménard** b & bp 27 Apr 1792, Chambly, QC. She married 24 Oct 1814, St. Mathias, QC, **Charles Hébert** (Jean-Baptiste Hébert & Marie Elisabeth Véronneau) b & bp 22 Dec 1794, Chambly, QC; d & bur 21 & 24 Mar 1874, Dunham, QC.

iv   **Marie Joseph Ménard** b & bp 8 & 9 May 1794, Chambly, QC.

v   **Marie Judith/Julie (?) Ménard** b & bp 15 & 16 Mar 1796, Chambly, QC.

vi   **Toussaint Ménard** b & bp 28 & 29 Mar 1798, Chambly, QC.

vii   **Pierre Ménard** b & bp 22 & 24 Mar 1800, Chambly, QC; d & bur there 6 & 7 Apr 1800.

viii   **Josephte Ménard** b & bp 29 & 30 Jul 1801, Chambly, QC. She married there 26 Aug 1822 **Jacob Ail** (Jean Ail & Marie Collingham, of Ulster, Flanders) who was of age at his marriage.

ix   **Augustin Ménard** b & bp 24 & 25 Jan 1807, St. Luc, QC.

x   **Jean-Baptiste Ménard** b & bp 31 Jan & 9 Feb 1809, St. Luc, QC.

xi   **Clémence Ménard** b & bp 21 & 14 Mar 1811, Chambly, QC; d & bur there 13 & 14 Jun 1811.

xii   **Emilie Ménard** b & bp 21 & 22 Apr 1812, Chambly, QC; d & bur there 13 & 14 May 1812.

xiii   **Marguerite Ménard** was over 21 when she married 17 Jul 1842, St. Armand, QC, **Joseph Bonneau** (Louis Bonneau & Marie Anne Paul), also over 21.

3.8   **MONTY, Marie** b & bp 18 Oct 1770, Chambly, QC; d between 1808 and 1812. She married 25 Sep 1787, Chambly, QC, **Jacques Goguet** (Jacques Goguet & Marie Louise Laporte dit Labonté) b & bp 1 & 2 Mar 1765, St. Ours, QC; m (2) as a widower 18 Nov 1811, Châteauguay, QC, Marie Louise Galipeau (Basile Galipeau & Louise Hamel).

When this couple's marriage contract was signed in Chambly, QC, on 24 Sep 1787 before the notary Antoine Grisé, Jacques Goguet was a farmer in St. Mathias, QC. He was also a farmer in Châteauguay, QC, and in Beauharnois, QC, after 1801. He apparently left Canada after his second marriage for in 1826, at the marriage of his daughter Josephte (xii), it was said that he had been absent from the country for several years, leaving his minor daughter to the guardianship of her brother Jacques (iii). This surely suggests that his absence was meant to be permanent, or at least of indefinite length. I have not found any record of his later activities.

Jacques Goguet was a brother of Joseph Goguet, husband of Madeleine Monty (8.7), and of François Goguet, husband of Catherine Monty (8.8), and an uncle of Marie Geneviève Goyette, wife of François Xavier Monty (3.9.3). The family name gradually changed to Goyet, Goyette.

Children:

i   **Marie Goguet** b & bp 15 & 16 Sep 1788, St. Mathias, QC; d & bur there 1 & 2 Sep 1789.

ii   **Marie Anne Goguet** b & bp 20 & 21 Jan 1790, Chambly, QC; d & bur 13 & 14 Nov 1790, St. Mathias, QC.

iii   **Jacques Goguet** b & bp 2 & 3 Oct 1791, St. Mathias, QC; d & bur 24 & 26 Jan 1863, Beauharnois, QC. He married 4 Feb 1811, Châteauguay, QC, **Josephte Leboeuf** (Charles Leboeuf & Archange Hébert) bp there 17 Jun 1789; d & bur 2 & 4 Dec 1867, Beauharnois, QC.

iv   **Joseph Goguet** b & bp 19 & 21 May 1793, St. Mathias, QC. He married 12 Nov 1810, Châteauguay, QC, **Véronique Fournier** (Pierre Fournier & Véronique Robert) b & bp there 15 Sep 1794.

v   **Augustin Goguet** b & bp 17 & 18 Mar 1795, St. Mathias, QC; d & bur there 8 & 9 Aug 1795.

vi   **Geneviève Goguet** b & bp 2 & 3 Jul 1796, St. Mathias, QC; d & bur there 31 Dec 1801 & 1 Jan 1802.

vii   **Marie Louise Goguet** b & bp 28 & 29 Mar 1798, St. Mathias, QC. She married 17 Jul 1815, St. Mathias, QC, **Joseph Balthazar** (Jean-Baptiste Balthazar & Louise Larocque) b & bp there 2 & 3 Jul 1793.

viii   **Louis Goguet/Goyette** b & bp 22 & 23 Mar 1799, St. Mathias, QC. He married 30 Oct 1830, River Raisin, MI, **Frances Moore** (Louis Moore & Marie Moreau) b 7 Feb 1807, Detroit, MI; m (1) François Bourdeau (Louis Bourdeau & Susanne Gaillard).

ix   **François Goguet** b & bp 3 & 4 Oct 1801, St. Mathias, QC.

x   **Marie Goguet** b 1803?; d 8 Mar 1806, Châteauguay, QC, at the age of 3.

xi   **Jean-Baptiste Goguet** b & bp 22 & 23 Jul 1805, Châteauguay, QC; d there 2 Aug 1805.

xii   **Josephte Goguet** b & bp 10 & 11 Aug 1806, Châteauguay, QC. She married 10 Jan 1826, Beauharnois, QC, **Jean-Baptiste Branchaud** (Jean-Baptiste Branchaud & Rose Tessier) b & bp 24 & 25 Sep 1801, Châteauguay, QC; d & bur 26 & 28 Jan 1860, Beauharnois, QC.

xiii   **Augustin Goguet** (twin) b & bp 11 Feb 1808, St. Luc, QC; d & bur there 11 & 14

Feb 1808.

    xiv   **Paul Goguet** (twin) b & bp 11 Feb 1808, St. Luc, QC; d & bur there 11 & 14 Feb 1808.

3.9   **MONTY, Jean-Baptiste** b & bp 18 Apr 1774, Chambly, QC; d & bur 1 & 3 Mar 1825, Iberville, QC. He married 17 Feb 1794, Chambly, QC, **Françoise Ménard** (Joseph Ménard & Marie Jeanne Aupry) b & bp there 1 & 2 Apr 1771; d & bur 1 & 3 Sep 1834, Iberville, QC.

    Jean-Baptiste Monty was originally a farmer in St. Mathias, QC, and after 1799 at the Mille Roches in the seigneury of Bleury, near St. Luc, QC. His wife was a sister of Julien Ménard, husband of Julie Amable Monty (3.7).

    A large number of Jean-Baptiste Monty's descendants reside in the United States, especially in Michigan where his son François Xavier (3.9.3) emigrated in the 1840s and adopted the surname of Montie which his own descendants still bear. In New England, especially in Massachusetts and Rhode Island, there are also a number of descendants of Jean-Baptiste's grandson Guillaume/William (3.9.2.2) who came to the United States in the mid-1860s. Their surname is either Monty or Monte.

Children:

3.9.1	Françoise	1794-1818&1844-1873
3.9.2	Jean-Baptiste	1796-1821-1827
3.9.3	François Xavier/Francis	1798-1818-1879
3.9.4	Marguerite	1800-1829&1835-1881
3.9.5	Théotiste	1802-1830-1834
3.9.6	Marie Louise	1804-1821-1825
3.9.7	Marie	1806-1825-1883
3.9.8	Rosalie/Sophie	1809- -1810
3.9.9	Ambroise	1812- -1812

3.10   **MONTY, Anonymous** bur 1 Feb 1776, Chambly, QC.
This child was stillborn.

3.11   **MONTY, Antoine** b & bp 25 & 27 May 1779, Chambly, QC; d & bur there 30 & 31 Dec 1779.

4.1   **MONTY, Joseph** b & bp 26 Jul 1760, Chambly, QC; d there 27 Jul 1760.

4.2   **MONTY, François** b & bp 18 Nov 1761, Chambly, QC.
    This child presumably died before the birth in July 1764 of a younger brother also named François (4.4). No death record for either child has been found. There is some evidence however that private Francis Monty (4.4) who served in the Continental Army during the American Revolution may have been born around 1761: he was the oldest son of Lt Francis Monty, according to affidavits signed on 15 Aug 1846 by both his brother Joseph Monty (4.8) and his son Christopher Monty (4.4.3) so would of necessity have been born before Jacques/James Monty (4.3). More precisely, he was said to be 24 years old in 1785 (John Andrew Bilow, "Census of Canadian Refugees in New York State in 1784, 1785, 1787," *French Canadian and Acadian Genealogical Review*, IX, 256). There remains however the problem of a second child who was named François at his baptism in 1764. It is possible that he was misnamed and that his father's name was substituted for his own, as happened on rare occasions, but I have no indication that that was the case here. For the moment I am leaving the list of François Monty's children as it is.

4.3   **MONTY, Jacques/James** b & bp 26 & 29 Jan 1763, Chambly, QC; d 9 Jul 1819, Peru, NY. He married **Anny Taylor** of Peekskill, NY, who predeceased her husband.
    François Monty's third son, named Jacques André at his baptism, was named at different times Jacques, Jacque, Jaque, Jack, or James Monty or Montey while serving in the Conti-

nental Army during the American Revolution and for a few years afterwards. In later years he was more commonly known as James Monty.

The few facts we know about his early life are contained mainly in his army records, in his pension application of 25 Apr 1818, and in an affidavit he signed the same day in support of his brother Amable's application in the Clinton Co., NY, Court of Common Pleas. From these we learn that he left Canada with his family in early 1776, enlisted as a private in the spring of 1776 in Col. James Livingston's First Canadian regiment, in which his father also served, and was transferred at a later, unspecified date to Capt. Olivie's company, Col. Moses Hazen's Second Canadian regiment. He participated in the battles of White Plains (1776), Fort Stanwix (1777), Saratoga (1777), Stillwater, (1777), Rhode Island (1778), Elizabethtown (1780), and Yorktown (1781), and was discharged in New Windsor, NY, in June 1783 after having served for seven years.

Jacques/James Monty's movements immediately after the war are uncertain, as is the date of his marriage. It is possible that he was the unnamed son of Lt. Francis Monty who left Poughkeepsie, NY, on 26 Jul 1783 with a group of Canadians under the leadership of Benjamin Mooers to establish a settlement on the shores of Lake Champlain. Yet he does not appear in the September 1784 census of soldiers and refugees in that area. There was present however in Albany, NY, in 1785 a 25-year-old Canadian, Jack Monty, who had left Canada in 1776. And a Jaque Monty was living with a wife and child on Lake Champlain on 11 Aug 1787 (John Andrew Bilow, "Census of Canadian Refugees in New York State, 1784, 1785, 1787," in *French Canadian and Acadian Genealogical Review,* IX, 242-253). One month later, in the balloting of 10 Sep 1787, James Monty was granted by the state of New York 500 acres of bounty land in the Refugee Patent (lot 186 of 80 acres and lot 250 of 420 acres). The following year, on 10 Mar 1788, he and his wife Anny were living near his father and brothers in the Point au Roche Patent (Clinton Co. Deeds, Book B).

He did not remain long in New York state at this time. He assigned his bounty land warrant to Benjamin Mooers on 22 Jan 1790 (#13420) and was living with his wife, a son under the age of 16, and a daughter, age unspecified, in Vergennes, VT, at the time of the 1790 census. The family was in Fishkill, NY, in 1800 and in Plattsburgh, NY, in 1810 (US censuses). That year his household included one son between the ages of 16 and 26, one son between the ages of 10 and 16, two daughters under the age of 10, and one female (his wife?) over the age of 45. Nothing more is heard of James Monty's wife or daughters. He was a widower at his death and was survived only by his sons Christopher, James, and Matthew, according to the testimony of his nephew John Monty Jr. (4.11.1) (Appendix I).

It was from Plattsburgh that James Monty applied on 23 Mar 1818 for a pension under the act of 18 Mar 1818. "I am," he stated, "in very indigent circumstances & am in need of assistance from the country for support & have no property where-with to support myself." No mention is made of a wife or children. A pension of $8 per month, retroactive to 23 Mar 1818, was allowed and certificate #1423 was issued in the name of James Montey on 30 Jun 1818. The War Department papers also refer, without elucidation, to an Invalid Pension (file #43017) and a Survivor's pension (S43017).

James Monty died the following year. Since he was intestate, his son James was named administrator of his estate in Plattsburgh on 25 Oct 1819 (Clinton Co. Surrogate's Court).

Children:

4.3.1	Christopher	1786?-	-1861
4.3.2	James	1797?-	-
4.3.3	Matthew	1798?-	-

4.4   **MONTY, François/Francis Jr**. b & bp 13 Jul 1864, Chambly, QC; d 10 Aug 1818, Plattsburgh, NY. He married **Mary Heath** (Joseph Heath & _____) b 1763?; d between 1810 and 1818.

Francis Monty Jr. left numerous descendants, several of whom have attempted to trace his and his children's lives. Very few primary documents have emerged, and no marriage record. Even the date of his birth/baptism is open to question (see my comments at 4.2). To document his life, one must rely for the most part on War Department records of his army service during the Revolutionary War and on Clinton Co., NY, court records detailing his and his family's situation after the war. Even then one must proceed with caution. His brother Joseph Monty (4.8) and his son Christopher Monty (4.4.3) both testified in Plattsburgh, NY, on 15 Aug 1846 that Francis Monty died on 10 Aug 1818. That is the date generally agreed upon. Yet the Saturday, 29 Aug 1818 issue of the *Plattsburg Republican* reported: "Drowned, off the point of Cumberland Head, on Sunday last, by the upsetting of a canoe, Francis Monty, a soldier in the regiment of Canadian refugees." The 10th of August fell on a Monday in 1818. "Sunday last" could apply, depending on the date the item was filed with the newspaper, to the 9th, 16th, or 23rd of the month. There are no guarantees.

The dates of birth of his wife and children are almost all derived from secondary sources. For his children, the outline provided by his daughter Barbary (4.4.5) in an affidavit of 9 Oct 1856 (Appendix I) is a good point of departure. She names not only her sisters' spouses (though unfortunately not her brothers' or her own) but also the children of those who were already deceased. In those cases where her statements could be checked against official or primary documents they have proved to be generally true, the major exception being the date of death of her grandfather. I have little cause to doubt her accuracy in identifying her siblings, both living and deceased.

Francis Monty Jr. served as a private in Capt. Lawrence Olivie's company, Col. Moses Hazen's Second Canadian regiment, during the Revolutionary War and was discharged in June 1783 at Pompton, near Fishkill, NY. The War Department records do not indicate the date of his enlistment nor do they contain any details of his engagements. After the war he settled on the shores of Lake Champlain where he was living in September 1784 with a wife and child. The following year Francis Monty, a 25-year-old former soldier, his 22-year-old wife, and an unnamed 2-year-old child were drawing provisions from the Contractor's stores on Lake Champlain. In another census taken in August 1787, François Monty's family (as distinct from Lt. Monty's family, listed separately) consisted of four persons (John Andrew Bilow, "Census of Canadian Refugees in New York State, 1784, 1785, 1787," *French Canadian and Acadian Genealogical Review*, IX, 242, 246, 253). This is the only instance I have found in the United States of the use of his French name. On other occasions he is named Francis or Francis Jr.

In the balloting for bounty land of 10 Sep 1787, Francis Monty Jr. was granted five hundred acres (lot 66 of 80 acres and lot 131 of 420 acres) in the Refugee Patent on Lake Champlain. He immediately sold the 80-acre lot to Harry Hardie and later transferred to Benjamin Mooers his Bounty Land Warrant (#13427) on 21 Sep 1790. He was not however a head of household in the 1790 census. His family may have been living in another household, perhaps his father's in Champlain, NY, or even in Fishkill, where two children were born in 1787 and 1792. He was in Champlain in 1800, with four male dependents under the age of 26, four female dependents under the age of 16, and one female (presumably his wife) between the ages of 26 and 45. In 1810 his household in Plattsburgh included his wife, five male dependents, and five female dependents (US censuses). He was a farmer there at his death.

Francis Monty Jr. died before his application for a veteran's pension could be processed. Many years later his son Christopher, who had been named administrator of his estate in the Clinton Co. Surrogate's Court in January 1819, applied on behalf of his father's heirs for a pension due the survivors of Revolutionary War soldiers. He attested on 15 Aug 1846 that "soon after the passage of the pension act of 1818, [Francis Monty Jr.] made application for a pension through the Agency of the Honorable Reuben H. Walworth & gave, as deponent was informed, his discharge & other papers relative to his services to him to send on to Washington. No certificate was received in his life time." There followed a lengthy series of court depositions, requests, and letters between the heirs of Francis Monty Jr. and the Pension Commission of the State of New York. The claim was finally denied in June 1847 on the grounds that the act of 1818 applied to veterans alone and not to their heirs, while the act of 7 Jun 1832, which did make provision for survivors, applied only to veterans alive on that date and to their families (File #R-7317).

More interesting to the genealogist is what all these documents reveal about the family. And also what remains unclear. On 4 Jul 1846 a decision of the Circuit Court in Plattsburgh (Appendix II) affirmed that "It was proven to the Satisfaction of Said Court that Francis

Monty was a Revolutionary Soldier of the United States, and that he died at the Town of Plattsburgh in the Said County of Clinton on the 10th day of August 1818; that he left no widow, that he left Six children who are all over the age of twenty one years and that they are his only Surviving children whose names are as follows, Christopher Monty, Abram Monty, Betsey Ward, Fanny Miller, Barbara Monty, and Margaret Frederic." At first glance this would imply that Johanna, Mary, and Joseph had predeceased their father. A closer reading suggests merely that six of Francis Monty's children, who by then were all over the age of 21, were still alive on 4 Jul 1846 while the other three had died before that date. I believe the second interpretation is the correct one and that the switch from past tense ("left") to present ("are") was quite deliberate. It accounts for the fact, among others, that Abraham Monty, who was 18 years old at his father's death, could be listed among Francis Monty's over-21-years-old surviving children.

Francis Monty Jr.'s wife Mary Heath was 22 years old in 1785, according to that year's census of Canadian soldiers and refugees on Lake Champlain (Bilow, p. 246). She was still alive in 1810 but predeceased her husband if indeed he "left no widow."

Children:

4.4.1	Johanna	1783?-	-
4.4.2	Joseph	-	-
4.4.3	Christopher	1787?-	-
4.4.4	Jane Ann	1792-	-1856
4.4.5	Barbary	-	-
4.4.6	Betsey	-	-
4.4.7	Abraham	1800-1822-1877	
4.4.8	Margaret	1803?-	-
4.4.9	Mary	-	-

4.5   **MONTY, Amable/Abraham** b around 1765; d between 1830 and 1840. He married **Barbary** ____ b 1763?

There are few certainties concerning Amable/Abraham Monty and his family. No birth, marriage, or death records have been found. His identification as François/ Francis Monty's son is based on an affidavit in the Clinton Co. Court of Common Pleas in Plattsburgh, NY, of 25 Apr 1818 by James Monty (4.3) concerning his brother Amable and on a later affidavit of 9 Oct 1856 by Mrs. Barbary (Monty) Morrison (4.4.5) referring to her uncle "Abraham Monty son of L[t] Monty" (Appendix I). His name is Amable in all documents pertaining to his service in the Continental Army during the American Revolution and in the 1800 census in Champlain, NY. Later censuses and civil documents in Plattsburgh name him Abraham. From what we know of either Amable or Abraham Monty, I have no reason to doubt that they are the same man.

The date of Amable Monty's birth is problematic. I have found only two references to his age, both in Court of Common Pleas documents supporting his application for a veteran's pension. In the first, dated 23 Mar 1818, he was said to be "about fifty four years." Two years later, on 3 Oct 1820, he was "aged sixty years." Yet since four of his siblings were born between 1760 and 1764, according to the records of St. Joseph's church in Chambly, QC, he could not have been born before 1765, a date which I submit with no great degree of conviction: he would have been rather young to have enlisted in 1776. In my more imaginative moments I wonder if Amable Monty could have been the child born on 13 Jul 1764 whose name in the baptismal record was entered mistakenly as François (see my comments at 4.2). But I have no proof.

Amable Monty first summarized his army career in an affidavit submitted to the Court of Common Pleas on 23 Mar 1818: "I was a private in the company commanded by Captain Olivie in Col Moses Hazen's Regiment in the service of the United States in the Continental Establishment called the Congress Regiment in the War of the Revolution that I enlisted in the Army of the United States at Albany the spring that the army which had been under the command of General Montgomery retreated from Canada which I believe was in the spring of 1776 in the Regiment of Col Livingston & was afterward transferred to the Regiment of Col

Hazen that I served seven years & upwards & I was discharged in New Windsor in the State of New York in the spring or summer after Peace was made with Great Brittain ..." A later declaration before the same Court, on 3 Oct 1820, states that "he joined Livingstons Regiment in Canada in 1774 [sic] and retreated with the army from Canada and enlisted in Captain Livingstons Company in the same Regiment for during the War and after the taking of Burgoyne [Saratoga, 1777] he served in the Armoreurs Shop untill about three years and was then transferred into Captain Olives Company in Col Hazens Congress Regiment and continued to serve therein to the end of the War and was discharged at New Windsor about June 1783 and was during his service in the Battles of the taking of Burgoyne." The War Department records also specify that while in Col. James Livingston's regiment he served in the companies of Captains Bird and Livingston.

Amable Monty's movements in the next few years are uncertain. Neither he nor Abraham Monty appears in the 1784 or 1785 censuses of Canadian soldiers and refugees on Lake Champlain, although Abraham Monty was elected on 3 April 1786 as one of three constables in the newly-created town of Plattsburgh, NY (*History of Clinton and Franklin Counties*, Philadelphia, 1880, p. 188). The following year, in the balloting of 10 Sep 1787, Amable Monty was allotted 500 acres of bounty land (lot 149 of 80 acres and lot 246 of 420 acres) in the Refugee Patent. He was in Champlain, NY, in 1800 (US census) but again in Plattsburgh in 1811 when a tax of 11¢ was levied on his real estate assessed at $50 (*History of Clinton and Franklin Counties*, p. 187). From there he also petitioned Congress, unsuccessfully, in 1814, 1815, 1816, 1817, and 1818, for "Compensation for supplies furnished in revolutionary war." He received however a veteran's pension (certificate #1422, dated 30 Jun 1818) of $8 per month, with arrears to 23 Mar 1818, the date of his application. His heirs also received a survivor's pension (certificate #S43012) after his death.

According to an affidavit 3 Oct 1820 in the Clinton Co. Court of Common Pleas, the 60-year-old Amable Monty was then a resident of Beekmantown, NY. He declared: "I am by occupation a farmer but am almost blind and therefore unable to labor. My family consists of my wife Barbery Monty aged about fifty seven and my son Benjamin Monty aged about thirteen a healthy Boy." His personal assets, excluding clothing and bedding, were valued at $20.56: one small cow ($15), one hen, six chicken, and two shoats ($2.25), 6 plates, 6 cups and saucers, 1 pot, and 1 tea kettle ($2.12), a pair of andirons and one water pail ($1.00), and 3 tea spoons (19¢). He owned no real estate. Nevertheless there is mention in the Deeds records in Clinton Co. of a sale to Abraham Monty from John Monty in 1826, and a return to Abram E. Monty in 1828 of property previously deeded by him to his son-in-law Joseph W. Baker, husband of his daughter Barbary.

The date of Amable Monty's death is no better known than that of his birth. He is mentioned in the 1830 US census in Plattsburgh but does not appear in the 1840 list of surviving Revolutionary War veterans.

His 57-year-old wife was named Barbery in his 1820 affidavit but Barbary in the 1856 deposition of her niece Mrs. Barbary (Monty) Morrison (4.4.5) (Appendix I). Later scribes often changed the name to the more common form Barbara.

Children:

4.5.1	John	1796?-	-	
4.5.2	Phoebe	-	-	
4.5.3	Julia	-	-	
4.5.4	Ann	1802?-	&	-1873
4.5.5	Barbary	-	-	
4.5.6	Benjamin	1807-	-1828	

4.6   **MONTY, Antoine** b & bp 8 & 9 May 1766, Chambly, QC.

4.7   **MONTY, Mary/Marie Madeleine** b & bp 10 & 12 Jul 1767, Chambly, QC; d between 1843 and 1856, probably in Chazy, NY. She married 17 Aug 1784, Albany, NY, **Louis Alexandre/Lewis Lizotte** (Joseph Lizotte & Marie Thérèse Lebel) b & bp 14 & 15 Dec 1752, St. Roch des Aulnaies, QC; d 23 Aug 1829, Chazy, NY.

This woman was named Marie Madeleine at her baptism but was known in the United States, where she came with her parents in 1776, as simply Mary or Polly. She married under the name of Polly Monty. When she later applied as Mary Lisote for a widow's pension on 3 Aug 1838 there was much concern about the disparity in names. Several relatives were called upon to testify that the marriage had indeed taken place on 17 Aug 1784 in Albany, NY, and that the torn fragment submitted in evidence was part of the original marriage certificate which had in times past been seen and read in its complete form by a number of individuals. Mary Lisote herself explained in an affidavit of 5 Jun 1839 in Clinton Co. Court before Judge Henry D. Dickenson that "her true name was, when she was married Mary Monty, but she was called and known by the name of Polly Monty at the time she was married to the said Lewis Lisote, that being a nickname, or a substitute for Mary, that being the reason why the name Polly appears in the annexed certificate." Her brother Joseph Monty (4.8) attested in the same Court that he had been present at the marriage and that his sister Mary was indeed Louis Lizotte's widow.

A widow's pension of $80 per year, with arrears to 4 Mar 1836, was then is-sued on 18 Sep 1839 (certificate #4221). According to the 1840 census of "Pensioners of the Revolutionary War," Mary Monty was then living in her son Joseph Lizotte's household in Chazy. A few years later a new request was made, under the Act of Congress of 3 Mar 1843. It was allowed, and certificate W24533 was issued in December 1843, again at the rate of $80 per year. She does not appear in any 1850 census and may have died before then. She was certainly deceased in November 1856 according to the testimony of her nephew John Monty (Appendix I).

Louis/Lewis Lizotte (also Lisot, Lisote, Lizot, Lezotte, Lezett, etc.) came to the United States in the early years of the American Revolution, enlisted as a private in Capt. Gilbert's company, Col. Moses Hazen's Second Canadian regiment, in Boston, MA, in December 1777, and was discharged on 30 Jun 1783 in New Windsor, NY, after having served for 5½ years (War Department Records). He was thus a comrade-at-arms of several Montys.

Louis Lezett and his wife were in Albany in September 1784 but soon settled on Lake Champlain where they were living in 1785 and 1787 (John Andrew Bilow, "Census of Canadian Refugees in New York State, 1784, 1785, 1787," *French Canadian and Acadian Genealogical Review*, IX, 242, 246, 253). In the balloting for bounty land on 10 Sep 1787 Louis Lisot was granted 500 acres in the Refugee Patent (lot 78 of 80 acres and lot 62 of 420 acres). The following year Lewis Lezotte was made constable of the first Court of Justice in Plattsburgh, NY (John W. Barber and Henry Howe, *Historical Collection s of the State of New York*, p. 109).

It appears that, like most former soldiers and refugees, Louis Lizotte preferred the shores of Lake Champlain to the undeveloped lands in the Refugee Patent. Thus when a further grant of 100 acres was issued on 22 Jan 1790 (Warrant #13340) it was assigned to Benjamin Mooers. A few years later the assessment roll in Champlain, NY, for the year 1798 notes the presence of "Louis Lizotte on Monty's Bay, 50 acres, adjoining François Monty, one log house ($2), value $200." In this area, which became the town of Chazy in 1804, the median house value at the time was $10, and none was valued under $2 (Nell Jane Barnett Sullivan and David Kendall Martin, *History of the Town of Chazy, Clinton County, NY*, p. 70). Louis Lizotte was perhaps one of the poorest refugees in the area.

His financial situation does not appear to have improved in the following years. A list of his total assets, filed on 3 Oct 1820 in the Clinton Co. Court of Common Pleas, is revealing: "Real estate: None — Personal estate excepting necessary & clothing: One old [illegible] $0.75; 2 tea cups & saucers $0.12; 2 old knives & forks $0.25; 1 old ax $0.50," for a total value of $1.62. That paints a grim picture of his domestic arrangements, even if one takes into consideration the tendency in all such documents to stress poverty and need. In the meantime, though, his application for a veteran's pension, made from Chazy on 26 Mar 1818, had been allowed on 6 Apr 1818 at the rate of $96 per year (certificate #67).

Children:

i   **Mary Lizotte** b 1788?, Chazy, NY; d after 1856. She married a first cousin **Christopher Monty** (4.3.1).

ii   **Louis/Lewis Lizotte** b 1792?, Chazy, NY; d 17 Sep 1877, Altona, NY. He married (1) around 1817 **Miranda Clark** b 1799?; d 26 Nov 1841, Chazy, NY, at the age of 42.

        He married (2) 1844? **Eleanor/Ellen** _____ b 1826?, Canada.

iii   **Joseph Lizotte** b 1793?, Chazy, NY. He married 1819? **Sophia Belanger** (Julian Victor Belanger & Marguerite Vigeant dit Taupier) b 1798?, Champlain, NY.

4.8   **MONTY, Joseph** b 1768?; d 20 Nov 1853, Chazy, NY. He married there 16 Jun 1808 **Mary Defayette/Fayette/Lafayette** b 1788?, QC; d between 1860 and 1870.

No record of Joseph Monty's birth or baptism has been found in Chambly, QC, where his siblings were born, or in the surrounding parishes. He may have been born in 1768 (he was 52 years old when he made a deposition on 3 Oct 1820 in the Clinton Co. Court of Common Pleas in Plattsburgh, NY) or 1773 (he was 67 in 1840, according to the Pension List of the state of New York), or even 1775 (he was 75 in the 1850 US census in Chazy, NY, and 78 years and 3 months old at his death). Given his enlistment in the American army in 1780, the earlier date seems more probable.

War Department records indicate that Joseph Monty served as a private, a musician, in Capt. Lawrence Olivie's company, Col. Moses Hazen's Second Canadian regiment. He enlisted in Fishkill, NY, in the spring of 1780 and remained in the same regiment until his discharge at New Windsor, NY, in June 1783. The following year he was in Albany, NY, for the wedding of his sister Mary/Marie Madeleine (4.7). His name does not appear on any of the early censuses of Canadian soldiers/refugees in New York State. Yet he was allotted on 10 Sep 1787 500 acres of bounty land in the Refugee Patent on Lake Champlain (lot 137 of 80 acres and lot 67 of 420 acres), for which letters patent were apparently never issued. A later Bounty Land Warrant (#13473), issued in his name on 22 Jan 1790 for 100 acres, was assigned to Benjamin Mooers.

I strongly suspect that Joseph Monty was in fact the same person as the mysterious "Julian Monty," a former soldier who was residing on Lake Champlain in 1784 and 1785, when he was 16 years old (John Andrew Bilow, "Census of Canadian Refugees in New York State, 1784, 1785, 1787," *French Canadian and Acadian Genealogical Review*, XI, 242, 246). He is never again mentioned in any document I have seen and is not found in the lists of Revolutionary War veterans eligible for Bounty land. I think it is more than coincidental that whenever the name of Joseph Monty is found, Julian is absent, and vice-versa. I have no proof, though, that the two names represent a single individual.

Joseph Monty was married in Chazy on 16 Jun 1808 by Justice of the Peace Nathan Carver. He applied from there on 4 Apr 1818 for a pension as a Revolutionary War veteran, which was granted on 15 Jul 1819 at the rate of $96 per annum, with arrears to 4 Apr 1818 (certificate #12258). He later stated in an affidavit of 3 Oct 1820 before the Court of Common Pleas in Plattsburgh, NY, that he was a 52-year-old farmer and that he had bought the preceding year 52½ acres of land in the Point au Roche Patent for $6 per acre, with a mortgage covering the full cost of purchase. No other real estate is listed. His personal property, excluding bedding and clothing, but including kitchen utensils, two cows, one hog, six sheep, and an ox, had a total value of $48.43. He owed $745 to eight creditors, including "about $400" due Benjamin Mooers, probably for his mortgage. His family consisted of his wife Mary, 32, and his children Julia, 11, Joseph, 9, Mary, 6, Rose, 2, and Edward, 18 months.

He remained in Chazy until his death and was buried there in the Ingraham Cemetery. His will, dated 12 Nov 1853 and probated in the Clinton Co. Surrogate's Court on 16 Jan 1854, directed that his wife Mary receive one third of his personal and real property as well as all arrears due him on his veteran's pension. The remainder would be divided equally between his children Julia Luck, Joseph Monty, Mary Savage, Rosalie Monty, Edward Monty, Lafayette Monty, Laura Trombley, Dewitt C. Monty, Loisa Savage, Moses Monty, William Monty, Lucy Ann Clough, and Wellington Monty. The real estate, which consisted of about 100 acres in Chazy, in lot #1 of the Point au Roche Patent, did in fact remain in the family well into the 20th century.

Marie Defayette (also Fayette, Lafayette) was 32 years old in 1820, according to her husband's affidavit on 3 October of that year. Later documents place her birth between 1788 and 1792. The earliest record may be the most reliable, although any date between 1788 and 1792 is possible.

On 10 Jun 1854 Mrs. Mary Monty applied from Chazy for a widow's pension, based on her husband's service in the American Revolution. This was granted on 25 Mar 1854 at the rate of $96 per year with arrears to 20 Nov 1753, the date of Joseph Monty's death (certificate # 3909). The following year, on 24 Mar 1855, she again petitioned "for the purpose of obtaining the Bounty Land to which she was entitled under the act approved March 3^d 1855." She then received 60 acres of land under Warrant #172. She was still a farmer in Chazy in 1860, at the age of 72, but does not appear in later censuses. She may have died before 1870.

Children:

4.8.1	Julia	1809?-	&1850-1912
4.8.2	Joseph	1810-	-1890
4.8.3	Mary	1814-1845-1901	
4.8.4	Rosalie/Rosella	1816-1845?-1901	
4.8.5	Edward	1817-1846-1904	
4.8.6	Lafayette	1822-	-1906
4.8.7	Laura	1823?-1849?-	
4.8.8	DeWitt Clinton (twin)	1827-	&1883-1898
4.8.9	Louisa (twin)	1827-	-1912
4.8.10	Moses	1830-1861?-1918	
4.8.11	William	1832?-	-
4.8.12	Lucy Ann	1834?-1853?-	
4.8.13	Wellington	1836?-	-1906

4.9 **MONTY, Catherine** b & bp 31 Jul & 6 Aug 1769, Chambly, QC; d 9 Apr 1840, Chazy, NY. She married there in the fall of 1790 and again in a Catholic ceremony on 12 May 1791, St. Hyacinthe, QC, **Clément Gosselin** (Gabriel Gosselin & Geneviève Crépeau) b & bp 12 Jun 1747, Ile d'Orléans, QC; m (1) 22 Jan 1770, Ste Anne de la Pocatière, QC, Marie Dionne (Germain Dionne & Louise Bernier); m (2) 15 Jan 1787, Longueuil, QC, Charlotte Ouimet (Ignace Ouimet & Amable Prairie); d 9 Mar 1816, Beekmantown, NY.

Catherine Monty came to the United States with her parents as a young child in 1776 and settled with them after the Revolutionary War on Lake Champlain in the area which later became Chazy, NY. She and her husband moved to Canada soon after their marriage and lived there for some twenty-five years before returning to Clinton County, NY, in 1815, shortly before his death. As the widow of a Revolutionary War veteran, she received a widow's pension (certificate #16655) which was transferred after her own death to her sole surviving child, Marie Geneviève/Jane Gosselin (xii), wife of Lewis Monty (4.3.1.1). She was living with that couple in Chazy in 1830 (US census).

The following summary of Clément Gosselin's life is based in large part on Ernest L. Monty's article on "Major Clément Gosselin" in the *French Canadian and Acadian Genealogical Review*, I, 27-44. Additional information concerning the Gosselin-Monty marriage can be found in the Pliny Moore papers cited in Nell Jane Barnett Sullivan and David Kendall Martin's *A History of the Town of Chazy, Clinton County., NY*, pp. 39sq.

Clément Gosselin was a farmer in Ste Anne de la Pocatière, QC, at the time of the American invasion of Canada in 1775. He immediately espoused the American cause, preaching rebellion and recruiting men for the invading army. He enlisted in Gen. Montgomery's army in Quebec in December 1775, participated in the attack on Quebec on 31 Dec 1775, and was promoted to Captain on 4 Mar 1776 in Col. Moses Hazen's Second Canadian regiment, in which rank he served until the end of the war. When the American forces retreated from Quebec in the spring of 1776, Clément Gosselin remained in the vicinity of Ste Anne de la Pocatière, still harassing the British and promoting the American cause, for which activities he was imprisoned in Quebec at the end of 1777. His imprisonment lasted no more than a few months: by March 1778 he had rejoined his regiment in White Plains, NY. He returned to Canada later that year and also in 1780 on several missions as an agent and courier. He was wounded at Yorktown on 4 Oct 1781 but remained in his command until June 1783 when he was brevetted a Major and mustered out of the army. Along with his brother Louis Gosselin, his father-in-law Germain Dionne, and his future father-in-law François/Francis Monty, he was a charter member of the Society of the Cincinnati.

Clément Gosselin first settled after the war on the shores of Lake Champlain in upper New York State where, in September 1784, the Gosslin (sic) family consisted of man, wife, and three children. His first wife died soon thereafter. He remarried in Longueuil, QC, on 15 Jan 1787 but continued to live on Lake Champlain: his family in August 1787 again consisted of five members (John Andrew Bilow, "Census of Canadian Refugees in New York State, 1784, 1785, 1787," *French Canadian and Acadian Genealogical Review*, XI, 242, 252). In the balloting of 10 Sep 1787, he was allotted 1,000 acres of bounty land (lots 27 and 50 of 80 acres each and lots 16 and 29 of 420 acres each) in the Refugee Patent, somewhat inland from the lake. He did not live there: on 7 Nov 1788 he gave Pliny Moore a power of attorney to sell this land (it was sold to Jacques Rouse on 30 May 1789 for 50 pounds, New York currency) and to purchase lot #3 in the Wheeler Douglass Patent, just north of Chazy Landing where he was already residing. There he built a barn, kept cows, and grew crops. On 7 Mar 1788, he became the first Major of the state militia for Clinton County and, on 28 October of that year, was made foreman of the grand jury in Plattsburgh, NY. A few years later, when he received on 22 Jan 1790 another 300 acres of bounty land in the Ohio Valley from the federal government (Warrant # 885), he again sold the land. It appears that he was even then planning to leave the Lake Champlain area for his near neighbor Murdoch McPherson, a former Lieutenant in Col. Hazen's regiment, had already written to Judge Pliny Moore on 20 Dec 1789 that "when he [Major Gosselin] will leave the place shall move there myself" (Sullivan and Martin, p. 48).

In the meantime Clément Gosselin's second wife had died in Longueuil, QC, on 9 Nov 1789, shortly after the birth of the couple's second child. He remained on Lake Champlain and married his third wife, Catherine Monty, in the early fall of 1790 before Justice of the Peace Murdoch McPherson.

Most genealogists claim that this marriage took place on 8 Nov 1790, although no record of it is extant to my knowledge. I believe however that it must have taken place at least one month earlier for on 8 Oct 1790 the resident Catholic priest on Lake Champlain, Father Pierre Huet de la Valinière, was already complaining to Judge Moore about perceived irregularities and asking "Whether it belong to one judge to mary [sic] secretly and in the night the members of one congregation of which the Minister is not absent." The judge's reply, dated 6 Nov 1790, refers to Clément Gosselin's marriage in the past tense: it was an accomplished fact and completely legal under the laws of the state of New York. Nevertheless he tried to soothe the irate priest by explaining that the Major was "under a Necessity to go into Canada sooner than the rights [rites] of your Church would allow for this Marriage." Father Huet was not appeased and, in a letter of 21 Nov 1790, accused the "impious Clement Gosselin" of having deceived Murdoch McPherson and dishonored "two families viz. the family of Gosselin and that of Mr. Demoty [sic], for now no honest person will have any acquaintance with them, nor keep any conversation with any of the both maried persons, they not being maried at all, wherefore their life is but a public concubinage according to our laws" (Sullivan and Martin, pp. 40-41).

I do not know if the situation as described by Father Huet is quite accurate. By all accounts he was a quarrelsome person, a trouble-maker wherever he went. All the children of François/Francis Monty for whom marriage records exist were married by Justices of the Peace rather than by Catholic priests. There is no evidence of ostracism in their cases. On the other hand, if Clément Gosselin and his wife were still in New York State in late November 1790, two months after claiming the need for immediate departure, another reason suggests itself for an early marriage: their first child was born on 15 May 1791.

At all events Clément Gosselin and Catherine Monty were in Canada by the early spring of 1791 (the dispensation of the banns given by the Vicar General is dated 15 Apr 1791) and were married anew on 12 May 1791 in Notre Dame church in St. Hyacinthe, QC. He was a carpenter there until around 1802 when the family moved to St. Luc, QC. There he bought land, worked as both carpenter and black-smith, and was also the parish cantor from 1802 to 1814. He then sold his land on 13 Mar 1815 and returned to the New York State where he died a few months later.

Clément Gosselin and Catherine Monty (or rather Mounty, as she was usually named in Canadian records) had at least fifteen children though only one, Marie Geneviève (xii), lived beyond infancy. There may have been a few more children: given the couple's history, I am suspicious of the four-year gap in births between 1806 and 1810.

Children:

i   **Clément Gosselin** b & bp 15 & 16 May 1791, St. Hyacinthe, QC; d & bur there 5 & 8 Jun 1791.

ii   **Anonymous Gosselin** b 10 Mar 1792, St. Hyacinthe, QC; d & bur there 10 Mar 1792.

iii   **Anonymous Gosselin** b 12 Dec 1792, St. Hyacinthe, QC; d & bur there 12 & 13 Dec 1792.

iv   **Anonymous Gosselin** b 12 Dec 1793, St. Hyacinthe, QC; d & bur there 12 Dec 1793.

v   **Catherine Apolline Gosselin** b & bp 17 & 18 Sep 1794, St. Hyacinthe, QC; d & bur there 18 & 19 Sep 1794.

vi   **Catherine Apolline Gosselin** b & bp 26 & 27 Jun 1795, St. Hyacinthe, QC; d & bur there 8 & 10 Aug 1795.

vii   **Anonymous Gosselin** b 16 Apr 1796, St. Hyacinthe, QC; d & bur there 16 Apr 1796.

viii   **Ferdinand Gosselin** b & bp 31 Jul 1798, St. Jean-Baptiste, QC; d & bur there 16 & 18 Aug 1798.

ix   **Pierre Jacques Gosselin** b & bp 29 Jul 1799, St. Hyacinthe, QC; d & bur there 14 & 15 Aug 1799.

x   **Jean-Baptiste Gosselin** b & bp 22 & 23 Jul 1802, St. Luc, QC; d & bur 28 & 30 Jul 1802, St. Luc & L'Acadie, QC.

xi   **Marguerite Apolline Gosselin** b & bp 10 Oct 1803, St. Luc, QC; d & bur there 13 & 14 Oct 1803.

xii   **Marie Geneviève/Jane Gosselin** b & bp 19 & 20 Sep 1804, St. Luc, QC; d 28 Feb 1891, Chazy, NY. She married **Lewis Monty** (4.3.1.1).

xiii   **Jean-Baptiste Gosselin** b & bp 8 Oct 1806, St. Luc, QC; d & bur there 8 & 9 Oct 1806.

xiv   **Marie Gosselin** b & bp 20 Jun 1810, St. Luc, QC; d & bur there 20 & 21 Jun 1810.

xv   **Michel Gosselin** b & bp 14 Oct 1811, St. Luc, QC; d & bur there 14 & 16 Oct 1811.

4.10   **MONTY, Placide** b & bp 8 Oct 1770, Chambly, QC; d 15 Feb 1847, Burlington, VT. He married 25 Dec 1807, Chazy, NY, **Susan Labare/Suzanne Lebert** (Jacques Lebert & Marie Anne Audet dit Lapointe) b & bp 1 Jan 1786, L'Acadie, QC; d & bur 1 & 3 Oct 1854, Addison, VT & Plattsburgh, NY.

Placide Monty was less than six years old when he followed his family to the United States in the spring of 1776. In spite of his widow's statement of 18 Apr 1853 before the Addison Co. Probate Court in Vergennes, VT, that he "was a private in Capt Francis Montys Co. Col Hazens Regiment and served as such from the commencement to the close of the Revolutionary war," a claim often repeated, his army records and his own affidavit of 3 Oct 1820 before the Clinton Co. Court of Common Pleas in Plattsburgh, NY, clearly indicate that he enlisted in the spring of 1780 in Fishkill, NY, as a musician in Capt. Lawrence Olivie's company, Col. Moses Hazen's Second Canadian regiment, and remained in the army until his discharge in June 1783 in New Windsor, NY. Even then, he would have been rather young at his enlistment and probably served as a drummer boy or a fifer. Note also that François/Francis Monty's daughter-in-law also promoted him to a captaincy he never held. He was a Lieutenant when he was discharged in January 1881, a few months after his son's enrollment.

Soon after his discharge from the army, Placide Monty established residence on Lake Champlain. He was there in August 1784 (John Andrew Bilow, "Census of Canadian Refugees in New York State, 1784, 1785, 1787," *French Canadian and Acadian Genealogical Re-*

view, IX, 242) and was listed among those entitled to receive bounty land from the state of New York in the balloting of 10 Sep 1787. He received on 11 Jan 1790 a Bounty Land Warrant (#13434) for 100 acres, which he assigned to Benjamin Mooers on 22 Jan 1790 for $325.

Placide Monty does not appear in any US census prior to his marriage. He may have been counted in 1790 and 1800 as a member of his father's household. He was a resident of Chazy, NY, in 1810 (US census), in April 1818 when he applied for a pension as a veteran of the Revolutionary war, and in October 1820 when he filed an affidavit in support of his claim before the Clinton Co. Court of Common Pleas in Plattsburgh, NY. A pension of $8 per month, retroactive to 6 Apr 1818, was granted on 23 Jul 1819 (certificate #13169).

In his deposition of 3 Oct 1820, he declared that he was a farmer in Chazy and that he had bought two months previously 54½ acres of land in the Point au Roche Patent in Clinton Co. for $6 per acre. The purchase price was covered by a mortgage. His personal property, excluding clothing and bedding, had a total value of $34. It included, besides a cow worth $18, his most valuable personal asset, "one Potash Kettle with a hole in it," "five Pail Kettle," one "Tea Kettle and small pot," a "Little Bake pan," "six small plates, 1 tea pot, 4 cups and saucers," "two spoons and 6 knives and forks," "one old Table made of a piece of split pine," and "one Pail and one Wash tub made of the end of a Bucket." His family consisted of his wife Susan, 32, and his children Placid, 10, Susan, 8, Emelia, 6, Betsey, 5, and Francis, 16 months. We can deduce that his daughter Louise, born in 1810, was then deceased and that Dominique and Mary, named in the 1856 affidavit (Appendix I) of their cousin John Monty Jr. (4.11.1), were born after October 1820.

Placide Monty remained in Clinton County for most of his life. In Chazy he was not only a farmer but a producer of potash, an important cash by-product of felling trees to clear the land (Nell Jane Barnett Sullivan and David Kendall Martin, *A History of the Town of Chazy, Clinton County, NY*, p. 108). He was in Beekmantown, NY, in 1830 and in Plattsburgh, NY, in 1840. Several real estate transactions are recorded in the Clinton Co. Register of Deeds in 1830, 1840, and 1841. He was still a resident of Plattsburgh in 1845 but apparently soon moved to Vermont where he died two years later, according to his widow's deposition of 7 Apr 1853 in the Addison Co., VT, Probate's Court. No trace of his burial has been found.

His wife's maiden name is generally Susan Labare in the United States but Suzanne Lebert at her baptism, at the baptism of her daughter Louise in Canada, and in the French record of her burial in Plattsburgh. After her husband's death she lived for a few years in Addison, VT, in the household of her daughter Elizabeth and son-in-law Francis Lashway. It is from Vergennes, VT, that she applied in April 1853 for a widow's pension on the basis of her husband's service during the American Revolution. Her brother-in-law John Monty (4.11) confirmed her statements in an affidavit of 3 May 1853 submitted to Thomas B. Watson, Judge of Clinton Co., who declared the evidence satisfactory on 14 May 1853. Certificate #1185 was then issued on 6 Aug 1853 for a widow's pension at the rate of $96 per year, retroactive to 3 Feb 1853. Susan Labare died the following year in Vermont but was buried in the cemetery of St. Peter's Catholic Church in Plattsburgh under the name of Suzanne (Lebert) Monty.

Children:

4.10.1	Placide	1809?-	-
4.10.2	Louise	1810-	-
4.10.3	Susan	1812?-	-
4.10.4	Amelia/Emelia	1814?-	-1899
4.10.5	Elizabeth/Betsey	1815?-1835?-1887	
4.10.6	Francis/Frank	1819-	-1896
4.10.7	Dominique	-	-
4.10.8	Mary	-	-

4.11   **MONTY, John** b between 1771 and 1774, QC; d & bur Mar 1861, Beekmantown & Chazy, NY. He married **Sarah Clark** b around 1793; d & bur Feb 1858, Beekmantown & Chazy, NY, at the age of 65.

There are several problems associated with John Monty's place and date of birth. He was said to have been born in Canada though there is no record there of his birth. Some American records indicate that he was born around 1771 while others show that he was born around 1774. Both dates present difficulties.

The 1771 date of birth can be found in some of the earliest documents: John Monty's depositions before the Court of Common Pleas in Plattsburgh, NY, on 4 Apr 1818 when he was 47 years old and on 3 Oct 1820 when he was 49 years old. Another deposition of 9 Sep 1856 shows that he was then 84 years old (War Department Records). He would thus have been born around 1771 or 1772. The difficulty here is that his brother Placide (4.10) was born on 8 Oct 1770 and his sister Cunégonde (4.12) on 11 Feb 1772. This hardly leaves time for a birth in 1771 unless either John or his sister, or both, were born prematurely. He could also be a twin whose birth went unrecorded. Neither solution is very convincing.

The 1774 date of birth is based principally on the inscription on his tombstone in the Ingraham Cemetery in Chazy, NY: "John MONTY / Died Mar 1861 /AE 87 Ys / Sarah / His Wife / Died Feb 1858 / AE 65 Ys." This is consistent with the 1840 Pensioners' census in Beekmantown, NY, when he was 66 years old, the 1850 census there, when he was 76 years old, and a deposition of 2 Mar 1854 in Plattsburgh before Justice of the Peace Isaac Aldridge when the 80-year-old John Monty supported the claim to a Revolutionary War pension of his brother Joseph's (4.8) widow (War Department Records). The difficulty here is that if John Monty was indeed born around 1774, he was extraordinarily young to enlist in the Continental army in the spring of 1780, which appears to be undeniable (see below). His date of birth then is still open to question.

Another problem arises from the fact that a John Monty, son of "Francis and Josephine (Berjevin) [sic] Monty" was baptized "conditionally" near Fishkill, NY, on 5 Oct 1781 by Father Ferdinand Farmer (Barbara B. O'Keefe, "List of Baptisms Registered in St. Joseph's Church, Philadelphia, from January 1, 1776 to October 21, 1781," *Records of the American Catholic Historical Society*, II, 274). Unfortunately Father Palmer did not provide either the age or the date of birth of the child. I find it difficult to accept, though, that a child would be given in 1781 the same name as an older brother who was still alive. I have come to believe that the son baptized in 1781 was indeed the John Monty who had been born in Canada between 1771 and 1774 and lived to 1861. Yet I wonder why, if born in Canada, he was not baptized in a Catholic church there as were most of his siblings through 1775.

For the rest, my major sources of information include John Monty's army records, his 1818 and 1820 applications for a veteran's pension along with supporting affidavits, a few other depositions where he testified on his siblings' behalf, his 1856 application for additional bounty land, US censuses from 1800 through 1850 as well as the testimony of his niece Mrs. Barbary (Monty) Morrison (4.4.5) in 1856 (Appendix I).

According to his affidavit of 4 Apr 1818 in the Clinton Co. Court of Common Pleas, John Monty enlisted as a private in the Revolutionary Army in the spring of 1780 in Fishkill, served as a musician (drummer boy or fifer?) in Capt. Lawrence Olivie's company, Col. Moses Hazen's Second Canadian regiment, until the end of the war, and was discharged in New Windsor, NY, in June 1783. He soon joined his parents on Lake Champlain for he appears in the September 1784 census of Canadians living in the area. He is not however on the August 1787 list, though he may then have been included in his father's seven-member household (John Andrew Bilow, "Census of Canadian Refugees in New York State, 1784, 1785, 1787," *French Canadian and Acadian Genealogical Review*, IX, 242, 253). Nor is he mentioned as a head of household in the 1790 US census.

Yet he was present on Lake Champlain during this time and was granted by the state of New York, at the balloting of 10 Sep 1787, 500 acres of bounty land in the Refugee Patent on Lake Champlain (lot 80 of 80 acres and lot 480 of 420 acres). Under the Congressional Land Ordinance of 1785, he also received in January 1790 an additional 100 acres in the same area.

He was a resident of Champlain, NY, in 1800 and of Chazy in 1810 and 1820 (US censuses). An Act of Congress of 18 Mar 1818 entitled him to a pension, for which he applied on 4 Apr 1818. Certificate #12257 was then issued on 15 Jul 1819, allowing him a pension of $8 per month payable semi-annually, with arrears to 4 Apr 1818.

In connection with this pension application, need had to be established. This was done on 3 Oct 1820 in a deposition before the Clinton Co. Court of Common Pleas where he declared that "I am by occupation a farmer & have a wife Sarah Monty and six children the oldest twelve years, who all live with me and are dependant upon me for support — the names and ages of my children are as follows John Monty Junr aged twelve years is a weakly child. Amanda Monty aged ten years. Joseph Monty aged nine years. Lewis Monty aged six years. Hannah Monty aged four years. Sarah Monty aged about seven months. All tolerably healthy."

He had few assets to support his family. His only real estate consisted of 52½ acres in lot #1 in the Point au Roche Patent which he had bought the previous year for $6 per acre, with a mortgage covering the entire cost of purchase. His personal assets, including one cow ($15) and one small hog ($1.50), were valued at $34.07 while his debts to nine different individuals totaled $125.35. A month later the schedule was revised: a $60 pair of oxen was added to the assets, but the debts now came to $153.37.

The land acquired in 1819 was sold in 1830. John Monty was then living in Beekmantown, NY, where he remained until his death. In 1850, the last year in which he appears in a US census, his land holdings were valued at $150. His household included not only his wife Sarah and son Nico (Nicholas) but also his son Joseph (whose own land was valued at $1,600) and family of six. It is probable that while John Monty was still the titular head of the household the actual reins of ownership had passed on to his son Joseph.

On 9 Sep 1856 John Monty applied for additional bounty land under the Act of Congress of 3 Mar 1855, as amended on 14 May 1856. He again reviewed his army career but changed the date and place of his enlistment. Some seventy years after the fact he claimed that "his father Lieut. Monty enlisted him when a youth in Albany on or about the (not recollected) day of (not recollected) AD. 1776." The year and place of his enrollment is clearly wrong. He nevertheless received 60 acres of land on his claim #257.157.

That is the last document I have seen pertaining directly to John Monty. Although I have not found him in the 1860 US census, I have no real cause to doubt the date of death inscribed on his tombstone in the Ingraham Cemetery in Chazy.

I have been unable to find Sarah Clark's family. I do not doubt her date of death as inscribed on her tombstone and, for lack of any other concrete evidence, assume that her age at death is approximately correct: she was 55 years old in 1850 (US census). She was in any event much younger than her husband, by 10 to 20 years according to the 1810-1840 censuses and by nineteen years in 1850. She was born in New York State according to this last census. Her children, however, indicated in later censuses that she was born in New York, Vermont, Massachusetts, or Connecticut. None of this is very satisfactory.

Children:

4.11.1	John Jr.	1808- -1880
4.11.2	Amanda	1810?- -
4.11.3	Joseph	1811?- -1892
4.11.4	Louis/Lewis	1815-1838-1910
4.11.5	Hannah E.	1816?-1838?-
4.11.6	Sarah	1820-1843?&1875-1903
4.11.7	Nicholas	1834-1860?-1916

4.12   **MONTY, Cunégonde** b & bp 11 & 12 Feb 1772, Chambly, QC; d & bur there 26 & 27 Aug 1772.

4.13   **MONTY, Pierre** b & bp 8 Aug 1773, Chambly, QC.
     No further trace of this child has been found. He is not mentioned among his father's descendants by either Mrs. Barbary (Monty) Morrison (4.4.5) or John Monty Jr. (4.11.1) in their depositions of October and November 1856 (Appendix I). He may have died in infancy.

4.14   **MONTY, Charlotte Michel** (sic) b & bp 27 Oct 1775, Chambly, QC.
     No further trace of this child has been found. She is not mentioned among her father's descendants by either Mrs. Barbary (Monty) Morrison (4.4.5) or John Monty Jr. (4.11.1) in

their depositions of October and November 1856 (Appendix I). She may have died in infancy.

4.15   **MONTY, Louisa/Lizzy?** bp 5 Oct 1781, near Fishkill, NY.

Louisa Monty's baptismal record is found in the Registers of St. Joseph's Catholic church in Philadelphia, PA, in which it is noted that Father Ferdinand Farmer baptized "conditionally" on 5 Oct 1781, near Fishkill, NY, a number of soldiers' children among whom John Monty (probably 4.11) and Louisa Monty, daughter of "Francis and Josephine (Berjevin) [sic] Monty" (Barbara B. O'Keefe, "List of Baptisms Registered in St. Joseph's Church, Philadelphia, from January 1, 1776 to October 21, 1781," *Records of the American Catholic Historical Society*, II, 274). Unfortunately Father Farmer failed to mention either the age or date of birth of the child.

There may be a later reference to this daughter of François/Francis Monty in the 1856 deposition of John Monty Jr. (4.11.1) before the Clinton Co. Court of Common Pleas in Plattsburgh, NY (Appendix I). He mentions a "Lizzy Monty dead daughter of Lt. Monty." Her name appears at the end of the text, inserted above the line, almost as an afterthought, as if John Monty Jr. had remembered her existence only with difficulty. In any event, since neither husband nor children are mentioned, the implication is that she did not marry. The nickname Lizzy might well stand for Louisa. I know of no other daughter whose name it could represent.

5.1   **MONTY, Marie Thérèse** b & bp 2 Mar 1761, Chambly, QC; d & bur there 15 & 17 May 1770.

5.2   **MONTY, Louise** b & bp 12 & 15 Sep 1762, Chambly, QC; d & bur 28 & 29 Mar 1813, St. Mathias, QC. She married there 24 Apr 1780 **Louis Barré** (Jean-Baptiste Barré & Agathe Larocque) b & bp 11 Jan 1757, Chambly, QC; m (2) 9 Sep 1828, St. Mathias, QC, Louise Guillon/Guyon (Antoine Guillon & Marie Louise Dubé), widow of François Demers dit Chedeville; m (3) 19 Sep 1836, St. Césaire, QC, Josette Tétreau (Louis Tétreau & Magdeleine Leduc), widow of Jean-Baptiste Auclair; d & bur 29 & 30 Sep 1839, St. Mathias, QC.

Louis Barré was a farmer in St. Mathias, QC. He was a brother of Elisabeth Barré, wife of Louis Monty (5.7), of Jean-Baptiste Barré, husband of Marie Elisabeth Monty (5.3), and of Marie Barré, wife of Charles Binet/Vinet (6.iii), all of whom lived in the same locality. This has led to errors at times in the baptismal records of St. Mathias where an in-law's name was substituted for the real parent's. Subsequent death or marriage records generally clarify the situation.

Children:
- i   **Louis Barré** b & bp 1 & 2 Dec 1781, St. Mathias, QC; d & bur 15 & 18 Feb 1845, St. Jean-Baptiste, QC. He married (1) there 16 Nov 1812 **Marie Louise Leclair** (Jean Leclair & Josephte Dansereau) b & bp 20 & 21 Jul 1789, Verchères, QC; d & bur 3 & 5 Jul 1824, St. Jean-Baptiste, QC.

  He married (2) 9 Aug 1825 St. Jean-Baptiste, QC, **Marguerite Jourdain** (Alexis Jourdain & Madeleine Lussier) b & bp there 20 Jan 1803; m (2) there 17 Feb 1846 Hilaire Dalpé dit Pariseau (Michel Dalpé dit Pariseau & Louise Danserault); d & bur 21 & 25 Oct 1873, St. Jean-Baptiste, QC.
- ii   **Marie Amable Barré** b & bp 1 Mar 1783, St. Mathias, QC. She married there 26 Jul 1813 **Louis Robert Desforges** (Louis Robert Desforges & Marie Martiale Donat) b & bp there 13 & 14 Sep 1788.
- iii   **Louise Barré** b & bp 27 & 28 Apr 1785, St. Mathias, QC; d & bur there 6 & 9 Dec 1862. She married 25 Oct 1819, Marieville, QC, **Louis Barrière** (René Barrière dit Langevin & Agathe Laporte) b & bp 9 & 10 Jun 1768, Chambly, QC; m (1) 13 Feb 1792, St. Mathias, QC, Marguerite Daigneau (Joseph Daigneau & Marie Anne Benoit); d & bur there 4 & 6 May 1852.
- iv   **Jean-Baptiste Barré** b & bp 22 & 23 Jul 1787, St. Mathias, QC. He married there 1 Jul 1811 **Marie Françoise Ostiguy** (Jean-Marie Ostiguy & Charlotte Massé) b &

bp 30 Sep & 1 Oct 1793, Chambly, QC.

v   **Charlotte Barré** b & bp 8 & 9 Aug 1789, St. Mathias, QC; d & bur 24 & 26 Sep 1868, Marieville, QC. She married 11 Aug 1806, St. Mathias, QC, **Antoine Benoit** (Joseph Benoit & Josephte Gauthier dit St. Germain) bp 21 Dec 1781, Chambly, QC; d & bur 27 & 29 Nov 1859, Marieville, QC.

vi   **Jean Pascal Barré** b & bp 8 Apr 1792, St. Mathias, QC; d & bur 22 & 24 May 1871, Richelieu, QC. He married 4 Apr 1837, Chambly, QC, **Charlotte Dussault** (Joseph Dussault & Elisabeth Ouimet) b & bp 26 & 28 Feb 1795, Beloeil, QC; d & bur 12 & 15 Jul 1867, Marieville, QC.

vii   **Charles Barré** b & bp 21 Aug 1794, St. Mathias, QC. He married there 11 Feb 1822 **Angèle Lasnier** (François Xavier Lasnier & Marie Amable Benjamin) b & bp there 5 & 6 Apr 1804.

viii   **Marguerite Barré** b & bp 9 May 1797, St. Mathias, QC. She married there 22 Jan 1821 **Louis Frégeau** (Jean-Baptiste Frégeau & Josette Lague) b & bp 26 & 27 Jan 1793, St. François de la Rivière du Sud, QC.

ix   **Marie Adélaïde Barré** b & bp 14 & 15 Jun 1799, St. Mathias, QC; d & bur 8 & 10 Jan 1876, St. Césaire, QC. She married 14 Feb 1820, St. Mathias, QC, **Pierre Barrière** (Louis Barrière & Marguerite Daigneau) b & bp there 8 Dec 1795.

x   **Pierre Barré** b & bp 25 Jun 1802, St. Mathias, QC. He married there 24 Jan 1826 **Marguerite Josephte Barrière** (Louis Barrière & Marguerite Daigneau).

xi   **David Barré** b & bp 16 & 17 Apr 1806, St. Mathias, QC; d & bur 25 & 27 Jun 1855, St. Césaire, QC. He married 22 Apr 1828, St. Mathias, QC, **Louise Rocheleau** (Pierre Rocheleau & Charlotte Patenaude) b & bp there 2 Mar 1810; d & bur 13 & 14 Apr 1891, Rougemont, QC.

5.3   **MONTY, Marie Elisabeth/Isabelle** bp 20 Aug 1764, Chambly, QC; d & bur 1 & 3 Dec 1841, St. Mathias, QC. She married there 8 Jan 1787 **Jean-Baptiste Barré** (Jean-Baptiste Barré & Agathe Larocque) b & bp 11 & 12 Apr 1761, Chambly, QC; d & bur 16 & 18 Jan 1842, St. Mathias, QC.

Jean-Baptiste (also Jean) Barré was a farmer in St. Mathias, QC. He was a brother of Elisabeth Barré, wife of Louis Monty (5.7), of Louis Barré, husband of Louise Monty (5.2), and of Marie Barré, wife of Charles Binet/Vinet (6.iii), all of whom lived in the same locality. This has led to errors at times in the baptismal records of St. Mathias where an in-law's name was substituted for the real parent's. Subsequent death or marriage records generally clarify the situation.

Children:

i   **Elisabeth Barré** b & bp 20 Nov 1787, St. Mathias, QC.

ii   **Marie Barré** b 1788?; d & bur 7 & 8 Jan 1805, St. Mathias, QC, at the age of 16.

iii   **Marie Desanges Barré** b & bp 8 Aug 1789, St. Mathias, QC; d & bur there 11 & 12 Feb 1791.

iv   **Jean-Baptiste Barré** b & bp 23 & 24 Feb 1792, St. Mathias, QC; d & bur 11 & 14 May 1877, Richelieu & Marieville, QC. He married 17 Feb 1824, Chambly, QC, **Catherine Harbec/Harbeck** (Joseph Harbec & Marie Anne Fréchette) b & bp there 25 & 26 Nov 1803.

v   **Joseph Barré** b & bp 25 & 26 Nov 1793, St. Mathias, QC; d & bur 29 Apr & 1 May 1835, St. Jean, QC. He married 24 Jun 1828, Napierville, QC, **Lucie Laroche** (Noël Laroche & Louise Gosselin).

vi   **Elisabeth Barré** b & bp 4 & 5 Sep 1795, St. Mathias, QC; d & bur 19 & 22 Mar 1879, St. Jean, QC. She married 8 Feb 1825, St. Mathias, QC, **Antoine Foisy** (Antoine Foisy & Charlotte Blanchard) b & bp 23 & 24 Feb 1797, Beloeil, QC.

vii   **Marie Desanges/Marie Angélique Barré** b & bp 23 & 24 Aug 1797, St. Mathias, QC; d & bur there 2 & 3 May 1798.

viii   **Pierre Barré** b & bp 27 & 28 Apr 1799, St. Mathias, QC.

ix   **David Barré** b 1800?; d & bur 12 & 13 Feb 1804, St. Mathias, QC, at the age of 4.

x   **Augustin Barré** b & bp 27 & 28 Aug 1801, St. Mathias, QC; d 14 Nov 1858,

Marieville, QC; bur there (French Baptist Cemetery) 16 Nov 1858. He married 15 Nov 1830, St. Jean-Baptiste, QC, **Angélique Vadnais** (Emmanuel Vadnais & Angélique Pratte) b & bp there 20 Oct 1809; d & bur 14 & 16 Mar 1861, Marieville, QC.

xi   **David Joseph Barré** b & bp 14 Jul 1805, St. Mathias, QC; d & bur 3 & 5 Jul 1853, Marieville, QC. He married there 25 Oct 1831 **Emérentienne/Mérentienne Careau** (Pierre Careau & Marie Victoire Tétreau) b & bp there 14 & 15 Mar 1812; m (2) there 24 Feb 1857 François Vigeant (Jean-Baptiste Vigeant & Judith Massé); d & bur there 19 & 22 Apr 1878.

5.4   **MONTY, Marie Anne** b & bp 4 Apr 1766, Chambly, QC; d & bur there 2 & 5 Jun 1770.

5.5   **MONTY, Pierre Honoré** b & bp 26 Jun 1767, Chambly, QC.

5.6   **MONTY, Félicité** b & bp 15 & 16 Jul 1769, Chambly, QC; d & bur there 23 & 29 Sep 1770.

5.7   **MONTY, Louis** b & bp 15 & 16 Jun 1771, Chambly, QC; d & bur 2 & 5 Oct 1833, Marieville & Chambly, QC. He married 4 Oct 1790, St. Mathias, QC, **Elisabeth Barré** (Jean-Baptiste Barré & Agathe Larocque) b 1768?; d & bur 12 & 14 Mar 1845, St. Mathias, QC, at the age of 77.

Louis Monty was a farmer in St. Mathias, QC. He drowned in the Richelieu River. His wife was a sister of Louis Barré, husband of Louise Monty (5.2), of Jean-Baptiste Barré, husband of Marie Elisabeth Monty (5.3), and of Marie Barré, wife of his cousin Charles Binet/Vinet (6.iii).

Children:

5.7.1	Louis	1791-1811-1867
5.7.2	Thomas	1792-1812&1829-1866
5.7.3	Anonymous	1794- -1794
5.7.4	Joseph	1796-1816-1830
5.7.5	Alexis	1798-1825-1868
5.7.6	Angélique	1800- -1801
5.7.7	Jacques	1801-1823-1855
5.7.8	Anonymous	1803- -1803
5.7.9	Marie Josephte	1803- -1804
5.7.10.	Isaac	1805-1832-1874
5.7.11	Angélique	1807-1829-1843

5.8   **MONTY, Joseph** b & bp 29 Apr 1773, Pointe Olivier (St. Mathias) and Chambly, QC; d & bur 10 & 11 Jul 1776, Pointe Olivier (St. Mathias) and Chambly, QC.

5.9   **MONTY, Marie** b & bp 27 Nov 1774, Chambly, QC; d & bur 29 Feb & 2 Mar 1860, Marieville, QC. She married (1) 29 Jul 1793, St. Mathias, QC, **Pierre Gervais** (Gabriel Gervais & Marie Amable Babeu) b & bp 8 & 9 May 1763, Laprairie, QC; d & bur 26 & 28 Feb 1820, St. Mathias, QC.

She married (2) 27 Jul 1824, St. Mathias, QC, **Antoine Mauray** (Antoine Mauray & Rose/Rosalie Hébert) b & bp 4 & 7 Nov 1773, Chambly, QC; m (1) 17 Oct 1803, St. Mathias, QC, Louise/Euphrosine Alain (Charles Alain & Magdeleine Bissonet).

Pierre Gervais was a farmer in St. Mathias, QC.

Antoine Mauray (also Morais, Maurais, Mauret) was a laborer in St. Mathias at his marriage to Marie Monty and a resident of Marieville, QC, at her death.

Children:

i   **Pierre Gervais** b & bp 1 & 2 May 1794, St. Mathias, QC. He married there

25 Nov 1822 **Marie** ____.

ii **Marie Sophie Gervais** b & bp 16 Dec 1795, St. Mathias, QC. She married there 27 Nov 1815 **Joseph Fortier** (Noël Fortier & Geneviève Barré) b & bp 2 Dec 1795, St. Mathias, QC.

iii **Joseph Gervais** b & bp 8 & 11 Mar 1797, St. Mathias, QC. He married 8 Sep 1829, Marieville, QC, **Emilie Messier** (Jean-Baptiste Messier & Louise Ledoux) b & bp there 23 & 24 Jun 1812.

iv **Jean-Baptiste Gervais** b & bp 21 & 22 Jul 1798, St. Mathias, QC; d & bur there 16 & 17 Feb 1799.

v **Louis Gervais** b & bp 30 Mar 1800, St. Mathias, QC; d & bur there 6 & 7 Feb 1804.

vi **Amable Gervais** b & bp 4 & 5 Dec 1801, St. Mathias, QC. She married there 30 Sep 1823 **Joseph Lefebvre** (François Lefebvre & Josette Desmarais) b & bp 24 Sep 1801, St. Hyacinthe, QC.

vii **Abraham Gervais** b & bp 16 Mar 1803, St. Mathias, QC; d & bur there 26 & 27 Feb 1804.

viii **Marie Louise Gervais** b & bp 19 Jul 1804, St. Mathias, QC.

ix **Josephte Gervais** b & bp 25 & 26 May 1806, St. Mathias, QC; d & bur there 19 & 21 Aug 1806.

x **Josephte Gervais** b & bp 29 & 30 Apr 1807, St. Mathias, QC; d & bur there 26 & 27 Jul 1807.

xi **Jean-Baptiste Gervais** b & bp 2 Jul 1808, St. Mathias, QC. He married (1) 6 Nov 1838, Marieville, QC, **Rosalie Massé dit Sancerre** (Charles Massé dit Sancerre & Rosalie Marcoux) b & bp there 21 Nov 1816; d & bur there 8 & 10 Apr 1843.

  He married (2) 30 Oct 1843, Marieville, QC, **Céleste Benoit** (Charles Benoit & Marguerite Robert) b & bp there 6 Mar 1814.

xii **Edouard Gervais** b & bp 20 Aug 1809, St. Mathias, QC; d & bur there 1 & 2 Sep 1809.

xiii **Josephte Gervais** b & bp 13 Jan 1811, St. Mathias, QC; d & bur 24 & 26 Jul 1878, Ste Brigide, QC. She married 27 Oct 1829, Chambly, QC, **Isaac Racine** (Urbain Racine & Ursule Demers) b & bp there 5 Mar 1810; d & bur 5 & 7 Mar 1889, Ste Brigide, QC.

xiv **Mathias Gervais** b & bp 12 & 13 Jun 1812, St. Mathias, QC; d & bur 13 & 15 May 1876, Ste Brigide, QC. He married 6 Mar 1848, Ste Brigitte des Saults, QC, **Adélaïde Paquet** (Mathias Paquet [adoptive father] & Julie Davignon) b 1826?; d & bur 19 & 21 Aug 1867, Ste Brigide, QC, at the age of 41.

xv **Louis Gervais** b & bp 21 & 22 Nov 1813, St. Mathias, QC; d & bur 29 & 31 Jan 1834, Chambly, QC.

xvi **Barthélemy Gervais** b & bp 23 & 24 Jul 1815, St. Mathias, QC; d & bur there 17 & 19 Dec 1816.

xvii **Eléonore Gervais** b & bp 2 & 3 Nov 1816, St. Mathias, QC; d & bur there 18 & 20 Apr 1817.

5.10   **MONTY, Joseph** b & bp 14 & 15 Aug 1776, Pointe Olivier & Chambly, QC; d & bur 16 & 18 Dec 1812, St. Mathias, QC. He married there 23 Nov 1801 **Marie Louise Vary** (Charles Vary & Marie Anne Goyet) b & bp 30 Jan 1777, Boucherville, QC; m (2) 10 Jan 1814, St. Mathias, QC, Pierre Veilleux/ Varieur (Pierre Veilleux & Françoise Fortier); d & bur there 9 & 11 Aug 1842.

Joseph Monty was a farmer in St. Mathias, QC.

Children:

5.10.1	Joseph	1802-1822-1823
5.10.2	Jean-Baptiste	1803- -1823
5.10.3	Marie Louise	1805-1826-
5.10.4	François David	1807- -1807
5.10.5	Céleste	1808-1826&1848-1976

5.11   **MONTY, Claire** b & bp 20 & 23 Aug 1778, St. Mathias, QC; d & bur there 23 & 24 Jun 1784.

5.12   **MONTY, Marie Amable** b & bp 20 & 21 May 1780, St. Ma-thias, QC; d & bur there 15 & 16 May 1781.

5.13   **MONTY, Marie Amable** b & bp 3 & 7 Jul 1782, St. Mathias, QC; d & bur there 14 Jul 1784.

5.14   **MONTY, Charlotte** b & bp 21 & 22 Jul 1784, St. Mathias, QC; d & bur there 12 & 14 Apr 1849. She married 17 Feb 1817, Chambly, QC, **Ignace Benoit** (Daniel Benoit dit Livernois & Marguerite Neveu) b & bp 16 Mar 1780, St. Mathias, QC; m (1) 10 Nov 1812, Marieville, QC, Ursule Boulay (Joseph Boulay & Angélique Dussault); d & bur 17 & 19 Dec 1850, St. Mathias, QC.
        Ignace Benoit was a farmer in Marieville and St. Mathias, QC.

Children:
i   **Ignace Benoit** b & bp 15 & 16 May 1819, Marieville, QC; d & bur there 19 & 21 May 1860. He married 12 Oct 1841, St. Mathias, QC, **Emilie Stebenne** (Charles Stebenne & Marie Elisabeth/Isabelle Ostilly/Ostiguy) b & bp 9 & 10 May 1823, Marieville, QC.
        He was a widower when he married (2) 15 Nov 1858, Marieville, QC, **Josephte Guertin** (Noël Guertin & Marie Josephte Brodeur) b & bp 27 Aug 1818, Beloeil, QC; m (1) there 18 Oct 1836 Flavien Pion (Jean-Baptiste Pion & Marguerite Renaud); m (3) 27 Feb 1865, St. Hilaire, QC, Paschal Authier, widower of Eléonore Adam; d & bur 8 & 11 Nov 1893, St. Hyacinthe, QC.
ii   **Honoré Benoit** b & bp 6 & 7 May 1820, Marieville, QC; d before 1880. He married 8 Nov 1842, St. Mathias, QC, **Prudence Desnoyers** (François Desnoyers & Prudence Goyette) b & bp 20 & 21 Aug 1824, St. Mathias, QC; d 12 May 1904, St. Joseph, KS.
iii **Onézime Benoit** b & bp 3 & 4 Oct 1821, Marieville & St. Mathias, QC; d & bur 11 & 13 May 1899, Marieville, QC. She married 27 Feb 1843, St. Mathias, QC, **François Xavier Desroches** (Paul Desroches & Josephte Perron) b & bp 25 & 26 Oct 1818, Marieville, QC; d & bur there 7 & 12 Mar 1887.
iv   **Guillaume Benoit/William Bennet** b & bp 12 & 13 Aug 1823, Marieville, QC. He married 29 Aug 1858, Stanstead, QC, Marie Giroux, widow of Joseph Gendreau.

8.1   **MONTY, Clément** b & bp 5 & 7 Mar 1764, Chambly, QC; d & bur 18 & 21 Mar 1825, St. Mathias, QC. He married 7 Nov 1786, Chambly, QC, **Marie Louise Ledoux** (François Ledoux & Louise Catudal) b & bp there 11 Nov 1767; d & bur 19 & 21 Jan 1844, Iberville, QC.
        Clément Monty was a farmer in St. Mathias, QC. His son Clément left around 1864 for Wisconsin where a large number of his descendants still reside.

Children:

8.1.1	Marie Louise	1787- -1790
8.1.2	Marie	1789-1813-1877
8.1.3	Michel	1791- -1813
8.1.4	Madeleine	1794-1814-1817
8.1.5	Catherine	1797-1816-1877
8.1.6	Amable	1799-1816-
8.1.7	Clément	1802-1831-1892
8.1.8	Marie Pélagie	1805- -1819
8.1.9	Marie Louise	1808-1834-1891

8.2   **MONTY, Marie Louise** b & bp 8 & 9 May 1766, Chambly, QC; d & bur 18 & 20 Dec 1834, Iberville, QC. She married (1) 13 Oct 1783, Chambly, QC, **François Ledoux** (François Ledoux & Marguerite Delandes dit Champigny) b & bp 17 Aug 1762, St. Antoine sur Richelieu, QC; d & bur 22 & 23 Nov 1786, Chambly, QC.

She married (2) 11 Jan 1790, St. Mathias, QC, **Joseph Larivière** (Joseph Larivière & Madeleine Porche) b 1759?, QC; d & bur 10 & 12 Feb 1813, St. Mathias, QC, at the age of 54.

François Ledoux was a half-brother of Marie Louise Ledoux, wife of Clément Monty (8.1).

Joseph Larivière was a farmer in St. Mathias, QC, for most of his married life.

Children:

i   **Anonymous Ledoux** b 26 Nov 1784, Chambly, QC; d & bur there 26 & 28 Nov 1784.

ii   **François Ledoux** b & bp 20 & 21 Sep 1786, Chambly, QC; d & bur there 5 & 12 Feb 1787.

iii   **Joseph Larivière** b & bp 20 & 21 Jan 1791, Chambly, QC; d & bur 9 & 11 May 1857, Iberville, QC. He married 1 Aug 1814, St. Mathias, QC, **Marie Louise Guillot** (Louis Guillot & Marie Beauvais) b & bp 2 & 3 Mar 1795, Chambly, QC.

iv   **Jean-Baptiste Larivière** b & bp 16 & 17 Aug 1793, Chambly, QC. He married (1) there 5 Feb 1816 **Marie Haché** (Pierre Haché & Louise Joubert) b & bp 20 & 21 Sep 1796, St. Mathias, QC; d & bur there 8 & 10 Dec 1817.

He married (2) 14 Aug 1820, St. Mathias, QC, **Louise Goguet** (Augustin Goguet & Marie Gaudrault) b & bp there 14 Oct 1800; d & bur there 11 & 13 Oct 1821.

v   **Louis Larivière** b & bp 13 & 14 Jul 1795, St. Mathias, QC; d & bur there 30 Jul & 1 Aug 1795.

vi   **Philibert/Philippe Larivière** b & bp 15 & 17 Aug 1796, St. Mathias, QC; d & bur 3 & 5 May 1874, Mont St. Grégoire, QC. He married (1) 14 Feb 1820, St. Mathias, QC, **Marguerite Davignon** (Joseph Davignon & Angélique Payant) b & bp there 9 Dec 1803; d & bur 7 & 9 Apr 1821, Marieville, QC.

He married (2) 14 Aug 1823, Marieville, QC, **Marie Desanges Lussier/Lucier** (Antoine Lussier & Agathe Janelle) b & bp 7 & 8 Jan 1806, Longueuil, QC; d & bur 21 & 23 Feb 1861, Mont St. Grégoire, QC.

He married (3) 21 Feb 1870, Mont St. Grégoire, QC, **Lucie Déry** (Louis Déry & Charlotte Vincelette) b & bp 20 Jul 1802, Chambly, QC; m (1) 21 Nov 1826, Marieville, QC, Pierre Vient (Louis Vient & Marie Latour).

vii   **Marguerite Larivière** b & bp 27 & 28 Dec 1798, St. Mathias, QC; d & bur 17 & 19 Dec 1856, Mont St. Grégoire, QC. She married 10 Nov 1817, St. Mathias, QC, **Jean-Baptiste Lareau** (Noël Lareau and Marguerite Racine) b & bp 27 Apr 1797, Chambly, QC; d & bur 7 & 10 Nov 1851, Mont St. Grégoire, QC.

viii   **Michel Larivière** b & bp 12 & 13 Jun 1802, St. Luc, QC. He married (1) 29 Jan 1828, St. Mathias, QC, **Flavie Harbec** (Jean-Baptiste Harbec & Catherine Guillot) b & bp 16 & 17 Mar 1810, Chambly, QC; d & bur 16 & 18 Mar 1851, Mont St. Grégoire, QC.

He married (2) 7 Feb 1853, Mont St. Grégoire, QC, **Geneviève Davignon** (Charles Davignon & Geneviève Bertrand) b & bp 28 Feb 1802, St. Mathias, QC; m (1) there 2 Aug 1819 Jean-Baptiste Barrière (Louis Barrière & Marguerite Daigneau); d & bur 26 & 28 Jul 1866, Mont St. Grégoire, QC.

8.3   **MONTY, Philibert/Philippe** b & bp 2 Jun 1768, Chambly, QC; d & bur 24 & 26 Mar 1839, Iberville, QC. He married 25 Feb 1805, St. Mathias, QC, **Josephte Neveu** (Louis Neveu & Marie Bessette) b & bp 22 & 23 Feb 1785, Chambly, QC; d & bur 31 Mar & 3 Apr 1869, Roxton Falls, QC.

Philibert Monty (Philbert at his baptism) was named Philippe at his marriage and at his death and Philibert generally on family occasions such as the births of his children and the marriages of siblings. Although he named one of his own sons Philibert in 1815, Philippe became the more common appellation after 1820.

Philibert/Philippe Monty was a farmer in St. Mathias, QC, until at least 1830. He was a resident of Iberville, QC, however at his death while his widow was living with her daughters Martine, Adélaïde, and Julie in Christieville, QC, in 1851 (Canadian census).

Children:

8.3.1	Clément	1805-1842-1874
8.3.2	Louise	1807-1836-1888
8.3.3	Josephte	1809-1846-1850
8.3.4	Lucille/Lucie	1810- -1813
8.3.5	Isabelle	1812- -1813
8.3.6	Florence/Flore	1813-1839-1876
8.3.7	Philippe/Philibert	1815- -1875
8.3.8	Jean-Baptiste	1816-1850-1888
8.3.9	Angélique	1818- -1909
8.3.10	Moyse/Eusèbe	1820- -1821
8.3.11	François/Frank	1822-1844&1850-1893
8.3.12	Marguerite	1825- -1825
8.3.13	Joseph Trefflé	1826- -1826
8.3.14	Edesse	1827- -1925
8.3.15	Martine	1830-1865-1904
8.3.16	Adèle/Adélaïde?	1831?- -
8.3.17	Julie	1837?- -

8.4 **MONTY, Bruno** b & bp 5 & 6 Oct 1771, Chambly, QC; d & bur there 22 & 23 Aug 1772.

8.5 **MONTY, Marie Geneviève** b & bp 27 & 30 Sep 1773, Chambly, QC; d & bur there 19 & 21 Oct 1773.

8.6 **MONTY, Félicité** b & bp 20 & 24 Nov 1774, Pointe Olivier & Chambly, QC; d & bur 17 & 19 Jul 1776, Pointe Olivier & Chambly, QC.

8.7 **MONTY, Madeleine** b & bp 23 & 25 Jun 1777, Chambly, QC; d & bur 31 Jul & 2 Aug 1848, Iberville, QC. She married 1 Aug 1796, St. Mathias, QC, **Joseph Goguet/Goyette** (Jacques Goyet & Marie Louise Laporte dit Labonté) b & bp 17 & 18 Jun 1775, Chambly, QC; d & bur 4 & 6 Jul 1861, Iberville, QC.

Joseph Goguet was a farmer in St. Mathias, QC, until 1807, according to his children's baptismal records. In the following years his children were baptized either in Iberville or in St. Luc, QC. He was retired and living in Iberville when his wife died in 1848 and was also living there in his son Edouard's household in 1851. His and his sons' surname had by then become Goyette (Canadian census).

Joseph Goguet was a brother of Jacques Goguet, husband of Marie Monty (3.8), and of François Goguet, husband of Catherine Monty (8.8) and an uncle of Marie Geneviève Goyette, wife of François Xavier Monty (3.9.3).

Children:

i **Madeleine Goguet** b & bp 22 Mar 1797, St. Mathias, QC. She married 16 Jan 1815, St. Luc, QC, **Jean-Baptiste Bénac** (Joseph Bénac & Marie Jeanne Jacques) b & bp 24 Jul & 15 Oct 1793, Cap St. Ignace, QC.

ii **Joseph Goguet** b & bp 26 & 27 Feb 1799, St. Mathias, QC; d & bur 6 & 9 Mar 1824, Iberville, QC.

iii **Marguerite Goguet** b & bp 15 & 16 Dec 1801, Chambly, QC. She married 18 Feb

1822, St. Luc, QC, **Pierre Massé** (François Massé & Geneviève Herbec) b & bp 8 & 9 Nov 1795, Chambly, QC.

iv   **François Goguet** b & bp 13 & 14 Apr 1804, St. Mathias, QC; d & bur 30 & 31 May 1804, Marieville, QC.

v   **Edouard Goguet/Goyette** b & bp 23 & 25 May 1805, St. Luc, QC; d & bur 27 & 29 Dec 1876, Iberville, QC. He married 22 Jan 1827, St. Mathias, QC, **Angèle Massé** (François Massé & Geneviève Herbec) b & bp there 2 & 3 Oct 1801; d & bur 29 Sep & 2 Oct 1882, Iberville, QC.

vi   **Jacques Goguet/Goyette** b & bp 25 & 27 Oct 1807, St. Mathias, QC; d & bur 30 Jun & 2 Jul 1889, St. Alexandre, QC. He married (1) 18 Nov 1828, Iberville, QC, **Sophie Lériger dit Laplante** (Pierre Lériger dit Laplante & Catherine Bessette) b 1813?; d & bur 6 & 8 Oct 1866, St. Alexandre, QC.

    He married (2) 21 Nov 1871, St. Alexandre, QC, **Adeline Bessette** (Adrien Bessette & Justine Robert) b & bp there 24 & 25 Nov 1854.

vii   **Philippe Goguet/Goyette** b & bp 6 & 7 Nov 1809, St. Mathias, QC; d & bur 14 & 16 Sep 1889, St. Sébastien, QC. He married (1) 15 Oct 1833, Iberville, QC, **Eléonore Ménard** (Antoine Ménard & Josephte Provost) b & bp 13 & 14 Jan 1817, Longueuil, QC; d & bur 31 Jul & 2 Aug 1843, Iberville, QC.

    He married (2) 27 Jan 1846, Iberville, QC, **Domitilde Hamel** (Pierre Hamel & Emilie Nadeau) b & bp 28 & 29 Mar 1824, St. Mathias, QC; d & bur 5 & 6 Feb 1882, St. Sébastien, QC.

viii   **Michel Goguet/Goyette** b & bp 3 Jan 1812, St. Mathias, QC; d & bur 5 & 7 Sep 1897, St. Alexandre, QC. He married (1) 6 Oct 1835, Iberville, QC, **Marguerite Bernier** (Isidore Bernier & Adélaïde Decelles) b & bp 14 & 18 May 1820, St. Luc, QC; d & bur 20 & 22 Sep 1846, Iberville, QC.

    He married (2) 19 Feb 1849, Iberville, QC, **Domitilde/Mathilde Bessette** (Edouard Bessette & Angèle Davignon) b 1830?; m (1) 28 Jul 1846, Iberville, QC, Joseph Joubert (Joseph Joubert & Anne Girouard); d & bur 1 & 3 May 1854, St. Alexandre, QC, at the age of 24.

    He married (3) 4 Feb 1856, St. Alexandre, QC, **Lucie Massé** (Jean-Baptiste Massé & Hormisdase Amédée).

ix   **Moïse Goguet/Goyette** b & bp 15 & 16 Feb 1814, St. Luc, QC. He married 14 Aug 1838, Chambly, QC, **Marcelline Vincelette** (Jean-Marie Vincelette & Scholastique Robert) b & bp there 10 Dec 1820.

x   **Angèle Goguet** b & bp 13 & 14 Jul 1820, St. Luc, QC.

8.8   **MONTY, Catherine** b & bp 10 & 12 Feb 1780, Chambly, QC. She married 24 Sep 1798, St. Mathias, QC, **François Goguet/Goyette** (Jacques Goyet & Marie Laporte dit Labonté) b & bp 2 & 3 Aug 1777, Chambly, QC.

François Goguet was a farmer in St. Mathias, QC, St. Luc, QC, and later in Iberville, QC. His surname had become Goyette by 1851 (Canadian census).

François Goguet was a brother of Jacques Goguet, husband of Marie Monty (3.8), and of Joseph Goguet, husband of Madeleine Monty (8.7), and an uncle of Marie Geneviève Goyette, wife of François Xavier Monty (3.9.3).

Children:

i   **François Goguet/Goyette** b & bp 30 Jun 1799, St. Mathias, QC; d & bur 28 & 30 Jan 1855, Mont St. Grégoire, QC. He married (1) 7 Feb 1820, St. Mathias, QC, **Martine Balthazar** (Amable Balthazar & Catherine Kinseller) b & bp there 29 & 30 Jan 1806; d & bur 25 & 27 Apr 1826, Marieville, QC.

    He married (2) 14 Feb 1831, Marieville, QC, **Euphrosine Bédard** (Louis Bédard & Marguerite Renault) b & bp there 7 Jul 1812; m (2) 12 May 1862, Mont St. Grégoire, QC, Noël Bertrand (Noël Beaulieu dit Bertrand & Thérèse Duclos), widower of Domitilde Messier.

ii   **Amable Goguet/Goyette** b & bp 8 & 9 Mar 1801, Marieville, QC. He married (1) 31 May 1836, St. Valentin, QC, **Marguerite Beaudriau** (Amable Beaudriau dit

Labonté & Marguerite Ménard) b & bp 15 May & 29 Sep 1810, Lacolle & Chambly, QC.

He was a widower when he married (2) 3 Mar 1851, Roxton Falls, QC, **Elisabeth Morin** (Jacques Morin & Hélène Gagnon), widow of Pierre Langevin.

iii   **Joseph Goguet** b & bp 4 & 6 Feb 1803, St. Luc, QC.

iv   **Clément Goguet/Goyette** b & bp 13 & 14 May 1805, St. Luc, QC. He married 6 Sep 1825, St. Mathias, QC, **Emilie Lareau** (Laurent Lareau & Cathe-rine Hébert) b & bp there 13 Mar 1805.

v   **Marie Louise Goguet** b & bp 3 & 4 Jun 1807, St. Mathias, QC.

vi   **Etienne Goguet** b & bp 6 & 7 Nov 1809, St. Mathias, QC; d & bur there 20 & 21 Nov 1815.

vii   **Lucie Goguet** b & bp 26 & 27 May 1812, St. Mathias, QC.

viii   **Edouard Goguet/Goyette** b & bp 26 Jul 1814, St. Mathias, QC. He married 14 Feb 1843, St. Valentin, QC, **Eusébie/Eusebia Gibeau** (Louis Gibeau & Suzanne Allard) b & bp 15 & 16 Jun 1827, Napierville, QC.

ix   **Maurice Goguet** b & bp 17 Nov 1816, Marieville, QC.

x   **Abraham Goguet/Goyette** b & bp 4 & 5 May 1819, St. Luc, QC. He married 7 Sep 1850, Granby, QC, **Eugénie Lagarde** (Joseph Lagarde & Julie Pagé) b & bp 9 Apr 1832, St. Marc sur Richelieu, QC.

xi   **Augustin Goguet/Goyette** b & bp 23 & 24 Mar 1821, St. Mathias, QC. He married 18 Jun 1850, Iberville, QC, **Victoire Choquette** (François Choquette & Victoire Morissette) b & bp 1 May 1832, St. Mathias, QC.

xii   **Julie Goguet** b & bp 17 Jul 1825, St. Mathias, QC; d & bur there 9 & 11 Nov 1826.

8.9   **MONTY, Marguerite** b & bp 15 & 16 Sep 1782, Chambly, QC; d & bur 25 & 27 Apr 1831, St. Mathias, QC. She married there 8 Jan 1811 **Michel Bérard** (Louis Bérard & Geneviève Roy) bp 7 Mar 1761, Verchères, QC; m (1) 27 Jan 1783, Varennes, QC, Marie Archange Renault (Charles Renault & Marie Joseph Maçon/Masson), widow of Louis Petit; d & bur 8 & 9 Jun 1852, Iberville, QC.

Michel Bérard was a carpenter in St. Mathias, QC, while married to Marguerite Monty.

8.10   **MONTY, Marie Archange** b & bp 17 & 18 May 1789, St. Ma-thias, QC; d & bur there 3 & 4 Aug 1790.

13.1   **MONTY, Catherine** b & bp 29 Apr 1772, Longueuil, QC; d & bur there 21 & 22 Jun 1837. She married (1) 14 Feb 1792, Chambly, QC, **Joseph Lareau** (Joseph Lareau & Marie Paquet dit Larivière) b & bp there 18 & 19 Feb 1770; d & bur 11 & 12 Jan 1811, Longueuil, QC.

She married (2) 17 Oct 1814, Chambly, QC, **Charles Mauray**.

Catherine Monty's marriage contract with Joseph Lareau was signed in Chambly, QC, on 7 Feb 1792 before the notary Antoine Grisé (Notarial Archives, Montreal, QC). He was a farmer in Chambly through at least 1803. By 1807 however he was a farmer in Longueuil, QC, where he remained until his death. He was a brother of Brigitte Lareau, wife of Antoine Monty (13.3).

Charles Mauray (also Murray, Moré, Morer, Maurais) was a farmer in Chambly at his marriage to Catherine Monty. He later became a farmer in Longueuil where he remained at least until her death in 1837. The marriage record in Chambly does not name his parents.

Children:

i   **Anonymous Lareau** b 21 Nov 1792, Chambly, QC; d & bur there 21 Nov 1792.

ii   **Catherine Lareau** b & bp 10 & 11 Dec 1793, Chambly, QC. She married there 13 Nov 1809 **Pierre Surprenant** (Charles Surprenant & Suzanne Audet) b & bp 18 & 19 Jan 1782, Laprairie, QC; d & bur 17 & 19 Jun 1867, Iberville, QC.

iii   **Joseph Lareau** b & bp 16 & 17 Mar 1795, Chambly, QC; d & bur 8 & 10 Mar 1877, Lacolle, QC. He married 29 Jul 1823, Chambly, QC, **Josephte Bigonesse** (Jean-Baptiste Bigonesse & Josephte Dubuc) b & bp there 8 Sep 1802; d & bur 11

& 13 Apr 1880, Lacolle, QC.

iv   **Marie Lareau** b & bp 12 & 13 Oct 1796, Chambly, QC; d & bur 26 & 28 Dec 1871, Laprairie, QC. She married 14 Feb 1814, Longueuil, QC, **Toussaint Sorel** (Jean-Baptiste Sorel dit Léveillé & Marie George) b 1788?; d & bur 12 & 14 Jan 1846, Longueuil, QC, at the age of 58.

v   **Marguerite Lareau** b & bp 8 & 9 Mar 1798, Chambly, QC; d & bur 20 & 22 Mar 1819, St. Luc, QC. She married 17 Jul 1815, Longueuil, QC, **Jacques Hébert** (Augustin Hébert & Marie Louise Baillargeon) b & bp there 5 & 6 Feb 1787; m (2) 1 May 1820, St. Luc, QC, Françoise Grégoire dit Lajeunesse (René Grégoire dit Lajeunesse & Marie Anne Jardet); d & bur 7 & 9 Jul 1864, St. Alexandre, QC.

vi   **Elisabeth Lareau** b & bp 5 Jan 1800, Chambly, QC; d & bur 19 & 21 Mar 1872, St. Hubert, QC. She married 9 Oct 1827, Longueuil, QC, **François Moquin** (Raphaël Moquin & Archange Parent) b & bp 5 & 6 Oct 1792, Laprairie, QC; d & bur 12 & 14 Dec 1872, St. Hubert, QC.

vii   **Joseph Lareau** b 24 Feb 1802, Longueuil, QC; d & bur there 27 & 28 Feb 1802 at the age of 3 days.

viii   **Marie Josephte Lareau** b & bp 31 Aug & 1 Sep 1803, Chambly, QC; d & bur there 18 & 20 Oct 1882. She married 25 Sep 1821, Longueuil, QC, **Alexis Bertrand** (Simon Bertrand & Josephte Dasylva) b & bp 28 Oct 1795, Chambly, QC; d & bur there 13 & 15 Oct 1859.

ix   **Julienne Lareau** b & bp 25 & 26 Sep 1807, Chambly, QC; d & bur 23 & 25 Jun 1857, Mont St. Grégoire, QC. She married 13 Oct 1829, Longueuil, QC, **Louis Patenaude** (Amable Patenaude & Marie Charron) b & bp there 1 & 2 May 1803; d & bur 15 & 18 Dec 1880, Bromont (West Shefford), QC.

13.2   **MONTY, Félicité** b & bp 31 Mar & 1 Apr 1774, Longueuil, QC; bur there 13 Aug 1774.

13.3   **MONTY, Antoine** b & bp 15 Aug 1775, Chambly, QC; d & bur 26 & 28 Nov 1864, St. Hubert, QC. He married 24 Nov 1794, Chambly, QC, **Brigitte Lareau** (Joseph Lareau & Marie Noël Paquet dit Larivière) b & bp there 6 & 7 Jan 1778; d & bur 25 & 27 Nov 1837, Longueuil, QC.

Antoine Monty was a blacksmith in Chambly, QC, at the baptism of his daughter Marguerite in 1798. From 1800 on he was a farmer in Longueuil, QC, and was still living there in 1851 as a widower in the household of his son Stanislas (13.3.17) (Canadian census). He may have moved to St. Hubert, QC, in the early 1860s when his son established residence in that parish.

Brigitte Lareau was a sister of Joseph Lareau, husband of Catherine Monty (13.1).

Children:

13.3.1	Antoine	1795-1820-1869
13.3.2	Marguerite	1798-1821-1853
13.3.3	Amable	1800- -1800
13.3.4	Angélique	1800- -1800
13.3.5	Desanges	1804-1824-1883
13.3.6	Marcel	1805-1831-1893
13.3.7	Sophie	1806- -1822
13.3.8	Basile	1808-1832-
13.3.9	Joseph	1810- -
13.3.10	Hyacinthe	1811-1836&1859-1884
13.3.11	Rachel/Marie	1813-1839-1891
13.3.12	Flavie	1814- -
13.3.13	Henriette	1815- -
13.3.14	Eric	1817- -
13.3.15	Narcisse	1818- -
13.3.16	Adolphe	1820- -

13.4   **MONTY, Marie Joseph** b & bp 20 May 1777, Chambly, QC; d & bur there 10 & 12 Dec 1842. She married there 16 Nov 1801 **Toussaint Trudeau** (Toussaint Trudeau & Geneviève Patenaude) b & bp 5 Mar 1773, Longueuil, QC; d & bur 7 & 10 Jan 1844, Chambly, QC.

Toussaint Trudeau (also Truteau) was a farmer in Chambly, QC.

Children:
i   **Toussaint Trudeau** b & bp 13 & 14 Oct 1802, Chambly, QC; d & bur there 28 & 30 Oct 1802.
ii   **Toussaint Trudeau** b & bp 4 Jan 1804, Chambly, QC; d & bur there 29 & 30 Jan 1820.
iii   **Marie Trudeau** b & bp 11 Apr 1806, Chambly, QC.
iv   **Ambroise/Amable Trudeau** b & bp 10 Nov 1807, Chambly, QC; d & bur there 2 & 4 Feb 1820.
v   **François Trudeau** b 1808?; d & bur 23 & 24 Oct 1834, Chambly, QC, at the age of 25.
vi   **Joseph Trudeau** b & bp 18 & 19 Jul 1809, Chambly, QC; d & bur there 11 & 12 Aug 1809.
vii   **Antoine Trudeau** b & bp 25 & 26 Sep 1810, Chambly, QC.
viii **Etienne Trudeau** b & bp 23 Oct 1812, Chambly, QC; d & bur there 27 & 30 Jan 1820.
ix   **Narcisse Trudeau** b & bp 6 & 7 Jul 1815, Chambly, QC. He married there 1 Feb 1842 **Domitilde Marcil** (Antoine Marcil & Julie Fréchette) b & bp there 30 Apr 1820.
x   **Hermine Trudeau** b & bp 12 May 1818, Chambly, QC; d & bur there 4 & 8 Feb 1820.
xi   **Flavie Trudeau** b & bp 6 Apr 1820, Chambly, QC. She married there 12 Jan 1841 **Joseph Scott** (André Scott & Sophie Demers) b & bp there 17 & 18 Jun 1817.
xii   **Etienne Trudeau** b & bp 30 & 31 Jul 1825, Chambly, QC.

13.5   **MONTY, Elisabeth/Isabelle** b & bp 5 Jan 1780, Chambly, QC; d & bur there 10 & 12 Dec 1822. She married there 29 Sep 1800 **Pascal/Paschal Guertin** (Joseph Guertin & Geneviève Leclerc) b & bp 4 & 5 Nov 1775, Longueuil, QC; m (2) 15 Nov 1824, Laprairie, QC, Rose Couture (Joseph Couture & Marie Louise Lemieux), widow of Pierre Hébert; d & bur 10 & 12 May 1848, Chambly, QC.

Elisabeth Monty was named Isabelle at several of the births and marriages of her children as well as at her widower's second marriage.

Pascal Guertin (Paschal Hiertin at his marriage to Elisabeth Monty) was a farmer in Chambly, QC.

Children:
i   **Joseph Guertin** b & bp 18 Mar 1802, Chambly, QC.
ii   **Elizabeth/Isabelle Guertin** b & bp 24 & 25 Feb 1804, Chambly, QC; d between 1827 and 1830. She married 14 Oct 1823, Chambly, QC, **David Morisset** (Jean-Baptiste Morisset & Louise Prévost) b & bp there 11 Dec 1798; m (2) 8 Nov 1830, Ste Martine, QC, Céleste Dame (Jean-Baptiste Dame & Geneviève Fréchette); d & bur there 12 & Oct 1847.
iii   **Adélaïde Guertin** b & bp 7 & 8 Apr 1805, Chambly, QC; d 1892, Brown Co., WI. She married 11 Oct 1825, Chambly, QC, **David Fournier** (Claude Fournier & Louise Pelletier) b & bp there 3 & 5 Mar 1805; d 14 Sep 1868, Howard, WI.
iv   **Pierre Guertin** b & bp 2 Aug 1806, Chambly, QC; d & bur there 31 Aug & 1 Sep 1806.
v   **Pierre Guertin** b & bp 18 & 19 Sep 1807, Chambly, QC; d 6 Sep 1871, Kankakee, IL. He married 31 Jan 1832, Chambly, QC, **Julienne Piédalue** (Charles Piédalue &

Marie Anne Fréchet) b & bp there 27 & 28 Feb 1808.

vi   **Geneviève Guertin** b & bp 17 Apr 1809, Chambly, QC; d & bur there 14 & 15 Oct 1810.

vii   **Anastasie Guertin** b & bp 18 & 19 Sep 1810, Chambly, QC. She married there 5 Nov 1833 **François Lamarre** (Denis Lamarre & Marguerite Ménard) b & bp 8 & 9 Feb 1812, Laprairie, QC.

viii   **Alexis Guertin** b & bp 7 & 8 Mar 1812, Chambly, QC. He married (1) 23 Nov 1835, Laprairie, QC, **Félicité Boyer** (Jean-Baptiste Boyer & Josephte Binet) b & bp there 24 Aug 1814; d & bur 7 & 9 Aug 1847, Chambly, QC.

     He married (2) 15 Feb 1848, Laprairie, QC, **Louise Couture** (François Couture & Barbe Amable Bouchard) b & bp there 7 & 9 Dec 1829.

ix   **Casimir Guertin** b & bp 2 & 3 Mar 1813, Chambly, QC; d & bur there 19 & 20 Jan 1817.

x   **Catherine Guertin** b 1814?; d & bur 9 & 11 Oct 1870, Bedford, QC, at the age of 55. She married (1) 28 Sep 1830, Chambly, QC, **François Xavier Scott** (André Scott & Marie Trahant) b & bp there 12 & 14 Mar 1804; d & bur ? & 27 Nov 1836, Laprairie, QC.

     She married (2) 24 Nov 1840, Chambly, QC, **Toussaint Lamoureux** (Michel Lamoureux & Marie Moquin) b & bp there 7 Aug 1815; d & bur 11 & 13 Jan 1889, Marieville, QC.

xi   **Antoine Guertin** b & bp 25 & 26 Oct 1815, Chambly, QC. He married 21 Oct 1833, Laprairie, QC, **Anastasie Couture** (François Couture & Barbe Amable Bouchard) b & bp there 24 Mar 1813; d & bur 30 Sep & 2 Oct 1895, Montreal, QC.

xii   **Benoit/Bénony Guertin** b & bp 21 Jan 1819, St. Mathias, QC; d & bur 30 Mar & 3 Apr 1819, Chambly, QC.

xiii   **Domitilde Guertin** b & bp 4 & 5 Feb 1820, St. Mathias, QC. She married 10 Oct 1837, Chambly, QC, **Antoine Huet** (Michel Huet & Rosalie Brouil-let).

xiv   **Pascal Guertin** b & bp 17 & 18 Apr 1821, Chambly, QC; d & bur there 29 & 31 Aug 1829.

13.6   **MONTY, Geneviève** b & bp 11 & 12 Feb 1782, Chambly, QC; d & bur 4 & 6 Dec 1862, Longueuil, QC. She married 1 Jul 1805, Chambly, QC, **François Moquin** (Pierre François Moquin & Josephte Daigneau) b & bp 7 & 8 Nov 1777, Laprairie, QC; d & bur 27 & 29 Apr 1848, Longueuil, QC.

François Moquin (Pierre François at his baptism) was a farmer in Longueuil, QC.

Children:

i   **François Moquin** b & bp 11 & 12 May 1806, Laprairie, QC. He married (1) 27 Sep 1831, Longueuil, QC, Marie **Pigeon** (Jacques Pigeon & Marie Gagnon) b & bp 6 Jan 1812, Montreal, QC; d & bur 1 & 3 Dec 1846, Longueuil, QC.

     He married (2) 7 Feb 1848, Chambly, QC, **Monique Deschamps** (Jean-Baptiste Deschamps & Marguerite Cusson).

ii   **Paul/Hippolyte Moquin** b & bp 24 & 25 Dec 1807, Longueuil & Laprairie, QC. He married 4 Oct 1836, Chambly, QC, **Clémence Vincelet** (Jacques Vincelet & Théotiste Fréchette) b & bp there 11 & 12 Aug 1821.

iii   **Geneviève Moquin** b & bp 2 Oct 1809, Longueuil and Laprairie, QC. She married 14 Feb 1831, Longueuil, QC, **Joseph Hély dit Berton** (Pierre Hély dit Berton & Marie Deniger) b & bp there 18 & 19 Sep 1803; m (1) there 8 May 1827 Marguerite Racine (Laurent Racine & Marie Anne Robert).

iv   **Pierre Moquin** b & bp 27 & 28 Feb 1812, Longueuil and Laprairie, QC. He married 3 Oct 1843, Chambly, QC, **Domitilde Vincelet** (Jacques Vincelet & Théotiste Fréchette) b & bp there 24 Sep 1823.

v   **Edesse Moquin** b & bp 23 & 24 Aug 1813, Longueuil and Laprairie, QC; d before 1865. She married 25 Oct 1842, Longueuil, QC, **Isaac Ouimet** (Joseph Ouimet & Judith Chamberland) m (2) 20 Jan 1865, Henryville, QC, Elizabeth Porter (William Porter & ____); m (3) 16 Nov 1868, L'Acadie, QC, Eliza Gagné (Antoine Gagné

& Hélène Bérubé).

vi   **Agathe/Anastasie Moquin** married 6 May 1834, Longueuil, QC, **Luc Arelle** (François Arelle & Françoise Beaudin) b 1810?, QC; d & bur 19 & 23 Dec 1889, St. Chrysostôme, QC, at the age of 79.

vii   **Emérence/Emérente/Emérentienne Moquin** b & bp 4 Mar 1815, Laprairie, QC; d & bur 13 & 16 Jul 1896, L'Acadie, QC. She married 7 Jul 1840, Longueuil, QC, **Narcisse Chouinard** (François Chouinard & Marie Corache) b & bp 20 & 23 Nov 1816, L'Acadie, QC; d & bur there 10 & 12 May 1883.

viii   **Catherine Moquin** b & bp 5 May 1816, Laprairie, QC; d & bur 26 & 27 Nov 1843, St. Rémi, QC. She married 25 Feb 1840, Longueuil, QC, **Toussaint Racine** (Charles Racine & Catherine Baillargeon) b & bp 6 & 7 Jan 1813, Laprairie, QC; d & bur there 6 & 7 Dec 1883.

ix   **Jean-Baptiste Moquin** b & bp 18 & 19 Jul 1817, Longueuil, QC.

x   **Joseph Moquin** b & bp 3 & 4 Feb 1819, Longueuil, QC; d & bur 1 & 3 Apr 1877, Laprairie, QC. He married (1) 3 Jul 1849, Longueuil, QC, **Elmire Lecompte** (Pierre Lecompte & Marie Anne Bouthillier) b & bp there 15 Nov 1829; d & bur there 16 & 18 Apr 1857.

     He married (2) 11 Oct 1858, Longueuil, QC, **Marie Surprenant** (Jean-Baptiste Surprenant & Anastasie Racine).

     He married (3) 21 Sep 1868, Laprairie, QC, **Marie Honorée/Honorine Bétourné/Bétournay** (André Bétourné & Josephte Trudeau) b & bp 8 & 9 Dec 1837, Longueuil, QC; m (2) 21 Jan 1888, Montreal, QC, François David, widower of Marie Claire Payrand (?); d & bur 12 & 14 Apr 1899, Longueuil, QC.

xi   **Jean-Baptiste Moquin** b & bp 24 & 25 Nov 1820, Longueuil & Laprairie, QC.

xii   **Julienne Moquin** b & bp 18 & 19 May 1822, Longueuil, QC; d 29 Apr 1903, Cohoes, NY. She married 29 Nov 1849, Montreal, QC, **Joseph Vadeboncoeur** (Joseph Fourré dit Vadeboncoeur & Rose St. Michel) b 1819?, QC.

xiii   **Bibiane/Caroline Moquin** b & bp 1 Dec 1824, Longueuil & Laprairie, QC. She married 28 Sep 1853, Montreal, QC, **Roch Civadier** (Joseph Civadier & Marguerite Comette).

xiv   **Flavie Moquin** b & bp 8 Sep 1827, Longueuil, QC; d & bur there 9 & 11 Feb 1830.

13.7   **MONTY, Marie Louise** b & bp 21 & 22 Nov 1783, Chambly, QC. She married there 14 Aug 1809 **Joseph Surprenant** (Charles Surprenant & Suzanne Audet) b & bp 15 May 1786, L'Acadie, QC.

     Joseph Surprenant was a brother of Pierre Surprenant, husband of Catherine Lareau (13.1.i). He was a resident of L'Acadie, QC, at the birth of his first child and from at least 1813 on a farmer in Chambly. He and his wife were still living there when their daughter Christine (ii) married in 1845. I have been unable to trace them or their children any further.

Children:

i.   **Joseph Surprenant** b & bp 30 & 31 Oct 1810, St. Luc, QC; d & bur 4 & 5 Sep 1834, Chambly, QC.

ii   **Christine Surprenant** b & bp 24 & 25 Mar 1813, Chambly, QC. She married there 29 Jul 1845 **David Darche** (François Darche & Marie Jetté) b & bp there 12 Jul 1822; d & bur there 23 & 26 Aug 1895.

iii   **Eusèbe Surprenant** b & bp 9 & 11 Jan 1820, Chambly, QC.

iv   **Casimir Surprenant** b & bp 12 Aug 1823, Chambly, QC; d & bur there 16 & 18 May 1824.

v   **Marie Domitilde Surprenant** b & bp 1 Nov 1825, Chambly, QC.

13.8   **MONTY, Amable** b & bp 15 Aug 1785, Chambly, QC; d & bur 11 & 13 Jul 1847, Montreal, QC. She married 25 Nov 1805, Chambly, QC, **Antoine Papineau** (Antoine Papineau & Josephte Benard) b & bp 11 & 12 Apr 1786, Montreal, QC; d & bur 16 & 18 Jan 1841, St. Polycarpe, QC.

Antoine Papineau was a farmer in Chambly, QC, through 1821 and an innkeeper in Montreal, QC, in 1823 and 1826. By 1833 he had become a farmer in St. Polycarpe, QC.

Children:

i   **Anastasie Papineau** b & bp 30 Oct 1806, Chambly, QC; d & bur 19 & 21 Sep 1875, St. Polycarpe, QC. She married 3 Feb 1823, Montreal, QC, **Louis Lamarre** (Alexis Lamarre & Marie Aupry) b & bp 17 Jun 1801, Chambly, QC.

ii   **Marie Amable Papineau** b & bp 15 Nov 1807, Chambly, QC; d & bur 30 Nov & 3 Dec 1855, Montreal & St. Polycarpe, QC. She married (1) 30 Jan 1826, Montreal, QC, **François Gareau dit Vadeboncoeur** (Joseph Gareau dit Vadeboncoeur & Marie Louise Goyet [also Juillet]) b & bp there 6 & 7 Jul 1799; d & bur 18 Jun 1832, St. Polycarpe, QC.

        She married (2) 3 Jun 1833, St. Polycarpe, QC, **Edouard Vincelet** (Jean-Marie Vincelet & Marie Brigitte Guyon/Dion) b & bp 14 & 15 Dec 1801, Chambly, QC; d & bur 28 & 29 Jul 1834, Montreal, QC.

        She married (3) 3 Mar 1840, Montreal, QC, **Benjamin Métayer** (Joseph Métayer & Thérèse Gareau) b & bp there 18 & 19 Dec 1811; d & bur there 3 & 5 Jan 1846.

        She married (4) 9 Feb 1847, Montreal, QC, **Frédérick Limoges** (Joseph Limoges & Louise Hagne) m (1) 7 Oct 1844, Montreal, QC, Anastasie De-roin (Louis Deroin & Marie Santel).

iii   **Antoine Papineau** b & bp 1 May 1809, Chambly, QC. He married 20 Nov 1837, St. Eustache, QC, **Marie Louise McKay** (Stephen McKay & Françoise Globensky).

iv   **Adélaïde Papineau** b & bp 15 Feb 1811, Chambly, QC. She married 14 Feb 1831, Montreal, QC, **Joseph Brabant** (Jean-Baptiste Brabant & Josephte Ekemberque).

v   **Elisabeth Papineau** b & bp 28 May 1812, Chambly, QC; d & bur there 16 & 17 Jul 1812.

vi   **Zoé Papineau** b & bp 20 Sep 1813, St. Mathias, QC; d & bur 10 & 11 Aug 1814, Chambly, QC.

vii   **Zoé Papineau** b & bp 16 & 17 Oct 1814, Chambly, QC; d & bur 2 & 4 Mar 1908, Montreal, QC.

viii   **Florence Papineau** b & bp 4 & 5 Oct 1815, Chambly, QC.

ix   **Flavie Papineau** b & bp 25 Nov 1816, Chambly, QC; d & bur 18 & 20 Feb 1854, St. Polycarpe, QC. She married there 30 Oct 1837 **Ambroise Beautron dit Major** (Etienne Beautron dit Major & Catherine Tessier) b & bp 24 & 27 Mar 1810, St. Benoit, QC; m (2) there 11 Oct 1856, St. Polycarpe, QC, Judith/Marie Julie Poirier (Jean-Baptiste Poirier dit Lafleur & Catherine Giroux).

x   **Anatalie Papineau** b & bp 7 & 8 Mar 1818, Chambly, QC; d & bur there 3 & 5 Apr 1819.

xi   **Joseph Papineau** b & bp 15 & 16 May 1821, Chambly, QC; d & bur there 25 & 27 Jun 1821.

13.9   **MONTY, Joseph** b & bp 10 Feb 1788, Chambly, QC; d & bur there 11 & 14 Mar 1862. He married (1) there 2 Jul 1810 **Marguerite Beauvais** (François Xavier Beauvais & Angélique Herbec) b & bp there 18 Dec 1792; d & bur there 20 & 24 Apr 1860.

He married (2) 28 May 1861, Marieville, QC, **Marie Proteau** (Jean-Marie Proteau & Marie Meunier) b & bp 4 Dec 1797, Chambly, QC; m (1) there 3 May 1813 François Séguin (Simon Séguin & Catherine Sicotte); m (2) Joseph Frichet (Pierre Frichet & Monique Piédalue), widower of Desanges Hébert and Geneviève Lamoureux); d & bur 8 & 10 Jan 1886, Mont St. Grégoire, QC.

Joseph Monty was a farmer in Chambly, QC. Most of his children left for Illinois with their families in the late 1850s. Only two, Marcelline (13.9.8) and Marguerite (13.9.13), remained in Canada.

Children of the first marriage:

13.9.1	Céleste	1811-1830-1891
13.9.2	Joseph	1813-1834-1883
13.9.3	Anastasie	1814- -1816
13.9.4	Domitille/Matilda	1816-1835-1886
13.9.5	Eugène/Eusèbe	1819- -1820
13.9.6	Cyril	1821- -1821
13.9.7	Anastasie	1822-1848-
13.9.8	Marcelline	1824-1850-1895
13.9.9	Aurélie	1827-1846&1870-1898
13.9.10	Aglaé	1829-1851-
13.9.11	Pierre Alfred	1831- -1831
13.9.12	Marie Onésime	1832- -1832
13.9.13	Marguerite	1834-1854-1868
13.9.14	Victoire	1835- -

13.10   **MONTY, Euphrosine** b & bp 9 Aug 1790, Chambly, QC. She married there 30 Oct 1809, Chambly, QC, **Etienne/Stephen Sénécal** (Etienne Sénécal & Marie Louise Lague) b & bp there 28 & 29 Sep 1787.

Etienne Sénécal was originally a farmer in Chambly, QC, and in the 1820s in Marieville, QC, and St. Césaire, QC. When his daughter Adélaïde was buried in Iberville, QC, in 1827, he was a carpenter, staying for only a few days in St. Jean, QC. There is no mention of a permanent residence. I believe the family had already left for the United States for, according to his naturalization papers of 1 Sep 1851 in Jefferson Co., NY, Etienne Sénécal was 38 years old when he emigrated. He first settled in Burlington, VT, where a son, Leon (xii) was born in 1829. He was a laborer there in 1830 before moving to Alexandria, NY, where he and his wife lived from at least 1840 until at least 1860 (US censuses). They may have died around Alexandria or Redwood, NY, where several of their children resided, though no record of their death or burial has been found.

Children:
i   **Etienne/Stephen Sénécal/Senecal** b & bp 24 & 25 Jan 1811, Chambly, QC; d 22 Jun 1894, NY. He married around 1835 **Esther Phaneuf** (Jean Phaneuf & Joséphine Dubois) b 1820?, QC; d & bur 23 & 26 Jul 1909, Redwood, NY, at the age of 89.
ii   **Marie Rachel Sénécal** b & bp 5 Jun 1812, Chambly, QC.
iii   **Mathilde Sénécal** b & bp 12 & 13 Mar 1814, Chambly, QC.
iv   **Hyacinthe Sénécal** b & bp 11 & 12 Aug 1815, Chambly, QC.
v   **Joseph Sénécal/Senecal** b & bp 2 Mar 1817, Chambly, QC; d & bur 2 & ? Aug 1898, Buffalo & Redwood, NY. He married 18 Jan 1839, **Mary Catherine Tisserand** (_____ Tisserand & Catherine _____) b 12 Aug 1824, France; d 29 Oct 1917, Grenadine Island, Ontario, Canada.
vi   **Jean-Baptiste Emilien Sénécal** b & bp 26 & 27 Jun 1818, Chambly, QC.
vii   **Marie Flavie Sénécal** b & bp 12 & 13 Mar 1820, Chambly, QC.
viii   **Marie Angélique Sénécal** b & bp 15 & 16 May 1822, Marieville, QC.
ix   **William Sénécal/Senecal** b 1823?, QC; d 1878. He married around 1845 **Mary Grappotte** (François Augustin/Augustus Grappotte & Marianne Ragot) b 14 Jul 1824, France; d 3 Feb 1898, Redwood, NY.
x   **Patrice Sénécal** b & bp 11 & 16 Mar 1824, St. Césaire, QC.
xi   **Adélaïde Sénécal** b Sep 1825; d & bur 13 & 15 Dec 1827, Iberville, QC, at the age of 2 years and 3 months.
xii   **Leon Senecal** b 1829, Burlington, VT. He married around 1854 **Frances Grappotte** (François Augustin/Augustus Grappotte & Marianne Ragot) b 1831?, France.

13.11   **MONTY, Angélique** b & bp 25 Sep 1792, Chambly, QC; d & bur there 23 & 24 Dec 1814. She married there 21 Feb 1814 a first cousin once removed, **Joseph Gélineau** (Joseph Gélineau & Angélique Monty [1.9]) b & bp there 13 & 14 May 1788; m there

(2) 28 Jul 1817 Charlotte Cognac (Barthélemy Cognac & Charlotte Denicourt); d & bur there 23 & 24 Dec 1823.

   Joseph Gélineau was a farmer in Chambly, QC.

Child:

 i **Joseph Gélineau** b & bp 15 Dec 1814, St. Mathias, QC; d 28 Sep 1887, Chambly, QC; bur there 30 Sep 1887 (St. Stephen Anglican Cemetery). He married 2 Mar 1835, Christ Church Cathedral (Anglican), Montreal, QC, **Elizabeth Stoddard/ Stoddart** (John Stoddart & Catherine Montgomery) b & bp 9 May & 13 Jul 1817, Chambly, QC; d & bur 15 & 19 Apr 1890, Kankakee, IL & Chambly, QC (St. Stephen Anglican Cemetery).

13.12   **MONTY, Casimir** b & bp 26 & 27 Sep 1794, St. Mathias, QC; d & bur there 18 & 19 Mar 1797.

3.1.1   **MONTY, Claude** b & bp 24 & 25 Jun 1788, Chambly, QC; d & bur there 2 & 4 August 1788.

3.1.2   **MONTY, Catherine** b 1789?, Clinton Co., NY; bp 18 Jul 1796, Chambly, QC; d & bur 28 & 30 Jan 1878, Ange Gardien, QC. She married (1) 15 Oct 1805, Marieville, QC, **Pierre Larivée** (Joseph Larivée & Marie Levasseur) b & bp 10 & 11 Nov 1784, Verchères, QC; d & bur 16 & 17 Jul 1832, Marieville, QC.

She married (2) 23 Jul 1833, St. Césaire, QC, **Louis Duclos** (Antoine Duclos & Marie Macelot) b & bp 30 Sep 1793, St. Mathias, QC; m (1) 19 Oct 1819, St. Jean-Baptiste, QC, Catherine Ménard (François Ménard & Marie Anne Forand); d & bur 2 & 4 Jun 1883, Ange Gardien, QC.

Catherine Monty was baptized in Chambly, QC, on the same day in 1796 as her younger siblings Jean-Baptiste, Marie Anne, and Joseph. She was then said to be 8 years old. At her death in January 1878 she was said to be 92 years old. She would then have been born in 1786, 1787, or 1788. Yet she could not have been born in 1788, since her brother Claude was born in June of that year. I do not find it plausible either that she was born in 1786 or 1787 for her parents would certainly have taken advantage of their stay in a Catholic parish to have had her baptized in 1788 at the same time as her younger brother Claude. Thus the suggested date of 1789.

Pierre Larivée was a farmer in Marieville, QC. The surname became Larrivée in the mid-19th century.

Louis Duclos was a farmer in St. Césaire, QC at his marriage to Catherine Monty. He was retired in Ange Gardien, QC, when she died.

Children:

i   **Pierre Larivée/Peter Larabee** b & bp 28 & 29 Oct 1806, Marieville, QC; d before 20 Nov 1879, Deer River, NY. He married 7 Nov 1826, Marieville, QC, **Marie Desanges Desautels** (Etienne Desautels & Marie Desanges Moquin) b & bp 13 & 14 Nov 1811, Chambly, QC; d 1880?, West Carthage, NY.

ii   **Marie Catherine Larivée** b & bp 29 Oct 1808, Marieville, QC. She married there 27 Jun 1825 **Edouard Bobo dit Fleury** (Jacques Bobo dit Fleury & Victoire Delubac dit St. Jean).

iii   **Céleste Larivée** b & bp 16 & 17 May 1810, Marieville, QC; d & bur 31 Mar & 2 Apr 1835, St. Césaire, QC. She married 23 Nov 1830, Marieville, QC, **Christophe Daudelin** (Noël Daudelin & Marie Anne Fuger dit Champagne) b & bp 30 Sep 1804, Varennes, QC; m (2) 3 Nov 1835, St. Césaire, QC, Marie Anne Dufresne (Jean-Baptiste Dufresne & Marie Louise Gri-gnon), widow of Joseph Dansereau and of Michel Chabot.

iv   **André Larivée** b & bp 26 Mar 1812, Marieville, QC. He married (1) 14 May 1833, St. Jean-Baptiste, QC, **Adélaïde Davignon** (Alexis Davignon & Madeleine Bonneville) b & bp 24 & 25 Sep 1801, Chambly, QC; m (1) 22 Jan 1822, Marieville, QC, Pierre Viens (Pierre Viens & Marie Elisabeth/Isabelle Gorgette dit Basile).

         He was a widower when he married (2) 26 May 1845, St. Césaire, QC, **Marguerite Rainaud/Rénaud** (Michel Rénaud & Félice Ledoux) m (1) 22 Feb 1841, St. Césaire, QC, Jean-Baptiste Lacasse (Jean-Baptiste Lacasse & Marguerite Roy).

v   **Agathe Larivée** b & bp 5 & 6 Feb 1814, Marieville, QC. She married 3 Jul 1832, Marieville, QC, **André Jodoin**/Jodouin (René Jodoin & Amable Babin) b 1811?, QC; d & bur 17 & 19 Nov 1859, Farnham, QC, at the age of 48.

vi   **François Xavier Larivée** b & bp 10 & 11 May 1816, Marieville, QC.

vii   **Angélique Larivée** b & bp 15 Sep 1818, Marieville, QC; d & bur there 21 & 23 Jul 1864. She married there 9 Sep 1835 **Louis Vigeant** (François Vigeant & Marie Louise Béïque) b & bp 5 Jul 1792, Chambly, QC; m (1) 17 Aug 1812, St. Mathias, QC, Marguerite Stebenne (Louis Stebenne & Marie Desanges Mailloux); d & bur 23 & 16 Feb 1872, Marieville, QC.

viii   **Joseph Larivée** b & bp 9 & 11 Mar 1821, Marieville, QC. He married there 21 Feb 1843 **Marie Léocadie Quimineur/Kimineur** (Antoine Quimineur & Geneviève Silvallier).

ix   **Fabien Larivée** b & bp 20 Jan 1823, Marieville, QC. He married 28 Oct 1845, Iberville, QC, **Adélaïde Choinière** (Joseph Choinière & Marie Tessier).

x   **Isaac Larivée** b & bp 2 & 9 Nov 1825, Marieville, QC; d & bur 28 & 29 Jul 1909, Farnham, QC. He married there 15 Oct 1850 **Françoise Chamberland** (Antoine Chamberland & Marguerite Gagné) b & bp 5 & 6 Aug 1807, St. Hyacinthe, QC; m (1) 4 Jul 1825, St. Césaire, QC, Michel Végiard (Michel Végiard & Hélène Béchand); d & bur 4 & 7 Oct 1886, Farnham, QC.

xi   **Louis Abraham Larivée** b & bp 5 & 6 May 1828, Marieville, QC. He married **Rosalie Garnie** (Augustin Garnie & Cécile Bessette).

xii   **Aurélie Larivée** b & bp 15 Jul 1831, Marieville, QC; d & bur 17 & 19 Sep 1898, Ange Gardien, QC. She married 2 Nov 1852, Farnham, QC, **Michel Garnie/Garny** (Augustin Garnie & Cécile Bessette) b & bp 28 Aug & 1 Oct (sic) 1826 St. Césaire, QC; m (1) there 13 May 1851, Marguerite Fortin (Jérémie Fortin & Marguerite Blanchet); d & bur 4 & 6 Aug 1897, West Farnham & Ange Gardien, QC.

3.1.3   **MONTY, Jean-Baptiste/John** b 12 Apr 1790, Grand Isle, VT; bp 18 Jul 1796, Chambly, QC; d & bur 16 & 18 Sep 1868, Colchester, VT. He married (1) **Mary Elizabeth ____** b 1775?; d 2 Jun 1842, Colchester, VT, at the age of 67.

He married (2) around 1842 **Marguerite/Margaret Landry** (Jean-Baptiste Landry & Josephte Mimo) b & bp 3 & 4 Jun 1820, L'Acadie, QC; d 26 Feb 1869, Colchester, VT.

There are few certainties concerning Jean-Baptiste/John Monty. Few primary records have been found, and even these give contradictory information. His baptismal record, for example, shows that he was 6 years old when he was baptized as Jean-Baptiste Monty in Chambly, QC, in 1796. Yet the Vital Records of Colchester, VT, would have him born in 1784: he was 84 years, 5 months, and 4 days old at his death. John Monty's tombstone in the Munson Cemetery in Colchester also has "Æ 84." I find it highly improbable that he was born in 1784, two years before his parents' marriage, and that the priest who baptized him could not see the difference between a 6- and a 12-year-old child. I think the error arose when the American authorities accepted without further inquiry the date of the baptismal certificate as the date of birth. The 1796 baptismal record shows otherwise.

It is uncertain how long Jean-Baptiste/John Monty remained in Canada with his parents. No trace of him is found in the United States before the 1820 census in Grand Isle, VT, though he had returned to the United States soon enough to participate in the War of 1812: the Veterans of the War of 1812 erected a small flag near his tombstone in the Munson Cemetery in Colchester. He settled after the war in South Hero, VT, and lived there until at least 1830. He moved to Colchester before his father's death there in 1839 and was named administrator of his estate on 5 Sep 1840 in the Chittenden Co., VT, Probate Court on 5 Sep 1840 (#1050). He was then and until his death a farmer in Colchester (US censuses). Oddly enough, there are two records of his death in the Colchester Vital Records. According to the first, John Monty, son of Claudius Monty, born in Grand Isle, died on 16 Sep 1868. According to the other, John Monty, husband of Elizabeth Monty, died on 18 Sep 1868 and was buried in Colchester. I take it that the latter record refers to burial rather than death — although that is also the date given on his tombstone. He was of course the widower of Elizabeth, but still the husband of Margaret Landry who died the following year.

The identity of John Monty's first wife, Mary Elizabeth, is unknown. I have found no marriage record in Vermont or elsewhere while her death certificate does not include her parents' names. We know from her son John Monty Jr.'s death record that her name was Mary Elizabeth Monty, but that is most probably her married name. If not, then she may have been a relative, perhaps a cousin or second cousin, though I know of no Elizabeth, Betsey, or Mary Monty of that generation who is otherwise unaccounted for.

Another thing gives me pause: she was 67 years old at her death, according to the Colchester Vital Records. Her tombstone in the Munson Cemetery there, which lies between her father-in-law's and her husband's, reads "Elizabeth / wife of John Monty / died June 2, 1842 /

Æ67." She would then have been 15 years older than her husband and her only known children would have been born when she was 44 and 48 years old. It is rather strange, though there is some sort of confirmation in the 1840 census when she was said to be between 60 and 70 years old.

John Monty's second wife, Margaret Landry, was a sister of Emilie/Emily Landry, wife of Joseph Monty (3.1.5). She was 47 years old at her death in February 1869, according to the Colchester Vital Records. The inscription on her tombstone in the Champlain Cemetery there reads however: "Margaret / wife of John Monty Sr. / 1828-1870." Both dates appear to be incorrect. Much more work needs to be done on the entire family.

Children of the first marriage:

| 3.1.3.1 | John Jr. | 1819-1838?-1879 |
| 3.1.3.2 | Claudius | 1823-1845?-1906 |

Children of the second marriage:

3.1.3.3	Benjamin Franklin	1843-1873-1926
3.1.3.4	Napoleon Bonaparte	1845-1869?-1927
3.1.3.5	William F.	1847- -1859
3.1.3.6	Infant girl	1848- -1848
3.1.3.7	Boardman	1850- -1864
3.1.3.8	Mary Ann	1855- -1864
3.1.3.9	Augusta Louisa	1858-1882-1947

3.1.4   MONTY, Marie Anne b 1792?, Clinton Co., NY; bp 18 Jul 1796, Chambly, QC; d & bur 3 & 5 May 1881, Dunham, QC. She married 4 Oct 1814, Marieville, QC, **Antoine Gaboriau dit Lapalme** (Laurent Gaboriau dit Lapalme & Marie Ursule Robert dit Lafontaine) b & bp 4 & 5 Sep 1786, St. Mathias, QC; d & bur 21 & 23 Mar 1853, Farnham, QC.

Marle Anne Monty was 4 years old at her Catholic baptism in Chambly, QC, in 1796. That is probably a more accurate indication of her date of birth than the age of 92 ascribed to her at her death.

Antoine Gaboriau was originally a farmer in Marieville, QC. By 1836, at the marriage of his daughter Marie Anne (i), he was a farmer in Farnham, QC, where he remained until his death. His surname sometimes appears as Gabriot dit Lapalme, Lapalme, or even, as at his death, Lapanne.

Children:

i   **Marie Anne Gaboriau dit Lapalme** b & bp 24 Nov 1815, Marieville, QC. She married 11 Jul 1836, St. Césaire, QC, **Olivier Courtemanche** (Jean-Baptiste Courtemanche & Angélique Giard) b & bp 21 Dec 1803, Beloeil, QC; m (1) 7 Jan 1832, St. Jean-Baptiste, QC, Céleste Pépin (Antoine Pépin & Marie Anne Bain); d & bur 18 & 20 Oct 1881, Dunham, QC.

ii   **Antoine Gaboriau dit Lapalme** b & bp 30 & 31 Oct 1820, Marieville, QC; d & bur 6 & 8 Nov 1892, Frelighsburg & Dunham, QC. He married 18 Oct 1842, Marieville, QC, **Sophie Delubac dit St. Jean** (François Delubac dit St. Jean & Archange Gendron) b & bp 7 Sep 1813, Longueuil, QC; d & bur 3 & 5 Aug 1895, Frelighsburg & Dunham, QC.

iii   **Marie Catherine Gaboriau** b & bp 23 & 24 Feb 1823, Marieville, QC; d & bur there 5 & 7 Feb 1826.

3.1.5   MONTY, Joseph b 1793?, Champlain, NY; bp 18 Jul 1796, Chambly, QC; d 30 Jun 1861, Milton, VT. He married **Emilie/Emily Landry** (Jean-Baptiste Landry & Josephte Mimo) b & bp 23 & 25 Jul 1807, L'Acadie, QC; d 17 Sep 1876, Roxbury, VT.

Joseph Monty was 3 years old at his Catholic baptism in Chambly, QC, in 1796. Later records indicate that he was slightly older: he was 59 years old in 1850 and 70 years old in 1860 (US censuses, Milton, VT). Yet the Vermont Vital Records show that Joseph Monty, who died at age 74 in Milton on 30 Jun 1861, was born in 1787 in Champlain, NY. As in the case of his brother Jean-Baptiste/John (3.1.3), I prefer to trust the baptismal record: it would be unlikely that the priest who baptized Joseph Monty would mistake a 9-year-old child for a 3-year-old.

Joseph Monty took part in the War of 1812, having enlisted in Vermont on 4 Oct 1813 in Capt. Langworthy's Company, Col. Clark's Rifle Corps, and on 12 Feb 1814 in Capt. J. Brooks' Company, US Artillery. He and his wife settled in South Hero, NY, after the war and had in 1820 two unnamed children, a boy and a girl, both under the age of 10. They are never mentioned in later censuses and may have died in childhood. From 1840 through 1860 Joseph Monta or Montee was a farm laborer in Milton (US censuses). Yet he was Joseph Monty at his death.

Emilie Landry was a sister of Marguerite Landry, wife of Jean-Baptiste/John Monty (3.1.3).

3.1.6   **MONTY, Marguerite** b & bp 10 & 11 Oct 1796, Chambly, QC; d & bur 2 & 3 May 1876, Sutton, QC. She married 29 May 1820, Marieville, QC, **François Bonneville dit Bouteille** (François Bonneville dit Bouteille & Elisabeth Delubac dit St. Jean) b & bp 15 & 16 Jun 1800, Longueuil, QC; d & bur 11 & 13 Aug 1880, Ange Gardien, QC.

François Bonneville was originally a farmer in Marieville, QC. By 1850 he had moved to St. Césaire, QC, where he remained until at least 1862. He was a retiree in Ange Gardien, QC, at the time of his death. He should not be confused with Antoine Bouteille dit Bonneville, husband of another Marguerite Monty (13.3.2).

Children:

i   **Anonymous Bonneville dit Bouteille** b 28 Sep 1820, Marieville, QC; d & bur there 28 & 29 Sep 1820.

ii   **François Xavier Bonneville dit Bouteille** b & bp 14 Sep 1823, Marieville, QC. He married 9 Jan 1843, St. Césaire, QC, **Marguerite Roy** (Joseph Roy & Marie Archange Ledoux) b 1820?; d & bur 6 & 8 Oct 1865, Sutton & Dunham, QC, at the age of 45.

iii   **Catherine Bonneville dit Bouteille** b & bp 10 & 11 May 1825, Marieville, QC; d & bur 26 & 28 Aug 1851, St. Césaire, QC. She married there 6 May 1851 **Abraham Roy** (Joseph Roy & Marie Archange Ledoux) b & bp there 9 & 11 Apr 1823; m (1) there 23 Feb 1846 Angèle Ménard (Pierre Ménard & Marguerite Pépin); m (3) there 27 Nov 1854 Louise Tétreau (Dominique Tétreau & Charlotte Lussier); d & bur 17 & 20 Jan 1891, Ange Gardien, QC.

iv   **Etienne Bonneville dit Bouteille** b & bp 11 & 12 Jul 1827, Marieville, QC. He married 16 Apr 1850, Chambly, QC, **Julie/Sophie Lamoureux** (Alexis Lamoureux & Archange Cognac) b & bp there 13 & 14 Mar 1834; d & bur 26 & 31 Jan 1876, Thorndike, MA & Chambly, QC.

v   **Pierre Bonneville dit Bouteille** b & bp 23 & 24 May 1829, Marieville, QC. He married 13 May 1862, St. Pie, QC, **Adèle Bonvouloir** (Pierre Bonvouloir & Justine/Félicité Fontaine) b & bp 9 & 10 Jan 1842, Mont St. Grégoire, QC; d & bur 9 & 11 Sep 1868, Ange Gardien, QC.

vi   **Jean-Baptiste Bonneville dit Bouteille** b & bp 5 & 6 Dec 1830, Marieville, QC. He married 19 Feb 1855, St. Césaire, QC, **Julie Auclair/Oclaire** (Charles Oclaire & Julie Loisel) b & bp 25 Mar 1836, St. Jean-Baptiste, QC; d & bur 7 & 9 Sep 1879, Ange Gardien, QC.

vii   **Zoé Bonneville dit Bouteille** b & bp 8 & 9 Mar 1832, St. Jean-Baptiste, QC; d & bur 20 & 22 Apr 1854, St. Césaire, QC.

viii   **Joseph Bonneville dit Bouteille** b & bp 31 Aug & 1 Sep 1833, Marieville, QC.

3.1.7   **MONTY, Suzanne** b & bp 10 & 13 Nov 1798, Chambly & St. Mathias, QC.

3.1.8   **MONTY, Benjamin** married **Mary Provost**.

I know little of these two people beyond the bare fact of their existence, attest-ed to in the 1960s by Sarah Almina Monty (3.1.3.3.3), Benjamin Monty's grand-niece. I have been able to verify in most cases the accuracy of her recollections but can find no other trace of this couple. It may be that they both died young for their daughter Sarah lived most of her life with the family of her uncle Jean-Baptiste/John Monty (3.1.3).

Child:

3.1.8.1	Sarah Ann	1854?-	-1872

3.3.1   **MONTY, Charlotte** b & bp 29 & 30 Jan 1791, Chambly, QC; d & bur 28 Feb & 1 Mar 1812, St. Luc & St. Mathias, QC. She married 22 Jan 1810, Chambly, QC, **Jean Vanier** (Jean-Baptiste Vanier & Marguerite Brisset) b & bp there 4 & 5 Oct 1788; m (2) 16 Jun 1817, St. Constant, QC, Josette Bourdeau (Joseph Bourdeau & Catherine Poissant); m (3) there 29 Jan 1821 Catherine Longtin (Antoine Longtin & Josette Dupuis); m (4) 18 Feb 1833, Ste Martine, QC, Françoise Asselin (Joseph Asselin & Catherine Aguenier).

Jean Vanier (Vagnier at his marriage) was a farmer and laborer in St. Luc, QC, at his first marriage, a farmer in St. Constant, QC, at his second and third marriages, a farmer in St. Rémi, QC, at his fourth, and a laborer in St. Urbain, QC, in 1891 (Canadian census).

Children:

i   **Jean-Baptiste Vanier** b & bp 30 Apr 1810, St. Luc, QC.

ii   **Charlotte Vanier** b & bp 17 Feb 1812, St. Luc, QC; d & bur 1 & 4 Mar 1873, St. Constant, QC. She married there 18 Sep 1826 **Toussaint Antoine Cusson** (Antoine Cusson & Marie Anne Roy) b & bp there 31 Oct & 1 Nov 1803; d & bur there 5 & 7 Jul 1879.

3.3.2   **MONTY/MONTEE, Joseph** b & bp 29 Feb & 1 Mar 1792, Chambly, QC; d & bur 21 & 23 Apr 1869, Glens Falls, NY. He married 25 Nov 1816, St. Luc, QC, **Victoire/Victoria Perrault** (Antoine Perrault & Marie Bissonet) b & bp 2 & 3 Aug 1796, L'Acadie, QC; d & bur 27 & 29 Nov 1873, Glens Falls, NY.

Joseph Monty was originally a farm laborer in St. Luc, QC, and from 1824 to 1838 a farm laborer/farmer in Iberville, QC. He moved before 1840 to Glens Falls, NY, where he was a cooper (US and state censuses), and was naturalized in Warren Co., NY, as Joseph Montee on 24 Oct 1860. He and his wife were buried in St. Alphonsus Cemetery in Glens Falls.

Children:

3.3.2.1	Joseph	1817-1841?-1874
3.3.2.2	Laurent	1818- -
3.3.2.3	Hubert/Albert	1819- -1860
3.3.2.4	Victoire	1821- -1821
3.3.2.5	George	1822- -
3.3.2.6	Victoire	1824- -1825
3.3.2.7	Sophie	1826- -1826
3.3.2.8	Raymond	1827- -1828
3.3.2.9	Benjamin/Bénoni	1829- -1833
3.3.2.10	Anonymous	1831- -1831
3.3.2.11	Pierre	1832- -1832
3.3.2.12	Anonymous	1833- -1833
3.3.2.13	Judith/Julie	1834- -1834
3.3.2.14	Anonymous	1835- -1835
3.3.2.15	Emilie/Amelia	1836-1857-
3.3.2.16	Edward/Romuald	1838-1860-1877

3.3.3   **MONTY, Félicité** b & bp 8 & 9 Oct 1793, Chambly, QC; d & bur 22 & 24

May 1794, St. Mathias, QC.

3.3.4   **MONTY, Antoine** b & bp 8 & 9 Jun 1795, Chambly, QC; d & bur there 16 & 17 Aug 1795.

3.3.5   **MONTY, Antoine** b 1796?; d 1830/1831. He married 1 Feb 1819, St. Luc, QC, **Adélaïde Massé** (Charles Massé/Macé & Marie Louise Carrière) b & bp 11 & 12 Mar 1801, Chambly, QC.

Antoine Monty was of age when he married in February 1819. He was then born between the death in August 1795 of an older brother also named Antoine and February 1798. Since his brother Jacques was born in 1797, the only possible year of birth is 1796. He was a laborer in St. Luc, QC, in 1819. After 1824 he was a resident of Iberville, QC, where the records describe him as either a laborer or farmer. His last child was born posthumously on 1 Mar 1831, thus the assumption of his death in 1830 or early 1831.

I have not found Adélaïde Massé in Canada after 1832. It is possible that she came to the United States with her son Antoine's family in the mid-1840s. She may have been the Adeline Masse (though reportedly born in NY) who was living in his household in Essex, NY, in 1850 and/or the 65-year-old Canadian Adeline Monta (sic) who was a member of his household in Schuyler Falls, NY, in 1860 (US censuses). In neither guise does she appear with his family in 1865. She may have died before then.

Children:

3.3.5.1	Antoine	1819-1842-1910	
3.3.5.2	Narcisse	1821-	-1822
3.3.5.3	Jean-Baptiste	1822-	-
3.3.5.4	Adélaïde	1824-	-1824
3.3.5.5	Marguerite	1825-	-
3.3.5.6	Emilie	1827-	-
3.3.5.7	Céleste	1831-	-1832

3.3.6   **MONTY/MONTEE, Jacques/Jacob** b & bp 4 Jul 1797, Chambly, QC. He married 20 May 1822, L'Acadie, QC, **Marguerite Dufault** (Joseph Dufault & Marie Marier) b & bp there 19 Aug 1806; d 1885/1886, Glens Falls, NY.

The history of this family is particularly troublesome due to a large number of name changes. Joseph Monty (3.3) and Marie Louise Goguet had a son in 1797 who was named Jacques at his baptism. In 1822 a Jean Monty, son of Joseph Monty and Marie Louise Goguet (who so far as I know never had a son named Jean or Jean-Baptiste) married Marguerite Dufault who, as the wife of *Jacques* Monty, a farmer and/or laborer in Iberville, Napierville, and St. Jean, QC, bore him eight children between 1824 and 1837. The marriage record obviously misstated the groom's name.

The family disappears from Canadian records after 1837. There was however in Addison Co., VT, in 1840 a Jacob Mounty (sic) whose household included, in addition to his wife, three sons between the ages of 5 and 20. In 1850, Jacob Monte (sic) was a laborer in Glens Falls, NY, and included in his household his wife Margaret, daughters Margaret and Rosa, and mother-in-law Mrs. Mary DeFoe (Marie Marier, widow of Joseph Dufault). By 1855 the family name had become Montee. The state census also adds that the family had been in Glens Falls since 1847 and that daughter Margaret had been born in Vermont.

I conclude that Jacques Monty and Marguerite Dufault left Canada between 1837 when a son (3.3.6.8) was born there and June 1840 (US census). They stayed in Vermont until at least the birth of their daughter Margaret (3.3.6.9) and probably until 1847 (1855 state census). A final move took them to Glens Falls, NY, where the youngest child was born (1850 US census).

Jacob Montee was a laborer in Glens Falls until at least 1860 (US censuses). He may have died before 1865 for Mrs. Margaret Montee was then living in the household of her daughter Margaret (3.3.6.9) and son-in-law John LaFountain in Glens Falls. She had had twelve children (state census). She was still a resident of Glenn Falls at her death. Her daughter Rosa was appointed administrator of her estate in the Warren Co., NY, Surrogate's Court on 4 Feb 1886.

Children:

3.3.6.1	Jacques/Jacob	1824-	-1899
3.3.6.2	Jean-Baptiste	1826-	-
3.3.6.3	Alfred	1828-	-
3.3.6.4	Jacques Frédéric	1829?-	-1832
3.3.6.5	Gabriel	1831-	-1832
3.3.6.6	Adélaïde	1833-	-1834
3.3.6.7	Jean/John	1835-1857&1898?-1907	
3.3.6.8	Edmond	1837-	-
3.3.6.9	Margaret	1842/44-1857-1921	
3.3.6.10	Rosalie/Rosa	1849-1863-1914	

3.3.7   **MONTY, Marie Amable** b & bp 13 & 16 Jun 1799, Chambly, QC; d & bur there 28 & 29 Jun 1800.

3.5.1   **MONTY, Pierre** b & bp 9 May 1788, Chambly, QC; d & bur there 14 & 17 Dec 1788.

3.5.2   **MONTY, Pierre** b & bp 5 & 6 Jun 1789, Chambly, QC; d & bur there 23 & 24 Jun 1789.

3.5.3   **MONTY, Marguerite** bp 12 Sep 1791, St. Régis, QC; d & bur 23 & 24 Aug 1792, Chambly, QC, at the age of one.

3.5.4   **MONTY, Charlotte** b & bp 5 & 6 Nov 1792, Chambly, QC; d & bur 29 & 30 Jul 1836, Iberville, QC. She married 18 Feb 1822, St. Luc, QC, **Jean François Dallaire** (Jean-Baptiste Dallaire & Anne Harris) m (2) 17 Apr 1837, Iberville, QC, Marie Louise Brosseau (Etienne Brosseau & Marie Archange Girouard), widow of Louis Caillé.

Jean François Dallaire (also Jean Daller/D'Aller, Jean-Baptiste Dallaire) was a minor at his first marriage. His occupations varied. He was a clerk in Iberville, QC, at the birth of his daughter Marie in 1822, a farmer at her death in 1823, and a laborer a few weeks later at the birth of his son Paul Léon.

Children:
  i   **Marie Dallaire** b & bp 9 & 11 Dec 1822, Iberville & St. Luc, QC; d & bur there 3 & 4 Oct 1823.
  ii **Paul Léon Dallaire** b & bp 27 Nov & 4 Dec 1823, Iberville, QC.

3.5.5   **MONTY, Jean-Baptiste** b & bp 6 Jun 1794, Chambly, QC; d & bur there 15 & 16 Jun 1794.

3.5.6   **MONTY, Louis** b & bp 12 Jun 1795, St. Mathias, QC.
This child presumably died before a younger brother of the same name (3.5.15) was born on 11 Jul 1806.

3.5.7   **MONTY, Jean-Baptiste** b & bp 21 & 22 Jun 1796, Chambly, QC; d & bur there 30 Jun & 1 Jul 1796.

3.5.8   **MONTY, Antoine** b & bp 13 & 14 Jun 1797, St. Mathias, QC; d & bur there 2 & 3 Jul 1797.

3.5.9   **MONTY, Marie Marguerite** b & bp 24 & 25 Jun 1798, St. Mathias, QC; d & bur there 5 & 6 Jul 1798.

3.5.10　　　　**MONTY, Marie Madeleine** b & bp 5 Jul 1799, St. Mathias, QC; d & bur there 1 & 3 Aug 1799.

3.5.11　　　　**MONTY, Marie Angélique** b & bp 4 & 5 Aug 1800, St. Mathias, QC; d & bur there 13 & 14 Aug 1800.

3.5.12　　　　**MONTY, Marguerite** b & bp 9 Jul 1802, L'Acadie, QC; d & bur 20 & 21 Jul 1802, St. Luc, QC.

3.5.13　　　　**MONTY/MONTA, Jean-Baptiste/John** b & bp 16 Sep 1803, St. Luc, QC. He married **Marie/Mary Labonté** b 1822?, QC.

Jean-Baptiste Monty was known in Vergennes, VT, where his children were born, as John Monta. He was a laborer there in 1850, when his much younger wife was 28 years old (US census). I have been unable to find the couple in later censuses. Only their son Joseph was still in Vergennes in 1860.

Children:

3.5.13.1	Mary Jane	1839?- -
3.5.13.2	Joseph	1844?-1865?-1894
3.5.13.3	Abigail	1846?- -
3.5.13.4	Ellen	1852-1873-

3.5.14　　　　**MONTY, Pierre** b & bp 22 & 23 Sep 1804, St. Luc, QC; d & bur 7 & 8 Oct 1804, St. Mathias, QC.

3.5.15　　　　**MONTY, Louis** b & bp 11 & 12 Jul 1806, St. Luc, QC; d & bur 22 & 23 Jul 1806, St. Mathias, QC.

3.5.16　　　　**MONTY, Pierre** b & bp 18 Sep 1807, St. Luc, QC; d & bur 2 & 3 Oct 1807, St. Mathias, QC.

3.5.17　　　　**MONTY, Marie Agnès** b & bp 15 & 17 May 1809, St. Luc, QC. She married 25 May 1830, St. Jean, QC, **Pierre Roy** (Pierre Roy & Thérèse Lisotte) b & bp 20 Jan 1806, Yamaska, QC.

Pierre Roy was a laborer in Iberville, QC, at his marriage.

Child:

i　　**Pierre Roy** b & bp 31 Dec 1831 & 4 Jan 1832, St. Jean, QC; d & bur 12 & 13 Jun 1832, Iberville, QC.

3.9.1　　　　**MONTY, Françoise** b & bp 21 & 22 Nov 1794, Chambly, QC; d & bur 24 & 26 Jun 1873, Iberville, QC. She married (1) 23 Nov 1818, St. Luc, QC, **Etienne Tougas** (Jean-Baptiste Tougas & Marguerite Benjamin dit St. Aubin) b & bp 20 & 21 Nov 1797, Chambly, QC; d & bur 7 & 9 Dec 1829, Iberville, QC.

She married (2) 19 Feb 1844, Iberville, QC, **Isaac Deneau** (Jacques Deneau & Elizabeth Boyer) b & bp 23 Jan 1797, St. Philippe, QC; m (1) there 20 Nov 1820, Marguerite Robert (Isaac Robert & Catherine Martin); d & bur 5 & 8 May 1876, Iberville, QC.

Etienne Tougas was originally a carpenter in St. Luc, QC, where his first two children were born. He was then a farmer in Marieville, QC, for a few years and in Iberville, QC, from 1824 until his death. He was a brother of Noël Tougas, husband of Marie Monty (3.9.7).

Isaac Deneau was a farmer in Iberville.

Children:

i　　**Etienne Tougas** b & bp 24 Oct 1819, St. Luc, QC; d & bur 16 & 20 May 1873, Iberville, QC. He married there 28 Jan 1840 **Mathilde Beaudry** (Jean-Baptiste

Beaudry & Josephte Brien) b 1821?, St. Charles, QC.

ii   **Abraham Tougas** b & bp 4 & 6 Jan 1821, St. Luc, QC; d & bur 24 & 26 Mar 1822, Marieville, QC.

iii   **Magloire/Abraham Tougas** b & bp 2 & 6 Oct 1822, Marieville, QC; d & bur there 21 & 23 Jun 1823.

iv   **Ambroise Tougas** b & bp 21 & 23 May 1824, Iberville, QC; d & bur 7 & 9 Oct 1893, Stanbridge, QC. He married (1) 30 May 1848, Iberville, QC, **Angèle Audet** (Laurent Audet dit Lapointe & Sophie Bessette) b 1826?; d & bur 31 Jan & 3 Feb 1851, Henryville, QC, at the age of 25.

        He married (2) 17 May 1852 QC, Henryville, QC, **Marie Dagesse** (Louis Dagesse & Archange Robidoux).

v   **Moyse Tougas** b & bp 10 & 11 Dec 1827, Iberville, QC. He married there 11 Nov 1856 **Odile Bourdon** (Hilaire Bourdon & Domitilde Thibodeau).

3.9.2   **MONTY, Jean-Baptiste** b & bp 14 & 16 Apr 1796, Chambly, QC; bur 1 Aug 1827, Iberville, QC. He married 1 Oct 1821, St. Luc, QC, **Catherine Morin** (Alphonse Morin & Elisabeth Brosseau) b & bp 23 & 24 Mar 1801, L'Acadie, QC; m (2) 20 Nov 1832, Iberville, QC, Louis Charpentier (Louis Charpentier & Louise Rougier).

Jean-Baptiste Monty was a farmer in Iberville, QC. The burial record does not specify the date of death; it states only that he had died a few days previously. His widow was a resident of Marieville, QC, at her second marriage. She lived until at least 1863 when she was godmother to her granddaughter Marie Piette (3.9.2.3.v).

Children:

3.9.2.1	Domitille	1822-1842-1903
3.9.2.2	Guillaume/William	1826-1847&1867-
3.9.2.3	Victoire	1828-1853-1899

3.9.3   **MONTY/MONTIE, François Xavier/Francis** b & bp 1 Jun 1796, Chambly, QC; d 22 June 1879, Ecorse, MI. He married 26 Jan 1818, St. Luc, QC, **Marie Geneviève/Mary Goyette** (Louis Goyette & Geneviève Vigeant) b & bp 2 & 3 Jul 1795, St. Mathias, QC; d 17 May 1880, Ecorse, MI.

François Xavier Monty was a farmer in St. Luc, QC, from 1818 to 1822 and in Iberville, QC, from 1824 to at least 1832. By the late 1840s he was a farmer in Ecorse, MI, where he and his wife became known as Francis and Mary Monti, Monte, or Montie (US censuses). The surname Montie predominated and was generally used by their descendants.

Children:

3.9.3.1	François Xavier	1818- -1820
3.9.3.2	Louis	1820-1847-1891
3.9.3.3	Jean-Baptiste/John B.	1822-1849-1888
3.9.3.4	Marie/Mary	1824-1856-1893
3.9.3.5	Abraham/Abram	1826- &1861?-1881
3.9.3.6	Antoine	1828-1857-1894
3.9.3.7	Marie Angèle/Angela	1830-1856-1914
3.9.3.8	Céleste	1832- -1855

3.9.4   **MONTY, Marguerite** b & bp 30 May & 3 Jun 1800, St. Mathias, QC; d & bur 6 & 9 Feb 1881, Ste Angèle, QC. She married (1) 3 Mar 1829, Iberville, QC, **Jean-Baptiste Choquette** (François Choquette & Charlotte Lebeau) b & bp 16 & 17 Feb 1800, St. Mathias, QC; m (1) 7 Jul 1822, Marieville, QC, Marie Anne Jetté (Louis Jetté & Marie Davignon); bur 18 Apr 1832, Iberville, QC.

She married (2) 2 Mar 1835, Iberville, QC, **Alexis Boulay** (Joseph Boulay & Angélique Dussault) b & bp 18 & 20 May 1792, St. Mathias, QC; m (1) there 19 Sep 1814 Marie Anne Lasnier (François Lasnier & Marie Benjamin dit St. Aubin); d & bur 23 & 24 Mar 1876, Ste Angèle, QC.

Jean-Baptiste Choquette was a farmer in Iberville, QC. The date of his death is omitted from the burial record which states merely that he was 32 years old and the husband of Marguerite Monti (sic).

Alexis Boulay (also Boulé, Boulais) was a resident of Marieville, QC, when he married Marguerite Monty. He was retired in Ste Angèle, QC, at his death.

3.9.5 **MONTY, Théotiste** b & bp 25 & 26 Jun 1802, St. Luc, QC; d & bur 31 Aug & 1 Sep 1834, Iberville, QC. She married there 16 Nov 1830 **Joseph Duquet** (Joseph Duquet & Marie Josephte Brosseau) b & bp 31 Jan & 1 Feb 1799, L'Acadie, QC; m (2) 2 Jun 1835, Henryville, QC, Julie Roy (Alexis Roy & Marie Boudreau).

Joseph Duquet (also Duquette) was a farmer in Iberville and in Henryville, QC.

Children:

i **Anastasie Duquet** b & bp 16 & 19 Dec 1831, Iberville, QC. She married 6 Nov 1855, Henryville, QC, **Joseph Laroche** (Joseph Laroche & Euphrosine Simard) b & bp 25 & 26 Mar 1826, Iberville, QC; d & bur 23 & 25 Aug 1866, Henryville, QC.

ii **Joseph Duquet** b & bp 18 & 19 Dec 1833, Iberville, QC. He married 27 May 1856, Henryville, QC, **Aurélie Chicoine** (Jean-Baptiste Chicoine & Marguerite Beaulac dit Desmarais) b & bp there 3 & 7 Feb 1838.

3.9.6 **MONTY, Marie Louise** b & bp 24 & 25 Jun 1804, St. Luc, QC; d & bur 16 & 18 Nov 1825, Iberville, QC. She married 6 Feb 1821, St. Luc, QC, **Jean-Baptiste Strachan** (Arthur Strachan & Marie Angélique Racine [2.viii]) b & bp 26 & 27 Dec 1796, Chambly, QC; m (2) 9 Feb 1830, Iberville, QC, Clotilde Comette (Etienne Comette & Elisabeth Giroux); d & bur 2 & 4 May 1860, Henryville, QC.

Jean-Baptiste Strachan (also Stracken, Straughan) was a farmer in Iberville, QC, at his marriages.

Children:

i **Marguerite Strachan/Stroken** b & bp 29 Nov 1821, St. Luc, QC. She married 5 Feb 1839, Iberville, QC, **Pierre Ménard** (Louis Ménard & Marie Lefort) b & bp 28 Jun 1811, Chambly, QC.

ii **Jean-Baptiste Strachan** b & bp 25 & 26 Mar 1824, Iberville, QC.

3.9.7 **MONTY, Marie** b & bp 8 & 9 Oct 1806, St. Luc, QC; d & bur 9 & 12 Feb 1883, Iberville, QC. She married there 11 Oct 1825 **Noël Tougas** (Jean-Baptiste Tougas & Marguerite Benjamin dit St. Aubin) b & bp 22 & 23 Dec 1800, St. Mathias, QC; d & bur 8 & 10 Aug 1866, Iberville, QC.

Noël Tougas was a brother of Etienne Tougas, husband of Françoise Monty (3.9.1). He was a laborer in Iberville, QC, at his marriage and a farmer or farm hand there and in the vicinity for most of his life. The family moved several times between 1835 and 1844, according to the 1851 Canadian census in Christieville, QC, which specifies each child's place of birth, but had returned to Iberville by 1844.

Children:

i **Marie Joseph Tougas** b & bp 20 & 21 Jul 1827, Iberville, QC; d & bur there 28 & 30 Jun 1828.

ii **Marie Tougas** b & bp 14 & 16 Sep 1829, Iberville, QC; d & bur there 30 Jun & 2 Jul 1851.

iii **Noël Tougas** b & bp 11 & 19 Jun 1831, Henryville & Iberville, QC; d & bur there 27 & 30 Apr 1861.

iv **Magloire Tougas** b & bp 18 & 25 Nov 1833, Henryville & St. Valentin, QC.

v **William Tougas** b 1835?, Stanbridge, QC.

vi **Emilie Tougas** b & bp Feb & 6 May 1839, St. Armand & Ormestown Twp, QC; d & bur 27 & 28 Nov 1844, Iberville, QC.

vii   **Ambroise Tougas** b 1842?, Stanbridge, QC. He married 24 Oct 1864, St. Jean, QC, **Hermine Valière** (Louis Valière & Marguerite Gendreau).

viii   **Magloire Tougas** b & bp 6 & 29 Mar 1843, Eastern Townships, QC; d & bur 29 & 31 Jul 1903, Iberville, QC. He married 26 Sep 1876, St. Pie, QC, **Asilda/Exilda Rouleau** (Jean-Baptiste Rouleau & Tharsile Daunais) b & bp 6 & 8 Jul 1843, St. Pie, QC; d & bur 15 & 18 Jan 1911, Iberville, QC.

ix   **Adélaïde Tougas** b & bp 10 & 12 Sep 1844, Iberville, QC; d & bur there 7 & 9 May 1867.

x   **Joseph Octave Tougas** b & bp 27 & 29 Nov 1847, Iberville, QC. He married 21 Apr 1873, St. Alexandre, QC, **Marie Bergeron** (Damien Bergeron & Mathilde Ménard).

xi   **Alexandre Tougas** b & bp 2 & 4 Mar 1851, Iberville, QC.

3.9.8   **MONTY, Rosalie/Sophie** b & bp 15 Aug 1809, St. Luc, QC; d & bur 30 Jan & 1 Feb 1810, St. Luc & St. Mathias, QC.

A daughter of Jean-Baptiste Monty and Françoise Ménard was baptized as Rosalie in St. Luc, QC, on the day of her birth in August 1809. Another child, who died at the end of January 1810 at the age of 5½ months, was buried in St. Mathias, QC, under the name Sophie. Barring twins, of whom there is no sign, they must be the same child.

3.9.9   **MONTY, Ambroise** b & bp 15 Jun 1812, St. Mathias, QC; d & bur there 3 & 4 Jul 1812.

4.3.1   **MONTY, Christopher** b around 1786, NY; d 10 Jun 1861, NY. He married a first cousin, **Mary Lizotte** (Louis Lizotte & Marie Madeline/Mary Monty [4.7]) b around 1788, Chazy, NY.

Christopher Monty's date of birth is somewhat problematic. The suggested date is based on the 1850 census in Essex, NY, when he and his wife were 64 and 62 years old respectively. That is consistent with the span of years shown in the censuses of 1800 in Vergennes, VT, of 1810 in Plattsburgh, NY, and of 1820 and 1840 in Chazy, NY. Three records however point to an earlier birth year. He was born between 1770 and 1780 according to the 1830 census in Chazy, in 1778 according to the 1855 state census in Essex when he was 77 years old (a statement I can easily disregard since it contains a number of provable errors), and in 1776 according to the inscription on his tombstone in the Riverside Cemetery in Plattsburgh. It reads: "Christopher Monty / Veteran of the War of 1812 / Died / June 10, 1861 / AE 85" (Northern New York State Tombstone Transcription Project). This can only refer to Christopher, son of Jacques/James Monty, since we know from the testimony of Mrs. Barbary Morrison (4.4.5) that her brother Christopher (4.4.3), the only other Christopher Monty of the appropriate age, had died before 1856 (Appendix I). The age of the deceased, though, is almost certainly incorrect: his father was only 13 years old in 1776. The early censuses appear to be more accurate.

Christopher Monty was a private in Capt. Green's company of the New York Militia during the Battle of Plattsburgh in early September 1814 and was allowed $84 on his claim (#4477) for losses incurred in the war (Pension Files, War of 1812). He was a farmer in Chazy before moving around 1841 to Essex. He had been living there for fourteen years in 1855 and was a shoemaker, but perhaps not a very successful one: the log house in which he, his wife, and his daughter Harriet's family lived was valued at only $20 (state census). Both he and his wife were alive in October 1856 according to the testimony of his cousin John Monty Jr. (4.11.1) (Appendix I).

The list of children below is certainly incomplete. In 1820, for example, there were five children in Christopher Monty's household: two males and one female under the age of 10 and two males between the ages of 10 and 16. In 1830, he was the head of a household of thirteen, though I suspect that this also included his son Christopher's (4.3.1.2) family. Another son, Lewis Monty (4.3.1.1.) was living next door. In 1840, there still resided in Chazy with Christopher Monty Sr. and his wife one male child (John?) between the ages of 10 and 15 and one female child (Harriet?) between the ages of 15 and 20.

Children:

4.3.1.1	Lewis	1806?-1828?-
4.3.1.2	Christopher	1810?- -
4.3.1.3	Harriet	1822?- -1886
4.3.1.4	John	1828?-1854?& &1886-

4.3.2   **MONTY, James** b between 1797 and 1808, Clinton Co., NY; d between 1870 and 1875, Essex, NY. He married **Charlotte Richard** (____ Richard & Mary ____) b Mar 1807, QC; d & bur 21 & 23 Aug 1900, Essex, NY.

The year of James Monty's birth varies considerably from census to census. I tend to believe in an early date, perhaps 1801 as recorded in the 1850 US census in Essex, NY, or even before 1800, for in the US census of that year in Fishkill, NY, his father counted in his household two sons (James and Matthew?) under the age of 10. An early date of birth would also explain how he could be appointed administrator of his father's estate on 25 Oct 1819 (Clinton Co., NY, Surrogate's Court). James Monty was then a laborer in Plattsburgh, NY. He moved to Essex around 1840 and had been a farmer there for fifteen years in 1855, living in a log house valued at $150. He prospered. His real estate was valued at $1,400 in 1860 while in 1865 his family was living in a frame house valued at $1,300. He was still farming in Essex in 1870 but was no longer alive in 1875 (US and state censuses).

Charlotte Richard's date and place of birth are taken from the 1900 US census in Essex. Other censuses place her birth between 1809 and 1812 while the notice of her death and burial in the *Ticonderoga Sentinel* of 3 Aug 1900 simply refers to her as "Mrs. Monty, an elderly lady..." who died at the home of her daughter Mrs. Alexander Cross. She had originally lived after her husband's death with her son James in Essex but was a member of the Cross family there in 1900 (US and state censuses).

Children:

4.3.2.1	James	1835?- -1898
4.3.2.2.	Lois	1836-1860?-1926
4.3.2.3	Warren	1839?-1865-1871
4.3.2.4	Harriet	1847?- -
4.3.2.5	Mary/Milly	1851?- -

4.3.3   **MONTY, Matthew** b 1798?, Clinton Co., NY; d between 1850 and 1856. He married before 1820 **Salome/Siloma Clark** b 1801?, NY.

Matthew Monty was a farmer in Beekmantown, NY, from at least 1820 when he and his wife already had one child. His assumed date of birth is derived from the 1850 census in Beekmantown when he was 52 years old. He died before November 1856 according to the affidavit of his cousin John Monty (4.11.1) who then named thirteen of his surviving children (Appendix I).

Seven of theses children, Matilda, Henry, David, Hepsabeth, Allen, Melvin, and Amelia were still at home in 1850 (US census). The older children named by John Monty had probably married by then or moved away from the area. They scattered even more after their father's death. I can find only Jane (4.3.3.5) in Clinton Co., NY, in 1860, and she soon left with her husband for New Hampshire. Others were living in Vermont, Massachusetts, Illinois, or Wisconsin. In some cases I know nothing beyond the names provided by John Monty.

I have added one child however to the list of Matthew Monty's children: Matthew Monty (4.3.3.3?) whose history in Bennington Co., VT, in the 1840s and 1850s suggests strongly that he was the brother of Abraham Monty (4.3.3.4) who married there and was a resident there through at least 1850. I hesitate to rely solely on circumstantial evidence, yet it seems preferable at this time to err on the side of inclusiveness.

Siloma Clark was 49 years old in 1850 and was born in New York State according to the census of that year in Beekmantown. In 1870 she was living in Stamford, VT, in the household of Joseph Reed, husband of her daughter Amelia (4.3. 3.14). Her surname was Monta, a variant also applied to her sons in Vermont.

Children:

4.3.3.1	Katy	-	-
4.3.3.2	Ginnie	-	-
4.3.3.3?	Matthew	1824-1845?-1883	
4.3.3.4	Abraham	1825-1845-1903	
4.3.3.5	Jane Ann/Geneviève	1826?-	-1905
4.3.3.6	Polly/Mary	1827?-1847-1859	
4.3.3.7	Eunice	-	-
4.3.3.8	Matilda	1829?-	-
4.3.3.9	Henry William	1833?-	-
4.3.3.10	David Wright	1834-1855-1912	
4.3.3.11	Hepsabeth	1837?-	-
4.3.3.12	Charles Allen	1841-1860-1891	
4.3.3.13	Melvin J.	1842?-1866?&1886-	
4.3.3.14	Amelia	1847-1864?-1916	

4.4.1   **MONTY, Johanna** b 1783?, Clinton Co., NY; d before 1846. She married **Abraham Monty**.

No birth, marriage, death, or burial record has been found for either Johanna Monty or Abraham Monty. The family connection was established by Mrs. Barbary (Monty) Morrison (4.4.5) who referred to her sister Johanna Monty, wife of Abraham Monty, in an affidavit of 9 Oct 1856 before the Clinton Co. Court of Common Pleas in Plattsburgh, NY (Appendix I). Given the age of her oldest child, she was probably the 2-year-old child of Mr. and Mrs. Francis Monty who were living on Lake Champlain in 1885 (John Andrew Bilow, "Census of Canadian Refugees in New York State, 1784, 1785, 1787," *French Canadian and Acadian Genealogical Review*, IX, 246).

Johanna Monty was deceased in October 1856 and had left the five children listed below, according to her sister Barbary's testimony (Appendix I). An earlier reference to the heirs of Francis Monty Jr. in the records of the Circuit Court in Plattsburgh implies that Johanna Monty died before July 1846 and even suggests that she predeceased her father. The judges affirmed on 4 Jul 1846 that Francis Monty, who died on 10 Aug 1818 "left Six children who are all over the age of twenty one years and that they are his only Surviving children whose names are as follows. Christopher Monty, Abram Monty, Betsey Ward, Fanny Miller, Barbara Monty, and Margaret Frederic" (Appendix II). At issue was the question of whether Francis Monty's living children were eligible to receive benefits derived from the Revolutionary War pension he had applied for before his death. The judges' opinion thus touched on both the past (1818) and the present (1846) and is somewhat ambiguous. It is not clear whether they listed only with those children who were still alive in 1846 or all who were alive at the time of their father's death. Johanna had certainly died before 1846. It is possible that she predeceased her father.

Abraham Monty's parentage is unknown. It would seem plausible that he was a relative of some kind. He is mentioned as the husband of Johanna Monty but not individually as a descendant of François/Francis Monty in the 1856 affidavits of Mrs. Barbary Morrison and John Monty Jr. (4.11.1) (Appendix I). This could mean either that his father, the primary heir, was still alive or that Abraham Monty belonged to another branch of the Monty family. I am somewhat leery about his name: François/Francis Monty's own son (4.5), though named Abraham in the 1810 and 1820 census in Plattsburgh as well as in Mrs. Barbary Morrison's affidavit of 1856, was nevertheless named Amable at his birth, in the 1800 census in Champlain, NY, and in all 1818 and 1820 papers dealing with his pension as a Revolutionary War veteran. Abraham is a later creation. The same change could also have occurred in Johanna Monty's husband's name.

In this connection I have been tempted to see in her husband a cousin once removed, Amable Monty (1.2), son of Amable Monty and Marie Angélique Létourneau. He would have been much older than his wife, which gives me pause. More importantly, I cannot find any trace of either spouse, individually or together, in New York State (though their children all apparently married and lived there in the 1830s and 1840s). Amable Monty himself was present in Canada at two of his sisters' marriages in 1779 and 1798 but seems never to have married or died there. The only record I have found which may pertain to him is that of the burial on 30 Jan 1802 in St. Luc, QC, of an anonymous female child born on Lake Champlain on 12 Jan 1802 and privately baptized at home. The parents are Amable Monty, a farmer on Lake Champlain, and Josette Monty (maiden name, as is customary in Canadian records). It could be that Josette was conceived to be French equivalent of Johanna, a name seldom found in French Canada.

But that is very little to go on. I can only hope that some future researcher may discover the missing link. In the meantime I have proceeded on the assumption that Johanna Monty's husband was a descendant of Jean Monty though, through necessity, the numbers assigned to their own descendants reflect her lineage rather than his.

Children:

4.4.1.1	Elizabeth	1802-	-1892
4.4.1.2	Abraham	1808-	-1852
4.4.1.3	Margaret	1811?-	&1836-1882
4.4.1.4	Francis/Frank	1814-1835?&1874?-1906	
4.4.1.5	Lucina	1816?-	-

4.4.2   **MONTY, Joseph** b Clinton Co., NY; d before 1846.

This man's name and those of his children are taken from an 1856 affidavit before the Clinton Co. Court of Common Pleas in Plattsburgh, NY, by his sister Mrs. Barbary Morrison (4.4.5). Joseph Monty was then deceased (Appendix I). Another court document (Appendix II) implies that Joseph Monty was no longer alive on 4 Jul 1846 when the judges of the Clinton Co. Circuit Court in Plattsburgh, NY affirmed on the basis of Christopher Monty's (4.4.3) testimony that Francis Monty Jr. (4.4) had only six surviving children. Joseph Monty is not included among them. There is some ambiguity though (See discussion at 4.4.1). It may be that he had even predeceased his father. I know nothing more about him.

Children:

4.4.2.1	John	1818?-	-
4.4.2.2	Joseph	-	-
4.4.2.3	Andrew	-	-

4.4.3   **MONTY, Christopher** b 1787?, Clinton Co., NY; d between 1850 and 1856. He married **Catherine Miller** b 1802?, Canada.

Christopher Monty, a farmer in Plattsburgh, NY, was 63 years old and his wife 48 in 1850 (US census). Neither appears in later censuses. He died before October 1856, probably in Plattsburgh, according to the testimony of his sister Mrs. Barbary Morrison (4.4.5) who also provided a list of his children (Appendix I).

He had been named administrator of his father's estate in 1819 by the Clinton Co. Surrogate's Court in Plattsburgh. As such he filed a number of petitions in 1846 and 1847, based on the Act of 7 Jun 1832, to secure for his father's heirs the pensions which may have been due on account of their father's service during the American Revolution. The claim was eventually denied since Francis Monty Jr. had died before the passage of the enabling legislation, but the numerous letters and affidavits which it engendered sheds much needed light on Christopher Monty's siblings. One opinion rendered by the judges of the Clinton Co. Circuit Court on 4 Jul 1846 establishes that six siblings, Christopher Monty, Abram Monty, Betsey Ward, Fanny Miller, Barbara Monty, and Margaret Frederic were still alive, while three others, Johanna, Joseph, and Mary were then deceased. The document provides some guidance not only as to the dates of the women's marriages but also as to a few deaths. Though it may be ambiguous (see my discussion at 4.4.1), it is nevertheless a valuable document and is transcribed in Appendix II.

Children:

4.4.3.1	Mary	1817?-	-1886
4.4.3.2	Julia	1821?-1836?-1871?	
4.4.3.3	Frederick	1829?-	-
4.4.3.4	Jane	-	-
4.4.3.5	Ann	1833?-	-
4.4.3.6	Andrew	1835-	-

4.4.4 **MONTY, Jane Ann** b 15 Jun 1792, Fishkill, NY; bp 1850, Plattsburgh, NY; d & bur there 19 & 20 May 1856. She married **John Miller/Jean-Baptiste Meunier dit Lafleur** (Jean Meunier dit Lafleur & Marie Anne Demers) b & bp 17 Sep 1782, Chambly, QC; d & bur 30 Aug & 1 Sep 1850, Plattsburgh, NY.

The baptismal record of Jane Monty in St. John the Baptist Catholic church in Plattsburgh, NY, is the source of much information concerning this couple. It reads: "Jane born 15 June 1792 was this day received into the Church. She is daughter of Francis Monté (sic) and was born in Fishkill St. of NY. Wife of John Miller who died here 30 August '50 and was buried in [illegible] on 1 Sept. Her godfather André Bird & godmother Mary Miller" (no day or month, 1850, p. 17). She was thus baptized after her husband's death, in the fall or early winter of 1850, and her godparents were her daughter Mary and her son-in-law Andrew Bird. André (sic) Bird was again present at her burial a few years later though the French records of St. Peter's Catholic church in Plattsburgh refer to Jeanne Monty, widow of the deceased Jean-Baptiste Lafleur.

These name and surname changes can be confusing, especially since Jane Ann Monty was known at her children's baptisms in Canada as Geneviève Monty, Johanna Mounty (sic), or Jeanne Monty. Her husband, named Jean-Baptiste Meunier or Jean-Baptiste Meunier dit Lafleur at his baptism and at the baptisms of his children in Canada, was generally known in the United States as John Miller, a direct translation of Meunier. The only exception I have seen is in his wife's French burial record where he was named Jean-Baptiste Lafleur.

John Miller was a farmer in Plattsburgh in 1850 when only his wife Jane and 18-year-old son Robert were members of his household (US census). He had been a laborer/farmer in Plattsburgh in 1815, 1819, and 1821 and in Saranac, NY, in 1823, according to his children's baptismal records in Chambly and Laprairie, QC. I know very little more about this family. The names of the eleven children who were still alive in October 1856 are taken from their aunt Mrs. Barbary Morrison's affidavit (Appendix I). Only François (ii) is missing.

Children:
   i   **John Miller/Jean-Baptiste Meunier** b & bp 1 Jan 1812 & 12 Jun 1815, Plattsburgh, NY & Chambly, QC.
   ii   **François Miller/Meunier** b & bp 1 Mar 1813 & 12 Jun 1815, Plattsburgh, NY & Chambly, QC.
   iii   **Mary Miller/Marie Meunier** b & bp 17 Sep 1814 & 12 Jun 1815, Plattsburgh, NY & Chambly, QC. She married **Andrew/André Bird**.
   iv   **Maria Miller/Marie Anne Meunier** b & bp 22 Dec 1816 & 2 Apr 1819, Plattsburgh, NY & Chambly, QC.
   v   **Joseph Miller/Meunier** b & bp 4 Nov 1819 & 9 Mar 1821, Plattsburgh, NY & Chambly, QC.
   vi   **Abraham Miller/Amable Meunier** b & bp 11 Oct 1821 & 13 Feb 1823, Saranac, NY & Laprairie, QC.
   vii   **Benjamin Miller**
   viii   **Anthony Miller**
   ix   **Elizabeth Miller**
   x   **Catherine Miller**
   xi   **Matilda Miller**
   xii   **Robert Miller** b 1832?, Plattsburgh, NY.

4.4.5 **MONTY, Barbary/Barbara** married between 1846 and 1856 ___ Morri-

son.

Mrs. Barbary Morrison's deposition of 9 Oct 1856 before the Clinton Co. Court of Common Pleas in Plattsburgh, NY (Appendix I) is the source of much information concerning the descendants of Francis Monty Jr., some of which cannot be found elsewhere. What could be verified has proved to be generally accurate, with a few exceptions I have noted. The name of her husband however is not included, which has made the search for his identity very difficult. I have not been successful.

It has been suggested that Barbary Monty was born around Plattsburgh. It is very possible, although I have been unable to find even indirect confirmation. She apparently married after 4 Jul 1846 when the Clinton Co. Circuit Court in Plattsburgh accepted proof that "Barbara Monty" was a surviving daughter of Francis Monty Jr. (Appendix I). Since that document refers to her sisters under their married names, it can be assumed she was then still single. She was married and living in Plattsburg when she testified before Judge Ellsworth in October 1856.

4.4.6   **MONTY, Betsey** married before 1846 **John Ward**.

The evidence concerning this couple is taken from two court documents in Plattsburgh, NY. In the first, dated 4 July 1846, it was proved to the satisfaction of the Clinton Co. Circuit Court that Betsey Ward was a surviving daughter of Francis Monty Jr. (Appendix II). In the second, dated 9 Oct 1856, her sister Mrs. Barbary Morrison (4.4.5) testified that "Betsey Ward (daughter of Francis Monty, son of L^t. Monty) who married John Ward" was still alive (Appendix I). It has been suggested that she was born around 1796, although I have been unable to find any record of her birth, marriage, or death. Nor have I found any trace of the Ward family in Clinton Co., NY.

4.4.7   **MONTY/MONTEE, Abraham** b 21 Apr 1800, Plattsburgh, NY; d 14 Feb 1877, Macomb, IL. He married 3 Feb/22 Apr 1822, Plattsburgh, NY, **Hester Ann Wilson** b there 3 Mar 1805; d 5 Nov 1882, Macomb, IL.

Abraham Monty/Montee is the ancestor of the Montee family whose history has been traced by Betty Ramsey in her *Monty-Montee History* (Fairview, UT, 1981). I have summarized her findings in several instances, added new information in others, and refer the reader to her work when I can find no confirmation from primary sources.

Much of what we know about Abraham Monty/Montee's life derives from the War Department records concerning his military service during the War of 1812, his application with supporting affidavits for a pension based on that service, and the correspondence this generated in the 1870s (photocopies in Ramsey, pp. 207 sq). He signed A. Montee. But there is little agreement between his statements and the records of the Adjutant General's Office. Abraham Montey (such is his name in the AGO files) enlisted in Plattsburgh, NY, in Capt. Jonathan Brooks' Company, US Artillery, on 14 Feb 1814 (AGO) or 22 Feb 1815 (A. Montee); he was absent as a deserter from Capt. L. Churchill's Company from 27 Apr to 9 Jul 1816 (AGO) or was in hospital for two months at Governor's Island (A. Montee); he deserted from Ft. Columbus on 11 Oct 1817 (AGO) or was discharged for disability in Plattsburgh in the fall of 1817 (A. Montee). Since he was unable to produce the discharge or other papers which would prove his claims, a pension was denied on the grounds that he was a deserter. I do not know where the truth lies: there are several inconsistencies in both sets of statements. It does seem odd, as Mrs. Ramsey notes, that a former deserter would later apply for a military pension, even at a distance of fifty years. It could perhaps be a case of mistaken identity though I know of no other Abraham Monty/Montey/Montee from Plattsburgh who was engaged in the War of 1812.

Abraham Monty or Montey married in Plattsburgh on either 3 Feb or 22 Apr 1822 (both dates are found in his affidavits). He remained there until at least May 1832 and then moved to Ohio where he made several real estate transactions and eventually owned a sawmill in Wyandot County. It is there that the surname Montee was first applied to his family, in the 1850 US census in Pitt Twp, OH. He moved to Illinois a few years later and was a farmer in Chalmers Twp, IL, in 1860 and in Emmet Twp, IL, in 1870. By 1875 the family was in Macomb, IL, where Hester Ann Wilson was still living in 1880 (US and state censuses). She died two years later and was buried alongside her husband in the Old Macomb Cemetery. Their tombstones bearing the names of "Abram MONTEE" and "HESTER ANN, wife of ABRAM MONTEE" are still standing.

Children:

4.4.7.1	Sarah Emily	1823-1841-1900
4.4.7.2	Mary Elizabeth	1825-1845-1907
4.4.7.3	Theodore	1827-1850&1853-1921
4.4.7.4	William	1829-1851-1890
4.4.7.5	Edward	1832-1853-1908
4.4.7.6	James Wilson	1834-1855-1914
4.4.7.7	Nancy	1836-1857-
4.4.7.8	Charles	1839-1861-1865
4.4.7.9	Francis Marion/Frank	1840-1861-1925
4.4.7.10	Catherine	1842-1862-
4.4.7.11	Hester Ann Eliza	1845- -1859
4.4.7.12	Clois Finley	1848-1867&1925-1927

4.4.8   **MONTY, Margaret** b 1803?, Clinton Co., NY; d between 1850 and 1856. She married **Joseph Frederick** b 1793?, QC; d 21 Feb 1890, Beekmantown, NY.

Margaret Monty was 47 years old in 1850 when she was living with her 57-year-old husband and children in Plattsburgh, NY (US census). She was deceased in October 1856 according to the deposition of her sister Mrs. Barbary Morrison (4.4.5) in the Clinton Co. Court of Common Pleas in Plattsburgh, (Appendix I), from which are taken the names of her surviving children.

Joseph Frederick (also Frederic) was a farm laborer in Plattsburgh until at least 1870 and was living in 1880 with his son Frank in Beekmantown, NY (US censuses). In the notice of his death in the *Plattsburgh Sentinel* of 21 Mar 1890, it is said that he was 104 years old at his death. That may be an exaggeration: none of the censuses from 1830 to 1880 indicate that he was born earlier than 1790 or later than 1795. The approximate year of birth I suggest above is based on his age of 57 in the 1850 census in Plattsburgh.

Children:

i   **Joseph Frederick** b 1820?, Plattsburgh, NY. He married 1845? **Ruth ____** b 1827?, VT.

ii   **Francis/Frank Frederick** b Feb 1821, Plattsburgh, NY. He married **Margaret ____** b 1828?, Canada.

iii   **Angeline Frederick** b Aug 1823, Plattsburgh, NY.

iv   **Margaret Frederick**

v   **Mary Ann Frederick**

vi   **Samuel Frederick** b 11 Apr 1832, Plattsburgh, NY; d & bur there 13 & 15 Jun 1916 at the age of 84 years, 2 months, and 2 days. He married 1855? **Catherine Houston** b 12 Aug 1832, Ireland; d 6 Sep 1918, Plattsburgh, NY.

vii   **Betsey Frederick** b 1835?, Plattsburgh, NY.

viii   **John Frederick** b 1837?, Plattsburgh, NY.

ix   **Charlotte Maria Frederick** b 1841?, Plattsburgh, NY. She married 1859? **Simeon Mooso** b 1840?, NY.

x   **Charles Edward Frederick** b 1842?, Plattsburgh, NY; d & bur there between 1890 and 1898. He married 1871? **Lavonia ____** b 1848?, NY.

xi   **Jane Ann Frederick** b 1846?, Plattsburgh, NY.

4.4.9   **MONTY, Mary** married **Joseph Houd** or **Houde**.

According to the sworn deposition of her sister Mrs. Barbary Morrison (4.4.5) on 9 Oct 1856 before the Clinton Co. Court of Common Pleas in Plattsburgh, NY (Appendix I), "Mary Monty the daughter of Francis Monty son of L^t. Monty, who married Joseph Houd" was then still alive. Yet when the Clinton Co. Circuit Court in Plattsburgh had affirmed on 4 Jul 1846 that Francis Monty Jr. at his death had "left Six children ... and that they are his only Surviving children" (Appendix II), Mary Monty was not listed under either her married or maiden name. Since the court's judgment was based at least in part on the testimony of her brother Christopher (4.4.3), I do not know how to explain the discrepancy. Nor have I found any other mention of this family in New York State.

4.5.1   **MONTY, John** b 1796?, NY. He married **Mary** ____ b 1812?, NY.

John Monty and his wife were residents of Chazy, NY, until at least 1840. They then moved to Saranac, NY, where John Monty, a farmer, owned real estate valued at $300 in 1850. He was then 54 years old and his wife Mary 38. They were still in Saranac in 1860 but do not appear there in later US censuses.

Children:

4.5.1.1	John	1825-1845?-
4.5.1.2	Eleanor	1832?- -

4.5.2   **MONTY, Phebe** married **Joseph Latray**.

From the deposition of her cousin Mrs. Barbary Morrison (4.4.5) in the Clinton Co. Court of Common Pleas in Plattsburgh, NY, on 9 Oct 1856 (Appendix I), it appears that Phebe Monty, wife of Joseph Latray, was still alive in 1856. I know nothing more about this family.

4.5.3   **MONTY, Julia** married **Peter Thouville**.

From the deposition of her cousin Mrs. Barbary Morrison (4.4.5) in the Clinton Co. Court of Common Pleas in Plattsburgh, NY, on 9 Oct 1856 (Appendix I) it appears that Julia Monty, wife of Peter Thouville, was still alive in 1856. I know nothing more about this family.

4.5.4   **MONTY, Ann** b 1802?, Plattsburgh, NY; d there 23 Apr 1873 at the age of 71. She married before 1820 **Levi Prindle** b 1784?; d 1 May 1844, Plattsburgh, NY, at the age of 60.

She may have married (2) between 1844 and 1850 ____ **Hubbard**.

Ann Monty and her husband were buried in the Gilliland Cemetery in Plattsburgh, NY. The inscription on the PRINDEL (sic) tombstone shows that "Levi Prindel / Died / May 1, 1844 / Aged 60 Y'rs" and that "Ann Monty / Relict of Levi Prindel / Died / Apr 23, 1873 / Aged 71 Y'rs." Prindel may indeed have been the original spelling of their surname. At least that is how it appears in the *Plattsburgh Republican* of 26 Feb 1820 when Levi Prindel signed a petition urging the reelection of New York Governor DeWitt Clinton. In later years the form Prindle was used almost exclusively.

The existence of Ann Monty's possible second husband is suggested by the 1850 and 1860 censuses in Beekmantown, NY, where the Prindle children's mother is named Mrs. Ann Hubbard. In neither case is a Mr. Hubbard present. Yet in October 1856, in a deposition before the Clinton Co. Court of Common Pleas in Plattsburgh, NY, Mrs. Barbary Morrison (4.4.5) identifies her cousin Ann, daughter of Abraham Monty, as the wife of Levi Prindle only (Appendix I). A second marriage, if it existed, may have been short-lived and soon forgotten.

From the scanty information provided in the 1820 through 1840 censuses in Plattsburgh, NY, it appears that Ann Monty and Levi Prindle married before 1820 and that by 1840 they had had at least two sons and six daughters. Two other children were born around 1841 and 1843, according to the 1850 census in Beekmantown, NY. Mrs. Ann Hubbard was then living with her children Levi, Ann E., Melissa, and William H. Prindle in the household of her daughter Jane Ann and son-in-law Stephen Lewis.

Children:
i   **Jane Ann Prindle** b 3 Sep 1821, Plattsburgh, NY; d there 26 Feb 1876. She married 1841? **Stephen K. Lewis** (Eli Lewis & Hopeful/Hope Finch) b 24 May 1822,

Beekmantown, NY; m (2) his sister-in-law Ann Eliza Prindle (iii); d 12 Nov 1902, Schuyler Falls, NY.

ii   **Levi Prindle** b 1831?, Plattsburgh, NY; d 1 Mar 1880, Beekmantown, NY, at the age of 48. He married **Delia** ___ b 1841?, NY.

iii   **Ann Eliza/Aneliza Prindle** b 21 Jan 1834, Plattsburgh, NY; d 29 Dec 1890 Schuyler Falls, NY. She married **Stephen K.** Lewis (Eli Lewis & Hopeful/Hope Finch) b 24 May 1822, Beekmantown, NY; m (1) Jane Ann Prindle (i); d 12 Nov 1902, Schuyler Falls, NY.

iv   **Josephus Prindle** b 1838?, Plattsburgh, NY; d there 25 Feb 1875.

v   **Melissa Prindle** b 1841?, Plattsburgh, NY. She married around 1859 **John Moore** b 1837?, NY.

vi   **William H. Prindle** b 1843?, Plattsburgh, NY.

4.5.5   **MONTY, Barbary** married **Joseph Baker**.

Barbary Monty, daughter of Abraham Monty, married Joseph Baker according to the October 1856 affidavit of her cousin Mrs. Barbary Morrison (4.4.5) in the Clinton Co. Court of Common Pleas in Plattsburgh, NY (Appendix I). There is scant evidence however of the couple's presence in the area, and that only through land transactions between Joseph W. Baker and Abraham Monty (4.5) in 1826 and 1828 (Clinton Co. Deeds, book K, p. 403 and book N, p. 405) and between Joseph W. Baker and John Monty (4.5.1) in 1829 (book O, p. 1).

It is possible that Joseph Baker moved to Ohio in the early 1830s and raised a family there. The 1850 census in Turtle Neck, OH, shows that a Joseph Baker, 55, born in Vermont, and his wife, Barbara, 44, born in New York, had three children born in New York: Louisa, 27, Mary, 21, and Josephine, 18, and three children born in Ohio: John S., 15, Charlotte A., 12, and Sarah J., 9. Several of the children married in Shelby Co., OH. The Paulding Co., OH, Death Records also show that Barbra (sic) Baker, a widow born in New York State, died on 10 Jun 1886 at the age of 81 years, 6 months, and 3 days. That could easily apply to Barbary Monty. Yet there are too many discrepancies in the intervening years to make a sure identification possible.

The same is true of the information Betty Ramsey provided in her *Monty Montee History*, pp. 155-156, on the basis of statements by Amy Lee Jacobs (Mrs. Ralph Tibbs), a granddaughter of Charlotte Ann Baker and Martin Van Buren Jacobs. I have been unable to confirm them.

4.5.6   **MONTY, Benjamin** b 9 Apr 1807, Clinton Co., NY; d 11 Jun 1828, Plattsburgh, NY, at the age of 21 years, 2 months, and 2 days. He married a cousin once removed **Margaret Monty** (4.4.1.4).

Benjamin Monty's date of birth is derived from the inscription on his tombstone in the Riverside Cemetery in Plattsburgh, NY. I know of his marriage only through the 1856 affidavit of his cousin Mrs. Barbary Morrison (4.4.5) in the Clinton Co. Court of Common Pleas in Plattsburgh (Appendix I).

4.8.1   **MONTY, Julia/Julie** b 1809?, Chazy, NY. She married (1) **Antoine/Anthony Savage** (Thomas Savage & Marguerite Marney dit Richelieu) in a civil wedding which was revalidated in a Catholic ceremony on 6 Jul 1845, Coopersville, NY.

She was a widow when she married (2) 19 May 1850, Coopersville, NY, **Samuel Luck/Locke** (Samuel Locke & Marie Cousineau) b & bp 24 & 25 Nov 1804, Montreal, QC; m (1) Saley (Sally?) Lussier (Jean-Baptiste Louis Lussier & Marie Jeanne Anderson); d between 1860 and 1870.

Julia Monty (Julie at both her marriages) was 11 years old when her father applied on 3 Oct 1820 for a pension as a Revolutionary War veteran and 41 years old at her second marriage. Her first husband, named Antoine Savage at the revalidation of their marriage in 1845, was known as Anthony Savage in 1840 when he and his wife had three children under the age of 5, two boys and a girl (US census, Beekmantown, NY).

The Savage and Monty families of Clinton Co., NY, were related in several ways: Antoine Savage's brother Louis married as his second wife Julia's sister Mary Monty (4.8.3), his nephew Charles Savage married Julia's sister Louisa Monty (4.8.9), while his son Thomas (4.8.1.i) married a second cousin Julia Monty (4.11.3.2).

Samuel Luck (Jean Samuel Locke at his baptism) was a shoemaker in Beekmantown when he married Julia Monty. They remained there for a time after their marriage but were living on her son Thomas Savage's farm in Chazy, NY, in 1860. She was a widow in 1870 and was living alone in Chazy in 1880, the "owner of a rented farm" (US censuses).

Children:

i   **Thomas Madison Savage** b 28 Oct 1837, Beekmantown, NY; d 5 Jan 1902, Lowell, MA. He married 1872? **Julia Monty** (Joseph Monty [4.11.3] & Marguerite Grégoire) b 13 Jul 1842, Beekmantown, NY; d 7 Apr 1912, Lowell, MA.

ii   **Rosalie/Rosella Savage** b 1838?, Beekmantown, NY.

iii   **Joel Savage** b 1840?, Beekmantown, NY.

iv   **George Savage** b 1841?, Beekmantown, NY; d & bur 9 & 10 Feb 1845, Beekmantown & Chazy, NY, at the age of 4.

v   **Mary Arvilla Savage** b & bp 15 Feb 1844 & 19 Jan 1845, Chazy & Coopersville, NY; d & bur 1930, Plattsburgh, NY. She married 1867? **Levi W. Lewis** (Stephen K. Lewis & Jane Ann Prindle [4.5.4.i]) b 1842?, Plattsburgh, NY; d & bur there 1924.

vi   **Honoré Savage** b & bp 9 Dec 1845 & 5 Mar 1846, Chazy & Coopersville, NY.

vii   **Laura Ann Savage** b & bp 20 Jan & 5 Jun 1847, Chazy & Coopersville, NY; d between 1920 and 1930. She married 1885? **William H. Waterson** (Joseph Waterson & Elizabeth English) b 17 Feb 1846, Chelsea, VT; d 20 Jun 1928, Dracut, MA.

viii   **Julia Calista Luck** bp 8 Jun 1851, Coopersville, NY.

4.8.2   **MONTY, Joseph** b Jul 1810, Chazy, NY; d there 12 Apr 1890 at the age of 79 years and 9 months. He married **Victoria Trombly** (Lewis Trombly/Louis Tremblay & Victoria Marne/Marney) b 1824, Chazy, NY; d there 6 Nov 1860 at the age of 36.

Joseph Monty was a lifelong resident and farmer in Chazy, NY. He and his wife were buried in the Trombly's Bay Cemetery there.

Children:

4.8.2.1	Augustus Lafayette	1848-	-1854
4.8.2.2	Victoria	1850-1869-1912	
4.8.2.3	Caroline E.	1852-	-1870
4.8.2.4	Celia/Cécilienne	1854-	-
4.8.2.5	Delia/Adeline	1856-	-
4.8.2.6	Amelia	1858?-	-1884

4.8.3   **MONTY, Mary** b 15 Jun 1814, Chazy, NY; d & bur there 11 & 13 Feb 1901. She married 21 Dec 1845, Coopersville, NY, **Lewis/Louis Savage** (Thomas Savage & Marguerite Marney dit Richelieu) b & bp 19 Sep 1798 & 29 Jun 1799, Clinton Co., NY & Chambly, QC; m (1) 31 Dec 1820, Plattsburgh, NY, Marguerite Gauthier/Margaret Gokey); d & bur 11 & 13 Apr 1864, Chazy, NY.

Lewis Savage (Louis Sauvage in French documents) was related to a number of Monty families: his brother Antoine Savage had married Julia Monty (4.8.1); his nephew Thomas Savage married Julia Monty (4.11.3.2) while a son of his first marriage, Charles Savage, married his second wife's sister, Louisa Monty (4.8.9). He was a farmer in Chazy, NY, and was buried, as were both his wives, in the Trombly's Bay Cemetery there.

Children:

i   **Mary Frances Savage** b & bp Jun & 15 Aug 1847, Chazy & Coopersville, NY; d 10 Aug 1919, West Chazy, NY. She married 7 May 1784, Plattsburgh, NY, **James Mousseau** (Maxim Mousseau & Marceline Chartier) b 1852?, Beekmantown, NY.

ii   **William DeWitt Savage** b & bp 27 May & 15 Aug 1850, Chazy & Coopersville,

NY; d 23 Sep 1916, Plattsburgh, NY. He married 1874 **Marie Genevieve/Mary J. Robarge** (Pierre/Peter Robarge & Marie Henriette Tremblay/ Mary Trombly) b 29 Dec 1852, Chazy, NY; d & bur 22 & 24 Dec 1928, Plattsburgh, NY.

iii   **Henrietta L. Savage** b 20 Sep 1856, Chazy, NY; d there 6 Oct 1856.

4.8.4   **MONTY, Rosalie/Rosella** b 20 May 1816, Chazy, NY; d 1 Jul 1901, Burlington, VT. She married 1845? a second cousin once removed, **Claudius Monty** (3.1.3.2).

Children:

3.1.3.2.1	Wilbur E.	1845-1868?-1934
3.1.3.2.2	Infant	1849- -1849
3.1.3.2.3	Ellen Nora/Elnora	1855?-1873-1932

4.8.5   **MONTY, Edward** b Apr 1817, Plattsburgh, NY; d 20 Aug 1904, Beekmantown, NY, at the age of 87. He married 15 Nov 1846, Cohoes, NY, **Jicey/Joyce Murphy** b there Nov 1817; d & bur 14 & 16 May 1904, Beekmantown & Chazy, NY, at the age of 86.

     Edward Monty was a farmer in Chazy, NY, until at least 1870 and in Beekmantown, NY, from at least 1880 on (US censuses). Both he and his wife were buried in the Ingraham Cemetery in Chazy. Her tombstone names her Joyce Murphy, wife of Edward Monty. She was known during her lifetime however as Jicey.

Children:

4.8.5.1	John E.	,	1847- -1895
4.8.5.2	Oreon		1850-1891-1930
4.8.5.3	Ella/Ellen		1853?-1876&1885?-
4.8.5.4	Etta		1857- -1942
4.8.5.5	Ida B.		1861?- -1879

4.8.6   **MONTY, Lafayette** b 22 Oct 1822, Chazy, NY; d there 5 Aug 1906.

     Lafayette Monty was a farmer in Chazy, NY, and was buried in the Ingraham Cemetery there. He did not marry.

4.8.7   **MONTY, Laura/Lura** b Oct 1823, Chazy, NY. She married **George Trombly/Tremblay** (François/Francis Tremblay & Marie Gendron) b 1820?, Chazy, NY; d 1 Jun 1857, Chazy, NY, at the age of 37.

     Very little is known about Laura or Lura Monty. Her name varies. She certainly married before 1854 for she was named Lura Trombly in her father's will of 12 Nov 1853. George Tremblay and his wife Laure Monty were the parents of three children who were baptized in St. Joseph's church in Coopersville, NY, in May 1857 and when he died a few weeks later his wife was named Laure Monty. Nevertheless her cousin John Monty Jr. (4.11.1) attested on 3 Nov 1856 in the Clinton Co. Court of Common Pleas in Plattsburgh, NY, that "Lucy Monty ... married George Trombly" (Appendix I). It is one of the very few errors I have found in that deposition. It is surely an inadvertent mistake since John Monty also states in the same document that Lucy Ann Monty (4.8.12) was the wife of Charles Clough, which is correct.

     The family may have lived away from the Chazy/Plattsburgh area after George Trombly's death, for I can find no references to Laura Monty or her children until 1900 when Lura (sic) Monty, a 76 year-old widow born in October 1823, was living with her brother Moses (4.8.10) in Chazy (US census). Yet when the estate of another brother, Wellington (4.8.13), was settled a few years later, her name was Laura Jones (*Plattsburgh Sentinel*, 14 Jun 1907). I know nothing about a possible second marriage, and nothing about her children beyond their baptisms in 1857.

Children:

i   **Charles Trombly/Tremblay** b & bp 9 Oct 1850 & 21 May 1857, Chazy & Coopersville, NY.

ii   **Lucie Trombly/Tremblay** b & bp 7 Oct 1852 & 21 May 1857, Chazy & Coopersville, NY.

iii   **Marie Anne Trombly/Tremblay** b & bp 13 Sep 1856 & 21 May 1857, Chazy & Coopersville, NY.

4.8.8   **MONTY, DeWitt Clinton** (twin) b 6 Feb 1827, Chazy, NY; d 3 Mar 1898, Jessup, IA. He married (1) **Susan Augusta Bromley** (Harvey Bromley & Elizabeth Howe) b 24 Aug 1843, Plattsburgh, NY; d & bur 1880, Parkersburg, IA.

He married (2) 29 Apr 1883, Parkersburg, IA, **Mary Appa/Mame A. Bromley** (John Harvey Bromley & Hannah Roberts) b 10 Aug 1854, Plattsburgh, NY; m (2) 20 Jan 1903, Jessup, IA, Flavel W. Harris (Nathan Wait Harris & Charity Emeline Wadsworth), widower of Lydia Jane Prentice; bur 1933, Perry Twp, IA.

Dewitt Clinton Monty was a hotel keeper in Plattsburgh, NY, in 1850 and was then single. I have been unable to locate him in 1860. It appears though, from information supplied by his daughter Nellie for the 1925 Iowa State census, that he and Sarah A. Bromley were married in Minnesota. They may have lived there for a while but were in Monticello, IA, in 1866 at the birth of a child. He was a drover there in 1870 and a restaurateur in Parkersburg, IA, in June 1880 when he was a widower (US censuses). Since his wife Susan died in 1880 according to the inscription on her tombstone in the Oak Hill Cemetery there, she must have died in the early months of that year.

DeWitt Clinton Monty was a merchant in Parkersburg at his second marriage in 1883, more specifically a grocer and restaurateur according to the *Iowa Gazetteer and Business Directory, 1884-1885*, and a hotel keeper in Jessup, IA, at his death. The Buchanan Co., IA, Death Records note that he died at the age of 71 years and 25 days and that he was buried in Parkersburg.

Mary Appa Bromley was a niece of Susan A. Bromley. She was a dressmaker in Jessup in 1900 and continued to live there following her second marriage. When she and Flavel W. Harris divorced a few years after 1910, she resumed her first husband's surname and was known in 1920 and 1930 as Mrs. Mame A. Monty (US censuses). She was also buried under that name in the Cedar Crest Cemetery near Jessup, in Perry Twp, IA.

Children of the first marriage:

4.8.8.1	Nellie Augusta	1866-1884-1947	
4.8.8.2	Kittie	1875?-	-

Children of the second marriage:

4.8.8.3	Anonymous son	1884-	-1884
4.8.8.4	Frank Clinton	1887-	-1902

4.8.9   **MONTY, Louisa** (twin) b 6 Feb 1827, Chazy, NY; d & bur 9 & 12 Oct 1912, North Andover, MA & Chazy, NY. She married between 1850 and 1854 **Charles Savage** (Louis Savage & Marguerite Gauthier/Margaret Gokey) b Apr 1827, NY.

Louisa Monty was single and living in her father's household in Chazy, NY, in 1850. She married between then and 12 Nov 1853 when her father named her Loisa Savage in his will (Clinton Co. Surrogate's Court, Plattsburgh, NY, 16 Jan 1854). Her husband was a farmer in Chazy and Beekmantown, NY, until at least 1880. He was retired in 1900 and had moved away. He was then living with his wife, son, and daughter Laura in Dracut, MA, and with his wife and son "Kirtland" in Lowell, MA, in 1910 (US censuses). Louisa Monty died two years later at her home in North Andover and was buried in the Ingraham Cemetery in Chazy (*Plattsburgh Sentinel*, 18 Oct 1912).

Charles Savage became his own father's brother-in-law through his marriage: Louis Savage had married in 1845 as his second wife Mary Monty (4.8.3), Louisa's sister.

Children:

i   **Lewis Courtland Savage** b Aug 1858, Beekmantown, NY.

ii   **Henrietta Louisa Savage** b & bp 16 Feb & 6 Jun 1864, Beekmantown & Coopers-

ville, NY.
iii   **Laura/Lauretta Savage** b & bp Sep 1871 & 28 Jun 1872, Chazy & Coopersville, NY.

4.8.10   **MONTY, Moses** b 21 May 1830, Chazy, NY; d there 14 Sept 1918. He married around 1861 **Sophia Brunelle** (Alex Brunelle & ____) b 2 April 1838, QC; d & bur 21 & 23 Feb 1908, Chazy, NY.

Moses Monty was a lifelong resident and farmer in Chazy, NY, and was buried alongside his wife in the Ingraham Cemetery there. The dates of their birth and death, taken from the inscriptions on their tombstone, vary only slightly from the dates found in censuses from 1850 through 1910 and are probably reasonably accurate.

The date of the couple's marriage is unclear. Sophia Brunell (sic) was a 22-year-old domestic in Mrs. Mary Monty's household in Chazy in June 1860 and presumably still single. She and Moses Monty may have married between then and the birth of a daughter in September of that year. On the other hand the 1900 census in Chazy indicates that they had then been married for thirty-eight years, which would place their marriage in 1862.

There has been some speculation that Moses Monty was the father of Edna Monty, an 8-year-old child living in his mother's household in Chazy in 1860 and an 18-year-old living in his brother Lafayette's household there in 1870. In neither case is her relationship to the head of the household made clear. She may well be the 90-year-old Mrs. Edna Baxter of Plainfield, MA, who claimed in 1942 to be Elrick Monty's (4.8.10.2) half-sister and sole heir. The Clinton Co., NY, Surrogate's Court denied the relationship and, since Elrick Monty had died intestate, divided his entire estate among his first cousins, his nearest relatives. That judgment was at first reversed by the Appellate Division of the Supreme Court but later reaffirmed by the Court of Appeals: Mrs. Baker was not a member of Elrick Monty's immediate family and was not entitled to any share of his estate (*Plattsburgh Daily Press*, 28 Nov 1942). Her parents are still unknown.

Children:

4.8.10.1	Ettie R.	1860-	-1874
4.8.10.2	Elrick W.	1863-	-1941

4.8.11   **MONTY, William** b 1832?, Chazy, NY. He married **Caroline** ____ b 1836?, NY; d 16 Jul 1860, Chazy, NY, at the age of 24.

William Monty was an 18-year-old laborer on his father's farm in Chazy, NY, in 1850 and a farmer there in June 1860 when his wife Caroline was 23 years old (US censuses). The date of her death is taken from her tombstone in the Riverview Cemetery in Chazy.

I have been unable to find William Monty after his wife's death though it appears, from a list of heirs and relatives of his brother Wellington Monty (4.8.13) which appeared in the *Plattsburgh Sentinel* of 14 Jun 1907 that he was still alive on that date. He may be the 30-year-old William H. Monty who enlisted in the Union Army in Plattsburgh, NY, on 27 Nov 1863 and served in the 118th New York Infantry Regiment during the Civil War. He may also be the William Monty born in Chazy, NY, around 1831, husband of Philomene Bosca/Bousquet (second wife?) who lived in Lowell, MA, in the 1870s and 1880s and in Deerfield, NH, until at least 1900 and left numerous descendants. His parentage though has eluded me.

4.8.12   **MONTY, Lucy Ann** b 1834?, Chazy, NY. She married between 1850 and 1854 **Charles P. Clough** (David Clough & Rebecca ____) b 1836?, Peru, NY; d 10 Jan 1903, Burlington, VT.

Lucy Ann Monty was a 16-year-old girl living with her parents in Chazy, NY, in 1850. As a married woman in Peru, NY, in 1860, she was 26 years old. I would trust these two censuses rather than the 1900 one in Burlington, VT, according to which she was born in July 1831 and had been married for 51 years. This last cannot be true: since she was still single in June 1850, she must have married between then and 12 Nov 1853 when her father referred to her in his will as Lucy Ann Clough, wife of Charles Clough (Clinton Co. Surrogate's Court, Plattsburgh, NY, 16 Jan 1854).

The 1900 census also appears to be in error when it indicates that Charles Clough was born in January 1830. According to earlier censuses in Peru and in Burlington, he was 14 years old in 1850, 24 in 1860, and 34 in 1870. He was a harness maker in Peru until 1869 or 1870 and then in Burlington, VT, where he spent the rest of his life (US censuses; Burlington, VT, City Directories).

Children:

i   **William B. Clough** b Nov 1855, Peru, NY. He married 3 Dec 1882, Burlington, VT, **Addie A. Thayer** (Martin Thayer & Roxana Spear) b there 11 Nov 1865.

ii   **Emmet R. Clough** b 1857?, Peru, NY.

iii   **Harry B. Clough** b Aug 1861, Peru, NY. He married 9 Mar 1886, Burlington, VT, **Katherine A./Katie Sullivan** (Daniel Sullivan & Mary _____) b there Oct 1865; d between 1903 and 1920.

iv   **Ida/Ada Rebecca Clough** b Feb 1864, Peru, NY. She married 8 Feb 1887, Burlington, VT, as his second wife **David Carpenter** (Joseph Carpenter & Emily Russell) b Apr 1850, Essex, NY.

v   **David F. Clough** b Dec 1866, Peru, NY. He married 22 Aug 1889, Burlington, VT, **Mary Counter** (Lewis Counter & Mary Pratt) b there Oct 1872.

vi   **Harriet/Hattie E. Clough** b Apr 1869, Peru, NY. She married 10 Oct 1892, Burlington, VT, **Thomas F. Russell** (James E. Russell & Mary A. _____) b there 23 Feb 1864.

vii **Lillie Clough** b 16 Feb 1871, Burlington, VT.

viii **Charles Clough** b 6 Sep 1873, Burlington, VT.

ix **Frederick Clough** b 5 Apr 1876, Burlington, VT.

x   **Jed Clough** b 7 May 1879, Burlington, VT.

4.8.13   **MONTY, Wellington** b 1836?, Chazy, NY; d 3 Apr 1906, Chazy, NY, at the age of 70.

Wellington Monty was a lifelong resident and farmer in Chazy, NY. The year of his birth is based on the inscription on his tombstone in the Ingraham Cemetery there. According to various State and US censuses in Chazy, though, he may have been born as early as 1832 and as late as 1839. He did not marry and his brother Moses (4.8.10) was appointed administrator of his estate in the Clinton Co. Surrogate's Court in Plattsburgh, NY, on 11 Apr 1906.

4.10.1   **MONTY, Placide** b 1809?, Chazy, NY.

Placide Monty was 10 years old when his father applied on 3 Oct 1820 for a pension as a Revolutionary War veteran (Clinton Co. Court of Common Pleas, Plattsburgh, NY). He could not however have been born in 1810 for his sister Louise (4.10.2) was born in June of that year. He was still alive in 1856 according to the testimony of his cousin John Monty Jr. (4.11.1) (Appendix I).

4.10.2   **MONTY, Louise** b & bp Jun 1810 & 21 Jan 1811, Chazy, NY & St. Luc, QC.

This child was not listed among Placide Monty's children when he applied on 3 Oct 1820 for a pension as a Revolutionary War veteran (Clinton Co. Court of Common Pleas, Plattsburgh, NY). She presumably died in infancy.

4.10.3   **MONTY, Susan** b 1812?, Chazy, NY; d before 1856.

Susan Monty was 8 years old when her father applied on 3 Oct 1820 for a pension as a Revolutionary War veteran (Clinton Co. Court of Common Pleas, Plattsburgh, NY). Her cousin John Monty Jr. (4.11.1) testified in his 3 Nov 1856 affidavit in the Clinton Co. Court of Common Pleas that she had married but was then deceased and had left two children whose names he did not know (Appendix I).

4.10.4   **MONTY, Amelia/Emelia** b 1814?, Chazy, NY; d 10 Mar 1899, Plattsburgh, NY. She married **Joseph Latray** b 27 Oct 1808; d 5 Jan 1848, Plattsburgh, NY, at the age of 39 years, 2 months, and 8 days.

Emelia Monty was 6 years old when her father applied on 3 Oct 1820 for a pension as a Revolutionary War veteran (Clinton Co. Court of Common Pleas, Plattsburgh, NY). Her cousin John Monty Jr. (4.11.1) refers to her as "Parmelia Monty who married Joseph Latra" (Appendix I) though she was named Amelia in all censuses from 1850 on and was buried as "Amelia Monty / His [Joseph Latray's] Wife / 1816-1899" in the Riverside Cemetery in Plattsburgh. The (probably erroneous) year of birth inscribed on the tombstone reflects information already included in the *Plattsburgh Sentinel* of 17 Mar 1899: Mrs. Amelia Latray was 83 years old at her death. I would rather trust here her father's declaration of 1820 and the 1850 US census in Plattsburgh which shows she was then 36 years old. She remained in Plattsburgh, making a home for her unmarried children, until her death (US censuses).

The dates of Joseph Latray's birth and death are taken from the inscription on his tombstone in the Riverview Cemetery in Plattsburgh. He was then identified as "Capt. Joseph Latray." He may have been an officer in the army or militia but more possibly a boat captain on Lake Champlain.

Children:

i   **Phoebe Latray** b 1834?, Plattsburgh., NY; bur there (Riverside Cemetery) 1878. She married around 1852 **Andrew S. Gregory** b 1831?, CT.

ii   **Roxena/Rosina Latray** b 1843?, Plattsburgh, NY; d between 1910 and 1920. She married 1891, as his third wife, **John Thomas Toulman** b 10 Nov 1840, Somersetshire, England; d 13 Jan 1920, Whitehall, NY.

iii   **Susan Latray** b 1845?, Plattsburgh, NY; bp there (St. John the Baptist Catholic church) 22 Sep 1850 at the age of 5.

iv   **Joseph Latray** b 1848?, Plattsburgh, NY; bp there (St. John the Baptist Catholic church) 22 Sep 1850 at the age of 2.

4.10.5   **MONTY, Elizabeth/Betsey** b 1815?, Chazy, NY; d 13 May 1887, Vergennes, VT. She married around 1835 (marriage revalidated in St. Joseph's Catholic Church, Burlington, VT, on 16 Aug 1851) **Francis/Frank Lashway/Lashua** b 1813?, NY; d 27 Feb 1892, Vergennes, VT.

Betsey Monty was 5 years old when her father applied on 3 Oct 1820 for a pension as a Revolutionary War veteran (Clinton Co. Court of Common Pleas, Plattsburgh, NY). She was generally named Elizabeth in US censuses, in the record of the revalidation of her marriage in 1851, and at her death.

She and her husband remained in New York State, where their first four children were born, until at least 1845 before moving to Addison, VT. Francis Laushway (sic) was 37 years old in 1850. He was a shoemaker in Addison in 1850 and 1860 and in Vergennes, VT, in 1870 and 1880 (US censuses). In these later censuses he was known as Frank Laushway, Lasway, or Lashua. Yet both his and his wife's death records bear the surname Lashway. In addition, he was named François Xavier Langevin at the revalidation of his marriage in 1851 and François Langevin when he attended the funeral of his mother-in-law Susan Labare in Plattsburgh on 30 Oct 1854 (Records, St. Peter's church, p. 124). That is probably the original family name, especially since Laushway appears to have been a common enough English version of Langevin. As for his children and grandchildren, the Vermont Vital Records alternate between Lashway and Lashua, with the latter becoming predominant after the mid-1870s.

Children:

i   **Francis/Frank Lashway/Lashua** b 1837?, NY. He married 1864? **Julia** _____ b 1845?, VT.

ii   **Susan Lashway/Lashua** b 1840?, NY.

iii   **Elizabeth Lashway/Lashua** b 1842?, NY.

iv   **James Lashway/Lashua** b 1845?, NY.

v   **Sarah Lashway/Lashua** b 19 Jun 1848, Addison, VT; d 14 Aug 1895, Vergennes, VT. She married around 1868 **Philip Pilon** b 20 Nov 1846, Roxton Falls, QC; d & bur 8 & 10 Feb 1938, Jericho & Vergennes, VT.

4.10.6   **MONTY, Francis/Frank** b Jun 1819, Chazy, NY; d & bur 7/8 & 11 Jan 1896, Plattsburgh, NY. He married **Matilda Rougier** b May 1821, QC; d & bur 23 & 25 Oct 1913, Plattsburgh, NY.

Francis Monty was 16 months old when his father applied on 3 Oct 1820 for a pension as a Revolutionary War veteran (Clinton Co. Court of Common Pleas, Plattsburgh, NY). He was still named Francis in the 1850 census in Plattsburgh but Frank in all later documents I have seen. He was in turn a sailor, a steam boat engineer, and a laborer there until his death (US & state censuses). There is a slight question about his exact date of death. The burial records of St. Peter's Church in Plattsburgh indicate that he had died on 7 Jan 1896 and was buried on 11 Jan 1896. The letters of administration issued to Mrs. Matilda Monty on 10 Jan 1896 by the Clinton Co. Surrogate's Court in Plattsburgh show on the other hand that Frank Monty had died on 8 Jan 1896. Either date is possible.

It is all the more puzzling then to find in the McLellan Cemetery Records of Clinton Co., NY, a tombstone in Plattsburgh's Old Catholic Cemetery with the inscriptions "Frank MONTY / Died Jan 4, 1885 / AE. 77" and "Matilda / His Wife" (no date of death). At first glance this could not apply to the present couple since this Frank Monty was still living in Plattsburgh with his wife Matilda in 1892 (state census). Yet I can find no other couple in the area to whom both names and dates would apply. Furthermore, no other Mrs. Matilda Monty is listed in the McLellan Records of the Old Catholic Cemetery although we know from the *Plattsburgh Sentinel* of 24 Oct 1913 that Frank Monty's wife was to be buried there on the following day. I tend to believe that the date of death inscribed on Frank Monty's tombstone was simply misread. It may be too late however to double-check the McLellan Records: in an incredible act of official vandalism, a large portion of the cemetery was bulldozed in 1983 and the tomb markers destroyed or scattered (*Plattsburgh Press Republican*, 8, 9, 10, and 13 Jun 1983). Though an attempt at restoration was made in 1989, many if not most tombstones were never recovered. Unless further evidence is found, there will always be a question about that inscription.

The date and place of birth of Matilda Rougier are taken from the 1900 US census in Plattsburgh. Earlier censuses indicate she was born between 1820 and 1825 while the *Plattsburgh Sentinel* of 24 Oct 1913 reported that she was 90 years old at her death. That newspaper is also the source for the dates of her death and burial.

Children:

4.10.6.1	Joseph	1842?- -
4.10.6.2	James R.	1846-1871?-
4.10.6.3	Daniel	1848?- -
4.10.6.4	Elizabeth	1850- -
4.10.6.5	Eliza	1852- -
4.10.6.6.	Louisa	1855-1878-
4.10.6.7	Marie Judith	1857- -
4.10.6.8	Jane	1858?- -
4.10.6.9	Robert F.	1859-1883?-1934
4.10.6.10	Emilie	1861- -
4.10.6.11	Carrie	1863?-1881&1903- -
4.10.6.12	George	1866-1893?&1925-1939

4.10.7   **MONTY, Dominique**

Dominique Monty was not listed among Placide Monty's children when the latter applied on 3 Oct 1820 for a pension as a Revolutionary War veteran (Clinton Co. Court of Common Pleas, Plattsburgh, NY) and was probably born after that date. He was still alive on 3 Nov 1856, according to the affidavit of his cousin John Monty Jr. (4.11.1) (Appendix I). I know nothing more about him.

4.10.8   **MONTY, Mary** married **Francis Hulgate** or **Holgate**.

Mary Monty was not listed among Placide Monty's children when he applied on 3 Oct 1820 for a pension as a Revolutionary War veteran (Clinton Co. Court of Common Pleas, Plattsburgh, NY) and was probably born after that date. She was alive in 1856 and married to a Francis Hulgate (perhaps Holgate), according to the affidavit of her cousin John Monty Jr. (4.11.1) (Appendix I). I have no further information on this couple.

4.11.1   **MONTY, John Jr.** b 1808?, Chazy, NY; d Jan 1880, Monona, IA. He married **Cornelia Merrihew** b 1808?, VT.

John Monty Jr. was 12 years old when his father applied on 3 Oct 1820 for a pension as a Revolutionary War veteran (Clinton Co. Court of Common Pleas, Plattsburgh, NY). He was an innkeeper in Chazy, NY, until at least November 1856 when he testified in the Clinton Co. Court of Common Pleas concerning François/Francis Monty's descendants (Appendix I). He left the area soon afterwards and was in Iowa when his daughter Angelina died in 1863. His sons Claudius and Charles were also in Iowa in the early 1860s. The family may have moved as a group or individually, within a few years of each other. John Monty, who was a carpenter and joiner in Monona, IA, in 1870, was then living with his son Charles' family. He was described as a farmer though in the 1880 Mortality schedule there while his widow was a member of her son Claudius' household in McGregor, IA (US censuses). Both he and his wife were buried in the old Monona, IA, Cemetery.

Cornelia Merrihew's year of birth is derived from the 1850 US census in Chazy, NY, when she was 42 years old. All censuses agree that she was born in Vermont. Her surname is found in her son Claudius' death record in Seattle, WA.

Children:

4.11.1.1	Charles Quincy	1834-1856?-1907
4.11.1.2	Sophronia	1836- -1845
4.11.1.3	Claudius	1838- &1876-1924
4.11.1,4	Albert W.	1840?-1861&1898?-1912
4.11.1.5	Angelina/Angeline	1846- -1863

4.11.2   **MONTY, Amanda** b 1810?, Chazy, NY.

Amanda Monty was 10 years old when her father applied on 3 Oct 1820 for a pension as a Revolutionary War veteran (Clinton Co. Court of Common Pleas, Plattsburgh, NY).

4.11.3   **MONTY, Joseph** b 1811?, Chazy, NY; d there 9 Apr 1892 at the age of 81. He married **Margaret Grégoire/Gregware** b 1820?; d 28 Feb 1899 at the age of 79.

Joseph Monty was 9 years old when his father applied on 3 Oct 1820 for a pension as a Revolutionary War veteran (Clinton Co. Court of Common Pleas, Plattsburgh, NY). He was a farmer in Beekmantown, NY, until at least 1870 and from at least 1880 on in Chazy, NY (US censuses). He and his wife were buried in the Ingraham Cemetery there.

Margaret (also Marguerite) Grégoire/Gregware was born between 1820 and 1823 in Canada, Vermont, New York, or more generally the United States according to various US and state censuses from 1850 to 1892. Her parents were born in Canada (1880 census). She apparently left Chazy shortly after her husband's death for her will, dated 25 Aug 1893 and probated on 27 Mar 1899 in the Clinton Co. Surrogate's Court in Plattsburgh, was signed in Compton, NH, where her daughter Cornelia was then living. She probably did not intend to return to her former home: her household furniture and agricultural implements were to be sold at auction on 20 Nov 1893 following a notice in the *Plattsburgh Sentinel* of 10 Nov 1893. I do not know where she died. She may have been living in Chazy, home of her son George and of her daughter Eleanor, or in Lowell, MA, where her daughters Julia, Mary, and Cornelia were residing in 1899.

Children:

4.11.3.1	George W.	1838-1859?-1923
4.11.3.2	Julia	1842-1872?-1912
4.11.3.3	Eleanor	1844-1864?&1881?-1931

4.11.3.4	Mary	1846-1873-1935
4.11.3.5	Cornelia E.	1849-1873?-1935
4.11.3.6	Lilice A.	1851- -1853
4.11.3.7	Lucretia	1853- -1854

4.11.4   **MONTY, Louis/Lewis** b 15 Apr 1815, Chazy, NY; d & bur 19 & 21 Dec 1910, Benton Harbor, MI. He married 26 Dec 1838, Clinton Co., NY, **Harriet Leware (?)** b 27 Oct 1819, Lacolle, QC; d & bur 27 & 29 Dec 1914, Benton Harbor, MI.

Louis (also Lewis) Monty was a farm laborer in Beekmantown, NY, in 1850, a hired man in Plattsburgh, NY, in 1860, and a farm laborer again in Beekmantown in 1870 (US censuses). In spite of his age (he was 47 though he admitted to only 42) he enlisted in August 1862 in Plattsburgh as a private in Co. H, 118th New York Infantry Regiment in which he served until 15 Jan 1865. He was "wounded in back by shell" and received a pension which was later transferred to his widow.

Lewis Monty and his family had moved to Michigan in the mid-1870s. He was a laborer in Benton, in 1880 and a farmer there in 1900. He was living in retirement in Benton Harbor, MI, in 1910 (US censuses) and was buried there, as was his wife, in Crystal Spring Cemetery.

Much of my knowledge concerning his family is derived from information communicated to me by his great-grandson Mr. Bertram E. Monty of Marysville, WA (4.11.4.6.9.1). Lewis Monty's obituary in Benton Harbor is especially valuable in providing the exact dates of his birth and marriage, the married names of five of his surviving daughters, and his wife's maiden name, Leware. This should be conclusive: since she was still alive at her husband's death one would assume that she had made sure that her surname was correctly stated. Yet I am unsure. I have been unable to find any Leware family in Clinton Co., NY, in the early 19th century. It may be that Lewis Monty's wife was a member of one of the Laware families in the area. More disturbing is the fact that two very different surnames, Wood and Sears, have shown up in documents pertaining to her children and grandchildren.

Harriet Wood was the mother of Hiram Monty (4.11.4.6) according to his biography in the 1926 *History of Snohomish County, Washington,* II, 786. She was also the mother of George Barnes Monty (4.11.4.8) according to his death record in Tacoma, WA, in 1928. Yet that was hardly a generally accepted fact in the family: when Hiram Monty died in 1934, his son Guy (4.11.4.6.9) reported his grandmother's maiden name as "unknown."

The wife of Lewis Monty is also listed as Harriet Sears in the DAR Lineage book on evidence supplied by her granddaughter Halo Hibbard, daughter of Sarah Louise Monty (4.11.4.10). Since she made it clear in a letter to the US Pension Office of 28 Nov 1914 that her own source of information about the Monty family was her grandmother Harriet, it is difficult to disregard her statements concerning Harriet herself. The name of Harriet Sears is also found in Nell Jane Barnett Sullivan and David Kendall Martin's *History of the Town of Chazy, Clinton Co., NY,* of 1970 and in Virginia Easley DeMarce's "Canadian Participants in the American Revolution" of 1980, both evidently based on Halo Hibbard's statements. Yet her own father, Daniel I. Hibbard, who in 1914 provided the vital information in his mother-in-law's death certificate, including the precise date and place of her birth, was unable to supply her parents' names or surnames. There is some doubt then about the source of his daughter's information.

Whatever her surname, all censuses agree that Harriet, wife of Louis/Lewis Monty, was born in Canada and that both her parents were of foreign origin. The 1900 US census in Benton, MI, specifies that her father was born in Germany and her mother in Canada, and that she had arrived in the United States in 1830.

Lewis Monty's obituary notice states that he was survived by eight of his eleven children. Only seven however are named: "Mrs. Frank Marmell of Oakland, Calif; Hiram E. of Cicero, Wash; George B. of Tacoma, Wash; Mrs. H. W. Foster of West Medford; Mrs. R. M. Wells and Mrs. D. I. Hibbard of this city, and Mrs. Freeman Bury of Coloma." The missing child is undoubtedly Lillia/Martha (Mrs. Samuel Hayward) of Nooksack, WA, who died in 1936. As for the others, I have been unable to identify Mrs. Frank Marmell who could be either Delia (4.11.4.1) or Melissa (4.11.4.2), either of whom could have married before 1870.

Children:

4.11.4.1	Delia	1840?- -
4.11.4.2	Melissa	1844?- -
4.11.4.3	Leroy	1846?- -
4.11.4.4	William Henry	1847?-1875-1899
4.11.4.5	Della A./Athalinda	1849-1865?-1931
4.11.4.6	Hiram/Myron	1851-1871-1934
4.11.4.7	Lillia/Martha	1854-1875-1936
4.11.4.8	George Barnes	1856-1889-1928
4.11.4.9	Frances H.	1860-1882&1892-
4.11.4.10	Sarah Louise	1862-1882-1925
4.11.4.11	Mary Elizabeth/Libby	1866?-1886-1946

4.11.5   **MONTY, Hannah E.** b 1816?, Chazy, NY. She married 1838? a cousin once removed, **Calvin A. Lezott/Lezotte** (Louis Lizotte [4.7.ii] & Miranda Clark) b 17 Jun 1818, Chazy, NY; d there 13 Jun 1888.

Hannah Monty was 4 years old when her father applied on 3 Oct 1820 for a pension as a Revolutionary War veteran (Clinton Co. Court of Common Pleas, Plattsburgh, NY). Yet all censuses in Chazy, NY, from 1850 through 1910 point to an 1818 year of birth. The 1900 census specifies that she was born in May 1818. That is quite possible though, for lack of an actual birth record, I prefer to rely on the earliest possible document. She remained in Chazy after her husband's death and was living there in 1900 and 1910 in the households of her daughters Carrie (iv) and Katie (viii) and their husbands. She had had nine children of whom five were still alive in 1910 (US censuses). She presumably died not much later. I have been unable however to find her tombstone in the Riverview Cemetery in Chazy where her husband and at least five of her children were buried.

Calvin Lezott was a brother of Louis/Lewis Alexandre Lezotte/Leazotte, husband of Jane Ann Monty (4.3.3.5) and a grandson of Mary/Marie Madeleine Monty (4.7) and Louis Alexandre/Lewis Lizotte. He was a farmer in Chazy, NY (US censuses). The spelling of his surname varies: Lezott, Lezotte, or Leazott. The most proper form is probably Lezott found on his and his children's tombstones in the Riverview Cemetery in Chazy.

Children:

i   **Lucretia Lezott** b 3 May 1839, Chazy, NY; d there 3 Apr 1840.

ii   **William C. Lezott** b 3 Mar 1843, Chazy, NY; d there 20 Oct 1907. He married July 1869 **Helen Goodrow** (Peter Goodrow & Amelia Ploof) b 12 Jan 1853, Champlain, NY; d 15 Nov 1929, Chazy, NY.

iii   **Charles Lezott** b 1845?, Chazy, NY.

iv   **Caroline/Carrie Lezott** b 1847?, Chazy, NY. She married 19 Aug 1877, Lowell, MA, **Walter S. Jewett** (Aaron Jewett & Mary Steward) b 17 Dec 1844, Solon, ME; m (1) there 1 May 1870 Matilda A. Hunnewell (Samuel Hunnewell & Mary S. Hopkins).

v   **Darius Lezott/Lezotte** b 1848?, Chazy, NY; d 26 Jan 1925, Orange, MA. He married 1876? **Mattie/Matilda ____** b 1860?, NY.

vi   **Nellie M./Helen Lezott** b 14 Jun 1853, Chazy, NY; d there 29 Jun 1931. She married 2 Jul 1881, Champlain, NY, **Elmer Lucius Hayes** (Lucius Darius Hayes & Sarah Ann Phillips) b there 31 Mar 1860; d 29 Apr 1945, Chazy, NY.

vii   **George L. Lezott** b 3 Mar 1860, Chazy, NY; d there 10 Sep 1867.

viii   **Katherine E./Katie Lezott** b 1864, Chazy, NY; d there 1923. She married 1891? as his second wife **George Hubert Sumner** b 27 Jul 1850, Canada; d 10 Jul 1925, Chazy, NY.

4.11.6   **MONTY, Sarah** b 27 Jan 1820, Chazy, NY; d 1 Aug 1903, Boyer, IA, at the age of 83 years, 6 months, and 4 days. She married (1) Clinton Co., NY, **Robert Weslie Oliver** (Alfred Oliver & Huldah Wormwood) b 2 Feb 1824, Clinton Co., NY; d 13 Jan 1872,

Woodbine, IA.

She married (2) 8 Oct 1875, Woodbine, IA, **David Jennings** b 1804?, PA; m (1) 1836?, Holmes Co., OH, Mary/Mariah Young; d 23 Feb 1888, Harrison Co., IA.

Robert Weslie Oliver was a sawyer in Peru, NY, in 1850 and a railroad worker in Burke, NY, in 1860 before moving to Iowa in the early 1860s. He may have stayed for a time in Monona, IA, where two of his daughters married in 1865 and 1866, though he was a railroad foreman in Woodbine, IA in 1870 (US censuses). Both he and his wife were buried in the Woodbine Cemetery.

David Jennings was a blacksmith. He lived with his first wife in Bloom, OH, in 1850 and 1860 and in Franklin, IA, in 1870. By 1880 he was in Jefferson, IA, where his household included his second wife Sarah and her children Lucy, Alfred M., and Robert L., all given the surname Jennings (US censuses). He may have legally adopted the Oliver children though I doubt it. In all other documents I have seen, including their marriage records, they continued to use the surname Oliver. Their mother, Sarah Monty, was also named Sarah Oliver at her death.

Children of the first marriage:

i   **Sarah A. Oliver** b Mar 1845, Clinton Co., NY. She married (1) 1863?, NY, **William Jackson** (William Jackson & Sarah Mary Deuel) b 1840?, Chateaugay, NY.

   She married (2) **Edward Bishop** (Daniel Bishop & Hannah ____) b Oct 1832, Plymouth, VT; m (1) Harriet ____ .

ii **Ann Eliza Oliver** b 10 Oct 1847, Clinton Co., NY. She married 1 Jan 1866, Monona, IA, **Marion H. Keene**; b 1840?, NY; d between 1870 and 1880.

iii **Lavina Corlista Oliver** b 13 Aug 1848, Peru, NY; d 21 Feb 1926, Council Bluffs, IA. She married 18 Jun 1870, Dunlap, IA, **William H. Collins** b 4 Mar 1849, PA; d 23 Aug 1890, Woodbine, IA

iv **Nancy Jane Oliver** b 29 Apr 1850, Peru, NY; d 4 Feb 1923, Spokane, WA. She married 27 Aug 1865, Monona, IA, **Albert Jennings** b Jun 1837, OH; d 14 Jan 1933.

v   **Lucy F. Oliver** b 14 Mar 1853, Peru, NY; d 22 Mar 1891, Woodbine, IA. She married there 28 Jun 1882 **George Cox** (George Cox & Mary Canady) b 20 Aug 1863, Boone Co., IN; d 29 Jan 1936, Woodbine, IA.

vi **Alfred M. Oliver** b Oct 1859, Burke, NY; d 3 Mar 1926. He married 6 Oct 1881, Magnolia, IA, **Amanda C. Cox** (George Cox & Mary Canady) b 1865, Boone Co., IN; bur 1917, Woodbine, IA, Cemetery.

vii **Robert Leslie Oliver** b 13 Jul 1863, Burke, NY; d & bur 7 & 9 Feb 1942, Woodbine, IA. He married 1 Jun 1882, Missouri Valley, IA, **Minnie Winifred Kinney** (Edward Kinney & Anna McCracken) b 25 Apr 1862, Pontiac, IL; d 22 Jan 1938, Woodbine, IA.

4.11.7   **MONTY, Nicholas** b Mar 1834, Beekmantown, NY; d 24 Mar 1916, Plattsburgh, NY. He married 1860? **Amelia Beaulieu/Emilie Deshudons** (Joseph Dehudon/ Hudon dit Beaulieu & Félicité Hende/Hinde) b & bp 17 Jul 1829, Laprairie, QC; d & bur 13 & 15 Aug 1918, West Plattsburgh, NY.

Nicholas Monty ("Neco" in the 1850 US census in Beekmantown, NY) and his wife Amelia had been married for forty years in 1900. He was a day laborer in Chazy, NY, in 1860 and a brickyard worker in Essex Junction, VT, in 1870 (though his wife and daughter Florence were still in Chazy). He was a laborer living with his family in Plattsburgh, NY, in 1880. That is the last time I have seen husband and wife together. Nicholas Monty was a laborer in Plattsburgh 1900 and was still a resident there at his death. Mrs. Amelia Monty, on the other hand, was living with her children but no husband in Beekmantown, NY, in 1892 and in the household of her daughter Alice (4.11.7.4) and her son-in-law George L. Gregory in Plattsburgh in 1900 and 1910 (US and state censuses). Both husband and wife were buried in the Gregory plot in the West Plattsburgh Union Cemetery in Morrisonville, NY.

Nicholas Monty's wife was baptized as Emilie, daughter of Joseph Deshudons (aka Dehudon, Hudon dit Beaulieu, Bolya, Bolia) and of Félicité Hinde (aka Hende, Hand, Henne).

She was generally known as Amelia in the United States, though Mille Bolya in the 1850 census in Chazy where she was staying with her parents and Melie Beaulieu at the baptisms of two of her children in Coopersville, NY, in 1867.

Children:

4.11.7.1	Eloi	1864- -
4.11.7.2	Florence Elsie	1867-1893-1893
4.11.7.3	Eldon E.	1872-1895?-1945
4.11.7.4	Alice Drusella	1874-1897?-1935

5.7.1   **MONTY, Louis** b & bp 26 Jul 1791, St. Mathias, QC; d & bur 29 & 31 Oct 1867, St. Mathias & Richelieu, QC. He married 11 Feb 1811, St. Mathias, QC, **Julie/Judith Messier** (Augustin Messier & Marie Véronique Mongeau) b & bp 23 Dec 1789, Varennes, QC; d & bur 31 Oct & 3 Nov 1865, St. Mathias & Richelieu, QC.

Louis Monty was a farmer in St. Mathias, QC. He became the guardian of his nieces Julienne (5.7.4.2) and Eudoxie (5.7.4.3) after the death of his brother Joseph in 1830. His wife was named Marie Judith at her baptism but was known as Julie as an adult.

Children:

5.7.1.1	Louis	1812-1832&1869-1877
5.7.1.2	Jean-Baptiste	1814-1838-1887
5.7.1.3	Marie Olive	1815-1835-1878
5.7.1.4	Marie Céleste	1816-1838&1839-1858
5.7.1.5	Michel	1817-1839-1907
5.7.1.6	Esther	1820- -1821
5.7.1.7	Flavie	1822-1841-1886
5.7.1.8	Clémence	1823-1845-1895
5.7.1.9	Honoré	1825-1847-1860
5.7.1.10	Adèle	1828-1846-1889
5.7.1.11	Timothée	1830- -1830
5.7.1.12	Prudent	1832-1852-1901

5.7.2   **MONTY, Thomas** b & bp 21 & 22 Dec 1792, St. Mathias, QC; d & bur 4 & 6 Jun 1866, St. Jean-Baptiste, QC. He married (1) 10 Aug 1812, St. Mathias, QC, **Catherine Benoit** (Paul Benoit & Isabelle Chaume) b & bp there 27 & 28 Nov 1794; d & bur 15 & 17 Jun 1826, St. Jean-Baptiste, QC.

He married (2) 10 Feb 1829, St. Jean-Baptiste, QC, **Agathe Hamel** (François Hamel & Marguerite Dubois) b & bp there 26 & 28 Apr 1809; d & bur 29 Feb & 2 Mar 1904, Marieville, QC.

Thomas Monty was a laborer in St. Mathias, QC, when his oldest child was born in 1813. From 1815 on he was a farmer in St. Jean-Baptiste, QC, where he retired a few years before his death.

Children of the first marriage:

5.7.2.1	Thomas	1813- -1856
5.7.2.2	Louis	1815- -
5.7.2.3	Anonymous	1817- -1817
5.7.2.4	Charlotte	1818- -1822
5.7.2.5	Catherine	1821-1865-1870
5.7.2.6	André	1823-1847-

Children of the second marriage:

5.7.2.7	Domitille	1829- -1830
5.7.2.8	Amable	1831-1854-1893
5.7.2.9	Louis	1836- -1859
5.7.2.10	Joseph	1837-1861-1908

5.7.2.11	Anonymous	1840- -1840
5.7.2.12	Marie Agathe	1844-1872-
5.7.2.13	Elise/Isabelle	1846-1869-1934
5.7.2.14	Antoine Jean-B. Charles	1848- -1854
5.7.2.15	Didace	1851-1875&1893-1909
5.7.2.16	Marie Louise Euphrosine	1853- -1858

5.7.3   **MONTY, Anonymous** b 4 Oct 1794, St. Mathias, QC; d & bur there 4 & 5 Oct 1794.

5.7.4   **MONTY, Joseph** b & bp 23 & 24 Jul 1796, St. Mathias, QC; d & bur 22 & 24 Sep 1830, St. Jean-Baptiste, QC. He married 19 Feb 1816, Marieville, QC, **Charlotte Tétreau** (Joseph Tétreau & Charlotte Lachapelle) b & bp 8 Jun 1796, St. Mathias, QC; d & bur 23 & 25 Apr 1829, St. Jean-Baptiste, QC.
    Joseph Monty was baptized under the name Joseph Jacques, although he does not appear to have ever used his second name. He was a farmer in St. Jean-Baptiste, QC, where his children were born. His brother Louis Monty (5.7.1) became the guardian of his daughters Julienne/Julie and Eudoxie after his death.

Children:
5.7.4.1	Joseph	1818- -1818
5.7.4.2	Julienne/Julie	1822-1836-1865
5.7.4.3	Eudoxie	1823-1840-1910
5.7.4.4	Marie	1829- -1829

5.7.5   **MONTY, Alexis** b & bp 24 & 25 Mar 1798, St. Mathias, QC; d & bur 13 & 15 Apr 1868, Ste Brigide, QC. He married 4 Oct 1825, Marieville, QC, **Scholastique Tessier** (Joseph Tessier & Marie Louise Tétrault) b & bp 23 Feb 1805, St. Mathias, QC; d & bur there 10 & 12 Sep 1857.
    Alexis Monty was a farmer in St. Mathias, QC, until at least 1857. By 1867 he had become a farmer in Ste Brigide, QC. His wife was a sister of Césarie Tessier, wife of Clément Monty (8.3.1).

Children:
5.7.5.1	Marie	1827-1849-
5.7.5.2	Scholastique	1829- -1910
5.7.5.3	Julie	1831- -
5.7.5.4	Alexis	1834- -1835
5.7.5.5	Louis	1836-1869-1882
5.7.5.6	Jacques	1839- -1839
5.7.5.7	Joseph	1842-1867&1877-1918
5.7.5.8	Joséphine	1847- -1848

5.7.6   **MONTY, Angélique** b & bp 16 Apr 1800, St. Mathias, QC; d & bur there 13 & 14 Jan 1801.

5.7.7   **MONTY, Jacques** b & bp 30 Aug 1801, St. Mathias, QC; d & bur 8 & 11 Dec 1855, St. Césaire, QC. He married 20 Jan 1823, Marieville, QC, **Charlotte Messier** (Joseph Messier & Charlotte Ledoux) b & bp 28 May 1805, St. Mathias, QC; d & bur 5 & 7 Oct 1882, St. Césaire, QC.
    Jacques Monty was originally a farmer in St. Mathias, QC, and from at least 1827 on in St. Césaire, QC.

Children:
| 5.7.7.1 | Léon | 1824-1846-1868 |
| 5.7.7.2 | Zoé | 1825-1845-1897 |

5.7.7.3	Michel	1827- -1832
5.7.7.4	Magloire	1829- -1832
5.7.7.5	Nazaire	1831- -1848
5.7.7.6	Adélaïde	1832- -1832
5.7.7.7	Onésime	1833-1853&1870-1900
5.7.7.8	Joseph	1835-1873-1914
5.7.7.9	Elise	1836- -1889
5.7.7.10	Adeline	1838- -1838
5.7.7.11	Vénérance	1839-1860&1891-1926
5.7.7.12	Adèle	1841- -1842
5.7.7.13	Ignace	1843- -1853
5.7.7.14	Philomène	1844-1863-1884
5.7.7.15	Jacques	1848-1872-1924

5.7.8   **MONTY, Marie Josephte** b & bp 12 & 14 Oct 1803, Chambly, QC; d & bur 2 & 4 Feb 1804, St. Mathias, QC.
See my note at 5.7.9

5.7.9   **MONTY, Anonymous** b 21 Oct 1803, St. Mathias, QC; d & bur there 21 & 22 Oct 1803.
Both this child and Marie Josephte Monty (5.7.8) are said in their baptismal and/or burial records to be children of Louis Monty and Elisabeth Barré, which is clearly impossible given their dates of birth. One or both sets of records must be wrong.

5.7.10   **MONTY, Isaac** b & bp 21 & 22 Jul 1805, St. Mathias, QC; d & bur 25 & 27 Nov 1874, Valcourt, QC. He married 8 May 1832, St. Mathias, QC, **Esther Girard** (Michel Girard & Charlotte Benoit) b 1814?, QC; m (2) 1 Oct 1883, St. Césaire, QC, Louis Gobeille/Gobeil (Marc Antoine Gobeille & Marguerite Pouliot), widower of Sophie Provost, Césaire Grisé, and Léocadie Bolduc; d & bur 5 & 7 Aug 1891, Ange Gardien, QC, at the age of 77.
Isaac Monty (François Isaac at his baptism) was a farmer in St. Césaire, QC, until at least 1849, and in Ange Gardien, QC, in the early 1850s (1851 Canadian census; 1852 baptism of his daughter Rose Anne). He moved to the United States perhaps as early as 1860 and was a laborer in Pembroke, NH, in 1870 (US census). He and his wife returned to Canada a few years later though most of their children remained in the United States.

Children:
5.7.10.1	Harline/Aurélie	1833- -
5.7.10.2	Moïse	1835-1860-1917
5.7.10.3	Michel/Mitchell	1836-1863-1911
5.7.10.4	Adeline	1839-1853-
5.7.10.5	Louis	1841-1869-1914
5.7.10.6	Esther	1843- -
5.7.10.7	Napoléon	1845- -1846
5.7.10.8	Nathalie/Mary N.	1847-1864?-1914
5.7.10.9	Adélaïde	1849- -
5.7.10.10	Rose Anne	1852-1867?-

5.7.11   **MONTY, Angélique** b & bp 14 Jul 1807, Marieville, QC; d & bur 11 & 13 Mar 1843, Mont St. Grégoire, QC. She married 17 Feb 1829, St. Mathias, QC, **Pierre Raymond Messier** (Jean-Baptiste Messier & Louise Ledoux) b & bp 30 & 31 Aug 1806, Marieville, QC; m (2) 29 Oct 1844, Mont St. Grégoire, QC, Apolline Touchet (Pierre Touchet & Marie Sansoucy); d & bur 6 & 8 Aug 1884, Ste Brigide, QC.
Pierre Messier was originally a farmer in St. Mathias, QC, and later in Marieville, Mont St. Grégoire, and Ste Brigide, QC.

Children:

i   **Marie Isabelle Messier** b & bp 17 Dec 1829, St. Mathias, QC; d & bur 17 & 20 Sep 1912, Marieville, QC. She married 2 Oct 1860, St. Mathias, QC, a first cousin once removed **Joseph Rainville** (Louis Rainville and Marie Olive Monty [5.7.1.3]) b & bp there 5 Jan 1836; d & bur 7 & 9 May 1912, Marieville, QC.

ii   **Catherine Messier** b & bp 14 & 15 Jul 1832, St. Mathias, QC; d before Sep 1837.

iii   **Norbert Messier** b & bp 14 & 15 Jun 1833, Marieville, QC. He married 23 Feb 1857, Dunham, QC, **Séraphine Auclaire** (Joseph Auclaire & Marie Larose) b & bp 22 Mar 1832, St. Césaire, QC.

iv   **Sophronie Messier** b & bp 27 Apr & 2 May 1835, Marieville, QC; d & bur 25 May 1862, Ste Brigide, QC. She married there 7 Nov 1859 **Louis Landry** (Hubert Landry & Emelie Ethier) b & bp 25 Aug 1833, St. Valentin, QC; d & bur 5 & 6 Sep 1863, Ste Brigide, QC.

v   **Adèle Messier** b & bp 1 & 3 Jul 1836, Marieville, QC. She married 4 Oct 1859, Ste Brigide, QC, **Pierre Landry** (Hubert Landry & Emelie Ethier) b & bp 23 Nov 1836, St. Valentin, QC; d & bur 27 & 31 Jul 1914, Sweetsburg & Ste Brigide, QC.

vi   **Catherine Messier** b & bp 31 Aug & 1 Sep 1837, Marieville, QC; d & bur there 9 & 11 Oct 1838.

vii   **Timothée Messier** b & bp 27 & 28 Jan 1839, Marieville, QC; d 9 Jul 1918, QC. He married 27 Oct 1863, St. Mathias, QC, a cousin once removed, **Marie Hermine Choquette** (Ambroise Choquette & Marie Céleste Monty [(5.7.1.4]) b & bp 18 & 19 Aug 1840, Marieville, QC.

viii   **Jacques Messier** b & bp 3 & 10 Apr 1841, Marieville, QC; d & bur 1 & 3 Mar 1843, Mont St. Grégoire, QC.

ix   **Victoire Messier** b & bp 11 & 15 Feb 1843, Mont St. Grégoire, QC; d & bur there 23 & 25 Jun 1843.

5.10.1   **MONTY, Joseph** b & bp 20 & 21 Aug 1802, St. Mathias, QC; d & bur there 18 & 20 Feb 1823. He married there 12 Aug 1822 **Adélaïde Harbec/Arbec** (Jean-Baptiste Harbec & Catherine Guillot) b & bp 30 Sep & 1 Oct 1804, Chambly, QC; m (2) 5 Jul 1825, St. Mathias, QC, Ambroise Bessette (François Bessette & Marie Fonteneau); m (3) 21 Sep 1852, Iberville, QC, Ambroise Vigeant (Ambroise Vigeant & Agathe Goddu), widower of Marguerite Demers; d & bur 14 & 16 Jun 1888, Iberville, QC.

Joseph Monty was a farmer in St. Mathias, QC.

5.10.2   **MONTY, Jean-Baptiste** b & bp 2 Sep 1803, St. Mathias, QC; d & bur there 24 & 26 May 1823.

Jean-Baptiste Monty was a farmer in St. Mathias, QC.

5.10.3   **MONTY, Marie Louise** b & bp 3 & 4 Nov 1805, St. Mathias, QC. She married there 30 Oct 1826 **Michel Decelle** (Basile Decelle & Charlotte Colette) b & bp 8 & 9 Sep 1805, Chambly, QC.

Michel Decelle (also Decelles, Descelles) was a farmer in Chambly, QC, where he was still living with his family in 1851 (Canadian census). I have not found any later trace of him there and suspect that he and his family left Canada not long afterwards. His daughter Mathilde married in Waltham, MA, in 1857 and at least one son, Basile, was working in Worcester, MA, in 1870 and 1880. Michel Decelle, retired, and his wife Louisa were living in Woonsocket, RI, in 1880 (US censuses).

Children:

i   **Louise Decelle** b & bp 18 Dec 1826, Chambly, QC. She married there 14 Jan 1845 **Camille Courtemanche** (Joseph Courtemanche & Julie Harbec) b & bp there 25 & 27 Aug 1820.

ii   **Clémence Decelle** b & bp 27 & 28 Oct 1828, Chambly, QC.

iii   **Julie Decelle** b & bp 13 & 14 Jul 1830, Chambly, QC; d & bur there 30 Nov & 2 Dec 1832.

iv   **Marie Mathurine Decelle** b & bp 2 Jan & 31 May 1832, Chambly, QC.

v   **Basile Decelle/Desell** b & bp 3 & 4 Mar 1834, Chambly, QC. He married **Philomene** ____ b 1837?, QC.

vi   **Marie Joséphine Decelle** b & bp 10 Mar 1836, Chambly, QC.

vii   **Mathilde/Matilda Decelle** b & bp 1 & 3 Feb 1838, Chambly, QC; d 29 Apr 1913, Worcester, MA. She married 6 Feb 1857, Waltham, MA, **Prosper Perreault** (René Prosper Perreault & Archange Desseingue) b 24 Jul 1837, QC; d 1 Sep 1907, Worcester, MA.

viii   **Marie Decelle** b & bp 8 & 12 Jul 1840, Chambly, QC.

ix   **Charlotte Decelle** b & bp 21 Feb 1843, Chambly, QC; d & bur there 9 & 11 Nov 1846.

x   **Joseph Decelle** b & bp 17 & 19 Jul 1846, Chambly, QC.

xi   **Julienne Decelle** b & bp 5 & 8 Jun 1850, Chambly, QC.

5.10.4   **MONTY, François David** b & bp 9 Apr 1807, St. Mathias, QC; d & bur there 29 & 30 Jul 1807.

5.10.5   **MONTY, Céleste** b & bp 15 Oct 1808, St. Mathias, QC; d & bur 9 & 11 Mar 1876, St. Sébastien, QC. She married (1) 6 Feb 1826, St. Mathias, QC, **Michel Larocque** (Michel Larocque & Marie Anne Troie) b & bp 30 Oct 1799, Chambly, QC.

She was a widow when she married (2) 1 Feb 1848, Henryville, QC, **Joseph Samson** (Etienne Samson & Marguerite Picard dit Destroismaisons) b & bp 31 Oct 1816, St. Pierre de la Rivière du Sud, QC; d 7 bur 3 & 5 Sep 1872, St. Sébastien, QC.

Michel Larocque, a farmer and master blacksmith, lived in St. Mathias, QC, until at least 1836 and in Henryville, QC, from at least 1839 on.

Joseph Samson and his wife were residents of Henryville at the births of their children. He was a farmer in St. Sébastien, QC, at his death.

Children:

i   **Virginie Larocque** b & bp 8 & 9 Mar 1827, St. Mathias, QC; d & bur 12 & 14 Oct 1864, St. Sébastien, QC. She married 12 May 1857, Henryville, QC, **Charles Patenaude** (Charles Patenaude & Marguerite Hains) b & bp 8 Nov 1821, St. Luc, QC; m (1) 26 Jan 1847, Henryville, QC, Angélique Dufresne (Pierre Dufresne & Emilie Deslauriers); m (3) 12 Feb 1866, St. Alexandre, QC, Virginie Gadouas (Médard Gadouas & Catherine Poissant); d & bur 24 & 26 Nov 1875, St. Sébastien, QC.

ii   **Olympe Anastasie Larocque** b & bp 28 & 29 Jun 1828, St. Mathias, QC.

iii   **Marie Henriette Larocque** b & bp 20 & 21 Dec 1829, St. Mathias, QC. She married 20 Sep 1852, Stanbridge, QC, **Joseph Pratte** (Théodore Pratte & Marie Martin) b & bp 2 & 3 May 1830, St. Jean-Baptiste, QC.

iv   **Hélène Larocque** married 25 Jan 1848, Henryville, QC, **Jean-Baptiste Chicoine** (Jean-Baptiste Chicoine & Marguerite Beaulac dit Desmarais) b & bp 29 Dec 1823 & 5 Sep 1824, Swanton, VT & St. Jean-Baptiste, QC.

v   **Louise Joséphine Larocque** b & bp 30 & 31 May 1832, St. Mathias, QC. She married 27 Feb 1854, Henryville, QC, **Jean-Baptiste Massé** (Jean-Baptiste Massé & Françoise Brosseau) b & bp 10 & 11 Mar 1833, St. Mathias, QC.

vi   **Michel Joseph Larocque** b & bp 18 & 19 Mar 1834, St. Mathias, QC; d & bur 17 & 19 Dec 1910, Windsor, QC. He married 7 Jan 1857, Stanbridge, QC, **Marie Carpentier** (François Xavier Carpentier & Marie Côté).

vii   **Edmond Larocque** b & bp 25 Mar 1836, St. Mathias, QC.

viii   **Simon Larocque** b & bp 16 & 18 Mar 1839, Henryville, QC. He married 4 Nov 1862, Stanbridge, QC, **Angèle Cadoret** (Hilaire Cadoret & Emilie Bernard) b & bp 26 May & 22 Jun 1844, Henryville, QC.

ix   **Alfred Larocque** married 18 Nov 1862, Stanbridge, QC, **Rosalie Audette** (Toussaint Audette & Emilie Vincent).

x   **Marie Philomène Larocque** b & bp 13 & 14 Sep 1843, Henryville, QC; d & bur there 27 & 28 Aug 1849.

xi   **Adèle Larocque** married 6 Apr 1867, St. Sebastien, QC, **Etienne Lussier** (Amable Lussier & Marie Savaria) m (1) 25 Apr 1853, St. Jean, QC, Aurélie Ferland (Louis Ferland & Suzanne Granger).

xii   **Florence Samson** b & bp 24 May 1848, Henryville, QC. She married 1 Oct 1872, St. Sébastien, QC, **Alfred Fournier** (Thomas Fournier & Salomé Therrien) b & bp 30 & 31 Mar 1845, Henryville, QC.

xiii   **Aurélie Samson** b & bp 12 Aug 1851, Henryville, QC; d & bur 13 & 14 Oct 1886, Bedford, QC. She married 21 Feb 1870, St. Sébastien, QC, **Joseph Cyr** (Joseph Cyr & Flavie Campbell) b 1848?, QC; m (2) 25 Nov 1889, St. Alexandre, QC, Emma Bourdeau (Joseph Bourdeau & Emelie Audet); d & bur 12 & 14 Nov 1914, Bedford, QC, at the age of 66.

xiv   **Joseph Samson** b & bp 20 Feb 1853, Henryville, QC; d & bur 10 & 13 Dec 1920, Stanbridge, QC. He married 15 Sep 1873, Iberville, QC, **Malvina Fréchette** (David Fréchette & Olive Corriveau) b 9 Oct 1855, QC; d & bur 22 Mar & 7 May 1940, Pike River & Stanbridge, QC.

5.10.6   **MONTY, Louis** b & bp 16 Aug 1810, St. Mathias, QC; d & bur there 8 & 9 Aug 1854. He married there 28 Sep 1830 **Josephte Foisy** (Claude Foisy & Ursule Barsalou) b & bp 2 Feb 1811, Chambly, QC; m (2) 22 Nov 1869, Richelieu, QC, **Louis Monty** (5.7.1.1); d & bur 20 & 22 Jan 1878, Ottawa, Ontario, Canada.

Louis Monty was a farmer in St. Mathias, QC. His widow's second husband, also named Louis Monty, was his first cousin once removed. She was staying in Ontario with her son Louis Dosithée (5.10.6.8) when she died and was buried in Notre Dame Cemetery in Ottawa, Canada.

Children:

5.10.6.1	Joséphine	1831-1854-1915
5.10.6.2	Joseph Louis	1833-1856-1888
5.10.6.3	Cordélie	1835-1853-
5.10.6.4	Damien	1838-1862&1866-1917
5.10.6.5	Narcisse Euphémien	1840- -1842
5.10.6.6	Marie Aglaé	1843-1863-1898
5.10.6.7	Jean-Marie Claude	1845- -1860
5.10.6.8	Louis Dosithée	1846- &1906-1919
5.10.6.9	Eustache	1848-1872-1902
5.10.6.10	Marie Heldrida	1851- -1857

8.1.1   **MONTY, Marie Louise** b & bp 3 & 4 Aug 1787, Chambly, QC; d & bur 17 & 18 Nov 1790, St. Mathias, QC.

8.1.2   **MONTY, Marie** b & bp 8 & 9 Jul 1789, Chambly, QC; d & bur 16 & 18 Aug 1877, Mont St. Grégoire, QC. She married 11 Jan 1813, St. Mathias, QC **Pierre Gamache** (Pierre Gamache & Cécile Davignon) b & bp 22 & 23 Apr 1785, Chambly, QC; m (1) 22 Nov 1810, Marieville, QC, Marie Desanges Janelle (François Janelle & Marie Reine Patenaude); d & bur 22 & 24 Sep 1858, Mont St. Grégoire, QC.

Pierre Gamache was a farmer in Marieville, QC, and in Mont St. Grégoire, QC, after the creation of the parish of St. Grégoire in 1841. He was a brother of Noël Gamache, husband of Amable Monty (8.1.6) and a half-brother of Osithe Gamache, wife of Clément Monty (8.1.7).

Children:

i   **Pierre Gamache** b & bp 19 & 20 Oct 1813, St. Mathias, QC; d & bur 24 & 27 Feb 1891, Mont St. Grégoire, QC. He married 26 Feb 1838, Marieville, QC, **Marie Lacombe** (François Lacombe & Charlotte Balthazar) b & bp 6 Mar 1818, St. Mathias, QC; d & bur 21 & 23 Sep 1895, Mont St. Grégoire, QC.

ii   **Clément Gamache** b & bp 19 Jun 1815, Marieville, QC; d & bur 13 & 16 Sep

1903, St. Alexandre, QC. He married there 7 Nov 1837 **Nathalie/Anathalie/Athalie Robert** (Jacques Robert & Geneviève Grenier) b & bp there 9 & 10 Nov 1818; d & bur 28 Sep & 1 Oct 1903, St. Alexandre, QC.

iii **Noël Gamache** b Jun 1818, QC; d & bur 24 & 26 Nov 1907, Mont St. Grégoire, QC, at the age of 89 years and 5 months. He married (1) there 1 Oct 1844, **Céleste Quintin** (Paul Quintin & Catherine Fréchette) b & bp 23 Sep 1822, St. Mathias, QC; d & bur 28 & 30 Dec 1852, Mont St. Grégoire, QC.

He married (2) 28 Sep 1863, Mont St. Grégoire, QC, **Prospère Robert** (Jacques Robert & Geneviève Grenier) b & bp 24 & 25 Jun 1823, Marieville, QC; d & bur 9 & 12 Jun 1893, Mont St. Grégoire, QC.

iv **Domitilde Gamache** b & bp 4 & 5 Jul 1820, Marieville, QC; d & bur there 10 & 12 Jun 1822.

v **Michel Gamache** b & bp 17 & 18 Aug 1822, Marieville, QC; d & bur 25 & 27 Jan 1893, Cookshire & Iberville, QC. He married 5 Nov 1844, Iberville, QC, **Marcelline Ménard** (Louis Ménard & Marie Lefort) b & bp there 14 & 15 Feb 1826; d & bur there 17 & 19 Aug 1864.

vi **Edouard Gamache** b & bp 29 & 31 Oct 1824, Marieville, QC; d & bur 5 & 7 Dec 1904, Cookshire, QC. He married 3 Oct 1848, Mont St. Grégoire, QC, **Onésime Fréchette** (Joseph Fréchette & Geneviève Lamoureux) b 16 Jan 1826, QC; d & bur 1 & 4 Dec 1925, Cookshire, QC, at the age of 99 years, 10 months, and 15 days.

vii **Marie Gamache** b & bp 24 & 25 Feb 1827, Marieville, QC; d & bur 9 & 11 Feb 1898, St. Alexandre, QC. She married 19 Jan 1847, Mont St. Grégoire, QC, **Alexis Jetté** (Toussaint Jetté & Josephte Benjamin) b & bp 19 & 20 May 1825, Marieville, QC; d & bur 2 & 4 Feb 1914, St. Alexandre, QC.

viii **Salomé Gamache** b & bp 12 & 13 Sep 1829, Marieville, QC. She married 13 Feb 1849, Mont St. Grégoire, QC, **Pierre Choquet/Choquette** (Pierre Choquet & Léocadie Carreau) b 12 Apr 1830, St. Jean, QC; m (2) as a widower 11 Aug 1856, St. Alexandre, QC, Marie Mochon (Joseph Mochon & Julienne Provost); m (3) there 23 Jul 1867 Mathilde Grégoire (Jean-Baptiste Grégoire & Rosalie Ponton); d & bur 2 & 5 Nov 1878, Bennington, VT & St. Alexandre, QC.

ix **Octave Gamache** b & bp 30 Jun & 1 Jul 1832, Iberville, QC. He married 26 Oct 1852, Mont St. Grégoire, QC, **Marie Quintin** (Antoine Quintin & Lucie Benjamin) b & bp 13 Oct 1834, Iberville, QC; d & bur 13 & 15 Apr 1871, Holyoke, MA & Iberville, QC.

8.1.3 **MONTY, Michel** b & bp 26 & 28 Oct 1791, Chambly, QC; d & bur 21 & 23 Jul 1813, St. Mathias, QC.

8.1.4 **MONTY, Madeleine** b & bp 11 & 12 Nov 1794, St. Mathias, QC; d & bur there 28 & 30 May 1817. She married there 18 Apr 1814 **Louis Lareau** (Noël Lareau & Marguerite Racine) b & bp 4 & 5 Aug 1793, Chambly, QC; m (2) 9 Oct 1820, St. Mathias, QC, Charlotte Bessette (Clément Bessette & Marie Louise Choquette); d & bur 31 Jul 1832, Iberville, QC.

Louis Lareau was a farm laborer in St. Mathias, QC, at his first marriage and at the births of his children. He and his brother Jean-Baptiste Lareau married two cousins, Madeleine Monty and Marguerite Larivière, daughter of Joseph Larivière and Marie Monty (8.2).

Children:

i **Marguerite Lareau** b & bp 24 Nov 1814, St. Mathias, QC; d & bur 21 & 23 Oct 1879, Iberville, QC. She married there 5 Oct 1830 **Jean-Baptiste Bertrand** (Jean-Baptiste Bertrand & Marie Anne Lebeau) b & bp 26 Sep 1807, St. Mathias, QC; d & bur 27 Feb & 2 Mar 1886, Iberville, QC.

ii **Noël Lareau** b & bp 27 & 28 Apr 1817, St. Mathias, QC; d & bur there 9 & 11 Jun 1817.

8.1.5 **MONTY, Catherine** b & bp 22 & 23 Jul 1797, St. Mathias, QC; d & bur 2

& 4 Jan 1877, Iberville, QC. She married 22 Jan 1816, St. Mathias, QC, **Joseph Boucher** (Joseph Boucher & Marie Anne Lareau) b & bp there 11 & 13 Mar 1796; d & bur 3 & 5 Aug 1865, Iberville, QC.

Joseph Boucher was a laborer and farmer in St. Mathias, QC, until at least 1827 and in Iberville, QC, from at least 1830. He was retired there at his death.

Children:

i   **Joseph Boucher** b & bp 3 Mar 1817, St. Luc, QC. He married 26 Feb 1838, St. Mathias, QC, **Rosalie Tétreau** (Jean-Baptiste Tétreau & Julie Guertin) b & bp there 25 & 26 Jul 1819.

ii   **Edouard Boucher** b & bp 9 & 10 Aug 1818, St. Mathias, QC; d & bur 12 & 14 Mar 1898, Iberville, QC. He married there 3 Jul 1838 **Mathilde/Martine Goyette** (François Goyette & Louise Bessette) b 1821?, QC; d & bur 4 & 9 Mar 1903, Iberville, QC, at the age of 82.

iii   **Ambroise Boucher** b & bp 7 Dec 1820, Chambly, QC; d & bur 20 & 23 Jan 1904, Iberville, QC. He married there 10 Feb 1846 **Ovide Bessette** (François Bessette & Marguerite Régnier) b & bp 24 Mar 1827, St. Mathias, QC; d & bur 22 & 24 Jul 1915, Iberville, QC.

iv   **Monique Boucher** b & bp 6 Jul 1822, St. Mathias, QC. She married 6 Feb 1844, Iberville, QC, **Pierre Dandurand** (Germain Dandurand & Suzanne Boivin) b & bp there 23 & 24 Dec 1823.

v   **Michel Boucher** b & bp 29 Sep 1824, St. Mathias, QC; d & bur 22 & 26 Jan 1903, Mont St. Grégoire, QC. He married 10 Feb 1852, Iberville, QC, **Céleste Guillot** (Etienne Guillot & Céleste Plante) b & bp there 4 Feb 1830; d & bur 1 & 3 Mar 1914, St. Jean & Mont St. Grégoire, QC.

vi   **Martine Boucher** b & bp 11 & 12 Jan 1827, St. Mathias, QC; d & bur 17 & 19 May 1905, Mont St. Grégoire, QC. She married 22 Jul 1845, Iberville, QC, **Eusèbe Fréchette** (Joseph Fréchette & Geneviève Lamoureux) b & bp 18 & 19 Jan 1824, Marieville, QC; d & bur 10 & 12 May 1905, Mont St. Grégoire, QC.

vii   **Marcel Boucher** b & bp 17 Oct 1830, Iberville, QC; d & bur there 16 & 18 Aug 1888. He married 3 Feb 1857, St. Liboire, QC, **Marie Sylvestre** (Alexis Amable Sylvestre & Angèle Voligny) b 1835?, QC.

viii   **Céleste Boucher** b & bp 15 Feb 1834, St. Jean, QC; d & bur 16 & 18 Feb 1876, St. Jean & Mont St. Grégoire, QC. She married 19 Sep 1870, Iberville, QC, **Napoléon Calcagno** (Jean-Baptiste Calcagno & Angélique Laporte) b & bp 1 & 2 Feb 1830, St. Jean, QC; d & bur 27 & 29 Apr 1882, Montreal & Mont St. Grégoire, QC.

ix   **Jean-Baptiste Boucher** b & bp 26 & 27 Jul 1836, St. Jean, QC; d & bur 17 & 20 Jan 1919, Mont St. Grégoire, QC. He married 14 Oct 1862, Ste Brigide, QC, **Célina Bazinet** (Pascal Bazinet & Aurélie Lareau) b 9 Sep 1844, QC; d & bur 16 & 18 Feb 1915, Mont St. Grégoire, QC.

x   **Cécile Boucher** b & bp 20 & 21 Nov 1840, Iberville, QC; d & bur 1922, Mont St. Grégoire, QC. She married 4 Mar 1867, Iberville, QC, **Alphée Tétrault/Tétreault** (Edouard Tétreault & Marie Anne Normandin) b & bp 20 & 21 Jan 1842, St. Mathias, QC; d & bur 1914, Mont St. Grégoire, QC.

8.1.6   **MONTY, Amable** b & bp 6 & 7 Oct 1799, St. Mathias, QC. She married there 11 Nov 1816 **Noël Gamache** (Pierre Gamache/Camarse dit St. André & Cécile Davignon) b & bp there 17 & 18 Oct 1798.

Noël Gamache (Camarse at his baptism) was a farmer in Marieville, QC, at the births of his children. I have found no trace of this family beyond 1833, when Noël Gamache was godfather in St. Luc, QC, to his nephew Clément Monty (8.1.7.2). He was a brother of Pierre Gamache, husband of Marie Monty (8.1.2) and a half-brother of Osithe Gamache, wife of Clément Monty (8.1.7).

Children:

i   **Noël Gamache** b & bp 10 & 11 Jan 1818, Marieville, QC.

ii   **Pierre Bénoni Gamache** b & bp 4 & 6 Jun 1819, Marieville, QC.

iii   **Adélaïde Gamache** b & bp 31 Jan & 4 Feb 1821, Marieville, QC.

iv   **Rose Gamache** b & bp 1 & 2 Sep 1822, Marieville, QC; d & bur there 30 Sep & 2 Oct 1822.

8.1.7   **MONTY, Clément** b & bp 27 Jul 1802, St. Mathias, QC; d 6 Nov 1892, Bear Creek, WI. He married 19 Jul 1831, St. Mathias, QC, **Osithe Gamache** (Pierre Gamache & Marie Reine Dame) b & bp there 17 & 18 Mar 1813; d 15 Jan 1891, Bear Creek, WI.

Clément Monty was a farmer in Iberville, QC, until the mid-1860s when he left with his family for the United States. They may have stayed in New Hampshire for a few years before moving on to Wisconsin. One son, Clément, settled permanently in New Hampshire while two others, who had children there between 1864 and 1866, joined their father and siblings in Bear Creek, WI, in 1867. The men all had adjoining farms there in 1870 (US census). Clément Monty and his wife remained there until their deaths and were buried in the St. Rose Cemetery in Clintonville, WI.

Osithe Gamache was a half-sister of Pierre Gamache, husband of Marie Monty (8.1.2) and of Noël Gamache, husband of Amable Monty (8.1.6). She is sometimes confused with a younger sister named Céleste (b & bp 27 & 28 Apr 1814, St. Mathias, QC). It was Osithe and not Céleste who married Clément Monty.

Children:

8.1.7.1	Osithe	1832- -1832
8.1.7.2	Clément	1833-1856?-1894
8.1.7.3	Marcel	1834- -1838
8.1.7.4	Michel/Mitchell	1836-1864-
8.1.7.5	Amédée/Charles	1837-1865-
8.1.7.6	Jean-Baptiste/John B.	1839-1865?-1891
8.1.7.7	Isaïe	1840- -1841
8.1.7.8	Joseph	1842- -1842
8.1.7.9	Philomène	1843-1863-1903
8.1.7.10	Marie Reine	1845- -1846
8.1.7.11	Mathilde/Matilda	1847- -1911
8.1.7.12	Joseph Abraham	1850-1870-1910
8.1.7.13	Edesse Virginie	1852- -1852
8.1.7.14	Camille	1853- -1896
8.1.7.15	Julie/Julia	1855- -1936

8.1.8   **MONTY, Marie Pélagie** b & bp 27 & 28 Jun 1805, St. Mathias, QC; d & bur there 2 & 4 Mar 1819.

8.1.9   **MONTY, Marie Louise** b & bp 10 & 11 Jun 1808, St. Mathias, QC; d & bur 18 & 20 Feb 1891, Iberville, QC. She married there 4 Feb 1834 **Abraham Cabana** (Joachim Cabana & Amable Chagnon) b & bp 10 & 11 Oct 1810, Verchères, QC; d & bur 21 & 24 May 1884, Iberville, QC.

Abraham Cabana was originally a miller in Chambly, QC, and later in St. Mathias, QC. By 1851 he was a farmer in Iberville, QC (Canadian census), and remained there until his death.

Children:

i   **Abraham Cabana** b & bp 22 & 23 Apr 1833, Chambly, QC. He married (1) 30 Jul 1860, Iberville, QC, a third cousin **Célina Surprenant** (Pierre Surprenant dit Lafontaine & Catherine Lareau [13.1.ii]) b 1829?, QC; d & bur 4 & 6 Dec 1872, St. Jean, QC, at the age of 43.

He married (2) 28 Jul 1873, Napierville, QC, **Philomène Hébert** (Antoine Hébert & Nathalie Henault) b & bp there 19 & 20 Jan 1837.

ii   **Joseph Eudore Cabana** b & bp 13 Dec 1836, Chambly, QC; d & bur 19 & 22 Mar

1877, Iberville, QC.

iii   **Janvier Cabana** b & bp 2 & 3 Jan 1841, St. Mathias, QC; d & bur there 24 & 25 Feb 1842.

iv   **Ambroise Cabana** b & bp 19 & 20 Apr 1839, Chambly, QC; d & bur 20 & 23 Oct 1905, Montreal, QC. He married 1 Aug 1864, Iberville, QC, **Rose Delima Pepin** (Laurent Pepin & Emérence Goyette) b & bp there 8 Jun 1847.

v   **Joseph Jacob Cabana** b & bp 28 Apr 1843, St. Mathias, QC; d & bur 8 & 11 Jul 1865, Iberville, QC. He married 12 Oct 1863, St. Mathias, QC, **Emelie Forti/Fortier** (Antoine Forti/Forty & Josephte Mailloux); b & bp 15 & 16 Nov 1839, Chambly & St. Mathias, QC; m (2) 18 Aug 1876, Chambly, QC, Joseph Talbot dit Gervais (Jean-Baptiste Talbot dit Gervais & Basilie [?] Robert), widower of Marie Delima Demars.

vi   **Marie Alodie/Mélanie/Mélodie Cabana** b & bp 9 Apr 1845, St. Mathias, QC. She married 13 Apr 1874, Iberville, QC, **Damase Vézina** (Prisque Vézina & Françoise Auger) b 1851?, QC.

vii   **Alphonse Cabana** b & bp 10 & 11 Jun 1848, St. Mathias, QC.

viii   **Azilda/Ezilda Cabana** b 30 Aug 1851, QC. She married 27 Dec 1886, Iberville, QC, **François Xavier Brière** (Louis Brière & Ursule Guillet) b & bp 25 & 27 Jan 1845, Marieville, QC; m (1) there 30 Jul 1867 Aurélie Choinière (Antoine Choinière & Rosalie Gladu).

ix   **Alfred Cabana** b 16 Apr 1854, QC.

8.1.10   **MONTY, Rosalie/Marie Rose** b & bp 14 Apr 1812, St. Mathias, QC; d & bur 7 & 9 Jun 1902, Chambly, QC. She married 14 Jun 1831, St. Mathias, QC, **Joseph Charoux** (André Charoux & Agathe Balthazar) b & bp there 27 & 28 Mar 1806; d & bur 23 & 26 May 1885, Chambly, QC.

Rosalie Monty (baptismal name) was named Marie Rose Monty in her marriage record and Rose in the Canadian censuses of 1851 and 1901. She was otherwise known as Rosalie.

Joseph Charoux (also Charroux) was a shoemaker first in Iberville, QC, and after 1843 in St. Mathias, QC. He was a laborer there in 1851 (Canadian census) but a resident of Chambly, QC, when his daughter Marie (viii) married in 1878.

Children:

i   **Joseph Charoux** b & bp 12 Apr 1832, Iberville, QC. He married 27 May 1861, Chambly, QC, **Emélie Guillet** (Hyacinthe Guillet & Emélie Dié) b & bp 26 & 27 Jan 1839, Marieville, QC.

ii   **Rosalie Charoux** b & bp 21 Sep 1833, St. Jean, QC; d & bur 6 & 9 May 1917, Montreal, QC.

iii   **Abraham Charoux** b & bp 2 & 3 Jan 1836, Iberville, QC. He married there 17 Feb 1857 **Céleste Balthazar** (Jean-Baptiste Balthazar & Catherine Bou-cher) b & bp 6 Sep 1834, St. Jean, QC.

iv   **Hermine Charoux** b & bp 22 & 23 Jun 1838, Iberville, QC; d & bur there 15 & 17 Mar 1842.

v   **Philomène Charoux** b 1840?

vi   **Marie Adeline/Célina Charoux** b & bp 14 Jan 1843, Iberville, QC; d & bur 5 & 7 Apr 1852, St. Mathias, QC.

vii   **Justin Charoux** b & bp 29 & 30 Jul 1844, St. Mathias, QC.

viii   **Marie Françoise Charoux** b & bp 4 & 5 Mar 1846, St. Mathias, QC; d & bur 3 & 6 Jun 1907, Chambly, QC. She married there 7 Oct 1878 **Léonidas Davignon** (Gonzague Davignon & Elisabeth Lemaire) b & bp there 5 Mar 1855; d & bur there 21 & 24 Dec 1899.

ix   **Adolphe Charoux** b & bp 25 Jun & 3 Jul 1848, Iberville, QC.

x   **Joséphine Charoux** b & bp 28 & 29 Jul 1850, St. Mathias, QC; d & bur 21 & 25 Sep 1873, Wilton, NH & Chambly, QC.

xi   **Alphonse Charoux** b & bp 18 & 19 Nov 1852, Iberville, QC; d & bur 27 & 28 Jan 1854, St. Mathias, QC.

xii   **Marcelline Charoux** b & bp 10 & 11 Jan 1855, Iberville, QC; d & bur 10 & 14 Apr 1884, Chambly, QC. She married there 27 Sep 1875 **Adolphe Racicot** (Antoine Racicot & Adèle Halde) b & bp 31 Aug & 1 Sep 1851, Mont St. Hilaire, QC; m (2) 30 Apr 1888, Chambly, QC, Agnès Davignon (Eusèbe Davignon & Edesse Lavoie); d & bur 28 & 31 Mar 1926, Montreal & Chambly, QC.

8.3.1   **MONTY, Clément** b & bp 24 Nov 1805, St. Mathias, QC; d & bur 30 Apr & 2 May 1874, Roxton Falls, QC. He married 9 Aug 1842, Iberville, QC, **Césarie Tessier** (Joseph Tessier & Marie Louise Tétrault) b & bp 10 & 12 Jan 1820, Marieville, QC; d 25 Feb 1903, Norwich, CT.

Clément Monty was a farmer in Iberville, QC, until 1850, in Henryville, QC, in 1851 and 1853 and in Iberville again in 1858. He moved to Roxton Falls, QC, in 1859 or early 1860 and remained there until his death. His widow and surviving children all emigrated and settled in Connecticut around 1890. Their children in turn later scattered among the New England States. None of their direct descendants can be found in Canada.

Césarie Tessier was a sister of Scholastique Tessier, wife of Alexis Monty (5.7.5). She arrived in the United States in 1890 and was living in 1900 in the household of her daughter Marie Louise in Norwich, CT. The US census of that year notes that she had had thirteen children of whom four, Philippe, Marie Louise, Césarie, and Albina, were still alive. She was buried in the Sacred Heart Cemetery in Norwich.

A note of caution: many family historians have said that she was born on 10 Jan 1832. That assertion, based on the data in her death record, is wrong. Even if we disregard her baptismal record, her marriage record clearly shows that she was over 21 years old in 1842.

Children:

8.3.1.1	Anonymous	1844-	-1844
8.3.1.2	Anonymous	1845-	-1845
8.3.1.3	Philippe/Philip	1846-1870?-	
8.3.1.4	Joseph	1848-	-1888
8.3.1.5	Anonymous	1850-	-1850
8.3.1.6	Marie Louise	1851-1881-	
8.3.1.7	Césarie	1853-1881-1912	
8.3.1.8	Albina	1858-1882-1948	
8.3.1.9	Anonymous	1860-	-1860
8.3.1.10	Anonymous	1861-	-1861

8.3.2   **MONTY, Louise** b & bp 3 & 4 Jun 1807, St. Mathias, QC; d 18 Dec 1888, Swanton, VT. She married 22 Aug 1836, Iberville, QC, **Jean-Baptiste Lareau** (Antoine Lareau & Isabelle Hébert) b & bp 11 & 12 Feb 1806, St. Mathias, QC.

This family never stayed long in any one place. According to the baptismal and marriage records of his children, Jean-Baptiste Lareau was a farmer in Iberville, QC, until at least 1840, a laborer in Mont St. Grégoire, QC, in 1844, a laborer at the Baie Missisquoi, QC, in 1846, a resident of the United States in 1848 and 1849, a farmer in Stanbridge, QC, in 1861, and a resident of Roxton Falls, QC, in 1865 and 1868. He was present at his son Edouard's marriage in Bedford, QC, in 1870. I have found no further records in Canada.

The couple may have moved to the Swanton, VT, area. John Baptista Larreau (sic) and Aloysia Monti (sic) were godparents in Swanton to several grandchildren in the 1870s and 1880s (Baptismal records, St. Mary's Catholic Church). Their children Elzéar (iii), Marie (iv), Edward (vi), and Margarita (v) were living there and their daughter Margarita also died there the same year as her mother "Maria Aloysia Monti", spouse of "John Baptista Larreau" (Death Records, St. Mary's Catholic Church).

Children:

i   **Mathilde Lareau** b & bp 17 & 18 Apr 1838, Iberville, QC. She married 11 Jan 1864, Stanbridge, QC, **Cléophas Clopin** (Jean-Baptiste Clopin & Mathilde Couturier).

ii **Jean-Baptiste Lareau** b & bp 7 & 11 Jan 1840, Iberville, QC; d & bur 31 Mar & 3 Apr 1940, Manchester, NH. He married 21 Feb 1865, Roxton Falls, QC, **Adeline Richer** (Onésime Richer & Vitaline Daniel) b & bp 23 & 24 Dec 1845, St. Pie, QC.

iii **Elzéar Lareau** b & bp 24 & 27 Jul 1842, St. Jean, QC. He married 22 Sep 1868, Roxton Falls, QC, **Azilda Jacques** (Joseph Jacques & Marie Gaulin).

iv **Marie Lareau** b & bp 7 & 8 May 1844, Mont St. Grégoire, QC. She married 9 Jul 1861, Stanbridge, QC, **David Cadoret** (Jean-Baptiste Cadoret & Françoise Duguay) b 1840?, QC.

v **Marguerite Adèle/Margarita Lareau** b & bp Sep & 11 Oct 1846, Iberville, QC; d 5 Dec 1888, Swanton, VT. She married **Joseph Choignière/Choinière**.

vi **Edouard/Edward Lareau** b & bp 25 Oct 1848 & 14 Jan 1849, US & Iberville, QC; d 4 Sep 1907, New Bedford, MA. He married 9 Aug 1870, Bedford, QC, **Joséphine Gaboriau** (Timothée Gaboriau & Marie Robert) b & bp 16 Feb 1851, St. Valentin, QC; d 22 Dec 1929, Ashland, MA.

8.3.3   **MONTY, Josephte** b & bp 9 Feb 1809, St. Mathias, QC; d & bur 24 & 26 Nov 1850, Iberville, QC. She married there 23 Nov 1846 **Daniel O'Brien** (Patrick O'Brien & Helen O'Connell, of County Cork, Ireland).

Daniel O'Brien, a laborer in Iberville, QC, was of age at his marriage.

Children:

i **Anonymous O'Brien** b 13 Nov 1848, Iberville, QC; d & bur there 13 & 15 Nov 1848.

ii **Philippe/Philibert O'Brien** b & bp 22 Nov 1850, Iberville, QC; d & bur there 14 & 15 Nov 1851.

8.3.4   **MONTY, Lucille/Lucie** b & bp 19 & 20 Aug 1810, Marieville, QC; d & bur 4 & 5 Nov 1813, St. Mathias, QC.

8.3.5   **MONTY, Isabelle** b & bp 16 Mar 1812, St. Mathias, QC; d & bur there 25 & 26 Jan 1813.

8.3.6   **MONTY, Florence/Flore** b & bp 9 & 10 Sep 1813, St. Mathias, QC; d & bur 13 & 15 Feb 1876, St. Jean, QC. She married 26 Nov 1839, Iberville, QC, **Nazaire Thuot** (Toussaint Thuot & Josephte Rémillard) b 1814?; m (2) 7 Nov 1881, St. Jean, QC, Séraphine Champagne (Antoine Champagne & Julienne Barrière), widow of Louis Gagnon; d & bur 13 & 15 Feb 1896, Iberville, QC, at the age of 82.

Nazaire Thuot was a farmer in St. Mathias, QC, at his first marriage but soon moved to Iberville, QC, where he was a farmer or laborer at the births of his children. From at least 1863 on he was a boatman on the Richelieu River. His first wife Florence Monty had been baptized under the name of Flore Monti (sic).

Children:

i **Marie Josephte Thuot** b & bp 18 & 19 Aug 1840, Iberville & St. Jean, QC.

ii **Sophie Thuot** b & bp 11 & 12 May 1842, St. Jean, QC.

iii **Marie Adèle Thuot** b & bp 27 & 28 Jan 1846, Henryville, QC. She married 29 Jan 1862, Iberville, QC, **Joseph Berger** (Louis Berger & Louise Laporte).

iv **Adélard Thuot** b & bp 2 & 3 May 1848, Iberville, QC. He married there 8 Jan 1867 **Marie Joséphine Provost** (Toussaint Provost & Françoise Bourgeois) b & bp there 8 & 9 Mar 1846.

v **Marie Malvina Thuot** b & bp 18 & 22 Dec 1850, Iberville, QC.

vi **Nazaire Thuot** b 1853?; d & bur 6 & 8 Jul 1863, Iberville, QC, at the age of 10.

8.3.7   **MONTY, Philippe/Philibert** b & bp 23 & 24 Feb 1815, St. Ma-thias, QC; d & bur 1 & 3 Jul 1875, Roxton Falls, QC.

The only time Philippe Monty was named Philibert was at his baptism. In all the numerous occasions when he was a witness to marriages and deaths in his family or acted as a godfather, he was called Philippe. He did not marry.

8.3.8   **MONTY, Jean-Baptiste** b & bp 1 & 2 Dec 1816, St. Mathias, QC; d & bur 12 & 15 Mar 1888, Sutton, QC. He married 29 Oct 1850, Iberville, QC, **Félicité Corriveau** (Charles Corriveau & Angèle Giasson) b & bp there 5 & 6 Apr 1831.

  Jean-Baptiste Monty was a farmer in Stanbridge, QC, at his marriage and until 1867. In 1868 he was an artisan in Bedford, QC, and in 1870 a merchant there. I do not know where he spent the years between then and his death. He was buried as "John Baptiste Montie, son of Philip and Josette Montie" by the Methodist minister in Sutton, QC, where his oldest son was living. In fact the two witnesses signed Marie Montie and John Montey, most probably his daughter-in-law Mary Como and son Jean-Baptiste/John B. Monty (8.3.8.1). There is no mention of his wife though she was still alive when her son Henry (8.3.8.9) married in 1892.

Children:

8.3.8.1	John B./Jean-Baptiste	1852-1880-1937
8.3.8.2	Charles Philippe	1854- -1859
8.3.8.3	François Napoléon	1856- -1870
8.3.8.4	Marie Jeanne Félicité	1858-1883-
8.3.8.5	Charles	1860-1883-1948
8.3.8.6	Céleste	1862-1878-
8.3.8.7	Jacques Philippe/Jake/Jacob	1864-1888-
8.3.8.8	George Edouard	1866-1907-1954
8.3.8.9	Henry/Henri Michel	1868-1892-
8.3.8.10	Marie Louise Eugénie	1870- -1870
8.3.8.11	Joséphine/Josie L.	1873-1891-
8.3.8.12	Lucie Anna	1876- -1877

8.3.9   **MONTY, Angélique** b & bp 10 Oct 1818, Marieville, QC; bur 14 May 1909, St. Jean, QC.

  Angélique Monty did not marry. Her burial record does not indicate the date of her death.

8.3.10   **MONTY, Moyse/Eusèbe** b & bp 18 & 19 Sep 1820, St. Mathias, QC; d & bur there 27 Feb & 1 Mar 1821.

  This child's baptismal record bears the name of Moyse Monty. He was buried at the age of 5½ months as Eusèbe Monty.

8.3.11   **MONTY, François/Frank** b & bp 27 & 28 Feb 1822, L'Acadie, QC; d 20 Nov 1893, New Bedford, MA. He married (1) 19 Feb 1844, St. Jean, QC, **Osithe Piédalue** d & bur 2 & 3 Feb 1848, St. Jean, QC.

  He married (2) 11 Feb 1850, Iberville, QC, **Aurélie Bourgeois** (Blaise Bourgeois & Josephte Bélanger) b & bp 14 & 15 Nov 1829, L'Acadie, QC; d 4 Jun 1913, New Bedford, MA.

  François Monty was a laborer in Iberville, QC, until at least 1850 and from 1853 through 1871 a resident of St. Armand, Stanbridge, and Bedford, QC. The entire family then left Canada for New Bedford, MA, where Frank Monty was a mill operator and teamster. His widow Aurélie Bourgeois (also known as Henrelie or Orelie in US censuses) remained there after his death (US censuses).

  Osithe Piédalue's surname is uncertain. Her marriage record, while referring to "Osithe connue sous le nom de Piédalue," does not include her parents' names. Yet there was a witness named Alexis Poirier who was identified as a brother of the bride! The two copies of her burial record are no more informative. The original church record, in a perhaps significant departure from common French Canadian usage, identifies her as "Osithe Monty, épouse de François Monty." The copy made for the civil authorities has "Osithe Piédalue." In neither case is her age at death indicated. I have not been able to find her parents and tend to believe that she was an illegitimate child whose parents French Canadian sources never identify. She was of age at her marriage.

Children of the first marriage:

8.3.11.1	François	1845-	-1845
8.3.11.2	Joseph	1846-	-1847
8.3.11.3	Anonymous	1848-	-1848

Children of the second marriage:

8.3.11.4	Aurélie	1850-1871-
8.3.11.5	François/Frank	1853-1887-1916
8.3.11.6	Philippe/Philip	1855-1880-1929
8.3.11.7	Edward	1857-1887?-1908
8.3.11.8	Jean-Baptiste/John B.	1859-1880&1894-
8.3.11.9	Adèle	1860-1920-
8.3.11.10	Joseph Ambroise	1863- -1865
8.3.11.11	Clément	1865- -1865
8.3.11.12	Siffroid George	1866- -1867
8.3.11.13	Marie Rosalie/Mary	1867-1890&1916&1917-
8.3.11.14	Malvina	1870-1893-
8.3.11.15	Josephine	1872-1890-1947

8.3.12   **MONTY, Marguerite** b & bp 17 & 21 Mar 1825, St. Mathias, QC; d & bur there 10 & 12 Jul 1825.

8.3.13   **MONTY, Joseph Trefflé** b & bp 29 & 30 Apr 1826, St. Mathias, QC; d & bur there 12 & 14 Sep 1826.

8.3.14   **MONTY, Edesse** b & bp 8 Sep 1827, Iberville, QC; d & bur 25 & 28 Jan 1925, St. Hyacinthe, QC.
     Edesse Monty did not marry.

8.3.15   **MONTY, Martine** b & bp 19 & 20 Apr 1830, Iberville, QC; d & bur 10 & 13 May 1904, St. Jean, QC. She married 13 Jan 1865, Roxton Falls, QC, **François Xavier Robidoux** (François Xavier Robidoux & Julie Bachand) b & bp 21 Nov 1840, St. Pie, QC; d & bur 27 & 30 Dec 1922, Roxton Pond & St. Jean, QC.
     François Xavier Robidoux was a farmer in Roxton Falls, QC, until about 1872, and in Roxton Pond, QC, a few years later. By 1890 he was a farmer in St. Jean, QC.

Children:
- i   **Anonymous Robidoux** b 6 Mar 1866, Roxton Falls, QC; d & bur there 6 & 8 Mar 1866.
- ii   **Charles Robidoux** b & bp 3 & 8 Dec 1867, Roxton Falls, QC; d between 1910 and 1920, Manchester, NH. He married 27 May 1890, St. Luc, QC, **Marie Louise Deland** (Alfred Deland & Hermine Toupin) b & bp 9 & 10 Nov 1868, Farnham, QC.
- iii   **Marie Rebecca Robidoux** b & bp 28 & 30 Oct 1869, Roxton Falls, QC; d & bur 11 & 13 Jan 1875, Roxton Pond & Roxton Falls, QC.
- iv   **Alfred Robidoux** b & bp 8 & 12 Jun 1871, Roxton Falls, QC. He married 8 May 1906, Roxton Pond, QC, **Rose Alba Belisle** (Joseph Belisle & Rose Alba Robidoux) b & bp there 2 & 6 Mar 1887.
- v   **Félix Robidoux** b & bp 25 & 29 Dec 1872, Roxton Falls, QC.
- vi   **Calixte Robidoux** b & bp 14 & 18 Oct 1874, Roxton Pond, QC. He married (1) 26 Oct 1897, St. Jean, QC, **Vitaline Rancourt** (Isaïe Rancourt & Delphine Boutin) b & bp 21 Nov 1870, Napierville, QC; d & bur there 5 & 8 Feb 1940.
     He married (2) 4 Nov 1947, Napierville, QC, **Marie Louise Hermine Baril** (Joseph Baril & Corinne Beaudry) b & bp 12 & 13 Feb 1886, Iberville, QC; m (1)

there 15 Sep 1908 Joseph Bergeron (Damien Bergeron & Mathilde Ménard); m (2) 17 Jul 1926, St. Alexandre, QC, Jean-Baptiste Martel (Dosithée Martel & Virginia Latimore), widower of Rose Anna Fontaine & Albina Bessette; bur 1950, St. Alexandre, QC.

vii   **Marie Louise Robidoux** b & bp 22 & 29 Jul 1877, Roxton Pond, QC. She married 8 Feb 1910, St. Jean, QC, **Victor Blais** (Alfred Blais & Marie Marchand) b & bp 13 & 14 May 1884, Napierville, QC.

8.3.16   **MONTY, Adèle/Adélaïde?** b 1831?, QC.

Adèle Monty, a sister of the bride, was present in November 1846 at the marriage of Daniel O'Brien and Josephte Monty (8.3.3). She is most probably the same woman as the 20-year-old Adélaïde who was living with her mother Josepthe Neveu and sisters Martine (8.3.15) and Julie (8.3.17) in Iberville, QC, in 1851 (Canadian census). I know nothing more about her.

8.3.17   **MONTY, Julie** b 1837?, QC.

Julie Monty was 14 years old in 1851 when she was living with her mother Josephte Neveu and sisters Martine (8.3.15) and Adélaïde (8.3.16?) in Iberville, QC (Canadian census). She had been present a few years earlier at the marriage of her sister Josephte (8.3.3.) in November 1846. I know nothing more about her.

13.3.1   **MONTY, Antoine** b & bp 13 & 14 Feb 1795, Chambly, QC; d & bur 1 & 3 Nov 1869, Laprairie, QC. He married there 6 Nov 1820 **Marie Anne Perras** (Jean-Baptiste Perras & Geneviève Vincent) b & bp there 2 Jan 1800; d & bur there 17 & 20 Jun 1870.

Antoine Monty was originally a farm laborer in Longueuil, QC, and a farm laborer and/or farmer in Laprairie, QC, after 1821.

Children:

13.3.1.1	Cyrille	1821-	-1842
13.3.1.2	Antoine	1822-	-1832
13.3.1.3	Sophie	1823-1846-1849	
13.3.1.4	Anonymous	1825-	-1825
13.3.1.5	Mathilde	1827-1849-1857	
13.3.1.6	Octave	1829-	-1830
13.3.1.7	Henriette	1830-	-1831
13.3.1.8	Denise	1833-1858-1915	
13.3.1.9	Marie Anne	1834-1862-1871	
13.3.1.10	Philomène	1835-	-1852
13.3.1.11	Elmire	1840-	-1929
13.3.1.12	Hermine	1843-1867-1922	

13.3.2   **MONTY, Marguerite** b & bp 20 Apr 1798, Chambly, QC; d & bur 31 Aug & 2 Sep 1853, Mont St. Grégoire, QC. She married 24 Jul 1821, Longueuil, QC, **Antoine Bouteille dit Bonneville** (Antoine Bouteille dit Bonneville & Geneviève Benoit) b & bp there 2 & 3 Dec 1799; d & bur 11 & 15 Feb 1848, Mont St. Grégoire, QC.

Antoine Bouteille dit Bonneville (also Bonneville dit Bouteille) was originally a farmer in Marieville, QC, and after 1841 in Mont St. Grégoire, QC. He drowned in the Richelieu River. Bonneville appears to have become the dominant surname over time. He was married for example as Antoine Bouteille dit Bonneville but was buried as simply Antoine Bonneville. The same trend is also found in his children's lives.

Caution should be taken not no confuse this family with that of François Bonneville dit Bouteille, husband of another Marguerite Monty (3.1.6).

Children:

i   **Antoine Bouteille dit Bonneville** b & bp 6 & 7 June 1822, Longueuil, QC.

ii   **Adélaïde Bouteille dit Bonneville** b Jan 1824; d & bur 26 & 28 Feb 1825, Marieville, QC, at the age of 13 months.

iii   **Nazaire Bouteille dit Bonneville** b & bp 26 & 27 Mar 1825, Marieville, QC; d & bur there 29 & 30 Jul 1825.

iv   **Adolphe Bouteille dit Bonneville** b & bp 21 & 22 Apr 1826, Marieville, QC; d & bur 21 & 23 Mar 1899, Bromont (West Shefford), QC. He married 19 Nov 1855, Mont St. Grégoire, QC, **Elmire Dextrase** (Michel Dextrase & Françoise Paquet) b & bp 21 Oct 1835, Iberville, QC.

v   **Marie Césarie Bouteille dit Bonneville** b & bp 17 & 18 Dec 1827, Marieville, QC; d & bur 27 & 30 Jun 1852, Mont St. Grégoire, QC. She married there 25 Nov 1850 **Julien Vincelette** (Antoine Vincelette & Esther Comeau) b & bp 15 & 16 May 1833, Marieville, QC.

vi   **Noël Bouteille dit Bonneville** b & bp 14 & 15 Jul 1829, Marieville, QC.

vii   **Alexandre Bouteille dit Bonneville** b & bp 28 & 31 Oct 1830, Marieville, QC; d & bur 30 Mar & 1 Apr 1849, Mont St. Grégoire, QC.

viii   **Flavien Bouteille dit Bonneville** b & bp 6 & 8 Jul 1832, Marieville, QC.

ix   **Flavie Bouteille dit Bonneville** b & bp 10 & 11 Feb 1834, Marieville, QC; d & bur 2 & 4 Aug 1853, Mont St. Grégoire, QC.

x   **Vital Bouteille dit Bonneville** b & bp 27 & 28 May 1835, Marieville, QC.

xi   **Henriette Bouteille dit Bonneville** b & bp 31 May & 1 Jun 1836, Marieville, QC; d & bur there 21 & 23 Jan 1838.

xii   **Denise Bouteille dit Bonneville** b & bp 8 & 9 Feb 1838, Marieville, QC.

xiii   **Napoléon Bouteille dit Bonneville** b & bp 26 & 28 May 1839, Marieville, QC.

xiv   **Edmond Bouteille dit Bonneville** b & bp 24 & 25 Mar 1841, Marieville, QC; d & bur there 28 & 29 Mar 1841.

13.3.3   **MONTY, Amable** (twin) b & bp 13 & 15 Mar 1800, Chambly, QC; d & bur 11 & 12 Sep 1800, Longueuil, QC, at the age of 6 months.

Amable Monty's burial record names him Antoine by error. Antoine Monty (13.3.1) in fact lived to age 74.

13.3.4   **MONTY, Angélique** (twin) b & bp 13 & 15 Mar 1800, Chambly, QC; d & bur 23 & 25 Mar 1800, Longueuil, QC.

13.3.5   **MONTY, Desanges/Mary** b & bp 19 & 20 Jan 1804, Chambly, QC; d 10 Mar 1883, Cornwall, VT. She married 22 Jun 1824, Longueuil, QC, **Amable Patenaude/ Patnaud/Patenode** (Amable Patenaude & Marie Charron) b & bp there 12 & 13 Sep 1800; d 5 Mar 1881, Cornwall, VT.

This woman was baptized as Marie Desanges Monty, though all Canadian records refer to her simply as Desanges Monty. In American records she is named either Mary or Desange. She and her husband were buried in St. Mary's Cemetery in Middlebury, VT.

Amable Patenaude was a brother of Louis Patenaude, husband of his wife's first cousin Julienne Lareau, daughter of Joseph Lareau and Catherine Monty (13.1). He was a farmer in Longueuil, QC, until 1831, in Marieville, QC, from 1832 through 1841, and in Mont St. Grégoire, QC, from 1843 through 1846. He emigrated around 1848 and was a laborer in Cornwall, VT, in 1850. Eleven of his children were then with him and his wife (only Amable, Cyrille, and Hyacinthe were missing). He remained in Cornwall as a farm laborer or farmer (US censuses) and a carpenter, according to his death record. His surname varies from Patenaude in Canada to Patnaud in US censuses and Patenode at his death (Vermont Vital Records).

Children:

i   **Amable Patenaude** b & bp 19 & 20 Sep 1824, Longueuil, QC.

ii   **Calixte Patenaude/Corliss Patnaud/Patenode** b & bp 2 & 3 Apr 1826, Longueuil & Laprairie, QC; d 2 Mar 1906, Cornwall, VT. He married (1) 11 Jul 1851, Burlington, VT, **Marie Lefebvre** (Louis Lefebvre & Emelie Patenaude) b 24 Feb 1832, QC; d 25 May 1870, Cornwall, VT.

iii   **Scholastique Patenaude/Patnaud** b & bp 10 Feb 1828, Laprairie, QC; d 6 Mar 1851, Cornwall, VT.

iv   **Alexandre Patenaude/Alexander Patnaud** b & bp 24 May 1829, Longueuil, QC.

v   **Octave Patenaude/Patnaud** b & bp 17 & 18 Jan 1831, Longueuil, QC; d 14 Feb 1905, Ticonderoga, NY. He married (1) 9 Oct 1853, Burlington, VT, **Sophronie Thibodeau** (Jean-Baptiste Thibodeau & Marie Lapointe) b 1833?, QC; d 28 Sep 1871, Schroon Lake, NY.

     He married (2) 8 Dec 1889, Schroon Lake, NY [possibly a rehabilitation in the Catholic Church of an earlier marriage] **Leonora Beaulieu** b May 1855, QC.

vi   **Cyrille Patenaude** b & bp 8 & 9 Oct 1832, Marieville, QC; d & bur there 18 & 19 Oct 1832.

vii   **Hyacinthe Patenaude** b & bp 28 Oct 1833, Marieville, QC; bur South Cemetery, Cornwall, VT.

viii   **Gédéon Patenaude/Patnaud** b & bp 13 & 14 Nov 1835, Marieville, QC; d 30 Apr 1855, Cornwall, VT.

ix   **Mathilde/Matilda Patenaude** b & bp 13 Sep 1837, Marieville, QC.

x   **Mederise Patnaud** (Ethelrise at her baptism) b & bp 19 & 25 Aug 1839, Marieville, QC; d 25 Apr 1869, Brandon, VT. She married 1855? **Joseph Bushey** b 9 May 1820, QC; m (1) 8 Jan 1845, Rutland, VT, Betsey Melissa Manley; d 17 Jun 1871, Brandon, VT.

xi   **Emery Patnaud** (Rémy at his baptism) b & bp 13 & 14 Jul 1841, Marieville, QC; d & bur 19 & 22 Oct 1911, East Shoreham, VT. He married 1870? **Jeanette M. Lapell** (Peter Lapell & Mary Eunice Patenaude) b 6 Dec 1854, Shoreham, VT; d there 18 Sep 1924.

xii   **Marie Célina Patenaude/Patnaud** b & bp 6 & 11 Mar 1843, Mont St. Grégoire, QC; d 9 Jul 1861, Cornwall, VT.

xiii   **Narcisse Patenaude/Nelson Patnaud** b & bp 17 Dec 1844, Mont St. Grégoire, QC; d 10 Sep 1863, Cornwall, VT.

xiv   **Noël Patenaude/Patnaud** b & bp 24 & 25 Dec 1846, Mont St. Grégoire, QC; d 6 Aug 1852, Cornwall, VT.

13.3.6   **MONTY, Marcel** b & bp 26 Apr 1805, Chambly, QC; d & bur 9 & 12 Jun 1893, Mont St. Grégoire, QC. He married 10 Oct 1831, Longueuil, QC, **Flavie Baillargeon** (Jean-Baptiste Baillargeon & Marie Marsil) b & bp there 4 & 5 Aug 1812; d & bur 22 & 24 Dec 1888, Mont St. Grégoire, QC.

     Marcel Monty was a farmer in Longueuil, QC, in 1832, in Marieville, QC, from 1835 through 1840, and in Mont St. Grégoire, QC, after 1841. He was retired in 1881 (Canadian census).

Children:

13.3.6.1	Flavie	1832- -1843
13.3.6.2	Denise	1835-1862-1874
13.3.6.3	Marcel	1837- -1843
13.3.6.4	Emery	1840-1865-1930
13.3.6.5	Ulric	1841?-1867-
13.3.6.6	Adèle	1842-1863-1911
13.3.6.7	Rémi	1844- -
13.3.6.8	Odile	1845-1867-1934
13.3.6.9	Vitaline	1847-1870-1930
13.3.6.10	Euphémie	1850- -1850
13.3.6.11	Bénonise	1850- -1851
13.3.6.12	Joseph	1852-1871&1878-1905

13.3.7   **MONTY, Sophie** b & bp 11 Nov 1806, Chambly, QC; d & bur 14 & 15 May 1822, Longueuil, QC.

13.3.8 **MONTY, Basile** b & bp 9 May 1808, Chambly, QC. He married 5 Jun 1832, Longueuil, QC, **Anastasie Dumas** (Joseph Dumas & Desanges Benoit) b & bp 10 Jul 1808, Chambly, QC; d & bur 14 & 16 Apr 1888, Rockville & Manteno, IL.

Basile Monty was a farmer in Laprairie, QC, in 1832, in Longueuil, QC, in 1837, in St. Rémi, QC, from 1838 to 1842. He was back in Longueuil in 1843 and remained there until at least 1849. He apparently left Canada before the 1851 census was taken and was by the early 1850s a farmer in Rockville, IL. He and his wife were still living there in 1880 (US censuses). She was buried in St. Joseph's Cemetery in Manteno, IL.

Children:

13.3.8.1	Basile	1832- -1832
13.3.8.2	Emery	1835-1863-1915
13.3.8.3	Philomène/Fanny	1837-1855-1922
13.3.8.4	Olive/Marie Ovide	1838-1870-1925
13.3.8.5	Euphémie/Phebe	1840- &1883?-
13.3.8.6	Kiese/Calixte	1841-1866-1923
13.3.8.7	Sophie/Sophia	1843-1865-1919
13.3.8.8	Désiré Isaïe	1845-1867-1912

13.3.9 **MONTY, Joseph** b & bp 18 Mar 1810, Chambly, QC.

13.3.10 **MONTY, Hyacinthe** b & bp 13 May 1811, Chambly, QC; d & bur 26 & 29 Dec 1884, Bromont (West Shefford), QC. He married (1) 15 Feb 1836, Longueuil, QC, **Marie Louise Lefebvre** (Louis Lefebvre & Marguerite Brossard) b & bp 21 Feb 1818, La-prairie, QC; d & bur 13 & 16 Oct 1857, Chambly, QC.

He married (2) 22 Nov 1859, Laprairie, QC, **Esther Brossard** (Pascal Bros- sard & Marie Boyer) b & bp there 23 & 24 May 1827; d & bur 19 & 22 Nov 1901, Granby, QC.

Hyacinthe Monty was a farmer in several parishes in the Richelieu valley during his lifetime: in Longueuil, QC, from 1836 to 1841, in Mont St. Grégoire, QC, from 1842 to 1848, in Chambly, QC, from 1849 to 1868, in St. Césaire, QC, after 1869, and in Bromont (West Shefford), QC, in the 1880s. His widow lived in Granby, QC, after his death.

Children of the first marriage:

13.3.10.1	Adeline	1836-1856-1864
13.3.10.2	Marie Louise	1838- -1856
13.3.10.3	Hyacinthe	1839- -1839
13.3.10.4	Henriette	1840-1859-1861
13.3.10.5	Delphine	1842- -1859
13.3.10.6	Flavie	1844-1863-1929
13.3.10.7	Hyacinthe Zéphirin	1845- -
13.3.10.8	Solyme	1847-1877-1934
13.3.10.9	Odile	1849- -1880
13.3.10.10	Moïse	1851- -
13.3.10.11	Marie	1852- -1853
13.3.10.12	Hyacinthe Isidore	1853- -1854
13.3.10.13	Louis	1855- -1855
13.3.10.14	Théophile	1856- -1856

Children of the second marriage:

13.3.10.15	Marie Esther	1860-1880-1884
13.3.10.16	Adélard	1862-1885-1927
13.3.10.17	Octave	1863-1893-1936
13.3.10.18	Arthur	1865-1889-
13.3.10.19	Hormisdas	1867-1899-
13.3.10.20	Bercéus	1869-1900-1930
13.3.10.21	Albina Angelina	1870-1904-1914

13.3.11 **MONTY, Rachel/Marie** b & bp 27 Feb 1813, Chambly, QC; d & bur 10 & 12 Dec 1891, St. Thomas d'Aquin, QC. She married 25 Nov 1839, Longueuil, QC, **Jean-Baptiste Riendeau** (François Joachim dit Riendeau & Catherine Moquin) b & bp 26 & 27 Feb 1817, Laprairie, QC.

Rachel Monty's name varied according to locality. It was Rachel when she was born and married in Canada but Marie or Mary when she was living and when she died in New Hampshire.

Her husband was named François in their marriage record. That is incorrect: his father's name was obviously substituted for his own. On all other occasions, from his baptism (Jean-Baptiste, son of François Joachim dit Riendo) and his children's baptisms and marriages to his wife's death, he was invariably named Jean-Baptiste.

Jean-Baptiste Riendeau was a farmer in St. Rémi, QC, for a few years after his marriage and in Mont St. Grégoire, QC, from at least 1844 on before moving to Nashua, NH, in the early 1860s. He was not with his family there however in 1870 and may have been deceased. His wife was then head of a household which included her four youngest children and three nieces, children of her brother Stanislas (13.3.17). She was a widow in 1880, still living in Nashua with her son Joseph (vii) and his wife Mary (US censuses). I do not know when she returned to Canada. It appears from her burial record that she had resided with her son Alfred (iii) in St. Thomas d'Aquin in St. Hyacinthe Co., QC, for a while before her death.

Children:

i   **Jean-Baptiste Riendeau** b & bp 3 Jun 1842, St. Rémi, QC. He married 23 Apr 1866, Nashua, NH, **Célanise Lalemand** b 1844?, QC.

ii   **Médérise Riendeau** b & bp 16 & 17 Apr 1844, Mont St. Grégoire, QC; d & bur 20 & 21 Aug 1878, Nashua, NH. She married there 23 Apr 1866 **Pierre Jeannotte** (Augustin Jeannotte & Angèle Paquet).

iii   **Alfred Riendeau** b & bp 25 Jul 1845, Mont St. Grégoire, QC; d & bur 24 & 27 Jul 1929, St. Thomas d'Aquin, QC. He married 14 Aug 1864, Nashua, NH, **Joséphine Théotiste Leblanc** (François Leblanc & Théotiste Rodier) b & bp 10 & 11 Oct 1848, St. Hyacinthe, QC; d & bur 16 & 19 Mar 1908, St. Thomas d'Aquin, QC.

iv   **Marie Euphémie Riendeau** b & bp 1 Mar 1847, Mont St. Grégoire, QC.

v   **Callixte Riendeau** b & bp 24 & 25 Apr 1848, Mont St. Grégoire, QC.

vi   **Narcisse Riendeau** b 1851?, QC; d & bur 6 & 9 Dec 1933, Nashua, NH. He married there 24 Feb 1873 **Sophie Salvail/Salvaille** (Pierre Salvaille & Aurélie Bibeau) b & bp 19 & 20 Nov 1854, Drummondville, QC; d & bur 15 & 18 Aug 1930, Nashua, NH.

vii   **Mathilde/Matilda Riendeau** b 1853?, QC. She married 25 Oct 1875, Nashua, NH, **Victor Gauvin** (Pierre Gauvin & Louise Perreault) b & bp 8 Aug 1855, St. Barnabé Sud, QC.

viii   **Joseph Riendeau** b & bp 24 & 28 Oct 1855, Mont St. Grégoire, QC. He married 11 Dec 1879, Nashua, NH, **Marie Sylvestre** (Achille Sylvestre & Marie Fiset) b & bp 8 & 9 Sep 1862, St. Cuthbert, QC; d & bur 28 Feb & 4 Mar 1914, Nashua, NH.

ix   **Marie Delima Riendeau** b & bp 4 & 6 Sep 1857, Mont St. Grégoire, QC. She married 27 Jan 1873, Nashua, NH, **François Xavier Bernard** (Calixte Bernard & Angèle Benoit) b & bp 7 Nov 1851, La Présentation, QC.

13.3.12   **MONTY, Flavie** b & bp 1 & 3 Sep 1814, Longueuil, QC.

13.3.1.3   **MONTY, Henriette** b & bp 27 & 28 Oct 1815, Longueuil & Laprairie, QC.

13.3.14   **MONTY, Eric** b & bp 5 Feb 1817, Longueuil & Laprairie, QC.

13.3.15   **MONTY, Narcisse** b & bp 25 & 26 Apr 1818, Longueuil & Laprairie, QC.

13.3.16   **MONTY, Adolphe** b & bp 12 & 13 Oct 1820, Longueuil & Laprairie, QC.

13.3.17   MONTY, Stanislas b & bp 7 & 8 Feb 1823, Longueuil & Laprairie, QC; d & bur 8 & 9 Jan 1895, Nashua, NH. He married 24 Nov 1846, Chambly, QC, **Adeline Patenaude** (Louis Patenaude & Marguerite Bourke/Bourg) b & bp there 7 Jan 1827; d & bur 27 & 29 Jun 1898, Nashua, NH.

Stanislas Monty (Vinceslas at his baptism) was a farmer in Longueuil, QC, through at least 1860, in St. Hubert, QC, from 1863 through 1867, and in Richelieu, QC, in 1870. I do not know when he moved to New Hampshire. I can find him in neither the 1880 US census nor the 1881 Canadian census. However three of his daughters, Philomène, Denise, and Marie, were already living in Nashua, NH, in 1870 and, according to his naturalization papers of 1883, his son Joseph had arrived in the United States in 1871. He may have emigrated around that time. He was retired in Nashua at his death and was buried in the St. Louis Cemetery there.

Children:

13.3.17.1	Bénonise/Belonise	1847- -1926
13.3.17.2	Philomène	1849-1874-1927
13.3.17.3	Joseph	1850- -1850
13.3.17.4	Anonymous	1851- -1851
13.3.17.5	Denise	1852-1877-1931
13.3.17.6	Marie Adelphie	1854-1879-1886
13.3.17.7	Rose/Rosalie	1856-1882-1936
13.3.17.8	Joseph Antoine	1860- -1885
13.3.17.9	Marie Malvina	1863- -
13.3.17.10	Louis	1865-1890&1913-1944
13.3.17.11	Exeline/Alexandrine	1867-1889-1946
13.3.17.12	Louise	1870-1894-1949

13.9.1   MONTY, Céleste b & bp 21 & 22 Jul 1811, Chambly, QC; d & bur 13 & 15 Jun 1891, Rockville & Manteno, IL. She married 16 Nov 1830, Chambly, QC, **Pierre Lamarre** (Alexis Lamarre & Marie Aupry) b & bp there 27 & 28 Aug 1808; d & bur 3 & 5 Feb 1898, Bourbonnais & Manteno, IL.

Pierre Lamarre was a brother of Louis Lamarre, husband of his wife's first cousin Anastasie Papineau, daughter of Amable Monty (13.8). He was a farmer first in Marieville, QC, and later in Mont St. Grégoire and Iberville, QC, before settling as a farmer in Rockville, IL, around 1856 (US censuses). He and his wife were buried in St. Joseph's Cemetery in Manteno, IL.

The surname in Illinois remained Lamarre on occasion but was more often spelled Lamare or Lamore, especially in the children's generation.

Children:

i   **Adèle/Adélaïde Lamarre** b & bp 9 & 10 Mar 1831, Chambly, QC; d & bur 15 & 17 Dec 1918, Rockford & Bourbonnais, IL She married (1) 16 Oct 1849, Iberville, QC, **François Xavier Bessette** (François Bessette & Julie Patenaude) b & bp 24 & 25 Jan 1833, Marieville, QC; d 25 Jul 1854, Bourbonnais, IL.

She married (2) 14 Apr 1855, Kankakee Co., IL, **John B./Jean-Baptiste Boucher** (Joseph Boucher & Marie ____) b 1825?, QC; d & bur 21 & 23 Sep 1898, Bourbonnais, IL, at the age of 73.

She married (3) around 1909, Kankakee Co., IL, **John Prairie/Jean Isaac Piédalue** (Leon Piédalue dit Prairie & Edesse Trudeau) b & bp 28 & 29 Nov 1829, Chambly, QC; m (1) 27 Oct 1851, IL, Will Co., IL, Aurelia Paquette (Geoffrey Paquette & Marie Aurore Dumas); d & bur 3 & 4 Jun 1911, Bourbonnais, IL.

ii   **Martine Lamarre** b & bp 12 Jul 1835, Marieville, QC; d & bur 17 & 18 Apr 1843, Mont St. Grégoire, QC.

iii   **Octave Lamarre/Lamore** b & bp 17 & 25 Apr 1838, Marieville, QC; d 12 Sep 1918, Kankakee, IL. He married 14 Jul 1861, Kankakee Co., IL, **Philomène**

Brouillette (Jacob Brouillette & Eudoxie Roireau dit Laliberté) b Jan 1839, QC; d & bur 1907, Kankakee, IL.

iv **Praxède/Sadie Lamarre** b & bp 16 May & 13 Jun 1840, Marieville, QC; d & bur 3 & 5 Feb 1916, Rockville & Manteno, IL. She married **James Black** b Oct 1831, Scotland; d & bur 30 Aug & Sep 1891, Rockville & Manteno, IL.

v   **Aglaé Lamarre** b & bp 19 & 22 Oct 1841, Marieville, QC; d & bur 20 & 21 Jan 1842, Mont St. Grégoire, QC.

vi **Camille Lamarre** b & bp 14 & 18 Dec 1842, Mont St. Grégoire, QC.

vii **Célina Lamarre** b 9 Feb 1845, Iberville, QC; d & bur there 12 & 20 Feb 1845.

viii **Théophile Trefflé Lamarre/Lamore** b & bp 30 Mar & 1 Apr 1847, Iberville, QC; d & bur 3 & 5 Jun 1891, Rockville & Manteno, IL. He married 24 Sep 1867, Manteno, IL, **Mary/Marie Sophie Trudeau** (Pierre Trefflé Trudeau & Sophie Bertrand) b & bp 26 & 27 Jan 1850, Chambly, QC; d & bur 10 & 11 Feb 1909, Kankakee & Manteno, IL.

ix **Camille Lamarre/Lamore** b & bp 27 & 28 Jul 1849, Iberville, QC; d 10 May 1927, Bourbonnais, IL. He married (1) there 26 Nov 1878 **Philomène Allard** (Louis Allard & Aurélie/Henrelie Blais) b & bp 27 Sep 1851, St. Paulin, QC; d & bur 10 & 12 Jul 1892, Bourbonnais, IL.

He married (2) 13 Feb 1901, Bourbonnais, IL, **Philomène Bonneville** (Hippolyte Bonneville & Elisabeth Mongeau) b there 1856; d & bur there 1930.

x   **Emma Lamarre/Lamore** b Jun 1855?, QC; d 28 Mar 1912, Kankakee, IL. She married 7 Sep 1868, Kankakee Co., IL, **Charles Deveraux** (Martin Deveraux & Ellen McCullough) b & bp 23 & 26 Feb 1843, Henryville, QC; d & bur 3 & 5 Mar 1910, Kankakee and Manteno, IL.

13.9.2   **MONTY, Joseph** b & bp 18 Mar 1813, Chambly, QC; d & bur 30 Mar & 2 Apr 1883, Montreal, QC. He married 22 Sep 1834, Chambly, QC (St. Stephen's Anglican Church), **Elizabeth/Isabel McCoig** b 1813?, QC; d 1891, Goodland, IN.

Joseph Monty was a laborer and farmer in Chambly, QC, in the early years of his marriage. He was a miller in Beloeil, QC, at the births of two children in 1841 and 1843 before returning to Chambly. He was a farmer there in 1851 when his wife Isabell was 38 years old (Canadian census). His family left for Illinois in the mid-1850s though it is unclear whether Joseph Monty came with them. George W. Smith implies that he did not: "In 1854, at the age of eighteen, Joseph Monty [Jr.] came to Kankakee County, Illinois, with his mother" (*History of Illinois and her People*, VI, 286). Joseph Monty Sr. was certainly not with his wife and children in Kankakee, IL, in 1860 or in Goodland, IN, in 1870 (US censuses), though he was in Canada for his father's funeral in Chambly on 14 Mar 1862. The only record of his presence in Illinois is the 1880 US census in Kankakee where he was living with his wife. Later that year he returned to Canada to stay for a time with his sister Marcelline (13.9.8) and her family. He died in Montreal's St-Jean-de-Dieu Hospital and was buried in its cemetery.

Elizabeth McCoig was identified only as a "spinster of Chambly" at her marriage. She was also named Isabell or Isabelle McCuaig, McQuade, or McKuett in various other records. In the United States her name was Isabel, Isabella, Isabell, or Isabelle. She returned to Indiana after 1880 and spent her last years in the household of her son Joseph in Goodland.

Children:

13.9.2.1	Joseph	1836-1874-1916
13.9.2.2	Margaret	1838-1860-1928
13.9.2.3	Malvina/Melvina	1841-1858-1888
13.9.2.4	Treffley/J.B. Trefflé	1843-1866-
13.9.2.5	William	1845- -1935
13.9.2.6	Alexandre Théodore	1847- -1849
13.9.2.7	Matilda	1850- -
13.9.2.8	Euphemia	1853- -

13.9.3   **MONTY, Anastasie** b & bp 9 Dec 1814, Chambly, QC; d & bur there 20 &

13.9.4   **MONTY, Domitille/Matilda** b & bp 23 & 24 Nov 1816, Chambly, QC; d 27 Oct 1886, Chicago, IL. She married 27 Jan 1835, Chambly, QC, **Jean-Baptiste Bigonesse/ John Bigoness** (Jean-Baptiste Bigonesse & Josephte Dubuc) b & bp there 21 & 22 Sep 1804; d & bur 22 & 24 Apr 1897, Chicago & Evanston, IL.

Jean-Baptiste Bigonesse was a farmer and innkeeper in Chambly, QC, until shortly after the birth of his son Napoleon in 1847. He then moved to Illinois where a child was born in 1849 or 1850. John Bigones (sic) was a master mason in Kankakee, IL, in 1860 and a stone mason (named John Begnoss) in Chicago, IL, in 1870. Ten years later he was a store clerk living in Milwaukee, WI, with his wife and sons Napoleon (vii) and Charles (xi) (US censuses). He did not stay there long. His wife died in Chicago a few years later and his obituary in the *Chicago Tribune* of 21 Apr 1897 implies that he had lived there continuously for forty-eight years. He and his wife were buried, along with several of their children, in the Calvary Cemetery in Evanston, IL.

Jean-Baptiste Bigonesse was a brother of Josephte Bigonesse, wife of Domitille Monty's first cousin, Joseph Lareau, son of Catherine Monty (13.1). He and his wife had had twelve children, eight of whom survived him (*Chicago Tribune*, 21 Apr 1897). They are Octave (ii), Dora (iv), Dorothy (v), Napoleon (vii), Albine (viii), Ida (ix), Charles (xi) and one other. Their surname is generally recorded as Bigoness. Their names however often underwent a variety of changes. I have indicated with a dash the various names/nicknames under which they appear in US censuses and between parentheses the names found in their Canadian baptismal records.

Children:

i   **Philomène (Marie Philomène) Bigonesse** b & bp 1 & 2 Apr 1836, Chambly, QC.

ii   **Octave Bigonesse/Bigoness** b & bp 4 Jan 1838, Chambly, QC; d & bur 13 & 16 Sep 1909, Kankakee & Momence, IL. He married 8 Nov 1861, Newton Co., IN, **Martha Jane Veatch** (George Veatch & Eliza Caroline Berringer) b 1844?, IN.

iii   **Cordelia (Marie Cordélie) Bigonesse** b & bp 24 & 25 Mar 1839, Chambly, QC.

iv   **Dora/Dorey (Marie Elise Dorimène) Bigonesse** b & bp 12 & 13 Jan 1841, Chambly, QC; d & bur Jun/Jul & 2 Jul 1925, Chicago & Evanston, IL. She married 1868? **Antoine Fortin** b 1843?, Canada; d & bur 9 & 12 Oct 1897, Chicago & Evanston, IL, at the age of 54.

v   **Dorothy/Hattie (Marie Sophie Dorothée) Bigonesse** b & bp 14 Dec 1842, Chambly, QC; d & bur 31 Aug & 2 Sep 1926, Chicago & Evanston, IL. She married 1890? ____ **Valiquette**.

vi   **Arthur (Jean-Baptiste Arthur) Bigonesse/Bigoness** b & bp 23 Oct 1844, Chambly, QC; d & bur 12 & 14 Jun 1889, ? & Evanston, IL. He married 1876? **Catherine Matthews** b 1857?, IL; m (2) 1891? Frederick Kettle (William Kettle & Frederika ____); d 30 Apr 1920, Chicago, IL.

vii   **Napoleon (Alexis Napoléon) Bigonesse/Bigoness** b & bp 2 & 4 May 1847, Chambly, QC; d & bur 25 & 27 Mar 1900, Chicago & Evanston, IL.

viii **Albine/Albena Bigonesse** b 1850?, IL; d & bur 3 & 6 July 1926, Chicago & Evanston, IL. She married 1874? **Eugene A. Fortin** b 1844?, Canada; d & bur ? & 19 Jun 1920, Evanston, IL.

ix   **Ida Bigonesse** b 1852?, IL; d & bur Nov & 1 Dec 1920, Chicago & Evanston, IL. She married **James C. Hoskins** b 1847?, Ireland; d & bur 31 Mar & 4 Apr 1897, Chicago & Evanston, IL.

x   **Louisa Bigonesse** b 1858?, Kankakee, IL.

xi   **Charles Bigonesse/Bigoness** b 19 May 1860, Kankakee, IL; d & bur 5 & 7 Feb 1934, Chicago & Evanston, IL. He married 26 Apr 1884 **Mary Gleason** b Feb 1866, IL.

13.9.5   **MONTY, Eugène/Eusèbe** b & bp 4 & 5 Jul 1819, Chambly, QC; d & bur there 2 & 4 Feb 1820.

This child was named Eugène at his baptism and Eusèbe at his death at the age of 7 months.

13.9.6 **MONTY, Cyril** b & bp 30 & 31 Jul 1821, Chambly, QC; d & bur there 29 Aug & 1 Sep 1821.

13.9.7 **MONTY, Anastasie** b & bp 22 Oct 1822, Chambly, QC; d Ferrisburgh, VT. She married 26 Sep 1848, Mont St. Grégoire, QC, **Antoine Ainse** (Jean-Baptiste Ainse & Josephte Sansouci) b & bp 25 & 26 Mar 1824, St. Mathias, QC; d Vergennes, VT.

Antoine Ainse (also Hains, Hins, Inse) was a farmer in Mont St. Grégoire, QC, until at least 1851 (Canadian census). He then moved to Ferrisburgh, VT, where he was a farmer in 1870 and 1880. The three children of his deceased daughter Margaret were then also living in his household (US censuses).

Child:

i **Marguerite/Margaret Ainse** b & bp 17 & 18 Nov 1849, Mont St. Grégoire, QC; d 23 Oct 1876, Vergennes, VT. She married 26 Dec 1865, Cornwall, VT, **Alphonse/ Alonzo Pigeon** (Paul Napoléon Pigeon & Marie Amélie Baril) b & bp 24 Oct 1847, Laprairie, QC; m (2) 19 Apr 1883, Vergennes, VT, Zéphirine Malo (Isidore Milo & Lucie Gravelle); d between 1897 and 1900.

13.9.8 **MONTY, Marceline** b & bp 10 Nov 1824, Chambly, QC; d & bur there 8 & 11 Sep 1895. She married there 16 Apr 1850 **Moïse Raymond** (François Raymond & Adélaïde Ouimet) b & bp there 9 & 10 Jun 1825; d & bur there 14 & 17 Jun 1897.

Moïse Raymond was a farmer in Chambly, QC, where he and his family occupied the house built by his wife's grandfather Antoine Monty (13) in 1786. It was still in the possession of Raymond descendants in the last decade of the 20th century.

Children:

i **Marie Odile Raymond** b & bp 11 & 12 Feb 1851, Chambly, QC; d & bur there 12 & 14 Mar 1858.

ii **Marie Cordélie Raymond** b Sep 1852; d & bur 22 & 23 Mar 1858, Chambly, QC, at the age of 5 years and 6 months.

iii **Moïse Henri Elzéar Raymond** b & bp 16 Nov 1854, Chambly, QC; d & bur 6 & 9 Mar 1925, Montreal & Chambly, QC. He married 18 Sep 1883, Chambly, QC, **Marie Mélanie Trudeau** (Joseph Onésime Trudeau & Dosi-thée/Dorothée Langevin) b & bp there 6 Oct 1862.

iv **Joseph Amable Raymond** b & bp 29 Jan 1857, Chambly, QC. He married 22 Jul 1878, Laprairie, QC, **Marie Rose Bourdon** (Pierre Bourdon & Emérence Poupart) b & bp there 20 & 22 Nov 1860.

v **Napoléon/Julien Napoléon Raymond** b & bp 23 & 24 Mar 1859, Chambly, QC; d & bur 25 Feb & 16 Apr 1936, Iberville & Chambly, QC. He married 3 Feb 1885, St. Mathias, QC, **Rose Anna Morier** (Charles Morier & Eugénie Foisy) b & bp 4 & 5 Aug 1861, Chambly, QC.

vi **Aimé Raymond** b & bp 30 Sep & 1 Oct 1860, Chambly, QC; d & bur 3 & 6 Jul 1933, Rougemont & Chambly, QC. He married (1) 26 Sep 1882, Chambly, QC, **Marie Anne Brouillet** (Cyprien Brouillet & Ann Thistlewait) b & bp there 7 & 8 Dec 1856; d & bur there 27 & 29 Feb 1896.

He married (2) 22 Aug 1896, St. Césaire, QC, **Rose Anna/Rosanna Leroux dit Cardinal** (Antoine Leroux dit Cardinal & Delima Régnier dit Brillon) b & bp there 7 May 1859; m (1) there 28 Jan 1879 Elie Choquette (Napoléon Choquette & Thérèse McDoff); d & bur 1 & 4 Feb 1941, Montreal & Chambly, QC.

vii **Adélard/Elzéar Raymond** b & bp 6 & 7 Aug 1862, Chambly, QC; d & bur there 19 & 22 Jan 1940. He married (1) there 28 Sep 1891 **Marie Louise Lagüe** (Edmond Lagüe & Clémence Dubuc) b & bp there 11 May 1868; d & bur there 24 & 26 Mar 1901.

He married (2) 19 Apr 1910, Chambly, QC, **Olivine/Joséphine Fournier** (Charles Fournier & Vitaline Monsey) b & bp there 23 & 24 Feb 1879.

viii **Raymond Antoine Raymond** b & bp 21 & 26 Mar 1865, Chambly, QC. He married 14 Oct 1890, Richelieu, QC, **Délia Ostiguy** (Pierre Ostiguy & Desanges Ashby) b 10 Jul 1869, QC; d & bur 27 & 28 Feb 1940, Chambly, QC, at the age of 70.

ix **Marcelline Marguerite Raymond** b & bp 13 Nov 1866, Chambly, QC; d & bur 13 & 16 Oct 1899, St. Mathias, QC. She married 30 Sep 1884, Chambly, QC, **Alfred Morier** (Charles Morier & Eugénie Foisy) b & bp there 12 & 13 Dec 1859; m (2) 20 Oct 1902, St. Jean-Baptiste, QC, Louise Cordélie Albertine Robert (Joseph Samuel Robert & Cordélie Gingras), widow of Joseph Lavoie; d & bur 14 & 17 May 1922, St. Mathias, QC.

13.9.9 **MONTY, Aurélie** b & bp 9 & 10 Feb 1827, Chambly, QC; d 9 May 1898, Chicago, IL. She married (1) 6 Oct 1846, Chambly, QC, a second cousin **Jacques Thomas Lasnier/Jacob Lanier** (Jacques Lasnier & Eléonore Piédalue) b & bp 21 Dec 1818, Marieville, QC.

She was a widow when she married (2) 27 Dec 1870, Kankakee Co., IL, **Joseph Hungviller** b 1830?, France.

Jacques Thomas Lasnier was a grocer in St. Mathias, QC, at his marriage and an innkeeper in Mont St. Grégoire, QC, in 1848. He then signed Jacques T. Lanier. He soon emigrated with his family to Bourbonnais, IL, for his first child died there in 1851. He was then known as Jacob Lanier.

Joseph Hungviller (also Hingviller) was a 30-year-old laborer in Kankakee, IL, in 1860 (US census).

Children:
i **Marie Aglaé Ezilda Lasnier** b & bp 27 & 29 Oct 1848, Mont St. Grégoire, QC; d 1 Nov 1851, Bourbonnais, IL.
ii **Hector Lasnier** b 1852, Bourbonnais, IL; d there Sep 1853 at the age of one.
iii **Joseph Hector Lasnier** b Dec 1856, Bourbonnais, IL; d there 28 Nov 1857 at the age of 11 months.

13.9.10 **MONTY, Aglaé** b & bp 3 Sep 1829, Chambly, QC; d between 1873 and 1880, Martinton, IL. She married 3 Mar 1851, Chambly, QC, **Henry Deland dit Champigny** (Henry Deland dit Champigny & Adélaïde Moreau) b & bp 14 Apr 1829, St. Luc, QC; d 4 Dec 1885, Martinton, IL.

Henry Deland, who was originally a farmer in Chambly, QC, emigrated in the late 1850s. He was naturalized in Kankakee, IL, on 10 Sep 1868 but spent most of his life in Iroquois Co., IL. He was a farmer in Buchanan, IL, in 1860 and in Martinton, IL, in 1870 and 1880. He was a widower in 1880 (US censuses). A few years later he shot himself accidentally and died instantly.

Children:
i **Henry Philippe Deland** b & bp 17 & 18 Dec 1851, St. Luc, QC.
ii **Alphonsine/Marie Aglaé Alphonsine Deland** b & bp 23 & 24 May 1854, St. Luc, QC. She married 24 Jan 1876, Kankakee Co., IL, **Antoine Dolphis Fortier** (Isaac Fortier & Léocadie Bouré/Bouret) b & bp 19 & 20 Oct 1850, St. Léon, QC.
iii **Marie Albine Deland** b & bp 5 & 6 Sep 1855, Chambly, QC; d & bur 13 & 14 Mar 1860, Iroquois Co., IL.
iv **Josephine Deland** b 1859?, Iroquois Co., IL.
v **Azelia/Marie Azéline Mélanie Deland** b & bp 1 & 2 Sep 1860, Iroquois Co., IL.
vi **Joseph Alfred Trefflé Deland** b & bp 19 Dec 1861 & 5 Jan 1862, Iroquois Co., IL.
vii **Annie/Anna Deland** b Apr 1866, Martinton, IL; d 22 Aug 1944, Kankakee, IL. She married 4 Apr 1888, Beaverville, IL, **John H. Gernon** (John Hall Gernon & Magdeleine Cousineau) b Aug 1850, QC; d 19 Jun 1926, Kankakee, IL.

viii   **Alfred W. C. Deland** b 1873?, Martinton, IL.

13.9.11   **MONTY, Pierre Alfred** b & bp 30 & 31 May 1831, Chambly, QC; d & bur there 28 & 31 Jul 1831.

13.9.12   **MONTY, Marie Onésime** b & bp 7 & 8 Aug 1832, Chambly, QC; d & bur there 22 & 23 Aug 1832.

13.9.13   **MONTY, Marguerite** b & bp 25 & 26 Aug 1834, Chambly, QC; d & bur there 21 & 23 Apr 1868. She married there 3 Jul 1854 **Hubert Forget dit Despaty** (Michel Despaty & Claire Tremblay) b & bp 17 Jun 1836, St. Luc, QC; m (2) 11 Nov 1869, Richelieu, QC, Célina Loiselle (Godfroid Loiselle & Onésime Ashby); d & bur 25 & 29 Mar 1909, Chambly, QC.

    Hubert Despaty was originally a farmer in St. Luc, QC, and later in Chambly, QC, from about 1859 on. Despaty (also Depaty and Despatis) was the surname commonly used during Marguerite Monty's lifetime. Forget became predominant in the 1870s.

Children:
- i   **Azilda Marguerite Forget dit Despaty** b & bp 17 Oct 1854, Laprairie, QC; d & bur 27 & 30 May 1904, Richelieu, QC. She married 10 Oct 1881, St. Luc, QC, **Joseph Nazaire Loiselle** (Godfroid Loiselle & Onésime Ashby) b & bp 6 & 8 Jan 1854, Mont St. Grégoire, QC; m (2) 30 Oct 1906, Iberville, QC, Marie Louise Loiselle (Joseph Loiselle & Marguerite Laroche); d & bp 6 & 9 Aug 1934, Richelieu, QC.
- ii   **Arthur Forget dit Despaty** b & bp 27 Sep 1855, Laprairie, QC.
- iii   **Rose Anna Forget dit Despaty** b & bp 22 & 23 Jul 1857, St. Luc, QC; d 13 Feb 1945, Chambly, QC. She married there 16 Jul 1877 **Noël Lareau** (Flavien Lareau & Julie Gauthier) b & bp there 22 & 23 Feb 1852; d & bur there 27 & 30 Oct 1924.
- iv   **Hubert Dosithée Forget dit Despaty** (twin) b & bp 1 & 2 Apr 1859, Chambly, QC; d & bur 19 & 23 Jan 1893, Laprairie & Chambly, QC. He married 8 Jul 1889, Chambly, QC, **Adeline O'Regan** (Humphrey O'Regan & Delphine Dufresne) b & bp 12 & 14 Jun 1856, Laprairie, QC.
- v   **Hugo/Hugues Joseph Forget dit Despaty** (twin) b & bp 1 & 2 Apr 1859, Chambly, QC; d & bur there 6 & 9 Jan 1915. He married 7 Aug 1882, Marieville, QC, **Eliza Loiselle** (Nazaire Loiselle & Marie Lebeau) b 1860?, Marieville, QC; d & bur 19 & 21 Jul 1883, Chambly, QC, at the age of 23.
- vi   **Marie Rose de Lima Forget dit Despaty** b & bp 1 Dec 1860, Chambly, QC; d & bur 10 & 12 Nov 1924, St. Jean, QC. She married 8 Oct 1877, Chambly, QC, **Camille/Emile Deneau/Denault** (Julien Denault & Josette Provost) b & bp there 23 & 24 May 1852; d & bur 14 & 16 Jan 1923, St. Jean, QC.
- vii   **Alphonse Forget dit Despaty** b & bp 9 & 10 Oct 1862, Chambly, QC; d & bur there 22 & 23 Jun 1866.
- viii   **Marguerite Georgina Forget dit Despaty** b & bp 15 Jan 1865, Chambly, QC; d & bur 7 & 8 Apr 1869, St. Luc & Chambly, QC.
- ix   **Henri Forget dit Despaty** b & bp 30 & 31 Mar 1867, Chambly, QC; d & bur there 23 & 25 Nov 1916. He married there 5 Jul 1893 **Georgine/Georgiana Gosselin** (Pierre Gosselin & Céleste Sabourin) b 1871?, QC; m (2) 20 Jul 1920, Montreal, QC, Etienne Barré (Paschal Barré & Pélagie Gervais), widower of Hosanna Beaudin; d & bur 29 Jan & 1 Feb 1928, Montreal & Chambly, QC, at the age of 57.

13.9.14   **MONTY, Victoire** b & bp 8 & 9 Nov 1835, Chambly, QC.

3.1.3.1   **MONTY, John Jr.** b Jan 1819, Grand Isle, VT; d 16 Nov 1879, Colchester, VT, at the age of 60 years and 10 months. He married 1838? **Elsie** ____ b 1820?, VT; d 15 Jan 1890, Colchester, VT.

John Monty Jr. was a farmer in Colchester, VT, whose real estate was valued at $1,000 in 1850, $1,600 in 1860, and $2,300 in 1870 (US censuses). He left a widow but no children (Chittenden Co. Probate Court, Burlington, VT, 26 Nov 1879) and was buried in the Munson Cemetery in Colchester alongside his grandfather Claude Monty, his parents, and his daughter Loisa S.

His wife Elsie (also Elsey, Elsa, Elcy) was born in Vermont and was a year or two younger than her husband (US censuses). The inscription on her tombstone in the Champlain Cemetery in Colchester reads: "Elsie / wife of / John Monty Jr. / 1820-1890." Yet she was 71 years old at her death, according to the Colchester Vital Records.

Child:

3.1.3.1.1	Loisa S.	1839-	-1840

3.1.3.2   **MONTY, Claudius/Cloude** b 23 Mar 1823, South Hero, VT; d 14 Oct 1906, Colchester, VT. He married 1845? **Rosalie/Rosella Monty** (Joseph Monty [4.8] & Mary Defayette) b 20 May 1816, Chazy, NY; d 1 Jul 1901, Burlington, VT.

Claudius Monty was living with his parents in his paternal grandfather's household in South Hero, VT, in 1830. He moved shortly thereafter with his family to Colchester, VT, where his first two children were born and where he was a farmer in 1850. A few years later a daughter was born in Milton, VT, where Claudius Monty was a carpenter and joiner, an occupation he pursued till the end of his life. He was still in Milton in 1860 but had returned to Colchester by 1870. He and his wife had been married for fifty-five years in 1900 and had had four children of whom two were still alive (US censuses).

His name and surname vary. Censuses generally refer to Claudius Monty, but also to Claudius Monta (1870) and Cloud Monta (1900). The Colchester Vital Records named him Claudius Montey at his death, though he was buried there in the Champlain Cemetery as Cloude Montey. Several years later, a petition for the settlement of his estate before the Chittenden Co. Probate Court (17 Oct 1917, #9543), named him Claude Monty. The variations continued into the next generation.

Children:

3.1.3.2.1	Wilbur E.	1845-1868?-1934
3.1.3.2.2	Infant son	1849- -1849
3.1.3.2.3	Ellen Nora/Elnora	1855?-1873-1932

3.1.3.3   **MONTY, Benjamin Franklin** b 12 Jul 1843, Colchester, VT; d there 6 Oct 1926. He married 8 Jan 1873, Belmont, NY, **Almira Hannah Shutts** (Jehiel Shutts & Mary A. ____) b 15 Apr 1845, Ellenburg, NY; m (1) 1860? Leonard E. Blatchley (John Blatchley & ____); m (2) around 1866 Edward J. Clark; d 25 Dec 1933, Los Angeles, CA.

Benjamin Monty enlisted on 15 Oct 1861 in the 6th Vermont Infantry Regiment and served in Company I (Capt. Frank Butterfield) until his discharge at Brattleboro, VT, on 28 Oct 1864. According to his discharge papers, "Said Benjamin Monty was born in Colchester in the State of Vermont, is Eighteen years of age [in fact he was 18 at his enlistment, 21 in 1864], Five feet Six inches high, Dark complexion, Blue eyes, Dark hair, and by occupation, when enrolled, a Farmer."

Benjamin Monty returned to farming after the war. He was a farmer in Colchester, VT, with real estate valued at $4,000 in 1870, and remained there until his death (US censuses). His tombstone in the Champlain Cemetery in Colchester reads "Benjiman [sic] F. Monty / July 12 1843 – Oct. 6 1926."

Almira Shutts' first husband had also been a farmer in Colchester. Leonard Blatchley had enlisted in the 1st Vermont Cavalry in August 1862 and died of typhoid fever in City

Point, VA, on 6 Jul 1864. She soon remarried and had a 13-year-old son, Joseph J. Clark, who was living in her third husband's household in Colchester in 1880 (US census). After Benjamin Monty's death she moved to California to be with her two daughters and was buried in Forest Lawn Memorial Park in Glendale, CA. Her name and dates of birth and death were nevertheless inscribed on Benjamin Monty's tombstone in Colchester.

The surname Monty was generally used during Benjamin Monty's lifetime. Monta is seen in only a few instances, after 1900. His sons however became known as Emery and Harley Monta.

Children:

3.1.3.3.1	Emma Bernice (twin)	1874-1898&	-1958
3.1.3.3.2	Emery Bernard (twin)	1874-1898-1950?	
3.1.3.3.3	Sarah Almina/Mina	1876-1914-1970	
3.1.3.3.4	Harley Clarence	1890-1814-1959	

3.1.3.4   **MONTY, Napoleon Bonaparte** b 30 Mar 1845, Colchester, VT; d 20 Jan 1927, Montpelier, VT. He married 1869? **Jane Gonyou** (Franklin Gonyou & Julia ____) b Sep 1849, Burlington, VT; m (2) 25 May 1895, Roxbury, VT, Charles A. Fisk (Charles B. Fisk & Betsy ____).

Napoleon Bonaparte Monty served as a private in the 2nd Vermont Infantry Regiment from 29 Aug 1864 to 31 Jul 1865 and later received an invalid pension (certificate #407485 dated 1 Jun 1877). He was a farm laborer in Colchester, VT, in 1870, a laborer in Roxbury, VT, in 1880, and a laborer in Montpelier, VT, from at least 1890 on (US censuses and 1890 Veterans Schedule).

There is one anomaly in the 1900 census. In spite of her second marriage in 1895 as the divorced wife of Napoleon B. Monty, Jane Gonyou was yet listed as the wife of both husbands. In both cases she was 50 years old, born in Vermont in September 1849 of parents born in French Canada, and had had one child, still living. The only difference: she had been married to Napoleon B. Monty for 31 years, and to Charles Fisk for 6 years. In later censuses, Napoleon Monty, divorced or single, was living alone in Montpelier while Charles and Jane Fisk continued to reside in Roxbury.

Child:

3.1.3.4.1	Nellie A.	1873-1897-1963

3.1.3.5   **MONTY, William F.** b 20 Mar 1847, Colchester, VT; d there 4 Jun 1859.

William F. Monty drowned when his canoe capsized in the Lamoille River. He was buried in the Champlain Cemetery in Colchester, VT.

3.1.3.6   **MONTY, Infant** (female) b Aug? 1848, Colchester, VT; d there 2 Oct 1848, at the age of 2 months.

This infant daughter of John and Margaret Monty was buried in the Champlain Cemetery in Colchester, VT.

3.1.3.7   **MONTY, Boardman** b 1850?; d 9 Nov 1864, Colchester, VT, at the age of 14.

Boardman Monty died of typhoid fever and was buried in the Champlain Cemetery in Colchester, VT. He does not appear with his family there in the 1860 census where a 10-year-old Samuel Monty, otherwise unknown, is included. It is probable that these two names represent the same child.

3.1.3.8   **MONTY, Mary Ann** b 1855?; d 24 Nov 1864, Colchester, VT, at the age of 9.

Mary Ann Monty died of typhoid fever and was buried in the Champlain Cemetery in Colchester, VT.

3.1.3.9 **MONTY, Augusta Louisa** b 12 Mar 1858, Colchester, VT; d 1947, Miami, FL. She married 30 Nov 1882, Colchester, VT, **Henry Thomas Ballard** (Benjamin S. Ballard & Lepha Rogers) b 5 Nov 1830, Georgia, VT; m (1) 1858? Judith Harrington Brooks (Smith A. Brooks & Alma Kibbe); d 16 Jan 1907, Burlington, VT.

Augusta Monty was 24 years old at her marriage and was consistently named Mrs. Augusta L. Ballard after her marriage. She is almost certainly the same person as the 2-year-old Louisa Monty who was living with her parents in Colchester, VT, in 1860 and the 11-year old Augusta living in 1870, after her parents' deaths, in her brother Benjamin's (3.1.3.3) household there (US censuses). If any uncertainty remains, it is due to the fact that the Colchester Vital Records name the child who was born to John and Margaret Monty on 12 Mar 1858 Julia Ann Monty, a name which does not to my knowledge reappear anywhere in connection with that family. I tend to believe an error was made in the birth record, or that the name originally given this child was later entirely disregarded.

Henry Ballard, a widower, was a laborer in Georgia, VT, in 1880 and a milk dealer in Colchester, VT, two years later, at his marriage to Augusta Monty. His widow was living with her stepson Smith S. Ballard and his family in Montpelier, VT, in 1920 and in Miami, FL, in 1930 (US censuses).

3.1.8.1 **MONTY, Sarah Ann** b 1854?; d 20 Mar 1872, Colchester, VT, at the age of 19.

Sarah Ann Monty (1854-1872) was buried in the Champlain Cemetery in Colchester, VT, and shares a tombstone with her aunt "Margaret / wife of / John Monty Sr." (3.1.3). She was living in her uncle's household in Colchester in 1860 and was keeping house there for her cousins Benjamin (3.1.3.3) and Augusta (3.1.3.9) Monty in 1870 (US censuses).

3.3.2.1 **MONTY/MONTEE, Joseph** b & bp 23 May & 1 Jun 1817, St. Luc, QC; d & bur 1 & 3 Aug 1874, Glens Falls, NY. He married 1841? **Mary Elizabeth Lambert** (Laurent Lambert & Marie Anne Lemire) b & bp 19 Jan 1820, Maskinongé, QC; d & bur 27 & 29 Aug 1887, Glens Falls, NY.

Joseph Monty came to Glens Falls, NY, in 1835 and was naturalized as Joseph Montee in Queensbury, NY, on 9 Sep 1840. He was in turn a cooper, a boatman, and again a cooper in that town, where the first eight of his children were born. The family may also have resided for a few years in the early 1860s in Syracuse, NY, where the youngest child was born. Joseph Montee was again in the Queensbury/Glens Falls area in 1870 and remained there until his death (US and state censuses). He and his wife were buried in St. Alphonsus Cemetery in Glens Falls.

It should be noted that while all civil records in New York State concerning this family carry the surname Montee, as do the tombstones in St. Alphonsus Cemetery, the vast majority of records in the church of St. Alphonsus are under the Monty surname.

Children:

3.3.2.1.1	Joseph	1842?- -1922
3.3.2.1.2	Mary Elizabeth	1844-1861-1910
3.3.2.1.3	Edmond	1846- -1919
3.3.2.1.4	Nelson/Narcisse	1848-1879-1905
3.3.2.1.5	Harriet	1851-1872-1931
3.3.2.1.6	Victoria/Mary V.	1853-1877-1915
3.3.2.1.7	Benoni	1856- -1878
3.3.2.1.8	Adeline	1859- -
3.3.2.1.9	Edgar M.	1864-1894-1948

3.3.2.2 **MONTY, Laurent** b & bp 26 Oct 1818, St. Luc, QC.

3.3.2.3 **MONTY/MONTEE, Hubert/Albert** b & bp 24 Oct 1819, St. Luc, QC; d & bur 13 & 15 Feb 1860, Glens Falls, NY. He married **Léocadie/Adaline Lavoie** (Joseph Lavoie & Marie Louise Charbonneau) b & bp 23 & 24 Nov 1825, L'Acadie, QC; d & bur 5 &

7 Feb 1906, Luzerne & Glens Falls, NY.

The identification of Hubert Monty, son of Joseph Monty and Victoire Perrault, with Albert Montee of Glens Falls, NY, has not been established through any primary document but rather through a series of coincidences which, cumulatively, become convincing. For these and for the later history of the family I am indebted in large part to Mr. Robert B. Rodriguez of Albuquerque, NM, one of Albert Montee's descendants.

Hubert Monty probably came to the United States with his parents around 1839. He was naturalized in Glens Falls on 12 Jul 1852 under the name of Albert Monte but became known in that community, where he was a cooper, as Albert Montee (US and state censuses). He was buried under that name and surname in St. Alphonsus Cemetery in Glens Falls. His descendants, with few exceptions, have retained that surname.

Albert Montee's wife was named Marie Léocadie Lavoie at her baptism and was generally known in the United States as Lucadia or Lucy during his lifetime. She chose to be known, though, after his death as Adaline or Adeline. That is the name found not only in all later censuses but also in the Warren Co., NY, Surrogate's Court where Mrs. Adaline Montee was named co-executrix of her husband's estate on 7 Mar 1860, at the death of Mrs. Adeline Montee in Luzerne, and at the funeral of Adeline Lavoie in St. Alphonsus Church in Glens Falls. The inscription on the MONTEE tombstone in St. Alphonsus Cemetery in Glens Falls refers however to "Elocadie Lavois [sic]," wife of Albert Montee.

Children:

3.3.2.3.1	Mary	1845-1865?-1918
3.3.2.3.2	Sophronia	1848- -1869
3.3.2.3.3	Albert	1850- -1927
3.3.2.3.4	George Edward	1853-1883-1926
3.3.2.3.5	Samuel	1854?- -1933
3.3.2.3.6	Josephine	1855-1878-1885
3.3.2.3.7	Philomene Melina	1858- -

3.3.2.4　　**MONTY, Victoire** b & bp 27 Jun 1821, St. Luc, QC; d & bur there 28 & 30 Jun 1821.

3.3.2.5　　**MONTY, George** b & bp 24 & 26 May 1822, St. Luc & L'Acadie, QC.

3.3.2.6　　**MONTY, Victoire** b & bp 4 & 11 Apr 1824, Iberville, QC; d & bur there 8 & 10 Mar 1825.

3.3.2.7　　**MONTY, Sophie** b & bp 5 & 12 Feb 1826, Iberville, QC; bur there 21 May 1826.

3.3.2.8　　**MONTY, Raymond** b & bp 4 Sep 1827, Iberville, QC; d & bur there 3 & 5 Feb 1828.

3.3.2.9　　**MONTY, Benjamin/Bénoni** b & bp 3 & 4 Mar 1829, Iberville, QC; d & bur there 6 & 7 Mar 1833.

This child was named Benjamin at his baptism but was buried, as the 4-year-old son of Joseph Monty and Victoire Perrault, under the name Bénoni.

3.3.2.10　　**MONTY, Anonymous** b & d Apr 1831, Iberville, QC; bur there 11 Apr 1831.

This child died immediately after birth, according to the burial records of the church of St. Athanase in Iberville, QC. The date of birth however is not stated.

3.3.2.11　　**MONTY, Pierre** b & bp 25 Apr 1832, Iberville, QC; d & bur there 26 & 27 Apr 1832.

3.3.2.12   **MONTY, Anonymous** b 7 Mar 1833, Iberville, QC; d & bur there 7 Mar 1833.

3.3.2.13   **MONTY, Judith/Julie** b & bp 2 & 3 Feb 1834, St. Mathias, QC; d & bur 26 & 27 Mar 1834, Iberville, QC.
Named Judith at her baptism, this child was buried at the age of two months under the name of Julie.

3.3.2.14   **MONTY, Anonymous** b 25 Apr 1835, Iberville, QC; d & bur there 25 Apr 1835.

3.3.2.15   **MONTY/MONTEE, Emilie/Amelia** b & bp 3 May 1836, Iberville, QC. She married 24 Feb 1857, Glens Falls, NY, **Pierre Boucher/Peter Butcher** (Charles Boucher & Ursule Dubord dit Latourelle) b 1827?, QC.
Emilie Monty came to the United States with her parents around 1839 and was known thereafter as Amelia Montee. Her husband, named Pierre Boucher at their marriage, was known as Peter Butcher in 1860 when he was a 33-year-old boatman in Glens Falls, NY (US census). He was also known as Peter Butcher on 7 Mar 1860 when he posted bond for the administrators of the estate of his brother-in-law Albert Montee (3.3.2.3) in the Warren Co., NY, Surrogate's Court. I have been unable to find any further trace of the family in either Canada or the United States.

3.3.2.16   **MONTY/MONTEE, Edward/Romuald** b & bp 13 & 14 Jun 1838, Iberville, QC; d & bur 21 & 23 Jan 1877, Glens Falls, NY. He married there 3 Jan 1860 **Philomène Bessette** b 1838?, QC; d & bur 19 & 21 Mar 1880, Glens Falls, NY, at the age of 42.
The child baptized as Romuald Monty came to the United States as an infant around 1839 and was henceforth known as Edouard Monty (at his marriage for example) or more commonly Edward Montee. He became a cooper in Glens Falls, NY, was naturalized, and continued to live in his father's household with his family until at least 1865 when his wife was 27 years old. In 1870 Edwin (sic) Montee was a cooper in East Greenwich, NY, though the family had returned to Glens Falls a few years before his death (US and state censuses). Both he and his wife were buried there in St. Alphonsus Cemetery.
Philomène Bessette was known in the United States under a variety of names: Philomene or Philomène Besset, Bessette, or Bessé in the church records of her marriage and of her children's baptisms, Salomi or Saloma Montee in US and state censuses, and Philome Montee in her will, dated the very day of her death. Her assets were bequeathed equally to her three surviving children: Nelson and Louis, who were left to the guardianship of Louis Lee, and Josephine who was left to the guardianship of John Beaudette (Warren Co., NY, Surrogate's Court, 7 Dec 1880). The other children had presumably predeceased their mother.

Children:

3.3.2.16.1	Marie Victoire	1860-	-
3.3.2.16.2	Edward	1863-	-
3.3.2.16.3	Nelson	1865-	-
3.3.2.16.4	Philomène Onésime	1867-	-1872
3.3.2.16.5	Lewis/Louis Arthur	1869-	-1949
3.3.2.16.6	Anonymous	1872-	-1874
3.3.2.16.7	Josephine	1874-1892-1956	
3.3.2.16.8	George Henry	1876-	-

3.3.5.1   **MONTY, Antoine** b & bp 22 Dec 1819, St. Luc, QC; d 1910?, NY. He married 8 Nov 1842, St. Jean, QC, **Adélaïde/Adeline Miron** (Joseph Miron & Charlotte Provost) b & bp 1 & 2 Jul 1826, Iberville, QC; d 1 Jun 1911, Plattsburgh, NY.
Antoine Monty was a laborer in St. Jean, QC, at his marriage and a resident of St. Luc, QC, at the baptism of his first child in 1843. He then moved to New York State before the birth of his son Antoine in July 1844. For the rest of his life, he moved from place to place in

Clinton, Essex, and Warren counties: he was a bloomer in Essex in 1850, a blacksmith in Redford in 1854, a resident of Plattsburgh in 1859, a bloomer in Schuyler Falls in 1860, a bloomer in Willsboro in 1865, a laborer in Glens Falls in 1870, a laborer in Crown Point in 1880, and a laborer in Ticonderoga in 1892 and 1900. A few years later, when he and his wife celebrated their fiftieth wedding anniversary, they were living with their daughter Sarah's family in Plattsburgh (*Plattsburgh Sentinel,* 15 Nov 1907) while in April 1910 they were living in the household of their son Nelson in Peru, NY. They had had eleven children of whom six were then still alive (US and state censuses). Antoine Monty died within the next few months for he predeceased his wife who died in Plattsburgh at the home of her daughter Julia (*Ticonderoga Sentinel,* 8 Jun 1911).

Temporary changes in surname accompanied these changes in locality. From Monty in 1850, it became Monta in 1860, Monte in 1865, Montee in 1870, Montey in 1880 before returning to Monty in 1892 and later years (US and state censuses).

Children:

3.3.5.1.1	Adélaïde	1843-	-
3.3.5.1.2	Antoine	1844-1863?-1937	
3.3.5.1.3	Sophie	1845-	-
3.3.5.1.4	Fred	1848?-	-
3.3.5.1.5	Rosalie	1850-	-
3.3.5.1.6	Joseph	1852-1876?-1929	
3.3.5.1.7	Nelson	1854-1880?-1937	
3.3.5.1.8	Edmond	1856-	-
3.3.5.1.9	Sarah/Cécile/Celina	1859-1878-1917	
3.3.5.1.10	Ellen	1861-1876?&1887?-	
3.3.5.1.11	Julia B.	1863-1879&1882&1906?&1917-	

3.3.5.2   **MONTY, Narcisse** b & bp 20 & 21 Apr 1821, St. Luc, QC; d & bur there 9 & 11 Jun 1822.

3.3.5.3   **MONTY, Jean-Baptiste** b & bp 16 & 17 Jun 1822, St. Luc, QC.
This child is occasionally confused with his second cousin Jean-Baptiste Monty (3.9.3.3), son of François Xavier Monty and Marie Goyette, who was also born in St. Luc, QC, in 1822 but lived most of his life in Michigan where he was known as John B. Montie.
I have not found any marriage or death records in Canada for the present Jean-Baptiste Monty. If he survived infancy he may have come to the United States in the 1840s as did his widowed mother and brother Antoine (3.3.5.1). There are a few men named John Monty/Monte/Montee born in Canada in the 1820s who later lived in New York State and whose parentage I have been unable to determine. He may have been one of them.

3.3.5.4   **MONTY, Adélaïde** b & bp 30 Apr & 12 May 1824, Iberville, QC; d & bur there 15 & 20 May 1824.

3.3.5.5.   **MONTY, Marguerite** b & bp 10 Jul 1825, Iberville, QC.

3.3.5.6   **MONTY, Emilie** b & bp Sep and 14 Oct 1827, Iberville, QC.
Emilie Monty was one month old at her baptism.

3.3.5.7   **MONTY, Céleste** b & bp 1 and 20 Mar 1831, Iberville, QC; d & bur there 9 & 10 Mar 1832.

3.3.6.1   **MONTY/MONTEE, Jacques/Jacob** b & bp 19 & 23 May 1824, Iberville, QC; d & bur 3 & 5 May 1899, Glens Falls, NY. He married **Elizabeth Lansing** (?) b between 1824 and 1828; d 1889?, Glens Falls, NY.
Jacques Monty arrived in the United States with his family in the 1840s and was known thereafter as Jacob Montee. He was a boatman in Glens Falls, NY, until at least 1892

when his son Joseph and daughter Emma were members of his household (US and state censuses).

There is much uncertainty about his wife: her maiden name, her place of birth, her age, and the date of her death. Censuses refer to her of course as Elizabeth Montee. Her will of 15 Nov 1888 is also in that name. On four occasions that I know of, though, an attempt was made at identifying her by her maiden name. The results are disconcerting. She was Elisabeth L. Ansugne at the baptism of her daughter Susan, Elisabeth Leroux/Lemoyne at the baptism of her son Joseph, Elisabeth Lenseygne at the baptism of her daughter Adeline (all of these in the French records of St. Alphonsus Church in Glens Falls), and Elizabeth Lansing in the marriage record of her daughter Emma in 1919 (Warren Co. Marriage Records, #3108). I have been unable to trace her under any of these or similar surnames.

She may have been born in either Canada (1860, 1865, 1875 US and state censuses), or in New York State (1870 and 1880 US censuses) and could have been born in 1824 (1880), 1825 (1870), 1826 (1865), or 1828 (1860 and 1875). I have not found a record of either her death or burial. I suspect that she died not too long before the executor of her will, Daniel L. Robertson, filed it for probate on 16 Sep 1889. There was some delay when it was discovered that a guardian needed to be appointed for "Adelaide Hoag" – in fact Mrs. Adeline (Montee) Hoag – who was still a minor. Mrs. Elizabeth Montee's will was then entered in the Warren Co. Surrogate's Court on 30 Dec 1889.

Children:

3.3.6.1.1	Emma	1852?-	&1919-1929
3.3.6.1.2	Josephine	1853-1877?&1890-1931	
3.3.6.1.3	Henry/William Henry	1856?-1876?-1894	
3.3.6.1.4	Susan	1858-1877?-1929	
3.3.6.1.5	Joseph Louis	1861-	-
3.3.6.1.6	Adelaide	1863-	-
3.3.6.1.7	Adeline	1870-1886-	

3.3.6.2   **MONTY, Jean-Baptiste** b & bp 20 Jan 1826, Iberville, QC.

3.3.6.3   **MONTY, Alfred** b & bp 18 & 19 Aug 1828, Napierville, QC.

3.3.6.4   **MONTY, Jacques Frédéric** b 1829?; d & bur 6 & 7 Mar 1832, Iberville, QC, at the age of 3.

3.3.6.5   **MONTY, Gabriel** b & bp 15 & 16 Feb 1831, Iberville, QC; d & bur there 14 & 16 Mar 1832.

3.3.6.6   **MONTY, Adélaïde** b & bp 31 Jan & 2 Feb 1833, Iberville, QC; d & bur there 9 & 11 Mar 1834.

3.3.6.7   **MONTY/MONTEE, John/Jean** b & bp 30 & 31 Jan 1835, St. Jean, QC; d & bur 30 May & 1 Jun 1907, Glens Falls, NY. He married (1) there 31 Aug 1857 **Malvina Adele Sansouci** b 1844?, QC; d 19 Nov 1889, Glens Falls, NY, at the age of 45.

He married (2) 1898? **Marie Louise Dufour** (Cyrille Dufour & Marie Anne Esmond) b & bp 25 Mar 1852, Chicoutimi, QC; m (1) there 25 Nov 1872 Guillaume Dubée (Guillaume Dubée & Marie Louise Godreau); d & bur 10 & 13 Sep 1924, Glens Falls, NY.

Jean Monty came to Glens Falls, NY, with his parents in the late 1840s and was naturalized in Queensbury, NY, on 12 Jul 1852. He was henceforth known as John Montee save in the French records of St. Alphonsus Church in Glens Falls where he was named Jean-Baptiste Monty at his first marriage. As John Montee he served during the Civil War as a private in Co. B, 175th New York Infantry Regiment from 20 Sep 1864 to 8 Sep 1865. On his return to Glens Falls he was in turn a boatman, a cooper, and a drayman (US and state censuses). He was buried there in St. Alphonsus Cemetery as were both his wives.

John Montee and his second wife had been married for two years in 1900 (US census).

Her baptismal name was Marie Louise Dufour. In Glens Falls records, though, she was variously known as Louise, Louisa, Mary L., or Marie L. She had arrived in the United States around 1881 and had had four children from her first marriage, two of whom, Adelard/Delor and Arthur J. Dubee, are mentioned in John Montee's will of 25 May 1904 (Warren Co., NY, Surrogate's Court, 25 Jul 1907).

Child of the first marriage:

3.3.6.7.1   Charles B.   1879-   -

3.3.6.8   **MONTY, Edmond** b & bp 25 & 26 May 1837, Iberville, QC.

3.3.6.9   **MONTY/MONTEE, Margaret** b 1842 or 1844, VT; d & bur 28 Apr & 2 May 1921, Glens Falls, NY. She married there 31 Aug 1857 **John LaFountain/Jean-Baptiste Robert dit Lafontaine** (Calixte Robert & Emilie Sancoucy) b & bp 27 Feb 1839, St. Jean-Baptiste, QC; d & bur 23 & 26 Dec 1917, Glens Falls, NY.

Margaret Montee's date of birth is uncertain. She was 8 years old in 1850, according to the US census in Glens Falls, NY. That is the earliest record we have, and would normally be the most authoritative. However all later censuses point to an 1844 year of birth as do her burial record in St. Alphonsus Church and the inscription on her tombstone in St. Alphonsus Cemetery. Either 1842 or 1844 is a possible year of birth.

She was most probably born in Vermont as is indicated in almost all censuses, and probably in Addison Co. where her parents were living in 1840 (US census). She moved with them to Glens Falls in 1847 and lived there for most of her life.

Jean-Baptiste Robert, who was living with his parents in St. Alexandre, QC, in 1851 (Canadian census), was generally known in New York State as John Lafountain. He was a cooper in Glens Falls in the early years of his marriage, in Fort Ann, NY, in 1870, and again in Glens Falls from at least 1880 on. He had also served during the Civil War in Co. D, 175th New York Infantry Regiment from 24 Sep 1864 to 30 Jun 1865. By 1910 he and his wife had had eleven children of whom six, John, Lucy, Azilda, Cordelia, Edward, and Angelina, were still alive (US and state censuses).

His surname varies. Censuses generally name him John Lafountain or LaFountain though he was named John Spring when he was a member of his father-in-law's household in Glens Falls in 1860. The records of St. Alphonsus Church there, which almost invariably adhere to the original French names and surnames, refer to him as J. B. Robert at the baptism of his first child and as Jean or Jean-Baptiste Lafontaine at the births and marriages of the others and at his and his wife's deaths. The name on his tombstone in St. Alphonsus Cemetery though is "John LaFountain." His descendants used the surname Lafountain.

Children:
i   **Mélie Onésime Lafountain** b & bp 16 May 1858, Glens Falls, NY; d before 1860.
ii   **John Lafountain** b May 1859, Glens Falls, NY; d & bur there 1 & 4 Nov 1929. He married there 13 Mar 1886 **Rebecca Vadeboncoeur/Hart** (François Vadeboncoeur & Olive Roger) b & bp 15 & 16 Feb 1868, St. Etienne des Grès, QC; d & bur 19 & 23 Jun 1941, Glens Falls, NY.
iii   **Lucy Lafountain** b & bp 9 & 25 Aug 1861, Glens Falls, NY; d & bur 7 & 10 Dec 1938, Queensbury, NY. She married (1) May 1877, North Granville, NY, **Arni J. Warner** b 14 Aug 1853, NY; d 31 Mar 1920, Keene, NY.
     She married (2) 9 Aug 1930, Glens Falls, NY, **Joseph/Octave Hubert Nadeau** (Rémi Nadeau & Philomène Bérubé) b & bp 30 Jun & 1 Jul 1869, Rivière du Loup, QC.
iv   **Louise Lafountain** b Sep 1863, Glens Falls, NY; d before 1870.
v   **Azilda/Ozilda Lafountain** b & bp 3 Apr & 6 May 1866, Glens Falls, NY; d & bur there 13 & 16 Mar 1935. She married there 25 Feb 1884 **Alexis Fortuna Vadeboncoeur/Alexander Hart** (François Vadeboncoeur & Olive Roger Ouellette) b & bp 3 Jun 1865, St. Etienne des Grès, QC; d & bur 20 & 23 Aug 1935, Glens Falls, NY.
vi   **Philomène Domithille Lafountain** b & bp 16 & 31 May 1868, Glens Falls, NY; d

before 1870.

vii **Cordelia Lafountain** b & bp 15 Sep & 24 Oct 1870, Glens Falls, NY; d & bur there 26 & 29 Dec 1941. She married there 1885? **James Richardson** (Henry Richardson & Mary M. ____) b Nov 1865, NY.

viii **Edward Napoleon Lafountain** b & bp 23 Feb & 7 Mar 1874, Glens Falls, NY; d & bur there 28 & 31 Jan 1944. He married 23 Nov 1893, Hudson Falls, NY, **Emma Laberge/Labarge** (Louis Laberge & Marie Césarie/Sarah Lapanne) b & bp 20 Aug & 12 Sep 1872, Hudson Falls & Glens Falls, NY; d & bur 3 & 7 Mar 1961, Glens Falls, NY.

ix **Angelina Elmire Lafountain** b & bp 8 May & 13 Jul 1878, Glens Falls, NY; d 18 Sep 1951. She married 1896? **Bradford George Moulton** (George Henry Moulton & Zorada Ann Rose) b 1865?, Fort Ann, NY; d 1939.

3.3.6.10 **MONTEE, Rosalie/Rosa/Rose** b 1849?, Glens Falls, NY; d & bur there 23 & 25 May 1914. She married there 4 May 1863 **Alexander Bovair/Boisvert** (Alexandre Boisvert & Madeleine Lavallée) b & bp ? Oct & 26 Nov 1840, ? & Iberville, QC, d & bur 29 & 31 Mar 1925, Glens Falls, NY.

Rosa Montee was a 1-year-old child in 1850 when she was living in Glens Falls, NY, with her parents. Later censuses place her birth between 1844 and 1852 though they all agree that she was born in New York State. If so, she must have been born after her parents' arrival in Glens Falls in 1847. The year of birth on her tombstone in St. Alphonsus Cemetery there, 1847, may well be correct. Her burial record in St. Alphonsus Church however, which shows her to be 69 years old in 1914, must be incorrect.

Her name varies somewhat. She was named Rosa or Rose in censuses. She was also identified as Rose Montee on the tombstone she shares with her husband. On other occasions, at her marriage and death and on the baptismal records of her children, her name is Rosalie.

Alexandre Boisvert was one month old at his baptism and was living with his parents in St. Alexandre, QC, in 1851 (Canadian census). When he came to the United States around 1854 both his name and surname generally changed. Although he was still Alexandre Boisvert in the records of St. Alphonsus Church in Glens Falls, several US and state censuses name him Alex, Aleck, or Alexander Bover, Bovar, Bovitt, or more frequently Bovair. The surname Bovair became permanent and is inscribed on his and his wife's tombstone in St. Alphonsus Cemetery in Glens Falls.

Alex Bovair remained in Glens Falls for many years after his marriage. He was a day laborer there in 1870, a tinsmith in 1880, and a laborer again in 1892. By 1900, when he and his wife had had eleven children of whom seven were still alive, he was a farmer in South Glens Falls (Moreau Twp), NY. He was living in 1920 in his son Fred's household in Glens Falls (US and state censuses).

Children:

i **George Edward Bovair** b & bp 11 Apr & 2 May 1864, Glens Falls, NY; d before 1870.

ii **Angelina Azilda Bovair** b & bp Jan & 6 May 1866, Glens Falls, NY; d & bur there 19 & 21 May 1869.

iii **Charles Bovair** b & bp 16 & 24 May 1868, Glens Falls, NY.

iv **Fred/Alfred Alexander Bovair/Bover** b & bp 10 Jun & 3 Jul 1870, Glens Falls, NY; d & bur there 7 & 11 Oct 1950. He married there 13 Nov 1892 **Josephine Chabot/Shepard** b 1872?, NY; d & bur 23 & 28 May 1944, Glens Falls, NY, at the age of 72.

v **Emma Bovair** b & bp 31 May & 18 Jun 1873, Glens Falls, NY. She married there 13 Jul 1898 **Roman Lee Pidgeon** b 17 Mar 1873, NY.

vi **William Alexander Bovair** b & bp 4 Apr & 20 May 1877, Glens Falls, NY; d & bur there 5 & 8 Nov 1915. He married there 26 Dec 1896 **Marie Melina Paradis** (Frank Paradis & Rosalie Hébert) b & bp there 12 Jun & 6 Jul 1871.

vii **Marie Valida Bovair** b & bp 16 Sep & 19 Oct 1879, Glens Falls, NY; d & bur there 27 & 30 Aug 1956. She married there 21 Oct 1897 **Eugene A. Vadebon-**

coeur/Hart (François Vadeboncoeur/Hart & Olive Roger Ouellette) b & bp 27 & 28 Feb 1876, St. Etienne des Grès, QC; d & bur 28 & 31 Jan 1957, Glens Falls, NY.

viii **Elizabeth Bovair** b & bp 16 Mar & 3 Apr 1881, Glens Falls, NY; d & bur there 5 & 8 Apr 1963. She married (1) there 30 Oct 1899 **Benjamin Johns** (William Johns & Sarah ____) b May 1878, Moreau Twp, NY; d between 1920 and 1930.
　　　She married (2) 19 Nov 1932, Glens Falls, NY, **William A. Taylor** (____ Taylor & Adeline ____) b 1869?, NY; m (1) 1890? Margaret ____ .

ix **Marie Anna Eliza Boisvert** b & bp 20 Jun & 1 Jul 1884, Glens Falls, NY; d & bur there 16 & 18 Nov 1886.

x **Jerome Arthur Boisvert** b & bp 20 Dec 1885 & 17 Jan 1886, Glens Falls, NY; d & bur there 5 & 7 Feb 1887.

xi **Gertrude Pauline Bovair** b & bp 20 Jul & 3 Aug 1889, Glens Falls, NY; d between 1917 and 1920. She married 1 Jan 1907, Glens Falls, NY, **William Cole Benedict** (Nicholas Benedict & Cordelia ____) b 30 Oct 1884, NY; m (2) 1923? Margaret ____ .

3.5.13.1　　　**MONTA, Mary Jane** b 1839?, Vergennes, VT. She married there 13 Dec 1856 **John Ayres/Ayers**, b 1837?, Waltham, VT.
　　Mary Jane Monta was 11 years old in 1850 when she was living with her parents in Vergennes, VT, and 22 years old in 1860 when she was the wife of John Ayers (sic), a 23-year old laborer there (US censuses). They had been married there on 13 Dec 1856 by the Rev. H. F. Leavitt under the names of Mary Monte and John Ayres (Vermont Vital Records). I have been unable to find them after 1860.

Child:
i　　**Annis Ayres** b 5 Jul 1857, Vergennes, VT.

3.5.13.2　　　**MONTA, Joseph** b 19 ???, 1844, Vergennes, VT; d & bur 21 & 23 May 1894, Burlington, VT. He married 1865? **Mary Croto** (Henry Croto & Mary Almond or Aleman) b 1 Jul 1849, Vergennes, VT; d 22 Jun 1924, Burlington, VT, at the age of 74 years, 11 months, and 21 days.
　　The incomplete date of Joseph Monta's birth is taken from the very faint inscription on his tombstone in Mount Calvary Cemetery in Burlington, VT. It corresponds to the year of birth found in earlier documents. His wife's year of birth, as stated on the tombstone, is less certain. It shows her dates as 1843-1924. It may be a misreading. I would rather trust the death record which states her age quite specifically.
　　Joseph Monta was a railroad brakeman in Burlington from the early days of his marriage. His widow continued to live there after his death, first with her daughter Louisa and later with her son Joseph. She had had six children, all of whom were still living in 1900 (US censuses). All but Delphine were buried alongside their parents in the Monta lot in Mount Calvary Cemetery and share their parents' tombstone.

Children:

3.5.13.2.1	Sophia	1866-1885-1916
3.5.13.2.2	Joseph John	1867-1903-1934
3.5.13.2.3	Delphine	1869-1891-1965
3.5.13.2.4	Mary Anne/Nettie	1872-1890-1952
3.5.13.2.5	Margaret Adele	1873-1896-1956
3.5.13.2.6	Louisa	1876-1898-1925

3.5.13.3　　　**MONTA, Abigail** b 1846?, Vergennes, Vt.
　　Abigail Monta was a 4-year-old child living with her parents in Vergennes, VT, in 1850 (US census).

3.5.13.4　　　**MONTA, Ellen** b & bp Jul 1852 & 8 Feb 1853, Vergennes & Burlington, VT. She married Aug 1873, Burlington, VT, **Joseph Fagga** (John Fagga & Mary ____) b

1849?, White Creek, NY.

Ellen Monta was baptized as Hélène Monty at the age of 7 months. Her name was Ellen at her marriage and at the births of her children though she was known as Mrs. Helen Fagga, widow of Joseph, in the Burlington, VT, City Directories from at least 1920 on. Her husband, who was 24 years old at his marriage, was a laborer in Burlington, VT, until at least 1891 (City Directories).

Children:

i   **Rosa Fagga** b 22 Jul 1875, Burlington, VT. She married there 16 Dec 1892 **James Francis** (Decatur/Caleb O. Francis & Rosa Blair) b there 4 Jul 1872.

ii   **William J. Fagga** b Dec 1877, Burlington, VT. He married (1) there 12 Mar 1896 **Mary Francis** (Decatur/Caleb O. Francis & Rosa Blair) b there 20 Feb 1879.

    He was a widower when he married (2) 18 Aug 1908, Burlington, VT, **Salina Hanse** (Joseph Hanse & Hannah Perry) b May 1882, Swanton, VT.

iii   **Anonymous (female) Fagga** b & d 22 Mar 1881, Burlington, VT.

iv   **Anonymous (male) Fagga** b & d 6 Aug 1882, Burlington, VT.

v   **Infant (male)** Fagga b 7 Aug 1884, Burlington, VT.

vi   **Mary L. Fagga** b 1886?, Burlington, VT. She married there 17 Nov 1908 **Harris Austin Sprague** (Frederick Sprague & Cora Clamore) b 13 Mar 1884, Grand Lake Stream, ME.

vii   **Josephine Fagga** b 1888?, Burlington, VT. She married there 23 Sep 1906 **Stephen Lovejoy Boyd** (William H. Boyd & Mrs. Minnie Lovejoy) b there 5 Oct 1887.

3.9.2.1   **MONTY, Domitille** b & bp 6 & 7 Oct 1822, St. Luc, QC; d 18 Jul 1903, Hudson Falls, NY. She married 11 Jan 1842, Iberville, QC, **Michel Audet dit Lapointe** (Jean-Baptiste Audet dit Lapointe & Marguerite Nolin) b & bp 13 May 1816, St. Luc, QC; d before 1880.

Michel Audet was a laborer in Iberville, QC, until 1846 and in Dunham, QC, from 1847 until at least 1869 when he and his wife were godparents to one of their grandchildren there. I have been unable to find his death record and do not if he came to the United States with his family in the 1870s and died there or if his family left Canada after his death. In 1880 his widow was living with two of her children, Emilie (vi) and Louis (x), in her son Daniel's (vii) household in Sandy Hill, the present-day Hudson Falls, NY (US census). She was buried there in St. Paul Cemetery, as were at least three of her children and their spouses.

The family's surname in Canada was commonly Audet or Audet dit Lapointe. In the United States the surname Lapointe or Lapoint was used almost exclusively.

Children:

i   **Michel Audet dit Lapointe** b & bp 28 & 30 Oct 1842, Iberville, QC. He married 7 Jan 1868, Dunham, QC, **Célina Boucher** (Antoine Boucher & Emérence Bélanger) b & bp 28 & 30 Aug 1849, Dunham & Stanbridge, QC.

ii   **Suzanne/Susan Audet dit Lapointe** b & bp 13 & 14 Jul 1844, Iberville, QC; d 25 Mar 1925, Hudson Falls, NY. She married 14 Nov 1859, Dunham, QC, **Edouard Mailhot/Edward Mayotte** (Joseph Mailhot & Céleste Duclos) b 1840?, QC; d 25 Aug 1907, Hudson Falls, NY, at the age of 67.

iii   **Marguerite Audet dit Lapointe** b & bp 10 & 12 Jan 1846, Iberville, QC. She married 8 Jul 1867, Dunham, QC, **Jean-Baptiste Chalifoux** (Pierre Chalifoux & Angèle Viens) b & bp 24 Jun 1845, Sorel, QC.

iv   **Marie Audet dit Lapointe** b & bp 17 Oct 1847 & 20 Feb 1848, Dunham & Stanbridge, QC; d 5 Apr 1920, Winchendon, MA. She married 8 Jul 1867, Dunham, QC, **Antoine Braconnier** (Joseph Braconnier & Rose Sancoucy dit Contré) b May 1838, QC; m (1) 11 Oct 1862, Dunham, QC, Louise Lafrenière (François Lafrenière & Rose Hébert); d 28 Mar 1904, Winchendon, MA.

v   **Jean-Baptiste Audet dit Lapointe** b & bp 2 Feb 1850, Dunham, QC; d & bur 11 & 14 Jan 1929, Hudson Falls, NY. He married 16 Jun 1868, Dunham, QC, **Sophronie Courtemanche** (Olivier Courtemanche & Marie Anne Lapanne/Gaboriau dit Lapalme) b & bp 15 & 16 Mar 1851, Farnham, QC; d & bur 29 Sep & 2 Oct 1926, Hudson Falls, NY.

vi   **Emilie Audet dit Lapointe** b & bp 13 & 14 May 1851, Dunham, QC.

vii   **Daniel Audet dit Lapointe/LaPoint** b & bp 13 & 17 Feb 1856, Dunham, QC. He married (1) 10 Oct 1878, Glens Falls, NY, a third cousin **Josephine Monty** (3.3.2.3.6).

        He married (2) 13 Aug 1887, Hudson Falls, NY, **Adélaïde Terrien/Thérien** (Jean-Baptiste Terrien & Adélaïde Anne Robillard) b & bp 2 Jun & 8 July 1855, Glens Falls, NY.

viii **Joseph Audet dit Lapointe** b & bp 6 & 7 Oct 1857, Dunham, QC.

ix   **Edouard Audet dit Lapointe** b & bp 19 & 22 Nov 1859, Dunham, QC; d & bur there 27 & 29 Mar 1860.

x   **Louis Audet dit Lapointe** b & bp 12 & 15 Mar 1861, Stanbridge, QC; d & bur 1 & 4 Apr 1956, Hudson Falls, NY. He married 1883? **Marie Bombardier** (Jean-Baptiste Bombardier & Emerentienne/Emerance Campbell) b 1866?, Hudson Falls, NY; d & bur there 9 & 11 Jul 1936 at the age of 70.

3.9.2.2   **MONTY/MONTE, Guillaume/William** b & bp 19 & 20 Feb 1826, Iberville, QC. He married (1) there 12 Jan 1847 **Olive Boucher** (Louis Boucher & Olive Adam) b & bp 28 & 29 Aug 1828, St. Mathias, QC; d & bur 25 & 27 May 1865, Dunham, QC.

      He married (2) 17 Jun 1867, Southbridge, MA, **Hermine St. Martin** (Felix St. Martin & Catherine Lavallee) b & bp 25 Jun 1836, Sorel, QC; m (1) _____ Cursey or Coursey; d 19 Dec 1899, Woonsocket, RI.

      According to his children's baptismal records, Guillaume Monty was a resident of Iberville, QC, in 1848, of Stanbridge, QC, in 1849, and of Iberville again in 1850. He was a farmer in St. Alexandre, QC, between 1853 and 1856 and in Iberville in 1858. He was living in Dunham, QC, at his first wife's death in 1865 but soon moved his family to Southbridge, MA, where Guillaume Monte (sic) was a laborer at his second marriage. His name and surname vary considerably after that. As William Monta he was a laborer in Westborough, MA, in 1870 (US census) though he was named either Guillaume or William Monte or Monty in the records of his children's births and marriages there. The family moved a few years later to neighboring Woonsocket, RI, where William Monty was a laborer in 1880 (US census). His last two children were born there, and some married there. As a result there is a strong presence of that family, under both the Monty and Monte surnames, in both Rhode Island and Massachusetts.

      I know of Hermine St. Martin's first marriage only through the record of her second marriage where she was named Ermine Cursey, daughter of Felix and Catherine Martin. Her maiden name was St. Martin however at the births of her children and at her death.

      It is to be noted that three of the children living in the Monta household in 1870, Louis, Joseph, and Melina Monta, all born in Massachusetts from 1859 to 1863, can not be the children of William Monta. In spite of the surname they were given then, they were most probably the children of Hermine St. Martin and her first husband.

Children of the first marriage:

3.9.2.2.1	Louis	1848-	-1848
3.9.2.2.2	Olive	1849-	-1849
3.9.2.2.3	Guillaume (twin)	1850-	-1854
3.9.2.2.4	John/Jean-Baptiste (twin)	1850-1878?-	
3.9.2.2.5	Joseph	1853-	-1853
3.9.2.2.6	Médérise	1854-1872&1919-1934	
3.9.2.2.7	William/Guillaume	1856-1882-1926	
3.9.2.2.8	Mary Jane	1858-1877-1946	
3.9.2.2.9	Victoire	1862-	-1866
3.9.2.2.10	Julie	1864-1881-1923	

Children of the second marriage:

3.9.2.2.11	Felix Joseph	1868-1898-1940
3.9.2.2.12	William	1869- -1870
3.9.2.2.13	Napoleon	1871?- -
3.9.2.2.14	Zoe	1873-1909-1932
3.9.2.2.15	Frederick	1879-1901&1947-1948

3.9.2.3 **MONTY, Victoire** b & bp 3 & 4 Feb 1828, Iberville, QC; d & bur 13 & 15 Mar 1899, Frelighsburg, QC. She married 7 Feb 1853, Dunham, QC, **Léon Piette** (Pierre Piette & Josephte Bélanger) b 1834?; d & bur 24 & 26 Feb 1866, Dunham, QC, at the age of 32.

Léon Piette was a laborer in Dunham, QC.

Children:
i **Maxime Piette** b & bp 31 Mar & 2 Apr 1853, Dunham, QC. He married there 20 Apr 1874 **Philomène Chaussé** (François Chaussé & Angèle Hêtu) b & bp 16 & 17 Feb 1852, St. Félix de Valois, QC; d & bur 13 & 16 Apr 1896, Frelighsburg, QC.

ii **Joseph Piette** married 24 Nov 1874, Bedford, QC, **Sophie Hébert** (Augustin Hébert & Sophie Bellerose) b & bp 20 & 21 Jun 1857, Dunham, QC.

iii **Léon Piette** b & bp 24 & 26 Aug 1855, Dunham, QC; d & bur 8 & 12 Mar 1921, Frelighsburg, QC. He married 11 May 1874, Dunham, QC, **Delima Alma Godin** (Jules Godin & Angèle Allard) b & bp 3 Aug 1852, Ste Mélanie, QC; d & bur 24 & 28 Jan 1935, Frelighsburg, QC.

iv **Moïse Piette** b & bp 23 Jun 1860, Dunham, QC; d & bur 8 & 11 Feb 1935, Dunham & Frelighsburg, QC. He married 4 Mar 1878, Dunham, QC, **Marie Godin** (Jules Godin & Angèle Allard) b & bp 20 Jul 1854, St. Félix de Valois, QC; d & bur 19 & 21 Oct 1924, Frelighsburg, QC.

v **Marie Piette** b & bp 6 & 14 Jun 1863, Dunham, QC. She married there 12 Aug 1878 **André Hébert** (Augustin Hébert & Sophie Bellerose).

vi **Jean-Baptiste Piette** b & bp 25 & 27 Feb 1866, Dunham, QC. He married there 11 Jun 1883 **Angèle Godin** (Jules Godin & Angèle Allard) b 18 Nov 1863, QC.

3.9.3.1 **MONTY, François Xavier** b & bp 13 & 14 Jul 1818, St. Luc, QC; d & bur there 26 & 28 Dec 1820.

3.9.3.2 **MONTY/MONTIE, Louis** b & bp 23 & 24 Feb 1820, St. Luc, QC; d 13 May 1891, Ecorse, MI. He married 31 Aug 1847, Detroit, MI, **Frances/Françoise Pilon** (Augustin Pilon & Marie Metay) b there 23 Feb 1830; d 1910, Ecorse, MI.

Louis Monty came to the United States with his parents in the mid-1840s and was a farmer in Ecorse, MI, in 1850. He was named Louis Monti then, and Louis Montie in later years. He and his wife had no children but had with them in 1880 an adopted son Simon Peter Drouillard who later married their niece Julia/Judith Montie (3.9.3.5.1) and provided a home for Frances Pilon after her husband's death (US censuses). Louis Montie was buried in St. Francis Xavier Cemetery in Ecorse.

The date of Frances Pilon's death is taken from Christian Denissen, *Genealogy of the French Families of the Detroit River Region, 1701-1936*, II, 855. She was a sister of Peter Pilon, husband of Marie/Mary Monty (3.9.3.4), and of Anthony Pilon, husband of Marie Angèle/Angela Monty (3.9.3.7).

3.9.3.3 **MONTY/MONTIE, Jean-Baptiste/John Baptist** b & bp 14 & 16 Apr 1822, St. Luc, QC; d 28 Jan 1888, Ecorse, MI. He married there 9 Jan 1849 **Emily/Axie Amelia Goodell** (Jonas Goodell & Angelica Saliot) b 15 May 1824, Detroit, MI; d 31 Aug 1916, Ecorse, MI.

Jean-Baptiste Monty came to the United States with his parents in the mid-1840s and was a blacksmith in Ecorse, MI, in 1850 (Jean B. Monti) and 1860 (John B. Monter [sic]). He later became known as John Baptist or John B. Montie and was buried in St. Francis Xavier Cemetery in Ecorse as John B. Montie. His widow, who was living alone in Ecorse in 1900 and 1910, had had ten children of whom nine were alive in 1910 (US censuses).

Children:

3.9.3.3.1	Louisa Angelica (twin)	1849-1870-1926
3.9.3.3.2	Philomene Elizabeth (twin)	1849-1875-1927
3.9.3.3.3	Alexander Francis Xavier	1851- -1935
3.9.3.3.4	Elijah John	1853-1882& -1933
3.9.3.3.5	Richard Anthony	1855-1877-1946
3.9.3.3.6	William Henry	1857-1881-1902
3.9.3.3.7	John Baptist	1859-1887-1934
3.9.3.3.8	Francis Jonas	1861-1885-1923
3.9.3.3.9	Emma Ellen	1863-1887-1952
3.9.3.3.10	Albert L.	1866-1894-1930

3.9.3.4   **MONTY, Marie/Mary** b & bp 22 Apr 1824, Iberville, QC; d 20 Dec 1893, Ecorse, MI. She married there 29 Nov 1856 **Peter Pilon** (Augustin Pilon & Marie Metay) b & bp 23 & 28 Jul 1832, Detroit, MI; m (2) 1894? Elizabeth ____; d 1921, Ecorse, MI.

Peter Pilon (also Pelo, Pelon) was a farm laborer in Ecorse, MI, in 1860 and a laborer there in 1900 when he and his second wife, Elizabeth, had been married for six years. In 1920 he was living in the household of Simon Peter Drouillard, husband of his niece Julia Montie (3.9.3.5.1) (US censuses). The date of his death is taken from Denissen, *Genealogy of the French Families ...*, II, 855.

He was a brother of Frances Pilon, wife of Louis Monty/Montie (3.9.3.2), and of Anthony Pilon, husband of Marie Angèle/Angela/Angeline Monty (3.9.3.7).

3.9.3.5   **MONTY/MONTIE, Abraham/Abram** b & bp 29 Apr & 29 May 1826, Iberville, QC; d 1881, St. Charles, MI. He married (1) **Elizabeth Drouillard** (Jean-Baptiste Drouillard & Elizabeth Lebeau) b & bp 30 Nov & 10 Dec 1811, Detroit, MI; m (1) there 2 Sep 1834 Denis Leblanc (Peter Francis Leblanc & Theresa Bourassa); d there 12 Mar 1860.

He married (2) 1861? **Virginia Lacroix** (Charles Lacroix & Marie Rose Bélanger) b 7 Apr 1840, Ecorse, MI; d & bur there 1 & 4 Jun 1913.

Abraham Monty came to Michigan with his parents in the mid-1840s and was known in turn as Abraham Monti (1850), Abe Monte (1860), and Abram Montie (1870 and 1880). He was a farmer in Ecorse, MI, until the mid-1870s and a laborer in St. Charles, MI, in 1880 (US censuses). His descendants used the Montie surname.

His widow moved to Detroit, MI, after his death and was living there with her sons Anthony and Charles in 1890 (City Directory). Ten years later she was a member of her son Charles' household in Springwells, MI. She had had thirteen children of whom six, Julia, Noah, Anthony, Virginia, Charles, and Matilda, were then still alive. In 1910 she was staying in Detroit with her daughter Virginia Josephine and son-in-law Peter Klasen (US censuses).

There is some question about her place of birth. Some censuses, and even her death record, state that she was born in Canada. Yet her parents were already in Ecorse in 1840. The 1850 census there also indicates that while her 13-year-old brother Charles had been born in Canada, the 9-year-old Virginia and an 8-year-old sister had been born in Michigan. I tend to believe the earliest document in this regard.

Children of the second marriage:

3.9.3.5.1	Julia/Judith	1862-1883-1944
3.9.3.5.2	Elizabeth	1863?-1882-1884
3.9.3.5.3	Louis	1864- -1864
3.9.3.5.4	Cecilia	1866- -1866
3.9.3.5.5	Noah	1868-1888-
3.9.3.5.6	Antoine/Anthony	1870-1892-1959
3.9.3.5.7	Virginia Josephine	1872-1902-
3.9.3.5.8	Charles Peter	1873-1899-
3.9.3.5.9	Francis	1875- -1877

| 3.9.3.5.10 | Augustus | 1877?- | - |
| 3.9.3.5.11 | Matilda | 1881-1905?- | |

3.9.3.6   **MONTY/MONTIE, Antoine** b & bp 11 & 20 Jun 1828, Iberville, QC; d 27 Feb 1894, Ecorse, MI. He married there 28 Jan 1857 **Catherine Bondy/Bondie** (Gabriel Bondy & Catherine Lafoy) b & bp 31 Oct & 8 Nov 1937, Detroit, MI; d 31 Oct 1897, Ecorse, MI.

Antoine Monty came to Michigan with his parents in the mid-1840s and was a farm laborer living with his parents in Ecorse, MI, in 1850. He remained a farmer in Ecorse his entire life and was known in various censuses as Antoine Monti (1850), Monte (1860), and later Montie (1870 and 1880). His descendants continued to use the Montie surname.

He and his wife were buried in St. Francis Xavier Cemetery in Ecorse.

Children:
3.9.3.6.1	Philomene	1859-1890-1893
3.9.3.6.2	Alexander A.	1861-1890-1924
3.9.3.6.3	Joseph	1863-1907-1947
3.9.3.6.4	John A.	1866-1894-1932
3.9.3.6.5	Charles Louis	1868- -1868
3.9.3.6.6	Leonora/Angeline	1870- -1887
3.9.3.6.7	Gabriel	1871-1910-1942
3.9.3.6.8	Peter R.	1875-1901&1908-1918

3.9.3.7   **MONTY, Marie Angèle/Angela/Angeline** b & bp 3 & 4 Aug 1830, Iberville, QC; d & bur 28 & 31 Jan 1916, River Rouge & Ecorse, MI. She married 30 Sep 1856, Ecorse, MI, **Antoine/Anthony Pilon/Pelon** (Augustin Pilon & Marie Metay) b & bp 13 & 14 Jan 1835, Detroit, MI; d 1911, MI.

Marie Angèle Monty (baptismal name) came to the United States with her parents in the mid-1840s. Her name and surname then varied. She was Angel Monti in the 1850 census in Ecorse, MI, Angela Monty at her marriage, and Angeline Pelo or Pelon after her marriage.

Antoine Pilon (baptismal name) was a brother of Frances Pilon, wife of Louis Monty (3.9.3.2), and of Peter Pilon, husband Marie/Mary Monty (3.9.3.4). He was known as Antoine Pilon in the 1850 census in Ecorse, Anthony Pilon at his marriage, Antheno Pelo in 1860, and Antoine Pelong (sic) or Pelon from 1880 through 1910. He was a farmer in Ecorse in 1860 and in Berlin, MI, in 1880, and a resident of Bay City, MI, in 1894. By 1910, he and his wife were living in River Rouge, MI, with their widowed son Antoine Pelon Jr. (US and state censuses). The date of his death is taken from Denissen, *Genealogy of the French Families ...*, II, 856.

Child:
    i   **Antoine Pilon/Pelon** b Jul 1857, Ecorse, MI. He married (1) 1882? **Angeline** ____ b Jun 1866, MI; d between 1900 and 1910.
         He married (2) between 1910 and 1920 **Maggie** ____ b 1871?, MI.

3.9.3.8   **MONTY, Céleste** b & bp 28 & 29 Aug 1832, Iberville, QC; d 4 Jun 1855, Ecorse, MI.

4.3.1.1   **MONTY, Lewis** b 1806?, Clinton Co., NY; d between 1870 and 1880, probably in Chazy, NY. He married a first cousin one removed **Marie Geneviève/Jane Gosselin** (Clément Gosselin & Catherine Monty [4.9]) b & bp 19 & 20 Sep 1804, St. Luc, QC; d 28 Feb 1891, Chazy, NY.

I have no direct proof of Lewis Monty's parentage for his name does not appear in the lists of the descendants of François/Francis Monty which were sworn to in 1856 by Mrs. Barbary Morrison (4.4.5) and John Monty Jr. (4.11.1) (Appendix I). John Monty Jr. refers to him only as the spouse of "Gennie [Gosselin] who married Louis Monty." One obvious reason for the omission could be that Lewis Monty was not a descendant, though I consider that rather improbable: there was no other Monty family in Clinton Co., NY, around the time of his birth. Another, more probable reason could be that his father was still alive in 1856. The father, but not the children, would then appear as a descendant of François/Francis Monty in his relatives' affidavits. On that basis, Christopher Monty (4.3.1) is the only possible father of Lewis Monty: he was the only son or grandson of François/Francis Monty who could have married before 1810 and who was still alive in 1856. Christopher Monty did in fact have two sons born between 1804 and 1810 according to the 1820 census in Chazy, NY. One of these is Christopher (4.3.1.2); the other, unidentified till now, would be Lewis.

Lewis Monty's date of birth is uncertain: it fluctuates between 1804 and 1808 in various records, though he was always said to be a few years younger than his wife. He married a few years before 1830 for in the census of that year in Chazy he and his wife had a son under the age of 5. He was then a farmer whose land adjoined that of Christopher Monty Sr. and remained a farmer in Chazy until at least 1870. He was deceased in June 1880 (US censuses). The name Louis Monti was used in the French records of St. Joseph's Church in Coopersville, NY. John Monty Jr. (4.11.1) had Louis Monty in his affidavit of 3 Nov 1856 (Appendix I). On all other records I have seen he was Lewis Monty.

Marie Geneviève Gosselin came to Beekmantown, NY, with her parents in 1815 and was henceforth known as Jane ("Gennie" in John Monty's affidavit is an exception). She lived in Chazy after her marriage and was still living there in her own home when she was brutally assaulted by a would-be burglar and died as a result of her injuries a few weeks later (*Plattsburgh Sentinel*, 28 Feb 1891 and 6 Mar 1891).

Children:

4.3.1.1.1	Son	1828?- -
4.3.1.1.2	Jane	1832?- -
4.3.1.1.3	Lydia	1838?-1860?-1918
4.3.1.1.4	Joseph	1842?- -
4.3.1.1.5	Sylvia	1843?- -
4.3.1.1.6	William	1846?- -

4.3.1.2   **MONTY, Christopher** b around 1810, Clinton Co., NY. He married **Sophia Auclair** b between 1808 and 1815, QC.

Christopher Monty's birth record has not been found. Various censuses place his birth in Clinton Co., NY, between 1808 and 1812. He may have lived at least temporarily in Canada, near Iberville, QC, where he was a laborer in 1833 according to his son Oliver's baptismal record. He was a farmer in Chazy, NY, in 1840 and in Essex, NY, from 1845 through at least 1855, and a brick mason in Lewis, NY, from 1860 through 1875 (US and state censuses). I have not found him in later censuses. He may have died between 1875 and 1880 when his surviving children were either living independently with their own families or in the household of their unmarried brother William (4.3.11.4).

Sophia (also Sophy, Sophie) Auclair was born in Canada between 1805 and 1815 according to most US and state censuses. She is not listed with her family in the 1875 state census in Lewis, NY, and was probably deceased at that time.

Children:

4.3.1.2.1	Thomas	1830?-	-
4.3.1.2.2	Oliver	1833-	-
4.3.1.2.3	Henry	1839?-1869-	
4.3.1.2.4	William	1840?-	-1897
4.3.1.2.5	Mitchell	1841?-	-
4.3.1.2.6	Sophia	1843-	-1920
4.3.1.2.7	Jane	1845?-	-
4.3.1.2.8	Caroline Adeline/Carrie A.	1848?-1894-1925	
4.3.1.2.9	Jerome	1852?-1878?-	

4.3.1.3   **MONTY, Harriet** b 1827?, Clinton Co., NY; d 24 Apr 1886, Westport,

NY. She married **Julius Blongy/Bélanger** (Julian Bélanger & Mary Labare/Lebert) b 1827?, Chazy, NY; d & bur 15 & 17 Jun 1913, Westport, NY, at the age of 85.

Harriet Monty's year of birth is quite uncertain. She was 23 years old in 1850, 30 in 1860, 40 in 1870, and 53 in 1880 (US censuses). Some say she was 64 years old at her death, thus born around 1822. Unfortunately the inscription on her tombstone in Hillside Cemetery in Westport, NY, is so faint as to be illegible. I would rather rely here on the 1850 census.

The same uncertainty applies to her children's dates of birth and death. My sources, in addition to censuses, are the records of St. Catherine of Sienna Church in Keeseville, NY, transcriptions of Blongy tombstones in Hillside Cemetery in Westport, and a few obituaries in the *Essex County Republican* of Keeseville and in the *Sentinel* of Ticonderoga, NY. Many of these are contradictory so that certainty of any kind is difficult to achieve.

Julius Blongy (also Blungy, Blonge, Belonga, Belongy, etc.) came to Essex Co., NY, around 1847 and remained in the area for the rest of his life, save for the period between 26 Aug 1864 and 5 Jun 1865 when he served in the Union Army as a private in Company E, 2nd New York Cavalry Regiment. He was a farm laborer/farmer in Essex until at least 1865 and a laborer in Willsboro, NY, and Ticonderoga in 1870 and 1880. He lived in his son Charles' household in Westport after his wife's death (US and state censuses) and was buried there in Hillside Cemetery.

The different spellings of the surname noted above are only a few of the many variants encountered. Although Blongy became the standard form of the surname, several of the children were baptized and/or married in Keeseville, NY, as children of Julien or Julian Bélanger. That is undoubtedly the original patronymic: his Canadian grandfather, Julien Bélanger, a veteran of the American Revolution, was one of the early settlers in Clinton Co., NY, and a neighbor of the Montys there.

Children:

i   **Lucy Blongy** b Sep 1847, Essex, NY; d there 2 Apr 1851, at the age of 3 years and 7 months; bur Westport, NY.

ii   **Henry Blongy** b Feb 1850, Essex, NY; d there 31 Mar 1851; bur Westport, NY.

iii   **Mary Blongy** b 1851?, Essex, NY.

iv   **Martha Jane Blongy** b Jan 1852, Essex, NY; bp 22 Sep 1870, Keeseville, NY; d 11 Nov 1883 at the age of 31 years and 10 months; bur 1883, Westport, NY. She married 22 Sep 1870, Keeseville, NY, **Octave Vézina** (Michel Vézina & Angèle Trudelle) b & bp 15 Jun 1852, Quebec, QC.

v   **Joseph Blongy** b 1854, Essex, NY; d between 1855 and 1860.

vi   **Lucy A. Blongy** b 1856?, Essex, NY; bp 22 Sep 1870, Keeseville, NY, at the age of 14; d Dec 1947, Westport, NY. She married 1882? **Fred Wymette/Ouimette** b Jan 1860, NY.

vii   **Charles Howard Blongy** b 1858?, Essex, NY; bp 22 Sep 1870, Keeseville, NY; d 16 May 1936, Rutland, VT; bur 1936, Westport, NY. He married 1890? **Huldah Mary Lobdell** (Richard Lobdell & Eleanor Ann Manning) b Dec 1866, Saranac, NY; d & bur 31 Jan & ? 1935, Westport, NY.

viii   **Pauline A./Polly Blongy** b 15 Aug 1859, Essex, NY; bp 22 Sep 1870, Keeseville, NY; d 4 Aug 1916, Rockingham, VT. She married 1876? **Adolphus Fredette** (Peter/Pierre Fredette & Rose Cross/Rosalie Lacroix) b 16 Apr 1845, Essex, NY; d 19 Deb 1917, Rockingham, VT.

4.3.1.4   **MONTY, John** around 1828, Clinton Co., NY. He married (1) between 1850 and 1855 **Amelia** _____ b 1833?, Canada.

He married (2) **Martha** _____ b 1831?, NY; d & bur 1876, Essex, NY, at the age of 45.

He married (3) 4 Aug 1886, Burlington, VT, **Adeline Primo** m (1) _____ St. Antoine.

There is little that is certain about John Monty and his life. His date of birth is only approximate, based on the 1850 US census in Essex, NY, when he was 22 years old. Five years later, though, he was only 25 years old (state census) while in 1886, at the time of his third marriage, he was said to be 54 years old.

None of his marriages is well documented. According to the 1855 New York State census he had then been a laborer in Essex for ten years and had a 22-year-old wife Amelia. I do not find them in the United States in 1860. They may have lived in Canada for a while for their daughter's marriage record notes that she was born there.

John Monty was a laborer in Westport, NY, in 1870 and had a 9-year-old son born in New York State. His wife Martha was then 37 years old (US census). The inscription on her tombstone in Whallon's Bay Cemetery in Essex reveals only that Martha MONTEY, wife of John, died in 1876 at the age of 45.

I know of John Monty's third wife, Mrs. Adeline (Primo) St. Antoine, only through their marriage record. They were divorced before 1900 when John Monty, a carpenter in Westport, was a boarder in John Goodrow's household (US census)

Child of the first marriage:

4.3.1.4.1	Amelia	1855?-1877-

Child of the second marriage:

4.3.1.4.2	George	1861?- -

4.3.2.1   **MONTY, James** b 1835?, Clinton Co., NY; d May 1898, Essex, NY. He married **Nancy M. ____** b 1837, Clinton Co., NY; d & bur 1885, Essex, NY.

James Monty was 15 years old in 1850. He was then living with his parents in Essex, NY, and remained there as a farmer until his death (US and state censuses). According to the *Ticonderoga Sentinel* of 19 May 1898, he died suddenly of heart disease in the second week of May 1898.

The years of his wife Nancy's birth and death are taken from the inscription on her tombstone in Whallon's Bay Cemetery in Essex.

Child:

4.3.2.1.1	James Jacob	1872-1895?-

4.3.2.2   **MONTY, Lois** b 3 Jun 1836, Clinton Co., NY; d & bur 10 & 22 Jan 1926, Westport & Essex, NY. She married 1860? **Alexander Cross/Alexis Lacroix** (Jean-Baptiste Lacroix & Catherine Thérien) b & bp 11 Jul 1831, Napierville, QC; d & bur 12 & ? Mar 1901, Essex, NY.

Alexander (also Aleck, Alex, Alexis) Cross arrived in the United States as a child around 1836 and was a laborer in Essex Co., NY, for most of his life. He and his wife had been married for forty years in 1900 and had had seven children of whom five were still alive. He was then retired and living in Essex, NY. His widow later made her home with her daughter and son-in-law Lottie and William Benway in Westport, NY (US censuses).

Lois Monty and Alexander Cross were both buried in the Old Burt Cemetery near Essex, as were their sons Gilbert (ii) and James (vii) and their daughter-in-law Lulu Jerdo.

Children:

i   **Warren Oliver Cross** b & bp 14 Aug 1864 & 7 Jun 1866, Essex & Keeseville, NY. He married 1887? **Sarah E. ____** b 1867?, NY.

ii   **Gilbert A. Cross** b & bp 19 Jan & 7 Jun 1866, Essex & Keeseville, NY; d & bur ? & 23 Apr 1884, Willsboro & Essex, NY.

iii   **Elizabeth Cross** b 1868?, Essex Co., NY. She married (1) 14 Aug 1895, Willsboro, NY, **John Ledoux.**
        She married (2) 1901? **____ Edgerly.**

iv   **Henry W. Cross** b & bp Sep & 13 Oct 1869, Willsboro & Keeseville, NY. He married 18 Jan 1893, Willsboro, NY, **Margaret Benway** (Joseph Benway & Edla ___) b Jul 1874, Essex Co., NY.

v   **John Cross** (twin) b & bp 23 May 1872 & 20 Mar 1873, Willsboro & Keeseville, NY.

vi   **Lottie/Charlotte Cross** (twin) b 23 May 1872, Willsboro, NY. She married there 28 Dec 1892 **William Joseph Benway** b 17 Nov 1872, NY.

vii   **James Burton Cross** b 2 Oct 1875, Willsboro, NY; d & bur 5 & 7 Nov 1936, Whallonsburg & Essex, NY. He married 4 Jan 1899, Willsboro, NY, **Lulu Mary Jerdo** (Sorell S. Jerdo & Martina/Martenia Grassett) b 1880, Essex, NY; bur there 1965.

4.3.2.3   **MONTY, Warren** b 1839?, Clinton Co., NY; d & bur 4 & 6 Apr 1871, Keeseville, NY. He married February 1865 (Catholic revalidation, 30 Apr 1866, Keeseville, NY) **Caroline Labarge** (Louis/Lewis Labarge & Maria/Mérence Denis) b 1840?, Essex Co., NY; m (2) 1 Jan 1874, Keeseville, NY, Félix Massé/Mossey/Mossy, widower of Emilie Mathon; d 23 Apr 1891, Willsboro, NY, at the age of 51.

Warren Monty was 11 years old in 1850 when he was living with his parents in Essex, NY (US census) and 23 years old on 8 Aug 1862 when he enlisted in the Union Army, Company F, 118th New York Infantry Regiment. He was made corporal on 23 Nov 1863, became a POW in Fair Oaks, VA, on 27 Oct 1864 (paroled), and was mustered out on 13 Jun 1865 in Richmond, VA. He was a farmer in Essex in 1865 and a laborer there in 1870 (US and state censuses). His veteran's pension (certificate #152375), for which he had applied on 5 Dec 1870, shortly before his death, was transferred to his widow on her application of 15 Jun 1871 (#196939).

Child:
4.3.2.3.1   Nellie A.   1867-1886-1940

4.3.2.4   **MONTY, Harriet** b 1847?, Essex, NY.

Harriet Monty was an 8-year-old child living with her parents in Essex, NY, in 1855. She was still with them there in 1870, at the age of 23 (US and state censuses).

4.3.2.5   **MONTY, Mary/Milly** b 1851?, Essex, NY.

Mary Monty was a 4-year-old child living with her parents in Essex, NY, in 1855. She was also with them there at age 9 in 1860 and at age 13 in 1865 though named Milly Monty (US and state censuses).

4.3.3.1   **MONTY, Katy** married **Joseph W. Clark**.

Katy (Catherine?) Monty, daughter of Matthew Monty, was deceased in November 1856 according to John Monty's (4.11.1) affidavit before the Clinton Co. Court of Common Pleas in Plattsburgh, NY (Appendix I). The names of her husband and children are also found in that document. I know nothing more about the family.

Children:
   I   **Matthew Clark**
   ii   **Cornelius Clark**
   iii   **Eliza Clark**
   iv   **Edward Clark**
   v   **Sophrone Clark**
   vi   **Joseph Clark**
   vii   **Leonard Clark**

4.3.3.2   **MONTY, Ginnie** married ____ **Payne**.

Ginnie (Genevieve?, Jane?) Monty, daughter of Matthew Monty, married a Mr. Payne and was still alive in November 1856 according to John Monty's (4.11.1) affidavit before the Clinton Co. Court of Common Pleas in Plattsburgh, NY (Appendix I). She was not with her parents in the 1850 US census in Beekmantown, NY, and had probably married before then. I know nothing more about her or her husband.

4.3.3.3   **MONTY/MONTE/MONTA, Matthew** b 1 Jan 1824, Beekmantown, NY; d 4 Jun 1883, Pownal, VT. He married around 1845 **Parmelia Bennett** (Josiah C. Bennett & Cyrena/Sirena Estes) b 24 Jan 1830, Pownal, VT; d there 15 Jan 1879.

This entry is tentative. I have no direct evidence that this man was the son of Matthew Monty and Salome Clark. Yet there is a good deal of circumstantial evidence that he was a brother of Abraham Monty (4.3.3.4) who resided in Bennington Co., VT, in the 1840s and early 1850s. Matthew Monta and his son Samuel were also in Stamford, VT, in 1870 when the widowed Mrs. Salome Monta (sic) was also living there in the household of her daughter and son-in-law Amelia (4.3.3.14) and Joseph Reed.

Matthew Monta (also Monte, Montee, Montey) was a carpenter in Pownal, VT, in 1850 and 1860, a farmer living without his wife in Stamford, VT, in 1870, and a laborer in Pownal in 1880 (US censuses). The date and place of his birth are taken from his death record. He died of consumption as did his divorced wife and his two sons.

Parmelia Bennett was a sister of Freelove Amy Bennett, wife of Abraham Monty/Montee (4.3.3.4).

Children:

4.3.3.3.1	Charles Otis	1846-	-1866
4.3.3.3.2	Sylvia Ann	1850-1868-	
4.3.3.3.3	Samuel B.	1855-	-1886

4.3.3.4　　　**MONTY/MONTEE, Abraham** b 16 Sep 1825, Clinton Co., NY; d 16 Feb 1903, Hudson, SD. He married 16 Oct 1845, Pownal, VT, **Freelove Amy Bennett** (Josiah C. Bennett & Cyrena/Sirena Estes) b there 19 Dec 1828; d 17 Mar 1900, Hudson, SD.

Abraham Montee was a wanderer for a large part of his life, as shown by the births of his children in several states as well as by his whereabouts in various censuses. He first moved to Vermont, where his first three children were born, and was a farmer in Bennington, VT, in 1850. During the next decade his children were born in New York and Wisconsin though by 1860 he was a farmer in New Boston, IL. A daughter was born there in 1862. He soon moved again and was a resident of Poweshiek Co., IA, when he enlisted in Iowa City, IA, as Abram Montee on 5 Jan 1864 in Co. B, 28th Iowa Infantry Regiment. He served until 31 Jul 1865 when he was mustered out in Savannah, GA. He then returned to Iowa, where the last three children were born, and was in 1870 a farmer in Washington Twp, IA. His real estate was then valued at a respectable $2,540. He nevertheless moved on again and by 1875 was a farmer in Eden, Dakota Territory. He settled there with his wife and several of his children and purchased 160 acres of farm land on 20 Feb 1877 (South Dakota Land Patents). He was a farmer in Hudson (Eden Twp) in 1880 and remained there until his death (US and Dakota Territory censuses).

The date of Abraham Monty's marriage is usually given as 5 Oct 1846. I have been unable to find a marriage record and am relying on the marriage announcement in the *Vermont Gazette* of Bennington, VT, of 11 Nov 1845: "In Pownal, on the 16th ult. By Sebastian Wagar, esq., Abraham Monty and Freelove Bennett, both of Pownal."

Freelove Bennett was a sister of Parmelia Bennett, wife of Matthew Monta (4.3.3.3).

Children:

4.3.3.4.1	Melvin Josiah	1846?-1868-1894/95
4.3.3.4.2	Clara/Clarissa	1848?-1862?&1879-1930
4.3.3.4.3	Moses Paige	1849?- -
4.3.3.4.4	Eunice Clarinda	1853-1870-1881
4.3.3.4.5	Thirza	1855-1873?-
4.3.3.4.6	Matthew Perry	1856-1891-1919
4.3.3.4.7	Mary Jane	1859?- -
4.3.3.4.8	Ella May/Nellie	1862-1883-1922
4.3.3.4.9	Austie Emma	1866-1885-1939
4.3.3.4.10	Florence Jeanette	1868-1885&1902?-1953
4.3.3.4.11	Margaret Elinor Anna	1869?-1884-

4.3.3.5　　　**MONTY, Jane Ann** b 1826?, Chazy, NY; d 3 Jul 1905, Sterling Junction, MA. She married a second cousin **Louis/Lewis Alexandre Lezotte/Leazott** (Louis Lizotte

[4.7.ii] & Miranda Clark) b 1822?, Chazy, NY; d 29 Aug 1884, Nashua, NH, at the age of 62.

Jane Ann Monty (also Jane, Jane A.) was named Geneviève Monty when five of her children were baptized in 1854 in the French Catholic church in Coopersville, NY. Her surname, which is generally Monty in New York State, is occasionally Montee in New Hampshire. Her husband's name alternates between Louis A. and Lewis A. while his surname varies with time, from Lizotte, Lezott, and Lezotte in New York State to Leazott and Leazotte in New Hampshire. His obituary in the *Plattsburgh Sentinel* of 2 Sep 1884 is in the name of Lewis Leazott while his brother Calvin, husband of Hannah Monty (4.11.5), used the surname Lezott.

Louis Lezott was a farmer in Chazy, NY, in 1850, when his wife was 24 years old, and until at least 1870 (US censuses). He moved with his family to Nashua, NH, in the early 1870s and, according to the marriage records of his sons William, George, and Joseph, was a laborer there in 1872, a teamster in 1874, and a laborer again in 1882. He was a jobber in 1880 (US census). All but one of his fourteen children survived him (*Plattsburgh Sentinel*, 2 Sep 1884).

Jane Ann Monty remained in Nashua for several years after her husband's death and was still a resident there in October 1897 at her son Bert's (xiii) second marriage. I have not found her there in the 1900 census. She may have moved to Massachusetts before then.

Children:

i   **Melvin James Lizotte/Lezotte** (twin) b & bp 22 Sep 1848 & 7 Jan 1854, Chazy & Coopersville, NY.

ii   **Melvina Jeanne Lizotte/Lezotte** (twin) b & bp 22 Sep 1848 & 7 Jan 1854, Chazy & Coopersville, NY.

iii   **Joseph Lezotte/Leazott/Leazotte** b & bp 4 Apr 1850 & 7 Jan 1854, Chazy & Coopersville, NY. He married (1) 1868? **Amelia Feriole** (Alexander Feriole & Mary ____) b 1846?, Chazy, NY; d between 1880 and 1882, Nashua, NH.

He married (2) 18 May 1882, Nashua, NH, **Margaret O'Harrin** (Thomas O'Harrin & Johanna ____) b Jan 1860, Ireland; d between 1910 and 1920, Nashua, NH.

iv   **William W. Lezotte/Leazott/Leazote** b & bp 1851? & 7 Jan 1854, Chazy & Coopersville, NY; d between 1900 and 1913, Nashua, NH. He married there 11 Oct 1872 **Delphine Blow** (Antoine Blow & Olive Messot) b Apr 1853, Altona, NY.

v   **Sophie Lezotte** b & bp 1851? & 7 Jan 1854, Chazy & Coopersville, NY.

vi   **George Willis Lezotte/Leazotte** b 14 Apr 1853, Chazy, NY; d 6 Dec 1941, Puyallup, WA. He married (1) 8 Feb 1874, Nashua, NH, **Lorancy Lavoneray** (Charles Lavoneray & Jane Putnam) b 1856?, Altona, NY; d around 1895, MN.

He married (2) 1896?, Staples, MN, **Sarah Belle Van Patten** (Nicholas Van Patten & Nancy Elizabeth ____) b 1872?, Mitchell Co., IA; d 12 Aug 1943, Puyallup, WA', at the age of 71.

vii   **Julius Lezotte** b 1855?, Chazy, NY.

viii   **Susan S. Lezotte** b 7 Mar 1856, Chazy, NY; d 5 Mar 1928, Weare, NH. She married 1878?, NH, **Orvis P. Philbrick** (David Philbrick & Martha Patience Stearns) b 28 Aug 1847, Barton, VT; m (1) Eliza Melvina Cowdrey; d 20 Nov 1914, Weare, NH.

ix   **Ada A. Lezotte** b Dec 1859, Chazy, NY.

x   **Anna S. Lezotte** b 1862?, Chazy, NY.

xi   **Virginia/Jennie R. Lezotte/Leazotte** b 1863?, Chazy, NY. She married 11 Dec 1882, Nashua, NH, a third cousin, **George Lizotte** (Joseph Lizotte & Susan Lebert) b 1857?, Altona, NY.

xii   **Matthew Leazotte** b Apr 1865, Chazy, NY. He married 11 Nov 1887, Nashua, NH, **Jennie Gerbruck** (Isaac Gerbruck & ____) b Oct 1865, Canada.

xiii   **Bert L./Albert Leazotte** b 1867? Chazy, NY. He married (1) 12 Sep 1894, Hudson, NH, **Sarah Sharbono/Charbonneau** (Frank Sharbono/Charbonneau & Margaret ____) b 1873?, Sciota, NY.

He was a widower when he married (2) 5 Oct 1897, Nashua, NH, **Mary Lary**

(George Lary & Julia ____) b 1868? Petersville, New Brunswick; m (1) and divorced ____ Howe.

xiv   **Victor Leonard Leazott/Leazotte** b Mar 1870, Chazy, NY; d 15 Jan 1946, Fitchburg, MA. He married 14 Mar 1893, Nashua, NH, **Nellie G. McSorley** b 1871?, New Brunswick, Canada.

He married (2) 1896? **Lena M. Henry** (John Henry & Charlotte Smith) b Feb 1875, St. George, New Brunswick, Canada; m (1) George Reynolds; d 5 Mar 1915, Fitchburg, MA.

He married (3) 23 Dec 1915, Fitchburg, MA, **Ethel M. Sidebottom**.

He married (4) around 1927 **Lillian Cummings** b 1886?, MA; m (1) 1907? ____ Washburn.

4.3.3.6   **MONTY, Polly/Mary** b 1827?, Beekmantown, NY; d 9 Nov 1859, Lincoln, VT. She married 31 Mar 1847, Essex, NY, **Eli Willard Benway** b 25 Apr 1825, Lincoln, VT; m (2) 20 Jun 1865 Mary Jane Colt; d 15 Oct 1897, Independence, KS.

Mary Monta, wife of Eli Benway, was buried in the Monkton, VT, Cemetery. She was named Polly Monty at her marriage as well as in the November 1856 affidavit of John Monty Jr. (4.11.1) (Appendix I), though Mary Benway when she was living with her husband and two children in Essex, NY, in 1850. She was named Charlotte Monty, though, in the biographical sketch of her son Eli James Benway in Theodore M. Stuart's *Past and Present of Lucas and Wayne Counties, Iowa* , II, 270-271. I believe that to be simply an error. There is no evidence that she was named Charlotte or Lottie in her lifetime, and there is no evidence of any Charlotte or Lottie Monty marrying an Eli Benway.

Eli Benway was a blacksmith in Essex, NY, for about ten years after his marriage before moving to Vermont around 1858. He was a resident of Northfield, VT, when he enlisted as a private in Co. F, 12th Vermont Infantry Regiment on 20 Aug 1862. He received a disability discharge on 20 Jan 1863 but reenlisted on 23 Jul 1864 in Co B, 1st Heavy Artillery Regiment from which he was mustered out on 25 Aug 1865. He soon left Vermont for the first child of his second marriage was born in Illinois in 1868. He was a farmer and blacksmith in Mason City, IL, in 1870 and a blacksmith in Independence, KS, in 1880 (US censuses). The List of Pensioners on the rolls of Montgomery Co., KS, in 1883 shows that he was a receiving a veteran's disability pension of $18 per month.

Children:
i   **Eli James Benway** b 1 Jan 1848, Essex, NY. He married 24 Dec 1868, Mason City, IL, **Maria Richman** (Bryan Richman & Ann Colby) b 7 Dec 1850, Peoria, IL.
ii   **John Benway** b 1849?, Essex, NY.
iii   **Henry C. Benway** b Aug 1851, Essex, NY. He married 2 Oct 1876, Mason City, IL, **Nina Blatchley** (George Blatchley & Delilah Green) b Sep 1853, IL.

4.3.3.7   **MONTY, Eunice**

Eunice Monty was alive in 1856 according to the testimony of John Monty Jr. (4.11.1) (Appendix I). She was not living in her father's household in Beekmantown, NY, in 1850 (US census) and may have left home or married before then.

4.3.3.8   **MONTY, Matilda** b 1829?, Beekmantown, NY.

Matilda Monty was 21 years old in 1850 when she was living with her parents in Beekmantown, NY (US census). She was still alive in 1856 according to the testimony of John Monty Jr. (4.11.1) (Appendix I).

4.3.3.9   **MONTY, Henry** b 1833?, Beekmantown, NY.

Henry Monty was a 17-year-old child living with his parents in Beekmantown, NY, in 1850 (US census) and was still alive in 1856 according to the testimony of John Monty Jr. (4.11.1) (Appendix I).

He is not found in later years in New York State and may well be the Henry/W. Henry/Henry William Monte/Montey, born in New York State between 1832 and 1839, who lived in Racine Co., WI, from at least 1870. He had married Adeline Gonyou or Ganyou in 1860 in West Chazy, NY, and had twelve children of whom ten are known: William, Walter, and Frank who were born in the 1860s either in New York State or in Wisconsin, and Mina/Minnie, Matthew, Eugene, Aaron Henry, Clarence, Hattie, and Anna, all born in Wisconsin in the 1870s and early 1880s. There are numerous records of his presence in Wisconsin. They give no clue however as to his parents or siblings and do not provide enough solid information to identify him as the son of Matthew Monty.

4.3.3.10   **MONTY/MONTA, David Wright** b Sep 1834, Beekmantown, NY; d 1 Feb 1912, Forsyth, MT. He married 7 Jul 1855, Williamstown, MA, **Mary Eliza Reed** (Horace Reed & Susan ____) b there Mar 1840; d 7 Sep 1913, Forsyth, MT.

David Monty led a rather nomadic existence in his early years. He lived with his parents in Beekmantown, NY, until at least 1850 and then moved to Williamstown, MA, where he was a laborer at his marriage. His first child was born in Canada in 1858 but died two years later in Bennington, VT, where her father was a laborer. He was a farmer in Williamstown on 11 Oct 1861 when, as David W. Monta, he enlisted as a private in Co. H, 27th Massachusetts Infantry Regiment. Two of his children were born there in 1863 and 1865 and another four in Sugar Grove, IA, where he was a farm laborer from 1870 through 1875. Then on to Minnesota where, on 15 May 1877, David W. Monta was given title to an 80-acre homestead (Minnesota Land Records, New Ulm office, Doc. #2721). He did not remain there long, for his last child was born in Wisconsin in 1878.

There the family settled for the next twenty-seven years. David Monta was a carpenter in Pewaukee, WI, in 1880 and was retired in 1900, living with his wife and a 9-year-old grandson Harry Griffith (parents still unidentified) in Superior, WI. He was a laborer in Genesee, WI, in 1905, but was staying on his son Frank's ranch in Forsyth, MT, in 1910, when six of his ten children were still alive (US and state censuses). He and his wife were both buried in the Forsyth Cemetery.

The dates on David W. Monta's tombstone, 1837-1912, reflect the data in his death record: he was 75 years old at his death. I believe that is wrong. He was 15 years old in June 1850 and was born in either late 1834 or early 1835 according to all subsequent censuses, including that of 1910. The month and year of birth I am using are taken from the 1900 census.

Children:

4.3.3.10.1	Susan	1858- -1860
4.3.3.10.2	David Edward	1863-1885?-
4.3.3.10.3	Allen Elsworth	1865-1886-1944
4.3.3.10.4	Eva L.	1870- -
4.3.3.10.5	Frank H.	1872-1903?&1913?-
4.3.3.10.6	Carrie (twin)	1875?- -
4.3.3.10.7	Cora (twin)	1875?- -
4.3.3.10.8	Frederick Otic	1878-1899-

4.3.3.11   **MONTY, Hepsabeth** b 1837?, Beekmantown, NY; d between 1910 and 1920, Williamstown, MA. She married (1) around 1858 ____ **Humphrey.**

She married (2) 1865? **James Franklin Holgate/Hulgate** b 1842?, NY; d May 1923, Williamstown, MA, at the age of 81.

Hepsabeth Monty was 13 years old in 1850 when she was living with her parents in Beekmantown, NY. Later censuses would have her born in 1838 or 1839, though she was generally three years older than her second husband. Her first husband is known only through the presence of his children Ida (i) and Charles (ii) Humphrey in their stepfather's household in Chazy, NY, 1870 (US census). Their mother had married between November 1856 when she was still single (Appendix I) and 1859 when her daughter Ida was born.

She married a second time around 1865 for she and James Holgate had been married for thirty-five years in 1900. His name and surname varied somewhat over the years. His surname was Hulgate in New York State but Holgate in Massachusetts. His name was either Franklin or Frank until 1880 but James or James Franklin after that time. He had enlisted in the Union Army as Frank Hulgate at age 21 on 25 Jul 1862 and served in Co. B, 118th New York Infantry Regiment until his discharge on 18 May 1865 in Albany, NY. He was a sawyer in Chazy in 1870, a shoemaker in Tewksbury, MA, in 1880, and a sawyer in Williamstown, MA, in 1900 and later years. He was a widower there in 1920 (US censuses). An item in the *North Adams Transcript* of 18 May 1948 recalled his death in Williamstown "25 Years Ago."

Children:
  i   **Ida Humphrey** b 1859?, WI.
  ii   **Charles H. Humphrey** b Jan 1861, NY. He married 15 May 1887, Williamstown, MA, **Annie ____** b Jul 1861, Ireland.
  iii **Cora May Holgate** b 1869?, Chazy, NY.
  iv **George William Holgate** b 11 Oct 1876, MA.
  v   **Frances Myrtle Holgate** b Jul 1879, Tewksbury, MA.

4.3.3.12   **MONTY, Charles Allen** b 11 Oct 1841, Beekmantown, NY; d 15 Oct 1891, Billerica, MA. He married 3 Jul 1860, Kenosha, WI, **Minerva Jane Berry/Barry** (Henry Barry & Sarah ____) b Sep 1842, Lockport, IL; d 19 Jan 1914, Lowell, MA.

Charles Allen Monty left New York State for the Midwest in the late 1850s and was a blacksmith in Racine, WI, at his marriage under the name of Allen Monty. All his children though were born in the East, his first in New York State, the second in Montreal, QC, and a third in DePeyster, NY, where Charles Monty was a shoemaker in 1870. He moved to Massachusetts a few years later: one daughter married in Lawrence, MA, in 1878 and Charles A. Monty was a shoemaker in Billerica, MA, in 1880. His widow remained there until at least 1900 when three of her six children were still alive (US censuses). In 1902, though, she was living in West Boylston, MA (City Directory) and in 1910 was a servant in a private family in Sterling, MA (US census).

The Kenosha Co., WI, Marriage Register refers to Allen Monty's bride as Minerva Barry, daughter of Henry and Sarah Barrah (sic). All other references I have seen say Berry.

Children:
4.3.3.12.1	Mary	1861?-1878-
4.3.3.12.2	Marguerite Mathilde	1867-1881&1894-1934
4.3.3.12.3	Charles Allen	1869-1887&1890-1939
4.3.3.12.4	Abigail	1871?- -
4.3.3.12.5	Florence Edith	1881-1898?-

4.3.3.13   **MONTY, Melvin J.** b 1842?, Beekmantown, NY; d between 1900 and 1910, Charlevoix, MI. He married (1) around 1866 **Emily Jane Richardson** (Asa Richardson & Susan Piper) b 1835?, Chazy, NY; d 2 May 1877, Elk Rapids, MI, at the age of 42.

He married (2) 27 Feb 1886, Charlevoix, MI, **Eliza A. Kerry** b Oct 1844, England.

Melvin Monty was an 8-year-old child living with his parents in Beekmantown, NY, in 1850 and was 19 years old when he enlisted on 15 May 1861 in Plattsburgh, NY, as a private in Co. K, 16th New York Infantry Regiment. After the war he and his wife apparently lived for a time in Massachusetts where a child was born in 1867. In June 1870 however Melvin Montee (sic) was a sawmill worker staying with his wife Emily and son Walter in the household of his brother-in-law Amos Richardson in Banks Twp, MI. A month later, at the birth of his daughter Louise, he was a farmer in Norwood, MI. He soon moved on: he was a laborer in Elk Rapids, MI, at the birth of his son William in 1877, a lumberman boarding with the Westgate family in Jordan, MI, in 1880, an engineer in Charlevoix, MI, at his second marriage, and a day laborer there in 1900. His widow Eliza was still living there in 1910 (US censuses).

There is some uncertainty about Emily Jane Richardson's dates of birth and death. I am using here the information found in the Antrim Co., MI, Death Records: she died in childbirth on 2 May 1877 at the age of 42. The inscription on her tombstone in the Norwood Cemetery however indicates that she died on 1 May 1877 at the age of 39 years, 10 months, and 1 day.

The censuses of 1900 and 1910 present another problem. In 1910 Mrs. Eliza Monty, who was then living with a 13-year-old adopted daughter, Katherine, indicated that, while she had been married only once, she had had two children, both of whom were still alive. In 1900, however she had stated that she had never had any children. Thus the 14-year-old Nellie who was then living in her father's household cannot be Eliza's daughter. Neither can she be the daughter of Emily Richardson who had died in 1877. I believe that the reference to Eliza Kerry's children in 1910 is to two adopted daughters, Nellie and Katherine.

Children of the first marriage:

4.3.3.13.1	Walter Sidney	1867-1895?-
4.3.3.13.2	Louise/Minnie	1870-1891&1904?-
4.3.3.13.3	William	1877- -

4.3.3.14   **MONTY, Amelia** b 14 Aug 1847, Beekmantown, NY; d 8 Jan 1916, Williamstown, MA. She married around 1864 **Joseph Reed** (William Reed & Betsey ____) b Oct 1846, Williamstown, MA; d 15 Nov 1921, Brooklyn, NY.

Joseph Reed and his wife lived in Bennington Co., VT, for several years after their marriage. He was a laborer in Stamford, VT, in 1870 when his household included his mother-in-law Mrs. Salome Monta (sic). He returned to Williamstown, MA, a few years later and was a farm laborer/farmer there in 1880 and later years. By 1910 he and his wife had had fourteen children of whom eight were then still alive (US censuses). They were both buried in Eastlawn Cemetery in Williamstown.

Children:

i   **Frank/Fred? Reed** b 1864?, VT.

ii   **Nettie G. Reed** b 11 Feb 1867, VT; d 22 Dec 1943, Hillsdale, NY. She married 1882? **Florian A. Bills** (Alexander Bills & Mary Demanche) b Mar 1859, Alsace-Lorraine, France; d 1921, Hillsdale, NY.

iii   **Minnie Reed** b 1869?, VT.

iv   **Lillian/Lillie Reed** b Oct 1870, VT. She married 1887? **Charles Morgan** b Sep 1859, VT.

v   **William Reed** b 1875?, Williamstown, MA; d there 9 Jan 1897.

vi   **Joseph Reed** b 1877?, Williamstown, MA.

vii   **Bessie M. Reed** b 11 Nov 1879, Williamstown, MA.

viii   **Walter Reed** b Mar 1882, Williamstown, MA.

ix   **Gracie Reed** b 13 Feb 1884, Topsfield, MA.

x   **Donald Reed** b 14 June 1886, Williamstown, MA. He married **Alice** ___ b 1884?, VT.

xi   **Jessie Reed** b Jun 1890, Williamstown, MA.

xii   **Loula Reed** b Mar 1892, Williamstown, MA.

4.4.1.1   **MONTY, Elizabeth** b Sep 1802, Clinton Co., NY; d 4 Jan 1892, Plattsburgh, NY, at the age of 89 years and 4 months. She married before 1820 **Eli Prindle** b 1773?, CT; d 10 Jul 1862, Plattsburgh, NY, at the age of 89.

The marriage of Elizabeth Monty and Eli Prindle is mentioned in the 1856 affidavit of Mrs. Barbary (Monty) Morrison (4.4.5) in the Court of Common Pleas in Plattsburgh, NY (Appendix I). Their dates of birth and death are taken from the inscriptions on their tombstones in Riverside Cemetery in Plattsburgh. His date of birth may only approximate. In none of the early US censuses is it said that Eli Prindle was born before 1775 (generally born after 1780). He also claimed to be 80 years old in 1860, just two years before his death. One thing remains constant: he was generally 20 or more years older than his wife who was born in the first decade of the nineteen century.

Eli Prindle was a soldier in the War of 1812 during the Battle of Plattsburgh (1814) and was allowed $50.00 on his claim for compensation (New York Military Equipment Claims, War of 1812, #4,878). He was an agricultural worker or laborer in Plattsburgh from at least 1820 on. By 1840, he and his wife had had at least one son and four daughters, in addition to Abram (i), known only through the inscription on his tombstone in Riverside Cemetery. My list of children is thus incomplete. Only Permelia, Harriet, and John were living in their father's household in 1850, and only John and the newly married Harriet in 1860 (US censuses).

Children:

i **Abram Prindle** b Nov 1825, Plattsburgh, NY; d there 21 Apr 1827 at the age of 1 year and 5 months.

ii **Permelia Prindle** b 1838?, Plattsburgh, NY.

iii **Harriet Prindle** b 1842?, Plattsburgh, NY. She married 1859/1860 **John Mitchell** b 1839?, NY.

iv **John Prindle** b 1844?, Plattsburgh, NY; d 18 Dec 1890, Glover, VT, at the age of 46. He married **Carrie** ____ b Jun 1853, VT.

4.4.1.2   **MONTY, Abraham** b 5 May 1808, Plattsburgh, NY; d there 5 Aug 1852. He married **Harriet Wait** (Daniel Wait & Polly Cogswell) b 29 Dec 1810, Plattsburgh, NY; d there 14 Dec 1852.

Abraham Monty was a teamster in Plattsburgh, NY, in 1850 (US census). Much of what I know concerning his immediate family is derived from a late 19th-century list of family members which was found in 1979 in a Bible once belonging to his granddaughter Mary Elizabeth Monty (4.4.1.2.2.4). This lady's grandson, Mr. Robert Leland Smith of San Antonio, TX, in turn made the document available to Mrs. Betty Ramsey who reproduced it in her *Monty-Montee History*. It is invaluable in providing precise dates of birth and deaths (up to 1885) for Abraham Monty, his wife, and their children. It both confirms and expands the basic list in Mrs. Barbary Morrison's affidavit of October 1856 (Appendix I).

Children:

4.4.1.2.1	Henry	1825- -1852
4.4.1.2.2	John C.	1827-1853&1870?-1892
4.4.1.2.3	Adam Wait	1829- -1829
4.4.1.2.4	Charles S.	1830- -1887
4.4.1.2.5	Mary Ann	1832- -
4.4.1.2.6	George	1834- -
4.4.1.2.7	Abraham B.	1836- -
4.4.1.2.8	Harriet	1838- -1841
4.4.1.2.9	Daniel M.	1840-1865&1886-1896
4.4.1.2.10	Laura A.	1842-1863-
4.4.1.2.11	Harriet/Hattie E.	1844-1867-1902
4.4.1.2.12	Benjamin K.	1846-1864-1885

4.4.1.3   **MONTY, Margaret** b 1811?, NY; d 15 Sep 1882, Plattsburgh, NY. She married (1) a first cousin once removed **Benjamin Monty** (4.5.6) (Amable/Abraham Monty & Barbary ____) b 9 Apr 1807, Clinton Co., NY; d 11 Jun 1828, Plattsburgh, NY, at the age of 21 years, 2 months, and 2 days.

She married (2) 1836 **Nehemiah Marvin** (Seth Marvin & Sarah/Susan Gilcrease) b 19 May 1809, Walpole, NH; d 18 May 1875, Plattsburgh, NY.

Margaret Monty's age varies somewhat from census to census. She was 39 in 1850 and 49 in 1860 but only 56 in 1870. I believe the earlier censuses may be more trustworthy. The notice of her death in the *Plattsburgh Sentinel* of September 1882 however would place her birth even earlier: she was said to be 73 years old at her death.

Benjamin Monty was buried in Riverside Cemetery in Plattsburgh, NY. I know of his marriage only through the 1856 affidavit of Mrs. Barbary Morrison (4.4.5) (Appendix I).

Nehemiah Marvin was a carpenter in Plattsburgh (US censuses).

Children of the second marriage:

i **William Henry Marvin** b 12 Oct 1838, Plattsburgh, NY; d 1860?, Burlington, Vt.

ii **Hannah Marvin** b 16 Apr 1841, Plattsburgh, NY; d before 1850.

iii **John Adams Marvin** b 5 Dec 1843, Plattsburgh, NY; d before 1850.

iv **George Henry Marvin** b 14 Jul 1845, Plattsburgh, NY; d 2 Apr 1882, Hardwick,

VT. He married 3 Aug 1872 **Emma J. Sternberg** b 1857?, NY.

v   **Susan Johanna Marvin** b 20 Nov 1847, Plattsburgh, NY.

vi **John Nehemiah Marvin** b 7 Sep 1850, Plattsburgh, NY. He married 2 Feb 1876, Clinton Co., NY, **Sarah Gertrude Shepherd** (William Shepherd & Luthera Daggett) b Dec 1852, Champlain, NY.

4.4.1.4   **MONTY, Francis/Frank** b 22 Mar 1814, NY; d 14 Jan 1906, St. Charles, MN. He married (1) around 1835 **Louisa ____** b 22 Aug 1814, NY; d 13 Sep 1872, St. Charles, MN, at the age of 58 years and 22 days.

He married (2) 1874?, **Mary ____** b Dec 1825, NY.

Francis Monty was a grocer in Mooers, NY, in 1850 but soon left for Minnesota where he settled with his first wife and children in Olmsted Co. in 1856 (Joseph A. Leonard, *History of Olmsted County, Minnesota*, p. 420). He bought three lots of land near St. Charles, MN, on 1 Aug 1859 (Minnesota Land Record, Winona Office) and became a farmer there. He and his second wife had been married for twenty-six years in 1900 (US censuses).

The dates of Francis Monty's birth and death and those of his wife Louisa are taken from the records of Hillside Cemetery in St. Charles, MN.

Children of the first marriage:

4.4.1.4.1	Mary	1836?- -
4.4.1.4.2	Eliza	1838-1854-1923
4.4.1.4.3	Hannah (twin)	1844- -
4.4.1.4.4	William Henry (twin)	1844-1876-1911

4.4.1.5   **MONTY, Lucina** b 1816?, NY. She married **Peleg Tabor Stafford** (Rowland Stafford & Phebe Tabor) b 21 Aug 1799, Plattsburgh, NY; m (1) 25 Nov 1818 Lillie/Lillis Purse; d 28 Feb 1861, Plattsburgh, NY, at the age of 61 years, 6 months, and seven days.

This woman is often named Lucinda. The three contemporary documents I have seen: the 1850 and 1860 censuses in Plattsburgh, NY, and the 1856 affidavit of her aunt Mrs. Barbary (Monty) Morrison (4.4.5) all show that her name was Lucina. The year of her birth is uncertain however: she was 34 in 1850 though only 42 in 1860 (US censuses). I have been unable to find her in later years.

Peleg Stafford was a pattern maker in Plattsburgh in 1850 and a machinist there in 1860 (US censuses). He was buried in the Stafford Cemetery in Beekmantown, NY, along with his parents, his first wife Lillis, two children of his first marriage, and numerous relatives.

Children:

i   **James Pierce Stafford** b 21 Jun 1840, Plattsburgh, NY; d 1921, East Burke, VT. He married 1861? **Mary Jane Emerson** (Samuel Emerson & Lettie McGregor) b 20 Jun 1840, Hemmingford, QC; d 1927, East Burke, VT.

ii   **Melissa Jane Stafford** b 1 Jun 1842, Plattsburgh, NY.

iii **William Stafford** b 8 Apr 1844, Plattsburgh, NY.

iv   **Adelaide/Adeline Stafford** b 7 Jul 1846, Plattsburgh, NY.

v   **Charles Stafford** b 12 Dec 1849, Plattsburgh, NY.

vi   **Eliza Stafford** b 1851?, Plattsburgh, NY.

vii **Mary Stafford** b 30 Sep 1854, Plattsburgh, NY.

viii **Helen Elizabeth Stafford** b 13 Sep 1856, Plattsburgh, NY.

ix   **Robert Stafford** b 2 May 1858, Plattsburgh, NY.

4.4.2.1   **MONTY, John/Jonas** b 1818?, Clinton Co., NY; d between 1870 and 1880. He married **Marie Louise Ménard** (Joseph Ménard & Marie Louise Lussier) b & bp 17 & 18 May 1824, Laprairie, QC; m (2) after 1880 Charles Dupee; d 5 Feb 1900, Cadyville, NY.

John Monty (or Jonas as he was called in several US and state censuses) was a laborer in Clinton Co., NY, at the births of his first two children, in Essex, NY, from 1845 until at least 1859, and in Franklin, NY, in 1860. By 1870 he was a farmer in West Plattsburgh, NY. All of these censuses point to 1818 as the year of his birth.

His widow was still living in Plattsburgh as Mrs. Mariell Monty in 1880 (US census). I know of her second marriage only through her obituary in the *Plattsburgh Sentinel* of 16 Feb 1900. That item also includes a list of her six surviving children: Mary Louise, Julia, Amelia, Henry, William, and Ella. It does not mention Charles Henry (4.4.2.1.10) whom I have nevertheless included since he was identified at his second marriage as the son of Jonas Monty and Mary Louise Miner (sic). Yet questions remain. See my discussion at 4.4.2.1.10.

4.4.2.1.1	Mary Louise	1842-1860?-1914
4.4.2.1.2	Julia A.	1844-1866?-
4.4.2.1.3	Joseph	1846- -1865
4.4.2.1.4	Amelia	1848?-1867?-1911
4.4.2.1.5	Henry	1851-1869?&1908?-1932
4.4.2.1.6	William	1854?- -
4.4.2.1.7	George	1854- -
4.4.2.1.8	Edward	1856-1878?-
4.4.2.1.9	Francis	1857?- -
4.4.2.1.10	Charles Henry	1858?- &1924-1931
4.4.2.1.11	William	1859-1879?-
4.4.2.1.12	Ella	1862-1881?&1897?-1927

4.4.2.2   **MONTY, Joseph**
Joseph Monty was alive in 1856, according to the testimony of his aunt Mrs. Barbary (Monty) Morrison (4.4.5) (Appendix I).

4.4.2.3   **MONTY, Andrew**
Andrew Monty was alive in 1856, according to the testimony of his aunt Mrs. Barbary (Monty) Morrison (4.4.5) (Appendix I).

4.4.3.1   **MONTY, Mary** b 1817?, Clinton Co., NY; d 9 May 1886, Plattsburgh, NY, at the age of 69. She married **James Griffin** b 9 Jan 1815, Plattsburgh, NY; d & bur there 20 & 22 Dec 1889.

James Griffin was a lifelong resident of Plattsburgh, NY. He was a grocer there until at least 1860 and a saloon keeper in later years (US censuses). He was survived by his three daughters (*Plattsburgh Sentinel*, 27 Dec 1889).

Children:
i   **Ellen Griffin** b 1837?, Plattsburgh, NY. She married **Charles Howland** b 1823?, VT.
ii   **Henry Griffin** b 1844?, Plattsburgh, NY; d there 8 Jul 1882. He married 1865? **Mary ____** b 1847?, NY.
iii **Eliza Griffin** b 1846?, Plattsburgh, NY. She married around 1867 **Giles Morrill** (Harmon Morrill & Olive ____) b 1844?, Plattsburgh, NY; d there 12 Dec 1874.
iv   **Albertine Griffin** b Mar 1848, Plattsburgh, NY; d 5 Dec 1934, NY. She married 1868? **John Morrill** (Harmon Morrill & Olive ____) b May 1845, Plattsburgh, NY; d 23 Oct 1923, Poughkeepsie, NY.
v   **Andrew Griffin** b 1853?, Plattsburgh, NY; d there 4 Dec 1876, at the age of 26.

4.4.3.2   **MONTY, Julia** b 1821?, Plattsburgh, NY; d there 3 Feb 1891. She married 1836? **Paul Montville** b 1814?, Canada; d probably Fall/Winter 1913, Plattsburgh, NY.

Julia Monty's year of birth is uncertain. She was born around 1821 according to the 1850, 1860, and 1870 censuses in Plattsburgh, NY, where she was living with her husband and children. Yet the report of her death in the *Plattsburgh Sentinel* of 6 Feb 1891 states that she died at the age of 73, which would place her birth in 1818. It is possible, though I prefer to rely here on the earlier reports of her age.

Paul Montville was 26 years old when he was naturalized in Plattsburgh on 6 Oct 1840. He was a teamster, laborer, or truck man there until he retired to live with his sons James (xiii) and Paul (xii) in 1900 and 1910 (US censuses). The year of his birth varies considerably from census to census, ranging from 1811 to 1818. I am using the date derived from his 1840 naturalization papers, which may be the most reliable. I have found no death, burial record, or even an obituary in the *Plattsburgh Sentinel* which had nonetheless reported on 15 Aug 1913 that "Paul Montville, sr. [was] seriously ill at the home of his son" and that there was "no hope of his recovery." On 19 Jun 1919 the *Sentinel* also recalled that the centenarian Paul Montville had died a few years earlier at the age of 103.

Many years later, in a section entitled "Press Files of 25 Years Ago," the *Plattsburgh Daily Press* of 7 Dec 1938 reprinted at least part of the original obituary. It mentions that Paul Montville was 106 (sic) years old at his death but does not include the exact date of death. It does however identify his surviving children: "two sons Paul Montville, Jr., of this city, and William Montville, of this city; five daughters, Mrs. Albert Case [Christiana] and Mrs. B. Myers [Mary], of this city, Mrs. Jennie Armstrong, Mrs. Nellie Brown and Mr. and Mrs. Kitty [Catherine?] Graham, of New York City."

Children:
i   **Herman Montville** b Jan 1837, Plattsburgh, NY; d between 1910 and 1920. He married 1863? **Matilda Fulton** (John Fulton & Hannah _____) b Jan 1843, Plattsburgh, NY; d & bur there 9 & 12 Jul 1924.
ii   **Frederick/Fred Montville** b 1841?, Plattsburgh, NY; d between 1900 and 1910. He married 1868? **Anna Cater** b May 1851, NY; d 28 Jul 1930, Plattsburgh, NY.
iii **Jane/Genevieve Montville** b & bp Jan 1842 & 14 Oct 1849, Plattsburgh, NY. She married _____ **Armstrong**.
iv   **Calliste Montville** b & bp Jan 1845 & 14 Oct 1849, Plattsburgh, NY.
v   **Christiana Montville** b 25 Dec 1845, Plattsburgh, NY; d & bur there 24 & 26 Nov 1919. She married **Albert Case** b 15 Mar 1843, VT; d 6 Mar 1910, Plattsburgh, NY.
vi   **Catherine Montville** b & bp Sep 1847 & 14 Oct 1849, Plattsburgh, NY.
vii **Pauline/Apolline Montville** b & bp Jun & 14 Oct 1849, Plattsburgh, NY.
viii **William Montville** b & bp 24 May 1851 & 14 Jan 1856, Plattsburgh, NY; d there 23 Jun 1920. He married 1875? **Mary Desloyer** b Sep 1861, NY.
ix   **Catherine Montville** b & bp 1 Sep 1853 & 14 Jan 1856, Plattsburgh, NY.
x   **Mary Montville** b & bp 24 Sep 1855 & 14 Jan 1856, Plattsburgh, NY; d & bur there 14 & 17 Aug 1920. She married there 1873 **Bonaparte M. Myers** b Apr 1850, NY; d & bur 15 & 20 Feb 1918, Plattsburgh, NY.
xi   **Ellen Montville** b 1858?, Plattsburgh, NY.
xii **Paul Montville Jr.** b Feb 1860, Plattsburgh, NY. He married (1) 1883? and divorced 24 Jul 1909, Plattsburgh, NY, **Louisa Laporte** (Theodore Sorel dit Laporte & Marie/Mary ___) b 1867?, Clinton Co., NY.
     He married (2) 31 Jul 1909, Plattsburgh, NY, **Alice Laware** (Louis Laware & Philomene Akey) b Oct 1869, Saranac, NY; m (1) 1890? and divorced 18 Aug 1908, Plattsburgh, NY, _____ Recour/Recor.
xiii **James Montville** b Jan 1863, Plattsburgh, NY; d there 21 Apr 1909. He married 1886? **Elizabeth Lavine** (Albert Magloire Lavigne/Lavine & Rosella Loiseau/ Loiseux/Bird) b Feb 1869, NY; m (2) John Schweitzer; d & bur 12 & 17 Oct 1922, Morrisonville, NY.
xiv **Nellie/Ella Montville** b & bp 12 May 1865 & 7 Jun 1875, Plattsburgh, NY. She married _____ **Brown.**

4.4.3.3   **MONTY, Frederick** b 1829?, NY.

Frederick Monty was a 21-year-old blacksmith in Plattsburgh, NY, in 1850 (US census) and was alive in 1856, according to the deposition of his aunt Mrs. Barbary (Monty) Morrison (4.4.5) (Appendix I). I am sure of nothing more. The following is only a possibility which might bear investigation.

He may be the Frederick Monty, husband of Jane McAlan, whose children Mary and Frederick, born in 1852 and 1853, were baptized on 14 Jan 1856 in St. Peter's Catholic Church in Plattsburgh. If so he may have died before 1860. He is not found in any of that year's censuses while Mrs. Jane Monty was then living in the Clinton Co. Poor House in Beekmantown, NY, with a 9-year-old daughter Jane, a 6-year-old son Benjamin, and a 1-year-old daughter Margaret (US census). A guardian was appointed for the two younger children in 1868 (Letters of Guardianship, Clinton Co., book D, pp. 54, 64), perhaps after their mother's death?

4.4.3.4   **MONTY, Jane** married **Joseph Meso** (?).

Jane Monty died before October 1856, leaving one child, Joseph, according to the deposition of her aunt Mrs. Barbary (Monty) Morrison (4.4.5) (Appendix I). Her husband's surname is very difficult to decipher in that document: it could be Meso, Mero, or even Ness. In none of these versions or their variants, Mooso, Mousseau, Miro, Miron, etc., have I been able to identify the family.

Child:
    i   **Joseph Meso** (?)

4.4.3.5   **MONTY, Ann** b 1833?, Plattsburgh, NY.

Ann Monty was a 17-year-old girl living with her parents in Plattsburgh, NY, in 1850 (US census). She was alive in 1856, according to the testimony of her aunt Mrs. Barbary (Monty) Morrison (4.4.5) (Appendix I).

4.4.3.6   **MONTY, Andrew** b 17 Mar 1835, Plattsburgh, NY; bp 9 Oct 1878, Montreal, QC. He married **Sally Ann Huestis** (Timothy Huestis & Betsey Connors Crossman) b 1834?, Crown Point, NY.

Andrew Monty was 15 years old in 1850 when he was living with his parents in Plattsburgh, NY. The precise date of his birth is taken from his baptismal record in St. Ann's Church in Montreal, QC, where he was identified as the son of Christopher Monty and Catherine Miller of Plattsburgh. He had been a boatman in Crown Point, NY, in 1865 and until at least 1875 (US and state censuses). I have found no later reference to him or his wife either in the United States or Canada, though two of their children, James Andrew and Mary, lived in Essex Co., NY, and their youngest son was with his uncle Daniel Huestis in Bridport, VT, in 1880.

Sally Ann Huestis was 16 years old when she was living with her parents in Crown Point in 1850 (US census). Later records show that she may have been born from 1834 to 1840.

Children:

4.4.3.6.1	Caroline Anna	1860?- -
4.4.3.6.2	James Andrew	1861-1886-1934
4.4.3.6.3	Olive N.	1865- -
4.4.3.6.4	John	1867?- -
4.4.3.6.5	Mary	1869-1887-1891
4.4.3.6.6	Elizabeth/Betsey	1871?- -
4.4.3.6.7	Alphons/Alpheus	1872- -1894

4.4.7.1   **MONTEE, Sarah Emily/Emiline** b 7 Feb 1823, Plattsburgh, NY; d 31 Dec 1900, Vernon Center, MN. She married 11 Apr 1841, Crawford Co., OH, **Abram/Abraham Malcolm Fraser** (Alexander Fraser & Hannah Christina Swisher) b 10 Jan 1821, OH; d 3 Apr 1896, Vernon Center, MN.

Abram (also Abraham, Abe) Fraser moved from Ohio to Illinois in the mid-1850s and a few years later to Minnesota where he settled permanently. He was a farmer in Waverly, MN, in 1870 and in Fraser, MN, in 1880. His widow remained in the area and was living in

June 1900 in Vernon Center, MN, in the household of her daughter Elnora (iii) and son-in-law George W. Robinson. She had had ten children of whom eight were still alive (US censuses).

Children:

i   **Francis F. Fraser/Frazer** b 1843?, OH; d 7 Mar 1895, Preston, MN. He married 5 Mar 1864, Fillmore Co., MN, **Julia A. Eddy** (George W. Eddy & Betsey Wheeler) b 20 Jul 1845, Cattaraugus Co., NY.

ii   **Annetta Fraser** b 1845?, OH. She married 1860? **Thomas VanWinkle** (Alexander VanWinkle & Sally/Sarah Jane Green) b 13 Oct 1840, Schuyler Co., IL.

iii   **Elnora Gertrude Fraser** b 24 Feb 1846, Little Sandusky, OH; d 7 Aug 1933, Lime Twp, MN. She married 11 Dec 1867, Nashville, MN, **George Washington Robinson** (Andrew S. Robinson & Mary Magdelena Wait) b 5 Feb 1842, Hollidaysburg, PA; d 29 Nov 1915, Vernon Center, MN.

iv   **Edwina Virginia Fraser** b 1848?, OH; d around 1890. She married 1864? **Thomas F. Talbot** (Thomas Talbot & Mary Reeve) b 25 Oct 1844, London, England; m (2) 1891? Helena Hanson; m (3) 1893? Amelia Dumke (Michael Dumke & Ernestine ____); m (4) 21 May 1901 Olivia ____, widow of Silas Moreland; d & bur 8 & 10 Jan 1910, Sleepy Eye, MN.

v   **Eugene A. Fraser** b 1852?, OH. He married 20 Aug 1874, Henry Co., MO, **Mary VanWinkle** (Alexander VanWinkle and Sally/Sarah Jane Green) b 1855?, Schuyler Co., IL.

vi   **Emily Irene Fraser** b Jun 1855, IL. She married 27 May 1873, Martin Co., MN, **James Ashworth** b Nov 1849, England.

vii   **Joseph A. Fraser** b 25 Dec 1857, IL; d 14 Jan 1949, Grand Rapids, MN. He married 8 Jan 1888, Martin Co., MN, **Vina/Lavina Shaw** (Samuel Shaw & Josephine Freeman) b 1862?, IL; d between 1894 and 1900.

viii   **Estella N. Fraser** b 1861?, Martin Co., MN. She married 30 Nov 1882, Fraser Twp, MN, **Charles T. Montgomery**.

ix   **Minnie/Minnesota Orella Fraser** b 15 Mar 1864, Welcome, MN; d 1935, Washburn Co., WI. She married 31 Jan 1889, Mankato, MN, **Arthur Eugene Briggs** (David B. Briggs & Julia Ann Lamphies) b 14 Jan 1862, Mauston, WI; d 20 Jan 1932, Stinnet, WI.

x   **Sidney Ralph Fraser** b 31 Aug 1869, Blue Earth Co., MN; d 27 Nov 1962, Tacoma, WA. He married 1893 **Florence Estelle Buck** (Thomas Buck & Mary ____) b 13 Jul 1876, Oshkosh, WI; d 10 May 1941, Tacoma, WA.

4.4.7.2   **MONTEE, Mary Elizabeth** b 5 Dec 1825, Plattsburgh, NY; d 8 Dec 1907, Riverside, CA. She married 4 Dec 1845, Wyandot Co., OH, **George Alford Cover** (Joseph Cover & Susannah Koch) b 2 Jun 1824, Graceham, MD; d 23 Jun 1900, Riverside, CA.

Mary Elizabeth Montee was a young child when her parents moved from New York State to Ohio in the early 1830s. She married there and lived for a while in Upper Sandusky, OH, where her husband was a blacksmith in 1850. The family then moved to Illinois. George Cover was a farmer in Macomb, IL, in 1860 and remained there until the early 1890s. By 1900 he was a farmer in Riverside, CA, where his son Theodore had settled some years previously (US censuses).

Children:

i   **William Oscar Cover** b 6 Dec 1846, Wyandot Co, OH; d there 16 Dec 1850.

ii   **Infant Cover** b & d 1847, Wyandot Co., OH.

iii   **Theodore Mortimer** b 14 Sep 1848, Wyandot Co., OH; d 15 Dec 1915, Long Beach, CA. He married 30 Dec 1869, Blandinsville, IL, **Clara Viola Logan** (Samuel Logan & Paulina Girton) b there 19 Sep 1851; d 17 Dec 1905, Riverside, CA.

4.4.7.3   **MONTEE, Theodore Commodore** b 8 May 1827, Plattsburgh, NY; d & bur 3 & 5 Jan 1921, McCune, KS. He married (1) 9 May 1850, Wyandot Co., OH, **Phebe Coberly** b 1830?; d between 1850 and 1853, McDonough Co., IL.

He was a widower when he married (2) 24 Nov 1853, McDonough Co., IL, **Nancy Brundage** (Solomon Brundage & Mary Jane Alexander) b 17 Apr 1833, Sangamon Co., IL; m (1) 25 Sep 1851 Joel Edmonston (James Edmonston & Polly _____); d 26 Dec 1906, McCune, KS.

Theodore C. Monty came to Ohio as a child with his family around 1833 and was living with his 20-year-old wife Phebe in his father's household in Pitt Twp, OH, in 1850. He moved shortly thereafter to McDonough Co., IL, where his first wife died. He was a mason in Bethel Twp, IL, in 1860 and a farmer there until the early 1880s when he became a farmer in Sheridan Twp, KS. He remained there until his second wife's death but was staying in Osage, KS, with his daughter Anna and her husband in 1910 and with his son Delmer in Neosho, KS, in 1920 (US censuses).

Children of the second marriage:

4.4.7.3.1	Rosetta	1854-	-1854
4.4.7.3.2	George Edward	1856-1880-1921	
4.4.7.3.3	Joseph M.	1858-	-1861
4.4.7.3.4	James A.	1861-1880-1905	
4.4.7.3.5	Mary Elizabeth	1863-1885-1961	
4.4.7.3.6	Anna/Phebe Ann	1865-1894?-1950	
4.4.7.3.7	John Francis/Frank	1868-1894-1946	
4.4.7.3.8	Theodore Elmer	1870-	-1873
4.4.7.3.9	Dora A.	1873-	-1874
4.4.7.3.10.	Della (twin)	1876-	-1876
4.4.7.3.11	Delmer (twin)	1876-1899?-1964	

4.4.7.4   **MONTEE, William** b 21 Jun 1829, Plattsburgh, NY; d 20 Sep 1890, Nevada, OH. He married 16 Jan 1851, Wyandot Co., OH, **Lorinda Coons** (Thomas Coons & Susan Brower) b Jul 1835, NY; d & bur 29 Apr & 3 May 1910, Upper Sandusky & Nevada, OH.

William Montee came to Ohio with his parents as a young child around 1833 and was a laborer on his father's farm in Pitt Twp, OH, in 1850. It is possible that he joined his relatives in Illinois for a few years in the early 1850s: his daughter Oella was buried there in 1854. All of his other known children were born in Little Sandusky, OH, where he was a farmer in 1860. He enlisted in the Union Army in September 1862 in Co. K of the 123rd Ohio Infantry Regiment and was discharged in August 1865 in Washington, DC. On his return home he became a hotel keeper, first in Little Sandusky and a few years later in Nevada, OH. He was the owner of the Kerr House there in 1880 (US censuses). Both he and his wife were buried in the Nevada Cemetery.

Lorinda (at times Lorenda) Coons lived after her husband's death with her daughter Anna, her only surviving child, in Little Sandusky in 1900 and in Upper Sandusky in 1910 (US censuses).

4.4.7.4.1	Oella	1852-	-1854
4.4.7.4.2	Mary E.	1854-	-1862
4.4.7.4.3	Anna E.	1856-1871-	
4.4.7.4.4	John H.	1873-	-
4.4.7.4.5	Randolph B.	1875?-	-

4.4.7.5   **MONTEE, Edward** b 5 May 1832, Plattsburgh, NY; d 20 Nov 1908, Little Sandusky, OH. He married there 13 Nov 1853 **Caroline Kotterman** (Michael Kotterman/Cotterman & Sarah King) b 21 Jul 1835, Perry Co., OH; d 31 Jul 1895, Little Sandusky, OH, at the age of 60 years and 10 days.

Edward Montee came to Ohio with his parents as an infant and spent most of his life in Little Sandusky, OH, though he joined his parents in Macomb, IL, for a few years between 1855 and 1861. He was a laborer there in 1860. He then returned to Little Sandusky where he was a blacksmith in 1870 and a Justice of the Peace in 1880. He had also built a brick factory there in the 1870s and served as Justice of the Peace for thirty years (*Biographical Memoirs of Wyandot County, Ohio*, pp. 292-293). He was retired and staying in his son Francis' household there in 1900 (US censuses). He and his wife were buried in Oak Hill Cemetery in Upper Sandusky, OH.

Children:

4.4.7.5.1	Alice Lodema	1854-1873-1880
4.4.7.5.2	David Leroy	1856-1876-1920
4.4.7.5.3	Francis Edward/Frank E.	1858-1878-1924

4.4.7.6 **MONTEE, James Wilson** b 25 Jul 1834, Little Sandusky, OH; d 24 Jan 1914, Cherokee, KS. He married 19 Dec 1855, Upper Sandusky, OH, **Harriet Lucinda Robinson** b 9 Feb 1832, Erie Co., PA; d 21 Jun 1898, Cherokee, KS.

James Wilson Montee left Ohio for Illinois a few years after his marriage and was a farmer in Doddsville (Bethel Twp), IL, in 1860 and in Macomb, IL, in 1870. In the mid-1870s he became a farmer in Cherokee, KS, where he remained until his death (US censuses). Both he and his wife were buried in the Cherokee Cemetery.

Children:

4.4.7.6.1	Leafie Elnora	1856-1877-1929
4.4.7.6.2	Charles Clifford	1860-1883-1929
4.4.7.6.3	James Wilson Jr.	1862-1893-1956
4.4.7.6.4	Harriet Ann	1864-1892-1944
4.4.7.6.5	Francis Abraham	1867-1894-1912
4.4.7.6.6	William Arthur	1869-1892-1965

4.4.7.7 **MONTEE, Nancy** b 13 Oct 1836, Little Sandusky, OH. She married 15 Oct 1857, McDonough Co., IL, **John Muse** b 1837?, PA.

Nancy Montee and her 23-year-old husband, a laborer born in Pennsylvania, were members of her father Abraham Montee's household in Macomb, IL, in 1860. John Muse was a farmer there in 1880 (US censuses). I have no certain knowledge of the family's later history.

Children:

i	**William E. Muse** b 1862?, McDonough Co., IL.
ii	**John Muse** b 1868?, McDonough Co., IL.
iii	**Emma Muse** b 1871?, McDonough Co., IL.

4.4.7.8 **MONTEE, Charles** b 7 Jul 1839, Little Sandusky, OH; d 24 Mar 1865, Macomb, IL. He married 14 Feb 1861, McDonough Co., IL, **Nancy Jane Lauderman/ Lowderman** (John Lowderman/Louderman/Lauderman & Jane Stradley) b 1842?, IN; m (2) 24 Dec 1869, McDonough Co., IL, L. W. Dickenson.

Charles Montee died at the age of 27 and was buried in the Old Macomb Cemetery (Betty Ramsey, *Monty-Montee History*, p. 216).

Nancy J. Lowderman was an 8-year child living with her father and stepmother in Henry Twp, IN, in 1850. Her surname was Louderman in 1860 (US censuses) though she married Charles Montee as Nancy J. Lauderman. She was "Mrs. Jane Montee" at her second marriage.

Children:

4.4.7.8.1	Hester	1862?-	-
4.4.7.8.2	Susan/Susie E.	1864-	-1941

4.4.7.9 **MONTEE, Francis Marion** b 25 May 1840, Little Sandusky, OH; d & bur 4 & 6 May 1925, Pittsburg, KS. He married 18 Aug 1861, Macomb, IL, **Mary Emilene Pur-**

dum (Samuel Purdum & Elizabeth Ann Tullis) b 6 Feb 1844, McDonough Co., IL; d & bur 8 & 10 Nov 1927, Pittsburg, KS.

Francis Marion Montee came to Illinois with his parents in the early 1850s and was a farmer in Macomb, IL, until about 1874 when he moved to Crawford Co., Kansas. He was a farmer and cattle breeder there in Sheridan Twp until at least 1910 and was living in retirement in Pittsburg, KS, in 1920 (US censuses). He and his wife were buried in Mount Olive Cemetery in Pittsburg.

Children:

4.4.7.9.1	Anna Alice	1862-1879-1946
4.4.7.9.2	Emma Harriet	1863-1882-1946
4.4.7.9.3	Mary Elizabeth	1865-1888-1940
4.4.7.9.4	Francis Edward	1867-1887&1902-1925
4.4.7.9.5	Albert A.	1868-1891&1904-1946
4.4.7.9.6	Charles Finley	1870-1897&1911-1928
4.4.7.9.7	James Walter	1872-1898-1950
4.4.7.9.8	Samuel Theodore	1875-1899&1913-1967
4.4.7.9.9	William Valentine	1877-1899-1969
4.4.7.9.10	Florence Ætna	1879-1917-1962
4.4.7.9.11	Nellie Almeta	1881-1904-1954
4.4.7.9.12	Dolly May	1884-1909-1962
4.4.7.9.13	Clarence Martin	1886-1908-1967

4.4.7.10   **MONTEE, Catherine** b 12 Feb 1842, Crawford Co., OH; d between 1870 and 1880. She married 16 Feb 1862, McDonough Co., IL, **William H. Coons** (William Coons & Christiana Smith) b 1844?, OH; m (2) Mary ____.

William Coons was 6 years old in 1850 when he was living with his parents in Pitt Twp, OH. He and his wife Catherine remained in Illinois for a few years after their marriage for their first child was born there. Their youngest child however was born in Ohio, perhaps in Little Sandusky where William H. Coons was a farmer in 1870. Catherine Montee may have died there before 1880 when William H. Coons, a saloon keeper, was living with a 29-year-old wife named Mary and the children of his first marriage in Nevada, OH (US censuses).

Children:

i   **Mary Emma Coons** b 1862?, IL.
ii   **George Edward Coons** b 1864?, OH or IL.
iii   **Joseph A. Coons** b 1866?, OH.

4.4.7.11   **MONTEE, Hester Ann Eliza** b 7 Nov 1845, Wyandot Co., OH; d & bur 1859, Schuyler Co., IL, at the age of 14.

4.4.7.12   **MONTEE, Clois Finley** b 25 Mar 1848, Little Sandusky, OH; d & bur 23 & 26 Jul 1927, Breezy Hill & Pittsburg, KS. He married (1) 31 Dec 1867, McDonough Co., IL, **Mary Catherine Ritter** (Samuel Ritter & Martha Ann Henley) b 26 Jan 1851, Macomb, IL; d 25 Sep 1916, Pittsburg, KS.

He married (2) around 1925 **Jane** ____ b 1856?, England; m (1) 1878? John Reddy.

Clois (Cloys at his marriage) Montee was a farmer in Macomb (Emmet Twp), IL, in 1870. He remained in Illinois until at least the birth of his daughter Lillie Gay in 1875 but moved before 1879 to Crawford Co., KS, where his daughter Rosa May was born. He was a farmer in Sheridan Twp, KS, in 1880 and in Baker Twp, KS, in 1900 and 1910. He was retired in 1920 and living next door to his son Charles Edward in Washington Twp, KS (US censuses). He and his first wife were buried in West Union Cemetery in Pittsburg, KS.

I have not found the record of Clois Monty's second marriage. He married Mrs. Jenny Reddy in 1925 according to Betty Ramsey's *Monty-Montee History*, p. 505. The reference must be to Mrs. Jane Reddy who, at the age of 64, was living in Crawford Co. in 1920 with her husband John and adopted son George. Ten years later, when she was living with this son,

George Reddy, in Tulsa, OX, she was a widow named Mrs. Jane Montee (US censuses).

Children of the first marriage:

4.4.7.12.1	Charles Edward	1868-1893&1909?-1945
4.4.7.12.2	William Henry	1870-1907-1961
4.4.7.12.3	Louis Melvin	1872-1892-1945
4.4.7.12.4	Ollie Etta	1873-1892?-1965
4.4.7.12.5	Lillian Gay	1875-1893-1907
4.4.7.12.6	Rosa May	1879-1896-1980
4.4.7.12.7	George Clois	1880-1902-1947
4.4.7.12.8	Amanda Florence	1882-1913?-1959
4.4.7.12.9	Emma Elizabeth	1886-1904-1927
4.4.7.12.10	David A.	1889-1909-1974

4.5.1.1 **MONTY/MONTA, John S.** b Aug 1825, Chazy, NY. He married **Jane A.** ____ b Apr 1826, NY.

The date of birth of John Monty (Monta in Onondaga and Oswego Counties, NY) is taken from the 1900 US census in Hannibal, NY. He had been a farmer in DeWitt, NY, in 1850 and 1860 and in Hannibal from at least 1870 on. In 1900 he and his wife had had eleven children of whom three, John, Amanda, and either Sarah or Joel, were still alive (US censuses). He and his wife may have died before 1910: neither appears in that year's census though their son John was still on the family farm.

Children:

4.5.1.1.1	John S.	1845- -
4.5.1.1.2	Sarah P.	1855?- -
4.5.1.1.3	Joel H.	1859- -
4.5.1.1.4	Amanda	1866-1894?-

4.5.1.2 **MONTY, Eleanor** b 1832?, Chazy, NY.

Eleanor Monty was living with her parents in Saranac, NY, in 1850 when she was 18 years old. She was also with them there in 1860, though named Ellinor (US censuses).

4.8.2.1 **MONTY, Augustus/Auguste Lafayette** b & bp 19 Jun & 23 Jul 1848, Chazy & Coopersville, NY; d 28 Jun 1854, Chazy, NY.

Augustus L. Monty (Auguste Lafayette at his baptism) was buried in Trombly's Bay Cemetery in Chazy, NY.

4.8.2.2 **MONTY, Victoria/Marie Victoire** bp 1 Nov 1850, Coopersville, NY; d 17 [a] Oct 1912, Plattsburgh, NY. She married there 5 Mar 1869 **Solomon Manor** (Pascal Ménard/ Manor & Sophie/Sophia Noiseux) b 1849?, Beekmantown, NY; d 18 Apr 1893, Plattsburgh, NY.

Neither the date nor place of birth is mentioned in Marie Victoire Monty's baptismal record. Since her name does not appear in the 1850 US census in Chazy, NY, she was probably born in the summer or fall of that year. She was 9 years old in 1860 and 19 in 1870 (US censuses). The inscription on her tombstone in the Ingraham Cemetery in Chazy, "Victoria Monty / 1848-1912," must be wrong as to the year of her birth.

Solomon Manor was a 1-year-old child living with his parents in Beekmantown, NY, in 1850 and a 21-year-old farmer staying in his father-in-law's household in Chazy in 1870. He does not appear with his family in 1880 though he was living in Plattsburgh, NY, and listed in the Veterans' Schedule in 1890: he had served during the Civil War in Co. B of the 193rd New York Infantry Regiment from 22 Feb 1865 to 18 Jan 1866 (US censuses). He was 44 years old at his death (*Plattsburgh Sentinel*, 21 Apr 1893) and was buried in the Old Catholic Cemetery in Plattsburgh.

Children:

i **Minnie/Amelia Victoria Manor** b & bp 5 Apr & 26 Jun 1870, Chazy & Coopersville, NY; d & bur 21 & 24 Jun 1953, Plattsburgh & Mooers, NY. She married 1888? **Rufus Palmer** (William Palmer & Jerusha (?) _____) b Oct 1844, Mooers, NY; d between 1900 and 1910.

ii **Joseph Manor** b Dec 1873, Chazy, NY; d there 11 Sep 1879 at the age of 5 years and 9 months.

4.8.2.3   **MONTY, Caroline** b & bp 21 Apr & 13 Jun 1852, Chazy & Coopersville, NY; d 26 Jul 1870, Chazy, NY.

Caroline Monty was buried in Trombly's Bay Cemetery in Chazy, NY.

4.8.2.4   **MONTY, Celia/Cécilienne** b & bp 21 Sep & 29 Oct 1854, Chazy & Coopersville, NY.

This child was named Cécilienne at her baptism and Celia in 1860 and 1870 when she was living with her family in Chazy, NY (US censuses).

4.8.2.5   **MONTY, Delia/Adeline** b & bp 11 Sep 1856 & 9 May 1857, Chazy & Coopersville, NY.

This child was named Adeline at her baptism and Delia in 1860 and 1870 when she was living with her family in Chazy, NY. She may be the 23-year-old Delia Monty, single, who was a cotton mill worker in Lowell, MA, in 1880 (US censuses). Her father is said to have been born in New York State but her mother in New Hampshire, which gives me pause.

4.8.2.6   **MONTY, Amelia** b 1858?; bur 22 Apr 1884, Coopersville, NY, at the age of 26.

The records of St. Joseph's Church in Coopersville, NY, include only the names of Amelia Monty's parents, her age at death, and the date of her burial. That woman however does not appear with her family in any US or state census that I have seen. I suspect that there may have been a mistake in her age, her parentage, or perhaps her name. There is a big question mark here.

4.8.5.1   **MONTY, John E.** b Nov 1847, Chazy, NY; d & bur there 28 & 30 Apr 1895 at the age of 47 years and 5 months. He married around 1873 **Lucy E. Mayo** (John B. Mayo [Jean-Baptiste Mailloux] & Emeline Ratell) b Feb 1854, Franklin Co., NY; d 14 Jan 1929, Chazy, NY, at the age of 74 years and 11 months.

John E. Monty was a sawmill worker in Chazy, NY, in 1870 and a carpenter in Ticonderoga, NY, in 1875 and in Chazy in 1880 and 1892 (US and state censuses). He and his wife were buried in the Ingraham Cemetery in Chazy.

Children:

4.8.5.1.1	Adeline/Addie	1875-	-1879
4.8.5.1.2	Mary Tessy/Jessie M.	1878-	-1879
4.8.5.1.3	Willis Ellsworth	1883-	-

4.8.5.2   **MONTY, Oreon** b May 1850, Chazy, NY; d & bur 10 & 12 Jun 1930, Beekmantown & Chazy, NY. He married 28 Oct 1891, Beekmantown, NY, **Emma Linda Craft** (Stephen Craft & Celinda A. Hall) b Jun 1865, Isle La Motte, VT; d & bur 21 & 24 Nov 1938, Beekmantown & Chazy, NY.

Oreon Monty was a sawmill worker in Chazy, NY, in 1870 and a farmer in Beekmantown, NY, from at least 1880 on (US censuses). His name varies somewhat: Oreon, Orion, Orin, and even Owen in the announcement of his marriage in the *Plattsburgh Sentinel* of 6 Nov 1891. It is Oreon on his tombstone in the Ingraham Cemetery in Chazy, where he and his wife were buried.

Children:

4.8.5.2.1	Edward Stephen	1893-1917-1972

4.8.5.3   MONTY, Ella/Ellen b Aug 1853, Chazy, NY. She married (1) 16 May 1876, Providence, RI, **John Kirkpatrick** (James Kirkpatrick & Isabella ____) b 1853?, Raleigh, NC.

She married (2) around 1885 **John Hay**.

This woman was named Ellen when she was living with her parents in Chazy, NY, in 1860 and 1870. She married however as Ella Monty and was known thereafter as Mrs. Ella Kirkpatrick and Mrs. Ella Hay. Her first husband, John Kirkpatrick, was a harness maker in Providence, RI, at his marriage, when he was 23 years old, and in Springfield, MA, in 1880. He may have died shortly before or after the birth of his third child for in 1900 Mrs. Ella Hay was living in Manhattan, NY, with three children, Edward and Etta Kirkpatrick and a 14-year-old Stewart Hay. She was a dressmaker in Manhattan, married, but with no husband present. In 1910 and 1920 she was a widow living in Clarkstown, NY, with her son Stewart Hay and her widowed daughter Mrs. Etta Borman (US censuses).

Children:
 i   **Edward Monty Kirkpatrick** b 23 Apr 1877, NY; d Aug 1979, Allendale, NJ. He married before 1918 **Catherine** ____ b 15 Apr 1894, NY; d Jul 1982, Allendale, NJ.
 ii   **Isabella Kirkpatrick** b 7 Jul 1879, Newport, RI.
 iii   **Etta M. Kirkpatrick** b 16 Apr 1883, NY; d Apr 1969, Rockland Co., NY. She married around 1902 **Charles Borman**.
 iv   **Ernest Stewart Hay** b 15 Jan 1886, NY.

4.8.5.4   MONTY, Etta b Jul 1857, Chazy, NY; d & bur 8 & 10 Nov 1942, Plattsburgh & Chazy, NY. She married 1909? **William A. Smith** b 1860?, NH; d between 1910 and 1920.

Etta Monty was single and living in her father's household in Beekmantown, NY, in 1900. In June 1910 she had been married for less than a year to the 60-year-old William A. Smith, a real estate dealer in Lowell, MA. It was a first marriage for both. She was a widow in 1920, an upholsterer who owned her own business in Lowell. She then returned to Beekmantown and was living in 1930 as the head of her own household in the home of her brother Oreon (4.8.5.2) (US censuses). She was buried alongside her parents in the Ingraham Cemetery, in Chazy, NY.

4.8.5.5   MONTY, Ida B. b 1861?, Chazy, NY; d 28 Aug 1879, Beekmantown, NY, at the age of 18.

Ida B. Monty was buried alongside her parents in the Ingraham Cemetery in Chazy. NY.

4.8.8.1   MONTY, Nellie Augusta b 9 Sep 1866, Monticello, IA; d 9 Oct 1947, Los Angeles, CA. She married 27 Aug 1884, IA, **John Alexander Zook** (Jacob C. Zook & Elizabeth Goodman) b 13 Apr 1861, Maquoketa, IA; d 27 Apr 1929, Waterloo, IA.

This couple may have lived for a few years after their marriage in Cherokee, IA, where their oldest child was born. John Zook was a plumber in East Waterloo, IA, in 1891 and a plumber/plumbing contractor in Waterloo, IA, from at least 1894 on. His widow was still living there in 1930 (US censuses). He was buried in the Fairview Cemetery in East Waterloo.

Children:
 i   **Beatrice Katherine Zook** b Jun 1889, Cherokee, IA. She married 8 Nov 1911, Waterloo, IA, **Roscoe Delzen Tiffany** (Douglas F. Tiffany & Ella Rinebarger) b 19 Jun 1883, Barreman, IL; d 29 Nov 1961, Los Angeles, CA.
 ii   **Marguerite Elizabeth Zook** b 19 Dec 1891, East Waterloo, IA; d Apr 1987, Corpus Christi, TX. She married 1 Mar 1916, Waterloo, IA, **Henry Kirk Wall** (Charles Joseph Wall & Louisa ____) b 1 Jan 1892, Logan, MO; d Nov 1970, Carthage,

MO.

iii **Earl A. Zook** b 10 Jan 1894, Waterloo, IA; d 14 Apr 1972, Los Angeles, CA. He married 17 Sep 1919, Waterloo, IA, **Dorothy M. Doherty** (Thomas Doherty & Eudora/Dora A. Young) b Jan 1900, Cedar Rapids, IA; d between 1925 and 1930, Waterloo, IA.

iv **Irene M. Zook** b 16 Aug 1896, Waterloo, IA.

v **Robert Monty Zook** b 18 Jan 1899, Waterloo, IA; d 2 Nov 1972, Los Angeles, CA. He married 1925? **Hazel _____** b 12 Apr 1903, IA; d 9 Oct 1978, Los Angeles, CA.

vi **Jack L. Zook** b 14 May 1901, Waterloo, IA; d Jun 1978, Las Vegas, NV. He married 31 Dec 1921, Waterloo, IA, **Esther A. Tetro** (Ward Tetro & Mabel Nabel) b 6 Sep 1901, IA; d Dec 1987, Las Vegas, NV.

4.8.8.2 **MONTY, Kittie** b 1875?, IA.

Kittie Monty was a 5-year-old child living with her father in Parkersburg, IA, in 1880 (US census).

4.8.8.3 **MONTY, Anonymous** (male) b 17 Nov 1884, Parkersburg, IA; d there 17 Nov 1884.

4.8.8.4 **MONTY, Frank Clinton** b 2 May 1887, Allison, IA; d 15 Jan 1902, Jesup, IA.

4.8.10.1 **MONTY, Ettie R.** b 2 Sep 1860, Chazy, NY; bp 28 Aug 1870, Coopersville, NY; d 1 Apr 1874, Chazy, NY.

This child's name and dates of birth and death are taken from the inscription on her tombstone in the Ingraham Cemetery in Chazy, NY, where she was buried alongside her parents and brother. Yet she was named Hattie in the 1870 census in Chazy and Marie Joséphine when she was baptized at the age of 10 in St. Joseph's Church in Coopersville, NY.

4.8.10.2 **MONTY, Elrick W.** b 4 Nov 1863/1867, Chazy, NY; bp 28 Aug 1870, Coopersville, NY; d & bur 27 & 29 May 1941, Chazy, NY.

The inscription on Elrick W. Monty's tombstone in the Ingraham Cemetery in Chazy, NY, indicates that he was born on 4 Nov 1867. I seriously doubt it for all US and state censuses from 1870 through 1900 point to 1863 as the year of his birth. He was also 8 years old when he was baptized (as Frédéric Monty) in 1870 in St. Joseph's Church in Coopersville, NY. It is only in later censuses that his presumed year of birth changes: 1865 in 1910 and 1920; 1867 in 1925 and 1930. I would rather trust the earlier documents.

Elrick (also Elric) Monty was a farmer in the Ingraham district of Chazy, NY. He did not marry.

4.10.6.1 **MONTY, Joseph** b 1842?, Plattsburgh, NY.

Joseph Monty was an 8-year-old child living with his parents in Plattsburgh, NY, in 1850 (US census). He does not appear with his family in any later census.

4.10.6.2 **MONTY, James R.** b Apr 1846, Plattsburgh, NY. He married 1871? **Frances/Fanny Methot/Matott** (Francis Methot & Frances Bourdeau/Bordeau) b & bp Oct 1849 & 12 Jan 1850, Champlain & Coopersville, NY; d 15 Jul 1905, Altona, NY.

James R. (occasionally Jacob R.) Monty was a farmer in Mooers, NY, until at least 1892 and in Altona, NY, in 1900 when he and his wife had been married for 28 years. He was still a farmer in Altona in 1910 but was retired in 1920 and living in his son Orville's household there in 1920 (US and state censuses).

Frances Methot (Françoise at her baptism) was a fist cousin of Sarah Thompson, wife of Joseph Monty (4.3.1.1.4). She was buried in St. John's Old Catholic Cemetery in Plattsburgh, NY, as "Fannie H. Matott / Wife of James R. Monty."

Children:

4.10.6.2.1	Francis	1872- -1873
4.10.6.2.2	Frederick Benjamin	1873-1902-1919
4.10.6.2.3	Elizabeth C.	1883-1902?-
4.10.6.2.4	James R.	1886- -1888
4.10.6.2.5	Carrie Louise	1888-1908-1911
4.10.6.2.6	Thomas	1890-1915-1919
4.10.6.2.7	Orville James	1894-1920-1959

4.10.6.3   **MONTY, Daniel** b 1848?, Plattsburgh, NY. He married between 1870 and 1880 **Mary E.** ____ b 1856?, VT.

Daniel Monty was a 2-year-old child living with his parents in Plattsburgh, NY, in 1850. He was a sailor there in 1870, when he was still single, and a laborer there in 1880, when his wife Mary E. was 24 years old (US censuses). I have found no further trace of this family.

4.10.6.4   **MONTY, Elizabeth Anne** b & bp 14 & 15 Sep 1850, Plattsburgh, NY; d & bur 27 & 30 May 1938, Vergennes, VT. She married 1869 **Jeremiah James Bartley** (James Bartley & Anna ____) b Jun 1840, Vergennes, VT; d there 1916.

Elizabeth Anne Monty (Isabelle at her baptism in St. John the Baptist Catholic Church in Plattsburgh, NY) came to Vergennes, VT, as a girl of 16 and stayed with relatives, probably her aunt Elizabeth Monty (4.10.5), until her marriage in 1869. She remained there after her husband's death and the deaths of three of her nine children (*Plattsburgh Daily News*, 21 May 1938).

Jeremiah Bartley was a Civil War veteran who had served as a private in Co. K, 2nd Vermont Infantry from 1 Oct 1861 until his discharge on 2 May 1863. He was a worker in Vergennes for most of his life and was retired there in 1910 (US censuses).

Children:
i   **John F. Bartley** b Oct 1869, Vergennes, VT; d before 1938. He married 1902? **Mary H.** ____ b 1870?, Canada.
ii   **James Bartley** died before May 1938.
iii   **William Joseph Bartley** b 25 Apr 1875, Vergennes, VT.
iv   **Charles Henry Bartley** b 18 Mar 1877, Vergennes, VT; d between 1946 and 1952, Bennington, VT. He married 1916? **Myrtle J. Floyd** (George Floyd & Della M. ____) b 25 Mar 1897, Westport, NY; d 29 Mar 1996, Bennington, VT.
v   **Agnes Louise Bartley** b Nov 1879, Vergennes, VT. She married 1908? **Norbert Patrick Hebert** (Jean Hebert & Elmire Demers) b 10 Jan 1878, Clinton Co., NY.
vi   **Chester A. Bartley** b Dec 1881, Vergennes, VT; d before May 1938..
vii   **Mary E. Bartley** b 7 Oct 1883, Vergennes, VY; d there Mar 1980.
viii   **Thomas Howard Bartley** b 14 Nov 1885, Vergennes, VT; d there 15 Nov 1966.
ix   **Daniel Harry Bartley** b 8 Oct 1890, Vergennes, VT; d there May 1980.

4.10.6.5   **MONTY, Eliza** b & bp 22 & 28 Oct 1852, Plattsburgh, NY.

Eliza Monty was living with her parents in Plattsburgh, NY, in 1860 but does not appear with them in 1870 (US censuses).

4.10.6.6   **MONTY, Louisa** b & bp 16 Jun & 1 Jul 1855, Plattsburgh, NY. She married there 22 Aug 1878 **Sidney Gibbs** b 1852?, NY.

Sidney Gibbs was a 28-year-old peddler living with his wife and daughter in Stony Point, NY, in 1880 (US census).

Child:
i   **Lena B. Gibbs** b Sep 1879, Stony Point, NY.

4.10.6.7   **MONTY, Marie Judith** b & bp 14 & 27 Sep 1857, Plattsburgh, NY.

This child's name and date of birth are taken from her baptismal record in St. Peter's Church in Plattsburgh, NY. She does not appear with her parents in the 1860 census there and may have died before then. It is also quite possible that she was listed in that census as the 2-year old Jane Monty (4.10.6.8) for whom I have found no baptismal record, which is rather unusual in this family. For lack of any solid evidence either way the two children are considered here to be distinct individuals.

4.10.6.8 **MONTY, Jane** b 1858?, Plattsburgh, NY.

Jane Monty was a 2-year-old child living with her parents in Plattsburgh, NY, in 1860 and was still with them in 1870, though not in 1880 (US censuses). She may well be the child who was baptized as Marie Judith Monty (4.10.6.7).

4.10.6.9 **MONTY, Robert F.** b & bp 5 & 20 Nov 1859, Plattsburgh, NY; d & bur 13 & 16 Feb 1934, Hartford, CT. He married 1883? **Agnes C. Rice** (James Rice & Eliza Ann ____) b Apr 1856, White Plains, NY; d & bur 6 & 9 Feb 1933, Hartford, CT.

This man's date of birth is taken from the records of St. Peter's Catholic Church in Plattsburgh, NY, where he was named Joseph Hubert Monty. He must be the same child as the 7-month-old Robert who was living with his parents in Plattsburgh in June 1860. All subsequent censuses and records name him Robert or Robert F. Monty.

Robert Monty moved away from Plattsburgh in the 1870s and lived in various localities (Harrison, NY, in 1880, Manhattan, NY, in 1900; Essex, CT, in 1910) before settling in Hartford, CT, where he was a mechanic in a typewriter factory in 1920 and a typewriter repairman in 1930. He and his wife had been married for seventeen years in 1900 (US censuses). They were both were buried in Old North Cemetery in Hartford.

Children:

4.10.6.9.1	Clara	1886- -1954
4.10.6.9.2	Alvin French	1889-1912?-1928
4.10.6.9.3	Robert	1891- -1892
4.10.6.9.4	Mary Agnes/Mae	1894-1922?-

4.10.6.10 **MONTY, Emilie** b & bp 15 Aug & 8 Sep 1861, Plattsburgh, NY.

This child does not appear with her parents in the 1870 US census in Plattsburgh, NY, and may have died before then.

4.10.6.11 **MONTY, Carrie** b 1863?, Plattsburgh, NY. She married (1) there 26 Sep 1881 **Thomas Beashau/Burgess/Baillargeon** (Thomas Beashau/Baillargeon & Julia/Julie Beausoleil) b & bp 2 & 6 May 1859, Keeseville, NY.

She married (2) 18 Jul 1903, Plattsburgh, NY, **Albert A. Owens** b 1884?, KY.

She married (3) between 1913 and 1918 **Orlando Cox** (John Cox & Mariah ____) b Jun 1859, Chazy, NY; m (1) 2 Jan 1884, West Chazy, NY, Laura Randlett; m (2) 3 Nov 1889, Schuyler Falls, NY, Emma L. Booth (Jeremiah Booth & Elizabeth ____); d & bur 28 & 31 Mar 1940, Plattsburgh, NY.

Carrie Monty was 18 years old at her first marriage. She had been named Clarissa as an 8-year old child living with her parents in Plattsburgh, NY, in 1870. Her name is Carrie in almost all the other documents I have seen. There are two exceptions: she was named Mrs. Clara Owens in 1910 when she was living with her second husband in her mother's household in Plattsburgh, and Mrs. Carolyn Cox in the May 1938 obituary of her sister Elizabeth (4.10.6.4) in the *Plattsburgh Daily Press*.

There are two records of Carrie Monty's first marriage. The Vergennes, VT, Vital Records show that she married Thomas Beashau, a 22-year-old resident of that town. The French records of St. Peter's Catholic Church in Plattsburgh, the bride's place of residence, name her groom Thomas Baillargeon. That is also the surname found in his baptismal records in St. John the Baptist Church in Keeseville, NY. Censuses, though, offer a number of variants. He was Thomas Biajo when living with his parents in Chesterfield, NY, in 1860, Thomas Beasy in Ausable, NY, in 1870, and Thomas Beashau when he was a factory worker in Vergennes in

1880, shortly before his marriage (US censuses). I have not found him in any later census. He may have been listed under yet another variant, possibly Burgess, his son's surname in the Rhode Island Birth Records and in the Clinton Co., NY, Marriage Records, or even Bergiss, his wife's surname at her second marriage.

Mrs. Carrie Bergiss married Albert A. Owens in St. John's Church in Plattsburgh (*Plattsburgh Sentinel*, 24 Jul 1903) and was living with him and their 6-year-old son Robert Owens in her mother's household in Plattsburgh in 1910. Albert Owens, born in Kentucky, was then a 26-year-old machinist working in an automobile shop (US census). I am a bit skeptical about his age as stated but have found nothing more about him to either prove or disprove it.

Carrie Monty married for a third time in the mid-1910s: she was named Mrs. Orlando Cox when her son Robert Franklin Burgess signed his World War I Draft Registration Card on 10 Sep 1918. She and her third husband, who had previously been a farmer in Schuyler Falls, NY, were living in Plattsburgh in 1920. She was also there in 1930 but without a husband, while Orlando Cox was again in Schuyler Falls (US censuses). She survived him.

Children:
i   **Robert Franklin Burgess** b 20 Jan 1899, Providence, RI; d 18 Jul 1971, Plattsburgh, NY. He married there 17 Sep 1924 **Gertrude Rita Rothermel** (Maurice Rothermel & Mary Boyle) b 1903?, Carbondale, PA.
ii   **Robert Owens** b 1904?, Plattsburgh, NY.

4.10.6.12   **MONTY, George** b & bp 3 & 18 Feb 1866, Plattsburgh, NY; d & bur there 6 & 8 Aug 1939. He married (1) 1893? **Mary Rachel Larose** (Edouard/Edward Octave Larose & Margaret Gareau/Gorow) b 27 Mar 1866, Plattsburgh, NY; m (2) there 13 Mar 1911 Simon Edward Meads (Richard Meads & Lydia Levinight); d & bur there 17 & 19 Dec 1928.

He married (2) 9 Mar 1925, Plattsburgh, NY, **Emma Parrish** (Stephen Parrish & Sarah Allen) b Jan 1868, Arnold, NY; m (1) 1894? Alexander Stay (Daniel C. Stay & Elizabeth Frazier); d & bur 1 & 3 Jun 1926, Plattsburgh, NY.

George Monty spent his early years with his parents in Plattsburgh, NY, and was a laborer there in 1900 when he and his wife Rachel had been married for seven years. Their son George and daughters Lillian and Loretta were with them (US censuses). These daughters, as well as their younger sister Bessie, were later identified at their marriages as the daughters of George Monty and Mary Larose or Mrs. Mary Meads. It is thus perplexing to find that when he married Emma Parrish in 1925 and Mary Larose married Simon Meads in 1911 they both claimed to be marrying for the first time. It cannot be inadvertent. Indeed the report of George Monty's marriage to Emma Parrish in the *Plattsburgh Sentinel* of 10 Mar 1925 made a point of stating "It is Monty's first marriage." His earlier marriage may have been annulled on grounds which escape me. He was a mason in Plattsburgh at his second marriage to the widow of Alexander (sometimes Alex, Aleck) Stay. He was buried in the Old Catholic Cemetery in Plattsburgh (*Plattsburgh Daily Press*, 7 & 8 Aug 1939).

Mary Rachel Larose remained with her daughters in Plattsburgh where Simon E. Meads was a sergeant in the Plattsburgh Barracks. They were both buried in the Post Cemetery there.

Children of the first marriage:
4.10.6.12.1	George	1894-1917?-
4.10.6.12.2	Margaret Lillian	1896-1914&1919?-
4.10.6.12.3	Loretta	1899-1921-
4.10.6.12.4	Bessie Mary	1902?-1919-

4.11.1.1   **MONTY, Charles Quincy** b 29 Sep 1834, Chazy, NY; d 19 Dec 1907, St. Paul, MN. He married 1856?, NY, **Polly C. Trombly** (Francis Trombly & Mary Gregory/Grégoire) b 6 Jan 1841, St. Lawrence Co., NY; d & bur 9 & 11 Sep 1938, Monona, IA.

This couple moved from New York State to Luana, IA, before the birth there of their son Charles in 1865. Five years later Charles Monty was a saloon keeper in Monona, IA. He soon became a farmer and raised his family on a 30-acre farm near Monona which he bought on 24 Sep 1872 and sold on 18 Jan 1901. He and his wife, who had been married for forty-four years in 1900, remained in Monona until at least 1905 (US and state censuses). When he died two years later, though, he and his wife were staying in St. Paul, MN, with their daughter Sophrona and her husband Robert Love.

Polly Trombly lived with several of her children after her husband's death. She was with her daughter Sophrona in St. Paul in 1910 and with her son Charles in Minneapolis, MN, in 1920 when she was acting as housekeeper for George A. Shilson, Charles' former brother-in-law. By 1925 she had returned to Monona where her son William was a member of her household. She was also in Monona in 1930 but was living with her daughter Polly and son-in-law Harry Pomeroy (US and state censuses). She and her husband were buried in the Monona Cemetery.

Children:

4.11.1.1.1	Claudius/Claude A.	1861-1887-1920
4.11.1.1.2	Sophrona/Sophia	1862-1882-1952
4.11.1.1.3	Charles W.	1865-1889?&1929?-1948
4.11.1.1.4	Polly C.	1867-1892-1954
4.11.1.1.5	Frank A.	1874-1903?-1957
4.11.1.1.6	Mary Catherine	1875-1896-1955
4.11.1.1.7	William Lee	1882- -1957

4.11.1.2   **MONTY, Sophronia** b 13 Aug 1836, Chazy, NY; d there 22 Jan 1845, at the age of 8 years, 5 months, and 8 days.

Sophronia Monty was buried in the Ingraham Cemetery in Chazy, NY.

4.11.1.3   **MONTY, Claudius** b 9 May 1838, Chazy, NY; d & bur 5 & 8 Jan 1924, Seattle, WA. He married (1) NY, **Sarah C. Trombly** (Lewis Trombly & Almeda Scott) b 1841?, Chazy, NY; d & bur 1872, Monona, IA, at the age of 30 years, 10 months, and 5 days.

He married (2) 29 Jun 1876, Clayton Co., IA, **Mary Lowcock** (William Lowcock & ____ Walker) b 5 Oct 1848, England; d & bur 7 & 11 Jan 1937, Seattle, WA.

Claudius Monty was a railroad bridge builder and carpenter. From New York State, where his first child was born, he followed the railroads westward. He was in Luana, IA, for the birth of a child in 1864, in Wisconsin for the birth of another in 1872, in Iowa again at his second marriage and until at least 1880, and in the Dakota Territory in 1884 for the birth of another child. He apparently remained there for several years and was a bridge carpenter in Madison, SD, in 1900. By 1920 he and his wife Mary were living in Seattle, WA, in the household of their daughter Ellen Ruth and son-in-law John W. Austen. His widow was also living with them there in 1930 (US censuses). They were both buried in Seattle's Evergreen Park Cemetery.

Sarah C. Trombly died following the birth of her daughter Lilly Sarah in March 1872 and was buried in the Monona, IA, Cemetery. The assumed year of her birth above is derived from her age at death. I am somewhat uneasy though about it: she was only 5 years old in 1850 when she was living with her parents in Chazy, NY (US census). It is possible that she was even younger than indicated on her tombstone.

Mrs. Ellen Austen (4.11.1.3.5) provided the information on her mother's death certificate, including Mary Lowcock's date of birth and the names of her parents, which are not found on her marriage record.

Children of the first marriage:

4.11.1.3.1	Louis Albert/Lewis	1860-1882-1922
4.11.1.3.2	Almeda	1862- -
4.11.1.3.3	Etta Estella	1864-1883-1925
4.11.1.3.4	Lilly Sarah	1872-1901?-

Children of the second marriage:

| 4.11.1.3.5 | Ellen Ruth | 1877-1903?- |
| 4.11.1.3.6 | Grace E. | 1884-   - |

4.11.1.4   **MONTY, Albert W.** b 1840?, Chazy, NY; d 21 Sep 1912, Melrose, MA. He married (1) 28 Dec 1861, Lowell, MA, **Elizabeth A. Flynn** (Thomas Flynn & Rebecca Wiseman) b 11 Oct 1842, Cornwall, Ontario, Canada; d 22 Jul 1893, Lowell, MA.

He married (2) 1898?, MA, **Ida M.** ___ b Dec 1859, MA.

Albert Monty was a 21-year-old operative in Lowell, MA, at his first marriage and a 23-year-old manufacturer there when he enlisted on 15 Jul 1863 as a private in the 12th Massachusetts Infantry Regiment. He was discharged for disability on 8 Dec 1863 and returned to Lowell where he was trader/dealer in leather goods. He moved to Boston, MA, in 1886 and was a leather merchant there in 1900, when he and his wife Ida had been married for two years. Ten years later he was a leather goods salesman in Melrose, MA. His widow lived there until at least 1933 (US censuses; Lowell, Boston, and Melrose City Directories).

Child of the first marriage:
| 4.11.1.4.1 | Luella/Lulu M. | 1866-   -1920 |

4.11.1.5   **MONTY, Angelina/Angeline** b 1846, Chazy, NY; d 11 Oct 1863, Monona, IA, at the age of 17.

Angelina Monty was a 4-year-old child living with her parents in Chazy, NY, in 1850 (US census). She was buried as Angeline Monty in the Monona, IA, Cemetery.

4.11.3.1   **MONTY, George W.** b Oct 1838, Beekmantown, NY; d & bur 31 Mar & 3 Apr 1923, South Lyndeboro, NH & Chazy, NY. He married 1859? **Adeline Bousquet/Bosca** (MichelBousquet/Mitchel Bosca & Zoé Bourassa) b & bp 7 & 8 Mar 1838, La Présentation, QC; d 19 Oct 1909, Chazy, NY.

George Monty was a farmer in Beekmantown, NY, in 1860 and 1870 and in Chazy, NY, in 1880. He then moved to Massachusetts where several of his children married in the 1880s and 1890s and where the two youngest died in 1888. While most of his children remained in Massachusetts, George Monty returned to Chazy in the mid-1890s and was again a farmer there in 1900. He and his wife had then been married for forty-one years. His daughter Myrtle and son-in-law Irving S. White were with him in Chazy in 1910, shortly after his wife's death, while in 1920 he was living in their household in Lyndeborough, NH (US censuses). He died in their home in South Lyndeboro, NH (*Plattsburgh Sentinel,* 6 Apr 1923) but was buried in the Ingraham Cemetery in Chazy alongside his wife and two younger sons.

George W. Monty's wife was named Adeline Bousquet at her baptism. In the United States her surname varied. It was usually Bosca though other phonetic renderings of the French Bousquet were also used. Her obituary in the *Plattsburgh Sentinel* of 22 Oct 1909, for example, refers to Adeline Boskey.

Children:
4.11.3.1.1	Joseph Howard	1859-1883-
4.11.3.1.2	George B.	1862-1893-
4.11.3.1.3	Lillian E./Lillie	1863-1889-
4.11.3.1.4	Edward A./Doward A.	1867-1893&1915-1936
4.11.3.1.5	Frank D./Franklin	1868-1899-
4.11.3.1.6	Mary Adeline/Addie M.	1870-1888&1903?-
4.11.3.1.7	Myrtle Violet	1874-1894-1961
4.11.3.1.8	Julius D.	1875- -1888
4.11.3.1.9	Charles F.	1878- -1888

4.11.3.2   **MONTY, Julia** b 13 Jul 1842, Beekmantown, NY; d 7 Apr 1912, Lowell, MA. She married 1872? a second cousin **Thomas Madison Savage** (Antoine Savage & Julia Monty [4.8.1]) b 28 Oct 1837, Beekmantown, NY; d 5 Jan 1902, Lowell, MA.

Julia Monty and Thomas M. Savage's dates of birth and death are found on their tombstone in the Ingraham Cemetery in Chazy, NY.

Thomas M. Savage was a farmer in Chazy before moving with his family to Lowell, MA, around 1892. He was a teamster there in 1900 when he and his wife had been married for twenty-eight years. Their four children were then all still living with them. The family scattered soon after that, perhaps as a result of his death. While the widowed Julia Monty and her daughter Ida May were still in Lowell in 1910, her son Ira was a farm laborer in Chazy, her son Asa J. was a shoe factory worker in Lynn, MA, and her son Austin was a public school teacher in Manchester, CT (US censuses).

Children:
i **Ida May Savage** b Jan 1874, Chazy, NY.
ii **Ira M. Savage** b Feb 1875, Chazy, NY.
iii **Asa Joseph Savage** b 4 Oct 1877, Chazy, NY.
iv **Austin Anthony Savage** b 6 Sep 1879, Chazy, NY; d 21 Nov 1955, Wallingford, CT.

4.11.3.3 **MONTY, Eleanor** b & bp 4 Nov 1844 & 12 May 1868, Beekmantown & Coopersville, NY; d 16 Jun 1931, West Chazy, NY. She married (1) 1864? **Julius Abare** (Isaac Abare & Mary Baker/Bélanger) b 1834, Chazy, NY; d 14 Nov 1873, at the age of 39.

She married (2) 1881? **Abner Loomis** (James Loomis & Permessa Bugbee) b 9 Jul 1842, Champlain, NY; d 14 Oct 1917, Chazy, NY.

Julius Abare and his wife left Chazy, NY, after the birth of their daughter in 1865 and were living in 1870 in Lowell, MA, where he was a mill worker (US census). I do not know if he died there or if the family had returned to Chazy before his death. He was buried in Riverview Cemetery in Chazy.

The widowed Mrs. Eleanor Abare was Postmistress of the Ingraham Post Office on Monty's Bay in 1876 and early 1877 (Nell Sullivan & David Martin, *A History of the Town of Chazy, Clinton Co., NY*, p. 185) and was living in her father's household in Chazy in 1880. She soon remarried: in 1900 she and Abner Loomis had been married for nineteen years. They continued to stay on her father's farm which had been deeded to her after his death in 1892. Abner Loomis, who had been Postmaster of the Ingraham Post Office from 1889 to 1894 (Sullivan & Martin, p. 185), was a farmer in Chazy in 1900 and retired in 1910 (US and state censuses). He was buried in the Abare family plot in Riverview Cemetery in Chazy along with his wife, her first husband, and their daughter Gertrude Abare.

Child:
i **Gertrude H. Abare** b 10 Oct 1865, Chazy, NY; d there 25 Sep 1885.

4.11.3.4 **MONTY, Mary** b 29 Aug 1846, Beekmantown, NY; d 5 May 1935, West Chazy, NY. She married 17 Dec 1873, Chazy, NY, **John B. Sabre/Jean-Baptiste Savaria** (Joseph Savaria & Marie Anne Gobert) b & bp 17 Nov & 17 Dec 1846, St. Valentin, QC; d & bur 24 & 27 Apr 1909, Lowell, MA & Chazy, NY.

Mary Monty's dates of birth and death are taken from the inscription on her tombstone in Riverview Cemetery in Chazy, NY, where she and her husband were buried.

The *History of Clinton and Franklin Counties, New York*, pp. 326-327, has a biography of John B. Sabre which, apart from an erroneous date of birth, appears to be fairly accurate. He came to the United States as a child with his parents, enrolled in the Union Army in Vermont in 1862, reenlisted in 1864, and engaged in trade after the war in Rhode Island and Vermont before settling in Ellenburg, NY, in 1873. He was a hay and grain dealer there until at least 1880 and later in Chazy and in Lowell, MA, where he also had a livery stable (US censuses; Lowell City Directories). His widow was living with her sister Julia (4.11.3.2) in Lowell in 1910, though she had formed the intention, according to her husband's obituary in the *Plattsburgh Sentinel* of 7 May 1909, of making her home with her sister Eleanor (4.11.3.3) in Chazy. She was in fact a resident of West Chazy in 1930 (US censuses).

4.11.3.5 **MONTY, Cornelia E.** b Jan 1849, Beekmantown, NY; d 25 Mar 1935,

Syracuse, NY. She married 1873? **George W. Fifield** (Herod Fifield & Betsey Clark) b 23 May 1845, Thornton, NH; d 26 Aug 1910.

George W. Fifield was a carpenter and farmer in Thornton, NH, until at least 1880 and a carpenter in Lowell, MA, in 1900 when he and his wife had been married for twenty-seven years. He was retired in 1910 and was staying with his wife in their son's household in Southington, CT (US censuses).

Cornelia Monty lived with her son after her husband's death and moved with him to Syracuse, NY, in the mid-1910s (US censuses; *Syracuse Herald*, 25 Mar 1935). Both she and her husband were buried in Campton, NH.

Child:

i   **Harry Leland Fifield** b 20 Nov 1880, Thornton, NH; d 19 Aug 1948, Syracuse, NY. He married (1) and divorced before 1920 ____.
He married (2) **Bertha Cynthia Baron** (Frederick Abbott Baron & Mary D. Hanson) b 1883?, Lowell, MA; d 1 Jan 1959, Syracuse, NY.

4.11.3.6   **MONTY, Lilice A,** b Apr 1851, Beekmantown, NY; d there 7 Jan 1853 at the age of 1 year and 9 months.

Lilice Monty was buried in the Ingraham Cemetery in Chazy, NY.

4.11.3.7   **MONTY, Lucretia** b Dec 1853, Beekmantown, NY; d there 11 Mar 1854 at the age of 3 months.

Lucretia Monty was buried in the Ingraham Cemetery in Chazy, NY.

4.11.4.1   **MONTY, Delia** b 1840?, Beekmantown, NY.

Delia Monty was a 10-year-old child living with her parents in Beekmantown, NY, in 1850 (US census). She does not appear with her family in later censuses and may have died before 1860. If she survived and married before then, she may be the daughter identified only as "Mrs. Frank Marmell [perhaps Marnell] of Oakland, Calif," in her father's obituary. But that name could also apply to her sister Melissa (4.11.4.2). I have been unable to find the couple.

4.11.4.2   **MONTY, Melissa** b 1844?, Beekmantown, NY.

Melissa Monty was a 6-year-old child living with her parents in Beekmantown, NY, in 1850 and a 17-year-old in Plattsburgh, NY, in 1860 (US censuses). She does not appear with her family in later years and may have married before 1870. In that case she may be the daughter identified only as "Mrs. Frank Marmell [perhaps Marnell] of Oakland, Calif," in her father's obituary. But that name could also apply to her sister Delia (4.11.4.1). I have been unable to find the couple.

4.11.4.3   **MONTY, Leroy** b 1846?, Beekmantown, NY.

Leroy Monty was a 4-year-old child living with his parents in Beekmantown, NY, in 1850 and in Plattsburgh, NY, in 1860. He enlisted on 4 Aug 1862 as a private in Co. H, 118th New York Infantry Regiment and received a disability discharge on 5 Jan 1863. He must have rejoined the army a few years later for he was a soldier in the Plattsburgh Barracks in 1870 (US censuses). I have been unable to find him after that date except, perhaps, on two occasions where William Henry Monty (4.11.4.4) appears to be a substitute for Leroy Monty. I am beginning to believe that the two names represent the same individual and will discuss my reasons in the following section. For the present I am treating Leroy and William Henry Monty as two separate individuals.

4.11.4.4   **MONTY, William Henry** b 1847?, Beekmantown, NY; d 2 Jul 1899, Everett, WA. He married 8 Aug 1875, St. Joseph, MI, **Louisa Ann Rectenwalt/Rectenvault** (John Stanley & Louise Rectenvault) b 9 Jan 1861, KY or IL; m (2) 3 Nov 1900, Everett, WA, James McGuire; d & bur 2 & 8 Apr 1928, Seattle & Everett, WA.

William Henry Monty's place in the family tree is far from clear-cut. He does not appear in any census with Louis/Lewis Monty's family. His marriage record does not include his parents' names. The tombstone of W. H. Monty in Evergreen Cemetery in Everett, WA, does not include dates of birth or death. It identifies him solely as a veteran of Co. I, 118th New York Infantry. Unfortunately the only Monty to serve in Co. I of that Regiment was thirty years old when he enlisted on 27 Nov 1863 and would have been born several years before Louis/Lewis Monty's marriage. Some researchers have concluded that William Henry was not his son.

Yet I hesitate to dismiss him. We know that his path westward followed very closely that of Louis/Lewis Monty's family: he moved from Clinton Co., NY to Berrien Co., MI, at the same time as that family, had his marriage witnessed by George B. Monty (4.11.4.6) and Frances H. Monty (4.11.4.9), both children of Louis/Lewis Monty, and moved to the same area of the Washington Territory and at about the same time as several of Louis/Lewis Monty's children. More tellingly, both the *Arlington Times* of 8 Jul 1899 and 9 Dec 1899 and the *Snohomish County Tribune* of 7 Jul 1899, which reported on his death and the ensuing murder trial of Simon J. Fox (also Focks), identify him as the brother of Hiram Monty (4.11.4.6) and George B. Monty (4.11.4.8). I find it hard to believe that his relatives, who attended the trial (see below), would have allowed a false relationship to be maintained throughout.

I know nothing of William Henry Monty before his marriage when he was a sawyer in St. Joseph, MI. He was known as William H. Monty, a 33-year-old worker in a sawmill in Muskegon, MI, in 1880 (US census). Three children were born in Michigan before the family moved to the Washington Territory at some time before the 1887 census. Henry Monty, as he came to be known, lived first on a farm near Silvana and then in Everett, where he was a mill hand. He was shot on 1 Jul 1899 by Simon J. Fox or Focks in a domestic dispute and died in the Everett Hospital the next day.

Two documents from 1899 and 1900 raise the possibility that his real, or official, name may have been other than William or Henry. The first is a report in the Arlington *Times* of 9 Dec 1899 on the conviction of Simon J. Focks for the "killing of L. L. Monty, which took place the 1st of last July." The article goes on to say that "The dead man had a brother living in Tacoma [George], who is a member of the firm of Monty & Gunn, and another brother living in Arlington [Hiram], both of whom were present at the trial." Prior to the trial, the *Snohomish County Tribune* of 7 Jul 1899 as well as the *Arlington Times* of 8 Jul 1899 had identified the victim as "Henry Monty." The surname of the assailant also was changed, from Fox in July to Focks in December, but in all other aspects of the case, including the character of the victim and the events leading to the shooting, the facts are similar. The name change could be a simple journalistic mistake. Or perhaps the trial brought the new names to light. I have been unable to find a transcript of the case. But then we meet another unexplained coincidence: the initials L. L. are those of a Civil War veteran, Lahen (sic) LeRoy Monty of Washington State who had served in Co. H, 118th New York Infantry and whose petition for an invalid pension was filed on 2 Mar 1891 (#997407). The Civil War Pension Index shows that after his death the guardian of his minor children, Louisa A. Monty, also petitioned from Washington State on behalf of these children (#711.625, filed on 10 Jan 1900). There are too many coincidences here. The matter must be studied further.

The names of Louisa Ann Rectenwalt's parents and her date of birth are taken from her death certificate. Unless the scribe inadvertently omitted her father's surname and included her mother's married name in the space reserved for her maiden name, she was an illegitimate child about whom I have been able to find little more. She was born in Kentucky, according to her death certificate. Yet the record of her first marriage states she was born in Illinois. Either is possible.

Children:

4.11.4.4.1	Lillie M.	1879-	-
4.11.4.4.2	Louisa/Louise A.	1881?-	-1934
4.11.4.4.3	Myrtle B.	1884-1905?-	
4.11.4.4.4	Florence	1886?-1905-	
4.11.4.4.5	Lewis/Louis Leroy	1889-1924?-1962	

4.11.4.4.6	Frank Milton	1891-1917&1920?-1956
4.11.4.4.7	William Henry	1895-1918&1923-

4.11.4.5   **MONTY, Della Athalinda** b Jun 1849, Beekmantown, NY; bur 8 Feb 1931, Benton Harbor, MI. She married 1865? **Richard M. Wells** (John Wells & Julia Clark) b Jul 1845, Plattsburgh, NY; bur 25 Apr 1924, Benton Harbor, MI.

This woman was known as Atlin and Athalinda Monty when living with her parents in Beekmantown and Plattsburgh, NY, in 1850 and 1860 and as Altralinda (sic) Della Wells at her burial. On other occasions from 1870 through 1920 she was known as Mrs. Della, Della A., or D.A. Wells. She had been married for thirty-five years in 1900 (US census).

Richard M. Wells and his wife remained in New York State for a few years after their marriage before moving West around 1869. He was a shoe maker in Lake Mills, IA, in 1870. A few years later he settled in Berrien Co., MI, where he had a variety of occupations. He was a farmer in St. Joseph, MI, in 1880, a carpenter in Benton, MI, at the birth of a son in 1885, and a real estate agent in Benton Harbor, MI, in 1900 and 1910. He was living in retirement there with his wife in 1920 (US censuses). They were both buried in Morton Hill Cemetery in Benton Harbor.

Children:
  i   **Cora E. Wells** b 1866?, NY. She married 21 Apr 1889, Benton Harbor, MI, and divorced 18 Oct 1895, Livingston, MT, **William Apsley Blackburn** (Thomas Blackburn & Diana C. Baer) b 9 Dec 1864, Lockhaven, PA; m (2) 26 Oct 1904, Butte, MT, Mrs. Ollie Belle Barry; d 31 Jul 1939, Missoula, MT.
  ii **Cary E. Wells** b 1868?, NY.
  iii **Elmer Wells** b 1871?, IA.
  iv **Bessie V. Wells** b 1 Sep 1879, St. Joseph, MI; d 28 Oct 1955, Los Angeles, CA. She married 1908? **Howard Bailey** b 1875?, NY.
  v   **John E. Wells** b 26 Feb 1885, Benton Harbor, MI.
  vi **William A. Wells** b 29 Mar 1889, Benton Harbor, MI; d 7 Aug 1948, Butte, MT. He married 1919? **Ella F. ____** b 1896?, MT; d 29 Dec 1945, Butte, MT, at the age of 49.

4.11.4.6   **MONTY, Hiram/Myron** b 8 Nov 1851, Beekmantown, NY; d & bur 11 & 14 Aug 1934, Everett & Arlington, WA. He married 25 Nov 1871, St. Joseph, MI, **Anna Louise Danielson** (Daniel Danielson & Christine ____) b 11 Dec 1853, Mariestad, Sweden; d & bur 19 & 22 Feb 1928, Cicero & Arlington, WA.

The marriage record of Hiram Montey (sic) and Anne L. Daugleson (sic) in St. Joseph, MI, does not include their parents' names. Nevertheless it seems clear from the 1911 obituary notice of Lewis Monty in Benton Harbor, MI, which lists among his sons "Hiram E. Monty, of Cicero, Wash." and from Hiram's own death certificate in Everett, WA, that he was indeed the son of Louis/Lewis Monty and his wife Harriet. These two items were sent to me by Hiram's grandson, Bertram E. Monty (4.11.4.6.9.1), to whom I am also indebted for much of the information concerning this family.

Hiram Monty does not appear with his family in any census in New York State. There is however a 10-year-old Myron living with his parents in Plattsburgh, NY, in 1860 and a 21-year-old Myron Monty who was a soldier in the Plattsburgh Barracks in 1870 (US censuses). Myron Monty does not appear in any later document that I have seen. I believe that Myron became Hiram when he moved to Michigan and that they are one and the same person.

I do not know what caused the name change. Hiram Monty was a farmer in St. Joseph, MI, at his marriage and a laborer in Benton Harbor in 1880 (US census). He later worked in a saw mill and was a grocer in St. Joseph at the birth of a son in 1882. According to Bertram E. Monty he also trapped muskrats in Mississippi and traveled to Tacoma, WA, in 1884 to work on the railroad. His family joined him soon after the birth of his son Glenn in 1885 and lived on a 160-acre homestead in Trafton (Cicero after 1902), WA, as early as 1887 (Washington Territory census). He cleared the land, planted crops, expanded into the dairy business, and left his three surviving sons a very prosperous farm at his death.

Anna Louise Danielson came to the United States as a young child around 1865: according to her death certificate she had lived in this country for sixty-nine years.

Children:

4.11.4.6.1	Clarence A.	1875-	-1876
4.11.4.6.2	Perley B.	1876-	-1878
4.11.4.6.3	Milton M.	1878-	-1879
4.11.4.6.4	Etta/Emetta	1880-1907&1910-1916	
4.11.4.6.5	George B. (twin)	1882-1905&1911-1953	
4.11.4.6.6	Anonymous (twin)	1882-	-1882
4.11.4.6.7	Glenn Lewis	1885-	-1944
4.11.4.6.8	Clayton B.	1889-	-1893
4.11.4.6.9	Guy	1892-1920-1952	
4.11.4.6.10	Hiram Jr.	1894-	-1973
4.11.4.6.11	Laona Mae	1897-	-1903

4.11.4.7   **MONTY, Lillia/Martha** b Mar 1854, Plattsburgh, NY; d 21 Mar 1936, Nooksack, WA. She married 12 Mar 1875, Ayer, MA, **Samuel Parker Hayward** (Cyrus Hayward & Olive Parker) b Jul 1849, Pepperell, MA.

This woman was named Martha in 1860 when, at the age of 6, she was living in Plattsburgh, NY, in her father's household. However she was named Lillia at her marriage at the age of 21 as well as in the 1900 US census in Benton Harbor, MI, where she was staying with her parents. In other censuses, in Pepperell, MA, in 1880, in Seattle, WA, in 1910, and in Nooksack, WA, in 1920, she was named Lillian A. or Lillie. I cannot account for the name change.

Samuel P. Hayward was a papermaker in Pepperell, MA, at his marriage and a preacher there in 1880. In later censuses, including the 1900 one in Peoria, IL, where he was a boarder while his wife was in Michigan with her parents, he was described as a minister or clergyman. The 1930 census in Nooksack specifies that he was a clergyman serving the Seventh Day Adventist Church. This couple had no children.

4.11.4.8   **MONTY, George Barnes** b 12 Oct 1856, Plattsburgh, NY; d & bur 5 & 7 Jul 1928, Tacoma, WA. He married 23 May 1889 **Eunice Belle Rank** (George W. Rank & Elizabeth Detwiler) b 13 Oct 1866, Mt. Carmel, IL; d 30 Aug 1939, Chattanooga, TN.

George Monty came to Michigan with his parents in the mid-1870s and was a grocery store clerk in Benton Harbor, MI, in 1880. He moved in the mid-1880s to Tacoma, WA, where he was a partner in the firm of MONTY & GUNN, retail grocers (US censuses).

Child:

4.11.4.8.1	George Rank	1901-1923?-1980

4.11.4.9   **MONTY, Frances H.** b Mar 1860, Plattsburgh, NY. She married (1) 23 Oct 1882, St. Joseph, MI, **Clarence A. Sales** b 1858?, VT.

She married (2) 22 Dec 1892, Chicago, IL, **Henry William Foster** (William Hale Foster & Sarah Maria Clark) b 2 Nov 1863, Athol, MA; m (1) 3 Jun 1886, Orange, MA, Lulu M. Hadley (Horace W. Hadley & Sedelia M. Boleyn).

Frances H. Monty was a 3-month-old infant when she was listed with her parents in the June 1860 census in Plattsburgh, NY. She came with them to Michigan in the mid-1870s and was a resident of Benton Harbor, MI, at her first marriage. Clarence A. Sales was then a 24-year-old engineer in Chicago, IL. I know nothing more about him.

Frances Monty moved East soon after her second marriage. Henry Foster was a machinist in Bridgeport, CT, in 1900, a commercial traveler in Medford, MA, in 1910, a salesman there in 1920, and a sales manager in Boston, MA, in 1930. The couple had no children (US censuses).

4.11.4.10   **MONTY, Sarah Louise** b 27 Sep 1862, Plattsburgh, NY; d 1925, Benton

Harbor, MI. She married 2 Apr 1882, St. Joseph, MI, **Daniel Ide Hibbard** (Mortimer Dormer Hibbard & Mary Rice Green) b 18 Oct 1847, Spring Hill, OH; d 1922, Benton Harbor, MI.

Daniel Hibbard was a hotel keeper in St. Joseph, MI, at his marriage, a dairyman in Benton Harbor, MI, in 1900 and a salesman there in 1910. He was retired there in 1920 (US censuses).

Children:

i   **Edward Leroy Hibbard** b 9 Oct 1882, Benton Harbor, MI; d Niles, MI. He married 6 Aug 1906, St. Joseph, MI, **Myrtle Paskel** (George Paskel & Adeline _____) b 30 Jun 1886, Jackson, MI; d 10 Jan 1989, South Bend, IN.

ii   **Halo Hibbard** b 31 Dec 1884, Benton Harbor, MI; d 1953. She married 17 Oct 1907, Berrien Co., MI, and divorced before 1910 **George R. Hull.**

4.11.4.11   **MONTY, Mary Elizabeth/Libby/Marie E.** b 7 Jul 1866, Plattsburgh, NY; d 29 Nov 1946, Benton Harbor, MI. She married there 16 Jun 1886 **Freeman Green Bury** (Freeman Green Bury & Anna Fredricke Breithaupt) b there 15 Oct 1861; d there 20 Apr 1958.

This woman was known under a variety of names. She was Elizabeth and Mary E. Monty when living with her parents in 1870 and 1880, Libby Monty at her marriage, Mrs. Libbie Bury in 1900, Mrs. Marie Bury in 1910 and 1930, and Mrs. Marie Elizabeth Bury in 1920 (US censuses).

Freeman Bury was a farmer in Benton Twp, MI, at his marriage and until at least 1900 and in Bainbridge Twp, MI, in 1910 and 1920. By 1930 he and his wife had moved to Benton Harbor where he was a cook in a canning factory. He and his wife had no children of their own but had a 9-year-old adopted daughter, Helen, in 1910 (US censuses).

4.11.7.1   **MONTY, Eloi** b & bp 23 Jul 1864 & 3 Nov 1867, ? & Coopersville, NY.

The date but not the place of Eloi Monty's birth is indicated in his baptismal record. It was probably in Clinton Co., NY, where his parents lived at various times in Chazy, Beekmantown, and Plattsburgh. He was no longer alive in 1870.

4.11.7.2   **MONTY, Florence Elsie** b & bp 9 Oct & 3 Nov 1867, Chazy & Coopersville, NY; d 11 Sep 1893, Lowell, MA. She married there 1 Feb 1893 **Herman L. Bryant** (William Bryant & Diadama/Dana Kingsley) b 1868?, Cutler, ME; m (2) 1905? Mattie P. Vaughn (Stephen Vaughn & Sarah J. _____).

Florence E. Monty was a bookkeeper in Lowell, MA, at her marriage while Herman L. Bryant was a 25-year-old mill worker there. He later lived with his second wife in Old Orchard Beach, ME (US censuses).

4.11.7.3   **MONTY, Eldon E.** b Jun 1872, Chazy, NY; d 5 Jun 1945, Chelmsford, MA. He married 1895? **Mabel _____** b Mar 1872, NY.

Eldon E. Monty lived in Plattsburgh and Beekmantown, NY, until at least 1892. He moved to Dracut, MA, before the birth of his first child and remained there until at least 1900 when he was a box maker there. He and his wife had then been married for five years. They moved to Lowell, MA, before the birth of their second child. Eldon Monty was a box maker there in 1910 and a chauffeur there when he signed on 12 Sep 1918 his World War I Draft Registration card. He then named as his closest relative his daughter Edith. His wife may have died before then, or they may have separated: in 1920 Eldon E. Monty, still a chauffeur in Lowell, living alone in lodgings, was still considered to be married (US and state censuses). I know nothing more about his wife.

Eldon E. Monty remained in Lowell until at least 1938 (City Directories). In 1942 he was in neighboring Chelmsford where he ran a filling station (Lowell Suburban Directory). That is where he died on the street, a short distance from his home where he lived alone. According to the *Lowell Sun* of 6 Jun 1945 and 7 Jun 1945, it was suspected at first that he was the victim of a hit-and-run driver. When the autopsy report indicated that his "death [was] caused by injuries sustained in a manner unknown," the Massachusetts State detectives were called in. I have not been able to find in the newspaper how the case was finally resolved.

Children:

4.11.7.3.1	Earl Frank	1898-1924-1978
4.11.7.3.2	Edith	1902-1922-1982

4.11.7.4   **MONTY, Alice Drusella** b Aug 1874, Plattsburgh, NY; d & bur 1935, Plattsburgh & West Plattsburgh, NY. She married 1897? **George L. Gregory** (Richard Gregory & Sarah ___) b Apr 1872, Andes, NY; d & bur 7 & 9 May 1941, Plattsburgh & West Plattsburgh, NY, at the age of 69.

Alice Drusella Monty and her husband, a bartender in Plattsburgh, NY, had been married for 3 years in 1900. They remained in that city where he was a laborer in 1910, a mill hand in 1920, a farmer in 1925, and a farm laborer in 1930 (US & state censuses) and were buried along with their child in the West Plattsburgh, NY, Union Cemetery. The year of her death is taken from the inscription on her tombstone.

Child:

i   **Edwin Benedict Gregory** b 19 Jul 1903, Plattsburgh, NY; d & bur 1903, Plattsburgh & West Plattsburgh, NY.

5.7.1.1   **MONTY, Louis** b & bp 16 Jun 1812, St. Mathias, QC; d & bur 21 & 23 Dec 1877, Richelieu, QC. He married (1) 7 Feb 1832, Marieville, QC, **Esther Boulais** (Antoine Boulais & Cécile Goguet) b & bp there 22 Apr 1815; d & bur 3 & 5 Oct 1868, Richelieu, QC.

He married (2) 22 Nov 1869, Richelieu, QC, **Josephte Foisy** (Claude Foisy & Ursule Barsalou) b & bp 2 Feb 1811, Chambly, QC; m (1) 28 Sep 1830, St. Mathias, QC, **Louis Monty** (5.10.6); d & bur 20 & 22 Jan 1878, Ottawa, Ontario, Canada.

Louis Monty was a farmer in Marieville, QC, until at least 1858 and later in Richelieu, QC, where his first wife died. He and his second wife may have lived for a few years in the early or mid-1870s in Holyoke, MA, for Josephte Foisy was said to be residing there at the marriage of her son Eustache Monty (5.10.6.9) in 1872. Several of Louis Monty's children from his first marriage, including Honoré/Henry (who had arrived in the United States in 1869), Adélaïde, Marie, Emérite, and Nérée, were also living there in the 1870s and 1880s. Louis Monty was nevertheless a farmer in Richelieu at his death. His widow was staying in Ottawa, Ontario, probably in the household of her son Louis Dosithée Monty (5.10.6.8), when she died. She was buried in Notre Dame Cemetery in Ottawa.

Children of the first marriage:

5.7.1.1.1	Esther	1832- -1903
5.7.1.1.2	Clémence	1835- -1836
5.7.1.1.3	Elmire	1837-1883-
5.7.1.1.4	Louis	1839- -1841
5.7.1.1.5	Philomène	1842- -1843
5.7.1.1.6	Honoré/Henry	1843-1864-1914
5.7.1.1.7	Adélaïde	1845-1864-1892
5.7.1.1.8	Marie	1847-1870-
5.7.1.1.9	Emérite	1848-1885-1902
5.7.1.1.10	Marie Cordélie	1851- -1856
5.7.1.1.11	Nérée	1853-1882-1916
5.7.1.1.12	Célina Joséphine	1855- -1930
5.7.1.1.13	Louis	1858- -1858

5.7.1.2   **MONTY, Jean-Baptiste** b & bp 21 & 22 Jan 1814, St. Mathias, QC; d & bur 5 & 9 May 1887, New York, NY & St. Mathias, QC. He married 20 Oct 1838, St. Mathias, QC, **Césarie Cordélia Davignon** (Joseph Davignon & Marie Victoire Vandandaigue) b & bp there 10 Nov 1814; d & bur 31 Aug & 5 Sep 1883, New York, NY & St.

Mathias, QC.

Jean-Baptiste Monty was a farmer and later a merchant in St. Mathias until at least 1875. He apparently moved to New York City in the early 1880s for he was a merchant there at his wife's death in 1883 as well as at his own death in 1887. At least three of his children were living there at the time.

Children:

5.7.1.2.1	Louis Joseph	1839-1859-
5.7.1.2.2	Marie Louise Virginie	1841-1862-1862
5.7.1.2.3	Marie Emélie	1843- -1853
5.7.1.2.4	Achille	1845- -
5.7.1.2.5	Alphonsine Elise	1846- -
5.7.1.2.6	Philomène T. Eulalie	1848- -
5.7.1.2.7	M. Emerante Eloyse	1849- -
5.7.1.2.8	Mathilde H. Rose/Matilda	1853-1875-
5.7.1.2.9	Rose Ameline	1854- -
5.7.1.2.10	Frederick E./Frédéric	1857-1892?-

5.7.1.3 **MONTY, Marie Olive** b & bp 8 Apr 1815, St. Mathias, QC; d & bur 16 & 19 Oct 1878, Richelieu, QC. She married 2 Mar 1835, St. Mathias, QC, **Louis Rainville** (Louis Rainville & Desanges Massé) b & bp there 19 & 20 Mar 1805; m (1) there 20 Sep 1825, Josephte Benoit (Hippolyte Benoit & Josephte Davignon); d & bur 1 & 3 Sep 1881, Richelieu, QC.

Louis Rainville was a farmer in St. Mathias, QC, until at least 1865 and then in Richelieu, QC.

Children:

i   **Joseph Rainville** b & bp 5 Jan 1836, St. Mathias, QC; d & bur 7 & 9 May 1912, Marieville, QC. He married 2 Oct 1860, St. Mathias, QC, a first cousin once removed, **Marie Isabelle Messier** (Pierre Messier & Angélique Monty [5.7.11]) b & bp there 17 Dec 1829; d & bur 17 & 20 Sep 1912, Marieville, QC.

ii **Marie Arsène Rainville** b & bp 12 Feb 1837, St. Mathias, QC; d & bur 9 & 11 Dec 1898, Richelieu, QC.

iii **Eusèbe Rainville** b & bp 18 & 19 Jan 1839, St. Mathias, QC. He married there 7 Oct 1861 **Rosalie Bessette/Besset** (Solyme Bessette & Judith Marcoux) b & bp 21 Jun 1842, Marieville, QC.

iv **Henry Polydore Rainville** b & bp 6 & 7 Feb 1841, St. Mathias, QC; d & bur 28 & 30 Jan 1882, Richelieu, QC. He married 17 Sep 1861, Marieville, QC, **Anastasie Messier** (Jean-Baptiste Messier & Emilie Mathy) b & bp there 22 Sep 1833; d & bur 6 & 8 May 1874, Richelieu, QC.

v   **Eudoxie Rainville** b & bp 16 May 1842, St. Mathias, QC. She married there 14 Feb 1865 **Toussaint Legrain** (Toussaint Legrain & Lucie Meu-nier); b & bp there 24 Dec 1846.

vi **Olivier Rainville** b & bp 16 Jan 1844, St. Mathias, QC. He married there 19 Jan 1863 **Marie Virginie Bessette** (Marcel Bessette & Théotiste Legrain) b & bp there 18 & 19 Feb 1845.

vii **Marie Emérite Rainville** b & bp 2 & 3 Oct 1845, St. Mathias, QC. She married 15 Jul 1872, Richelieu, QC, **Pierre Beaudry** (Pierre Beaudry & Marie Préfontaine) b 23 Sep 1840, QC.

viii **Jean-Baptiste Rainville** b & bp 22 & 23 Jan 1847, St. Mathias, QC; d & bur 19 & 24 Feb Woonsocket, RI & Richelieu, QC. He married 12 Oct 1868, Richelieu, QC, **Philomène Desmarais** (Honoré Desmarais & Ursule Massé) b & bp 18 & 19 Sep 1844, St. Mathias, QC.

ix **Adèle Rainville** b & bp 29 & 30 Oct 1848, St. Mathias, QC; d & bur 3 & 5 Jun 1915, Magog, QC. She married 23 Oct 1871, Richelieu, QC, **Mathias Meunier** (Michel Meunier & Victoire Brodeur) b & bp 24 Nov 1842, Marieville, QC; d &

bur 2 & 5 Apr 1916, Magog, QC.

x   **Charles Rainville** b & bp 14 & 15 May 1850, St. Mathias, QC; d & bur there 28 & 29 Dec 1850.

xi   **Rosalie Rainville** b & bp 8 & 9 Oct 1851, St. Mathias, QC; d & bur 27 & 29 Apr 1930, Sherbrooke, QC. She married 21 Apr 1873, Richelieu, QC, **Joseph Cho-quette** (Solomon Choquette & Flavie Benoit) b & bp 29 Apr 1845, Henryville, QC; d & bur 7 & 10 Jan 1929, Sherbrooke, QC.

xii   **Moïse Rainville** b & bp 22 Aug 1853, St. Mathias, QC. He married 5 Feb 1895, Hébertville, QC, **Alphéda Simard** (Ferdinand Simard & Aglaé Lavoie) b 28 Jan 1864, QC.

xiii   **Henry Alphonse Rainville** b 1855; d & bur 11 & 13 Dec 1858, St. Mathias, QC, at the age of 3.

xiv   **Anonymous Rainville** b 1 Jan 1858, St. Mathias, QC; d & bur there 1 & 2 Jan 1858.

xv   **Félix Rainville** b & bp 23 & 24 Feb 1859, St. Mathias, QC; d & bur 11 & 13 Aug 1912, Richelieu, QC. He married 28 Nov 1882, St. Damase, QC, **Marie Beaure-gard** (François Xavier Jarred dit Beauregard & Aurélie Vandal/Vandale) b & bp 1 & 2 Feb 1860, St. Simon, QC.

5.7.1.4   **MONTY, Marie Céleste** b & bp 27 May 1816, St. Mathias, QC; d & bur 4 & 6 Jul 1858, St. Alexandre, QC. She married (1) 9 Jan 1838, St. Mathias, QC, **Joseph Fabien Gauthier** (Augustin Gauthier & Josette Petit dit Beauchemin) b May 1815?; d & bur 9 & 11 Mar 1838, Marieville, QC, at the age of 22 years and 10 months.

She married (2) 8 Oct 1839, St. Mathias, QC, **Ambroise Choquette** (François Cho-quette & Angélique Beauvais) b & bp there 8 & 9 Feb 1812; m (2) there 13 Oct 1862 Flavie Bessette (Julien Bessette & Marguerite Lareau); m (3) 13 Nov 1871, Iberville, QC, Célina Bousquet, widow of Marcel Sicotte; d & bur 30 Jan & 1 Feb 1887, Ange Gardien, QC.

Marie Céleste Monty's first husband, Joseph Fabien (also Flavien) Gauthier, was a farmer in Marieville, QC. The burial record states erroneously that his wife was Marguerite Monty. At her second marriage, Marie Céleste Monty and her brother Michel (5.7.1.5) mar-ried on the same day a brother and sister, Ambroise and Adélaïde Choquette. Ambroise Cho-quette was then a farmer in St. Mathias, QC. He was also a farmer in Iberville, QC, from about 1842 to 1850, in St. Alexandre, QC, from 1851 (Canadian census) to at least 1858, and once again, by 1869, in Iberville.

Children:

i   **Adeline Choquette** b 1839?, QC; d & bur 5 & 7 Aug 1853, St. Alexandre & Iber-ville, QC, at the age of 14.

ii   **Marie Hermine Choquette** b & bp 18 & 19 Aug 1840, Marieville, QC. She mar-ried 27 Oct 1863, St. Mathias, QC, a first cousin once removed, **Timothée Messier** (Pierre Messier & Angélique Monty [5.7.11]) b & bp 27 & 28 Jan 1839, Marieville, QC.

iii   **Marie Caroline Choquette** b & bp 28 Jul 1842, St. Jean, QC.

iv   **Marie Célina Choquette** b & bp 13 & 14 May 1845, Iberville, QC; d & bur there 2 & 4 May 1846.

v   **Adèle Choquette** b & bp 13 & 14 Jul 1847, Iberville, QC; d & bur 18 & 21 Jan 1929, Ange Gardien, QC. She married 19 Oct 1869, St. Jean-Baptiste, QC, **Joseph Viens/Vient** (Emmanuel Vient & Marie Jeanne L'Homme) b & bp there 22 & 23 Apr 1838; m (1) 3 Mar 1862, St. Mathias, QC, Philomène Jarret (François Jarret & Victoire Métras); d & bur 25 & 28 Nov 1927, Ange Gardien, QC.

vi   **Louis Choquette** b & bp 5 & 6 Nov 1850, Iberville, QC.

vii   **Marie Azilda Choquette** b & bp 30 Jun & 1 Jul 1858, St. Alexandre, QC.

5.7.1.5   **MONTY, Michel** b & bp 15 & 16 Dec 1817, St. Mathias, QC; d & bur 17 & 19 Dec 1907, Marieville, QC. He married 8 Oct 1839, St. Mathias, QC, **Adélaïde Cho-quette** (François Choquette & Angélique Beauvais) b & bp 4 Sep 1816, Marieville, QC; d &

bur there 15 & 17 Jun 1892.

Michel Monty was a farmer in St. Mathias, QC, when he married and in St. Jean-Baptiste, QC, from at least 1841 through at least 1860. By 1881, though, he was a farmer in Marieville, QC, where he remained until his death (Canadian censuses). He and his sister Marie Céleste (5.7.1.4) had married on the same day a sister and brother, Adélaïde and Ambroise Choquette.

Children:

5.7.1.5.1	Adeline/Delima	1841-	-1843
5.7.1.5.2	Michel	1842-	-1856
5.7.1.5.3	Louis Michel	1859-1882-1941	

5.7.1.6   **MONTY, Esther** b & bp 24 Nov 1820, St. Mathias, QC; d & bur there 21 & 22 Mar 1821.

5.7.1.7   **MONTY, Flavie** b & bp 28 Feb 1822, St. Mathias, QC; d & bur 17 & 20 Oct 1886, St. Jean-Baptiste, QC. She married 20 Oct 1841, St. Mathias, QC, **Jacques Bédard** (Joseph Bédard & Catherine Guillet/Diette) b & bp 27 & 28 Jan 1817, Chambly, QC; d & bur 23 & 25 Jul 1870, St. Jean-Baptiste, QC.

Jacques Bédard was a farmer in St. Césaire, QC, originally and in St. Jean-Baptiste, QC, from 1855 on.

Children:
i   **Adélaïde/Adèle Bédard** b & bp 31 Aug 1842, Marieville, QC; d & bur 14 & 18 Oct 1909, Central Falls, RI & St. Jean-Baptiste, QC.
ii   **Angèle Bédard** b & bp 11 Jan 1844, St. Césaire, QC.
iii   **Aurélie Cordélie Bédard** b & bp 16 Aug 1845, St. Césaire, QC.
iv   **Jacques Bédard** b & bp 21 & 22 Jun 1847, St. Césaire, QC. He married 6 Oct 1868, St. Jean-Baptiste, QC, **Philomène Burelle** (Joseph Burelle & Amable Desautels) b & bp 22 Aug 1847, Chambly, QC; d & bur 30 May & 2 Jun 1919, Marieville, QC.
v   **Elias Bédard** b & bp 10 & 11 Mar 1849, St. Césaire, QC; d & bur 22 & 24 Jun 1932, St. Jean-Baptiste, QC. She married there 28 Apr 1873 **Delphis/Edouard Adelphe/Dolphis Chagnon** (Elie Chagnon & Olympe Fréchette) b & bp there 25 & 26 Oct 1852; d & bur 16 & 24 Dec 1928, Notre Dame du Bon Conseil & St. Jean-Baptiste, QC.
vi   **Philomène Bédard** b & bp 28 Dec 1850, St. Césaire, QC; d & bur 19 & 22 Mar 1905, Montreal, QC.
vii   **Joseph Bédard** b & bp 15 & 16 Sep 1852, St. Césaire, QC. He married 4 Mar 1878, St. Jean-Baptiste, QC, **Alphonsine Quintal** (Pierre Quintal & Rosalie Nadeau) b & bp there 9 Jun 1858.
viii   **Célestin Bédard** b & bp 4 & 5 May 1854, St. Césaire, QC. He married 3 Nov 1875, Marieville, QC, **Mélina D'Auray/Doré** (Charles Casimir Doré & Louise Messier) b & bp there 28 Jul 1851.
ix   **Marie Bédard** b & bp 24 Aug 1855, St. Jean-Baptiste, QC.
x   **Louis Pierre Bédard** b & bp 13 & 14 Jan 1858, St. Jean-Baptiste, QC. He married 2 May 1887, St. Damase, QC, **Marie Louise Carrière** (Hercule Carrière & Julie Privé).
xi   **Joseph Marie Henry Bédard** b & bp 5 & 6 Jul 1859, St. Jean-Baptiste, QC.
xii   **Marie Célina Rosalba Bédard** b & bp 28 & 29 Sep 1861, St. Jean-Baptiste, QC.
xiii   **Flavie Bédard** b & bp 31 Mar & 1 Apr 1863, St. Jean-Baptiste, QC. She married there 19 Jan 1885 **Louis Azarie Moreau dit Dejourdy** (Joseph Moreau dit Dejourdy & Césarie Barbeau) b & bp there 18 May 1860.
xiv   **Azilda Bédard** b & bp 25 Oct 1864, Marieville, QC. She married 25 Sep 1897, St. Jean-Baptiste, QC, **Joseph Charles Edouard Chabot** (Edouard Chabot & Hermine

Beauregard) b & bp there 23 & 24 Jun 1863; m (1) 21 Jan 1890, St. Hyacinthe, QC, Joséphine Fréchette (Eusèbe Fréchette & Emelie Côté).

5.7.1.8   **MONTY, Clémence** b & bp 8 Dec 1823, St. Mathias, QC; d & bur 24 & 27 Feb 1895, St. Alexandre, QC. She married 22 Jul 1845, St. Mathias, QC, **Jean-Baptiste Dandurand** (Germain Dandurand & Suzanne Boivin) b & bp 1 & 2 Jan 1818, St. Luc, QC; m (1) 5 Jan 1839, Iberville, QC, Rose Guilmin (François Guilmin & Rose Lavallée); d & bur 11 & 13 Sep 1906, Ste Sabine, QC.

Jean-Baptiste Dandurand (Jean-Baptiste Janvier at his baptism) was a farmer in Iberville, QC, at both his marriages and later in Stanbridge, QC, and St. Alexandre, QC. He was still living there in 1901, though he was a resident of Ste Sabine, QC, at his death a few years later.

Children:
i   **Virginie Dandurand** b & bp 2 & 4 Jan 1847, Stanbridge, QC; d & bur there 19 & 21 May 1877. She married there 6 Feb 1872 **Trefflé Morin** (François Morin & Judith Galipeau) b & bp 11 & 12 Aug 1844, Iberville, QC; m (2) 4 Feb 1878, Stanbridge, QC, Onésime Daigneau (Alexis Daigneau & Onésime Jetté); d & bur there 4 & 7 Jan 1921.

ii   **Adélaïde Dandurand** b & bp 13 & 14 Aug 1848, Stanbridge, QC; d & bur there 18 & 19 Oct 1849.

iii   **Célina Dandurand** b & bp 30 Apr & 1 May 1850, Stanbridge, QC; d & bur 1 & 3 Jun 1919, Sweetsburg & St. Alexandre, QC. She married 6 Feb 1872, Stanbridge, QC, **Alexandre Brault/Breault** (Joseph Brault & Marie Sénésac) b & bp there 13 & 14 Dec 1851; d & bur 28 & 30 Apr 1913, St. Alexandre, QC.

iv   **Jean-Baptiste Dandurand** b & bp 1 Feb 1852, Stanbridge, QC. He married there 18 Oct 1887 **Marie Arzélie Galipeau** (Pierre Galipeau & Elisabeth Hamel) b 8 May 1853, QC.

v   **Isaïe Dandurand** b & bp 21 & 22 Nov 1853, Stanbridge, QC. He married 18 Oct 1875, Ange Gardien, QC, **Malvina Mercure** (Pierre Mercure & Marguerite Roy) b & bp 21 & 22 Apr 1855, St. Césaire, QC; d & bur 2 & 4 Aug 1883, Ange Gardien, QC.

vi   **Joseph Dandurand** b & bp 1 & 2 Sep 1855, Stanbridge, QC; d & bur 21 & 23 Jan 1937, Stanbridge & St. Alexandre, QC. He married 6 Jun 1887, St. Alexandre, QC, **Marie Hormisdas Plante** (Moïse Plante & Céleste Bonneau).

vii   **Octavie Dandurand** b & bp 8 & 9 Jun 1857, Stanbridge, QC; d & bur 30 Jan & 4 May 1936, Franklin, VT & Stanbridge, QC. She married 10 Oct 1882, St. Alexandre, QC, **Ephrem Bouchard** (Joseph Bouchard & Marie Rose Morin) b & bp 3 & 4 Dec 1852, Stanbridge, QC.

viii   **Marie Delima Dandurand** b & bp 26 & 27 Feb 1859, Stanbridge, QC.

ix   **Narcisse Dandurand** b & bp 27 & 28 Feb 1861, Stanbridge, QC.

x   **Honoré Dandurand** b & bp 20 & 21 Dec 1862, Stanbridge, QC; d & bur there 24 & 27 Jan 1938. He married there 8 Feb 1887 **Rosa/Rose Delima Lasnier** (Solyme Lasnier & Marie Benjamin) b & bp there 19 & 20 Mar 1870.

xi   **Azilda Dandurand** b & bp 13 & 15 Dec 1864, Stanbridge, QC; d & bur 18 & 21 Jul 1885, St. Alexandre, QC.

5.7.1.9   **MONTY, Honoré** b & bp 7 & 8 Nov 1825, St. Mathias, QC; d & bur 5 & 9 Oct 1860, Marieville, QC. He married 28 Sep 1847, St. Mathias, QC, **Célina Massé** (Honoré Massé & Emélie Martel) m (2) 11 Oct 1869, Richelieu, QC, Joseph Tétreau (Augustin Tétreau & Geneviève Gaudreau), widower of Céleste Besset and of Marie Vigeant.

Honoré Monty was a school teacher in Montreal, QC, at his marriage. A year later he was a teacher in St. Mathias, QC, and a notary's clerk there in 1853. He then moved to Marieville, QC, where he was a notary in 1856 and a Clerk of Court in 1858. He was a member of the *Chambre des notaires* for the District of St. Hyacinthe, QC, at the time of his death.

Célina Massé was a minor at her first marriage. At her second, she was a resident of

Richelieu, QC, where Joseph Tétreau was a farmer.

Children:

5.7.1.9.1	Alexander B./Honoré	1848-1869&1887-1916
5.7.1.9.2	Marie Elia Célina	1850- -1852
5.7.1.9.3	Flavien	1853- -1853
5.7.1.9.4	Edouard Flavien Frédéric G.	1857- -1857
5.7.1.9.5	Jacques François X. Arthur	1858- -1859
5.7.1.9.6	Marie Elia Célina	1860- -1861

5.7.1.10 **MONTY, Adèle** b & bp 23 & 24 Apr 1828, St. Mathias, QC; d & bur 2 & 5 Sep 1889, Richelieu, QC. She married 23 Feb 1846, St. Mathias, QC, **Charles Gervais** (Charles Gervais & Josette Tessier) b & bp 26 Apr 1823, Montreal, QC; d & bur 19 & 21 Apr 1914, Richelieu, QC.

Charles Gervais was a farmer in St. Mathias, QC, until at least 1868 and in Richelieu, QC, from at least 1870 on.

Children:

i   **Philomène Gervais** b & bp 16 & 17 Jan 1847, St. Mathias, QC; d & bur 12 & 14 Aug 1918, St. Luc, QC. She married 16 Oct 1871, Richelieu, QC, **Joseph Charles Harbec** (Charles Harbec & Judith Lefebvre) b & bp 27 Oct 1834, Chambly, QC; d & bur 12 & 15 Jan 1923, St. Jean & St. Luc, QC.

ii   **Christine Gervais** b & bp 25 & 26 Sep 1848, St. Mathias, QC; d & bur 6 & 8 Mar 1897, Chambly, QC. She married 29 Sep 1868, St. Mathias, QC, **Stanislas Meunier** (François Stanislas Meunier & Priscille Lacombe) b & bp there 8 & 9 Jun 1844; m (2) 8 Apr 1907, Montreal, QC, Célanie Guilbault, widow of François Boucher.

iii **Prudent Gervais** b & bp 9 & 10 May 1850, St. Mathias, QC; d & bur there 10 & 12 Dec 1852.

iv   **Charles Olivier Gervais** b & bp 5 & 7 Mar 1852, St. Mathias, QC; d & bur 28 Mar & 2 Apr 1888, St. Jean, QC. He married there 22 May 1877 **Alphonsine Lanoue** (Julien Lanoue & Rosalie Thibodeau) b & bp there 15 & 16 Mar 1855; d & bur there 27 & 30 Nov 1905.

v   **Moïse Gervais** b & bp 22 Aug 1853, St. Mathias, QC.

vi   **Adélaïde Gervais** b & bp 25 & 26 Mar 1854, St. Mathias, QC; d & bur 14 & 18 Mar 1929, Montreal & Chambly, QC. She married 27 May 1879, Richelieu, QC, **Pierre Saül Hardy** (Sévère Hardy & Emélie Labelle) b & bp 29 Jun 1857, Ste Thérèse, QC; d & bur 6 & 9 Dec 1940, St. Jean & Chambly, QC.

vii **Alphonse Frédéric Gervais** b & bp 13 & 15 Apr 1856, St. Mathias, QC; d & bur 22 & 25 Nov 1931, St. Jean, QC. He married there (1) 27 Oct 1891 **Evelina Bisaillon** (Joseph Bisaillon & Victoire/Victoria Monroe) b & bp there 19 & 20 Jul 1867; d & bur there 20 & 23 Mar 1897.

He married (2) 17 Oct 1898, St. Jean, QC, **Léontine Bessette** (Damase Bessette & Tharsile Massé) b & bp 1 Apr 1855, Iberville, QC; m (1) there 15 Feb 1873 Narcisse Bousquet (Louis Bousquet & Zoé Bisaillon); d & bur 31 Aug & 4 Sep 1939, St. Jean, QC.

viii **Frédéric Gervais** b & bp 16 Nov 1859, St. Mathias, QC; d & bur there 22 & 23 Jan 1860.

ix   **Louis Arthur Gervais** b & bp 8 & 9 Sep 1861, Marieville, QC; d & bur 13 & 16 Feb 1863, St. Mathias, QC.

x   **Honoré Achille Hippolyte Gervais** b & bp 13 & 15 Aug 1863, St. Mathias, QC; d & bur 8 & 11 Aug 1915, Montreal, QC. He married there 17 May 1887 **Albina Robert** (Joseph Robert & Olympe Berlinguet) b & bp there 2 & 3 Mar 1863; d & bur there 4 & 7 Feb 1940.

xi   **Marie Adrienne Blanche Hortense Gervais** b & bp 28 & 29 Nov 1865, Marieville, QC; d & bur 31 Aug & 2 Sep 1924, Montreal, QC. She married 25 Feb 1889,

Richelieu, QC, **Eusèbe Lanoue** (Julien Lanoue & Rosalie Thibodeau) b & bp 2 & 3 Dec 1849, St. Jean, QC; m (1) there 14 Aug 1871 Joséphine Monette (Julien Monette & Julienne Tétrault); d & bur 6 & 9 Dec 1916, Montreal & St. Jean, QC.

xii   **Romuald Adrien Ladislas Gervais** b & bp 2 & 5 Feb 1868, St. Mathias & Chambly, QC.

xiii   **Maximilien Gervais** b 2 Feb 1869, QC; d & bur 14 & 16 Mar 1906, Richelieu, QC. He married there 28 Jan 1890 **Alexina Lussier** (Théodore Lussier & Octavie Lefrançois) b & bp there 21 Apr 1870; d & bur there 16 & 18 Apr 1918.

xiv   **Elisée Horace Gervais** b & bp 30 Oct & 1 Nov 1870, Richelieu, QC; d 4 Nov 1960, St. Jean, QC. He married (1) 31 Aug 1897, Marieville, QC, **Clara Henriette Ledoux** (Stanislas Ledoux & Henriette Archambault) b 8 Nov 1872?, QC; d & bur 4 & 7 Apr 1917, St. Jean, QC, at the age of 46.

He married (2) 29 Sep 1947, Marieville, QC, **Alice Blandine Desautels** (Jean-Baptiste Desautels & Azilda Bergeron) b & bp 25 Aug 1877, St. Césaire, QC; m (1) there 16 Aug 1898 Joseph Nicholas Ledoux (Stanislas Ledoux & Henriette Archambault); d & bur 3 & 6 May 1959, Marieville, QC.

5.7.1.11   **MONTY, Timothée** b & bp 4 & 5 Apr 1830, St. Mathias, QC; d & bur there 6 & 7 Apr 1830.

5.7.1.12   **MONTY, Prudent** b & bp 16 & 17 Jul 1832, Marieville, QC; d 19 Sep 1901, Woonsocket, RI. He married 4 Feb 1852, Longueuil, QC, **Onésime Daignault** (Basile Daignault & Julienne Vandandaigue) b & bp there 17 Sep 1832; d & bur 17 & 20 Mar 1914, Chambly, QC.

Prudent Monty was originally a farmer in St. Mathias, QC. He emigrated with his family around 1871 and was for many years a mill worker in Holyoke, MA, before moving to Woonsocket, RI. He was a gardener there in 1900, living in the household of his daughter Celia and son-in-law Joseph Lussier. He and his wife had had eleven children of whom six were then alive (US censuses).

Onésime Daignault (Marie Elénise Deniau at her baptism) was a granddaughter of François Deniau and Marguerite Monty (1.16) and thus her husband's third cousin. She remained in the United States for several years after his death and was living in her son John B. L. Monty's household in Bristol, CT, in 1910 (US census). She returned to Canada a few years later and was staying with her daughter Hermine and son-in-law Alphonse Brunelle in Chambly, QC, at her death.

Children:

5.7.1.12.1	Eudoxie	1853-1876&1885-1945
5.7.1.12.2	Marie Louise Eliane	1854- -1854
5.7.1.12.3	Louis Michel Théophile	1855- -
5.7.1.12.4	John B. L./Jean-Bapt. Léonidas	1856-1877&1901?&1914-1914?
5.7.1.12.5	Louis Charles	1858-1879-1935
5.7.1.12.6	Celia/Cecilia	1861-1881&1928-1941
5.7.1.12.7	Hermine	1863-1886&1906-1941
5.7.1.12.8	Georges Alfred	1865- -1865
5.7.1.12.9	Salvina	1871- -1874
5.7.1.12.10	Avelina	1872- -1872
5.7.1.12.11	Edward	1873-1897-

5.7.2.1   **MONTY, Thomas** b & bp 30 Jun & 1 Jul 1813, St. Mathias, QC; d & bur 6 & 8 May 1856, St. Jean-Baptiste, QC.

Thomas Monty was a laborer living in his father's household in St. Jean-Baptiste, QC, in 1851 (Canadian census). He did not marry.

5.7.2.2   **MONTY, Louis** b & bp 12 May 1815, St. Jean-Baptiste, QC.

This child presumably died before May 1836 when a half-brother also named Louis

(5.7.2.9) was baptized in Marieville, QC.

5.7.2.3   **MONTY, Anonymous** (male) b 2 Aug 1817, St. Jean-Baptiste, QC; d & bur there 2 Aug 1817.
This child was stillborn.

5.7.2.4   **MONTY, Charlotte** b & bp 6 & 7 Oct 1818, St. Jean-Baptiste, QC; d & bur there 26 & 28 Feb 1822.
The 1822 burial record of a 3-year-old daughter of Thomas Monty and Catherine Benoit bears the name of Catherine Monty. This must be an error for their daughter Catherine (5.7.2.5) was only 8 months old in February 1822. The reference must be to their daughter Charlotte who would then have been 3 years old and of whom no further trace is found.

5.7.2.5   **MONTY, Catherine** b & bp 22 Jun 1821, St. Jean-Baptiste, QC; d & bur 15 & 17 Jan 1870, Ange Gardien, QC. She married there 27 Nov 1865 **François Adam** (François Adam & Amable Choquette) b & bp 1 Mar 1822, St. Mathias, QC; m (1) there 10 Jan 1843 Catherine Lagüe (Toussaint Lagüe & Charlotte Ponton); m (3) 6 Feb 1872, Ange Gardien, QC, Sophie Daigneau (Jacques Daigneau & Joséphine Gauvin); m (4) 22 Aug 1898, Farnham, QC, Sophie Dion, widow of Julien Leduc and of Narcisse Laporte.
François Adam was a farmer in Ange Gardien, QC.

5.7.2.6   **MONTY, André** b & bp 11 Oct 1823, St. Jean-Baptiste, QC; d between 1883 and 1900. He married 15 Feb 1847, St. Jean-Baptiste, QC, **Marie Louise Touchette** (Simon Touchette & Angélique Dion) b & bp there 26 & 27 Sep 1821; d & bur 28 & 29 Mar 1907, Farnham, QC.
André Monty was a farmer in St. Jean-Baptiste, QC, at his marriage, in St. Césaire, QC, from 1848 through at least 1859, and in Ange Gardien, QC, in the late 1860s and 1870s. He and his wife were residents of Bromont (West Shefford), QC, at the death of their son Augustin in 1883.
Louise Touchette came to the United States in 1897, perhaps after her husband's death and was in 1900 a widow living in her son Thomas' household in New Bedford, MA. She had had ten children of whom six were still alive (US census). She was still in New Bedford in 1902 (City Directory).

Children:

5.7.2.6.1	Marie Louise	1848-1869-1869
5.7.2.6.2	Louis	1849-1875-1924
5.7.2.6.3	Cordélie	1851- -
5.7.2.6.4	André	1852-1873-1911
5.7.2.6.5	Malvina	1854- -1870
5.7.2.6.6	Thomas	1855-1876&1894-1918
5.7.2.6.7	Marie Aurélie Henriette	1857- -
5.7.2.6.8	Alexina	1859?-1886-
5.7.2.6.9	Augustin	1860?- -1883

5.7.2.7   **MONTY, Domitille** b & bp 14 & 15 Dec 1829, St. Jean-Baptiste, QC; d & bur there 23 & 25 May 1830.

5.7.2.8   **MONTY, Amable** b & bp 20 Jan 1831, Marieville, QC; d & bur 18 & 21 Nov 1893, St. Jean-Baptiste, QC. He married 27 Feb 1854, St. Césaire, QC, **Julienne Beaumont** (Louis Couillard dit Beaumont & Josephte Duchesneau) b & bp 19 Jan 1830, St Charles sur Richelieu, QC; m (1) there 10 Oct 1848 Louis Dussault (Louis Dussault & Rose Léveillé); d between 1881 and 1893.
Amable Monty was a blacksmith in St. Césaire, QC, at his marriage and in Abbotsford, QC, until at least 1871 (Lovell's Directory). He, or maybe only his wife and children, then moved to the United States for his last child was born in Massachusetts around 1873. He was

not with his family in 1880 when Mary Monti (sic) and seven of her children, Raoul, Trefflé, Arthur, Solyme, Raymond, Mary, and Mitchell, were living in Webster, MA (US census). His wife Julienne and children Raoul, Trefflé, Arthur, Malvina, Solyme, and Raymond were with him, though, in 1881 when he was a farmer in St. Eugène de Grantham, QC (Canadian census). This must have been a temporary stay. At least six of his surviving children returned to Massachusetts and some married there in the early 1880s. By 1891, Amable Monty, a blacksmith in Granby, QC, was again without a family (Canadian census). He was a blacksmith in St. Jean-Baptiste, QC, at his death.

Julienne Beaumont predeceased her husband. I have not found her death record in either Canada or the United States. She had been named Julienne Couillard at her baptism but Julienne Beaumont at her marriage and at the baptisms and marriages of her children.

Children:

5.7.2.8.1	Amédée	1855-1873?-1913
5.7.2.8.2	Raoul	1859-1881-1946
5.7.2.8.3	Télesphore	1860- -1863
5.7.2.8.4	Trefflé	1862-1883&1919-
5.7.2.8.5	Arthur	1863- -1893
5.7.2.8.6	Marie Malvina	1865-1887-1919
5.7.2.8.7	Solyme	1866- -
5.7.2.8.8	Raymond Euclide	1869- -
5.7.2.8.9	Marie Georgine	1871- -1872
5.7.2.8.10	Mitchell	1873?- -

5.7.2.9   **MONTY, Louis** b & bp 19 May 1836, Marieville, QC; d & bur 17 & 19 Apr 1859, St. Jean-Baptiste, QC.

5.7.2.10   **MONTY, Joseph** b & bp 24 Oct 1837, St. Jean-Baptiste, QC; d & bur there 14 & 16 Mar 1908. He married there 5 Feb 1861 **Marcelline Burelle** (Joseph Burelle & Amable Desautels) b & bp there 3 Apr 1841; d & bur there 24 & 26 Nov 1917.

Joseph Monty was a farmer in St. Jean-Baptiste, QC.

Children:

5.7.2.10.1	Euphrasie	1862-1894-1941
5.7.2.10.2	Achille/Archie	1864-1907-
5.7.2.10.3	Arzélie	1865- -1869
5.7.2.10.4	Evelina	1867- -1943
5.7.2.10.5	Wilfrid	1869-1919-1959
5.7.2.10.6	Victoria	1871-1892-1910
5.7.2.10.7	Rosine/Rosalba	1873- -1875
5.7.2.10.8	Albani/Albini	1874- -1955
5.7.2.10.9	Antoine	1877- -1877
5.7.2.10.10	Clara Hermina Aglaé	1878-1908-1940
5.7.2.10.11	Marie Louise Anne/Dorilla	1881- -1883

5.7.2.11   **MONTY, Anonymous** b 4 Aug 1840, St. Jean-Baptiste, QC; d & bur there 4 & 5 Aug 1840.

5.7.2.12   **MONTY, Marie Agathe** b & bp 22 May 1844, St. Jean-Baptiste, QC. She married there 12 Feb 1872 **Jean-Baptiste Choquette** (Hubert Choquette & Marie Breault) b & bp 22 & 23 Jul 1854, Mont St. Grégoire, QC.

Jean-Baptiste Choquette was a laborer in St. Césaire, QC, until at least 1879, after which date the family seems to disappear from Canada. It is said that Jean-Baptiste Choquette was in Moosup, CT, in the late 19th century but I have found no evidence of the family's presence there.

Children:
i   **Marie Louise Anne Choquette** b & bp 2 & 3 Jul 1873, St. Jean-Baptiste, QC.
ii   **Jean-Baptiste C. Adélard Choquette** b & bp 5 & 6 May 1875, Marieville, QC.
iii   **Adélard Choquette** b & bp 30 & 31 Mar 1879, St. Césaire, QC.

5.7.2.13   **MONTY, Elise/Isabelle** b & bp 19 & 20 Sep 1846, St. Jean-Baptiste, QC;
d & bur 6 & 8 Jan 1934, St. Mathias, QC. She married 5 Jul 1869, St. Jean-Baptiste, QC,
Hubert Daignault (Pierre Daignault & Séraphine Robert) b & bp there 9 Jun 1837; m (1)
there 16 Feb 1863 Aglaé Fontaine (Joseph Fontaine dit Bienvenue & Euphémie Choinière); d
between 1891 and 1895.

     This woman was known as Isabelle at her baptism and at her burial. She signed her
marriage record however as Elisa Monty (though the text itself refers to Elise Monty) and was
known as Elise in Canadian censuses as well as at the births and deaths of her children.

     Hubert Daignault (also Daigneau, Dagneau dit Laprise) was a farmer in St. Jean-
Baptiste, QC. He was alive in 1891 at the death of his daughter Pluvine (iii) but was deceased
three years later at the death of his daughter Arsélia (i). His widow remained in St. Jean-
Baptiste with her children until at least 1901 but was living with her sons in St. Mathias, QC,
in 1911 (Canadian censuses).

Children:
i   **Marie Azélia/Arsélia Daignault** b & bp 10 Apr 1870, St. Jean-Baptiste, QC; d &
      bur there 19 & 21 Aug 1894.
ii   **Marie Flavine Daignault** b & bp 26 Jul 1871, St. Jean-Baptiste, QC.
iii   **Marie Pluvine Daignault** b 1873?; d & bur 1 & 3 Jul 1891, St. Jean-Baptiste, QC,
      at the age of 18.
iv   **Albert Daignault** b 24 Oct 1879, QC. He married (1) 19 Nov 1928, Chambly, QC,
      Laura Léveillé (Charles Cognac dit Léveillé & Virginie Lariche) b & bp there 24
      Jan 1884; d & bur 13 & 15 Feb 1930, Ste Angèle & Chambly, QC.
      He married (2) 10 Oct 1931, Ste Angèle, QC, **Rose Amande Mailloux** (Honoré
      Mailloux & Hermine Barré) b & bp there 27 & 29 Jul 1879.
v   **George Daignault** b & bp 23 Apr 1883, Milton, QC. He married 1907? **Alberta
      Ashby** (Napoléon Ashby & Clarinda Fournier) b & bp 12 & 13 Feb 1887, Marie-
      ville, QC.

5.7.2.14   **MONTY, Antoine Jean-Baptiste Charles** b & bp 12 & 13 Aug 1848, St.
Jean-Baptiste, QC; d & bur there 22 & 23 Mar 1854.

5.7.2.15   **MONTY, Didace** b & bp 17 & 18 Jun 1851, Marieville, QC; d & bur 19 &
22 Oct 1909, St. Jean-Baptiste, QC. He married (1) there 19 Jan 1875 **Aglaé Leroux** (François Leroux & Sophie Blanchard) b & bp 17 Apr 1848, St. Césaire, QC.

     He was a widower when he married (2) 17 Jun 1893, North Grosvenordale, CT, **Geor-
giana Gagné** (Pierre Gagné & Marie Daigle) b & bp 2 Mar 1867, Armagh, QC; m (1) 1 Jan
1886, Rochester, NH, Pierre Prince (Joseph Prince & Hermine Poirier).

     Didace Monty was a farmer in Milton, QC, at his marriage and apparently remained
there until about 1885, even when his children were baptized in other localities. In 1887,
though, he was a laborer in St. Jean-Baptiste, QC, where a child was stillborn. According to
the 1900 US census in Plainfield, CT, Didace Montie (sic) and his family arrived in the
United States in 1888 (although a daughter, Emma, was born in Canada in 1890). I do not
know when he returned to Canada. He survived his second wife and was a *bourgeois* in St.
Jean-Baptiste at his death. Most of his children, though, remained in New England.

Children of the first marriage:

5.7.2.15.1	Hormisdas	1876- -1904
5.7.2.15.2	Delphis Frank	1877-1920-1947
5.7.2.15.3	Dorilla	1880-1911-
5.7.2.15.4	Maranda	1881-1900?& -

5.7.2.15.5	Leandra Leopoldine/Lora	1882-	-
5.7.2.15.6	Adélard	1885-	-
5.7.2.15.7	Anonymous	1887-	-1887
5.7.2.15.8	Emma	1890-	-

Children of the second marriage:

5.7.2.15.9	Rena/Marie Regina	1894-1913?-1983
5.7.2.15.10	Joseph	1896- -1959
5.7.2.15.11	Polydore	-1926-

5.7.2.16   **MONTY, Marie Louise Euphrosine** b & bp 7 & 8 Jun 1853, St. Jean-Baptiste, QC; d & bur there 20 & 22 Apr 1858.

5.7.4.1   **MONTY, Joseph** b & bp 1 & 2 Feb 1818, St. Jean-Baptiste, QC; d & bur there 4 & 6 Feb 1818.

5.7.4.2   **MONTY, Julienne/Julie** b & bp 11 & 12 May 1822, St. Jean-Baptiste, QC; d & bur 10 & 12 Feb 1865, Iberville, QC. She married 11 Oct 1836, St. Mathias, QC, **Edouard Besset** (Julien Besset & Marguerite Larault) b & bp there 2 May 1816; d & bur 11 & 13 Dec 1882, St. Luc & Iberville, QC.

Edouard Besset (also Bessette) was originally a farmer in St. Mathias, QC, and from 1843 on in Iberville, QC. He was living in 1881 in his son Alfred's household in St. Luc, QC (Canadian census).

Children:
i   **Edouard Besset** b & bp 5 Nov 1839, St. Mathias, QC.
ii   **Joseph Besset** b & bp 3 May 1841, St. Mathias, QC; d & bur 19 & 21 Jul 1916, St. Jean & Iberville, QC. He married 16 Feb 1863, Iberville, QC, **Marie Anne Brosseau** (Noël Brosseau & Marie Anne Chaumière) b & bp there 29 Mar 1841; d & bur 13 & 15 Jan 1920 Montreal & Iberville, QC.
iii   **Edouard Besset/Bessette** b & bp 31 Mar & 1 Apr 1843, Iberville, QC. He married there 12 Jan 1869 **Euphrosine Bessette** (François Bessette & Julie Patenaude) b & bp there 27 & 28 June 1845.
iv   **Pierre Besset** b & bp 27 & 29 Jun 1845, St. Jean, QC; d & bur 2 & 4 Feb 1851, Iberville, QC.
v   **Alfred Besset** b & bp 24 & 25 Jul 1848, Iberville, QC. He married (1) 1872? **Anastasie Souci** b 1852?, QC; d & bur 6 & 9 Mar 1885, St. Luc, QC, at the age of 33.
    He married (2) 5 Nov 1885, St. Jean, QC, **Malvina Frederick** (Joseph Frederick & Louise Collet).
vi   **Delphine Besset** b & bp 22 & 23 Apr 1850, Iberville, QC.
vii   **Pierre/Peter Besset** b & bp 20 & 21 Jul 1852, Iberville, QC. He married 1879? **Rebecca ____** b Mar 1855, QC.
viii   **Charles Besset** b & bp 13 & 14 May 1854, Iberville, QC.
ix   **Alphonse Besset** b & bp 16 & 17 Jun 1860, Iberville, QC.
x   **Marie Médérise Besset** b & bp 25 & 26 Oct 1863, Iberville, QC; d & bur there 20 & 22 Oct 1864.

5.7.4.3   **MONTY, Eudoxie** b & bp 24 Oct 1823, St. Jean-Baptiste, QC; d & bur 26 & 29 Jun 1910, Holyoke & South Hadley Falls, MA. She married 18 Feb 1840, St. Mathias, QC, **Honoré Besset** (Louis Clément Besset & Marie Louise Terrien) b & bp 1 Mar 1821, St. Luc, QC; d between 1888 and 1900.

Honoré Besset (also Bessette) was originally a farmer and laborer in Iberville, QC. He was also a boatman there in 1862 and a farmer and carpenter in 1870 though a resident of Holyoke, MA, in 1872 when his daughter Eudoxie (vii) married. He was back in Iberville by 1881 (Canadian census) and was present at his son Honoré's second marriage there in 1888. He died before 1900 for his widow was then living with her daughter Marie Louise and son-in-law Louis Bibeau in Holyoke. She continued to reside with them until her death (US censuses).

Children:
- i   **Eudoxie Besset/Bessette** b & bp 18 & 19 Sep 1841, Iberville, QC; d & bur there 14 & 15 Jul 1842.
- ii   **Honoré** (also **Clément H.**) **Besset/Bessette** b & bp 28 May 1843, Iberville, QC; d & bur 13 & 16 May 1898, St. Jean, QC. He married there (1) 4 Sep 1876, **Marie Rousseau** (Léon Rousseau & Zoé Mondona) b & bp there 28 Feb & 1 Mar 1858; d & bur there 24 & 28 Dec 1882.

    He married (2) 9 Jan 1888, Iberville, QC, **Elise/Marie Louise Lareau** (Honoré Lareau & Emélie Tétreault) b & bp there 14 & 15 Jul 1854.
- iii   **Marie Besset/Bessette** b & bp 7 & 8 Jun 1845, Iberville, QC; d & bur there 4 & 6 Sep 1845.
- iv   **Adée Louise Besset/Bessette** b & bp 17 & 18 Oct 1846, Iberville, QC.
- v   **Moïse Besset/Bessette** b & bp 28 & 29 Sep 1848, Iberville, QC. He married there 2 Feb 1874 **Virginie Forand** (Charles Forand & Sophie Jarry) b & bp there 22 & 28 Jul 1850.
- vi   **Marie Mélinda Besset/Bessette** b & bp 15 & 16 Sep 1850, Iberville, QC.
- vii   **Eudoxie Besset/Bessette** b & bp 29 Jun 1852, Iberville, QC. She married there 19 Nov 1872 **Israël Labelle** (Joseph Labelle & Zéphirine Dorion) b & bp 22 & 28 Jul 1850, St. André Est, QC.
- viii   **Athanase Delphis Besset/Bessette** b & bp 10 & 11 Jun 1854, Iberville, QC; d & bur there 7 & 8 Nov 1855.
- ix   **Stanislas Besset/Bessette** b & bp 8 Jul 1856, Iberville, QC; d & bur there 4 & 5 May 1858.
- x   **Marie Virginie Osanna Besset/Bessette** b & bp 20 & 22 May 1858, Iberville, QC.
- xi   **Athanase Besset/Bessette** b & bp 7 Apr 1860, Iberville, QC; d & bur there 17 & 19 Jun 1860.
- xii   **Marie Louise Azllda/Mary L. Besset/Bessette** b & bp 18 & 19 Jul 1862, Iberville, QC. She married 1885? **Louis Bibeau** b Jan 1859, QC.
- xiii   **Hercule Besset/Bessette** b & bp 13 & 14 Oct 1866, Iberville, QC.
- xiv   **Joseph Alexandre Besset/Bessette** b & bp 27 & 28 Feb 1870, Iberville, QC; d & bur there 31 Mar & 1 Apr 1870.

5.7.4.4   **MONTY, Marie** b & bp 2 & 3 Jan 1829, St. Jean-Baptiste, QC; d & bur there 12 & 14 Sep 1829.

5.7.5.1   **MONTY, Marie** b & bp 18 & 19 Jul 1827, St. Mathias, QC; d between 1880 and 1883. She married 28 Nov 1849, St. Mathias, QC, **Alexis Jérémie Adam dit Laramée** (François Adam dit Laramée & Amable Choquet) b & bp 17 Jul 1824, Marieville, QC; m (1) 3 Feb 1845, St. Mathias, QC, Sophie Gendron (Joseph Gendron & Marie Laguna).

Marie Monty was living with her husband Jeremiah Adams (sic) in Chicopee, MA, in 1880 (US census) but was deceased at the marriage of her daughter Virginie (iv) in 1883.

Her husband was named Alexis Jérémie Adam at his baptism and appears to have used both names at will. He married his first wife under the name of Alexis Adam, but both their children had Jérémie Adam as father. He was Jérémie when he married Marie Monty, Alexis when their first child was baptized, and Jérémie again at the younger children's baptisms. He was a farmer in St. Mathias, QC, until at least 1864 and may have emigrated in the late 1860s or early or 1870s: he was a resident of Salem, MA, when his son Alexis (ii) married in 1872. By 1880 Virginie (iv), Arthur (viii), and Mary (i), along with her husband and four children, were all living with their parents in Chicopee. Jeremiah Adams was a farmer there (US census). He was also there when his daughter Virginie married in 1883. I have been unable to trace him further.

Children:

i   **Marie/Mary Adam** b & bp 31 Jul & 3 Aug 1851, St. Mathias, QC; d 15 Jul 1888, Holyoke, MA. She married 1871?, QC, **Joseph Magneron dit Lajeunesse** (Jean-Baptiste Magneron dit Lajeunesse & Théotiste Miron) b & bp 20 & 21 May 1847, St. Jacques l'Achigan, QC; m (2) Camille Belland; d Mar 1894.

ii   **Alexis/Alphonse Adam** b & bp 2 & 3 Jan 1853, Marieville, QC; d & bur 30 Dec 1942 & 2 Jan 1943, Chambly, QC. He married (1) 5 Jan 1872, St. Basile, QC, **Malvina Picard** (Noël Picard & Catherine Lagüe) b 1845?, QC; d & bur 29 Nov & 1 Dec 1925, St. Basile, QC, at the age of 80.

He married (2) 8 Jul 1926, St. Basile, QC, **Rose Adeline Lalumière** (Eusèbe Lalumière & Philomène Letourneau) b & bp 5 Mar 1862, St. Bruno, QC; d & bur 19 & 21 Dec 1937, St. Basile, QC.

iii   **Marie Azilda Adam** b & bp 14 & 15 Oct 1854, St. Mathias, QC.

iv   **Philomène Adam** b & bp 14 Jul 1856, St. Mathias, QC; d & bur there 1 & 2 Sep 1858.

v   **Virginie Adam** b & bp 10 & 11 Mar 1858, St. Mathias, QC; d & bur 13 & 15 Dec 1932, Chambly, QC. She married 5 Feb 1883, St. Basile, QC, **Joseph Noreau/Norault** (David Noreau/Norault & Josette Dubé) b & bp 16 & 18 Apr 1861, St. Bruno, QC.

vi   **Noël Adam** b & bp 25 & 26 Dec 1859, St. Mathias, QC; d & bur there 31 Jan & 1 Feb 1860.

vii   **Rosalie Adam** b & bp 5 Jan 1861, St. Mathias, QC.

viii   **Joseph Arthur Adam** b & bp 12 Oct 1862, St. Mathias, QC; d & bur there 5 & 7 Apr 1864.

ix   **Arthur Edmond Adam** b & bp 22 & 23 Oct 1864, St. Mathias, QC.

5.7.5.2   **MONTY, Scholastique** b & bp 30 Jul 1829, St. Mathias, QC; d & bur 8 & 10 Jun 1910, St. Jean QC.

Scholastique Monty did not marry.

5.7.5.3   **MONTY, Julie** b & bp 4 Jul 1831, St. Mathias, QC.

5.7.5.4   **MONTY, Alexis** b & bp 11 Jul 1834, St. Mathias, QC; d & bur there 9 & 10 Feb 1835.

5.7.5.5.   **MONTY, Louis** b & bp 29 & 30 Dec 1836, St. Mathias, QC; d & bur 7 & 9 May 1882, Ste Brigide, QC. He married there 25 Oct 1869 **Eulalie Quimineur/Quimeneur/Kymineur dit Laflamme** (Charles Quimineur dit Laflamme & Anastasie Bédard) b & bp 25 Mar 1847, Marieville, QC; d & bur 27 & 29 Dec 1914, Ste Brigide, QC.

Louis Monty was a farmer in Ste Brigide, QC, until about 1872 when he and his family first moved to the United States. In the ensuing years the family apparently moved back and forth between the two countries, with children born in Connecticut in 1873 and 1878 and the others in Canada. Louis Monte (sic) himself was a woolen mill worker in Norwich, CT in 1880 (US census) though he died in Canada two years later.

After her husband's death Eulalie Quimineur (also Quimeneur, Kymineur, and Kimineur dit Laflamme) returned to Connecticut with her children and was a resident there when her daughter Rose Anna married in 1891. She may have returned as early as 1885: that is when her son Louis claimed in his naturalization papers of 17 Oct 1904 to have arrived in the United States. She was in Canada though in 1901 when she was living in St. Césaire, QC, next door to her daughter Emma and son-in-law Arthur Gendron (Canadian census). She was back in Norwich a few years later and was in 1910 the head of a household which included her son Louis and his wife as well as her widowed daughter Rose Anna and four grandchildren. According to that year's US census, she had had seven children of whom four, Rose Anna, Joseph Hormidas, Emma, and Louis, were still alive. The following year she was living in Ste Brigide, QC, with her daughter Emma and son-in-law Arthur Gendron (Canadian census). She died and was buried there under the name of Eulalie Laflamme.

Children:

5.7.5.5.1	Rose Anna	1870-1891-1912
5.7.5.5.2	Joseph Hormidas/Peter H.	1873-1908-1959
5.7.5.5.3	Charles Auguste	1875- -1875
5.7.5.5.4	Edna	1878?- -
5.7.5.5.5	Emma/Marie Anna	1880-1899-1980
5.7.5.5.6	Louis	1882-1909-

5.7.5.6   **MONTY, Jacques** b & bp 25 Jul 1839, St. Mathias, QC; d & bur there 25 & 26 Jul 1839.

5.7.5.7   **MONTY, Joseph** b & bp 24 & 25 Sep 1842, St. Mathias, QC; d & bur 15 & 18 Mar 1918, St. Jean, QC. He married (1) 12 Aug 1867, Ste Brigide, QC, **Dorothée Tétrault** (Hubert Tétrault & Victoire Blanchette) b & bp 12 & 19 Nov 1847, Mont St. Grégoire, QC; d & bur 6 & 8 May 1875, Ste Brigide, QC.

He married (2) 22 Jan 1877, St. Luc, QC, **Mathilde Papineau** (David Papineau & Agathe Demers) b & bp 1 & 3 Dec 1843, Chambly, QC; d & bur 1 & 3 Jul 1922, St. Jean, QC.

Joseph Monty was a farmer in Ste Brigide, QC, at his first marriage, in Ste Angèle, QC, in 1868, and in Ste Brigide again in 1870. He may have worked in the United States for a few years for his son Aimé was born there around 1874. He was back in Ste Brigide though when his first wife died in 1875. He remained in Canada and was a carpenter in St. Jean, QC, at his second marriage, a farmer in St. Luc, QC, in 1881 and 1891, a teamster in St. Jean in 1901, and a milkman there in 1911 (Canadian censuses).

Children of the first marriage:

5.7.5.7.1	Joseph Pierre	1868- -1875
5.7.5.7.2	Ephrem	1870-1900-1925
5.7.5.7.3	Aimé	1874?- -1932

Children of the second marriage:

5.7.5.7.4	Joseph	1879-1904-1917
5.7.5.7.5	Henri David	1882- -

5.7.5.8   **MONTY, Joséphine** b & bp 14 May 1847, St. Mathias, QC; d & bur there 3 & 4 Nov 1848.

5.7.7.1   **MONTY, Léon** b & bp 12 & 13 Mar 1824, St. Mathias, QC; d 9 Feb 1868, Holyoke, MA. He married 17 Feb 1846, St. Césaire, QC, **Mathilde Mongeau** (Jean-Baptiste Mongeau & Madeleine Montplaisir) b & bp 29 & 30 Nov 1826, St. Jean-Baptiste, QC; d & bur 30 Jul & 1 Aug 1915, Holyoke & South Hadley Falls, MA.

Léon Monty was a farmer in St. Césaire, QC, until the early 1860s and a laborer in Holyoke, MA, at the birth of a daughter there in May 1863.

Mathilde Mongeau remained in the Holyoke area with her children after her husband's death and by 1910 was living in South Hadley, MA, with her granddaughter Julia Monty (5.7.7.1.4.1) and her husband William Fleming (US censuses). She was buried in Notre Dame Cemetery in South Hadley Falls, MA, in the Rébétez family plot alongside her daughter Alphonsine (5.7.7.1.2) and son-in-law Julien Pierre Rébétez.

Children:

5.7.7.1.1	Louis Arthur	1847- -1850
5.7.7.1.2	Alphonsine	1848-1869-1880
5.7.7.1.3	Dorie Mathilde/Louisa D.	1850-1889-
5.7.7.1.4	Jean-Baptiste/John	1852-1874-1906
5.7.7.1.5	Marie	1854-1876-1891
5.7 7.1.6	Félix	1856- -1856

5.7.7.1.7	Eli Joseph	1857-1883-1907
5.7.7.1.8	Isaïe Louis	1860-1886-1903
5.7.7.1.9	Laura Valarie	1863-1882&1886?&1909?-1923

5.7.7.2   MONTY, Zoé b & bp 8 & 9 Aug 1825, St. Mathias, QC; d 9 Feb 1897, Holyoke, MA. She married 8 Apr 1845, St. Césaire, QC, **Charles Ménard dit Bellerose** (Joseph Ménard dit Bellerose & Apolline Legros dit St. Pierre) b & bp 15 Jan 1824, St. Hyacinthe, QC; m (2) 8 Apr 1899, St. Pie, QC, Rosalie Labonté (David Baudriault dit Labonté & Isabelle Lucier), widow of François Messier.

Charles Ménard was a farmer in St. Césaire, QC, at his first marriage. The family moved soon after the birth of the youngest child to Holyoke, MA, where several children married in the 1870s and 1880s. Zoé Monty was buried in South Hadley Falls, MA. Charles Ménard returned to Canada after her death and was living in St. Césaire with his second wife in 1901 (Canadian census).

Children:

i   **Charles Ménard** b & bp 4 Jul 1846, St. Césaire, QC.

ii   **Frédéric/Uldéric Ménard** b & bp 19 & 20 May 1848, St. Césaire, QC. He married (1) Feb 1871, Holyoke, MA, **Clara Viger** (Charles Viger & Elise ____) b 1853?, QC; d 1896, Holyoke, MA.

    He married (2) 24 Oct 1897, Holyoke, MA, **Eva Moreau** (Moïse Moreau & Marie Ethier) b & bp 13 & 14 Dec 1859, St. Alexandre, QC, widow of ____ Aubrey.

iii **Adolphe Ménard** b & bp 30 May 1850, St. Césaire, QC; d 1910, Northampton, MA. He married 16 Jul 1872, Holyoke, MA, **Marcelle/Marceline Moquin** (Michel Moquin & Rosalie Bouteille dite Bonneville) b & bp 12 & 13 May 1849, St. Mathias, QC; d 1918, Holyoke, MA.

iv   **Claudia Ménard** b & bp 22 May 1852, St. Césaire, QC. She married there 7 Feb 1871 **Amédée Gingras** (Jean-Baptiste Gingras & Domitilde Larocque) b & bp 2 & 3 Mar 1848, St. Jean-Baptiste, QC.

v   **Eloïse Ménard** b & bp 10 Aug 1854, St. Césaire, QC.

vi   **Alida Ménard** married 20 Jan 1874, St. Césaire, QC, **Adolphe Ouimet** (Alexis Ouimet & Mathilde Gaucher) b & bp 27 May 1852, St. Pie, QC.

vii **François/Frank Ménard/Maynard** b & bp 13 & 14 Oct 1856, St. Césaire, QC. He married 31 Jan 1881, Holyoke, MA, **Hermaline/Armelia Pelland** (Paul Pelland/Pailland & Marie Mender) b Jul 1856, QC; d 1915, West Springfield, MA.

viii **Malvina Ménard** b & bp 30 Nov 1858, St. Césaire, QC. She married there 20 Nov 1884 **Israël Charron dit Cabana** (Hilaire Charron dit Cabana & Louise Gingras) b & bp 23 Aug 1854, St. Pie, QC.

ix   **Vénérance/Honorée Alexina Ménard** b & bp 20 Dec 1860, St. Césaire, QC. She married there 7 Jan 1884 **Joseph Ménard** (Antoine Ménard & Henriette Trouillet) b & bp 28 Apr 1859, Abbotsford, QC; m (2) as a widower 26 Nov 1910, Springfield, MA, Zénobie Chapdelaine.

x   **Anthyme Sylvestre Ménard** b & bp 30 & 31 Dec 1862, St. Césaire, QC; d 1905, Holyoke, MA. He married 27 Aug 1888, Springfield, MA, **Osia E. Gelineau** (Charles W. Gelineau & Marie Louise Levesque) b Sep 1871, Webster, MA.

xi   **Amanda Ménard** b & bp 17 & 18 Oct 1864, St. Césaire, QC.

5.7.7.3   MONTY, Michel b & bp 3 May 1827, St. Césaire, QC; d & bur there 16 & 18 Jun 1832.

5.7.7.4   MONTY, Magloire b & bp 7 & 8 Mar 1829, St. Césaire, QC; d & bur there 8 Mar 1832.

5.7.7.5   MONTY, Nazaire b & bp 9 & 10 Jan 1831, St. Césaire, QC; d & bur there 21 & 23 Oct 1848.

5.7.7.6   **MONTY, Adélaïde** b & bp 15 Jul 1832, St. Césaire, QC; d & bur there 31 Jul & 2 Aug 1832.

5.7.7.7   **MONTY, Onésime** b & bp 26 & 28 Jun 1833, St. Césaire, QC; d & bur 25 & 27 Dec 1900, Ange Gardien, QC. She married (1) 8 Nov 1853, St. Césaire, QC, **Pierre Goddu** (Pierre Goddu & Céleste Messier) b & bp 21 Jan 1832, St. Hyacinthe, QC; d & bur 15 & 17 Mar 1858, St. Césaire, QC.

She married (2) 25 Apr 1870, St. Césaire, QC, **Pierre St. Jacques dit Cheval** (François St. Jacques dit Cheval & Madeleine Durocher) b & bp 17 Jan 1809, La Présentation, QC; d & bur 16 & 18 Mar 1905, Ange Gardien, QC.

Onésime Monty's first husband, Pierre Goddu (also Godu), was a farmer in St. Césaire, QC. Her second husband, Pierre St. Jacques, was also originally a farmer in St. Césaire and in 1893 a farmer in Ange Gardien, QC. He was a resident of Holyoke, MA, in 1898 when his son Pierre (v) married and of Ange Gardien in 1901 when he was a member of his son Charles' (iv) household (Canadian census). His signature varies. It is generally Pierre St. Jacques, with an occasional Pierre Cheval.

Children:
- i   **Marie Onésime Goddu** b & bp 27 Aug 1854, St. Césaire, QC; d & bur there 25 & 26 Mar 1856.
- ii   **Pierre Goddu** b & bp 8 Mar 1856, St. Césaire, QC. He married there 28 Feb 1876 **Arcélia Gaudreau** (Edouard Gaudreau & Adèle Gingras) b & bp there 20 Apr 1858.
- iii   **Emilie Goddu** b & bp 4 & 5 Jan 1858, St. Césaire, QC. She married there 8 Feb 1876 **Louis Napoléon Dubreuil** (Louis Dubreuil & Priscille Daigneau) b & bp there 21 & 24 Aug 1856.
- iv   **Charles St. Jacques/Cheval** b & bp 5 Mar 1871, St. Césaire, QC; d & bur 7 & 10 Feb 1908, Ange Gardien, QC. He married there 13 Feb 1893 **Eudoxie Paquette** (Amable Paquette & Marie Brosseau) b Mar 1875?, QC; d & bur 3 & 5 Dec 1906, Ange Gardien, QC, at the age of 31 years and 9 months.
- v   **Pierre/Peter St. Jacques** b & bp 21 & 22 Mar 1877, St. Césaire, QC. He married (1) 27 Jul 1898, St. Hyacinthe, QC, **Alexine/Alexandrine Barré** (Abraham Barré & Victoire Gauvin) b & bp 28 & 30 Sep 1883, Ange Gardien, QC; d between 1900 and 1908, Holyoke, MA.
  He married (2) 1908?, Holyoke, MA, **Georgianna Grenier** b 1882?, QC.

5.7.7.8   **MONTY, Joseph** b & bp 7 Jul 1835, St. Césaire, QC; d & bur 19 & 23 Jun 1914, Ange Gardien, QC. He married 24 Feb 1873, Holyoke, MA, **Delphine Lussier/Lucier** (Antoine Lussier & Agathe Fréchette) b & bp 18 Aug 1836, Marieville, QC; d & bur 13 & 16 Oct 1919, Abbotsford & Ange Gardien, QC.

Joseph Monty arrived in the United States in the 1860s and was a thread mill worker in Holyoke, MA, in 1870 and a saloon keeper there in 1880 (US censuses). He was retired and living with his wife in the village of Canrobert, QC, in 1901 and 1911 (Canadian censuses). They apparently had had no children.

Delphine Lussier was a half-sister of Joseph Lussier, husband of Celia Monty (5.7.1. 12.6).

5.7.7.9   **MONTY, Elise** b & bp 28 Nov 1836, St. Césaire, QC; d & bur there 7 & 9 Nov 1889.

5.7.7.10   **MONTY, Adeline** b & bp 10 Jul 1838, St. Césaire, QC; d & bur there 16 & 17 Aug 1838.

5.7.7.11   **MONTY, Vénérance** b & bp 20 & 21 Aug 1839, Marieville, QC; d & bur 22 & 24 Dec 1926, St. Hyacinthe & Abbotsford, QC. She married (1) 20 Feb 1860, St.

Césaire, QC, **Pierre Gaudreau** (Louis Gaudreau & Louise Tétreau) b & bp 27 & 28 Jun 1835, St. Pie, QC.

She was a widow when she married (2) 21 May 1891, St. Hyacinthe, QC, **Justin Pierre Rébétez** (Victor Rébétez & Marie Anne Cogniat) b 12 May 1837, Geneva, Switzerland; m (1) 13 Jul 1869, Holyoke, MA, **Alphonsine Monty** (5.7.7.1.2); d & bur Jul 1906, Holyoke & South Hadley Falls, MA.

Vénérance Monty's first husband, Pierre Gaudreau, was a farmer in St. Césaire, QC. They had no children. She was a resident of Abbotsford, QC, at her second marriage (according to her Canadian marriage record) or a teacher in St. Pie, QC (according to the Massachusetts Marriage Records). She returned to Canada after her second husband's death and was living in 1911 with the family of her niece Laure Monty (5.7.7.15.2) in Montreal, QC (Canadian census).

Justin Pierre Rébétez had arrived in the United States as a young man in 1852 and was a wire mill worker in Holyoke, MA, until at least 1900 (US censuses). He was buried in Notre Dame Cemetery in South Hadley Falls, MA.

5.7.7.12   **MONTY, Adèle** b & bp 3 & 4 Jul 1841, St. Césaire, QC; d & bur there 7 & 8 Apr 1842.

5.7.7.13   **MONTY, Ignace** b & bp 15 Mar 1843, St. Pie, QC; d & bur 14 & 16 Jul 1853, St. Césaire, QC.

5.7.7.14   **MONTY, Philomène** b & bp 22 Sep 1844, St. Césaire, QC; d & bur 31 Mar & 3 Apr 1884, Three Rivers, MA & Abbotsford, QC. She married 20 Apr 1863, St. Césaire, QC, **Toussaint Stebenne/Thomas Stebbins** (Toussaint Stebenne & Adélaïde Béïque) b & bp 25 Feb 1842, St. Mathias, QC; m (2) 13 Sep 1886, St. Hyacinthe, QC, Rose Delima Morin (Pierre Morin & Tharsile Levasseur); d & bur 19 & 23 Dec 1924, Abbotsford, QC.

This family's history is particularly complex due to an unusual number of moves between Canada and the United States, with names and surnames changing according to the country of residence. Toussaint Stebenne was a resident of Holyoke, MA, when he married Philomène Monty in Canada. When they lived in Massachusetts after their marriage, he was almost invariably named Thomas Stebbins while his wife was given a number of aliases, from Phylimene and Filmene to Ella and Ellen.

Thomas Stebbins was a carpenter in Holyoke when his first four children were born. It appears that he had intended to settle there: the 1870 US census notes that his real estate holdings were valued at $2,300, an unusual amount in an era and place where recent immigrants seldom held any real property. He nevertheless returned to Canada for a while: Toussaint Stebenne was a farmer in St. Césaire, QC, when a child was born there in 1872. Two years later Thomas Stebbins was back in Holyoke where he was a mill worker at the births of children from 1874 through at least 1878. Then back to Canada: Toussaint Stebenne was a farmer in Abbotsford, QC, at the births of two children in 1881 and 1883. The following year however Thomas Stebbins was again in the United States when his wife died in Three Rivers, MA. He returned to Abbotsford, remarried in 1886 as Toussaint Stebenne, started a new family, and remained there until his death.

Needless to say that with all these peregrinations and name changes the list of Philomène Monty's children below is most probably incomplete.

Children:

i   **Rosanna Stebbins** b 1864?, Holyoke, MA.

ii   **Napoleon Stebbins** b 30 Dec 1868, Holyoke, MA; d there 1 Oct 1869.

iii   **Theodore Stebbins** b 21 Sep 1869, Holyoke, MA; d there 30 Sep 1869.

iv   **Alfred/Wilfrid Stanislas Stebbins/Stebenne** b 17 Jul 1870, Holyoke, MA; d & bur 13 & 14 Jun 1872, St. Césaire, QC.

v   **Homer Arthur Stebbins** b & bp 28 & 29 Jun 1872, St. Césaire, QC. He married 3 Sep 1894, Holyoke, MA, **Rose Alma Georgina Saurette/Sorette** (Trefflé Sorette & Exilda Lemonde) b & bp 4 & 5 Feb 1874, St. Pie, QC.

vi   **George Stebbins** b Jul 1874, Holyoke, MA. He married there 1 Jul 1895 **Corinne St. Peter** (Joseph St. Peter & Josephine Boyer) b Aug 1877, QC.

vii   **Laure Rosa Stebbins/Stebenne** b 10 Jun 1877, Holyoke, MA. She married 5 Aug 1901, Abbotsford, QC, **Pierre Gaudreau** (Joseph Gaudreau & Adeline Frégeau) b & bp 16 & 21 May 1876, St. Césaire, QC; d & bur 21 & 24 May 1938, Montreal & Abbotsford, QC.

viii   **Cora L. Stebbins/Stebenne** b 1 Apr 1878, Holyoke, MA; d & bur 19 & 23 Mar 1936, St. Hyacinthe, QC. She married 16 Jun 1908, Abbotsford, QC, **Ovide Larivière** (Augustin Larivière & Marie Azilda Laflamme) b & bp 5 & 6 May 1880, St. Hyacinthe, QC; d & bur there 7 & 11 Apr 1932.

ix   **Marie Corinne Stebenne** b & bp 20 Apr 1881, Abbotsford, QC; d & bur there 23 & 25 April 1881.

x   **Marie Louise Stebenne** b & bp 3 Feb 1883, Abbotsford, QC. She married there 28 Aug 1903 **Euclide Brodeur** (Herménégilde Brodeur & Exilda Côté) b & bp 3 & 4 Jan 1880, St. Alphonse, QC.

5.7.7.15   **MONTY, Jacques** b & bp 12 Mar 1848, St. Césaire, QC; d & bur 24 & 27 Nov 1924, Sorel & Montreal, QC. He married 17 Jun 1872, St. Pie, QC, **Rose Adèle Beauchemin** (Henri Petit dit Beauchemin & Césarie Hamel) b & bp 7 Mar 1848, Beloeil, QC; d & bur 6 & 9 Nov 1912, Montreal, QC.

Jacques Monty (Jacques Adolphe at his baptism) was a merchant in St. Césaire, QC, at his marriage but soon moved to Montreal, QC, where he was a traveling salesman. At the time of his death he was staying with his daughter Lilia and son-in-law Dr. Joseph Guertin, in Sorel, QC. He, his wife and several of their children were buried in the Côte-des-Neiges Cemetery in Montreal.

Children:

5.7.7.15.1	Rodolphe	1873-1899-1928
5.7.7.15.2	Laure	1875-1898-1954
5.7.7.15.3	Marie Alphonsine Alice	1877 -1877
5.7.7.15.4	Lilia/Lelia Cordelia	1878-1903-
5.7.7.15.5	Corinne	1880-1905-1912
5.7.7.15.6	Charles Emile	1883- -1932
5.7.7.15.7	Alice Eveline Cora	1885- -1885
5.7.7.15.8	Alice Sara Bertha	1886- -

5.7.10.1   **MONTY, Harline/Aurélie** b & bp 29 & 31 May 1833, St. Césaire, QC.

Isaac Monty's first child was named Marie Harline at her baptism. At the age of 18, though, when she was living with her parents in Ange Gardien, QC, in 1851, she was called Aurélie (Canadian census).

5.7.10.2   **MONTY, Moïse** b & bp 20 & 22 Jan 1835, St. Césaire, QC; d & bur there 13 & 19 Apr 1917. He married 20 Feb 1860, Abbotsford, QC, **Joséphine Charron** (Joseph Charron & Adélaïde Colin) b & bp 30 Jun 1841, Chambly, QC; d & bur 20 & 22 Oct 1914, Suncook, NH.

Moïse Monty was originally a farmer in Abbotsford, QC. He emigrated in 1878, settled in Pembroke (Suncook Village), NH, and was naturalized in Concord, NH, on 2 Nov 1892. He was a restaurateur at the death of his son Louis in 1899, a saloon keeper in 1900, and a liquor dealer in 1910 (US censuses). He was buried however in Canada, while his wife and several of their children were buried in St. John the Baptist Cemetery in Suncook, NH.

Children:

5.7.10.2.1	Moïse	1861-1887-
5.7.10.2.2	Louis	1863- -1864
5.7.10.2.3	Arthur	1865-1890-1951
5.7.10.2.4	Louis	1867-1891-1899

5.7.10.2.5	Anonymous	1869- -1869
5.7.10.2.6	Delima	1872-1889-1948
5.7.10.2.7	Anna	1874-1891-1915
5.7.10.2.8	Joseph	1876-1895-1945

5.7.10.3   **MONTY/MONTE, Michel/Mitchell/Michael** b & bp 22 & 24 Sep 1836, St. Césaire, QC; d 24 Mar 1911, West Warwick, RI. He married 18 Oct 1863, Southbridge, MA, **Marie Gaudreau** (Louis Gaudreau & Marguerite ____) b 2 May 1840, QC; d 10 Nov 1912, West Warwick, RI.

Michel Monty (Mitchell and at times Michael Monte or Monti in the United States) led a wandering life. He was born in Canada, married in Massachusetts, had children in Connecticut around 1863, in New Hampshire around 1864, in Canada in 1865, in New Hampshire in 1867, in Massachusetts in 1868, in Connecticut again from 1869 to 1879, and in Rhode Island from 1880 on. Even within that state his life was rather nomadic. He was a farm laborer in Glocester in 1880, a farmer in Coventry at the birth of a child in 1890, and a farmer in West Warwick in 1900 (US censuses). Both he and his wife were buried in St. Joseph's Cemetery in Arctic, RI. His children generally used the surname Monte.

Children:

5.7.10.3.1	Israel	1863?- -
5.7.10.3.2	Delima	1864?- -
5.7.10.3.3	Edmond/Edmund	1865-1890?-1933
5.7.10.3.4	Adelaide	1867-1885-1941
5.7.10.3.5	Emma	1868- -
5.7.10.3.6	Celinda/Celina	1869-1897&1911-1935
5.7.10.3.7	Elizabeth/Lizzie	1870-1889-1940
5.7.10.3.8	Annie/Zénaïde	1872-1899-1939
5.7.10.3.9	Louis/Lewis	1876?-1899-1918
5.7.10.3.10	Alphonsine	1877-1897-1938
5.7.10.3.11	Jean-Baptiste/John	1879&1896&1915&1928-1929
5.7.10.3.12	Felix	1880- -1944
5.7.10.3.13	Alexander	1882-1905?-1957
5.7.10.3.14	Michel/Mitchell	1884-1915-
5.7.10.3.15	Marie Louise	1886-1908?-1972
5.7.10.3.16	Delima	1890-1916-1956

5.7.10.4   **MONTY, Adeline** b & bp 5 & 6 Jun 1839, St. Césaire, QC; d between 1868 and 1877. She married 18 Jan 1853, St. Césaire, QC, **Joseph Catudal dit St. Jean** (Joseph Catudal dit St. Jean & Suzanne Pépin) b & bp there 19 Sep 1828.

Adeline Monty was deceased when her son Emery (iii) married in May 1877.

Joseph Catudal dit St. Jean was originally a farmer in Ange Gardien, QC, then in Abbotsford, QC, from 1857 to about 1869, and finally in Milton, QC, where he was present at his daughter Médérise's (iv) marriage in 1892. The family name appears to have shifted gradually from Catudal to St. Jean, though not with any consistency. Both surnames are found well into the 20th century.

Children:

i   **Joseph Catudal dit St. Jean** b & bp 9 & 10 Dec 1853, St. Césaire, QC.

ii   **Ephrem Catudal dit St. Jean** b & bp 1 & 2 Mar 1857, Abbotsford, QC.

iii   **Emery Catudal dit St. Jean** b & bp 31 Dec 1858 & 1 Jan 1859, Abbotsford, QC; d & bur 14 & 16 Aug 1934, Adamsville, QC. He married (1) 15 May 1877, Abbotsford, QC, **Rosalie Desranleau** (Damase Desranleau & Adeline Ledoux) b & bp there 15 & 16 Oct 1857; d & bur 1 & 3 Jun 1920, Adamsville, QC.

He married (2) 14 Feb 1931, Granby, QC, **Roseline McLean** (Pierre Brouillet dit McLean & Roseline Choinière) b & bp 18 & 21 Apr 1867, St. Césaire, QC; m (1) 29 Oct 1884, Ste Angèle de Monnoir, QC, Damase Martel (Joseph Martel &

Marie Elmire Boulais).

iv   **Médérise Catudal dit St. Jean** b & bp 18 & 19 Jan 1861, Abbotsford, QC. She married 9 Nov 1892, Milton, QC, **Alfred Choquette** (Bruno Choquette & Sophie Parent) b & bp 3 & 5 Apr 1859, Ange Gardien, QC; d & bur ? & 22 Dec 1928, Granby, QC.

v   **Adeline Catudal dit St. Jean** b & bp 10 & 11 Apr 1863, Abbotsford, QC.

vi   **Moïse Catudal dit St. Jean** b & bp 6 & 8 Jan 1865, Abbotsford, QC; d & bur there 6 & 8 Oct 1865.

vii   **Edmond Catudal dit St. Jean** b & bp 14 & 15 Jul 1866, Abbotsford, QC. He married 8 Jan 1901, Granby, QC, **Arzélie Charron**, widow of Paul Ruel.

viii   **Rose Anna/Rosanna Catudal dit St. Jean** b & bp 17 & 18 Aug 1868, Abbotsford, QC; d & bur 15 & 17 Jan 1949, Valcourt, QC. She married 13 Sep 1887, Milton, QC, **Georges Robichaud** (Pierre Robichaud & Rebecca Lanctôt) b & bp 27 May & 3 Jun 1866, Valcourt & Stukely, QC; d & bur 14 & 17 Oct 1934, Valcourt, QC.

5.7.10.5   **MONTY, Louis** b & bp 23 & 24 Mar 1841, St. Césaire, QC; d & bur 12 & 15 Jan 1914, Valcourt, QC. He married 28 May 1869, Concord, NH, **Aurélie Rodier/Royer** b 3 Jun 1846, QC; d & bur 1 & 3 May 1915, Valcourt, QC.

Louis Monty was a farmer in Valcourt, QC, for most of his life and had retired there before his death. He also spent some years in the United States. He was a cotton mill worker in Pembroke, NH, in 1870, living with his wife and son Louis in his father's household there, though his younger children were born in Valcourt from 1871 through 1884. The family may have come back to New Hampshire in 1886 when one daughter was born and another died in Pembroke. A third daughter also married there in 1890. The other children married in Valcourt, which suggests that the family had returned to Canada at some time in the early 1890s. They were all there save Rose Anna (5.7.10.5.3) in 1901 and 1911 (Canadian censuses).

Aurélie Rodier was occasionally named Royer in both Canadian and American documents.

Children:

5.7.10.5.1	Louis	1869-1895&1904-1923
5.7.10.5.2	Napoléon	1871-1895&1912-1945
5.7.10.5.3	Rose Anna/Rosa	1873-1890-
5.7.10.5.4	Malvina	1875- -1886
5.7.10.5.5	Trefflé	1878-1902&1929?-1955
5.7.10.5.6	Charles	1880-1905-1946
5.7.10.5.7	Albina	1882-1907-1928
5.7.10.5.8	Ludovic	1884-1908-
5.7.10.5.9	Adélaïde	1886- -1902

5.7.10.6   **MONTY, Esther** b & bp 6 Sep 1843, St. Césaire, QC.

Esther Monty was living with her parents in Ange Gardien, QC, in 1851 (Canadian census).

5.7.10.7   **MONTY, Napoléon** b & bp 18 Jun 1845, St. Césaire, QC; d & bur there 13 & 14 Sep 1846.

This child was named Napoleon at his baptism but was buried at the age of 1 under the name of Paul Léon.

5.7.10.8   **MONTY, Nathalie/Mary N.** b & bp 15 & 19 Jun 1847, St. Césaire, QC; d & bur 30 Jan & 2 Feb 1914, Suncook, NH. She married 1864? **Octave Desroches** (Louis Desroches & Catherine Cardinal) b & bp 6 & 7 Jun 1843, St. Césaire, QC; d & bur 27 & 29 Mar 1904, Suncook, NH.

Octave Desroches (also Desrocher, Desroche, Stone) arrived in the United States in 1860 and was living in 1870 as Octave Stone with his wife Mary and two children in his father-in-law's household in Suncook, NH. He was a cotton mill worker there until at least 1880 but a boarding house owner in 1900 when he and his wife had been married for thirty-six years. They had had ten children of whom eight were still alive (US censuses). Both of them and at least six of their children were buried in St. John the Baptist Cemetery in Suncook.

The family surname varied considerably. The records of St. John the Baptist Church generally use Desroches or Desroche with an occasional Desrocher. US censuses alternate between Stone in 1870, Deroch in 1880, Desrouchie in 1900, and Stone again in 1910. A few years later three sons signed their World War I Draft Registration cards as George Henry Desroche, John Desrocher, and Joseph William Desroches. I have indicated below the most common surname(s) I have found for each child.

Children:

i   **Octave Desroches** b Feb 1867, Suncook, NH; d & bur there 18 & 20 Nov 1916. He married there 27 Apr 1901 **Catherine Hinds** (Charles August Hinds & Mary Aluta Bend) b Jun 1876, VT.

ii   **Mary/Marie Desroches** b 1869?, Suncook, NH.

iii **Louis Desroches/Stone** b 1872?, Suncook, NH. He married 22 Jan 1895, Hooksett, NH, **Rosa/Rose de Lima Rhéaume** (François Xavier/Frank Rhéaume & Philomène/Phebe Lemieux) b & bp 30 Jan 1875, St. Rémi, QC.

iv   **George Henry Desroches/Desroche** b & bp 14 & 22 May 1876, Suncook, NH; d & bur there 9 & 13 Apr 1957. He married there 3 Jan 1905 **Adgive Flore Desmarais** (Alfred Desmarais & Sophie Crevier) b & bp 7 Aug 1874, St. François du Lac, QC; d & bur 6 & 9 Sep 1950, Suncook, NH.

v   **Josephine Desroches/Desrocher** b & bp 5 & 6 May 1878, Suncook, NH; d & bur there 1 & 5 May 1937. She married there 20 Sep 1897 **John Plourde** (Olivier Plourde & Marie Bourgouin) b 3 Jan 1877, Frenchville, ME; m (2) 12 Nov 1938, Manchester, NH, Florida Baril (Léon Baril & Aurélie Cora Lambert); d & bur 27 & 31 Mar 1950, Suncook, NH.

vi   **Sarah Jeanne Desroches** b & bp 14 & 15 Mar 1880, Suncook, NH; d & bur there 1 & 4 May 1925.

vii **John/Jean-Baptiste Desroches** b & bp 17 & 18 Mar 1882, Suncook, NH; d & bur there 18 & 21 Mar 1936.

viii **Joseph William Desroches** b 14 Aug 1883, Suncook, NH; d & bur there 24 & 28 May 1956.

5.7.10.9   **MONTY, Adélaïde** b & bp 1 & 2 Jul 1849, St. Césaire, QC.

Adélaïde Monty was living with her parents in Ange Gardien, QC, in 1851 (Canadian census).

5.7.10.10   **MONTY, Rose Anne** b & bp 8 & 10 Aug 1852, Ange Gardien & St. Césaire, QC. She married 1867? **Orman J. Gregory/Grégoire** (Joseph Grégoire & Emma Sénécal) b Aug 1844, St. Jean, QC; d 20 Feb 1891, Franklin, NH, at the age of 46 years and 6 months.

Orman J. Gregory was a tannery worker in Franklin, NH, in 1870 and 1880 (US censuses) and a farmer there in later years. His name varies. It is Elmer and Erman in the 1870 and 1880 censuses, though rather consistently Orman or Ormand in the New Hampshire Vital Records, including his own death record. That is the name I have adopted, though with less than full confidence. The names of his parents and his approximate date of birth are also taken from his death record. I have been unable to confirm the information through Canadian records.

Rose Anne Monty was still living in Franklin with five of her children in 1910 (US census). I have not found her in later years. She may have died before 1920.

Children:

i   **Addie Gregory** b 23 Oct 1868, Franklin, NH. She married 1929?, **Frank P. Chesley** (Josiah C. Chesley & Almira ____) b Jun 1864, Concord, NH; m (1) 1886? Bridget ____.

ii   **Joseph Gregory** b 22 Aug 1869, Franklin, NH. He married there 29 Aug 1896 **Corinne Pereault** (Pierre Paul Fidèle Pereault & Justine Hêtu) b & bp 20 & 21 Aug 1864, L'Assomption, QC.

iii   **Phoebe Gregory** b Jul 1871, Franklin, NH. She married there 22 Feb 1892 **Auguste Pereault** (Pierre Paul Fidèle Pereault & Justine Hêtu) b & bp 6 Mar 1869, L'Assomption, QC.

iv   **Mary Ellen/Marie Hélène Gregory** b 29 Aug 1873, Franklin, NH. She married there 27 Aug 1897 **Ernest Gaudet** (Gédéon Gaudet & Clarisse/Claire Leblanc) b 1866?, QC.

v   **John Gregory** b 19 Sep 1875, Franklin, NH. He married there 20 Aug 1906 **Laura Emma Rocheleau** (Olivier Rocheleau & Aurélie Gaudette) b & bp 19 May 1880, St. Léonard d'Aston, QC.

vi   **Warren Gregory** b 4 Feb 1879, Franklin, NH. He married there 15 Feb 1915 **Ida Marie Beauchêne** (Joseph Beauchêne & Lucy Bean) b Aug 1882, VT.

vii   **Fred Richard Gregory** b 4 Feb 1882, Franklin, NH; d Sep 1973, Manchester, NH. He married 1917? **Annie E. ____** b 6 Jan 1883, NY; d Jan 1968, Manchester, NH.

viii   **Rose B. Gregory** b 25 Jun 1887, Franklin, NH. She married there 9 Jan 1911 **Harry Percy Young** (Alexander S. Young & Ella Piper) b 18 Apr 1886, Laconia, NH; d Jan 1972, Keene, NH.

5.10.6.1   **MONTY, Joséphine** b & bp 4 Sep 1831, St. Mathias, QC; d & bur 25 & 27 Sep 1915, Chambly, QC. She married there 4 Dec 1854 **Matthew Ingledew** (George Ingledew & Mary Ann ____) b 10 May 1835, Canada; d & bur 30 Oct & 2 Nov 1904, Chambly, QC.

Matthew Ingledew was a farmer in Chambly, QC, and had lived there since at least 1851 (Canadian census). He and his wife were married there in St. Stephen's Anglican Church, where their children were also baptized. He was buried in St. Stephen's Cemetery while Joséphine Monty was buried in the cemetery of St. Coeur de Marie Catholic Church.

Children:

i   **George Ingledew** b 1855?; d & bur 23 & 24 Dec 1855, Chambly, QC.

ii   **Mary Anne Josephine Ingledew** b & bp 23 Dec 1856 & 4 Jan 1857, Chambly, QC.

iii   **Charles Ingledew** b & bp 3 Sep & 28 Nov 1858, Chambly, QC.

iv   **George Louis Ingledew** b & bp 11 Jun & 1 Jul 1860, Chambly, QC.

v   **Margaret Ingledew** b & bp 3 & 21 Jul 1862, Chambly, QC.

vi   **Elizabeth Matilda Ingledew** b & bp 24 Sep 1864 & 22 Jan 1865, Chambly, QC.

5.10.6.2   **MONTY, Joseph Louis** b & bp 9 & 10 Sep 1833, St. Mathias, QC; d & bur 18 & 20 Apr 1888, St. Césaire, QC. He married 15 Apr 1856, Marieville, QC, **Adèle Nadeau** (Louis Nadeau & Cécile Bérard) b & bp there 23 Oct 1832; d & bur 3 & 6 Oct 1902, St. Césaire, QC.

Joseph Monty was a farmer in St. Césaire, QC. His widow was staying with her children Rémi, Sylvia, and Adolphe in Ste Angèle, QC, in 1891 (Canadian census).

Children:

5.10.6.2.1	Marie Ezilda	1857- -1858
5.10.6.2.2	Mathilde	1858-1878-1916
5.10.6.2.3	Antoine	1861-1886-1925
5.10.6.2.4	Sergius	1863- -1874
5.10.6.2.5	Rémi	1869-1893&1919-1948
5.10.6.2.6	Aloïsia	1871-1887-1901
5.10.6.2.7	Sylvia	1873-1893-1946
5.10.6.2.8	Adolphe/Adolph	1875- -

5.10.6.3   **MONTY, Cordélie** b & bp 24 Oct 1835, St. Mathias, QC. She married there 18 Jul 1853 **Edouard Auguste Bugaud** (Julien Bugaud & Périne Berton).
Edouard Auguste Bugaud was a resident of Montreal, QC, at his marriage.

5.10.6.4   **MONTY, Damien** b & bp 22 Nov 1838, St. Mathias, QC; d & bur ? & 23 Mar 1917, St. Jean, QC. He married (1) 24 Feb 1862, St. Mathias, QC, **Marie Zoé Célina Séguin** (Jean-Baptiste Séguin & Zoé Vigeant) b & bp 6 Jul 1841, Marieville, QC; d & bur 17 & 20 Nov 1862, St. Mathias, QC.
He married (2) 30 Jan 1866, St. Luc, QC, **Sophie Célina Papineau** (François Papineau & Adélaïde Molleur) b & bp there 16 Aug & 23 Sep 1839; d & bur 7 & 10 Apr 1920, St. Jean, QC.
Damien Monty was a farmer in various localities in the Richelieu valley: in St. Mathias until 1868, in Richelieu in 1869 and 1871, in St. Luc from 1873 through 1879, and in St. Jean in the 1880s. He was still living there with his second wife in 1901 and 1911 (Canadian censuses).

Child of the first marriage:
5.10.6.4.1	Marie Célina	1862-	-1863

Children of the second marriage:
5.10.6.4.2	Louis Henri Damien	1866-	-1876
5.10.6.4.3	Marie Louise Célina	1867-	-1936
5.10.6.4.4	Marie Clara Elia	1869-1888-	
5.10.6.4.5	Joseph Louis Rémi	1871-	-1940
5.10.6.4.6	David Emilien Damien	1873-	-1876
5.10.6.4.7	Rose Anna	1875-1896-	
5.10.6.4.8	Adeline	1877-1919-	
5.10.6.4.9	Joséphine Catherine Elisabeth	1879-	-
5.10.6.4.10	Evangéline Georgiana	1882-	-1884

5.10.6.5   **MONTY, Narcisse Euphémien** b & bp 28 Dec 1840, St. Mathias, QC; d & bur there 2 & 3 Jan 1842.

5.10.6.6   **MONTY, Marie Aglaé** b & bp 11 & 12 Feb 1843, St. Mathias, QC; d & bur 2 & 4 Feb 1898, Ottawa, Ontario, Canada. She married 3 Nov 1863, St. Mathias, QC, **Pierre Antoine Trudeau** (Antoine Trudeau & Geneviève Trudeau) b & bp 28 Jan 1840, Chambly, QC; m (2) 12 Apr 1904, Dorval, QC, Adèle Leclerc (Théodore Leclerc & Joseph Blondin); d & bur 20 & 22 Apr 1933, Ottawa, Ontario, Canada.
Pierre Trudeau was a boatman at his marriage to Marie Aglaé Monty. He had been a cabinet maker in Ottawa, Ontario, Canada, for sixty years at his death.

5.10.6.7   **MONTY, Jean-Marie Claude** b & bp 5 & 6 Jan 1845, St. Ma-thias, QC; d & bur there 28 & 30 Apr 1860.

5.10.6.8   **MONTY, Louis Dosithée** b & bp 24 & 26 Sep 1846, St. Mathias, QC; d & bur 25 & 28 May 1919, Montreal, QC. He married (1) **Marie Aubé** b 24 Dec 1844, QC; d & bur 19 & 22 Jul 1905, Montreal, QC, at the age of 60 years and 7 months.
He married (2) 28 Apr 1906, Montreal, QC, **Adeline Dionne** (Jacques Dionne & Eme-lie Côté) b & bp 11 & 12 Aug 1851. Montmagny, QC; m (1) Jean-Baptiste Paré; m (2) 22 Aug 1881, Montreal, QC, Euclide Martin (Tertullien Martin & Dorothée Aubé), widower of Rachel Plessis-Belair; d & bur 8 & 10 May 1922, Ottawa, Ontario & Montreal, QC.
This man was named Dosithée at his baptism but was generally known as an adult as Louis D. or Louis Dosithée Monty. He was a teamster in St. Jean, QC, at the birth of his first child in 1871 but soon moved to Ottawa, Ontario, where his younger children were born. He was a grocer there in 1881 and a furniture maker in 1891. He returned to the Province of Que-bec a few years later and was a carpenter in Montreal, QC, in 1901 and 1911 (Canadian cen-

suses).

Children of the first marriage:

5.10.6.8.1	Joseph Louis	1871-1901-1916
5.10.6.8.2	Anne Agnès Alphonsine	1872- -
5.10.6.8.3	Napoléon Alphonse	1874- -
5.10.6.8.4	Alfred Dollard	1875- -
5.10.6.8.5	Emile Herménégilde	1878-1903-
5.10.6.8.6	Alphonse Léopold	1881- -1908

5.10.6.9   **MONTY, Eustache** b & bp 5 & 6 Sep 1848, St. Mathias, QC; d & bur 27 & 30 Jan 1902, Montreal, QC. He married 21 Oct 1872, St. Césaire, QC, **Aloysia Tétreau** (François Tétreau & Julie Roy) b & bp there 29 Jun 1851; d & bur 26 & 28 Nov 1931, Montreal, QC.

Eustache Monty (Prudent Eustache at his baptism) was a grocer in Montreal, QC. His wife was named Marie Cordélie Elisa at her baptism, although Aloysia (also Aloïsia, Louisa) was most commonly used in later years.

Children:

5.10.6.9.1	Louis Eustache	1873-1899-1933
5.10.6.9.2	Georges Napoléon	1875-1904-
5.10.6.9.3	Marie Louise	1877- -1878
5.10.6.9.4	Marie Onalda	1878-1909-1933
5.10.6.9.5	Marie Louise Albina	1880- -1939
5.10.6.9.6	Joseph Ismaël	1882-1906-1930
5.10.6.9.7	Pierre Emile	1884- -1885
5.10.6.9.8	Marie Anne (twin)	1886- -1886
5.10.6.9.9	Anonymous (twin)	1886- -1886
5.10.6.9.10	Marie Joséphine	1887- -1887

5.10.6.10   **MONTY, Marie Heldrida** b & bp 7 Apr 1851, St. Mathias, QC; d & bur there 8 & 9 Oct 1857.

8.1.7.1   **MONTY, Osithe** b 19 Aug 1832, QC; d & bur 4 & 5 Sep 1832, Iberville, QC, at 15 days of age.

8.1.7.2   **MONTY, Clément** b & bp 7 & 8 Aug 1833, St. Luc, QC; d 10 Oct 1894, Merrimack, NH. He married around 1856, probably in New Hampshire (Catholic rehabilitation 11 Jun 1859, St. Mathias, QC) **Rosalie/Rose St. Jean** b Jul 1840, QC.

Clément Monty was a laborer on his father's farm in Iberville, QC, in 1851 (Canadian census) but soon left for Manchester, NH, where he arrived in October 1852 (Naturalization papers, Manchester, 2 Mar 1875). It was probably there he married and his first two children were born. The family returned in 1858 or 1859 to Canada, where the couple's marriage was rehabilitated and two more children were born in 1860 and 1862. The younger children were all born in New Hampshire. Clément Monty was a laborer in Manchester in 1880 and later in Merrimack, NH. His widow was still living there in 1900. She had had twelve children of whom six, Louis, Rose, Clément, William, Mary J., and Edward were then alive (US censuses).

Children:

8.1.7.2.1	Louis	1856-1877?-
8.1.7.2.2	Rosalie/Rose	1857-1876-
8.1.7.2.3	Clément	1860- -
8.1.7.2.4	William	1862-1883&1887-
8.1.7.2.5	Mary J.	1863?-1883-
8.1.7.2.6	John	1864?- -1881

8.1.7.2.7	Charles	1870-	-1892
8.1.7.2.8	George	1873?-	-1899
8.1.7.2.9	Frank	1876-	-1877
8.1.7.2.10	Edward	1880-	-

8.1.7.3   **MONTY, Marcel** b & bp 19 Nov 1834, Iberville, QC; d & bur there 24 & 26 Apr 1838.

8.1.7.4   **MONTY, Michel/Mitchell** b & bp 6 Jun 1836, Iberville, QC; d between 1880 and 1900. He married 1 Feb 1864, Mont St. Grégoire, QC, **Mathilde/Matilda Bertrand** (Noël Beaulieu dit Bertrand & Domitilde Messier) b & bp 20 & 21 May 1842, Mont St. Grégoire, QC; d 26 Nov 1929, Savanna, IL.

Michel Monty emigrated shortly after his marriage. He lived for a few years in New Hampshire where his first two children were born before moving to Bear Creek, WI, where he settled near his father and several siblings. He was a farmer there in 1870 and 1880. I have not found his death record. By 1900 however his widow and at least four of his children were living in Savanna, IL. Only his oldest son Peter appears to have remained in Wisconsin (US censuses).

Children:

8.1.7.4.1	Peter/Mitchell	1864?-1910?-1946
8.1.7.4.2	Matilda	1865?- -
8.1.7.4.3	Francis/Frank	1868-1892-1944
8.1.7.4.4	Phoebe	1871?- -
8.1.7.4.5	Victoria Rosella	1873-1890?-1957
8.1.7.4.6	Agnes	1874- -1950
8.1.7.4.7	Genevieve	1876-1897-1931
8.1.7.4.8	Henry Louis	1879-1912?-1958

8.1.7.5   **MONTY, Amédée/Charles** b & bp 20 & 21 Jun 1837, Iberville, QC. He married 16 Oct 1865, St. Jean, QC, **Julie/Julia Ménard** (Pierre Ménard & Marie Benoit) b & bp there 9 & 10 Sep 1848; m (2) 1904? _____ Trumbla/Trembla; d & bur 1937, Clintonville, WI.

Amédée Monty apparently followed his father and brothers to the United States soon after his marriage and like them became a farmer in Bear Creek, WI, in the late 1860s. In 1880, the couple then known as Charles and Julia Monty had only one child living with them, the 6-year-old John. I have not found them in any later state or US census. Nor have I found Charles Monty's death or place of burial. The following information is derived mainly from a tombstone in the St. Rose Cemetery in Clintonville, WI, marked "MONTY, Children of C. & J. / Harrine, Paine, Charley, Julia / Mary, Johnnie, Carmilite / Julia (TRUMBLA) 1849-1937 / Mary A. 1881-1903 / dau of Charles & J."

It would seem at first that Trumbla would be Julia's maiden name. On the basis of the 1910, 1920, and 1930 censuses in Clintonville, I believe rather that it was her second husband's surname. In 1910 Mrs. Julia Trumbla, 60 years old, born in Canada, a widow who had had twelve children of whom none was alive, had been married for only six years. This of itself argues for a second marriage. She was still in Clintonville in 1920, the head of a household which included several lodgers. Ten years later, at age 82, Mrs. Julia Trembla (sic), who had first married at age 18, was living in Clintonville with her niece Mrs. Mary Miller, daughter of Alfred Lareau and Philomène Monty (8.1.7.9). Though I have been unable to find a record of Julia Ménard's second marriage, or even the name of her second husband, the link with Amédée/Charles Monty seems clear enough.

The list of children, derived in large part from cemetery inscriptions, is certainly incomplete (there should be twelve names) and the names may be inexact. Johnnie probably refers to John (8.1.7.5.1) who was living with his parents in Bear Creek, WI, in 1880 (US census). Mary A. (8.1.7.5.2) and Mary (8.1.7.5.8) however appear to be two different persons. In any case they were all deceased in 1910 (US census).

Children:

8.1.7.5.1	John	1874?-	-
8.1.7.5.2	Mary A.	1881-	-1903
8.1.7.5.3	Alfred	1883-	-1904
8.1.7.5.4	Harrine	-	-
8.1.7.5.5	Paine	-	-
8.1.7.5.6	Charley	-	-
8.1.7.5.7	Julia	-	-
8.1.7.5.8	Mary	-	-
8.1.7.5.9	Carmilite	-	-

8.1.7.6   **MONTY, Jean-Baptiste/John B.** b & bp 3 Feb 1839, Iberville, QC; d 9 Jul 1891, Clintonville, WI. He married around 1865 **Lucadia Boudreau** (?) b Feb 1851.

This couple lived originally in New Hampshire, possibly Keene, where their first child was born. A second child was born around 1868 in Bear Creek, WI, where John Monty was a farmer. He remained in the area until his death and was buried in St. Rose Cemetery in Clintonville, WI.

His widow lived in her son John Julius' household there until at least 1910 (US censuses). Several entries on the Internet show that her name was Lucadia Boudreau, that she was born on 17 Feb 1851 in Canada, and that she died on 9 Mar 1912 in Clintonville. I have been able to verify only two items: her given name in censuses from 1870 through 1910 is somewhat close to Lucadia (or Léocadie if she was of French descent), and she was born in February 1851 (1900 census). That census, though, says she was born in New York State, while the others indicate that she was born in Canada. In the absence of any birth/baptism, marriage, or death/burial record, even her maiden name is in question. She may belong to one of the Bourdeau families of Canada who had daughters named Léocadie born in 1851.

Children:

8.1.7.6.1	John Julius	1866?-1903-1947
8.1.7.6.2	Charles	1868?- -
8.1.7.6.3	Ursula	1873?- -
8.1.7.6.4	Josephine	1874-1892-1922
8.1.7.6.5	George William	1877-1901-1957
8.1.7.6.6	Frederick John	1879-1903&1928-1965
8.1.7.6.7	Joseph	1881- -
8.1.7.6.8	Nicholas W./Nic	1883-1903?-1970
8.1.7.6.9	Charles J.	1885-1912-1965
8.1.7.6.10	Edward	1887- -1887
8.1.7.6.11	Hazel	1888- -
8.1.7.6.12	Julia Mary	1891-1918?-

8.1.7.7   **MONTY, Isaïe** b & bp 22 & 23 Dec 1840, Iberville, QC; d & bur there 12 & 13 Aug 1841.

8.1.7.8   **MONTY, Joseph** b & bp 23 May 1842, Iberville, QC; d & bur there 21 & 23 Aug 1842.

8.1.7.9   **MONTY, Philomène** b & bp 29 & 30 Jul 1843, Iberville, QC; d 20 Feb 1903, Waupaca Co., WI. She married 26 Oct 1863, Mont St. Grégoire, QC, **Alfred Lareau** b 2 Apr 1845, QC; d 3 Jan 1904, Waupaca Co., WI.

French Canadian church records apply the euphemism "de parents inconnus" (of unknown parents) to illegitimate children. At his marriage Alfred, "fils mineur de parents inconnus," was given no surname. I am using here the surname found on the family tombstone which marks his, his wife's and six of his children's graves in St. Rose Cemetery in Clintonville, WI. Two of his sons, Charles and Joseph, were also known as Lareau in the 1900 US census. On the other hand, earlier censuses refer to Fred Lorow and Fred Larue.

Philomène Monty and her husband left Canada for New Hampshire shortly after their marriage for their two oldest children were born there. The family soon moved again and settled in the mid-1860s in Bear Creek, WI, alongside numerous Monty relatives: in 1880 John Monty, Clement Monty, Michel Monty, Charles Monty, and Fred and Philomene Larue all had adjoining farms (US censuses). The Lareau family is not found in Bear Creek however in 1900. The dates of death of Fred Lareau and his wife are taken from the inscriptions on their tombstone. That is also my only source of information about their children Clarisse, John B., Maggie, M. Claire, and Mathilda.

Children:

i   **Philomene Lareau** b 1864?, NH.

ii   **Alfred Lareau** b 10 Mar 1866, NH; d 20 Jan 1889, Waupaca Co., WI.

iii   **Ruth Lareau** b 1867?, Bear Creek, WI.

iv   **Charles Lareau** b Nov 1869, Bear Creek, WI; bur 26 Jul 1930, Green Bay, WI. He married 1894? **Clara Miller** (____ Miller & Alma ____) b May 1873, WI.

v   **Edmund Lareau** b 1871/72?, Bear Creek, WI.

vi   **Joseph Lareau** b Jun 1873, Bear Creek, WI.

vii   **Clarisse Lareau** b 6 Mar 1875, Bear Creek, WI; d there 27 Jan 1880.

viii   **Mary Lareau** b 1877?, Bear Creek, WI. She married there 1906? **Benjamin/Bernard Edward Miller** b 9 Nov 1880, MN.

ix   **John B. Lareau** b 7 Dec 1878, Bear Creek, WI; d there 21 Jan 1880.

x   **Maggie Lareau** b 21 Jan 1881, Waupaca Co., WI; d there 24 Jun 1881.

xi   **M. Claire Lareau** b 17 Aug 1882, Waupaca Co., WI; d there 6 Sep 1882.

xii   **Emma Lareau** b 1884?, Waupaca Co., WI. She married 1908? **George William Spang** (Joseph Spang & Amelia ____) b 7 Dec 1882, WI; d Oct 1966, Clintonville, WI.

xiii   **Mathilda Lareau** b 5 Jan 1887, Waupaca Co., WI; d there 20 Jan 1889.

8.1.7.10   **MONTY, Marie Reine** b & bp 1 Jul 1845, St. Luc, QC; d & bur 13 & 15 Jul 1846, Iberville, QC.

8.1.7.11   **MONTY, Mathilde/Matilda** b & bp 29 & 30 Jun 1847, Iberville, QC; d & bur there 11 & 13 Sep 1911.

Mathilde Monty came to Bear Creek, WI, with her parents in the mid-1860s and lived there on her father's farm, as Matilda Monty, until his death in 1892. She and her sister Julia (8.1.7.15) stayed in Clintonville, WI, until at least 1900 (US censuses) but then returned to Canada where they were living in St. Jean, QC, in 1911 (Canadian census).

8.1.7.12   **MONTY, Joseph Abraham** b & bp 17 Mar 1850, Iberville, QC; d & bur 5 & 7 May 1910, Deer Creek & Bear Creek, WI. He married 25 Dec 1870, Hortonville, WI, **Mary Jane Bricco/Marie Geneviève Bricault** (Paul/Solomon Bricault/Bricco & Sarah Tuft) b & bp 23 Oct 1854, Henryville, QC; d 11 Nov 1943, Bear Creek, WI.

Joseph Abraham Monty's date of birth is based on his baptismal record in the church of St. Athanase in Iberville, QC. The date of 17 Mar 1851 found on his death certificate and reproduced on his tombstone in St. Mary's Cemetery in Bear Creek, WI, cannot be correct.

Joseph Abraham Monty came to Wisconsin with his parents in 1864 and became a farmer in Maple Creek and later Deer Creek, WI (US censuses). He continued to use the surname Monty though some of his children later switched to Monte. As a result, while his own death certificate is in the name of "Joseph Monty Sr.," his wife's death certificate, based on information provided by her son Ben Monte, is in the name of "Mary Jane Monte," spouse of "Joseph Monte." But then her tombstone in St. Mary's Cemetery in Bear Creek is inscribed "Mary Jane Monty."

Children:

8.1.7.12.1   William   1871-   -1872

8.1.7.12.2	Alexander Joseph	1873-1893&1951-1958
8.1.7.12.3	Sarah Anne	1875-1892-1933
8.1.7.12.4	Sadie Exelda	1877-1899-1978
8.1.7.12.5	Saul Solomon	1879-1905-1966
8.1.7.12.6	Joseph Abraham	1881-1906-1983
8.1.7.12.7	Edward	1883- -1883
8.1.7.12.8	Elizabeth Jane	1885-1905-1959
8.1.7.12.9	Vincent	1887-1914-1963
8.1.7.12.10	Benjamin Bernard	1889-1913-1962
8.1.7.12.11	Abraham Arthur	1891-1917& & & -1975
8.1.7.12.12	Mary Beulah	1893-1911-1976
8.1.7.12.13	Vivien Gertrude	1895-1918-1919
8.1.7.12.14	Adeline	1897-1917-1980
8.1.7.12.15	Marie Antoinette	1899-1922-1987

8.1.7.13   **MONTY, Edesse Virginie** b & bp 26 & 27 Feb 1852, Iberville, QC; d & bur there 16 & 17 Jun 1852.

8.1.7.14   **MONTY, Camille** b & bp 26 Aug 1853, Iberville, QC; d & bur 1896, Clintonville, WI.
        Camille Monty came to Bear Creek, WI, with his parents in the mid-1860s and was buried with them in St. Rose Cemetery in Clintonville, WI. He was a deaf mute (1880 census).

8.1.7.15   **MONTY, Julie/Julia** b & bp 6 & 7 May 1855, Iberville, QC; d & bur 8 & 9 Oct 1936, Montreal, QC.
        Julie Monty came to Bear Creek, WI, with her parents in the mid-1860s and lived there on her father's farm, as Julia Monty, until his death in 1892. She and her sister Matilda (8.1.7.11) stayed in Clintonville, WI, until at least 1900 (US censuses) before returning to Canada. They were living together in St. Jean, QC, in 1911 (Canadian census).

8.3.1.1   **MONTY, Anonymous** b 17 May 1844, Iberville, QC; d & bur there 17 & 20 May 1844.

8.3.1.2   **MONTY, Anonymous** b 4 Apr 1845, Iberville, QC; d & bur there 4 & 7 Apr 1845.

8.3.1.3   **MONTY, Philippe/Philip** b & bp 19 Jun 1846, Iberville, QC; d between 1910 and 1920. He married 1870? **Mary L. Higgins** b Feb 1855, CT.
        Philippe Monty came to the United States as a young man in 1867 and soon married, probably in Connecticut where his wife was born. I do not know where the couple resided immediately after their marriage: their first known child was born in New York State in 1878. The others were born in Roxton Pond, QC, where Philippe Monty was a blacksmith. The family returned to the United States around 1897 and stayed for a few years in Norwich, CT, where Philip Monty continued working as a blacksmith. He and his wife had been married for 30 years in 1900 and had had thirteen children of whom six were still alive. The family moved to Scotland, CT, a few years later. Philip Monty was a farmer there in 1910 but was deceased in 1920 when his widow was keeping house in Willimantic, CT, for her son Philip, daughter Anna, and grandson George Gadua. She was in turn a member of her son Philip's household in Brookline, MA, in 1930 (US censuses).

Children:
8.3.1.3.1	Elizabeth	1878-1898-
8.3.1.3.2	Amelda/Amanda	1880-1900-
8.3.1.3.3	Emma Louise	1882-1901-
8.3.1.3.4	François X. Philippe Alfred	1884- -

8.3.1.3.5	Adelina	1885- -1886
8.3.1.3.6	Georges Elphège	1887- -1888
8.3.1.3.7	Philip Adélard	1889-1911?&1924-1975
8.3.1.3.8	Rose Alba Priscilla	1891- -1891
8.3.1.3.9	Eva Anastasia/Anna	1892-1911-
8.3.1.3.10	Rose Adeline	1894- -

8.3.1.4   **MONTY, Joseph** b & bp 6 May & 9 Jul 1848, Iberville, QC; d & bur 28 & 30 Jun 1888, Roxton Pond, QC.
Joseph Monty did not marry.

8.3.1.5   **MONTY, Anonymous** b 10 Apr 1850, Iberville, QC; d & bur there 10 & 12 Apr 1850.

8.3.1.6   **MONTY, Marie Louise/Mary** b & bp 24 Jun 1851, Henryville, QC. She married 25 Jan 1881, Roxton Falls, QC, a widower, **Michel Gaudreau** (Augustin Gaudreau & Anne Lasablonnière) b & bp 2 & 3 Sep 1847, Ste Scholastique, QC; m (1) 17 Jan 1870, Ste Adèle, QC, Arthémise Vézeau (François Vézeau & Anastasie Boileau).
Michel Gaudreau was a farmer in Roxton Falls, QC, before moving his family to Connecticut in the 1890s. His widow, who was living with her mother Césarie Tessier in Norwich, CT, in 1900, had had five children of whom two were still alive (US census).

Children:
i   **George Gaudreau** b & bp 13 & 14 Sep 1882, Roxton Falls, QC. He married 23 May 1903, Norwich, CT, a second cousin, **Cordelia Monty** (8.3.8.5.1).
ii   **Eugène Gaudreau** b & bp 30 & 31 Aug 1884, Roxton Falls, QC; d & bur there 25 & 27 Jan 1885.
iii **Aimé Gaudreau** b & bp 19 & 21 Dec 1885, Roxton Falls, QC.
iv   **Philippe Gaudreau** b & bp 25 & 27 Mar 1887, Roxton Falls, QC.

8.3.1.7   **MONTY, Césarie** b & bp 11 & 13 Dec 1853, Henryville, QC; d 24 Jun 1912, Taftville, CT. She married 8 Feb 1881, Roxton Falls, QC, **Stanislas Beautron dit Major** (Henry Beautron dit Major & Félonise Caron) b & bp 2 & 3 Dec 1852, St. Hughes, QC; d 14 Jul 1918, Norwich, CT.
Césarie Monty was buried in Sacred Heart Cemetery in Norwich, CT.
Stanislas Major was a farmer in Roxton Falls, QC, until at least April 1891 (Canadian census). His last child, though, was born the following year in Norwich, CT, where her father was a mill operative. According to the 1900 US census, he and his wife had had eight children of whom three, Clara, Matilda, and Laura, were then alive.

Children:
i   **Clément Major** b & bp 1 & 2 Nov 1881, Roxton Falls, QC; d & bur there 4 & 6 Nov 1881.
ii   **Clara Major** b & bp 11 Aug 1883, Roxton Pond, QC; d 7 Nov 1918, Taftville, CT. She married 10 Nov 1902, Norwich, CT, **Roderick Joseph/Joseph Frédéric Bernard** (Egiste Bernard & Marguerite Tétreault) b & bp 17 & 18 Jun 1883, St. Pie, QC; m (2) 1920 Exilda ____ ; d 15 Aug 1968, Windham, CT.
iii **Alida Major** b & bp 6 & 9 Aug 1885, Roxton Falls, QC; d & bur there 31 May & 2 Jun 1886.
iv   **Marie Flora Major** b & bp 27 Mar & 3 Apr 1887, Roxton Falls, QC.
v   **Clément Stanislas Major** b & bp 9 & 14 Apr 1889, Roxton Falls, QC.
vi   **Matilda Major** b & bp 30 Jul & 1 Aug 1890, Roxton Falls, QC; d & bur 27 & 30 Nov 1953, Taftville, CT. She married 14 Sep 1908, Norwich, CT, **Joseph Jean-Baptiste Gauvin** (Joseph Gauvin & Julia Despres) b 2 Feb 1890, Danielson, CT; d & bur 12 & 16 Jul 1969, Taftville, CT.
vi   **Rose Hermina Flora/Laura Major** b 4 Dec 1892, Taftville, CT.

8.3.1.8 **MONTY, Albina** b & bp 3 & 4 Mar 1858, Iberville, QC; d 22 Jul 1948, New Bedford, MA. She married 9 Jan 1882, Roxton Falls, QC, **Joseph Brodeur** (Paul Brodeur & Dorothée Ayotte dit Malo) b & bp 12 Sep 1856, St. Damase, QC; d between 1932 and 1937, New Bedford, MA.

Joseph Brodeur was a farmer in Granby, QC, until 1897. He then emigrated with his family and was a cotton mill worker in Norwich, CT, in 1900. A few years later he moved to New Bedford, MA, where he was still living in 1932 (US censuses; New Bedford City Directories). By 1937, though, Mrs. Albina Brodeur was a widow (New Bedford City Directory).

Children:
- i **Télesphore J./Joseph Clément Télesphore Brodeur** b & bp 18 & 19 May 1883, Granby, QC; d between 1937 and 1941, New Bedford, MA. He married 9 May 1910, Granby, QC, **Exilia Mathilda Paquette** (Joseph Paquette & Mathilde Barsalou) b & bp there 30 & 31 Jan 1884.
- ii **Marie Elmire Amelda Brodeur** b & bp 16 & 20 Feb 1885, Granby, QC.
- iii **Philip H./Herménégilde Philippe Azarie Brodeur** b & bp 28 Nov 1886, Granby, QC. He married 1908? **Eva** _____ b 1886?, NH; d 30 Nov 1931, New Bedford, MA.
- iv **Emma Rose/Alma Brodeur** b & bp 10 & 11 Nov 1888, Granby, QC; d 19 Dec 1978, Cranston, RI. She married 31 May 1915, New Bedford, MA, **Joseph Whalley** (Joseph Whalley & Rose Ann Shevlin) b 3 Jun 1888, Padiham, England; m (1) 25 Nov 1912, New Bedford, MA, Amanda Caissy (Simon Caissy & Marguerite Bourgeois); d 30 Sep 1962, North Smithfield, RI.
- v **Louis Polydore/Paul Brodeur** b & bp 30 Jun & 1 Jul 1890, Granby, QC. He married (1) 28 Jun 1910, New Bedford, MA, **Mary Adeline Sevigny** (Luke Sevigny & Marie Filion) b Jul 1885, Fall River, MA; d before 1920.
  He married (2) 1926? **Rose/Rosanna** _____ b 1880?, MA; d 9 Jul 1931, New Bedford, MA.
- vi **Clément Augustin Brodeur** b & bp 28 Aug 1891, Granby, QC; d Oct 1962, New Bedford, MA. He married there 26 Apr 1920 **Olivine E. Gingras** (Philippe Gingras & Edwidge St. Onge) b 31 Aug 1888, Taftville, CT; d Nov 1965, New Bedford, MA.
- vii **Silvère Louis Brodeur** b & bp 20 & 21 Jun 1894, Granby, QC; d between 1952 and 1955. He married around 1931, New Bedford, MA, **Bernadette P. Antaya** (Paul Antaya & Desanges Cournoyer) b 1897?, MA.
- viii **Paul Oscar Uldéric Brodeur** b & bp 2 Jul 1895, Granby, QC; d & bur there 1 & 2 Oct 1895.
- ix **Maria Brodeur** b & bp 9 & 10 Sep 1896, Granby, QC; d Jun 1971, New Bedford, MA. She married 1923? **Albert Varieur** (Octave Varieur/Veilleux & Josephine Sabourin) b & bp 29 Jun & 1 Jul 1893, Magog, QC; m (1) 27 Jan 1913, New Bedford, MA, Aurore/Aura Riendeau (Dieudonné Riendeau & Cordelia Perron); d Aug 1967, Acushnet, MA.
- x **Elida Brodeur** b 1 May 1898, Norwich, CT.
- xi **Georgiana Brodeur** b 12 Feb 1900, Taftville, CT.
- xii **George Alfred Brodeur** b 18 Aug 1901, Taftville, CT.

8.3.1.9 **MONTY, Anonymous** b May 1860, Roxton Falls, QC; bur there 7 May 1860.

8.3.1.10 **MONTY, Anonymous** b Jun 1861, Roxton Falls, QC; bur there 7 Jun 1861.

8.3.8.1 **MONTY, John B./Jean-Baptiste** b & bp 28 Feb & 10 Mar 1852, Stanbridge, QC; d 10 Apr 1937, Norwich, CT. He married 5 Feb 1880, Richford, VT, **Mary Como/Comeau** (John Como & Mary Joy) b 23 Aug 1863, East Berkshire, VT; d 9 Jan 1916, Norwich, CT.

John B. Monty was named Jean-Baptiste at his baptism and in French Canadian church records though John in the 1891 and 1901 Canadian censuses. He was a farmer in Sutton, QC, until about 1903 when the family moved to the Norwich, CT, area. He was a factory worker there, known as John or John B. Monty (City Directories).

Mary Como's surname was Como in the United States but Comeau in Canada. The date and place of her birth are taken from her death record. Other documents seem to indicate that she was born in Sutton but I have found no record of it there. She was buried in St. Joseph's Cemetery in Norwich.

Children:

8.3.8.1.1	Eugene Napoleon	1881-1904?-
8.3.8.1.2	Georgiana	1883- -1885
8.3.8.1.3	Louis/Lewis Joseph/Homer	1886-1915?-1963
8.3.8.1.4	Arthur/Henri William	1889- -
8.3.8.1.5	Charles	1891- -
8.3.8.1.6	John A./Joseph Amédée	1892-1913?-1955
8.3.8.1.7	George Omer/Homer	1894- -

8.3.8.2   **MONTY, Charles Philippe** b & bp 15 & 18 Apr 1854, Stanbridge, QC; d & bur there 31 Jul & 2 Aug 1859.

8.3.8.3   **MONTY, François Napoléon** b & bp 8 & 13 Jul 1856, Stanbridge, QC; d & bur 11 & 12 Sep 1870, Bedford, QC.

8.3.8.4   **MONTY, Marie Jeanne Félicité** b & bp 14 Apr & 2 May 1858, Stanbridge, QC. She married 3 Apr 1883, Richford, VT, **Pierre/Peter Touchette** (Elie Touchette & Domitilde/Mathilde Barrès) b 1855?, Sutton, QC; d & bur there 21 & 23 Nov 1883, at the age of 28.

Mary Monty, a 25-year-old daughter of John and Fidelia (sic) Monty, was a resident of Sutton, QC, when she married 27-year-old Peter Twochette (sic), son of Eli (sic) and Mathilda Twochette, who was a railroad employee there. When he died just eight months later the burial record in St. André's Church in Sutton does not mention his wife's name, as would normally be the case if he were either married or widowed. Instead, he is identified simply by reference to his parents. I cannot explain the anomaly unless the marriage was for some reason annulled. I have found no later trace of Mary Monty or Marie Jeanne Félicité Monty.

8.3.8.5   **MONTY, Charles** b & bp 3 & 5 May 1860, Stanbridge, QC; d & bur 1948, Windham Co, CT. He married 1 Sep 1883, Richford, VT, **Joséphine Comeau/Como** (Alexandre Comeau & Olive Nault) b 1869?, Franklin, VT.

Charles Monty (Joseph Charles at his baptism) first married Josephine Como before a Protestant minister in Richford, VT, then had the marriage revalidated in the Catholic church in Sutton, QC, on 15 Dec 1885 (bride: Joséphine Comeau). He was a farmer/farm laborer there until 1902 before moving to Norwich, CT, where his daughter Cordelia married in May 1903. In 1910, 1920, and 1930, he was a cotton mill worker in Plainfield, CT (US censuses).

Josephine Como, born in Vermont, was 1 year old in 1870 when she was living with her parents in Franklin, VT, and 10 years old in 1880 when she was living with them in Morristown, VT. She was ten years younger than her husband in the US censuses of 1910 and 1920. The date found in the 1901 Canadian census in Sutton, 16 May 1867, is most probably wrong (as are seven of the eight dates of birth it ascribes to Charles Monty and his children).

Children:

8.3.8.5.1	Cordelia	1886-1903-1950
8.3.8.5.2	Charles Edward/Edouard	1888-1914?-1966
8.3.8.5.3	George	1890-1911?-1958
8.3.8.5.4	Joséphine	1891-1911?-
8.3.8.5.5	Dona/Donat/Robert	1894- -1959

| 8.3.8.5.6 | Arthur Ovila | 1897-   -1966 |
| 8.3.8.5.7 | Yvonne Alida | 1899-1919?-1987 |

8.3.8.6 **MONTY, Céleste/Alice** b & bp 14 & 17 Aug 1862, Stanbridge, QC. She married 28 Jul 1878, Sutton, QC, **Jérôme/Jérémie Vadeboncoeur/Verboncoeur/Goodheart** (Julien Vadeboncoeur/Goodheart & Clara Raymond) b 1854?, Highgate, VT.

The records of St. André Church in Sutton, QC, include the marriage, on 28 Jul 1878, of Céleste Monty and Jérémie Vadeboncoeur. The bride and groom however signed Alice Montey and Jérôme Varboncoeur. Their names and surnames constantly vary. They were Céleste Monty and Jérôme Vadeboncoeur at their children's baptisms, Jerome and Ellis Goodheart in the 1881 Canadian census in Sutton, Jerome and Alice Goodhart (sic) when he registered their daughter Georgiana's birth in Norwich, CT, in 1903, and Jeremiah and Alice Verboncoeur in the 1910 US census in New Bedford, MA.

He was a 27-year-old farmer in Sutton in 1881 (Canadian census) and a laborer in Richford, VT, at the birth of his son Charles in 1899. It is unclear from the other children's baptismal records if they were born in Sutton or in Richford. The 1910 US census in New Bedford, MA, where Jeremiah Verboncoeur was a watchman, noted that his children George, Georgiana, Lucie, and Charles were all born in Vermont, which is what I have indicated, though with no great degree of confidence. I have been unable to trace the family beyond 1910.

Children:
i   **Joseph Napoléon Vadeboncoeur** b & bp 21 Apr & 5 May 1881, Sutton, QC.
ii   **Jérôme Vadeboncoeur** b & bp 12 & 16 Sep 1883, Sutton, QC.
iii **George Vadeboncoeur/Verboncoeur** b 1888?, Richford (?), VT.
iv   **Georgiana Vadeboncoeur/Verboncoeur** b & bp 5 Jan & 1 Nov 1891, Richford, VT (?) & Sutton, QC.
v   **Lucie/Lucy Vadeboncoeur/Verboncoeur/Goodheart** b 4 Jun 1893, Richford, VT; d 25 Jan 1958, Queens, NY. She married 19 Feb 1912, MA, **Albert Alexander Perrenod** (Luc Perrenod & Lucille A. Montandon) b 6 Apr 1868, Neuchâtel, Switzerland; m (1) 22 Dec 1890, Bridgetown, Barbados, Millicent Mary Letitia Plimmer (Thomas Swithen Plimmer & Margaret Ann Osmond); d 1939, NY.
vi   **Anonymous Vadeboncoeur** b 22 Aug 1895; d & bur 22 & 25 Aug 1895, Richford, VT (?) & Sutton, QC.
vii **Charles Henri Vadeboncoeur/Verboncoeur** b & bp 12 Jun & 2 Jul 1899, Richford, VT & Sutton, QC.

8.3.8.7 **MONTY, Jacques Philippe/Philip/Jacob** b & bp 18 & 20 Nov 1864, Stanbridge, QC. He married 10 Nov 1888, Richford, VT, **Clara Shover** (Peter Shover & Delia Laplant) b 26 Mar 1867, Montgomery, VT; d 17 Dec 1958, Plainfield, CT.

There are many variations of this couple's names and surnames. They married as Philip Monty (Jacques Philippe at his baptism) and Clara Shover. At their children's baptisms in Sutton, QC, his name is either Jacques or Philippe Monty and hers Clara Chauvin. They were Jake and Clara Monte in the 1891 Canadian census there but Philip and Clara Monte in the 1901 census. Yet when a child died in Norwich, CT, in 1903 his parents were Jake Monty and Clara Sholda. They were also known in US censuses as Jacob and Clara Monty.

Philip Monty was a resident of Richford, VT, at his marriage though a farmer in Sutton in 1891 and 1901 (Canadian censuses). The family may have moved back and forth between Canada and the United States. His children were all baptized in Sutton, a few miles north of the border, though the four oldest later claimed they had been born in Vermont (1910, 1920, 1930 US censuses). The family moved to Connecticut in the early years of the 20th century and was living in Norwich when son Francis died in January 1903. Jacob Monty was a farmer in Scotland, CT, in 1910 and in Plainfield, CT, 1920 and 1930 (US censuses).

Children:
| 8.3.8.7.1 | Henry John B. | 1889-   -1985 |

8.3.8.7.2	Philippe	1893-	-1893
8.3.8.7.3	Joseph Eusèbe	1895-	-1981
8.3.8.7.4	Napoléon	1897-	-
8.3.8.7.5	François/Francis	1899-	-1903
8.3.8.7.6	Rose	1902-1923?-1928?-1983	
8.3.8.7.7	Julia C.	1908-	-1987

8.3.8.8 **MONTY, George Edouard** b & bp 7 Nov 1866 & 6 Jan 1867, VT (?) & Iberville, QC; d 15 Jan 1954, Scotland, CT. He married 13 Nov 1907, Baltic, CT, **Adonalda/Donalda Goddu/Gadue** (Antoine Goddu & Anastasie Gauthier) b & bp 16 Jun 1879, Beloeil, QC; d 1944, Scotland, CT.

George E. Monty's baptismal record shows that his parents were of Stanbridge, QC, in January 1867. He may have been born in Vermont, as noted in the US censuses of 1910, 1920, and 1930, which would explain the unusual delay between birth and baptism. On the other hand when George Monte was a farmer in Sutton, QC in 1891 and 1901 the Canadian censuses show that he was born in the Province of Quebec. Either is possible. He left for Connecticut with his brothers in the early 1900s and became a farmer in Scotland, CT, where he was again known as George Monty (US censuses). The date of his marriage, found in family history, is only partly confirmed by the 1910 census: he and his wife had been married for only two years. Yet they had a 4-year-old son.

His wife's name and surname vary. She was Marie Louise Octavie Analda Goddu at her baptism, Donalda Godu in the 1881 Canadian census in Beloeil, QC, Donalda Gadue in the 1900 US census in Norwich, CT, and Mrs. Adonalda Monty in the censuses of 1910, 1920, and 1930 in Scotland, CT.

Children:
8.3.8.8.1	William	1906-	-1983
8.3.8.8.2	Phyllis	1909-	-1979
8.3.8.8.3	Mary A.	1910-	-1981
8.3.8.8.4	George Edward	1912-	-
8.3.8.8.5	Henry M.	1914-	-1977
8.3.8.8.6	Josephine R.	1918-	-

8.3.8.9 **MONTY/MONTIE, Henry/Henri Michel** b & bp 21 & 28 Jun 1868, Highgate, VT & Stanbridge, QC; d between 1930 and 1936, CT. He married 4 Jan 1892, Sutton, QC, **Bridget Turgeon** (Peter Turgeon & Bridget Eagleton) b 12 Mar 1876, Spencer, MA; d 27 Jun 1936, Norwich, CT.

This couple's marriage record bears the names of Henri Monty (Henri Michel at his baptism) and Brigitte Turgeon. Their signatures however are clearly Henry Monty and Bridget Turgeon. He was generally named Henry Monty and his wife Brigitte at the baptisms of their children in Sutton, QC, where he was a farmer. Yet the 1891 and 1901 Canadian censuses there name him Henry Monte. When the family moved to Norwich, CT, at some time between then and the birth of Cecilia in 1906, he and his wife became known as Henry Montie and Bridget Sturgeon. And although two censuses (1910 and 1930) still carry the surname Monty, the Connecticut Vital Records consistently show the children's surname as Montie.

Henry Montie was a blacksmith in Norwich until at least 1911 and was a house carpenter there in 1920. In 1930 he and his wife were living with their youngest child, Frances, in Killingly, CT (US censuses). My list of children is certainly incomplete: according to William George's birth record in 1910 he was the couple's tenth child.

Children:
8.3.8.9.1	Marie Félicité	1894-1914-1979
8.3.8.9.2	Josephine Bridget	1894-1914-
8.3.8.9.3	Henry George	1896-1919?-1971
8.3.8.9.4	Esther	1897- -1915
8.3.8.9.5	Rose Anna	1901-1919-1991

8.3.8.9.6	Cecilia	1906-	-1986
8.3.8.9.7	William George	1910-	-1993
8.3.8.9.8	Frances Faith	1914-	-

8.3.8.10 **MONTY, Marie Louise Eugénie** b & bp 12 & 13 Nov 1870, Bedford, QC; d & bur there 4 & 7 Dec 1870.

8.3.8.11 **MONTY, Joséphine/Josie L.** b & bp 24 & 25 May 1873, Bedford, QC. She married 13 May 1891, Richford, VT, **Henry R. Barup** (Samuel Barup & Mary Judd) b there Sep 1867.

According to her marriage record Josie L. Monty was born in Sutton, QC. Her baptismal record however states that she was born in Bedford, QC. Her husband was a farmer in Richford, VT, at his marriage and in 1900 (US census). He and his wife Josephine had then had but one child who was no longer alive. I know nothing more about the family.

Child:
i   **George Barup** b 18 Jan 1893, Richford, VT; d there 28 Jan 1893.

8.3.8.12 **MONTY, Lucie Anna** b & bp 18 & 25 Dec 1876, Bedford, QC; d & bur there 6 & 8 Jan 1877.

8.3.11.1 **MONTY, François** b & bp 21 Aug 1845, St. Jean, QC; d & bur there 23 & 24 Aug 1845.

8.3.11.2 **MONTY, Joseph** b & bp 30 Nov & 1 Dec 1846, Iberville, QC; d & bur there 30 Jan & 1 Feb 1847.

8.3.11.3 **MONTY, Anonymous** b 2 Feb 1848, St. Jean, QC; d & bur there 2 & 3 Feb 1848.

8.3.11.4 **MONTY, Aurélie** b & bp 29 & 31 Oct 1850, Iberville, QC. She married 1 Aug 1871, Bedford, QC, **Joseph Pascal Benoit** (Christophe Benoit & Anastasie Hamel) b & bp 7 & 10 Jun 1849, Franklin Co., VT & Stanbridge, QC; d 15 Jun 1923, New Bedford, MA. .

Joseph Benoit was born in Vermont according to a number of US censuses, and particularly in Swanton or St. Albans, according to his children's birth records in Massachusetts. Yet his parents were of St. Armand, QC, when he was baptized in Stanbridge, QC. He was a blacksmith in Bedford, QC, at his marriage but appears never to have stayed very long in any one locality: according to the place of birth of his children, he was in New Bedford, MA, in 1872, in Bedford, QC, in 1874, in New York State in 1877, in Farnham, QC, in 1880, in Granby, QC, in 1882, and in New Bedford again in 1885 and later years. He was a blacksmith there. He and his wife had had fourteen children of whom eight, Joseph, Edouard, William J., Philip, Lena, Emma, Ida, and Regina, were alive in 1900 (US censuses).

Children:
i   **Joseph Benoit** b 3 Jun 1872, New Bedford, MA.
ii   **Edouard François/Edward Benoit** b & bp 2 & 13 Mar 1874, Bedford, QC; d Feb 1964. He married 10 May 1894, New Bedford, MA, **Minnie Hanlon** (Warren Hanlon & Mary Torpes) b May 1877, MA.
iii   **William J. Benoit** b Apr 1877, NY.
iv   **Philip/Pascal Philippe Benoit** b & bp 25 & 27 May 1880, Farnham, QC. He married (1) 20 Jun 1904, New Bedford, MA, **Dina Rosa Millet** (Joseph Millet & Ida French) b there 29 June 1887.
      He was a widower when he married (2) 2 Feb 1910, New Bedford, MA, **Mary T. Connelly** (William Connelly & Julia A. Calnan) b there Aug 1880.
v   **Véronique Eugénie Malvina Benoit** b & bp 19 & 22 May 1882, Granby, QC; d before 1900.

vi   **Marie J. Benoit** b 1 Oct 1885, New Bedford, MA; d before 1900.

vii   **Lena Benoit** b 7 May 1888, New Bedford, MA.

viii   **George J. Benoit** b 18 Mar 1890, New Bedford, MA; d before 1900.

ix   **Mary Emma/Marie E. Benoit** b 23 Jul 1891, New Bedford, MA; d 27 Jan 1968, Fall River, MA. She married 8 Dec 1908, New Bedford, MA, **Thomas Henry Arsenault/Aceino** (Charles Arsenault & Anna Augusta Steeves) b 12 Jan 1888, Hopewell Hill, New Brunswick, Canada; d 27 Jan 1925, Dodgeville, MA.

x   **Ida Benoit** b 2 Oct 1893, New Bedford, MA.

xi   **Regina E. Benoit** b 23 Oct 1895, New Bedford, MA.

8.3.11.5   **MONTY, François/Frank Jr.** b & bp 25 & 26 Mar 1853, St. Armand & Stanbridge, QC; d & bur 1916, New Bedford, MA. He married 10 Jan 1887, Holyoke, MA, **Arthémise Geoffrion** (Jean-Baptiste Geoffrion & Lucie/Lucy Petit dit Beauchemin) b & bp 5 & 6 May 1852, Beloeil, QC; d 16 Aug 1916, New Bedford, MA.

François Monty arrived in the United States in 1871 and was naturalized as Frank Monty on 11 Nov 1897 in Boston, MA. He was a baker in New Bedford, MA, at his marriage, a painter in 1889 and 1890, and the owner of a livery stable there in 1900. In 1910 he was described as a teamster (US censuses). He and his wife were buried in the Old Sacred Heart Cemetery in New Bedford.

Children:

8.3.11.5.1	Armosa/Harmosa	1887-1907-1964
8.3.11.5.2	Almo	1889- -1904
8.3.11.5.3	Hector Louis	1890-1922-
8.3.11.5.4	Blanche Y.	1894-1914-1977

8.3.11.6   **MONTY, Philippe/Philip** b & bp 20 & 22 Nov 1855, Stanbridge, QC; d 25 May 1929, New Bedford, MA. He married there 15 Apr 1880 **Azilda Dufresne** (Damase Dufresne & Elisabeth Bourassa) b & bp 13 May 1860, St. Alexandre, QC; d 1918, New Bedford, MA.

Philippe Monty came to the United States with his parents in 1871, was naturalized in 1890, and was henceforth known as Philip Monty. He was a barber in New Bedford, MA. He and his wife had eight children of whom five were still alive in 1910. After her death he stayed for a few years with his son Arthur in the household of his daughter Bertha and son-in-law Arthur Frigault in New Bedford (US censuses).

Children:

8.3.11.6.1	Philip	1881-1916-
8.3.11.6.2	Marie Azilda	1883-1916-1949
8.3.11.6.3	William Wilfred	1885-1903?&1926-1961
8.3.11.6.4	Malvina A.	1886- -1887
8.3.11.6.5	Alphonse	1888- -1888
8.3.11.6.6	Bertha/Berthe Arthémise	1891-1913-
8.3.11.6.7	Billian	1896- -
8.3.11.6.8	Arthur J.	1902?-1929-

8.3.11.7   **MONTY, Edward** b & bp 11 & 13 Jun 1859, Henryville, QC; d 1908, Fairhaven, MA. He married 1887? **Albina V. Cloutier** (Louis Cloutier & Josephine ____) b Dec 1866, Albany, NY; m (2) Cortland, NY, George Lane.

Edward Monty came to New Bedford, MA, with his parents in 1871 and was naturalized in the Bristol Co. Superior Court in Taunton, MA, in 1883 (#1342). His marital history is murky. I have not found his marriage record and know of his marriage mainly through his children's birth and death records. Nor is he listed with his wife in either US censuses or in New Bedford City Directories where he was described variously as an oiler, speeder tender, or clerk residing at the same address as his widowed mother. His date of death is taken from the Massachusetts Death Index.

Mrs. Albina Monty had been married for 13 years in 1900 and had had eight children, of whom five were still alive. She was then head of her household in New Bedford. Ten years later she was a widow living in Cortland, NY, with her daughter Lillian (8.3.11.7.2) and her husband George Truman. She remarried in the next few years and was living with her second husband George Lane and a granddaughter Marie Pacentini (8.3.11.7.7.i) in Cortland in 1920 (US censuses). She was also there when she was mentioned in the 1930 "Mothers Pilgrimage, WWI" as the mother of the deceased Sgt Arthur P. Monty (8.3.11.7.6).

Children:

8.3.11.7.1	Anonymous	1889-	-1889
8.3.11.7.2	Lillian Josephine	1890-1909-1954	
8.3.11.7.3	Joseph François	1892-	-1894
8.3.11.7.4	Florence	1893-1912?-1980	
8.3.11.7.5	Joseph T.	1894-	-
8.3.11.7.6	Arthur P.	1897-	-1918
8.3.11.7.7	Rose	1898-1915?-1968	
8.3.11.7.8	Alfred Joseph/Fred	1899-1924?-1987	

8.3.11.8   **MONTY, Jean-Baptiste/John B.** b & bp 21 & 30 Jan 1859, Stanbridge, QC; d 23 Jun 1926, Pawtucket, RI. He married (1) 5 Sep 1880, New Bedford, MA, **Malvina Hubert** (Jean-Baptiste Hubert & Marie Tremblay) b 1860?, QC; d 29 Dec 1891, Fall River, MA, at the age of 31.

He married (2) 22 May 1894, Fall River, MA, **Marianne Pelletier** (Théodule Pelletier & Catherine Geoffroy) b & bp 24 Jul 1858, Ste Mélanie, QC; bur 7 May 1950, Pawtucket, RI.

Jean-Baptiste Monty came to the United States with his parents in 1871. He was a cotton mill worker in New Bedford, MA, for a few years in the early 1880s and later in Fall River, MA, where most of the children of his first marriage were born. His first child however was born in Bromont (West Shefford), QC.

John B. Monty was still in Fall River in 1900 but moved before 1910 to Pawtucket, RI, where he was a cotton mill worker and later a barber (US censuses; City Directories). He and his second wife were buried in Notre Dame Cemetery in Pawtucket. They had had four children, all of whom were deceased in 1910 (US census).

Children of the first marriage:

8.3.11.8.1	Anna/Mariana/Mary Ann	1881-1908-	
8.3.11.8.2	Josephine A.	1884-	-1886
8.3.11.8.3	François Arthur	1886-	-1889
8.3.11.8.4	Alfred Noel	1888-1908-	
8.3.11.8.5	Malvina Josephine	1890-	-1986
8.3.11.8.6	Hector	1891-1910-1918	

Child of the second marriage:

8.3.11.8.7	Anonymous	1897-	-1897

8.3.11.9   **MONTY, Adèle** b & bp 30 Sep & 12 Oct 1860, Stanbridge, QC. She married 27 Dec 1920, New Bedford, MA, **Dominic/Dominique St. Pierre/St. Peter** (Ferdinand St. Pierre/ St. Peter & Elodie Lizotte) b & bp ? & 25 May 1865, Frenchville, ME.

The records of St. Luce's Catholic Church in Frenchville, ME, do not indicate Dominic St. Pierre's date of birth. He was probably baptized a few days after birth as his siblings had been. His name and surname vary. He was Dominic St. Pierre at his baptism, Dominic St. Peter when he was living with his parents in Lyndon, ME, in 1870, Dominique St. Peter when he was with them in Caribou, ME, in 1880 (US censuses), and Dominique St. Pierre at his marriage to Adèle Monty.

8.3.11.10   **MONTY, Joseph Ambroise** b & bp 18 Jan 1863, Stanbridge, QC; d & bur there 4 & 6 Mar 1865.

8.3.11.11   **MONTY, Clément** b & bp 7 & 8 Mar 1865, Stanbridge, QC; d & bur there 7 & 9 Sep 1865.

8.3.11.12   **MONTY, Siffroid George** b & bp 30 & 31 Jul 1866, Stanbridge, QC; d & bur there 3 & 5 Feb 1867.

8.3.11.13   **MONTY, Marie Rosalie/Mary** b & bp 8 & 14 Dec 1867, Bedford & Stanbridge, QC. She married (1) 3 Feb 1890, New Bedford, MA, **Zotique Dionne** (Edouard Dionne & Bibiane Molleur) b Dec 1867, QC; d 1905, New Bedford, MA.
    She married (2) 6 Mar 1916, New Bedford, MA, **Albert Pepin** (Jules Pepin & Tharsile Hébert) b & bp 21 Aug 1863, St. Pie, QC; m (1) 6 May 1889, Lowell, MA, Rosanna Garand (Joseph Garand & Emerence Barrette); d 1916, New Bedford, MA.
    She married (3) 11 Jun 1917, New Bedford, MA, **Joseph Adélard Robert** (Moïse Robert & Adélaïde Rémillard) b & bp 30 Dec 1860, Napierville, QC; m (1) 21 Jun 1886, New Bedford, MA, Régina Grégoire (Pierre Grégoire & Marie Cyr); m (2) 5 Aug 1907, Fairhaven, MA, Valérie Leboeuf (Louis Leboeuf & Mathilde Gauthier).
    Marie Rosalie Monty (baptismal name) married her Zotique Dionne, a carder in New Bedford, MA, as Mary Monty. I have not found his birth record. It is probable he was born in the area around Iberville, QC, where his parents married in January 1867 and where a younger brother was born in 1869. He was a 13-year-old child living there with his parents in 1881 (Canadian census). He came to the United States in 1884 and was naturalized before 1900. He and his wife had then had five children of whom the three listed below were still alive. His widow was still living with her children in New Bedford in 1910 (US censuses).
    She married her second husband, Albert Pepin, as Rosalie Monty.
    She also married under that name her third husband, Joseph Adélard Robert. In the 1920 and 1930 US censuses in New Bedford, though, their names are Joseph A. and Mary Roberts. He had arrived in the United States in 1878 and was a weaver in New Bedford (US censuses).

Children:
i   **George Dionne** b Feb 1893, New Bedford, MA.
ii   **Emile Arthur Dionne** b 10 Nov 1894, Belleville, Ontario, Canada.
iii **Eva Dionne** b 3 Nov 1898, New Bedford, MA; d there 16 Nov 1976. She married there 5 Mar 1917 **William Joseph Cocker** (John Cocker & Rose Donahue) b 1 Apr 1888, Ashton Under Lyne, Lancashire, England.

8.3.11.14   **MONTY, Malvina** b & bp 5 & 6 Jan 1870, Bedford, QC. She married 29 Aug 1893, New Bedford, MA, **Wenceslas Côté** (Hilaire Côté & Philomène Hébert) b 1869? Wenceslas Côté was 24 years old at his marriage.

8.3.11.15   **MONTY, Josephine** b 27 May 1872, New Bedford, MA; d there 24 Jan 1947. She married there 9 Jun 1890 **Victor Adrien Loranger** (Sévère Loranger & Eleonore Lesieur) b & bp 29 & 30 Mar 1867, Yamamiche, QC; d 8 Aug 1916, New Bedford, MA.
    Victor A. Loranger came to the United States in 1882 and was a baker in New Bedford, MA, at his marriage. He was a teamster there at the births of his children and until his death. The 1900 census specifies that he was working in a livery stable, perhaps that of Frank Monty (8.3.11.5), his brother-in-law and neighbor. By 1910 he and his wife had had seven children of whom six were still alive (US censuses). They were both buried, as were three of their children, in the New Sacred Heart Cemetery in New Bedford.

Children:
i   **Josephine Loranger** b 10 Mar 1892, New Bedford, MA; d there 26 Dec 1971. She married there 23 Nov 1914 **Napoléon Coderre** (Paul Coderre & Aurélie Dufresne) b & bp 13 & 14 Aug 1890, Farnham, QC.
ii   **Alice A. Loranger** b 14 Jun 1894, New Bedford, MA; d there 31 Dec 1988.

iii   **Bertha Loranger** b 10 Nov 1895, New Bedford, MA; d there 1 Jun 1994. She married there 30 Jun 1919 **Henry Roberts** (Samuel Roberts & Lydia Doucette) b 22 Aug 1894, Fall River, MA; d Oct 1968, New Bedford, MA.

iv   **Adrien Loranger** b 27 Apr 1897, New Bedford, MA; d there 15 Oct 1962. He married there 1923 **Grace Fauteux** (Henry A. Fauteux & Laura _____) b there 22 May 1904; d 15 Jun 1995, Wareham, MA.

v   **Arthur Loranger** b Jan 1899, New Bedford, MA; d & bur there 1933.

vi   **Armosa/Edna Loranger** b 1900?, New Bedford, MA.

vii   **François Loranger** b 1902, New Bedford, MA; d & bur there 1903.

13.3.1.1   **MONTY, Cyrille** b & bp 20 & 21 Apr 1821, Longueuil, QC; d & bur there 21 & 23 May 1842.

13.3.1.2   **MONTY, Antoine** b & bp 14 May 1822, Laprairie, QC; d & bur there 10 & 12 Jan 1832.

13.3.1.3   **MONTY, Sophie** b & bp 21 & 22 Sep 1823, Laprairie, QC; d & bur there 25 & 28 Mar 1849. She married there 23 Feb 1846, **Joseph Archambault** (Joseph Archambault & Suzanne Chartier) b & bp 25 Feb 1811, Pointe aux Trembles, QC; m (1) 15 Sep 1834, Longue Pointe, QC, Marie Olive Trudeau (Benjamin Trudeau & Catherine Vinet).
Joseph Archambault was a farmer in Longue Pointe, QC. He survived Sophie Monty.

Children:

i   **Sophie Azilda Archambault** b & bp 12 Dec 1846, Montreal, QC; d & bur 9 & 12 Sep 1879, Laprairie, QC. She married 21 Nov 1871, Laprairie, QC, **Louis Tougas** (Louis Tougas & Madeleine Perras) b & bp there 22 & 23 Dec 1838; m (1) there 27 Nov 1860, Philomène Surprenant (Joseph Surprenant & Emilie St. Gemme Beauvais); d & bur 20 & 22 Jul 1920, St. Rémi, QC.

ii   **Joseph Bénoni Archambault** b & bp 3 & 4 May 1848, Montreal, QC. He married 24 Oct 1871, Laprairie, QC, **Marie Caroline Rousseau** (Luc Rousseau & Angélique Alloire) b & bp 23 & 24 Sep 1848, Laprairie, QC; d & bur 29 May & 2 Jun 1924, Montreal, QC.

13.3.1.4   **MONTY, Anonymous** b 12 Sep 1825, Laprairie, QC; d & bur there 12 & 13 Sep 1825.

13.3.1.5   **MONTY, Mathilde** b & bp 14 Sep 1827, Laprairie, QC; d & bur 20 & 22 Jun 1857, Mont St. Grégoire, QC. She married 1 May 1849, Laprairie, QC, **Isaïe Bisaillon** (Alexis Bisaillon & Josette Marotte dit Labonté) b & bp there 7 & 8 Dec 1821; m (2) 1 Feb 1859, Mont St. Grégoire, QC, Scholastique Laporte (Etienne Laporte & Marie Ledoux); d 23 Aug 1895, Woonsocket, RI.
Isaïe Bisaillon was a farmer in Mont St. Grégoire, QC, until at least 1875, when a child of his second marriage was born. He moved to Woonsocket, RI, shortly afterwards and was a laborer there in 1880 (US census). He and his second wife were buried in Precious Blood Cemetery in Woonsocket.

Children:

i   **Antoine Isaïe Bisaillon** b & bp 8 & 9 Jul 1850, Laprairie, QC. He married 7 Jan 1873, Waterloo, QC, **Marie Eliza/Elizabeth Gervais** (Nicolas Gervais & Emilie Daniel) b & bp 7 Sep 1851, St. Dominique, QC.

ii   **Marie Mathilde Bisaillon** b & bp 7 & 8 Feb 1852, Laprairie, QC; d & bur 28 & 30 Jan 1858, Mont St. Grégoire, QC.

iii   **Denise Bisaillon** b & bp 3 & 4 Apr 1854, Laprairie, QC; d 18 Oct 1945, Woonsocket, RI. She married 7 Feb 1876, Waterloo, QC, **Alfred Beaudry** (Alexis Beaudry & Adélaïde Tétreau) b & bp 14 & 15 Mar 1848, Stanbridge, QC; m (1) 15 Sep 1873, Waterloo, QC, Mary Jane Barrett (Michael Barrett & Mary Morris); d 14

Nov 1930, Woonsocket, RI.

13.3.1.6   **MONTY, Octave** b & bp 1 & 2 Apr 1829, Laprairie, QC; d & bur there 12 & 14 Dec 1830.

13.3.1.7   **MONTY, Henriette** b & bp 14 & 15 Sep 1830, Laprairie, QC; d & bur there 1 & 3 Aug 1831.

13.3.1.8   **MONTY, Denise** b & bp 12 & 13 May 1833, Laprairie, QC; d & bur 10 & 12 Jul 1915, Longueuil & St. Bruno, QC. She married 19 Oct 1858, Laprairie, QC, a second cousin, **Evariste Moquin** (François Moquin & Elisabeth Lareau) b & bp 9 Aug 1832, Longueuil, QC; d & bur 14 & 16 Nov 1894, Longueuil & St. Bruno, QC.

Evariste Moquin's maternal grandparents were Joseph Lareau and Catherine Monty (13.1). He was a farmer in Longueuil, QC, at his marriage and later in St. Bruno, QC, where all his children were born. He was retired in Longueuil, QC, at his death.

Children:
i   **Ernestine Moquin** b & bp 5 & 6 Apr 1860, St. Bruno, QC; d & bur there 22 & 26 Apr 1869.
ii   **Evariste Moquin** b & bp 19 Jun 1861, St. Bruno, QC; d & bur there 19 & 21 Aug 1879.
iii   **Flavien Hormisdas Moquin** b & bp 30 & 31 Jan 1863, St. Bruno, QC; d & bur there 4 & 7 Jan 1886.
iv   **Malvina Denyse Moquin** b & bp 28 Sep 1864, St. Bruno, QC; d & bur there 1 & 2 May 1865.
v   **Amédée Moquin** b & bp 25 & 26 May 1867, St. Bruno, QC; d & bur 19 & 21 Oct 1901, Longueuil, QC. He married 30 Aug 1893, Montreal, QC, a first cousin, **Nélida St. Yves** (Télesphore St. Yves & Marie Anne Monty [13.3.1.9]) b & bp 2 & 3 Mar 1870, Laprairie, QC; d & bur 31 Aug & 2 Sep 1909, Longueuil, QC.
vi   **Alfred Joseph Moquin** b & bp 28 Sep & 3 Oct 1868, St. Bruno, QC; d & bur 6 & 8 May 1949, Malone & Ft. Covington, NY. He married 31 May 1896, Ft. Covington, NY, **Justina Marie Brault** (Moïse Brault & Octavie Gendron) b & bp 21 & 22 Nov 1872, St. Etienne, QC; d 8 Feb 1952, Malone, NY.
vii   **Georges Aimé Moquin** b & bp 13 & 14 Aug 1871, St. Bruno, QC; d & bur 14 & 17 Jun 1926, Montreal, QC. He married there 9 Jun 1915 **Maria Lucia Clavet** (Etienne Zéphirin Clavet & Lucie/Lucia Galarneau).
viii **Marie Georgina Moquin** b & bp 6 & 7 Nov 1872, St. Bruno, QC; d & bur there 24 & 25 Jun 1873.
ix   **Joseph Urgel Moquin** b & bp 6 & 8 Nov 1874, St. Bruno, QC.
x   **Almaïs Emma Moquin** b & bp 10 & 12 Sep 1876, St. Bruno, QC; d & bur there 24 & 26 Jan 1887.

13.3.1.9   **MONTY, Marie Anne** b & bp 30 Oct & 1 Nov 1834, Laprairie, QC; d & bur there 17 & 20 Mar 1871. She married there 24 Jun 1862 **Télesphore St. Yves** (Pierre St. Yves & Marie Compain) b & bp there 21 Aug 1835; m (2) 28 Oct 1872, St. Luc, QC, Martine Langevin dit Lacroix (Ambroise Langevin dit Lacroix & Rosalie Provost); d & bur 7 & 9 Jul 1903, Longueuil, QC.

Télesphore St. Yves was a laborer and farmer in Laprairie, QC.

Children:
i   **Marie Emilie/Emelia St. Yves** b & bp 13 Oct 1868, Laprairie, QC. She married 21 Nov 1892, Longueuil, QC, **Napoléon Brunelle** (Adolphe Brunelle & Angèle Bouthillier) b & bp 15 & 17 Jul 1864, Laprairie, QC; d & bur 14 & 17 Feb 1933, Montreal & St. Lambert, QC.
ii   **Nélida St. Yves** b & bp 2 & 3 Mar 1870, Laprairie, QC; d & bur 31 Aug & 2 Sep 1909, Longueuil, QC. She married 30 Aug 1893, Montreal, QC, a first cousin

Amédée Moquin (Evariste Moquin & Denise Monty [13.3.1.8]) b & bp 25 & 26 May 1867, St. Bruno, QC; d & bur 19 & 21 Oct 1901, Longueuil, QC.

13.3.1.10   **MONTY, Philomène** b & bp 14 & 18 Dec 1835, Chambly, QC; d & bur 21 & 23 Jul 1852, Laprairie, QC.

13.3.1.11   **MONTY, Elmire** b & bp 10 Apr 1840, Laprairie, QC; d & bur 1 & 2 Mar 1929, Montreal & Longueuil, QC.
Elmire Monty did not marry.

13.3.1.12   **MONTY, Hermine** b & bp 24 & 25 Nov 1843, Laprairie, QC; d & bur 13 & 16 Feb 1922, Montreal & Longueuil, QC. She married 19 Nov 1867, Laprairie, QC, a third cousin, **Alfred Patenaude** (Michel Patenaude & Anastasie Daignault) b & bp 28 & 29 Jul 1842, Longueuil, QC; d & bur there 28 & 30 Jun 1900.
Alfred Patenaude, whose maternal grandparents were François Deniau and Marguerite Monty (16.10), was named Michel Joseph Wilfred at his baptism. In all other circumstances, including his marriage and death and the births of his children, he was named Alfred. He was a farmer in Longueuil, St. Hubert, and Laprairie, QC, in the early years of his marriage and a merchant in Longueuil in 1876. By 1894, he was a merchant in Montreal, QC.

Children:
i   **Alfred Patenaude** b & bp 16 & 17 Sep 1868, Laprairie, QC; d & bur 14 & 16 Apr 1914, Montreal & Longueuil, QC. He married 12 May 1897, Montreal, QC, **Marie Louise Messier** (Etienne Messier & Théotiste Mongeau) b & bp 3 Oct 1870, Varennes, QC; m (2) 11 Sep 1916, Montreal, QC, Ferdinand Poirier (Ferdinand Poirier & Hermine Provencher), widower of Laura Bérubé; d & bur there 11 & 13 Feb 1937.
ii   **Louis Ernest Patenaude** b & bp 20 & 24 Feb 1870, Laprairie & Chambly, QC; d & bur 5 & 6 Mar 1870, Laprairie, QC.
iii   **Michel Ernest Patenaude** b & bp 1 & 2 Apr 1876, Longueuil, QC; d & bur 5 & 7 Aug 1902, Montreal & Longueuil, QC.
iv   **Marie Anne Patenaude** b & bp 22 & 23 Sep 1878, Longueuil, QC; d & bur there 23 & 25 Jan 1882.
v   **Marguerite Blanche Patenaude** b & bp 18 & 19 Oct 1882, Longueuil, QC; bur there 16 Oct 1952.
vi   **Evariste Basile Patenaude** b & bp 26 & 27 May 1884, Longueuil, QC. He married 17 May 1904, Montreal, QC, **Anne Lafrenière** (Désiré Lafrenière & Tharsile Bergeron) b & bp there 8 Jan 1882.

13.3.6.1   **MONTY, Flavie** b & bp 9 & 10 Aug 1832, Longueuil, QC; d & bur 25 & 27 Mar 1843, Mont St. Grégoire, QC.

13.3.6.2   **MONTY, Denise** b & bp 3 Oct 1835, Marieville, QC; d & bur 9 & 11 Apr 1874, Iberville & Mont St. Grégoire, QC. She married 7 Jan 1862, Mont St. Grégoire, QC, **Didace Dextraze** (Pierre Dextraze & Charlotte Robidoux) b & bp 6 & 8 Dec 1838, Marieville, QC; m (2) 25 Jun 1877, Iberville, QC, Marie Bessette (Noël Bessette & Martine Gamache); d & bur 9 & 11 Nov 1909, Mont St. Grégoire, QC.
Didace Dextraze (also Destras, Dextrase) was a farmer in Iberville and Mont St. Grégoire, QC.

Children:
i   **Elzéar Dextraze** b & bp 8 & 9 Apr 1864, Mont St. Grégoire, QC. He married 21 Apr 1884, Iberville, QC, **Marie Emélie/Emmeline McNulty** (Joseph McNulty & Hermine Boucher) b & bp 17 & 22 Nov 1862, Mont St. Grégoire, QC.
ii   **Delia/Marie Rose Dextraze/Dextras** b & bp 16 & 18 Sep 1865, Iberville, QC; d & bur 1955, Woonsocket, RI. She married 22 Sep 1885, Woonsocket, RI, **Edéas Al-**

fred Choquette (Alfred Choquette & Philomene Esinhart) b & bp 10 Jan 1864, Mont St. Grégoire, QC; d 10 Apr 1906, Woonsocket, RI.

iii **Joseph Aldore Dextraze** b & bp 13 May 1867, Mont St. Grégoire, QC.

iv **Alphonse Grégoire Dextraze** b & bp 1 & 2 Jan 1869, Mont St. Grégoire, QC; d & bur 20 & 23 Oct 1905, Farnham, QC. He married 20 Apr 1891, Ste Brigide, QC, **Victoria Laroche** (Narcisse Laroche & Aurélie Trahan) b & bp there 14 & 18 Dec 1870; m (2) 9 Jan 1911, Farnham, QC, Auguste Lussier (Gédéon Lussier & Adeline Poudrette dit Lavigne), widower of Odile Belisle.

v **Ulric Dextraze/Dextras** b & bp 7 & 9 Jan 1871, Iberville, QC; bur 1935, Woonsocket, RI. He married there 17 Aug 1891 **Marie Louise Corinne Côté** (Joachim Côté & Philomène McCarthy) b & bp 26 & 27 Mar 1870, St. Cuthbert, QC; d 23 Jun 1922, Woonsocket, RI.

vi **Alcide Dextraze** b & bp 3 & 5 Nov 1872, Mont St. Grégoire, QC; d & bur there 1949. He married there 24 Oct 1898 **Laura Angelina Choquette** (Gédéon Léon Choquette & Malvina Ponton) b & bp there 13 & 14 Oct 1877; d & bur there 1951.

vii **Denise Elmina/Hermina Dextraze** b & bp 8 & 10 Apr 1874, Iberville & Mont St. Grégoire, QC. She married 21 Oct 1889, Marieville, QC, **David Ferguson** (William Ferguson & Isabella Scott) b 16 Jan 1868, Durham, QC; bp 5 Aug 1880, Acton Vale (Protestant Church), QC.

13.3.6.3 **MONTY, Marcel** b & bp 7 & 9 Jun 1837, Marieville, QC; d & bur 6 & 8 Apr 1843, Mont St. Grégoire, QC.

13.3.6.4 **MONTY, Emery** b & bp 16 & 17 May 1840, Marieville, QC; d & bur 18 & 20 Aug 1930, Ste Brigide, QC. He married 14 Nov 1865, Mont St. Grégoire, QC, **Aglaé Lareau** (Joseph Lareau & Flavie Lalanne) b & bp 30 Sep & 3 Oct 1847, Mont St. Grégoire & Mont St. Hilaire, QC; d & bur 27 & 29 Apr 1914, Ste Brigide, QC.

Emery Monty (Emery Uldéric at his baptism) was a farmer in Ste Brigide, QC. His wife was a sister of Guillaume Lareau, husband of Vitaline Monty (13.3.6.9), and of Azilda Lareau, second wife of Joseph Monty (13.3.6.12).

Children:

13.3.6.4.1	Marie Eva	1867- -1867
13.3.6.4.2	Eva	1868-1895-1952
13.3.6.4.3	Zénaïde	1870-1890&1909-1946
13.3.6.4.4	Rosilda	1871-1896-
13.3.6.4.5	Delima/Rose de Lima	1874-1898-1957
13.3.6.4.6	Edéas	1876-1898-
13.3.6.4.7	Anselme	1877- -1879
13.3.6.4.8	Emile	1880-1911-1942
13.3.6.4.9	Hilaire	1882-1907-1949
13.3.6.4.10	Albert	1883-1911-1918
13.3.6.4.11	Ovila	1885-1919-1935

13.3.6.5 **MONTY, Ulric** b 1841?, QC. He married 12 Nov 1867, Mont St. Grégoire, QC, **Adélaïde Kaigle** (Frederick Kaigle & Apolline Lalanne) b & bp there 13 & 14 Apr 1849.

Ulric Monty was a farmer in Mont St. Grégoire, QC, until at least 1878. Two years later, when he was 39 years old, he was a teamster in Elizabethtown, Dakota Territory (US census) but was again a farmer in Mont St. Grégoire in 1881 (Canadian census). I have not found him or his wife in later years in either Canada or the United States. The family may have returned to South Dakota: one daughter certainly and the other probably lived and died there.

Children:

13.3.6.5.1	Alma	1876-1896?-1934
13.3.6.5.2	Rose Emma/Rosa	1878- -

13.3.6.6   **MONTY, Adèle** b & bp 23 & 27 Feb 1842, Mont St. Grégoire, QC; d & bur there 3 & 6 Jul 1911. She married there 3 Feb 1863 **Cléophas Quintin** (Eusèbe Quintin & Marguerite Bessette) b & bp 27 & 28 Jul 1840, Marieville, QC; d & bur 24 & 26 Dec 1900, Mont St. Grégoire, QC.

Cléophas Quintin was a farmer in Mont St. Grégoire, QC.

Children:

i   **Cléophas Quintin** b & bp 5 & 6 Dec 1863, Mont St. Grégoire, QC; bur there 1950. He married 26 May 1891, Iberville, QC, **Angèle Brun** (Siméon Brun & Zoé Pinsonneault) b & bp 15 Nov 1865, St. Valentin, QC; d & bur 27 & 30 Mar 1937, St. Jean & Mont St. Grégoire, QC.

ii   **Albina Quintin** b & bp 6 & 7 Jun 1865, St. Alexandre, QC; d & bur there 2 & 5 Oct 1917. She married 5 Oct 1885, Mont St. Grégoire, QC, **Marcel Gamache** (Marcel Gamache & Marie Dion) b & bp there 4 & 6 Dec 1857; d & bur 24 & 27 May 1939, St. Alexandre, QC.

iii   **Regina/Marie Rose Reine Quintin** b & bp 4 & 5 Oct 1866, Mont St. Grégoire, QC. She married there 2 Sep 1889 **Arthur Davignon** (Gédéon Léon Davignon & Eleonore/Léonie Quintin) b & bp there 26 Apr & 1 May 1870.

iv   **Ulric Quintin** b & bp 4 Jan 1868, Mont St. Grégoire, QC; d & bur there 21 & 22 Jan 1868.

v   **Zéphirin Quintin** b & bp 29 & 31 Jan 1869, Mont St. Grégoire, QC.

vi   **Agnès Quintin** b & bp 26 & 31 Jul 1870, Mont St. Grégoire, QC; d & bur there 8 & 10 Jul 1878.

vii   **Ezilda Quintin** b & bp 5 & 8 Mar 1872, Mont St. Grégoire, QC; d & bur there 29 May & 1 Jun 1873.

viii **Philias Quintin** b & bp 14 & 15 Apr 1873, Mont St. Grégoire, QC; bur there 1961. He married (1) 25 Sep 1893, St. Alexandre, QC, **Rose Quintin** (Moïse Quintin & Emilie Choquette) b & bp there 21 & 22 Jul 1873; d & bur 3 & 7 Jun 1927, St. Jean & Mont St. Grégoire, QC.

He married (2) 2 Jun 1928, Mont St. Grégoire, QC, **Donalda Hortense Tétreault** (Eugène Tétreault & Vizana Tétreault) b & bp 30 Apr 1896, Marieville, QC.

ix   **Ezilda Quintin** b & bp 18 & 19 Oct 1874, Mont St. Grégoire, QC; d & bur there 15 & 16 Oct 1882.

x   **Georgiana Quintin** b & bp 23 & 24 Apr 1876, Mont St. Grégoire, QC; d & bur there 9 & 11 Jul 1888.

xi   **Theodore Quintin** b & bp 12 & 14 Apr 1878, Mont St. Grégoire, QC; d Nov 1968, Newport, VT. He married 9 Jan 1900, New Bedford, MA, **Ida Agnès Corbin** (Pierre Corbin & Méthailde Racine) b & bp 31 May 1881, St. Leonard, New Brunswick, Canada.

xii   **Adélard Quintin** b & bp 18 & 20 Apr 1879, Mont St. Grégoire; d & bur there 23 & 25 Oct 1882.

xiii **Honorius Quintin** b & bp 6 & 8 Aug 1880, Mont St. Grégoire, QC; d & bur there 8 & 9 Mar 1891.

xiv   **Alma Quintin** b & bp 6 & 7 Nov 1881, Mont St. Grégoire, QC; bur there 1969. She married there 19 Feb 1906 **Modeste Herménégilde Fortier** (Joseph Fortier & Euphémie Kaigle) b & bp there 15 & 16 Apr 1878.

xv   **Alonzo Frédéric D. Quintin** b & bp 25 & 26 Apr 1883, Mont St. Grégoire, QC; bur there 1967. He married there 19 Oct 1909 **Marie Aglaé Bessette** (Amédée Bessette & Adeline Carreau) b 1882?, QC; bur 1957, Mont St. Grégoire, QC, at the age of 75.

xvi   **Joseph Réséda Quintin** b & bp 16 & 17 Nov 1885, Mont St. Grégoire, QC; d & bur there 7 & 9 Mat 1902.

13.3.6.7   **MONTY, Rémi** b & bp 3 & 4 Feb 1844, Mont St. Grégoire, QC.

Rémi Monty was living with his parents in Mont St. Grégoire in 1851 (Canadian census).

13.3.6.8   **MONTY, Odile** b & bp 16 & 17 Aug 1845, Mont St. Grégoire, QC; d & bur 4 & 7 May 1934, St. Majorique de Grantham, QC. She married there 26 Feb 1867 **Clément Gamache** (Marcel Gamache & Céleste Boucher) b & bp 27 & 28 Jul 1839, Iberville, QC; d & bur 4 & 8 Jan 1918, St. Majorique de Grantham, QC.

Clément Gamache was a farmer in Mont St. Grégoire, QC, at his marriage and also at times in Iberville, Richelieu, St. Alexandre, and Ste Brigide, QC. He moved to New Bedford, MA, in 1890 to work as a laborer and was by 1900 a naturalized American citizen. He nevertheless returned to Canada during the next few years and was a farmer in St. Majorique de Grantham, QC, in 1911 (Canadian census) and at his death.

Nine of this couple's fourteen children were still alive in 1900 (US census). Most returned to Canada in the first decade of the twentieth century and settled there permanently. Only two remained in New Bedford: Odena (v) and Didace/Didas (vi). Another son, Theodore (vii), lived a few years in Canada before moving to Rhode Island where he died.

Children:

i   **Clément Gamache** b & bp 22 & 23 Nov 1867, Mont St. Grégoire, QC. He married 17 Aug 1891, New Bedford, MA, **Eva Jetté** (Joseph Jetté & Célina Larocque) b & bp 18 & 20 Mar 1870, Ste Brigide, QC; d & bur 27 & 30 Aug 1935, Dunham, QC.

ii   **Marie Louise/Delima Gamache** b & bp 28 Aug 1869, Iberville, QC; d & bur 22 & 24 Aug 1870, Mont St. Grégoire, QC.

iii   **Théodore Achille Gamache** b & bp 10 & 11 Feb 1871, Mont St. Grégoire, QC; d & bur there 17 & 19 Nov 1873.

iv   **Polidore Gamache** b & bp 12 & 16 Sep 1872, Richelieu, QC; d & bur 10 & 12 Feb 1924, Drummondville, QC. He married 22 Feb 1900, New Bedford, MA, **Julie Bessette** (Joseph Edmond Bessette & Julie Massé) b & bp 15 Mar 1871, Mont St. Grégoire, QC.

v   **Odena/Audéna Gamache** b & bp 22 May 1874, Richelieu, QC. She married 16 Jan 1899, New Bedford, MA, **Joseph Dextrase** (Dosithée Dextrase & Rose Bessette).

vi   **Didace Gamache** b & bp 26 Jun 1876, Iberville, QC. He married 16 Jan 1899, New Bedford, MA, **Rose Anne/Rosanna Brunelle** (Magloire Brunelle & Rose/Rosalie Gagnon) b & bp 27 Dec 1875 & 2 Jan 1876, Iberville, QC.

vii   **Théodore Gamache** b & bp 18 & 19 Apr 1878, Mont St. Grégoire, QC; d 29 Jul 1924, Woonsocket, RI. He married 30 Oct 1899, New Bedford, MA, **Arzelia Benjamin** (Prosper Benjamin & Alphonsine Ponton) b 20 May 1881, Holyoke, MA; d 5 Apr 1961, Woonsocket, RI.

viii   **Alphonse Gamache** b & bp 3 & 4 May 1879, St. Alexandre, QC; d & bur there 12 & 13 May 1879.

ix   **Henri Victor Gamache** b & bp 10 & 16 May 1880, St. Alexandre, QC; d before June 1900.

x   **Alphonse Gamache** b & bp 1 & 2 Apr 1882, Mont St. Grégoire, QC. He married **Marie Rose Hamel** (Alexis Hamel & Marie Larivière) b & bp 21 & 23 Mar 1887, Beloeil, QC.

xi   **Rose Alba Gamache** b & bp 23 Aug 1883, Iberville, QC. She married 24 Oct 1911, St. Majorique de Grantham, QC, **Alfred Gagné/Gagnier** (Jean-Baptiste Gagnier & Julienne Fréchette) b & bp 30 Nov & 1 Dec 1881, St. François du Lac, QC.

xii   **Théophitus/Joseph Otiochus Gamache** b & bp 27 Feb & 2 Mar 1885, Iberville, QC. He married 1 Feb 1915, St. Majorique de Grantham, QC, **Clérina Charland** (Nérée Charland & Hildegarde Provençal) b & bp 19 & 20 Sep 1893, Drummondville, QC.

xiii   **Marie Clarinda Gamache** b & bp 18 & 19 Sep 1886, Ste Brigide, QC. She married 28 Jun 1910, St. Majorique de Grantham, QC, **Joseph Cusson** (Jean-Baptiste Cusson & Elmire Chicoine) b & bp 7 & 8 Mar 1885, Milton, QC.

xiv **Isaïe Gamache** b & bp 25 & 26 Apr 1889, Ste Brigide, QC; d before June 1900.

13.3.6.9   **MONTY, Vitaline** b & bp 11 & 24 Nov 1847, Mont St. Grégoire, QC; d 31 Oct 1930, Woonsocket, RI. She married 4 Oct 1870, Mont St. Grégoire, QC, **Guillaume Lareau** (Joseph Lareau & Flavie Lalanne) b & bp there 26 Sep 1849; d 10 May 1921, Woonsocket, RI.

Guillaume Lareau was a brother of Azilda Lareau, second wife of Joseph Monty (13.3.6.12) and of Aglaé Lareau, wife of Emery Monty (13.3.6.4). He was a farmer in Mont St. Grégoire, QC, and, for a few years, in Ste Brigide, QC, before emigrating in 1890. He became a mill worker in Woonsocket, RI, and was naturalized there in 1898. He was known as Guillaume Laroe in the 1910 and 1920 US censuses, a surname which at least two of his sons adopted. His tombstone in Precious Blood Cemetery in Woonsocket, where his wife is also buried, is inscribed though with the original Lareau surname.

Children:

i   **Guillaume Lareau** b & bp 21 Jul 1871, Mont St. Grégoire, QC; d & bur there 19 & 21 Aug 1875.

ii   **Odena Anna Lareau** b & bp 14 & 16 May 1873, Mont St. Grégoire, QC; bur 1954, Woonsocket, RI. She married there 21 Jun 1896 **Joseph Athanase Gendron** (Aimé Gendron & Vitaline Auger) b & bp 13 Mar 1869, St. Casimir, QC; d 24 Aug 1946, Woonsocket, RI.

iii   **Dorile Guillaume Lareau** b & bp 8 & 9 Dec 1875, Ste Brigide, QC. He married (1) 21 Jun 1896, Woonsocket, RI, **Marie Louise Forcier** (Olivier Forcier & Elisa Letendre) b & bp 1 Dec 1878, St. Louis de Bonsecours, QC; d 24 Feb 1913, Woonsocket, RI.

     He married (2) 15 Jan 1918, Woonsocket, RI, **Helen/Hélène Bérard** (Ephraïm/ Ephrem Bérard & Julie Valois) b & bp there 4 & 5 Sep 1882; d there Oct 1970.

iv   **Achille Lareau** b & bp 8 & 9 Sep 1877, Ste Brigide, QC. He married 7 Jan 1901, Woonsocket, RI, **Clara Boyer** (Benjamin Boyer & Eulalie Deslauriers) b Sep 1876, Montréal, QC.

v   **Henri Alphonse Lareau** b & bp 22 & 24 Mar 1879, Mont St. Grégoire, QC; d & bur there 19 & 21 Apr 1879.

vi   **Alida Lareau** b & bp 3 & 4 Feb 1884, Mont St. Grégoire, QC; d 1915. She married 18 Sep 1906, Woonsocket, RI, **Georges Hamel** (Antoine Hamel & Adeline Pion).

vii   **Eugene Laroe/Eugène Avila Lareau** b & bp 22 & 23 Jul 1885, Mont St. Grégoire, QC. He married 1905? **Josephine O'Hara** (Patrick O'Hara & Ann McGullin) b 12 Feb 1885, Medway, MA.

viii **Marie Anne Armandine Lareau** (twin) b & bp 15 & 16 Apr 1889, Mont St. Grégoire, QC; d Oct 1972, Staten Island, NY. She married 1 Jun 1911, Woonsocket, RI, **Robert Vincent Thorpe** (George Thorpe & Mary McGlynn) b 25 Feb 1889, RI; d Sep 1973, Roscoe, NY.

ix   **Hervé Joseph Lareau/Laroe** (twin) b & bp 15 & 16 Apr 1889, Mont St. Grégoire, QC; d 24 Jan 1954, Woonsocket, RI. He married there 3 Jun 1918 **Mary Genevieve McGarity** (Michael McGarity & Ellen ____) b there 23 May 1894; d 16 Dec 1988, Esmond, RI.

13.3.6.10   **MONTY, Euphémie** (twin) b & bp 26 Dec 1850, Mont St. Grégoire, QC; d & bur there 29 & 31 Dec 1850.

13.3.6.11   **MONTY, Bénonise** (twin) b & bp 26 Dec 1850, Mont St. Grégoire, QC; d & bur there 1 & 2 Feb 1851.

13.3.6.12   **MONTY, Joseph** b & bp 13 Sep 1852, Mont St. Grégoire, QC; d & bur 21 & 24 Jan 1905, Montréal & Mont St. Grégoire, QC. He married (1) 26 Sep 1871, Mont St. Grégoire, QC, **Esther Letertre** (Athanase Letertre & Mathilde Lalanne) b & bp there 9 & 10 Jul 1854; d & bur there 6 & 8 Jan 1875.

He married (2) 16 Sep 1878, Mont St. Grégoire, QC, **Azilda/Elisa Lareau** (Joseph Lareau & Flavie Lalanne) b & bp there 16 Jul 1860; m (2) there 28 Nov 1907 Nazaire Quintin (Eusèbe Quintin & Marguerite Bessette), widower of Azilda Lalanne; d & bur there 13 & 16 Oct 1929.

Joseph Monty was a farmer in Mont St. Grégoire, QC.

His second wife was a sister of Aglaé Lareau, wife of Emery Monty (13.3.6.4) and of Guillaume Lareau, husband of Vitaline Monty (13.3.6.9). Her second husband was the brother of Cléophas Quintin, husband of her sister-in-law Adèle Monty (13.3.6.6).

Children of the first marriage:

13.3.6.12.1	Anonymous	1873-	-1873
13.3.6.12.2	Philias	1874-1901&1904-1953	

Child of the second marriage:

13.3.6.12.3	Marie Anne	1889-1908&1915-1953

13.3.8.1   **MONTY, Basile** b & bp 19 & 20 Aug 1832, Laprairie, QC; d & bur 8 & 10 Oct 1832, Longueuil, QC.

13.3.8.2   **MONTY, Emery** b & bp 23 & 24 Jun 1835, Longueuil, QC; d & bur 5 & 8 Mar 1915, Rockville & Manteno, IL. He married 28 Dec 1863, Kankakee, IL, a first cousin **Matilda Paquette** (Godfroy Paquet & Marie Aurore Dumas) b & bp 16 Sep 1835, Chambly, QC; d & bur 8 & 10 Jul 1905, Rockville & Manteno, IL.

Emery Monty and Matilda Paquette (Marie Domitille Paquet at her baptism) were both grandchildren through their mothers of Joseph Dumas and Marie Desanges Benoit of Chambly, QC. The Paquet/Paquette family came to Kankakee Co., IL, in the 1840s while Emery Monty arrived there with his parents in the early 1850s. He became a farmer in Rockville, IL, and lived there most of his life, with the exception of a few months in the spring of 1865 when he served in Co. D, 15th Illinois Infantry Regiment and a few years around 1900 where he was in Dodds, IL. He had returned to Kankakee however before his wife's death in 1905 and was living in 1910 in the household of his daughter Ida and his son-in-law Arthur Reed in Manteno, IL (US censuses). Both he and his wife were buried in St. Joseph's Cemetery in Manteno.

Children:

13.3.8.2.1	Johanna/Cordelia	1865?-	-1877
13.3.8.2.2	Emery Alonzo	1867-	-1867
13.3.8.2.3	Ida Olive	1868-1891-1920	
13.3.8.2.4	Dora Adeline	1870-1891-1940	
13.3.8.2.5	Edgar Wesley	1874-1898-1948	
13.3.8.2.6	Alonzo Duff	1877-1907-1958	
13.3.8.2.7	Lucy Juliette	1879-1904-1950	

13.3.8.3   **MONTY, Philomène/Fanny** b & bp 2 & 3 Mar 1837, Longueuil, QC; d 2 Aug 1922, Manteno, IL. She married 9 Sep 1855, Kankakee Co., IL, **Charles Wesley Beedy** (Daniel A. Beedy & Sarah Johnson) b Jul 1832, Orleans Co., VT; d 10 Jul 1913, Manteno, IL.

Philomène Monty arrived in the United States with her parents in the 1850s and was living in her father's household in Rockville, IL, in 1860 as the 23-year-old Philomen Monty (US census). It would then appear that she was still single. In spite of this I believe she was the Fanny Muncy (sic) who had married Charles Wesley Beedy in Kankakee Co., IL, in 1855. She was identified in the 1900 US census in Northfield Twp, IL, as "Fanny Montie," wife of W. C. Beedy, to whom she had been married for 45 years. Mrs. Wesley Beedy of Manteno, IL, was further identified as the sister of Emery Monty (13.3.8.2) in the latter's 1915 obituary. And when Mrs. Fanny Beedy died a few years later, her death record noted that she was the daughter of Ed (sic) Montie and that she had been born in Canada on 2 Mar 1837, the exact date of birth of Philomène Monty, daughter of Basile Monty, according to the records of St.

Antoine de Pades Church in Longueuil, QC. In spite of the change from Philomène to Fanny (perhaps a nickname or a perceived English version of the French name) and a few other inconsistencies, such as her father's name in her death certificate, it seems most probable that Charles Wesley Beedy's wife was indeed Philomène Monty, daughter of Basile Monty.

Charles Wesley Beedy's date of birth is taken from the 1900 US census in Northfield Twp, IL. He had no stated occupation and was probably retired: he had been a farmer in Reed, IL, in 1860 and in Peotone, IL, in 1870 and 1880. I do not know how long he and his wife stayed in Northfield Twp. By 1910, they were living with their children Minnie and Walter in Manteno and remained there until their deaths (US censuses). They were buried there in Manteno's Elmwood Cemetery.

Children:

i   **Lillian Aurelia Beedy** b 31 Aug 1856, IL; d 31 Aug 1923, Manteno, IL. She married 7 Nov 1877, Kankakee Co., IL, **George Walter Hatch** (Charles P. Hatch & Lydia Taylor) b 28 Apr 1851, Hardwick, VT; d 12 Nov 1931, Manteno, IL.

ii   **Izora Phoebe Beedy** b 25 Jun 1858, Manteno, IL; d 18 Jun 1945, Chicago, IL. She married 6 Jan 1876, Kankakee Co., IL, **John Pascal Hatch** (Charles P. Hatch & Lydia Taylor) b 5 Sep 1853, Hardwick, VT; d & bur 24 & 27 Sep 1927, Chicago & Manteno, IL.

iii   **Walter D. Beedy** b Mar 1860, Reed, IL; d 27 Mar 1944, Kankakee, IL. He married 18 Mar 1901, Cook Co., IL, **Myrtle Boynton** (Clarence A. Boynton & Irena C. Nelson) b May 1881, Will Co., IL.

iv   **Agnes Beedy** b Apr 1863, Will Co., IL; d 1955, Kankakee Co., IL. She married there 14 Dec 1881 **Frank Beauregard** (Pierre/Peter Jarret dit Beauregard & Elizabeth Pion dit Fontaine) b Feb 1859, Rockville, IL; d 16 Jun 1939, Kankakee Co., IL.

v   **Oscar Nathan Beedy** b Mar 1867, Will Co., IL; d 20 Sep 1948, Chicago, IL. He married 1 Dec 1897, Cook Co., IL, **Catherine/Kittie McFadden** (Patrick McFadden & Anna Barrett) b 21 Nov 1870, Chicago, IL.

vi   **Mattie/Martha J. Beedy** b May 1870, Peotone, IL; d 8 Aug 1942, Manteno, IL. She married 3 Sep 1890, Cook Co., IL, **Henry D. Crawford** (William Crawford & Abigail ____) b Nov 1862, Peotone, IL; d between 1910 and 1920.

vii   **Minnie Beedy** b Jul 1872, Peotone, IL; d 8 May 1946, Chicago, IL.

viii   **Albert Vincent Beedy** b 25 Dec 1875, Peotone, IL; d 14 Mar 1954, Blue Island, IL. He married 3 Jul 1899, St. Joseph, MI, **Emma M. Newman** (John Newman & ___) b May 1877, IL.

13.3.8.4   **MONTY, Olive/Marie Ovide** b & bp 11 Nov 1838, St. Rémi, QC; d 28 Aug 1925, La Crosse, IN. She married 10 Mar 1870, Kankakee Co., IL, **Noah Yando** b Nov 1845, NY; d around 1913.

Olive Monty (Marie Ovide at her baptism) came to the United States with her parents in the 1850s and was living in her father's household in Rockville, IL, in 1860.

Noah Yando was a farm laborer/farmer in Rockville in 1870 and 1880, and a farmer in Monee, IL, in 1900. He was also described as a farmer in 1910 when he was living in Gardner, ND, with his daughter Dora (ii) and her husband Irvin Magruder. His wife, though, had remained in Illinois and was staying with her son Edgar (v) in Monee. She was a widow in 1920, living in the household of her daughter Agnes (iii) and son-in-law Thomas Tucker in Dewey, IN (US censuses). She survived her husband by twelve years and was buried in St. Joseph's Cemetery in Manteno, IL.

Children:

i   **Ophelia Yando** b Aug 1870, Rockville, IL; d 24 Nov 1935, Evergreen Park, IL. She married 24 May 1899, Will Co., IL, **Obediah Lancaster** (Hugh Lancaster & Elizabeth A. McGruder) b Dec 1849, Bourbonnais, IL; m (1) 24 May 1871, Kankakee Co., IL, Sarah Ellen Redman (David Marr Redman & Sarah Ann Yetter); d 27 Nov 1917, Bradley, IL.

ii   **Dora Yando** b 28 Feb 1872, Rockville, IL; d & bur 13 & 16 Mar 1959, Kankakee, IL. She married 2 Dec 1891, Chicago, IL, **Irvin C. Magruder** (Noah Magruder & Mary E. Redman) b 11 May 1868, Rockville, IL; d & bur 12 & 16 Feb 1942, Bradley & Kankakee, IL.

iii   **Agnes P. Yando** b May 1873, Rockville, IL; d & bur 1952, LaCrosse, IN. She married 22 Feb 1892, Cook Co., IL, **Thomas Edgar Tucker** (Thomas Tucker & Ann ____) b Jul 1866, IL; d & bur 1933, LaCrosse, IN.

iv   **Noah Jerry Yando** b 22 May 1875, Rockville, IL; d 13 Oct 1935, Chicago Heights, IL. He married 1905? **Winifred Laughlin** (Hannibal Laughlin & Rosa ____) b Jan 1884, IL; d 5 Dec 1949, Cook Co., IL, at the age of 65.

v   **Edgar John Yando** b 14 Dec 1876, Rockville, IL; d & bur 14 & 17 Jul 1956, Bradley & Kankakee, IL. He married 1903? **Mary Boehl** (August Boehl & Wilhelmina Klein) b Feb 1880, Will Co., IL.

vi   **Ezra Peter Yando** b 21 Apr 1878, Rockville, IL; d 22 Dec 1962, Monee, IL. He married there 1905? **Emma Diercks** (Heinrich F. Diercks & Emma Boehl) b there 15 Mar 1882; d there 28 Nov 1973.

vii   **Mary Regina Yando** b Dec 1879, Rockville, IL; d & bur 1963, Peotone & Wilton Center, IL. She married 23 Sep 1914, Forsyth, MT, **August Henry Boehl** (August Boehl & Wilhelmina Klein) b 15 Jul 1863, Monee, IL; d & bur 10 & 14 Aug 1938, Forsyth, MT.

viii   **Rosa Yando** b 5 Mar 1881, Rockville, IL; d 27 Sep 1970, San Mateo Co., CA. She married **Robert Davis**.

13.3.8.5   **MONTY, Euphémie/Phoebe** b & bp 9 & 10 Feb 1840, St. Rémi, QC; d between 1920 and 1930, Chicago, IL. She married (1) and divorced ____.
She married (2) 1883? **Clet Santy** b Jan 1851, Canada.

Euphémie Monty came to the United States with her parents in the early 1850s and was living in 1860 and 1870 in her father's household in Rockville, IL. She was then named Phoebe. She was still living with her parents and using her maiden name in 1880 though she was then divorced (US censuses). I know nothing of her first husband.

She and Clet (also Clay) Santy, a laborer in Chicago, IL, had been married for seventeen years in 1900. After that their history is rather confusing. They were known as Clet and Phoebe Sanctuaire in 1910, the last time I have seen them together. In 1920 Clet Santy was living a few streets away from Mrs. Febe (sic) Santy who was staying with her nephews George and Frank Letourneau (13.3.8.7.i and 13.3.8.7.v). She claimed to be a widow. Yet Clet Santy was an inmate in the Oak Forest, IL, Infirmary in 1930 and claimed in turn to be a widower (US censuses). I have not found any death or burial records and have come to wonder if widowhood was not used as a substitute for divorce or separation.

13.3.8.6   **MONTY/MONTIE, Kiese/Calixte** b & bp 26 & 27 Oct 1841, St. Rémi, QC; d & bur 10 & 12 May 1923, Kankakee & St. Anne, IL. He married 28 May 1866, Bourbonnais, IL, a second cousin once removed, **Aglaé/Agnes Bessette** (François Xavier Bessette & Adèle Lamarre) b & bp 18 Aug 1850, Iberville, QC; d & bur 27 & 30 Mar 1920, Kankakee & St. Anne, IL.

The child baptized in Canada as Evariste Monty became known in Illinois, where he came with his parents in the early 1850s, under a variety of names: Casse, Calixte, Calice, Kaiser, Keise, Kice, Keese, Kiese (this last being the name on his tombstone in the Catholic Cemetery of St. Anne, IL). His surname also varies, either Monty or Montie, with no discernable sequence. Generally his daughters were known as Monty while his sons adopted the surname Montie.

He served during the Civil War as a private in Co. I, 76th Illinois Infantry Regiment from 31 Jul 1862 to 23 May 1865. On his return to Illinois he became a farmer in various communities in Kankakee Co.: Rockville, Manteno, Limestone, Waldron, and Aroma until at least 1910. He was retired in Kankakee, IL, in 1920 (US censuses). Both he and his wife were buried in the Catholic Cemetery in St. Anne.

His wife was named Aglaé Bessette at her baptism and marriage and at some of her children's marriages. On other occasions and on her tombstone she was named Agnes.

Children:

13.3.8.6.1	Agnes	1867-1892-1940
13.3.8.6.2	William	1868-1895-1944
13.3.8.6.3	Ida May	1869-1891-
13.3.8.6.4	Noah	1873-1895-1903
13.3.8.6.5	Julia Phoebe	1874-1894&1948-1972
13.3.8.6.6	Frank Lawrence	1876-1904-1945
13.3.8.6.7	Alfred	1879- -1903
13.3.8.6.8	Arthur Harry	1884-1906-1970
13.3.8.6.9	Meddie	1884- -1888
13.3.8.6.10	Alex M./Alexander	1888-1912-1968

13.3.8.7   **MONTY, Sophie/Sophia** b & bp 24 & 25 Dec 1843, Longueuil & Laprairie, QC; d 30 Sep 1919, Chicago, IL. She married 9 Oct 1865, Bourbonnais, IL, **Désiré Létourneau** (Michel G. Létourneau & Julie Jaret dit Beauregard) b 7 Jul 1844, QC; d 3 Dec 1908, Chicago, IL.

Désiré Létourneau (also Letourno) came to the United States as a child in the late 1840s and was living on his father's farm in Bourbonnais, IL, in 1850 and 1860. He enlisted in the Union Army on 24 Jul 1862 and served as a private in Co. D of the 76th Illinois Infantry Regiment. On his return home he became a farmer in Rockville, IL, in 1870 but soon left for Chicago, IL, where he was a butcher in 1880 and 1900 (US censuses). He had received, on his application of 9 May 1892, a veteran's invalid pension (certificate #617,686) which was transferred to his widow at his death (certificate #998,453).

Children:

i   **George Letourneau** b 1866?, Rockville, IL.

ii   **Alfred/Fred Letourneau** b Mar 1867, Rockville, IL; d 28 Nov 1943, Cook Co., IL. He married 5 Apr 1893, Kankakee Co., IL, **Rose Alba Maisonneuve** b 1875?, Canada; d 15 Apr 1950, Cook Co., IL.

iii   **Walter Letourneau** b Dec 1869, Rockville, IL; d there 12 Jan 1874.

iv   **Alexander Letourneau** b Feb 1872, IL; d 9 Oct 1913, Chicago, IL. He married 1902? **Adelphia/Delia Callahan** (Peter J. Callahan & Sarah Ellen Hensen) b 1877?, Jackson Co., Il.

v   **Frank Letourneau** b 18 Dec 1877, IL.

vi   **William Letourneau** b 1 Apr 1879, IL. He married 1902? **Helen/Nellie ____** b 1885?, OH.

vii   **Mary Letourneau** b Apr 1881, Chicago, IL.

viii   **Edward Letourneau** b 25 Jan 1889, Chicago, IL.

13.3.8.8   **MONTY, Désiré Isaïe** b & bp 29 & 30 Oct 1845, Longueuil, QC; d 20 Sep 1912, Aurora, KS. He married 29 Jan 1867, Bourbonnais, IL, **Caroline Hébert** (Jean-Baptiste Hébert & Sophia/ Sophie C. Richard) b there 30 Jun 1850; d 8 May 1938, Aurora, KS.

The inscription on D. Monty's tombstone in St. Peter's Cemetery in Aurora, KS, shows that he was born on 2 Nov 1845. That is the date generally accepted by family historians. I prefer to rely on the records of St. Antoine de Pade's Church in Longueuil, QC, which show that Isaïe Montigny, son of Basile Montigny and Anastasie Dumas, was baptized in Longueuil on 30 Oct 1845 when he was one day old (1845, baptism #159). Montigny is one of several surnames which were occasionally attached to the Monty family in Canada. I have no doubt that Basile Montigny was in fact Basile Monty and that his son Isaïe later became the husband of Caroline Hébert. Indeed Sophie Richard referred several times to her son-in-law as Isaïe Monty in her Memoirs ("Journal of Sophie Richard," 1878-1880, pp. 3, 4). She was one of the few to do so. He was generally known as Désiré in the United States.

Désiré Isaïe Monty came to the United States with his parents in the early 1850s and was a farmer in Rockville, IL, until early 1879 when he moved first to Nelson, KS, and shortly thereafter to Aurora, KS, where his last five children were born. He was a farmer there until his death (US censuses).

Caroline Hébert was still living on her late husband's farm in Aurora, KS, with her sons Peter and Henry in 1920 and with her son Henry's family in 1930 (US censuses). She and her husband were buried in St. Peter's Cemetery there.

Children:

13.3.8.8.1	Anonymous	1869- -1869
13.3.8.8.2	Emery	1869-1894?-1941
13.3.8.8.3	Nellie/Nelida M.	1871-1892-1963
13.3.8.8.4	Matilda Ann/Annie	1873-1898?-1972
13.3.8.8.5	Peter Edward	1875- -1928
13.3.8.8.6	Israel Oswald	1877- -1879
13.3.8.8.7	John Achille	1878-1903?-1966
13.3.8.8.8	George E.	1881-1913?-1975
13.3.8.8.9	Fred	1883-1909-1975
13.3.8.8.10	Laura	1885-1906-1978
13.3.8.8.11	Philip/Phillip Joseph	1889-1919?-1982
13.3.8.8.12	Henry A.	1896-1917-1943

13.3.10.1   **MONTY, Adeline** b & bp 30 Oct 1836, Laprairie, QC; d & bur 19 & 20 Jun 1864, Chambly, QC. She married there 4 Feb 1856 **Alexis Thuot** (Michel Thuot & Catherine Jetté) b & bp there 23 & 24 Apr 1827; m (2) there 22 Feb 1865 Marcelline Demers (François Demers & Euphrosine Chartier); m (3) there 17 Jan 1871 Philomène Bouthillier (Etienne Bouthillier & Catherine Lamoureux); d & bur there 15 & 17 Apr 1905.

Alexis Thuot (Alexandre at his baptism) was a farmer in Chambly, QC.

Children:
i   **Aldéric Thuot** b & bp 13 Dec 1856, Chambly, QC.
ii   **Joseph Thuot** b & bp 1 Apr 1858, Chambly, QC.
iii   **Alphonse Thuot** b & bp 15 & 16 Feb 1860, Chambly, QC; d & bur 23 & 27 May 1935, Montreal, QC. He married **Marie Louise Archambault** (Gilbert Archambault & Elise Pelletier) b & bp 13 Jun 1862, St. Paul, QC; d & bur 1 & 4 Jul 1933, Montreal, QC.
iv   **Alexis Thuot** b & bp 23 Jun 1861, Chambly, QC; d & bur there 28 & 29 Jun 1861.
v   **Adeline Thuot** b & bp 30 Nov & 1 Dec 1862, Chambly, QC. She married there 12 Jul 1887 **Philippe Fortier** (Louis Fortier & Adeline Grisé).
vi   **Jérémie Thuot** b & bp 6 Jun 1864, Chambly, QC.

13.3.10.2   **MONTY, Marie Louise** b & bp 23 Apr 1838, Chambly, QC; d & bur there 10 & 12 Apr 1856.

13.3.10.3   **MONTY, Hyacinthe** b & bp 12 & 13 Sep 1839, Longueuil & Laprairie, QC; d & bur 16 & 17 Sep 1839, Longueuil, QC.

13.3.10.4   **MONTY, Henriette** b & bp 9 Aug 1840, Longueuil, QC; d & bur 10 & 12 Aug 1861, Chambly, QC. She married there 25 Oct 1859 **Jean-Baptiste Racicot** (Toussaint Racicot & Catherine Ethier) b & bp 29 & 30 Jan 1840, Boucherville, QC.

Jean-Baptiste Racicot was originally a farmer in Chambly, QC, and after his wife's death in Boucherville, QC. He was deceased when his son Alphonse married in 1884.

Children:
i   **Hyacinthe Racicot** b & bp 27 & 28 Mar 1860, Chambly, QC.
ii   **Alphonse Racicot** b 28 Apr 1861, QC; d & bur 16 & 18 Apr 1904, Varennes, QC, at the age of 43. He married there 29 Jan 1884 **Alphonsine Jodoin** (Théophile Jodoin & Angèle Savaria) b & bp there 15 Nov 1862; d & bur there 6 & 7 Sep 1909.

13.3.10.5   **MONTY, Delphine** b & bp 13 & 19 Jun 1842, Mont St. Grégoire, QC; d & bur 27 & 30 Sep 1859, Chambly, QC.

13.3.10.6   **MONTY, Flavie** b & bp 6 & 7 Apr 1844, Mont St. Grégoire, QC; d & bur 21 & 24 Aug 1927, Waterloo & Bromont, QC. She married 16 Jun 1863, Chambly, QC, **Jérémie Demers** (François Demers & Anne Masseleau) b & bp there 26 Jun 1844; d & bur 27 & 29 Jul 1920, Waterloo & Bromont, QC.

Jérémie Demers was a farmer in Chambly, QC, until the mid-1870s when he moved to Bromont, QC. He was a farmer there until at least 1901 but was retired in Waterloo, QC, in 1911 (Canadian censuses).

Children:

i   **Joseph Jérémie Demers** b & bp 25 & 26 Mar 1864, Chambly, QC.

ii   **Marie Flavie Eulalie Demers** b & bp 2 May 1866, Chambly, QC; d & bur 11 & 13 Nov 1929, Waterloo, QC. She married 19 Nov 1888, Bromont, QC, **Joseph Edouard Girard** (Célestin Girard & Basilice Blain) b & bp 31 Mar & 1 Apr 1855, St. Césaire, QC; d & bur 24 & 26 Jun 1926, Waterloo, QC.

iii   **Joséphine Exina/Alexina Demers** b & bp 13 & 14 Dec 1867, Chambly, QC. She married 31 Aug 1887, Bromont, QC, **Honoré/Henry Dextradeur** (Honoré Dextradeur/Destradeur/Dockstader & Denise Bédard) b & bp 25 Aug 1862, St. Alexandre, QC.

iv   **Rose Anna Demers** b & bp 14 & 15 Aug 1869, Chambly, QC. She married 30 Aug 1898, Bromont, QC, **Zoël Lavallée** (Joseph Lavallée & Lucie Daigneault) b & bp 31 Mar & 1 Apr 1875, St. Joachim de Shefford & Waterloo, QC; d & bur 16 & 19 Nov 1925, Waterloo, QC.

v   **Joséphine Delia Demers** b & bp 26 Jul 1871, Chambly, QC; d & bur 17 & 19 Feb 1884, Bromont, QC.

vi   **Marie Louise Albina Demers** b & bp 25 Aug 1872, Chambly, QC; d & bur 27 & 29 Jan 1877, Bromont, QC.

vii   **Paméla Demers** b & bp 26 & 27 Mar 1874, Chambly, QC; d & bur 19 & 22 Feb 1933, Montreal & Granby, QC. She married 6 Feb 1899, Bromont, QC, **Edmond Dextradeur** (Honoré Dextradeur/Destradeur/Dockstader & Denise Bédard) b & bp there 6 & 7 Jul 1872; m (1) 30 Oct 1893, Granby, QC, Corinne Beaulac (François Beaulac & Arzélie Bousquet); m (3) 25 Oct 1938, St. Hyacinthe, QC, Léopoldine Grisé (Godfroy Grisé & Sara Duclos), widow of Arthur Aubry.

viii   **Marie Emma Georgiana Demers** b & bp 4 & 5 Nov 1875, Bromont, QC; d & bur there 8 & 10 Feb 1877.

ix   **Médéas Demers** married 30 May 1898, Waterloo, QC, **Hermina Fortin** (Joseph Fortin & Julie Laflamme).

x   **Joseph Adélard Demers** b & bp 18 & 20 Mar 1877, Bromont, QC.

xi   **Paul Emile Demers** b & bp 4 & 6 Oct 1878, Bromont, QC; d & bur there 13 & 15 Jul 1882.

xii   **Alphonse Demers** b & bp 19 & 23 May 1880, Bromont, QC. He married there 2 Jul 1900 **Jeanne Henriette/Jennie Déry** (Antoine Déry & Delia Barber) b & bp 7 Sep 1883 & 1 Jan 1886, US & Granby, QC.

xiii   **Eliza Demers** b & bp 13 & 15 Mar 1882, Bromont, QC. She married there 24 Sep 1900 **Gédéon Poirier** (Joseph Poirier & Clarisse Huot) b & bp 20 & 24 Jan 1875, Bromont, QC.

xiv   **Anonymous Demers** b 1 Mar 1885 Bromont, QC; d & bur there 1 & 2 Mar 1885.

xv   **Ada Emma Demers** b & bp 13 & 19 Jun 1887, Bromont, QC; d & bur 31 Oct & 2 Nov 1918, Waterloo, QC. She married 11 Sep 1905, Bromont, QC, **William Arthur/Guillaume Potvin** (Jean Potvin & Emilie Grégoire) b & bp 5 Apr 1882, Adamsville, QC; m (2) 9 Jul 1923, Granby, QC, Georgina Côté (Théophile Côté & Philomène Bail).

xvi   **Clara Demers** b & bp 25 & 28 Oct 1888, Bromont, QC. She married there 12 Feb

1906 **Armand Potvin** (Paul Potvin & Célina Lessard) b & bp 28 & 29 Jan 1887, Granby, QC.

13.3.10.7   **MONTY, Hyacinthe Zéphirin** b & bp 26 Jul 1845, Mont St. Grégoire, QC.

13.3.10.8   **MONTY, Solyme** b & bp 4 & 5 Apr 1847, Iberville, QC; d & bur 26 Feb & 1 Mar 1934, Chambly, QC. He married 2 Apr 1877, Montreal, QC, a first cousin **Marie Louise Boutheiller** (Louis Boutheiller & Marguerite Lefebvre) b & bp 1 Oct 1850, Longueuil, QC; d & bur 25 & 27 Apr 1915, Chambly, QC.
        Solyme Monty was a farmer in Chambly, QC. His mother Marie Louise Lefebvre and his wife's mother were sisters.

Children:
13.3.10.8.1	Arthur	1878-	-
13.3.10.8.2	Joseph Albert	1880-1916-1970	

13.3.10.9   **MONTY, Odile** b & bp 9 Apr 1849, Chambly, QC; d & bur 24 & 26 Jan 1880, Bromont, QC.

13.3.10.10   **MONTY, Moïse** b & bp 21 Jun 1851, Chambly, QC.

13.3.10.11   **MONTY, Marie** b & bp 25 Dec 1852, Chambly, QC; d & bur there 16 & 17 Feb 1853.

13.3.10.12   **MONTY, Hyacinthe Isidore** b & bp 10 & 11 Dec 1853, Chambly, QC; d & bur there 13 & 15 Aug 1854.

13.3.10.13   **MONTY, Louis** b & bp 25 Mar 1855, Chambly, QC; d & bur there 1 & 3 Aug 1855.

13.3.10.14   **MONTY, Théophile** b & bp 4 Jul 1856, Chambly, QC; d & bur there 22 & 24 Aug 1856.

13.3.10.15   **MONTY, Marie Esther** b & bp 23 & 24 Nov 1860, Chambly, QC; d & bur 27 & 29 Aug 1884, Bromont, QC. She married there 9 Feb 1880 **Napoléon Poirier** (Moïse Poirier & Arcène Hélie) b & bp there 18 & 23 Nov 1859; m (2) 16 Jan 1888, Roxton Falls, QC, Clara Victoria Martin (Michel Martin & Mathilde Gauvin).
        Napoléon Poirier was a farmer in Bromont, QC, until at least 1901 (Canadian census). He was a brother of Julienne Poirier, wife of André Monty (5.7.2.6.4).

Children:
i   **Napoléon/Ernest Poirier** b & bp 15 & 18 Mar 1881, Bromont, QC; d & bur there 4 & 5 May 1881.
ii   **Marie Oliva Poirier** b & bp 15 & 16 Nov 1883, Bromont, QC; d 14 Nov 1969, Chicago, IL. She married 29 May 1906, Montreal, QC, **Joseph René Ayotte** (Joseph Elzéar Ayotte & Marie Elmire Normandin) b & bp there 24 Sep 1884; d 20 Jan 1977, Burlington, IA.

13.3.10.16   **MONTY, Adélard** b & bp 27 & 28 Apr 1862, Chambly, QC; d & bur 9 & 14 Mar 1927, Roxton Pond, QC. He married 22 Jun 1885, Granby, QC, **Marie Anne Hélène/ Anna Bourbeau** (Narcisse Bourbeau & Marie Célina/Mary Farrell) b & bp 15 & 22 Apr 1864, Bromont, QC; d 25 Nov 1944, Roxton Pond, QC.
        Adélard Monty was originally a farmer in Waterloo, QC, but later operated a saw mill and tool-making plant in Roxton Pond, QC, which he had bought from his brother Arthur (13.3.10.18) in 1899. His wife's name varies: Marie Anne Hélène at her baptism, Marie Anne

at her marriage, but Anna at the births and marriages of her children as well as at her burial.

Children:

13.3.10.16.1	Horace	1886-1917-1951
13.3.10.16.2	Clara	1887-1910-1962
13.3.10.16.3	Marie Rose Laura	1889- -1889
13.3.10.16.4	Harold	1890- -1935
13.3.10.16.5	Maurice/Raphaël François	1891- -
13.3.10.16.6	Lucrèce Alice	1893-1920-
13.3.10.16.7	Berthe Yvonne	1895- -
13.3.10.16.8	Anne Antoinette	1896- -1897
13.3.10.16.9	Augustine Grâce Lena	1898- -1899
13.3.10.16.10	Edgar	1899- -1959
13.3.10.16.11	Victor	1901-1931-
13.3.10.16.12	Gertrude	1902- -1985
13.3.10.16.13	Paul Emile	1905- -1931
13.3.10.16.14	Etienne Lucienne Adélard	1908- -1908

13.3.10.17   **MONTY, Octave** b & bp 8 & 9 Oct 1863, Chambly, QC; d & bur 1 & 3 Jul 1936, Granby, QC. He married there 20 Jun 1893 **Emeline/Eliza Emilie Gannon** (Michael Gannon & Mary Wallace) b & bp there 18 Oct & 15 Nov 1863; d & bur there 24 & 26 Dec 1917.

Octave Monty was originally a farmer in Granby, QC, but a clerk there in 1911 (Canadian censuses). His wife, named Eliza Emilie at her baptism, was known as Emeline at her marriage and at her death.

Children:

13.3.10.17.1	Eveline Eva	1895- -1895
13.3.10.17.2	Ivan Bertrand Lloyd	1896-1924&1942-
13.3.10.17.3	Gwendolyn	1898- -
13.3.10.17.4	Gerald Augustin	1900- -1900
13.3.10.17.5	Hildred Alexandra Octavia	1902- -

13.3.10.18   **MONTY, Arthur** b & bp 7 & 8 Dec 1865, Chambly, QC. He married 28 Oct 1889, Granby, QC, **Anna Paré** (Louis Paré & Brigitte Leblanc) b & bp 8 & 15 Sep 1872, Granby, QC.

Arthur Monty was a merchant in Granby, QC, at the births of his first three children. He then lived for a few years with his family in Roxton Pond, QC, where he had bought in 1895 a saw mill and tool-making plant. These he sold in 1899 to his brother Adélard (13.3.10.16) and returned to Granby where he was again a merchant in 1901 and 1911 (Canadian censuses).

Children:

13.3.10.18.1	Blanche	1890-1913-
13.3.10.18.2	Arthur Nestor	1892- -1895
13.3.10.18.3	Bernadette	1894-1932-
13.3.10.18.4	Amintha	1896-1924-1936
13.3.10.18.5	Graziella	1898-1930-
13.3.10.18.6	Laurence	1904-1936-
13.3.10.18.7	Marcel	1908-1939-
13.3.10.18.8	Thérèse	1910- -

13.3.10.19   **MONTY, Hormisdas** b & bp 30 & 31 Mar 1867, Chambly, QC. He married 10 Jul 1899, Granby, QC, **Elizabeth Sheridan** (Francis Sheridan & Mary Butler) b & bp 22 & 28 Apr 1872, Granby, QC.

Hormisdas Monty (Louis Isidore Hormisdas at his baptism) was a merchant in Granby,

QC.

Children:

13.3.10.19.1	Lloyd	1901-	-
13.3.10.19.2	Gerald Rosario	1903-	-1903
13.3.10.19.3	Viola	1906-1936-	
13.3.10.19.4	Anonymous (male)	1908-	-1908
13.3.10.19.5	Eileen	1911-1937-	
13.3.10.19.6	Anonymous (female)	1914-	-1914

13.3.10.20 **MONTY, Bercéus** b & bp 7 & 10 Jan 1869, St. Césaire, QC; d & bur 19 & 21 Feb 1930, Granby, QC. He married 19 Jun 1900, Waterloo, QC, **Louise Hélène Tartre** (Raphaël Tartre & Mélina Hébert) b & bp there 2 & 7 Apr 1878; d 2 Apr 1960, QC. Bercéus Monty was a merchant in Granby, QC.

Children:

13.3.10.20.1	Gabrielle	1901-	-
13.3.10.20.2	Madeleine Elizabeth	1903-1939-	

13.3.10.21 **MONTY, Albina Angelina** b & bp 22 & 24 Sep 1870, St. Césaire, QC; d & bur 4 & 7 Dec 1914, Montreal, QC. She married there 31 May 1904 **Lionel Ayotte** (Joseph Elzéar Ayotte & Marie Elmire Normandin) b & bp there 12 & 13 Mar 1881; m (2) there 22 Dec 1914 Berthe Paquette (James Paquette & Azilda Gratton); m (3) 6 Jul 1937, James Bay, QC, Marie Anne Henriette Hudon (J. Elzéar Hudon & Emilie Gagné); d 1 May 1958, Montreal, QC.

13.3.17.1 **MONTY, Bénonise/Belonise** b & bp 28 & 29 Aug 1847, Longueuil, QC; d & bur 29 Apr 7 1 May 1926, Nashua, NH.
This woman was named Bénonise at her baptism but was also known as Bellenize, Milenese, or Melenese Monty in various US censuses and as Belonise Monty in the burial records of St. Louis de Gonzague Church in Nashua, NH. She had come to Nashua with her parents in 1871 and remained single, residing first with them and later with the families of her sisters Philomène (13.3.17.2) and Louise (13.3.17.12) (US censuses).

13.3.17.2 **MONTY, Philomène** b & bp 30 & 31 Jan 1849, Laprairie, QC; d & bur 13 & 16 May 1927, Nashua, NH. She married there 5 Oct 1874 **Joseph Pierre Paul** (Moïse Paul Hus & Judith Chalifoux) b & bp 7 Apr 1852, Sorel, QC; d & bur 23 & 25 May 1928, Nashua, NH.
Joseph Paul arrived in the United States as a young man and was naturalized in 1890. He was a laborer in Nashua, NH, at his marriage and at the births of most of his children, a merchant there in 1892, a saloon keeper in 1900, and a watchman in 1920 (US censuses).

Children:

i **Marie Louise Paul** b & bp 14 Jun 1875, Nashua, NH; d & bur there 27 & 30 Oct 1946. She married there 24 Aug 1896 **Alphonse Eugène Morissette** (Calixte Morissette & Lucille/Adela Smith) b 7 May 1870, Bromptonville, QC.

ii **Rose Delima Paul** b & bp 28 Dec 1877, Nashua, NH; d & bur there 20 & 21 Feb 1881.

iii **Moïse Paul** b & bp 22 Mar 1880, Nashua, NH; d & bur there 12 & 13 Feb 1881.

iv **Joseph Siméon Paul** b & bp 26 & 27 Mar 1882, Nashua, NH; d & bur there 16 & 18 Feb 1935. He married there 1 Sep 1919 **Leda Laquerre** (Télesphore Laquerre & Georgiana Baudet) b Mar 1883, QC.

v **Edward/Pinee? Paul** b & bp 19 Oct 1884, Nashua, NH; d & bur there 18 & 20 Apr 1887.

vi **Pierre Paul** b & bp 23 Jun 1886, Nashua, NH; d & bur there 6 & 7 Apr 1887.

vii **Olina Paul** b 27 Nov 1887, Nashua, NH; d there 23 & 26 Mar 1979. She married there 29 Jan 1912 **Charles Eugène Boucher** (Timothée Boucher & Zehna Rioux) b & bp 25 Nov 1881, Trois Pistoles, QC.

viii **Alma Paul** b & bp 10 & 11 Dec 1891, Nashua, NH. She married 1911? **Joseph P. Gendron** (Octave Gendron & Eulalie Caouette) b & bp 9 & 15 Nov 1811, St. François & St. Pierre de la Rivière du Sud, QC.

ix **Amédée Paul** b & bp 6 & 10 Jan 1892, Nashua, NH. He married **Ruth** ____ b 17 May 1895; d Jul 1985, Hudson, NH.

13.3.17.3   **MONTY, Joseph** b & bp 6 & 10 Oct 1850, Longueuil, QC; d & bur there 18 & 20 Nov 1850.

13.3.17.4   **MONTY, Anonymous** b 3 Dec 1851, Longueuil, QC; d & bur there 3 & 5 Dec 1851.

13.3.17.5   **MONTY, Denise** b & bp 29 & 30 Dec 1852, Longueuil & Chambly, QC; d & bur 21 & 24 Nov 1931, Nashua, NH. She married there 4 Feb 1877 **Siméon Doucet** (Pierre Doucet & Julie Prince) b Jan 1854, Windsor, QC; d & bur 1 & 4 Feb 1914, Nashua, NH.

Denise Monty came to New Hampshire with her parents in 1871. Her husband Siméon Doucet (also Doucette) had arrived in the United States in 1876 and lived in Nashua, NH, for most of his married life. He was a laborer there in 1880, a railroad man in 1900, and a lighting plant employee in 1910. Only five of their children, Adeline, Desneiges, Frank, Philip, and Alfred, were then still alive (US censuses).

The family surname is constantly Doucet in the New Hampshire Vital Records. A few censuses however and several Nashua City Directories list family members under the surname Doucette.

Children:

i   **Adeline Doucet** b & bp 8 Aug 1878, Nashua, NH; d & bur there 27 & 30 Aug 1954. She married there 16 Feb 1903 **Joseph Thériault** (Félix Thériault & Adeline Gagnon) b 22 Jul 1880, QC; d & bur 17 & 20 Sep 1923, Nashua, NH.

ii   **Desneiges Doucet** b & bp 2 Mar 1880, Nashua, NH; d & bur there 9 & 12 Jun 1920.

iii   **Francis Joseph Siméon/Frank Doucet** b & bp 27 Jun 1882, Nashua, NH; d there 25 Jan 1948.

iv   **William Doucet** b May 1884, NH; d & bur 31 Oct & 1 Nov 1885, Newmarket, NH, at the age of 1 year and 5 months.

v   **Chloise Doucet** b 2 Mar 1888, Nashua, NH; d before 1900.

vi   **Philippe/Philip J. Doucet** b 28 Aug 1889, Nashua, NH; d & bur 3 & 7 Jan 1974, Milford & Nashua, NH. He married 26 Nov 1919, Nashua, NH, **Louisa/Marie Louise Martin** (John/Jean-Baptiste Martin & Delia Raymond) b & bp there 4 & 6 Jul 1888; d & bur there 8 & 12 May 1972.

vii   **Alfred Doucet** b & bp 30 Jun 1890, Nashua, NH; d & bur there 28 Jun & 1 Jul 1947. He married there 21 Nov 1921 **Evelina Louise Morin** (Joseph Morin & Hermine Daudelin) b & bp there 28 May 1888; d & bur there 22 & 24 Dec 1938.

viii   **Joseph Doucet** b & d 1 Feb 1892, Nashua NH.

ix   **Anonymous Doucet** (stillborn) b & d 6 Aug 1892, Nashua, NH.

x   **Anonymous Doucet** b 9 Aug 1896, Nashua, NH; d & bur there 9 & 10 Aug 1896.

xi   **Louis Raoul Romeo** Doucet b & bp 24 Jul 1898, Nashua, NH; d & bur there 28 & 29 Jul 1898.

13.3.17.6   **MONTY, Marie Adelphie** b & bp 9 Apr 1854, Longueuil, QC; d & bur 6 & 8 Sep 1886, Nashua, NH. She married there 27 Oct 1879 **Cyrille Salvail** (Pierre Salvail & Aurélie Bibeau) b & bp 20 & 21 Dec 1852, Drummondville, QC; m (2) 26 Sep 1893, Nashua, NH, Philomène Leazotte (Jean-Baptiste Leazotte & Marie Corbin); d & bur there 1 & 6 Oct 1932.

Marie Adelphie Monty came to the United States with her parents in 1871 but returned to Canada after her marriage. She and Cyrille Salvail lived for a few years in St. Germain de Grantham, QC, where he was a farmer in 1881 (Canadian census) and where their two oldest children were born, before settling permanently in Nashua, NH, in 1885. He was a saloon keeper there in 1900, a liquor dealer in 1910, and was retired in 1920. He had been naturalized in 1891 (US censuses).

Cyrille Salvail's sister Sophie married Marie Adelphie Monty's first cousin, Narcisse Riendeau (13.3.11.vi).

Children:

i   **Marie Amelie Salvail** b & bp 4 Nov 1881, St. Germain de Grantham, QC; d 14 Aug 1944, Nashua, NH. She married 1904? **Walter Rémi Avard** (Théophile Avard & Adeline Morel) b & bp 23 Sep 1878, Nashua, NH; d 15 Feb 1968, Goffstown, NH.

ii   **Joseph Noé Salvail** b & bp 4 Jun 1883, St. Germain de Grantham, QC; d & bur 9 & 11 Jan 1962, Nashua, NH.

iii   **Henry Salvail** b & bp 29 Mar 1886, Nashua, NH.

13.3.17.7   **MONTY, Rose/Rosalie** b & bp 22 Jun 1856, Longueuil, QC; d & bur 16 & 19 Dec 1936, Nashua, NH. She married there 20 Feb 1882 **Francis/Frank Pombrio/Pontbriand** (Joseph Pontbriand & Angèle Lepine) b & bp 5 & 7 Jun 1857, Altona & Coopersville, NY; m (1) 14 Aug 1876, Grand Isle, VT, Eliza Tait (John Tait & Celia Moss); d & bur 23 & 26 Dec 1933, Nashua, NH.

Rose Monty was named Marie Rosalie at her baptism and either Rose, Rosalie, or Rosanna at her marriage and at the births of her children.

Francis/Frank Pombrio (occasionally Pontbriand) was a brother of Maxime Pombrio, husband of Exeline Monty (13.3.17.11). He was a railroad man at his marriage, a miller in the mid-1880s and the 1890s, and a teamster in Nashua, NH, until at least 1930 (US censuses). His children generally used the surname Pombrio though one of his sons, William (iv) was known as William Pontbriand at his death.

Children:

i   **Rose Anna Pombrio** b & bp 30 Mar & 1 Apr 1883, Nashua, NH; d & bur there 29 Apr & 2 May 1967.

ii   **Joseph Simeon Pombrio** b & bp 20 Feb 1885, Nashua, NH; d & bur there 27 & 29 Apr 1953. He married there 22 Aug 1910 **Sadie Boulay** (Victor Boulay & Exilia Lemery) b & bp there 13 & 14 Apr 1889; d there Sep 1977.

iii   **Edward Pombrio** b & bp 13 & 14 Mar 1888, Nashua, NH; d & bur there 31 Jan & 3 Feb 1953. He married there 4 Sep 1912 **Florence Maud Mansur** (George H. Mansur & Elizabeth M. Berry) b 20 Feb 1886, West Groton, MA; d Apr 1984, South Newbury, NH.

iv   **William Charles Pontbriand/Pombrio** b & bp 29 Jun 1890, Nashua, NH; d there Oct 1969. He married there 1920? **Agnes L. Sullivan** (David Sullivan & Mary White) b there 9 Jan 1898; d there Jan 1988.

v   **Marie Pombrio** b 6 Feb 1896, Nashua, NH; d & bur there 6 & 7 Feb 1896.

13.3.17.8   **MONTY, Joseph Antoine** b & bp 3 Oct 1860, Longueuil, QC; d & bur 18 & 21 Feb 1885, Nashua, NH.

Joseph Monty arrived in the United States in 1871 and was naturalized on 27 Oct 1883 in Nashua, NH. He did not marry.

13.3.17.9   **MONTY, Marie Malvina** b & bp 2 & 3 Jan 1863, Laprairie, QC.

13.3.17.10   **MONTY, Louis** b & bp 11 & 12 May 1865, Longueuil, QC; d 10 Apr 1944, Nashua, NH. He married (1) there 9 May 1890 **Emma Dutilly** (Augustin Dutilly & Louise Payent dit St. Onge) b & bp 1 & 2 Oct 1865, St. Hyacinthe, QC; d & bur 19 & 20 Mar 1908, Nashua, NH.

He married (2) 28 Oct 1913, Nashua, NH, **Sarah/Sadie Prescott** (Luther Prescott & Sophie Armand) b 1877?, NY; d & bur 1 & 3 Feb 1939, Nashua, NH, at the age of 61.

Louis Monty was a clerk in Nashua, NH, at his first marriage and at the birth of a son in 1891. In later years, in US censuses from 1900 on and in Nashua City Directories from 1901 through 1938, he was generally described as a sawyer, a carpenter, or a wood worker. For a few years in the beginning of the 1930s he was also the sexton of St. Patrick's Church in Nashua.

Children of the first marriage:

13.3.17.10.1	Olier/Oliver	1891-1916-1918
13.3.17.10.2	Raymond Leo Henri	1903-1931-1991
13.3.17.10.3	Leo F.	1905-1949-1986

13.3.17.11   **MONTY, Exeline/Alexandrine** b & bp 9 Mar 1867, St. Hubert, QC; d & bur 3 & 6 Feb 1946, Nashua, NH. She married there 19 Aug 1889 **Maxime Pontbriand/ Pombrio** (Joseph Pontbriand & Angèle Lepine) b & bp 27 Jul & 2 Sep 1864, Chazy & Coopersville, NY; d & bur 23 & 26 May 1934, Nashua, NH.

This woman was named Marie Alexandrine at her baptism though she was commonly known as Exeline or Hexaline in New Hampshire where she arrived with her parents around 1871. The name Alexandrine also appears in the records of a few of her children's baptisms in St. Louis de Gonzague Church in Nashua, NH.

Maxime Pontbriand/Pombrio was a brother of Francis Pombrio, husband of Rose Monty (13.3.17.7). He was a railroad employee in Nashua at his marriage, a miller in 1890 and 1891, a laborer in 1893, a teamster in 1894, a laborer again in 1897, and a bookkeeper in a coal office in 1910 and 1920. He was retired in 1930 (US censuses).

His surname varies according to sources but tended to become Pombrio over time. It was Pontbriand at his marriage and at the births of his children though Pombrio in US censuses. The Nashua City Directories generally list him and his children under Pontbriand until 1923 and under Pombrio after that year. In a few cases, Pombrio later reverted to Pontbriand.

Children:

i   **Louis Pontbriand** b & bp 4 & 5 Jun 1890, Nashua, NH; d & bur there 31 Dec 1894.

ii   **Oliver Pombrio/Joseph Olivier Pontbriand** b & bp 12 Oct 1891, Nashua, NH; d 15 Sep 1918, France; bur 16 Sep 1921, Nashua, NH.

iii   **Joseph Romeo Pontbriand** b & bp 22 & 23 Apr 1893, Nashua, NH; d & bur there 5 & 7 Jun 1894.

iv   **Albert Pontbriand/Pombrio** b & bp 30 Jul 1894, Nashua, NH.

v   **Leo Pontbriand/Pombrio** b & bp 14 &15 Aug 1897, Nashua, NH; d & bur there 22 & 26 Apr 1973. He married 14 Jan 1943 **Anna L./Marie Lucie Archambault** (Arthur Archambault & Mary Jane/Jennie/Eugenie Marotte) b & bp 14 & 21 Feb 1900, Nashua, NH; m (1) 15 Mar 1921 John Joseph Burns (Henry M. Burns & Celia L. ____); d 2 Jul 1982, Nashua, NH.

vi   **Homer/Joseph Omer Pontbriand/Pombrio** b & bp 21 & 22 Jan 1899, Nashua, NH; d & bur there 30 Dec 1963 & 4 Jan 1964. He married 1928? **Laura Demers** b 1894?, WI.

vii   **Olivine Beatrice Pontbriand/Pombrio** b & bp 19 & 20 Oct 1905, Nashua, NH; d Jan 1981, Orange Center, MA. She married 8 Jul 1941, Nashua, NH, **Kenneth Mansur** (Charles Mansur & Fanny Short) b 12 Jan 1909, MA; d Oct 1978, Hudson, NH.

13.3.17.12   **MONTY, Louise** b & bp 2 & 3 Nov 1870, Richelieu, QC; d & bur 27 & 30 Aug 1949, Nashua, NH. She married there 5 Feb 1894 **Olivier Desclos** (Ovide Desclos & Adeline Lafond) b & bp 26 & 27 Apr 1868, St. Paulin, QC; d & bur 17 & 20 Jul 1917, Nashua, NH.

Louise Monty (Marie Louise at her baptism) came to the United States with her parents in 1871 and was naturalized in 1888. By 1910 she and her husband had had eight children, all boys, all still alive (US censuses).

Olivier (also Oliver) Desclos (occasionally Duclos, Declos) arrived in the United States in 1883 and became a shoemaker in Nashua, NH. The 1900 and 1910 censuses say more precisely that he was a trimmer in a shoe factory. He, his wife, and several of their children were buried in St. Louis de Gonzague Cemetery in Nashua.

Children:

i   **Ernest Francis Desclos** b & bp 9 & 10 Jul 1894, Nashua, NH; d & bur there 29 Aug & 1 Sep 1955. He married 2 Jun 1925, St. Hyacinthe, QC, **Germaine Hébert** (Joseph Hébert & Eléonore Brodeur) b & bp there 22 Sep 1896; d & bur 27 & 30 Jul 1987, Daytona Beach, FL & Nashua, NH.

ii   **Leo Arthur Desclos** b & bp 3 & 4 Sep 1896, Nashua, NH; d 2 Feb 1988, Pittsfield, NH. He married **Kathryn T. ____** .

iii   **Emile Silvio Desclos** b & bp 16 & 18 Aug 1898, Nashua, NH; d there Dec 1973. He married (1) there 14 Oct 1933, **Marie Irène Poirier** (David Poirier & Augustine Ouellette).

     He married (2) 28 Jun 1947, Nashua, NH, **Rose Delima Gagnon** (Alfred Gagnon & Victorine Chassé) b & bp there 4 Sep 1901; m (1) 1920? Napoleon L. Pelletier (Timothy Pelletier & Leda ____); d Apr 1983, Nashua, NH.

iv   **Edmond Stanislas Desclos** b & bp 25 Jun 1900, Nashua, NH; d Jan 1976, Pascoag, RI.

v   **Patrick/Patrice Osias Desclos** b & bp 17 & 18 Mar 1902, Nashua, NH; d 12 Jan 1975, Danvers, MA. He married 25 Jan 1936, Nashua, NH, **Marie Lucille Douville** (Edward Douville & Angelina Hamel) b & bp there 25 & 26 Mar 1911; d 25 Nov 1992, Danvers, MA.

vi   **Paul Ovide Desclos** b & bp 3 & 5 Jun 1904, Nashua, NH; d & bur there 16 & 18 Mar 1936.

vii   **Louis Euclide Hector Desclos** b & bp 18 & 19 Aug 1906, Nashua, NH. He married there 20 Sep 1925 **Alice Lavoie** (William J. Lavoie & Wildrey (?) Deboisbriand) b 1906?, NH.

viii   **Norman Olivier Desclos** b & bp 14 & 16 Jan 1910, Nashua, NH; d & bur there 10 & 13 Oct 1987. He married 15 Sep 1934, Manchester, NH, **Jeanne L. Berube** (Elie Bérubé & Marie Anne Lacroix) b there 4 Jul 1915; d & bur 6 & 9 Apr 1987, Nashua, NH.

13.9.2.1   **MONTY, Joseph** b & bp 15 & 19 Jun 1836, Chambly, QC; d 17 Jan 1916, Goodland, IN. He married 29 Jan 1874, Kankakee Co., IL, **Hilda Bloom** (Henry Sterling Bloom & Elizabeth Ann Kerns) b Apr 1849, Rockville, IL; d 4 Mar 1940, Kankakee, IL.

Joseph Monty arrived in the United States with his parents in the mid-1850s and was a resident of Wilmington, IL, when he enlisted on 1 Aug 1862 as a private in Co. F, 64th Illinois Infantry Regiment. He moved to Indiana after his discharge on 3 May 1865 and was living in 1870 with three of his siblings in his mother's household in Goodland, IN. He was a farmer there in 1870 and 1880, and a retired farmer in 1900 and 1910. He and his wife had had no children (US censuses. See also George W. Smith, *History of Illinois*, p. 286).

Hilda Bloom moved back to Illinois after her husband's death and lived in Kankakee, IL, with relatives until her death.

13.9.2.2   **MONTY, Margaret** b & bp 30 Aug 1838, Chambly, QC; d 8 Mar 1928, Custer, IL She married 12 Nov 1860, Kankakee Co., IL, **William Trainer** (William Trainer & Margaret Moore) b 30 Dec 1834, Isle of Man; d between 1900 and 1910, Custer, IL.

Margaret Monty (Marie Marguerite at her baptism) came to Illinois with her parents in the mid-1850s. William Trainer, who had arrived in the United States in 1853, was a farmer in Custer Twp, IL, until at least 1900. Margaret Monty, who was a widow in 1910, continued to live there, in her son Archibald's household, until her death (US censuses). According to the 1900 census, she had had ten children of whom five were still alive.

Information about William Trainer's parents and birth was found in *The History of Will County, Illinois*, pp. 876-877.

Children:
i   **Mary Trainer** b 1865?, Custer, IL.
ii   **William Trainer** b Jul 1867, Custer , IL.
iii   **Frances Trainer** b Oct 1869, Custer, IL.
iv   **Archibald Trainer** b 16 Feb 1876, Custer, IL; d Feb 1968, Wilmington, IL.
v   **Emma Trainer** b 19 Jan 1879, Custer, IL; d 6 Jun 1972, Cadillac, MI. She married 22 Mar 1898, Will Co., IL, **Charles E. Taylor** (Anthony G. Taylor & Eliza I. Hicks) b there 5 Jul 1873; d 1955, Missaukee Co., MI.

13.9.2.3   **MONTY, Malvina/Melvina** b & bp 2 & 6 Feb 1841, Beloeil, QC; d 13 Dec 1888, Grantsburg, WI. She married 4 Jul 1858, Kankakee Co., IL, **Samuel D. Rice** (Henry L. Rice & Mary Deneen) b 23 Mar 1835, Cleveland, OH; d 13 Jul 1910, Grantsburg, WI.

Malvina Monty (Marie Malvina at her baptism) came to Illinois with her parents in the mid-1850s. Her name in various American records appears as both Malvina and Melvina, with no discernable sequence, though she was named Melvina Rice at her death.

Samuel D. Rice was a farmer in Rockville, IL, in 1860. He enlisted in the Union Army in August 1862 and served as a private in Co. F, 64th Illinois Infantry Regiment until 3 Feb 1863. He returned to Rockville, where his first child was born in 1865 but moved the following year to Polk Co., WI, where a second child was born, and around 1868 to Burnett Co., WI, where the last three children were born. He was a farmer in Grantsburg, WI, in 1870 and until his death (US censuses). He and his wife were both buried in Riverside Cemetery in Anderson Twp, WI.

Children:
i   **Mary Belle Rice** b 4 Feb 1865, IL.
ii   **Frederick W. Rice** b 1 Jan 1867, Sterling, WI.
iii   **Nettie V. Rice** b 14 Nov 1869, Trade River, WI.
iv   **Daniel Rice** b 7 Jun 1873, Trade River, WI.
v   **Ruth M. Rice** b 12 Jul 1880, Trade River, WI.

13.9.2.4   **MONTY, Treffley/Jean-Baptiste Trefflé** b & bp 14 & 15 Mar 1843, Beloeil, QC; d between 1916 and 1920. He married 4 Jul 1866, Kankakee Co., IL, **Ellen Rowe** (William A. Rowe & Mary Ann Ten Eyck) b 18 Sep 1842, Rockville, IL; d Jan 1924, Polk Co., WI.

Treffley Monty (Jean-Baptiste Trefflé at his baptism) came to Illinois with his parents in the mid-1850s. He moved to Polk Co., WI, soon after his marriage and was a farmer in Sterling, WI, from 1870 until his death. His widow remained on the farm until her death (US censuses).

Treffley Monty was also active in community affairs. As T. F. Monty, he served as the Sterling Town Chairman on at least six occasions between 1875 and 1916 and was the Sheriff of Polk Co. in 1880-82 and 1893-94 (*Polk County Centennial Official Directory, 1853-1953*, compiled by E. E. Husband, 1953).

Children:

13.9.2.4.1	Cassius W.	1867-1899-
13.9.2.4.2	Walter C.	1871- -
13.9.2.4.3	Minnie Mary	1874-1896&1912-
13.9.2.4.4	Rutherford/Ruford George	1876-1894?-

13.9.2.5   **MONTY, William** b & bp 10 & 11 Jul 1845, Chambly, QC; d 12 Jun 1935, Custer, IL.

William Monty (named Guillaume at his baptism but William as early as the 1851 Canadian census in Chambly, QC), came to Illinois with his parents as a child in the mid-1850s and was living in 1860 with his mother and sister Euphemia in the household of his brother-in-law Samuel D. Rice (13.9.2.3) in Rockville, IL (US census). He was a resident of Rockville when he enlisted on 27 Feb 1864 as a private in Co. F, 64th Illinois Infantry Regiment in which he served until 11 Jul 1865. He later received an invalid pension (#1175253) for which he had applied on 8 Oct 1869. He was a farmer in Goodland, IN, in 1870, living with three of his siblings in his mother's household (US census).

I have found little trace of William Monty's movements after that time. His listing in the Veterans Schedule of the 1890 census in Muskegon Co., MI, adds nothing to the information given above. In 1920 he was an inmate, single, in the National Military Home in Malibu, CA (US census).

13.9.2.6   **MONTY, Alexandre Théodore** b & bp 18 & 20 Oct 1847, Cham-bly, QC; d & bur there 29 & 31 Mar 1849.

13.9.2.7   **MONTY, Matilda** b & bp 2 & 3 Mar 1850, Chambly, QC.
Matilda Monty (Henriette Mathilde at her baptism) came to the United States with her parents in the mid-1850s and was living with her sister Margaret (13.9.2.2) in the household of William Trainer Sr. in Wilmington, IL, in 1860 and in her mother's household in Good-land, IN, in 1870 (US censuses).

13.9.2.8   **MONTY, Euphemia** b & bp 19 Nov 1853, Chambly, QC.
Euphemia Monty (Catherine Euphémie at her baptism) came to Illinois as a child in the mid-1850s and was living in the household of her brother-in-law Samuel D. Rice (13.9.2.3) in Rockville, IL, in 1860, in her mother's household in Goodland, IN, in 1870, with her parents in Kankakee, IL, in 1880, and in the household of her brother Joseph (13.9.2.1) in Goodland, IN, in 1900. She was a dressmaker then as well as in 1920 when she was living in Tempe, AZ. She did not marry (US censuses).

3.1.3.1.1   **MONTY, Loisa S.** b Jan 1839, Colchester, VT; d there 23 May 1840, at the age of 16 months.

Loisa S. Monty was buried in the Munson Cemetery in Colchester, VT, alongside her father and paternal grandparents.

3.1.3.2.1   **MONTY/MONTA/MONTEY, Wilbur E.** b 24 Dec 1845, Colchester, VT; d & bur there 10 & 13 May 1934. He married 1868?, West Milton, VT, **Louisa Corno** (Joseph Corno & Juliet Provost) b 10 Feb 1853, Westford, VT; d 6 Mar 1926, Colchester, VT.

Wilbur E. Monty was a farmer in Milton, VT, when he enlisted as a private on 7 Aug 1864 in Co. F, 8th Vermont Infantry Regiment. He served until 1 Jun 1865 and then returned to Milton where he married and his first child was born. A few years later he moved to Colchester, VT, his birthplace, and was a farmer there until at least 1920. In 1930 he was living, or perhaps only staying temporarily, in the household of his daughter Etta and son-in-law Brion B. Small in Bridgton, ME. He and his wife had been married for thirty-two years in 1900 (US censuses). They were both buried in the Champlain Cemetery in Colchester alongside his father Cloud and their daughter Elener (sic) Montey Hanson.

Wilbur Monty's surname varied, without any discernable pattern: it was generally Monty (enlistment papers, births of children, 1860, 1880, and 1930 censuses, 1934 probate of his will) though Monta in the 1870 and 1900 censuses, and Montey in the 1920 census and on the large tombstone inscribed MONTEY in the Champlain Cemetery.

Children:
3.1.3.2.1.1	Electa	1870-1888&1911-
3.1.3.2.1.2	Emerette/Etta	1875-1895&1929-
3.1.3.2.1.3	Eleanor/Elenor	1880-1895-1910

3.1.3.2.2   **MONTY, Infant** d 30 Aug 1849, Colchester, VT.

This child's tombstone in the Champlain Cemetery in Colchester, VT, reads simply "Infant son of C. & R. Monty died Aug. 30, 1849."

3.1.3.2.3   **MONTY, Ellen Nora/Elnora** b 1855?, Milton, VT; d 22 Feb 1932, Burlington, VT. She married 30 Oct 1873, Milton, VT, **John Leach** (John Leach & Eliza ____) b 1849? Ireland.

Ellen Nora Monty was 18 years old at her marriage. John Leach was then a 24-year-old laborer in Colchester, VT. He was a marble worker in Burlington, VT, in 1880 and a City Water Works employee there in 1900. His widow was living there in the household of her daughter Bertha (vi) and son-in-law Louis Archambault in 1920 (US censuses).

Children:
i   **Rosilla/Lilly Leach** b Nov 1874, Colchester, VT.
ii   **Lucretia Leach** b 25 Nov 1875, Colchester, VT. She married 25 Jun 1901, Burlington, VT, **Albert Edward Wakefield** (James Wakefield & Lavina ____) b there Aug 1867.
iii **Bernard C. Leach** b 25 May 1877, Colchester, VT. He married 19 Jul 1900, Burlington, VT, **Minnie B. Sweeney** (John Sweeney & Mary DeForest) b Mar 1883, Richmond, VT.
iv   **Louisa Leach** b 1879, Burlington, VT.
v   **John Leach** b May 1880, Burlington, VT. He married 1903? **Anna M.** ____ b 1886?, PA.
vi   **Bertha Leach** b 2 Feb 1885, Burlington, VT; d there Dec 1975. She married there 22 Aug 1904, **Louis Archambault** (Charles Archambault & Adeline Laplante) b there Aug 1870.

3.1.3.3.1   **MONTY/MONTA, Emma Bernice** (twin) b 18 Jan 1874, Colchester, VT;

d 11 Sep 1958, Los Angeles, CA. She married (1) 16 Apr 1898, Colchester, VT, **Charles Eugene McNall** (Rodney W. McNall & Sarah Jane Crockett) b there 1 Dec 1860; m (1) there 6 Apr 1881 Jennie Sophia Coon (Oliver E. Coon & Lucretia Baldwin); m (2) 29 Feb 1888, Georgia, VT, Edna R. Gale (Stephen Gale & Augusta Caswell); d 23 Sep 1903, Colchester, VT.

She married (2) **Charles Nelson Miller**.

Eugene McNall was a farmer in Colchester, VT. His second wife was the sister of Nettie B. Gale, wife of Emery Monta (3.1.3.3.2).

I know of Emma Bernice Monty's second marriage only through the statement of her sister Sarah Almina (3.1.3.3.3).

3.1.3.3.2 **MONTA, Emery Bernard** (twin) b 18 Jan 1874, Colchester, VT; d around 1950, Claremont, NH. He married 1 Nov 1898, Colchester, VT, **Nettie B. Gale** (Stephen Gale & Augusta Caswell) b there Oct 1875.

Emery Bernard Monta was a farmer in Colchester, VT, at his marriage and a laborer in a brick yard there in 1900. He moved before 1909 to Claremont, NH (City Directory). In 1920 he was a deputy sheriff in Sullivan county, NH, and the sheriff there in 1930 (US censuses). According to his sister Sarah Almina (3.1.3.3.3) he died there around 1950.

Child:

3.1.3.3.2.1	Francis	1912-	-1986

3.1.3.3.3 **MONTY/MONTE, Sarah Almina/Mina S.** b 5 Aug 1876, Colchester, VT; d 4 Oct 1970, Los Angeles, CA. She married there 14 Feb 1914 **Edward Delor Yarter** (Antoine Yarter/Guertin & Sara Côté) b & bp 22 Jul & 9 Aug 1868, Kingsbury & Glens Falls, NY; m (1) 1888? Mary ____; d 29 Dec 1938, Los Angeles, CA.

Mina Monte was a nurse in Los Angeles, CA, in 1900 and 1910.

Edward D. Yarter (Joseph Adelard at his baptism) was a carpenter in Williamstown, MA, who had been married for twelve years to his wife Mary in 1900. He was living with her and two of their children in Los Angeles, CA, in 1910. .After his second marriage he was a carpenter in Eagle Rock, CA, in 1920 and in Los Angeles in 1930 (US censuses).

Child:

i   **Monty Herbert Yarter** b 2 Oct 1918, Los Angeles, CA; d there 17 Oct 1982. He married there 8 Dec 1940 **Laurita C. Chilson** (Daniel Gipson Chilson & Laura May Alexander) b 12 Jul 1921, San Diego, CA; d 18 Feb 2003, Pima, AZ.

3.1.3.3.4 **MONTA, Harley Clarence** b 20 Jan 1890, Colchester, VT; d there 21 Apr 1959. He married 25 Mar 1914, Burlington, VT, **Ada Morrow** (Samuel Morrow & Alberta McBride) b 28 Dec 1890, Colchester, VT; d 23 Mar 1968, Burlington, VT.

Harley Clarence Monta was a farmer in Colchester, VT.

Children:

3.1.3.3.4.1	Robert Morrow	1915-1936&	-
3.1.3.3.4.2	Thelma Ethel	1918-1945-	
3.1.3.3.4.3	Harlene Cecelia	1920-	-2007
3.1.3.3.4.4	Shirley Elizabeth	1923-1944-	
3.1.3.3.4.5	Wesley Clarence	1925-	-
3.1.3.3.4.6	Margaret Eileen	1932-1958-	

3.1.3.4.1 **MONTY, Nellie A.** b Dec 1873, Roxbury, VT; d 18 Mar 1963, Montpelier, VT. She married there 26 Oct 1897 **Edward Gill** (John Gill & Ann ___) b Nov 1872, VT; d 21 Jul 1945, Montpelier, VT.

Edward Gill was a grocer in Montpelier, VT, at his marriage and until at least 1920. By 1930 he was the owner of the Strand Theater in that city. This couple had no children (US censuses).

3.3.2.1.1   **MONTEE, Joseph** b 1842?, Glens Falls, NY; d & bur there 19 & 21 Oct 1922 at the age of 80.

Joseph Montee Jr. was 8 years old in 1850 when he was living with his parents in Glens Falls, NY. He was a boatman there in 1860 and 1870 but was described in 1875, when he was staying in his widowed mother's household there, as a gold miner whose usual place of employment was California. He was a lead miner in St. Elmo, CO, in 1910, and a retiree in Redondo Beach, CA, in 1920 (US and state censuses). He apparently returned to Glens Falls shortly thereafter for his will of 1 Apr 1922 identifies him as a resident of that town (Warren Co., NY, Surrogate's Court, 1 Nov 1922). He was buried in St. Alphonsus Cemetery there.

3.3.2.1.2   **MONTEE, Mary Elizabeth** b Jul 1844, Glens Falls, NY; d & bur there 17 & 20 Jun 1910. She married there 5 Aug 1861 **Marc Labonté/Michael LaBounty** b 1835?, Canada; d & bur 24 & 27 Mar 1908, Glens Falls, NY, at the age of 72.

This couple married as Elizabeth Monty and Marc Labonté in St. Alphonsus Church in Glens Falls, NY. He continued to be known as Marc or Mark Labonté in the baptismal, marriage, and burial records of his children there and also in his own burial record as Mark Labonté. All censuses however name him Michael LaBounty. He was a boatman in Glens Falls from 1870 on (US censuses) and was buried there, as was his wife, in St. Alphonsus Cemetery.

His wife's name appears in the St. Alphonsus records as Elizabeth, Marie Elizabeth, Isabelle, or Marie Isabelle Monty, while US and state censuses name her Mary E. Monte, Monty, or Montee before her marriage and Elizabeth, Mary, or Mary E. LaBounty after 1861. By 1900 she had had fourteen children of whom only five, Joseph, Louis, Adele, Lawrence, and Milla were still alive.

Children:

i   **Joseph E. LaBounty** b Nov 1865, Glens Falls, NY.

ii   **Louis E. LaBounty** b & bp 26 Mar & 5 May 1867, Glens Falls, NY; d & bur there 23 & 26 Apr 1910. He married there 8 Apr 1896 **Louise Elizabeth Beausoleil/Goodson** (Olivier Beausoleil & Julia Hoag/Hogue) b & bp there 8 & 16 Sep 1866; d & bur 30 Apr & 3 May 1948, New York City & Glens Falls, NY.

iii   **Adele Velina/Lena/Eveline LaBounty** b & bp 8 Dec 1868 & 24 Jan 1869, Glens Falls, NY; d & bur 27 Jun & 1 Jul 1929, Lyndhurst, NJ & Glens Falls, NY.

iv   **Narcisse Alexis/Alexandre LaBounty** b & bp 22 Feb 1871, Glens Falls, NY; d & bur there 7 Apr 1872.

v   **Narcisse Alfred LaBounty** b & bp 28 Jun & 12 Jul 1874, Glens Falls, NY; d before 1900.

vi   **Edgar LaBounty** b & bp 30 Oct 1876, Glens Falls, NY; d before 1900.

vii   **Lawrence Theodore LaBounty** b & bp 3 & 6 Oct 1878, Glens Falls, NY; d & bur 2 & 5 Oct 1938, Nutley, NJ & Glens Falls, NY. He married 5 Jul 1899, Glens Falls, NY, **Ida May Sansouci** (Nazaire Sansouci & Elenora _____) b Sep 1878, North Adams, MA; d & bur 24 & 27 May 1911, Glens Falls, NY.

viii   **Joseph LaBounty** b & bp 13 Nov 1880, Glens Falls, NY; d there 13 Nov 1880.

ix   **Marie LaBounty** b & bp 5 Oct 1881, Glens Falls, NY; d there 5 Oct 1881.

x   **Milla/Millie Elizabeth LaBounty** b & bp 10 Dec 1882 & 7 Jan 1883, Glens Falls, NY. She married there 29 Oct 1903 **Lawrence Frederick Coon** (Louis Coon & Lucy Stoddard) b 23 Apr 1884, NY.

xi   **Child LaBounty** b & bp 7 Jan 1886, Glens Falls, NY.

3.3.2.1.3   **MONTEE, Edmond** b 21 Jan 1846, Glens Falls, NY; d & bur there 23 & 26 Mar 1919. He married **Hattie A./Adeline Girard** (William/Guillaume Girard & Elizabeth Goyette) b & bp 12 & 30 Jun 1861, Glens Falls, NY; d there 5 Jun 1896.

Edmond Montee was in turn a cooper, a boatman, a laborer, and a tax collector in Glens Falls, NY (US and state censuses). He and his wife were buried there in St. Alphonsus Cemetery.

Children:

3.3.2.1.3.1	Bertha A.	1885-1920-
3.3.2.1.3.2	Anna Pearl (twin)	1888-1919-
3.3.2.1.3.3	Lena V. (twin)	1888-1912-

3.3.2.1.4 **MONTEE, Nelson/Narcisse** b & bp 24 Jul & 21 Aug 1848, Glens Falls & Hudson Falls, NY; d & bur 4 & 7 Aug 1905, Glens Falls & South Glens Falls, NY. He married 13 Nov 1879, Glens Falls, NY, **Hannah O'Hearn** (Patrick O'Hearn & Mary Driscoll) b there 5 Jan 1852; d & bur 9 & 11 Feb 1896, Lake George & South Glens Falls, NY.

Nelson Montee was a teamster and laborer in Glens Falls, NY (US and state censuses). He was named Nelson Monte at his baptism in St. Mary's/St. Paul's Church in Hudson Falls, NY, Nelson Montee in all civil records I have seen, but Narcisse Monty in the French records of St. Alphonsus Church in Glens Falls, notably at the baptisms of his children and at his death. He was buried alongside his wife and two of his children in St. Mary's Cemetery in South Glens Falls, NY.

Children:

3.3.2.1.4.1	William Henry	1881- -1906
3.3.2.1.4.2	Mary Elizabeth	1883-1911-1954
3.3.2.1.4.3	Joseph Frederick	1887- -1918
3.3.2.1.4.4	Alice Margaret	1888- -1962
3.3.2.1.4.5	Catherine Mary Anne/Marion	1890- -1890

3.3.2.1.5 **MONTEE, Harriet** b & bp 16 Jan & 11 May 1851, Glens Falls & Hudson Falls, NY; d & bur 4 & 6 Nov 1931, Glens Falls, NY. She married there 6 Aug 1872 **Edward Willard/Ouellet** (Joseph Willard/Ouellet & Julia Lesage) b 1849?, Vergennes, VT; d & bur 8 & 10 Nov 1922, Glens Falls, NY, at the age of 73.

This woman was named Harriet Monte at her baptism in St Mary's/St. Paul's Church in Hudson Falls, NY, Henriette Monty at her marriage to "Edouard Ouellet" in St. Alphonsus Church in Glens Falls, NY, at the baptisms of their children, and at her burial there, and either Harriet or Hattie Montee in all other documents I have seen.

Her husband's name and surname also vary. He was Edward Wilette when living with his parents in Vergennes, VT, in 1850 (US census), Edouard or Edward Ouellet or Ouellette in the baptismal, marriage, and burial records of St. Alphonsus Church, and Edward Willard in New York State civil records. He was a stone mason in Glens Falls in 1900, a brick mason in 1910, and a factory watchman in 1920 (US censuses). He and his wife were buried there in St. Alphonsus Cemetery.

Children:

i　**Frederick Edward Willard** b & bp 9 & 11 May 1873, Glens Falls, NY; d & bur there (as Alfred Edouard) 28 & 29 Nov 1873 at the age of 6 months.

ii　**Mary Isabelle Willard** b & bp 20 & 25 Apr 1875, Glens Falls, NY; d before 1900.

iii　**Josephine Eveline Willard** b & bp 26 Jul & 3 Aug 1879, Glens Falls, NY; d Jul 1969, Poughkeepsie, NY. She married 21 May 1903, Glens Falls, NY, **Charles Dennis Callahan** (John Callahan & Nora Ready) b there 19 Nov 1876; d & bur 17 & 19 Jan 1929, Glens Falls & South Glens Falls, NY.

iv　**Francis Edgar/Frank Willard** b & bp 19 & 27 Mar 1881, Glens Falls, NY; d & bur 15 & 19 Aug 1940, South Glens Falls, NY. He married 24 Feb 1902, Glens Falls, NY, **Helen Elizabeth McCarthy** b there 15 Aug 1879; d there 1937.

v　**Nellie L./Helene Louise Willard** b & bp 17 Mar & 1 Apr 1883, Glens Falls, NY; d & bur 13 & 15 Mar 1909, Schenectady & Glens Falls, NY. She married 22 Oct 1902, Glens Falls, NY, **Joseph Theophile Beaudet** (Julian Beaudet & Odile Anna Lagace) b & bp there 6 & 8 Oct 1880; m (2) 14 Feb 1911, Gardner, MA, **Mary Elizabeth Montee** (3.3.2.1.4.2); d & bur 23 & 26 Feb 1958, Glens Falls, NY.

vi　**Elizabeth Willard** b 26 Oct 1890, Corinth, NY; d & bur 22 & 24 Jul 1979, Plattsburgh & Glens Falls, NY. She married 16 Nov 1910, Glens Falls, NY, **Thomas A. Cronin** (James Cronin & Anna Payton) b & bp there 3 & 17 May 1885; d & bur 23 & 24 Oct 1964, Cohoes & Glens Falls, NY.

3.3.2.1.6   **MONTEE, Victoria/Mary V.** b 1853, Glens Falls, NY; d & bur 31 Aug & 3 Sep 1915, Schenectady & Glens Falls, NY. She married 3 Apr 1877, Glens Falls, NY, **David Drolette** (Joseph Drolette & Philinda ____) b Apr 1850, Vergennes, VT; d & bur 1933, Schenectady & Glens Falls, NY.

The year of Victoria Montee's birth is taken from the inscription on her tombstone in St. Alphonsus Cemetery in Glens Falls, NY. She was 7 years old in 1860 but 61 years old at her death according to the records of St. Alphonsus Church there. She had six children of whom only two, Harvey and Marion, were still alive in 1900 (US censuses). She was usually named Victoria or Mary V. though Victorine at her marriage in St. Alphonsus Church and Victoire at the baptisms of her children there.

David Drolette (also Drolet, Drollette, Droulettte, Drulette) was a laborer in Glens Falls in 1892, in Fort Edward, NY, in 1900, and in Glens Falls again in 1905. He moved to Schenectady, NY, at some time before 1910 and remained there until his death. He was a laborer and factory worker there, though retired in 1930 (US and state censuses). The year of his death is found on his tombstone in Glens Falls' St. Alphonsus Cemetery.

Children:
i   **Harvey Edmund Drolet/Drolette** b & bp 4 & 19 Jan 1879, Glens Falls, NY.
ii   **Marion V. Drolet/Drolette** b Nov 1884, Glens Falls, NY. She married 1909? **George F. Murray** b 1884?, NY.
iii   **Joseph Howard Drolet** b & bp 29 Feb & 4 Mar 1888, Glens Falls, NY; d before 1900.

3.3.2.1.7   **MONTEE, Benoni** b & bp 4 & 14 Jun 1856, Glens Falls, NY; d & bur there 11 & 12 Mar 1878.

Benoni Montee's dates of birth, baptism, death, and burial are taken from the records of St. Alphonsus Church in Glens Falls, NY. The tombstone of Bonie (sic) Montee in St. Alphonsus Cemetery shows however that he died on 17 Mar 1877 at the age of 22.

3.3.2.1.8   **MONTEE, Adeline** b & bp 10 & 11 Apr 1859, Glens Falls, NY.

Adeline Montee does not appear with her parent in censuses later than 1860 and may have died before 1870.

3.3.2.1.9   **MONTEE, Edgar M.** b & bp 7 Mar 1864 & 12 Sep 1865, Syracuse & Glens Falls, NY; d & bur 12 & 15 May 1948, Glens Falls, NY. He married there 5 Sep 1894 **Ellen/Nelly Cronin** b Jan 1865?, England (Wales); d & bur 10 & 13 Sep 1948, Glens Falls, NY.

Edgar M. Montee (Moïse Edgar at his baptism) spent most of his life in Glens Falls, NY, as a cigar factory worker, a postman, and for twenty-eight years a Prudential Life Insurance Co. agent (US and state censuses). According to his obituary in the Glens Falls *Post-Star* of 13 May 1948, he had also joined his brother Joseph (3.3.2.1.1) for a few years as a miner in St. Elmo, CO.

The date of birth of Ellen Cronin (Nelly Cronin at her marriage) is taken from the 1900 US census, which corresponds with the ages stated in later censuses. She was said to be 87 years old at her death, though I believe it unlikely that she was born in 1861. She and her husband were buried in St. Alphonsus Cemetery in Glens Falls.

Children:

3.3.2.1.9.1	Joseph Harold	1896- -1902
3.3.2.1.9.2	Evelyn Rose	1898-1918-1947

3.3.2.3.1   **MONTEE, Mary** b Jan 1845, Glens Falls, NY; d & bur there 8 & 11 Mar

1918. She married 1865?, **Frank/François Xavier LaRose** (Joseph Flavien LaRose & Charlotte Houle) b & bp 7 & 8 Jan 1946, St. Hyacinthe, QC; d & bur 7 & 10 Feb 1919, Glens Falls, NY.

Frank LaRose (François Xavier at his baptism and in the records of St. Alphonsus Church in Glens Falls, NY) arrived in the United States as a child around 1850 and became a cooper in Glens Falls. He and his wife had been married for thirty-five years in 1900 and had had fourteen children of whom seven, Ada, Alfred, Emily, Henry, Mattie, Arthur, and Leroy Edward were then still alive (US and state censuses). They were both buried in St. Alphonsus Cemetery in Glens Falls.

Children:
i   **Ada/Addie LaRose** b Nov 1866?, Glens Falls, NY; d & bur there 23 & 25 Nov 1939 at the age of 74. She married there 24 Oct 1889 **Hurst Wallace** (James Wallace & Helen ____) b Feb 1865?, Chester, NY; d & bur 2 & 5 Feb 1935, Glens Falls, NY, at the age of 71.

ii   **Marie Josephine Eva/Josie LaRose** b & bp 9 Feb & 3 Mar 1867, Glens Falls, NY; d there 14 Feb 1890.

iii   **Frederic Albert/Fred A. LaRose** b & bp 7 Feb & 2 Mar 1870, Glens Falls, NY; d & bur 30 Apr & 2 May 1931, Hudson Falls, NY. He married 1891? **Zia Mae Wells** b 1876?, NY.

iv   **Jerome LaRose** b & bp 6 & 25 Feb 1872, Glens Falls, NY; d before 1900.

v   **Emily C./Clara Amelia LaRose** b & bp 23 Feb & 13 Aug 1874, Glens Falls, NY; d 1932?, CT. She married 26 Nov 1905, Glens Falls, NY, **Benjamin F. Burgoyne** (Peter Burgoyne & Helen Blakeley) b 1873?, VT.

vi   **Henry George LaRose** b 9 Jan 1876, Glens Falls, NY; d there 1 Dec 1929. He married 1905? **Celia Mosher** (Bardine George Mosher & Sophronia Newton) b 11 Apr 1880, Hadley, NY; d Oct 1968, Hudson Falls, NY.

vii   **Rosanna LaRose** b 1878?, Glens Falls, NY; d before 1900.

viii   **Mattie LaRose** b Feb 1879, Glens Falls, NY.

ix   **Elizabeth Delvina LaRose** b & bp 20 Jul & 4 Sep 1881, Glens Falls, NY; d there Feb 1890, at the age of 8.

x   **Arthur Francis/Frank LaRose** b & bp 8 & 13 Jan 1884, Glens Falls, NY; d Sep 1951, MA. He married 1917? **Emma Irene Cummings** b 1880?, MA.

xi   **Leroy Edward LaRose** b & bp 14 Mar & 29 Aug 1886, Glens Falls, NY; d Jan 1936, Hudson Falls, NY. He married 1921? **Mary E. Keech** b 30 Dec 1890, NY; d Oct 1978, Fort Edward, NY.

xii   **Marie Genevieve LaRose** b & bp 3 Jan & 10 Feb 1889, Glens Falls, NY.

3.3.2.3.2   **MONTEE, Sophronia** b 25 May 1848, Glens Falls, NY; d & bur there 25 & 27 May 1869.

Sophronia Montee was buried in St. Alphonsus Cemetery in Glens Falls, NY.

3.3.2.3.3   **MONTEE, Albert** b May 1850, Glens Falls, NY; d & bur there 22 & 25 Jan 1927 at the age of 78.

Albert Montee Jr. was one month old in June 1850 when he was living with his parents in Glens Falls, NY. He was a boatman there until at least 1880 and in later years a cooper (US and state censuses). He was buried in Glens Falls' St. Alphonsus Cemetery. He did not marry.

3.3.2.3.4   **MONTEE, George Edward** b around 1852, Glens Falls, NY; d & bur 15 & ? Feb 1926, Detroit, MI & Lake Luzerne, NY. He married 25 Oct 1883, Glens Falls, NY, **Margaret Menzies** (William Andrew Menzies & Elizabeth Greer) b 31 Aug 1860, Palmers Falls, NY; d & bur 11 & 14 Aug 1925, Albany & Lake Luzerne, NY.

George E. Montee's date of birth is uncertain. He was born in 1851 according to the inscription on his tombstone in the Holy Infancy Cemetery in Lake Luzerne, NY. Yet he was 3 years old in 1855 (state census) and 31 years old in October 1883 according to his marriage certificate (in the name of George E. Monty but with the signature Geo E. Montee). He may also have been born in February 1853, if one relies on the 1900 census in Luzerne, NY.

George Montee was a boatman in Glens Falls, NY, in 1870 and 1880. He then moved to Luzerne where he was a saloon keeper at his marriage and a hotel owner from at least 1910 on (US and state censuses). He died in Detroit, MI, while visiting his sons who had moved there some years earlier but was buried next to his wife in the Lake Luzerne Cemetery.

I am indebted to George E. Montee's grandson, Mr. Robert Rodriguez of Albuquerque, NM, for much information concerning this family.

Children:

3.3.2.3.4.1	Infant	1884- -1885
3.3.2.3.4.2	Walter Ambrose	1886-1920?-1945
3.3.2.3.4.3	Harold	1888- -1889
3.3.2.3.4.4	Harry Louis	1890-1916-1972
3.3.2.3.4.5	William Hurst	1892-1921-1961
3.3.2.3.4.6	Marie	1894- -1895
3.3.2.3.4.7	Helen Madeline	1898-1926?-1948
3.3.2.3.4.8	Pauline Elizabeth	1903-1927?-1966

3.3.2.3.5   **MONTEE, Samuel** b 1853/1854?, Glens Falls, NY; d & bur there 18 & 28 Jan 1933 at the age of 88. He may have married (1) **Julia** ____ b 1857?, NH.

He may have married (2) **Tressa?/Teresa?** ____ b 1854?, US.

I know little of Samuel Montee beyond what is found in US and New York State censuses, little of which has been verified. Albert and Lucadia Montee had living with them in Glens Falls, NY, in 1855 a 2-year-old son whose name in the state census I find illegible. The 1860 US census lists a 7-year-old son named Perot who is never heard from again. There then appears in 1870 a 17-year-old Samuel whose age from then on defies chronological time: he was 25 in 1880, 30 in 1892, 41 in 1900, 51 in 1905, 65 in 1920, and 74 in 1930, the only constant being that, when he was living in his father's or mother's household, he was younger than his brothers Albert and George E. and older than his sister Josephine. I believe that Perot and Samuel were the same person and that the year of birth indicated in the earlier censuses is the most likely to be accurate.

Samuel Montee's marital status is also difficult to fathom. He was single while living in Glens Falls until at least 1870. He was married though in 1880 when he and a 23-year-old Mrs. Julia Montee were servants in a private family in Lebanon, NH. He had returned to Glens Falls by 1888 (City Directories) and lived there as a laborer, hostler, and boatman until at least 1905. There is no hint of a wife until the 1905 state census when his mother's household included, along with her sons Albert and Samuel, a 51-year-old daughter-in-law, Tressa (?), perhaps Teresa, who could be the wife of either son. To the best of my knowledge, however, Albert Montee never married while in 1920 Samuel Montee, who was by then working in a lumber camp in Fort Ann, NY, was divorced. I know nothing more about this (possibly second) marriage. In 1930, when Samuel Montee was living in retirement in Glens Falls, he was once again listed as single (US and state censuses). And yet when he was buried in St. Alphonsus' Cemetery in Glens Falls, the records note that he was an 88-year-old widower.

3.3.2.3.6   **MONTEE, Josephine/Addie** b & bp 3 Oct & 5 Nov 1855, Glens Falls, NY; d & bur 21 & 23 May 1885, Hudson Falls, NY. She married 10 Oct 1878 , Glens Falls, NY, a third cousin **Daniel Lapointe/Lapoint** (Michel Audet dit Lapointe & Domitilde/ Matilda Monty [3.9.2.1]) b & bp 13 & 17 Feb 1856, Dunham, QC; m (2) 13 Aug 1887, Hudson Falls, NY, Adélaïde Thérien/Terrien (Jean-Baptiste Terrien & Adélaïde Anne Robillard).

Daniel Lapointe was a sawmill worker in Sandy Hill (Hudson Falls), NY, in 1880 and a merchant in Glens Falls, NY, in 1892 (US and state censuses). Only his daughter Amelia was then living with him and his second wife. I have been unable to trace the family further.

Children:

i   **Mary Amelia Lapointe/Lapoint** b July 1879, Hudson Falls, NY.

ii   **Alfred Daniel Lapointe/Lapoint** b & bp 24 & 26 Mar 1882, Hudson Falls & Glens

Falls, NY.

    iii   **Joseph Lapointe/Lapoint** b & bp 8 & 9 Nov 1884, Hudson Falls, NY.

3.3.2.3.7   **MONTEE, Philomene Melina** b & bp 25 May & 6 Jun 1858, Glens Falls, QC.

This child does not appear with her parents in the 1860 census in Glens Falls, NY, and may have died before then.

3.3.2.16.1   **MONTEE, Marie Victoire** b & bp 17 & 25 Nov 1860, Glens Falls, NY.

This child probably died in infancy. She does not appear with her parents in either the 1865 state census in Glens Falls, NY, or the 1870 US census in East Greenwich, NY.

3.3.2.16.2   **MONTEE, Edward** b & bp 6 & 11 Jan 1863, Glens Falls, NY.

Edward Montee was living with his parents in Glens Falls, NY, in 1865 and in East Greenwich, NY, in 1870 (state and US censuses). He is not mentioned as one of his mother's three surviving children in her will of 19 Mar 1880 and presumably died before then.

3.3.2.16.3   **MONTEE, Nelson** b Jan 1865, Glens Falls, NY.

Following his mother's death in 1880, Nelson Montee lived for a time with his guardian, Louis Lee, in Greenwich, NY. By 1900 he was a photographer in Mechanicville, NY, where he remained until at least 1930. He did not marry (US censuses).

3.3.2.16.4   **MONTEE, Philomène Onésime** b & bp 30 Mar & 12 Apr 1867, Glens Falls, NY; d & bur there 26 & 27 Aug 1872.

3.3.2.16.5   **MONTEE, Lewis/Louis Arthur** b & bp 18 & 24 Jul 1869, Glens Falls, NY; d & bur there 5 & 7 Apr 1949.

Lewis Montee (Louis Arthur at his baptism) lived with his guardian Louis Lee, in Greenwich, NY, after his mother's death and remained in Washington Co., NY, until at least 1920. He was a paper mill worker in Queensbury, NY, though, in 1930 (US censuses). He did not marry.

3.3.2.16.6   **MONTEE, Anonymous** b Dec 1872, Glens Falls, NY; d & bur there 12 & 14 Jun 1874, at the age of 18 months.

This unnamed child was buried in St. Alphonsus Cemetery in Glens Falls, NY.

3.3.2.16.7   **MONTEE, Josephine Hermine** b & bp 2 Mar & 14 Jun 1874, Glens Falls, NY; d & bur there 3 & 6 Apr 1956. She married there 9 Sep 1892 **Peter/Pierre Beaudin** (Paul Beaudin & Caroline Boisvert/Greenwood) b & bp there 16 & 20 Mar 1870; d & bur there 15 & 18 Oct 1943.

Peter Beaudin (Pierre in the records of St. Alphonsus Church in Glens Falls, NY) was a commercial traveler in Glens Falls until at least 1920 and an eyeglass salesman there in 1930. In 1910, he and his wife had had nine children of whom six, Aurelia, Beatrice, Genevieve, Viola, Paul, and Agnes, were still alive (US censuses).

Children:
    i   **Caroline Marie Beaudin** b & bp 12 & 13 Nov 1892, Glens Falls, NY; d before 1910.
    ii   **Jean Narcisse Beaudin** b & bp 9 & 11 Mar 1894, Glens Falls, NY; d & bur there 8 & 9 Jul 1894.
    iii   **Leo Louis Etienne Beaudin** b & bp 5 & 8 Sep 1895, Glens Falls, NY; d before 1910.
    iv   **Aurelia/Marie Aurélie Beaudin** b & bp 30 Jul & 2 Aug 1896, Glens Falls, NY; d & bur there 12 & 14 Oct 1918.
    v   **Beatrice P. Beaudin** b 6 Nov 1898, Glens Falls, NY; d & bur there 1 & 4 Jun 1985. She married there 16 Jun 1927 **William Farnum Haviland** (Roger F. Haviland &

Ida Sarah Hall) b 31 Mar 1899, Kingsbury, NY; d & bur 12 & 15 Jan 1971, Glens Falls, NY.

vi   **Genevieve Josephine Beaudin** b & bp 12 & 17 Feb 1901, Glens Falls, NY; bur there 10 Jun 1963. She married there 28 Apr 1934 **Robert Bress** (Joseph Bress & Esther Simard) b 1 Sep 1897, NY; d & bur 23 & 27 Mar 1977, Cohoes & Glens Falls, NY.

vii   **Viola F. Beaudin** b 20 Jun 1903, Glens Falls, NY; d & bur 6 & 9 Dec 1993, Queensbury & South Glens Falls, NY. She married 24 Jun 1929, Glens Falls, NY, **Robert James Shanahan** (Edward Shanahan & Mary Riley) b 27 Dec 1896, Fort Edward, NY; d & bur 27 & 30 Mar 1966, Glens Falls & South Glens Falls, NY.

viii   **Paul Edward Beaudin** b & bp 17 & 29 Apr 1906, Glens Falls, NY; d there Jul 1973. He married (1) there 1931 **Laura Carpenter**.

He married (2) **Frances E. O'Connell** (James O'Connell & Mary ____) b 29 Aug 1909, Glens Falls, NY; d there 16 Jan 2002.

ix   **Agnes Cecile/Cecilia Beaudin** b & bp 6 & 15 Mar 1908, Glens Falls, NY; d & bur there 3 Jan & 24 Apr 2003. She married there 23 Jun 1928 **Leroy/Roy B. Akins** (Burton Akins & Helen Buckley) b & bp there 7 Apr 1903 & 1 Sep 1908; d & bur there 7 & 10 Jun 1976.

x   **Florence Alice Beaudin** b & bp 15 & 20 Nov 1910, Glens Falls, NY; d & bur there 1 & 3 Oct 1990. She married there 17 Oct 1950 **William Cunningham** (William Cunningham & Mary Conroy) b 7 Dec 1906; d & bur 25 & 28 Nov 1963, Glens Falls, NY.

xi   **Robert Peter Beaudin** b & bp 26 Dec 1913 & 4 Jan 1914, Glens Falls, NY; d 22 Jan 1986, Ticonderoga, NY. He married **Marian E. Spring** (Arthur D. Spring & Merle Kirby) b 13 Jan 1918, Ticonderoga, NY; d 28 Dec 2003, Chambersburg, PA.

3.3.2.16.8   **MONTEE, George Henry** b & bp 26 Sep & 13 Nov 1876, Glens Falls, NY.

George Henry Montee was not included among his mother's three surviving children in her will of 19 Mar 1880 and presumably died before then.

3.3.5.1.1   **MONTY, Adélaïde** b & bp 20 Aug & 1 Sep 1843, St. Luc, QC.

This child was not with her parents in Essex, NY, in 1850 (US census) and may have died before then.

3.3.5.1.2   **MONTY, Antoine** b 31 Jul 1844, Black Brook, NY; d 6 Jan 1937, Ticonderoga, NY. He married 1863? **Marguerite/Margaret Miron/Miro/Merrow** (Joseph Germain Miron & Emelie/Amelia Coulombe) b & bp 3 & 4 Aug 1841, St. Jean, QC; d 9 Feb 1926, Ticonderoga, NY.

Antoine Monty moved rather often in his early years. He was living with his parents in Essex, NY, in 1850 and in Schuyler Falls, NY, in 1860. After his marriage he was a bloomer in Willsboro, NY, in 1865, a sawyer in Glens Falls, NY, in 1870, a hammersmith in Crown Point, NY, in 1880, and a laborer in Ticonderoga, NY, in 1892 and until the end of his life. He and his wife had been married for thirty-seven years in 1900 and had had eight children, of whom six were then still alive (US and state censuses). Antoine Monty and his wife were both buried in the Ironville Cemetery in Crown Point (*Ticonderoga Sentinel,* 11 Feb 1926 and 7 Jan 1937).

Marguerite Miron (Marie Marguerite at her baptism) came to the United States as a child with her parents and was living with them in Champlain, NY, in 1850 and 1860 (US censuses). Her name then and in later censuses was consistently Margaret. Yet the records of St. Mary's Church in Ticonderoga refer to Marguerite, wife of Antoine Monty, and her obituary in the *Ticonderoga Sentinel* of 11 Feb 1926 refers to "Mrs. Marguerite (Merrow) Monty." The family surname, Miron in Canada, became most often Miro or Mero in New York State, and occasionally Merrow.

Children:

3.3.5.1.2.1	Rose F./Rosa	1864-1883?-1908?
3.3.5.1.2.2	William H.	1865-1895-1913
3.3.5.1.2.3	Laura Ann	1867-1884&1916& -1952
3.3.5.1.2.4	Alvina	1870-1896&1944-1944
3.3.5.1.2.5	George	1873- -1873
3.3.5.1.2.6	Charles A.	1874-1901?-1940
3.3.5.1.2.7	John Henry	1876-1898?-1953
3.3.5.1.2.8	Margaret	- -

3.3.5.1.3   **MONTY, Sophie** b & bp 14 & 15 Mar 1845, Coopersville, NY.
This child was not with her parents in Essex, NY, in 1850 (US census) and may have died before then.

3.3.5.1.4   **MONTY, Fred** b 1848?, NY.
Fred Monty was a 2-year-old child living with his parents in Essex, NY, in 1850 (US census). He does not appear with them in later years and may have died in childhood.

3.3.5.1.5   **MONTY, Rosalie** b & bp Apr & 14 Oct 1850, Essex & Coopersville, NY.
Rosalie Monty was a 2-month-old infant living with her parents in Essex, NY, in June 1850 (US census) and was 6 months old at her baptism. She does not appear with her parents in later years and may have died in childhood.

3.3.5.1.6   **MONTY, Joseph** b & bp 6 Feb & 13 Apr 1852, Rouses Point & Coopersville, NY; d 30 May 1929, Moriah, NY. He married 1876? **Célina Robert** (Moïse Robert/ Moses Robare & Josephine Patenaude) b 6 Apr 1853, Keeseville, NY; d 11 Oct 1933, Port Henry, NY.
Joseph Monty and Célina Robert (also Robare, Robard) were first married by a Justice of the Peace and had their marriage rehabilitated in Our Lady of Lourdes Catholic Church in Schroon Lake, NY, on 18 Feb 1890. The date of their original wedding is uncertain: according to the 1900 US census in Saratoga, NY, they had then been married for 24 years. But the 1910 census in Moriah, NY, indicates that they had then been married for 30 years. The date in the earlier census is perhaps more probable: their first child was born in February 1880.
Joseph Monty never remained long in any locality. As a child he moved with his parents within New York State from Rouses Point to Schuyler Falls (1860), to Willsborough (1865), and to Glens Falls (1870). His first child was born in Crown Point, NY. The next four however were born in Vermont where their father was a laborer in Colchester and in Waterbury. The family soon came back to New York State: Joseph Monty and Célina Robert were again residents of Crown Point when their marriage was rehabilitated in 1890. He was a laborer there in 1892, a railroad worker in Saratoga in 1900, an engineer on the state road in Moriah in 1910, and a teamster doing highway work in Port Henry in 1920. His widow was living in 1930 in the household of her son Anderson in Moriah (US and state censuses).

Children:
3.3.5.1.6.1	Edward D.	1880-1904-1948
3.3.5.1.6.2	Sarah/Cécile	1883-1900?-
3.3.5.1.6.3	Harriet/Henriette Hélène	1885-1906?-
3.3.5.1.6.4	Napoleon Joseph	1886-1913-1966
3.3.5.1.6.5	Rollin/Riley	1889-1915&1919-
3.3.5.1.6.6	George Philémon	1892- -
3.3.5.1.6.7	Cora Florence	1894-1909&1916-1945
3.3.5.1.6.8	Anderson Walter	1896-1919-1971
3.3.5.1.6.9	Joseph Dewey	1898- -

3.3.5.1.7   **MONTY, Nelson/Narcisse** b & bp 5 & 12 Feb 1854, Redford, NY; d & bur 15 & 17 Apr 1937, Plattsburgh & Peru, NY. He married 1880? **Mary Sinclair/St. Clair** (Thomas St. Clair & Betsey ____) b 1862?, Crown Point, NY; d & bur 2 & 5 Sep 1929, Peru, NY.

NY.

Nelson Monty (Narcisse at his baptism) was living with his parents in Glens Falls, NY, in 1870. He was a married man in 1880, an iron worker staying in a boarding house in North Hudson, NY. His wife though was not with him: the 18-year-old Mrs. Mary Monty was living next door. The couple remained in New York State, where their two oldest children were born, until the late 1880s when Nelson Monty (also Montey) became a farmer in Middlebury, VT. He stayed there until at least 1900, when he and his wife had been married for twenty years. They may have returned to New York State shortly after then: their last child was born in Ticonderoga, NY. By 1910 he was a farmer in Peru, NY, where he remained until his death (US and state censuses). He and his wife were buried in the Peru Village Cemetery.

Mary Sinclair's date of birth is uncertain. Most censuses from 1870 on indicate that she was born in 1862. Yet the 1900 census notes that she was born in December 1865, while the inscription on her tombstone reads "1859-1929." She was 69 years old at her death according to the *Plattsburgh Sentinel* of 6 Sep 1929.

Children:
3.3.5.1.7.1	Bertha Jane	1883-1903?-1910
3.3.5.1.7.2	Nellie	1886- -1895
3.3.5.1.7.3	Louis	1889- -1911
3.3.5.1.7.4	Anonymous	1890- -1890
3.3.5.1.7.5	Ethel Parmelee	1896-1914&1946-1974
3.3.5.1.7.6	Sarah Ellen	1898-1917-1991
3.3.5.1.7.7	Aileen Frances	1901-1918&1924&1929?-1987

3.3.5.1.8   **MONTY, Edmond** b & bp 5 & 8 June 1856, Redford, NY.

This child was not with his parents in Schuyler Falls, NY, in 1860 (US census) and may have died before then.

3.3.5.1.9   **MONTY, Sarah/Cécile/Celina** b & bp 16 Mar & 29 May 1859, Plattsburgh & Redford, NY; d & bur 22 & 24 Aug 1917, Plattsburgh, NY. She married there 24 Aug 1878 **Peter/Pierre Bourgerie** (Antoine Bourgerie & Emilie ____) b there 1855?; d & bur there 27 & 30 Mar 1940 at the age of 84.

This woman's name appears in various forms. She was Cécile at her baptism, Celina at her marriage, and Celia, Cecilia, or Sarah in various US and state censuses. Sarah became prevalent over time. That was her name at her children's marriages and whenever she appeared as the wife of Peter Bourgerie in the Plattsburgh, NY, newspapers, including the announcement of her death in the *Plattsburgh Sentinel* of 24 Aug 1917. She, her husband, and several of their children were buried in St. Peter Cemetery in Plattsburgh.

Peter/Pierre Bourgerie (also Bourgery, Burgery, Bougerie, Busherie) was a trucker in Plattsburgh. He was survived by his daughter Eva (iv) of Rockland, MA, and his son William (ii) of Albany, NY (*Plattsburgh Daily Press*, 28 & 30 Mar 1940).

Children:
i   **Lillian Mary/Marie Eulalie Bourgerie** b & bp 21 May & 29 Jun 1879, Plattsburgh, NY; d & bur there 6 & 9 Jun 1934. She married 1899? **Frederick/Fred Raby** (Milo Raby & Margaret ____) b 31 Dec 1876, Plattsburgh, NY; d & bur there 1 & 4 Sep 1935.

ii   **William A. Bourgerie** b 1880?, Plattsburgh, NY. He married there 8 Feb 1916 **Delia Barker** (Pascal Barker & Pauline Robinson) b 1872?, Keeseville, NY; m (1) ____ Beckwick; d & bur 19 & 22 Aug 1936, Albany, NY.

iii   **Marie Elmina/Mina Bourgerie** b & bp 18 & 29 Apr 1882, Plattsburgh, NY. She married 1901? as his second wife **Joseph H. Baker** b 1868?, MA.

iv   **Eva Bourgerie** b & bp 22 & 31 Jan 1890, Plattsburgh, NY; d & bur there 26 & 28 Oct 1918. She married there (1) 15 Apr 1912 **August Henry Overbeck** (William F. Overbeck & Augusta R. Beyerdorf) b Jul 1882, Baltimore, MD.

She married (2) 10 May 1917 **Nelson John Barber** (Theophile Barber/Babin &

233

Orelia/Aurélie Hebert) b & bp 4 & 29 Apr 1877, Keeseville, NY; d & bur 1 & 5 May 1947, Plattsburgh, NY.

v **George Bourgerie** b & bp 29 May & 7 Jun 1896, Plattsburgh, NY; d & bur there 24 & 26 Oct 1918.

3.3.5.1.10 **MONTY, Ellen** b & bp 24 Jan & 3 Feb 1861, Dannemora, NY. She married (1) 1876? **Alexander Lafountain** (Seymour Lafountain & Sophie ____) b 1854?, Champlain, NY.

She married (2) 1887? **James A. Orkins** (Anson A. Orkins & Maria ____) b May 1854, Benson, VT; d 6 Sep 1926, Ticonderoga, NY.

Ellen Monty (Helene at her baptism), her 26-year-old husband Alex Lafountain, and their two children were staying in 1880 in her father's household in Crown Point, NY. In 1892 she was living with her second husband and the two children of her first marriage in Ticonderoga, NY, where James A. Orkins was a grocer. He was also described as a merchant in 1900 when he and his wife had been married for thirteen years, and a butcher there in 1920 (US and state censuses).

Children:
i **Ida/Adela Lafountain** b & bp 10 May & 23 Dec 1877, VT & Plattsburgh, NY.
ii **Cora Lafountain** b 1879?, Essex Co., NY. She married 23 Sep 1895, Ticonderoga, NY, **William Austin Gale** (Daniel Amory Gale & Rosetta Cynthia Austin) b 21 Sep 1872, Sudbury, VT; d & bur 13 & 15 Apr 1924, Ticonderoga, NY.

3.3.5.1.11 **MONTY, Julia B.** b & bp 1 Jul & 20 Sep 1863, Essex Co. & Keeseville, NY; d between 1917 and 1920. She married (1) 8 Aug 1879, Burlington, VT, **Henry Demport**.

She married (2) 6 Aug 1882, Crown Point, NY, **Nelson Eugene Porter** (Nelson Porter & Eleanor Burns) b 10 Jan 1846, Ticonderoga, NY; m (2) 1900? Esther ____ ; d between 1910 and June 1914.

She married (3) 1906? **Eli Balch** (Seth Balch & Cordelia ____) b Feb 1863, St. Lawrence Co., NY; m (1) 1883? Mary ____ ; d 1 Sep 1913, Plattsburgh, NY.

She married (4) 14 Jul 1917, South Glens Falls, NY, **Charles H. Sleight** (George G. Sleight & Catherine Dicker) b Jan 1848, Pleasant Valley, NY; m (1) 1873? Mary Jane Rose.

Mrs. Julia B. Demport was living with her infant son in her father's household in Crown Point, NY, in June 1880 (US census). Her husband was absent or may already have been deceased.

Nelson Eugene Porter had served in the Union Army during the Civil War in Co. E, 2nd New York Cavalry Regiment and received a pension on 28 May 1880 (Civil War Pension Index). He was a blacksmith in Stillwater, NY, in 1870 but a resident of Ticonderoga at his first marriage and until at least 1890. He was a machinist in Saratoga Springs, NY, in 1900, when he and his second wife Esther had been married for less than a year, and a patternmaker for G.E. in Schenectady, NY, in 1910 (US censuses). He died a few years later and on 24 Jun 1914 Julia Monty, by then Mrs. Julia Balch, applied for a pension as the widow of a Civil War Veteran. I do not know if she ever received that pension: a counter-claim was filed on 27 Oct 1915 by Nelson Potters's second wife, Mrs. Esther Porter.

Julia Monty had been married for four years to Eli Balch, a railroad brakeman in Plattsburgh, NY, in 1910. She had had three children, all of whom were still alive, though only one, Frederick Porter, was living with her and her husband (US census). She left Plattsburgh after Eli Balch's death and was a dressmaker in Queensbury, NY, when she married Charles H. Sleight who was a farmer there. She died before 1920 when he was a widower (US censuses).

Children:
i **Henry Francis Demport/Denport** b & bp 20 May 1880 & 26 Jul 1881, Crown Point & Ticonderoga, NY.
ii **Frederick Eugene Porter** b 2 Dec 1889, Ticonderoga, NY; d May 1953, Albany,

NY. He married 8 Nov 1912, Plattsburgh, NY, **Nina Maude Thornhill** (Stephen W. Thornhill & Emma Cordelia Perkins) b 20 Oct 1894, Ogdensburg, NY; d 6 Jun 1978, Dunedin, FL.

3.3.6.1.1   **MONTEE, Emma** b 1852?, Glens Falls, NY; d & bur there 23 & 26 Oct 1929 at the age of 78. She married (1) ___ and was divorced 5 Apr 1888, Saratoga Springs, NY.

She married (2) 29 Nov 1919, Glens Falls, NY, **Joseph Neddo** (Raymond Neddo & Mary B____) b Jun 1870, Canada.

I know of Emma Montee's first marriage only through a notation on her second marriage record showing the date of a previous divorce. She is also identified in that document as the daughter of Jacob Montee and Elizabeth Lansing. She had obviously taken back her maiden after her divorce: she was known as Emma Montee not only in her mother's will of 15 Nov 1888 but also in the 1892 state census in Glens Falls, NY, where she was a member of her father's household.

Joseph Neddo (also Neddow, Nadeau) had arrived in the United States around 1885 and was a laborer in Newcomb, NY, in 1900 and 1910. He was a laborer in Glens Falls at his marriage and until at least 1930 (US censuses).

3.3.6.1.2   **MONTEE, Josephine** b Oct 1853, Glens Falls, NY; d & bur there 17 & 20 Jan 1931. She married (1) 1877? (Catholic "blessing of previous marriage" on 29 May 1880 in St. Alphonsus Church, Glens Falls, NY) **Joseph Didier Paul Arele** (Didier Arele & Lisa Lamoureux) b & bp 20 Apr & 4 May 1858, Glens Falls, NY; d between June 1880 and April 1883.

She married (2) 11 Nov 1890, Glens Falls, NY, **Edward Benson** (Daniel Benson & Sarah ___) b Feb 1862, NY; d between 1900 and 1920.

Joseph Arele was a boatman living with his wife and children in his father-in-law's household in Glens Falls, NY, in 1880 (US census). He was deceased when his third child was baptized in April 1883.

Edward Benson was a laborer in Glens Falls in 1892 and in Kingsbury, NY, in 1900 (US and state censuses). He was away from his household in 1910 when his wife was in Glens Falls with her sons Edward and Dewey Benson. She remained in Glens Falls and was a widow in 1920 when she was a member of her son Edward's household there and in 1930 when she was living in the household of a grandson-in-law William Corbett and his wife Josephine, daughter of Eliza Arele (i) and Moses Mayotte.

Children :

1	**Elizabeth/Eliza Arele** b May 1878, Glens Falls, NY; d & bur there 22 & 24 Dec 1921. She married 1895? **Moïse/Moses Mayotte** (also **Mailhot**).
ii	**John Arele** b 1879, Glens Falls, NY.
iii	**Joseph Napoleon Arele** b & bp 13 & 29 Apr 1883, Glens Falls, NY.
iv	**Edward V. Benson** bp 26 Apr 1892, Glens Falls, NY; d & bur 27 & 30 Jul 1957, Canandaigua, NY, at the age of 65. He married 2 Jul 1921, Glens Falls, NY, **Helen E. Labram** (William Labram & Anna Gates) bp 16 Mar 1892, Methodist Church, Glens Falls, NY.
v	**Lisa Maria Benson** b & bp 13 Mar & 7 Apr 1895, Glens Falls, NY.
vi	**Dewey Benson** b & bp 20 Jul & 7 Aug 1898, Hudson Falls, NY; d & bur 4 & 6 Jan 1945, Glens Falls, NY. He married there 21 Sep 1918 **Ada Gilman** (Lee Gilman & Georgiana Fredette) b 23 Apr 1901, Rutland, VT; d Aug 1973, Glens Falls, VT.

3.3.6.1.3   **MONTY/MONTEE, Henry/William Henry** b 1856?, US; d & bur 26 & 28 Dec 1894, Glens Falls, NY. He married 1876? **Louisa Poirier/Peer/Pair** b Jun 1861, Highgate, VT.

Henry Montee was 4 years old in 1860 when he was living with his parents in Glens Falls, NY. His place of birth is uncertain: various US and state censuses in Glens Falls show that he was born in Massachusetts, Wisconsin, or New York State. I do not know where his parents were in 1856: they were not listed in the 1855 state census in Glens Falls, though they had children there in 1853 and 1858. I think it is significant that the 1860 and 1865 censuses single him out as the only child in the family born outside the state of New York. But whether he was born in Massachusetts or Wisconsin is an open question.

Henry Montee was a laborer in a sawmill in Glens Falls in 1880, when his oldest child was 3 years old, and remained there until the late 1880s. He then moved to Keene, NH, where he was a laborer in 1890 at the birth of his son Carl and a mechanic in 1894 at the marriage of his daughter Elizabeth. His surname in New Hampshire had by then reverted to Monty while his given name was variously Henry, W. Henry, or William Henry. He may have returned to Glens Falls shortly before his death for he was a resident of Warren Co., NY, at his death (Warren Co., NY, Probate records, Book G, p. 142).

His widow remained in Keene where she was running a boarding house in 1900. She had had seven children of whom four, Elizabeth, William, Fred, and Carl, were still alive (US census). Her surname varies: it is Poirier in the French records of her children's baptisms in St. Alphonsus Church in Glens Falls but Peer in the New Hampshire birth record of her son Carl, and Pair in the New Hampshire marriage record of her daughter Elizabeth. I have not found her birth or marriage records in Vermont or New York under any of these surnames.

Children:

3.3.6.1.3.1	Elizabeth Julia	1877-1894-
3.3.6.1.3.2	Charles	1879- -
3.3.6.1.3.3	Arthur	- -1897
3.3.6.1.3.4	William Henry	1882-1907-
3.3.6.1.3.5	Jacques	1884- -
3.3.6.1.3.6	Joseph Alfred/Fred	1887-1913?-1952?
3.3.6.1.3.7	Carl Alvin	1890- -1943

3.3.6.1.4   **MONTEE, Susan** b & bp 10 Oct 1858 & 1 Jan 1859, Glens Falls, NY; d & bur there 25 & 27 Jun 1929. She married 1877? **Richard Lord** b Aug 1854, NY.

Richard Lord was a foundry worker in Glens Falls, NY, until at least 1920 and was still living there, with no stated occupation, in 1930. He and his wife had been married for twenty-three years in 1900 and had had ten children of whom six, Isabelle, James Henry, Gertrude, Josephine, Andrew, and Frank were then still alive (US censuses).

Children:

i   **Elizabeth/Isabelle Lord** b & bp Mar 1878 & 8 May 1881, Glens Falls, NY. She married there 10 Jun 1903 **Charles Wesley Martindale** (John Martindale & Mary Annas) b 14 Oct 1878, Kingsbury, NY.

ii   **Joseph Edward Lord** b & bp 27 Apr & 3 Dec 1882, Glens Falls, NY; d before 1900.

iii   **James Henry Lord** b 6 Feb 1885, Waterford, NY; d Sep 1967, Saratoga Co., NY. He married 22 Apr 1908, Glens Falls, NY, **Gertrude Van Wagner** (Lewis Van Wagner & Mary A. Smith) b 1881?, NY.

iv   **Gertrude Lord** b & bp 21 Jul & 14 Aug 1887, Glens Falls, NY.

v   **Josephine Mary Lord** b & bp 20 May & 24 Jun 1891, Glens Falls, NY; d there Nov 1979. She married there 21 Jun 1911, **George Leslie Bullard** (Truman Bullard & Elizabeth Chadwick) b 11 Aug 1885, Luzerne, NY; d 1951, Glens Falls, NY.

vi   **Andrew Lord** b & bp 13 & 25 Sep 1892, Glens Falls, NY; d & bur there 26 & 28 Oct 1914.

vii   **Joseph Etienne Owen/Oliver Lord** b & bp 28 Mar & 5 May 1895, Glens Falls, NY; d & bur there 14 & 16 Sep 1895 at the age of 6 months.

viii   **Frank Clifford Lord** b & bp 7 Nov & 20 Dec 1896, Glens Falls, NY; d 1954, Pinellas Co., FL.

3.3.6.1.5   **MONTEE, Joseph Louis** b & bp 18 Sep & 27 Oct 1861, Glens Falls, NY.

Joseph Montee was a sawyer in Glens Falls, NY, in 1892, still single and living in his father's household there (state census). I have been unable to trace him further.

3.3.6.1.6 **MONTEE, Adelaide** b Dec 1863, Glens Falls, NY.

Adelaide Montee was an 18-month-old child living with her parents in Glens Falls, NY, in June 1865 (state census). She does not appear with her family at any later date and may have died before 1870.

3.3.6.1.7 **MONTEE, Adeline** b & bp 30 May & 18 Sep 1870, Glens Falls, NY. She married there 5 Jan 1886 **Joseph Hoag**.

I know little of this woman beyond her baptism and marriage in St. Alphonsus Church in Glens Falls, NY. She was named Adelaide Hoag in her mother's will of 15 Nov 1888 and was still a minor on 30 Dec 1889 when the Warren Co. Surrogate's Court appointed James H. Bain as her guardian. I have been unable to trace her or her husband any further.

3.3.6.7.1 **MONTEE, Charles B.** b & bp 5 Jul & 11 Sep 1879, Glens Falls, NY.

Charles B. Montee (Charles Jean Baptiste at his baptism) was a laborer in Glens Falls, NY, in 1905 (state census). He was named co-executor of his father John Montee's will on 25 Jul 1907 in the Warren Co., NY, Surrogate's Court.

3.5.13.2.1 **MONTA, Sophia** b & bp 1 and 14 Mar 1866, Burlington, VT; d & bur 1916, Troy, NY & Burlington, VT. She married 29 Oct 1885, Burlington, VT, **William Walter Scott** (William Scott & Margaret Bain/Baines) b there 25 Feb 1857.

The year of Sophia Monta's death is taken from the tombstone she shares with her parents and several siblings in Mount Calvary Cemetery in Burlington, VT.

William W. Scott was a bookbinder in Burlington at his marriage and until at least 1900. He then moved with his family to Troy, NY, where he was a factory worker in 1910. He and his wife had had three children of whom two, William A. and Joseph B, were then still alive. As a widower in 1920, William W. Scott was living in his son William A. Scott's household in Troy (US censuses).

Children:
i   **William Arthur Scott** b 25 Jul 1886, Burlington, VT. He married 1907? **Abbie Hayner** (Ellis D. Hayner & Elizabeth _____) b Jun 1889, Troy, NY.
ii   **Joseph B. Scott** b 13 Dec 1887, Burlington, VT.
iii   **Eugene Scott** b 28 Apr 1901, Burlington, VT; d before 1910.

3.5.13.2.2 **MONTA, Joseph John** b & bp 28 & 29 Nov 1867, Burlington, VT; d there 10 Mar 1934. He married 29 Jun 1903, Middlebury, VT, **Mary Harriette/Hattie Daniels** (Edward Daniels & Mary Alice Nichols) b there 3 Oct 1884.

Joseph John Monta was a marble worker in Middlebury, VT, at his marriage. He and his wife apparently soon parted: not once are they found together in any census from 1910 through 1930. Mrs. Hattie Monta was living with her daughter, but without her husband, in Middlebury in 1910 and was in 1920 and 1930 a housekeeper and companion to two widows in Brooklyn, NY, and Bennington, VT. Joseph Monta had returned to Burlington, VT, where he was a marble cutter (US censuses). He was buried in the Monta lot in Mount Calvary Cemetery in Burlington where he shares a tombstone with his parents and four of his sisters.

Child:
3.5.13.2.2.1   Helen Mary   1904-   -

3.5.13.2.3 **MONTA, Delphine** b 14 Sep 1869, Burlington, VT; d Jul 1965, MI. She married 18 Aug 1891, Burlington, VT, **Halsey Hathaway** (Sylvester Hathaway & Harriet Thomas) b 1871, AuSable, NY; d & bur 11 & 14 Mar 1931, Thomasville & Clintonville (AuSable), NY, at the age of 60.

The year of Halsey Hathaway's birth is taken from the inscription on his tombstone in the Old Clintonville Cemetery in AuSable, NY. He was a farmer in AuSable, his place of birth, when he married. His daughter however was born in Burlington, VT, where he was a laborer and produce dealer until at least 1909 (City Directories). The following year he and his wife were cooks in a private school in North Elba, NY. They then returned to AuSable where Halsey Hathaway was a farmer in 1920 and 1930 (US censuses). According to his obituary in the *Plattsburgh Sentinel* of 20 Mar 1931, he was also known as a cattle dealer.

Delphine Monta sold the farm after her husband's death and lived for some years in Burlington before joining her daughter's family in Michigan where she died. I have no certain knowledge that she was in fact buried next to her husband in the Old Clintonville Cemetery where her tombstone was inscribed, probably at the time of her husband's death, "Delphine E. / HATHAWAY / 1869-19 ." The year of her death may have been added after the transcription was made in July 1962.

Child:

i   **Grace May Hathaway** b 24 May 1893, Burlington, VT; d 24 Mar 1961, Kenockee Twp, MI. She married 5 Dec 1916, Burlington, VT, **Arthur Leonard Louks** (George R. Louks & Alvina Green) b 22 Apr 1886, Lincoln, MI; d 18 Jan 1973, Yale, MI.

3.5.13.2.4   **MONTA, Mary Anne/Nettie** b & bp 4 & 5 Feb 1872, Vergennes & Burlington, VT; d & bur 1952, Burlington, VT. She married there 24 Jun 1890 **Edward J. Walker** (Joel Walker/Marcheterre & Caroline Latourelle) b & bp 12 Jul & 25 Aug 1869, Keeseville, NY; d & bur 1943, Burlington, VT.

This woman was named Marie Anne at her baptism, Mary Anne at her marriage, Mary or Nita at the births of her children, but invariably Nettie in US censuses as well on her tombstone in Mount Calvary Cemetery in Burlington, VT. .

Edward J. Walker was baptized as Edmond Joël Marcheterre, which surname was commonly used in New York State. In Vermont however both he and his father were generally known as Walker, a loose translation from the French, the major exception being the French records of St. Joseph's Church in Burlington which continued to use the surname Marcheterre (as also the surname Monty even when civil records say Monta). As for the change from Edmond to Edward, I cannot explain it save in terms of a personal preference. Again with the exception of the church records in Burlington, he was known in Vermont as Edward.

Edward J. Walker was a carpenter/builder/building contractor in Burlington (US censuses; City Directories). Both he and his wife were buried there in the Monta lot in Mount Calvary Cemetery where they share a tombstone with her parents and four of her siblings. I have no reason to doubt the accuracy of the tombstone inscriptions in regard to the years of their deaths. They show however that both were born in 1871 which is clearly wrong.

Children:

i   **Edward Joseph Walker** b 15 Mar 1891, Burlington, VT. He married 1920? **Helen M. ____** b 1891?, Ireland.

ii   **Raymond J. Walker** b 24 Sep 1899, Burlington, VT; d Aug 1987, Tampa, FL. He married 1928?, **Mabel ____** b 1901?, MA.

iii   **Harvey L. Walker** b 29 Oct 1901, Burlington, VT; d there 1 May 1906.

iv   **Lucille Abigail Walker** b 19 Dec 1905, Burlington, VT; d 5 Mar 1983, Anaheim, CA. She married **Herbert Rockwell Blanchard** (Wallace J. Blanchard & Carrie E. Baldwin) b 7 Jul 1908, Boston, MA; d 21 Apr 1984, Anaheim, CA.

v   **Leona Walker** b 1908?, Burlington, VT.

vi   **Clarence J. Walker** b 16 Jul 1911, Burlington, VT; d 29 Jul 1993, Hartford, CT. He married **Edna Denski** (Joseph Denski & Catherine Broska) b 13 Jun 1918, West Suffield, CT.

3.5.13.2.5   **MONTA, Margaret Adele** b & bp 5 & 7 Dec 1873, Burlington, VT; d & bur there 1956. She married there 23 Jun 1896 **Mitchell Nelson Hamlin** (Théophile Hamlin & Mathilde Filion) b 10 Aug 1874, Port Douglass, NY; d & bur 1940, Burlington, VT.

I am using here the names found in the Vermont Vital Records, which correspond to those in the US censuses. The records of St. Joseph's Church in Burlington, VT, however show that Marguerite Adèle (baptismal name) married Herménégilde Hamelin. Mitchell Hamlin was a cotton mill worker in Burlington for most of his married life, save for a brief period around 1907 and 1908 when two children were born in New York State (US censuses). He and his wife were buried along with several of her relatives in the Monta lot in Burlington's Mount Calvary Cemetery.

Children:

i   **Florence Hamlin** b 18 Jul 1897, Burlington, VT.
ii **Cecilia Adeline Hamlin** b 1 Feb 1899, Burlington, VT.
iii **Edith Dorothy Hamlin** b 24 Jan 1901, Burlington, VT; d 28 Oct 1993, Riverside Co., CA. She married 1924? **Louis Herman Wheel** (Moses Wheel & Rosalie ___) b 27 Aug 1900, Burlington, VT; d Feb 1978, Burbank, CA.
iv **Hazel May Hamlin** b 20 May 1903, Burlington, VT.
v   **Harold John Hamlin** b 22 Nov 1904, Burlington, VT; d 10 Dec 1985, Saint Cloud, FL.
vi **Roy/LeRoy Hamlin** b 1907?, NY.
vii **Leslie John Hamlin** b 26 Sep 1908, NY; d 26 Jan 1983, Orange, CA.
viii **Walter Hamlin** b 20 Nov 1912, Burlington, VT; d Mar 1982, Ashland, OR.

3.5.13.2.6   **MONTA, Louisa** b & bp 21 Apr & 1 May 1876, Burlington, VT; d & bur there 1925. She married there 22 Nov 1898 **Eugene Edmond VanClette/VanCleet** (Meddy Van Clette [Amédée Vincelette] & Mary Elizabeth Gauthier) b 17 Aug 1875, Cornwall, VT; m (2) 1901?, Agnes Marie ____ .

The year of Louisa Monta's death is taken from the inscription on her tombstone in Mount Calvary Cemetery in Burlington, VT. She was buried in the Monta plot as Louisa Vanclett, daughter of Joseph Monta and Mary Croto. Her husband's surname varied somewhat. It was VanClette in the Vermont Vital Records: at his birth, first marriage, and at the birth of his child. He later more commonly used the surname VanCleet: such is his signature, for example, on his World War I Registration Card. The original surname, Vincelette, was used to my knowledge only in the French records of St. Joseph's Church in Burlington, VT.

Eugene VanClette was a cotton mill worker in Burlington in 1900 when his household included his mother-in-law Mrs. Mary Monta and his brother-in-law Joseph Monta (3.5.13.2.2). His marriage was obviously short-lived for while Mrs. Louisa VanSleet (sic) was still living with her mother and brother in Burlington in 1910, he was an attendant in the State Hospital in Taunton, MA, and had been married for nine years, presumably to a second wife (US censuses). Eight years later, when he signed his World War I Registration Card, he was a special patrolman for the Brooklyn, NY, Police Department, whose nearest relative was his wife, Mrs. Agnes Marie VanCleet.

Child:

i   **Anonymous VanClette** b & d 29 Mar 1899, Burlington, VT.

3.9.2.2.1   **MONTY, Louis** b & bp 10 Jan 1848, Stanbridge, QC; d & bur 23 & 27 Feb 1848, St. Luc, QC.

3.9.2.2.2   **MONTY, Olive** b & bp 5 & 6 Apr 1849, Stanbridge, QC; d & bur there 31 Oct & 2 Nov 1849.

3.9.2.2.3   **MONTY, Guillaume** (twin) b & bp ? & 3 Sep 1850, St. Alexandre & St. Jean, QC; d & bur 22 & 24 Jul 1854, St. Alexandre, QC.

Guillaume Monty's baptismal record does not include the date or place of his birth. His twin brother however was born in St. Alexandre, QC, according to the birth record of his daughter Emma (3.9.2.2.4.2) in 1884.

3.9.2.2.4   **MONTY/MONTEE, John/Jean-Baptiste** (twin) b & bp ? & 3 Sep 1850, St. Alexandre & St. Jean, QC. He married 1878? **Lucy E. Winter** (Charles Winter & Clara F. ____) b Apr 1858, Gorham, ME; d 8 Jun 1906, Farmington, NH.

Jean-Baptiste Monty's baptismal record does not include the date or place of his birth. The latter is found in his daughter Emma's birth record. He came to the United States in the 1860s and was a farm laborer living in his father's household in Westborough, MA, in 1870. He soon moved to Farmington, NH, where he was a shoe shop worker/shoemaker until at least 1900. He and his wife had then been married for twenty-two years (US censuses). This family's surname in the New Hampshire Vital Records is constantly Montee.

Children:

3.9.2.2.4.1	Carrie M.	1881-1900-
3.9.2.2.4.2	Emma L.	1884-1905-1971
3.9.2.2.4.3	Florence M.	1887- -

3.9.2.2.5   **MONTY, Joseph** b & bp 11 & 12 Apr 1853, St. Alexandre, QC; d & bur there 19 & 20 Oct 1853.

3.9.2.2.6   **MONTY, Médérise** b & bp 28 & 29 Oct 1854, St. Alexandre, QC; d & bur 13 & 15 Mar 1934, Montreal, QC. She married (1) 17 Aug 1872, Southbridge, MA, **Elie Bouvier** (Pierre Bouvier & Josette Arpin) b & bp 4 & 5 Mar 1851, St. Ours, QC; d between December 1892 and April 1893.

She married (2) 22 Nov 1919, Montreal, QC, **Herménégilde Pilon** (Hyacinthe Pilon & Emelie Vallée) b & bp 23 & 24 Mar 1864, Rigaud, QC; m (1) there 26 Oct 1855 Rosalie Lalonde (Jacques Lalonde & Philomène Gauthier); d & bur 9 & 11 May 1928, Montreal & Rigaud, QC.

Elie Bouvier was a carpenter in Southbridge, MA, at his marriage, a resident of St. Ours, QC, at the birth of a daughter in 1875, a tinsmith in Contrecoeur, QC, at the birth of another child in 1876, and a tinsmith and/or farmer in Marieville, QC, from 1877 until at least May 1891 (Canadian census). He was a tinsmith in the Hochelaga district of Montreal when his daughter Emelia (i) died in December 1892 but was deceased at the death of his daughter Rose Alba (viii) in April 1893.

Herménégilde Pilon (Joseph Napoléon Erménégilde at his baptism) was a farmer in Rigaud, QC, at his first marriage. He was a resident of Outremont, QC, when he married Médérise Monty.

Children:

i   **Emelia Bouvier** b & bp 16 & 17 Jan 1875, St. Ours, QC; d & bur 29 & 31 Dec 1892, Montreal, QC.

ii   **Louise Olympe Bouvier** b & bp 7 Oct 1876, Contrecoeur, QC. She married 11 Jun 1895, St. Ours, QC, **George Dansereau** (Félix Dansereau & Virginie Casavant) b & bp there 18 & 19 Jul 1872.

iii **Arthur Adélard Bouvier** b & bp 8 & 9 Aug 1877, Marieville, QC. He married 27 Nov 1899, L'Epiphanie, QC, **Eva Chaillé/Oliva Chailly** (Olivier Chaillé & Philomène Dinel) b & bp 28 Apr 1881, St. Roch de l'Achigan, QC.

iv   **Rose Anna Sophie Bouvier** b & bp 15 Jul 1879, Marieville, QC; d & bur there 2 & 5 Feb 1938. She married there 1 Mar 1897 **Adélard Racicot** (Antoine Racicot & Sophie Trahan) b & bp there 21 Oct 1874; d & bur there 28 & 30 Jun 1920.

v   **Ernest Bouvier** b May 1880, QC.

vi   **Regina Bouvier** b & bp 10 & 11 May 1881, Marieville, QC; d & bur there 18 & 19 Aug 1881.

vii **Joseph Elie Ulric Bouvier** b & bp 27 Jun 1882, Marieville, QC.

viii **Victoria/Rose Alba Bouvier** b & bp 17 & 18 Nov 1883, Marieville, QC; d & bur there 23 & 25 Apr 1893.

ix   **Maximilienne Bouvier** b & bp 10 & 15 Feb 1885, Marieville, QC; d & bur 24 & 27 Apr 1917, Montreal, QC. She married there 19 Apr 1904 **Louis Guibord** (Marcel Guibord & Delima Plante) b & bp there 23 Jul 1882; m (2) there 27 Sep 1919 Nadia Sauvé (Noé Sauvé & Emilie Vinet).

x   **Flavie Aurore Bouvier** b & bp 20 & 21 Mar 1886, Marieville, QC; d & bur there 29 & 30 Jun 1886.

xi   **Raoul Isola Bouvier** b & bp 27 & 28 Feb 1887, Marieville, QC; d & bur there 29 & 30 Jul 1887.

xii   **Delia Antonia Bouvier** b & bp 6 & 7 Mar 1888, Marieville, QC; d & bur there 18 & 19 May 1889.

xiii   **Emile Isola Bouvier** b & bp 27 & 28 Jun 1889, Marieville, QC. He married 7 Jan 1914, Montreal, QC, **Léonide Lamoureux** (Ulric Lamoureux & Philomène Dubeau) b & bp there 31 May & 1 Jun 1893.

xiv   **Hermine Bouvier** b & bp 25 & 26 Oct 1890, Marieville, QC.

3.9.2.2.7   **MONTY/MONTE, William/Guillaume** b & bp 24 Aug 1856, St. Alexandre, QC; d & bur 9 & 11 Mar 1926, Westborough, MA. He married (1) there 23 Aug 1882 **Catherine E. Kearns** (Michael Kearns & Bridget Gradie) b 11 Jan 1856, Worcester, MA; d 7 Jan 1884, Westborough, MA.

He married (2) around 1915 **Margaret L. Brady** (John Brady & Margaret _____) b Jun 1864, Worcester Co., MA.

Guillaume Monty (baptismal name) came to the United States as a child and was thereafter called William Monty or more often Monte. He remained in Westborough, MA, where he was a shoe or boot maker throughout his life (US censuses; City Directories).

Child of the first marriage:
3.9.2.2.7.1   William   1883-   -1886

3.9.2.2.8   **MONTY/MONTE, Mary Jane** b & bp 15 & 16 Aug 1858, Iberville, QC; bur 6 Nov 1946, Westborough, MA. She married there 3 Jun 1877 **Frank Weston Taft** (Solomon Jewett Taft & Sarah A. Forbush) b 22 Jul 1857, Boston, MA.

Marie Monty (baptismal name) came to the United States as a child with her family in the late 1860s and was known in 1870, when she was living in her father's household in Westborough, MA, as Mary Monta (US census). She married however under the name of Mary Monte and was known as a married woman as either Mary J. or Mary Jane Taft.

Frank W. Taft was a resident of Westborough, MA, at his marriage and a boot maker there at the births of children in 1877, 1879, and 1883. The family also lived for a time in Marlborough, MA, where he was a shoe worker in 1880. He was a prison officer in Somerset, MA, in 1920 and retired in Boston, MA where he and his wife were living in 1930 with their daughter Bertha and son-in-law Lucien Robbins (US censuses).

Children:
i   **Bertha Monte Taft** b 10 Dec 1877, Westborough, MA. She married 1899? **Lucien Noyes Robbins** (Joseph N. Robbins & Esther _____) b 18 Apr 1874, MO; d Oct 1963, MA.

ii   **Ernest Jewett Taft** b 18 Feb 1879, Westborough, MA; d there Feb 1880.

iii   **Sarah Louise Taft** b 21 Dec 1880, Marlborough, MA; d 26 May 1971, Medford, MA. She married 30 Jan 1901, Charlton, MA, **Alfred Raymond Bennett** (Alfred R. Bennett & Abigail L. Hodgdon) b 3 Nov 1875, East Boothbay, ME; d 3 Nov 1966, Boston, MA.

iv   **Emory Wood Taft** b 30 Jan 1883, Westborough, MA.

v   **Frances E. Taft** b 1887?, MA.

3.9.2.2.9   **MONTY, Victoire/Victoria** b & bp 29 Jan 1862, Stanbridge, QC; d & bur 25 & 27 Feb 1866, Dunham, QC.

This child was named Victoire at her baptism and Victoria at her death at the age of four.

3.9.2.2.10   **MONTY, Julie** b & bp 16 & 17 Sep 1864, Dunham, QC; d 1923, New Bedford, MA. She married 25 Oct 1881, Woonsocket, RI, **Eusèbe Gosselin** (Eusèbe Gosselin & Olympe Dufresne) b Mar 1861, QC; d 1937, New Bedford, MA.

Julie Monty came to the United States as a child in the late 1860s. Her birth, marriage, and burial records all refer to her as Julie Monty. Only in US censuses was she named Julia.

Eusèbe Gosselin came to the United States as a child around 1868 and was a 20-year-old mill worker in Woonsocket, RI, at his marriage. He was a laborer there until at least 1893 before moving to New Bedford, MA, where he was a barber/hairdresser from at least 1898 on. By 1900 he and his wife had had two children only one of whom, Joseph, was still alive (US censuses; Woonsocket and New Bedford City Directories). They were buried in the New Sacred Heart Cemetery in New Bedford, along with their son Joseph and an unidentified Laura, probably the deceased child mentioned in the 1900 and 1910 censuses.

Children:

i   **Joseph I. Gosselin** b 2 Jan 1883, Woonsocket, RI; d & bur 1943, New Bedford, MA. He married there 31 Oct 1911 **Armoza Lafrance** (Alphonse Lafrance & Caroline Fecteau) b 1 Dec 1886, Fairhaven, MA; d 13 Mar 1965, San Diego, CA.

ii   **Unidentified (Laura?) Gosselin** d before 1900.

3.9.2.2.11   **MONTY, Felix Joseph** b 8 Mar 1868, Southbridge, MA; d 31 Aug 1940, Woonsocket, RI. He married there 20 Sep 1898 **Ella Daigle** (Nazaire Daigle & Stephanie Fontaine) b 1871?, Woodstock, VT; d 16 Jan 1905, Woonsocket, RI, at the age of 33.

Felix J. Monty did not remarry after his wife early death. He was a machinist in Woonsocket, RI, in 1910 and 1920, and was in the State Infirmary in Cranston, RI, in 1930 (US censuses). He was buried in Precious Blood Cemetery in Woonsocket.

Children:

3.9.2.2.11.1	Harold Roger	1899-	-1972
3.9.2.2.11.2	Regina	1901-	-1905
3.9.2.2.11.3	Wallace E.	1904-1947-1984	

3.9.2.2.12   **MONTY, William** b 20 Apr 1869, Southbridge, MA; d 31 Jul 1870, Westborough, MA.

3.9.2.2.13   **MONTY, Napoleon** b Dec 1870, Westborough, MA.

Napoleon Monty was a teamster in Woonsocket, RI, in 1900 (US census).

3.9.2.2.14   **MONTY, Zoe** b 31 Aug 1873, Woonsocket, RI; d 20 Jan 1932, Woonsocket, RI. She married there 20 Apr 1909 **Napoleon Ayotte** (Norbert Ayotte & Hermine Drainville/Rainville) b & bp 4 Nov 1869, St. Barthélemy, QC.

Napoleon Ayotte (Joseph Napoléon at his baptism) was a carpenter in Woonsocket, RI, in 1900. He had arrived in the United States in 1880 and was a naturalized American citizen. He moved to Blackstone, MA, with his family in the late 1910s and was a house carpenter and building contractor there in 1920 and 1930 (US censuses).

Children:

i   **Lucien Ayotte** b 22 Aug 1910, RI; d 5 Dec 1996, Woonsocket, RI.

ii   **Simone G. Ayotte,** b 19 Oct 1911, RI; d 26 Jul 2005, Methuen, MA.

iii   **Madeleine Ayotte** b Apr 1913, RI.

3.9.2.2.15   **MONTY, Frederick** b & bp 18 Sep & 5 Oct 1879, Woonsocket, RI; d 18 Mar 1948, Bellingham, MA. He married (1) 2 Jul 1901, Woonsocket, RI, **Lucina Darche** (François Jean Marie Georges Darche & Azilda Vigeant dit Taupier) b 14 Sep 1877, QC; d 31 Dec 1941, Bellingham, MA.

He married (2) 10 May 1947, Woonsocket, RI, **Marie Louise Lachance** (Octave Lachance & Geneviève Champagne) b & bp 13 May 1883, St. Gabriel de Brandon, QC; m (1)

1903? William/Guillaume Marcil; d 26 Mar 1963, Woonsocket, RI.

Frederick Monty was originally a worker in Woonsocket, RI, where his first three children were born. The family then moved to Bellingham, MA, though he continued to work as a machinist in Woonsocket (US censuses; Woonsocket City Directories). He and both of his wives were buried there in Precious Blood Cemetery.

Lucina Darche was married in St. Anne's Catholic Church in Woonsocket under the name of Anna Marie Louise Lucina Darche. In all other documents I have seen, from the 1881 Canadian census in St. Mathias, QC, where she was a 4-year-old child living with her parents to the record of her burial in Woonsocket, she was named simply Lucina.

Children of the first marriage:

3.9.2.2.15.1	Albert	1902?- -
3.9.2.2.15.2	Mary A.	1903?- -
3.9.2.2.15.3	Gertrude Cecile	1905-1927-1974
3.9.2.2.15.4	Aline C.	1907-1938?-1991
3.9.2.2.15.5	Bernard R.	1909- & -1995
3.9.2.2.15.6	Madeline/Madeleine	1912- -1988
3.9.2.2.15.7	Georgette	1914-1937-2005
3.9.2.2.15.8	Emile D.	1916-1944-1988

3.9.3.3.1   **MONTIE, Louisa Angelica** (twin) b & bp 1 & 2 Nov 1849, Ecorse, MI; d there 4 Aug 1926. She married there 1 Nov 1870 **Gideon Sanch/Gédéon Sanche** (Augustin Anselme/Sam Sanche & Scholastique Bélanger) b & bp 8 & 9 Jan 1848, St. Augustin, QC; d 10 Mar 1926, Ecorse, MI.

Gédéon Sanche arrived in the United States as a young man around 1865 and became known generally as Gideon Sanch. He was first a laborer in Ecorse, MI, and then a butcher there from at least 1900 on. He and his wife had six children of whom four, Ellen, Melvena, John B., and Edith, were still alive in 1900 (US censuses). He and his wife were buried in St. Joseph Cemetery in Ecorse.

Children:

i   **Ellen E. Sanch** b 6 Jul 1871, Ecorse, MI; d 17 Sep 1947, Los Angeles Co., CA. She married 1898? **Thomas LeBlanc** (Thomas LeBlanc & Adeline Mc Quillen) b 8 Oct 1870, Ecorse, MI; d 7 Feb 1944, Los Angeles Co., CA.

ii   **Melvena Sanch** b 28 May 1873, Ecorse, MI; d 10 Apr 1956, Los Angeles, CA. She married 1894? **Francis Columbus Drouillard** (Toussaint Drouillard & Susanne Paré/Susan Parry) b & bp 13 & 29 Apr 1866, Ecorse, MI.

iii   **John Baptist Augustus Sanch** b 8 Aug 1876, Ecorse, MI; d 10 May 1938, Pittsfield, MI. He married 31 Dec 1902 **Eugenia Laura/Jennie Chase** (Jacob Chase & Joanna ____) b 16 May 1885, Canada; d 13 Oct 1931, Mooreville, MI.

iv   **Edith Sanch** b Nov 1879, Ecorse, MI.

v   **William Albert Sanch** b & bp 25 Aug & 2 Sep 1883, Ecorse, MI; d before 1900.

3.9.3.3.2   **MONTIE, Philomene Elizabeth** (twin) b & bp 1 & 2 Nov 1849, Ecorse, MI; d there 4 Apr 1927. She married there 6 Sep 1875 **Charles Louis Ouellette** (Patrick Ouellette & Margaret Longtin) b 1 Aug 1848, Detroit, MI; d 1930, Ecorse, MI.

Charles Ouellette (also Ouelette) was a house carpenter in Ecorse, MI (US censuses).

Children:

i   **Edward Albert Ouellette** b 11 Jun 1876, Ecorse, MI. He married 1903? **Anna Mabel Somers** (Thomas H. Summers/Somers & Mary ____) b Dec 1879, Ecorse, MI.

ii   **Emma Ouellette** b Feb 1878, Ecorse, MI. She married 1906?, as his second wife **Alfred Herman Leblanc** (Abraham Leblanc & Felicity/Phyllis Paré) b 26 Jun 1867, Ecorse, MI; d 15 Jul 1956.

iii   **John Elijah Ouellette** b 28 Jul 1879, Ecorse, MI. He married 1909? **Florence ____** b 1889?, OH.

    iv   **Charlotte Susan Ouellette** b 2 Jan 1884, Bay City, MI; d 5 Jun 1944. She married 14 Nov 1907, Detroit, MI, **Wilbur Charles Price** b there 19 Dec 1883; d 1959.

3.9.3.3.3   **MONTIE, Alexander Francis Xavier** b & bp 6 & 8 Jul 1851, Ecorse, MI; d 1935. He married **Minnie Strang** b 1856; d 1936.

    Alex Montie was a member of his father's household in Ecorse, MI, in 1860 (US census). I have been unable to trace him in later years and know of his marriage and death only through Christian Denissen's *Genealogy of the French Families of the Detroit River Region, 1703-1936*, II, 856.

3.9.3.3.4   **MONTIE, Elijah John** b & bp 20 & 23 Mar 1853, Ecorse, MI; d there 1 Jul 1933. He married (1) there 26 Sep 1882 **Mary Ferstl** (John Ferstl & Catherine Steinburger) b there 22 Aug 1861; d 31 Oct 1952, Wyandotte, MI.

    He was divorced when he married (2) between 1910 and 1920 **Theresa ____** b 1887?, MI.

    Elijah Montie held a variety of occupations in Ecorse, MI. He was a laborer in 1900, a saloon keeper in 1910, a school janitor in 1920 when his wife Theresa was 32 years old, and a railroad watchman in 1930 (US censuses).

    Mary Ferstl was said to be a widow in 1910 when she was living with her daughter Ellen in Wyandotte, MI, in 1910 (US census). That is obviously incorrect.

Children of the first marriage:

3.9.3.3.4.1	Elijah John	1884-1909-1970
3.9.3.3.4.2	Joseph Gabriel	1885- -1885
3.9.3.3.4.3	Ellen Laura	1891-1909&1911-1949

3.9.3.3.5   **MONTIE, Richard Anthony** b & bp 6 & 10 Feb 1855, Ecorse, MI; d there 4 Jul 1946. He married there 12 Feb 1877 **Eliza Cicotte** (Joseph Cicotte & Domitilla/Matilda Leblanc) b there 25 Dec 1857; d there 9 Feb 1931.

    Richard Montie was a laborer in Ecorse, MI, at his marriage, a farmer in 1889 at the birth of his son Charles Benjamin, and a railroad worker from at least 1900 on. He was retired in 1930 (US censuses). Both he and his wife were buried in St. Francis Xavier Cemetery in Ecorse.

Children:

3.9.3.3.5.1	Estella Anna	1878-1898-1954
3.9.3.3.5.2	Richard Columbus	1881-1907-1927
3.9.3.3.5.3	Isabella/Bella	1883-1902-1977
3.9.3.3.5.4	Joseph Edward	1886-1911-1975
3.9.3.3.5.5	Charles Benjamin	1889-1916-1924

3.9.3.3.6   **MONTIE, William Henry** b & bp 4 & 8 May 1857, Ecorse, MI; d & bur there 10 & 13 Nov 1902. He married there 1 Jun 1881 **Aurelia Emily/Amelia Cicotte** (John Baptist Cicotte & Josephine Zoe Metay) b & bp there 18 & 30 Aug 1861; d there 21 Jul 1921.

    William Montie was a laborer in Ecorse, MI, at his marriage, a sawyer in 1888 at the birth of his daughter Emma Eliza, a hotel keeper in 1900, and a saloon keeper at his death. His widow was living there in 1910 in the household of her daughter Emma and son-in-law Fred Droste. She had had five children of whom the four named below were still alive. In 1920, in a reversal of roles, she was the head of a household which included her former son-in-law and his second wife, two grandchildren, and a child of Fred Droste's second marriage.

Children:

3.9.3.3.6.1	Maud	1882-1901-
3.9.3.3.6.2	Louisa Genevieve/Viva	1883-1903-
3.9.3.3.6.3	William John	1885-1909-

3.9.3.3.6.4   Emma Eliza   1888-1907-1910

3.9.3.3.7   **MONTIE, John Baptist** b & bp 24 & 28 Nov 1859, Ecorse, MI; d there 30 Sep 1934. He married there 21 Jun 1887 **Ellen Dubeau** (John Baptist Dubeau & Archange Paré) b & bp there 2 & 7 Apr 1866.
     John Baptist Montie was a sawyer in Ecorse, MI, in 1900 and a carpenter there from at least 1910 through 1930 (US censuses).

Children:
3.9.3.3.7.1   Elsie M./Helen Marie   1888-1907-
3.9.3.3.7.2   John Baptist   1892-1916&1935-1969

3.9.3.3.8   **MONTIE, Francis Jonas** b & bp 18 Aug & 1 Sep 1861, Ecorse, MI; d 2 May 1923, Detroit, MI. He married 25 Aug 1885, Ecorse, MI, **Susan Bondie** (Antoine Bondie & Maria Smith) b there May 1864.
     Francis Montie was a foreman and superintendent in various enterprises in Ecorse, MI. His widow was still living there in 1930 with the family of her daughter Ada and son-in-law Adray Labadie (US censuses).
     Francis Montie was buried in Holy Cross Cemetery in Detroit, MI.

Children:
3.9.3.3.8.1   Francis Xavier   1887-1910-
3.9.3.3.8.2   Leo Anthony   1889-1911-1933
3.9.3.3.8.3   Louis Russell   1894-   -1894
3.9.3.3.8.4   Ada Suzanne   1897-1919-

3.9.3.3.9   **MONTIE, Emma Ellen** b & bp 18 & 30 Aug 1863, Ecorse, MI; bur 1952, Port Huron, MI. She married 17 Jan 1887, Ecorse, MI, **Gustavus A. Rogers** (John Rogers & Julia Lavaley) b 10 Aug 1857, St. Clair Co., MI; d 30 Oct 1905, Port Huron, MI.
     Gustavus A. Rogers was a marine engineer in Port Huron, MI. His widow remained there with her children until at least 1910. By 1920 though she was in Detroit, MI, with her three youngest children while in 1930 she was living in South Bend, IN, with her daughter Achthah and son-in-law Elmer Prue (US censuses). She and her husband were buried in Mount Hope Cemetery in St. Clair Co., MI.

Children:
i   **Blanche Rogers** b 3 Dec 1887, Port Huron, MI; d 27 Jul 1941, Marine City, MI. She married 30 Nov 1907 **Russell Frank Ouellette** (François Ouellette & Catherine Lavely) b 10 May 1888, Marine City, MI; d there 28 Jul 1946.
ii   **Gustavus A. Rogers** b 6 Apr 1892, Port Huron, MI; d 19 May 1971, Allen Park, MI. He married 1919? **Leona May Collins** (Charles Collins & Cecilia ____) b Jan 1898, Toledo, OH; d 1936.
iii   **Albert Lewis Rogers** b 8 Nov 1894, Port Huron, MI; d 27 Sep 1974, Lincoln Park, MI. He married **Harriet ____**.
iv   **John B. Rogers** b 27 Sep 1897, Port Huron, MI; d 6 Aug 1982, Southfield, MI. He married **Florence E. ____** b 5 Feb 1902; d 27 Jan 1990, Garden City, MI.
v   **Achthah/Achtha/Asthah Rogers** b 6 Nov 1899, Port Huron, MI; d 16 Oct 1986, South Bend, IN. She married 1923? **Elmer Ernest Prue** (Frank Prue & Carrie ___) b 20 Apr 1896, Detroit, MI; d 13 Apr 1971, South Bend, IN.

3.9.3.3.10   **MONTIE, Albert L.** b & bp 16 & 21 Mar 1866, Ecorse, MI; d there 29 Dec 1930. He married there 5 Nov 1894, Ecorse, MI, **Julia Ann McQuade** (Owen McQuade & Julia Foley) b there 24 Aug 1870.
     Albert Montie was a laborer in Ecorse, MI, for most of his life and was living in retirement there with his wife in April 1930 (US censuses). He was buried in St. Mary's Cemetery in Rockwood, MI, while his wife was buried in Holy Sepulcher Cemetery in Southfield,

MI.

Children:

| 3.9.3.3.10.1 | Albert John | 1896-1919-1936 |
| 3.9.3.3.10.2 | Earl Eugene | 1899-1921&1927-1978 |

3.9.3.5.1 **MONTIE, Julia/Judith** b Sep 1862, Ecorse, MI; d & bur there 1944. She married there 23 Jan 1883 **Simon Peter Drouillard** (Simon Solomon/Samuel Drouillard & Sarah Ann Metay) b there 10 May 1862; d & bur there 1940.

This woman married under the name of Judith Montie. Yet all the censuses and Vital Records I have seen, both before and after her marriage, name her Julia. I believe that to be correct.

Simon Drouillard was described in the 1880 census in Ecorse as the adopted son of Lewis (3.9.3.2) and Frances Montie. In 1900, when the widowed Frances (Pilon) Montie was living in Simon Drouillard's household, she was termed his stepmother, which is less likely.

Simon Drouillard was in turn a laborer, a farmer, and a carpenter in Ecorse, MI (US censuses). Both he and his wife were buried there in St. Francis Xavier Cemetery.

Children:

i   **Anonymous** (female) **Drouillard** b & d 8 Nov 1883, Ecorse, MI.

ii   **Elizabeth M. Drouillard** b Dec 1885, Ecorse, MI; d & bur 1951, Algonac, MI. She married 16 Nov 1904, Ecorse, MI, **Nelson M. Genaw** (Gregory Genaw & Mary Ann Sharrow) b 30 Aug 1882, Clay, MI; d 28 Oct 1946, Algonac, MI.

iii **Frances L. Drouillard** b 21 Jun 1888, Ecorse, MI. She married 24 Jul 1906, Algonac, MI, **David G. Genaw** (Gregory Genaw & Mary Ann Sharrow) b 28 Sep 1889, Clay, MI.

iv   **Josephine V. Drouillard** b May 1890, Ecorse, MI. She married 1912? **Evelyn Saavedra** b 1886?, Spain; d 1934, at the age of 48.

v   **Gertrude S. Drouillard** b Sep 1894, Ecorse, MI. She married 1915? **Lorenzo Louis Gee** (Laurent/Lawrence Gee & Philomene/Felicity Summerfield) b 11 Apr 1890, Wyandotte, MI.

vi   **Arthur Drouillard** b 17 January 1896, Ecorse, MI; d there 28 Jan 1896.

3.9.3.5.2 **MONTIE, Elizabeth** b 1863?, Ecorse, MI; d 1884. She was 18 years old when she married 10 Jan 1882, Ecorse, MI, **Philip Bouley** (Charles Bouley & Marie Poupard) b 8 Aug 1861, Rockwood, MI.

The year of Elizabeth Montie's death is taken from Christian Denissen's *Genealogy of the French Families ...*, II, 856.

Philip Bouley (also Bulley, Bully) was a laborer in Rockwood, MI, at his marriage and in Ash, MI, in 1900. He was a farmer in Berlin Twp, MI, in 1910 when his household included his widowed mother and his daughter's family (US censuses). I have not found him in later censuses.

Child:

i   **Ida Bouley/Bulley** b 5 May 1884, MI; d Sep 1968, Monroe, MI. She married 1904? **Benjamin Barron** (Eli Barron & Philomena Mercure) b 3 Mar 1879, Newport, MI.

3.9.3.5.3 **MONTIE, Louis** b & d 1864, Ecorse, MI (Denissen, *Genealogy of the French Families ...*, II, 856).

3.9.3.5.4 **MONTIE, Cecilia** b & d 1866, Ecorse, MI (Denissen, *Genealogy of the French Families ...*, II, 856).

3.9.3.5.5 **MONTIE, Noah** b 28 Jun 1868, Ecorse, MI; d between 1910 and 1920, Detroit, MI. He married there 6 Nov 1888 **Mary Elizabeth Sarazin** (John Sarazin & ____) b Aug 1866, MI; d 1927, Detroit, MI.

Noah Montie was a carpenter in Detroit, MI, until at least 1910 (US censuses). He died in 1925 and was buried in the Holy Cross Cemetery in Detroit, according to Denissen, *Genealogy of the French Families ...*, II, 857. I believe that year of death to be wrong: Mrs. Mary E. Montie was already a widow in 1920 (US census).

Children:

3.9.3.5.5.1	Martha	1889-1910-
3.9.3.5.5.2	Joseph	1891- -1916
3.9.3.5.5.3	Alfred Octave	1892- -1901
3.9.3.5.5.4	Albert Felix	1893-1917& -1971
3.9.3.5.5.5	Edward Charles	1895-1920?-
3.9.3.5.5.6	Lillian Elenor	1896-1919?-1980
3.9.3.5.5.7	John L.	1898- -1898
3.9.3.5.5.8	Viola Mary	1899-1924?-1971
3.9.3.5.5.9	Frances	1901- -1902
3.9.3.5.5.10	George Ernest	1903- -
3.9.3.5.5.11	Walter	1905- -1991
3.9.3.5.5.12	Donald Elmer (twin)	1907-1935-1981
3.9.3.5.5.13	Dorothy Ellen (twin)	1907- -1908
3.9.3.5.5.14	Rose Maria Agnes	1909- -

3.9.3.5.6   **MONTIE, Antoine/Anthony** b 13 Jun 1870, Ecorse, MI; d there 25 Jan 1957. He married 9 Feb 1892, Detroit, MI, **Edwidge/Addie Lacroix** (Emmanuel Lacroix & Elizabeth Foster) b & bp 30 May & 8 Jun 1871, Ecorse, MI; d there 26 Mar 1947.

Antoine Montie was a wood turner in a shipyard in Detroit, MI, at his marriage, in Springwells, MI, in 1900, in Algonac, MI, in 1910, and in Ecorse, MI, in 1920 and later years (US censuses). He and his wife were buried in the Michigan Memorial Cemetery in Flat Rock, MI.

Children:

3.9.3.5.6.1	Irene Marie	1894-1922-1977
3.9.3.5.6.2	Thomas Levi	1896- -
3.9.3.5.6.3	Marie Edith	1901-1925-1986
3.9.3.5.6.4	Dora E.	1904- -1982
3.9.3.5.6.5	Bernard Robert	1910-1933&1940-1973
3.9.3.5.6.6	Virginia	1914-1933-1980

3.9.3.5.7   **MONTIE, Virginia Josephine** b & bp 28 Jan & 1 Feb 1872, Ecorse, MI. She married 9 Sep 1902, Delray, MI, **Peter Klasen** (Nicholas Klasen & Elizabeth Eiden) b 4 Jun 1865, Detroit, MI; d & bur there 30 Mar & 2 Apr 1920.

Peter Klasen was a house painter in Detroit, MI, in 1900 and a contractor there in 1910 when his mother-in-law Virginia Lacroix was a member of his household (US censuses). He was buried in Detroit's Holy Cross Cemetery.

Children:

i   **Margaret M. Klasen** b 6 Aug 1903, Detroit, MI.
ii   **Gertrude J. Klasen** b 1904?, Detroit, MI.

3.9.3.5.8   **MONTIE, Charles Peter** b 22 Jul 1873, Wayne Co., MI. He married 28 Nov 1899, Delray, MI, **Charlotte Atwood** (Charles Atwood & Minnie Deneau/Deneaux) b 21 Mar 1883, Springwells, MI; d & bur 19 & 21 Aug 1947, Ecorse, MI.

Charles Montie was a machinist in Delray, MI, at his marriage and in Springwells, MI, and Ecorse, MI, in later years. He was a shipyard carpenter in Ecorse in 1920 and a machinist in a lumber yard there in 1930. His household then included a 14-year-old adopted son, George Montie, born in Michigan of Belgian parents (US censuses).

Charlotte Atwood survived her husband and all but two of her children, Arthur and

Bernadette (*Detroit News*, 20 Aug 1947).

Children:

3.9.3.5.8.1	Arthur Aloysius	1900-1920-1959
3.9.3.5.8.2	Wilfrid	1903- -1903
3.9.3.5.8.3	Marcella	1904- -1905
3.9.3.5.8.4	Bernadette Gertrude	1907-1933-1999
3.9.3.5.8.5	Levi Joseph	1909- -1916

3.9.3.5.9   **MONTIE, Francis** b May 1875, St. Charles, MI; d there 30 Mar 1877 at the age of 1 year and 10 months.

3.9.3.5.10   **MONTIE, Augustus** b 1877?, St. Charles, MI.
Augustus Montie was a 3-year-old child living with his parents in St. Charles, MI, in 1880 (US census).

3.9.3.5.11   **MONTIE, Matilda** b Jan 1881, St. Charles, MI. She married 1905? **John McEachan** b 1870?, Canada.
Matilda Montie and her husband apparently lived in Canada for a time after their marriage for their first child was born there. The family was back in the United States however by 1912 when a son was born in Detroit, MI. John McEachan was a 50-year-old teamster there in 1920 and a 59-year-old lumber yard laborer in 1930 when he and his wife had been married for twenty-five years (US censuses).

Children:
i   **Jessie McEachan** b 1908?, Canada.
ii   **Allen P. McEachan** b 10 Apr 1912, Detroit, MI; d 18 Jul 1980, Melvindale, MI.
iii **John Lawrence McEachan** b 16 Jun 1914, Detroit, MI; d 10 Oct 1973, Eustis, FL. He married **Mary Helen ____** b 26 Nov 1916; d 30 Nov 1997, Eustis, FL.

3.9.3.6.1   **MONTIE, Philomene** b 6 Apr 1859, Ecorse, MI; d there 27 Mar 1893. She married there 2 Jun 1890 **Henry LeBlanc** (Thomas LeBlanc & Thecla Bourassa) b 17 Sep 1844, Detroit, MI; m (2) 8 May 1894, Ecorse, MI, Marie Philomene Bondie/Bondy; d & bur there 21 & 25 Apr 1910.
Henry LeBlanc, a farmer in Ecorse, MI, was a half-brother of Lillian LeBlanc, wife of Alexander A. Montie (3.9.3.6.2). He and his first wife were buried in St. Francis Xavier Cemetery in Ecorse.

Child:
i   **Anonymous Leblanc** b & d 17 Jun 1891, Ecorse, MI.

3.9.3.6.2   **MONTIE, Alexander A.** b 8 Jul 1861, Ecorse, MI; d there 8 Dec 1924. He married there 17 Feb 1890 **Lillian Adeline LeBlanc** (Thomas LeBlanc & Adeline/Ida McQuillan) b there 29 Mar 1869; d & bur 21 & 25 Jan 1916, River Rouge & Wyandotte, MI.
Alex A. Montie was a farmer in Ecorse, MI, until at least 1910 and a laborer in a chemical plant in River Rouge, MI, in 1920 (US censuses).
Lillian LeBlanc, a half-sister of Henry LeBlanc, husband of Philomene Montie (3.9.3.6.1), was buried in Mt. Carmel Cemetery in Wyandotte. MI.

Children:

3.9.3.6.2.1	Thomas Antoine	1891-1920?-
3.9.3.6.2.2	Ellen	1892- -1896
3.9.3.6.2.3	Eli/Isaac	1895- -1899
3.9.3.6.2.4	George Sylvester	1896-1916?-1965
3.9.3.6.2.5	Walter E.	1898- -1899

3.9.3.6.2.6	Charlotte Adelina	1899-	-1996
3.9.3.6.2.7	Anna Ida	1901-	-1993
3.9.3.6.2.8	Anonymous	1904-	-1904

3.9.3.6.3 **MONTIE, Joseph** b & bp 27 Sep & 4 Oct 1863, Ecorse, MI; d 14 Aug 1947, Wyandotte, MI. He married 29 Jan 1907, River Rouge, MI, **Lillian Rose LeBlanc** (Samuel LeBlanc & Delia Dugrey) b 24 Jan 1880, Ecorse, MI; d 23 Jan 1956, Wyandotte, MI.

Joseph Montie was a farmer in Ecorse, MI, in 1910, a retired farmer at the birth of a child in 1917, and a laborer there in 1920 and in Lincoln Park, MI, in 1930 (US censuses). Both he and his wife were buried in Mount Carmel Cemetery in Wyandotte, MI.

Lillian Rose LeBlanc was a sister of Victor LeBlanc, husband of Emma Ida Montie (3.9. 3.6.4.1).

Children:
| 3.9.3.6.3.1 | Beatrice | 1907-1926-1983 |
| 3.9.3.6.3.2 | Adele Catherine | 1917-1958- |

3.9.3.6.4 **MONTIE, John A.** b & bp 18 & 22 Jul 1866, Ecorse, MI; d there 31 Jul 1932. He married there 5 Feb 1894 **Philomene/Phyllis Ida Bourassa** (Alexander Bourassa & Elizabeth Bondie) b & bp there 23 & 25 Jul 1875; d there 1963.

John A. Montie lived in Ecorse, MI, for most of his life, first as a farmer until at least 1910, as a retiree in 1920, and then as a packer in an alkali plant in 1930 (US censuses). Both he and his wife were buried in St. Francis Xavier Cemetery there.

Children:
3.9.3.6.4.1	Emma Ida	1895-1915-1988
3.9.3.6.4.2	Eleanor	1898-1915&1922-1971
3.9.3.6.4.3	Albert J.	1900-1920?-1979
3.9.3.6.4.4	Walter Alexander	1902-1923-1994
3.9.3.6.4.5	Vina E./Melvina	1904-1923-1988
3.9.3.6.4.6	Mabel G.	1907-1937-1988

3.9.3.6.5 **MONTIE, Charles Louis** b & bp 19 May 1868, Ecorse, MI; d there 1868 (Denissen, *Genealogy of the French Families ...*, II, 856).

3.9.3.6.6 **MONTIE, Leonora/Angeline** b & bp 9 & 16 Jan 1870, Ecorse, MI; d there 8 Oct 1887.

This child appears under the name of Angeline in the 1880 US census in Ecorse, MI. In all other records her name is Leonora.

3.9.3.6.7 **MONTIE, Gabriel** b & bp 9 & 12 Nov 1871, Ecorse, MI; d there 1942. He married there 22 Nov 1910 **Olive Steffes** (Anthony Steffes & Alice ____) b 1889?, MI.

Gabriel Montie was a plant foreman in Ecorse, MI, at his marriage, when his bride was 21 years old, and a chemical plant worker in 1920 and 1930. His wife was then still alive (US censuses). He was buried in St. Francis Xavier Cemetery in Ecorse.

Children:
3.9.3.6.7.1	Edward Gabriel	1913-	-2008
3.9.3.6.7.2	Margaret	1914-1934-	
3.9.3.6.7.3	Robert Donald	1919-	-1980
3.9.3.6.7.4	Mary Jane	1924-	-

3.9.3.6.8 **MONTIE, Peter R.** b & bp 24 & 26 Sep 1875, Ecorse, MI; d & bur there 23 & 26 Nov 1918. He married (1) there 8 Jan 1901 **Mary Josephine Labadie** (Joseph Labadie & Julia Bondie) b & bp there 6 May & 27 Jun 1880; d & bur there 2 & 5 Jul 1907.

He married (2) 27 Oct 1908, Ecorse, MI, **Anna Champagne** (William Champagne &

Mary Cicotte) b there Aug 1885; m (2) 1921? John St. Amant.

Peter Montie was a farmer in Ecorse, MI, at his first marriage, a sawmill worker there in 1910, and a laborer there when he died.

In 1930 Anna Champagne had been married for nine years to John St. Amant whose household in Ecorse also included his stepdaughters Hazel and Myrtle Montie (US censuses).

Child of the first marriage:

3.9.3.6.8.1	Anonymous	1907-	-1907

Children of the second marriage:

3.9.3.6.8.2	Richard Herbert	1909-	-1910
3.9.3.6.8.3	Hazel Elizabeth	1912-1934-1979	
3.9.3.6.8.4	Myrtle Frances	1914-1936-	

4.3.1.1.1   **MONTY, ____** (male) b between 1825 and 1830, Chazy, NY.

Lewis Monty and his wife had a son of less than 5 years in 1830. He was between 10 and 15 years old in 1840 (US censuses, Chazy, NY).

4.3.1.1.2   **MONTY, Jane** b 1832?, Chazy, NY.

Jane (also M. Jane, Mary J., Mary Jane) Monty was 18 years old in 1850 when she was living with her parents in Chazy, NY. She was still single and living in her mother's household there in 1880 (US censuses).

4.3.1.1.3   **MONTY, Lydia** b 1838?, Chazy, NY; d & bur 15 & 17 Nov 1918, Mechanicville, NY. She married 1860? **Andrew Dusham/Ducharme** (François Ducharme & Marie Riel dit Lirlande) b 1840?, NY; d 20 Aug 1927, Mechanicville, NY.

Lydia Monty was 12 years old in 1850 when she was living with her parents in Chazy, NY. Later censuses point to many different years of birth: she may have been born around 1830, 1832, 1833, or 1840 and was either the same age as, ten years younger than, or ten years older than her husband. Her age at death is no better known: she was either 81 years old, according to the records of the Cassidy Funeral Home in Mechanicville, NY, or 89 years old, according to the inscription on her tombstone in Hudson View Cemetery there.

Similar uncertainties surround her husband's age. Andrew Dusham (André Ducharme in the French records of St. Joseph's Church in West Chazy, NY) might have been born in 1829, 1830, 1840, 1841, or 1843, according to various censuses, or in 1837, according to the inscription on his tombstone in Hudson View Cemetery in Mechanicville. He was a farm laborer in Chazy and West Chazy until at least 1910 and then moved to Mechanicville with his wife to stay with their daughter Anna and her husband. He was still living there in his son-in-law Leonard Rood's household in 1930. In 1900, he and his wife had been married for forty years (US censuses).

Children:

i   **Martha Dusham** b 1867?, Chazy, NY.

ii   **Anna L. Dusham** b 1871?, Chazy, NY; d & bur 11 & 14 Oct 1928, Mechanicville, NY. She married 1898? **Leonard Rood** b May 1876, Beekmantown, NY.

iii   **Elsie/Elsa Dusham** b Jul 1876?, Chazy, NY. She married there 29 Jul 1895 **Edward Abare** b Aug 1873?, NY.

4.3.1.1.4   **MONTY, Joseph** b 1842?, Chazy, NY; d between 1892 and 1910. He married **Sarah Thompson** (William Thompson & Betsey/Elizabeth Methot) b 1852?, Champlain, NY; d 29 Aug 1924, Chazy, NY.

Joseph Monty, who was 8 years old in 1850, was a farmer and laborer in Chazy, NY, until at least 1892. I do not find the family there in the 1900 US census though Mrs. Sarah Monty, a widow, was holding household there in 1910 for her sons Thomas and William. She had had seven children of whom six were still alive (US and state censuses).

Sarah Thompson, a first cousin of Frances/Fanny Methot, wife of James R. Monty

(4.10.6.2), was 18 years old in 1870 (US census). She died at the home of her son Charles in Chazy (*Plattsburgh Sentinel*, 2 Sep 1924).

Children:

4.3.1.1.4.1	Henry W.	1873?- -
4.3.1.1.4.2	Nellie J.	1877?- -
4.3.1.1.4.3	Joseph Willis	1879-1899?-1946
4.3.1.1.4.4	Thomas	1882-1910-
4.3.1.1.4.5	Ellis	1885?- -
4.3.1.1.4.6	Charles H.	1886-1909-1962
4.3.1.1.4.7	William	1889-1919-1965

4.3.1.1.5　　　**MONTY, Sylvia** b 1843?, Chazy, NY.
　　　Sylvia Monty was a 7-year-old child living with her parents in Chazy, NY, in 1850. She does not appear with them in 1860 (US censuses).

4.3.1.1.6　　　**MONTY, William** b 1846?, Chazy, NY. He married **Catherine/Katie Graves** (James Graves & Marceline ____) b 1846?, Beekmantown, NY; m (1) Damase Martin (Antoine Martin & Angélique ____).
　　　William Monty was a 4-year-old child living with his parents in Chazy, NY, in 1850 and was a farm laborer there in 1880 when his wife was 34 years old (US censuses). The couple apparently moved in the 1880s to Grand Isle, VT, for Mrs. Kate Monty was living there in 1890 when she was identified as the former widow of Demas (sic) Martin, a private in Co. F, 96th New York Infantry Regiment, who was killed in action in Cold Harbor, VA, on 3 Jun 1864 (Veterans Schedule). I have found no later reference to William Monty or his wife.

Children:

4.3.1.1.6.1	Ada	1873-1891?/1894-1956
4.3.1.1.6.2	Anna/Hannah	1875-1889& -1940
4.3.1.1.6.3	William Alexander	1883-1910-1947

4.3.1.2.1　　　**MONTY, Thomas** b 1830?, Chazy, NY. He married **Mary Ariel/Riel** b 1839?, Canada.
　　　Thomas Monty was 20 years old in 1850 when he was living with his parents in Essex, NY. According to later censuses though he may have been born as late as 1837. By June 1855 he and his 17-year-old wife Mary were living in Lewis, NY, in a modest frame house valued at $100. He was then a laborer and in 1860, a bloomer there. He may have lived for a short time in Vermont: although he was a member of his father's household in Lewis in 1865, the state census notes that he was married and usually employed in Vermont. His wife and children were not with him. In fact one child was baptized a few months later, on 1 Jan 1866, in Stanbridge, QC.
　　　The family soon returned to New York State where all the other children were born. Thomas Monty was a laborer in Elizabethtown, NY, in 1870, a collier in 1875, and a farmer in 1880. The family moved to Wisconsin in the mid-1880s for several children married there from 1889 on, generally under the surname Montay. Thomas Montai (sic), a widower, was living in Wausau, WI, in 1900 with five of his children who were still single.
　　　Mary Ariel (also Riel, Rielle, Arieu) is generally said to have been born in Canada. In two state censuses in Lewis, though, her place of birth is said to be Clinton Co., NY.

Children:

4.3.1.2.1.1	Amos	1856?- -
4.3.1.2.1.2	William	1858?-1889-
4.3.1.2.1.3	Henry C.	1861-1889&1895-
4.3.1.2.1.4	Willis	1864?- -
4.3.1.2.1.5	Elizabeth	1865-1883?-
4.3.1.2.1.6	Mary	1868?-1892-

4.3.1.2.1.7	Emily/Millie	1872?- -
4.3.1.2.1.8	Albert J.	1874-1894-
4.3.1.2.1.9	Bertrand/Bert	1876- -
4.3.1.2.1.10	John T.	1879-1901-
4.3.1.2.1.11	Alicia	1881- -
4.3.1.2.1.12	Catherine	1882-1903-1925

4.3.1.2.2 **MONTY, Oliver** b & bp 20 May 1833, Iberville, QC.

Although born in Canada, Oliver Monty (Olivier at his baptism) was brought up in Chazy, NY. He moved to Essex, NY, with his parents in the mid-1840s and was a laborer there in 1850, living in his father's household (US census). I have not found him in any later census.

4.3.1.2.3 **MONTY, Henry** b 1839?, Chazy, NY; d between 1900 and 1905. He married Jul 1869, NY, **Betsey/Bessie** _____ b May 1853, Essex Co., NY; m (2) 1905?, John Betters; d 25 Jan 1927, Black Brook, NY.

Henry Monty was an 11-year-old child living with his parents in Essex, NY, in 1850. He was a farm laborer in Lewis, NY, in 1860 and 1865, a laborer in 1870 and a blacksmith there in 1880. By 1900 he was a plaster mason in North Elba, NY. He and his wife had had three children, only one of whom, Mary Jane, was still alive (US and state censuses).

Mrs. Bessie Betters had been married to her second husband for five years in 1910 and lived with him in Black Brook, NY, until her death (US censuses).

Children:
4.3.1.2.3.1	Mary Jane/Jennie	1870-1888-1929
4.3.1.2.3.2	Sophia	1872- -
4.3.1.2.3.3	Carrie	1873- -

4.3.1.2.4 **MONTY, William** b 1840?, Chazy, NY; d & bur ? & 13 Dec 1897, Moriah & Lewis, NY.

William Monty came to Essex Co., NY, with his parents in the mid-1840s and was a teamster and/or laborer in Lewis, NY, through most of his life. He did not marry but appears to have become the "head of the family" after his father's death: his household in 1880 included not only his sister Caroline (4.3.1.2.8) but also the wife and child of his brother Jerome (4.3.1.2.9). His sister was in turn keeping house for him in Lewis in 1892 (US and state censuses). He had moved to Moriah, NY, a short time before his death (*Ticonderoga Sentinel*, 16 Dec 1897).

4.3.1.2.5 **MONTY, Mitchell** b 1841?, Chazy, NY.

Mitchell Monty came to Essex Co., NY, with his parents on the mid-1840s and was living with them in Essex, NY, in 1850 and 1855, when he was 14 years old (US and state censuses). I have not found him in later years.

4.3.1.2.6 **MONTY, Sophia** b & bp 9 Mar & 9 Jul 1843, Chazy & Coopersville, NY; d & bur 17 & 20 May 1920, Moriah, NY.

Sophia Monty came to Essex Co., NY, with her parents in the mid-1840s and was a member of her father's household in Essex and Lewis, NY, until at least 1875 (US and state censuses). She did not marry and died at the home of her sister Caroline (4.3.1.2.8) in Moriah, NY (*Ticonderoga Sentinel*, 27 May 1920).

4.3.1.2.7 **MONTY, Jane** b 1845?, Essex, NY.

Jane Monty was a 5-year-old child living with her parents in Essex, NY, in 1850. She was also with them in 1855 but does not appear with her family after that date (US and state censuses).

4.3.1.2.8 **MONTY, Caroline Adeline/Carrie A.** b 1848?, Essex, NY; d 1925,

Moriah, NY. She married Jan 1894 **Nathan A. Gale** b Feb 1843, NH; m (1) Susan E. ____; d 28 Feb 1916, Moriah, NY.

Adeline Monty was a 2-year-old child living with her parents in Essex, NY, in 1850. She was named Caroline in the 1855 state census there and in censuses until 1870, after which time she was known as Carrie or Carrie A. Monty. She stayed in her father's household in Essex and in Lewis, NY, and later in her brother William's (4.3.1.2.4) household in Lewis until her marriage. She then lived in Moriah, NY, where Nathan A. Gale was a farmer (US and state censuses). The announcement of their marriage is found in the *Ticonderoga Sentinel* of 22 Jan 1894.

4.3.1.2.9   **MONTY, Jerome** b 1852?, Essex, NY. He married 1878? **Ella** ____ b 1863?, NY.

Jerome Monty was a 3-year-old child living with his parents in Essex, NY, in 1855. He moved with them to Lewis, NY, before 1860 and remained there until at least 1880 when he was a brick mason residing with his 17-year-old wife and one-year-old son in the household of his brother William (4.3.1.2.4) (US and state censuses). I have found no later trace of this family.

Child:
4.3.1.2.9.1   Harry B.   1879-   -

4.3.1.4.1   **MONTY, Amelia** b 1855?, QC. She married 2 Mar 1877, Fall River, MA, **Louis Nadeau** (Grégoire Nadeau & Zoé Langlois) b & bp 27 & 28 Dec 1848, Marieville, QC.

Amelia Monty was 22 years old at her marriage. Louis Nadeau was then a clerk in Fall River, MA. I have found no trace of this couple after the birth of their son.

Child:
i   **Louis J. Nadeau** b 8 Apr 1877, Fall River, MA.

4.3.1.4.2   **MONTY, George** b 1861?, NY.

George Monty was a 9-year-old child living with his parents in Westport, NY, in 1870 (US census).

4.3.2.1.1   **MONTY, James Jacob** b 17 Nov 1872, Essex, NY; d between 1927 and 1930. He married 1895? **Elizabeth Anna Johnpeer** (Joseph Johnpeer & Pauline Shappy) b May 1876, Willsborough, NY; d 6 May 1949, Bridgeport, CT.

James Monty was a farmer in Essex, NY, in 1900, when he and his wife had been married for five years. He moved to Vermont in early March 1902 (*Ticonderoga Sentinel*, 13 Mar 1902) and was a farmer in Castleton and Fair Haven, VT, when his two youngest children were born in 1904 and 1906. He was a machine operator in Bridgeport, CT, when he signed his World War I Draft Registration card in 1917 and a factory worker there until at least 1926 (US censuses; City Directories). His widow continued to live in the area until her death.

Children:

4.3.2.1.1.1	Herbert W.	1895-	-
4.3.2.1.1.2	Ethel	1897-	-1925
4.3.2.1.1.3	Meta Elizabeth	1904-1921?-1949	
4.3.2.1.1.4	Helen Evelyn	1906-1925&1943-1973	

4.3.2.3.1   **MONTY, Nellie A.** b & bp 28 Sep & 15 Nov 1867, Essex & Keeseville, NY; d & bur 8 & 10 Jul 1940, Ticonderoga & Willsboro, NY. She married 21 Oct 1886, Willsboro, NY, **Thomas F. Burroughs** (Horatio Burroughs & Anna Faye) b 1867, Port Kent, NY; d & bur 1953, Ticonderoga & Willsboro, NY.

Thomas Burroughs was a 3-year-old child living with his parents in Chesterfield, NY, in 1870. He was a boatman in Essex, NY, in 1910, a shipyard worker in Shelburne, VT, in 1920, and a paper mill worker in Ticonderoga, NY, in 1930 (US censuses). He and his wife were buried in Calvary Cemetery in Willsboro, NY.

Children:
- i **Mary E./Nellie Burroughs** b & bp 12 & 27 Nov 1887, Essex, NY; d Mar 1973, Hannacroix, NY. She married 15 Sep 1909, Essex, **NY, Joseph Warren Good** (Joseph Good & Adeline Milo) b 17 Feb 1888, Lyon Mountain, NY.
- ii **Horace James Burroughs** b & bp 7 & 20 Sep 1903, Essex, NY; d Aug 1975, Ticonderoga, NY. He married **Florence Helen Trieb** (Baltasar/Balthasar Trieb & Katharine Myers) b 5 Aug 1908, Jericho, VT; d 21 Dec 2000, Ticonderoga, NY.
- iii **Anna Carolina Burroughs** b & bp 25 & 28 Oct 1906, Essex, NY; d 26 Nov 1988, Glens Falls, NY. She married 5 Sep 1932, Ticonderoga, NY, **Howard Maheu** (____ Maheu & Nellie E. Lonergan) b 14 Jan 1906, NY; d Oct 1986, Glens Falls, NY.

4.3.3.3.1   **MONTA, Charles Otis** b 7 Nov 1846, Pownal, VT; d & bur there 19 & 26 Jan 1886.

Charles Otis Monta was a farmer in Pownal, VT. He was buried in the Garden Cemetery there.

4.3.3.3.2   **MONTA, Sylvia Ann** b 10 May 1850, Pownal, VT; d there between 1878 and 1880. She married 26 Mar 1868, Bennington, VT, **Leander Thompson** (Barber Thompson & Sarah A. Brown) b 1842?, Pownal, VT.

Leander Thompson was an 8-year-old child living with his parents in Pownal, VT, in 1850 (US census). He enlisted in the Union Army on 27 Aug 1862 and was a Sergeant in Co. A, 14th Vermont Regiment until his discharge on 30 Jul 1863. He returned to his father's farm in Pownal and was a farmer there until at least 1890. He was a widower in 1880 (US censuses; 1890 Veterans Schedule).

Note: this couple's oldest child, Louie, was a 1-year old male in 1870 and an 11-year-old female in 1880. I have been unable to trace him/her any further.

Children:
- i **Louie Thompson** b 1869?, Pownal, VT.
- ii **Clayton L. Thompson** b Dec 1870, Pownal, VT. He married there 25 Feb 1897 **Blanche Alice Peckham** (Joseph I. Peckham & Adelia Downs) b there Jan 1878.
- iii **Maude Lena Thompson** b 20 Oct 1872, Pownal, VT; d & bur 1957, Bennington, VT. She married 11 Apr 1893 **David Edward Bushnell** (David Bushnell & Lenora A. Barber) b 5 Sep 1868, Bennington, VT; d & bur there 1946.
- iv **Sarah A. Thompson** b 25 Sep 1874, Pownal, VT.
- v **Julie Thompson** b May 1878, Pownal, VT.

4.3.3.3.3   **MONTA, Samuel B.** b 12 Oct 1855, Pownal, VT; d there 11 May 1886. He married around 1878 **Susan Lurana Proud** (Zara/Zerah Potter Proud & Larana/Lurana Mason) b 17 Oct 1858, Bennington, VT.

Samuel B. Monta (also Monte) was a laborer in Pownal, VT, at the births of his children and more specifically a farm laborer in 1880 (US census). He died of consumption.

Children:

4.3.3.3.3.1	Anonymous	1879-	-1879
4.3.3.3.3.2	Maud A.	1881-	-
4.3.3.3.3.3	Blanche	1883-	-1891

4.3.3.4.1   **MONTEE, Melvin Josiah** b 1846?, VT; d 1894/1895. He married 31 Jul 1868, Guthrie Co., IA, **Martha E. Jackson**.

Melvin J. Montee was a 4-year-old child living with his parents in Bennington, VT, in 1850 (US census). He was with them as they moved every few years from Vermont to New York to Wisconsin to Illinois in 1860 and finally to Iowa in the early 1860s. He was a resident of Poweshiek Co, IA, when he enlisted with his father in the Union Army in Iowa City, IA, on 5 Jan 1864. He served as a private in Co. B, 28th Iowa Infantry Regiment, until 18 Jul 1865 when he was mustered out in Washington, DC. He returned to Iowa and married there, though he soon left for the Dakota Territory. He and his wife were among the early homesteaders in Union Co., with land in Alcester Twp as well as in Meridan Twp, where a patent for an 80-acre homestead was issued on 10 Dec 1874 in the name of Martha E. Montee.

The couple otherwise kept a very low profile. I have been unable to find them in any census in Iowa or South Dakota. Melvin Josiah Montee nevertheless applied on 22 Dec 1893 (#188460) for an invalid pension based on his Civil War services. He received it (certificate #1077596) for only a short period of time. By 1895 Mrs. Martha E. Montee began receiving a widow's pension (certificate # 570570).

4.3.3.4.2   **MONTEE, Clara/Clarissa** b 1848?, VT?; d 26 Feb 1930, Hudson, SD. She married (1) 1862? **George Dixon** (William Dixon & Jane ____) b 1843?, England; d 1878?, Eden, SD.

She married (2) Dec 1879, Lincoln Co., SD, **John Smith** b Nov 1847, Canada; d 24 Jun 1939, Hudson, SD.

It is difficult to determine Clara Montee's date and place of birth. She was 2 years old in 1850 when she was living with her parents in Bennington, VT. She had been born in Vermont. Other censuses indicate that she was born between 1846 and 1849 in New York (1860, 1870), Massachusetts (1880, 1920), or Maine (1900, 1910). I have no reason to believe that her parents ever resided in Massachusetts or Maine. I am relying here on the information provided in the earliest census.

Clara Montee moved several times as a child, from Vermont to New York, Wisconsin, Illinois, and, in the mid-1860s, Iowa. She probably married there: her first husband, George Dixon, a 17-year-old resident of Poweshiek Co., IA, in 1860, was a farmer in Washington Twp, IA, in 1870 and 1871 (US censuses; birth record of his second child). The family then left for the Dakota Territory where a third child was born in 1874.

John Smith arrived in the United States in 1868 and became a farmer in Eden, SD, where he was still living in 1930 (US censuses). He and his wife were buried in the Hudson, SD, Cemetery.

Children:
i   **Alice J. Dixon** b May 1869, Dallas Co., IA; d 29 Jul 1937, MT. She married 1889? **Edgerton E. Gibson** (William Henry Gibson & Mary Iles) b 29 May 1865, Rochester, NY; d 25 Oct 1938, MT.

ii   **Anna Margaret Dixon** b 25 May 1871, Dallas Co., IA; d 23 Sep 1948, Santa Barbara, CA. She married 26 Jan 1890, Hudson, SD, **William Albert Iles** (John Iles & Ann Gauntlet) b 29 Jun 1863, Ontario, Canada; d 1 Jun 1934, Santa Barbara, CA.

iii   **Carrie Viola Dixon** b 15 Sep 1875, Eden, SD; d 5 Jan 1914, Belfield, ND. She married 22 Feb 1893, Hudson, SD, **John William Doty** (David Charles Doty & Mary Hopkins) b 9 Aug 1868, Cambridge, IA; d 3 Apr 1944, Belfield, ND.

iv   **George Wilber Dixon** b 5 Jan 1878, Eden, SD; d 31 May 1929, Union Co., SD. He married 20 Jan 1909, Hudson, SD, **Lillian M. Vipond** (John Vipond & Jane Raisbeck) b 27 Sep 1877, WI; d Aug 1970, Hawarden, IA.

v   **Roy Smith** b 3 Oct 1880, Eden, SD; d May 1965, SD. He married 1905? **Cora Belle Miner** (William Louis Miner & Desire Electa Gates) b 29 Mar 1881, Eden, SD; d 1971.

vi   **Ross Esmond Smith** b 3 Apr 1883, Eden, SD; d Oct 1972, Hawarden, IA. He married 18 Jul 1906, Hudson, SD, **Myrtle Lenore Miner** (William Louis Miner & Desire Electa Gates) b 8 Jul 1885, Eden, SD; d Jan 1974, Hudson, SD.

vii   **Leon Dick Smith** b 10 May 1886, Eden, SD; d Sep 1966, Hudson, SD. He married 31 Oct 1927, Madison, SD, **Myrtle E. Lentz** (Frank Lentz & Emma ____) b 30 Jun 1907, Baker, SD; d Jul 1974, Hawarden, IA.

4.3.3.4.3   **MONTEE, Moses Paige** b 1849?, Bennington, VT; d between 1877 and

1880. He married **Mary Sanders Knight** (John Knight & Christina ____) b 15 Feb 1855, Montreal, QC; m (2) 1882? August/Gus Lesemann (Henry Lesemann & Anna ____); d 12 May 1924.

Moses P. Monty was a one-year-old child living with his parents in Bennington, VT, in 1850. He moved West with them through several states and was living on his father's farm in Washington Twp, IA, in 1870. He left a few years later for the Dakota Territory where his oldest child was born. The two youngest however were apparently born in Kansas. Yet in 1880 his 25-year-old widow was staying with two of her daughters in the household of her brother William Knight in Virginia Twp, SD (US censuses).

Mary Knight had been married to her second husband, a railroad engineer in San Marcial, NM, for eighteen years in 1900. She had had six children of whom five, including three from her second marriage, were still alive (US census).

Children:

4.3.3.4.3.1	Mary	1875?-	-
4.3.3.4.3.2	Corta (twin)	1878?-	-
4.3.3.4.3.3	Cuba (twin)	1878?-	-

4.3.3.4.4 **MONTEE, Eunice Clarinda** b 31 Mar 1853, NY; d 28 May 1881, Eden, SD. She married 27 Jan 1870, Dallas Co., IA, **Peterson Pierce** (Thomas Pierce & Elizabeth ____) b Mar 1848, PA; d Niobrara, NE.

Clarinda Montee left New York State as a child and moved with her parents to Wisconsin, Illinois, and Iowa. She married there and was staying with her 22-year-old husband, Peterson Pierce, on her father's farm in Washington Twp, IA, in June 1870 (US census). Her first child was born there, though she and her husband moved to Eden, SD, before the birth of their second child in 1875.

Peterson Pierce was a farmer in Eden for most of the rest of his life. By 1930 however he was living in Niobrara, NE, where his son Arthur (iv) had moved around 1926 (US censuses). He had been a private in Co. H, 47th Illinois Infantry Regiment during the Civil War, a fact noted on his tombstone in L'Eau Qui Court Cemetery in Niobrara.

Children:

i   **Eva Pierce** b 1872?, Dallas Co., IA.

ii   **Nora/Eleonora Pierce** b 27 Mar 1875, Eden, SD. She married 1899? **John Brown** b Jan 1875, IA.

iii   **Thomas Willard Pierce** b 15 Feb 1877, Eden, SD; d 19 Feb 1951, Stutsman Co., ND. He married 1905? **Mabel A.** ____ b 31 Jul 1883, IA; d 5 Oct 1962, Stutsman Co., ND.

iv   **James Arthur Pierce** b 9 May 1879, Eden, SD; d & bur 1963, Niobrara, NE. He married 3 Jan 1911, Hudson, SD, **Bertha Solem** b 27 Oct 1892, Norway; d & bur Jun 1983, Niobrara, NE.

4.3.3.4.5 **MONTEE, Thirza** b 28 Apr 1855, WI. She married 1873? **William Knight** (John Knight & Ellen/Elinor McFallen) b 10 Jan 1839, Waterville, ME; d 9 Nov 1909, Hudson, SD.

Thirza (also Thirsey, Thursa, Thursey) Montee was living with her parents in Mercer Co., IL, in 1860 and in Dallas Co., IA. in 1870. She probably married in the Dakota Territory soon after her family's arrival there in the early 1870s. William Knight's family had already relocated there in the 1860s. He was a farmer in Eden, SD, in 1870 and 1880 and in Hudson, SD, in 1900, when he and his wife had been married for twenty-seven years. They had had three children, all of whom were then still alive. Thirza Montee continued to live in Hudson with her son Archie until at least 1930 (US censuses) and was still living there at the death of her sister Austie Emma (4.3.3.4.9) in 1939.

Children:

i   **Archie/Archer Knight** b 1 Jul 1873, Hudson, SD.

    ii   **Mary Knight** b 1874?, Hudson, SD.

    iii   **Fern Knight** b Dec 1879, Hudson, SD.

4.3.3.4.6   **MONTEE, Matthew Perry** 6 Jul 1856, NY; d 4 Apr 1919, Brainerd, MN. He married 7 Apr 1891, Boyer, IA, **Harriet Eleanor/Ella Cone** (Hiram Cone & Harriet Jane Mansfield) b Mar 1872, MO.

Matthew Montee led a somewhat nomadic existence. Various US and state censuses show him living with his parents in Mercer Co., IL, in 1860, in Dallas Co., IA, in 1870, and in Eden, SD, in 1880. He also worked for a time in Kansas before his marriage according to family history: he was a surveyor of timber lands for the railroad, which might explain his later peregrinations. He returned to Iowa where he married in 1891, moved back to South Dakota where his oldest child was born in 1893, and then again to Iowa for the birth of a child in Sioux Co. in 1894. In 1895, though, he was working in Harrison Co., IA. But not for long. His third child was born in Missouri in 1896, and the fourth in Nebraska in 1899. There he remained for at least two years: he was a teamster in Yankee Hill, NE, in 1900. The family then returned to South Dakota where three children were born between 1901 and 1904, before moving on to Minnesota where the last two were born. Matthew Montee had perhaps decided to settle down there: in 1910 he was a farmer in Aitkin Co. (Haugen Twp), MN. He and his wife had then had eight children, all of whom were still alive. He was a resident of McGregor, MN, at his death.

His widow soon left Minnesota: she was living with her children Perry, Mary, Ethel, and Joy in New London, IA, in 1920, and with the two youngest there in 1925. She was an inmate of the Henry Co. Home in Center Twp, IA, in 1930 (US and state censuses).

Children:

4.3.3.4.6.1	Tracy D.	1892-1919?-1934
4.3.3.4.6.2	Jesse Abram	1894-1920& -1961
4.3.3.4.6.3	Hobart Cecil	1896-1922&1939?-1949
4.3.3.4.6.4	Floy	1899- -
4.3.3.4.6.5	Paige	1901?- -1919
4.3.3.4.6.6	Perry	1903?-1927?-
4.3.3.4.6.7	Mary	1904?- -
4.3.3.4.6.8	Ethel	1908?- -
4.3.3.4.6.9	Joy M.	1912-1928?&1936?-2002

4.3.3.4.7   **MONTEE, Mary Jane** b 1859?, WI. She married **John Doherty**.

Mary Jane Montee was a 1-year-old child living with her parents in Mercer Co, IL, in 1860. She moved with them to Washington Twp, IA, before 1870 and to the Dakota Territory in the early 1870s. She was a hotel cook in Eden, SD, in 1880, single, and still staying with her parents (US censuses). I know of her marriage only through Betty Miller Ramsey who also states in her *Monty-Montee History,* p. 145, that Mary Jane Montee died in her early twenties and left no children.

4.3.3.4.8   **MONTEE, Ella May/Nellie** b 11 Aug 1862, Mercer Co., IL; d & bur 8 & ? Aug 1922, Hawarden, IA & Hudson, SD. She married 29 Apr 1883, Niobrara, NE, **Isaac Armstrong** (James Armstrong & Catherine Shupe) b 9 Dec 1853, OH; d & bur 1912, Hudson, SD.

Ella May Montee left Illinois shortly after birth and moved with her parents to Washington Twp, IA, in 1870 and the Dakota Territory in the early 1870s. She was staying in 1880 with her sister Eunice Clarinda (4.3.3.4.4) and brother-in-law Peterson Pierce in Eden, SD. Isaac Armstrong was then a farmer in York Co., NE, living in his brother William's household.

After their marriage the couple remained in Nebraska for a few years before moving on to Kansas, where a child was born in 1887, and then to Iowa, where two others were born in 1889 and 1891. By 1900 Isaac Armstrong was a day laborer in Hudson, SD. He and his wife had then had six children of whom the five listed below were still alive. Both he and his wife were rural mail carriers in Hudson in 1910. She left the area after his death and was the owner of a boarding house in Kansas City, KS, in 1920 (US censuses). She then moved on to Hawarden, IA, where her son Charles (ii) had settled, before her own death two years later. Both she and her husband were buried in the Hudson Cemetery.

Children:

i   **Alta L. Armstrong** b 22 Feb 1884, Creighton, NE; d 21 Dec 1964. She married 1905?, Hudson, SD, **Adam Clinton Pixley** (James Harvey Pixley & Henrietta Hommel) b 27 Dec 1875, York, OH.

ii   **Charles/Charlie Ross Armstrong** b 2 Sep 1885, Creighton, NE; d 12 Dec 1965, Walla Walla, WA. He married 24 Feb 1909, Hudson, SD, **Nora Rolfine Anderson** (Andrew Matthew Anderson & Marie Rasmussen) b there 19 Jun 1890; d 17 Jun 1948, Custer Co., SD.

iii   **Elsie L. Armstrong** b May 1887, KS; d 12 Jun 1934, Yankton, SD. She married 25 Apr 1909, Hudson, SD, **Allen Bedford Clement** (Philip Henry B. Clement & Harriet Allen) b there 11 Jun 1885; d 17 Sep 1944, Rapid City, SD.

iv   **Guy Raymond Armstrong** b 4 Jul 1889, Woodbine, IA.

v   **Carl Just Armstrong** b 5 Jun 1891, Woodbine, IA.

4.3.3.4.9   **MONTEE, Austie Emma** b 1 Jul 1866, Woodbine, IA; d & bur 10 & 13 Sep 1939, Wessington Springs, SD. She married 25 Aug 1885, Niobrara, NE, **James A. Holcomb** (Ruben T. Holcomb & Sarah E. Wilderman) b 16 Dec 1856, Green Co., WI; d & bur 31 Dec 1937 & 3 Jan 1938, Wessington Springs, SD.

Emma Montee was living with her parents in Dallas Co. (Washington Twp), IA, in 1870 and in Eden, SD, in 1880. She and her husband were early homesteaders in Wessington Springs, SD. James Holcomb was a farmer there in 1900 and 1910, an operative in 1920, and a retiree in 1930 (US censuses). He and his wife were buried there in Prospect Hill Cemetery as were their son Robert (viii) and their daughter-in-law Julia Hill, wife of Wendell Holcomb (x).

Children:

i   **Ruby Florence Holcomb** b 27 Jun 1886, Wessington Springs, SD; d 30 Sep 1972, Woonsocket, SD. She married Mar 1908, Wessington Springs, SD, **Burton Leroy Morehead** (Oliver Morehead & Frances Diana Pierson) b 16 Nov 1885, Jerauld Co., SD; d 19 Apr 1961, Hennepin Co., MN.

ii   **Ernest Perry Holcomb** b 16 Dec 1887, Wessington Springs, SD; d 26 Jul 1961, Los Angeles, CA. He married 18 Feb 1914, Wessington Springs, SD, **Edna Hazel Eagle** (William Strite Eagle & Emma Rose Thomas) b 12 Mar 1890, Dale Twp, SD; d 5 Jan 1957, Wessington Springs, SD.

iii   **Jennie May Holcomb** b 2 Sep 1889, Wessington Springs, SD; d Nov 1980, Central City, IA. She married 19 Dec 1912, Wessington Springs, SD, **William Curtis Falcon** (Clement Falcon & Minnie _____) b 24 Mar 1888, Marion, IA.

iv   **Lottie Holcomb** (twin) b 1891, Wessington Springs, SD; d there 1891 at one day of age.

v   **Lettie Holcomb** (twin) b 1891, Wessington Springs, SD; d there 1891 at 3 days of age.

vi   **Myra Austie Holcomb** b 5 Dec 1893, Wessington Springs, SD; d & bur 9 & 12 May 1973, Riverside, CA. She married 10 Apr 1915, Huron, SD, **Floyd David Pierce** (Claynoid N. Isreal & Belle Irwin) b 8 Mar 1895, Canton, KS; m (2) Wilma I. Favrhow; d 24 Oct 1986, Fontana, CA.

vii   **Harley James Holcomb** b 20 Oct 1896, Wessington Springs, SD; d 12 Aug 1970, Los Angeles, CA. He married 1926? **Edna Pauline O'Brien** (Joseph O'Brien & Mary Bachmore) b 11 Aug 1897, Jerauld Co., SD; d 8 May 1982, Los Angeles, CA.

viii   **Robert Holcomb** b Jan 1901, Wessington Springs, SD; d & bur there Mar 1901 at the age of 2 months.

ix   **Walter Montee Holcomb** b 10 Jul 1904, Wessington Springs, SD; d 4 May 1943,

Columbus, OH. He married 1927? **Emily Elizabeth Pilling** (Albert Pilling & Elizabeth Clarke) b 10 Nov 1907, Plymouth, MA; d 4 Jun 1980, Los Angeles, CA.

x **Wendell Earl Holcomb** b 7 Jan 1907, Wessington, Springs, SD; d 29 Dec 1977, Compton, CA. He married (1) 26 Dec 1929, Belle Fourche, SD, **Julia Nancy Hill** (_____ Hill & Jessie _____) b Feb 1909, Billings Co., ND; d & bur 13 & ? Jan 1933, Wessington Springs, SD.

He married (2) 10 Feb 1934, Plankinton, SD, **Eva Dodd** (Joseph S. Dodd & Mary E. Aubrey) b 1905?, IL.

xi **Marion Elizabeth Holcomb** b 31 May 1911, Wessington Springs, SD; d there 29 Sep 1999. She married 6 Apr 1929, Canton, SD, **Burl Powell** (Joshua Dwyer Powell & Evaline Augusta Hackett) b 16 Jun 1908, Jerauld Co., SD; d 28 Mar 2004, Wessington Springs, SD.

4.3.3.4.10 **MONTEE, Florence Jeanette/Nettie** b 15 Sep 1868, Adel, IA; d 2 Jun 1953, Santa Barbara, CA. She married (1) 26 Sep 1885, Niobrara, NE, **George Gilman**.

She was divorced when she married (2) 1902? **Frank Hamilton** b May 1859, IL; m (1) 1893? Christine _____; d between 1920 and 1930.

Florence Montee came to the Dakota Territory with her parents in the early 1870s and was living in her father's household in Eden Twp, SD, in 1880. In 1885 however, just prior to her first marriage, she was staying in Creighton, NE, with her sister Maggie (4.3.3.4.11) and her brother-in-law Eugene Perry. She was then known as Nettie, as also at first marriage. On other occasions, her name as an adult was Florence.

She and George Gilman may have lived in Kansas for their son was born there. She divorced after five years of marriage and was again a member of her father's household in Hudson, SD, in 1900 (US census).

She and Frank Hamilton, a cook in Hudson, had been married for eight years in 1910. In 1920 he was a carpenter and she a nurse in Armour, SD. Ten years later, after his death, she was a practical nurse in Santa Barbara, CA, where she was keeping house for her divorced son Vernon and her grandson Roy (US and state censuses). She remained in Santa Barbara until her death.

Child:

i **Vernon Sears Gilman** b 8 Jul 1886, Fargo Springs, KS; d 3 Sep 1956, Santa Barbara, CA. He married 26 Nov 1907, Canton, SD, **Minnie O. Anderson** b 24 Mar 1880, IA; d 21 Aug 1970, Los Angeles, CA.

4.3.3.4.11 **MONTEE, Margaret Elinor Anna** b 1869?, IA. She married 7 Nov 1884, Niobrara, NE, **Eugene/Gene Perry** b Aug 1858, IA; d between 1900 and 1910.

This woman's name and date of birth vary considerably from census to census. Anna Montee was a one-year-old child living with her parents in Washington Twp, IA, in 1870 while Margaret Montee was 10 years old when living with them in Eden, SD, in 1880. Mrs. Maggie Perry was 17 years old however in 1885, while Mrs. Margaret Perry was 29 years old in 1900. Mrs. Margarite Perry was 38 years old when, as a widow, she was a member of her daughter Carrie Alma and son-in-law William Snyder's household in Meadow Twp, SD (US and state censuses). The date of birth inferred from the earliest census may be the most reliable.

Eugene Perry was a farmer in Creighton, NE, in 1880 and 1885, and in Jefferson Twp, NE, in 1900 (US and state censuses). In between times, though, the family obviously moved around quite a bit: of the three children listed in the 1900 census the first was born in Nebraska, the second in Oklahoma, and the third in Kansas.

Children:

i **Alma/Carrie Alma Perry** b May 1885, Creighton, NE. She married 1904? **William Snyder** b 1883?, MN.

ii **Harry L. Perry** b 8 Sep 1887, OK; d Jul 1974, Kansas City, MO. He married 25 Feb 1908, Gettysburg, SD, **Agnes Irene Nutter** (John Thomas Nutter & Sarah Ann

Shackleton) b 22 Dec 1889, Walworth Co., SD; d Feb 1980, Sheridan Co., NE.
iii   **Gertrude Perry** b Apr 1891, KS.

4.3.3.10.1   **MONTY/MONTE, Susan** b Jul 1858, Canada; d 27 May 1860, Bennington, VT, at the age of 1 year and 10 months.

4.3.3.10.2   **MONTA, David Edward** b Apr 1863, Williamstown, MA; d between 1920 and 1930, probably in WI. He married 1885? **Rosamund Anna/Annie Stubbs** (John Stubbs & Mary A. ____) b Oct 1860, England; d May 1932, Kenosha, WI.

David E. Monta came to Iowa with his parents in the late 1860s and to Pewaukee, WI, between 1875 and 1878. He was a farm laborer there in 1880. He may have moved to Waukesha, WI, where his wife's family had settled in the 1850s, around the time of his marriage. He was a stone mason and plasterer there at the births of his children. By 1900, when he and his wife had been married for fifteen years, he was a contractor in Genesee, WI. He was a stone mason there in 1905 and 1910 and a machinist in Kenosha, WI, in 1920. He died within the next decade: his widow was living in 1930 with her daughter Myrtle in Kenosha (US and state censuses). Mrs. Anna Monta died there in her daughter's home two years later (*Waukesha Freeman*, 12 May 1932).

Children:

4.3.3.10.2.1	Infant (female)	1885-	-
4.3.3.10.2.2	Myrtle Pearl	1889-	-
4.3.3.10.2.3	Frederick William/Fred W.	1894-1917-1964	

4.3.3.10.3   **MONTA, Allen Elsworth** b May 1865, Williamstown, MA; d 8 Jan 1944, Kitsap Co., WA. He married 20 Jun 1886, Knapp, WI, **Effie Florence Phillips** (Thomas J. Phillips & Mattie A. Tinker) b Oct 1869, Durand, WI; d 13 Mar 1946, Tacoma, WA.

Allen E. Monta came to Iowa with his parents in the late 1860s and to Pewaukee, WI, between 1875 and 1878. He was a farm worker there in 1880, a laborer in Knapp, WI, in 1886, and a laborer in Superior, WI, in 1900. He soon moved again: his sons Albert and Howard were born in Washington State and Idaho respectively, while in 1910 he was a factory worker in Portland, OR. By then he and his wife had had nine children of whom six, including the five named below, were still alive. The family returned to Wisconsin before 1920. Allen Monta was then a machinist in Milwaukee, WI, and a brass mill worker in Pleasant Prairie, WI, in 1930 (US censuses). I do not know when he and his wife moved back to Washington State.

Children:

4.3.3.10.3.1	Fred W.	1887-1916?-
4.3.3.10.3.2	Clarence Henry	1892-1916?-1960
4.3.3.10.3.3	Mabel	1898- -
4.3.3.10.3.4	Albert R.	1903?-1924?-
4.3.3.10.3.5	Howard R.	1905-1920?-1988

4.3.3.10.4   **MONTA, Eva L.** b Mar 1870, Sugar Grove, IA.

Eva L. Monta was living with her parents in Pewaukee, WI, in 1880. I have been unable to find her in later censuses. I suspect, but cannot prove, that she was the mother of the 9-year-old Harry Griffith who was staying in Superior, WI, in June 1900 with his maternal grandparents David and Mary Monta (US censuses). His parents' whereabouts are unknown.

4.3.3.10.5   **MONTA, Frank H.** b Jun 1872, Sugar Grove, IA. He married (1) 1903? ____ .

He was a widower when he married (2) 1913? **Elizabeth Emma Pennant** (John Pennant & Elizabeth Emma Rogers) b 28 Aug 1879, England; d & bur 27 & 30 Mar 1939, Tacoma, WA.

Frank Monta was a teamster, single, living in his father's household in Superior, WI, in

1900. Ten years later he was a rancher in Forsyth, MT, a widower who had been married for seven years and whose household included both his parents. He may have left the area after his parents' deaths in the early 1910s. He was a carpenter in Tacoma, WA, in 1920 and a shingler there in 1930, when he and his second wife had been married for about seventeen years (US censuses).

Children of the second marriage:

4.3.3.10.5.1	William	1913?-	-
4.3.3.10.5.2	John David	1918-	-1995
4.3.3.10.5.3	Mary E.	1922?-	-

4.3.3.10.6   MONTA, Carrie (twin) b 1875?, Sugar Grove, IA.
Carrie Monta was a 5-year-old child living with her parents in Pewaukee, WI, in 1880 (US census).

4.3.3.10.7   MONTA, Cora (twin) b 1875?, Sugar Grove, IA.
Cora Monta was a 5-year-old child living with her parents in Pewaukee, WI, in 1880 (US census).

4.3.3.10.8   MONTA, Frederick Otic b 8 Feb 1878, Pewaukee, WI. He married 14 Dec 1899, West Superior, WI, **Bertha Julia Hoffman** (Stephen Hoffman & Bertha Nelson) b there 1877?
Fred Otic Monta was a nailer in West Superior, WI, at his marriage, a machinist in Superior, WI, in 1910, and a factory worker there on 1 Jan 1920 when his wife was 42 years old (US censuses). I have been unable to trace him, his wife, or his child any further.

Child:

4.3.3.10.8.1	Lyla M.	1906?-	-

4.3.3.12.1   MONTY, Mary b 1861?, Mooers, NY. She married 26 Oct 1878, Lawrence, MA, **Allen Abercrombie** (John Abercrombie & Flora McKee) b 1857?, Holyoke, MA.
Mary Monty was a 9-year-old child living with her parents in DePeyster, NY, in 1870 (US census) and probably moved with them to Massachusetts shortly before her marriage. Two records of it exist, one in Lawrence, MA, and the other in Methuen, MA (Massachusetts Marriage Records, vol. 298, pp. 207, 240). They agree that the marriage took place on 26 Oct 1878 in Lawrence and that the 18-year-old bride, Mary Monty, born in Mooretown (sic), NY, was the daughter of Charles and Minerva Monty while the 21-year-old groom, Allen W. or H. Abercrombie, born in Holyoke, MA, was the son of John Abercrombie and Flora McKee. He was an operative in Methuen, MA.
It is then somewhat disconcerting to find that Allen H. Abercrombie, who had been living in Lawrence, MA, with his parents John and Flora Abercrombie since at least 1860, was still living with them in 1880 as a 23-year-old single man (US censuses). It is possible that the marriage was short-lived, though I have found no death, or even divorce, records for a Mrs. Mary (Monty) Abercrombie. Neither have I found any further mention of Allen or Mary Abercrombie in later censuses. This remains a minor mystery.

4.3.3.12.2   MONTY, Marguerite Mathilde b 8 Nov 1867, Montreal, QC; d 15 Sep 1934, Nashua, NH. She married (1) 25 Dec 1881, Billerica, MA, **Foster Beale Putney** (Asa G. Putney & Sophronia A. Edmands) b there 7 Nov 1851; d there 9 Nov 1891.
She married (2) 2 Jun 1894, Laconia, NH, **Allen Hurlbert** (S. Meyers Hurlbert & Sarah Frances Allen) b May 1869, Hartford, CT; d between 1923 and 1928, Nashua, NH.
Marguerite Monty was the only child of her family to have been born in Canada. She was with her parents in De Peyster, NY, in 1870 and in Billerica, MA, in 1880. Her first husband, Foster B. Putney, was a farmer there (US censuses).
Her second husband, Allen Hurlbert, was born in Hartford, CT, according to his marriage record and in Connecticut generally according to the 1870 census in Hartford. I have ac-

cepted this though there may be some doubt: a few later censuses say he was born in Massachusetts where his parents generally resided and where his siblings were born. He was an optician residing in Laconia, NH, at his marriage and until 1899, in Chelmsford, MA, in 1900 and for a few years thereafter, and in Nashua, NH, from at least 1910 on (US censuses). He was still living there with his wife in 1923 though Mrs. Marguerite M. Hurlbert was a widow in 1928 (Nashua City Directories).

Children:

i   **Laura Minerva Putney** b 22 Oct 1882, Billerica, MA; d 27 Jan 1919, Nashua, NH. She married 7 Feb 1910, Manchester, NH, **William Stephen Gilbody** (William Gilbody & Agnes Bridget Leahy) b 29 Jan 1888, MA; d 7 May 1946, Nashua, NH.

ii   **Mary Matilda Putney** b 21 Jun 1884, Billerica, MA; d 7 Nov 1947, San Francisco, CA. She married (1) 1904?, NH, **Ralph Arnold Lewis** (Freeman A. Lewis & Delia Hannah Larabee) b 12 Feb 1880, Medford, MA; m (2) 1923?, Frances Arnette; d 10 Oct 1933, Chicago, IL.

      She married (2) 1925?, CA, **David Rufus Halliday** (____ Halliday & ____ O'Brien) b 10 Aug 1876, CA; d 22 May 1950, San Francisco, CA.

iii   **George Foster Putney** b 1 May 1886, Billerica, MA; d 1919, Nashua, NH. He married around 1917 **Elizabeth/Bessie McKay** b 1891?, Canada.

iv   **Arthur Allen Putney** b 13 Jan 1888, Billerica, MA. He married 1910? **Iva Lillian Crane** (Simon D. Crane & Mary J. B. Colby) b 16 Apr 1889, Pembroke, NH.

v   **Foster Beale Putney** b 5 Jun 1892, Billerica, MA; d 28 May 1967 Denver, CO. He married (1) 1913, Lowell, MA, **Florence S. Page** (Charles W. Page & Almira Bailey) b 1 Feb 1894, Worcester, MA; d between 1920 and 1930.

      He married (2) 12 Jan 1930, Alamogordo, NM, **Euna Valeria Bradford** (Frederick Monroe Bradford & Maggie Lou McNatt) b there 28 Apr 1906; d 14 Mar 1985, Denver, CO.

vi   **Francis Allen Hurlbert** b 9 Mar 1895, Laconia, NH; d 26 Nov 1949, Pasadena, CA. He married 4 Nov 1922, Hinsdale, NH, **Maude Eleanor Hildreth** (Clarence Raymond Hildreth & Helen N. Swanson/Hilma Natalie Svenson) b 8 Jun 1896, Brattleboro, VT; m (2) 26 Jan 1966, Pasadena, CA, Daniel Greenleaf Emery (Edgar Emery & Florence M. Carter); d 23 Apr 1989, Los Angeles, CA.

vii   **Harriet Marguerite Hurlbert** b 29 Jul 1896, Lakeport, NH; d Mar 1986, Warwick, RI. She married 4 Nov 1919, Nashua, NH, **Merton Walter Glidden** (Lewis C. Glidden & Rose ____) b 23 Jan 1893, Bethel, ME; d 24 Jul 1977, San Diego, CA.

viii   **Helen Louise Hurlbert** b 11 Jan 1899, Laconia, NH; d 18 Jul 1957, Nashua, NH. She married there 16 Jan 1919 **Otto Agaton Halquist** (Argeton (?) Halquist & ____) b 12 Sep 1890, Nashua, NH.

ix   **Mildred Hurlbert** b 1 Jun 1900, Chelmsford, MA; d & bur 25 & 28 Apr 1947, Brookline, MA, & Nashua, NH. She married 1923? **Kenneth Russell Douglass** (Frank Douglass & Magdeline ____) b 19 Feb 1894, Worcester, MA; d 4 Sep 1983, Barnstable, MA.

x   **Madeline Hurlbert** b 23 Aug 1903, Chelmsford, MA; d 2 Dec 1969, Milford, NH. She married 1927? **Walter L. Everett** (Frank S. Everett & Florence B. Perkins) b 9 Apr 1895, Nashua, NH.

4.3.3.12.3   MONTY, Charles Allen b Jan 1869, DePeyster, NY; d 23 Dec 1939, Glendale, NH. He married (1) 26 Oct 1887, Nashua, NH, **Rose A. Reynolds** (Ai A. Reynolds & Melvina Leazott) b Aug 1869, Chazy, NY; d 8 Jul 1889, Nashua, NH.

    He married (2) 12 Nov 1890, Gilford, NH, **Nellie F. Dockham** (Alonzo Dockham & Clara J. Bean) b 14 Jul 1874, Lowell, MA; d 9 Sep 1954, Laconia, NH.

    Charles Allen Monty moved with his parents to Billerica, MA, in the mid-1870s, and later to Nashua, NH, where he was a railroad employee in 1887. Three years later, at the time of his second marriage, he was a laborer in Gilford, NH, and a farmer there in 1893 and 1895 when two of his children were born. He returned to Massachusetts with his family shortly thereafter and was a shoe salesman in Billerica, MA, in 1900, a teamster in Bedford, MA, in 1910, and a laborer in a lumber yard in Lowell, MA, in 1920. The family then moved back to Gilford, where Charles A. Monty was a caretaker on a chicken farm in 1930 (US censuses).

Child of the first marriage:

4.3.3.12.3.1	Frank	1888- -

Children of the second marriage:

4.3.3.12.3.2	Louis B.	1893-1917?&1927?-1966
4.3.3.12.3.3	Edith	1895- -
4.3.3.12.3.4	Clara Jane	1903-1931-1985
4.3.3.12.3.5	John A.	1904?-1927?-

4.3.3.12.4   **MONTY, Abigail** b 1871?, NY.

Abigail Monty was a 9-year-old child living with her parents in Billerica, MA, in 1880 (US census).

4.3.3.12.5   **MONTY, Florence Edith** b 21 Oct 1881, Billerica, MA; d between 1914 and 1920. She married 1898? **William A. Moore** b Feb 1872, MA.

Florence Monty and her husband had been married for two years in 1900. William Moore was then a painter in Billerica, MA. He was also a house painter in Oxford, MA, in 1910 and in Worcester, MA, in 1920 when he was a widower and in 1930 (US censuses).

Children:

i   **Ruth Moore** b Dec 1898, Billerica, MA. She married 1918? **William F. Whalen** (John Whalen & Mary ____) b 25 Jul 1895, Worcester, MA.

ii   **Edwin A. Moore** b May 1900, Billerica, MA.

iii   **Norman W. Moore** b 1901?, MA.

iv   **Laura S. Moore** b 1902?, MA.

v   **George A. Moore** b 1904?, MA.

vi   **Freeman A. Moore** b 18 Feb 1907, West Boylston, MA; d & bur 27 & 29 Apr 1992, Worcester, MA. He married 1943? **Anna M. Raulinaitis** (Joseph Raulinaitis & Agota Mathewson) b 29 Sep 1912, Lithuania; d & bur 21 & 24 Sep 2005.

vii   **Hazel F. Moore** b May 1909, Oxford, MA.

viii   **Doris E. Moore** b 1912?, Worcester Co., MA.

ix   **Beatrice Moore** b 1914?, Worcester Co., MA.

4.3.3.13.1   **MONTY, Walter Sidney** b 18 Feb 1867, Bernardston, MA; d between 1920 and 1930, probably in Muskegon, MI. He married 1895? **Jeannette A./Jeannie Sanford** (Daniel Francis Sanford & Barbara Woodside) b Aug 1878, Canada.

Walter Monty came to Michigan as a toddler and was living with his parents in Banks Twp, MI, in 1870. He was a laborer in Bear Creek Co., MI, in 1900, when he and his wife had been married for five years, and in Muskegon, MI, in 1920. No children are mentioned. His widow was still in Muskegon in 1930 (US censuses).

4.3.3.13.2   **MONTY, Louise/Minnie** b 14 Jul 1870, Norwood, MI. She married (1) 17 Sep 1891, Boyne, MI, **Edward C. Newman** (William C. Newman & Louise Oates) b Jul 1864, KY.

She married (2) 1904? **Jacob Frank Van Ry** (Frank Van Ry & Cordelia ____) b 22 Aug 1868, Holland, MI; m (1) 1888? Mary Alice McGinnis; m (3) Dora ____ ; d 19 Nov 1944, San Francisco, CA.

This woman was named Louise at her birth and at her first marriage. After that time I have seen only Mrs. Minnie Newman (1900 census in Charlevoix, MI) or Van Ry (1910 census in Holland, MI, and 1920 census in Los Angeles, CA).

Edward C. Newman was a house painter in Charlevoix, MI, at his marriage and in 1930 (US census)

Jacob Van Ry was a sailor in Holland MI, when he and his first wife had been married for twelve years. He was a repairman there in 1910 when he and his second wife had been married for six years. They were both in Los Angeles, CA, in 1920, though divorced. By 1930 he and his third wife, Dora, were living in San Francisco (US censuses).

Children:

i   **Ivan F. Newman** b 8 Aug 1893, Charlevoix, MI; d Jan 1946, Holland, MI. He married 1910? **Johanna A. Blok** (Gerrit Blok & Gertrude ____) b Aug 1892, Holland, MI; d & bur there 12 & 14 Oct 1961.

ii   **Chloris L. Newman** b 13 June 1896, Charlevoix, MI; d 2 Mar 1963, Los Angeles Co., CA. She married 1911? **Hale Asa Studebaker** (William Studebaker & Claudia Lorena Wood) b 5 Mar 1889, Riverside, CA; d 27 Jan 1963, Los Angeles Co., CA.

iii   **Richard E. Van Ry** b 7 Oct 106, Holland, MI; d 2 Jul 1971, Tulare Co., CA.

4.3.3.13.3   **MONTY, William** b 2 May 1877, Elk Rapids, MI.
William Monty was living in the household of his maternal uncle Amos Richardson in Banks Twp, MI, in 1880 (US census).

4.4.1.2.1   **MONTY, Henry** b 3 Sep 1825, Plattsburgh, NY; d there 3 Mar 1852. He married **Catherine ____** b 1827?, England.
The dates of Henry Monty's birth and death are taken from a 19th-century list of descendants of Abraham Monty (4.4.1.2) which was found in a family Bible and reproduced by Betty Ramsey in her *Monty-Montee History*, p. 632. Henry Monty was a sawyer in Plattsburgh, NY, in 1850 when his wife Catherine was 23 years old (US census).

Child:

4.4.1.2.1.1   Ann Eliza   1851?-   -

4.4.1.2.2   **MONTY, John C.** b 16 Apr 1827, Plattsburgh, NY; d 8 Jun 1892, Glens Falls. He married (1) 2 Jun 1853, Sandy Hill, NY, **Mary E. Stowell** (Henry Stowell/Stoel & Mercy Tubbs) b 1835?, Schroon, NY; d & bur 1869, Glens Falls & Fort Edward, NY.
He married (2) 1870? **Mary Elizabeth Nulty** b Feb 1845, Washington Co., NY; bur 1923, Fort Edward, NY.
John C. Monty left Plattsburgh, NY, for Washington Co., NY, in the late 1840s and was a resident of Sandy Hill, NY, at his marriage. He was a laborer and later a foreman in a sawmill there before moving to Glens Falls, NY, and becoming a businessman. In 1870 and 1880 he was the owner of a lumber company there and vice-president of a stone quarry (US and state censuses). He and both his wives were buried in the Union Cemetery in Fort Edward, NY.
Mary Stowell (also Stoel), was 20 years old in 1855 (state census).
Mary Elizabeth Nulty lived in Sandy Hill (renamed Hudson Falls in 1910) after John Monty's death and until at least 1920 (US censuses).

Children of the first marriage:

4.4.1.2.2.1	Harriet M.	1856-1881-1933
4.4.1.2.2.2	William Henry	1858-1884?-
4.4.1.2.2.3	Benjamin Frank	1860-1898?-
4.4.1.2.2.4	Mary Elizabeth	1863-1889-1938
4.4.1.2.2.5	Julia Anna	1866-1900?-1938

4.4.1.2.3   **MONTY, Adam Wait** b 2 May 1829, Plattsburgh, NY; d there 26 Jul 1829.
The dates of Adam Wait Monty's birth and death are taken from a 19th-century list of descendants of Abraham Monty (4.4.1.2) which was found in a family Bible and reproduced by Betty Ramsey in her *Monty-Montee History*, p. 632.
There is a tombstone in Riverside Cemetery in Plattsburgh, NY, however, which reads: "In memory of / an infant babe / son of Abram & Harriet MONTY, / who died July 28, 1830,

aged 5 months." It is barely possible that a still unidentified child was born between May 1829 and September 1830. It is more probable, I believe, that one of the dates either on the tombstone or in the family Bible is incorrect. Which one(s)? I do not know.

4.4.1.2.4   **MONTY, Charles S.** b 14 Sep 1830, Plattsburgh, NY; d 29 Jun 1887, Rutland, VT. He married **Kate/Catherine Southard** b 1832?, NY; d 30 Aug 1883, Rutland, VT, at the age of 51.

Charles Monty was a baker in Plattsburgh, NY, in 1850 and was still single. He soon married and moved to Rutland, VT, where his son was born in 1854. He was still there when he enlisted in the Union Army on 19 Dec 1863. He served as a private in the 9th Vermont Infantry Regiment until 7 Aug 1865. In 1870 he was a sawyer in Glens Falls, NY, and in 1880 a teamster in Rutland (US censuses). He, his wife, and his son were buried in Rutland's Evergreen Cemetery.

Child:
4.4.1.2.4.1   William H.   1854-1884-1901

4.4.1.2.5   **MONTY, Mary Ann** b 4 Jun 1832, Plattsburgh, NY.

Mary Ann Monty was living with her parents in Plattsburgh, NY, in 1850 (US census) and was still alive in 1856, according to the affidavit of Mrs. Barbary Morrison (Appendix I).

4.4.1.2.6   **MONTY, George** b 26 Oct 1834, Plattsburgh, NY.

George Monty was living with his parents in Plattsburgh, NY, in 1850 (US census) and was still alive in 1856, according to the affidavit of Mrs. Barbary Morrison (Appendix I).

4.4.1.2.7   **MONTY, Abraham B.** b 26 Aug 1836, Plattsburgh, NY.

Abram Monty was living with his parents in Plattsburgh, NY, in 1850 (US census) and was still alive in 1856, according to the affidavit of Mrs. Barbary Morrison (Appendix I).

4.4.1.2.8   **MONTY, Harriet** b 27 Aug 1838, Plattsburgh, NY; d there 28 Feb 1841.

4.4.1.2.9   **MONTY, Daniel M.** b 2 Mar 1840, Plattsburgh, NY; d 21 Dec 1897, Sandy Hill, NY. He married there (1) 10 Dec 1865 **Louise S./Sarah Louisa Parry** (Joseph Parry & Mary Louisa Yves) b 21 Oct 1844, Fort Edward, NY; d 19 May 1876, Sandy Hill, NY.

He married (2) 17 Feb 1886 **Carrie M./Mary Caroline Barkley** (Alexander Barkley & Margaret A. Reid) b 30 Jun 1846, Argyle, NY; m (1) 14 Nov 1866, William McLaren (William McLaren & _____); d 10 Oct 1935, Bristol, VT.

Daniel Monty left Plattsburgh, NY, after his parents' deaths in 1852 to stay with his brother John C. Monty (4.4.1.2.2) in Sandy Hill, NY. He was a laborer there in 1860, a bookkeeper in 1870, and a businessman in later years (US censuses; Cuyler Reynolds, ed., *Hudson-Mohawk Genealogical and Family Memoirs*, III, 1051-1052). His and Louise Parry's dates of birth and death are taken from the inscription on their tombstone in the Union Cemetery in Fort Edward, NY. Daniel's date of birth there is the same as in the 19th-century list of descendants of Abraham Monty (4.4.1.2) reproduced in Betty Ramsey's *Monty-Montee History*, p. 632. The *Hudson-Mohawk ... Memoirs* however claim that he was born on 1 Mar 1840 and died on 23 Dec 1896 (III, 1051) and that Sarah Louisa Parry was born on 25 Oct 1844 (III, 1188).

Carrie Barkley continued to live in Sandy Hill (renamed Hudson Falls in 1910) after her second husband's death and until at least 1920 (US censuses). Information about her family and first marriage can be found in the *Hudson-Mohawk ... Memoirs*, III, 1052.

Children of the first marriage:
4.4.1.2.9.1   Joseph Parry   1866-1895-1914
4.4.1.2.9.2   Elizabeth   1869-1896-
4.4.1.2.9.3   Fannie Louise   1872-1900?-

4.4.1.2.10   **MONTY, Laura A.** b 27 Jun 1842, Plattsburgh, NY. She married 13 Oct 1863, Rutland, VT, **Edward Fenn** (Abner Fenn & Louisa Abigail Graves) b 1832?, VT; d between 1891 and 1900.

Laura Monty left Plattsburgh, NY, after her parents' deaths in 1852 and moved to Sandy Hill, NY, where her older brother John C. Monty (4.4.1.2.1) was living. She was a servant in a hotel there in 1860 but was a resident of Rutland, VT, when she married a few years later.

Edward Fenn was a 31-year-old clerk in Rutland at his marriage and a druggist from 1870 until at least 1892 (US censuses; Rutland City Directories). His widow was living in Rutland in 1900 with her children Fred and Edith. She had had seven children of whom only three were then still alive (US censuses).

Children:

i   **Charles E. Fenn** b 6 Oct 1864, Rutland, VT. He married 1888? **Sally S. ____** b 1869?, KY.

ii   **Carrie L. Fenn** b 1869?, Rutland, VT. She married there 17 Oct 1888 **Frederic K. Ma....**

iii   **Mary F. Fenn** b 1872?, Rutland, VT.

iv   **Fred Thomas Fenn** b 24 May 1878, Rutland, VT.

v   **Cassie B. Fenn** b 1880?, Rutland, VT; d there 20 Aug 1897 at the age of 17.

vi   **Edith L. Fenn** b 7 Aug 1883, Rutland, VT.

4.4.1.2.11   **MONTY, Harriet E./Hattie** b 24 May 1844, Plattsburgh, NY; d 11 Apr 1902, Rutland, VT. She married 2 Oct 1867 **John H. Thompson** (Caleb Thompson & Martha Haskins) b 18 Jan 1830, Fort Ann, NY; d 2 Jan 1908, Pittsford, VT, at the age of 77 years, 11 months, and 16 days.

Harriet Montey (sic) was a 5-year-old child living with her parents in Plattsburgh, NY, in 1850 (US census). The precise date of her birth is taken from a 19th-century list of the descendants of Abraham Monty (4.4.1.2) which was reproduced in Betty Ramsey's *Monty-Montee History*, p. 632. The tombstone of Hattie E. Monty Thompson in Evergreen Cemetery in Rutland, VT, however, bears the dates 1846-1902.

She and her husband probably remained in New York State for a few years after their marriage for their only child was born there in 1869. By 1880 however John H. Thompson was a truck man in Rutland, as also in 1900 when his household included his wife, son and daughter-in-law, and three grandchildren all born in Vermont (US censuses). He was buried alongside his wife in Rutland's Evergreen Cemetery but again the tombstone inscription appears to be in error. It reads 1832-1908.

Child:

i   **George Baker Thompson** b 15 Feb 1869, Fort Ann, NY; d 5 Jun 1908, Rutland, VT. He married 5 May 1892 **Josephine Alice Bussell** b Aug 1871, Plattsburgh, NY.

4.4.1.2.12   **MONTY, Benjamin K.** b 18 Jan 1846, Plattsburgh, NY; d 19 Apr 1885, Ellendale, ND. He married 23 Mar 1864, Sandy Hill, NY, **Anna M. Wade** (Hiram Wade & Marion ____) b 1845?, Schroon. NY; d 17 Sep 1895, ND.

Benjamin Monty left Plattsburgh, NY, after his parents' deaths in 1852 and lived for a time in the household of his brother John C. Monty (4.4.1.2.2) in Sandy Hill, NY. He enlisted from there as a private in Co. E, 96th New York Infantry Regiment on 10 Feb 1862, reenlisted in the same company on 29 Feb 1864, and was mustered out as a Sergeant 1st Class on 6 Feb 1866 in City Point, VA. He returned to Sandy Hill and was a carpenter there until at least 1872. He then moved to Grand Haven, MI, where he was a farmer at the birth of a child in 1874 and a carpenter in 1877 and 1880 when two other children were born. The family moved again a few years later: Benjamin K. Monty was residing in North Dakota when he applied on

7 Mar 1885 for an invalid pension based on his Civil War service. He died a month later and was buried in the Ellendale, ND, Cemetery under a headstone provided for Union Civil War veterans. His pension was transferred to his widow (certificate #279144) and after her death to their minor children (certificate #442905).

Children:

4.4.1.2.12.1	Clara L./Lula	1867?-	-
4.4.1.2.12.2	George H.	1870-	-
4.4.1.2.12.3	Bertha A.	1872?-	-
4.4.1.2.12.4	Grace E.	1874-	-
4.4.1.2.12.5	Jennie H.	1877-	-
4.4.1.2.12.6	William Harper	1880-1900-1947	

4.4.1.4.1   **MONTY, Mary** b 1836?, Clinton Co., NY.

Mary Monty was a 14-year-old girl living with her parents in Mooers, NY, in 1850 (US census).

4.4.1.4.2   **MONTY, Eliza** b 1 Apr 1838, Chazy, NY; d 31 Aug 1923, Hennepin Co., MN. She married 2 Dec 1854, Hamilton, Ontario, Canada, **Alfred P. Stearns** (Henry Stearns & Louisa/Lois T. Smith) b 9 Jan 1830, Grafton, NH; d 13 Dec 1922, Winona Co., MN.

Albert P. Stearns was a railroad worker in Mooers, NY, in 1850 and continued working for the railroad for over thirty years. He also became a farmer and community leader in Olmsted County, MN, where he bought land in 1856 and settled near his wife's family. He was a farmer in Dover, MN, in 1860 and almost continuously until 1906 when he sold his property and moved to St. Charles, MN. He and his wife were living there in retirement in 1910 and 1920 (US censuses; Joseph A. Leonard, *History of Olmsted County, Minnesota*, pp. 419-420).

Children:

i   **Frank Henry Stearns** b 29 Nov 1855, Lewiston, MN; d 21 Apr 1951, St. Charles, MN. He married 1878? **Etta C./Ester C. Weeks** (Willard Weeks & Emily Lochsan) b 24 May 1855, Kinsman, OH; d 2 Aug 1935, St. Charles, MN.

ii   **Louise/Louisa Stearns** b 1862, Dover, MN; d & bur 25 & ? Apr 1943, Dubuque, IA. She married 1882? **Vernon B. Tooke** (David Tooke & Arianna O'Reilley) b 1859, MN; d & bur 1947, Dubuque, IA.

iii   **May Eliza Stearns** b 10 Feb 1877, Dover, MN; d 11 May 1969, Hennepin Co., MN. She married 1901? **Albert Charles Kaufman** (August Kaufman & Anne _____) b 9 Feb 1873, La Crosse, WI; d 3 Aug 1948, Hennepin Co., MN.

4.4.1.4.3   **MONTY, Hannah** (twin) b 15 Feb 1844, Clinton Co., NY.

Hannah Monty was a 7-year-old child living with her parents in Mooers, NY, in 1850 (US census)

4.4.1.4.4   **MONTY, William Henry** (twin) b 15 Feb 1844, Clinton Co., NY; d 24 Mar 1911. He married 12 Jul 1876, **Laura Holbrook Coburn** (Othniel Dinsmore Coburn & Helen Maria Cobb) b 28 Jan 1848, Dracut, MA; d 26 May 1938, Los Angeles, CA.

William Monty came to Minnesota with his parents around 1856 and was living in 1860 on his father's farm in Dover, MN. He was a railroad employee in St. Paul, MN, in 1880 and a train conductor there in 1900 when he and his wife had been married for twenty-four years. He was buried near his parents in Hillside Cemetery in St. Charles, MN. His widow soon left for California and was living in Long Beach, CA, in 1920 and in Santa Barbara, CA, in 1930 (US censuses).

Child:

4.4.1.4.4.1	Frank Densmore	1879-1904?-1950

4.4.2.1.1   **MONTY, Mary Louise** b Aug 1842, Clinton Co., NY; d 13 Aug 1914,

Plattsburgh, NY. She married 1860? **Irving W. Mastick/Mastic** (Asa Mastick & Anna ____) b May 1839, Essex Co., NY; d 25 Sep 1907, Plattsburgh, NY.

Mary L. Monty was a single woman living with her parents in Franklin, NY, in June 1860. She must have married soon after that date for her two oldest children were born around 1860 and 1861.

Irving W. Mastick was an iron worker in Plattsburgh, NY, in 1880 and a day laborer there in 1900. He and his wife had then had nine children of whom six, Ella, Ida, Earl, Walter, Myra, and Charles were still alive (US censuses).

The family surname changed over time, though not always consistently. It was Mastick until about 1880. In later years it was usually Mastic, as in the obituaries of "Mr. I. W. Mastic" and "Mrs. Mary L. Mastic" in the *Plattsburgh Sentinel* of 27 Sep 1907 and 14 Aug 1914. Yet their tombstone in Riverside Cemetery in Plattsburgh, NY, is inscribed MASTICK. Their sons in turn carried the Mastic surname.

Children:
i **Ella L. Mastic** b 1860?, Essex, NY. She married 15 Jul 1888, Bloomingdale, NY, **Fred H. Berkley** (Roderick Berkley & Hannah/Anna ____) b Aug 1867, Westford, VT.
ii **Ida C. Mastic** b Jun 1861, Essex, NY; d 30 Sep 1918, Plattsburgh, NY. She married 1883? **Burton Grant Rockwell** (Jabez Grant Rockwell & Louisa McEuen) b July 1857, Alburgh, VT; d Aug 1902, Plattsburgh, NY.
iii **Addie Mastic** b 1864?, Plattsburgh, NY; d 11 Jan 1900, Chester, MA. She married 1882?, Plattsburgh, NY, **Frank W. Gooley** (Peter Gooley & Marie Armour) b Oct 1861, AuSable Forks, NY; m (2) 1900? Lillian Goulah; d 11 Nov 1926, Pittsfield, MA.
iv **Earl W. Mastic** b 1869?, Plattsburgh, NY. He married 1927? as his second wife **Emma** ____ b 1877?, NY.
v **Walter J. Mastic** b Sep 1872, Plattsburgh, NY. He married 1894? **Carrie A.** ____ b May 1875, NY.
vi **Myra L. Mastic** b Mar 1874, Plattsburgh, NY; d there 31 May 1917. She married **Joseph Greenough** (Joseph Greenough & Emily ____) b Feb 1878, Bristol, VT.
vii **Carrie M. Mastic** b 1877?, Plattsburgh, NY; d before 1900.
viii **Charles Frederick/C. Fred Mastic** b 13 Feb 1879, Plattsburgh, NY; d & bur 24 & 26 Dec 1930, Plattsburgh & Peru, NY. He married 28 Nov 1901, Plattsburgh, NY, **Marie M. Opray/Aupray/Aupré** (Dennis Opray/Denis Aupré & Hermina/Ermine Jarvis/Hermine Gervais) b & bp 28 Jan & 17 Mar 1880, Peru & Keeseville, NY; d Sep 1969, Plattsburgh, NY.

4.4.2.1.2   **MONTY, Julia A.** b & bp 4 Dec 1844 & 19 Mar 1845, Clinton Co. & Coopersville, NY; d between 1920 and 1930. She married 1866?, NY, **Charles Newel Park** (Charles Park/Parks & Aseneth Beede) b 23 Feb 1841, Hyde Park, VT; d 4 Mar 1917, St. Anthony, ID.

Charles Newel Park was a resident of Franklin, NY, when he enlisted in the Union Army on 25 Sept 1861. He reenlisted on 14 Dec 1863 and served as a private in Co. E, 60th New York Infantry Regiment until his discharge on 20 Jun 1865. He married soon after his return to Upper New York State and was a laborer and saw mill worker in Plattsburgh, NY, in 1870 and 1880. He moved West in the 1880s, first to Clark Co., SD, where he was residing in 1890, and later to Idaho. In 1910, when he was a farmer in Ora, ID, he and his wife had been married for forty-three years and had had six children, all of whom were still alive. Mrs. Julia A. Park joined her daughter Jeannette in St. Anthony, ID, after her husband's death and was living in her household there in 1920 (US and state censuses).

Children:
i **Pearl S. Park** b 23 Oct 1866, Plattsburgh, NY; d 3 Sep 1923, Blackfoot, ID. He married 1905? **Janet B.** ____ b 1880?, WI.
ii **Lillie Ann Park** b 25 Feb 1871, Plattsburgh, NY; d 21 Mar 1939, St. Anthony, ID.

She married 8 Nov 1890, Clark Co., SD, **Edward Olsen Frok/Froke** (Ole Christensen Froke & Anne Marie Asbjoiusen) b 18 Nov 1863, Waterville, IA; d 25 Dec 1932, St, Anthony, ID.

iii   **Elmina Park** b 1878?, Plattsburgh, NY.

iv   **Cora Park** b Mar 1880, Plattsburgh, NY.

v   **Jeannette/Janet A. Park** b 28 Oct 1883, Plattsburgh, NY; d 9 Sep 1936, St. Anthony, ID. She married (1) 1901? **Guy Earl Duffus** (John R. Duffus & Jennie Shearer) b 23 Mar 1879, Poweshiek Co., IA; d 26 Mar 1959, Riverside Co., CA.

She married (2) 20 May 1926, Rexburg, ID, **Rudolph F. Kersten** (Herman Kersten & Susanna _____) b 6 Jan 1878, MN; d 30 Jun 1937, St. Anthony, ID.

4.4.2.1.3   **MONTY, Joseph** b & bp 8 Jun & 8 Sep 1846, Essex & Coopersville, NY; d 15 Jan 1865, Fort Fisher, GA.

Joseph Monty was a farmer in Franklin, NY, when he enlisted on 7 Sep 1864 in Plattsburgh, NY, as a private in Co. G, 142nd New York Infantry Regiment. He died in action and was first interred near Kennesaw Mountain, GA. His remains were later transferred to the National Cemetery in Marietta, GA (grave #558).

4.4.2.1.4   **MONTY, Amelia** b & bp 1848? & 23 Oct 1851, Essex & Coopersville, NY; d 2 Dec 1911, Chester, NY, at the age of 63. She married 1867? **Alexander St. Dennis** (Louis St. Dennis & Hannah Varno) b Mar 1840, Plattsburgh, NY; m (2) 29 Apr 1912, Pottersville, NY, Alice Southwick (Albert Southwick & Allie _____), widow of _____ Monroe.

Amelia Monty was named Emelie at her baptism when she was 3 years old, but Milla when she was living with her parents in Essex, NY, in 1855 and Amelia in all other records I have seen. She was also named Amelia when she was buried in the Bird Pond Road Cemetery in Chester, NY.

Alexander St. Dennis was a farmer in Chester, NY, until at least 1910. He and his wife Amelia had been married for thirty-three years in 1900 and had had six children of whom only two, Burton and Lowell, were still alive. He was a resident of Pottersville, NY, at his second marriage.

Children:

i   **Ida L. St. Dennis** b Apr 1870, Chester, NY; d before 1900.

ii   **Burton Leroy St. Dennis** b Dec 1872, Chester, NY. He married 1897? **Laura E. _____** b Dec 1876, NY.

iii   **Alexander St. Dennis** b 1876?, Chester, NY; d before 1900.

iv   **Jerome St. Dennis** b Oct 1879, Chester, NY; d before 1900.

v   **Lowell E. St. Dennis** b Aug 1881, Chester, NY. He married 2 Oct 1910, Pottersville, NY, **Winifred Barlow** (William Barlow & _____ King) b 1887?, Hague, NY.

4.4.2.1.5   **MONTY, Henry** b & bp 14 Jul & 23 Oct 1851, Essex & Coopersville, NY; d 28 Feb 1932, Schenectady, NY. He married (1) 1869? **Jane Pauline White** (Silas P. White & Susan _____) b Feb 1851, Clinton Co., NY; d 18 Oct 1901, Plattsburgh, NY, at the age of 50.

He married (2) 1908? **Alice _____** b 1860s, NY; m (1) 1890? James Hughes.

Henry Monty (Honoré at his baptism) was a farmer in West Plattsburgh, NY, in 1870 and a bloomer and laborer in Plattsburgh, NY, 1880 and 1900. By then he and his wife Jane had been married for thirty-one years and had had eleven children of whom six, Susan, Eleanor, Laura, Clinton, Frances, and Edward, were still alive (US censuses).

By 1910 he was a farm laborer in Beekmantown, NY, and had been remarried for two years. His household consisted of his second wife Alice and two sons of her first marriage (US census). This is the only evidence I have of Henry Monty's second marriage. He was living alone in the Clinton Co. Home in Beekmantown in 1925 (state census) and was a resident of Plattsburgh when his sister Ella (4.4.2.1.12) died in early 1927 (*Plattsburgh Sentinel*, 4 Mar 1927). He died in the home of his son Edward in Schenectady, NY (*Plattsburgh Daily Press*, 1 Mar 1932).

Children of the first marriage:

4.4.2.1.5.1	Susan E.	1869-1886?-1961	
4.4.2.1.5.2	Charlotte/Lottie J.	1871?-	-1890
4.4.2.1.5.3	Jonas	1874?-	-
4.4.2.1.5.4	Charles	1876?-	-
4.4.2.1.5.5	Eleanor A.	1878-1901-	
4.4.2.1.5.6	Laura	1880-1895-1942	
4.4.2.1.5.7	Clinton	1882-1905?-	
4.4.2.1.5.8	Bessie May	1886-	-1894
4.4.2.1.5.9	Frances Hazel	1889-1907?&1923-	
4.4.2.1.5.10	Edward Monroe	1891-1911&	-1978

4.4.2.1.6 MONTY, William b 1854?, Essex, NY.

William Monty was a one-year-old child living with his parents in Essex, NY, in 1855 (state census). I suspect that this is the same child as George (4.4.2.1.7) who was born in June 1854 according to his baptismal record of March 1855 but is not listed in the state census of June 1855. Neither William nor George is present with the family in the 1860 US census.

4.4.2.1.7 MONTY, George b & bp 13 Jun 1854 & 7 Mar 1855, Essex & Keeseville, NY.

See 4.4.2.1.6 above.

4.4.2.1.8 MONTY, Edward b & bp 4 Sep & 22 Oct 1856, Essex & Keeseville, NY; d between 1882 and 1892. He married 1878? **Rose Walker** (Charles Walker & Sophia ____) b 1849?, Beekmantown, NY; d & bur 31 Dec 1931 & 2 Jan 1932, Cadyville & West Plattsburgh, NY, at the age of 82.

Edward Monty was a laborer in Plattsburgh, NY, in 1880, when he and his wife had a one-year-old child. Rose Walker remained in Plattsburgh after his death and was living with her two children in her father's household there in 1892. She was a farmer in her own right in Plattsburgh in 1900, and also in 1910 when her household included her daughter Clara and son-in-law Cleve Akey and their children. She was in turn a member of their household in 1920 and 1930 (US and state censuses). She was buried in the Union Cemetery in West Plattsburgh, NY (*Plattsburgh Daily Press*, 2 Jan 1932).

Children:

4.4.2.1.8.1	Mary Louisa	1879-	-
4.4.2.1.8.2	Clara N.	1883-1903?-	

4.4.2.1.9 MONTY, Francis b 1857?, Essex, NY.

Francis Monty was a 13-year-old child living with his parents in West Plattsburgh, NY, in 1870 (US census).

4.4.2.1.10. MONTY, Charles Henry b 1858?, Essex, NY; d 1931. He married (1) ____.

He married (2) 21 Apr 1924, Plattsburgh, NY, **Laura Delia Comstock** (Allan Comstock & Elizabeth Fuller) b 7 May 1870, Wilmington, NY; m (1) 1888, Nathan Spear (Elias Spear & Susan ____); d & bur 6 & 10 Sep 1943, Essex Junction, VT & Plattsburgh, NY.

I know little about Charles Henry Monty beyond what is contained in the record of his second marriage: he was a 66-year-old widower, son of Jonas Monty and Mary Louise Miner, a laborer in Plattsburgh, NY, born in Essex, NY, when he married the 53-year-old widow Laura Delia Spear, daughter of Allan Comstock and Elizabeth Fuller, born in Wilmington, NY, and residing in Plattsburgh (Clinton Co., NY, Marriage Records, #6441). The year of his death is found in Mrs. Laura Spear Monty's obituary: "In 1924 she married Henry Monty whose death occurred in 1931" (*Plattsburgh Press Republican*, 9 Sep 1943). Yet neither Henry nor Mrs. Laura Monty has been found in any 1930 US census.

I have also been unable to find a trace of Charles Henry Monty, son of John/Jonas Monty and Mary Louise Miner/Manor/Mainard/Ménard. He does not appear in any census with them as a child or independently as a single, married, or widowed adult. Neither is he mentioned in Marie Louise Ménard's obituary as a surviving child (*Plattsburgh Sentinel*, 16 Feb 1900). There is a remote possibility that Charles Henry Monty and Henry Monty (4.4.2.1.5) were the same man. The discrepancy in ages however gives me pause. It would also have been Henry's third marriage, not his second as stated in the marriage record. I have no satisfactory solution to the problem.

The year of Laura Comstock's first marriage is taken from her obituary in the *Plattsburgh Press Republican*. It also states that she was born on 7 May 1869, which I believe to be an error: she was only one month old in June 1870 (US census, Wilmington, NY).

4.4.2.1.11　　**MONTY, William** b 2 Apr 1859, Merrillsville, NY; d & bur 6 & 9 Jun 1949, Plattsburgh (Cadyville), NY. He married 1880, **Lillian Wood** (Joseph Wood & Terressa R. Walker) b Jan 1859, AuSable, NY; d & bur 24 & 26 Sep 1929, Plattsburgh (Cadyville), NY.

William Monty was a laborer in the Cadyville area of Plattsburgh, NY, in 1880 and until at least 1892 and a farmer there in 1900 and until at least 1920. He was also active in community affairs and was a Supervisor of the Town of Plattsburgh for several years. While continuing to live on the farm, which was operated by son Neil in 1925 and later, he was also a deputy sheriff for a number of years (US and state censuses). He and his wife were buried in the family plot in the Cadyville Cemetery (*Plattsburgh Sentinel*, 27 Sep 1929; *Plattsburgh Press Republican*, 17 Jun 1949).

Children:

4.4.2.1.11.1	Warren J.	1880-	-1903
4.4.2.1.11.2	Fred Lester	1887-	&1928-1971
4.4.2.1.11.3	Neil James C.	1891-	-1970
4.4.2.1.11.4	Alverda	1901?-1921-1961	

4.4.2.1.12　　**MONTY, Ella** b Apr 1862, NY; d & bur 3 & 5 Mar 1927, Glens Falls & Cadyville, NY. She married (1) 1881? **John Miller**.

She married (2) 1897? **George Baker** (David Baker & Eveline _____) b Jan 1879, Plattsburgh, NY.

Ella Monty was a single woman living with her widowed mother in Plattsburgh, NY, in 1880. When the latter died in February 1900, her daughter was named Mrs. John Miller (*Plattsburgh Sentinel*, 16 Feb 1900). Yet it appears from the US census taken a few months later that Ella Monty and George Baker, a laborer in Plattsburgh, had already been married for three years. They were living with the three Miller children listed below in the household of Ella's stepfather, Charles Dupee. They were still in the Plattsburgh area in 1910 and in Cadyville, NY, when John Miller (iii) died in 1916. They moved a few years later, first to Fort Ann, NY, where George Baker was a railroad worker in 1920, and then to Glens Falls, NY, where she died. She was buried in the family plot in Cadyville *(Plattsburgh Sentinel*, 4 Mar 1927). George Baker remained in Glens Falls and was a paper mill worker there in 1930 (US censuses).

One unusual fact about Ella Monty, which was noted with amusement in the *Plattsburgh Sentinel* of 26 Oct 1900: when her son Fred Miller married Carrie Baker, George Baker's sister, he became his own mother's brother-in-law.

Children:

 i **Fred Miller** b Nov 1881, Plattsburgh, NY. He married 18 Oct 1900, Morrisonville, NY, **Caroline/Carrie Baker** (David Baker & Eveline _____) b Apr 1882, Plattsburgh, NY; d before 1910.

 ii **Jennie Miller** b 1886?, Plattsburgh, NY. She married 1905? **Lawrence Edgar Osborne** b 6 Jun 1881, Rutland, VT.

 iii **John Miller** b 1888?, Plattsburgh, NY; d there (Cadyville) 26 Jun 1916, at the age

4.4.3.6.1   **MONTY, Caroline Anna** b 1860?, Essex Co., NY.

Caroline A. Monty was a 5-year-old child living with her parents in Crown Point, NY, in 1865. She was also a member of her father's household there in 1870 and 1875 but was named Anna (US and state censuses).

4.4.3.6.2   **MONTY, James Andrew** b May 1861, Crown Point, NY; d & bur 14 & 17 Mar 1934, Whitehall & Crown Point, NY. He married 24 Jun 1886, Montreal, QC, **Ervie Olive/Eva Huestis** (Daniel Huestis & Olive S. Lapham) b Jul 1860, Bridport, VT.

James A. Monty and Ervie Olive Huestis were first cousins, his mother and her father being children of Timothy Huestis and Elizabeth (Betsey) Connors Crossman. They married in the Presbyterian Crescent Church in Montreal, QC.

James A. Monty was a laborer in Crown Point, NY, in 1880, a boatman in Bridport, VT, in 1886 and 1888 and in Waterford, NY, in 1900. He was a dairy farmer in Whitehall, NY, in 1920 and 1930, when he was a widower (US censuses). He was buried in Forestdale Cemetery in Crown Point (*Ticonderoga Sentinel*, 22 Mar 1934).

Children:

4.4.3.6.2.1	Ersie	1888- -
4.4.3.6.2.2	Carl K.	1900?-1924?-1950

4.4.3.6.3   **MONTY, Olive N.** b May 1865, Crown Point, NY.

Olive N. Monty was a one-month-old infant living with her parents in Crown Point, NY, in June 1865. She was also with them there in 1870 and 1875 (US and state censuses). I have been unable to find her in later years in spite of a tantalizing item in the *Ticonderoga Sentinel* of 6 Mar 1902: "Miss Olive Monty left Monday for Plattsburg [sic], after a six months' stay in Crown Point."

4.4.3.6.4   **MONTY, John** b 1867?, Crown Point, NY.

John Monty was a 3-year-old child living with his parents in Crown Point, NY, in 1870. He was also with them there in 1875 (US and state censuses).

4.4.3.6.5   **MONTY, Mary** b 1869, Crown Point, NY; d there 28 Jan 1891 at the age of 21. She married 25 Apr 1887, Plattsburgh, NY, **Leonard A. Johnson**.

Mary Monty was 1 year old in 1870 when she was living with her parents in Crown Point, NY (US census). The date of her death is taken from her tombstone in the Brick Cemetery there. Her husband was a resident of New York City (*Plattsburgh Sentinel*, 29 Apr 1887).

4.4.3.6.6   **MONTY, Elizabeth/Betsey** b 1871?, Crown Point, NY.

Betsey Monty was a 4-year-old child living with her parents in Crown Point, NY, in 1875 (state census).

4.4.3.6.7   **MONTY, Alphons/Alpheus** b Nov 1872, Crown Point, NY; d 18 Nov 1894, Saratoga Springs, NY, at the age of 22.

Alphons Monty was 2 years and 7 months old on 1 Jun 1875 when he was living with his parents in Crown Point, NY. He was named Alpheus in 1880 when he was staying with his uncle Daniel Huestis in Bridport, VT (US and state censuses) and at his death.

4.4.7.3.1   **MONTEE, Rosetta** b 28 Aug 1854, Macomb, IL; d there Sep 1854.

4.4.7.3.2   **MONTEE, George Edward** b 27 Jul 1856, Macomb, IL; d 27 Dec 1921, Columbus, KS. He married 1 Apr 1880, Bethel, IL, **Hannah Catherine/Kate Shoopman** (Jacob Sylvester Shoopman & Mary Jane Driscal/Driskell) b there 25 Nov 1860; d 28 Mar 1915, McCune, KS.

George E. Montee was originally a farmer in McDonough Co. (Bethel Twp), IL, before moving to Kansas in 1883 or 1884. He was a farmer in Sheridan, KS, in 1885, a livery man there in 1900, and a farmer there again in 1905. During this time the family had left Kansas only briefly: a daughter, Mary Myrtle, was born in Nebraska in 1892. George Montee returned to Nebraska in the late 1900s and was a farmer in Hall Co. (Cameron Twp), NE, in 1910. Five years later he was a farmer in McCune, KS. He remained in Kansas after his wife's death and was living alone in Columbus, KS, in 1920 (US and state censuses).

Children:

4.4.7.3.2.1	Lennie	1881- -1881
4.4.7.3.2.2	Theodore Edward	1882-1905?-1921
4.4.7.3.2.3	Lee Jacob	1885-1910-1963
4.4.7.3.2.4	Della Mae	1887-1907?-1980
4.4.7.3.2.5	Nellie Maude	1889- -1890
4.4.7.3.2.6	Charles	1891- -1892
4.4.7.3.2.7	Mary Myrtle	1892-1909-1972
4.4.7.3.2.8	Nancy Ellen	1894-1918-1933
4.4.7.3.2.9	Hazel Irene	1900-1918?-1953
4.4.7.3.2.10	John S.	1902-1922-1933

4.4.7.3.3   **MONTEE, Joseph M.** b 6 Dec 1858, Macomb, IL; d there 26 Sep 1861.

4.4.7.3.4   **MONTEE, James A.** b 18 Mar 1861, Macomb, IL; d 23 Jun 1905. He married 26 Dec 1880, McDonough Co. (Lamoine Twp), IL, **Catherine Mildred Dunsworth** (Thomas Dunsworth & Elizabeth Adelia Tuggle) b there 3 May 1864; m (2) 25 Apr 1887, Lane Co., KS, Nathan Hurt Moore (Ephraim Riley Moore & Rachel Ann Murphey); d 31 Jul 1952, Fredonia, KS.

James A. Montee was a resident of Bethel Twp, IL, at his marriage, which was obviously short-lived. Less than five years later, on 1 Mar 1885, he was said to be a single man, a farmer living in his father's household in McCune, KS (state census). He was buried in the McCune Cemetery.

4.4.7.3.5   **MONTEE, Mary Elizabeth** b 9 Sep 1863, Macomb, IL; d & bur 18 & 23 Sep 1961, Colorado Springs, CO. She married 22 Dec 1885, Cherokee Co., KS, **Stephen B. Crum** (John Crum & Mary Ann Getz) b 19 Oct 1850, Tiffin, OH; d & bur 20 & 24 May 1924, Colorado Springs, CO.

Stephen B. Crum was a farmer in Sheridan Twp, KS, until at least 1900. He moved a few years later to El Paso Co., CO, where he was a farmer in 1910 and 1920. His widow was still living there in 1930 (US censuses).

Children:

i   **Freddie Crum** b 24 Oct 1890, Sheridan Twp, KS; d there 11 Feb 1892.

ii   **Vernie Frank Crum** b 5 Aug 1893, Sheridan Twp, KS; d & bur 22 & 26 Jan 1972, Colorado Springs, CO. He married there 11 Dec 1912 **Esther Leora Terrill** (Henry Curtis Terrill & Susanna Chambers) b 16 Aug 1893, Oswego, KS; d & bur 14 & 17 Jan 1980, Colorado Springs, CO.

iii   **William Bryan Crum** b 29 Aug 1896, Sheridan Twp, KS; d 24 Oct 1955. He married 30 Mar 1915, Colorado Springs, CO, **Elsie Octavia Johnson** (Oneas Mitten Johnson & Viola Barnes) b 4 Oct 1897, Columbus, KS; d 4 Oct 1955.

iv   **Ernest Orville Crum** b 3 Jan 1899, Sheridan Twp, KS; d Jan 1980, Naples, ID. He married 15 Apr 1922, Colorado Springs, CO, **Lillie/Lillian Rebecca Warren** b 19 Jul 1902, OK; d Mar 1980, Naples, ID.

4.4.7.3.6   **MONTEE, Anna/Phebe Ann** b 9 Nov 1865, Macomb, IL; d 1950, McCune, KS. She married as his second wife 1894? **Robert J. Swain** (James Swain & ____) b Nov 1849, Jerseyville, IL; d 1916, McCune, KS.

Robert Swain moved to Kansas in the 1870s and was a farmer in Sheridan Twp until at least 1895. He had married and been widowed between 1880 and 1885. In 1895 he and his second wife Anna included in their household an 11-year-old son, Lester, of his previous marriage. The family moved a few years later. Robert Swain was a miller in McCune, KS, in 1900 and a farmer there in 1910 and 1915 (US and state censuses).

Child:

i   **Alfred R. Swain** b 5 Oct 1898, McCune, KS; d 7 May 1975, Pasadena, TX. He married 1915? **Hazel M. _____** b 1898?, KS.

4.4.7.3.7   **MONTEE, John Francis/Frank** b 11 Mar 1868, Macomb, IL; d 13 Jun 1946, Cherokee, KS. He married there 6 Mar 1894 **Anna Mary Morrison** (Robert Morrison & Emily Chadsey) b 26 Oct 1867, Montezuma, IA; d 24 Jun 1924, Cherokee, KS.

Frank Montee was a resident of McCune, KS, and Annie Morrison a resident of Cherokee, KS, at their marriage. They lived for a few years in the Indian Territory of Oklahoma, where their first two children were born but soon returned to Kansas where they remained until their deaths. Frank Montee was a livery stable owner in Scammon, KS, in 1900 and in Cherokee, KS, in 1910. By 1915 he was a coal miner in Cherokee and a mine foreman there in 1920 (US and state censuses). He and his wife were buried in the Cherokee City Cemetery.

There is an unusual circumstance about this marriage. The Crawford Co. Marriage Register includes two marriages for this couple. The first took place in 1894 as indicated above before a minister of the Methodist Episcopal Church. The second occurred on 14 Dec 1914 when Frank Montee, 47, and Mrs. Anna Montee, 47, both of Cherokee, were wed before a probate judge in Girard, KS. They may have needed to rectify some irregularity in the first ceremony. Or perhaps they simply renewed their vows. The records do not say.

Children:

4.4.7.3.7.1	Robert Leslie	1895-1916-1978
4.4.7.3.7.2	Leila Emma	1896-1921-1976
4.4.7.3.7.3	Percy Clinton	1900-1923-1988
4.4.7.3.7.4	Dorothy	1902-1917-1982
4.4.7.3.7.5	Mark S.	1903-1926-1994
4.4.7.3.7.6	Thomas Omer	1906-1928-1968

4.4.7.3.8   **MONTEE, Theodore Elmer** b 6 Feb 1870, Macomb, IL; d there 2 Dec 1873.

4.4.7.3.9   **MONTEE, Dora A.** b 7 Sep 1873, Macomb, IL; d there 28 Nov 1874.

4.4.7.3.10   **MONTEE, Della** (twin) b 4 Feb 1876, Macomb, IL; d there 15 Jul 1876.

4.4.7.3.11   **MONTEE, Delmer** (twin) b 4 Feb 1876, Macomb, IL; d 24 Nov 1964, San Diego, CA. He married 1899? **Rose Lucas** (Isaac Lucas & Mary Mc Queen) b 1 Jun 1876, Columbus, IN; d 22 Jun 1963, San Diego, CA.

Delmer Montee and his wife had been married less than a year in June 1900 when he was working on his father's farm in McCune, KS. He was a livery man in Sheridan, KS, in 1910 and a farmer in Neosho, KS, in 1920 and 1930 (US censuses). The family later moved to California, probably before 1936 when a child married there.

Children:

4.4.7.3.11.1	Theodore Isaac	1901-1929?-1982
4.4.7.3.11.2	Robert Earl	1903-1927-1981
4.4.7.3.11.3	Jess Frank/Jack	1905-1928-1983
4.4.7.3.11.4	Ray	1907- -1909
4.4.7.3.11.5	Edythe Mary	1912-1934-2006
4.4.7.3.11.6	Bessie A.	1915-1936-2003

4.4.7.4.1   **MONTEE, Oella** b 1852; d & bur 1854, Schuyler Co., IL.
I know of this child only through Betty Ramsey's *Monty-Montee History*, p. 168.

4.4.7.4.2   **MONTEE, Mary E.** b May/Jun 1854, OH; d & bur Apr 1862, Little Sandusky, OH.
Mary Monty (sic) was 6 years old in June 1860 when she was living with her parents in Little Sandusky, OH (US census). According to the inscription on her tombstone in the Little Sandusky Cemetery, she was 7 years, 1 month, and 14 days old when she died in April 1862.

4.4.7.4.3   **MONTEE, Anna E.** b 5 Apr 1856, Little Sandusky, OH. She married 9 Oct 1871, Wyandot Co., OH, **William M. Welch** (William Welch & Margaret A. Smith) b 13 Jun 1851, Antrim, OH; d 17 Oct 1883, Nevada, OH.
Mrs. Anna E. Welch was living with her two children in her father's household in Nevada, OH, in 1880 while her husband, a 29-year-old farm laborer, was staying in the household of his brother James A. Welch in Antrim Twp, OH. As a widow she lived with her widowed mother in Little Sandusky, OH, in 1900 and in Upper Sandusky, OH, in 1910. Both her own children were then still alive (US censuses).
William Welch was buried in the Nevada Cemetery. The dates of his birth and death are found in the *History of Wyandot County* (1884), p. 732.

Children:
i   **Charles William Welch** b 10 Apr 1872, Antrim Twp, OH. He married (1) 21 Sep 1893, Wyandot Co., OH, **Callie/Selena California Putnam** (David Putnam & Lydia Ann Morehart) b 22 Apr 1866, Hancock Co., OH; d 18 Dec 1908, Marion, OH.
       He married (2) 1 May 1909, Epworth, OH, **Myrtle C. Gordon** b 1881?, OH.
ii   **Ralph E. Welch** b 14 Feb 1875, Antrim Twp, OH. He married (1) 16 Sep 1896, Wyandot Co., OH, **Floy E. Walterhouse** (Israel Walterhouse & Lucinda Bunn) b 4 Sep 1877, Little Sandusky, OH; d there 27 Jul 1906.
       He married (2) 11 Mar 1908, Upper Sandusky, OH, **Frances Isabel Culver** (John Culver & Nancy E. Irvin) b there 8 Dec 1880; m (1) there 21 Apr 1901 Albert Bahr (Conrad Bahr & Lena Hill).

4.4.7.4.4   **MONTEE, John H.** b 11 Dec 1873, Little Sandusky, OH; d between 1884 and 1900.
John H. Montee was living with his parents in Nevada, OH, in 1880 and was still alive when the *History of Wyandot County* was published in 1884 (p. 720). He was deceased in June 1900 when his mother had only one surviving child, her daughter Anna (US censuses).

4.4.7.4.5   **MONTEE, Randolph B.** b 1875?, Little Sandusky, OH; d between 1880 and 1884.
Randolph B. Montee was a 5-year-old child living with his parents in Nevada, OH, in 1880 (US census). He was deceased however when the *History of Wyandot County* was published in 1884: his parents then had only two surviving children, Anna (4.4.7.4.2) and John (4.4.7.4.3).

4.4.7.5.1   **MONTEE, Alice Lodema** b 17 Jul 1854, Little Sandusky, OH; d & bur 7 & ? Sep 1880, Galion & Upper Sandusky, OH. She married 27 Feb 1873, Wyandot Co., OH, **Milton Naylor** (John Nailor & Sarah A. _____) b Apr 1849, Marion, OH; m (2) 1882? Anna _____.
Alice Monty was living in June 1880 with her husband and 6-year-old son in Galion, OH. She died a few months later and was buried in Oak Hill Cemetery in Upper Sandusky, OH, in the same lot as her parents and grandparents.
Milton Naylor was a carpenter in Galion in 1880 and later in Marion, OH, until at least 1920. In 1900 he and his second wife, Anna, had been married for eighteen years and had had

seven sons of their own (US censuses). Alice Montee's son was not then living with his father. I have been unable to find the child after 1880.

Child:

    i   **Edward Naylor** b 1874?, OH.

4.4.7.5.2   **MONTEE, David Leroy** b 7 Aug 1856, Little Sandusky, OH; d there 29 Aug 1920. He married 2 Sep 1876, Wyandot Co., OH, **Mary Jane Sheets** (Peter Sheets & Margaret Spong) b there 17 Aug 1860; d 14 Apr 1930, Bucyrus, OH.

    David Montee was a farm worker and laborer in Little Sandusky, OH, throughout his life. He and his wife were buried in the Little Sandusky Cemetery.

Children:

4.4.7.5.2.1	Margaret Ellen	1877-1899-1967
4.4.7.5.2.2	Myrta Edna	1880-1897-1967
4.4.7.5.2.3	Emma B.	1882-1904-1973
4.4.7.5.2.4	Frances Belle	1883-1903-1977
4.4.7.5.2.5	Grover Cleveland	1887- -1956
4.4.7.5.2.6	Fowler C.	1890-1917&1927?-1972
4.4.7.5.2.7	Lorin Edward	1892-1915-1961
4.4.7.5.2.8	Iva M.	1896- -1977
4.4.7.5.2.9	Robert L.	1898-1921-1983
4.4.7.5.2.10	Villa Faye	1901-1917&1921?-1971
4.4.7.5.2.11	Mary B.	1903-1920?-1983

4.4.7.5.3   **MONTEE, Francis Edward/Frank E.** b 24 Nov 1858, Macomb, IL; d & bur 13 & 15 May 1924, Little Sandusky & Upper Sandusky, OH. He married 14 Apr 1878, Wyandot Co., OH, **Magdalena/Lena Weist** (Christopher Weist & Mary Ann Wilt) b 25 Jun 1861, Cardington, OH; d & bur 16 & 18 Sep 1939, Upper Sandusky, OH.

    Frank Montee was born in Illinois during his parents' brief period of residence there between 1857 and 1862. He moved with them to Little Sandusky, OH, where he became a farmer and remained until his death. His widow was still living there in 1930 (US censuses).

    Frank E. Montee and Magdalena Weist Montee were both buried alongside his parents in Oak Hill Cemetery in Upper Sandusky, OH.

Children:

4.4.7.5.3.1	Stella Mae	1878-1895-1922
4.4.7.5.3.2	Charles Edward	1880-1905-1965
4.4.7.5.3.3	Ralph Francis	1883-1909-1935
4.4.7.5.3.4	Alice Lodema	1886-1904-1965

4.4.7.6.1   **MONTEE, Leafie Elnora** b 21 Sep 1856, Little Sandusky, OH; d 24 Dec 1929, Stark, KS. She married 19 May 1877, Beulah, KS, **Benjamin F. Cummings** (Thomas Cummings & Ellen Cunningham) b Oct 1856, Camp Point, IL.

    Benjamin F. Cummings was a resident of Sheridan, KS, at his marriage, a farmer in Barton Co., MO, in 1880, and a farmer again in Sheridan in 1900, when his father-in-law James Montee was his landlord. In 1910 he was a painter/paperhanger in Erie, KS. He and his wife had had two children, both still alive. They also had an adopted child, James T., with whom Benjamin Cummings would make his home in Coffeeville, KS, after his wife's death (US censuses).

Children:

    i   **Hattie E. Cummings** b 1878?, MO.
    ii   **Jessie Cummings** b Sep 1881, MO. She married 1 Jun 1897, Neosho Co., KS, **George Barnhart** (Calvin Barnhart & Anne Moore) b Mar 1875, Walnut Grove, KS.

4.4.7.6.2   **MONTEE, Charles Clifford** b 22 Aug 1860, Bethel Twp, IL; d & bur 30 May & 2 Jun 1929, Pittsburg, KS. He married 3 Jul 1883, Girard, KS, **Daisy May Kelly** (George W. Kelly & Mary I. Thomas) b 29 May 1865, Lebanon, IL; d 6 May 1945, Pittsburg, KS.

Charles Clifford Montee was a teenager when his parents moved to Crawford Co., KS, where he spent the rest of his life. He was a farm laborer in Sheridan Twp in 1880 and a farmer there until at least 1920. He and his wife soon retired to neighboring Pittsburg, KS, where his widow was still living in 1930 (US censuses). They were both buried in Mount Olive Cemetery there.

Children:

4.4.7.6.2.1	Hattie May	1885- -1885
4.4.7.6.2.2	Charles Sylvester	1886-1909-1954
4.4.7.6.2.3	Nora Lee	1887-1915-1927
4.4.7.6.2.4	Iva Ruth	1891-1916-1985
4.4.7.6.2.5	Harry Earl	1896-1923-1960
4.4.7.6.2.6	Clair Edward	1902-1939-1980
4.4.7.6.2.7	Ruby Nadine	1911-1927&1974-

4.4.7.6.3   **MONTEE, James Wilson Jr**. b 22 Oct 1862, Macomb, IL; d & bur 26 & 30 Dec 1956, Los Angeles & Whittier, CA. He married 13 Dec 1893, Salem, OR, **Margaret Julia White** (Elijah H. White & Mary Ellen Mitchell) b 31 Mar 1870, Burnside, PA; d & bur 12 & 16 Oct 1962, Palm Springs & Whittier, CA.

James Wilson Montee Jr. had an extraordinarily varied and eventful life, as is documented in Betty Ramsey's *Monty-Montee History*, pp. 320-383. He was in turn a stage coach driver in Dodge City, KS, a homesteader in Ashland, KS, a photographer in Ohio, Kansas, Oregon, and California where he and his wife came after their marriage. By 1895 he was in the citrus business in Redlands, CA, where he was also a photographer in 1900. He next moved to Los Angeles, CA, where he was a house builder in 1920. He also found a new interest in aviation. He not only participated with his son Kenneth in founding the K. W. Montee Aircraft Co. but also learned how to fly and obtained his pilot's license in 1927 at the age of 65. He was indeed described in 1930, when he was 68 years old, as an aviator at Clover Field in Santa Barbara, CA (US censuses). His passion for flying never abated. Numerous newspapers around the country reported in 1947 on his flight in one of the early jet planes on his 85th birthday. They also noted his habit of taking his family on a flight over Los Angeles on his birthdays, the last such outing being just one year before his death, on his 93rd birthday.

Children:

4.4.7.6.3.1	Kenneth White	1897-1920-1926
4.4.7.6.3.2	Ralph Bunn	1899-1919?&1929?-1932
4.4.7.6.3.3	Harold Jack	1902-1922& -1965
4.4.7.6.3.4	Pauline Mildred	1911-1939-1989

4.4.7.6.4   **MONTEE, Harriet Ann/Hattie** b 22 Dec 1864, Macomb, IL; d 20 Oct 1944, La Cygne, KS. She married 1 Mar 1892, Cherokee, KS, **Stephen Marion Millard** (William Henry Millard & Elizabeth Henderson) b 30 Mar 1859, Pennville, MO; d 30 Oct 1943, La Cygne, KS.

Before his marriage Stephen Millard had been a whaler in the Pacific and Atlantic Oceans for seven years. Three of his letters to "Miss Hattie" are included in Betty Ramsey's *Monty-Montee History*, pp. 385-392. He was a resident of Cherokee, KS, at his marriage and a carpenter in Pittsburg, KS, in 1900. He then bought a farm in Lincoln Twp near La Cygne, KS, where he and his wife remained until their deaths (US censuses). They had no children.

4.4.7.6.5   **MONTEE, Francis Abraham** b 29 May 1867, Macomb, IL; d 12 Apr 1912, Anaheim, CA. He married 28 Jun 1894, Los Angeles, CA, **Katie/Cassie B./Katherine**

O'Donnell (Thomas O'Donnell & Anna _____) b Mar 1866, Columbus, OH; d 12 Apr 1912, Anaheim, CA.

Francis Abraham Montee had come to Cherokee, KS, with his parents in the mid-1870s and was living with them there in 1880. He may have accompanied, or perhaps followed, his brother James Wilson Montee (4.4.7.6.3) to Oregon in the early 1890s for he was a resident of Salem, OR, at his marriage. He remained in California, though, after his marriage and was a foreman in the Alpine Plaster Company in Los Angeles, CA, in 1900 and a farmer in Fullerton Twp, CA, in 1910 (US censuses). He was also a businessman owning several properties in Orange Co., CA. It was there he and his wife were murdered in a dispute over some land holdings near Anaheim, CA. They were both buried in Lee Mission Cemetery in Boyle Heights, CA, where they had lived. They had no children.

His wife's name varies. It was Katie when she was a child living with her parents in Columbus, OH, as well as at her marriage, Cassie B. in the 1900 and 1910 censuses in Los Angeles and Orange counties, and Katherine at her death.

4.4.7.6.6   **MONTEE, William Arthur** b 11 Nov 1869, Macomb, IL; d & bur 18 & 20 Aug 1965, Pleasanton & LaCygne, KS. He married 1 Mar 1892, Cherokee, KS, **Nora Julia Woodling** (Isaac Woodling & Mary Elizabeth Garwood) b there 16 Dec 1873; m (2) 25 Aug 1936, Las Animas, CO, H. Bert Siens; d & bur 2 & 4 Oct 1950, French Camp, CA.

William Arthur Montee came to Cherokee, KS, with his parents in the mid-1870s and was a coal miner in Sheridan, KS, in 1900. He left around 1907 for Rocky Ford, CO, where he was a carpenter and house builder, and also a farmer in 1910. He and his wife divorced before 1920. She was in Rocky Ford with their children in 1920 and 1930 while he returned to Kansas and bought a farm in Linn County (US censuses). He moved to Pleasanton, KS, a few years before his death.

Nora Julia Woodling's second marriage ended in divorce. She again took the Montee surname and spent her last years with her daughter Sylvia in Manteca, CA.

Children:

4.4.7.6.6.1	Donald R.	1893- -1893
4.4.7.6.6.2	Grace Elizabeth	1894-1914-1989
4.4.7.6.6.3	Clarence Arthur	1896- -1908
4.4.7.6.6.4	Lucy Harriet	1899- -1899
4.4.7.6.6.5	Goldie Juanita	1902-1924-1976
4.4.7.6.6.6	Sylvia Ruth	1904-1925-1984
4.4.7.6.6.7	William Albert	1908-1931&1958-1982

4.4.7.8.1   **MONTEE, Hester** b 1862?, Macomb, IL.

Hester Montee was an 8-year-old child living with her paternal grandparents in Macomb, IL, in 1870 (US census).

4.4.7.8.2   **MONTEE, Susan/Susie E.** b 24 Dec 1864, Macomb, IL; d 26 Jul 1941, Los Angeles, CA. She married 1885? **William B. Osborn** b Mar 1854, AR.

William Osborn was a saw mill worker in River Twp, AR, in 1900 when he and his wife had been married for fifteen years. They were still in Arkansas in 1910, running a boarding house in Brown Springs, AR, but later moved to Louisiana. William Osborn was a lumber mill worker in Pineville, LA, in 1920 (US censuses).

Children:
i   **Hattie R. Osborn** b May 1886, AR.
ii   **George Ransom Osborn** b 2 Sep 1888, AR. He married **Rosa E. _____** b 1897?, LA.
iii **William Montee Osborn** b 14 Mar 1891, Malvern, AR.

4.4.7.9.1   **MONTEE, Anna Alice** b 5 Jun 1862, Macomb, IL; d & bur 17 & 19 Dec 1946, Stillwater, OK. She married 4 Sep 1879, Cherokee, KS, **John Partee Hoke** (John I.

Hoke & Nancy Matilda Teague Bowman) b 27 Aug 1854, Taylorsville, NC; d & bur 26 & 28 Apr 1941, Stillwater, OK.

Anna Alice Montee came to Kansas with her parents in the mid-1870s and married there. Her husband was a farmer in Cherokee, KS, until the early 1890s when the family moved to Quay, OK. John Hoke was a farmer there in 1900 and 1910 but moved again before 1920 to Stillwater, OK, where he and his wife continued to reside until their deaths (US censuses).

Children:

i   **Addie May Hoke** b 23 May 1880, Cherokee, KS; d 31 May 1918, Stillwater, OK. She married 30 May 1897, Quay, OK, **William T. Beeler** (John J. Beeler & Mary E. Thomas) b 26 Apr 1872, Lancaster, MO; d 2 Dec 1960, Stillwater, OK.

ii   **John Francis Hoke** b 3 Feb 1882, Cherokee, KS; d there 4 Sep 1886.

iii   **Charles Edward Hoke** b 31 Aug 1883, Cherokee, KS; d Feb 1972, Siloam Springs, AR. He married 26 Oct 1910, Eufaula, OK, **Leah Caroline Brown** (Milton William Brown & Susanna Uhl) b 9 Mar 1885, Douglass, KS; d 27 Apr 1963, Siloam Springs, AR.

iv   **Harry Grover Hoke** b 19 Sep 1884, Cherokee, KS; d 21 Oct 1966, Stillwater, OK. He married 3 Sep 1912, Pittsburgh, PA, **Mabel Kate Charlton** (William Church Charlton & Kate Idella Morledge) b there 12 Apr 1885; d 6 May 1981, Stillwater, OK.

v   **Mary Matilda Hoke** b 18 Dec 1887, Sheridan, KS; d Oct 1980, Nevada, MO. She married 7 Jul 1917, Tulsa, OK, **Riley Elmer Andrew** (Ensley G. Andrew & Elizabeth J. Blair) b 24 Aug 1879, Warren, IN; m (1) 1904? Delight Mary Lynn (Benjamin Brothers Lynn & Nancy Louisa McMillan); d 10 Jan 1958, Nevada, MO.

vi   **George Albert Hoke** b 6 Feb 1889, Cherokee, KS; d Mar 1969, Norman, OK. He married **Lavalette Collins** (John H. Collins & Banner Hood) b 9 Oct 1888, Charlotte, NC.

vii   **Mac Hoke** b 27 May 1891, Cherokee, KS; d 19 Jun 1945, Portland, OR. He married 30 Dec 1914, Stillwater, OK, **Carrie Williamson** (Francis M. Williamson & Nettie Godard) b 24 Jan 1893, Galesburg, IL; d & bur 3 & 7 Jan 1992, Pendleton, OR.

viii   **Rhoda Charlotte Hoke** b 15 Dec 1892, Cherokee, KS; d 9 Jun 1983, Spearman, TX. She married 15 May 1919, Stillwater, OK, **Haden Bourland Hart** (Walter Bedford Hart & Margaret Elizabeth Bradshaw) b 6 Apr 1892, Montague, TX; d 11 Dec 1967, Gruver, TX.

ix   **Roy Theodore Hoke** b 31 Oct 1895, Quay, OK; d Sep 1987, Stillwater, OK. He married there 22 Aug 1917 **Estelle Roberts** b 11 Sep 1897, TN; d 23 Apr 1978, Stillwater, OK.

x   **Jesse Walter Hoke** b 7 Aug 1899, Quay, OK; d Nov 1981, Oklahoma City, OK. He married 21 Jun 1924, Clinton, OK, **Melba Remund** (George Remund & Bertha Radant) b 22 Sep 1903, Waseca, MN; d 9 Apr 2001, Oklahoma City, OK.

xi   **James T. Hoke** b 6 Feb 1902, Quay, OK; d Aug 1983, Green Valley, AZ. He married 20 Dec 1924, Stillwater, OK, **Marie Mayberry** b 9 Jun 1905, Claremore, OK; d Nov 1986, Tucson, AZ.

4.4.7.9.2   **MONTEE, Emma Harriet** b 3 Dec 1863, Macomb, IL; d & bur 21 & 23 Oct 1946, Coldwater & Uniontown, KS. She married 23 Feb 1882, Girard, KS, **James Edward Monroe Biles** (Alexander William Biles & Mary Jane Burrage) b 19 Feb 1855, Albermale, NC; d & bur 25 & 28 Oct 1942, Wellston & St. Louis, MO.

Emma Harriet Montee and her sister Mary Elizabeth (4.4.7.9.3) married two brothers. James Edward Biles was for many years a farmer in Uniontown, KS, before moving to another farm near Fort Scott, KS, where he and his wife lived for thirty years (US censuses; *The Western Star*, Coldwater, KS, 6 Nov 1942).

Children:

<table>
<tr><td>i</td><td>

Mary Emily/Mamie Biles b 9 Jan 1883, Pittsburg, KS; d & bur 2 & 4 Mar 1968, Coldwater & Crown Hill, KS. She married 20 Dec 1899, Fort Scott, KS, **Riley Davis Harris** (Thomas Harris & Lenora Sachet) b 12 May 1879, Rich Hill, MO; d & bur 3 & 6 Feb 1941, Coldwater & Crown Hill, KS.
</td></tr>
</table>

i **Mary Emily/Mamie Biles** b 9 Jan 1883, Pittsburg, KS; d & bur 2 & 4 Mar 1968, Coldwater & Crown Hill, KS. She married 20 Dec 1899, Fort Scott, KS, **Riley Davis Harris** (Thomas Harris & Lenora Sachet) b 12 May 1879, Rich Hill, MO; d & bur 3 & 6 Feb 1941, Coldwater & Crown Hill, KS.

ii **Flora Belle/Floy B. Biles** b 3 Jul 1884, Uniontown, KS; d Mar 1984, Coldwater, KS. She married 20 Jun 1907, St. Louis, MO, **Joseph Brauss** (Carl Brauss & ___) b 14 Dec 1880, Coblentz, Germany; d & bur 14 & 16 Jul 1947, St. Louis, MO.

iii **Maude Anna Biles** b 2 Mar 1887, Uniontown, KS; d & bur 23 & 26 Aug 1963, St. Louis, MO. She married there 19 Mar 1910 **Gustav A. Zell** (John Zell & Ann Rieke) b there 20 Nov 1886, m (1) Rose Goldkuhl; d & bur 26 & 29 Dec 1973, Branson & St. Louis, MO.

iv **Lloyd Montee Biles** b 31 Dec 1900, Uniontown, KS; d & bur 9 & 12 Mar 1980, Fort Scott & Uniontown, KS. He married 10 Oct 1923, Independence, MO, **Vera Lillian Martin** (James Hudson Martin & Myrtle May Barnett) b 13 Feb 1903, Hamilton, IA; d 2 May 1998, Redfield, KS.

v **Juanita Letitia Biles** b 22 Jul 1903, Uniontown, KS; d & bur 19 & 22 May 1928, Granite City, IL & St. Louis, MO. She married 17 Jul 1926, St. Louis, MO, **John Ignatius Mimlitz** (Matthew Mimlitz & Rose ____) b there 17 Aug 1900; m (2) Gladys Mueller; d & bur there 6 & 10 Dec 1957.

vi **Ferne Marion Biles** b 23 Feb 1906, Uniontown, KS; d & bur 17 & 21 Jul 1972, St. Louis, MO. She married there 23 Feb 1934 **Leroy Henry Temme** (Johann Herman David Temme & Wilhelmine Martha Louisa Paske) b there 27 Sep 1909; m (2) there 16 Aug 1973 Anna Louise Sauerwein, widow of John Wilson Jr.; d there 5 Jun 1991.

4.4.7.9.3   **MONTEE, Mary Elizabeth** b 31 Aug 1865, Macomb, IL; d & bur 17 & 18 Feb 1940, McAlester, OK. She married 1 Mar 1888, Cherokee, KS, **Rufus A. Biles** (Alexander William Biles & Mary Jane Burrage) b 7 Apr 1863, Albermale, NC; d & bur 9 & 11 Oct 1936, McAlester, OK.

Mary Elizabeth Montee and her sister Emma Harriet (4.4.7.9.2) married two brothers. Her own husband was a farmer in Cherokee, KS, until at least 1896, a baker in Joplin, MO, in 1900 and in McAlester, OK, in 1910, and a private businessman there in 1920. He was retired in 1930 (US censuses). Both he and his wife were buried in Oak Hill Cemetery in McAlester.

Children:

i **Francis Martin Biles** b 29 Mar 1889, Cherokee, KS; d there 22 Jun 1889.

ii **Dessie Elsie Biles** b 14 Nov 1890, Cherokee, KS; d 31 Oct 1954, McAlester, OK. She married (1) there 25 Oct 1910 **Hamilton Johnson** (Henry Viley Johnson & Rose Rarrish) b 28 Aug 1884, Georgetown, KY; d & bur 17 & ? May 1919, McAlester, OK & Georgetown, KY.
She married (2) Nov 1942 **William R. Hatfield**.

iii **Edith Montee Biles** b 25 Sep 1896, Cherokee, KS; d 12 Aug 1952. She married Nov 1940 **Marion Jasper Dean** (Morris Dean & Mariah Jasper) b 8 May 1881, Little Hickman, KY; m (1) 1907? Nora D. Coghill (James Spencer Coghill & Eliza Thorp); d 14 Jan 1961.

4.4.7.9.4   **MONTEE, Francis Edward** b 1 Aug 1867, Macomb, IL; d 30 Dec 1925, Pittsburg, KS. He married (1) 29 Dec 1887, McDonough Co., IL, **Annette Andrews** (James Andrews & Rosanna Bown) b 8 Jul 1869, Chalmers, IL; d 10 May 1957, Macomb, IL.

He was divorced when he married (2) 12 Mar 1902 Aurora, MO, **Olive E. Quinby** (Charles Quinby & Amelia Stanton) b 21 Dec 1881, NV; m (2) 1928, Los Angeles, CA, Freeman J. Neal (John F. Neal & Clara Reno Akin); d there 13 Feb 1964.

Francis Edward Montee came to Kansas with his parents in the mid-1870s and became a farmer in Cherokee, KS, where the children of his first marriage were born. He moved to Oklahoma after his second marriage and was in 1910 the president of a lumber company in Atoka, OK. He was an oil operator in Tulsa, OK, in 1920 (US censuses).

Annette Andrews returned to Illinois after her divorce and was staying with her children in her father's household in Chalmers, IL, in 1900 and 1910. She was living with her son Jesse in Emmet Twp, IL, in 1920 and, after his death, in Chalmers again in 1930 (US censuses).

Olive Quinby was living with her second husband and her son Stanton Montee in Los Angeles, CA, in 1930 (US census).

Children of the first marriage:

4.4.7.9.4.1	Jesse Howard	1888- -1925
4.4.7.9.4.2	Estella Gertrude	1890-1907-1935
4.4.7.9.4.3	Grace Fern	1893-1912-1956

Children of the second marriage:

4.4.7.9.4.4	Francis Edward	1907-1928?&	&	-1968
4.4.7.9.4.5	Stanton Quinby	1917-1944-1990		

4.4.7.9.5   **MONTEE, Albert A.** b 3 Dec 1868, Macomb, IL; d & bur 25 & 28 Mar 1946, Hepler & Walnut, KS. He married (1) 15 Oct 1891, Girard, KS, **Amanda Cooley** b 1871?

He married (2) 18 Jun 1904, Neosho, MO, **Lenora Hazel Harris** b 18 Jul 1886, Walnut, KS; d & bur 8 & 10 Jul 1923, Cherokee & Walnut, KS.

Albert A. Montee came to Kansas with his parents in the mid-1870s and was a resident of Cherokee, KS, at his first marriage when his bride 20 years old. He was a druggist in Girard, KS, in 1910 and a farmer in Sheridan Twp, KS, in 1920 and 1930 (US censuses).

Children of the second marriage:

4.4.7.9.5.1	Paul Leo	1905- -1906		
4.4.7.9.5.2	Gerald Fremont	1907-1930&1979-1999		
4.4.7.9.5.3	Mary Kathryn	1909-1928-1993		
4.4.7.9.5.4	Albert A.	1911-1945-1987		
4.4.7.9.5.5	Frederick Dale	1913-1979-2003		
4.4.7.9.5.6	Clarence Edward	1915-	&	-1973
4.4.7.9.5.7	Charlotte Louise	1920- -1997		

4.4.7.9.6   **MONTEE, Charles Finley** b 15 Jul 1870, Macomb, IL; d & bur 30 May & 1 Jun 1928, Pittsburg, KS. He married 18 Nov 1897, Plymouth, IL, **Ina Isabella Scott** (David Scott & Maria Poster) b Apr 1874, Lamoine Twp, IL; d 25 Feb 1910, Colchester, IL.

He married (2) 30 Apr 1911, Crawford Co., KS, **Eva Willey** (William H. Willey & Ida Hammond) b Jul 1885, Cherokee Co., KS.

Charles Finley Montee came to Kansas with his parents in the mid-1870s and was a pharmacist in Cherokee, KS, at his first marriage and until at least 1900. He then left to study medicine at the Barnes Medical School in St. Louis, MO. He practiced for a few years in Colchester, IL, where his children were born, before returning to Kansas soon after his first wife's death. He established a practice in Pittsburg, KS, and was also for a time the City's Health Officer and the Crawford Co. Coroner. His private life was apparently less successful: by 1920 he was divorced from his second wife (US censuses).

Children of the first marriage:

4.4.7.9.6.1	Dolly Isabelle	1907- -1907
4.4.7.9.6.2	Jewell Kenneth	1908-1930-1991

4.4.7.9.7   **MONTEE, James Walter** b 23 May 1872, Macomb, IL; d & bur 6 & 8 Sep 1950, Joplin, MO. He married 31 Jan 1898, Crawford Co., KS, **Letitia Schol Kennedy** (George Kennedy & Sarah Reaugh) b 12 Aug 1872, Jacksonville, IL; d & bur 6 & 8 Mar 1947, Joplin, MO.

James Walter Montee came to Kansas with his parents in the mid-1870s and became a pharmacist, businessman, and legislator in Crawford Co., KS. He was a pharmacist in Girard, KS, in 1910, a bank president there in 1920, and a pharmacist in Arcadia, KS, in 1930 (US censuses). Beginning in 1893 he served six terms as a Kansas State Representative (Republican) and two terms as a Senator. He moved around 1935 to Joplin, MO, where he established the Montee pharmacy (*The Joplin Globe*, 7 Sep 1950). He and his wife were buried in the Ozark Memorial Park Cemetery in Joplin, MO.

Child:

4.4.7.9.7.1	Sarah Frances	1907-1930-1978

4.4.7.9.8   **MONTEE, Samuel Theodore** b 27 Jan 1875, Cherokee, KS; d & bur 19 & 22 May 1967, Girard & Pittsburg, KS. He married (1) 24 May 1899, Galena, KS, **Freda Ada Downing** (Abraham Nelson Downing & Mattie/Martha A. Duvall) b 22 Mar 1879, Council Grove, KS; d & bur 8 & 11 May 1910, Pittsburg, KS.

He married (2) 28 Aug 1913, Carl Junction, MO, **Effie Luellen Vance** (Robert Bruce Vance & Effie _____) b 22 Jul 1884, St. Louis, MO; d 9 Mar 1988, Pittsburg, KS.

Theodore Montee was a street car conductor in Pittsburg, KS, in 1910 and 1920, and a real estate agent in Girard, KS, in 1930 (US censuses). He was also a partner in his brother James' drug store in Girard and, like his brother, was active in politics. He was the Crawford County Treasurer from 1923 to 1927. He and his first wife were buried in Mount Olive Cemetery in Pittsburg.

Children of the first marriage:

4.4.7.9.8.1	Ruth Duene	1901-1921-1995
4.4.7.9.8.2	Ralph Cyril	1903-1926?&1956-1975
4.4.7.9.8.3	Nadine Theodora	1905-1933-1999

Children of the second marriage:

4.4.7.9.8.4	Theodore Vance	1914-1946-
4.4.7.9.8.5	Norris Hadley	1919- -1943

4.4.7.9.9   **MONTEE, William Valentine** b 11 Jun 1877, Cherokee, KS; d & bur 27 & 31 Jan 1969, Billings, MT. He married 4 Oct 1899, Pittsburg, KS, **Elizabeth Norman** (Alfred Norman & Mary E. Matthews) b 29 Mar 1881, Wetmore, PA; d & bur 10 & 14 Jul 1934, Billings, MT.

William Valentine Montee was a farmer in Pittsburg, KS, until at least 1926. He moved in the late 1920s to Billings, MT, where he was a refinery worker in 1930 (US censuses). He and his wife were buried in Mountview Cemetery there.

Children:

4.4.7.9.9.1	Hazel Marie	1900-1922?&1950-1990
4.4.7.9.9.2	Florence Ætna	1902-1920-1975
4.4.7.9.9.3	Thelma Faye	1904-1924-1962
4.4.7.9.9.4	William Valentine	1906-1925-1994
4.4.7.9.9.5	Harold Clifton	1908-1931&1950-1974
4.4.7.9.9.6	Helen Veneta	1911-1932-2002
4.4.7.9.9.7	Clyde Merle	1912-1933-1973
4.4.7.9.9.8	Elizabeth Norma	1914-1935-2004
4.4.7.9.9.9	Marguerite Cecile	1918-1938-2001
4.4.7.9.9.10	Charles Finley	1920-1938&1962& -1999
4.4.7.9.9.11	Bernice Lavon	1922- -1984
4.4.7.9.9.12	Richard Wallace	1926- -1926

4.4.7.9.10   **MONTEE, Florence Ætna** b 9 Nov 1879, Cherokee, KS; d 4 May 1962, Topeka, KS. She married 20 Aug 1917, KS, **Jesse Wells Miley** (James W. Miley & Sarilda Hammond) b 13 Dec 1878, Farlington, KS; d & bur 14 & 17 Jan 1952, Topeka, KS.

Jesse Wells Miley was a public school teacher in Girard, KS, in 1910 and the Crawford County Superintendent of Schools there in 1918 and 1920. He was also the State Superintendent of schools in Topeka, KS, for a few years in the early and mid 1920s. By 1930 however he had returned to Crawford Co. and was president of an investment and loan company in Pittsburg, KS (US censuses). I do not know when the family moved permanently to Topeka. Both he and his wife were buried in Mount Hope Cemetery there.

Children:
i   **Dorothy Jean Miley** b 4 Sep 1919, Girard, KS; d 15 Nov 1998, Topeka, KS. She married **Everett A. Culbertson** (Jesse P. Culbertson & Blanche M. Leathem) b 8 Apr 1917, Kansas City, MO; d Jul 1989, Topeka, KS.
ii **Frances Marion Miley** b 22 May 1925, Topeka, KS; d & bur 15 & 19 Nov 2001, Rossville & Topeka, KS.

4.4.7.9.11   **MONTEE, Nellie Almeta** b 16 Oct 1881, Cherokee, KS; d & bur 13 & 15 Sep 1954, Winfield, KS. She married 10 Apr 1904, Girard, KS, **John Clement Starnes** (James Starnes & Mary Chapman) b 2 Feb 1877, Worthington, IN.
   John C. Starnes was a resident of Altamont, KS, at his marriage and a pharmacist in Winfield, KS, in 1920 (US census).

4.4.7.9.12   **MONTEE, Dolly May** b 7 Apr 1884, Cherokee, KS; d & bur 23 & 25 Aug 1962, Pittsburg, KS. She married 3 Aug 1909, Girard, KS, **Fred Muse** (John Muse & Almeda _____) b 8 Mar 1888, Clinton, MO; d & bur 27 & 29 Jul 1957, Pittsburg, KS.
   Fred Muse was a laborer in Wellington, KS, in 1900 and a farmer in Sheridan, KS, in 1915 and until at least 1930 (US and state censuses). I know of his daughter Edith's marriages only through Betty Ramsey's *Monty-Montee History*, p. 499.

Children:
i   **LeRoy Francis/Roy Muse** b 25 Feb 1910, Wellington, KS; d Feb 1984, Pittsburg, KS. He married 30 Sep 1934, Perry, OK, **Dorothy Imogene Scott** (Grover C. Scott & Maude A. Wells) b 7 Jul 1911, Sedan, KS; d 24 Apr 1994, Pittsburg, KS.
ii **Edith Maxine Muse** b 17 Apr 1917, Sheridan, KS. She married (1) 30 Dec 1936, **William McMurray**.
    She married (2) **William Willis Sullivan**.

4.4.7.9.13   **MONTEE, Clarence Martin** b 16 Feb 1886, Cherokee, KS; d & bur 6 & 8 Dec 1967, Pittsburg & Arcadia, KS. He married 1 Nov 1908, Arcadia, KS, **Sarah Catherine Mohon** (George Benjamin Mohon & Georgia M. Major) b 1 Apr 1889, Garland, KS; d & bur 23 & 26 Apr 1972, Hutchinson & Arcadia, KS.
   Clarence Montee was a physician in Pittsburg, KS (US censuses). He was also the mayor of the city from 1923 to 1927.

Children:
4.4.7.9.13.1	Mary Elizabeth	1909-1931-1999
4.4.7.9.13.2	Benjamin Mohon	1911-1931&1965-1992
4.4.7.9.13.3	Dennis Lee	1915-1937&1968-1984

4.4.7.12.1   **MONTEE, Charles Edward** b 28 Oct 1868, Macomb, IL; d 13 Sep 1945, Pittsburg, KS. He married (1) 20 Dec 1893, Liberty, NE, **Frances Isabella Kivett** (Richmond Kivett & Nancy Johnson) b there 20 Oct 1872; d & bur there 15 & ? Jun 1901.
   He married (2) 1909? **Ethel Maude Jackson** b 8 Mar 1889, Joplin, MO; d 23 May 1960, Pittsburg, KS.
   Charles E. Montee moved with his parents from Illinois to Crawford Co., KS, in the late 1870s, and from there left as a young man for Nebraska where he was a resident of Pawnee Co., at his first marriage. He was away from his family in 1900 when his wife and children were living in her mother's household in Liberty Twp, NE. Perhaps following his wife's

death in 1901, he returned to Kansas with his son (his surviving daughter remained in Nebraska with her maternal grandmother), remarried a few years later, and was a coal miner in Baker Twp, KS, in 1910 and in Washington, KS, in 1920. By 1930, when he and his second wife had been married for twenty-one years, he was a farmer in Ross Twp, KS (US censuses).

Children of the first marriage:

4.4.7.12.1.1	Nona Myrtle	1894-1917-1981
4.4.7.12.1.2	Earl Lester	1896-1918-1960
4.4.7.12.1.3	Wilma I.	1900- -1901

Children of the second marriage:

4.4.7.12.1.4	Francis Evelyn	1910- -1910
4.4.7.12.1.5	LaVaye Amelia	1911-1937&1945-1998
4.4.7.12.1.6	Mary E.	1915- -
4.4.7.12.1.7	Lillian Belle	1917-1934-1991
4.4.7.12.1.8	Angeline Irene	1926-1944& &1998-

4.4.7.12.2 **MONTEE, William Henry** b 30 Jun 1870, Macomb, IL; d & bur 5 & 8 Nov 1961, Cherokee, KS. He married 4 Dec 1907, Girard, KS, **Lucy Evans** (Edward Evans & Ann Ibbeson) b 11 Jan 1880, Collinsville, IL; m (1) 15 Sep 1896, Girard, KS, Hugh McNeilly; d 10 Sep 1959, Cherokee, KS.

William Henry Monty came to Crawford Co., KS, with his parents in the late 1870s. He was a coal miner in Baker Twp, Ks, in 1900 and a farmer in Sheridan Twp, KS, until at least 1930 (US censuses). He and his wife were buried in the McNeilly plot in the Cherokee City Cemetery in Cherokee, KS. One of his stepchildren, Margaret Ann McNeilly, later married his nephew Claude Franklin Jackson (4.4.7.12.5.iv).

Child:

4.4.7.12.2.1	Dorothy Lucille	1911- -1981

4.4.7.12.3 **MONTEE, Louis Melvin** b 14 Jun 1872, Macomb, IL; d & bur 25 & 26 Sep 1945, Pittsburg, KS. He married 26 Dec 1892, Girard, KS, **Alice Letitia Gray** (Riley Gray & Martha J. Munroe) b 5 Jul 1876, Crawford, MO; d 7 Aug 1947, Pittsburg, KS.

Louis Melvin Montee came to Kansas as a child with his parents and was a resident of Fleming, KS, at his marriage. He was a stableman in Baker Twp, KS, in 1900, a farmer in Cherokee, KS, in 1910 and 1920, and a miner in Sheridan, KS, in 1930 (US censuses). He and his wife were buried in West Union Cemetery in Pittsburg, KS.

Children:

4.4.7.12.3.1	Myrtle	1894-1918-1982
4.4.7.12.3.2	Blanche	1896- -1898
4.4.7.12.3.3	Earl Merle	1899-1919-1969
4.4.7.12.3.4	Archie	1901-1922?-1965
4.4.7.12.3.5	Riley Finley	1903-1923?&1945-1958
4.4.7.12.3.6	Rolla Ray	1905-1924-1994
4.4.7.12.3.7	Carl Robert	1907-1930-1982
4.4.7.12.3.8	Fern R.	1910-1929?-2001
4.4.7.12.3.9	Louis Glen	1912-1935-1973
4.4.7.12.3.10	Alice	1916- -
4.4.7.12.3.11	Woodrow Wilson	1918-1939&-1970-2002

4.4.7.12.4 **MONTEE, Ollie Etta** b 1 Nov 1873, Macomb, IL; d 6 Jan 1965, Sheridan, WY. She married 1892? **William Bennett** (Alva Hamilton Bennett & Nancy Jane Cox) b Jun 1870, Harrison Co., WV; d Apr 1914, Sheridan, WY.

William Bennett was living with his family in Cloud Co., KS, in 1880. He apparently remained in Kansas after his marriage for all of his children save the youngest were born in that state until 1910. Yet in 1900, when he and his wife had been married for eight years, he was a teamster in Ozark Twp, MO. The family moved to Wyoming before the birth of the youngest child in March 1914 and William Bennett's death one month later. His widow remained in the Acme Camp in Sheridan Co., WY, where several of her children worked in the coal mines (US and state censuses).

Children:

i   **Mary Bennett** b 1895?, KS; d 1896, KS, at the age of 18 months.

ii   **William Byron Bennett** b 6 Apr 1897, KS; d May 1978, Newcastle, WY. He married 1926? **Hazel Brandt** b 1896?, MN; d 12 Nov 1956, Sheridan, WY.

iii   **John Edward Bennett** b 19 Oct 1898, KS; d 12 Aug 1925, Sheridan Co., WY. He married 15 Jul 1924, Sheridan, WY, **Elizabeth Mae Renie** (George W. Renie & Elizabeth Dunn) b 1906?, Sheridan Co., WY.

iv   **Lottie Bennett** b 14 Sep 1900, KS; d 2 Jan 1992, Sheridan, WY. She married there 21 Jun 1916 **Caesar Migratti** b 24 Jun 1891, Turin, Italy; d 5 Feb 1979, Sheridan, WY.

v   **Archie Lee Bennett** b 6 Sep 1902, KS; d Feb 1983, Sheridan, WY. He married 5 Sep 1925, WY, **Doris I. Lytle** (James John Lytle & Elma Viola _____) b 5 Jul 1906, Dietz, WY; d Nov 1989, Sheridan, WY.

vi   **Nellie Mae/Mary N. Bennett** b 10 Jul 1906, KS; d 13 Mar 1985, Pasco, WA. She married 7 Jul 1925, Sheridan, WY, **William Woodhead** (George Woodhead & Agnes Holsten) b 18 Jul 1895, WY; d 9 Nov 1969, Pasco, WA.

vii   **Alice E. Bennett** b 4 Aug 1908, KS; d 11 Jul 1998, Great Falls, MT. She married (1) 1928? **Nick Koacella** (Betty Ramsey, *Monty-Montee History*, p. 538).

      She married (2) **Emmet Eldridge Anderson** (Charles Anderson & Sina _____) b 24 Mar 1889, Harlan, IA.

viii   **George Bennett** b 9 Sep 1910, KS; d 12 Aug 1972. He married (1) **Ruby** ____.

      He was divorced when he married (2) **Vern** ____ (Betty Ramsey, *Monty-Montee History*, p. 538).

ix   **Frances Bennett** b 13 Mar 1914, Acme, WY; d 20 Oct 2000, Great Falls, MT. She married 1932, Choteau, MT, **John D. Panos** b 28 Dec 1898, Greece; d 15 Jul 1970, Great Falls, MT.

4.4.7.12.5   **MONTEE, Lillie Gay** b 31 Mar 1875, Macomb, IL; d 5 Dec 1907, Girard, KS. She married 23 Apr 1893, Crawford Co., KS, **William Jackson** (Andrew Jackson & Eliza Jane _____) b Apr 1873, IN.

William Jackson was a resident of Sheridan, KS, at his marriage and a laborer in Baker Twp, KS in 1900 (US census). I have been unable to find him in later censuses. The family appears to have scattered after Lillie Montee's death for the children, when later encountered, were all living in Oklahoma in relatives' households or on their own. William Jackson may have died before 12 Sep 1918 for his son Alva Elmer (ii) then named his brother Clyde (iii) as his nearest relative (World War I Draft Registration card).

Children:

i   **Marie Jackson** b & d 1894, KS.

ii   **Alva Elmer Jackson** b 15 Jun 1899, Baker Twp, KS; d 7 Jan 1937.

iii   **William Clyde Jackson** (twin) b 22 Nov 1900, Baker Twp, KS. He married **Anna Goodman**.

iv   **Claude Franklin Jackson** (twin) b 22 Nov 1900, Baker Twp, KS; d Feb 1980, Pittsburg, KS. He married **Margaret Ann McNeilly** (Hugh McNeilly & Lucy Evans) b 12 Jul 1900, Baker Twp, KS; d 20 Apr 1999, Pittsburg, KS.

4.4.7.12.6   **MONTEE, Rosa May** b 18 Mar 1879, Cherokee, KS; d & bur 2 & 5 Jan 1980, Pittsburg & Girard, KS. She married 19 Dec 1896 **Charles Clinton Everitt** (Robert D. Everitt & Elizabeth Friend) b 12 Dec 1875, Good Hope, OH; d 6 Dec 1972, Girard, KS.

     Charles C. Everitt was a coal miner in Baker Twp, KS, in 1900, a deputy county clerk in Girard, KS, in 1910 and the Crawford Co. Treasurer in 1920 and 1930 (US censuses). He also served a term as County auditor in 1934-1936 before becoming a tax preparer in 1942. He was still working in that capacity a year before his death when he and his wife celebrated their 75th wedding anniversary (*Great Bend Daily Tribune*, Great Bend, KS, 2 Dec 1971).

Children:

i **Robert Clifford Everitt** b 2 Jul 1898, Cherokee, KS; d Jan 1982, Girard, KS. He married (1) 24 Feb 1918, Ft. Sill, OK, **Ida Elizabeth James** (George Washington James & Alice Ann Bercham) b 11 Sep 1898, Arcadia (Mulberry), KS; m (2) ____ Schwartz; d 29 Jul 1972, Redwood City, CA.

He married (2) 1938 **Edna Evelyn Farmer** (James A. Farmer & Audrey C. ____) b 14 Aug 1914, MO; d 14 Dec 1964 (Betty Ramsey, *Monty-Montee History*, p 548).

He married (3) 14 Mar 1964, Columbus, KS, **Kathryn/Catherine Elizabeth Gill** (John Thomas Gill & Safrona Ann/Fannie Dunaway) b 22 Nov 1912, Denver, CO; m (1) 17 Feb 1929, Drumright, OK, Amos Ishmal Felts (Pink Green Felts & Laura Melinda Campbell); m (2) Jun 1948, Tijuana, Mexico, James Franklin Nance (James Franklin Nance & Lucille H. Hyslop); d 20 Mar 1998, Joplin, MO.

ii **Frances Pauline Everitt** b 13 Mar 1900, Baker Twp, KS; d 21 Oct 1990. She married 2 Oct 1918 **Frederick Dewey Banks** (George Banks & Julia A. ____) b 22 Sep 1899, Girard, KS; d 18 Oct 1975, Olathe, KS.

iii **Marces Alta Everitt** b 7 Oct 1901, Chicopee, KS; d Feb 1992, Pittsburg, KS. She married there 26 Jan 1928 **August DeGasperi** (August DeGasperi & Mary ____) b there 10 Oct 1897; d there Aug 1966.

iv **Montee Clinton Everitt** b 18 Dec 1905, Pittsburg, KS; d there 9 Sep 1992. He married 31 Dec 1929 **Cova Sneed** (William H. Sneed & Addie Lucinda McKinney) b 8 Aug 1907, Clay Twp, MO; d 31 Dec 1987, Pittsburg, KS.

4.4.7.12.7 **MONTEE, George Clois** b 18 Sep 1880, Cherokee, KS; d 8 Jul 1947, Drexel, MO. He married 8 Oct 1902, Girard, KS, **Laura Irene Nankivell** (James Stephen Nankivell & Eliza Walker) b 12 Feb 1885, Pittsburg, KS; d 22 Jan 1948, Drexel, MO.

George C. Montee was a farmer in Baker Twp, KS, in 1910 and in Washington Twp, KS, in 1920 and 1930. He was described in 1930 as both a farmer and a miner (US censuses).

Children:

4.4.7.12.7.1	William Clois	1903-1923-1984
4.4.7.12.7.2	Anna Mae	1905-1939-
4.4.7.12.7.3	Ora George	1907-1926-2003
4.4.7.12.7.4	James Stephen	1910-1928-1997
4.4.7.12.7.5	George Henry	1917-1938-1986
4.4.7.12.7.6	Emiline Marie	1921- -1921
4.4.7.12.7.7	Edward Glen	1922-1943&2000-2001

4.4.7.12.8 **MONTEE, Amanda Florence** b 18 Jan 1882, Crawford Co., KS; d 19 Jun 1959, Pittsburg, KS. She married 1913? **Charles G. Prideaux** (Lewis William Prideaux & Mary A. ____) b 9 Oct 1883, Crawford Co., KS.

Charles G. Prideaux was a coal miner in Pittsburg, KS, in 1910 and in Arma, KS, in 1920 and 1930 when he and his wife had been had been married for sixteen years (US censuses).

Children:

i **Pauline Prideaux** b 26 Jun 1914, Arma, KS. She married **Wilburn Argalia Enke** (Jesse Enke & Iva Mae Burton) b 17 Apr 1909, Stotts City, MO; d 25 Nov 1983, Chicago, IL.

ii **Montee Charles Prideaux** b 5 Dec 1916, Arma, KS; d 24 Aug 1998, Girard, KS. He married 15 Apr 1941, Chicago, IL, **Marietta Thurman** (Thomas L. Thurman &

Willa _____) b 28 Jan 1919, OK; d & bur 1 & 5 Dec 2004, Chicago, IL & Girard, KS.

4.4.7.12.9   **MONTEE, Emma Elizabeth** b 22 Nov 1886, MO; d 4 May 1927, Kansas City, KS. She married 12 Aug 1904, Crawford Co., KS, **William Asbury Stout** (Asbury Thompson Stout & Carrie Belle Timmons) b 22 Feb 1880, Georgetown, IL; d 31 May 1957, Kansas City, MO.

I have doubts about this listing. Emma Elizabeth Montee is not listed as Clois Montee's daughter in any US or state census I have seen. Neither have I found her living as a child with another family. The fact that she was born in Missouri while all her alleged siblings were born in Kansas also gives me pause. Yet family history holds that she was indeed the daughter of Clois Montee and Mary Catherine Ritter. I am including her name here, but with very little conviction.

Emma Elizabeth Montee was a resident of Fleming, KS, at her marriage while her husband was a resident of Kansas City, MO. He was a railroad car inspector in Kansas City, KS, in 1920 and 1930 (US censuses).

Children:
i   **Ruby May Stout** b 9 May 1906, Kansas City, KS; d 14 Dec 1995, St. Charles, MO. She married 9 Nov 1925, Kansas City, KS, **Frank McCoy** (Byron McCoy & Freddie McNew) b there 23 Aug 1902; d 5 Jan 1989, Hayward, CA.
ii   **Elsie Pauline Stout** b 1 Sep 1907, Kansas City, KS. She married (1) 1924? **Walter Henry Fischer** (Henry Fischer & Anna C. Horn) b 30 Mar 1903, Kansas City, KS; d 14 Dec 1976, Edwardsville, KS.
     She was divorced when she married (2) 21 Apr 1956 **Frank Charles Fair** (Betty Ramsey, *Monty-Montee History*, p. 574).
iii **Blanche Marie Stout** b 10 Jan 1909, Kansas City, KS; d there Dec 1981. She married there 1928? **William Frederick O'Brien** (John O'Brien & Maude Bunce) b there 8 Oct 1908; d there Aug 1968.
iv   **Clois Stout** b 1913?, Kansas City, KS.

4.4.7.12.10   **MONTEE, David A.** b 4 Apr 1889, Chicopee, KS; d & bur 9 & 12 Jan 1974, Merrionette Park, IL & Girard, KS. He married 17 Feb 1909, Girard, KS, **May Theresa Horn** (George Horn & Margaret _____) b 3 Apr 1893, Streator, IL; d 12 May 1960, Chicago, IL.

David A. Montee was a resident of Pittsburg, KS, at his marriage and a coal mine worker in Washington Twp, KS, in 1920. He left Kansas after the births of his children and was a laborer for a farm company in Chicago, IL, in 1930 (US censuses). Both he and his wife were buried in Girard, KS.

Children:

4.4.7.12.10.1	Reba A.	1909- -1984
4.4.7.12.10.2	Ruth Evelyn	1910-1930-1974
4.4.7.12.10.3	David A.	1922-1943-1961

4.5.1.1.1   **MONTA, John S.** b Sep 1845, Onondaga Co., NY.

John Monta lived with his parents in DeWitt, NY, in 1850 and 1860, was a laborer on his father's farm in Hannibal, NY, in 1870, 1880, and 1900, and was a truck farmer there in 1910. He left the farm a few years later and was living in 1920 with his sister Amanda (4.5.1.1.4) in Fulton, NY, where he was a factory worker. He did not marry (US censuses).

4.5.1.1.2   **MONTA, Sarah P.** b 1855?, Onondaga Co., NY. She married between 1870 and 1878 _____ **Perry**.

Sarah Monta was a 5-year-old child living with her parents in DeWitt, NY, in 1860 and was also staying with them in Hannibal, NY, in 1870. She was still living there with them in 1880, but as a widow, Mrs. Sarah P. Perry. I have found no later trace of her. In 1900 only her son was living on his grandfather's farm in Hannibal (US censuses).

Child:

i   **Frank/Francis Perry** b Aug 1878, Oswego Co., NY; d & bur 27 & 28 Feb 1936, Fulton, NY. He married 1906? **Mary Moody** (William Moody & Laura ____) b 1891?, NY.

4.5.1.1.3   MONTA, Joel H. b 1859, Onondaga Co., NY.

Joel H. Monta was a 1-year-old child living with his parents in DeWitt, NY, in 1860. He was also with them in Hannibal, NY, in 1870 and 1880 when he was a farmer (US censuses). I have not found him in later years.

4.5.1.1.4   MONTA, Amanda/Mandy b May 1866, NY. She married 1894? as his second wife **William Jetto** b Apr 1866, NY.

Amanda Monta lived in Hannibal, NY, with her parents before her marriage and on a farm in Granby, NY, with her husband and three stepchildren in 1900. She was still with him there in 1910 when they had been married for sixteen years. William Jetto (also Jette) may have died in the next few years. By 1920 Mrs. Amanda Jetto was a mill worker living with her brother John Monta (4.5.1.1.1) in Fulton, NY, and in 1930 a scrub woman holding household there for her divorced nephew Frank Perry (4.5.1.1.2.i) (US censuses).

4.8.5.1.1   MONTY, Adeline/Addie M. b 24 May 1875, Ticonderoga, NY; d 19 Dec 1879, Chazy, NY, at the age of 4 years, 6 months, and 25 days.

Adeline Monty was less than a month old in June 1875 when she was living with her parents in Ticonderoga, NY (state census). The tombstone which she shares with her sister Jessie (4.8.5.1.2) in the Ingraham Cemetery in Chazy, NY, names her Addie M. Monty.

4.8.5.1.2   MONTY, Mary Tessy/Jessie M. b & bp 10 Jun 1878 & 28 Jun 1879, Chazy & Coopersville, NY; d 28 Dec 1879, Chazy, NY, at the age of 1 year, 6 months, and 17 days.

Mary Tessy Monty was baptized in St. Joseph's Church in Coopersville, NY. The tombstone which she shares with her sister (4.8.5.1.1) in the Ingraham Cemetery in Chazy, NY, names her Jessie M. Monty.

4.8.5.1.3   MONTY, Willis Ellsworth b & bp 20 Mar 1883 & 11 Aug 1884, West Chazy, NY; d Aug 1953, Silver Springs, MD.

Willis E. Monty was a student in Burlington, VT, in 1900 and a bookkeeper there in 1910 before moving to Washington D.C. around 1917 to work for the federal government. He was a clerk in 1920 and an attorney there in 1930 and later years (US censuses; *Plattsburgh Press Republican*, 3 Sep 1953). He did not marry.

4.8.5.2.1   MONTY, Edward Stephen b 11 Apr 1893, Beekmantown, NY; d Oct 1972, Plattsburgh, NY. He married 25 Jul 1917, Beekmantown, NY, **Ruby Inez Gonya** (Ira Gonya & Lottie Ladd Hunt) b there 26 Jul 1899; d & bur 11 & 14 May 1983, Plattsburgh, NY.

Edward Stephen Monty was a farmer and Justice of the Peace in Beekmantown, NY. His wife was a sister of Carl Darwin Gonya, husband of Florence Dorothy Monty (4.8.5.2.2). She was buried in Riverside Cemetery in Plattsburgh, NY (*Plattsburgh Press Republican*, 12 & 16 May 1983).

Children:

4.8.5.2.1.1	Joyce Shirley	1919-1944-
4.8.5.2.1.2	Doris Muriel	1921-1948-
4.8.5.2.1.3	Edward Oreon	1927-1947-1975

4.8.5.2.2   MONTY, Florence Dorothy b 28 Sep 1895, Beekmantown, NY; d & bur 5

& 8 May 1975, Plattsburgh & Beekmantown, NY. She married 7 May 1919, Plattsburgh, NY, **Carl Darwin Gonya** (Ira Gonya & Lottie Ladd Hunt) b 15 Jun 1894, Beekmantown, NY; d & bur 18 & 20 May 1941, Plattsburgh & Beekmantown, NY.

Carl Darwin Gonya, a brother of Ruby Inez Gonya, wife of Edward Stephen Monty (4.8.5.2.1), was a farmer and Justice of the Peace in Beekmantown, NY. He and his wife were buried in the Point au Roche Cemetery there (*Plattsburgh Daily Press*, 19 & 21 may 1941; *Plattsburgh Press Republican*, 7 May 1975).

Children:

i **Avis Helen Gonya** b 1921, Plattsburgh, NY; d there 1921.

ii **Willis Oreon Gonya** b 3 Dec 1931, Plattsburgh, NY. He married 15 Jul 1961, Glens Falls, NY, **Ruth Louise Mound** (Clifford Ernest Mound & Doris Josephine Pattee) b there 5 Jan 1939.

iii **Evelyn Emma Gonya** b 15 Apr 1933, Plattsburgh, NY. She married there 12 Sep 1959 **Robert Lorenzo Bennett** (Emanuel Bennett & Florence ____) b 23 Apr 1927, AuSable, NY.

4.10.6.2.1 **MONTY, Francis/Frank B.** b & bp 11 Jul & 15 Aug 1872, Wood's Falls & Ellenburg, NY; d & bur 31 Mar & 2 Apr 1873, Plattsburgh, NY.

Francis Monty was baptized in St. Edmund's Church in Ellenburg, NY, and was buried in the Old Catholic Cemetery in Plattsburgh, NY, as Frank B. Monty.

4.10.6.2.2 **MONTY, Frederick Benjamin/Fred B.** b & bp 31 Dec 1873 & 1 Mar 1874, Mooers & Plattsburgh, NY; d 11 Jun 1919, Plattsburgh, NY. He married 17 Sep 1902, Mooers Forks, NY, **Mary Beany** (John Beany & Sara Kennedy) b Oct 1871, Altona, NY; d & bur there 2 & 6 Jul 1950, at the age of 78.

Fred B. Monty was a farmer in Mooers, NY. His widow, a school teacher in Mooers and Altona, NY, was named administrator of his estate on 23 Jun 1919 in the Clinton Co. Surrogate's Court in Plattsburgh, NY, and continued to farm her husband's land after his death (US and state censuses). She and her husband were buried in Holy Angels Cemetery in Altona.

Children:

4.10.6.2.2.1	Cecil Joseph	1904-1928-1950
4.10.6.2.2.2	John Frederick	1907-1927-1977

4.10.6.2.3 **MONTY, Elizabeth C.** b Apr 1883, Mooers, NY. She married 1902? **Arthur Chapin Martin** (Willard Martin & Rosetta ____) b 28 Nov 1876, Hartford, VT; m (1) 1898? Anna ____ .

Arthur C. Martin was a brass molder in Hudson, NH. He had then been married for two years to his first wife Anna in 1900 and for eight years to Elizabeth Monty in 1910 (US censuses). He was still in Hudson, retired, in 1949 (City Directories).

Children:

i **Winifred F. Martin** b 1903?, Hudson, NH.

ii **Doris L. Martin** b 1905?, NY. She married 1930 **William J. Grant** b 1898?, NH; d between 1950 and 1954, Hudson, NH.

iii **Louis M. Martin** b 1907?, Hudson, NH.

iv **Roger J. W. Martin** b Oct 1909, Hudson, NH.

v **Janice R. Martin** b 1923?, Hudson, NH.

vi **Norma N. Martin** b Jun 1927, Hudson, NH.

4.10.6.2.4 **MONTY, James R.** b 1886, Mooers, NY; d & bur 31 Mar & 3 Apr 1888, Mooers & Plattsburgh, NY, at the age of 2.

James R. Monty was buried in the Old Catholic Cemetery in Plattsburgh, NY.

4.10.6.2.5   **MONTY, Carrie Louise** b 13 Apr 1888, Mooers, NY; d & bur 8 & 11 Jan 1911, Altona, NY. She married 15 Jun 1908, Champlain, NY, **Joseph Tallman** (Cyril Tallman & Matilda Perras) b & bp 5 Dec 1886 & 24 Jan 1887, Mooers, NY; m (2) Laura ____.

Carrie Monty and her husband had two children, both of whom died before June 1910 when Joseph Tallman was a laborer on his father-in-law's general farm in Altona, NY. She died the following year and was buried there in Holy Angels Cemetery.

Joseph Tallman left the area after Carrie's death and was a machinist in Barre, MA, on 1 Jan 1920 with a 27-year-old wife Laura and two children of his second marriage, both born in Massachusetts (US censuses).

4.10.6.2.6   **MONTY, Thomas** b & bp 8 Aug 1890 & 5 Apr 1891, Altona & Mooers Forks, NY; d 6 Sep 1919, Altona, NY. He married 19 Jan 1915, Mooers Forks, NY, **Gertrude E. Wood** (Melvin J. Wood & Philanda Marie Pratt) b Apr 1887, Altona, NY; d 6 Mar 1950, Danbury, CT.

Thomas Monty was a farmer in Altona, NY. His widow and children were on the farm there in 1920 and in Saranac Lake, NY, in 1930 (US censuses). They then moved at some time before 1945 to Danbury, CT (City Directories) and, with the exception of Willard who was serving in the US Army in Germany, were all still there when she died. She was buried with her husband in Holy Angels Cemetery in Altona, (*Plattsburgh Press Republican*, 9 Mar 1950).

Children:

4.10.6.2.6.1	James Willard	1915-1946?-1989	
4.10.6.2.6.2	Mildred Lona	1916?-	-
4.10.6.2.6.3	Thomas Gaylord	1917-	-1973
4.10.6.2.6.4	Melvin E.	1920-	-1980

4.10.6.2.7   **MONTY, Orville James** b & bp 15 Apr 1894 & 12 Mar 1895, Altona, NY; d 28 May 1959, Pinellas Co., FL. He married 1 Sep 1920, Altona, NY, and divorced Nov 1956, Pinellas Co., FL, **Anna L. Pyper** (Joseph Pyper & Zoe Gauthier) b 16 Oct 1886, Altona, NY; m (1) there 29 Aug 1911 Arthur W. Dame (William Dame & Florence Goff); d 8 Feb 1970, Auburn, NY.

Orville James Monty was a farmer in Altona, NY, for most of his life and was buried there in Holy Angels Cemetery.

Children:

4.10.6.2.7.1	Orville James	1921-1943-1987	
4.10.6.2.7.2	Dorothy	1926-	-
4.10.6.2.7.3	Elizabeth Ann	1931-	-

4.10.6.9.1   **MONTY, Clara** b Sep 1886, NY; d 1 Apr 1954, Hartford, CT.

Clara Monty was living with her parents in New York City in 1900 and was a hospital nurse in Manhattan, NY, in 1920 and 1930 (US censuses). She moved to Hartford, CT, and was a nurse there in the early 1930s (City Directories). She did not marry.

4.10.6.9.2   **MONTY, Alvin French** b 6 May 1889, White Plains, NY; d & b 1 & 4 Feb 1928, Hartford & Centerbrook, CT. He married around 1912 **Augusta Selner** (William Selner & Bridget ____) b 17 Oct 1895, Middlesex Co., CT; m (2) 1935 John Henry Westwood Jr. (John Henry Westwood & Ellen F. ____); d 28 Aug 1981, Windsor, CT.

Alvin F. Monty was a factory worker in Essex, CT, in 1910 when he was still single and a machinist in Hartford, CT, after his marriage. His widow was still living there with her two children in 1930 (US censuses).

Children:

4.10.6.9.2.1	Robert W.	1913-	-1994

4.10.6.9.2.2   Dorothy   1915?-   -

4.10.6.9.3   **MONTY, Robert** b 4 Aug 1891, New York City, NY; d there 20 Dec 1892.

4.10.6.9.4   **MONTY, Mary Agnes/Mae** b 25 May 1894, New York, NY. She married around 1922 **Edward Antonio Brulé** (Agapit Brulé & Rose Anna Provost) b & bp 30 & 31 Jul 1892, Sherbrooke, QC; m (2) Veronica Socha (Martin Socha & Annie ____); d 27 Feb 1972, Hartford, CT.

This woman's birth record is in the name of Agnes M. Monty. Nevertheless she was consistently known as May or Mary A. Monty when living with her family in New York and Connecticut and Mae after her marriage. She and her husband, who was a machinist/printer for the *Hartford Times*, had been married for eight years in 1930 (US censuses). She was still alive in 1942 when he signed as Edward Antonio Brule his World War II Draft Registration papers. That is also the name found on his World War I Draft Registration card. Nevertheless his baptismal name was simply Joseph Antonio. Edward was a later acquisition.

Child:
i   **Florence Brule** b 23 Jun 1924, Hartford, CT; d 5 Jun 1989, Branford, CT. She married **Donald M. Knibbs** (Milton Knibbs & Ruth Muir) b 9 May 1924, Farmington, CT; d 6 Nov 1993, New Britain, CT.

4.10.6.12.1   **MONTY, George** b & bp 20 Feb & 20 May 1894, Plattsburgh, NY. He married 1917? **Florence Meads** (Simon Edward Meads & ____) b 1895?, MD.

George Monty left home as a young man and was living in Baltimore, MD, when he signed in June 1917 his World War I Draft Registration card. His wife however was staying with her children in her mother-in-law's household in Plattsburgh, NY, in 1920. George Monty was absent. He was in Philadelphia when his mother died in 1928 (*Plattsburgh Sentinel,* 18 Dec 1928) and was still there with his wife in 1942 when he signed his World War II Draft Registration card.

George Monty and his wife had an unusual relationship: his mother, Mary Rachel Larose, had married as her second husband Simon Meads, his wife's father by a first marriage. They were then step-brother and sister.

Children:
4.10.6.12.1.1	Edward	1918-	-
4.10.6.12.1.2	Francis Leroy (twin)	1919-	-1920
4.10.6.12.1.3	Arthur L. (twin)	1919-	-

4.10.6.12.2   **MONTY, Margaret Lillian** b & bp 17 Aug & 4 Oct 1896, Plattsburgh, NY; d & bur there 14 & 16 May 1944. She married there (1) 16 Aug 1914 **Arthur Joseph Tuchschmidt** (Arnold J. Tuchschmidt & Rose Schmidt) b 16 Aug 1890, St. Louis, MO.

She married (2) 1924? **Carl Johnson** b 1896?, OH.

Arthur Joseph Tuchschmidt was a private in the Plattsburgh, NY, Army Barracks in 1910. At his marriage a few years later, he was a store clerk in Plattsburgh. He was still living there but alone in 1925 (US and state censuses).

Carl Johnson's name appears in the 1930 census as both a sergeant in the Plattsburgh, NY, Army Barracks and an odd-job laborer living in Peru, NY, with his wife Lillian and 5-year-old son Edward (US census). He survived his wife. She was buried in Mount Carmel Cemetery in Plattsburgh (*Plattsburgh Press Republican,* 15 May 1944).

Child:
i   **Edward George Johnson** b 1925?, Plattsburg, NY.

4.10.6.12.3   **MONTY, Loretta** b & bp 14 Sep & 15 Oct 1899, Plattsburgh, NY; d & bur 25 & 28 Feb 1979, Phoenix & Prescott, AZ. She married (1) 3 Jan 1921, Plattsburgh, NY, **Charles G. McKay** (Robert McKay & Mary Bennett) b Aug 1898, Long Island, NY; d before

1930.

She married (2) **Andreas Nottestad** (____ Nøttestad & Therese ____) b 25 Oct 1902, Hamar, Norway; d & bur 17 & 21 Jan 1974, Phoenix & Prescott, AZ.

Charles G. McKay was a private in the Plattsburgh, NY, Army Barracks at his marriage. He was not listed in the 1925 state census there with his wife and 3-year-old daughter and may have died before then.

Mrs. Loretta McKay was a widow living in Plattsburgh with her daughter in 1930 (US census) and was still there when her stepfather Simon Meads died in 1937 (*Plattsburgh Daily Press*, 1 May 1937). She remarried before 1944 when, as Mrs. Andreas Nottestad, she was a resident of Florence, CO (*Plattsburgh Press Republican*, 11 Mar 1944 and 15 May 1944). I do not know when she and her second husband moved to Arizona. They were both buried in the Prescott, AZ, National Cemetery.

Andreas Nottestad arrived in the United States as a 17-year old on 15 Jun 1920. He was a corporal in the Plattsburgh Army Barracks in 1930 (US census) and a sergeant there in the early 1930s, according to a few articles in the local newspaper.

Child:
  i   **Florence McKay** b 1922?, Plattsburgh, NY.

4.10.6.12.4   MONTY, Bessie Mary b 1902?, Plattsburgh, NY. She married there 2 Aug 1919 **John Francis Leppert** (Joseph Leppert & Elizabeth Carney) b 16 Sep 1892, New York, NY; d & bur 28 Nov & 2 Dec 1968, Plattsburgh & West Chazy, NY.

Bessie Mary Monty was 17 years old at her marriage. She was living in Plattsburgh, NY, when her stepfather Simon Meads died on 18 May 1937 (*Plattsburgh Daily Press*, 19 May 1937) but predeceased her husband.

John Francis Leppert was a clerk in the Plattsburgh Army Barracks when he married, and a Railroad freight clerk in Plattsburgh in 1925 and 1930 (US and state censuses) and later years. He was buried in St. Joseph's Cemetery in West Chazy, NY, where he had been living in retirement (*Plattsburgh Press Republican*, 30 Nov 1968).

Children:
  i   **George Arthur Leppert** b 1920?, Plattsburgh, NY. He married 18 Mar 1944, Childress, TX, **Jessie Jean Long** (Jessie Kirkwood Long & Mary Lee Martin) b 25 Oct 1926, Clay Co., TX.
  ii **Mary Elizabeth Leppert** b 20 Sep 1922, Plattsburgh, NY; d & bur 30 Aug & 1 Sep 1984, Plattsburgh & West Chazy, NY. She married **Howard E. Relation** (Herbert Relation & Mae K. Abood) b 19 Oct 1918, West Chazy, NY; m (2) there 1986 Morena Cecilia LaBarge (Edward LaBarge & Frances Lajoy), widow of Paul Emory Bretz; d & bur 27 Mar & Spring 2007, Plattsburgh & West Chazy, NY.

4.11.1.1.1   MONTY, Claudius/Claude A. b 6 Jun 1861, Jericho, NY; d & bur 6 & 9 Jan 1920, Council Bluffs, IA. He married 1887?, MN, **Mary E. Gilligan** b 18 Nov 1868, NY; d 18 Jun 1920, Council Bluffs, IA.

Claudius Monty was only a few years old when he came to Iowa with his parents and paternal grandparents. He was with them in Monona, IA, in 1870. He married, though, in Minnesota and was a railroad conductor in Austin Twp, MN, in 1900 when he and his wife had been married for thirteen years. He moved in 1907 to Council Bluffs, IA, where Claude A. Monty (rather than Claudius found in earlier records) was a conductor for the Great Western Railroad (US censuses). He died after a prolonged illness and was buried in St. Joseph's Cemetery in Council Bluffs (*Council Bluffs Nonpareil*, 7 Jan 1920). His wife and son were also buried in that cemetery.

Children:
| 4.11.1.1.1.1 | Lulu/Lulla B. | 1888-1911?-1953 |
| 4.11.1.1.1.2 | Francis/Frank D. | 1898- -1923 |

4.11.1.1.2   **MONTY, Sophrona E./Sophia** b 16 Jan 1862, Jericho, NY; d 29 Sep 1952, St. Paul, MN. She married 4 Sep 1882, Prairie du Chien, WI, **Robert H. Love** (William Love & Mary Jane Stinsen) b 10 May 1855, Ireland; d 29 Oct 1933, St. Paul, MN.

Sophrona Monty came to Iowa as an infant with her parents and was living with them in Monona, IA, in 1870 and 1880. Her name varies in each census, even after her marriage: it may be Sophronia, Sophrona, or Sophrone. She married however under the name of Sophia.

Robert H. Love had arrived in the United States as a youngster in 1869 and was naturalized in 1874. He was a railroad worker in Girard, IA, at his marriage but soon moved to St. Paul, MN. He was a switchman there in 1890-1891 (City Directories) and in 1900 and 1910, and a railroad conductor there in 1920 and 1930 (US censuses). Though he and his wife remained in St. Paul until their deaths, they were both buried in the Monona Cemetery alongside her brother Charles (4.11.1.1.3) and her sister Polly (4.11.1.1.4) and her husband.

Children:
  i   **Robert H. Love** b 27 Feb 1884, Clayton Co., IA; d 21 Jan 1938, St. Paul, MN. He married there 20 Sep 1905 **Catherine/Katherina Vilsmeyer** (Joseph Vilsmeyer & Anna ____) b 1886?, Minneapolis, MN.
  ii   **Marie Jessie Love** b 7 Mar 1888, IA; d 19 Mar 1970, Minneapolis, MN. She married 10 May 1904, St. Paul, MN, **George John Boehm** (John Boehm & Anna Stock) b 13 Aug 1879, Columbus, MN; d 18 Jun 1973, Chisago Co., MN.

4.11.1.1.3   **MONTY, Charles W.** b 20 Apr 1865, Luana, IA; d 16 May 1948, St. Paul, MN. He married (1) around 1889 **Rebecca Shilson** (Christian Shilson & Rosetta Pomeroy) b 18 Jan 1870, Winona Co., MN; m (2) 1897?, Horace Dudley Munger; m (3) 23 Jan 1913 William E. Dull (Simon B. Dull & Eva Miller), widower of Lucy L. Wymore.

He married (2) 1929? **Lillian ____** b 10 Aug 1870, IL; d 26 May 1959, St. Paul, MN.

Neither of Charles W. Monty's marriages is well documented. I have been unable to find records of either one. He also maintained in all censuses through 1920 that he was single, while his children, who were living with their mother and stepfather in 1900, were listed under their stepfather's surname. His great-granddaughter, Mrs. Carole Pecoraro of Pleasanton, CA, pointed me in the right direction. Further information about Rebecca Shilson can be found in the biography of William E. Dull in Ellery M. Hancock's *Past and Present of Allamakee County, Iowa*, p. 572.

Charles W. Monty's first marriage dissolved around the time of his youngest child's birth. While he was a laborer on his father's farm in Monona, IA, in 1900 his former wife was living with her three children and husband Horace Munger in Hayward, WI. Strangely enough, though, when Charles Monty was a stationary engineer in Minneapolis, MN, in 1920, he was living in the household of his ex-brother-in-law George A. Shilson, for whom his mother was housekeeper. He was said to be single (US censuses).

Charles W. Monty was a railroad flagman in St. Paul, MN in 1930, when he and his second wife, Lillian, had been married for one year (US census). He remained in St. Paul until his death but was buried in the Monona Cemetery alongside his sisters Sophrona (4.11.1.1.2) and Polly C. (4.11.1.1.4) and their husbands.

Rebecca Shilson is occasionally named Rebecca May, as in the 1880 census in Minneiska, MN, where she and her siblings were listed under their stepfather Thomas May's surname. She was in fact the daughter of Christian Shilson who died the very year of her birth. She had been married for three years to Horace Munger in 1900. He was then a farmer in Hayward, WI, and in Lenroot, WI, in 1910 (US censuses). She remarried shortly after his death on 11 Feb 1912 and was living with William E. Dull in Monona, IA, in 1920 and in Hayward, WI, in 1930 (US censuses).

Children of the first marriage:
4.11.1.1.3.1	Mabel	1890-1909-1977
4.11.1.1.3.2	Orpha	1894-1911-1968
4.11.1.1.3.3	Leon	1896-1920-1975

4.11.1.1.4   **MONTY, Polly C.** b 30 Jun 1867, Luana, IA; d 2 Jun 1954, Monona, IA. She married there 18 Jun 1892 **Harry E. Pomeroy** (Alvin Pomeroy & Betsey Fox) b 11 Sep 1870, Minneiska, MN; d & bur 29 Jan & 1 Feb 1961, Mason City & Monona, IA.

Harry Pomeroy and his wife first lived on a farm a few miles north of Monona, IA, before moving to Monona itself where he was a hostler in 1900. They were staying in Yellow Bank Twp, MN, on the farm of their brother-in-law Joseph Thill, husband of Mary C. Monty (4.11.1.6) in 1910, though this may have been only a short visit. The account of the Pomeroys' lives which appeared in the Monona *News* of 25 Jun 1942 on the occasion of their Golden Wedding Anniversary noted that they had lived near or in Monona ever since their marriage. Harry Pomeroy was a dray man there in 1920 and a brick and stone mason in 1930 (US censuses). They had no children. Following his wife's death Harry Pomeroy moved in 1956 to a Nursing Home in Mason City, IA, where he died (*Mason City Globe Gazette*, Jan 30, 1961). He was buried alongside his wife and several in-laws in the Monona City Cemetery.

4.11.1.1.5   **MONTY, Frank A./Francis** b 29 Jan 1874, Monona, IA; d 22 Jan 1957, Spring Valley, MN. He married 1903? **Mary V./Vennie/Vencentia Collins** (Michael Collins & Margaret Bohan) b 6 Oct 1878, Austin, MN; d 1 Apr 1968, Spring Valley, MN.

Francis Monty was living with his parents in Monona, IA in 1880. In all other US and state censuses as well as at his death, he was known as Frank or Frank A. Monty. He moved to Austin, MN, in the 1890s and enlisted there on 24 Apr 1898 as a private in Co. G. of the Minnesota Volunteers during the Spanish-American War. On his return to Austin he worked for the railroad, first as a brakeman in 1900 and then as a conductor in 1910 and 1920. He was also a conductor in LaCrosse, WI, in 1930 (US censuses). He remained in LaCrosse until at least 1938 but had moved to Spring Valley, MN, before his brother Charles (4.11.1.1.3) died in 1948. He and his wife spent the rest of their lives there.

The date of their marriage is unusually uncertain. They had been married for seven years in 1910 according to the census of that year but for thirty years in 1930 according to that year's census. Any date after June 1900, when both were single, would be possible. A marriage record is also needed to clarify the matter of Miss Collin's name. It was Mary V. when she was living with her parents in 1880 and 1900, Vincinna (?) in 1910, Vennie in 1920 and 1930 (US censuses), and "Vennie (Vencentia)" in the Minnesota Death records.

4.11.1.1.5.1	Robert J.	1904-	-1977
4.11.1.1.5.2	Lucille Margaret	1906-1925?&	-1985

4.11.1.1.6   **MONTY, Mary Catherine** b 7 Dec 1875, Monona, IA; d 30 Jan 1955, St. Cloud, MN. She married 6 May 1896, Monona, IA, **Joseph Thill** (John Thill & Barbara Steel) b Oct 1872, Luana, IA; d 7 Mar 1941, St. Cloud, MN.

This couple's marriage record in Allamakee Co., IA, shows the bride's name as Mamie C. Monty. That is the only time I have seen that nickname applied to her. She and Joseph Thill were married at the residence of the bride's mother in Monona, IA, and were to live after their marriage in Postville, IA. They did not long remain there. In 1900, Joseph Thill was a farmer in Rudd Twp, IA; in 1907, at his father-in-law's death, a resident of Ortonville, MN; and in 1910 a farm laborer in Yellow Bank Twp, MN. By 1930 he was a janitor in St. Cloud, MN (US censuses). He and his wife remained in St. Cloud and were buried there in North Star Cemetery.

Children:

i   **Frank Byron Thill** b 27 Feb 1897, IA; d & bur 26 & 30 Jan 1984, St. Cloud & South Minneapolis, MN. He married 1920? **Lenore A. ____** b 1901?, MN.

ii   **Roy Gilbert Thill** b 28 Sep 1899, Rudd Twp, IA; d 6 Nov 1936, St. Cloud, MN.

iii   **Harold G. Thill** b 4 Apr 1901, Rudd Twp, IA; d Apr 1959. He married 1924? **Clara M. ____** b 28 Sep 1905, MN; d 11 Apr 1998, Marinette, WI.

iv   **Joseph B. Thill** b 1 May 1904, IA; d 18 Aug 1986, St. Cloud, MN. He married 1929? **Marie Isabell ____** b 12 Nov 1909, Windom, MN; d 8 Apr 1998, Waite

Park, MN.

v   **Robert George Thill** b 9 Jun 1917, MN; d 14 Dec 1978, Sherburne Co., MN.

4.11.1.1.7   **MONTY, William Lee** b 2 Jan 1882, Monona, IA; d 16 May 1957, Minneapolis, MN.

William L. Monty was a farm laborer in Rudd Twp, IA, in 1900 (US census). He was a resident of St. Cloud, MN, at his father's death in 1907 and of Minneapolis, MN, when he signed on 12 Sep 1918 his World War I Draft Registration card. He was unemployed and named his mother as his nearest relative. He was indeed staying with her in Monona, IA, in 1925 and was still single (state census). Five years later, though, when he was a prisoner in the Minneapolis City Workhouse, the 1930 census notes that he had married at age 38. I have seen no evidence of such a marriage.

4.11.1.3.1   **MONTY, Louis/Lewis Albert** b 4 Jun 1860, Chazy, NY; d 3 Mar 1922, Marquette, IA. He married 7 Jan 1882, Prairie du Chien, WI, **Honora Leona/Nora Bender** (Charles Wesley Bender & Anna Calkins) b 13 Jul 1861, Waukson, IA; d Sep 1950, Dubuque, IA.

Louis Albert Monty came to Iowa with his parents as a young child and was a mechanic in McGregor, IA, at his marriage. He moved shortly thereafter to North McGregor (now Marquette) where he was a railroad bridge carpenter and builder in 1900 and 1920 (US censuses). He had in fact been an employee of the Milwaukee RR for forty-two years at his death. He was also quite active in the community and served as a councilman in Marquette for eight years and as a School Board member for fifteen years, including twelve years as President of the Board (*North Iowa Times*, McGregor, IA, Mar 1922).

Louis A. Monty was buried in Pleasant Grove Cemetery in McGregor. His widow left the area after his death and was living in 1930 with her daughter Lulu and her son-in-law Edward J. Palmer in Dubuque Co., IA (US censuses).

Children:

4.11.1.3.1.1	Harry Claudius	1883- -1884
4.11.1.3.1.2	Winifred Etta	1885-1904-1944
4.11.1.3.1.3	Flora Almeda	1887-1927?-
4.11.1.3.1.4	Lulu Jessie	1889-1914-

4.11.1.3.2   **MONTY, Almeda** b 18 Jun 1862; bur Monona, IA.

Almeda Monty probably died as an infant and was buried with her mother in the Monona, IA, Cemetery.

4.11.1.3.3   **MONTY, Etta Estella** b 17 Aug 1864, Luana, IA; d 9 Nov 1925, Spencer, SD. She married there 9 Oct 1883 **Thomas Liversage Callant** (John Callant/Kelland & Margaretta Liversage) b 21 Sep 1849, Bridgenorth, Shropshire, England; d 6 Oct 1925, Spencer, SD.

Etta Estella Monty was a resident of McGregor, IA, until at least January 1882, when she was a witness to the marriage of her brother Louis Albert in Prairie du Chien, WI. She moved to the Dakota Territory with her family shortly before her own marriage.

Thomas Callant had arrived in the United States with his family in the 1860s and was a farm laborer in Wagner, IA, in 1870. He then moved to the Dakota Territory where he was a farmer in Davison Co. in 1880. He was a drayman in Spencer, SD, in 1900 and 1910 and a teamster there in 1920 (US censuses).

Children:

i   **Mary Lillian Callant** b 6 Aug 1884, Spencer, SD; d 29 Jul 1957. She married 1901? **Ira C. Smith** (Chandler Raymond Smith & Mary Jane Goodrich) b Nov 1871, OH .

ii   **Ellen Margaretta Callant** b 2 Dec 1885, Spencer, SD; d & bur 26 & 29 Mar 1973, Lacey, WA. She married 26 Oct 1906, Spencer, SD, **Laurence Cleveland Hun-**

tamer (John Huntamer & Mary A. Hare) b 26 Oct 1885, Madison, SD; d & bur 19 & 22 Mar 1958, Lacey, WA.

iii   **Zoe Blanche Callant** b 28 Sep 1887, Spencer, SD; d 6 Aug 1957. She married 4 Jun 1914, Spencer, SD, **James Spencer Tuggle** (William S. Tuggle & Anna C. Railsback) b 22 Oct 1888, Gallatin, MO; d Jun 1973, Seattle, WA.

iv   **Anonymous Callant** b & d 6 Mar 1889, Spencer, SD.

v   **John Albert Callant** b 29 Apr 1890, Spencer, SD; d there Mar 1967. He married 23 Jun 1920, Farmer, SD, **Emma Tugel** (Gustav H. Tugel & Louise Juliane/Julia A. Myers) b 21 Sep 1893, Danvers, IL; d Apr 1985, Fort Wayne, IN.

vi   **Ida May Callant** b 8 Jan 1892, Spencer, SD; d there 14 May 1894.

vii   **Claudia Genevieve Callant** b 15 Apr 1896, Spencer, SD; d 5 Nov 1977, Olympia, WA. She married (1) 4 Aug 1925, Spencer, SD, **Elmer Ernest Jensen/Jenson** (Fred Martin Jensen & Alta Laura Bentley) b 23 Sep 1887, Montrose, SD.

She married (2) 23 Feb 1934 **Charles Norton Rhoads** (Murdoch Monroe Rhoads & Amanda Elizabeth Haralson) b 23 Oct 1893, Hamilton Co., TX; m (1) 6 Jun 1915 and divorced Vera Pearl Lindley; m (3) 26 Nov 1979, Mrs. Carol Richley; d 27 Jul 1980, Olympia, WA.

4.11.1.3.4   **MONTY, Lilly Sarah** b Mar 1872, WI; d between 1920 and 1930. She married 1901?, a widower, **Frank James Ginder** (Daniel Ginder & Elizabeth _____) b Oct 1866, Portage, WI; m (1) 1894? ____; d 2 May 1952, Medical Lake, WA.

Lilly Sarah Monty was living with her parents in McGregor, IA, in 1880 and came with them to the Dakota Territory in the early 1880s. She was a teacher in Madison, SD, in 1900 (US census).

James Ginder had arrived in the Dakota Territory with his parents in the 1870s and was a confectioner in Madison, SD, in 1900. He was then a widower who had first married, according to the 1930 census, at the age of 28. He and his second wife (named Lilly S. and Lillie S.) moved to Washington State after the birth of their first child. He was a butcher in Blaise, WA, in 1910 and in Prosser, WA, in 1920 and 1930. He was then again a widower (US censuses).

Children:
i   **Frances Grace Ginder** b 1 Jul 1902, Lake Co., SD.
ii   **Elizabeth V. Ginder** b 13 Feb 1907, Bellingham, WA.

4.11.1.3.5   **MONTY, Ellen Ruth** b Jul 1877, McGregor, IA; d 12 Mar 1944, Seattle, WA. She married 1903? **John William Austen** (John Austen & Rachel Horton) b 8 Jul 1878, Rochelle, IL.

Ellen Monty came to the Dakota Territory with her family in the early 1880s and, as Ruth E. Monty, still living in her father's household, was a teacher in Madison, SD, in 1900. In later censuses her name alternates between Ellen and Ruth E. She was Mrs. Ellen Austen when she gave the information included in her mother's death certificate in 1937 and Mrs. Ellen R. Austen at her death.

John Austen was in the banking business all his life. He was a bank cashier in New York Mills, MN, in 1900, and in Carney, OK, in 1910 when he and his wife had been married for seven years. He was working for the National City Bank in Seattle, WA, in 1918 and was a bank auditor there in 1920 and 1930 (US censuses).

4.11.1.3.6   **MONTY, Grace E.** b Jun 1884, SD.

Grace E. Monty was living in her father's household in Madison, SD, in 1900 (US census).

4.11.1.4.1   **MONTY, Luella/Lulu M.** b 6 Dec 1866, Lowell, MA; d there 20 Nov 1920.

This woman was named Luella at her birth and in the 1870 and 1880 censuses in Lowell, MA, where she was living with her parents. After that time, though, she was known as Lulu M. Monty. She remained in Lowell after her father had left the area and was in 1900 a stenographer boarding with a distant relative, Laura Ann Savage (4.8.1.vii) and her husband. She was a nurse in a doctor's office in 1910, and a supervising nurse in January 1920 (US censuses). She did not marry.

4.11.3.1.1   **MONTY, Joseph Howard** b Nov 1859, Chazy, NY; d between 1910 and 1917. He married 16 Sep 1883, Lowell, MA, **Delphine Brunelle** (Joseph Brunelle & Eleanor Plouffe) b Apr 1864, Sciota, NY.

Joseph Monty was a mill operative in Lowell, MA, at his marriage, a carder in a cotton mill in Billerica, MA, in 1900, and a cotton mill worker in Lowell in 1910. His wife, named Delphina at her marriage but Delphine and occasionally Della in other records, had five children of whom two, William A. and Theresa V., were still alive in 1900 (US censuses). She was a widow in 1917 and was living in Lowell with her daughter and son-in-law Theresa and Herbert Patterson (City Directory). She was also with them there in 1920 and in Milford, MA, in 1930 (US censuses).

Children:

4.11.3.1.1.1	Francis J.	1884- -
4.11.3.1.1.2	William Alphonse	1886-1918?-
4.11.3.1.1.3	Clifford	1888- -1888
4.11.3.1.1.4	Theresa V.	1891-1914-

4.11.3.1.2   **MONTY, George B.** b Jan 1862, Chazy, NY; d between 1930 and 1938. He married 16 Aug 1893, West Chazy, NY, **Emma Hall** (George Hall & Flavia Hall) b Jan 1873, NY; d & bur 2 & 7 Jun 1924, West Chazy, NY.

George B. Monty was a farmer in Chazy, NY. He retired before 1930 and was then living in the household of his daughter Helen and son-in-law Leon Powers (US and state censuses). He was deceased in 1938 when his sisters Lillian (4.11.3.1.3) and Myrtle (4.11.3.1.7) were the only two surviving children of George Monty and Adeline Bosca (*Lowell Sun*, 15 Jul 1938).

Children:

4.11.3.1.2.1	George D.	1894-1916-1974
4.11.3.1.2.2	Joseph Elias	1897- -1912
4.11.3.1.2.3	Helen Gertrude	1898-1919-1990
4.11.3.1.2.4	Charles	1901- -1902
4.11.3.1.2.5	Roy Kenneth	1906- -

4.11.3.1.3   **MONTY, Lillian E./Lillie** b & bp 21 Jun 1863 & 19 Oct 1884 (sic), Chazy & West Chazy, NY. She married 11 Jul 1889, Tewksbury, MA, **William Pringle** (George Pringle & Mary A. Maynard) b 23 Feb 1870, Wilmington, MA.

William Pringle was a farmer in Tewksbury, MA, at his marriage, a teamster there in 1900, and a farmer there in 1910 when he and his wife had had three children, only one of whom, Mildred, was still alive. He was a cotton mill worker in Lowell, MA, in 1920 before returning to Tewksbury where he was a laborer in 1930 (US censuses). He and his wife remained in Tewksbury where they celebrated Thanksgiving together in 1945 in their daughter's home (*Lowell Sun,* 24 Nov 1945). He was still a resident of Tewksbury when a sister, Mrs. Mary Ann Willard, died in 1955 (*Lowell Sun*, 7 Apr 1955).

Child:

   i   **Mildred N. Pringle** b 4 Mar 1897, Tewksbury, MA; d there 10 Aug 1980. She married 1919? **Harry William Patterson** (Eugene Patterson & Hattie ___) b 11 Jan 1896, Tewksbury, MA; d there 23 Oct 1974.

4.11.3.1.4   **MONTY, Edward A./Doward A.** b Apr 1867, Chazy, NY; d 9 Feb 1936, Lowell, MA. He married (1) 28 Dec 1893, Tewksbury, MA, **Nellie Fatu?** (Charles B. Fatu? &

Lizzie _____) b 1874?, Hallowell, ME.

He was divorced when he married (2) Jun 1915 **Lucy Donaghey** (Thomas H. Donaghey & Mary Ann Hill) b 31 Mar 1875, Lowell, MA; d & bur 27 & 31 Dec 1962, Methuen & Lowell, MA.

This man was known under a variety of names. He was Edward A. Monty as a child living with his parents in Beekmantown, NY, and in Chazy, NY, in 1870 and 1880. But when he married in 1893, the Tewksbury, MA, records which clearly identify him as the 27-year-old son of George W. and Adeline Monty name him Doward A. Monty, a farmer in Tewksbury. He was also known as Doward Monty, a teamster in Tewksbury, in the 1900 US census there. He had been married for seven years though his wife was not with him. Durward Monty was divorced in 1910 when he was living with his sister Lillian (4.11.3.1.4) and her husband in Tewksbury. He was a farm laborer.

There then appeared in the Lowell, MA, *Sunday Telegram* of 26 Jun 1915 an announcement of marriage intentions between Howard A. Monty and Lucy Donaghy (sic). The marriage did take place for in 1920 Durward A. Monty, a laborer on a truck farm in Lowell, was head of a household which included not only his wife Lucy but several Donaghey in-laws. He was again known as Doward A. Monty in 1930 when he was a laborer for the city of Lowell (US censuses) and at his death, as reported in the 1937 Lowell City Directory. At her own death, though, Lucy Donaghey was the widow of Howard Monty (*Lowell Sun*, 29 Dec 1962). It seems clear that all these names represent the same person.

The *Lowell Sun* of 26 Jun 1894 offers an intriguing item: "It is stated that Doward A. Monty of Tewksbury Center has had fortune smile upon him in the shape of a $75,000 legacy." I do not know of any close relative who could have left him such a substantial sum of money. It may have come to him through his wife. Or it may have been only a rumor. The *Sun* never followed through on the story and his subsequent (apparent) lifestyle does not indicate any sudden influx of wealth.

I know nothing about his first wife Nellie (or perhaps Nettie) save what is contained in her marriage record: her parents, age, and place of birth. I have found no Fatu family in the United States and tend to believe her surname was in fact misheard or misspelled in the marriage record.

4.11.3.1.5   **MONTY, Frank/Franklin D.** b Jun 1868, Chazy, NY; d between 1910 and 1923. He married 1899, Lowell, MA, **Mrs. Mary S. Lee** b Feb 1866, NH.

Frank D. Monty was a house carpenter in Tewksbury, MA, at his marriage and in 1900, and a house carpenter in Lowell, MA, in 1910. I have seen the name Franklin D. only when he was a child living with his parents in 1870 and 1880 (US censuses). He may have died before 1920: I have not found him in any census of that year. He certainly died before 1923 for he predeceased his father who died in March of that year (*Plattsburgh Sentinel*, 6 Apr 1923).

4.11.3.1.6   **MONTY, Mary Adeline/Addie M.** b Jul 1870, Chazy, NY. She married (1) 16 Apr 1888, Lowell, MA, **James Kelly** (James Kelly & Bridget _____) b 1866?, England.

She married (2) 1903? **Charles Horace Williams** b 26 May 1873, Canada; m (1) 1894? Mary McDonald.

The Massachusetts Marriage Records show that James Kelley, son of James and Bridget Kelly, born in England, was a 22-year-old weaver in Lowell, MA, at his marriage (vol. 389, p. 167). When his daughter was born a few years later he was an operative in Lowell (Massachusetts Birth Records, vol. 413, p. 222). I know nothing more about him.

Mrs. Mary Kelly and her daughter Blanche, her only child, were living in her father George Monty's household in Chazy in 1900. By 1910 she had been married for seven years to Charles H. Williams. He was then a drug store clerk in Lowell, whose household included, in addition to his wife Addie M. and stepdaughter Blanche Kelley (sic), three children of his first marriage. He was a salesman in Lowell in 1920 (US censuses). I have not found the couple after 1922 when Charles H. Williams was a manager in Lowell (City Directory). Mary Adeline Monty was in any event deceased in 1938 when her sisters Lillian (4.11.3.1.3) and Myrtle (4.11.3.1.7) were the only surviving children of George Monty and Adeline Bosca (*Lowell Sun*, 15 Jul 1938).

Child:
    i   **Blanche Kelly** b 11 Dec 1891, Lowell, MA. She married ____ **Johnson**.

4.11.3.1.7   **MONTY, Myrtle Violet** b 22 Jan 1874, Chazy, NY; d 17 Feb 1961, Hillsborough Co., NH. She married 5 Dec 1894, Lowell, MA, **Irving S. White** (Sullivan White & Julia Ann Farrell) b 25 May 1869, Bridgewater, VT.

    Irving S. White was a laborer in Lowell, MA, at his marriage, a farm laborer on his father-in-law's farm in Chazy, NY, in 1910, a farm laborer in Lyndeborough, NH, in 1920, when his father-in-law was a member of his household, and also in 1930 (US censuses). He and his wife (named Myrtilla in 1880 when she was living in Chazy with her parents, Violet at her marriage, and Myrtle in the censuses of 1910, 1920, and 1930) were still in Lyndeborough in 1945 (*Lowell Sun*, 24 Nov 1945). He predeceased his wife who continued to live at home until she entered a nursing home in Milford some months before her death. She died en route to the Monadnock Community Hospital in Peterborough, NH (*Nashua Telegraph*, 18 Feb 1961).

4.11.3.1.8   **MONTY, Julius D.** b May 1875, Chazy, NY; d 2 Feb 1888, Wilmington, MA, at the age of 12 years and 8 months.

    Julius D. Monty was buried in the Ingraham Cemetery in Chazy, NY.

4.11.3.1.9   **MONTY, Charles F.** b Aug 1878, Chazy, NY; d 15 Jan 1888, Wilmington, MA, at the age of 9 years and 5 months.

    Charles F. Monty was buried in the Ingraham Cemetery in Chazy, NY.

4.11.4.4.1   **MONTY, Lillie M.** b Jun 1879, Muskegon, MI.

    Lillie M. Monty left Michigan as a young child and was living with her parents in Silvana, Washington Territory, in 1887. She was working in Ballard, WA, in 1900 and was in 1910 a member of her mother and stepfather's household in Everett, WA. She was still single (Washington Territory and US censuses).

4.11.4.4.2   **MONTY, Louisa/Louise A.** b 1881?, MI; d 19 Feb 1934, Everett, WA.

    Louisa Monty was 6 years old when she was living with her parents in Silvana, Washington Territory, in 1887. She was a member of her mother and stepfather's household in Everett, WA, in 1910 as well as in 1920 (Washington Territory and US censuses). She apparently never married.

4.11.4.4.3   **MONTY, Myrtle B.** b Nov 1884, MI. She married 1905? **Perry P. Smith** b 1883?, MI.

    Myrtle Monty left Michigan as a young child and was living with her family in Silvana, Washington Territory, in 1887. She was a domestic in Everett, WA, in 1900. She was listed twice in the 1910 US census, once with her 27-year-old husband and 4-your-old son in Granite Falls, WA, and again as a member of her mother and stepfather's household in Everett. But though she had been married for five years and her child was named Avey Smith, she was identified as Myrtle Monty. She was perhaps then in the process of separating from her husband: she was divorced in 1920 when she was living alone in Seattle, WA (Washington Territory and US censuses).

Child:
    i   **Avery Smith** b 1906?, WA.

4.11.4.4.4   **MONTY, Florence** b 1886?, Silvana, WA. She married 22 Aug 1905, Everett., WA, **Simon Frederick Fox** b 1877?, MI.

    Florence Monty was an infant living with her parents in Silvana, Washington Territory, in 1887 and was 23 years old on 15 Apr 1910 when, as Mrs. Waneta Fox, she was staying in her stepfather's household in Everett, WA. Her husband of four years was not present. There is another listing however in the 1910 census in Granite Falls, WA, which includes Simon F. Fox, a 33-year-old shingle mill worker, and his 24-year-old wife Florence to whom he had been married for five years (Washington Territory and US censuses). I believe both Mrs. Fox refer to the same woman. A double listing would not be too unusual. I cannot however explain the name Waneta which is not found in any other records connected with the Monty family. I have not found the couple in later censuses.

4.11.4.4.5   **MONTY, Lewis/Louis Leroy** b 12 Jan 1889, Silvana, WA; d 14 Nov 1962, Everett, WA. He married 1924? **Violetta Scott** (H. John Scott & G. Sophia ____) b Dec 1898, Grand Rapids, WI; m (1) 1916? Clair Adelbert Martin (Charles Martin & Lela ____).

Lewis Leroy Monty was a sailor for the Everett Packing Co. of Everett, WA, when he signed his World War I Draft Registration card in 1917. From at least 1920 on, though, he was a longshoreman in Everett. He and his wife had been married for six years in 1930 (US censuses).

4.11.4.4.6   **MONTY, Frank Milton** b 21 May 1891, Silvana, WA; d 27 Oct 1956, Everett, WA. He married (1) 6 Apr 1917 **Alice J. Hickey** (Philip J. Hickey & Nellie ____) b Apr 1897, Spokane, WA; d & bur 1918, Snohomish Co., WA.

He married (2) 1920? **Hazel E. ____** b 16 Aug 1898, WA; d 14 Jun 1968, Los Angeles, CA.

Frank M. Monty was staying with his son in his stepfather's household in Everett, WA, in 1920. His wife had died in childbirth and was buried in Mount Carmel Cemetery in Snohomish Co., WA. In 1930, when he and his second wife Hazel had been married for ten years, Frank Monty was a longshoreman in Beverly Park, WA (US censuses).

Child of the first marriage:
4.11.4.4.6.1   Frank Henry   1918-   -1990

4.11.4.4.7   **MONTY, William Henry** b 29 Apr 1895, Silvana, WA. He married (1) 3 Aug 1918 **Gladys Hoback** (Harry J. Hoback & Nellie Savageau) b 25 Sep 1900, Snohomish Co., WA; d 5 Aug 1968, Everett, WA.

He married (2) 26 Oct 1923, Everett, WA, **Mrs. Grace Berry** b 1887?, KS.

William Henry Monty was a mariner working for the Everett Tug & Barge Co. in Everett, WA, when he signed his World War I Draft Registration card on 5 Jun 1917. His first marriage appears to have been short-lived. By 1920 he and his wife Gladys, though still married, had separate residences in Everett where he was a lumber mill worker. In 1930 he was a longshoreman in Beverly Park, WA. With him were his second wife Grace, who was then 43 years old and had first married at the age of 19, and a 12-year-old child born in Montana named Joseph Monty (US censuses). There is no evidence that William Monty and his first wife ever had a son. Joseph Monty may have been the son of Mrs. Grace Berry's first marriage, formally or informally adopted by William H. Monty. Or he may have been simply adopted into the family. I do not know.

4.11.4.6.1   **MONTY, Clarence A.** b 3 Mar 1875, St. Joseph, MI; d 4 Jul 1876, Benton Harbor, MI.

4.11.4.6.2   **MONTY, Perley B.** b 6 Dec 1876, Benton Harbor, MI; d there 16 Aug 1878.

4.11.4.6.3   **MONTY, Milton M.** b 10 Dec 1879, Benton Harbor, MI; d there 12 Sep 1879.

4.11.4.6.4   **MONTY, Etta/Emetta** b 6 Aug 1880, Benton Harbor, MI; d 21 Jan 1916, Tonasket, WA. She married (1) 7 Jul 1907, Everett, WA, **John Van Rooy** (John Van Rooy & Matilda Delaurelle) b 27 Aug 1882, WI; m (2) 1911? Frieda Schultz; d 27 Aug 1951, Grays Harbor, WA.

She was divorced when she married (2) 23 Dec 1910, Republic, WA, **Roy/Leroy Brittain** (Wesley Francis Brittain & Sarah Elizabeth Voiles) b 29 Sep 1887, Parkman, WY; m (2) 1917? Doris Genevieve Knight; d 17 May 1962, Sequim, WA.

Etta Monty (Emetta at her birth) left Michigan as a child before 1887 and was living with her parents in Trafton, WA, in 1900. Her first marriage was obviously short-lived. By 1910 John Van Rooy was divorced and again living in his father's household in Trafton. Etta Monty was then teaching school under her maiden name in Okanogon Co., WA, where Roy Brittain was a guard in the Forest Service (Washington Territory and US censuses). She died of complications following childbirth and her child was raised by her paternal grandparents.

Roy Brittain soon remarried: by 1 Jan 1920 he and his second wife Doris had a 2-year-old son. He was then a farmer in Marcus, WA, and in 1930 a logger in Clallam Co., WA (US censuses).

Child:

i   **Virginia Brittain** b 23 Dec 1915, Tonasket, WA; d Jun 1986, Las Vegas, NV. She married 1936, Marcus, WA, **Bernard Ingvard Bakken** (Andrew Bakken & ____) b 8 Dec 1914, Fargo, ND; d 9 Apr 1982, Portland, OR.

4.11.4.6.5   **MONTY, George B.** (twin) b 19 Sep 1882, Benton Harbor, MI; d & bur 1 & 4 Nov 1953, Arlington, WA. He married (1) 1 Apr 1905, Snohomish Co., WA, **Evelyn Eleanor Richardson** (Crawford Richardson & Celina Amelia/Selina A. Eastwood) b Apr 1885, PA; m (2) 14 Nov 1906, Snohomish Co., WA, George Tripp.

He married (2) 20 Jun 1911, Tacoma, WA, **Jessie Marie Ralph** (Robert Ralph & Edith Mabel Doxey) b 11 Feb 1893, Midland, MI; d 5 Dec 1982, Arlington, WA.

George B. Monty left Michigan as a child before 1887 and was living with his parents in Trafton (later Cicero), WA, in 1900. He was a mechanic/millwright in a sawmill there in 1920 and 1930 (Washington Territory and US censuses) and later purchased land there. He retired in Arlington, WA, and was buried, as was his second wife, in the Arlington Municipal Cemetery.

Child of the first marriage:
4.11.4.6.5.1	Lester D.	1905-1927-1994

Children of the second marriage:
4.11.4.6.5.2	Geraldine L.	1912-1931-
4.11.4.6.5.3	Ralph Clayton	1914-1939-1974
4.11.4.6.5.4	Delores Mae	1922-1942-2003

4.11.4.6.6   **MONTY, Anonymous** (twin) b 19 Sep 1882, Benton Harbor, MI; d there 19 Oct 1882.

4.11.4.6.7   **MONTY, Glenn Lewis** b 3 Jun 1885, Benton Harbor, MI; d & bur 31 Mar & 3 Apr 1944, Cicero & Arlington, WA.

Glenn L. Monty (Glenndault Monta in his birth record) was a toddler when he came with his parents to the Washington Territory. He was a farmer on the family homestead in Cicero, WA (Washington Territory and US censuses). He did not marry.

There is a one-year discrepancy between the date of birth, 3 June 1885, shown in the Berrien Co., MI, Birth Records (Bk. C, p. 140) and later documents such as Glenn Lewis Monty's World War I Draft Registration card (born 3 Jun 1884) and his death certificate (#134) in Snohomish Co., WA (59 years old at death). The inscription on his tombstone in the Arlington, WA, Municipal Cemetery carries the dates 1884-1944. Either year is of course possible. I have chosen to trust the document closest in time to the actual birth. Also to be noted is that the 1900 US census in Trafton shows that the 14-year-old G. L. Montey (sic) was born in June 1885.

4.11.4.6.8   **MONTY, Clayton B.** b 15 Jul 1889, Trafton, WA; d there 4 Aug 1893.

4.11.4.6.9   **MONTY, Guy** b 24 Jan 1892, Trafton (now Cicero), WA; d & bur 21 & 25 Aug 1952, Fir Island & Arlington, WA. He married 24 Apr 1920, Everett, WA, **Mary Dell Watkins** (John H. Watkins & Georgiana Bush) b 12 Oct 1902, Skyhomish, WA; m (2) and divorced Lawrence William Hopkins (William F. Hopkins & Jennie Scott); m (3) 12 Sep 1958, Snohomish Co., WA Otto Rojahn (Richard Rojahn & Elizabeth _____); d 15 Dec 1967, Everett, WA.

Guy Monty was a dairy farmer on the family homestead in Cicero, WA, and was buried in the Arlington, WA, Municipal Cemetery.

Children:

4.11.4.6.9.1	Bertram Edgar	1920-1944-
4.11.4.6.9.2	Melvin Morris	1922-1943-1989

4.11.4.6.10   **MONTY, Hiram Jr.** b 10 Apr 1894, Trafton (now Cicero), WA; d 5 Mar 1973, Arlington, WA.

Hiram Monty Jr. was a dairy farmer on the family homestead in Cicero, WA, and was buried in the Arlington, WA, Municipal Cemetery. He did not marry.

4.11.4.6.11   **MONTY, Laona Mae** b 12 Mar 1897, Trafton, WA; d there 18 May 1903.

4.11.4.8.1   **MONTY, George Rank** b 27 Oct 1901, Tacoma, WA; d 2 Oct 1980, Long Beach, CA. He married 1923?, Tacoma, WA, **Lavinia Willeby** (Samuel E. Willeby & Mary V. Hamilton) b 21 Apr 1902, Darrington, WA; d 7 Nov 1984, Culver City, CA.

George Rank Monty was a salesman in Tacoma, WA, in 1921 (City Directory) and an auditor in Tacoma, WA, in 1930 when he and his wife had been married for seven years (US census). The family later moved to California.

Children:

4.11.4.8.1.1	Betty June	1924-1942?-2002
4.11.4.8.1.2	Janice Carol	1926- -
4.11.4.8.1.3	George Rank Jr.	1927-1947&1950-

4.11.7.3.1   **MONTY, Earl Frank** b 29 Jan 1898, Dracut, MA; d 28 Oct 1978, Lawrence, MA. He married Apr 1924, Lowell, MA, **Grace A. Brigham** b 4 Apr 1900, MA; d 7 Aug 1978, Lawrence, MA.

Earl Frank Monty was a truck driver in Lowell, MA, when he signed on 12 Sep 1918 his World War I Draft Registration card. He and his wife lived in Lawrence, MA, where he was a driver or chauffeur, in 1925 and later years (City Directories; US censuses).

Child:

4.11.7.3.1.1	Earl F.	1925- -1944/45

4.11.7.3.2   **MONTY, Edith** b 22 Feb 1902, Lowell, MA; d & bur 28 & 31 Jul 1982, Plattsburgh, NY. She married there 14 Aug 1922 **Roy G. Shelley** (Benjamin Shelley & Elvira Demarse) b 9 Mar 1901, West Plattsburgh, NY; d & bur 28 Nov & 1 Dec 1973, Plattsburgh, NY.

Edith Monty was in Lowell, MA, when her father signed his World War I Draft Registration card on 12 Sep 1918 but was staying with her aunt and uncle Alice Drusella Monty (4.11.7.4) and George L. Gregory in Plattsburgh, NY, in 1920. Roy Shelley was a truck driver there in 1930 (US censuses). He and his wife were both buried in Plattsburgh's Riverside Cemetery (*Plattsburgh Press Republican*, 30 Nov 1973 and 30 Jul 1982).

Child:

i   **Marjorie B. Shelley** b 13 Jan 1924, Plattsburgh, NY; d 10 Mar 2005, Bradenton, FL. She married Oct 1983, Plattsburgh, NY, **Robert J. Golden** (Leo J. Golden &

Phyllis A. Goodrow) b there July 1925.

5.7.1.1.1   **MONTY, Esther** b & bp 31 Dec 1832, Marieville, QC; d & bur there 14 & 16 Feb 1903.
Esther Monty did not marry.

5.7.1.1.2   **MONTY, Clémence** b & bp 16 Apr 1835, Marieville, QC; d & bur there 18 & 19 May 1836.

5.7.1.1.3   **MONTY, Elmire** b & bp 3 Feb 1837, Marieville, QC. She married 31 May 1883, Richelieu, QC, **Jérémie Larocque** (Jean-Baptiste Larocque & Marguerite Grenier) b & bp 6 & 7 Nov 1830, St. Mathias, QC; m (1) there 23 Feb 1857 Philomène Béïque (Louis Béïque & Elisabeth L'Homme); d & bur 7 & 9 May 1914, Marieville & St. Mathias, QC.
Jérémie Larocque was a blacksmith in St. Mathias, QC, at his first marriage and a farmer there in 1881 and later years. He was a farmer in Marieville, QC, in 1901 though he and Elmire Monty were back in St. Mathias in 1911 (Canadian censuses). She survived her husband.

5.7.1.1.4   **MONTY, Louis** b & bp 23 Aug 1839, Marieville, QC; d & bur there 4 & 8 Mar 1841.

5.7.1.1.5   **MONTY, Philomène** b & bp 2 Mar 1842, Marieville, QC; d & bur there 25 & 27 Dec 1843.

5.7.1.1.6   **MONTY, Honoré/Henry** b & bp 12 & 13 Dec 1843, Marieville, QC; d 1914, Waterbury, CT. He married 17 Oct 1864, St. Mathias, QC, **Adeline Bessette** (Solyme Bessette & Judith Marcoux) b & bp there 20 & 21 Jul 1844.
Honoré Monty was a farmer in St. Mathias, QC, until about 1869 when he moved to the United States. He was a cotton mill worker in Holyoke, MA, in 1870 and a dealer there in 1880. The family then moved to Waterbury, CT, where Honore Monty was employed from at least 1891 on as clerk, salesman, teamster, and, after 1901, carriage maker (US censuses; City Directories through 1914). His widow continued to live at their old address in 1915 and 1916 (City Directories).
According to the 1900 census in Waterbury, Adeline Bessette (Marguerite Adeline Besset at her baptism) had had twelve children of whom only two, Louis Alphonse and Flora, were then still alive.
One of her sisters, Agnès Bessette, married Nérée Monty (5.7.1.1.11) while another, Rosalie Bessette, married Eusèbe Rainville, son of Marie Olive Monty (5.7.1.3) and Louis Rainville.

Children:
5.7.1.1.6.1	Honoré Solyme	1865-	-1867
5.7.1.1.6.2	Louis Alphonse	1867-1890-	
5.7.1.1.6.3	Joséphat Arthur	1868-	-1869
5.7.1.1.6.4	Flora	1876-	-

5.7.1.1.7   **MONTY, Adélaïde** b & bp 11 & 12 Feb 1845, Marieville, QC; d 22 Jan 1892, Holyoke, MA. She married 26 Jan 1864, St. Mathias, QC, a second cousin **Edmond Choquette** (Edouard Choquette & Emérite Messier) b Jul 1838, QC; d 25 Jan 1929, Holyoke, MA.
Adélaïde Monty and Edmond Choquette shared a common ancestor in Augustin Messier, father of Julie Messier (5.7.1), Adélaïde Monty's paternal grandmother.
Edmond Choquette was a farmer in Marieville, QC, until 1869. The following June he was a cotton mill worker living in Holyoke, MA, with his wife Delia and his children Emma, Edmund, and Achille. He returned to Canada a few years later for two children were born in Chambly, QC, in 1874 and 1876. The family then came back to Holyoke before the birth of

the youngest child in 1881. Edmond Choquette worked there as a millwright until at least 1920 (US censuses).

Children:
i   **Emma Adélaïde Choquette** b & bp 17 & 18 Aug 1865, Marieville, QC. She married 13 Sep 1886, Holyoke, MA, **Joseph Desroches** (Edouard Desroches & Odile Martel) b & bp 7 & 9 Dec 1865, Ste Angèle & St. Césaire, QC.

ii   **Edmond/Edmund Choquette** b & bp 2 & 3 Dec 1866, Marieville, QC. He married 19 Dec 1891, Holyoke, MA, **Catherine Bigonesse/Bigness** (Léon Bigonesse & Zoé Beaudry) who was 22 years old at her marriage.

iii   **Achille Philias Choquette** b & bp 18 & 20 Dec 1868, Marieville, QC.

iv   **Rose Antoinette Choquette** b & bp 9 & 10 Aug 1874, Chambly, QC.

v   **Hélène Choquette** b & bp 28 May 1876, Chambly, QC; d 1925, Holyoke, MA. She married there 6 May 1901 **Alphonse Dubois** (Jean-Baptiste/John B. Dubois & Marie Anne Jeannotte) b & bp 2 Jan 1873, Beloeil, QC.

vi   **Laura Choquette** b May 1881, Holyoke, MA; d there 1956.

5.7.1.1.8   **MONTY, Marie** b & bp 10 & 11 Jan 1847, Marieville, QC. She married 8 Aug 1870, Richelieu, QC, a second cousin, **Joseph Larocque** (Isaac Larocque & Marie Messier) b Mar 1835, QC; m (1) 7 Jan 1861, St. Mathias, QC, Elmire Ostiguy (Mathias Ostiguy & Hortense Courtemanche).

Marie Monty and Joseph Larocque shared a common ancestor in Augustin Messier, father of Julie Messier (5.7.1), Marie Monty's paternal grandmother.

Joseph Larocque was originally a carter and carpenter in Richelieu, QC. He left around 1873 for Holyoke, MA, where he was a carpenter and where three children were born, returned to Canada in the early 1880s for the births of two more children, and then came back to Holyoke before the birth of his last child in 1886. He moved to Waterbury, CT, a few years later and was a laborer there in 1900. He and his wife had then had nine children of whom six, Joseph, Richard, Mary L., Lena, Phelix (Charles Philias), and Delore, were still alive (US censuses). He was a naturalized American citizen, as were his sons Joseph Jr. and Richard. Yet I have been unable to find him or his wife in the United States in later years and wonder if they did not return a final time to Canada with some of their children.

Children:
i   **Joseph Louis Alfred Larocque** b & bp 9 & 10 Nov 1871, Richelieu, QC; d 3 Mar 1952, Middletown, CT. He married 1904? **Sarah A. Durley** (William Durley & Dora ____) b Sep 1873, CT; m (1) 1893? James Conroy; d 17 Oct 1952, Waterbury, CT.

ii   **Pierre Richard Larocque** b & bp 21 & 22 Nov 1872, Richelieu, QC. He married 4 May 1898, Waterbury, CT, **Amanda Mathon** (Louis Mathon & Eloise Ayotte) b & bp 11 Apr 1876, Ste Geneviève de Batiscan, QC.

iii   **Mary L. Larocque** b Oct 1874, MA.

iv   **Henry Larocque** b 18 Sep 1877, Holyoke, MA; d before 1880.

v   **Odrick/Medrick Larocque** b 21 Feb 1880, Holyoke, MA; d before 1900.

vi   **Lena Larocque** b Apr 1882, QC.

vii   **Charles Philias/Phelix Larocque** b & bp 5 & 7 Jun 1883, Richelieu, QC.

viii   **Delore (Adelard?) Larocque** b 9 Mar 1886, Holyoke, MA.

5.7.1.1.9   **MONTY, Emérite/Mérite** b & bp 23 & 24 Sep 1848, Marieville, QC; d & bur 1 & 3 Aug 1902, St. Edouard de Napierville, QC. She married 24 Mar 1885, Montreal, QC, as his second wife **Moïse Sicotte/Moyse Chicotte** (Jean-Baptiste Chicotte & Marie Louise Robert) b & bp 27 & 28 Feb 1842, St. Edouard de Napierville, QC; m (3) 20 Feb 1906, St. Michel, QC, Hermine Martin (Toussaint Martin & Suzanne Laplante), widow of Adolphe Longtin; d & bur ? & 7 May 1928, Sherrington & St. Edouard de Napierville, QC.

Emérite Monty and Moïse Sicotte (Moyse Chicotte at his baptism) were both residents of Holyoke, MA, at their marriage. He was then a teamster there as also at the births of his daughters in 1888 and 1891. In 1889, however, when his son was born in St. Edouard de Napierville, QC, he was said to be a farmer there. He returned permanently to the area in the 1890s and was living with Emérite Monty and their children in St. Edouard de Napierville in 1901 and with his third wife in neighboring St. Michel, QC, in 1911 (Canadian censuses).

Children:

i   **Marie Cora/Ida Sicotte** b 24 Mar 1888, Holyoke, MA. She married 5 May 1908, St. Michel, QC, **Louis Victor/Hector Faille** (Narcisse Faille & Rose de Lima Houle) b & bp there 7 & 8 Nov 1880; m (1) 15 Sep 1902, St. Antoine Abbé, QC, Anésie Guérin (Amable Guérin & Eliza Lefebvre).

ii   **Rosario Sicotte** b & bp 13 & 15 May 1889, St. Edouard de Napierville, QC. He married 30 Jun 1915, St. Michel, QC, **Rose Alma Métras** (Philorum Métras & Joséphine Myre) b & bp 4 & 6 Jul 1887, St. Antoine Abbé, QC; m (1) 30 Oct 1905, St. Michel, QC, Alexandre Ricard (Louis Ricard & Martine Fortier).

iii   **Marie Evelina Sicotte** b 8 Oct 1891, Holyoke, MA. She married 23 Apr 1919, St. Michel, QC, **Rémi Pié/Pied** (Armand Pied & Odile Cardinal) b & bp there 17 Mar 1897.

5.7.1.1.10   **MONTY, Marie Cordélie** b & bp 13 & 14 Mar 1851, Marieville, QC; d & bur there 22 & 23 Apr 1856.

5.7.1.1.11   **MONTY, Nérée** b & bp 11 & 12 Aug 1853, Marieville, QC; d 17 Jul 1916, Cranston, RI. He married 30 May 1882, Holyoke, MA, **Agnès Bessette** (Solyme Bessette & Judith Marcoux) b & bp 14 & 15 Jun 1858, St. Mathias, QC.

Nérée Monty came to Holyoke, MA, as a child with his father and stepmother and was an agent there at his marriage. His first child was born in Canada though he was in Rhode Island at the birth of his daughter Ernestine in 1886 and in Waterbury, CT, when he was naturalized on 27 Oct 1892. He was a carpenter there from the early 1890s and until at least 1900. Only one of his nine children was then still alive. I have not found him in 1910 when his wife was staying in Pawtucket, RI, with her daughter Ernestine and son-in-law Philippe Viau. She had returned to Waterbury by 1917 and was staying with the Viau family as late as 1927 (US censuses; City Directories).

One of Agnès Bessette's sisters, Adeline Bessette, married Honoré Monty (5.7.1.1.6) while another, Rosalie Bessette, married Eusèbe Rainville, son of Marie Olive Monty (5.7.1.3) and Louis Rainville.

Children:

5.7.1.1.11.1	Louis Armin	1883-	-1884
5.7.1.1.11.2	Ernestine Agnès	1886-1909?-1969	
5.7.1.1.11.3	Anonymous	1888-	-1888

5.7.1.1.12   **MONTY, Célina Joséphine** b & bp 9 Oct 1855, Marieville, QC; d & bur 5 & 7 Feb 1930, Marieville & Richelieu, QC.

5.7.1.1.13   **MONTY, Louis** b & bp 6 Apr 1858, Marieville, QC; d & bur there 1 & 3 May 1858.

5.7.1.2.1   **MONTY, Louis Joseph** b & bp 21 Nov 1839, St. Mathias, QC. He married 1 Jun 1859, Montreal, QC, **Louise Adélaïde Azilda Plamondon** (Pierre Plamondon & Adélaïde Fernet) b & bp 19 & 20 Oct 1839, Montreal, QC.

Louis Joseph Monty (Louis Jean-Baptiste Joseph Donat at his baptism) was a merchant in Mont St. Grégoire, QC, when his son was born in 1860. He later was a partner with Elzéar Rainville in the firm of Monty & Rainville, general storekeepers, in Marieville, QC (Lovell's Directory, 1871). I have not found him in Canada in later years and strongly suspect that he emigrated during the 1870s along with his parents (both of whom died in New York City in the 1880s) and at least two and possibly three siblings, Achille (5.7.1.2.4), Mathilde

(5.7.1.2.8), and Frederick E. (5.7.1.2.10) who had come to the United States in the 1870s.

Child:
5.7.1.2.1.1   Joseph Louis/Lewis   1860-1881-

5.7.1.2.2   **MONTY, Marie Louise Virginie** b & bp 30 Sep & 3 Oct 1841, St. Mathias, QC; d & bur 31 Dec 1862 & 5 Jan 1863, Marieville & St. Mathias, QC. She married there 12 May 1862 **Félix Fontaine** (Félix Fontaine & Esther Dubuc) b & bp 19 & 20 Sep 1832, St. Charles, QC; m (2) 27 Jun 1869, Richelieu, QC, Marie Clara Limoges (Pierre Limoges & Lucie Viger); d & bur 20 & 22 Jun 1900, Rougemont, QC.
    Félix Fontaine was a notary in Marieville, QC.

Child:
i   **Marie Virginie Fontaine** b & bp 28 Dec 1862, Marieville, QC; d & bur 28 Dec 1862 & 5 Jan 1863, Marieville & St. Mathias, QC.

5.7.1.2.3   **MONTY, Marie Emélie** b & bp 22 May 1843, St. Mathias, QC; d & bur there 28 & 31 Aug 1853.

5.7.1.2.4   **MONTY/MONTE, Achille** b & bp 13 Feb 1845, St. Mathias, QC.
    Achille Monty (François Xavier Achille at his baptism) was in 1871 a member of the firm of Monty & D'Artois, "lumber merchants & general dealers in groceries, provisions, liquors, hardware, boots and shoes, crockery, etc." in West Farnham, QC (Lovell's Directory). I have not found him in either Canadian or American censuses after then.
    I suspect that he was the Achille Monte, born in Canada in February 1845, who had arrived in the United States in 1871 and was living on 7th Ave in Manhattan, NY, in 1900. He had been married for three years though his wife was not with him (US census). His occupation is illegible though I find it suggestive that his residence was within one block of the *Monti & Hudon* meat market owned since 1890 by Frederick E. Monti (5.7.1.2.10) and his brother-in-law Démétrius P. Hudon (5.7.1.2.8).

5.7.1.2.5   **MONTY, Alphonsine Elise** b & bp 14 Oct 1846, St. Mathias, QC.

5.7.1.2.6   **MONTY, Philomène Théodore Eulalie** b & bp 26 & 27 May 1848, St. Mathias, QC.

5.7.1.2.7   **MONTY, Marie Emerante Eloyse** b & bp 18 & 20 Jul 1849, St. Mathias, QC.

5.7.1.2.8   **MONTY, Mathilde Helwidge Rose/Matilda** b & bp 13 & 17 Jul 1853, St. Mathias, QC. She married there 15 Sep 1875 **Démétrius Pierre Hudon** (Hyacinthe Hudon dit Beaulieu & Vitaline Langlois) b & bp 10 Jan 1845, Rivière Ouelle, QC.
    Démétrius Pierre Hudon was a clerk in Montreal, QC, at his marriage. By 1890 he was the co-owner with his brother-in-law Frederick E. Monti (5.7.1.2.10) of a meat market, *Monti & Hudon*, on 7th Ave in Manhattan, NY. He and Frederick Monti also shared the same home address on 124th St. (New York City Directory). He was retired by 1910 and living with his wife Matilda in the Bronx, NY. It was from there he applied for naturalization on 28 Jun 1912 (New York Co., NY, Supreme Court Naturalization Petitions, vol. 69, p. 122). Demetrius and Matilda Hudon were still living in the Bronx in 1930 (US censuses). They had had no children.

5.7.1.2.9   **MONTY, Rose Ameline** b & bp 5 & 6 Nov 1854, St. Mathias, QC.

5.7.1.2.10   **MONTY/MONTE/MONTI, Frederick E./Frédéric** b & bp 29 Apr & 1 May 1857, St. Mathias, QC. He married 1892? **Lizzie R.** ____ b Jun 1856, MA.
    This man was named Emile Ulger Frédéric Monty at his baptism. Both his name and

surname varied along the years. He came to the United States around 1873 and was known in 1890, when he was the co-owner with his brother-in-law Demetrius P. Hudon (5.7.1.2.8) of the *Monti & Hudon* meat market on 7th Ave in Manhattan, NY, as Frederick E. Monti (New York City Directory, 1890). He was still single and shared a home address with his brother-in-law. In 1900, Frederick E. Monte was the owner of a "meat and provisions" market in Manhattan and was living there with his wife Lizzie. They moved to Massachusetts in the next several years. In 1910, when he and his wife had been married for eighteen years, Frederic Monti was a provisions merchant in Boston, MA (US censuses).

5.7.1.5.1   **MONTY, Adeline/Delima** b & bp 1 & 2 May 1841, St. Jean-Baptiste, QC; d & bur there 24 & 26 Nov 1843.

This child was named Marie Adeline at her baptism and Delima when she died at the age of 2½ years. There is no evidence of a twin birth.

5.7.1.5.2   **MONTY, Michel** b & bp 29 & 30 Mar 1842, St. Jean-Baptiste, QC; d & bur there 5 & 9 Dec 1856.

5.7.1.5.3   **MONTY, Louis Michel** b & bp 27 & 28 Jun 1859, St. Jean-Baptiste, QC; d & bur there 28 & 31 Mar 1941. He married 14 Feb 1882, St. Damase, QC, **Célina Jodoin** (Augustin Jodoin & Colette Allard) b & bp there 6 & 7 Dec 1861; d 17 Nov 1952, Marieville, QC.

Louis Monty (Louis Michel at his baptism) was a farmer in St. Jean-Baptiste, QC, for most of his life. I have seen no sign that he ever came to the United States and so am intrigued by the fact that three of his daughters, Alberta, Marie Anne, and Donalda, who were living with their parents in St. Jean-Baptiste in 1901 (Canadian census), married in Norwich, CT, between 1907 and 1914. There must be a connection, perhaps through one of the several Jodoin families of Connecticut. One daughter later returned to Canada with her husband; the other two remained in the United States. One son, Charles Emile, who was living with his parents in St. Jean-Baptiste in 1901 also made his life in the United States, in Vermont. The descendants of Louis Monty and Célina Jodoin are thus found in both Canada and the United States.

Children:

5.7.1.5.3.1	Evangéline	1883-1901-
5.7.1.5.3.2	Alberta/Celia Albertine	1884-1907-
5.7.1.5.3.3	Marie Anne Flore/Mary A.	1885-1907-1968
5.7.1.5.3.4	Charles Emile	1886-1924-1973
5.7.1.5.3.5	Donalda	1887-1914-1951
5.7.1.5.3.6	Michel Auguste	1888- -1910
5.7.1.5.3.7	Marie	1892- -1892
5.7.1.5.3.8	François Xavier Antoine	1894- -1896
5.7.1.5.3.9	Rosario Louis Philippe	1897- -1901
5.7.1.5.3.10	Alphonse	1898-1927-1971
5.7.1.5.3.11	Jean-Baptiste Polydore	1901-1924-

5.7.1.9.1   **MONTY, Alexander B./Honoré Bercéus** b & bp 30 & 31 Aug 1848, Chambly, QC; d 20 Dec 1916, Burlington, VT. He married (1) there 9 Jul 1869 **Mary Louisa Barbeau** (Joseph Barbeau & Marie Manville) b 1849? Keeseville, NY.

He was a widower when he married (2) 22 Apr 1887, Colchester, VT, **Domitilde/ Matilda Frégeau** (Michel Frégeau & Domitilde/Matilda Audet) b & bp 3 Mar 1851, St. Valentin, QC; m (1) 31 Jan 1875, Winooski, VT, Jean-Baptiste Livernois, widower of Marie Larochelle; d 25 Feb 1925, Lawrence, MA.

I have identified Alexander B. Monty, son of Honoré Monty and Célina Massé, whose naturalization papers of 2 Jul 1874 in the Superior Court of Hampden Co., MA, indicate that he was born in Canada on 30 Aug 1848, with Honoré Bérceus, son of Honoré Monty and Célina Massé, born that very day in Chambly, QC. There is no evidence of twins, of Honoré

Bercéus' death, nor of any child in that family named Alexander. I cannot explain the name change: the usual English version of Honoré is Henry.

At the time of their marriage both Alexander B. Monty and Mary Louisa Barbeau were residents of Holyoke, MA. He was a carpenter there at the birth of his first child in April 1870, and a store clerk in June of that year. He was also a resident of Holyoke when he was naturalized in 1874 and at the birth of his third child in April 1875. The second child however was born in 1872 in Colchester, VT, as well as the younger children. From about 1878 through 1890 the family lived in Winooski, VT, where Alexander (occasionally Alex) Monty was in turn a druggist's clerk, a laborer, a factory worker, and a carpenter. The family then moved to Lawrence, MA, where he was a mill worker in 1891 and 1893 at the births of his last two children and until at least 1900. He was still a mill worker in 1910, though living in Amesbury, MA. His widow was a patient in the Lawrence, MA, Tuberculosis Hospital in 1920 (US censuses).

Mary Louisa Barbeau (also Barbo, Barber) who was born in Keeseville, NY, according to her children's birth certificates, was 21 years old in 1870 (US census).

Children of the first marriage:

5.7.1.9.1.1	Emma M.	1870-1891-1956
5.7.1.9.1.2	Henry Joseph	1872-1895-
5.7.1.9.1.3	Alexander	1875- -1875
5.7.1.9.1.4	Ella Elizabeth	1878- -1923
5.7.1.9.1.5	Clara	1880-1901?-1971
5.7.1.9.1.6	Dora	1882-1909?-

Children of the second marriage:

5.7.1.9.1.7	Célina	1888- -1888
5.7.1.9.1.8	Mary	1889- -
5.7.1.9.1.9	Joseph	1890- -1890
5.7.1.9.1.10	Joseph	1891- -1891
5.7.1.9.1.11	Anonymous	1893- -1893

5.7.1.9.2   **MONTY, Marie Elia Célina** b & bp 4 & 5 Jul 1850, St. Mathias, QC; d & bur there 11 & 13 Mar 1852.

5.7.1.9.3   **MONTY, Flavien** b & bp 26 & 28 Mar 1853, St. Mathias, QC; d & bur there 25 & 26 Jun 1853.

5.7.1.9.4   **MONTY, Edouard Flavien Frédéric Gustave** b & bp 20 & 21 May 1857, Marieville, QC; d & bur there 30 May & 1 Jun 1857.

5.7.1.9.5   **MONTY, Jacques François Xavier Arthur** b & bp 7 & 8 Dec 1858, Marieville, QC; d & bur there 30 Dec 1859 & 1 Jan 1860.

5.7.1.9.6   **MONTY, Marie Elia Célina** b & bp 14 & 15 Nov 1860, Marieville, QC; d & bur there 8 & 9 Jan 1861.

5.7.1.12.1   **MONTY, Eudoxie** b & bp 10 Mar 1853, St. Mathias, QC; d 4 May 1945, St. Hyacinthe, QC. She married (1) 23 Oct 1876, Sherbrooke, QC, **Edouard Laroche** (Jean Laroche & Marguerite Laroche) b & bp 11 & 12 Aug 1838, Ste Croix, QC; d 3 Jun 1883, Holyoke, MA.

She married (2) 23 May 1885, Holyoke, MA, as his third wife **Louis Israël Morier** (Désiré Morier & Zoé Blanchard) b & bp 8 & 9 Sep 1836, St. Hilaire, QC; m (1) 26 Nov 1861, St. Jean-Baptiste, QC, Philomène Pepin (Cyprien Pepin & Domithilde Bertrand); m (2) _____ ; d & bur 9 & 12 Jun 1922, St. Hyacinthe, QC.

Edouard Laroche and Eudoxie Monty (Marie Julie Eudoxie at her baptism) moved to Holyoke, MA, soon after their marriage. He was a carpenter there. He died of consumption and was buried in Notre Dame Cemetery in South Hadley Falls, MA.

Eudoxie Monty was a dressmaker in Holyoke at her second marriage. She and Louis Morier, a paper mill employee, lived there until 1894 when they returned to Canada and settled in St. Hyacinthe, QC. Louis Morier was a farmer there in 1901 and retired in 1911 (Canadian censuses).

Children:

i   **George H. Laroche** b 5 Mar 1877, Holyoke, MA.

ii   **Frédéric A. Laroche** b 25 Oct 1880, Holyoke, MA.

iii   **Henry E. Laroche** b 15 Jan 1882, Holyoke, MA.

iv   **Eudore (Horace** at his birth) **Morier** b 16 Mar 1886, Holyoke, MA; d 28 Oct 1954, Montreal, QC. He married (1) **Flore/Marie Blanche Angéline Flora Leblanc** (Auguste Leblanc & Eulalie Lord) b & bp 28 Feb & 3 Mar 1893, Montreal, QC; d & bur 11 & 15 Oct 1928, Montreal & St. Hyacinthe, QC.
He married (2) 27 Oct 1932, Quebec, QC, **Marguerite Marie Evelyn Chabot** (Avila Chabot & Marguerite Viel) b Mar 1905, Winnipeg, Manitoba, Canada.

v   **Eva Morier** b 6 May 1888, Holyoke, MA. She married 22 Jun 1933, St. Hyacinthe, QC, **Augustin Médard Hormisdas Mageau** (Elie Mageau & Adeline Jubinville) b & bp 19 Oct 1884, St. Liboire, QC.

vi   **William Morier** b 18 Dec 1889, Holyoke, MA; d there 5 Mar 1892.

vii   **Edouard Morier** b 4 Jan 1893, Holyoke, MA. He married (1) 2 Aug 1921, St. Hyacinthe, QC, **Yolande Rachel Alida Picard** (Jean-Baptiste Picard & Clérinda Morin) b & bp there 18 Feb 1895; d & bur 30 Nov & 3 Dec 1921, Montreal & St. Thomas d'Aquin, QC.
He married (2) 15 Jan 1930, Montreal, QC, **Berthe Antonie Riendeau** (Dosithée Riendeau & Médérise Picard) b & bp 18 & 20 Jan 1902, Ste Madeleine, QC.

5.7.1.12.2   **MONTY, Marie Louise Eliane** b & bp 21 & 22 Apr 1854, St. Mathias, QC; d & bur there 27 & 28 Apr 1854.

5.7.1.12.3   **MONTY, Louis Michel Théophile** b & bp 21 & 22 Jun 1855, St. Mathias, QC.

Louis Michel Théophile Monty was not included among his parents' six surviving children in the 1900 census in Woonsocket, RI. Nor was he found in earlier US censuses. He may have died in Canada before his parents emigrated in 1871 or in the United States before 1880.

5.7.1.12.4   **MONTY, Jean-Baptiste Léonidas/John B. L.** b & bp 23 & 24 Jun 1856, Marieville, QC; d & bur 1914? Hartford & Bristol, CT. He married (1) 13 Aug 1877, Holyoke, MA, with a Catholic marriage on 25 Sep 1877, St. Hyacinthe, QC, **Alphonsine Lagüe** (Joseph Lagüe & Rosalie Plante) b Dec 1854, QC; d & bur 13 & 16 Apr 1894 Chicopee, MA & St. Mathias, QC, at the age of 39 years and 4 months.

He married (2) 1901? **Elmire** ____ b 1873?, MA.

He married (3) 23 Sep 1914, Bristol, CT, **Ethel M. Allen** (Seneca Allen & Florence Green) b 13 Jul 1888, Lincoln, VT.

Jean-Baptiste Léonidas Monty was known under several names. He signed as Oneil Monty the baptismal record of his nephew Adelbert Honoré Monty (5.7.1.12. 5.3) in 1883, as John B. L. Monty his naturalization papers on 26 Oct 1883 (Superior Court, Hampden Co., MA), and as J. B. L. Monty as witness to his mother's funeral in 1914. The two marriages records I have found however are in the name of Jean-Baptiste Monty, while he was identified as Jean-Baptiste Onile Monty at his first wife's death in 1894.

He was in 1880 and for several years a cotton mill worker in Holyoke, MA, and then a photographer in Chicopee, MA, from at least 1890 through 1894 and in Ware, MA, in 1900. He moved to Connecticut with his second wife and was a factory worker in Bristol, CT, in 1910 when his mother was a member of his household (US censuses). I have not found his death record. He probably died shortly after his third marriage, in the last months of 1914: the

1915 Bristol City Directory refers only to Ethel Monty, "widow John B. L." Family lore has it that he died in a hospital in Hartford, CT, and was buried in Bristol.

5.7.1.12.5 **MONTY, Louis Charles Alphonse** b & bp 2 Mar 1858, Chambly, QC; d 21 Oct 1935, Holyoke, MA. He married there 18 May 1879 **Azarise Gaucher** (Pierre Gaucher & Philomène Messier) b & bp 21 Feb 1862, St. Pie, QC; d 18 May 1954, Holyoke, MA.

Louis Monty came to Holyoke, MA, with his parents in 1871 and was naturalized there on 22 Oct 1887 in the Police Court of Hampden Co. He was a factory worker and tram conductor (US censuses). He and his wife were buried in the Monty family plot in Notre Dame Cemetery in South Hadley Falls, MA.

Azarise Gaucher (Marie Zéphirine Azarie at her baptism) came to Holyoke with her parents in 1870 and remained there for the rest of her life.

Children:

5.7.1.12.5.1	Elméria/M. Sylvia	1880- -1880
5.7.1.12.5.2	Rosario Armand	1881- -1910
5.7.1.12.5.3	Adelbert Honoré	1883-1906-1934
5.7.1.12.5.4	Blanche Dolora	1885-1911-1968
5.7.1.12.5.5	Léonie Rosaria	1888- -1892
5.7.1.12.5.6	Una Azarise	1889-1913-1965
5.7.1.12.5.7	Ernest Louis	1897-1930&1978-1985
5.7.1.12.5.8	Vincent Honoré	1906- -1998

5.7.1.12.6 **MONTY, Celia/Cecilia** b & bp 17 Jun 1861, Marieville, QC; d 11 Mar 1941, Woonsocket, RI. She married (1) 23 May 1881, Holyoke, MA, **Joseph Antoine Lussier/Lucier** (Antoine Lussier & Angélique Cusson) b & bp 4 & 5 May 1859, St. Pie, QC; d 10 Sep 1906, Woonsocket, RI.

She married (2) 1928, Woonsocket, RI, **Alexandre Goulet** (Louis Goulet & Marie Zoé Beauregard) b & bp 29 Sep 1858, St. Liboire, QC; m (1) 1878? Emilie ____ ; d 24 Jun 1938, Woonsocket, RI.

Celia Monty (Marie Elia Célia at her baptism) came to Holyoke, MA, with her parents in 1871 and was originally known there as Celia Monty (1880 census; marriage record). As time went on however she became more frequently known as Cecilia in US censuses as well as on her children's birth records and at her death. She was buried, as were both her husbands, in the Precious Blood Cemetery in Woonsocket, RI.

Joseph Lussier (often Lucier, as in his marriage record and the birth records of most of his children) was a half-brother of Delphine Lussier, wife of Joseph Monty (5.7.7.8). He had arrived in the United States with his parents in 1863 and was a mill worker in Holyoke in 1870 and at his marriage, and a carpenter there at the births of his first four children. He was also a carpenter in Woonsocket where the family moved around 1887. By 1900 he and his wife had had ten children of whom four, Henri, Hermina, William, and Oscar, were still alive. His widow remained in Woonsocket and was holding household there for her three youngest children in 1920 (US censuses).

Alexander Goulet (Michel Alexandre at his baptism) was a restaurant owner in Woonsocket in 1920, when his first wife was still alive. He was retired in 1930 (US censuses).

Children:

i   **Marie Lussier** b 10 Jun 1882, Holyoke, MA; d there 3 Jun 1882.

ii   **Diamond Lussier** b 13 Jan 1884, Holyoke, MA; d before 1900.

iii **Joseph Lussier** b 13 Dec 1884, Holyoke, MA; d there 14 Dec 1884.

iv **Joseph Henri Lussier** b 21 Dec 1886, Holyoke, MA.

v   **Hermina Lussier** b 1 Nov 1888, Woonsocket, RI. She married 1910? **Joseph Allard** (Léon Allard & ____) b 10 Sep 1890, QC; d Nov 1970, Woonsocket, RI.

vi **Emeline Monty Lussier** b 16 Mar 1891, Woonsocket, RI; d there 19 May 1891.

vii **William Lussier** b 31 May 1893, Woonsocket, RI. He married 1912? **Hazel** ____ b 1891?, MA.

viii   **Oscar Eugene Lussier** b 8 Jun 1898, Woonsocket, RI; d there Apr 1965. He married (1) there 8 Nov 1920 **Anna Maria Baxter** (Charles H. Baxter & Anna Roddy) b there Sep 1898.

He was a widower when he married (2) 11 Nov 1950, Woonsocket, RI, **Grace F. McCool** (George McCool & Mary Lloyd) b 17 Oct 1916, MA; d 31 May 2002, Woonsocket, RI.

ix   **Leon Lussier** b 14 Feb 1901, Woonsocket, RI; d there Sep 1977. He married there 7 Jun 1926 **Annette Richard** (Jean-Baptiste A. Richard & Olivine Dufresne) b there 28 Jul 1901; d there Aug 1986.

x   **Blanche Lussier** b & bp 15 Aug 1903, Woonsocket, RI; d 19 Mar 1990, Providence, RI. She married (1) 1925? **Wilfred Maillé** (Ulnéric Maillé & Hélène ___) b Oct 1896, Providence, RI.

She was a widow when she married (2) 22 May 1954, Woonsocket, RI, **Léon Arthur Laberge** (Arthur Laberge & Regina St. Onge) b & bp 20 Jan 1904, Lévis, QC; d 24 Jan 1980, Long Beach, CA.

5.7.1.12.7   **MONTY, Hermine/Hermina** b & bp 15 May 1863, St. Mathias, QC; d & bur 25 & 29 Dec 1941, Chambly, QC. She married (1) 1 Feb 1886, Holyoke, MA, **William Gaulin** (Clément Gaulin & Adélaïde Larivière dit Chapdelaine) b & bp 15 & 16 Feb 1853, St. David d'Yamaska, QC; m (1) 1 Sep 1873, Woonsocket, RI, Agnès Marcoux (Flavien Marcoux & Célina Bessette); d there 22 Dec 1900.

She married (2) 27 Nov 1906, Montreal, QC, **Alphonse Brunelle** (Joseph Brunelle & Philomène Lamoureux) b & bp 19 Feb 1864, Chambly, QC.

William Gaulin (Guillaume at his baptism) was a clerk in Woonsocket, RI, at his first marriage, a baker there in 1880 (US census), and a merchant in 1886 at his second marriage. His widow lived for a few years in New York City before returning to Canada where she and her second husband lived on a farm near Chambly, QC. Alphonse Brunelle survived his wife.

5.7.1.12.8   **MONTY, Georges Alfred/Prudent** b & bp 26 & 27 Jun 1865, St. Mathias, QC; d & bur 28 & 30 Sep 1865, St. Mathias & Richelieu, QC.

The records of St. Mathias, QC, include the birth on 26 Jun 1865 of Georges Alfred, son of Prudent Monty and Onésime Daignault, and the death of Prudent, son of the same couple, on 28 Sep 1865 at the age of 1 month and 15 days. On the face of it, this is an impossibility. One or the other of these accounts must be wrong.

5.7.1.12.9   **MONTY, Salvina** b & bp 13 & 15 Mar 1871, Holyoke, MA; d there 12 Jul 1874.

This child is named Salvina in the Holyoke, MA, records of her birth and death. She was nevertheless baptized in the Precious Blood Catholic Church there as Marie Louise Onésime Monty.

5.7.1.12.10   **MONTY, Avelina** b 13 Apr 1872, Holyoke, MA; d there 10 Jul 1872.

5.7.1.12.11   **MONTY, Edward** b & bp 18 Aug 1873, Holyoke, MA. He married 25 Jan 1897, Woonsocket, RI, **Malvina Beaudreau/Boudreau** (Félix Beaudreau and Marie Parenteau) b there 1872; d & bur there 1952.

Edward Monty was a streetcar conductor in Woonsocket, RI, in 1900 and was staying with his wife and daughters in his father-in-law's household there. In 1920 Malvina Beaudreau was divorced and living in Manville, RI, with her daughter Antoinette and son-in-law Emile Fortier. She was a widow in 1930, living with her daughter Beatrice and son-in-law Arthur McPherson in Woonsocket (US censuses). The years of her birth and death are taken from the tombstone inscription in the Precious Blood Cemetery there. The 1900 census however shows that she was born in June 1871.

Children:

5.7.1.12.11.1   Beatrice   1898-1922-

5.7.2.6.1   **MONTY, Marie Louise** b & bp 2 & 4 Jan 1848, St. Césaire, QC; d & bur 14 & 16 Nov 1869, Granby, QC. She married 1 Feb 1869, Ange Gardien, QC, **Joseph Messier** (François Messier & Esther Bonnette) b 1849?, QC; m (2) 30 Oct 1870, Granby, QC, Flavie Domingue (Solyme Domingue & Adèle Catudal).

At her marriage the bride signed Marie Monthy, the only time I have seen this variant of the surname in a signature. Her husband, who was 32 years old in 1881 (Canadian census), was a blacksmith in Farnham, QC, at his marriage. When his wife died a few months later he was a blacksmith in Granby, QC.

Child:

i   **Eugène Albert Messier** b & bp 5 & 16 Nov 1869, Granby, QC.

5.7.2.6.2   **MONTY, Louis** b & bp 7 & 8 Jul 1849, St. Césaire, QC; d & bur 28 Nov & 1 Dec 1924, St. Alphonse, QC. He married 8 Feb 1875, Ange Gardien, QC, **Célina Brouillet/ Brouillette** (François Brouillet & Mathilde Vient) b & bp 17 & 18 Apr 1856, St. Jean-Baptiste, QC.

Louis Monty was a farmer in Ange Gardien, QC, at his marriage and a farmer in St. Alphonse, QC, at the births of his first eight children. He was a mill worker for a few years in Dudley, MA, where two children were born in 1892 and 1895, though he was back in Canada for the births of the next two. He was again a farmer in St. Alphonse in 1901 and remained there until his death (Canadian censuses). He predeceased his wife.

Children:

5.7.2.6.2.1	Médérise	1875- -
5.7.2.6.2.2	Delia Rosanna	1877-1899?-1937
5.7.2.6.2.3	Marie Louise Rosanna	1879- -1881
5.7.2.6.2.4	Arthur Joseph	1881-1908-
5.7.2.6.2.5	Louis Joseph Henri	1883-1912-1958
5.7.2.6.2.6	Laura	1885-1907-
5.7.2.6.2.7	Aldéa Angélina	1887-1911-
5.7.2.6.2.8	Oliva	1890-1916-
5.7.2.6.2.9	Léa	1892-1913-
5.7.2.6.2.10	Joseph Louis	1895- -
5.7.2.6.2.11	George	1897-1923-
5.7.1.6.2.12	Anonymous	1899- -1899

5.7.2.6.3   **MONTY, Cordélie** b & bp 9 Apr 1851, St. Césaire, QC.

5.7.2.6.4   **MONTY, André** b & bp 9 Aug 1852, St. Césaire, QC; d & but 14 & 16 Aug 1911, Bromont, QC. He married there 26 Aug 1873 **Julienne Poirier** (Moïse Poirier & Arsène Héli) b 22 Jan 1856, QC; d & bur 20 & 22 Oct 1932, Montreal & Bromont, QC.

André Monty was a farmer in Bromont, QC. His wife was a sister of Napoléon Poirier, husband of Marie Esther Monty (13.3.10.15).

Children:

5.7.2.6.4.1	Marie Alphonsine	1874- -1874
5.7.2.6.4.2	Rose/Rosa	1875-1913-1917
5.7.2.6.4.3	Alphonsine	1878-1903-1936
5.7.2.6.4.4	Arthur	1880-1903-1904
5.7.2.6.4.5	Alphonse	1883-1911&1916-1939
5.7.2.6.4.6	Clara Eva	1886-1909-
5.7.2.6.4.7	Ernest	1888-1911-1959
5.7.2.6.4.8	Oscar Roméo André	1895-1920-
5.7.2.6.4.9	Albert Rosario	1898-1922-1955

5.7.2.6.4.10   Marie Ange Arsena   1901-   -

5.7.2.6.5   **MONTY, Malvina** b & bp 17 Mar 1854, St. Césaire, QC; d & bur 18 & 20 Feb 1870, Ange Gardien, QC.

5.7.2.6.6   **MONTY, Thomas** b & bp 14 & 16 Sep 1855, St. Césaire, QC; d 15 Jul 1918, Dartmouth, MA. He married (1) 11 Sep 1876, Waterloo, QC, **Emma Gervais** (Isaac Gervais & Louise Bourbeau) b & bp 31 Jul & 1 Aug 1851, Granby, QC; d & bur 10 & 13 Oct 1893, Waterloo, QC.

He married (2) 20 Sep 1894, Waterloo, QC, a sister-in-law, **Marguerite/Philomène Gervais** (Isaac Gervais & Louise Bourbeau) b & bp 1 Feb 1838, St. Césaire, QC; d 2 Jul 1918, Dartmouth, MA.

Thomas Monty was a farmer in Waterloo and Bromont (West Shefford), QC, before moving in 1896 to New Bedford, MA, where he was a mill worker and laborer in 1900 and 1910 (US censuses). He and his second wife were buried there in the New Sacred Heart Cemetery. His surname which was commonly spelled Monti in Canada reverted to Monty in Massachusetts.

Children of the first marriage:

5.7.2.6.6.1	Georgiana Eleonora	1877-	-1881
5.7.2.6.6.2	Ida	1879-1902?-1965	
5.7.2.6.6.3	Victoria Louise	1880-1910-	
5.7.2.6.6.4	Rose Anna/M. Dorila	1882-	-1883
5.7.2.6.6.5	Honora	1884-	-
5.7.2.6.6.6	Emma L.	1885-1910?-1956	
5.7.2.6.6.7	Thomas	1887-1908-	
5.7.2.6.6.8	Anselme Ulric	1889-1909-1918	
5.7.2.6.6.9	Ovilla	1891-1913-1976	

5.7.2.6 7   **MONTY, Marie Aurélie Henriette** b & bp 15 & 16 Apr 1857, St. Césaire, QC.

5.7.2.6.8   **MONTY, Alexina** b 1859?, QC. She married 22 Nov 1886, Montreal, QC, **John McCutcheon** (John McCutcheon & Elisabeth Laframboise) b 1861?, MA; d between 1916 and 1918, Nashua, NH.

I have not found Alexina Monty's baptismal record. She was of age at her marriage and was 51 years old in 1910 when she and her husband had been married for twenty-four years. She had had twelve children of whom four, John, Fred, Anna, and Rose, were still alive (US census, Nashua, NH).

The names of John McCutcheon's parents are taken from his marriage record, with the added information that they were from Chambly, QC. John McCutcheon himself, though, was born in Massachusetts according to the 1910 census in Nashua, NH, when he was 49 years old. He was a resident of Montreal, QC, at his marriage, a laborer in Farnham, QC, in 1890 and 1892, and a railroad employee in St. Césaire, QC, in 1894 and 1895. The family moved around 1897 to Nashua where he was a laborer and a brakeman for the Boston & Maine Railroad until at least 1916. Mrs. Alexina McCutcheon, who was a widow in 1918, remained in the city after her husband's death (City Directories) and was living there in 1920 with her daughters Rosa McCutcheon (iv) and Mrs. Anna Follansbee (iii) in the household of her son John (i) (US census).

Children:
    i   **John B. McCutcheon** b 26 May 1888, Montreal, QC. He married 1908? **Anne B. ____** b 11 Feb 1893, NH; d 28 Mar 1992, Nashua, NH.
    ii   **Joseph Henry McCutcheon** b & bp 16 & 20 Sep 1890, Farnham, QC; d & bur 3 & 4 Nov 1894, St. Césaire, QC.
    iii   **Alfred Romeo/Fred R. McCutcheon** b & bp 9 & 12 Jul 1892, Farnham, QC; d

May 1972, Nashua, NH. He married 1917? **Lydia Pelletier** (_____ Pelletier & Flavie _____) b 12 Sep 1891, NH; d Jan 1984, Nashua, NH.

    iv   **Marie Louise Anna McCutcheon** b & bp 5 & 6 Jun 1895, St. Césaire, QC. She married _____ **Follansbee.**

    v   **Rose D. McCutcheon** b 1898?, Nashua, NH.

5.7.2.6.9   **MONTY, Augustin** b 1860?; d & bur 31 May & 2 Jun 1883, Bromont, QC, at the age of 23.

5.7.2.8.1   **MONTY, Amédée** b & bp 18 & 19 Apr 1855, St. Jean-Baptiste, QC; d 22 Dec 1913, Taunton, MA. He married 1873? **Adeline Bourque** (Joseph Bourque & Marguerite Davignon) b & bp 19 & 20 Sep 1849, St. Césaire & Marieville, QC; d 21 Mar 1945.

According to his naturalization papers of 2 Aug 1890 in Providence, RI, Amédée Monty (Antoine Amable Amédée at his baptism) had arrived in the United States and settled in Ware, MA, in March 1872. He soon moved on: his first two children were born in Connecticut, the third in Massachusetts, and the last five in Rhode Island. He was a loom fixer in Manville, RI, in 1880, a mill worker in Woonsocket, RI, in 1881, and an overseer there in 1892. By 1900, when he and his wife had been married for twenty-seven years, he was a loom fixer in a cotton mill in Fall River, MA, and in 1910 a weaver in Woonsocket (US censuses). He died in Taunton, MA, and was buried in Notre Dame Cemetery in Fall River.

Adeline Bourque moved to Connecticut after her husband's death and was living in 1920 with her daughter Florilda and her husband in Plainfield, CT, and with her daughter Rosanna and her husband in Wauregan, CT, in 1930 (US censuses). The date of her death is found in an item from Fall River which was published on 22 Mar 1945 in the *Lowell Sun* of Lowell, MA. It does not mention the place(s) of death or burial.

Children:

5.7.2.8.1.1	Minnie/Melvine	1876?-1896-
5.7.2.8.1.2	Florant	1878?- -
5.7.2.8.1.3	Theodore Frederick	1879-1901-
5.7.2.8.1.4	Rosanna	1881-1898?-1954
5.7.1.8.1.5	Octavie Clara Eglantine	1885- -
5.7.2.8.1.6	Florilda	1888-1906&1911-
5.7.2.8.1.7	Eva Marie	1890- -1895
5.7.2.8.1.8	Oscar	1892- -1903

5.7.2.8.2   **MONTY/MONTIE, Raoul** b & bp 19 & 26 Apr 1859, Abbotsford, QC; d 26 Feb 1946, Woonsocket, RI. He married 24 Nov 1881, Webster, MA, **Helena/Ellen Labonté** (Philip Labonté & Susan _____) b Nov 1857, NH; d & bur 1925, Woonsocket, RI.

Raoul Monty came to the United States with his parents in the early 1870s and was naturalized in 1900. He was a cotton mill worker in Webster, MA, in 1880 but returned to Canada for a few months in 1881 when he was a blacksmith living with his parents in St. Eugène de Grantham, QC (Canadian census). He came back to Webster before the fall of that year and remained there for a few years after his marriage. A final move took him to Woonsocket, RI. He was a loom fixer there from at least 1897 until his retirement. In addition to the two children named below, he and his wife had another child, still unidentified, who was born and died between 1900 and 1910 (US censuses).

The family surname changed over the years. It was Monty rather consistently through the 1920s but became occasionally Monte and more frequently Montie in the 1930s and 1940s (US census; City Directories). Raoul Montie, his wife, his sons, and a daughter-in-law were all buried in Precious Blood Cemetery in Woonsocket under a MONTIE tombstone.

Children:

5.7.2.8.2.1	Leonard Felix	1885- -1943
5.7.2.8.2.2	Leo Louis	1897-1917&1944-1958

5.7.2.8.3   **MONTY, Télesphore** b & bp 12 & 13 Oct 1860, Abbotsford, QC; d & bur there 9 & 11 May 1863.

5.7.2.8.4   **MONTY, Trefflé** b & bp 17 & 19 Apr 1862, Abbotsford, QC; d between 1930 and 1937. He married (1) 30 Oct 1883, Webster, MA, **Célanie/Célina Belhumeur** (Antoine Belhumeur & Célina _____) b 1863?, QC; d 13 Mar 1919, Fall River, MA, at the age of 56.

He married (2) 28 Mar 1919, New Bedford, MA, **Mrs. Adélaïde/Adeline Duclos** b 1860? QC.

Trefflé Monty came to the United States in the early 1870s and was a mill operative in Webster, MA, in 1880. The following year he was a blacksmith living with his family in St. Eugène de Grantham, QC (Canadian census). He was back in Webster for his marriage in 1883 and the birth of a child in 1884 but moved to New Bedford, MA, before the birth of a second child in 1886. Two other children were born in Pascoag, RI, in 1893 and in Dudley, MA, in 1894. I do not know where the family spent the next fifteen years. Célanie Belhumeur died in Fall River, MA, in 1919 and he remarried a few weeks later in New Bedford. He was a weaver in a cotton mill there in 1920 and until at least 1930 (US censuses).

Mrs. Adélaïde (also Adeline) Duclos was a 59-year-old widow at her second marriage. She continued to live in New Bedford until at least 1937 (City Directories).

Children of the first marriage:

5.7.2.8.4.1	Rosalie	1884-	-1886
5.7.2.8.4.2	Louis Trefflé	1886-1910&1918-1968	
5.7.2.8.4.3	Louis	1893-	-1894
5.7.2.8.4.4	Joseph Louis	1894-	-1914

5.7.2.8.5   **MONTY, Arthur** b & bp 16 & 18 Jun 1863, Abbotsford, QC; d 29 Dec 1893, Bridgewater, MA.

Arthur Monty came to the United States with his parents in the early 1870s and was a cotton mill worker in Webster, MA, in 1880 (US census).

5.7.2.8.6   **MONTY, Marie Malvina** b & bp 5 & 22 Jan 1865, Abbotsford, QC; d 2 Sep 1919, Woonsocket, RI. She married there 8 Feb 1887 **Pierre Péloquin** (Nazaire/Nelson Péloquin & Philomène Latraverse) b & bp 15 Nov 1860, Sorel, QC; d 19 Nov 1946, Woonsocket, RI.

This woman was baptized as Marie Monty but was known as Mary when she was a cotton mill worker in Webster, MA, in 1880 (US census). She used the name Malvina however at her marriage and was known as such in all subsequent records.

Pierre Péloquin was a weaver in Woonsocket. He had arrived in the United States in 1876 and was naturalized in 1887 (US censuses). Both he and his wife were buried in Woonsocket's Precious Blood Cemetery.

Children:

i **Anita Peloquin** b 23 Feb 1888, Woonsocket, RI; d there 12 Mar 1952. She married there 28 Jun 1915 **Eugene A. Sauvageau** (Adelmar Sauvageau & Estelle Paquette) b & bp 17 & 18 Oct 1887, St. Charles des Grondines, QC; d 7 Aug 1957, Woonsocket, RI.

ii **Regina Peloquin** b 1 Apr 1890, Woonsocket, RI; d there 28 Mar 1989. She married there 2 Jun 1924 **Edward George Lafleur** (Oliver Lafleur & Georgianna Lareau) b 4 Jul 1893, Worcester, MA; d 17 Nov 1964, Woonsocket, RI.

iii **Oscar Peter Peloquin** b 12 Jan 1893, Woonsocket, RI; d 29 Apr 1968, Bristol, RI.

iv **Gerald Peloquin** b 26 Jul 1896, Woonsocket, RI; d there 18 Apr 1953. He married there 12 Apr 1920 **Loretta Yvonne Dulude** (Ovila Dulude & Louise Valois) b there 1 Mar 1897; m (2) there 15 Apr 1968 Leon Cayer (Joseph Cayer & Marie Buisse); d there 27 Mar 1971.

v **Marie V. C. Peloquin** b 30 Aug 1902, Woonsocket, RI; d there 19 Sep 1902.

5.7.2.8.7   MONTY, Solyme b & bp 20 & 28 Oct 1866, Abbotsford, QC.

Solyme Monty was a cotton mill worker in Webster, MA, in 1880 (US census) but was living with his parents in St. Eugène de Grantham, QC, in 1881 (Canadian census).

5.7.2.8.8   MONTY, Raymond Euclide b & bp 24 & 25 Apr 1869, Abbotsford, QC.

Raymond Monty was living with his mother in Webster, MA, in 1880 (US census) and with both his parents in St. Eugène de Grantham, QC, in 1881 (Canadian census).

5.7.2.8.9   MONTY, Marie Georgine b Feb 1871; d & bur 1 & 2 Apr 1872, St. Césaire, QC, at the age of 14 months.

5.7.2.8.10   MONTY, Mitchell b 1873?, MA.

Mitchell Monty was a 7-year-old child living with his mother in Webster, MA, in 1880 (US census). He was the only child in his family to be born in the United States. He was not with his parents in St. Eugène de Grantham, QC, when the Canadian census was taken the following year and may have died before then.

5.7.2.10.1   MONTY, Euphrasie b & bp 8 Jul 1862, St. Jean-Baptiste, QC; d & bur 6 & 9 Jun 1941, Marieville, QC. She married 7 Apr 1894, St. Jean-Baptiste, QC, **Grégoire Edmond Bédard** (Joseph Bédard & Célina Benjamin) b & bp 8 & 12 Apr 1864, Marieville, QC; m (1) there 9 Nov 1885 Henriette Langevin (Benjamin Langevin & Marie Galipeau); d & bur there 30 Sep & 2 Oct 1937.

Euphrasie Monty (Marcelline Euphrasie at her baptism) was also occasionally named Euphrosine at her children's baptisms.

Grégoire Bédard was a baker in Marieville, St. Jean, and Roxton Pond, QC, until at least 1895 and was a farmer in Roxton Pond in 1897 and subsequent years. His name then changed. He still signed Grégoire Bédard (his baptismal name) in 1895 at the baptism of a daughter but Edmond Bédard at the baptisms of his younger children. He was also known as Edmond Bédard at all their marriages and in the Canadian censuses of 1901 and 1911. His burial record is in the name of Grégoire Edmond Bédard.

Children:
  i   **Marie Anne Bédard** b & bp 30 Sep & 1 Oct 1895, Roxton Pond, QC. She married 11 Dec 1923, Marieville, QC, **Eugène Boucher** (Hormisdas Boucher & Joséphine Boucher) b & bp 4 & 6 Nov 1897, Mont St. Grégoire, QC.
  ii   **Philias Edmond Hervé Bédard** b & bp 28 & 31 Dec 1897, Roxton Falls, QC.
  iii   **Bernadette Bédard** b & bp 10 & 17 Sep 1899, Roxton Pond, QC. She married 4 Feb 1920, Marieville, QC, **Eugène Messier** (Louis Messier & Clara Phaneuf) b & bp there 13 Apr 1898.
  iv   **Auguste Antoine Bédard** b & bp 7 & 11 Dec 1900, Roxton Pond, QC.
  v   **Archibald Edmond Justin Bédard** b & bp 11 & 13 Apr 1902, Roxton Pond, QC; d & bur 24 & 27 Jan 1958, Marieville, QC. He married 4 Dec 1923, Iberville, QC, **Yvonne Lasnier** (Georges Lasnier & Odena Harbecq) b & bp 12 Nov 1903, Ste Brigide, QC; d 25 Sep 1974, Marieville, QC. .
  vi   **Marie Aurore Lumina Bella Bédard** b & bp 13 & 14 Oct 1903, Roxton Pond, QC. She married 22 May 1923, Marieville, QC, **Léo Ernest Brosseau** (Edouard Brosseau & Albina Choquette) b & bp 22 & 23 May 1899, Mont St. Grégoire, QC.
  vii   **Rodolphe Roméo Bédard** b & bp 6 & 7 Dec 1905, Roxton Pond, QC; d & bur there 20 & 22 Feb 1908.

5.7.2.10.2   MONTY, Achille/Archie b & bp 3 & 4 Feb 1864, St. Jean-Baptiste, QC; d before 1943. He married 25 Nov 1907, Granby, QC, **Antonia Poirier** (Adolphe Poirier & Rose Anna Desmarais) b & bp 1 Oct 1885, Ange Gardien, QC; m (2) 13 Sep 1943, Sherbrooke, QC, Joseph Beauregard (Honoré Beauregard & Brigitte Letourneau), widower of Emma Lalime.

Achille Monty (Louis Achille at his baptism) was a baker in St. Valérien, QC, at his marriage and in four other localities in the Richelieu Valley and the Eastern Townships before emigrating around 1916. In Newport, VT, where he was a farmer in 1920 and 1930, he was known as Archie Monty (US censuses).

Antonia Poirier (Marie Laura Antonia at her baptism) was a sister of Joseph Poirier, husband of Clara Hermina Monty (5.7.2.10.10).

Children:

5.7.2.10.2.1	Anonymous (male)	1908-	-1908
5.7.2.10.2.2	Anonymous (male)	1909-	-1909
7.7.2.10.2.3	Marie Jeanne	1913-	-1914
5.7.2.10.2.4	Anonymous (male)	1914-	-1914
5.7.2.10.2.5	Gilberta	1915-	-
5.7.2.10.2.6	Leonard	1928-	-

5.7.2.10.3 **MONTY, Arzélie** b & bp 28 & 29 Nov 1865, St. Jean-Baptiste, QC; d & bur there 23 & 25 Jun 1869.

5.7.2.10.4 **MONTY, Evelina** b & bp 20 & 22 Jul 1867, St. Jean-Baptiste, QC; d & bur there 16 & 18 May 1943.

5.7.2.10.5 **MONTY, Wilfrid** b & bp 3 Oct 1869, St. Jean-Baptiste, QC; d & bur 19 & 21 Apr 1959, Marieville, QC. He married 30 Sep 1919, Mont St. Grégoire, QC, **Marie Odéna Lalanne** (Pierre Lalanne & Elmire Massé) b & bp there 12 & 13 Mar 1872; d & bur 10 & 12 Dec 1934, Montreal & Mont St. Grégoire, QC.

Wilfrid Monty was a farmer in St. Jean-Baptiste, QC, at his marriage.

5.7.2.10.6 **MONTY, Victoria** b & bp 16 May 1871, St. Jean-Baptiste, QC; d & bur there 4 & 6 Sep 1910. She married there 29 Feb 1892 **Avila Lemonde** (Félix Lemonde & Célina Blanchard) b & bp there 9 & 11 Jan 1867; d & bur there 15 & 17 Feb 1939.

Avila Lemonde was a farmer in St. Jean-Baptiste, QC.

Children:

i   **Félix Avila Lemonde** b & bp 27 & 28 Apr 1893, St. Jean-Baptiste, QC. He married there 12 Oct 1914 **Amanda Grenier** (Emery/Méril Grenier & Azilda Roy) b Aug 1897, QC.

ii   **Graziella/Maria Victoria Graziella Lemonde** b & bp 27 & 28 Jan 1895, St. Jean-Baptiste, QC. She married there 3 Jul 1917 **Philippe Casavant** (Amanda Casavant & Emma Fréchette) b & bp there 3 Oct 1894.

iii **Emilien Lemonde** b & bp 13 & 14 Mar 1896, St. Jean-Baptiste, QC. He married (1) there 11 Sep 1923 **Aurore Véronneau** (Henri Véronneau & Antonia Belisle) b 28 Jul 1899, St. Hyacinthe, QC.

He was a widower when he married (2) 7 Dec 1968, Henryville, QC, **Marguerite Anne Tourangeau,** widow of Joseph Ouimette.

iv   **Achille Octave Lemonde** b & bp 18 & 19 May 1897, St. Jean-Baptiste, QC.

v   **Corinne Thérèse Lemonde** b & bp 28 & 29 Dec 1898, St. Jean-Baptiste, QC. She married 15 Mar 1934, Montreal, QC, **Joseph Frédéric Dalpé** (Moïse Dalpé & Caroline Larochelle) b & bp 13 & 14 Mar 1887, Dunham, QC.

vi   **Pierre Avila Lemonde** b & bp 4 & 5 Apr 1901, St. Jean-Baptiste, QC; d & bur there 7 & 8 Nov 1901.

vii **Agnès/Marie Rose Agnès Lemonde** b & bp 29 & 30 Oct 1902, St. Jean-Baptiste, QC. She married there 22 Aug 1923 **Joseph Wilfrid Casavant** (Amanda Casavant & Emma Fréchette) b & bp there 17 Jun 1901.

viii **Flore Hélène Lemonde** b & bp 3 & 4 Feb 1904, St. Jean-Baptiste, QC. She married there 8 Sep 1926 **Eugène Casavant** (Amanda Casavant & Emma Fréchette) b & bp there May 1903.

ix   **Gaston/François-Xavier Gaston Lemonde** b & bp 1 & 2 Dec 1905, St. Jean-Baptiste, QC. He married there 10 Jun 1950 **Marie Rose Vincelette** (Louis Vincelette & Emma Lafrance).

x   **Germaine Georgette Lemonde** b & bp 19 & 20 May 1908, St. Jean-Baptiste, QC. She married there 25 Oct 1933 **Albert Bernard** (Joseph Bernard & Maria Lauda Fafard) b & bp 8 & 9 Oct 1906, Ste Madeleine, QC.

5.7.2.10.7   **MONTY, Rosine/Rosalba** b & bp 6 Sep 1873, St. Jean-Baptiste, QC; d & bur there 28 & 29 May 1875.

This child was named Marie Rosine at her birth and Rosalba when she died at 20 months of age.

5.7.2.10.8   **MONTY, Albini** bp 15 Aug 1874, Marieville, QC; d & bur 4 & 7 Jan 1955, St. Jean-Baptiste, QC.

Albini Monty's baptismal record is found on a single sheet of paper inserted in the *Registres* of the church of Ste Marie de Monnoir in Marieville, QC, following a court order of 3 May 1918. It does not include his date of birth. He was of Granby, QC, when he was godfather to a niece, Cécile Adelina Poirier (5.7.2.10.10.iv), in 1912.

5.7.2.10.9   **MONTY, Antoine** b & bp 14 & 15 Oct 1877, St. Jean-Baptiste, QC; d & bur there 5 & 7 Dec 1877.

5.7.2.10.10   **MONTY, Clara Hermina Aglaé** b & bp 23 & 24 Nov 1878, St. Jean-Baptiste, QC; d & bur 1940 Burlington, VT. She married 5 May 1908, Milton, QC, **Joseph Poirier** (Adolphe Poirier & Rose Anna Desmarais) b & bp 13 & 14 Apr 1884, Ange Gardien, QC; d between 1920 and 1930.

This woman was named Hermina Clara Aglaé at her baptism and at her marriage. She was named simply Clara though at the baptisms of her children in Canada, in the 1930 US census in Newport, VT, and on her tombstone in Mount Calvary Cemetery in Burlington, VT.

Joseph Poirier was a farm laborer in several Canadian villages in the early years of his marriage before purchasing a farm in Newport, VT, where his wife and four children joined him in September 1914 (Immigration cards). Clara Monty was a widow living on the family dairy farm in Newport with eight of her children in 1930 (US census). By 1936 she was keeping house in Burlington, VT, for her son Audlard (sic) and her daughters Mabel, Marion, and Aldea (City Directories).

Children:
i   **Adelord J./Adélard Poirier** b & bp 7 & 8 May 1909, St. Alphonse, QC; d & bur 6 & ? May 1986, Milton & Burlington, VT.
ii   **Simonne Poirier** b & bp 14 May 1910, Marieville, QC.
iii   **Yvette Fleurange/Florange Poirier** b & bp 29 & 30 Jul 1911, Ange Gardien, QC.
iv   **Cécile Adelina Poirier** b & bp 29 Oct & 3 Nov 1912, Ange Gardien, QC; d & bur 26 & 27 Jan 1913, Sweetsburg, QC.
v   **Clara Malberge/Mabel Poirier** b & bp 23 & 26 Oct 1913, Adamsville, QC.
vi   **Angela Poirier** b 1915?, Newport, VT.
vii   **Marianna/Marion Poirier** b 1917?, Newport, VT.
viii   **Aldea Poirier** b 1918?, Newport, VT.
ix   **Aurore Poirier** b 1921?, Newport, VT.

5.7.2.10.11   **MONTY, Marie Louise Anne/Dorilla** b & bp 31 Aug & 1 Sep 1881, St. Jean-Baptiste, QC; d & bur there 5 & 7 Jan 1883.

This child was named Marie Louis Anne at her birth and Dorilla when she died at the age of 16 months. Since there is no evidence of twin births, the two names must refer to the same child.

5.7.2.15.1   **MONTY, Hormisdas Achille** b & bp 31 Mar 1876, Milton, QC; d & bur 6

& 8 Jul 1904, Beloeil, QC.

Hormisdas Monty came to the United States with his parents in 1888 and was naturalized in the Norwich, CT., Court of Common Pleas on 23 Oct 1900 as Armedon (?) Monty. His name in the 1902 Norwich, CT, City Directory was Almedas Monty, a barber. He did not marry.

5.7.2.15.2	**MONTY, Delphis Frank** b & bp 5 Sep 1877, St. Jean-Baptiste, QC; d 11 Aug 1947, Chicopee, MA. He married 17 May 1920, Moosup, CT, **Emma Loiselle** b 1881?, RI.

Delphis Frank Monty (François Delphis at his baptism) came to the United States with his parents around 1888 and was a mill worker in New Bedford, MA, in 1918 (World War I Draft Registration card), in Plainfield, CT, in 1920, and in Chicopee, MA, in 1930 when his wife Emma was 49 years old (US censuses). He continued to reside in Chicopee until his death, though he was working in a silk mill in Holyoke, MA, in 1942 when he signed his World War II Draft Registration card. His widow was still living in Chicopee in 1967 (City Directories).

5.7.2.15.3	**MONTY, Dorilla** b & bp 24 & 25 Jan 1880, Milton, QC. She married 17 Jan 1911, Taftville, CT, **Joseph Dominique Octave Desautels** (Octave Desautels & Rosalie Beaudry) b & bp 18 Jun 1881, St. Pie, QC.

Joseph Desautels had arrived in the United States in 1898 and was a cotton mill worker in Taftville, CT, at his marriage. He and his wife, who had come to Connecticut as a child in 1888 and was a weaver in Taftville in 1910 (US census), returned to Canada in 1912 (1913 Norwich City Directory). I have been unable to find them after that time.

5.7.2.15.4	**MONTY, Maranda** b Jul 1881, QC. She married 1900? (1) **Antoine/Anthony Allard** (Antoine Allard & Hélène Donais) b May 1880, QC; d between 1910 and 1920.
	She may have married (2) ____ **Taylor.**

Maranda Monty arrived in the United States with her parents around 1888 and was living in June 1900 in her father's household in Plainfield, CT. She must have married only a few months later for in 1910 she and Anthony Allard, a glazier in Central Falls, RI, had been married for ten years. They had had no children. Mrs. Maranda Allard, a widow, was lodging in Holyoke, MA, in 1920 (US censuses).

I have been unable to confirm her second marriage, known to me only through family lore.

5.7.2.15.5	**MONTY, Leandra Léopoldine/Lora** b & bp 5 & 8 Jul 1882, Upton, QC.
	Leandra Léopoldine Monty (baptismal name) was known as Lora Monty when she was living in her father's household in Plainfield, CT, in 1900 (US census).

5.7.2.15.6	**MONTY, Adélard** b & bp 16 & 17 Aug 1885, Milton, QC.
	Adélard Monty was not with his father in Plainfield, CT, in 1900 and may have died before then.

5.7.2.15.7	**MONTY, Anonymous** bur 3 Dec 1887, St. Jean-Baptiste, QC.
	This child was stillborn.

5.7.2.15.8	**MONTY, Emma** b Mar 1890, QC.
	Although her parents had come to live in the United States in 1888, Emma Monty was born in Canada according to the 1900 US census in Plainfield, CT, where she was living in her father's household. She was a witness to the marriage of her sister Dorilla (5.7.2.15.3) in Taftville, CT, in 1911. I know nothing more about her.

5.7.2.15.9	**MONTY, Rena/Marie Regina** b & bp 29 Mar 1894, North Grosvenordale, CT; d 13 Aug 1983, South Hadley, MA. She married 1913? **Joseph Ovila Bergeron** (Victor Bergeron & Melina ____) b 10 Sep 1894, Warwick, RI; d 30 Nov 1975, Holyoke, MA.

Rena Monty (Marie Regina at her baptism) and her husband, a mill worker in Winsted, CT, lived in Connecticut for several years after their marriage before moving to Massachusetts in the late 1920s. In 1930, when he and his wife had been married for seventeen years, Joseph Bergeron was a clerk in a meat market in Holyoke, MA (US censuses). He was however a resident of South Hadley, MA, at his death.

Children:

i   **Irene Ann Bergeron** b 26 Jul 1914, Plainfield, CT; d 24 Feb 2002, Holyoke, MA. She married (1) ____ **Vachon.**
    She married (2) 1966? **John William Lambert** (William Lambert & Mary Banyard) b 10 Mar 1918, Boston, MA; d 27 Jan 2003, Chicopee, MA.

ii **Alice Bergeron** b 14 Jun 1918, Winsted, CT; d 8 Jul 1989, Northampton, MA. She married **Michael Fesko** (John Fesko & Bertha ____) b 7 Feb 1912, MA; d 29 Sep 1987, South Hadley, MA.

iii **Joseph O. Bergeron** b 12 Jul 1921, CT; d 20 Jun 1984, Holyoke, MA.

iv **Theodore L. Bergeron** b 13 Feb 1924, CT; d 14 Dec 1995, Ormond Beach, FL. He married **June N. Baker** b Aug 1924.

5.7.2.15.10   MONTY, Joseph b 19 Jul 1896, Wauregan, CT; d 2 Oct 1959, Newtown, CT.

Joseph Monty did not marry. He was a resident of Winchester, CT, at his death.

5.7.2.15.11   MONTY, Polydore married 16 Feb 1926, Drummondville, QC, **Juliette Forcier** (Bonaventure Forcier & Alexandrina Théroux) b & bp 27 & 28 Sep 1903, St. Bonaventure d'Upton, QC.

Children:

5.7.2.15.11.1	Anonymous (male)	1927-	-1927
5.7.2.15.11.2	Mariette Jeannine Aurore	1928-1957-1993	
5.7.2.15.11.3	Gilles Eddy Doris	1933-	-
5.7.2.15.11.4	Yvon	-	-
5.7.2.15.11.5	Jean Guy Normand	1935-1957-2000	
5.5.2.15.11.6	Anonymous (female)	1938-	-1938

5.7.5.5.1   MONTY, Rose Anna/Rosanna b & bp 22 & 23 Aug 1870, Ste Brigide, QC; d & bur 23 & 25 Jul 1912, Ste Brigide & St. Césaire, QC. She married 7 Jul 1891, St. Césaire, QC, **Omer Brodeur** (David Brodeur & Euphrasie Guillet/Guillette) b & bp there 8 & 9 Mar 1869; d & bur there 15 & 17 Jun 1908.

Rose Anna Monty lived for several years in Norwich, CT, where her father was a mill worker in the 1870s and early 1880s. She returned to Canada with her family and was a resident of St. Césaire, QC, at her marriage.

Omer Brodeur was a farmer in Ange Gardien, QC, for a few years after his marriage and in St. Césaire after 1893. His widow was staying in 1910 with her children in her mother's household in Norwich, CT (US census) but she soon returned to Canada. She died there a few years later and her children remained there.

Children:

i   **Anonymous Brodeur** b 26 Jun 1892, Ange Gardien, QC; d & bur there 26 & 27 Jun 1892.

ii **Fidélia Brodeur** b & bp 10 & 12 Jun 1893, Ange Gardien, QC. She married 15 Jun 1914, St. Césaire, QC, **Phidias Beaudry** (Napoléon Beaudry & Célina Ashby) b 8 Nov 1890, QC.

iii **Omer Adrien/Adrian Brodeur** b & bp 4 & 6 Oct 1895, St. Césaire, QC.

iv **Florina Brodeur** b & bp 26 & 29 Jan 1898, St. Césaire, QC; d & bur there 15 & 17 Jan 1901.

v   **Marie Rose Anna Clarinda Brodeur** b & bp 24 & 26 Aug 1900, St. Césaire, QC.

vi   **Anonymous** (male) **Brodeur** b 16 May 1903, St Césaire, QC; d & bur there 16 May 1903.

vii **Blanche Antoinette Gertrude Brodeur** b & bp 23 & 24 Jan 1905, St Césaire, QC; d & bur there 27 & 28 Nov 1905.

viii **Rachel Brodeur** b & bp 3 & 4 Nov 1906, St. Césaire, QC. She married there 10 Apr 1928, **Donat/Joseph Lucien Donat Antonio Gagné** (Chrysostôme Gagné & Delia Roussel) b & bp there 8 & 9 Jul 1905.

5.7.5.5.2   MONTY, Joseph Hormidas/Peter H. b 17 Nov 1873, CT; d 3 Mar 1959, Glastonbury, CT. He married 7 May 1908, Providence, RI, **Sarah E. Jarvis** (Henry Jarvis & Elizabeth ____) b Dec 1882, Hamilton, NE; d 12 Sep 1965, Hartford, CT.

I have not found this man's birth record and am relying on information found in the World War I Draft Registration card signed by Peter Joseph Hormidas Monty in Willimantic, CT, on 12 Sep 1918. On other occasions, he used various combinations of these names. He was Hormidas Monte (sic) when living with his parents in Norwich, CT, in 1880; Joseph H. Monty at his marriage; Peter H. Monty in the 1910 and 1920 censuses in Jewett City and Sterling, CT; and Joseph H. Monty again in the 1930 census in Sterling and in both his and his wife's death records. He was a steam fitter in Jewett City in 1910, a worker in a dye plant in Sterling in 1920, and a piper there in 1930 (US censuses).

Children:
5.7.5.5.2.1	Joseph E.	1909- -
5.7.5.5.2.2	Harold J.	1912-1942-1994
5.7.5.5.2.3	Lillian	1916- -

5.7.5.5.3   MONTY, Charles Auguste b & bp 15 & 18 Sep 1875, Ste Brigide, QC; d & bur there 29 Sep & 1 Oct 1875.

5.7.5.5.4   MONTY, Edna b 1878?, CT.

Edna Monty was a 2-year-old child living with her parents in Norwich, CT, in 1880. She died before 1910 when her mother had only four surviving children, Rose Anna, Joseph, Emma, and Louis (US censuses).

5.7.5.5.5   MONTY, Emma/Marie Anna b & bp 19 Jan 1880, Ste Brigide, QC; d Dec 1980, Claremont, NH. She married 22 Jan 1899, **Arthur Joseph Gendron** (Joseph Gendron & Dorothée Bédard) b & bp 11 & 13 Feb 1877, Ste Brigide, QC; d before 1949.

This woman was baptized under the name of Marie Anna Monty but was known as Emma only a few months later when she was living with her parents in Occum, CT (1880 census). She continued to be known as Emma in Canadian and US censuses, at the births of her children, and at her death.

Her marriage was marked by several moves between Canada and the United States. Arthur Gendron was a farmer in St. Césaire in 1901 and until 1905. The family was in Connecticut though in 1906 and 1909, in Ste Brigide, QC, in 1911 and 1915, and in Vermont after May 1916 (QC and CT Birth Records; Immigration cards). Arthur Gendron was a farmer in Jay, VT, in 1918 when he signed his World War I Draft registration card and until at least 1930 (US censuses). His widow, Mrs. Emma Gendron, was living with her sons Arthur (i) and Fulgence (iii) in Claremont, NH, in 1949 (City Directory).

Children:
i   **Arthur Joseph Gendron** b & bp 28 & 29 Jul 1901, St. Césaire, QC; d May 1979, Claremont, NH. He married **Rose Ellen ____**.

ii   **Rose Delima Marie Gendron** b & bp 11 & 12 Apr 1903, St. Césaire, QC.

iii **Fulgence Gérard Gendron** b & bp 3 & 4 Mar 1905, St. Césaire, QC; d 4 Mar 1990.

iv   **Aldea E. Gendron** b 12 Oct 1906, CT; d 4 Mar 2008, Derby Line, VT. She married **Abel Cyrille Patenaude** (Augustin Patenaude & Octavie Routhier) b & bp 10 & 12

May 1907, St. Malo, QC; d 28 Feb 1996, Pinellas Co., FL.

v   **Alma R. Gendron** b 20 Mar 1909, Jewett City, CT; d & bur 1 & 4 Sep 2004, Rocky Hill, CT. She married **Albert D. Bouchard** (Joseph Bouchard & Oglore [?] Moreau) b 5 Sep 1907, New Bedford, MA; d 23 Oct 2003, Rocky Hill, CT.

vi   **Berthe/Bertha Eulalie Gendron** b & bp 24 & 25 May 1911, Ste Brigide, QC. She married _____ **Lanoue**.

vii   **Anonymous Gendron** b 21 Jul 1915, Ste Brigide, QC; d & bur there 21 & 22 Jul 1915.

vii   **Annette F. Gendron** b 11 Feb 1917, North Troy, VT; d & bur 11 & 15 Jan 2003 Lebanon & Claremont, NH. She married 1948? **Wilfred R. Joyal** (Omer/Homer Joyal & Delima _____) b 17 Feb 1906, Newport, VT; d 9 May 1984, Hartford, VT.

5.7.5.5.6   **MONTY/MONTE, Louis** b & bp 11 & 15 Oct 1882, Ste Brigide, QC; d between 1920 and 1923. He married 16 Nov 1909, Taftville, CT, **Alma Bénac** (Hubert Bénac & Médérise Marcoux) b & bp 1 Apr 1878, St. Alexandre, QC.

Louis Monty was a posthumous child. He originally came to the United States as a child with his widowed mother in 1885 but later returned to Canada and was staying with her in St. Césaire, QC, in 1901 (Canadian census). A few years later he was a resident of Griswold, CT, when he was naturalized as Louis Monte on 17 Oct 1904 in the Norwich, CT, Court of Common Pleas. Yet the Monty surname continued to be used: in his marriage record, in his World War I Draft Registration card of 12 Sep 1918, and in the Norwich Suburban Directories. Only two US censuses show variants: Louis Montie in Norwich in 1910 and Louis Monte in Jewett City, CT, in 1920.

Louis Monty was a mill hand in Jewett City at his marriage, a weaver in Norwich in 1910 (US census), a laborer in St. Césaire, QC, in 1911 (Canadian census), and a farmer in Ste Brigide at the births of his children in 1912 and 1916. According to the April 1917 Manifest of Border crossings from Canada to the US, though, when he was on his way to Connecticut with his wife and sons, his most recent occupation had been as a locomotive fireman in Montreal, QC. He was a fireman for an industrial plant in Jewett City in 1920 (US census). His widow, Mrs. Alma Monty was also the owner of a grocery store there in 1923 (Norwich Suburban Directory). I have been unable to trace her any further.

Children:

5.7.5.5.6.1	Lionel Fulgence	1912-	-1980
5.7.5.5.6.2	Wilfred Louis Alphonse	1916-	-

5.7.5.7.1   **MONTY, Joseph Pierre** b & bp 28 & 29 Jun 1868, Ste Angèle, QC; d & bur 17 & 18 May 1875, Ste Brigide, QC.

5.7.5.7.2   **MONTY, Ephrem** b & bp 27 & 29 May 1870, Ste Brigide, QC; d & bur 17 & 20 Aug 1925, Montreal & St. Luc, QC. He married there 11 Sep 1900 **Diana Dalpé dit Pariseau** (Honoré Dalpé dit Pariseau & Emma Filion) b & bp 6 & 8 Feb 1876, Montreal, QC; m (2) 22 Oct 1927, St. Luc, QC, Arthur Surprenant (François Surprenant & Julienne Lespérance), widower of Antonia Rémillard.

Ephrem Monty (Timothée Ephraïm at his baptism) was a laborer in St. Luc, QC, in 1901 and a hotel clerk in Montreal, QC, in 1911 (Canadian censuses). He and his wife (named Marie Louise Diane at her baptism) apparently had no children.

5.7.5.7.3   **MONTY, Aimé** b 1874?, US; d 16 Mar 1932, East Providence, RI.

Aimé Monty was a 7-year-old child living in his father's household in St. Luc, QC, in 1881. Unlike his brothers, he was born in the United States (Canadian census). He returned to the United States as an adult and was a machinist in Providence Co., RI, from at least 1904 until his death (US censuses; City Directories, Pawtucket and East Providence, RI). He did not marry.

5.7.5.7.4   **MONTY, Joseph** b & bp 12 & 13 Dec 1879, St. Luc, QC; d & bur 20 & 22

Feb 1917, St. Jean, QC. He married 10 Feb 1904, Montreal, QC, **Amanda Beausens dit Beauchamp** (Alexandre Beausens & Joséphine Bertrand) b & bp 17 & 18 Jun 1878, Iberville, QC; m (2) 24 Aug 1918, Montreal, QC, Camille Rhéaume (Jean-Baptiste Rhéaume & Malvina Brazeau), widower of Césarine Gauthier; d & bur there 19 & 21 Sep 1928.

Joseph Monty (Louis Joseph Monty at his baptism) was a laborer in St. Jean, QC, at his marriage and more specifically a teamster at the birth of his daughter in 1904. He was also a teamster there in 1911 but was separated from his wife who was living with her children in her mother's household in Montreal, QC (Canadian censuses) .

Children:

5.7.5.7.4.1	Mathilde Joséphine Irène	1904-1935-
5.7.5.7.4.2	Joseph Conrad	1906-1935-

5.7.5.7.5   **MONTY, Henri David** b & bp 31 Oct & 1 Nov 1882, St. Luc, QC.

Henri Monty was a teamster living with his parents in St. Jean, QC, in 1911 (Canadian census).

5.7.7.1.1   **MONTY, Louis Arthur** b & bp 2 May 1847, St. Césaire, QC; d & bur there 27 & 29 Jan 1850.

This child was named Louis Hercule at his death at the age of 2 years and 9 months.

5.7.7.1.2   **MONTY, Alphonsine** b & bp 21 & 22 Oct 1848, St. Césaire, QC; d 15 Sep 1880, Holyoke, MA. She married there 13 Jul 1869 **Justin Pierre Rébétez** (Victor Rébétez & Marie Anne Cogniat) b 12 May 1837, Geneva, Switzerland; m (2) 21 May 1891, St. Hyacinthe, QC, his first wife's aunt, **Vénérance Monty** (5.7.7.11); d Jul 1906, Holyoke, MA.

Justin Rébétez had arrived in the United States in 1852 and was a wire mill worker in Holyoke, MA (US censuses). He and Alphonsine Monty were buried in Notre Dame Cemetery in South Hadley Falls, MA. They had no children.

5.7.7.1.3   **MONTY, Dorie Mathilde/Dora/Louisa/Louise D.** b & bp 15 Jul 1850, St. Cesaire, QC. She married 12 Nov 1889, Montague, MA, as his second wife **John St. Germain** (Joseph St. Germain & Geneviève Laplante) b & bp 22 & 24 Apr 1844, St. Aimé, QC; m (1) 1876? _____ ; m (3) 1904? Josephine _____ .

This woman was known under a variety of names. She was baptized as Marie Mathilde Dorie Monty. As the 20-year-old daughter of the widowed Matilda Mongeau (her mother's maiden name) she was named Louisa Mongeau (!) in the 1870 US census in Holyoke, MA. She was a dressmaker named Louise D. Monty living in Mrs. Matilda Monty's house in Holyoke in 1888 (City Directory). She married under the name of Dorie Monty but was known as Dora in the 1900 US census in Montague, MA.

John St. Germain (Jean Baptiste at his baptism) was a brick maker in Montague at his second marriage and a laborer in a brick factory there 1900 and 1910. His wife Dorie probably died between 1900 and 1904 for by 1910 he and his third wife, Josephine, had been married for six years (US censuses).

5.7.7.1.4   **MONTY, Jean-Baptiste/John** b & bp 2 Sep 1852, St. Césaire, QC; d 24 Feb 1906, Holyoke, MA. He married there 9 Feb 1874 **Sarah McCabe** (James McCabe & Catherine Moran) b 1856?, Scotland; d 11 May 1891, Holyoke, MA, at the age of 35.

Jean-Baptiste Monty came to Holyoke, MA, as a child with his parents in the early 1860s and was naturalized as John Monty on 29 Oct 1883 in the Hampden Co. Superior Court in Springfield, MA. He was a thread mill worker in Holyoke in 1870 and a cotton mill worker there in 1880 (US censuses). I have not found him in 1900 when his surviving children were either living with relatives or boarding in Holyoke.

Children:

5.7.7.1.4.1	Julia	1874-1902-
5.7.7.1.4.2	Anonymous	1879- -1879

5.7.7.1.4.3	Emanuel/Manuel	1880-1902-1915
5.7.7.1.4.4	Adella	1881- -
5.7.7.1.4.5	John B.	1883-1911-
5.7.7.1.4.6	Albert Edward	1885-1907?&1918-1924
5.7.7.1.4.7	Sarah	1888- -1888
5.7.7.1.4.8	Michael	1890- -1890

5.7.7.1.5 **MONTY, Marie/Mary** b & bp 3 & 4 Jun 1854, St. Césaire, QC; d 3 Jun 1891, Holyoke, MA. She married there 4 Sep 1876 **Calixte Bibeau** (Cyprien Bibeau & Elizabeth Simmerrell) b Sep 1856, QC; m (2) 1892? Mrs. Mary Bodwin.

Marie Monty came to Holyoke, MA, with her parents in the early 1860s. Calixte Bibeau (also Bibo, Bebo) was a clerk in Holyoke, MA, at his first marriage and at the births of his children. In 1900, when he and his second wife had been married for eight years, he was a butcher there (US censuses).

Children:
i **Justin Bibeau** b 3 Nov 1877, Holyoke, MA; d there 23 Jul 1882.
ii **Lea Bibeau** b 27 Apr 1885, Holyoke, MA; d there 22 Aug 1967. She married there 1911? a widower **Alcide Chartier** (Louis Chartier & Esther Dufort) b & bp 26 Jan 1881, St. Roch, QC; m (1) Rosilda Plante (Napoleon Plante & Octavie Pelletier); d Jan 1967, Holyoke, MA.

5.7.7.1.6 **MONTY, Félix** b & bp 25 Aug 1856, St. Césaire, QC; d & bur there 10 & 12 Sep 1856.

5.7.7.1.7 **MONTY, Eli Joseph** b & bp 18 Nov 1857, St. Césaire, QC; d 1907, Holyoke, MA. He married there 6 Dec 1883 **Ellen/Nellie Fitzgerald** (Michael Fitzgerald & Ellen ____) b there 1855?; d there 1904.

Eli J. Monty (Joseph Elie at his baptism) arrived in Holyoke, MA, with his parents in the early 1860s. He had a variety of occupations, from livery stable worker in 1880 and bartender at his marriage to mill worker in later years (US censuses; Holyoke City Directories). His wife was 28 years old at her marriage.

Children:
5.7.7.1.7.1	Alfred	1884- -
5.7.7.1.7.2	Lena	1884?- -1888
5.7.7.1.7.3	Mary Agnes	1886-1911?-
5.7.7.1.7.4	Leon F.	1888- -1889
5.7.7.1.7.5	Mathilde	1889- -
5.7.7.1.7.6	Nellie	1890- -

5.7.7.1.8 **MONTY, Isaïe Louis** b & bp 5 May 1860, St. Cesaire, QC; d 17 Feb 1903, Holyoke, MA. He married there 29 Jan 1886 **Elizabeth/Eliza St. Jean** (François Xavier/Francis St. Jean & Sophie Harnois) b & bp 17 Jan 1865, Lavaltrie, QC.

Isaïe Monty (Joseph Isaïe at his baptism) arrived in Holyoke, MA, with his parents in the early 1860s. He was a bartender at his marriage, when his bride was 21 years old, a papermaker at the birth of his first child, and a bartender again at the births of his younger children. He married under the name of Isaïe Louis Monty but was more commonly known as Louis or Louis I. Monty (US censuses, Holyoke City Directories, death record). His widow remained in Holyoke with her two surviving daughters. She was a dressmaker there until at least 1930 (US censuses).

Children:
5.7.7.1.8.1	Blanche I.	1886- -1888
5.7.7.1.8.2	Aurora/Ora L.	1888- -
5.7.7.1.8.3	Ella Eva	1893- -

5.7.7.1.9   **MONTY, Laura Valarie** b 15 May 1863, Holyoke, MA; d & bur 29 Jan & 1 Feb 1923, Bridgeport, CT. She married (1) 13 May 1882, Holyoke, MA, **Regiald Hunter** (James Hunter & Alice ____) b 1861?, Springfield, MA.

    She married (2) 1886? **Albert Edwin/Edward Hackett** (Luther Hackett & Clara Jackson) b 26 Jul 1861, Haverhill, MA; d 14 Feb 1904, Holyoke, MA.

    She may have married (3) 1909? ____ **Moorehead**.

    This woman was named Valarie at her birth, Laura in the 1870 census in Holyoke, MA, and Valerie in the 1800 census there. Several Bridgeport, CT, City Directories also refer to her as Mrs. Viola Hackett. She married though under the name of Laura and was buried in Lakeview Cemetery in Bridgeport as Mrs. Laura Hackett.

    Her first husband, Regiald Hunter, was a 21-year-old papermaker in Holyoke at his marriage. I have not found him in Massachusetts after the birth of their son in 1883. By 1900 Laura Monty had been married for 14 years to Edward (sic) Hackett, a "city hospital engineer" in Holyoke and had had eleven children of whom six, all children of her second marriage, were still alive.

    Laura Valarie Monty moved to Bridgeport after her second husband's death and apparently remarried. She appears in the 1910 census there as Mrs. Laura Moorehead who had been married for a year to a third husband, unfortunately absent, and whose household included three daughters, Helen, Luella, and Irene Hackett. That marriage must have been short-lived: in 1920 it was Mrs. Viola (sic) Hackett, a widow, who was keeping house for her daughter Irene (US censuses).

Children:

i   **Robert R. Hunter** b 7 Sep 1883, Holyoke, MA; d before 1900.

ii   **Albert Edwin/Edward Hackett** b 8 Feb 1888, Boston, MA; d 29 Jun 1950, West Haven, CT. He married (1) 24 Jun 1911, Bridgeport, CT, **Bertha Georges** b 1891?, Hungary; d Dec 1931, Bridgeport, CT.

       He married (2) 8 Jun 1932, New York City, NY, **Juliette Amelie Dattler** (Gustav Dattler & Amelie ____) there 25 Oct 1901; d 28 Dec 1992, New Haven, CT.

iii   **William Joseph Hackett** b 11 Mar 1889, MA; d 21 Feb 1905, Holyoke, MA.

iv   **George Hackett** b 11 Sep 1890, MA; d 1 Aug 1891, MA.

v   **Clara/Clarissa Mae Hackett** b 30 Aug 1892, MA; d 24 Aug 1976, Springfield, MA. She married 1919? **Bradford John Crawford** (Bradford John Crawford & Nellie Wright) b 1 May 1890, Spencertown, NY; d 1 Apr 1963, Rocky Hill, CT.

vi   **Viola Blanche Hackett** b 1 Mar 1894, MA; d 1 Jun 1895, Lawrence, MA.

vii **Helen Frances Hackett** b 6 Jun 1895, Holyoke, MA; d 20 Jan 1990, Milford, CT. She married 10 Aug 1913, Bridgeport, CT, **Spurgeon Hewitt** (Zebah Hewitt & Amanda Hillson) b there 6 May 1889; d there 18 Jul 1959.

viii **Luella Hackett** b 8 Jun 1897, MA; d 1948, NJ. She married 1914? **Stephen John Goda** (John Goda & Mary ____) b 3 Nov 1890, Bronxville, NY.

ix   **Irene Charlotte Hackett** b 25 Jan 1900, Holyoke, MA; d 28 Aug 1988, Milford, CT. She married 1925? **Otto Edward Hitt/Hiitt** b 20 May 1882, Karlsruhe, Germany; d 20 Nov 1963, Bridgeport, CT.

5.7.7.15.1   **MONTY, Rodolphe** b & bp 30 Nov & 8 Dec 1873, Montreal, QC; d & bur 1 & 4 Dec 1928, St. Hyacinthe & Montreal, QC. He married 6 Jun 1899, St. Césaire, QC, **Eugénie Dorval** (Arthur Dorval & Hélène Préfontaine) b & bp there 27 Dec 1876 & 5 Jan 1877; d & bur 26 Feb & 1 Mar 1960, Montreal, QC.

    Rodolphe Monty (Jacques Misaël Rodolphe at his baptism) was an attorney, a partner in the law offices of Monty and Duranleau in Montreal, QC. He was a well known political figure and for a brief period in 1921 was Canadian Secretary of State in the government of the Conservative Prime Minister Arthur Meighen.

Children:

5.7.7.15.1.1   Eugénie Antoinette Hélène   1900-   -1901

5.7.7.15.1.2	Paul	1902-1929-1972
5.7.7.15.1.3	Dorval	1904- -1958
5.7.7.15.1.4	Henri	1906-1933-1976
5.7.7.15.1.5	Marguerite	1908-1939-1992
5.7.7.15.1.6	Maurice	1910- -1968
5.7.7.15.1.7	Estelle	1911-1943-1995
5.7.7.15.1.8	Jean	1913-1941&1955-1987
5.7.7.15.1.9	Jules	1914- -1919
5.7.7.15.1.10	Andrée	1917-1963-1992
5.7.7.15.1.11	Guy	1920-1947-

5.7.7.15.2   **MONTY, Laure** b & bp 18 & 22 Aug 1875, Montreal, QC; d & bur there 16 & 19 Aug 1954. She married there 22 Aug 1898 **Alfred Duranleau** (Napoléon Duranleau & Adélaïde Patenaude) b & bp 1 & 2 Nov 1871, West Farnham, QC; d & bur 14 & 17 Mar 1951, Montreal, QC.

Alfred Duranleau (Toussaint Alfred at his baptism) was an attorney and politician in Montreal, QC. He was a partner in the law offices of Monty & Duranleau and became a judge of the Superior Court in 1935. Both he and his wife were buried in the Côte-des-Neiges Cemetery in Montreal.

Children:

i   **Lucienne/Marie Adèle Laure Lucienne Duranleau** b & bp 4 & 6 Nov 1899, Montreal, QC; d there 24 Mar 1972. She married 1921? **Roméo Bienvenu** (Tancrède Bienvenu & Clara Martin) b & bp 26 & 28 Mar 1896, Montreal, QC; d there 1 Jan 1982.

ii   **Napoléon Alfred Armand Lucien Duranleau** b & bp 5 & 7 Sep 1901, Montreal, QC; d & bur there 7 & 9 May 1904.

iii **Clarinda Jeanne Rolande Duranleau** b & bp 8 & 10 Aug 1903, Montreal, QC; d & bur there 3 & 5 Nov 1904.

iv   **Philomène Albina Cécile Duranleau** b & bp 3 & 5 Aug 1905, Montreal, QC; d & bur there 1 & 2 Jan 1907.

v   **Adrien/Rodolphe Vianney Adrien Fernand Duranleau** b & bp 28 Dec 1906, Montreal, QC. He married 3 Feb 1934, Outremont, QC, **Madeleine/Marie Angeline Hermine Madeleine Gagnon** (Rodolphe Gagnon & Hermine Panneton) b & bp 29 & 30 Apr 1911, Montreal, QC.

vi   **René/Joseph Philias René Gaston Duranleau** b & bp 28 & 29 Apr 1908, Montreal, QC. He married (1) 9 Jan 1937, Outremont, QC, **Françoise/Marie Joséphine Imelda Françoise Barsalou** (Lionel Barsalou & Juliette Lanctôt).

He married (2) 26 Jul 1975, Westmount, QC, **Claire Janin** (Alban Janin & Alexina Grégoire), widow of David Nantel.

vii **Paul/Joseph Girard Roland Paul Duranleau** b & bp 5 & 6 Aug 1910, Montreal, QC. He married 11 May 1940, Longueuil, QC, **Yvette Dubuc** (Hilaire Dubuc & Lucie Lasnier) b & bp there 6 & 7 Aug 1921.

viii **Claire/Marie Paule Cécile Claire Duranleau** b & bp 2 & 3 Feb 1913, Montreal, QC. She married there 21 Apr 1934 **Jules Dupré** (Alfred Dupré & Méline ____).

ix   **Emile Lucien Aimé Duranleau** b & bp 27 Jan 1914, Montreal, QC.

5.7.7.15.3   **MONTY, Marie Alphonsine Alice** b & bp 1 & 10 May 1877, Montreal, QC; d & bur 20 & 22 Aug 1877, Montreal & St. Pie, QC.

5.7.7.15.4   **MONTY, Lilia Cordelia** b & bp 13 & 16 Jun 1878, Montreal, QC. She married there 20 Oct 1903 **Joseph Guertin** (Joséphat Guertin & Cordelia Handfield) b Aug 1877, QC.

Joseph Guertin was a physician and surgeon in Sorel, QC.

Children:

i   **Paul Emile Guertin** b & bp 23 & 24 Jul 1904, Sorel, QC. He married 14 Jul 1940, Montreal, QC, **Marie Paule Lafleur** (Télesphore Lafleur & Clémen-tine Frappier) b & bp there 26 Sep 1911.

ii   **Yvette Guertin** b & bp 19 & 20 Nov 1910, Sorel, QC.

iii   **Alfred Jules Marcel Guertin** b & bp 8 & 10 Jun 1917, Sorel, QC; d & bur there 21 & 23 Dec 1919.

5.7.7.15.5   **MONTY, Corinne** b & bp 13 & 15 Mar 1880, Montreal, QC; d & bur 25 & 28 Feb 1912, Milton, QC. She married 10 Oct 1905, Montreal, QC, **Raoul Armand Desrochers** (Charles Desrochers & Herminie Geoffrion) b & bp 5 Mar 1882, St. Charles, QC; m (2) 3 Jun 1924, Knowlton, QC, Liliane Davignon (Joseph Davignon & Nellie Pratte); d & bur 21 & 24 Jul 1929, St. Charles sur Richelieu, QC.

Corinne Monty's husband was named Joseph Arsène Armand Raoul Durocher at his baptism but Raoul Armand Desrochers at both his marriages and at his death. He was a physician in Milton, QC, throughout his first marriage, in Montreal at his second marriage, and in St. Charles sur Richelieu at his death.

Children:

i   **Charles Adélard René Desrochers** b & bp 18 & 19 Dec 1906, Milton, QC; d & bur there 13 & 15 Sep 1907.

ii   **Lucien/Joseph Jacques Jean René Lucien Desrochers** b & bp 1 & 3 May 1908, Milton, QC; d 8 Feb 1991, Montreal, QC. He married 22 May 1937, Westmount, QC, **Andrée Chase-Casgrain** (Alexandre Chase-Casgrain & Marguerite Pinson-nault) b & bp 7 & 13 Oct 1914, Montreal, QC; d 11 Feb 1981.

iii   **Thérèse/Marie Laure Albina Thérèse Desrochers** b & bp 21 & 23 Sep 1909, Milton, QC. She married 31 Jul 1944, Westmount, QC, **Foster Rolland Will** (John L. Will & Mary Ann Ashling) b 26 Dec 1903, England; d 4 Jul 1955.

iv   **Lilia Yvette Jeanne Desrochers** b & bp 19 & 24 Jun 1911, Milton, QC; d & bur 8 & 10 Nov 1913, Montreal, QC.

5.7.7.15.6   **MONTY, Charles Emile** b & bp 8 & 10 Jun 1883, Valleyfield, QC; d & bur 19 & 21 Mar 1932, Montreal, QC.

Charles Emile Monty was an attorney in Montreal, QC. He did not marry.

5.7.7.15.7   **MONTY, Alice Eveline Cora** b & bp 27 & 28 Jan 1885, Montreal, QC; d & bur 17 & 22 Jun 1885, Montreal & St. Pie, QC.

5.7.7.15.8   **MONTY, Alice Sara Bertha** b & bp 31 Aug & 1 Sep 1886, Montreal, QC.

5.7.10.2.1   **MONTY, Moïse** b & bp 13 & 15 Jun 1861, Abbotsford, QC. He married 16 May 1887, St. Césaire, QC, **Alphonsine Malo** (Pierre Malo & Adélaïde Loisel) b 18 May 1866, QC; d & bur 19 & 22 Sep 1925, St. Césaire, QC.

Moïse Monty was a weaver in St. Césaire, QC, at his marriage. His first child however was born in Suncook, NH. He and his wife probably remained in the area for a while: they were godparents in Suncook to their nephew Joseph Moïse Monty (5.7.10.2.4.2) in 1893 but had returned to Canada before the birth of a son in 1895. Moïse Monty was then a farmer in St. Césaire as also in 1901 and 1911 (Canadian censuses) and at the births of his younger children. He was still living there in 1936 at the marriage of his son Laurier.

Children:

5.7.10.2.1.1	Moïse Henri	1888- -1888
5.7.10.2.1.2	Eddy Edouard	1895-1917-
5.7.10.2.1.3	Bertha	1899-1919-1930
5.7.10.2.1.4	Laurier	1902-1936-
5.7.10.2.1.5	Rosario	1904-1930-1931
5.7.10.2.1.6	Laurence	1910-1930-1931

5.7.10.2.2   **MONTY, Louis** b & bp 26 & 27 May 1863, Abbotsford, QC; d & bur there 26 & 28 Mar 1864.

5.7.10.2.3   **MONTY, Arthur** b & bp 6 & 8 Mar 1865, St. Pie, QC; d & bur 11 & 14 Nov 1951, Abbotsford, QC. He married 24 Sep 1890, Suncook, NH, **Armidée Frégeau** (Louis Frégeau & Alphonsine Charron) b & bp 19 & 26 Feb 1873, Abbotsford, QC.

Arthur Monty was a laborer in Pembroke, NH, at his marriage. According to his naturalization papers of 25 Oct 1890 in Concord, NH, he had arrived in the United States on 4 Mar 1880 and had since resided in Pembroke. He and his wife seemingly returned to Canada before 1900. They are not found in the United States census of that year but were living with their son Napoléon in Abbotsford, QC, in 1901 and 1911 (Canadian censuses) and were still in Abbotsford when he married in 1913. In 1920, though, Arthur Monty and his wife were both working in a cotton mill in Manchester, NH (US census). I do not know when they returned to Canada.

Children:
5.7.10.2.3.1	Arthur	1891-	-1891
5.7.10.2.3.2	Napoléon	1892-1913-	

5.7.10.2.4   **MONTY, Louis/Lewis** b & bp 10 & 11 Jun 1867, Abbotsford, QC; d & bur 29 Nov & 1 Dec 1899, Allenstown & Suncook, NH. He married 12 Oct 1891, Suncook, NH, **Julia Ann Gately** (Matthew Gately & Annie _____) b Sep 1872, England; m (2) 1905? Arthur B. Foss; m (3) Duncan Bethune (_____ Bethune & Margaret McNichol).

Lewis Monty arrived in the United States in May 1880 and was naturalized on 30 Oct 1890 in Concord, NH. He was a mill worker in Pembroke and Allenstown, NH, and was buried in St. John the Baptist Cemetery in Suncook, NH.

The widowed Julia Gately (also Gatley, Gateley), who had arrived in the United States around 1888, was living with her four surviving children, Albert, Annie, George, and Agnes, in her mother's household in Suncook in 1900 (US census). In 1910, when she had been married to Arthur B. Foss, a farmer in Suncook, for four years, only one child, George, was a member of their household (the other children were sill living with their maternal grandmother in Suncook). In 1920 and 1930 Julia Gately and her third husband, Duncan Bethune, were cotton mill workers in Manchester, NH (US censuses).

Children:
5.7.10.2.4.1	Albert Joseph	1892-1918?-
5.7.10.2.4.2	Joseph Moïse	1893- -1896
5.7.10.2.4.3	Mary Anna L.	1894-1920-
5.7.10.2.4.4	George Arthur	1896-1928?&1961-1974
5.7.10.2.4.5	Agnes	1898-1930-

5.7.10.2.5   **MONTY, Anonymous** b 23 May 1869, Abbotsford, QC; d & bur there 23 & 25 May 1869.

5.7.10.2.6   **MONTY, Delima** b & bp 18 & 22 Jan 1872, Abbotsford & St. Césaire, QC; d & bur 5 & 8 Jul 1948, Suncook, NH. She married there 28 May 1889 **Alfred Chaput** (Denis Chaput & Esther Carlière) b 1860?, QC; d & bur 22 & 25 Jun 1932, Suncook, NH, at the age of 72.

Alfred Chaput and his wife (named Rose Anna Delima at her baptism) had both arrived in the United States around 1880. He was a weaver in Allenstown and Suncook, NH, until at least 1930 (US censuses). They were both buried in St. John the Baptist Cemetery in Suncook.

5.7.10.2.7   **MONTY, Anna** b & bp 19 & 22 Mar 1874, Abbotsford, QC; d & bur 24 & 28 Aug 1915, Suncook, NH. She married there 24 Aug 1891 **Ignace Rondeau** (Georges Rondeau & Aglaé Crépeau) b & bp 14 & 16 Mar 1867, St. Gabriel de Brandon, QC; d & bur 7 & 10 Apr 1947, Suncook, NH.

Anna Monty arrived in the United States with her parents in 1880 and resided in Suncook, NH, until her death. Her surname in the records of St. John the Baptist Church there is often Monti.

Ignace Rondeau (Joseph Digmas at his baptism) came to the United States in the 1880s and was a farmer in Suncook, NH, at his marriage. At the baptism of his first child in St. Gabriel de Brandon, QC, though, he was said to be a farmer in that parish. If so it was a temporary stay. All other children were born in New Hampshire and Ignace Rondeau became an American citizen in 1896. He was a day laborer in Suncook in 1900, and a mill worker there from at least 1910 through 1930 (US censuses). He and his wife and several children were buried there in St. John the Baptist Cemetery.

Children:

i   **George Rondeau** b & bp 14 & 15 Oct 1892, St. Gabriel de Brandon, QC; d & bur 4 & 7 Dec 1972, Manchester & Suncook, NH. He married 13 Aug 1917, Hooksett, NH, **Rosa Pepin** (Samuel Pepin & Laura/Lea ____) b there May 1895; d & bur 5 & 8 Mar 1961, Suncook, NH.

ii   **Joseph Alcide Rondeau** b & bp 11 Jun 1895, Suncook, NH; d & bur there 27 & 28 Oct 1895.

iii   **Siméon Rondeau** b & bp 3 Oct 1897, Suncook, NH; d & bur there 23 & 27 Oct 1971. He married there 23 Jun 1919 **Anna Ménard** (David Ménard & Emeline Bousquet) b & bp 16 & 19 Nov 1893, Richmond, QC; d & bur 29 Aug & 1 Sep 1980, Lebanon & Suncook, NH.

iv   **Yvonne Agnula Rondeau** b & bp 26 & 27 Dec 1899, Suncook, NH; d & bur there 1 & 3 Jan 1900.

v   **Agnula Albina Rondeau** b & bp 23 Jan 1901, Suncook, NH; d & bur 16 & 21 Jul 1997, Pembroke & Suncook, NH. She married 23 Apr 1936, Suncook, NH, **Eugene Ernest Letendre** (Odilon P. Letendre & Virginia Dubois) b & bp there 11 Feb 1901; d & bur there 25 & 27 Nov 1976.

vi   **Anonymous Rondeau** d & bur 14 Feb 1903, Suncook, NH.

vii   **Alcide Rondeau** b & bp 12 Jul 1906, Suncook, NH; d & bur there 9 & 14 Aug 1953. He married there 16 Jun 1930 **Emma Poisson** (David Poisson & Emma Tétreault) b & bp there 27 & 29 Nov 1904; d & bur 2 & 6 Apr 1964, Pembroke & Suncook, NH.

viii   **Glanda O. Rondeau** b & bp 25 Sep 1908, Suncook, NH; d & bur there 7 & 8 Nov 1944. She married there 9 Feb 1932 **Joseph François/Frank Joseph Baron** (Eustache Baron & Rosanna Dubé) b & bp 29 & 30 Nov 1898, Ste Clotilde de Horton, QC.

ix   **Oswald J. Rondeau** b & bp 27 Jun 1911, Suncook, NH; d & bur there 24 & 27 Jan 1975. He married (1) there 4 Jul 1931 **Antonia Champagne** (Joseph Champagne & Marie Louise Provoneau) b & bp 23 Dec 1908, St. Séverin de Prouxville, QC.
He married (2) **Rachel Daigle**.

x   **Walter J. Rondeau** b & bp 23 Jul 1914, Suncook, NH; d & bur 15 & 18 Nov 2003, Concord & Allenstown, NH. He married 20 Apr 1940, Suncook, NH, **Margaret Sadie Foote** (Henry Foote & Rose Anna Mitchell) b 30 Oct 1921, S. Johnstown, New Brunswick, Canada.

5.7.10.2.8   **MONTY, Joseph** b & bp 13 & 14 Jun 1876, Abbotsford, QC; d & bur 20 & 23 Jul 1945, Suncook, NH. He married 2 Jan 1895, Hooksett, NH, **Melina Rhéaume** (François Xavier/Frank Rhéaume & Philomène Lemieux) b & bp 5 & 6 Jan 1877, St. Rémi, QC; d & bur 2 & 7 Apr 1947, Suncook, NH.

Joseph Monty arrived in the United States with his parents in 1880 and was naturalized in 1897. In 1900 he was a weaver in Suncook, NH, and a loom fixer there in 1910 and through at least 1930 (US censuses). He and his wife were buried in St. John the Baptist Cemetery in Suncook.

Amelia/Melina Rhéaume came to the United States with her parents around 1888 and was naturalized in 1898. Her name varies. It was Amelia at her marriage, Mina at the births of some of her children, Melina in the US censuses and in two Probate Court records of 11 Sep 1945 and 22 Apr 1947 (Merrimack Co., NH, #44832 and #45619), and Malvina in her burial record.

Amelia Rhéaume's sister Rosa Rhéaume married Joseph Monty's cousin, Louis Desrochers/Stone (5.7.10.8.iii).

Children:

5.7.10.2.8.1	Eva Marguerite	1898-1919-1984
5.7.10.2.8.2	Arthur Henry	1899-1927-1941
5.7.10.2.8.3	Albert H.	1908-1931-1974
5.7.10.2.8.4	Lillian Flora	1910-1931-1986
5.7.10.2.8.5	Henri Leo	1915- -1916
5.7.10.2.8.6	Percy Alphee	1917-1942-1976

5.7.10.3.1   **MONTE, Israel** b 1863? He married **Mary Ann Corbin** b CT; d before 1910.

Israel Monte's place of birth is difficult to determine, for various censuses have him born in Canada (1870, 1930), Connecticut (1880, 1920), or Rhode Island (1910). I tend to disregard the 1870 and 1930 censuses since they contain some obvious errors of fact. He would then have been born in Connecticut, probably, or Rhode Island, possibly.

He was a 7-year-old child living with his parents in Putnam, CT, in 1870 and was a spinner or loom fixer in Connecticut or Rhode Island cotton mills for most of his life. He was in Glocester, RI, in 1880, in Arkwright, RI, in 1892 and 1894 (City Directories) as well as at the death of his son Michel in 1896, in Warwick, RI, in 1910 when he was a widower holding household for his children Israel Jr., Ada, William A, and Irene, in Jewett City, CT, in 1920 when he was living in his son Israel's household, and in Coventry, RI in 1930 when he was living with his sister Elizabeth (5.7.10.3.7) and his brother-in-law George Salois (US censuses).

I know nothing about Mary Ann Corbin save her name which is found in the baptismal records of two of her children in West Warwick, RI, and her place of birth which is noted in several censuses referring to her son Israel.

Children:

5.7.10.3.1.1	Israel Joseph	1888-1916?-1971
5.7.10.3.1.2	Rose Eda/Ada	1892- -
5.7.10.3.1.3	Michel	1896- -1896
5.7.10.3.1.4	William A.	1899?-1925?-
5.7.10.3.1.5	Irene	1901?- -

5.7.10.3.2   **MONTY/MONTI, Delima** b 1864?, NH.

Delima Monti was a 6-year-old child living with her parents in Putnam, CT, in 1870 (US census). She does not appear with them in later censuses and may have married or died before 1880. She was almost surely deceased in 1890 when a younger sister (5.7.10.3.16) was named Delima at her baptism.

5.7.10.3.3   **MONTY/MONTIE, Edmond/Edmund** b & bp 10 & 14 Sep 1865, Abbotsford, QC; bur 1933, Putnam, CT. He married 1890? **Rose Anna/Rosanna Paul** (Joseph Paul Hus & Emérence Gingras) b & bp 20 & 21 Dec 1871, St. Bonaventure, QC; d 9 Dec 1925, Putnam, CT.

Edmond Monty arrived in the United States with his parents the year of his birth and lived with them in Putnam, CT, in 1870 and in Glocester, RI, in 1880. He was a farmer in Glocester when his son Edward was born in 1893, a loom fixer in Coventry, RI, in 1900 when he and his wife had been married for ten years, a laborer in a box shop in Putnam, CT, in

1910, and a boiler tender in Glocester in 1920 (US censuses).

His name was most often Edmond, though occasionally Edmund. His surname varied: Monty at his baptism, Monti in 1870, Monte in 1880 and 1893, Montee in 1900 and 1910, and Montie in 1920. It was Montie at his and his wife's death. His tombstone in St. Mary's Cemetery in Putnam, where his wife and son Joseph are also buried, reads "EDMOND MONTIE / 1865-1933." His son Conrad also used the Montie surname.

Children:

5.7.10.3.3.1	Rosanna	1892-1912?-1976
5.7.10.3.3.2	Edward	1893- -1909
5.7.10.3.3.3	Joseph H.	1896- -1918
5.7.10.3.3.4	Henri A.	1901- -1901
5.7.10.3.3.5	Conrad T.	1904-1928?-1961

5.7.10.3.4 **MONTY/MONTE, Adelaide** b 5 Apr 1867, Concord, NH; d & bur 22 & 25 Aug 1941, Phenix, RI. She married 6 Apr 1885, West Warwick, RI, **Michel/Mitchell Salois** (Joseph Salois & Zoé Dupôt) b & bp 4 & 6 Mar 1864, Yamaska, QC; d & bur 22 & 26 Sep 1939, Phenix, RI.

This woman was named Adaline Monte in 1880 when she was living in her father's household in Glocester, RI (US census) but Adelaide Monty at her marriage. Her maiden name was Adelaide Monte according to her burial record. Other variants include Addie, Addela, Adelaid, or Delia (US censuses).

Michel (occasionally Mitchel or Mitchell) Salois (also Sallois, Salway, Saylois, or Sulway) arrived in the United States as a child in 1866 and was naturalized in 1890. He was a cotton weaver in Warwick, RI, in 1900 and 1910 and a road worker in West Warwick (Phenix), RI, in 1920 and 1930 (US censuses). He and his wife were buried in Notre Dame Cemetery in Phenix.

Children:

i   **Adelaide Salois** b & bp 5 & 8 Feb 1886, West Warwick, RI; bur there 1965. She married 27 Apr 1908, Phenix, RI, **Henry Lambert** b 15 Feb 1877, QC; bur 1959, West Warwick, RI.

ii   **Joseph Salois** b & bp 23 & 24 Feb 1887, Harris & West Warwick, RI; d & bur 24 & 26 Feb 1924, Phenix & Arctic, RI.

iii **Philorome/Phillip Salois** b & bp 4 & 7 Apr 1889, Harris & West Warwick, RI; d & bur 10 & 13 Mar 1943, Phenix, RI. He married there 20 Apr 1914 **Belzemire Bélanger** (Godefroi Bélanger & Caroline Blanchette) b & bp 10 & 11 May 1891, L'Islet, QC; d Jun 1982, West Warwick, RI.

iv   **Ernest Salois** b & bp 15 & 18 Oct 1891, Arctic, RI. He married 28 Nov 1929, West Warwick, RI, **Lauretta Bacon** (Joseph Bacon & Matilda Leclerc) b & bp 20 & 26 Oct 1902, Arctic, RI; m (2) 15 May 1945, Westover, MA, Robert Lamoureux; d 18 Nov 1971, Holyoke, MA.

v   **Donat Pierre Salois** b & bp 10 & 12 May 1895, West Warwick, RI; d & bur 2 & 6 Jul 1946, Newport & Phenix, RI. He married 27 Jun 1921, West Warwick, RI, **Rose Eva Rabouin** (Saul Rabouin & Georgianna Rondeau) b 26 Oct 1894, Warwick, RI; d 11 Aug 1988, Coventry, RI.

vi   **William Salois** b May 1898, West Warwick, RI.

vii **Blanche Salois** b 1901?, West Warwick, RI.

5.7.10.3.5 **MONTY/MONTE, Emma** b 1 Apr 1868, Southbridge, MA.

This child was living with her parents in Putnam, CT, in 1870 and in Glocester, RI, in 1880 (US census).

5.7.10.3.6 **MONTY/MONTE, Celinda/Celina** b 7 Oct 1869, Putnam, CT; bur 1935, West Warwick, RI. She married (1) there 11 Jan 1897 **Léonard Théroux** (Jean-Baptiste Théroux & Marie Adélaïde Salvas), b & bp 14 & 15 Mar 1868, St. Robert, QC; d 29 May 1909,

Providence, RI.

She married (2) 21 Jan 1911, West Warwick, RI, a widower, **Joseph Lebeau** (Isaac Lebeau & Marie Robert) b 29 Oct 1869, Warwick, RI; bur 1945, West Warwick, RI.

This woman's marriage records are in the name of Celina Monty. All census records I have seen however refer to her as Celinda Monti (1870) or Monte (1880), Celinda Theroux (1910), or Celinda Lebeau (1920, 1930). She was buried as Celinda Lebeau in St. Joseph's Cemetery in West Warwick, RI.

Mrs. Celinda Theroux, a childless widow, was working in 1910 in a cotton mill in Warwick, RI. Her next door neighbor then was Joseph Lebeau, a widower with four children, and a brother of Rosaline Lebeau, first wife of Jean-Baptiste Monty (5.7.10.3.11). He was a loom fixer in Warwick in 1910 and in West Warwick, RI, in 1930 (US censuses) and was buried in St. Joseph's Cemetery in West Warwick.

Child:
i   **Lillian Lebeau** b 1916?, RI.

5.7.10.3.7   **MONTY/MONTE, Elizabeth/Lizzie** b Oct 1870, CT; d 2 Feb 1940, West Warwick, RI. She married 4 Mar 1889, Warwick, RI, **George Hormisdas Salois** (Joseph Salois & Zoé Bibeau) b & bp 23 Feb 1862, St. Aimé, QC; bur 1932, West Warwick, RI.

Lizzie Monte was living with her parents in Glocester, RI, in 1880 (US census) and married Hormisdas Salois under that name. After her marriage, though, she was known as Elisa or Lisa, in the records of St. John the Baptist Church in West Warwick, RI, or as Elizabeth, in the US censuses in Coventry, RI, from 1900 through 1930. Only the presence of a brother-in-law, Israel Monte (5.7.10.3.1), in the household of George and Elizabeth Salois in 1930 allows me to equate this couple with the Lizzie Monte and Hormisdas Salois of earlier years.

George Salois was a cotton mill worker in Coventry. I do not know how Hormidas Salois (baptismal name) became George Hormisdas Salois. While all Catholic Church records in West Warwick name him Hormisdas, he was known as George in US censuses and George H. in West Warwick Directories. He was buried as George Hormisdas Salois in St. Joseph's Cemetery in West Warwick.

Children:
i   **George Hormisdas Salois** b & bp 23 & 26 Aug 1891, West Warwick, RI.
ii   **Marie Adée/Lydia Salois** b & bp 26 & 27 Sep 1896, West Warwick, RI. She married 10 May 1915, Phenix, RI, **Herbert G. Adams** (Augustus Adams & Mary ___) b 14 Sep 1889, Johnston, RI.
iii   **Florence Salois** b 1902?, RI.
iv   **Delia Salois** b 1906?, RI.

5.7.10.3.8   **MONTE, Annie/Zénaïde** b 7 Dec 1872, Putnam, CT; d & bur 18 & 21 Oct 1939, Howard & West Warwick (Arctic), RI. She married 13 Feb 1899, Warwick, RI, **Charles Rainville** (Siméon Rainville & Henriette Viens) b & bp 13 & 14 Aug 1875, Upton, QC; m (1) there 5 Feb 1894 Parmelia Grenier (Pierre Grenier & Félonise Goulet); m (3) 24 Feb 1941, West Warwick, RI, Marie Corona Paquin (Joseph Paquin & Delia ____); d there Nov 1966.

This woman was known as Annie Monte when she was living with her parents in Glocester, RI, in 1880, when she married, and when she was living with her husband in North Attleboro, MA, in 1910. She was named Zénaïde however in later censuses and was buried in St. Joseph's Cemetery in West Warwick, RI, as Zénaïde Rainville, wife of Charles Rainville.

Charles Rainville arrived in the United States in 1887 and was a carpenter in Ware, MA, when his first wife died on 25 Jun 1898. He and Annie Monte lived in Rhode Island, where their children were born, for a few years after their marriage. He was a carpenter in North Attleboro, MA, in 1910, in Bristol, RI, in 1920, and in West Warwick, RI, in 1930 (US censuses).

Children:

    i   **Florence A. Rainville** b 17 Jan 1900, Phenix, RI; d & bur 13 & 15 May 1985, Cranston & West Warwick, RI. She married 9 Nov 1925, West Warwick, RI, **Siméon Lachance** (Cléophas Lachance & Anna Dallaire) b 5 Jul 1896, East Providence, RI; d & bur 29 Sep & 1 Oct 1980, West Warwick, RI.

   ii   **Albert W. Rainville** b 1901?, RI.

5.7.10.3.9   **MONTE/MONTIE, Louis/Lewis** b 1876?, Putnam, CT; d & bur 19 & 20 Jan 1918, Pontiac & West Warwick (Arctic), RI. He married 13 Feb 1899, Natick, RI, **Marie Rainville** (Louis Rainville & Rosilda Théroux) b & bp 22 Jan 1882, West Warwick, RI; d before 1910.

    Lewis Monte was a 4-year-old child living with his parents in Glocester, RI, in 1880 (US census). His marriage record in St. Joseph's Church in Natick, RI, however is in the name of Louis Monte. I have not found him or his wife in any 1900 census but by 1910 the 35-year-old Louis Montie, a widower, was staying with his daughter Blanche in the home of his mother-in-law, Mrs. Rosilda Rainville, in Warwick, RI. His older daughter Eva was living with her paternal aunt and uncle Alphonsine (5.7.10.3.10) and William Forrest (US censuses).

    Louis Montie's tombstone in St. Joseph's Cemetery in West Warwick (Arctic) is inscribed: "LOUIS MONTIE / 1876-1918." All would be fine save for the records of the Potvin Funeral Home in West Warwick which show that Louis Monty (sic), husband of Marie Rainville, was born on 25 Nov 1873 and died on 19 Jan 1918 at the age of 44 years, 1 month, and 25 days. I cannot explain the discrepancy.

Children:

5.7.10.3.9.1	Eva	1900-1923-
5.7.10.3.9.2	Marie Rose Blanche	1901-1921-1949

5.7.10.3.10   **MONTY, Alphonsine** b 9 Jun 1877, Chestnut Hill, CT; d & bur 24 & 28 Mar 1938, Centreville & West Warwick (Arctic), RI. She married 11 Jan 1897, West Warwick, RI, **William George Forrest** (George Forrest & Sophie Rabouin) b 22 Mar 1873, Phenix, RI; d & bur 11 & 13 May 1942, Centreville & West Warwick (Arctic), RI.

    William Forrest (Guillaume Georges at his marriage) was an insurance agent in Warwick and West Warwick, RI. He and his wife had one child who was deceased in 1910. An adopted son was with them in West Warwick in 1930 (US censuses). They were both residents of Centreville, RI, at their deaths but were buried in St. Joseph's Cemetery in West Warwick (Arctic), RI.

5.7.10.3.11   **MONTE/MONTY/MONTIE, Jean-Baptiste/John** b 27 May 1879, Putnam, CT; bur 1929, West Warwick (Arctic), RI. He married (1) there 11 May 1896, **Rosaline Lebeau** (Isaac Lebeau & Marie Robert) b 29 Dec 1876, Warwick, RI.

    He married (2) 8 Nov 1915, RI, **Delia Phillips** b 1871?, VT; m (1) 16 Jun 1905, RI. Dennis E. Hosmer (Edwin E. Hosmer & Lucy M. ____).

    He married (3) 26 Mar 1928, West Warwick, RI, **Della Jacob** (Julien Jacob & Dosilda Baribeau) b 4 Mar 1882, Rutland, VT.

    This man's surname varies considerably. He was John Monte when living with his parents in Glocester, RI, in 1880 though Jean-Baptiste Monty in the records of his first and third marriages as well as of his daughter's marriage in 1916. He was John Monte when he married Delia Hosmer in 1915 but John Baptist Montie when he signed his World War I Registration card three years later. He was then a bartender in Arctic, RI, whose nearest relative was Mrs. Della (sic) Montie. In 1920, though, John Monty was a bartender in West Warwick, RI, with a 49-year-old wife named Delia (US censuses). And after all these variants, his tombstone in St. Joseph's Cemetery in West Warwick bears the surname MONTE.

    Rosaline Lebeau was a sister of Joseph Lebeau, second husband of Célina Monty (5.7.10.3.6).

    I have little sure information about his second and third wives. I know of Delia Phillips' marriages only through the Rhode Island Marriage Index and the 1920 census. I know of

Della Jacob's parents and date of birth only through the record of her marriage in St. John the Baptist Church in West Warwick.

There is a tombstone inscription in St. Joseph's Cemetery in West Warwick however which may be pertinent. It refers to Delia Monte, nee Jacobs (sic), born in 1871. There is no date of death. If the reference is to John Monte's second wife, then her maiden name was Jacobs and her first husband a Mr. Phillips. Without further evidence, this is only conjectural.

Child of the first marriage:

5.7.10.3.11.1	Dora	1897-1916-

5.7.10.3.12   **MONTE, Felix** b 15 Sep 1880, Putnam, CT; bur 1944, West Warwick, RI.

Felix Monte was a hotel clerk and bartender in Warwick, RI, in 1910, a dyer in a chemical plant in Coventry, RI, in 1920, and a print shop employee there in 1930 when he was living in his brother Alexander's household (US censuses). He was still in Coventry and still single in 1942 when he signed his World War II Draft Registration card. He was buried in St. Joseph's Cemetery in West Warwick, RI.

5.7.10.3.13   **MONTE, Alexander** b 26 Aug 1882, Putnam, CT; d & bur 1957, Coventry & West Warwick, RI. He married 1905? **Marie Bélanger** b 20 Aug 1881, QC; d & bur Sep 1973, Coventry & West Warwick, RI.

Alexander Monte was a farm laborer in Warwick, RI, in 1900 and a foreman in a grain mill in Coventry, RI, in 1910, when he and his wife had been married for five years, and until at least 1930 (US censuses). He was still in Coventry in 1942 when he signed his World War II Draft Registration card. He and his wife were buried in St. Joseph's Cemetery in West Warwick, RI.

Children:

5.7.10.3.13.1	Yvonne Blanche	1906-	-1975
5.7.10.3.13.2	Irene A.	1907-	-1998
5.7.10.3.13.3	Alma D.	1908-	-1993
5.7.10.3.13.4	Marie D. L.	1910-	-1910
5.7.10.3.13.5	Jeannette B.	1913?-	-
5.7.10.3.13.6	Cécile J.	1915-	-
5.7.10.3.13.7	William J.	1916-1938-1982	
5.7.10.3.13.8	Ann/Anne Mary	1918-	-
5.7.10.3.13.9	Gerard Joseph	1921-1945-1982	

5.7.10.3.14   **MONTIE/MONTY/MONTE, Mitchell** b & bp 28 & 30 Apr 1884, West Warwick (Lippitt), RI. He married 7 Jun 1915, Providence, RI, **Susan E. Boyd** (William J. Boyd & Susan ____) b Jan 1884, MA.

Mitchell Montie (Michel Monty at his baptism) had a variety of surnames, with Montie becoming predominant after 1920. It was Monte in 1900 when he was a cotton mill worker living in Warwick, RI, and in 1910 when he was a farm laborer in Coventry, RI, Montie at his marriage, Monte in 1920 when he was a mill worker in Johnston, RI, and Montie again in 1930 when he was a woolen mill worker in Cranston, RI (US censuses). Mitchell Montie and his wife Susan were still in Cranston in 1950 but had moved before 1956 to Providence, RI, where they were living in 1960 (City Directories). They apparently had no children.

5.7.10.3.15   **MONTY/MONTE, Marie Louise** b & bp 9 & 10 Apr 1886, West Warwick (Phenix), RI; d & bur 17 & 21 Sep 1972, Attleboro, MA & West Warwick, RI. She married 1908? **Antoine François Guindon** (Antoine Guindon & Celina Raboin) b 12 Nov 1885, Washington, RI; d & bur 9 & 12 Apr 1975, Attleboro, MA & West Warwick, RI.

This woman was named Marie Louise Monty at her baptism but Marie Monte when she was living with her parents in Warwick, RI, in 1900. She and her husband Anthony F. Guindon, a jeweler in Attleboro, MA, had been married for two years in 1910. In later years he was a resident of West Warwick, RI, while working for a jewelry company in Providence,

RI (US censuses; Providence Directories, 1912-1959). He and his wife were both residents of Attleboro, MA, at their deaths but were buried in St. Joseph's Cemetery in West Warwick.

5.7.10.3.16 **MONTY/MONTE, Delima** b & bp 17 Jun 1890, Coventry & West Warwick, RI; d & bur 11 & 14 Dec 1956, Yarmouth, MA & West Warwick, RI. She married 15 May 1916, West Warwick, RI, **Louis Jodoin** (Philéas Jodoin & Marie Robert) b 11 Aug 1882, Wauregan, CT.

Louis Jodoin was a jeweler in Attleboro, MA, in the early and mid-1910s (City Directories). He remained in Attleboro after his marriage and was a shop manager in 1918 (World War I Draft Registration card), a grocery store salesman in 1920, and a butcher in 1930 (US censuses). He owned his own shop there, Jodoin Market, in 1942 (World War II Draft Registration card). He predeceased his wife who was buried in St. Joseph's Cemetery in West Warwick, RI.

Child:
i   **Gerard L. Jodoin** 24 Mar 1917, RI; d 3 Mar 1997, Yarmouth, MA. He married **Eileen R. ____** b Jan 1920.

5.7.10.5.1 **MONTY, Louis** b 26 Dec 1869, Pembroke, NH; d & bur 25 & 27 Jan 1923, Valcourt, QC. He married (1) there 21 Oct 1895 **Louise Foisy** (Pierre Foisy & Eliza Beauregard) b & bp 3 May & 2 Jun 1872, Valcourt & Stukely, QC; d & bur 16 & 17 Apr 1897, Valcourt, QC.

He married (2) 15 Feb 1904, Shefford, QC, **Dorila Beauregard** (Honoré Beauregard & Hermine Daignault) b & bp 18 Feb 1883, Shefford, QC.

I have not found Louis Monty's birth or baptismal record. He was born in December 1869 according to the 1870 US census in Pembroke, NH. The day of his birth is found in the 1901 Canadian census in Valcourt (Ely Sud), QC. He soon went to Canada with his parents for a younger brother was born there in 1871. He may have returned to New Hampshire with them for a few years in the 1880s but was a farmer in Valcourt, QC, at his marriages and at the births of his children. He was retired there at his death.

Louise Foisy died in childbirth. She was a sister of Marie Rose Foisy and of Joséphine Foisy, Napoléon Monty's first and second wives (5.7.10.5.2).

Dorila Beauregard was a sister of Mathilde Beauregard, wife of Trefflé Monty (5.7.10.5.5). She survived her husband and was living in Drummondville, QC, when her daughter Marguerite married there in 1939.

Child of the first marriage:
5.7.10.5.1.1	Louise Yvonne	1897-1920-

Children of the second marriage:
5.7.10.5.1.2	Alice Estelle	1904-1924-1933
5.7.10.5.1.3	Justina Aldéa	1906-1923-
5.7.10.5.1.4	Jeannette Irène	1908-1925-
5.7.10.5.1.5	Urgèle Maurice	1910- -1924
5.7.10.5.1.6	Flore G./Fleurette	1912-1932-
5.7.10.5.1.7	George Emile	1914-1938-
5.7.10.5.1.8	Eugène Jean-Louis	1916-1938-
5.7.10.5.1.9	Cécile Yvette	1917-1941-
5.7.10.5.1.10	Marguerite Bertha	1919-1939-
5.7.10.5.1.11	Gilberte Hélène	1921-1944-
5.7.10.5.1.12	Paul Omer Roland	1922-1944-1998

5.7.10.5.2 **MONTY, Napoléon** b & bp 24 Aug 1871, Valcourt, QC; d & bur there 27 Jan & 17 Apr 1945. He married (1) there 12 Aug 1895 **Marie Rose Foisy** (Pierre Foisy & Eliza Beauregard) b 10 Jun 1874, QC; d & bur 5 & 7 Sep 1907, Valcourt, QC.

He married (2) 23 Dec 1912, Valcourt, QC, his sister-in-law **Joséphine Foisy** (Pierre

Foisy & Eliza Beauregard) b & bp there 24 & 27 Oct 1882; d & bur there 27 & 29 Apr 1950.

Napoléon Monty was a farmer in Valcourt, QC. Both his wives were sisters of Louise Foisy, first wife of Louis Monty (5.7.10.5.1).

Children of the first marriage:

5.7.10.5.2.1	Rose Alma	1896-1913-
5.7.10.5.2.2	Louis Oliva	1897- -1912
5.7.10.5.2.3	Clara Orespha	1899-1915-1916
5.7.10.5.2.4	Marie Flore/Florise	1901- -1923
5.7.10.5.2.5	Henri	1903-1923-1965
5.7.10.5.2.6	Juliette Dorila (twin)	1905-1925-
5.7.10.5.2.7	Georgiana Julienne (twin)	1905- -
5.7.10.5.2.8	Germaine	1907-1930-

5.7.10.5.3   **MONTY, Rose Anna/Rosa** b & bp 1 & 5 Sep 1873, Valcourt & Stukely, QC. She married 23 Nov 1890, Suncook, NH, **Elza Strickford/Antoine Elzéar Frappier** (Antoine Frappier & Elizabeth Lamarche) b & bp 22 Jun & 15 Jul 1866, Barnston & Stanstead, QC.

Marie Rose Anna Monty (baptismal name) was named Rosa when she married Elza Strickford and either Rose, Rose A., or Rosa in US and Canadian church records and censuses.

Her husband's name varies more significantly. He had been named Antoine Elzéar Frappier at his baptism but adopted the Strickford surname, as did his parents, when he arrived in New Hampshire. The change was not constant. He was known as Elza Strickford when he married in St. John the Baptist Church in Suncook, NH, yet his name was Elzéar Frappier when his daughters Emma Rose and Nellie Esther were baptized there a few years later. He was Elsah Strickford when he was a carriage painter in Bow, NH, in 1900, and Elisar (?) Frappier when he was a painter in Hatley, QC, in 1911 (US and Canadian censuses). After that time the surname Frappier was used in Canada and Strickford in the United States. Antoine Elie (sic) Frappier and his wife were in North Hatley when their daughter Claudia married in 1922 while Eliza Strickford was a resident of North Hatley when his brother Emmie Strickford died in 1932 (Manchester, NH, *Union Leader*, 25 Feb 1932).

Children:

i   **Emma Rose Frappier/Strickford** b & bp 19 Feb 1893, Suncook, NH; d & bur there 20 Feb 1893.

ii   **Nellie Esther Frappier/Strickford** b & bp 14 & 15 Jan 1894, Suncook, NH.

iii   **Jess/Jesse Frappier/Strickford** b Jun 1896, NH.

iv   **Claudia Frappier/Strickford** b Feb 1899, NH. She married 19 Dec 1922, North Hatley, QC, **Pierre/Peter Joseph Landry** (François Olivier Landry & Marie Guimond) b 27 Nov 1896, Fairfield, ME.

5.7.10.5.4   **MONTY, Malvina** b & bp 7 & 9 May 1875, Valcourt, QC; d & bur 26 & 27 Aug 1886, Pembroke & Suncook, NH.

5.7.10.5.5   **MONTY, Trefflé** b & bp 20 & 22 Apr 1878, Valcourt, QC; d & bur 5 & ? Mar 1955, Tewksbury, MA & Manchester, NH. He married (1) 23 Jun 1902, Shefford, QC, **Mathilde Beauregard** (Honoré Beauregard & Hermine Daignault) b & bp 11 & 12 Aug 1879, Shefford, QC; d 10 May 1927, Manchester, NH.

He married (2) 1929? **Mary P. ____** b 1889?, NH.

Trefflé Monty was a farmer in Valcourt, QC, until he left for Manchester, NH, in April 1923 with his wife Matilda and children Adolphe, Yvonne, Ernest, Maurice, and Céleste. He was a cotton mill worker there on 1 Apr 1930 when his second wife, Mary P, was 41 years old (US census).

Mathilde Beauregard was a sister of Dorila Beauregard, second wife of Louis Monty (5.7.10.5.1).

Children:

5.7.10.5.5.1	Adolphe Trefflé	1903-1928-1968
5.7.10.5.5.2	Yvonne	1904- -
5.7.10.5.5.3	Ernest Ovila	1908- -1986
5.7.10.5.5.4	Maurice	1911-1933-1975
5.7.10.5.5.5	Céleste Léa	1913- -
5.7.10.5.5.6	Alice Aline Florence	1914- -1917

5.7.10.5.6   **MONTY, Charles** b & bp 23 & 24 May 1880, Valcourt, QC; d & bur there 15 & 21 Nov 1946. He married there 6 Mar 1905 **Adèle/Adelle Fortier** (Alexandre Cyprien Fortier & Sophronie Brodeur) b Apr 1886, MA.

Charles Monty (Charles Joseph Victor Wilfrid at his baptism) was a blacksmith in Valcourt, QC, at his marriage and at the birth of his son there the following year. He and his wife soon emigrated for their second child was born in Fitchburg, MA. Charles Monty was a laborer there in 1910, living with his 25-year-old wife Adelle and two children in his father-in-law's household.

That is the last time I have seen husband and wife together. In 1920 Mrs. Adelle Monty was still in Fitchburg but with only her 8-year-old daughter Irene living with her. In 1930, she was in Burrillville, RI, with her daughter and son-in-law Irene and Théophile A. Racine (US censuses).

Children:

5.7.10.5.6.1	Joseph Edward	1906-1927?-1979
5.7.10.5.6.2	Yvonne	1908?- -
5.7.10.5.6.3	Irene	1911-1928?-1981

5.7.10.5.7   **MONTY, Albina/Apolline Georgina** b & bp 21 & 25 Jun 1882, Valcourt, QC; d & bur 29 Mar & 2 Apr 1928, Sherbrooke, QC. She married 8 Jan 1907, Valcourt, QC, **Hector Bachand** (Jean-Baptiste Bachand & Mélina Desautels) b & bp 24 & 25 Nov 1882, St. Liboire, QC.

This woman was baptized under the name of Marie Apolline Georgina Monty. She was nevertheless named Albina in the 1901 Canadian census in Valcourt, QC, and at her marriage. I cannot explain the name change.

Hector Bachand was a cheese maker in Valcourt at the births of his children there in 1908 and 1910, and in Sherbrooke, QC, at his wife's death in 1928.

Children:

i   **Marie Bernadette Béatrice Bachand** b & bp 24 & 25 Aug 1908, Valcourt, QC. She married 8 May 1929, Sherbrooke, QC, **Joseph Arthur St. Laurent** (Elzéar St. Laurent & Delia Raymond) b & bp there 5 Apr 1905.

ii   **Thérèse Marthe Bachand** b & bp 8 May 1910, Valcourt, QC.

5.7.10.5.8   **MONTY, Ludovic** b & bp 20 & 21 Mar 1884, Valcourt, QC. He married there 7 Jan 1908 **Anna Racicot** (Antoine Racicot & Hermine Proulx) b & bp there 10 & 11 Sep 1886.

Ludovic Monty was a farmer in Valcourt, QC, through 1915 and in Piopolis, QC, from at least 1918 through at least 1934. He and his wife were living in Milan, QC, at the marriage of their son Louis Lionel in 1949.

Children:

5.7.10.5.8.1	Horace	1909-1934-2000
5.7.10.5.8.2	Simone Clémentine	1910-1944-
5.7.10.5.8.3	Olida Agnès	1912-1937-
5.7.10.5.8.4	Cécile Liliose	1914-1938-
5.7.10.5.8.5	Blanche Aimée	1915- -

5.7.10.5.8.6	Marie Alice Aurélie	1918-1939-
5.7.10.5.8.7	Jean Ludovic	1921- -
5.7.10.5.8.8	René Wilfrid	1924- -
5.7.10.5.8.9	Louis Lionel Edmond	1926-1949-
5.7.10.5.8.10	Victor Edouard	1928- -

5.7.10.5.9   **MONTY, Adélaïde** b & bp 23/24 & 25 May 1886, Pembroke & Suncook, NH; d & bur 5 & 8 Aug 1902, Valcourt, QC.

The New Hampshire Vital Records show that Adelaide Monty was born on 23 May 1886 while the baptismal records of St. John the Baptist Catholic Church in Suncook, NH, have it that Marie Césarie Adélaïde Monty was born on 24 May. Either day is possible. I am disregarding the date of 15 May 1886 found in the 1901 Canadian census in Valcourt, QC, which also claims that she was born in the Province of Quebec.

5.10.6.2.1   **MONTY, Marie Ezilda** b & bp 18 & 20 Feb 1857, Marieville, QC; d & bur there 19 & 20 Jan 1858.

5.10.6.2.2   **MONTY, Mathilde** b & bp 31 Oct & 1 Nov 1858, Marieville, QC; d & bur 18 & 20 Mar 1916, St. Césaire, QC. She married there 15 Oct 1878 **Césaire Barrière** (François Barrière & Flavie Davignon) b & bp there 20 & 21 Nov 1859.

Césaire Barrière was a farmer in St. Césaire, QC, until at least 1911 (Canadian censuses). He survived his wife.

Children:
i   **Anonymous Barrière** d & bur 20 & 24 Mar 1882, Abbotsford, QC.
ii   **Arsélie/Arzelia Barrière** b & bp 26 & 27 Feb 1883, St. Césaire, QC. She married there 16 Feb 1904 **James Gilmour** (Thomas Gilmour & Eulalie Fleury) b Aug 1880, QC.

5.10.6.2.3   **MONTY, Antoine** b & bp 14 & 17 Jun 1861, Marieville, QC; d & bur 27 & 31 Aug 1925, St. Césaire, QC. He married there 11 May 1886 **Médérise Beauvais** (Abraham Beauvais & Adèle Nadeau) b & bp there 14 Jan 1862; d & bur there 26 & 28 Feb 1938.

Antoine Monty was an innkeeper in St. Césaire, QC, at the birth of his first child in 1887 and a farmer there in 1889 and later years. He was still a farmer there in 1911 (Canadian census) though he had retired before his death.

Children:
5.10.6.2.3.1	Joseph Louis Rémy	1887-1907-
5.10.6.2.3.2	Marie Louise Aldéa	1889- -1890
5.10.6.2.3.3	Alcide	1891- -1892
5.10.6.2.3.4	Albina	1893-1913-1926
5.10.6.2.3.5	Rose Alma	1895- -1910
5.10.6.2.3.6	Anonymous	1897- -1897
5.10.6.2.3.7	Sergius	1899-1925-1969
5.10.6.2.3.8	Joseph Georges	1901- -
5.10.6.2.3.9	Marie Emmela Sylvia	1904- -1904
5.10.6.2.3.10	Anonymous (male)	1907- -1907

5.10.6.2.4   **MONTY, Sergius** b & bp 24 & 25 Aug 1863, St. Césaire, QC; d & bur there 28 & 30 Mar 1874.

5.10.6.2.5   **MONTY, Rémi** b & bp 1 & 7 Mar 1869, St. Césaire, QC; d there 18 Nov 1948. He married (1) there 15 Aug 1893 **Roseline Brodeur** (David Brodeur & Adée Benoit) b & bp there 28 Feb 1878; d & bur there 14 & 16 Oct 1914.

He married (2) 5 Feb 1919, St. Jean, QC, a first cousin, **Adeline Monty** (Damien Monty [5.10.6.4] & Sophie Célina Papineau) b & bp 5 & 6 Jul 1877, St. Luc, QC.

Rémi Monty (Joseph Louis Rémi at his baptism) was a carpenter in Ste Angèle, QC, in 1891 (Canadian census) and a farmer in St. Césaire, QC, at his marriage. He moved around 1897 with his family to South Hadley, MA, where he was a farmer in 1900 and a milk peddler in 1910 (US censuses). He returned to St. Césaire shortly afterwards and was a farmer there in June 1911 (Canadian census). He remained there until his death.

Rémi Monty's first wife was a sister of Arthur Brodeur, husband of Aloïsia Monty (5.10.6.2.6) and of Emery Brodeur, husband of Sylvia Monty (5.10.6.2.7).

Children:

5.10.6.2.5.1	Laura Yvonne	1894-1914-
5.10.6.2.5.2	Joseph Amédée	1896-1917-1982
5.10.6.2.5.3	Rose Emma/Rosanna	1898-1916-
5.10.6.2.5.4	Rémi Louis	1899- -
5.10.6.2.5.5	Sylvia	1909-1930-
5.10.6.2.5.6	Médard	1911-1958-

5.10.6.2.6   **MONTY, Aloïsia** b & bp 5 & 7 Feb 1871, St. Césaire, QC; d & bur there 7 & 9 Nov 1901. She married there 13 Sep 1887 **Arthur Brodeur** (David Brodeur & Adée Benoit) b & bp there 22 Jul 1867.

Arthur Brodeur was originally a farmer in St. Césaire, QC, through at least 1901 (Canadian census). He apparently left the area after his wife's death and was living in Cobalt, Ontario, Canada, when two of his children married in 1920. He was a brother of Emery Brodeur, husband of Sylvia Monty (5.10.6.2.7), and of Roseline Brodeur, wife of Rémi Monty (5.10.6.2.5).

Children:

i   **Rémi Louis Brodeur** b & bp 19 & 20 Jul 1888, St. Césaire, QC; d & bur 4 & 6 Jul 1927, Timmins, Ontario, Canada. He married 9 Mar 1912, Cobalt, Ontario, Canada, **Emelia Pigeon** (Pierre Pigeon & Albertile Giroux) b 1883?, Montebello, QC; d & bur 1 & 5 Dec 1938, Ottawa, Ontario, Canada, at the age of 55.

ii   **Sylvia Yvonne Brodeur** b & bp 13 & 14 Apr 1890, St. Césaire, QC. She married there 24 Feb 1908 **Dieudonné/Donat Viens** (André Viens & Louise Ostiguy) b & bp there 25 & 28 Jun 1885; d & bur 4 & 6 Apr 1953, Beloeil & St. Césaire, QC.

iii   **Henri Louis Brodeur** b & bp 23 Aug 1891, St. Césaire, QC. He married 15 Sep 1914, Cobalt, Ontario, Canada, **Delia Côté** (François Xavier Côté & Ernestine Marquis) b 1889?, Salem, MA.

iv   **Georges Brodeur** b & bp 7 & 13 Jan 1893, St. Césaire, QC. He married 7 Feb 1921, Montreal, QC, **Anna Bella Gagné** (Napoléon Gagné & Anna Théroux) b & bp 24 Jul 1894, St. Hugues, QC.

v   **Uldège Brodeur** b & bp 2 Feb 1894 St. Césaire, QC. He married 14 Jan 1920, Ange Gardien, QC, **Marie Louise Héla Authier** (Donat Authier & Georgiana Benoit) b & bp 27 & 29 Dec 1900, Abbotsford, QC.

vi   **Rose Delima Brodeur** b & bp 13 & 14 Apr 1895, St. Césaire, QC.

vii   **Philias David Brodeur** b & bp 18 & 19 Oct 1896, St. Césaire, QC. He married there 12 Sep 1923 **Alexina Roy** (Frédéric Roy & Amanda Chabot) b & bp there 2 & 3 Aug 1904.

viii **Marie Anne/Anna Marie Brodeur** b & bp 11 & 16 Mar 1898, St. Césaire, QC. She married there 27 Sep 1920 **François Xavier Gariépy** (Joseph Gariépy & Marie Gervais).

5.10.6.2.7   **MONTY, Sylvia** b & bp 19 & 21 Mar 1873, St. Césaire, QC; d & bur there Jul 1946. She married 10 Jan 1893, St. Angèle, QC, **Emery Brodeur** (David Brodeur & Adée Benoit) b & bp 21 Oct 1871, St. Césaire, QC.

Emery Brodeur was a farmer in St. Césaire, QC. He was a brother of Roseline Brodeur, wife of Rémi Monty (5.10.6.2.5), and of Arthur Brodeur, husband of Aloïsia Monty (5.10.6.2.6).

Children:

i **Louis Rémi Brodeur** b & bp 15 & 17 Dec 1893, St. Césaire, QC; d & bur there 31 Jan & 1 Feb 1894.

ii **Arthur Brodeur** b & bp 26 & 28 Jul 1895, St. Césaire, QC. He married there 4 Feb 1920 **Marie Rosalie Albina Ménard** (William Ménard & Albina Gagné) b & bp there 12 & 14 Oct 1894.

iii **Honoré Brodeur** b & bp 7 & 10 Apr 1897, St. Césaire, QC; d Aug 1954, Abbotsford, QC. He married 14 Apr 1920, St. Césaire, QC, **Orida Gagné** (Joseph Gagné & Marie Bourbeau) b & bp there 2 & 3 Nov 1897.

iv **Emma Brodeur** b & bp 28 & 30 Sep 1898, St. Césaire, QC. She married there 4 Feb 1920 **Ernest Ovila Ménard** (Alexis Ménard & Alma Bourbeau) b & bp 24 & 27 Jan 1898, Abbotsford, QC.

v **Léona Brodeur** b & bp 22 & 23 Dec 1900, St. Césaire, QC. She married there 1 Dec 1920, **Hervé Robert** (Alfred Robert & Marie Rose Rocheleau) b & bp 22 & 23 Feb 1898, St. Pie, QC.

vi **Rose Anna Brodeur** b & bp 23 Sep 1902, St. Césaire, QC; d & bur there 30 Nov & 1 Dec 1903.

vii **Louis Adélard Brodeur** b & bp 12 Mar 1904, St. Césaire, QC; d & bur there 25 & 27 Feb 1911.

viii **Marie Louise Alma Brodeur** b & bp 20 Aug 1905, St. Césaire, QC; d & bur there 3 & 4 Dec 1906.

ix **Angela Clarinda Brodeur** b & bp 20 & 21 Nov 1907, St. Césaire, QC. She married there 12 Nov 1928 **Joseph Albert Adrien Paquette** (Arthur Paquette & Anna Dumontier) b & bp 11 & 12 Feb 1906, Berthierville, QC.

x **Hector Agénar/Agénor Brodeur** b & bp 17 & 18 Aug 1909, St. Césaire, QC; d & bur there 21 & 24 Feb 1930.

xi **Alméda Brodeur** b & bp 2 & 3 Sep 1912, St. Césaire, QC. She married there 15 Jul 1935 **Henri Paul Côté** (Henri Côté & Anna St. Pierre).

xii **Napoléon Armand Brodeur** b & bp 12 & 13 May 1914, St. Césaire, QC; d & bur there 19 & 20 Jan 1915.

xiii **Cécile Brodeur** b & bp 17 & 18 Oct 1918, St. Césaire, QC. She married (1) there 23 Aug 1943 **Euchariste Giroux** (Philippe Giroux & Aurore Roussel) b & bp there 16 & 18 Sep 1910.

 She married (2) 18 May 1959, St. Césaire, QC, **Jean-Marie Larose** (Edmond Larose & Rose Anna Robert), widower of Jeanne Pineault and of A. Michaudville; b & bp 16 & 17 Feb 1910, St. Alphonse de Granby, QC.

5.10.6.2.8 **MONTY, Adolphe/Adolph** b & bp 29 & 30 Jun 1875, St. Césaire, QC.

Adolphe Monty (Pierre Uldéric Adolphe at his baptism) was a schoolboy living with his widowed mother in Ste Angèle, QC, in 1891 (Canadian census). He soon joined his brother Rémi (5.10.6.2.5) in South Hadley, MA, and was a milk peddler there, named Adolphus Monty, in 1900 (US census). He was not in Massachusetts in 1910 but was a farm laborer in Amenia, ND, on 12 Sep 1918 when he signed as Adolph Monty his World War I Draft Registration card. He had been in the United States for twenty-eight years and had apparently never married. He was still in Cass Co., ND, in 1925 (state census).

5.10.6.4.1 **MONTY, Marie Célina** b & bp 8 & 9 Nov 1862, St. Mathias, QC; d & bur there 20 & 21 Mar 1863.

5.10.6.4.2 **MONTY, Louis Henri Damien** b & bp 27 Nov 1866, Marieville, QC; d & bur 19 Dec 1876 & 10 Apr 1877, St. Luc, QC.

The body of Henri Monty was placed in the crypt of St. Joseph's Church in Chambly, QC, on 21 Dec 1876 to await a Spring burial in St. Luc, QC.

5.10.6.4.3 **MONTY, Marie Louise Célina** b & bp 20 & 25 Dec 1867, St. Mathias,

QC; d & bur 11 & 13 Feb 1936, Montreal & St. Jean, QC.

Marie Monty was a dressmaker in Montreal, QC. She did not marry.

5.10.6.4.4   **MONTY, Maria Clara Elia** b & bp 26 & 27 Aug 1869, Richelieu, QC. She married 1 Oct 1888, Montreal, QC, **Ovila Thériault/Terriault** (Cléophas Terriault & Julie Boucher) b Feb 1867, QC; d & bur 3 & 6 Jul 1939, St. Jean, QC, at the age of 72 years and 4 months.

Ovila Thériault was a machinist in Montreal, QC, at his marriage and a master plumber there in 1911 (Canadian census). His surname then and on his burial record was Thériault. Yet both he and his father signed Terriault on his marriage record. He predeceased his wife.

5.10.6.4.5   **MONTY, Joseph Louis Rémi** b & bp 25 Aug & 3 Sep 1871, Richelieu, QC; d & bur 13 & 15 Aug 1940, St. Jean, QC.

Joseph Monty was a farmer in St. Jean, QC. He did not marry.

5.10.6.4.6   **MONTY, David Emilien Damien** b & bp 16 & 20 Jul 1873, St. Luc, QC; d & bur there 10 & 11 Dec 1876.

5.10.6.4.7   **MONTY, Rose Anna** b & bp 29 & 31 Mar 1875, St. Luc, QC. She married 28 Oct 1896, St. Jean, QC, **Arthur Langlois** (Samuel Langlois & Priscille Hébert) b & bp there 3 & 4 Oct 1868.

Arthur Langlois was a farmer in St. Jean, QC. He and his wife (named Joséphine Rose Anna at her baptism but most commonly known as simply Rose Anna Monty) were still residents of St. Jean when their daughter Simone married there in 1939.

Children:
- i **Samuel Arthur Langlois** b & bp 11 Mar 1898, St. Jean, QC. He married there 21 Sep 1926 **Lucienne Therrien** (Fabien Therrien & Emelie Deland) b & bp there 16 & 18 May 1902.
- ii **Célina Irène Victoire Langlois** b & bp 3 & 4 Feb 1900, St. Jean, QC.
- iii **René Jean Joseph Armand Langlois** b & bp 1 & 3 May 1902, St. Jean, QC. He married there 2 Dec 1939 **Jeanne d'Arc Aubré** (Pierre Aubré & Joséphine Duchesneau) b & bp 31 Aug & 1 Sep 1915, Lyster, QC.
- iv **Benoit Edouard Louis Charles Langlois** b & bp 15 & 16 Dec 1904, St. Jean, QC.
- v **Aline Anne Marguerite Langlois** b & bp 7 Jul 1907, St. Jean, QC. She married there 16 Dec 1935 **Joseph Albert Aubré** (Pierre Aubré & Joséphine Duchesneau) b & bp 1 Jul 1904, Lyster, QC.
- vi **Louis Charles Rodolphe Emilien Langlois** b & bp 26 & 27 Jul 1909, St. Jean, QC. He married 19 Jun 1935, St. Blaise, QC, **Cécile Lorrain** (Edouard Lorrain & Alice Samoisette) b & bp there 21 & 22 Jun 1913.
- vii **Jeanne Hélène Emma Langlois** b & bp 23 & 24 Jan 1912, St. Jean, QC. She married there 12 Sep 1934 **Armand Albert Samoisette** (Delphis Samoisette & Joséphine Fortin) b & bp 16 & 17 Feb 1911, St. Blaise, QC.
- viii **Antoinette Agnès Simone Langlois** b & bp 22 & 23 Jan 1914, St. Jean, QC. She married there 28 Oct 1939 **Fernand Bourret** (Argermire Bourret & Anna Trudel).

5.10.6.4.8   **MONTY, Adeline** b & bp 5 & 6 Jul 1877, St. Luc, QC. She married 5 Feb 1919, St. Jean, QC, her first cousin, **Rémi Monty** (5.10.6.2.5).

5.10.6.4.9   **MONTY, Joséphine Catherine Elisabeth** b & bp 5 Nov 1879, St. Luc, QC.

Joséphine Monty was a dressmaker, single, living in Montreal, QC, in 1911 in the household of her sister and brother-in-law Maria (5.10.6.4.4) and Ovila Thériault (Canadian census).

5.10.6.4.10   **MONTY, Evangéline Georgiana** b & bp 8 Apr 1882, St. Jean, QC; d &

bur 18 & 19 May 1884, St. Jean & St. Luc, QC.

5.10.6.8.1 **MONTY, Joseph Louis** b & bp 4 & 5 Apr 1871, Iberville, QC; d & bur 6 & 9 Feb 1916, Montreal, QC. He married there 10 Jun 1901, **Alice Huet** (Eusèbe Huet & Rose Delima Rollin) b bp there 16 & 18 Aug 1878.

Joseph Louis Monty (Joseph Louis Isidore at his baptism) was a typographer in St. Hyacinthe, QC, at the birth of his first child and in later years in Montreal, QC.

Children:

5.10.6.8.1.1	Alice Agnès Thérèse	1902-1937-
5.10.6.8.1.2	Lucien Ernest	1903-1929-
5.10.6.8.1.3	Anna Lucienne	1905- -
5.10.6.8.1.4	Gérard Paul Emile	1907- -

5.10.6.8.2 **MONTY, Anne Agnès Alphonsine** b & bp 22 & 23 Oct 1872, Ottawa, Ontario, Canada.

5.10.6.8.3 **MONTY, Napoléon Alphonse** b & bp 24 & 26 Apr 1874, Ottawa, Ontario, Canada.

5.10.6.8.4 **MONTY, Alfred Dollard** b & bp 31 Jul & 1 Aug 1875, Ottawa, Ontario, Canada.

5.10.6.8.5 **MONTY, Emile Herménégilde** b & bp 2 & 5 May 1878, Ottawa, Ontario, Canada. He married 12 Jun 1903, Montreal, QC, **Marie Dufort** (Louis Dufort & Emma Renaud) b & bp 4 & 5 Oct 1882, St. Paul l'Hermite, QC.

This couple's marriage record in St. Jean-Baptiste Church in Montreal, QC, correctly identifies the groom as Emile Monty, son of Louis Monty. The index however, which is based on an incorrect name in the margin of the text, shows that Marie Dufort's husband was Louis Monty. There is absolutely no question that her husband, and the father of her children, was Emile Monty.

Emile Monty was a clerk in Montreal at his marriage and at the births of his children through 1910. He was an insurance agent in 1911 (Canadian census).

Children:

5.10.6.8.5.1	Louis Emile Arthur	1904-	-
5.10.6.8.5.2	Emma Florence Agnès	1905-	-
5.10.6.8.5.3	Hervé	1906-1941-	
5.10.6.8.5.4	Lucienne Bernadette	1907-	-1908
5.10.6.8.5.5	Blanche Simone Elisabeth	1909-	-
5.10.6.8.5.6	Gabrielle Gertrude Emma	1910-	-1910
5.10.6.8.5.7	Pierre Emile Ernest	1911-	-
5.10.6.8.5.8	Jeanne Berthe	-1938-	

5.10.6.8.6 **MONTY, Alphonse Léopold** b & bp 14 & 17 Apr 1881, Ottawa, Ontario, Canada; d & bur 20 & 24 Feb 1908, Montreal, QC.

Alphonse Léopold Monty (Joseph Alphonse Urbain Léopold Monti at his baptism) was a journalist in Montreal, QC.

5.10.6.9.1 **MONTY, Louis Eustache** b & bp 22 & 24 Jul 1873, St. Césaire, QC; d & bur 27 & 30 Jan 1933, Montreal, QC. He married 24 Apr 1899, Chapeau, QC, **Estella Catherine McNeil** (Neil William McNeil & Teresa Catherine Grey) b & bp 9 Mar & 21 Apr 1878, Chapeau, QC; d 11 Jan 1965, Montreal, QC.

Louis Eustache Monty was a painter best known for his religious art which decorates many churches in both Canada and the American West and Midwest (Obituary notice in the *Bulletin des Recherches Historiques*, IV, 755).

Children:

5.10.6.9.1.1	Albert Aloysius	1900-	-1924
5.10.6.9.1.2	Marguerite Mathilde	1901-	-1921
5.10.6.9.1.3	Théodore	1902-1935-1988	
5.10.6.9.1.4	Thérèse	1903-	-1903
5.10.6.9.1.5	Reginald	1905-	-1905
5.10.6.9.1.6	Gérard Arthur	1906-1939-1977	
5.10.6.9.1.7	Gertrude Lilliane	1907-1930-	
5.10.6.9.1.8	François Napoléon	1909-	-1984
5.10.6.9.1.9	Estelle Hélène	1911-1939-1981	
5.10.6.9.1.10	Jean Pierre	1912-1943-1977	
5.10.6.9.1.11	Charles E. Neil	1914-1947-	
5.10.6.9.1.12	Lucille	1915-1943-1958	
5.10.6.9.1.13	Louis	1917-	-1918
5.10.6.9.1.14	Zita (twin)	1918-1947-	
5.10.6.9.1.15	Françoise Claire (twin)	1918-	-1919

5.10.6.9.2 **MONTY, Georges Napoléon** b & bp 4 & 7 Mar 1875, Montreal, QC. He married there 8 Aug 1904 **Marie Emma Paquin** (Paul Paquin & Mary O'Connell); b there 14 Oct 1876; d there 1956.

Georges Napoléon Monty was an accountant and businessman in Montreal, QC.

Children:

5.10.6.9.2.1	Paul Stanislas	1905-	-1990
5.10.6.9.2.2	Jeanne Aloysia	1906-	-1907
5.10.6.9.2.3	Blanche	1908-	-1908
5.10.6.9.2.4	Philibert Henri	1911-1944-1986	

5.10.6.9.3 **MONTY, Marie Louise** b & bp 6 Jun 1877, Montreal, QC; d & bur there 30 & 31 Jul 1878.

5.10.6.9.4 **MONTY, Marie Onalda** b & bp 23 & 25 Dec 1878, Montreal, QC; d & bur there 28 & 31 Aug 1933. She married there 29 Jul 1909 **Joseph Prégent** (Paul Prégent & Philomène Major) b 24 Mar 1882, Parry Sound, Ontario, Canada; m (2) 22 Jun 1935, Ste Thérèse, QC, Rosanna Reine Amiot dit Beaucage (Joseph Amiot dit Beaucage & Marguerite Sanche).

Joseph Prégent was a sanitation worker in Montreal, QC.

Children:

i   **Marguerite Rita Liliane Prégent** b & bp 19 & 20 May 1910, Montreal, QC.

ii   **Paul André Prégent** b & bp 8 & 10 Oct 1911, Montreal, QC.

iii   **Léona Marie Cordelia Prégent** b & bp 26 Dec 1912, Montreal, QC.

iv   **Wilfrid Gaston Lionel Prégent** b & bp 8 & 9 Feb 1914, Montreal, QC. He married there 11 Feb 1939 **Marie Desneiges Bernadette Tremblay** (François Tremblay & Marie Dufour).

v   **Françoise Alexina Thérèse Prégent** b & bp 4 & 5 Oct 1916, Montreal, QC; d & bur there 12 & 14 Sep 1917.

vi   **Graziella Pauline Prégent** b & bp 25 & 26 Apr 1918, Montreal, QC; d & bur there 28 & 30 Apr 1918.

vii   **Joseph Alexandre Napoléon Prégent** b & bp 27 & 28 Jul 1921, Montreal, QC; d & bur there 9 & 11 Aug 1921.

5.10.6.9.5 **MONTY, Marie Louise Albina** b & bp 20 & 21 Jul 1880, Montreal, QC; d & bur there 6 & 9 Mar 1939.

5.10.6.9.6   **MONTY, Joseph Ismaël** b & bp 21 & 23 Jul 1882, Montreal, QC; d & bur there 31 Oct & 3 Nov 1930. He married there 2 Jul 1906 **Annonciade Renaud** (Joseph Renaud & Marie Caisse) b & bp 1 May 1887, Montreal, QC; d & bur there 4 & 6 Jun 1917.

Joseph Monty was a city employee in Montreal, QC, at his marriage.

Children:

5.10.6.9.6.1	Gilberte	1908-	-1934
5.10.6.9.6.2	Roland Alfred	1908-	-1909
5.10.6.9.6.3	Juliette Madeleine	1909-1932-	
5.10.6.9.6.4	Marcel Paul Achille	1912-	-1913
5.10.6.9.6.5	Gérard Paul Emile	1914-	-1914

5.10.6.9.7   **MONTY, Pierre Emile** b & bp 3 Mar 1884, Montreal, QC; d & bur there 15 & 17 Sep 1885.

5.10.6.9.8   **MONTY, Marie Anne** (twin) b & bp 19 & 20 Feb 1886, Mont-real, QC; d & bur there 28 Feb & 1 Mar 1886.

5.10.6.9.9   **MONTY, Anonymous** (twin) b 19 Feb 1886, Montreal, QC; d & bur there 19 & 22 Feb 1886.

5.10.6.9.10   **MONTY, Marie Joséphine** b & bp 22 & 23 Feb 1887, Montreal, QC; d & bur there 1 & 3 Sep 1887.

8.1.7.2.1   **MONTY, Louis** b Jan 1856, Manchester, NH; d between 1910 and 1920. He married 1877? **Victoria/Victorine Baker** b Feb 1861, QC; d 8 Nov 1933, Manchester, NH.

Louis Monty and his wife had been married for twenty-three years in 1900. He was a laborer in Manchester, NH, until at least 1883, and from 1885 through at least 1910 a farmer/laborer in Bedford, NH. His widow was a mill worker in Manchester in 1920 but was staying with her daughter and son-in-law in Bedford in 1930. She had had six children of whom only one, Mary Ann, survived to maturity (US censuses).

Children:

8.1.7.2.1.1	Louis	1878-	-1883
8.1.7.2.1.2	William	1879-	-1883
8.1.7.2.1.3	Philip	1881-	-1882
8.1.7.2.1.4	Joseph	1883-	-1885
8.1.7.2.1.5	Mary Ann V.	1885-1904?-	

8.1.7.2.2   **MONTY, Rosalie/Rose/Rosa** b Dec 1857, Manchester, NH. She married there 5 Jul 1876 **Richard G. Hartman** (George Hartman & Johanna ____) b 1855?, Lawrence, MA.

Rosalie Monty was 18 months old when her parents' marriage was revalidated in St. Mathias, QC, in June 1859 (see 8.1.7.2) and 18 years old at her marriage under the name of Rose Monty.

Richard G. Hartman was a 21-year-old barber in Manchester, NH, at his marriage and a 26-year-old shop employee there in 1880 (US census). His wife was then named Rosa.

8.1.7.2.3   **MONTY, Clément** b & bp 7 & 9 Sep 1860, Mont St. Grégoire, QC.

Clément Monty came to Manchester, NH, as a child with his parents in the early 1860s and was a laborer living in his father's household there in 1880. He was a widower in 1910, when he was a hired hand on the farm of George C. Fulton in Manchester (US censuses). I know nothing about his marriage or possible family.

8.1.7.2.4   **MONTY/MONTE, William** b & bp 18 & 21 Sep 1862, Ste Brigide, QC; d between 1900 and 1915. He married (1) 20 Jun 1883, Manchester, NH, **Rebecca Daniels** (Charles Daniels & Matilda ____) b 1864?, Canada.

He married (2) 1 Oct 1887, Manchester, NH, **Amanda Dupont** (Denis Dupont & Adeline ____) b Jul 1864, QC.

William Monty came to the United States with his parents as an infant and became a carriage painter in Manchester, NH. He moved to Bedford, NH, after his second marriage and was a painter, pail maker, and laborer there until at least 1900. The family surname had then become Monte. The widowed Mrs. Amanda Monte was living in Manchester with her children Charles and Emily in 1915 and 1916, in Peabody, MA, in 1920, in Manchester again around 1924-1926, and in Brockton, MA, from at least 1929 until at least 1932 (US censuses; Manchester and Brockton City Directories).

Child of the first marriage:

8.1.7.2.4.1	William	1882-	-1883

Children of the second marriage:

8.1.7.2.4.2	William J.	1888-1909-
8.1.7.2.4.3	Edward Joseph Odilon	1890-1920?-
8.1.7.2.4.4	Emily	1895-1917?-
8.1.7.2.4.5	Charles Wilfred	1897-1919?-1966
8.1.7.2.4.6	Henry Ernest	1898- -1977

8.1.7.2.5   **MONTY, Mary J.** b 1863?, Keene, NH. She married 3 Jul 1883, Manchester, NH, **Lewis W. Adams** (George Adams & Charlotte ____) b 1863?, Leicester, MA.

Mary J. Monty and her husband were both 20 years old at their marriage. She was a widow living alone in Manchester, NH, in 1910 while in 1930 she was sharing a household in Merrimack, NH, with her brother Edward (8.1.7.2.10) (US censuses).

8.1.7.2.6   **MONTY, John** b 1864?, NH; d 19 Apr 1881, Manchester, NH, at the age of 16.

John Monty was a farm laborer living with his family in Manchester, NH, in 1880 (US census).

8.1.7.2.7   **MONTY, Charles** b 17 Jun 1870, Merrimack, NH; d there 19 May 1892. Charles Monty was buried in St. Joseph's Cemetery in Manchester, NH.

8.1.7.2.8   **MONTY, George** b 1873?, Manchester, NH; d 25 Apr 1899, Merrimack, NH, at the age of 26.

George Monty did not marry. He was buried in St. Joseph's Cemetery in Manchester, NH.

8.1.7.2.9   **MONTY, Frank** b Jan 1876, Manchester, NH; d there 18 May 1877, at the age of 16 months.

8.1.7.2.10   **MONTE/MONTY, Edward** b Mar 1880, Manchester, NH. He married **Marguerite/Margaret** ____ b 1873?, NY; d between 1920 and 1930.

Edward Monte was a farm laborer in Merrimack, NH, in 1900 and a tannery worker there in 1920 when his wife Margaret was 47 years old. He was still a laborer there in 1930, though a widower who shared a home with his widowed sister Mary J. (8.1.7.2.5) (US censuses).

8.1.7.4.1   **MONTY, Peter/Mitchell/Michel** b 1864?, NH; d & bur 1946, Clintonville, WI. He married 1910? **Bertha Bork** (Frederick Bork & Caroline ____) b 1866, Prussia (Pomerania); m (1) 1883? John Meggers; d & bur 1941, Clintonville, WI.

My identification of Peter Monty of Clintonville, WI, with Mitchell or Michel Monty, son of Michel Monty and Mathilde Bertrand, is based on the obituaries of his sister Mary

Genevieve (8.1.7.4.7) and of his brother Frank (8.1.7.4.3) in the *Savanna Daily Journal* of 27 Oct 1931 and 18 Aug 1944. Peter, Mary Genevieve, and Frank Monty were siblings.

Peter Monty of Clintonville, WI, the brother of Mary Genevieve and Frank Monty, has no known history prior to 1920 when he was a 50-year-old railroad employee in Clintonville. He was a 62-year-old railroad carpenter there in 1930 and had been married for twenty years. We also know that he had been born in New Hampshire of Canadian parents (US censuses). The inscription on his tombstone in Clintonville's Graceland Cemetery points to still another year of birth: 1867. All of these ages and dates are probably wrong: according to the 1870 census in Bear Creek, WI, only two of Mitchell Monty's children were born in New Hampshire, in 1864 and 1865. The third, born in Wisconsin in 1867, was Frank Monty.

Mitchel Monty on the other hand was living with his parents Mitchel and Matilda Monty in Bear Creek, WI, in 1870 when he was 6 years old. He had been born in New Hampshire. He was also in Bear Creek with his parents and numerous siblings in 1880 when he was 15 years old (US censuses). He then disappears and was not named as a brother of Frank and Genevieve Monty in their obituaries.

In spite of the 40-year gap between 1880 and 1920 when neither Peter nor Mitchell can be found, I believe that Mitchell/Michel Monty and Peter Monty were the same person. For lack of more precise information I am using the year of birth implied in the earliest record we have, the 1870 census, while accepting the year of death found on his tombstone.

The dates of Bertha Bork's birth and death are taken from the inscription on her tombstone in Graceland Cemetery in Clintonville. She had arrived in the United States with her parents around 1872 and had first married at age 16. She was divorced and living in Clintonville with her children William and Clara Meggers in 1910 (US censuses).

8.1.7.4.2   **MONTY, Matilda** b 1865?, NH.

Matilda Monty was 5 years old when she was living with her parents in Bear Creek, WI, in 1870. She was not among her parents' six surviving children in 1900 and presumably died before then (US censuses).

8.1.7.4.3   **MONTY, Francis/Frank** b 22 Jul 1868, Bear Creek, WI; d 15 Aug 1944, Savanna, IL. He married there 27 Sep 1892 **Matilda Raymond** (Moïse/Moses Raymond & Domithilde/Matilda Beauvais) b there Feb 1864; d there 26 Nov 1929.

Frank Monty was a rail sawyer in Savanna, IL, in 1900, a laborer there in 1910, and a machinist in 1920 and 1930. He and his wife had five children of whom three, John, Lucille, and Mary, were still alive in 1910 (US censuses). He was buried in St. John's Cemetery in Savanna (*Savanna Daily Journal*, 18 Aug 1944).

Children:

8.1.7.4.3.1	John F.	1893-	-
8.1.7.5.3.2	Jerome	1895-	-
8.1.7.4.3.3	Raymond E.	1899-	-
8.1.7.4.3.4	Lucille M.	1901-1922?-1985	
8.1.7.4.3.5	Mary Kathleen	1905-	-

8.1.7.4.4   **MONTY, Phoebe** b 1871?, Bear Creek, WI.

Phoebe Monty was a 9-year-old child living with her parents in Bear Creek, WI, in 1880. She was not among her parents' six surviving children in 1900 and presumably died before then (US censuses).

8.1.7.4.5   **MONTY, Victoria Rosella** b Aug 1873, Bear Creek, WI; d 21 Apr 1957, Palatine, IL. She married 20 Feb 1890, WI, **James D. Perry** b 18 Mar 1868, Fond du Lac, WI; d & bur 15 & 18 Feb 1938, Palatine, IL.

Victoria Monty and her husband lived in Wisconsin for a few years after their marriage before moving to Illinois in the mid-1890s. James D. Perry was a barber in Savanna, IL, in 1900, and in Palatine, IL, from about 1902 on (US censuses). He had five sons, two of whom, Orville and Eugene, predeceased him. He was buried in Hillside Cemetery in Palatine (*Chi-*

Children
   i   **Alva L. Perry** b 23 Jun 1891, Baraboo, WI; d & bur 14 & 17 Oct 1949, Palatine, IL. He married there 25 Sep 1912 **Laura E. Vehe** (John Charles Vehe & Caroline Umbdenstock) b there 15 Jan 1891; d & bur there 24 & 27 Sep 1955.

   ii   **Darrell R. Perry** b 9 Oct 1894, Chicago, IL; d & bur 24 & 27 Jan 1961, Chicago & Palatine, IL.

   iii **Orville Perry** d before 1938.

   iv **Eugene M. Perry** b 1904?, Palatine, IL; d before 1938.

   v   **Carl H. Perry** b 1906?, Palatine, IL.

8.1.7.4.6   **MONTY, Agnes** b 21 Jan 1874, Bear Creek, WI; d 8 Jun 1950, Chicago, IL.

Agnes Monty was living with her parents in Bear Creek, WI, in 1880, with her mother in Savanna, IL, in 1900, and with her sister Genevieve (8.1.7.4.7) and brother-in-law William D. Bishell in Savanna in 1910 and in Chicago, IL, in 1930. She was a saleslady there (US censuses). She did not marry.

8.1.7.4.7   **MONTY, Genevieve** b 22 Feb 1876, Bear Creek, WI; d & bur 26 & ? Oct 1931, Evanston & Savanna, IL. She married 25 Dec 1895, Chicago, IL, **William Dawson Bishell** (William Bishell & Elizabeth Dawson) b 14 May 1872, Caythorpe, Lincolnshire, England.

William Bishell came to the United States when he was about 14 years old and after a few years spent in farm work in Wisconsin and Illinois moved to Chicago, IL, where he became a barber. He and his wife then moved to Dubuque, IA, and stayed there for about three years before moving on again, this time to Savanna, IL. He was a barber there in 1900 and until at least 1920. By 1930, though, he was again a barber in Chicago. He and his wife had had three children, none of whom survived infancy (US censuses).

A sketch of William Bishell's early life is found in Newton Bateman et al's *History of Carroll County, Illinois*, p. 746. He survived his wife (*Savanna Daily Journal*, 27 Oct 1931).

8.1.7.4.8   **MONTY, Henry Louis** b 14 Apr 1879, Bear Creek, WI; d & bur 26 & 29 Oct 1958, Rockford & Savanna, IL. He married 1912?, Savanna, IL, **June V. Colebaugh** (James A. Colebaugh & Belle O. Johnson) b there 8 May 1888; d & bur 11 & 13 Nov 1941, Rockford & Savanna, IL .

Henry Monty was a cigar maker in Savanna, IL, in 1900 and 1910 before moving around 1918 to Rockford, IL, where he remained until his death. He was a metal worker there in 1930 (US censuses). Both he and his wife were buried in St. John's Cemetery in Savanna (*Savanna Daily Journal*, 4 Nov 1958).

Children:

| 8.1.7.4.8.1 | Donald William | 1913- | -1991 |
| 8.1.7.4.8.2 | Robert Louis | 1920- | - |

8.1.7.5.1   **MONTY, John** b 1874?, Bear Creek, WI; d before 1910.

John Monty was a 6-year-old child living with his parents in Bear Creek, WI, in 1880 (US census). He died before 1910 when none of his mother's children was still alive and was probably the Johnnie Monty whose name is found on a tombstone dedicated to the "Children of C. & J. MONTY" in St. Rose Cemetery in Clintonville, WI.

8.1.7.5.2   **MONTY, Mary A.** b 1881, Waupaca Co., WI; d there 1903.

The years of Mary A. Monty's birth and death are found on her tombstone in St. Rose Cemetery in Clintonville, WI.

8.1.7.5.3   **MONTY, Alfred** b 1883, Waupaca Co., WI; d there 1904.

The years of birth and death of Alfred Monty, "son of Charles & J." are found on the tombstone he shares with his grandfather Clément Monty (8.1.7) in St. Rose Cemetery in Clintonville, WI.

8.1.7.5.4 MONTY, Harrine (?) d before 1910.

Harrine (?) Monty's name is found on a tombstone dedicated to the "Children of C. & J. MONTY" in St. Rose Cemetery in Clintonville, WI. None of Charles Monty and Julie Ménard's children was alive in 1910 (US census).

8.1.7.5.5 MONTY, Paine d before 1910.

Paine Monty's name is found on a tombstone dedicated to the "Children of C. & J. MONTY" in St. Rose Cemetery in Clintonville, WI. None of Charles Monty and Julie Ménard's children was alive in 1910 (US census).

8.1.7.5.6 MONTY, Charley d before 1910.

Charley Monty's name is found on a tombstone dedicated to the "Children of C. & J. MONTY" in St. Rose Cemetery in Clintonville, WI. None of Charles Monty and Julie Ménard's children was alive in 1910 (US census).

8.1.7.5.7 MONTY, Julia d before 1910.

Julia Monty's name is found on a tombstone dedicated to the "Children of C. & J. MONTY" in St. Rose Cemetery in Clintonville, WI. None of Charles Monty and Julie Ménard's children was alive in 1910 (US census).

8.1.7.5.8 MONTY, Mary d before 1910.

Mary Monty's name is found on a tombstone dedicated to the "Children of C. & J. MONTY" in St. Rose Cemetery in Clintonville, WI. None of Charles Monty and Julie Ménard's children was alive in 1910 (US census).

8.1.7.5.9 MONTY, Carmilite (?) d before 1910.

Carmilite (?) Monty's name is found on a tombstone dedicated to the "Children of C. & J. MONTY" in St. Rose Cemetery in Clintonville, WI. None of Charles Monty and Julie Ménard's children was alive in 1910 (US census).

8.1.7.6.1 MONTY, John Julius b 1866?, Keene, NH; d & bur 1947, Clintonville, WI. He married there 13 Mar 1903 **Margaret Ellsbury** (Henry Ellsbury & Catherine ____) b there May 1876; d & bur there 1952.

John J. Monty was a 4-year-old child living with his parents in Bear Creek, WI, in 1870. He was the only child in the family to have been born in New Hampshire and had arrived in Wisconsin as a toddler before the birth of his brother Charles (8.1.7.6.2) around 1868 (US census). Thus the date of birth of January 1868 found in the 1900 US census (and also on his tombstone) must be in error.

John J. Monty was a teamster in Clintonville, WI, in 1900. He soon joined the police force there and was Chief of Police at his marriage and until 1 May 1938 (US censuses; Appleton, WI, *Post-Crescent*, Oct 4 & 17, 1938). The dates of his and his wife's deaths are taken from the inscriptions on their tombstone in Clintonville's Graceland Cemetery.

Children:

8.1.7.6.1.1	Milton John	1904-	-1906
8.1.7.6.1.2	Marshall G.	1906-1932-1978	
8.1.7.6.1.3	Margaret	1909-1937-	
8.1.7.6.1.4	John Henry	1913-	-1985
8.1.7.6.1.5	Ruth E.	1915-	-1916

8.1.7.6.2 MONTY, Charles b 1868?, Bear Creek, WI.

Charles Monty was a 2-year-old child living with his parents in Bear Creek, WI, in

1870 (US census). He does not appear with his family in 1880 and may have died before then, which would explain the name Charles given another child in May 1885 (8.1.7.6.9).

8.1.7.6.3 **MONTY, Ursula** b 1873?, Bear Creek, WI.

Ursula Monty was a 7-year-old child living with her parents in Bear Creek, WI, in 1880 (US census).

8.1.7.6.4 **MONTY, Josephine/Josie** b May 1875 Bear Creek, WI; d & bur ? & 24 Aug 1922, Clintonville, WI. She married there 31 Jul 1892 **Henry W. Rohrer** (Leonard Rohrer & Rosina Geiger) b 14 Feb 1871, Menasha, WI; d 16 or 17 Aug 1928, Appleton, WI.

I am uncertain about Josephine Monty's date of birth. The date I am using is taken from the 1900 US census with which all other censuses I have seen are in agreement. Yet her tombstone in Graceland Cemetery in Clintonville, WI, carries a birth date of 1874.

Henry Rohrer was a farm laborer/farmer in Clintonville (US censuses). He and his wife were buried in Graceland Cemetery along with their infant son Leo.

Children:

i   **Leo Rohrer** d & bur before 1900, Clintonville, WI.

ii   **Grace B. Rohrer** b 8 Aug 1898, Clintonville, WI; d & bur 30 Aug & 1 Sep 1973, Wisconsin Rapids, WI. She married 16 Apr 1920 **Lloyd Randall Barton** (William Otis Barton & Margaret Rose Cormican) b 10 Dec 1898, Grand Rapids, WI; d 9 Sep 1982, Wisconsin Rapids, WI.

iii   **Dola Rohrer** b 4 Dec 1899, Clintonville, WI; d there Nov 1985. She married 1921, Iola, WI, **Charles E. Plopper** (Elmer Plopper & Anna Brown) b 1 Mar 1900, Clintonville, WI; d there 19 Sep 1964.

iv   **Mildred Rohrer** b 14 Jun 1901, Clintonville, WI; d 29 Apr 1992. She married 1925 **Andrew Frank Holdmann** (Jacob Holdmann & Mary Sterr) b 18 Jan 1900, Wauwatosa, WI; d Feb 1968, Kenosha, WI.

v   **Gladys H. Rohrer** b 16 Sep 1903, Clintonville, WI; d 6 Dec 1997, Jefferson Co., WI. She married 29 Oct 1928, Waukegan, IL, **Lester E. Keller** (Otto F. Keller & Alice L.____) b 16 Apr 1906, Waupaca Co., WI; d 28 May 1989, Jefferson Co., WI.

vi   **Beatrice Rohrer** b 25 Feb 1907, Clintonville, WI; d 9 Aug 1989, Milwaukee, WI.

vii   **Helen Rohrer** b 5 Apr 1915, Clintonville, WI; d 11 Jul 1996, Milwaukee, WI. She married there 4 Jul 1941 **Richard Bosley** (____ Bosley & Clara Roetzer) b there May 1918.

8.1.7.6.5 **MONTY/MONTE, George William** b 7 May 1877, Bear Creek, WI; bur 1957, Clintonville, WI. He married there 13 Aug 1901 **Frieda/Freda Laura Schoepke** (August Schoepke & Frederika Mallow) b 23 Jul 1882, Marion, WI; d 24 Oct 1974, Clintonville, WI.

George Monty was a sawmill worker in Clintonville, WI, in 1900, a foreman in a lumber camp in Crandon, WI, in 1910, and a logging contractor in Presque Isle, WI, in 1920 (US censuses). After that time the family surname is often seen as Monte, as in the 1930 census in Kingsford, MI, where George W. Monte was an automobile worker and in the announcement in the *Appleton Post Crescent* of 11 Aug 1937 of Berdean Monte's marriage. Her parents, Mr. and Mrs. George W. Monte, were then residents of Embarrass, WI. Yet their tombstone in Clintonville's Graceland Cemetery bears the surname MONTY.

Children:

8.1.7.6.5.1	Violet Bernice	1902- -
8.1.7.6.5.2	Claude G.	1904-1923?-1961
8.1.7.6.5.3	Milton E.	1905- -1921
8.1.7.6.5.4	Howard Gladwyn	1907-1930-1994
8.1.7.6.5.5	George H.	1910-1938-1994
8.1.7.6.5.6	Berdean	1915-1937-1975

8.1.7.6.5.7	Keith Jack	1917-	-1987
8.1.7.6.5.8	Cleo Mae	1918-	-1920
8.1.7.6.5.9	Warren J.	1922-1945-2005	

8.1.7.6.6   **MONTY/MONTE, Frederick John/Fred** b 22 Feb 1879, Clintonville, WI; d 31 Mar 1965, Edmonds, WA. He married (1) 1 Jul 1903, Samoa, CA, **Ellen Catherine Lebeau** b 19 Dec 1884, Menominee, WI; d 31 Jan 1953, Portland, OR.

He was divorced when he married (2) 31 Aug 1928, Tacoma, WA, **Ruth Winifred Nelson** (Nels A. Nelson & Annie ____) b 10 Nov 1898, Superior, WI; d 24 Jan 1984, Seattle, WA.

Fred Monty was a sawmill hand in 1900 in Clintonville, WI. He left for the West Coast shortly afterwards and married his first wife there. By 1905, when his son was born in Everett, WA, the family surname had become Monte. The change became permanent. Fred Monte was a shingle mill filer in Snohomish Co., WA, in 1910 and a filer for a lumber company in Portland, OR, in 1920. He and his wife divorced in the next few years. He returned to Washington State, remarried, and was an inspector in a shingle mill in Tacoma, WA, in 1930. His former wife Ellen remained in Portland and was a musician there in 1930 (US censuses).

Child of the first marriage:
| 8.1.7.6.6.1 | Everett Delford | 1905-1932-1986 |

8.1.7.6.7   **MONTY, Joseph** b Mar 1881, Clintonville, WI.

Joseph Monty was living in his mother's household in Clintonville, WI, in 1900 (US census).

8.1.7.6.8   **MONTY/MONTE, Nicholas W./Nicolas** b 2 Aug 1883, Clintonville, WI; d 20 Dec 1970, Miles City, MT. He married 1913?, MT, **Marian Bircher** (Emil Bircher & Mary Bauer) b Dec 1892, Custer Co., MT; d there 12 Dec 1971.

Nicholas Monty was living in his mother's household in Clintonville, WI, in 1900. He left Wisconsin in the next few years and was a homesteader in Custer Co., MT, in 1910 under the name of Nicholas W. Monte. He was a stock and grain farmer there in 1920 and 1930 when he and his wife had been married for seventeen years (US censuses). The Monte surname, which his children used, became permanent..

Children:
8.1.7.6.8.1	Wayne W.	1914-1934-1987
8.1.7.6.8.2	Amos/Rex A.	1916-	-
8.1.7.6.8.3	Glenn W.	1917-	-1975

8.1.7.6.9   **MONTY/MONTE, Charles J.** b 6 May 1885, Clintonville, WI; d 7 Apr 1965, Los Angeles, CA. He married 29 Nov 1912, Hanley Falls, MN, **Laura R. Trovatten** (Halvor A. Trovatten & Kari Holte) b 18 Sep 1887, Yellow Medicine Co., MN; d & bur 21 & 24 Aug 1978, Gonvick, MN.

There is a minor discrepancy in the date of Charles J. Monte's death as recorded in Los Angeles, CA, (7 Apr 1965) and in the Social Security Death Index (Mar 1965). For lack of any other evidence, I am relying here on the original report rather than on the SSDI which is derivative.

Charles Monty was living in his mother's household in Clintonville, WI, in 1900 and was a laborer there in 1905 (US and state censuses). I do not know when he left for Minnesota. He was there for a few years after his marriage for his first two children were born there. He was a logging contractor in Presque Isle, WI, though, in 1920 and a farmer in Sandness Twp, MN, in 1930 (US censuses). His surname had then become Monte, a form which his son Claude also adopted. His widow, on the other hand, was known as Laura Monty at her death. Harold, Charles, and Keith also retained the Monty surname.

Children:

8.1.7.6.9.1	Harold Charles	1914-1942-1983
8.1.7.6.9.2	Claude Louis	1915-1949-1977
8.1.7.6.9.3	Corinne Harriet	1921-1946-
8.1.7.6.9.4	Lauraine Anna	1922-1951-2005
8.1.7.6.9.5	Charles Ralph	1924-1948-1982
8.1.7.6.9.6	Hugh Otis	1929- -1929
8.1.7.6.9.7	Keith Harland	1931- &1994-1995

8.1.7.6.10   **MONTY, Edward** b 6 Aug 1887, Clintonville, WI; d there 11 Sep 1887 at the age of 1 month and 5 days.
        Edward Monty shares a tombstone with his father in St. Rose Cemetery in Clintonville, WI.

8.1.7.6.11   **MONTY, Hazel** b Oct 1888, Clintonville, WI.
        Hazel Monty was living with her mother in Clintonville, WI, in 1900 and 1905 (US & state censuses).

8.1.7.6.12   **MONTY, Julia Mary** b Sep 1891, Clintonville, WI. She married 1918? **Arthur J. Wolf** (John Wolf & Mary ____) b 10 Feb 1894, Brillion, WI; d 15 May 1959.
        Arthur J. Wolf was a repairman and driver in Clintonville, WI, in 1917 (World War I Draft Registration card), a machinist in Milwaukee, WI, in 1920, and a millwright there in 1930 when he and his wife had been married for twelve years (US censuses).

Child:
i   **Arthur J. Wolf** b 15 Nov 1920, Milwaukee, WI. He married **Myrna A.** ____ b 20 Apr 1921, Caldwell, WI.

8.1.7.12.1   **MONTY, William** b 3 Dec 1871, Maple Creek, WI; d there 18 Jan 1872.

8.1.7.12.2   **MONTY, Alexander Joseph** b 4 Feb 1873, Maple Creek, WI; d 30 May 1958, Fergus Falls, MN. He married (1) 26 Aug 1893, Deer Creek, WI, **Emma Louise Joubert** (Joseph Joubert & Mary Lyons) b 26 Nov 1872, Outagamie Co., WI; d & bur 29 Aug & 1 Sep 1947, Motley, MN.
        He married (2) 1951, **Myrtle Louella Streit** b 17 Jun 1890; d 7 Jul 1993, Henning, MN.
        Alexander Joseph Monty was a farmer in Deer Creek, WI, at his first marriage and a laborer in Elderon, WI, in 1900 (US census). He left for North Dakota in 1906 and was a farmer in Fryburg Twp (Belfield), ND, for thirty-two years before moving to Minnesota. Details of the family's life in North Dakota can be found in *Echoing Trails: Billings County History*, p. 547. Alexander J. Monty and Emma Joubert were buried in Evergreen Cemetery in Motley, MN.

Children of the first marriage:
8.1.7.12.2.1	Floyd Francis	1895-1920-1921
8.1.7.12.2.2	Rachel M.	1896-1916?-1984
8.1.7.12.2.3	Roy Alexander	1897-1923&1965-1982
8.1.7.12.2.4	Florence Mary	1899-1920&1937-1975

8.1.7.12.3   **MONTY, Sarah Anne** b 15 Mar 1875, Maple Creek, WI; d 2 Sep 1933, Gillett, WI. She married 4 Jul 1892, Sugar Bush, WI, **Gilbert Anthony Mayo** (Matthew Mayou & Delphine Pelletier) b & bp 28 Mar & 22 Apr 1860, Altona & Coopersville, NY; d & bur 1 & 4 Oct 1943, Antigo & White Lake, WI.
        Gilbert Mayo was apparently an itinerant farmer, whose many moves are reflected in the birth places of his children in Wisconsin. They were born in turn in Waupaca Co., Outagamie Co., Langlade Co., Forest Co., and again in Langlade Co. in 1914. He was a farmer in Liberty, WI, in 1900, in Laona, WI, in 1910, and in Elton, WI, in 1920 (US censuses). He was

a resident of White Lake, WI, at his death and was buried in the Catholic Cemetery there (*Antigo Daily Journal*, 1 Oct 1943)

Sarah Ann Monty was originally buried in St. Mary's Cemetery in Bear Creek, WI. Her remains were later moved near her husband's in the Catholic Cemetery in White Lake.

Children:

i **Edna Mayo** b 16 Jul 1893, Northport, WI; d 8 Jun 1951, WA. She married 3 May 1915, WI, **Joseph J. Majeski** (William W. Majeski & Anna Buergermuster) b 2 Feb 1894, Lessor, WI; d 23 Apr 1977, Longview, WA.

ii **Marvel Mayo** b 15 Aug 1894, Northport, WI; d 31 Dec 1994, Centralia, WA. She married Sep 1912 **Andrew S. Londo** (Fred/Alfrederick A. Londo & Philomene Burbey) b 13 Apr 1876, Ahnapee, WI.

iii **Vaden Mayo** b 3 Apr 1896, Bear Creek, WI; d there 5 Apr 1898.

iv **Olive Mayo** b 16 Jul 1898, Bear Creek, WI; d 28 Sep 1975, Oconto Falls, WI. She married 28 Sep 1916, WI, **Thomas Edwin Graham** (David C. Graham & Bertha J. Hart) b 19 Nov 1892, Creston, IA.

v **Goldie Mary Mayo** b 27 Apr 1900, Liberty, WI; d 10 Jul 1982, Rhinelander, WI. She married 5 Jul 1919, WI, **Harold William Irick** (Allen W. Irick & Catherine ____) b 26 Apr 1897, Rhinelander, WI; d there 31 Mar 1953.

vi **Ivan Gilbert Mayo** b 23 Apr 1902, Kempster, WI; d 9 Jul 1987, Longview, WA. He married 1923? **Anna Josephine Wahlleithner** (Marcus Wahlleithner & Anna Babler) b 23 Jan 1908, Elton, WI; d 29 May 2004, Kelso, WA.

vii **Sylvia Theresa Mayo** b 8 Mar 1904, WI; d 8 Dec 2000, Pelkie, MI. She married 16 Jan 1926 **Richard Leonard Juetten** (Henry Peter Juetten & Emma M. Ramer) b 25 Dec 1902, WI; d 16 Feb 1969, Escanaba, MI.

viii **Fern Mayo** b 5 Aug 1906, Laona, WI; d Apr 1964. He married Aug 1936 **Genevieve** ____ b 29 Aug 1916; d 3 Oct 1997, Kelso, WA.

ix **Byron Mayo** b 23 Jun 1908, Laona, WI; d there 23 Oct 1908.

x **Leo Charles Mayo** b 24 May 1914, Laona, WI; d 1 May 2005, Longview, WA. He married **Maxine Pritchard** (William E. Pritchard & Josephine E. Suthard) b 3 Mar 1918, Cowlitz Co., WA; d 20 Dec 1989, Longview, WA.

8.1.7.12.4   **MONTY, Sadie Exelda** b 16 May 1877, Maple Creek, WI; d & bur 29 Mar & 1 Apr 1978, New London & Bear Creek, WI. She married 4 Oct 1899, Bear Creek, WI, **Joseph George Lehman** (Louis Alexander Lehman & Phoebe/ Philomene Bovette) b 14 Nov 1877, Deer Creek, WI; d & bur 26 & 29 Apr 1955, Bear Creek, WI.

This woman was known as Azelda or Exelia as a child and as Exelda Sadie Monty at her marriage. In later years she was known as Mrs. Sadie Lehman. Both she and her husband, a farmer in Deer Creek, WI, were buried in St. Mary's Cemetery in Bear Creek, WI.

Children:

i **Merlin Joseph Lehman** b & bp 9 & 29 Jul 1900, Deer Creek & Bear Creek, WI; d 17 Apr 1980, Appleton, WI. He married 30 Jun 1924, Bear Creek, WI, **Lila A. Bedor** (Edward Bedor & Ida Curtis) b 5 Feb 1905, Shiocton, WI; d 7 Apr 1975, Appleton, WI.

ii **Marie Antoinette/Antonia Lehman** b & bp & 7 May & 15 Jun 1902, Deer Creek & Bear Creek, WI; d 14 Feb 1999, Bear Creek, WI. She married 28 Jan 1924 **Clarence William Luebke** (John Luebke & Amelia A. ____) b 27 Aug 1901, Deer Creek, WI; d 9 May 1984, Bear Creek, WI.

iii **Rupert Louis Lehman** b & bp 3 & 17 Apr 1904, Deer Creek & Bear Creek, WI; d 14 Jul 1981, Menasha, WI. He married there 15 Jun 1926 **Hattie A. Kalinowski** (Frank Kalinowski & Agnes ____) b there 28 Aug 1905; d there 31 Mar 2001.

iv **Raymond Solomon Lehman** b & bp 29 May & 10 Jun 1906, Deer Creek & Bear Creek, WI; d 6 Feb 1985, Bear Creek, WI. He married there 4 Apr 1929 **Gladys H. Ramsdell** (Clancy Ramsdell & Martha Raisleo) b 16 Apr 1909, WI; d 31 Jul 2003, New London, WI.

v   **Florence Mary Lehman** b & bp 28 Mar & 10 Apr 1910, Deer Creek & Bear Creek, WI; d 21 Jul 2002, New London, WI. She married 3 Feb 1936, Appleton, WI, **Victor Elmer Morack** (Fred H. Morack & Margaret _____) b 24 Jun 1908, Oshkosh, WI; d 25 Mar 1995, New London, WI.

vi   **Gordon Conrad Lehman** b 16 Apr 1912, Deer Creek, WI; d 26 Jul 1971, Bear Creek, WI. He married there 20 Jun 1939 **Anna Marie Johnson** (Jacob Johnson & Anna McClone) b there 26 Aug 1911; d there 8 Oct 1990.

vii   **Leola Eleanor Lehman** b 25 Oct 1915, Deer Creek, WI. She married 28 Jul 1936, Bear Creek, WI, **Evan Raymond Jepson** (Albert L. Jepson & Margaret Dempsey) b 14 May 1906, Deer Creek, WI; d 11 May 1989, Clintonville, WI.

8.1.7.12.5   **MONTY, Saul Solomon** b 21 Apr 1879, Maple Creek, WI; d & bur 17 & 19 Feb 1966, Phelps, WI. He married 23 Oct 1905, Bear Creek, WI, **Jennie Kathryn Halverson** (Nero Halverson & Sophie Olson) b 5 May 1884, WI; d & bur 16 & 19 Apr 1969, Phelps, WI.

Saul Monty was a laborer on his father's farm in Deer Creek, WI, in 1900 and a farmer/teamster in Elderon Twp, WI, in 1910. He moved to Phelps, WI, a few years later and was a railroad section foreman there in 1920 and a sawmill worker in 1930 (US censuses). He remained there until his death and was buried, as was his wife, in the Phelps Cemetery.

Saul Solomon Monty's wife was, by all accounts, a sister of Antonette Henrietta Mary Halverson, wife of his brother Joseph Abraham Monty (8.1.7.12.6). According to the marriage records of St. Mary's parsonage in Welcome (Bear Creek), WI, however, Solomon Monty married on 23 Oct 1905 Jane Catherine Richard. I cannot explain the discrepancy.

Children:

8.1.7.12.5.1	Lloyd Solomon	1907-1937-1996
8.1.7.12.5.2	Abraham Joseph	1908-1934-1989
8.1.7.12.5.3	Carol Sophie	1909-1928?&1933-
8.1.7.12.5.4	Verne Vincent	1911-1941-1989
8.1.7.12.5.5	Algern/Algernon Lawrence	1913-1936&1952-1981
8.1.7.12.5.6	Edward Sylvester	1915-1944?-1954
8.1.7.12.5.7	Milton Benjamin	1916-1948-1988
8.1.7.12.5.8	Ruth Mary	1918- -2006
8.1.7.12.5.9	Vivian Shirley	1919-1939-
8.1.7.12.5.10	Eleanor Jennie	1921-1941-
8.1.7.12.5.11	Kenneth Charles	1922-1948-
8.1.7.12.5.12	Beverly Alice	1924-1950-
8.1.7.12.5.13	Russell John	1926- -

8.1.7.12.6   **MONTY, Joseph Abraham** b 22 Aug 1881, Maple Creek, WI; d 29 Apr 1983, New London, WI. He married 22 May 1906, Bear Creek, WI, **Antonette (Nettie) Henrietta Mary Halverson** (Nero Halverson & Sophia Olson) b 7 Jan 1889, WI; d & bur 7 & 11 Nov 1966, New London & Bear Creek, WI.

Joseph Abraham Monty Jr. was a farm laborer in Deer Creek, WI, in 1900 and in Elderon Twp, WI, in 1910, a farmer in Clintonville, WI, in 1920, and a farm manager in Deer Creek in 1930 (US censuses). He stayed on the farm until he retired in 1959 and turned the farm over to his son Lester (*Appleton Post Crescent*, 18 May 1966). He and his wife, who were residents of New London, WI, at their deaths, were both buried in St. Mary's Cemetery in Bear Creek, WI.

Nettie Halverson's place of birth is uncertain. On the occasion of her 60th wedding anniversary, the *Appleton Post Crescent* of 18 May 1966 stated that she was born on 7 Jan 1889 in Wittenberg, WI. When she died six months later, the same newspaper stated on 8 Nov 1966 that she was born in Elderon, WI. I have not found a record of her birth in either Shawano or Marathon county.

Children:

8.1.7.12.6.1	Earl Joseph	1907-1932-1959
8.1.7.12.6.2	Mary	1908- -1908
8.1.7.12.6.3	Raymond Lester	1909-1947-1997
8.1.7.12.6.4	Lester Leon	1911-1940-1979
8.1.7.12.6.5	Adeline Mae	1913- &1947-2005
8.1.7.12.6.6	Edna Anna	1915-1932&1972-2004
8.1.7.12.6.7	Orville	1916- -1916
8.1.7.12.6.8	Reynold Nathan	1917-1950-1999
8.1.7.12.6.9	Lorraine Elizabeth	1918-1941-
8.1.7.12.6.10	Delores Mary	1920-1938-2002
8.1.7.12.6.11	Llewellyn Vincent	1921-1943-2002
8.1.7.12.6.12	Marvin Norbert	1932- -1932

8.1.7.12.7   **MONTY, Edward** b 15 Sep 1883, Maple Creek, WI; d there 4 Oct 1883.

8.1.7.12.8   **MONTY, Elizabeth Jane** b 10 Feb 1885, Deer Creek, WI; d & bur 23 & 25 Mar 1959, Antigo & White Lake, WI. She married 28 Feb 1905, Welcome (Bear Creek), WI, **Francis Thomas/Frank Murray** (James Murray & Margaret Heffernan) b 30 Oct 1883, New London, WI; d & bur 28 Sep & 1 Oct 1952, Antigo & White Lake, WI.

Frank Murray was a farmer in Maple Creek, WI, until about 1920, when the family moved to White Lake, WI. Both he and his wife were buried in St. James' Cemetery there.

Children:

i   **James Bernard Murray** b 28 Dec 1905, Deer Creek, WI; d & bur 7 & 10 Oct 1983, Berwyn & Justice, IL. He married 3 Jan 1927, Chicago, IL, **Mathilda Sophia/Hilda Smith** (John Theodore Smith & Barbara Walters) b 21 May 1903, White Lake, WI; d & bur 1 & 3 Jan 1989, Berwyn & Justice, IL.

ii   **Gertrude Adeline Murray (Sister Alena)** b 9 Jun 1908, Maple Creek, WI; d & bur 7 & 9 Apr 1991, Manitowoc, WI.

iii   **Muriel Frances Murray** b 4 Oct 1909, Maple Creek, WI; d & bur 9 & 12 Jan 1993, Oshkosh, WI. She married 12 Feb 1941, White Lake, WI, **Anthony Jacob Kammerer** (Paul Peter Kammerer & Katherine Marie Bender) b 12 Aug 1902, Oshkosh, WI; d & bur there 2 & 6 Dec 1969.

iv   **Veronica Marian Murray** b 1 Nov 1910, Maple Creek, WI; d there 7 Aug 1911.

v   **Edwin Joseph Murray** b 14 Feb 1912, Maple Creek, WI; d 20 Dec 1981, Wittenberg, WI. He married 12 Feb 1941, White Lake, WI, **Gladys Ellen Fultz** (Everett Freeman Fultz & Bessie Fultz) b 24 Mar 1921, Columbus, OH; d 30 Nov 1971, Antigo, WI.

vi   **Vera Elizabeth Murray** b 12 Mar 1914, Maple Creek, WI; d & bur 9 & 11 Sep 1979, Antigo & Elton, WI. She married 4 Jan 1932, White Lake, WI, **Leonard Leo Nixon** (Leonard Leo Nixon & Anna Clara Cunningham) b there 5 Mar 1904; d 8 Jun 1989, Elton, WI.

vii   **Blanche Theresa Murray** b 6 Jun 1915, Maple Creek, WI; d 17 Apr 2004, Oshkosh, WI. She married there 21 Sep 1946 **William Robert Eschenbauch** (Allen John Eschenbauch & Frances Matilda Cochennette) b 10 Jul 1912, Arbor Vitae, WI; d 6 Nov 1976, Woodruff, WI.

viii   **Kenneth Ludwig Murray** b 24 May 1917, Maple Creek, WI; d & bur 19 & 22 Jul 2000, Appleton, WI. He married there 8 Oct 1947 **Bette Helen Aures** (Henry Aures & Helen Nichols) b there 24 Mar 1929; d there 7 Jul 2002.

ix   **Francis Vernon Murray** b 1 Feb 1919, Maple Creek, WI; d & bur 25 & ? Feb 1992, Iron Mountain, MI & White Lake, WI. He married 4 Sep 1948, White Lake, WI, **Lena May Hatfield** (James Jackson Hatfield & Clara Ruth Choate) b 9 May 1927, Hillsboro, KY.

x   **Leland William Murray** b 24 Jan 1921, White Lake, WI; d 15 Apr 2005, Casa Grande, AZ. He married 6 May 1943, White Lake, WI, **Audrey Mae Lambert**

(Robert Lee Lambert & Elizabeth Ann Creech) b 10 Jan 1924, Sciotoville, OH.

xi   **John Aloysius Murray** b & d 1 Jul 1923, White Lake, WI.

8.1.7.12.9   **MONTY/MONTE, Vincent** b 8 Jun 1887, Deer Creek, WI; d 26 May 1963, Rhinelander, WI. He married 8 Jun 1914, Bear Creek, WI, **Della Virginia Petit** (Joseph Petit & Elizabeth Trembly) b 6 Mar 1889, New London, WI; d 6 Jun 1976, Argonne, WI.

Vincent Monty was a farm laborer in Starks, WI, when he signed on 5 Jun 1917 his World War I Draft Registration card. In later hears he used the Monte surname. Vincent Monte was a farmer in Pelican, WI, in 1920 (US census) and remained in Oneida Co., WI, until the late 1920's when the family moved to Argonne, WI.

Children:

8.1.7.12.9.1	Jeanette	1916-1934&	-
8.1.7.12.9.2	Audrey Viola	1919-1939-1969	
8.1.7.12.9.3	Richard Vincent	1921-1943?-1999	
8.1.7.12.9.4	Joyce Patricia	1923-1942-1999	
8.1.7.12.9.5	Hugh Joseph	1925-1947-2003	
8.1.7.12.9.6	Roland Russell	1927-1956-1998	
8.1.7.12.9.7	Gordon Eugene	1929-1950?-	

8.1.7.12.10   **MONTY/MONTE, Benjamin Bernard** b 15 Apr 1889, Deer Creek, WI; d & bur 22 & 25 Aug 1962, New London & Bear Creek, WI. He married 10 Jan 1913, Bear Creek, WI, **Mable M. Long** (Michael Long & Bridget Flanagan) b 22 Sep 1889, Deer Creek, WI; d 2 Apr 1963, New London, WI.

Ben Monty was a farmer in Clintonville, WI, in 1920. He moved to New London, WI, in 1924 and became an automobile salesman there named Monte (US censuses; *Appleton Post Crescent*, 18 Nov 1924; *Oshkosh Daily Northwestern*, 24 Aug 1962). That change in the surname became permanent: his and his wife's tombstone in St. Mary's Cemetery in Bear Creek is clearly marked MONTE.

8.1.7.12.11   **MONTY/MONTE, Abraham Arthur** b 29 Aug 1891, Deer Creek, WI; d 12 Nov 1975, Texarkana, TX. He married (1) 17 Apr 1917, Bear Creek, WI, **Edna Llewella Tate** (William Tate & Elvira Terrell) b 2 Jul 1895, Bear Creek, WI; d & bur 15 & 21 Jan 1927, Wittenberg, TX & Clintonville, WI.

He married (2) and divorced **Irene Glover**.

He married (3) and divorced **Patricia Kirkpatrick** .

He married (4) **Beverly Mae Westerman** b 22 Oct 1908; d 5 Oct 1995, Huntsville, TX.

Abraham Arthur Monty was a hotel keeper in Bear Creek, WI, when he signed on 5 Jun 1917 his World War I Registration card. He lived there and in New London, WI, before moving to Wyoming and then to Hutchinson Co., TX, around 1926. His wife Edna was murdered during a robbery at the gas station which he operated in Wittenberg, TX (*Appleton Post Crescent*, 17, 20, 22, 28 Jan 1927). A. A. Monty returned to Texas after his wife's funeral. His surname there became Monte.

Child of the first marriage:

8.1.7.12.11.1	Ellis Joseph	1918-1937&	-2005

8.1.7.12.12   **MONTY, Mary Beulah** b 13 Jul 1893, Deer Creek, WI; d & bur 29 Sep & 1 Oct 1976, New London & Bear Creek, WI. She married 28 Jun 1911, Bear Creek, WI, **Carlton Richard Kempf** (August Kempf & Pauline Finger) b 21 Apr 1888, Maple Creek, WI; d 28 Mar 1964, New London, WI.

Carlton Kempf was a farmer in Deer Creek, WI, in 1920 and 1930 (US censuses). He, his wife, and their son August were buried in St. Mary's Cemetery in Bear Creek, WI.

Children:

i   **Donald Carlton Kempf** b 22 Apr 1913, Maple Creek, WI; d 15 Mar 1978, Bear Creek, WI. He married there 23 Nov 1937 **Helen Pearl Dempsey** (John M. Dempsey & Emma Welsch) b there Feb 1920.

ii   **Byron George Kempf** b 9 Jun 1918, Deer Creek, WI. He married (1) 30 May 1948, **Marian Schonthaler.**

       He was divorced when he married (2) **Earline Rush.**

iii   **August J. Kempf** b & d 28 Aug 1924, Outagamie Co., WI; bur 1924, Bear Creek, WI.

iv   **Hiram Albert Kempf** b 7 Jan 1928, Maple Creek, WI; d 27 Oct 1982, Los Angeles, CA. He married 25 Sep 1948 and divorced Nov 1971, Waupaca Co., WI, **Lulu Mae Christensen** b 1924?

8.1.7.12.13   **MONTY, Vivian Gertrude** b 29 Mar 1895, Deer Creek, WI; d 15 Apr 1919. She married 1 Jan 1918, WI, **George Humphrey.**

Vivian Monty was buried in St. Mary's Cemetery in Bear Creek, WI.

8.1.7.12.14   **MONTY, Adeline** b 25 Apr 1897, Deer Creek, WI; d 24 Jul 1980, Fond du Lac, WI. She married 1 Mar 1917, Shawano, WI, **John Constantine Rossey** (Constantine Rossey & Martha Fitzpatrick) b 8 Jun 1895, Royalton, WI; d 4 Aug 1978, Fond du Lac, WI.

The daughter of Joseph Monty and Mary Bricco who was born on 25 Apr 1897 is named Victoria in the Outagamie Co., WI, Register of Births. She was named Adeline however in all US and state censuses from 1900 on as well as at her marriage and death.

John C. Rossey was a machinist in Clintonville in 1917 and 1920 (US census). He and his wife were in Fond du Lac, WI, when they celebrated their 50th wedding anniversary (*Fond du Lac Commonwealth Reporter*, 6 Mar 1967). They were buried there in the Shrine of Rest Mausoleum.

Children:

i   **LaVerne Mary Rossey** b 17 Aug 1917, Shawano, WI; d & bur 1 & 5 Oct 2006, Fond du Lac, WI. She married 29 Feb 1932, Menominee, MI, **Leo Otto Reffke** (Gustav Albert Reffke & Lena I. Milheiser) b 25 Jan 1912, Appleton, WI; d 24 Sep 1991, Fond du Lac, WI.

ii   **Shirley Rossey** b 17 Dec 1920, Clintonville, WI; d & bur 14 & 21 Feb 1984, Milwaukee, WI. She married (1) 1937? **Jesse Gouley** (John Gouley & Margaret Benoit) b 18 Jun 1915, Marinette, WI; d 24 Aug 1998, Milwaukee, WI.

       She was divorced when she married (2) **Robert G. Kiebler** (____ Kiebler & Herena Podratz) b May 1923, WI.

iii   **Joseph Gustav Rossey** b 20 Jun 1924, Kaukauna, WI. He married (1) **Armella Losser.**

       He was divorced when he married (2) **Lorraine** ____ b Jan 1928.

iv   **John Rossey** b & d 13 Oct 1926, Appleton, WI.

v   **John James Rossey** b 17 Sep 1928, Appleton, WI; d 15 Apr 1981, Fond du Lac, WI. He married **Delores Schwartzburger.**

vi   **Eugene Edward/Gene E. Rossey** b 29 Nov 1930, Appleton, WI. He married **Margaret Effert** b Sep 1930.

8.1.7.12.15   **MONTY, Marie Antoinette** b 24 Aug 1899, Deer Creek, WI; d & bur 12 & ? Jun 1987, Oconto Falls & Bear Creek, WI. She married 27 Feb 1922, Milwaukee, WI, **Arthur J. Ziegelbauer** (John J. Ziegelbauer & Thecla F. Schaller) b there 1 Dec 1902; d & bur 2 & 5 Jan 1965, Appleton & Bear Creek, WI.

Arthur Ziegelbauer was a factory worker in Bear Creek, WI, in 1930 (US census) and the owner of an Auto Body Shop in Appleton, WI, at his death (*Oshkosh Daily Northwestern*, 4 Jan 1965). He and his wife were buried in St. Mary's Cemetery in Bear Creek, WI.

Children:

i   **Lila Mary Jane Ziegelbauer** b 13 May 1923, Bear Creek, WI; d 12 Aug 2007,

Oconto Falls, WI. She married 28 Aug 1943 **Lyle Edward Wolff** (Edward/Eddie Wolff & Gertrude Butters) b Jun 1923, WI.

ii   **Arthur John Ziegelbauer** b & d 1 Dec 1925, Bear Creek, WI.

8.3.1.3.1   **MONTY, Elizabeth** b May 1878, Whitehall, NY. She married 5 Sep 1898, Taftville, CT, **Noah D. Gauthier** (François Dasis Gauthier & Malvina Coderre) b & bp 24 & 25 Nov 1876, St. Césaire, QC.

Elizabeth Monty spent most of her youth in Roxton Pond, QC. She came back to the United States around 1897 and was staying with her husband Noel, a cotton mill comber, in her parents' home in Norwich, CT, in 1900 (US census).

Noah D. Gauthier (François Dasis Noé at his baptism) was known in the United States under several different names: Noel in the 1900 census, Noah in the census of 1910 when he was an overseer in a cotton mill in Plainfield, CT, Noah Dasis in his World War I Draft Registration card of 12 Sep 1918 when he was a plant foreman in Westbrook, ME, Noe or Noe D. in the Westbrook City Directories from 1919 through at least 1926, and Noah D. in those directories from 1934 through at least 1942.

Children:

i   **Hilda May Laure Gauthier** b 22 Oct 1901, Norwich, CT.

ii   **Stephanie L. Gauthier** b 1909?, Plainfield, CT. She married 14 Jun 1941, ME, **Anthony Palombo** (Joseph Palombo & Marie/Mary _____) b 24 Jul 1910, North Providence, RI; d Nov 1968.

8.3.1.3.2   **MONTY, Amelda/Amanda** b & bp 9 & 15 Feb 1880, Roxton Pond, QC. She married 21 Feb 1900, Taftville, CT, **Emules Dieudonné Letendre** (Peter Letendre & Udasie Obertin) b 4 May 1878, Sprague (Baltic Village), CT.

Amanda Monty (Clara Amanda at her baptism) arrived in the United States around 1897 and was staying with her husband in her father's household in Norwich, CT, in 1900. She had however married as Amelda Monty, which name is also found on her children's birth records and in the 1910, 1920, and 1930 censuses in Connecticut and Massachusetts. Mrs. Amelda Letendre, widow of Emules, was living in Gloucester, MA in 1951 (City Directory).

Emules Letendre was a silk mill worker in Norwich in 1900 and 1910, in Willimantic, CT, in 1920, and in New Bedford, MA, in 1930 (US censuses). When he signed his World War I Draft Registration card on 12 Sep 1918, however, he gave his occupation as "real estate."

Children:

i   **George Emules Letendre** b 3 Feb 1901, Taftville, CT; d 30 Aug 1985, Clearwater, FL. He married 1924? **Rose** _____ b 21 Sep 1901, MA; d 23 Jul 1982, Largo, FL.

ii   **Napoleon Oleas Clealand Letendre** b 29 Aug 1902, Taftville, CT; d 7 Jun 1966, San Francisco, CA.

iii   **Arzelia Amelda Letendre** b 14 Nov 1904, Taftville, CT.

iv   **Edwin Louis Letendre** b 18 May 1907, Taftville, CT; d 17 Jan 1996, Soulsbyville, CA.

8.3.1.3.3   **MONTY, Emma Louise** b & bp 9 & 12 Mar 1882, Roxton Pond, QC. She married 20 Aug 1901, Taftville, CT, **Frank Lamprey** (Joseph Lamprey & Mary White) b 1877?, Canada.

Emma Louise Monty arrived in the United States around 1897 and was living with her parents in Norwich, CT, in 1900 (US census). Her husband was a 24-year-old laborer there at his marriage. I have not found the couple in the United States after that time.

8.3.1.3.4   **MONTY, François Xavier Philippe Alfred** b & bp 1 & 3 Feb 1884, Roxton Pond, QC.

This child is not included among his parents' six surviving children in the 1900 US census in Norwich, CT, and probably died before then.

8.3.1.3.5 **MONTY, Adelina** b & bp 7 & 13 Dec 1885, Roxton Pond, QC; d & bur there 7 & 9 Oct 1886.

8.3.1.3.6 **MONTY, Georges Elphège** b & bp 10 & 16 Oct 1887, Roxton Pond, QC; d & bur there 19 & 21 May 1888.

8.3.1.3.7 **MONTY, Philip Adélard** b & bp 8 & 14 Jul 1889, Roxton Pond, QC; d 18 Feb 1975, Boston, MA. He married (1) around 1911 **Lucy/Lucelia Tarbox** (Edward David Tarbox & Lucy/Lucelia/Celia Lattimer) b Jan 1889, CT; m (2) 1927? William Loughborough (Evan S. Loughborough & Dorcas C. Whitford).

He married (2) 30 Jul 1924, Providence, RI, **Marion Dowdell** (James E. Dowdell & Lorinda Slayton) b 1 Oct 1890, Waltham, MA; d Mar 1969, Boston, MA.

Philip Monty (Adélard at his baptism) arrived in the United States around 1897 and was living with his parents in Norwich, CT, in 1900. He was a trainman staying with his widowed mother in Willimantic, CT, in 1920 while his wife Lucelia was staying with their three children in her own mother's household in Pawtucket, CT. The couple divorced soon after the birth of their fourth child. Philip Monty then moved to Massachusetts and was a janitor in Brookline, MA, in 1930 (US censuses).

Children of the first marriage:

8.3.1.3.7.1	Mary	1912?-	-
8.3.1.3.7.2	Mildred	1914?-	-
8.3.1.3.7.3	Stanley Edward	1918-1941-2002	
8.3.1.3.7.4	Ernestine	1922-	-

8.3.1.3.8 **MONTY, Rose Alba Priscilla** b & bp 17 Feb & 1 Mar 1891, Roxton Pond, QC; d & bur there 6 & 8 Oct 1891.

8.3.1.3.9 **MONTY, Anna/Eva Anastasia** b & bp 15 & 20 Apr 1892, Roxton Pond, QC. She married 29 May 1911, Baltic, CT, **Joseph Auguste Gadue** (Antoine Godhue/Gadue & Anastasie Gauthier) b 3 Dec 1872, QC; d 17 Aug 1963, Windham, CT.

This woman was named Marie Eva Anastasie at her baptism and Eva Anastasia at her marriage but was most commonly known in the United States, where she arrived around 1897, as Anna Monty (1900 and 1910 censuses in Norwich, CT) or Mrs. Anna Gadue (1920 census). She was then staying with her son, but without her husband, in her mother's household in Willimantic, CT.

Joseph Gadue was a laborer on his father's farm in Scotland, CT, in 1910 and a weaver in Willimantic when he signed on 12 Sep 1918 his World War I Draft Registration card. Mrs. Anna Gadue was his next-of-kin. They may have separated between then and 1920. His death record identifies him as the divorced husband of Mrs. Anna Gadue.

Child:

i **George Gadue** b 3 Jan 1916, CT; d 20 Oct 2001, Norwich, CT. He married **Bernadette Deslandes** (Pierre E. Deslandes & Marie Palmena Leblanc) b 21 Jul 1916, Baltic, CT; d 25 Jun 1995, Norwich, CT.

8.3.1.3.10 **MONTY, Rose Adeline** b & bp 24 Feb & 17 Mar 1894, Roxton Pond, QC.
Rose Monty came to the United States as a child and was living in her father's household in Norwich, CT, in 1900 and in Scotland, CT, in 1910 (US censuses).

8.3.8.1.1 **MONTY, Eugene Napoleon** b & bp 25 Jan & 27 Feb 1881, Sutton, QC; d between 1942 and 1948. He married 28 Mar 1904, Mansonville, QC, **Thankful Victoria Audette** (George W. Audette & Emily Cadorette) b 21 Dec 1883, Glen Sutton, QC; d 14 May 1973, Norwich, CT.

Eugene Monty (Eugène at his baptism; Eugene Napoleon at his marriage) was originally a farmer and carpenter in Mansonville, QC. He and his wife were married and his children were baptized in the Methodist Church there. He came to the United States with his family in August 1920 and was a building carpenter in Norwich, CT, until at least 1942 (1930 census; Norwich City Directories).

Mrs. Thankful Monty was a widow in 1948 (Norwich City Directory). She remained in the area and was a resident of Jewett City, CT, at her death.

Children:

8.3.8.1.1.1	Clayton Eugene	1905-	-1905
8.3.8.1.1.2	Bertha Amelia	1906-1929?-1980	
8.3.8.1.1.3	Melba Christina	1909-	-
8.3.8.1.1.4	Reginald Eugene	1911-	-1994

8.3.8.1.2   MONTY, Georgiana b & bp 5 Jul & 12 Aug 1883, Sutton, QC; d & bur there 29 & 31 Mar 1885.

8.3.8.1.3   MONTY, Louis/Lewis Joseph/Homer b & bp 29 Sep 1886 & 1 Nov 1891, Sutton, QC; d 30 May 1963, Norwich, CT. He married 1915? **Margaret Agnes McGrath** (John McGrath & Margaret Sullivan) b 5 Jun 1894, Dracut, MA; d 4 Jan 1983, Norwich, CT.

This man was known under a variety of names. He was Louis Joseph Monty at his baptism, Homer in the 1891 and 1901 Canadian censuses in Sutton, QC, as well as in the World War I Draft Registration card he signed in Sprague, CT, on 5 Jun 1917, Louis in the 1920 US census in Sprague, and Lewis the 1930 US census in Norwich, CT. He was naturalized there on 15 May 1934 as Lewis Joseph Monty (Certificate #4201) but signed his World War II Draft Registration card in 1942 as Louis Joseph Monty. On the other hand, the Norwich City Directories from 1936 through 1951 refer to Homer Monty, as do the Connecticut Death Records and the Social Security Death Index for both him and his wife. Since both Louis/Lewis Monty and Homer Monty were born the same day in the same Canadian village, had a wife named Margaret who had been born in Massachusetts in 1894, and had similarly-named children of the same age, it seems clear that both names refer to the same man.

Louis Joseph/Homer Monty arrived in the United States in 1905 and was a carpenter in Versailles, CT, in 1917, in Sprague in 1920, and in Norwich in 1930, when he and his wife had been married for fifteen years (US censuses). He was still a carpenter there in 1936 but a contractor in 1951 (City Directories).

Children:

8.3.8.1.3.1	Ruth M.	1916-	-1982
8.3.8.1.3.2	Louis Eugene	1919-	-
8.3.8.1.3.3	Dorothea	1927-	-
8.3.8.1.3.4	Barbara E.	1930-1951-	

8.3.8.1.4   MONTY, Arthur/Henri William b & bp 31 Jan 1889 & 1 Nov 1891, Sutton, QC.

This man was baptized as Henri William Monty. He was nevertheless named Arthur when he was living with his parents in Sutton, QC, in 1891 and 1901 (Canadian censuses) as well as in 1910 and 1920 when he was living in the household of his uncle Charles Monty (8.3.8.5) in Plainfield, CT. He had arrived in the United States in 1903 and was a mill worker there (US censuses). I have been unable to find him in later years.

8.3.8.1.5   MONTY, Charles b & bp 28 & 29 Oct 1891, Sutton QC.

Charles Monty's parents, according to his baptismal record in Sutton, QC, were Charles Monty and Marie Comeau. In fact Charles Monty's wife was Joséphine Comeau (8.3.8.5) who had given birth to a daughter in May 1891 and could not be the mother of another child born five months later. Marie Comeau was the wife of Jean-Baptiste Monty (8.3.8.1) who must be the true father. The scribe's error is perhaps understandable: eight cousins of various ages from five related families were baptized in Sutton on 29 Oct and 1 Nov 1891.

Charles Monty may have died before the date of the 1901 Canadian census: he was not living then with either set of possible parents.

8.3.8.1.6　　　　**MONTY, John A./Joseph Amédée** b & bp 11 Sep & 18 Nov 1892, Sutton, QC; d 26 Dec 1955, Norwich, CT. He married 1913? **Jessie Weir Goodfellow** (Robert Weir Goodfellow & Maud Adelia Tarrant) b 28 Jul 1893, Hinchinbrooke Twp, Ontario, Canada; d 2 Jun 1991, New London, CT.

The child baptized as Joseph Amédée Monty was named simply Joseph when he was living with his parents in Sutton, QC, in 1901 (Canadian census). He arrived in the United States around 1908 and was known as "Meddie John" when he was a cotton mill worker living in the household of his uncle Charles Monty (8.3.8.5) in Plainfield, CT, in 1910. He signed his World War I Draft Registration card on 5 Jun 1917, however, as John A. Monty and continued to be known under that name. He was a carpenter in Versailles, CT, in 1917, in Sprague, CT, in 1920, and in New London, CT., in 1930, when he and his wife and been married for sixteen years (US censuses). The couple later divorced and while John A. Monty and his children continued to use the surname Monty, his former wife was known at her death as Mrs. Jessie W. Montie, divorced wife of John Montie.

Children:

8.3.8.1.6.1	John W.	1914-	-1999
8.3.8.1.6.2	Douglas A.	1917-	-1917
8.3.8.1.6.3	Marian Elizabeth	1920-1942-1995	

8.3.8.1.7　　　　**MONTY/MONTE, George Omer/Homer** b & bp 4 Sep & 10 Oct 1894, Sutton, QC.

George Monty (George Omer at his baptism) was living with his parents in Sutton, QC, in 1901 (Canadian census). He was a single man, unemployed, when he signed as George Homer Monte his World War I Draft Registration card in New London Co., CT, on 5 Jun 1917. I know nothing more about him.

8.3.8.5.1　　　　**MONTY, Cordelia** b & bp 23 & 25 Mar 1886, Sutton, QC; d 6 May 1950, Griswold, CT. She married 23 May 1903, Norwich, CT, a second cousin, **George Clément Gaudreau** (Michel Gaudreau & Marie Louise Monty [8.3.1.6]) b & bp 13 & 14 Sep 1882, Roxton Falls, QC.

Cordelia Monty (Félicité Cordélia at her baptism) came to Connecticut with her parents in 1902 or 1903, shortly before her marriage. Her husband was a cotton mill worker in Norwich, CT, at his marriage and at the births of his children, and a farmer in Scotland, CT, in 1920 (US census). He predeceased his wife.

Children:

i　　**George Ovila Gaudreau** b 22 Jun 1904, Taftville, CT.

ii　　**Rose A. Gaudreau** b 8 Nov 1905, Occum, CT; d 21 May 1996, Manchester, CT. She married **Albert Riquier** b 4 Feb 1911, CT; d 23 Aug 1994, Windham, CT.

iii　　**Marie Gaudreau** b & d 21 Nov 1906, Taftville, CT.

iv　　**Joseph Gaudreau** b & d 23 Jul 1910, Norwich, CT.

v　　**Helen Gaudreau** b 9 Sep 1911, Taftville, CT; d & bur 12 & 18 Sep 2000, Sun City Center, FL & Windham, CT. She married **William Segal**.

vi　　**Louise M. Gaudreau** b Aug 1915, Scotland, CT.

vii　　**Dorothy Jeanette Gaudreau** b 23 Apr 1918, Willimantic, CT; d & bur 20 & 23 Jun 2005, Middletown & Griswold, CT. She married **George E. Barr** (Eusebe Barr & Emily ____) b 21 Feb 1914, Windham Co., CT; d 18 May 1968, Griswold, CT.

viii　　**Blanche A. Gaudreau** b 11 Dec 1920, Scotland, CT; d 2 Oct 2000, Norwich, CT. She married **Matthew Straub** (Frank Straub & Anna ____) b 27 Apr 1920, Wallingford, CT; d 12 Jan 2000, Norwich, CT.

ix　　**Wilfred A. Gaudreau** b 11 Dec 1924, CT; d 21 Aug 2001, Putnam, CT. He married 14 Jun 1981, Mansfield, CT, **Aleta March**.

8.3.8.5.2   **MONTY, Charles Edward/Edouard** b & bp 27 Feb & 19 Mar 1888, Sutton, QC; d 26 Jul 1966, Norwich, CT. He married 1914? **Philomène/Phoebe Véronneau** (François Xavier/Frank Véronneau & Célina/Salina Boulanger) b & bp 3 & 4 Jul 1894, Upton, QC; d 29 Jan 1965, Plainfield, CT.

Charles Edouard Monty came to the United States with his parents around 1902 and was a resident of Plainfield, CT, when he was naturalized in Windham Co., CT, on 13 May 1914 as Charles Edward Monty (Certificate #131). He was a weaver in a cotton mill in Plainfield in 1910, a prison guard in Wethersfield, CT, in 1920, and a cotton mill weaver in Plainfield again in 1930, when he and his wife had been married for sixteen years (US censuses). He was still a resident there at his death.

Philomène Véronneau came to the United States with her parents in 1897 and was known henceforth as Phoebe. She was naturalized in 1913.

Children:

8.3.8.5.2.1	Blanche	1915-	-1974
8.3.8.5.2.2	Joseph Armand	1918-1945&1977-2006	
8.3.8.5.2.3	Albert Charles	1921-1944?-2005	
8.3.8.5.2.4	Jeannette I.	1927-	-

8.3.8.5.3   **MONTY, George** b & bp 7 Mar & 27 Apr 1890, Sutton, QC; d 17 Feb 1958, Preston, CT. He married 1911? **Della** ____ b 1891?, QC.

George Monty's baptismal record of 17 Apr 1890 in St. André Church in Sutton, QC shows that he was born on 7 Mar 1890: "né le sept mars dernier." According to the 1901 Canadian census in Sutton, though, he was born on 23 Feb 1890. The "Record of births outside the United States" in the Norwich, CT, Vital Records then mentioned on 7 Mar 1903 a third date: George Monty, son of Charles Monty and Josephine Comeau, was born in Canada on 23 Dec 1889. None of these dates can be corroborated. I am relying here on the earliest record.

George O. Monty was a machinist living in Killingly, CT, with a wife and two children in 1917 (World War I Draft Registration card). A few years later, on 1 Jan 1920, when his wife Della was 28 years old, he was a machinist in Willimantic, CT. But by 1930, although they had been married for nineteen years, and were still married, they were living apart. He was a garage mechanic in Willimantic while she was an attendant in the Norwich State Hospital in Preston, CT. The children were with neither parent (US censuses).

George Monty moved to Massachusetts during the 1930s and was a foundry worker in Holyoke, MA, when he signed his World War II Draft Registration card in 1942. Since he then named as the person who would always be aware of his whereabouts his daughter Mrs. Beulah Capistrant, it would appear his wife was not with him. He was in any event divorced at his death when he was a resident of Windham, CT.

Children:

8.3.8.5.3.1	Roland	1913?-	-
8.3.8.5.3.2	Beulah A.	1914-1930?-1995	
8.3.8.5.3.3	David E.	1921-	-1996

8.3.8.5.4   **MONTY, Joséphine** b & bp 3 May & 1 Nov 1891, Sutton, QC; d between 1918 and 1930. She married 1911? **John Samuel Hollingworth** (____ Hollingworth & Mary ____) b 9 Feb 1888, Lonsdale, RI.

Joséphine Monty came to the United States with her parents in 1902 or 1903 and was living with them in Plainfield, CT, in 1910. All her children were born in Connecticut though her husband signed his World War I Draft Registration card on 5 Jun 1917 from North Oxford, MA, where he was a weaver. In 1930 John S. Hollingworth was a widower living with his three oldest children next door to his father-in-law in Plainfield,. His youngest child, Yvonne, was living with her maternal grandparents (US censuses).

Children:

i   **Beatrice Hollingworth** b 1912?, CT.
ii   **Blanche Hollingworth** b 1913?, CT.
iii **Samuel Hollingworth** b 1916?, CT.
iv **Yvonne Hollingworth** b 1918?, CT.

8.3.8.5.5   **MONTY, Dona/Donat/Robert** b & bp 10 Feb & 11 Mar 1894, Sutton, QC; d 1 Jun 1959, Putnam, CT. He married (1) **Minnie** ____ b 1895?, CT.

He married (2) **Lucy** ____.

This man's name alternates between Donat/Dona and Robert in both Canadian and American records. He was baptized as Donat Monty but named Robert in the 1901 Canadian census in Sutton, QC, where he was living with his parents. He came to the United States with them in 1902/1903 and was again named Robert in the 1910 US census in Plainfield, CT. Yet he signed his World War I Draft Registration card in Plainfield on 5 Jun 1917 as Dona Monty. He was also named Dona in the 1 Jan 1920 US census there, when his wife Minnie was 24 years old, and in his death record in Windham Co., CT. His deceased wife was named Lucy. I know nothing more about either of these women.

8.3.8.5.6   **MONTY, Arthur Ovila** b & bp 2 & 9 May 1897, Sutton, QC; d 9 Jun 1966, Augusta, ME.

Arthur Ovila Monty came to the United States with his parents in 1902 or 1903 and was a carder in a cotton mill in Plainfield, CT, in 1920. He was a resident of Moosup, CT, when he was naturalized on 17 Sep 1926 (Certificate #1168) and a cotton mill operative in New Bedford, MA, in 1930 (US censuses). He was a resident of Lisbon Falls, ME, at his death.

8.3.8.5.7   **MONTY, Yvonne Alida** b & bp 15 & 17 Sep 1899, Sutton, QC; d 20 Jan 1987, Plainfield, CT. She married 1919? **Joseph Alfred Piche** (Jeremiah/ Jerry Piche & Delia ____) b 10 Feb 1892, Moosup, CT; d 19 Sep 1975, Preston, CT.

Yvonne Monty (often Evon or Ivonne in US censuses) arrived in the United States with her parents in 1902 or 1903 and was naturalized in 1919. She and her husband, a textile worker in Plainfield, CT, had been married for eleven years in 1930 (US census) and were still residents there at their deaths.

Children:

i   **Rita Piche** b 1921?, Plainfield, CT.
ii   **Alida Piche** b 1924?, Plainfield, CT.

8.3.8.7.1   **MONTY, Henry John B.** b & bp 25 Dec 1889 & 29 Oct 1891, Montgomery, VT & Sutton, QC; d 21 Jul 1985, Norwich, CT.

Henry Monty was living with his parents in Sutton, QC, in 1901 (Canadian census) and returned with them to the United States in 1902 or 1903. He was with them in Scotland, CT, in 1910 and was a farm laborer/operator on his father's farm in Plainfield, CT, in 1920 and 1930 (US censuses). He was a farmer there until his death. He did not marry.

8.3.8.7.2   **MONTY, Philippe** b & bp 16 Feb & 11 Jun 1893, Richford, VT & Sutton, QC; d & bur 26 & 28 Jun 1893, Sutton, QC.

8.3.8.7.3   **MONTY, Joseph Eusèbe** b & bp 27 Jan & 7 Feb 1895, Richford, VT & Sutton, QC; d 25 Aug 1981, Norwich, CT.

Joseph Monty was living with his parents in Sutton, QC, in 1901 (Canadian census) and returned with them to the United States in 1902 or 1903. He was a member of his father's household in Scotland, CT, in 1910 and a farm operator on his father's farm in Plainfield, CT, in 1930 (US censuses). He was a farmer there until his death. He did not marry.

8.3.8.7.4   **MONTY, Napoléon** b & bp 25 Jul & 15 Aug 1897, Richford, VT & Sutton, QC.

Napoléon Monty was not with his parents in Sutton, QC, in 1901 (Canadian census) nor in later US censuses. He may have died in infancy.

8.3.8.7.5 **MONTY, François/Francis** b & bp 2 & 6 Aug 1899, Richford, VT & Sutton, QC; d 28 Jan 1903, Norwich, CT.

8.3.8.7.6 **MONTY, Rose** b & bp 20 Feb & 6 Apr 1902, Sutton, QC; d 18 Jan 1983, Norwich, CT. She married (1) 1923? **Daniel Downing**.

She married (2) 1928? **Edward T. Gadue** (Joseph Stanislas Taniste Gadue & Georgiana Mae Dubois) b Aug 1908, Scotland, CT.

Rose Monty was 19 years old at her first marriage. She and her second husband, Edward Gadue, had been married for two years in 1930 when he was a fireman in the State hospital in Plainfield, CT (US census).

Children:
  i   **Mary Elizabeth/Betty Downing** b 17 Nov 1925, Plainfield, CT; d & bur 7 & 9 Sep 2005, Salem & Preston, CT. She married (1) **Nathan T. Pell**.
    She married (2) **Richard L. Hardegen** b 31 Mar 1915; d 24 Mar 1978, Norwich, CT.
  ii   **Edward F. Gadue** b 15 May 1929, Norwich, CT; d 26 Feb 2005, Putnam, CT. He married 1952? **Grace M. Duquette**.
  iii   **Charles Henry Gadue** b 29 Dec 1932, Norwich, CT; d 17 May 2007, Arcadia, FL. He married **Ellen A. _____** b Feb 1943.
  iv   **Rose Marie Gadue** b Aug 1940, CT. She married **Rudolph Desjarlais** (Rudolph Desjarlais & Louise A. Cadieux) b Mar 1938.

8.3.8.7.7 **MONTY, Julia C.** b 29 Apr 1908, Scotland, CT; d 29 Jul 1987, Plainfield, CT. She married **Franklyn W. McWay** (Henry Christopher McWay & Hazel Bragg) b 11 Feb 1907, Worcester Co., MA; m (1) 1929? Cecilia _____; d 6 Jan 1985, Norwich, CT.

Franklyn McWay was a paper mill worker in Sterling, CT, in 1930. He and his 18-year-old wife Cecilia, who had been born in New York State of parents born in Italy and Germany, had a 5-month old son Franklyn (US census). That son could not be, as some would have it, a child of Julia C. Monty.

8.3.8.8.1 **MONTY, William** b 30 Mar 1906, Scotland, CT; d there 8 Mar 1983.

William Monty worked on his father's farm in Scotland, CT, in 1930 (US census) and was still a poultry farmer there at his death. He did not marry.

8.3.8.8.2 **MONTY, Phyllis** b 30 Mar 1909, Scotland, CT; d 20 Feb 1979, Windham Co., CT.

Philiset (sic) A. Monty was living with her parents in Scotland, CT, in 1920. This may well be a scribe's fanciful phonetic rendering of Félicité. She was named Phyllis Monty when she was a mill worker, still single, in Willimantic, CT, in 1930 (US census).

8.3.8.8.3 **MONTY, Mary A.** b 4 Oct 1910, Scotland, CT; d 8 Jul 1981, Hartford, CT. She married **Harold S. Sprague** (Elijah Sprague & Anna M. _____) b 11 Sep 1906, Green Cove Springs, FL; m (2) 27 Aug 1983, Manchester, CT, Estelle Virginia (Tony Virginia & Isabella _____), widow of Howard Lappen; d there 2 Oct 1995.

Harold Sprague was a life insurance agent in Meriden, CT, in 1930 (US census) and for many years in Manchester, CT. He was a Navy veteran of World War II (Hartford *Courant*, 4 Oct 1995).

Child:
  i   **Nelson J. Sprague** b May 1935, CT. He married Cosette _____ b 1937?

8.3.8.8.4   **MONTY, George Edward** b 13 Sep 1912, Scotland, CT.

George E. Monty was a laborer on his father's farm in Scotland, CT, in 1930 (US census) but an automobile serviceman when he enlisted in the US Army in Hartford, CT, on 5 May 1942. He was single (World War II Army Enlistment Records).

8.3.8.8.5   **MONTY, Henry M.** b 20 Jul 1914, Scotland, CT; d 6 Nov 1977, Manchester, CT. He married **Lucy Peila** (Martin Peila & Giovanna _____) b 17 Jan 1921, Manchester, CT; d & bur 5 & 9 Jan 2001, East Hartford & Manchester, CT.

Henry Monty was living on his father's farm in Scotland, CT, in 1930 (US census) but was a meat cutter in Manchester, CT, in the 1950s and 1960s (City Directories). His wife Lucy was buried in St. James Cemetery there.

Children:

8.3.8.8.5.1	Eugene H.	1951-	-
8.3.8.8.5.2	George M.	1955-	-

8.3.8.8.6   **MONTY, Josephine R.** b Feb 1918, Scotland, CT.

Josephine R. Monty was 1 year and 10 months old on 1 Jan 1920 when she was living on her father's farm in Scotland, CT. She was also living there in 1930 (US censuses).

8.3.8.9.1   **MONTY/MONTIE, Marie Félicité** b & bp 1 & 26 Jan 1894, Sutton, QC; d 30 Jan 1979, Euclid, OH. She married 19 Aug 1914, Norwich, CT, **Joseph A. Lede** (Emmanuel Lede & ____ Gray) b 1884?, St. Bartholomew, French West Indies; d 1 Feb 1962, Norwich, CT, at the age of 77.

This woman was known under a variety of names and surnames. She was Marie Félicité Monty at her baptism, Philisse Monte in the 1901 Canadian census in Sutton, QC, Phelisse Monty in the 1910 US census in Norwich, CT, and Marie P. Montie at her marriage. As a married woman she was Marie or M. Felicite Lede in the censuses of 1920 and 1930 in New London, CT, though Phyllis M., Felicite M., M. F. Phyllis, M. F. Philiset, etc. in the City Directories of New London and Revere, MA, where the family resided for a time.

Joseph Lede arrived in the United States in 1900 and was naturalized in Norwich on 4 June 1914. He was a seaman at his marriage, a US Navy Signal Quartermaster when a child was born in 1917, and a chief petty officer in the US Coast Guard in 1920 and 1930 (US censuses). He made his career in the Coast Guard and was most often stationed in New London, with occasional postings in Massachusetts and New York.

Children:

   i   **Joseph Henry Lede** b 1 Jun 1915, Norwich, CT; d Jun 1972.

   ii   **Faith Elizabeth Félicité Lede** b 3 May 1917, Norwich, CT; d 30 Nov 1999, Hudson, OH. She married ____ **Lucas**.

8.3.8.9.2   **MONTY/MONTIE, Josephine Bridget** b & bp 1 Dec 1894 & 7 Apr 1895 Sutton, QC. She married 4 Sep 1914, Norwich, CT, **Clarence Lougee Fowler** (Lyman George Fowler & Eva I. Patterson) b 11 Sep 1891, Hampden, ME; d 9 Jun 1982, Bangor, ME.

Josephine Bridget Monty's date and place of birth are taken from her baptismal record in Sutton, QC. According to her marriage record however she was born in Richmond, VT. There is no confirmation though in the Vermont Vital Records.

Her name and surname vary. She was Brigitte Monty at her baptism, Bridget Monte in the 1901 Canadian census in Sutton, QC, Bridget Monty in the 1910 US census in Norwich, CT, Josephine B. Montie at her marriage, Bridget J. Monte at the birth of her first child, and Mrs. Josephine Fowler in the 1920 and 1930 US censuses in Bangor, ME and Norwich, CT.

Clarence L. Fowler was a paper mill worker in Norwich at his marriage. The family stayed there until at least June 1917 when he signed his World War I Draft Registration card. A few months later, though, a child was born in Bangor, ME. Clarence Fowler was a paper mill worker there in 1920. He and his wife apparently separated in the mid or late 1920s. By 1930 Mrs. Josephine Fowler was living with her sister Rose (8.3.8.9.5) in Norwich and had a job there as a tabulator in a bottle factory. Her husband, a Railroad employee, was staying with his children in his father's household in Hamden, ME (US censuses).

Children:
i   **Henry Lyman Fowler** b 29 Mar 1915, Norwich, CT; d 9 Aug 1979, Bangor, ME. He married there 28 Jun 1946 **Florence V. Gerrish** m (2) there 18 Apr 1981 Linwood M. Moon (Everett H. Moon & Olive E. Phillips).

ii   **Iola Fowler** b Sep 1917, Bangor, ME.

iii **Pearl Fowler** b 18 Dec 1919, Bangor, ME; d there 8 Jan 1985. She married there 11 Jun 1938 **Warren L. Hurd** (Oakman Rooks Hurd & Iva Collins) b there 8 Dec 1916; d 4 Jan 2002, Holden, ME.

iv **Melvin C. Fowler** b 6 Nov 1921, Bangor, ME; d there 9 Dec 2004. He married there 10 May 1947 **Phyllis L. Ramsey** (Charles L. Ramsey & Vernie B. Worcester) b there Feb 1928.

8.3.8.9.3   **MONTY/MONTIE, Henry George** b & bp 1 Jan & 15 Mar 1896, Sutton, QC; d 22 Nov 1971, Norwich, CT. He married 1919? **Agnes V. McDermott** (Michael McDermott & Bridget ____) b 1895?, CT; d 17 Sep 1971, Norwich, CT, at the age of 76.

This man was baptized as Henry Télesphore George Monty but was known as Henry Monte in the 1901 Canadian census in Sutton, QC, and as Henry, Henry G., or Henry George Montie in the United States. He came to Norwich, CT, with his parents in the early 1900s and remained there until his death. He was a machinist in a paper mill in 1920, a building contractor in 1930 (US censuses), and a carpenter from at least 1933 on (Norwich City Directories).

8.3.8.9.4   **MONTY/MONTIE, Esther** b & bp 20 Nov & 26 Dec 1897, Sutton, QC; d 3 Dec 1915, Norwich, CT.

Esther Monte (Esther Monty at her baptism) was living with her parents in Sutton, QC, in 1901 (Canadian census). She came to Norwich, CT, with them in the early 1900s and was known in the 1910 census there as Esther Monty. She was buried in St. Joseph's Cemetery in Norwich however as Esther Montie.

8.3.8.9.5   **MONTY, Rose Anna** b & bp 29 Jan & 12 Feb 1901, Sutton, QC; d 27 Sep 1991, Putnam, CT. She married 1919 **Amédée/Amédé Joseph Lusignan** (Pierre/Peter Lusignan & Marie Louise Rousseau) b & bp 25 & 26 Feb 1898, Sutton, QC.

Rose Monty came to the United States with her parents around 1902 and was living with them in Norwich, CT, in 1910 (US census). It is probably there that she married Amédée Lusignan (Eddéas Amédé Ovila at his baptism) who had also come to the United States as a child with his parents. He was a carpenter in Uncasville, CT, and still single when he signed his World Ward Draft Registration card in New London, CT, on 12 Sep 1918. Two years later he was a married salesman in Montville, CT, and in 1930 a carpenter in Norwich. He and his wife had then been married for eleven years (US censuses). He predeceased his wife.

Child:
i   **Eunice Lusignan** b 1921?, New London Co., CT.

8.3.8.9.6   **MONTY/MONTIE, Cecilia** b 22 Jun 1906, Norwich, CT; d there 4 Mar 1986. She married **Earl Kibbe.**

Mrs. Cecilia (Montie) Kibbe survived her husband.

8.3.8.9.7   **MONTIE, William George** b 15 May 1910, Occum, CT; d 27 Jun 1993, Norwich, CT. He married **Marie ____.**

William Montie was a building carpenter in Norwich, CT, in 1930 when he was living with his sister Marie Félicité (8.3.8.9.1) and brother-in-law Joseph Lede (US census). He was also described as a carpenter at his death.

8.3.8.9.8   **MONTIE, Frances Faith** b 4 Aug 1914, Norwich, CT.

Frances Faith Montie was living with her parents in Norwich, CT, in 1920 and in Killingly, CT, in 1930 (US censuses). She was a clerk in Norwich in 1936 (City Directory).

8.3.11.5.1 **MONTY, Armosa/Harmosa** b 12 Dec 1887, New Bedford, MA; d there 15 Jul 1964. She married there 5 Aug 1907 **Arthur Ostiguy** (Honoré Ostiguy & Clarinda Barré) b & bp 30 & 31 Dec 1884, Richelieu, QC.
This woman was named Marie Armosa at her birth and Armosa at her marriage but Harmosa in many other records. Her tombstone in the Old Sacred Heart Cemetery in New Bedford, MA, where she was buried alongside her parents, also bears the name Harmosa.
Arthur Ostiguy (François Arthur at his baptism) arrived in the United States around 1904. He was a rigger in a shipyard in New Bedford, MA, in 1920 and a laborer for a wrecking company there in 1930 (US censuses). He was still living there in retirement in 1955 (City Directories).

Children:

i   **Raymond Ostiguy** b 16 May 1908, New Bedford, MA; d & bur 30 Aug & 5 Sep 1996, Meridien, MS & New Bedford, MA. He married **Cécile Lajoie** (Alphonse Lajoie & Joséphine Deschênes) b & bp 1 & 2 Oct 1913, Kamouraska, QC; d 6 Mar 1982, New Bedford, MA.

ii   **Lucy Blanche Ostiguy** b 2 Jul 1909, New Bedford, MA; d there 15 Jun 2000. She married **Edward H. Riendeau** (Théophile Riendeau & Delphine ____) b 16 Dec 1909, Fall River, MA; d Mar 1971.

iii **Wilfred L. Ostiguy** b Jun 1912, New Bedford, MA. He married there 1938? **Annie Taylor** (James Taylor & Molly Brown) b there 11 Nov 1913; d there 31 May 2005.

iv   **Norman Ostiguy** b 12 May 1917, New Bedford, MA; d there 18 Sep 1976. He married **Gilberte Marie Guenette** (Benjamin A. Guenette & Marie A. Laferrière) b 14 Sep 1918, New Bedford, MA; d there 24 Apr 1980.

v   **Rita F. Ostiguy** b Apr 1919, New Bedford, MA. She married there 1941 **Albert L. Deneault** (Serveul Deneault & Laura Dragon) b there 25 Jan 1914; d there 13 Apr 2003.

vi   **Anna Ostiguy** b Nov 1922, New Bedford, MA. She married **Alfred W. Dube** (Zéphirin Dube & Flora ____) b 2 Dec 1929, New Bedford, MA; d there 17 Jul 1998.

8.3.11.5.2 **MONTY, Almo** b 1 Apr 1889, New Bedford, MA; d there 23 Jul 1904.

8.3.11.5.3 **MONTY, Hector Louis** b 16 Jul 1890, New Bedford, MA. He married there 1922? **Eugenia Gagne** b 12 Oct 1898, MA; m (1) 1915? Arsène Durand (Arsène Durand & Mary____); d 6 Dec 1992, East Windsor, CT.
This man was occasionally known as Louis or Louis H. Monty but more often as Hector Monty. He was a teamster in New Bedford, MA, in 1910, a chauffeur there in 1920 when he was staying with his sister Blanche (8.3.11.5.4) and brother-in-law Wilfred Metthe, and a truck driver there in 1930, when he and wife had then been married for eight years (US censuses). The New Bedford City Directories show that Hector Monty was a truck driver there until at least 1943. His wife, "Eugenia Monty (Mrs. Hector)" was then the proprietor of the Plymouth Hotel in New Bedford and continued to be listed as the proprietor until at least 1949. By 1955 the hotel was under new ownership. At her death, the widowed Mrs. Eugenia Monty was a hotel owner in East Hartford, CT.

8.3.11.5.4 **MONTY, Blanche Y.** b 23 Nov 1894, New Bedford, MA; d there 9 Sep 1977. She married there 10 Jan 1914 **Wilfred Metthe** (David Metthe & Médérise Boivin) b there 2 Mar 1891.
Wilfred Metthe was a cotton mill worker in New Bedford, MA, in 1920 when his brother-in-law Hector Monty (8.3.8.5.3) was a member of his household. He was a salesman in 1930 (US censuses). He and his wife were still living there in 1955 (City Directories).

Children:

i   **Gerald D. Metthe** b 30 Nov 1914, New Bedford, MA; d there 29 Sep 1994. He married **Theresa C. _____** b Dec 1923.

ii   **Doris Metthe** b Feb 1919, New Bedford, MA.

8.3.11.6.1   MONTY, Philip b 3 Feb 1881, New Bedford, MA. He married there 6 Sep 1916 **Agnes Anna Maguire/McGuire** (Francis McGuire & Margaret Ann Druhan) b 1886?, Nova Scotia, Canada.

Philip Monty was a barber in New Bedford, MA, until at least 1940 and in Fairhaven, MA, from 1941 to at least 1949. Anna Maguire, who was 30 years old at her marriage, was later known as Mrs. Agnes or Agnes A. Monty (US censuses; City Directories).

8.3.11.6.2   MONTY, Marie Azilda b 28 Oct 1883, New Bedford, MA; d there 5 Nov 1949. She married there 19 Jun 1916 **John Thomas Sloane** (Arthur Sloane & Ann Gannon) b 13 Sep 1876, Darlington, England; d 14 May 1931, New Bedford, MA.

John Thomas Sloane arrived in the United States around 1890 and was naturalized in 1912. He was a merchant in New Bedford, MA, in 1918 and 1920 and a brick layer there in 1930 (World War I Draft Registration card; US censuses).

Child:

i   **Estelle Azilda Sloane** b 23 Oct 1918, South Dartmouth, MA. She married **Lester C. Smith** (Michael Thomas Smith & Delia Curley) b 23 Mar 1914, Gloucester, MA; d 11 Jan 2003, New Bedford, MA.

8.3.11.6.3   MONTY, William Wilfred b 31 Jan 1885, New Bedford, MA; d & bur there 20 & 24 Jul 1961. He married (1) 1903? **Julie Benoit** (William Benoit & Nathalie Gemme) b & bp 27 & 28 Feb 1880, Marieville, QC; d 7 Jun 1925, New Bedford, MA.

He married (2) 1926, New Bedford, MA, **Laura Roy** (Napoléon Roy & Malvina ___) b 6 Jul 1892, Waterbury, CT; d Dec 1967, New Bedford, MA.

William W. Monty (Wilfred Guillaume at his birth) was a cotton mill worker in New Bedford, MA, in 1910 when he and his first wife Julie had been married for seven years. He was also a cotton mill worker there in 1920 but the owner of a barber shop there in 1930. He and his second wife had then been married for four years (US censuses). He was buried in New Bedford's Sacred Heart Cemetery.

Children of the first marriage:

8.3.11.6.3.1	Elzéar Wilfred	1904-1927-1955
8.3.11.6.3.2	Lauretta/Laurette	1906- -1996
8.3.11.6.3.3	Jeannette	1910-1928-1999
8.3.11.6.3.4	Georgette	1913- -1994
8.3.11.6.3.5	Agnes Marie	1916-1935-2001
8.3.11.6.3.6	Joseph Adrien/Adrian	1919- -2004
8.3.11.6.3.7	Cora	1921-1941?-1994
8.3.11.6.3.8	Ernest W.	1923-1942?-1998

Children of the second marriage:

8.3.11.6.3.9	Linette T.	1928- -1983
8.3.11.6.3.10	Maurice A.	1932- -1980
8.3.11.6.3.11	Lionel/Leonel A.	1933- -

8.3.11.6.4   MONTY, Malvina A. b 19 Oct 1886, New Bedford, MA; d there 26 Feb 1887.

8.3.11.6.5   MONTY, Alphonse b 15 May 1888, New Bedford, MA; d there 3 Aug 1888.

8.3.11.6.6   MONTY, Bertha/Berthe Arthémise b 30 Sep 1891, New Bedford, MA.

She married there 1 Sep 1913 **Alfred David Frigault** (Octave Frigault & Celina Chartier) b 26 Sep 1890, Taftville, CT; d 1958 at the age of 68.

This woman was named Berthe Arthémise at her birth but was generally known as an adult as Bertha. Her husband Alfred Frigault (also Frégeault) was a salesman in New Bedford, MA, in 1920 and a grocer there in 1930 (US censuses).

Children:

i   **Marie Rose Simone Frigault** b 20 Apr 1916, New Bedford, MA; d there 23 Feb 1978. She married **Francis E. Mahoney** (____ Mahoney & Anne I. ____) b 17 Feb 1910, New Bedford, MA; d there 5 Mar 1978.

ii   **Normand Alfred Frigault** b 15 May 1920, New Bedford, MA; d 11 Sep 1982, Fall River, MA. He married **Louise Pimental** (John Pimental & Mary ____) b 19 Aug 1924, Bristol Co., MA.

iii **Roger George Frigault** b 1 Sep 1922, New Bedford, MA; d 1 Mar 1994, Pompano Beach, FL. He married 1948? **Lucille Dion** (Theodore Dion & Odélie/Odélide Champagne) b 28 Oct 1924, Lawrence, MA.

iv   **Therese Bertha Frigault** b 1 Dec 1928, New Bedford, MA; d 15 Jul 2005, Manchester, CT. She married 1951? **Robert Granger** (Jean L. Granger & Emelda ____) b Jan 1930, New Bedford, MA.

8.3.11.6.7   **MONTY, Billian** b Feb 1896, New Bedford, MA; d between 1900 and 1910.

This child was living with her parents in New Bedford, MA, in 1900 but was not included in 1910 among her parents' five surviving children (US censuses).

8.3.11.6.8   **MONTY, Arthur J.** b 1902?, New Bedford, MA. He married there 1929 **Mary E. Shevlin** (James Shevlin & Elizabeth ____) b 1894?, MA.

Arthur Monty, a cotton mill worker in New Bedford, MA, was 17 years old on 1 Jan 1920. In 1930, when he and his 36-year-old wife had been married for one year, he was a garage mechanic there (US censuses).

8.3.11.7.1   **MONTY, Anonymous** b & d 27 Jul 1889, New Bedford, MA.

8.3.11.7.2   **MONTY, Lillian Josephine** b 16 Aug 1890, Penacook, NH; d & bur 1 & 5 Apr 1954, Binghamton & Cortland, NY. She married 24 Dec 1909, Cortland, NY, **George William Truman** (Eri O. Truman & Mary Angie Stearns) b 24 Feb 1884, South Otselic, NY; d 27 Jun 1960, Cortland, NY.

Lillian Monty was apparently the only child in her family to have been born in New Hampshire. She was living with her mother in New Bedford, MA, in 1900 and moved to Cortland, NY, shortly before her marriage. She and her husband resided in that city except for a few years around 1920 when George Truman was a factory worker in Syracuse, NY. They had returned to Cortland, though, before 1930 (US censuses). Lillian Monty was buried there in St. Mary's Cemetery (*Syracuse Herald-Journal*, 3 Apr 1954).

Children:

i.   **Georgiana Lillian Truman** b 14 Mar 1911, Cortland, NY; d there 14 Dec 1982. She married (1) 1929? **Neil Craig** b 1906?, NY.
     She married (2) **Paul Smith**.

ii   **Louis Edward Truman** b 29 Jul 1912, Cortland, NY; d & bur there 8 & 11 Aug 1976. He married (1) 1929?, **Anna Davis** b 1911?, NY.
     He married (2) Cortland, NY, **Nora Marie Lewis** (Edmund C. Lewis & Nellie M. ____) b 2 Oct 1910, Solon, NY; m (1) ____ Allen; d 7 Mar 1981, Cortland, NY.

iii **Arthur Bert Truman** b 31 Jul 1917, Cortland, NY; d 21 Sep 1985, Jamaica, NY. He married **Eleanor Leacock**.

iv   **Willis Eri Truman** b 17 Jan 1920, Syracuse, NY; d & bur 2 & 6 Apr 1998, Syra-

cuse & Cortland, NY. He married **Kathryn H. Smith** (Floyd Smith & Elsie ___)
b 11 Apr 1923, PA; d & bur 13 & 15 Apr 1993, Syracuse & Cortland, NY.

v   **Lawrence Eugene Truman** b 18 May 1922, Virgil, NY; d 12 Aug 1943 over Germany.

vi   **Alice Lillian Truman** b 2 Oct 1924, NY; d 2 Jul 2002, Catskill, NY. She married ___ **Martin**.

vii   **Agnes Albina Truman** b Jun 1926, NY. She married **Walter Slosek** (Stanley Slosek & Caroline Mollek) b 22 Nov 1917, Utica, NY; d 25 Oct 1994, West Windfield, NY.

viii   **Dorothy Louise Truman** b 22 Jul 1928, NY. She married **Gary Terrell Bidwell** (Robert Bruce Bidwell & Margaret Helen Terrell) b 3 Aug 1923, Horsehead, NY; d 17 Aug 1980, Rome, NY.

ix   **Dolorita Ellen Truman** married **Douglas R. Fleming** (Charles Fleming & Lula H. ___) b 3 Nov 1924, Broome Co., NY; d 3 Feb 1964, Germany.

x   **George Louis Truman** b 21 Jan 1932, Cortland, NY; d 13 Dec 1995, Travis AFB, Fairfield, CA.

8.3.11.7.3   MONTY, Joseph François b Sep 1892; d 18 Dec 1894, New Bedford, MA.

Joseph François Monty was 2 years and 3 months old at his death. No place of birth is indicated in the Massachusetts Death Records.

8.3.11.7.4   MONTY, Florence b 27 Sep 1893, NY; d Mar 1980, Schenectady, NY.

She married 1912? **Nicola/Nicholas M. Costa** b 25 Nov 1884, Italy.

Alone of her siblings, Florence Monty was born in New York State. She was living with her mother in New Bedford, MA, in 1900 and may have returned with her to New York State after her father's death in 1908. She and her husband had been married for eighteen years in 1930 (US censuses).

Nicola Costa arrived in New York on 9 Jun 1903 and was generally known thereafter as Nicholas Costa. He did sign though in 1918 his World War I Draft Registration card as Nicholas M. Cost. He was then a delivery clerk for the Hudson Navigation Co. in Albany, NY. He was a Railroad stevedore there in 1920 and a delivery clerk in 1930 (US censuses).

Children:

i   **Florence Costa** b 1913?, NY. She married 1929? **Francis Brown** b 1911?, ME.

ii   **Anthony Costa** b Jul 1915, NY.

iii   **Alice Costa** b Jul 1919, Albany, NY.

iv   **Marie Costa** b 1921?, Albany, NY.

v   **Gladys Costa** b Feb 1930, Albany, NY.

8.3.11.7.5   MONTY, Joseph T. b 15 Oct 1894, New Bedford. MA.

Joseph T. Monty was not included among his mother's five surviving children in the 1900 US census in New Bedford, MA. He presumably died before then though I have not found his death in the Massachusetts Death Records.

8.3.11.7.6   MONTY, Arthur P. b Jan 1897, New Bedford, MA; d 4 Oct 1918, France.

Arthur Monty was a resident of Cortland, NY, when he enlisted in the 26th Infantry Division, US Army, during World War I. Sgt. Arthur P. Monty was killed in action and was buried in the Meuse-Argonne American Cemetery in Romagne-sous-Montfaucon, France.

8.3.11.7.7   MONTY, Rose b 13 Sep 1898, New Bedford, MA; d Feb 1968, Castle Creek, NY. She married around 1915 Pio Pacentini/Piacenteni b 17 Jan 1888, Veroli, Roma, Italy.

I have found very few records of this family, and all have slightly different forms of the surname. The most authoritative may be the Social Security record of Mrs. Rose Pacentini's death. Other variants include Piacentene, Piacenteni, Piaccenteni, Piaccentine.

Pio Piacenteni was a worker in Cortland, NY, when he signed his World War I Draft Registration card in 1918 and a grocery store owner in Homer, NY, in 1920 (US census).

Children:
i   **Mary/Marie Pacentini** b Oct 1915, Cortland, NY.
ii   **Edward Pacentini** b 1917?, Cortland, NY.
iii **Angelina Pacentini** b Jun 1919, Cortland Co., NY.

8.3.11.7.8   **MONTY, Alfred Joseph/Fred** b 14 Nov 1899, New Bedford, MA; d & bur 26 & 30 Jun 1987, Cortland, NY. He married 1924?, **Gladys Davis** (Fred Davis & Lina Deland) b 2 Feb 1905, NY; d Feb 1985, Homer, NY.

A 6-month-old Frederick Monty was living in his mother's household in New Bedford, MA, in 1900. The name must be a mistake, a substitute for the informal Fred, by which name Edward Monty's son was quite commonly known in later years (in numerous articles about his family in the *Syracuse Herald-Journal,* for example). On more formal occasions, such as in US censuses or in his death record, he was named Alfred or Alfred J. Monty.

Alfred J. Monty was a yeoman in the US Navy stationed in Newport, RI, in 1920, a drill operator in Cortland, NY in 1930 when he and his wife had been married for six years (US censuses), and a resident of Homer, NY, in later years. He was buried in St. Mary's Cemetery in Cortland (*Syracuse Post-Standard,* 29 Jun 1987).

Children:

8.3.11.7.8.1	Arthur P.	1927-1947?-	
8.3.11.7.8.2	Rose Gladys	1929-	-
8.3.11.7.8.3	Alfred J.	1930-	-1979
8.3.11.7.8.4	Marie	-	-
8.3.11.7.8.5	Elizabeth	-1951?-	
8.3.11.7.8.6	Angela	1937-	-
8.3.11.7.8.7	Edward	1943-	-

8.3.11.8.1   **MONTY, Anna/Mariana/Mary Ann** b & bp 31 Jul & 1 Aug 1881, Bromont (West Shefford), QC. She married 20 Jul 1908, Fall River, MA, **Herbert Thomas/ Hubert Bourassa** (Pierre/Peter Bourassa & Octavie Monast) b 26 Jul 1882, East Douglas, MA; d Dec 1966, Pawtucket, RI.

This woman was baptized as Marie Malvina Monty but was later known under a number of other names: Anna, Marianne, Anna M., and Mary A. in censuses from 1900 through 1930, Mariana at her marriage, Mary Ann in 1918 when her husband signed his World War I Draft Registration card, and Anna in 1942 when he signed his World War II Draft Registration card.

Herbert Thomas Bourassa's full name and place of birth are taken from his World War II Draft Registration card. He was known as Herbert in the 1900, 1920, and 1930 censuses in Pawtucket, RI, in his Draft Registration cards of 1918 and 1942, and in his death record. Yet he was named Hubert at his marriage and a few years later in the 1910 census in Pawtucket. He was a house painter there until at least 1946 (US censuses; Pawtucket City Directories).

Children:
i   **Octavie Lauretta/Loretta Bourassa** b 24 May 1909, Pawtucket, R.I; d 11 Nov 1997, Central Falls, RI.
ii   **Armande/Armandine Bourassa** b 1911?, Pawtucket, RI. She married 1936? **Alcide J. Champagne** (Alfred Champagne & Omeril _____) b 14 May 1906, MA; d 18 Jan 1977, Fall River, MA.
iii **Mary Ann Bourassa** b 1913?, Pawtucket, RI.
iv   **Lillian Bourassa** b Dec 1918, Pawtucket, RI. She married there 1942 **Paul Antoine Begin** (Edward Begin & Clara Groulx) b 15 Feb 1921, Manchester, NH; d 4 Aug 1997, Woonsocket, RI.
v   **Alberta Bourassa** b Feb 1921, Pawtucket, RI.

8.3.11.8.2   **MONTY, Josephine A.** b 15 Jan 1884, Fall River, MA; d 2 Apr 1886, New Bedford, MA.

8.3.11.8.3   **MONTY, François Arthur** b 4 Mar 1886, New Bedford, MA; d 23 Jun 1889, Fall River, MA.

8.3.11.8.4   **MONTY, Alfred Noel** b 24 Dec 1888, Fall River, MA. He married there 24 Nov 1908 **Anita A. Messier** (Joseph Messier & Albina Gendron) b 1889?, New Bedford, MA.

Alfred Monty was living with his father and stepmother in Fall River, MA, in 1900 (US census). He was married there in St. Roch Catholic Church, and his daughters were baptized there. I know little more about his family. He and his wife may have separated in the mid-1910s. The Pawtucket, RI, City Directories show that Alfred Monty was a barber there from at least 1916 through at least 1946. He acknowledged having a wife and child when he signed on 5 Jun 1917 his World War I Draft Registration card, but I can find no evidence that Anita Messier or her children were ever in Rhode Island. In January 1920, when she was 30 years old, she was staying with her daughter Irene in her father's household in Fall River (US census). Alfred Monty continued to live in Pawtucket, sharing a home with his father and his sister Malvina (8.3.11.8.5). She, and not his wife, was the person he named in his 1942 World War II Draft Registration card as the person who would always be aware of his address.

Children:
| 8.3.11.8.4.1 | Gertrude Anita Albina | 1910- | - |
| 8.3.11.8.4.2 | Irene Imelda | 1911- | - |

8.3.11.8.5   **MONTY, Malvina Josephine** b 20 Jan 1890, Fall River, MA; d Feb 1986, Pawtucket, RI.

Malvina Monty (Josephine Malvina in her birth record) was living with her father and stepmother in Fall River, MA, in 1900 and in Pawtucket, RI, in 1910 (US censuses). I have not found her in later censuses but the Pawtucket City Directories show that she continued to live there in her father's and then her brother Alfred's home until at least 1946.

8.3.11.8.6   **MONTY, Hector** b & bp 15 & 20 Dec 1891, Fall River, MA; d & bur 25 & 26 Oct 1918, Waterloo, QC. He married 9 Jun 1910, Bromont, QC, **Alphonsine Huot** (Octave Huot & Delphine Poirier) b 1888?, QC.

Hector Monty (Joseph Hector Thaddée at his baptism) was only two weeks old when his mother died. He was apparently sent to stay with his maternal relatives in Canada and was living in 1901 in the household of his maternal uncle Louis Hubert in Waterloo, QC (Canadian census). He was a farmer in Bromont, QC, at his death.

Alphonsine Huot was a 3-year-old child living with her parents in Brome, QC, in 1891 (Canadian census). She survived her husband.

Children:
8.3.11.8.6.1	Octave Pierre Hubert	1911-	-
8.3.11.8.6.2	Graziella	1913-1952-
8.3.11.8.6.3	Jean-Louis Joséphat	1915-1944-
8.3.11.8.6.4	Marcel	1916-1942-
8.3.11.8.6.5	Marie Jeanne	1919-1948-

8.3.11.8.7   **MONTY, Anonymous** (male) b & d 22 Dec 1897, Fall River, MA.
This child was stillborn.

13.3.6.4.1   **MONTY, Marie Eva** b & bp 3 & 4 Mar 1867, Ste Brigide, QC; d & bur there 9 & 11 Mar 1867.

13.3.6.4.2   **MONTY, Eva** b & bp 18 Jun 1868, Ste Brigide, QC; d & bur there 7 & 10 Feb 1952. She married there 25 Feb 1895 **Adélard Jetté** (Joseph Jetté & Célina Larocque) b & bp there 29 May & 6 Jun 1865; d & bur there 13 & 16 Aug 1915.

Adélard Jetté was a farmer in Ste Brigide, QC. His sister Eva Jetté was the wife of Clément Gamache (13.3.6.8.i), Eva Monty's first cousin.

Children:
- i   **Rose Amanda Aurore Jetté** b & bp 17 & 18 Apr 1896, Ste Brigide, QC; d & bur there 30 Apr & 2 May 1904.
- ii   **Marie Anne Jetté** b & bp 24 Jun 1897, Ste Brigide, QC. She married there 25 Jun 1917 **Rosario Martel** (Timothée Martel & Marie Leduc).
- iii   **Eva/Geniva Reséda Jetté** b & bp 29 & 30 Aug 1898, Ste Brigide, QC.
- iv   **Eliana Jetté** b & bp 22 & 23 Nov 1899, Farnham, QC. She married 19 May 1921, Ste Brigide, QC, **Léo Gladu** (Hormisdas Gladu & Malvina Dubuc) b & bp there 31 Mar & 1 Apr 1900; d 20 Aug 1987, St. Lambert, QC.
- v   **Léopold Jetté** b & bp 10 & 11 Mar 1904, Ste Brigide, QC. He married there 25 Jan 1928 **Marie Anne Massé** (Ernest Massé & Amanda Blanchette) b & bp there 1 Sep 1904.
- vi   **Aldéric Arthur Jetté** b & bp 29 Nov & 1 Dec 1906, Ste Brigide, QC.
- vii   **Bernadette Antoinette Jetté** b & bp 21 & 22 Mar 1910, Ste Brigide, QC. She married there 16 Aug 1932 **Armand Simard** (Edouard Simard & Rosalie Pepin) b & bp 16 & 17 Nov 1909, Farnham, QC.

13.3.6.4.3   **MONTY, Zénaïde** b & bp 17 & 19 Jun 1870, Ste Brigide, QC; d & bur 1 & 4 May 1946, QC. She married (1) 30 Sep 1890, Ste Brigide, QC, **Philias Goineau** (Eusèbe Goineau & Lucie Benoit) b & bp there 29 & 30 Sep 1868; d & bur there 25 & 28 Feb 1905.

She married (2) 25 Nov 1909, Ste Brigide, QC, **Isaac Choinière** (Isaac Choinière & Justine Lanctôt/Langdoc) b & bp 6 & 7 Dec 1875, St. Alphonse, QC; m (1) 23 Jan 1900, St. Césaire, QC, Césarie Morin (Timothée Morin & Césarie Casgrain); d & bur 12 & 15 Oct 1932, Iberville, QC.

Philias Goineau was a farmer in Ste Brigide, QC.

Isaac Choinière was also a farmer in Ste Brigide in 1909 and 1911 (Canadian census). He was an innkeeper in Iberville, QC, though, at his death. His mother's maiden name is uncertain. It was Lanctôt at his baptism but Langdoc when she died in 1877 and when her widower remarried in 1878, and Lacoste in 1900 in the record of Isaac Choinière's first marriage. The first two readings are probably closest to reality.

Children:
- i   **Médéric Edgar Goineau** b & bp 16 & 18 Sep 1892, Ste Brigide, QC. He married there 22 Jun 1919 **Yvonne Lemaire** (Eusèbe Lemaire & Azilda Brodeur) b & bp there 1 & 2 Sep 1896.
- ii   **Henri Oliva Goineau** b & bp 18 & 19 Feb 1899, Ste Brigide, QC. He married there 18 Aug 1920 **Noemi Paméla/Noemie Pratte** (Origène/Eugène Pratte & Louisa Vincelette) b & bp 26 & 27 Jan 1898, St. Jean-Baptiste, QC.
- iii   **Marie Rose Lorenza/Laurence Goineau** b & bp 16 & 17 Mar 1901, Ste Brigide, QC.
- iv   **Joseph Albert Goineau** b & bp 11 May 1902, Ste Brigide, QC; d & bur there 12 & 13 May 1902.

13.3.6.4.4   **MONTY, Rosilda** b & bp 31 Dec 1871 & 1 Jan 1872, Ste Brigide, QC. She married there 22 Sep 1896 **Alcide Bessette** (Isidore Bessette & Josephte Boulais) b & bp 7 & 11 Apr 1869, Ste Angèle, QC.

Alcide Bessette (Joseph Alcide Agapite at his baptism) was a farmer in Ste Angèle, QC. His wife, named Marie Albina Rosilda at her baptism, was generally known as Rosilda as an adult: at her marriage, in the Canadian censuses of 1901 and 1911, and at the baptisms of her daughters in 1905 and 1909. I have found the name Albina only once, at the baptism of her son in 1901.

Children:
i   **Emery/Irénée/René Bessette** b & bp 24 & 26 Jan 1901, Ste Angèle, QC; d & bur 3 & 6 Feb 1929, St. Jean & Ste Angèle, QC.
ii   **Marie Germaine Bessette** b & bp 12 & 13 Apr 1905, Ste Angèle, QC.
iii   **Armande Diana/Amande Bessette** b & bp 20 & 21 Dec 1909, Ste Angèle, QC. She married there 26 Jun 1937 **Paul Emile Hébert** (Joseph Hébert & Amanda Quintin) b & bp 15 & 16 Aug 1911, Mont St. Grégoire, QC.

13.3.6.4.5   **MONTY, Delima/Rose de Lima** b & bp 29 & 30 Dec 1874, Ste Brigide, QC; d 15 Jul 1957, QC. She married 18 Jan 1898, Ste Brigide, QC, **François Etienne Tarte/ Leterte** (Etienne Tarte/Leterte/Letertre & Marie Choquette) b & bp 3 & 5 Sep 1871, St. Alexandre, QC; d 13 Feb 1951, St. Jean, QC.

This woman was named Rose de Lima at her baptism and at the baptisms of two of her children. She married however under the name of Delima Monty and was known as such at the baptisms of most of her children as well as in the Canadian censuses of 1901 and 1911.

She and her husband lived in various communities in Southern Quebec. François Tarte (François Etienne Leterte at his baptism) was a farmer in Ste Sabine, QC, at his marriage, in St. Alexandre and West Shefford, QC, in 1901 and 1911 (Canadian censuses), in St. Césaire, QC, when his daughter Alma (i) married in 1923, and in St. Sébastien, QC, when his son Eugène (v) married in 1937.

Children:
i   **Alma Victoria Tarte** b & bp 16 & 17 Mar 1901, Ste Sabine, QC. She married 24 Oct 1923, St. Césaire, QC, **Joseph Ulric Bessette** (Félix Bessette & Georgiana Tétreau) b & bp 3 Nov 1900, Ste Angèle, QC.
ii   **Fortunat François Tarte** b & bp 14 & 15 Feb 1903, Ste Sabine, QC; d 23 Mar 1989, Burlington, VT.
iii   **Hormisdas Tarte** b & bp 28 & 29 Jan 1905, Ste Sabine, QC.
iv   **Odile Anna Tarte** b & bp 21 & 22 Jul 1906, Ste Sabine, QC.
v   **Eugène Adhémar Tarte** b & bp 14 & 15 Jul 1907, Ste Sabine, QC. He married 19 Oct 1937, St. Césaire, QC, **Marie Rose Anne Tremblay** (Arthur Tremblay & Albina Chabot) b & bp there 15 & 17 May 1913.
vi   **Bernadette Laurenza Tarte** b & bp 27 May 1910, Ste Sabine, QC.

13.3.6.4.6   **MONTY, Edéas** b & bp 4 & 5 Apr 1876, Ste Brigide, QC. He married 21 Jun 1898, Ste Brigide, QC, **Delima/Rose de Lima Martel** (Timothée Martel & Marie Josephte Leduc) b & bp there 22 & 26 Mar 1880; d & bur there 9 & 11 Oct 1954.

Edéas Monty was a farmer in Ste Brigide, QC. He survived his wife Delima (Rose de Lima at her baptism).

Children:

13.3.6.4.6.1	Marie Reine Olida/Irène	1903-1928-
13.3.6.4.6.2	Jeanne Eva	1904-1931-
13.3.6.4.6.3	Uldéric Emilien	1905- -1930
13.3.6.4.6.4	Yvonne Lorenza	1907-1929-
13.3.6.4.6.5	Hervé Raphaël	1909-1933-
13.3.6.4.6.6	Marie Jeanne Angela	1912-1931-2000
13.3.6.4.6.7	Noëlla Alva	1913-1934-
13.3.6.4.6.8	Thérèse	1916-1938-
13.3.6.4.6.9	Florent Emery	1919- -1927

13.3.6.4.7   **MONTY, Anselme** b & bp 16 & 17 Oct 1877, Ste Brigide, QC; d & bur there 12 & 14 Jan 1879.

13.3.6.4.8   **MONTY, Emile** b & bp 30 Jul & 1 Aug 1880, Ste Brigide, QC; d & bur there 4 & 6 Aug 1942. He married 29 May 1911, St. Alexandre, QC, **Jeanne Annette Tarte** (Joseph Tarte & Rosalie Savaria) b & bp there 28 Jun 1889; m (2) 10 Jul 1948, Farnham, QC, Conrad Bissonnette (Achille Bissonnette & Vitaline Chabot), widower of Olivine Lemaire.

    Emile Monty was a farmer in Ste Brigide, QC.

Children:

13.3.6.4.8.1	Lucette	1914-1933&	-
13.3.6.4.8.2	Gérard	1916-1939-	

13.3.6.4.9   **MONTY, Hilaire** b & bp 1 & 3 Jan 1882, Ste Brigide, QC; d 28 Aug 1949, St. Jean, QC. He married 19 Aug 1907, Ste Angèle, QC, **Elise Bienvenu** (Timothée Bienvenu & Adèle Loiselle) b & bp there 19 & 20 May 1888; d 5 Feb 1973, Ste Rose, QC.

    Hilaire Monty was a blacksmith in Ste Brigide, QC, at his marriage and until at least 1911 (Canadian census).

Children:

13.3.6.4.9.1	Simone	1908-1927-1973
13.3.6.4.9.2	Germain	1909-1935&1955-1962

13.3.6.4.10   **MONTY, Albert** b & bp 20 & 21 Mar 1883, Ste Brigide, QC; d & bur 19 & 22 Apr 1918, Bedford & Ste Brigide, QC. He married 18 Sep 1911, Clarenceville, QC, **Berthe St. Jean** (Alexis St. Jean & Edwidge Bergeron) b & bp there 5 & 7 Sep 1888; m (2) 17 Apr 1922, Sweetsburg, QC, Olivier Bergeron (François Bergeron & Louise Dion); d 28 Jan 1956, Farnham, QC.

    Albert Monty was a fur merchant in Bedford, QC.

Children:

13.3.6.4.10.1	Gérard Richard	1912-	-1913
13.3.6.4.10.2	Marguerite Hélène	1914-1940-	
13.3.6.4.10.3	Bernard	1915-1946-1993	
13.3.6.4.10.4	Rachel	1917-	-1945

13.3.6.4.11   **MONTY, Ovila** b & bp 29 & 30 Dec 1885, Ste Brigide, QC; d & bur there 23 & 26 Jan 1935. He married 26 Feb 1919, Mont St. Grégoire, QC, **Aldina Desroches** (Jean-Baptiste Desroches & Joséphine Boucher) b & bp there 22 & 23 Oct 1897; m (2) 6 Jul 1957, Iberville, QC, Edéas Dubuc (Charles Dubuc & Leodina Martel), widower of Rose Alba Daigneault; d there 29 Nov 1971.

    Ovila Monty was a farmer in Ste Brigide, QC.

Children:

13.3.6.4.11.1	Anonymous	1920-	-1920
13.3.6.4.11.2	Anicet	1921-1954-	
13.3.6.4.11.3	Jean-Paul	1925-1950-	
13.3.6.4.11.4	Anonymous	1930-	-1930
13.3.6.4.11.5	Marcelle	1931-1949-1992	
13.3.6.4.11.6	Alain	1933-	-1937

13.3.6.5.1   **MONTY, Alma** b & bp 28 & 29 May 1876, Mont St. Grégoire, QC; d 9 May 1934, Butte Co., SD. She married 1896? **Edward Alphonse Rail** (Alexis Rehel & Félicité Boucher) b & bp 14 & 23 Feb 1868, Cap d'Espoir, QC; d 17 Mar 1951, Stevens Co., WA.

    Alma Monty (Marie Ozias Alma at her baptism) was living with her parents in Elizabethtown, SD, in 1880 (US census). The following year she was in St. Grégoire, QC, with her parents and younger sister (Canadian census). I do not know when she returned to the United States. In 1900 she and her husband had been married for four years.

Edward Rail (Edouard Alphonse Rehel at his baptism) had arrived in the United States in 1886. He was a farmer in St. Onge, SD, in 1900, in Moreau, SD, in 1910 and in Butte Co. (Twp 14), SD, in 1930 (US censuses). He may have left South Dakota to live with his son and daughter-in-law in Washington State after his wife's death. He died there though he was buried alongside his wife in Gate of Heavens Cemetery in St. Onge.

Child:

i   **Ulric Alexis Rail** b 5 Jul 1899, St. Onge, SD; d 16 Jun 1982, Chewelah, WA. He married 25 Nov 1920, De Smet, SD, **Bertha Melstad** (Johnnas/John Munson Melstad & Synnive/Susie Houkaas) b 22 May 1888, Kingsbury Co., SD; d 10 Jun 1968, Stevens Co., WA.

13.3.6.5.2   **MONTY, Rose Emma/Rosa** b & bp 27 & 29 Jun 1878, Mont St. Grégoire, QC.

Rosa Monty (Rose Emma at her baptism) was living with her parents in Elizabethtown, SD, in 1880 (US census). The following year Rose Alma (sic) Monty was in St. Grégoire, QC, with her parents and older sister Alma (Canadian census). I have not found her, or her parents, in later US or Canadian censuses, though I am intrigued by a reference in the South Dakota Death Index, 1905-1955, to the death of a Rosellma Monty in Yankton Co., SD, on 15 Jan 1917.

13.3.6.13.1   **MONTY, Anonymous** b 20 Mar 1873, Mont St. Grégoire, QC; d & bur there 20 & 21 Mar 1873.

13.3.6.13.2   **MONTY, Philias** b & bp 27 & 28 Nov 1874, Mont St. Grégoire, QC; d & bur 3 & 6 Aug 1953, Montreal & Mont St. Grégoire, QC. He married (1) 8 Jan 1901, Mont St. Grégoire, QC, **Mathilde Brodeur** (Honoré Brodeur & Josette Girard) b & bp there 5 & 6 Jan 1877; d & bur there 24 & 26 Jul 1901.

He married (2) 9 Feb 1904, Farnham, QC, **Eliza Victorine Mercure** (Césaire Mercure & Joséphine Déragon) b & bp 28 Aug & 1 Sep 1881, Ange Gardien, QC.

Philias Monty (Joseph Athanase Philias at his baptism) was a farmer in St. Grégoire, QC, at his first marriage, a merchant there at his second, and a butcher in Montreal in 1911 (Canadian census). He apparently also went by the name of Philias Esdras Monty. That was his name, for example, when he and his wife Elisa (sic) Mercure were godparents to their nephew Gaston Davignon (13.3.6.13.3.i) in 1910. He signed though simply Philias E. Monty.

13.3.6.13.3   **MONTY, Marie Anne** b & bp 10 & 11 Aug 1889, Mont St. Grégoire, QC; d & bur there 5 & ? Dec 1953. She married (1) there 12 Aug 1908 **Rodolphe Davignon** (Edouard Davignon & Malvina Guillet) b & bp 3 & 6 Dec 1885, Marieville, QC; d & bur 3 & 6 May 1914, Iberville & St. Grégoire, QC.

She married (2) 20 Jan 1915, Iberville, QC, **Delphis Moreau** (Raphaël Moreau & Rose Roy) b & bp 29 Jul 1874, St. Jean, QC; m (1) 23 Jun 1903, Dunham, QC, Rosanna Santerre (Jean Santerre & Sophie Couture); d & bur 4 & 6 May 1942, Mont St. Grégoire, QC.

Rodolphe Davignon was a carpenter in Marieville, QC, at his marriage and an innkeeper in Iberville, QC at the birth of his son Gaston (i) in 1910.

Delphis Moreau was a farmer in St. Jean, QC, in 1901 (Canadian census) and at his first marriage in 1903. He was an agent there when he married Marie Anne Monty in 1915 and in innkeeper in Iberville, QC, when his son Gilles (ii) was born in 1916. By 1921, at the birth of his daughter Yolande (iii), he was a commercial agent in Sorel, QC. He and his wife were still residing there in 1928 at the death of her son Gaston Davignon.

Children:

i   **Gaston Laurent Esdras Davignon** b & bp 31 May & 2 Jun 1910, Iberville, QC; d & bur 15 & 19 Nov 1928, Quebec & Mont St. Grégoire, QC.

ii   **Gilles Yvon Alain Moreau** b & bp 22 & 25 Jun 1916, Iberville, QC; d & bur 1977, Mont St. Grégoire, QC. He married **Marthe Durand** b 1922.

iii   **Yolande Moreau** b & bp 17 & 18 Jun 1921, Sorel, QC; d & bur 22 & 23 Jan 1922, Sorel & Mont St. Grégoire, QC.

13.3.8.2.1   **MONTY, Johanna/Cordelia** b 1865?, IL; d 23 Apr 1877, Kankakee, IL.

Johanna Monty was a 5-year-old child living with her parents in Rockville, IL, in 1870 (US census). She was buried in St. Joseph's Cemetery in Manteno, IL, at the age of 12 under the name of Cordelia Monty.

13.3.8.2.2   **MONTY, Emery Alonzo** b Aug 1867, Bourbonnais, IL; d there 28 Oct 1867 at the age of 2 months.

"Emerie Lanzo Monti" was buried in the cemetery of the church of the Maternity of the Blessed Virgin Mary in Bourbonnais, IL.

13.3.8.2.3   **MONTY, Ida Olive** b 25 Nov 1868, Rockville, IL; d 6 Jan 1920, Kankakee, IL She married 18 Nov 1891, Rockville, IL, **Arthur E. N. Reed** (James Reed & Eliza Dycus) b there Sep 1870; d 30 Oct 1926, Manteno, IL.

Arthur E. N. Reed was a butcher in Manteno, IL, at his marriage, a livestock buyer in 1900 and 1910, and a jobber in 1920 (US censuses).

Children:
i   **Howard E. Reed** b 30 Jul 1893, Manteno, IL; d Sep 1975, Loveland, CO.
ii   **Lester A. Reed** b 26 Jan 1895, Manteno, IL; d & bur there 4 & 7 Oct 1981. He married 1926?, IL, **Marcella E. Schaal** (Ambrose Frederick Schaal & Mildred Rose/Millie Bossert) b 1906?, Kankakee Co., IL.
iii   **Edward/Eddie Reed** b 25 Apr 1897, Manteno, IL; d there 23 Jul 1991. He married 1925? **Grace Meyer** (August H. Meyer & Rosa R. Weber) b 20 Jan 1898, Manteno, IL; d there Jul 1987.

13.3.8.2.4   **MONTY, Dora Adeline** b 9 Jan 1870, Rockville, IL; d 15 Feb 1940, Los Angeles, CA. She married 4 Feb 1891, Rockville, IL, **Eugene O. Magruder** (Morton Magruder & Sisphina Sampsel) b there Jul 1869; d 11 Jul 1942, Los Angeles, CA.

Eugene Magruder was a farmer in Rockville, IL, at his marriage, owned a livery stable in Bradley, IL, in 1900, and was a real estate agent there at the birth of a son in 1904. He was a real estate agent in Kankakee, IL, in 1920 and in Chicago, IL, in 1930 (US censuses).

Eugene Magruder's first cousin, Irvin C. Magruder, married Dora Monty's first cousin, Dora Yando, daughter of Olive Monty (13.3.8.4) and Noah Yando.

Children:
i   **Oswald Harley Magruder** b 15 Jul 1895, Bradley, IL; d 23 Oct 1954, Los Angeles Co., CA.
ii   **Virgil Lionel Magruder** b 30 Dec 1904, Bradley, IL; d 30 Jun 1985, Sarasota Co., FL.

13.3.8.2.5   **MONTY, Edgar Wesley** b 18 Nov 1874, Rockville, IL; d & bur 29 Feb & 3 Mar 1948, Bradley & Kankakee, IL. He married 11 Jan 1898, Mount Vernon, IL, **Ethel M. Collins** (Elijah Collins & Sarah M. Donner) b there 26 Oct 1878; d & bur 28 & 30 Apr 1970, Kankakee, IL.

Edgar Monty was a farmer in Dodds, IL, in 1900 and in Bourbonnais, IL, in 1910 and 1920. In 1930 he was a sawyer in a furniture factory in Bradley, IL (US censuses) and remained there until his death.

Children:

13.3.8.2.5.1	Ruby Neal	1899-1921?-1945
13.3.8.2.5.2	Nina B.	1901- -1986
13.3.8.2.5.3	Walter E.	1903-1931-1971
13.3.8.2.5.4	Edgar Collins	1905- -1987

| 13.3.8.2.5.5 | Everell Alonzo | 1907-1931-1986 |
| 13.3.8.2.5.6 | Richard Wayne | 1915-1945- |

13.3.8.2.6 **MONTY, Alonzo Duff** b 29 Jan 1877, Rockville, IL; d 20 Aug 1958, Kankakee, IL. He married there 7 May 1907 **Lois Dolan** (James Dolan & Rennie ____) b 1884?, Dixon, IL.

Alonzo Monty was a farm hand in Manteno, IL, in 1900 and a streetcar employee in Kankakee, IL, at his marriage, when his bride was 23 years old. The marriage did not last long. Alonzo Monty was divorced in 1920, and even before that, his 1918 World War I Draft Registration card shows that his brother Edgar, not his wife, was his closest relative. He was then a railroad engineer in Kankakee as well as in 1920 and 1930 (US censuses). He was buried in St. Joseph's Cemetery in Manteno.

13.3.8.2.7 **MONTY, Lucy Juliette** b 5 Feb 1879, Rockville, IL; d 2 May 1950, Franklin Co., IL. She married 25 Dec 1904, Dodds, IL, **Herman Bradford** (John Bradford & Sarah Stockard) b 8 Jul 1875, Jefferson Co., IL; d 16 Mar 1929, Franklin Co., IL.

Herman Bradford was a farm laborer in Bourbonnais, IL, in 1900, a tanner in Dodds, IL, at his marriage, and a coal mine engineer in Benton, IL, in 1910 and 1920. His widow was still living there in 1930, keeping house for her two youngest children (US censuses).

Children:
i   **Vern Lyle Bradford** b 1904?, Franklin Co., IL.
ii   **Stella Bradford** b 20 Nov 1907, Franklin Co., IL; d 26 Apr 1982, Ziegler, IL. She married 1924? **Archie Sinclair Grammer** (John W. Grammer & Millie Ann Jones) b 15 Jan 1897, Benton, IL; d there 6 Nov 1952.
iii   **Royal Herman Bradford** b Mar/Apr 1910, Benton, IL. He married **Ruth** ____.
iv   **John Emery Bradford** b Mar 1915, Benton, IL; d there 19 Jul 1937.
v   **Wilma Lucille Bradford** b 10 Aug 1918, Benton, IL; d 19 Apr 1992, Ann Arbor, MI. She married **William Arthur Howard** b 11 Jul 1918, Pontiac, MI.

13.3.8.6.1 **MONTY, Agnes** b 20 Mar 1867, Rockville, IL; d & bur 13 & 16 Sep 1940, Kankakee, IL. She married 7 May 1892, St. Anne, IL, **John Cross** (Francis Cross & Annette Laroche) b 9 Sep 1863, Grimaud, Var, France; d 21 May 1934, Kankakee, IL.

Agnes Monty was born on 20 Mar 1870 according to her death certificate. It is probably incorrect. All evidence points to an earlier year of birth: Agnes Monty was 3 years old in 1870 and 13 years old in 1880 when she was living with her parents in Kankakee Co., IL (US censuses), 25 years old at her marriage in 1892, 26 years old when her first child was born in 1893, 33 years old in 1900 (US census), etc.

John Cross came to the United States from France as a child in 1867 or 1868 and was naturalized in 1885. Given his French birth, it is probable that his name was originally Jean Lacroix and that his father was François Lacroix. He was in fact named Jean Cross at the birth of his first child. He was a farmer in Kankakee, IL, at his marriage and in Aroma Park, IL, from at least 1897 through 1 Jan 1920. He seemingly returned to Kankakee shortly thereafter for when his mother-in-law died there in March 1920 "Mrs. Agnes Cross" was said be to a resident of that city. The family was also in Kankakee in 1930 (US censuses).

John Cross and his wife were buried in the St. Anne, IL, Township Cemetery.

Children:
i   **John Fred Cross** b 20 Mar 1893, Kankakee, IL; d 18 May 1959, Aroma Park, IL. He married 19 Mar 1917, Kankakee, IL, **Maude Laflamme** (George Laflamme & Corinna/Cora Delibac) b there 2 Dec 1893; d there 10 Jan 1972.
ii   **Deland Cross** b 12 Jul 1897, Aroma Park, IL; d 26 Mar 1962, Kankakee, IL. He married 25 Jul 1917, St. Anne, IL, **Beatrice Bourgeois** (Isaïe Bourgeois & Herminie Trudeau) b & bp there 15 Oct & 1 Nov 1896; d 29 Apr 1977, Clifton, IL.
iii   **Clifford Edward Cross** b 9 Apr 1899, Aroma Park, IL; d & bur 11 & 13 Apr 1963, Kankakee & St. Anne, IL.

iv　　**Paul A. Cross** b 17 Aug 1901, Aroma Park, IL; d 23 May 1981, Kankakee, IL. He married there 31 Dec 1930 **Bertha Dahling** (Adolph Dahling & Minnie Schmidt) b there 8 May 1900; d there 4 Sep 1983.

v　　**Clarence Henry Cross** b 16 Aug 1905, Aroma Park, IL; d 4 Aug 2004, Roan Mountain, TN. He married **Mary Louise Houde** (Eugene Houde & Mary Boudreau) b 9 Sep 1906, Kankakee Co., IL; d 1 Jul 1999, Kankakee, IL.

vi　　**Rollin Cross** b 15 Aug 1908, Aroma Park, IL; d 15 Aug 1976, Kankakee, IL. He married 3 Jul 1933, Crown Point, IN, **Beatrice A. Hooker** (Claude P. Hooker & Lulu Nance) b 11 Mar 1909, Kankakee, IL; d there 26 Dec 1986.

13.3.8.6.2　　　**MONTIE, William** b 19 Oct 1868, Rockville, IL; d 15 May 1944, Waukegan, IL. He married 6 Feb 1895, Aroma Park, IL, **Nellie M. Day** (Alexander Day & Catherine Stebben) b there 5 Jul 1877; d & bur 27 & 29 Jan 1947, Chicago & Aroma Park, IL.

William Montie was a farmer in Aroma Park, IL, at his marriage, a hospital attendant in Kankakee, IL, in 1900, a saloon keeper there in 1910, a farmer in Aroma Park in 1920, and a gardener in Chicago, IL, in 1930 (US censuses). He was a resident of St. Anne, IL, at the death of his sister Agnes (13.3.8.6.1) in 1940 and later moved to Waukegan, IL, following his retirement. He and his wife were buried in the Aroma Park Cemetery.

The inscription on his tombstone, according to which he was born on 19 Oct 1869, is surely incorrect: he was already 2 years old at the time of the 1870 census in Rockville, IL.

Children:

13.3.8.6.2.1	Vernie W.	1896-	-1994
13.3.8.6.2.2	Melvin C.	1900-	-1921
13.3.8.6.2.3	Elwood	1908-	-1985

13.3.8.6.3　　　**MONTY, Ida May** b Sep 1869, Rockville, IL. She married 4 Jul 1891, Kankakee, IL, **Alfred Noah Menard** (Prudent Menard & Henriette Fortin) b Jan 1866, Pilot, IL.

The date of Ida May Monty's birth is taken from the 1870 US census in Rockville, IL, which specifies that she was born the preceding September. The date of October 1870 recorded in the 1900 US census is surely wrong as to the year, and probably the month.

Alfred Menard was a farmer in Irwin, IL, at his marriage and in Otto, IL, in 1900. He was a farmer in Salix (Liberty Twp), IA, in 1910 and until at least 1925 (US and state censuses). I can trace him no further.

Children:

i　　**Alfred George Menard** b 25 Feb 1892, Irwin, IL; d 15 Mar 1969, San Diego Co., CA. He married 9 Jan 1912, Salix, IA, **Ida Lacroix** (Peter Lacroix & Josephine Handfield) b Aug 1886, Lakeport, IA.

ii　　**Laura Agnes Menard** b 8 Apr 1894, Irwin, IL; d Oct 1989, Sioux City, IA. She married 22 Sep 1912, Salix, IA, **Howard Belmont Low** (Edwin Herbert Low & Anna E. Lawson) b there 1 Jun 1894.

iii　　**Julia Cordelia Menard** b 23 Apr 1900, Otto, IL; d 14 Jan 1982, Boca Raton, FL. She married **George Dewey Hansen** (James J. Hansen & Nikoline? ____) b 30 Mar 1898, IA; d 4 Apr 1982, Boca Raton, FL.

iv　　**Child Menard** b after 1900; d before 1910.

13.3.8.6.4　　　**MONTIE, Noah** b May 1873, Manteno, IL; d & bur 1903, Kankakee Co. & St Anne, IL. He married 2 Jan 1895, Kankakee, IL, **Effie Kent** (Hamilton Kent & Cecelia/ Celia Hanks) b 30 Jun 1872, Iroquois Co., IL; m (2) 1909 Edgar J. Smith, widower of Grace Gratton; d & bur 29 Jun & 1 Jul 1933, Chicago & Kankakee, IL.

Noah Montie was a farmer in Waldron, IL, at his marriage, in St. Anne, IL, at the birth of his first child, and in Limestone, IL, in 1900 (US census). He was buried in St. Anne's Catholic Cemetery alongside his parents and siblings.

Effie Kent and her second husband, a Railroad freight handler in Kankakee, IL, had been married for a year in April 1910. Her children were with her, though listed under the Smith surname. In 1920 they had regained their Monty surname while living with their mother and stepfather in Bourbonnais, IL (US censuses). According to her obituary of 30 Jun 1933, Effie Kent died at the home of her son Harold in Chicago, IL. She was buried in the Mount Grove Cemetery in Kankakee.

Children:

13.3.8.6.4.1	Harold Jesse	1895-1921-
13.3.8.6.4.2	Claribel	1901-1920-1986
13.3.8.6.4.3	Noah Alfred	1903-1928?-1964

13.3.8.6.5   **MONTIE, Julia Phoebe** b 29 Jul 1874, Manteno, IL; d 19 Jan 1972, Decatur, IL. She married (1) 12 Sep 1894, St. Anne, IL, **Henry G. Look** (John Look & Fredericka Wynhoff) b 27 Dec 1866, Oak Creek, WI; d & bur 15 & 17 Mar 1945, Kankakee, IL.

She married (2) 1948, Chicago, IL, **Henry Christman** (Albert Christman & Annette Laroche) b 15 Dec 1869, IL; d 19 Feb 1953, Los Angeles, CA.

Henry G. Look was a farmer in Otto, IL, at his marriage and until at least 1920 and a cemetery caretaker there in 1930 (US censuses). He and his wife were buried in Mount Calvary Cemetery in Kankakee, IL.

Henry Christman was a half-brother of John Cross, husband of Julia Monty's sister Agnes (13.3.8.6.1).

Children:
- i   **Lawrence Henry Look** b 14 Aug 1895, Otto, IL; d 11 Dec 1929, Kankakee, IL.
- ii   **Edwin Alfred Look** b 1 May 1897, Otto, IL; d & bur 1 & 3 Oct 1933, Otto & Kankakee, IL.
- iii   **Lucille Rosella Look** b 10 Feb 1901, Otto, IL; d 28 Nov 1984, Thiensville, WI. She married 13 Apr 1944, Cook Co., IL, **Rudolf Ludwig Holmes** (Rudolf Holmes & Olga ____) b 14 Aug 1900, Chicago, IL; d 11 Oct 1964, Oshkosh, WI.
- iv   **Laura Marie Look** b & bp 8 Sep & 5 Oct 1902, Otto & Kankakee, IL; d 7 Aug 1999, Decatur, IL. She married 5 Apr 1934, Kankakee, IL, **Frank Josephus Madell** (Johannes Madell & Catherine Noe) b 30 Jul 1896, Oshkosh, WI; d 5 Jan 1985, Decatur, IL.
- v   **Alberta Agnes Frederika Look** b & bp 22 Dec 1909 & 2 Jan 1910, Kankakee, IL; d 5 Aug 1981, Alsip, IL. She married **Raymond F. O'Leary** (Edward O'Leary & Clara Frank) b 4 Nov 1905, Chicago, IL; d 28 Sep 1985, Alsip, IL.
- vi   **Dorothy Orena Louise Look** b 10 May 1912, Otto, IL. She married **Brown Aubrey Lee** (Arthur Franklin Lee & Annie Lee Jones) b 11 Apr 1911, Birmingham, AL; d 21 Dec 1985, Los Angeles, CA.

13.3.8.6.6   **MONTIE, Frank Lawrence** b 13 Apr 1876, Rockville, IL; d 3 Apr 1945, Rock Island, IL. He married 14 Jan 1904, Kankakee, IL, **Lillian Belle Fowler** (George Fowler & Althea Marshall) b 14 Nov 1879, Ganeer, IL; d 1927.

Frank Montie was a farmer in Waldron, IL, in 1900 and at his marriage, and a railroad fireman in Kankakee, IL, in 1920 (US censuses). He was buried in the Montie family plot in the Catholic Cemetery of St. Anne, IL, while Lillian Fowler was buried in her brother-in-law William Montie's (13.3.8.6.2) plot in Aroma Park, IL. I know of the year of her death only through the inscription on her tombstone there.

Children:

13.3.8.6.6.1	Elwyn Etheridge	1904-1928-1967
13.3.8.6.6.2	Agnes Althea	1907- -1932

13.3.8.6.7   **MONTIE, Alfred** b 6 Jul 1879, Manteno, IL; d & bur 27 Feb & 2 Mar 1903, Aroma Park & St. Anne, IL.

Alfred Montie was buried alongside his parents and siblings in the Catholic Cemetery in St. Anne, IL.

13.3.8.6.8 **MONTIE, Arthur Harry** (twin?) b 13 Jun 1884, Otto, IL; d & bur 2 & 6 Mar 1970, Chicago & St. Anne, IL. He married 25 Feb 1906, Kankakee, IL, **Edna Trudeau** (Cyrille Trudeau & Malvina Hebert) b May 1887, L'Erable, IL.

Arthur Harry Montie's date of birth is taken from his 1942 delayed birth certificate (#1685) which is also the date found in his 1918 World War I Draft Registration card. If that is correct, then he was a twin of Meddie (13.3.8.6.9). He was 21 years old at his marriage. His age, though, varies somewhat from census to census. He may have been born in 1883 (1900, 1910), 1885 (1920), or 1887 (1930). Some doubt remains.

Arthur Montie was a farmer in Waldron, IL, at his marriage and a salesman in Kankakee in 1910 and 1920. His wife and daughter were still there in 1930 while he was an inmate in the Vermillion Co. jail in Danville, IL (US censuses). He later moved to the Chicago, IL, area and was living in Evanston, IL, at the death of his sister Agnes (13.3.8.6.1) in 1940 and in Chicago at the death of his brother Alex (13.3.8.6.10) in 1968. He was buried in the Catholic Cemetery in St. Anne, IL. His wife had predeceased him.

Child:
| 13.3.8.6.8.1 | Lucille Lorine | 1908-1944-1999 |

13.3.8.6.9 **MONTIE, Meddie** (twin?) b 1884, Kankakee Co., IL; bur 1888, St. Anne, IL.

The years of Meddie Montie's birth and death are taken from the tombstone inscription in the Catholic Cemetery in St. Anne, IL, where he/she was buried alongside his/her parents and three brothers. If the year of birth is correct, then the child would have been a twin of Arthur above (provided of course that the date of his birth, 13 Jun 1884, based on a delayed birth certificate, is also correct).

13.3.8.6.10 **MONTIE, Alex M./Alexander.** b 14 Jul 1888, Kankakee, IL; d there 6 Dec 1968. He married 12 Dec 1912, Kankakee Co., IL, **Edna Lowe** b 1888?, IL.

Alex Montie was a laborer on his father's farm in Aroma Park, IL, in 1910 and an automobile salesman in Kankakee, IL, in 1920 and 1930. His wife, who survived him, was then 31 years old (US censuses). They apparently had no children. He was buried in the Kankakee Memorial Gardens.

13.3.8.8.1 **MONTY, Anonymous** b 1869?; d 22 Sep 1869, Bourbonnais, IL.

This child died before being named or baptized (Death Records, Maternity of the Blessed Virgin Mary Catholic Church, Bourbonnais, IL).

13.3.8.8.2 **MONTY, Emery** b 10 Dec 1869, Rockville, IL; d & bur 1941, Aurora, KS. He married 1894?, KS, **Elizabeth DeMars** (Henry/Honoré DeMars & Emma/Adelaide Letourneau) b Feb 1874, Aurora, KS; d & bur there 1961.

Emery Monty came to Kansas with his parents in 1879 and became a farmer in Aurora, KS. He and his wife, a sister of Edward DeMars, husband of Nelida Monty (13.3.8.8.3), had been married for six years in 1900 (US censuses). Both were buried in St. Peter's Cemetery in Aurora.

Children:
13.3.8.8.2.1	Emma Laura	1899-1925?-2001
13.3.8.8.2.2	Philip	1903- -1934
13.3.8.8.2.3	Marcelline Leona	1908- -1973
13.3.8.8.2.4	Irene Luella	1914-1937-2001

13.3.8.8.3 **MONTY, Nellie/Nelida M.** b 16 Oct 1871, Manteno, IL; d & bur 19 & 21 Nov 1963, Salina, KS. She married 22 Feb 1892, Aurora, KS, **Edward DeMars** (Henry/Honoré DeMars & Emma/Adelaide Letourneau) b there Jun 1872; d 24 Oct 1932, Salina, KS.

Nellie Monty (Nelida M. at her marriage) came to Kansas with her parents in 1879 and was living with them in Cloud Co. in 1880. Her husband Edward DeMars was a brother of Elizabeth DeMars, wife of Emery Monty (13.3.8.8.2). He was a farmer in Aurora, KS, at his marriage and until 1917 when the family moved to Salina, KS. He was a flour mill worker there in 1920 and a truck driver in 1930 (US censuses). He and his wife were buried, along with most of their children, in Salina's Mount Calvary Cemetery.

Children:

i   **Phillip Henry DeMars** b 13 Mar 1893, Aurora, KS; d 26 Apr 1937, KS. He married 1920? **Della Massey** (Jesse Massey & Rose ____) b 1901?, Lick Creek Twp, IA.

ii   **Emery Alfred DeMars** b 4 Jul 1894, Aurora, KS; d & bur 19 & 21 May 1957, Salina, KS. He married 1917? **Victoria Margaret Brosseau** (Arthur L. Brosseau & Louise ____) b 1 Dec 1895, Summit Twp, KS; d & bur 1 & 5 Apr 1977, Salina, KS.

iii   **Hector John DeMars** b 2 Sep 1898, Aurora, KS; d 5 Jul 1998, Salina, KS.

iv   **Dorothy/Dora Emma DeMars** b 31 Jan 1901, Aurora, KS; d Oct 1992, Salina, KS. She married **James C. Peterson** (James C. Peterson & Annie ___) b 16 Mar 1898, KS; d Jan 1982, Salina, KS.

v   **Rena/Lorena Ella DeMars** b 20 Aug 1902, Aurora, KS; d 7 Sep 1997, Salina, KS. She married there 16 Aug 1921 **Francis Theodore Walker** (Clarence Theodore Walker & Laura Louise Tinkler) b 30 Nov 1903, KS; d 9 Jun 1996, Salina, KS.

vi   **Alice Marcelline DeMars** b 19 Apr 1907, Aurora, KS; d 23 Dec 1932, Salina, KS. She married 1931? **Anthony Aloysius Wary** (Leon Peter Wary & Eliza Wolfeiffer) b 8 Nov 1891, Salina, KS; d & bur 28 Aug & 2 Sep 1960, Denver, CO & Salina, KS.

vii   **George William DeMars** b 22 Jul 1908, Aurora, KS; d 4 Nov 1991, Salina, KS. He married **Edna Mae Bradshaw** (Willard Bradshaw & Marjory Katherine Miller) b 4 Jul 1912, Covert, KS; d & bur there 4 & 8 May 1975.

viii   **Raymond Oswald DeMars** b Jun 1910, Aurora, KS; d there 1 May 1911.

ix   **Bernice Viola DeMars** b 17 May 1914, Concordia, KS; d & bur 21 & 23 Dec 2006, Salina, KS. She married **Gus W. Buchholz, Jr.** (Gus W. Buchholz & Eva ____) b 3 Oct 1912, KS; d 24 Mar 1979, Salina, KS.

x   **Alphonse Herman DeMars** b 10 Mar 1917, Salina, KS; d there 10 Apr 1991.

xi   **Vernon DeMars** b 28 Jun 1919, Salina, KS; d there 24 Oct 1995.

13.3.8.8.4   **MONTY, Matilda Ann/Annie** b 16 Aug 1873, Kankakee, IL; d & bur 6 & 9 Dec 1972, McPherson & Salina, KS. She married 1898, Aurora, KS, **Henry Lawrence** (Louis Lawrence & Josephine ____) b there 22 Feb 1873; d & bur 20 & 22 May 1957, Salina, KS.

Annie Monty came to Kansas as a child and was living with her parents in Nelson Twp, KS, in 1880. Her name varied after she married. It was Matilda in 1900, Annie M. in 1910, Anna in 1917 (Henry Lawrence's World War I Draft Registration card), and Matilda in 1920 and 1930 (US censuses). She was also named Matilda Ann in both her and her husband's obituaries in the *Salina Journal* of 6 Dec 1972 and 20 May 1957 while her tombstone in Salina's Mount Calvary Cemetery is in the name of Matilda A. Lawrence.

Henry Lawrence was a farmer in Colfax, KS, in 1900 when he and his wife had been married for two years. He was a laborer in Aurora, KS, in 1910 and in Salina, KS, in 1920 and 1930 (US censuses). He was buried in Mount Calvary Cemetery in Salina.

Children:

i   **John Lawrence** b 8 Nov 1899, Colfax, KS; d Jun 1984, Huntsville, AL. He married 1925? **Ethel Winans** (Joseph Everett Winans & Mary Edna Clayton) b 1 Aug 1902, Bennington, KS; d 1935, Salina, KS.

ii   **Ella Lawrence** b 13 Jul 1901, Cloud Co., KS; d Jan 1970, Denver, CO. She married ____ **Garnier**.

iii **Laura Lawrence** b 1903?, St. Joseph, KS; d 7 Apr 1962, Salina, KS. She married **Roy Serrault** (Dennis Serrault & Lula ____) b 8 May 1905, Cambria, KS; d 11 Dec 1990.

iv **Josephine Lawrence** b 1906?, Cloud Co., KS.

v **Philip Lawrence** b Feb 1909, Cloud Co., KS

vi **Della Lawrence** b 26 Nov 1913, KS; d Dec 1990. She married ____ **Bishop.**

vii **Lola Lawrence** b 12 Dec 1915, KS; d May 1978, Salina, KS. She married ____ **Buchenau.**

13.3.8.8.5 **MONTY, Peter Edward** b 13 May 1875, Kankakee Co., IL; d 13 Sep 1928, Aurora, KS.

Peter E. Monty came to Kansas with his parents in 1879 and became a farmer in Aurora, KS (US censuses). He remained single and was buried in St. Peter's Cemetery in Aurora alongside his parents.

13.3.8.8.6 **MONTY, Israel Oswald** b 24 Jan 1877, Rockville, IL; d 11 Mar 1879, Nelson, KS, at the age of 2 years and 2 months.

The dates of Israel Oswald Monty's birth and death are taken from his maternal grandmother Sophie Richard's *Journal* (1874-1878, p. 27; 1878-1780, p. 4). The 1880 Mortality Schedule for Nelson, KS, also noted his death in March 1879, shortly after his parents' arrival there.

13.3.8.8.7 **MONTY, John Achille** b 5 Dec 1878, Rockville, IL; d 13 Jul 1966, Clyde, KS. He married 1903? **Rosa/Rose Savoie** (Michael/Michel Maxime Savoie & Julia Lagesse) b 5 Nov 1883, Aurora, KS; d there 27 Dec 1951.

John Monty came to Kansas with his parents shortly after his birth and was living with them in Aurora, KS, in 1900. He was a farmer in Colfax, KS, in 1910, when he had been married for seven years, and also in 1920. In 1930 he was a farmer in Center Twp, KS (US censuses). He and his wife were both buried in St. Peter's Cemetery in Aurora.

John Monty and his brothers George, Philip, and Henry married four sisters, Rosa, Lola, Regina, and Delvina Savoie.

Children:

13.3.8.8.7.1	Laura D.	1905-1924-
13.3.8.8.7.2	Abner W.	1917-1942-1997

13.3.8.8.8 **MONTY, George E.** b 1 Nov 1881, Aurora, KS; d & bur 13 & 17 Mar 1975, Salina, KS. He married 1913? **Lola Savoie** (Michael/Michel Maxime Savoie & Julia Lagesse) b Aug 1895, Aurora, KS; d 26 Mar 1934, Salina, KS.

George E. Monty was a laborer on his father's farm in Aurora, KS, in 1910, a mill hand in Smoky Hill, KS, in 1920, and a miller in Salina, KS, on 1 Apr 1930 when he and his wife had been married for sixteen years (US censuses). They remained in Salina and were both buried there in Mount Calvary Cemetery.

George Monty and his brothers John, Philip, and Henry married four sisters, Lola, Rosa, Regina, and Delvina Savoie.

Children:

13.3.8.8.8.1	Eldon Lee	1914-1941-1995	
13.3.8.8.8.2	Alcid E.	1917-1939-1994	
13.3.8.8.8.3	George Désiré	1923-1949-2008	
13.3.8.8.8.4	Richard Eugene	1928-	-2007
13.3.8.8.8.5	Joan	1932-	-

13.3.8.8.9 **MONTY, Fred/Alfred** b 24 Sep 1883, Aurora, KS; d 24 Feb 1975, Wichita, KS. He married 22 Jun 1909, Aurora, KS, **Elizabeth Letourneau** (____ Letourneau & Marie ____) b there 12 Nov 1884; d 12 Apr 1958, KS.

Fred Monty was a farmer in Aurora, KS, in 1910, a machinist in Newton, KS, in 1920, and a garment cutter in Wichita, KS, in 1930 (US censuses). He and his wife remained in that city and were buried there in Calvary Cemetery.

Children:

13.3.8.8.9.1	Wilfred W.	1910-	-1982
13.3.8.8.9.2	Mildred Victorine	1920-1942-2008	
13.3.8.8.9.3	Armeline C.	1922-	-2002
13.3.8.8.9.4	Melvin E.	1923-	-1994
13.3.8.8.9.5	Robert Eugene	1926-	-2002

13.3.8.8.10   **MONTY, Laura** b Jan 1885, Aurora, KS; d 2 Aug 1978, Hays, KS. She married 13 Jan 1906, Aurora, KS, **Joseph LaBarge** (Peter Labarge & Olivine Bechard) b there 2 Dec 1882; d 22 Feb 1963, Plainville, KS.

I have not found a birth record for Laura Monty and am using the date of birth found in the 1900 census in Aurora, KS, when she was 15 years old. She was 21 years old at her marriage. I am reluctant to accept the date of birth of 13 Jan 1884 which most genealogists have adopted since it conflicts not only with her age in various censuses but also with the birth of an older brother in September 1883 (13.3.8.8.9).

Joseph LaBarge was a farmer in Damar, KS, until at least 1930 (US censuses). He and his wife were buried there.

Children:

i   **Clara LaBarge** b 2 Aug 1906, Damar, KS; d there 6 Apr 1980. She married there 15 Feb 1929 **Dolphis Senesac** (Adolphis Senesac & Exilda Hebert) b there 12 Feb 1902; d there 30 Apr 1969.

ii   **Lena LaBarge** b 5 Aug 1907, Damar, KS; d 9 Jul 1989, Chicago, IL. She married 1929? **Cyrille Manny** (Adelard/Adelor Manny & Silica St. Peter) b 27 Jun 1897, Graham Co., KS; d Feb 1964, IL.

iii   **Raymond LaBarge** b 3 Jan 1909, Damar, KS; d there 2 Aug 1978. He married there 17 Jun 1930 **Dorilda Irene Manny** (Adelard/Adelor Manny & Silica St. Peter) b there 24 Dec 1908; d there 24 May 1999.

iv   **Phillip E. LaBarge** b 14 Dec 1916, Damar, KS; d there 4 Aug 1999. He married there 31 Jan 1939 **Edmae Desbien** (Anthony Desbien & Louise Conyac/Coignac) b there 2 Dec 1920.

v   **Leonard LaBarge** b 5 Dec 1917, Damar, KS; d 27 Nov 1944, Belgium. He married **Caroline C. Newell** (George A. Newell & Malvina Mary Plante) b 18 Jan 1921, Damar, KS; m (2) 5 Apr 1955, Wichita, KS, Melvin Garrett; d & bur 28 Jul & 1 Aug 2008, Cassville, MO & Damar, KS.

vi   **Della LaBarge** b 9 Feb 1920, Damar, KS; d & bur 4 & 9 Feb 2004, Hays & Damar, KS. She married 10 May 1938, Damar, KS, **Casimir St. Peter** (William St. Peter & Roselda Louise Hebert) b 1917?, KS; d 8 Oct 1955, KS.

vii   **Hubert Oscar LaBarge** b 14 Dec 1921, Damar, KS; d 24 Nov 1999, Salina, KS. He married 8 Aug 1942, Damar, KS, **Evangeline Newell** (George R. Newell & Alma M. Brin) b there 15 May 1924; d & bur 11 & 15 Dec 2007, Salina, KS.

viii   **Dula LaBarge** b 12 Nov 1923, Damar, KS. She married there 24 Nov 1958 **Clarence H. Eichman** (Fred H. Eichman & Ethel Hedge) b 9 Aug 1921, Morlan, KS; d 28 Dec 2001, Damar, KS.

ix   **Vernon Lawrence LaBarge** b 11 Jan 1927, Damar, KS; d & bur 15 & 18 Mar 2008, Ellis, KS. He married there 11 Apr 1955 **Irene Marie Newell** (George R. Newell & Alma M. Brin).

x   **Delmer Clifford LaBarge** b 7 Feb 1929, Damar, KS; d & bur 21 & 26 Nov 2007, Hill City & Damar, KS. He married 18 Feb 1952, Damar, KS, **Marion V. Morin** (Joseph Morin & Lucille Harriet Desmarteau) b there 1 June 1931.

13.3.8.8.11   **MONTY, Philip/Phillip Joseph** b 8 Nov 1889, Aurora, KS; d 24 Feb 1982,

Concordia, KS. He married 1919? **Regina A. Savoie** (Michael/Michel Maxime Savoie & Julia Lagesse) b 8 Mar 1889, Aurora, KS; 26 Mar 1969, Clyde, KS.

Philip Monty was a farm laborer in Aurora, KS, in 1910 and, after his marriage, a farmer in Nelson Twp, KS, in 1920 and 1930 (US censuses). He was living in Clyde, KS, when his brother George (13.3.8.8.8) died in 1975. Both he and his wife were buried there in Mount Calvary Cemetery.

Philip Monty and his brothers John, George, and Henry married four sisters, Regina, Rosa, Lola, and Delvina Savoie.

Children:

13.3.8.8.11.1	Leonard A.	1922-1944-1989
13.3.8.8.11.2	Eldemore	1925- -2005
13.3.8.8.11.3	LaVerne C.	1926-1952-2003

13.3.8.8.12   **MONTY, Henry A.** b 15 Feb 1896, Aurora, KS; d there 8 Aug 1943. He married there 16 Jan 1917 **Delvina R. Savoie** (Michael/Michel Maxime Savoie & Julia Lagesse) b there 14 Jan 1897, KS; d 21 Nov 1978, Concordia, KS.

Henry Monty inherited his father's farm in Aurora, KS, and was living there with his wife and his widowed mother in 1920 and 1930 (US censuses). Both he and his wife were buried in St. Peter's Cemetery in Aurora.

Henry Monty and his brothers John, George, and Philip married four sisters, Delvina, Rosa, Lola, and Regina Savoie.

Children:

13.3.8.8.12.1	Maxine	1917?- -1918
13.3.8.8.12.2	Della Mae	1924-1945-2008
13.3.8.8.12.3	Annabel T.	1926-1946-
13.3.8.8.12.4	Donald Dean	1928-1949&1975-2006

13.3.10.8.1   **MONTY, Arthur** b & bp 2 Feb 1878, Chambly, QC.
Arthur Monty was a farmer living on his father's farm in Chambly, QC, in 1911. He was still single (Canadian census).

13.3.10.8.2   **MONTY, Joseph Albert** b & bp 13 Apr 1880, Longueuil, QC; d & bur 26 & 30 Jan 1970, Chambly, QC. He married 1 Jul 1916, St. Charles, QC, **Marie Rose Annette Lucier/Lussier** (Patrice Lucier & Basilice Desautels) b & bp there 3 & 4 Oct 1891; d & bur 13 & 17 Nov 1969, Chambly, QC.

Joseph Albert Monty was a farmer in Chambly, QC. His name appears on various records as Joseph Albert, Joseph, or Albert Monty while his wife was known as Marie Rose Annette, M. R. Annette, or simply Annette Lucier or Lussier.

Children:

13.3.10.8.2.1	Albert Solime	1917- -
13.3.10.8.2.2	Arsène Maurice	1920- -1949
13.3.10.8.2.3	Laurent	1921-1950-
13.3.10.8.2.4	Alphonse Rodolphe	1923- -1923
13.3.10.8.2.5	Georgette Julienne	1924-1948-

13.3.10.16.1   **MONTY, Horace** b & bp 23 May 1886, Waterloo, QC; bur 24 Dec 1951, Roxton Pond, QC. He married 3 Sep 1917, Acton Vale, QC, **Gertrude Cordeau** (Zacharie Cordeau & Philomène Charbonneau) b & bp there 24 & 26 Mar 1891; d 8 Feb 1984, Roxton Pond, QC.

Horace Monty was a merchant in Roxton Pond, QC.

Children:

13.3.10.16.1.1	Jeanne d'Arc Anna	1919-1944-

| 13.3.10.16.1.2 | Thérèse Simone Agathe | 1921- | - |
| 13.3.10.16.1.3 | Yvonne Exeline | 1922- | - |

13.3.10.16.2 **MONTY, Clara** b & bp 30 Oct & 4 Nov 1887, Waterloo, QC; d 1962, Montreal, QC. She married 19 Sep 1910, Roxton Pond, QC, **Horace Poirier** (Wilfrid Poirier & Emma Saurette dit Larose) b & bp 18 Aug 1886, St. Pie, QC.

Children:

i **Jean-Paul Gaston Poirier** b & bp 6 Aug 1911, Roxton Falls, QC; d Jul 1960, Montreal, QC. He married there 2 Sep 1936 **Blanche/Bianca Olga Alessandra Carli** (Vincenzo/Vincent Carli & Catterina/Catherine Servi) b & bp there 2 & 7 May 1911.

ii **Claire Amande Poirier** b & bp 2 & 3 Nov 1912, Roxton Falls, QC. She married 13 Jul 1940, Montreal, QC, **Albert Léon Lépine** (Joseph Gédéon Lépine & Elmire Ferland) b & bp 18 & 23 Aug 1914, Ottawa, Ontario, Canada.

iii **Marcel Lucien Poirier** b & bp 25 & 26 Jul 1915, Roxton Falls, QC. He married 23 Jun 1945, Montreal, QC, **Andrée Desjardins** (Roméo Desjardins & Antoinette Viger) b & bp there 30 & 31 Aug 1922.

iv **Germain Poirier** b 25 May 1917, Kindsaid, Saskatchewan, Canada; d 27 Feb 1974, Montreal, QC. He married there 8 Jan 1944 **Yvette Morin**.

v **Charles Emile Poirier** b 6 Feb 1919, Kindsaid, Saskatchewan, Canada; d 3 Jul 1992. He married Montreal, QC, **Pauline Chénier**.

vi **Lucien Edgar Poirier** b & bp 12 & 13 Oct 1921, Mont-Laurier, QC; d 13 Jun 1974. He married 30 May 1953, Ste Adèle, QC, **Claire Deslauriers** (Edouard Deslauriers & Adrienne Lavoie).

vii **Yves Luc Poirier** b & bp 16 Jul 1923, Roxton Pond, QC; d 10 Jan 1981, Montreal, QC. He married Montreal East, QC, **Jacqueline Lefebvre**.

viii **Jules Poirier** b 15 Aug 1926, Montreal, QC; d there 31 Mar 1977.

13.3.10.16.3 **MONTY, Marie Rose Laura** b & bp 11 & 19 Mar 1889, Waterloo, QC; d & bur there 26 & 28 Sep 1889.

13.3.10.16.4 **MONTY, Harold** b & bp 25 & 29 Jun 1890, Waterloo, QC; d & bur 9 & 12 Dec 1935, La Conception, QC.

Harold Monty (Jean-Baptiste Harold at his baptism) was the pastor of the Catholic parish of La Conception, QC, at his death.

13.3.10.16.5 **MONTY, Maurice/Raphaël François** b & bp 30 Nov & 1 Dec 1891, Waterloo, QC.

Joseph Raphaël François Monty, son of Adélard Monty and Anna Bourbeau, was born on 30 Nov 1891 and baptized the following day, according to the records of St. Bernardin Church in Waterloo, QC. That child is never again mentioned in connection with his family but is replaced in the 1901 Canadian census in Roxton Pond, QC, by a 9-year-old Maurice, born on 30 Oct (sic) 1891 and in 1911 by an 18-year-old Maurice, born in Oct 1893 (sic). Both names must refer to the same child, though I cannot explain the name change. Maurice Monty was a secular priest serving in Val David, QC, when his brother Horace (13.3.10.6.1) died in 1951.

13.3.10.16.6 **MONTY, Lucrèce Alice** b & bp 8 & 9 Jul 1893, Waterloo, QC. She married 20 Jul 1920, Roxton Pond, QC, **Zéphirin Israël Delorme** (Joseph Delorme & Henriette Gaudette) b & bp 3 & 5 Oct 1892, Waterloo, QC; d & bur 11 & 14 Jun 1927, Roxton Pond, QC.

Zéphirin Delorme was a notary public in Roxton Pond, QC. His widow was still living there when her brother Horace (13.3.10.16.1) died in 1951.

Children:

i   Marianne Rachel Cécile Delorme b & bp 4 & 5 Jun 1921, Roxton Pond, QC. She married there 16 Jun 1943 **Lucien Vincent Guillemette** (Alphonse Guillemette & Médiane Tétreault) b & bp 18 & 20 Feb 1917, Roxton Pond, QC.

ii   **Adrien Jean Luc Delorme** b & bp 1 & 2 Aug 1922, Roxton Pond, QC.

iii   **Simon Philippe Delorme** b & bp 20 Jul 1923, Roxton Pond, QC; d & bur there 31 Aug & 2 Sep 1924.

iv   **Françoise Gisèle Delorme** b & bp 18 & 19 Jan 1926, Roxton Pond, QC.

v   **Simone Delorme** married 28 Jul 1951, Roxton Pond, QC, **Jacques Paradis** (Paul Paradis & Maria Kennedy).

13.3.10.16.7   **MONTY, Berthe Yvonne** b & bp 5 & 10 Mar 1895, Waterloo, QC.

Berthe Yvonne Monty became a nun in the Order of St. Joseph where she was known as Sister St. Adélard. She survived her brother Horace (13.3.10.16.1).

13.3.10.16.8   **MONTY, Anne Antoinette** b & bp 24 Aug 1896, Waterloo, QC; d & bur 12 & 13 Aug 1897, Roxton Pond, QC.

13.3.10.16.9   **MONTY, Augustine Grâce Lena** b & bp 13 & 16 Jul 1898, Roxton Pond, QC; d & bur there 2 & 4 Feb 1899.

13.3.10.16.10   **MONTY, Edgar** b & bp 21 & 22 Aug 1899, Roxton Pond, QC; bur 25 Nov 1959, Lefaivre, Ontario, Canada.

Edgar Monty (Gilbert Edgar Clodimir at his baptism) was a Dominican priest.

13.3.10.16.11   **MONTY, Victor** b & bp 16 & 18 Jul 1901, Roxton Pond, QC. He married 16 Jun 1931, Montreal, QC, **Marguerite Bergeron** (Alphonse Bergeron & Blanche Gauthier) b & bp 16 Dec 1907, Montreal, QC; d 1 Jan 1988, Ste Rose, QC.

Victor Monty (Joseph Henri Victor at his baptism) was a notary public in Roxton Pond at his marriage and at the birth of his daughter in 1932. He was a notary public in Granby, QC, when his brother Horace (13.3.10.16.1) died in 1951.

Child:
13.3.10.16.11.1   Lise   1932-1953-

13.3.10.16.12   **MONTY, Gertrude** b & bp 29 & 31 Dec 1902, Roxton Pond, QC; d & bur there 1985.

Gertrude Monty (Marie Constance Gertrude Noëlla at her baptism) was a lifelong resident of Roxton Pond, QC. She did not marry. The date of her death is taken from the inscription on the MONTY tombstone in the Catholic Cemetery of Roxton Pond where she was buried alongside her parents and her brother Paul Emile (13.3.10.16.13).

13.3.10.16.13   **MONTY, Paul Emile** b & bp 15 & 16 Aug 1905, Roxton Pond, QC; d & bur there 30 Jun & 2 Jul 1931.

Paul Emile Monty (Joseph Ignace Paul Emile at his baptism) did not marry.

13.3.10.16.14   **MONTY, Etienne Lucien Adélard** b & bp 27 Feb 1908, Roxton Pond, QC; d & bur there 12 & 20 Apr 1908.

13.3.10.17.1   **MONTY, Eveline Eva** b & bp 29 & 31 Mar 1895, Granby, QC; d & bur there 12 & 14 Sep 1895.

13.3.10.17.2   **MONTY, Ivan Bertrand Lloyd** b & bp 7 & 11 Jun 1896, Granby, QC. He married (1) there 25 Jun 1924 **Mary Lyla Maud Averill** (Frank Averill & Helen/Nelly Pow) b there Mar 1901; d & bur there 2 & 4 Nov 1930, at the age of 29.

He married (2) 20 Jul 1942, Stukely, QC, **Marie Jeanne Emilia Courtemanche** (Uldéric Courtemanche & Emilia Gervais) b & bp there 19 & 25 Aug 1907.

Ivan Monty was named Bertrand Ivan Lloyd at his baptism. He signed his World War I recruitment papers on 24 Jun 1918 as Ivan Monty and the record of his first marriage in 1924 as Ivan Bertrand Lloyd Monty.

13.3.10.17.3   **MONTY, Gwendolyn** b & bp 24 & 26 Jun 1898, Granby, QC.
Gwendolyn Monty (Marie Flore Gwendolyn at her baptism) was living with her parents in Granby, QC, in 1901 and 1911(Canadian censuses).

13.3.10.17.4   **MONTY, Gerald Augustin** b & bp 15 & 20 Apr 1900, Granby, QC; d & bur there 27 & 28 Aug 1900.

13.3.10.17.5   **MONTY, Hildred Alexina Octavia** b & bp 12 & 14 Sep 1902, Granby, QC.

13.3.10.18.1   **MONTY, Blanche** b & bp 7 & 10 Aug 1890, Granby, QC. She married there 31 Mar 1913 **Alfred Homer Gervais** (Gilbert Gervais & Henriette Bertrand) b 4 Jul 1886, Westmeath, Ontario, Canada
Blanche Monty was named Anna Blanche Nélida at her baptism.

Children:
- i   **Louise Rachel Gervais** b & bp 15 & 20 Sep 1913, Hawkesbury, Ontario, Canada. She married 25 Jul 1942, Fort Coulonge, QC, **William Lionel Sauriol** (Isaïe Sauriol & Emma Leclair) b & bp there 19 & 26 May 1912.
- ii   **Jérôme Arthur Louis Gervais** b & bp 23 & 27 Sep 1914, Hawkesbury, Ontario, Canada; d 3 Nov 1996, Fort Coulonge, QC. He married 13 Jul 1957, Montreal, QC, **Gisèle Corbin** (Arthur Corbin & Corinne Lahaie) b & bp 6 & 8 Aug 1912, Outremont, QC; d 1989, Montreal, QC.
- iii   **Polydore Nestor Gervais** b & bp 7 & 11 Jun 1916, Hawkesbury, Ontario, Canada.
- iv   **Luc Emile Lloyd Gervais** b & bp 10 & 11 May 1919, Granby, QC; d 8 Jun 1967, Montreal, QC.
- v   **Jean Gilles Gervais** b & bp 9 & 13 Apr 1921, Fort Coulonge, QC.
- vi   **Roch Gervais** b 1925? He married 5 Sep 1949, Fort Coulonge, QC, **Theresa Marvela/Marvel Ward** (James Ward & Beatrice Dempsey) b & bp there 8 & 10 Apr 1927.
- vi   **Georgette Thérèse Gervais** b & bp 11 & 15 Jul 1928, Fort Coulonge, QC. She married 13 Oct 1952, Montreal, QC, **Earl Michael Ward** (James Ward & Beatrice Dempsey) b & bp 28 Nov & 1 Dec 1929, Fort Coulonge, QC.

13.3.10.18.2   **MONTY, Arthur Nestor** b & bp 22 & 24 Jul 1892, Granby, QC; d & bur there 5 & 6 Jan 1895.

13.3.10.18.3   **MONTY, Bernadette** b & bp 18 Mar 1894, Granby, QC. She married 5 Mar 1932, Montreal, QC, **Marc Antoine Ginchereau** (Zotique Ginchereau & Elise Mercier) b & bp there 19 & 20 Jan 1901.
Bernadette Monty was named Marie Rose Alba Bernadette at her baptism. Her husband was baptized as Joseph Olivier Marc Antoine Gaston Ginchereau.

13.3.10.18.4   **MONTY, Amintha** b & bp 1 & 3 Mar 1896, Roxton Pond, QC; d & bur 3 & 5 Aug 1936, Montreal, QC. She married 14 Oct 1924, Granby, QC, **John Athol Ede** (John William Ede & Margaret Levena Patteson/Pattison) b & bp 22 Jun 1896 & 7 Jan 1897, Montreal, QC.
Amintha Monty was named Marie Irène Amintha at her baptism. John Athol Ede was born in the St. Henri district of Montreal, QC, and was baptized by the minister of the Grace Baptist Church in Westmount, QC. He was again baptized in St. Patrick's Catholic Church in Montreal on 1 Oct 1924, a few weeks before his marriage. He survived his wife.

Child:
    i   **John Arthur Ede** b & bp 20 May & 1 Jun 1925, Montreal, QC.

13.3.10.18.5   **MONTY, Graziella** b & bp 18 & 20 Mar 1898, Roxton Pond, QC. She married 22 May 1930, Montreal, QC, **Roméo Brodeur** (Marc Aurèle Brodeur & Cordelia Martineau) b & bp there 8 & 9 Sep 1896.

    Graziella Monty was named Marie Amélie Graziella at her baptism. Her husband was baptized as Marc Roméo Brodeur. The names of the four children for whom I have no other information are taken from Louise Monty's *Généalogie de la famille Monty*, IV, 136.

Children:
    i   **Camille Yves Marc Brodeur** b & bp 4 & 5 Mar 1931, Montreal, QC.
    ii   **Marie Marthe Brodeur** b & bp 18 & 19 Jun 1932, Montreal, QC.
    iii   **Raymond Brodeur**
    iv   **Francine Brodeur**
    v   **Louise Monique Gisèle Brodeur** b & bp 10 & 15 Dec 1935, Montreal, QC.
    vi   **Jean Brodeur**
    vii **Denis Brodeur**

13.3.10.18.6   **MONTY, Laurence** b & bp 27 & 30 Mar 1904, Granby, QC. She married 13 Apr 1936, Montreal, QC, **Léopold Morin** (Ernest Morin & Maria Hubert) b & bp there 17 & 18 Sep 1900.

    Laurence Monty was named Marie Valéda Laurence Ernestine at her baptism. Her husband was baptized as Joseph Aldéric Edouard Léopold Morin.

13.3.10.18.7   **MONTY, Marcel** b & bp 1 Jan 1908, Granby, QC. He married 1 Jul 1939, Montreal, QC, **Marie Yvonne Plante** (Horace Plante & Wilhelmine Létourneau) b & bp 18 Dec 1906, Sorel, QC.

    Marcel Monty was named Joseph Arthur Marcel at his baptism. His wife was baptized as Marie Malvina Yvonne Plante.

13.3.10.18.8   **MONTY, Thérèse** b & bp 11 & 13 Mar 1910, Granby, QC.

    Thérèse Monty was named Marie Hélène Brigitte Thérèse at her baptism.

13.3.10.19.1   **MONTY, Lloyd** b & bp 1 & 2 Feb 1901, Granby, QC. He married **Berthe Duquette** (Edouard Duquette & Marie Louise Lecours) b & bp 2 & 6 Mar 1902, Bromont, QC.

    Lloyd Monty was named Augustin Nestor Lloyd at his baptism. His wife was baptized as Marie Antoinette Berthe Albertine Duquette.

Child:
13.3.10.19.1.1   Robert   -   -

13.3.10.19.2   **MONTY, Gerald Rosario** b & bp 1 Mar 1903, Granby, QC; d & bur there 8 & 9 Mar 1903.

13.3.10.19.3   **MONTY, Viola** b & bp 26 & 30 Sep 1906, Granby, QC. She married 30 Oct 1936, Montreal, QC, **Paul Mayers** (Ernest Mayers & Eugénie Lamothe) b & bp 21 & 23 Apr 1908, Montreal, QC.

    Viola Monty was named Mary Elmire Viola at her baptism.

13.3.10.19.4   **MONTY, Anonymous** (male) b 19 Sep 1908, Granby, QC; d & bur there 19 Sep 1908.

13.3.10.19.5   **MONTY, Eileen** b & bp 24 & 26 Feb 1911, Granby, QC. She married 17 Jun 1937, Montreal, QC, **Frank Raoul McCormack** (William McCormack & Lucy Agnes

Farr).

This woman, who married as Eileen Monty, was baptized as Françoise Mildred Hélène Monty. Only three months later, though, in the 1911 census in Granby, QC, her name was given as Eileen. She does not appear to have used the French version of her name.

13.3.10.19.6 **MONTY, Anonymous** (female) b 2 Jul 1914, Granby, QC; d & bur there 2 Jul 1914.

This child was stillborn.

13.3.10.20.1 **MONTY, Gabrielle** b & bp 2 & 3 Apr 1901, Granby, QC.

Gabrielle Monty was named Marie Cécile Françoise Gabrielle at her baptism.

13.3.10.20.2 **MONTY, Madeleine Elizabeth** b & bp 19 & 22 Nov 1903, Granby, QC. She married 10 Apr 1939, Outremont, QC, **Albert Donald Hillman** (Adolphe Hillman & Grace Patton) b & bp 26 May & 2 Jun 1895, Curran, Ontario, Canada; m (1) 20 Sep 1927, Montreal, QC, Maria Van Troyen (Pierre Van Troyen & Pauline Bori).

This woman signed her marriage record as Madeleine Elizabeth Monty. The text itself refers to Marie Cécile Madeleine Elizabeth Monty, her baptismal name.

13.3.17.10.1 **MONTY, Olier/Oliver** b & bp 17 Mar 1891, Nashua, NH; d & bur there 7 & 10 Oct 1918. He married there 9 May 1916 **Lea Plouffe** (François Plouffe & Julie Fortier) b & bp there 3 & 4 Jan 1894; m (2) there 15 Sep 1925 Jean/John S. Leblanc (Hubert Leblanc & Odile Lagesse); d & bur there 31 Dec 1994 & 4 Jan 1995.

Olier Monty (Louis Alphonse Olier at his baptism) was a harness maker in Nashua, NH, in 1910 and a shoemaker there in 1911 and later years (US censuses; Nashua City Directories). Although his name in the City directories was Oliver Monty, he signed his World War I Registration card as Olier Monty. The records of St. Louis de Gonzague Church in Nashua also refer to him consistently as Olier Monty.

Children:
13.3.17.10.1.1	Antoinette Corinne Jeannette	1917-	-1919
13.3.17.10.1.2	Claire Louise	1918-	-

13.3.17.10.2 **MONTY, Raymond Leo Henri** b & bp 17 Apr 1903, Nashua, NH; d & bur there 18 & 21 Jan 1991. He married there 29 Aug 1931 **Alice Breault** (Silas Breault & Zenobia Cadoret) b & bp there 17 Dec 1896; d & bur there 1 & 5 Apr 1977.

Raymond Monty was a mail carrier in Nashua, NH. He and his wife were buried there in St. Louis Cemetery.

13.3.17.10.3 **MONTY, Leo F.** b & bp 1 Oct 1905, Nashua, NH; d & bur there 15 & 18 Oct 1986. He married there 28 Apr 1949 **Angelina Miller** (Ernest Miller & Philomene Garant) b there 29 Jul 1913; d & bur there 17 & 18 Dec 1987.

Leo Monty (Joseph François Leo at his baptism) was a shoemaker in Nashua, NH. He and his wife were buried there in St. Louis Cemetery.

Child:
13.3.17.10.3.1	Infant	1951-	-1951

13.9.2.4.1 **MONTY, Cassius W.** b 6 Jan 1867, Sterling, WI. He married 22 Jun 1899, St. Croix Falls, WI, **Cora A. McGuire** (William F. McGuire & Mary A. ____) b 19 Jan 1872, Stillwater, MN.

Cassius W. Monty was a millwright in Sterling, WI, in 1900, and a teacher and millwright in St. Croix Falls, WI, at the birth of his daughter Ardis in September of that year. He was the County Superintendent of Schools there from 1900 to 1908, the principal of the Polk County Normal School in 1906 and 1910, the St. Croix Falls Village Supervisor in 1911 and 1912, and was still working in the public school system there in 1920. He was at the Southern

Wisconsin College and Training School in Dover, WI, in 1930 while his wife and children were still in St. Croix Falls (US censuses).

Children:

13.9.2.4.1.1	Ardis Aileen	1900-	-1954
13.9.2.4.1.2	Kenneth	1904-	-1938

13.9.2.4.2   **MONTY, Walter C.** b Jan 1871, Sterling, WI.

Walter Monty was a farmer in Sterling, WI, until at least 1920. He had not married and was living on the family farm with his widowed mother (US censuses).

13.9.2.4.3   **MONTY, Minnie May** b May 1874, Sterling, WI. She married (1) Nov 1896, Hudson, WI, **Charles Amel/Emil Berquist** b 1872?, MN; d 11 Dec 1951, Minneapolis, MN.

She married (2) 1912? **Harry Frank Beckmark/Backmark** (Lars P. Backmark & Mary ____) b 16 Mar 1884, Polk Co., WI.

Minnie May Monty's first husband was named Charles Amel Berquist at his marriage and at his death. In 1900, however, when they were living in St. Croix Falls, WI, he was named Emil Bergquist. He and his wife apparently separated after the birth of their youngest child in 1907. By 1910 Minnie Monty was living with her children in her father's household in Sterling, WI. She had had four children of whom the first three listed below were still alive. Ten years later she was living in Kendall, WI, with her second husband and daughters Evelyn Beckmark and Geneva and Irid Berquist.

Harry Frank Beckmark was a butter maker in Kendall, WI, when he signed on 12 Sep 1918 his World War I Draft Registration card. That appears to have been his chosen surname. His parents however used the surname Backmark.

Children:

i   **Geneva Evangeline Berquist** b 31 Mar 1897, WI or MN; d 14 Feb 1981, Los Angeles, CA. She married ____ **Grimshaw.**

ii   **Rowe Berquist** b 16 Feb 1900, WI; d 23 Mar 1974, Minneapolis, MN. He married 1926? **Lillian Buttenhoff** (____ Buttenhoff & ____ Kuntz) b 5 Dec 1895, MN; d 5 Jan 1974, Minneapolis, MN.

iii   **Irid Berquist** b 1907?, WI.

iv   **Evelyn Beckmark** b 1913?, WI.

13.9.2.4.4   **MONTY, Rutherford/Ruford George** b 20 Mar 1876, Sterling, WI. He married 1894? **Elama Mara Butler** (Harry Frederick Butler & Mary Ann Wamboldt) b 27 Mar 1873, Minneapolis, MN; d & bur 10 & 14 Nov 1970, Amery & Osceola, WI.

Rutherford (very often Ruford) Monty was a barber in Osceola Mills, WI, at the birth of his daughter in 1895 and a miller in Sterling, WI, in 1900, when he and his wife had been married for six years. He was a railroad agent in St. Croix Falls, WI, from at least 1910 until at least 1930 (US censuses).

Child:

13.9.2.4.4.1	Ethel Mona	1895-	-

3.1.3.2.1.1 **MONTY/MONTA, Electa** b 12 Aug 1870, Milton, VT. She married (1) 6 Feb 1888, Burlington, VT, **Henry Ira/Henri Bessette/Bassett** (Louis Bessette & Marie Lacroix) b & bp 7 May & 12 Jun 1864, Granby, QC; d & bur 1940, Burlington, VT.

She married (2) 24 Jun 1911, Portland, ME, **Horace M. Pratt** (James Pratt & Amy Tidd) b Oct 1856, Bloomfield, ME; m (1) 20 Dec 1899, Portland, ME, Mary E. Smith; d between 1920 and 1930.

Electa Monty's first husband was named Henri Bessette at his baptism but Ira Bessett in 1880 when he was working on his father's farm in Burlington, VT, Henry Bessette in St. Joseph's Catholic Church record of his marriage, Henry Basett in the Vermont Vital Records of that marriage, and Henry I. Basset or Bassett in US censuses. His tombstone in Mount Calvary Cemetery in Burlington is inscribed HENRY I. BESSETTE.

Henry Bassett was a house painter in Burlington at his marriage and a paper hanger there in 1900. He and his wife apparently separated in the mid to late 1890s and were living apart in 1900. Electa Monta even claimed to be single and had resumed her maiden name. Meanwhile their children Mable, Katie, Eddie, and Eugene were pupils in St. Joseph's Orphanage in Burlington. The three youngest children however were with their father in 1910 when he was a house painter in Burlington. He owned his own shop there in 1920 and was even styled a house "decorator" in 1930. His marital status is less clear: he was married in 1900, widowed in 1910, divorced in 1920, and widowed again in 1930 when he was staying with his daughter Katherine C. (ii) and her husband (US censuses).

I do not know when or why Electa Monta moved to Maine. She was a resident of South Portland, ME, at her marriage to Horace M. Pratt. It is possible that this was a third marriage: the Maine Marriage Index shows that on 24 Jun 1911 Horace M. Pratt married Electa R. Monta as well as Electa M. Sawyer, who could well be Mrs. Electa Monta Sawyer. I know nothing about this possible second husband.

Horace M. Pratt worked in a locomotive shop in Madison, ME, in 1880 and was a machinist in Portland from at least 1900 to at least 1920 (US censuses). His widow was still living there when her father's will was probated in Burlington in 1934 (Chittenden Co., VT, Probate Court, #12-929).

Children:
> i   **Mabel/Marie Amable Bessette** b & bp 23 & 31 Jan 1889, Burlington, VT; d 10 May 1979, Lynn, MA. She married 29 Aug 1909, Troy, NY, **Ernest Francis Robillard** (Joseph Robillard & Lucy L'Heureux) b 16 Jun 1886, Burlington, VT; d 19 Nov 1975, Warren, MA.
> ii   **Catherine/Katherine Céleste Bessette** b & bp 28 Mar & 24 Apr 1890, Burlington, VT. She married 1912? **Joseph H. Sears** (Theodore Sears & Ida ____) b 19 Nov 1887, Burlington, VT; d there Nov 1980.
> iii   **Edward/Henri Edouard Bessette** b & bp 24 Feb & 6 Mar 1892, Burlington, VT.
> iv   **Eugène Théophile Bessette** b & bp 25 Dec 1893 & 14 Jan 1894, Burlington, VT.

3.1.3.2.1.2 **MONTY, Emerette/Etta** b 11 Mar 1875, Colchester, VT. She married (1) 9 Jan 1895, Burlington, VT, **Olen Olsen** (Donald Olsen & Maria Hanson) b Feb 1864, Copenhagen, Denmark.

She married (2) 9 Dec 1929, Portland, ME, **Bion B. Small** (Benjamin Small & Catherine ____) b Oct 1855, Lubec, ME; m (1) 1877? Dora ____.

Olen Olsen (also Olson, Olesen) came to the United States in 1883 and was a laborer in Burlington, VT, at his marriage to Amarette Mounthy (sic). He was a weaver in Winooski, VT, in 1900 and in Pawtucket, RI, in 1910 (US censuses), and was still living there in 1922 according to the City Directory of that year.

Etta Monty was a resident of Bridgton, ME, at her second marriage and was living there with her new husband in 1930 when their household included her widowed father Wilbur Monty (US census). She was a resident of Portland, ME, when her father's died in 1934 (Chittenden Co., VT, Probate Court, #12-929).

Bion B. Small was an employee of the Boston & Maine Railroad (watchman and freight clerk) in South Portland, ME, until at least 1910. He was retired in 1920 and 1930 (US censuses; City Directories).

Children:
  i   **Olive Olsen** b Apr 1896, Winooski, VT.
  ii   **Albert Olsen** b Aug 1898, Winooski, VT.
  iii **Paulina Olsen** b Feb 1900, Winooski, VT.

3.1.3.2.1.3   **MONTY/MONTA/MONTEY, Eleanor/Elenor** b 26 Jul 1880, Colchester, VT; d 31 Mar 1910. She married 15 Oct 1895, Burlington, VT, **Peter Hanson** (Peter Hanson & Minnert Peterson) b Nov 1865, Denmark; d & bur 1935, Colchester, VT.

Eleanor Monty's name and surname varied somewhat in her lifetime. She married as Eleanor Monty but was known at the births of her children as Elenor Montey, Elenor Monty, and Eleanor Monta. She was buried in the Champlain Cemetery in Colchester, VT, as Elenor Montey Hanson.

Peter Hanson was a carpenter in Burlington, VT, at his marriage, a laborer in Winooski, VT, in 1900, a farmer in Colchester from at least 1902 to 1920, and a carpenter there in 1930 (US censuses). The year of his death is taken from the inscription on his tombstone in the Champlain Cemetery in Colchester.

Children:
  i   **Minnie Hanson** b 22 Mar 1900, Colchester, VT; d there 25 May 1900.
  ii   **Margaret Hanson** b 6 Oct 1902, Colchester, VT. She married ____ **Ladd**.
  iii **Harold Whittaker Hanson** b 7 Feb 1906, Colchester, VT; d Dec 1978, Grand Isle, VT.

3.1.3.3.2.1   **MONTA, Francis** b 22 Feb 1912, Claremont, NH; d Jan 1986, Glencliff, NH.

3.1.3.3.4.1   **MONTA, Robert Morrow** b 3 Feb 1915, Colchester, VT. He married (1) there 14 Oct 1936 **Dorothy Graves** (Claude Graves & Rosanna ____) b 5 Oct 1916, Burlington, VT; d 23 Mar 1986, Colchester, VT.

He married (2) **Julie Magoon**.

Robert Monta and his wife Julie were residents of Colchester, VT, at the death of his sister Harlene (3.1.3.3.4.3) in 2007 (*Burlington Free Press*, 15 Oct 2007).

Children of the first marriage:
3.1.3.3.4.1.1	Roy Emery	1937-	-
3.1.3.3.4.1.2	Nancy Elaine	-	-
3.1.3.3.4.1.3	Emily	-	-

3.1.3.3.4.2   **MONTA, Thelma Ethel** b 11 Mar 1918, Colchester, VT. She married 25 Nov 1945, Colchester, VT, **Douglas Norman Wright** (Norman B. Wright & Clara E. ____) b there 1917?

Douglas Wright was a 2-year-old child living with his parents in Colchester, VT, on 1 Jan 1920 (US census).

Children:
  i   **Lois Elaine Wright** b 1955?, VT. She married **Kermit Blaisdell** (Willard H. Blaisdell & Izola E. Spaulding) b Jan 1945, Enosburg Falls, VT.
  ii   **Martha Susan Wright** b 1958? VT. She married **Duane Allan Howard** b Nov 1948.
  iii **Norma Louise Wright** married **Kenneth R. Pullen** b 1945?
  iv   **Seth Andrew Wright** b 1960?, VT. He married **Wendy S. Rother** b 1960?

3.1.3.3.4.3   MONTA, Harlene Cecelia b 16 Apr 1920, Milton, VT; d & bur 12 & 16 Oct 2007, Burlington & Colchester, VT.

Harlene Cecelia Monta was buried in the Colchester, VT, Village Cemetery.

3.1.3.3.4.4   MONTA, Shirley Elizabeth b 3 Jun 1923, Colchester, VT. She married there 28 Dec 1944 **Leslie T. Casavant** (Caleb S. Casavant & Mabel J. ___) b 6 Jun 1921, Burlington, VT; d & bur 26 & 29 Apr 1997, Bristol, CT.

This couple lived in Bristol and Terryville, CT. Leslie Casavant, who predeceased his wife, was buried in Peacedale Cemetery in Bristol.

Children:

i   **Kathleen Ann Casavant** b May 1946. She married 3 May 1984, Bristol, CT, **William N. Winters** b 9 Jul 1939, Hartford, CT; d 18 Apr 1991, Bristol, CT.

ii   **Leslie Lynne Casavant** b Jun 1956. She married (1) 14 Oct 1978, Bristol, CT, **Stephen R. Paradise** (Joseph Francis Paradise & Joyce D. Williams) b Oct 1955. She married (2) 18 Sep 1992, Berlin, CT, **David L. Hawkins** b Mar 1955.

3.1.3.3.4.5   MONTA, Wesley Clarence b 10 Oct 1925, Colchester, VT.

Wesley C. Monta was living with his parents in Colchester, VT, in 1930 (US census).

3.1.3.3.4.6   MONTA, Margaret Eileen b 6 Jul 1932, Burlington, VT. She married 14 Jun 1958, Colchester, VT, **Paul C. Dunham** (Paul Clinton Dunham & Marion Elsie Strong) b 1931.

Children:

i   **Barbara Holly Dunham**

ii   **Bruce Matthew Dunham** married **Diane Margaret Roza**.

3.3.2.1.3.1   MONTEE, Bertha A. b & bp 12 Dec 1885, Glens Falls, NY. She married there 24 Feb 1920 **Arthur Goodness** (Joseph E. Goodness & Ida Ives) b 5 Jan 1900, Luzerne, NY; d 8 Sep 1988, Schenectady, NY.

Arthur Goodness was a mechanic in Glens Falls, NY, at his marriage and an electrician in Schenectady, NY, in 1930 (US census). He was a brother of Frank H. Goodness, husband of Anna Pearl Montee (3.3.2.1.3.2).

Child:

i   **Marie Goodness** b 1922?, Glens Falls, NY.

3.3.2.1.3.2   MONTEE, Anna Pearl (twin) b & bp 29 Nov & 23 Dec 1888, Glens Falls, NY. She married there 7 Jul 1919 **Frank H. Goodness** (Joseph E. Goodness & Ida Ives) b May 1895, Hadley, NY; m (1) 3 Sep 1916, Warrensburg, NY, Eleanor Donohue (Dennis Donohue & Agnes Cross); d between 1920 and 1930.

Frank Goodness was a brother of Arthur Goodness, husband of Bertha A. Montee (3.3.2.1.3.1). He was a chauffeur in Glens Falls, NY, at his first marriage and a carpenter there at his second. His widow was housekeeper in 1930 for her sister Lena (3.3.2.1.3.3) and brother-in-law Loren LaFay in Fort Edward, NY (US census).

3.3.2.1.3.3   MONTEE, Lena Victoria (twin) b & bp 29 Nov & 23 Dec 1888, Glens Falls, NY. She married there 28 Nov 1912 **Loren Fred LaFay/Laurent Alfred Lefebvre** (Fred LaFay/Alfred Lefebvre & Emma Perry/Hermine Perras) b & bp 28 Dec 1887 & 3 Jan 1888, Hudson Falls, NY; d May 1963, NY.

Lena Montee's husband was baptized in St. Paul's Catholic church in Hudson Falls, NY, under the name of Laurent Alfred Lefebvre, son of Alfred Lefebvre and Hermine Perras. He married under that name in St. Alphonsus church in Glens Falls, NY, as the son of Alfred and Emma Lefebvre. The French surname was also used at the baptisms of his first three children though all civil records I have seen name him Loren LaFay or occasionally LeFay.

Loren LaFay was an apprentice machinist in Hudson Falls NY, in 1910, a toolmaker in Albany, NY, in 1920, and a machinist in Fort Edward, NY, in 1930 (US censuses).

Children:

i   **Anna Ruth LaFay** b & bp 25 Aug & 14 Sep 1913, Hudson Falls & Glens Falls, NY; d & bur 27 & 30 Aug 1990, Fort Edward & Argyle, NY. She married (1) 22 Apr 1933, Hudson Falls, NY, **Edward Watson.**

      She married (2) **Owen E. Londrigan** (Maurice J. Londrigan & Maud E. _____) b 16 Dec 1919, Kingsbury, NY; d 14 Jun 1988.

ii   **Lena Monty LaFay** b & bp 27 Jun & 25 Jul 1915, Hudson Falls, NY.

iii   **Loren Edmund LaFay** b & bp 9 Oct & 4 Nov 1917, Hudson Falls, NY; d Feb 1966, Glens Falls, NY. He married **Josephine A. Marino** (Daniel Marino & Lucy _____) b 14 Jun 1918, Glens Falls, NY; d there 26 Apr 1997.

iv   **Joseph A. LaFay** b 28 Jan 1926, NY; d 8 Dec 1996, Hudson Falls, NY.

3.3.2.1.4.1   **MONTEE, William Henry** b & bp 11 & 15 May 1881, Glens Falls, NY; d & bur 30 Mar & 2 Apr 1906, Glens Falls & South Glens Falls, NY.

William H. Montee (Guillaume Henri at his baptism) was a laborer in Glens Falls, NY. He did not marry and was buried alongside his parents in St. Mary's Cemetery in South Glens Falls, NY.

3.3.2.1.4.2   **MONTEE, Mary Elizabeth** b & bp 18 & 25 Mar 1883, Glens Falls, NY; d & bur 17 & 20 Apr 1954, Albany & Glens Falls, NY. She married 14 Feb 1911, Gardner, MA, **Joseph Theophile Beaudet** (Julien/Julian Beaudet & Odile Anna/Odina Lagace) b & bp 6 & 8 Oct 1880, Glens Falls, NY; m (1) there 22 Oct 1902 **Nellie L. Willard** (Edward Willard & Harriet Montee); d & bur there 23 & 26 Feb 1958.

Mary Elizabeth Montee was a first cousin of Nellie Willard (3.3.2.1.5.v), her husband's first wife.

Theophile Beaudet was a clothing salesman in Glens Falls, NY, in 1900. He moved to Schenectady, NY, after his first marriage and was a resident there when his first wife died. He later returned to Glens Falls where he was an accountant in a paper mill in 1920 and a public accountant in 1930 (US censuses). He and both his wives were buried in St. Alphonsus Cemetery there.

Children:

i   **Julian Frederic Beaudet** b & bp 27 Apr & 7 May 1916, Glens Falls, NY; d there 14 Mar 1990. He married there 8 May 1939 **Mildred Alida Tripp** (Neil E. Tripp & Hazel V. McNutt) b 16 Apr 1917, Cayuga Co., NY.

ii   **Arthur Joseph Beaudet** b & bp 14 Dec 1917 & 6 Jan 1918, Glens Falls, NY; d 15 Aug 2005, Austin, TX. He married **Charlotte Editha McGann** b 23 Aug 1924; d 24 Dec 2005, Greensboro, NC.

3.3.2.1.4.3   **MONTEE, Joseph Frederick** b & bp 7 & 13 Feb 1887, Glens Falls, NY; d 9 Sep 1918, France.

Fred Joseph Montee was a salesman in Buffalo, NY, when he signed his World War I Draft Registration card on 5 Jun 1917. He was single. Corporal Joseph Frederick Montee died in France and was buried in the Oise-Aisne American Cemetery near Château-Thierry.

3.3.2.1.4.4   **MONTEE, Alice Margaret** b & bp 9 & 11 Sep 1888, Glens Falls, NY; d 27 Dec 1962, Albany, NY. She married 1916? **Leroy W. Allen** (Nelson Allen & Florence _____) b Aug 1886, Glens Falls, NY; d 1943.

Leroy W. Allen was a superintendent of the street railway in Glens Falls, NY, in 1920 and a sales clerk in Schenectady, NY, in 1930 when he and his wife had been married for fourteen years (US censuses). She was buried in Most Holy Redeemer Cemetery in Niskayuna, NY.

Child:

i   **Monty Leroy Allen** b 19 Jul 1917, Glens Falls, NY; d 16 Oct 1986, Delray Beach, FL.

3.3.2.1.4.5   **MONTEE, Catherine Mary Ann/Marion C.** b & bp 17 & 27 Jul 1890, Glens Falls, NY; d there 1 Sep 1890.

Catherine Mary Ann Montee (baptismal name) was six weeks old when she was buried under the name of Marion C. Montee in St. Mary's Cemetery in South Glens Falls, NY.

3.3.2.1.9.1   **MONTEE, Joseph Harold** b & bp 18 Oct & 8 Nov 1896, Glens Falls, NY; d there 11 Jul 1902.

This child was named Joseph Harold at birth. His tombstone in St. Alphonsus Cemetery in Glens Falls, NY, however is in the name of Harold J. Montee.

3.3.2.1.9.2   **MONTEE, Evelyn Rose** b & bp 20 & 24 Jul 1898, Glens Falls, NY; d there 19 Jun 1947. She married there 12 Jun 1918 **Francis Leo Lambert** (Ambrose H. Lambert & Adele Lapoint) b & bp there 30 Sep & 1 Oct 1895; d & bur there 1 & 4 Feb 1960.

Francis L. Lambert was a clerk in music store in Glens Falls, NY, in 1920 and the manager there in 1930 (US censuses). He and his wife were buried in St. Alphonsus Cemetery in Glens Falls.

Child:

i   **Leo Joseph Lambert** b & bp 26 Sep & 15 Oct 1922, Glens Falls, NY. He married there 28 Apr 1951, **Theresa Rainville** (Dominique Rainville & Emma Deapo) b there 1926?

3.3.2.3.4.1   **MONTEE, Infant** b Nov/Dec 1884; d 7 Nov 1885, Luzerne, NY, at the age of 10 (or 11) months and 27 (or 7) days.

This child was buried in the Holy Infancy Catholic Cemetery in Lake Luzerne, NY. The tombstone inscription however is so faint that the various transcribers have all read a different age at death. The only certainty is that the child was less than a year old.

3.3.2.3.4.2   **MONTEE, Walter Ambrose** b 20 May 1886, Luzerne, NY; d 10 Dec 1945, MI. He married 1920? **Rita Irene O'Hern** (Richard O'Hern & ____) b 14 Aug 1892, Byron, MI; d around 1955, Detroit, MI.

Walter Montee was a papermaker in Luzerne, NY, in 1905. He moved to Detroit, MI, and was working for the Ford Motor Co. there when he signed on 12 Sep 1918 his World War I Draft Registration card. In 1930, when he and his wife had been married for ten years, he was a car salesman there (US and state censuses).

Children:

3.3.2.3.4.2.1	Walter Richard	1924-1945-
3.3.2.3.4.2.2	Margaret M.	1926- -1988

3.3.2.3.4.3   **MONTEE, Harold** b 6 Apr 1888, Luzerne, NY; d there 16 Jun 1889 at the age of 1 year, 2 months, and 10 days.

3.3.2.3.4.4   **MONTEE, Harry Louis** b 23 Apr 1890, Luzerne, NY; d 28 Jan 1972, Seattle, WA. He married 17 Jan 1916, Detroit, MI, **Florence Emily Dietz** (Henry C. Dietz & Mary Elizabeth Lines) b there 4 Nov 1897; d 24 May 1966, Seattle, WA.

Harry L. Montee left New York State for Detroit, MI, in the early 1910s and was a timekeeper for the Ford Motor Co. there when he signed on 5 Jun 1917 his World War I Draft Registration card. He was a salesman there in 1920 and 1930 (US censuses).

Child:

3.3.2.3.4.4.1	Josephine Florence	1917-1938-1993

3.3.2.3.4.5 **MONTEE, William Hurst** b 6 Apr 1892, Luzerne, NY; d 1961, Grosse Pointe, MI. He married 2 Apr 1921, Detroit, MI, **Laura Roberts** (Benjamin Franklin Roberts & Laura Howard) b 1 Feb 1899, Cambria, WY; m (2) Lucius Gaylord Hulbert (Prescott Hulbert & Elizabeth _____); d 10 Oct 1993, Columbus, OH.

William Hurst Montee left New York State for Detroit, MI, in the early 1910s and worked there as an engineer in the automobile industry (US censuses).

Children:

3.3.2.3.4.5.1	June/Jane (twin)	1922-	-1928
3.3.2.3.4.5.2	Jean (twin)	1922-	-
3.3.2.3.4.5.3	Jacqueline	-	-

3.3.2.3.4.6 **MONTEE, Marie** b 18 Sep 1894, Luzerne, NY; d there Mar 1895 at the age of 6 months.

3.3.2.3.4.7 **MONTEE, Helen Madeline** b 31 Aug 1898, Luzerne, NY; d & bur 6 & ? Aug 1948, Albany and Lake Luzerne, NY. She married 1926? **John Roosevelt Rodriguez** (Armando Bernardo Rodriguez & Mary Ellen Kelly) b 21 Jun 1899, New York, NY; d & bur Aug 1972, Albany & Lake Luzerne, NY.

This woman was generally known as Madeline Montee though her formal signature was Helen Madeline Montee or Helen Madeline Rodriguez. She was a stenographer in Detroit, MI, in 1920 (US census) but was a resident of Albany, NY, when her father died in February 1926. She probably married later that year for, according to her son Robert's birth record of January 1934, she had then been a housekeeper, often a synonym for housewife, for eight years.

John R. Rodriguez' date of birth is taken from the Social Security Death Index. When he signed his World War I Draft Registration card in Nassau Co., NY, on 12 Sep 1918, however, he stated that he was born on 28 Jun 1899. Either date is possible. He was a printer in Nassau Co. in 1918 and continued working as a printer there and in Albany, where he moved soon after the birth of his first child. Both he and his wife were buried in Holy Infancy Catholic Cemetery in Lake Luzerne, NY.

Children:

i **George E. Rodriguez** b 8 Apr 1930, Lynbrook, NY; d 13 Mar 2003, Albany, NY. He married there **Joan Kelly**.

ii **John A. Rodriguez** b Jan 1932, Albany, NY.

iii **Robert Benedict Rodriguez** b 2 Jan 1934, Albany, NY. He married 19 Feb 1955, Del Rio, TX, **Maria Alicia Martinez**.

iv **Douglas William Rodriguez** b 14 Apr 1936, Albany, NY. He married **Joan _____** .

3.3.2.3.4.8 **MONTEE, Pauline Elizabeth** b 21 May 1903, Luzerne, NY; d 8 Jun 1966, Albany, NY. She married 1927? **Howard Crawford Bennett** b 17 Mar 1907, New York, NY; d 17 May 1946, Albany, NY.

Howard C. Bennett and his wife had been married for 3 years in 1930 (US census). He was a real estate agent in Albany, NY.

Children:

i **Norma Bennett** b 1 Feb 1929, Albany, NY; d there Dec 1968. She married **Joseph Nagengast** (Emil Nagengast & Sophia _____) b 29 Sep 1925, Albany, NY; d Nov 1980.

ii **Howard Bennett** b 1932, Albany, NY. He married **Millie _____** .

iii **Joyce Bennett** b 22 Mar 1937, Albany, NY; d & bur 27 & 30 Oct 2004, Liverpool & Clay, NY. She married **Robert P. Crannage** b 11 May 1936, Troy, NY; d & bur 5 & 10 Nov 2005, Liverpool & Clay, NY.

3.3.5.1.2.1   **MONTY, Rose F./Rosa** b Feb 1864, Essex Co., NY; d 1908?, at the age of 44. She married 1883? **Willard H. Hodskins** (Milton Hodskins & Emelie Church) b & bp 6 Dec 1860 & 9 Dec 1905, Essex Co. & Glens Falls, NY.

Willard H. Hodskins was a farm laborer in Westport, NY, in 1900 when he and his wife had been married for seventeen years. They had had four children who were still living with them in 1905 in Glens Falls, NY, where Willard Hodskins was a carpenter (US and state censuses). That was also the year when he and his sons Austin, Wesley, and Frederick were baptized on the same day in St. Alphonsus Catholic Church in Glens Falls.

Rose Monty died at the age of 44, according to her mother's obituary in the *Ticonderoga Sentinel* of 11 Feb 1926.

Children:
i   **Austin W. Hodskins** b & bp 28 Aug 1884 & 9 Dec 1905, Essex Co. & Glens Falls, NY; d & bur 17 & 20 Aug 1908, Glens Falls, NY.
ii   **Wesley C. Hodskins** b & bp 24 Mar 1886 & 9 Dec 1905, Crown Point & Glens Falls, NY. He married (1) 9 Dec 1909, Schroon Lake, NY, **Olive Lockwood** (Edward Linus Lockwood & Betsey R. Wilcox) b there Aug 1882; d & bur there 1911.
        He married (2) 31 May 1913, Elizabethtown, NY, **Marjorie McAuley** (Charles McAuley & Agnes Gardner) b there Mar 1893; d 10 Mar 1940, New York, NY.
iii   **Rose/Rosa Hodskins** b Feb 1888, NY. She married 15 Aug 1906, Glens Falls, NY, **Louis Richardson** (John Richardson & Eliza ____) b there 1 Dec 1874; d & bur there 21 & 24 Feb 1943.
iv   **Frederick/Fred Hodskins** b & bp 11 Jan 1890 & 9 Dec 1905, Essex Co. & Glens Falls, NY.

3.3.5.1.2.2   **MONTY, William H.** b 5 Jul 1865, Willsboro, NY; d & bur 31 Dec 1913 & 5 Jan 1914, Ticonderoga, NY. He married 25 Jun 1895, Vergennes, VT, **Sarah LaPorte** (Julius LaPorte & Matilda Daigneault) b there 1868?

William Monty was a teamster in Ticonderoga, NY, at his marriage. According to his obituary in the *Ticonderoga Sentinel* of 8 Jan 1914, he left no wife or children.

Sarah LaPorte was 2 years old when living with her parents in Vergennes, VT, in 1870 and 12 years old in 1880 (US censuses). Yet she was said to be 24 years old at her marriage. I am relying here on the earlier records.

3.3.5.1.2.3   **MONTY, Laura Ann** b & bp 19 Mar & 17 Sep 1867, Essex & Keeseville, NY; d 30 Mar 1952, Ticonderoga, NY. She married (1) 17 Sep 1884, Keeseville, NY, and divorced 10 May 1902, Saratoga, NY, **Napoleon Gaudreau/Goodrow** (Antoine Gaudreau & Louise ____).

She married (2) perhaps as early as 1902 but certainly on 13 Dec 1916, Ticonderoga, NY, **Lewis LaDuke** (Felix LaDuke & Harriet Wilson) b 1864?, Essex Co., NY; m (1) 1890? ____; d 17 Aug 1928, Ticonderoga, NY.

She married (3) between 1930 and 1937 **William Parsons** (John Parsons & Martha ____) b 1868?, NY; m (1) 1888? and divorced 1920, Essex Co., NY, Lillie ____; m (2) 11 Nov 1920, Jennie Pepper, widow of Charles Crossman; d & bur 16 & 18 Feb 1948, Ticonderoga, NY, at the age of 80.

The story of Laura Ann Monty's marriages is based to a large extent on indirect evidence. The 1916 record of her marriage to Lewis LaDuke notes that she was the divorced wife of Napoleon Goodrow. It also states she was a widow: he may have died before 1916. I know nothing more about him. His children consistently used the surname Goodrow.

The date of her second marriage is open to question. The Essex Co., NY, Marriage Records (#2251) indicate that Laura Monty Goodrow and Lewis LaDuke were married in Ticonderoga, NY, on 13 Dec 1916. Yet various issues of the *Ticonderoga Sentinel* from at least 1904 on refer to Mrs. Lewis LaDuke as either the mother of Goodrow children or the sister of William Monty (3.3.5.1.2.2). The 1910 US census in Ticonderoga specifies that Laura and Lewis LaDuke had been married for eight years. It may be that this marriage was a common-law one which was legalized in 1916, perhaps after Napoleon Gaudreau's death. Or it may be that the 1916 marriage was merely a Catholic validation of a pre-existing civil marriage. I do not know.

Lewis LaDuke was a 52-year-old widower when he married Laura Monty in 1916. He was a teamster in Ticonderoga in 1910 and 1920 and was buried there in Mount Hope Cemetery. His widow was living in Hudson Falls, NY, in 1930 (US censuses).

Laura Monty remarried before 1937 when her father died at the home of his daughter, Mrs. William Parsons of Ticonderoga. She was also in Ticonderoga when her son John L. Goodrow (iv) died in 1945. Yet when William Parsons died at a sister's home there in 1948, his wife Laura was said to be living in Poultney, VT (*Ticonderoga Sentinel*, 7 Jan 1937, 15 Nov 1945, and 19 Feb 1948). He was buried in Mount Hope Cemetery in Ticonderoga.

Children:

i. **William Goodrow** b 1885?, Essex Co., NY. He married 1921? **Elsie A.** ____ b 1895?, NY.

ii **Margaret Goodrow** b 1886?, Ticonderoga, NY. She married (1) 1906? and divorced 21 Dec 1915, Middlebury, VT, **Alexander Lewis** (Francis Lewis & Jennie ____) b 2 Dec 1882, NJ.
She married (2) 2 Dec 1916, Ticonderoga, NY, **Charles Richard Bishop** (Fred L. Bishop & Lillian ___) b 11 Sep 1892, Whitehall, NY; d Jun 1970, Scotia, NY.

iii **Laura Goodrow** b 1891?, Ticonderoga, NY. She married there 22 Apr 1911 **Silas DeRosia/Joseph Célestin Desrosiers** (Dosithée Louis Desrosiers & Elizabeth Nadeau) b & bp 17 & 18 Mar 1890, St. Eugène de Grantham, QC.

iv **John Louis Goodrow** b 15 Aug 1892, Crown Point, NY; d & bur 14 & 17 Nov 1945, Ticonderoga, NY. He married there 6 Nov 1916 **Emma Sartwell** (Frank C. Sartwell & Ida Minerva Burt) b there 22 Aug 1896; d there 23 Jan 1954.

v **George Leslie Goodrow** b & bp 8 Sep 1894 & 9 Feb 1899, Ticonderoga, NY. He married 1924? **Hazel** ____ b 8 Mar 1903, NY; d Mar 1986, Glens Falls, NY.

vi **Leonard Gaudreau** b & bp 16 Aug 1897 & 14 Aug 1898, Ticonderoga, NY; d there 15 Sep 1898.

3.3.5.1.2.4   **MONTY, Alvina** b & bp 6 & 10 Apr 1870, Glens Falls, NY; d 29 Nov 1944, Ticonderoga, NY. She married (1) there 30 Nov 1896 **Joseph A. Nadeau/Neddo** (Silas Neddo & Ellen Fernette) b & bp there 14 Jun & 9 Jul 1874; d & bur there 21 & 25 Mar 1940.

She married (2) 6 Aug 1944, Ticonderoga, NY, **William Alonzo Petty** (Charles L. Petty & Mary E. ____) b 11 Aug 1873, Essex Co., NY; m (1) 1896? Maud B. ____.

Alvina Monty's first husband was known as Joseph Neddo in the records of his baptism and marriage as well as in the 1900 US census in Ticonderoga, NY, where he was a teamster. In later censuses Joseph Nadeau was a teamster in Ticonderoga in 1910, a freight handler in a paper mill there in 1920, and a chemical plant laborer in 1930. His sons regularly used the surname Nadeau.

William Petty was an automobile salesman in Ticonderoga in 1930. He and his first wife Maud had been married for four years in 1900 (US censuses). He survived his second wife (*Ticonderoga Sentinel*, 30 Nov 1944).

Children:

i **Joseph Roland Nadeau** b & bp 27 Sep & 31 Oct 1897, Ticonderoga, NY. He married 28 Sep 1920, Glens Falls, NY, **Eva May Porter** (Clark Porter & Amanda Stephen) b Mar 1899, Schuylerville, NY.

ii **Silas William Nadeau** b & bp 26 Aug & 28 Sep 1902, Ticonderoga, NY; d there Apr 1966. He married **Gladys L. King** (Edward Francis King & Laura ____) b 1907?, Ticonderoga, NY; d & bur Nov 1929, Crown Point, NY, at the age of 22.

iii **Cyril Andrew Nadeau** b & bp 13 May & 3 Jun 1906, Ticonderoga, NY; d Oct 1976, Erie Co., NY. He married 1926? **Viola M.** ____ b 17 Aug 1906, Ticonderoga, NY; m (2) there 21 Dec 1946 William Noel (Frank Noel & Rhoda Fleming); d & bur 15 & 18 Dec 1993, Albany & Ticonderoga, NY.

3.3.5.1.2.5   **MONTY, George** b & bp 23 Apr & 3 Jul 1873, NY & Burlington, VT; bur 3 Oct 1873, Plattsburgh, VT.

3.3.5.1.2.6   **MONTY, Charles A.** b & bp 7 Sep 1874 & 1 Jan 1875, NY & Plattsburgh, NY; d & bur 31 May & 3 Jun 1940, Elizabethtown & South Glens Falls, NY. He married 1901? **Julia Agnes Cronin** b 1875?, NY; d & bur 17 & 19 Apr 1941, Elizabethtown & South Glens Falls, NY.

    Charles A. Monty was named Charles Antoine at his baptism in St. Peter's church in Plattsburgh, NY. He signed his World War I Draft registration card however as Charles Andrew Monty. All other references are to Charles or Charles A. Monty. He was a day laborer in Glens Falls, NY, in 1900, a barber there in 1910 when he and his 35-year-old wife had been married for nine years, a truck man in Ticonderoga, NY, in 1920, and a barber in Elizabethtown, NY, in 1930 (US censuses) and until his death. Both he and his wife were buried in St. Mary's Cemetery in South Glens Falls, NY. They had no children.

3.3.5.1.2.7   **MONTY, John Henry** b & bp 24 Nov 1876 & 29 Apr 1877, NY & Plattsburgh, NY; d & bur 18 Jan & 11 May 1953, Glens Falls & Queensbury, NY. He married 1898? **Melissa E. Stimpson** (Amos Stimpson & Matilda Covill) b 1876?, Essex Co., NY; d & bur 1942, Glens Falls & Queensbury, NY.

    John H. Monty was a house painter in Glens Falls, NY. He and his 34-year-old wife had been married for twelve years in 1910 and had had seven children of whom three, Nora, Edith, and John Jr., were still alive (US and state censuses). He and his wife were buried in Pineview Cemetery in Queensbury, NY.

Children:

3.3.5.1.2.7.1	Nora Malvina	1899-1922?-1988
3.3.5.1.2.7.2	Edith Mary	1900-1922?-1996
3.3.5.1.2.7.3	Ellen M.	1905- -1905
3.3.5.1.2.7.4	John Henry	1906-1928?-1983

3.3.5.1.2.8   **MONTY, Margaret** died before 1900.

    This child died in infancy according to her mother's obituary in the *Ticonderoga Sentinel* of 11 Feb 1926.

3.3.5.1.6.1   **MONTY, Edward D.** b & bp 14 Feb 1880 & 14 Nov 1885, Crown Point, NY & Burlington, VT; d & bur 23 & 26 Sep 1948, Port Henry & Crown Point, NY. He married 10 Nov 1904, Crown Point, NY, **Mae C. Richards** (Simon P. Richards & Emma Metcalf) b 10 Nov 1880, Schroon Lake, NY; d & bur 25 & 28 Dec 1936, Crown Point, NY.

    After spending his early years in Vermont, Edward Monty returned to New York State with his parents in 1889 or early 1890 and was living with them in Crown Point, NY, in 1892 and in Saratoga, NY, in 1900. He was a farm laborer/farmer in West Haven, VT, in 1910, in Moriah, NY, in 1920, and in Crown Point in 1930 (US and state censuses). He left Crown Point after his wife's death and was staying in his daughter Marguerite's home in Port Henry, NY, at the time of his death. Both he and his wife were buried in Fairview Cemetery in Crown Point (*Ticonderoga Sentinel*, 31 Dec 1936 and 30 Sep 1948).

Children:

3.3.5.1.6.1.1	Claude Orlin	1909- -1983
3.3.5.1.6.1.2	Marguerite	1915-1953-2002

3.3.5.1.6.2   **MONTY, Sarah/Cécile/Celia** b & bp 18 May 1883 & 14 Nov 1885, Colchester & Burlington, VT. She married 1900? **Fred Premo** b 16 Jun 1875, Canada.

    Sarah Monty (Cécile at her baptism) moved to Essex Co., NY, with her parents in 1889 or early 1890 and was living with them in Saratoga, NY, in 1900 (US census). She may have married in the summer or fall of that year, for her daughter Anna Loretta's birth record indicates that she was a second child. She was consistently named Sarah in civil records until at least 1918 though Silia and Celia in the 1920 and 1930 US censuses in Port Henry, NY. She was not mentioned among her older brother Edward's surviving siblings in the *Ticonderoga Sentinel* of 30 Sep 1948 and probably died before then.

Fred Premo was a laborer in Victory Mills, NY, at his daughter's birth in 1902, a weaver in Cohoes, NY, in 1910, a trainman in Port Henry in 1918 and 1920, and a caretaker there in 1930 (US censuses; World War I Draft Registration card).

Child:

i   **Anna Loretta Premo** b 15 Jun 1902, Victory Mills, NY; d Oct 1981, Port Henry, NY. She married 1926? **George William Abare** b 17 Dec 1892, Fitchburg, MA; d Feb 1973, Port Henry, NY.

3.3.5.1.6.3   **MONTY, Harriet/Henriette Hélène** b & bp 18 Sep & 14 Nov 1885, Colchester & Burlington, VT. She married 1906? **Duncan D. Cameron** (David R. Cameron & Anna Lyall) b Nov 1866, Greenwich, NY; bur there 1954? at the age of 88.

Harriet Monty (Henriette Hélène at her baptism) left Vermont at a very young age and was living with her parents in Crown Point, NY, in 1892 and in Saratoga, NY, in 1900. Her husband, described as a musician in the 1900 US census in Greenwich, NY, was a millwright in Mechanicville, NY, in 1910 when he and his wife had been married for four years. He was a carpenter in Hudson Falls, NY, in 1920 and 1930 (US and state censuses) and later moved to Glens Falls, NY: Mrs. Duncan Cameron was said to be living there at the death of her brother Edward (3.3.5.1.6.1) in September 1948 (*Ticonderoga Sentinel*, 30 Sep 1948). Duncan Cameron was buried in the Greenwich Cemetery along with his parents and numerous relatives.

Children:

i   **David D. Cameron** b 1 Apr 1908, Greenwich, NY; d Feb 1982, Ballston Spa, NY.
ii   **Marion Cameron** b 1910?, Greenwich, NY.
iii   **Earl D. Cameron** b 29 Jan 1918, Greenwich, NY; d 11 Feb 1973.

3.3.5.1.6.4   **MONTY, Napoleon Joseph** b & bp 30 Jun 1886 & 16 Feb 1890, Colchester, VT & Schroon Lake, NY; d & bur 22 & 26 Sep 1966, Whallonsburg & Port Henry, NY. He married 6 Jan 1913, Port Henry, NY, **Daffodil Maple** (Henry Maple & Winifred Sanders) b there 20 Jan 1894; d & bur 8 & 11 Nov 1955, Plattsburgh & Port Henry, NY.

Napoleon Monty came to New York State with his parents a few months prior to his baptism and was living with them in Crown Point, NY, in 1892, in Saratoga, NY, in 1900, and in Moriah, NY, in 1910. He was a railroad worker there until at least 1913 and in Port Henry, NY, from at least 1920 on (US and state censuses). He was still residing in Port Henry at the death of his brother Edward (3.3.5.1.6.1) in 1948 (*Ticonderoga Sentinel*, 30 Sep 1948) and was buried alongside his wife in St. Patrick's Cemetery there.

Children:

3.3.5.1.6.4.1	Altha Genevieve	1913-1932-1993
3.3.5.1.6.4.2	Cleo	1915- -2006
3.3.5.1.6.4.3	Gladys	1919-1947-1975
3.3.5.1.6.4.4	Ray R.	1922-1946-1964

3.3.5.1.6.5   **MONTY, Rollin/Riley** b & bp 23 Apr 1889 & 16 Feb 1890, Waterbury, VT & Schroon Lake, NY. He married (1) 23 Sep 1915, Providence, RI, and divorced there 6 Apr 1918 **Lillian Elvina Hodell** (John Emil Hodell & Johanna Caroline Hultgen) b there 11 Mar 1895; m (2) there 3 Aug 1920 Michael Andrew Squizzero (Pasquale Squizzero & Elizabeth ____); d Jul 1992, Cranston, RI.

He married (2) 21 Dec 1919, Westport, NY, **Mary Bowers** (Michael Bowers & Margaret Rawley) b 1886?, New York, NY.

Rollin Monty (Joseph Riley at his baptism) came to New York State with his parents soon after his birth and was living with them in Crown Point, NY, in 1892 and in Saratoga, NY, in 1900 (US censuses). His movements after that time are unclear. He was in Providence, RI, when he first married but did not stay there very long: he was a stationary engineer in Port Henry, NY, when he signed, as Roland (sic) Monty his World War I Draft Registration card on 5 Jun 1917 and an engineer in Westport, NY, at his marriage to the 33-year-old Mary Bowers in 1919. He apparently remained in Essex Co., NY, and was a resident of Schroon Lake, NY, when his brother Edward (3.3.5.1.6.1) died in 1948 (*Ticonderoga Sentinel*, 30 Sep 1948).

Two things though puzzle me. One is that he is not found, under any of his possible names or nicknames, in any census after 1900. The other is the public notice published in nine issues of the *Ticonderoga Sentinel* from April to September 1930 of a suit brought by Dora Monty in the Supreme Court of Essex Co., NY, for an annulment of her marriage to Rollin Monty. I do not know who she might be. It is possible that he had divorced, or separated from, his second wife and that Dora was a third wife. Or it could be that his second wife, named Mary at her marriage, was rather a Dora or Mary Dora. I have been unable to solve the mystery.

3.3.5.1.6.6 **MONTY, George Philemon** b & bp 29 Feb & 6 Mar 1892, Crown Point & Schroon Lake, NY.

This child does not appear with his parents in the 1900 US census in Saratoga, NY, and may have died before then.

3.3.5.1.6.7 **MONTY, Cora Florence** b & bp 4 Jan & 4 Mar 1894, Ticonderoga, NY; bur Dec 1945, Glens Falls, NY. She married (1) 29 Oct 1909, Port Henry, NY, and divorced 29 Jan 1916, Greenwich, NY, **John F. Smith** (Charles Smith & Caroline Sears) b Jun 1886, Port Henry, NY.

She married (2) 6 Feb 1916, Port Henry, NY, **Robert Melvin Richards** (Simon Richards & Emma E. Metcalf) b 3 May 1886, Schroon Lake, NY.

John F. Smith was an engineer in Port Henry, NY, at his marriage. His son Joseph was using his stepfather's surname in the 1920 and 1930 US censuses in Poultney and Benson, VT.

Robert M. Richards was a farmer in Orwell, VT, at his marriage, a teamster in Poultney, VT, in 1920, and a farmer in Benson, VT, in 1930 (US censuses).

Children:
i   **Joseph Smith Richards** b 1912?, NY.
ii   **Florence Kathleen Richards** b 1916?, Rutland Co., VT; d 1945, Glens Falls, NY. She married 1934 **Daniel Joseph Corentto** (Alexander Daniel Corentto & Rosa Maria Gallo) b 4 Mar 1911, Glens Falls, NY; m (2) there 9 Jun 1949 June Marilyn Tinney; d there 6 Jun 1991.
iii **Robert Merrill Richards** b 30 Aug 1918, Poultney, VT; d 19 Apr 1994, Glens Falls, NY. He married **Grace Lansing**.
iv   **Bertha Mae Richards** b 21 Jun 1926, Rutland Co., VT; d Mar 1984, Glens Falls, NY. She married ____ **Potter**.

3.3.5.1.6.8 **MONTY, Anderson/Andrew Walter** b & bp 26 May & 19 Jul 1896, Crown Point & Schroon Lake, NY; d Aug 1971, Ticonderoga, NY. He married 28 Apr 1919, Port Henry, NY, **Mildred LaRock** (Henry LaRock & Anna Maple) b 20 Feb 1900, Burlington, VT; d Oct 1975, Troy, NY.

Anderson Monty was baptized under the name of Andrew Walter Monty in Our Lady of Lourdes' church in Schroon Lake, NY. He was also known as Andrew in the 1920 US census when he and his wife were staying with his parents in Port Henry, NY. In all other censuses, in his World War I Draft Registration card, in his marriage record, and in the Social Security Administration files, his name was recorded as Anderson.

The Social Security Death Index shows that Anderson Monty was born on 26 May 1895. I believe that is wrong. His baptismal record and his World War I Draft Registration card as well as all the censuses I have seen indicate to the contrary that he was born in 1896.

Anderson Monty was a laborer in Moriah, NY, at his marriage. The following year, as Andrew Monty, he was a railroad worker in Port Henry, NY, and in 1930 a laborer again in Moriah, where his widowed mother was a member of his household (US censuses). He was a resident of Ticonderoga, NY, at the death of his brother Edward (3.3.5.1.6.1) in September 1948 (*Ticonderoga Sentinel*, 30 Sep 1948).

Children:

3.3.5.1.6.8.1	Walter J.	1920-	-1975
3.3.5.1.6.8.2	Mary	1925?-	-
3.3.5.1.6.8.3	David	1929-	-
3.3.5.1.6.8.4	Nancy	-	-

3.3.5.1.6.9   **MONTY, Joseph Dewey** b & bp 13 Sep & 16 Oct 1898, Crown Point & Schroon Lake, NY.

Joseph Monty (Joseph Dewey at his baptism) was living with his parents in Saratoga, NY, in 1900 (US census) but does not appear with them in later years. He may have died before 1910.

3.3.5.1.7.1   **MONTY, Bertha Jane** b & bp 14 Nov 1883 & 13 Jan 1884, Redford, NY; d 24 Dec 1910, Fort Edward, NY. She married 1903? **Bert Daniel Porter** (Daniel Porter & Nelly A. Seaver) b 9 Jul 1878, Northville, NY; m (2) before September 1918 Nora ____.

Bert D. Porter and his wife Bertha had been married for six years in April 1910. He was then a machinist in Fort Edward, NY, and in Kingsbury, NY, in 1920 (US censuses). He remarried before 12 Sep 1918 when he named his wife Nora as his nearest relative (World War I Draft Registration).

Child:

i   **Evan W. Porter** b 30 Jan 1904, Washington Co., NY; d 7 Feb 1968, San Bernardino Co., CA. He married 1929? **Anna V.** ____ b 1902?, NY.

3.3.5.1.7.2   **MONTY, Nellie** b 1 Nov 1886, NY; d 14 Jan 1895, Waterbury, VT.

3.3.5.1.7.3   **MONTY, Louis** b 18 Sep 1889, Waterbury, VT; d 21 Oct 1911, Peru, NY.

Louis Monty came to Peru, NY, with his parents in the early 1900s and was a laborer on his father's farm there in 1910 (US censuses). He died at the age of 21 years, 1 month, and 3 days (*Plattsburgh Sentinel*, 27 Oct 1911) and was buried in the Peru Village Cemetery.

3.3.5.1.7.4   **MONTY, Anonymous** b & d 18 Sep 1890, Waterbury, VT.

3.3.5.1.7.5   **MONTY, Ethel Parmelee** b & bp 20 Mar 1896 & 19 Jun 1915, Waterbury, VT & Keeseville, NY; d & bur 16 & 18 Jul 1974, Plattsburgh, NY. She married (1) 23 Jul 1914 and 19 Jun 1915 (Catholic ceremony), Keeseville, NY, **Alfred Andrew LaBounty** (Alexander/Alexis LaBounty & Martha Gumlaw/Marceline Gamelin) b & bp 23 Oct & 9 Nov 1891, Chesterfield & Keeseville, NY.

She was a widow when she married (2) 9 Jan 1946, Plattsburgh, NY, **Louis Zéphirin Defayette** (Albert Defayette & Catherine Lamoureux) b 16 Jun 1881, Redford, NY; m (1) there 29 Apr 1904 Marie Louise Bigras (Dominique/Dominic Bigras & Marguerite/Margaret Pelletier); d there 1960.

Alfred LaBounty was a laborer in Peru, NY, at his marriage. He moved to Vermont shortly after the birth of his first child and was a station porter for the Central Vermont RR in St. Albans, VT, when he signed on 5 Jun 1917 his World War I Registration card. The family soon returned to Clinton Co., NY. Alfred LaBounty was a laborer in Plattsburgh, NY, in 1920, a boatman in Keeseville, NY, in 1925, and a boatman in Peru in 1930 (US and state censuses).

Louis Defayette was a farmer in Redford, NY.

Children:

i   **Isabelle/Isabella LaBounty** b 6 Jul 1915, Plattsburgh, NY; d & bur 2 & 5 Feb 1990, Plattsburgh & Keeseville, NY. She married **Roger H. Robare** (William Robare & Jennie Weed) b 5 Aug 1914, Keeseville, NY; d & bur 4 & 7 Sep 1983, Plattsburgh & Keeseville, NY.

ii   **Frances Marion LaBounty** b 24 Jun 1917, St. Albans, VT; d 21 Jul 2005, Vergennes, VT. She married 1 Dec 1935 **Andrew J. Brileya** (Andrew Brileya & Cora ____) b 29 Jun 1914, VT; d 25 Apr 1997, Shoreham, VT.

iii   **Pascal/Paschal LaBounty** b 23 Apr 1919, Plattsburgh, NY; d there 29 Sep 2002. He married **Geraldine E. Sommers** b 17 Sep 1924; d 4 Dec 2004, Plattsburgh, NY.

iv   **Victoria LaBounty** b 1921?, Clinton Co., NY. She married **Francis Wilson Dyer** (James Wilson Dyer & Jennie/Genevieve Marie Theroux) b 20 Oct 1919, Keeseville, NY; d 5 Feb 1979, Plattsburgh, NY.

v   **Clayton C. LaBounty** b 23 May 1923, Keeseville, NY; d & bur 2 & 5 Aug 2000, Presque Isle & Ashland, ME. He married 23 Jul 1945 **Rosanna Labelle** (Angus Labelle & Olive ____) b 4 Dec 1921, Ashland, ME; d & bur 14 & 18 Dec 2001, Plattsburgh, NY.

vi   **Joyce A. LaBounty** b Feb 1926, Clinton Co., NY. She married 20 Oct 1945, Plattsburgh, NY, **Alton W. Bushey** (Phoenix A. Bushey & Edith M. Baldwin) b Jul 1925, Chazy, NY.

vii   **Gladys R. LaBounty** b 18 May 1927, Keeseville, NY; d there 9 Jul 1982. She married (1) **Robert L. Pafford** (Robert Leonard Pafford & Nannie Morris) b 15 Jun 1921, VA; d & bur 21 & 25 Jul 1972, ? & Arlington, VA.

       She married (2) **Robert A. Brackett** (John E. Brackett & Florence ____) b 2 Jan 1929, Saratoga Springs, NY; d & bur 1 & 4 Oct 1979, Plattsburgh, NY.

3.3.5.1.7.6   **MONTY, Sarah Ellen** b 30 Oct 1898, Waterbury, VT; d & bur 10 & 15 Jun 1991, Rouses Point & Plattsburgh, NY. She married 21 Apr 1917, Swanton, VT, **Philip A. McLeod** (Albert E. McLeod & Elmira/Myra Lesperance) b there 6 May 1895; d 6 Jun 1968, Plattsburgh, NY.

Philip A. McLeod was a printer in Swanton, VT, in 1920 (US census). He moved that year to Plattsburgh, NY, and was a linotype operator at the *Press Republican* there until a few months before his death (*Press Republican,* 7 Jun 1968).

Children:

i   **Lillian A. McLeod** b Nov 1917, Swanton, VT. She married 15 Nov 1944, Atlantic City, NJ, **Arthur James Russell** (Arthur James Russell & Katherine ____) b 27 Aug 1915, Fort Edward, NY; d 12 Jan 1993, Tacoma, WA.

ii   **Doris Elizabeth McLeod** b Feb 1920, Swanton, VT. She married Jun 1939 **Bert Allen Lighthall** (Willard Lighthall & Anna Mahan) b 2 Mar 1917, Bennington, VT; m (2) Sylvia Polhemus (Charles Polhemus & Gladys ____); d 12 Mar 1974, Albany, NY.

iii   **Philip A. McLeod Jr.** b May 1923, Plattsburgh, NY. He married June 1943, Clinton Co., NY, **Genevieve/Geneva Yanulavich** (Frank Yanulavich & Louisa ____) b 1923?, NY.

3.3.5.1.7.7   **MONTY, Aileen Frances** b 10 Apr 1901, Ticonderoga, NY; d 21 May 1987, Plattsburgh., NY. She married (1) there 27 Dec 1918 and divorced there 11 Mar 1922 **Herbert Charles Tharp** (James Albert Tharp & Florence Mary Smith) b 14 Aug 1892, Tipton Co., IN; m (2) 1922? Daisy ____ ; d Mar 1974, Elwood, IN.

       She married (2) 6 Feb 1924, Peru, NY, **Frank Eugene Lyon** (George Emory Lyon & Henrietta Weatherwax) b there 16 Nov 1898; d there 9 Nov 1946.

       She married (3) 1929? **Charles Carpenter** (Leslie Carpenter & Lavina Scripture) b 20 Feb 1905, Warrensburg, NY; d 30 Jan 1973, Plattsburgh, NY.

       Herbert Charles Tharp was a soldier stationed in Plattsburgh, NY, at his first marriage.

He returned to Indiana after his army service and settled with his wife Aileen in Kokomo, IN. He was an automobile factory worker there in 1920 and a poultry man in Indianapolis, IN, in 1930 when he and his second wife Daisy had been married for eight years (US censuses).

Aileen Monty had returned to New York State before the birth of her first child. Her second husband, Frank Eugene Lyon, was a machinist in Peru, NY, at his marriage and a sash maker there in 1925 (state census).

Charles Carpenter was a garage mechanic in Peru in 1930. His household included not only his wife Aileen, to whom he had been married for less than a year, but also two stepsons, Charles Tharp and Leonard Lyon (US census). He was still a resident of Peru at his death.

Children:
i   **Charles H. Tharp** b 31 Jan 1921, Clinton Co., NY; d 8 May 1993, Willsboro, NY. He married **Treva M. Perrotte** (Charles Perrotte & Eva Blow) b 20 May 1922, Mooers, NY; d 23 Sep 2002, Willsboro, NY.
ii   **Leonard E. Lyon** b Aug 1926, Peru, NY.
iii   **Lowell Carpenter** b 9 Jan 1933, Peru, NY. He married **Miretta Abigail Cannan** b 25 Jun 1931; d 4 Feb 1996, Charlotte, NC.
iv   **Ralph L. Carpenter** b 29 Jan 1934, Peru, NY; d 3 Jan 2003, Danbury, CT. He married 28 Apr 1956, Willsboro, NY, **Jeanne Young** (Deloid Young & Edna ____).
v   **Marilyn Carpenter** b 16 Dec 1941, Peru, NY. She married 1961 **Ronald Lee Kingsbury** (Ronald D. Kingsbury & Florence Gibson) b 19 Jan 1935, NY.

3.3.6.1.3.1   **MONTY, Elizabeth Julia** b & bp Apr 1877 & 27 Jan 1878, Glens Falls, NY. She married 10 Feb 1894, Keene, NH, **Anthony Oliver** (Daniel Oliver & Sophie Castor) b Dec 1867, Highgate, VT; m (2) 1903? Ellen/Nellie ____ ; d 4 May 1924, Keene, NH.

Julie Elizabeth Monty, daughter of Henry Monty and Louise Poirier, was 9 months old at her baptism in St. Alphonsus church in Glens Falls, NY. Her name was Julia in the 1880 census there, Elizabeth at her marriage, and Lizzie J. in the 1900 census in Keene, NH. She was then divorced and living in her mother's household.

Anthony Oliver was a laborer in Keene, NH, at his first marriage, a telephone lineman there in 1900, and a hotel worker in 1910 when he and his second wife Nellie had been married for seven years. In 1920 he was a china factory worker whose wife was named Ellen (US censuses).

Child:
i   **Anonymous Oliver** (female) b & d 17 Jan 1895, Keene, NH.

3.3.6.1.3.2   **MONTY, Charles** b & bp 26 Jul & 21 Oct 1879, Glens Falls, NY.

3.3.6.1.3.3   **MONTY, Arthur** b Glens Falls, NY; d 2 May 1897, Keene, NH.
Arthur Monty's death record does not include his age. It merely states that he was born in Glens Falls, NY, the son of William H. Monty and Louisa Peer.

3.3.6.1.3.4   **MONTY, William Henry** b & bp 22 Sep & 25 Nov 1882, Glens Falls, NY. He married 12 Mar 1907, Providence, RI, **Carrie Gertrude Woodward** (William A. Woodward & Sarah F. Tucker) b Dec 1879, Taunton, MA.

William Henry Monty was a railroad conductor residing in Taunton, MA, in 1910 and 1920 and in Mansfield, MA, in 1930 (US censuses). His wife was the sister of Luella B. Woodward who married his younger brother Carl (3.3.6.1.3.7).

Children:
3.3.6.1.3.4.1	Leon W.	1908-	-1999
3.3.6.1.3.4.2	Alvin William	1909-	-1978
3.3.6.1.3.4.3	Donald Ralph	1911-1939?-1988	
3.3.6.1.3.4.4	Austin H.	1913-1938-1993	

| 3.3.6.1.3.4.5 | Louise E. | 1914- | -1969 |
| 3.3.6.1.3.4.6 | Ursula | 1920- | - |

3.3.6.1.3.5   **MONTY, Jacques** b & bp 24 Jul & 14 Sep 1884, Glens Falls, NY.

3.3.6.1.3.6   **MONTY, Joseph Alfred/Fred** b & bp 30 Jul & 21 Aug 1887, Glens Falls, NY; d 1952?, Springfield, MA. He married 1913? **Mary D. Pair** (Albert Pair & Delia/Delima ____) b 26 Jul 1896, MA; d 12 Sep 1991, Springfield, MA.

Fred Monty moved to Keene, NH, with his parents soon after his birth and was living there in his widowed mother's household in 1900. After that date he was most commonly known as Joseph F. Monty. He was a farmer in Sidney, ME, in 1920, when his in-laws were members of his household, and a machine operator in Springfield, MA, in 1930. He and his wife had then been married for seventeen years (US censuses). The Springfield City Directories show that he was a steamfitter or plumber there until 1951 and that Mrs. Mary D. Monty was a widow in 1953.

Child:

| 3.3.6.1.3.6.1 | Mary L. | 1916-1937- |

3.3.6.1.3.7   **MONTY, Carl Alvin** b 26 Mar 1890, Keene, NH; d 7 Apr 1943, Springfield, MA. He married **Luella B. Woodward** (William Woodward & Sarah F. Tucker) b 22 Jul 1893, Taunton, MA; d 8 Feb 1974, Attleboro, MA.

Carl Monty came to Massachusetts with his family between 1900 and 1910 and was a plant foreman in Taunton, MA, in 1920. He was a machinist there until 1923 and a lather in Springfield, MA, from 1924 on (US censuses; Taunton City Directories; Springfield City Directories).

Luella B. Woodward was a resident of Mansfield, MA, at her death but was buried in Swan Point Cemetery in Providence, RI. She was a sister of Carrie G. Woodward, wife of William Henry Monty (3.3.6.1.3.4).

3.5.13.2.2.1   **MONTA, Helen Mary** b 7 Aug 1904, Middlebury, VT.

Helen Monta was living with her mother in Middlebury, VT, in 1910 and with her maternal aunt and uncle, Anna Daniels and Edward A. Tobin, in Bennington, VT, in 1920. By 1930 she was a public school teacher in Carmel, NY (US censuses).

3.9.2.2.4.1   **MONTEE, Carrie M.** b 2 Dec 1881, Farmington, NH. She married there 20 Oct 1900 **Leon Everett Gilman** (Warren L. Gilman & Annie B. ____) b there 24 Jun 1878.

This couple did not stay together very long. In 1910 Leon E. Gilman was living with his parents in Farmington, NH, while his wife and 9-year-old son were in Merrimac, MA, where Mrs. Carrie Gilman had a boarding house. I have not found her in later censuses though Leon Gilman, still living in Farmington, was divorced in 1920. He was there also in 1930 but was residing in 1942 in nearby Rochester, NH (US censuses; World War II Draft Registration card).

Child:

i   **George N. Gilman** b 1 Mar 1901, Farmington, NH; d 17 Oct 1992, Westmoreland, NH.

3.9.2.2.4.2   **MONTEE, Emma L.** b 7 Dec 1884, Farmington, NH; d Feb 1971, Manchester, NH. She married 21 May 1905, Farmington, NH, **Herbert Alfred Willey** (Peltiah Willey & Caroline ____) b 7 Dec 1881, Strafford Co., NH; d 1940, Miami, FL.

Herbert Alfred Willey worked in a shoe factory in Farmington, NH, in 1910 and in Haverhill, MA, in 1920. By 1930 he was a house carpenter in Miami, FL (US censuses). He and his wife apparently had no children.

3.9.2.2.4.3   **MONTEE, Florence M.** b 3 Sep 1887, Farmington, NH.

Florence Montee was living with her parents in Farmington, NH, in 1900 (US census).

3.9.2.2.7.1   **MONTE, William** b 29 Dec 1883, Westborough, MA; d there 20 Oct 1886.

3.9.2.2.11.1   **MONTY, Harold Roger** b 19 Dec 1899, Woonsocket, RI; d & bur 16 & 27 Jul 1972, Ormond Beach, FL & Arlington, VA. He married **Helen Marie** ____ b 9 Nov 1903; d & bur 18 & 21 Feb 1947, ? & Arlington, VA.

Harold Roger Monty, a former USN Lieutenant, and his wife Helen Marie were buried in the Arlington, VA, National Cemetery.

3.9.2.2.11.2   **MONTY, Regina** b 1901, Woonsocket, RI; d there 21 Oct 1905 at the age of four.

3.9.2.2.11.3   **MONTY-RACINE, Wallace E.** b & bp 31 Oct & 6 Nov 1904, Woonsocket, RI; d 13 Mar 1984, Norwalk, CT. He married 25 Oct 1947, Slatersville, RI, **Simone E. Brodeur** (Oscar Brodeur & Arzelia Fonteneau) b 23 Jul 1913, Woonsocket, RI; m (1) 12 Nov 1934, Slatersville, RI, George Albert Champagne (Oscar Champagne & Anna Ayotte); d 19 Sep 1999, Norwalk, CT.

Wallace E. Monty's mother having died soon after his birth he was brought up as their own son by Jean C. and Annie Racine whose surname he adopted. To my knowledge the name Wallace E. Monty appears only in his baptismal record in the church of St. Anne in Woonsocket, RI. He was known as Wallace Monty-Racine at his marriage in St. John the Evangelist Church in Slatersville, RI. All other records I have seen name him Wallace Racine.

3.9.2.2.15.1   **MONTY, Albert** b 1902?, Woonsocket, RI.

This child was 8 years old in 1910 when he was living with his parents in Bellingham, MA. He does not appear with them in any later census.

3.9.2.2.15.2   **MONTY, Marie A./Mary A.** b 1903?, Woonsocket, RI.

Marie A. Monty was a 7-year-old child living with her parents in Bellingham, MA, in 1910. She continued to reside there until at least 1930 (US censuses) while working as a bookkeeper in Woonsocket, RI, until at least 1938 (City Directories).

3.9.2.2.15.3   **MONTY, Gertrude Cecile** b 24 Jun 1905, Woonsocket, RI; d & bur 24 & 26 Nov 1974, Woonsocket, RI & South Bellingham, MA. She married 16 May 1927, Woonsocket, RI, **Laurent/Lawrence Florian Guay** (Alphonse Guay & Joséphine Latulipe) b 2 Dec 1904, Moose River, ME; d 12 Sep 1976, near Jackman, ME.

Laurent Florian Guay was known as either Laurent or Lawrence throughout his life, with no clear predominance of one name over the other. He was a house painter in Woonsocket, RI, in 1930 (US census) and a machinist there in the 1930s (City Directories). He and his wife moved to Bellingham, MA, at some time before 1951 and were still residents there at their deaths.

Gertrude C. Monty was buried in St. John the Baptist Cemetery in South Bellingham, MA (Records of the Menard Funeral Home in Woonsocket, RI).

Child:

   i   **Vivian M. Guay** b Apr 1929, Woonsocket, RI.

3.9.2.2.15.4   **MONTY, Aline C.** b 5 Mar 1907, Woonsocket, RI; d 2 Oct 1991, East Blackstone, MA. She married 1938? **Eugene Octave Thuot** (Edgar Thuot & Exina ____) b 18 Sep 1905, Woonsocket, RI; d 11 Jan 1985, East Blackstone, MA.

Aline Monty was for many years a bookkeeper in Woonsocket, RI, while residing with her husband, a plumber, in East Blackstone, MA (Woonsocket City Directories). She was buried in Precious Blood Cemetery in Woonsocket

Eugene Octave Thuot was buried in Swan Point Cemetery in Providence, RI.

3.9.2.2.15.5   MONTY, Bernard R. b 5 Aug 1909, Bellingham, MA; d 7 Aug 1995, Woonsocket, RI. He married 1951? as his second wife **Stasia P. Kaczor** (Stanislaw/Stanley Kaczor & Paulina/Pauline Wodynska) b 1923, Woonsocket, RI.

Bernard Monty was living with his parents in Bellingham, MA, in 1930 when he was a printer's apprentice in Woonsocket, RI (US census). He worked as a linotype operator in Waterville, ME, for a few years in the late 1930s and in Woonsocket in the early 1940s. He later became a businessman there, though still residing in South Bellingham, MA, and was by 1949 the executive president of Leclaire & Monty, Inc., which owned among other things a Studebaker car dealership and an appliance store (Waterville and Woonsocket City Directories). His widow lived in North Smithfield, RI, after his death.

I know nothing about his first marriage save that he was divorced, without dependants, when he enlisted in the US Army in Boston, MA, on 20 Mar 1941 (World War II Enlistment Records).

Child of the second marriage:
3.9.2.2.15.5.1   Bruce   1951?-   -

3.9.2.2.15.6   MONTY, Madeline/Madeleine L. b 26 Mar 1912, Bellingham, MA; d 15 Apr 1988, St. Cloud, FL. She married **Henry A. Graves** (Joseph Graves & Mary Antonia Berube) b 19 Jul 1910, Fitchburg, MA; d 30 Apr 1963, Woonsocket, RI.

This woman's name varies. She was Madeline when living with her parents in Bellingham, MA, in 1920 and 1930 (US censuses), Madeline or Madeleine L. in the City Directories of Woonsocket, RI, where she lived with her husband from at least 1936 on, Leonine Madeline in the Florida Death Index as well as in her obituary in the *Orlando Sentinel* of 18 Apr 1988, and Madeleine in the Social Security Death Index.

Henry A. Graves was a mill worker in Woonsocket, RI, in 1930 and until at least 1959 (US census; City Directories). He was buried there in Precious Blood Cemetery.

Children:
i   **Gerald L. Graves** b Jun 1937, Woonsocket, RI. He married **Nancy M. ____** b 1938.
ii   **Robert Graves** d 1991, Herndon, VA. He married **Joan Doe** b Jul 1942.
iii   **Adrian Graves** married **Elizabeth Soos**.
iv   **Thomas A. Graves** b Aug 1945, Woonsocket, RI. He married **Carmen Cavallaro** (Mario Cavallaro & Norma Larivière) b Jul 1947.
v   **Patricia M. Graves** b 1949, Woonsocket, RI; d & bur there 1967.

3.9.2.2.15.7   MONTY, Georgette b 19 Sep 1914, Bellingham, MA; d 5 Jul 2005, Colonial Heights, VA. She married 25 Nov 1937, South Bellingham, MA, **Henry O. Leveille** (Frederick Leveille & Wilhelmine Gagnon) b 1911?, Northbridge, MA.

Henry O. Leveille was a plumber in Woonsocket, RI, until at least 1943 (City Directories).

3.9.2.2.15.8   MONTY, Emile D. b & bp 18 & 21 Jul 1916, Bellingham, MA & Woonsocket, RI; d 27 Sep 1988, Titusville, FL. He married 14 Oct 1944, Woonsocket, RI, **Anita Hattie Parenteau** (Arthur Parenteau & Lucienne Fournier) b & bp there 27 Aug 1922; d 23 Apr 2007, Rockledge, FL.

Emile D. Monty was a businessman and real estate salesman in Woonsocket, RI (City Directories). He spent his retirement years in Florida.

3.9.3.3.4.1   MONTIE, Elijah John b & bp 23 & 26 Jan 1884, Ecorse, MI; d 3 Mar 1970, Belleville, MI. He married 16 Feb 1909, New Boston, MI, **Charlotte Marie Leblanc** (Charles Peter Leblanc & Emma Cicotte) b 7 Jun 1887, Sumpter, MI; d 27 Nov 1943, MI.

Elijah John Montie Jr. was a house carpenter in Ecorse, MI, at his marriage, a laborer or teamster at the births of his children through 1916, and a carpenter again in 1920. In 1930 he was a house carpenter in Wyandotte, MI (US censuses). He and his wife were buried in Mallet Cemetery (St. Stephen Catholic Cemetery) in New Boston, MI.

Children:

3.9.3.3.4.1.1	Charles Elijah	1909-	-
3.9.3.3.4.1.2	Gerald Joseph	1911-1932?&	-
3.9.3.3.4.1.3	Charlotte Anita	1913-	-
3.8.3.3.4.1.4	Elijah John	1916-1935?-1990	
3.9.3.3.4.1.5	Leonard Richard	1920-1941-2002	
3.9.3.3.4.1.6	Lionel Edmund	1921-	-1978
3.9.3.3.4.1.7	Richard Vernon	1935-	-1936
3.9.3.3.4.1.8	Richard C.	1939-	-1941

3.9.3.3.4.2   **MONTIE, Joseph Gabriel** b & bp 28 May & 7 Jun 1885, Ecorse, MI; d there 18 Nov 1885.

3.9.3.3.4.3   **MONTIE, Ellen Laura** b & bp 21 & 28 Jun 1891, Ecorse, MI; d 8 Jul 1949, Lindsey, OH. She married (1) 24 Nov 1909, Windsor, Ontario, Canada, **William Mack** (John Mack & Ella Noble) b 1875?

She married (2) 6 Dec 1911, Fremont, OH, **Marshall Gillmor** (Lester Gillmor & Grace Lytle) b there 4 Dec 1891; d 10 Jun 1965, Green Springs, OH.

William Mack was a 34-year-old resident of Ecorse, MI, when he married in 1909. The marriage was short-lived for in April 1910 Mrs. Ellen Mack was living without her husband in her mother's household in Ecorse.

Marshall Gillmor was a driver in Fremont, OH, at his marriage and a farmer in Riley Twp, OH, in 1920. He and his wife were in Ballville, OH, in 1930 (US censuses) and in Fremont again in 1942 when he signed his World War II Draft Registration card. He was then employed by a construction company in Sandusky, OH.

3.9.3.3.5.1   **MONTIE, Estella Anna** b & bp 6 & 17 Feb 1878, Ecorse, MI; d there 9 Oct 1954. She married there 26 Apr 1898 **Elmer Robert Labadie** (John Baptist Labadie & Mary Adelaide Lacroix) b & bp there 31 Jan & 3 Feb 1870; d there 19 Apr 1964.

Elmer R. Labadie had a varied career in Ecorse, MI. He was an agent at his marriage, a telegraph operator at the birth of his first child and until at least 1902, and a deputy sheriff in 1908. He was in the hardware business in 1910, in real estate in 1911, and in hardware again in 1913 when his wife was a storekeeper. In 1920 he was a Collector in the Revenue Office there and a real estate salesman in 1930 (Michigan Birth Records; US censuses).

Children:
i   **Everett Raymond Labadie** b 23 Aug 1899, Ecorse, MI; d 11 Sep 1990, Venice, FL. He married 21 Apr 1926, Windsor, Ontario, Canada, **Georgina E. Murray** (George S. Murray & Annie Byrnes) b there 18 Jul 1899; d 5 Feb 1993, Venice, FL.
ii   **Viola G. Labadie** b 6 Jan 1902, Ecorse, MI; d 6 Mar 1976, Wyandotte, MI.
iii   **Marie E. Labadie** b 4 Aug 1904, Ecorse, MI; d 27 Nov 1997, St. Petersburg, FL. She married **Albert Wesner**.
iv   **John Richard Labadie** b 1 Mar 1908, Ecorse, MI; d 2 Dec 1973, Lincoln Park, MI. He married **Hilda ____**.
v   **Bernadette E. Labadie** b 8 Jan 1911, Ecorse, MI; d 2 Oct 1991, Wyandotte, MI. She married **Clarence Mahalak** (Joseph Mahalak & Mary E. ____) b 18 Feb 1910, Wyandotte, MI; d there 29 Nov 1994.
vi   **Elmer J. Labadie** b 3 May 1913, Ecorse, MI; d 8 Sep 1977, Dearborn, MI. He married **Helen R. Miller** (Orrin Russell Miller & Bertha Luella Smith) b 18 Feb 1916, Lima, OH; d 12 Feb 2001, Clearwater, FL.
vii   **Norbert F. Labadie** b 4 Oct 1918, Ecorse, MI; d 12 Apr 1980, Detroit, MI. He married **Jean ____**.
viii   **Richard Benedict Labadie** b 22 Mar 1922, Ecorse, MI; d 20 Feb 1984, Lincoln

Park, MI. He married 30 May 1947 **Marguerite Catherine Adams** (Albert Adams & Anna Marie Burkhard) b 18 Aug 1922, Geistown, PA; d 16 Dec 1976, Ecorse, MI.

3.9.3.3.5.2   **MONTIE, Richard Columbus** b & bp 23 & 26 Jun 1881, Ecorse, MI; d there 16 Sep 1927. He married there 5 Feb 1907 **Ella Gertrude Marrier** (James Marrier & Catherine Conroy) b there Jul 1882.

Richard Montie was a merchant in Ecorse, MI, at his marriage and specifically a grocer at the birth of a child in 1916. He was still in Ecorse in 1920, though without a stated occupation, and was buried in St. Francis Xavier Cemetery there. His widow and daughter remained in Ecorse after his death (US censuses).

Child:
3.9.3.3.5.2.1   Helen Isabelle   1916-   -1934

3.9.3.3.5.3   **MONTIE, Isabella/Bella** b & bp 12 & 26 Nov 1883, Ecorse, MI; d 27 Sep 1977, Riverview, MI. She married 18 Sep 1902, Ecorse, MI, **Francis J. Durocher** (Joseph Durocher & Marguerite Dupuy/Margaret Dupuis) b 11 Jun 1873, Sandwich West, Ontario, Canada; d & bur 8 & 12 Feb 1912, Ecorse, MI.

There are conflicting reports of Isabella Montie's date of birth. I am using here the dates of birth and baptism found in the generally well-informed Christian Denissen's *Genealogy of the French Families of the Detroit River Region*, II, 857. Yet the Social Security Death Index has her birth on 26 Nov 1883 (perhaps confusing the date of baptism with the date of birth) while the Michigan Death Index shows that she was born on 25 Nov 1882. Her tombstone in St. Francis Xavier Cemetery in Ecorse, MI, bears the dates 1882-1977. She was a resident of Lincoln Park, MI, at her death.

Francis J. Durocher was a physician in Ecorse and was buried in St. Francis Xavier Cemetery there. His name in Michigan records was invariably Francis J. Durocher, which reflects the name François given him in the 1881 census in Sandwich West, Ontario, Canada. Yet the Birth Records there name him Joseph Albert Durocher (1873, #029993). I cannot explain the name change.

Children:
i   **Margaret Durocher** b 27 Jul 1904, Ecorse, MI.
ii   **Francis J. Durocher** b 31 May 1911, Ecorse, MI; d & bur there 1922.

3.9.3.3.5.4   **MONTIE, Joseph Edward** b & bp 11 & 17 Jan 1886, Ecorse, MI; d 25 Jul 1975, Dearborn, MI. He married 25 Sep 1911, Ecorse, MI, **Justina/Justine Gee** (Laurent/ Lawrence Gee & Philomene/Felicity Sumerfield) b Feb 1886, Wyandotte, MI.

Joseph Montie lived almost his entire life in Ecorse, MI, where he was in turn a grocery store clerk in 1910 and at the birth of a son in 1912, a village clerk in 1920, and a salesman in 1930 (US censuses). He was still a resident of Ecorse at his death.

Justina (also Justine, Jessie) Gee was a sister of Lorenzo Louis Gee, husband of Gertrude S. Drouillard (3.9.3.5.1.v).

Children:
3.9.3.3.5.4.1   Raymond Edward   1912-1936&   -1991
3.9.3.3.5.4.2   Marian   1922-   -1922

3.9.3.3.5.5   **MONTIE, Charles Benjamin** b & bp 10 & 18 Aug 1889, Ecorse, MI; d there 31 Mar 1924. He married there 4 Oct 1916 **Cora Thibault** (Francis Xavier Thibault & Marie Clark) b there 1890?; d & bur there 1947.

Benjamin Montie was a laborer in Ecorse, MI, at his marriage, when his bride was 26 years old, and a shipyard worker there in 1920. His widow was living with her son in her father's household in Ecorse in 1930 (US censuses). She and her husband were buried in St. Francis Xavier Cemetery there.

Child:
3.9.3.3.5.5.1   Milton Benjamin   1917-   -1986

3.9.3.3.6.1   **MONTIE, Maud** b Feb 1882, Ecorse, MI. She married there 28 Nov 1901 **Elmer Richard Goodell** (Gabriel Richard Goodell & Zoe Elizabeth Pitre) b & bp there 1 & 5 Apr 1875.

Elmer R. Goodell was a carpenter in Detroit, MI, at his marriage and a laborer in Ecorse, MI, at the birth of his son the following year. He was a deputy sheriff in 1910 and a grocer there when he signed on 12 Sep 1918 his World War I Draft Registration card. Then came an unusual move. In 1920, he was a grocer in Ballast Point, FL. I do not know how long the family stayed in Florida. By 1930 Elmer Goodell, a laborer, and his wife were again living in Ecorse, next door to their son Russell and his wife (US censuses).

Child:
i   **Russell R. Goodell** b 30 Aug 1902, Ecorse, MI; d 2 Jun 1973, Lincoln Park, MI. He married 1923? **Angeline** ____ b 6 Apr 1907, MI; d 17 Jun 1973, Lincoln Park, MI.

3.9.3.3.6.2   **MONTIE, Louisa Genevieve/Viva** b & bp 28 May & 3 Jun 1883, Ecorse, MI. She married there 24 Nov 1903 **Charles J. Tank** (Charles Tank & Caroline Bertine or Pitten) b Jan 1870, MI.

This woman appears in Michigan records under a variety of names. She was Louisa Genevieve at her birth, Viva in the 1900 US census in Ecorse, MI, as well as at the marriage and at the births of her first two children, Genevieve at the birth of a son in 1911, Genevieve Louisa at the birth of a daughter in 1913, Geneva in the 1920 US census, and then Jeneve in the 1930 US census.

Charles Tank had a number of occupations in Ecorse. He was a day laborer in 1900, a machinist at his marriage, a saloon keeper at the birth of a child in 1904, a machinist again at the birth of another child in 1908, a saloon worker in 1910, and a restaurateur at the births of two more children in 1911 and 1913. In 1920 he was a policeman and in 1930 a painter/contractor (US censuses).

Children:
i   **Charles Tank** b 12 Sep 1904, Ecorse, MI; d 7 Dec 1971, Lincoln Park, MI.
ii   **Vernon John Tank** b 31 May 1908, Ecorse, MI; d Jan 1964. He married 9 Oct 1948 **Esther M. Blood** (Harry E. Blood & Ada M. Jorgenson) b May 1926, Oshkosh, WI.
iii   **William Tank** b 29 Jul 1911, Ecorse, MI; d 21 Nov 1972, Trenton, MI.
iv   **Orellia Genevieve Tank** b 1 Nov 1913, Ecorse, MI; d 1 Jun 1983, San Bernardino Co., CA. She married **Edward Louis Mesler** (____ Mesler & ____ Sprague) b 17 Mar 1911, IL; d 25 Apr 1987, San Bernardino Co., CA.
v   **Lewis Tank** b 1918?, Ecorse, MI.

3.9.3.3.6.3   **MONTIE, William John** b & bp 7 & 8 Nov 1885, Ecorse, MI. He married 23 Nov 1909, Rockwood, MI, **Anna Bertha Gonyea/Gagnier** (Cyril Gonyea & Josephine Parent) b 5 May 1887, MI; bp 29 Nov 1895, Rockwood, MI.

William Montie was a riveter in a shipyard in Ecorse, MI, at his marriage and until at least 1920. He was a police officer in 1930 (US censuses). His wife's surname varies. She was Anna Gonia in the 1900 US census in Brownstown, MI, Annie B. Gonyea at her marriage, and Anna Gagnier or Gagner at the births of her children (Wayne Co., MI, Vital Records).

Children:
3.9.3.3.6.3.1   Cyril Ellsworth   1910-   -1971
3.9.3.3.6.3.2   Anonymous   1911-   -1911
3.9.3.3.6.3.3   Emma Josephine   1912-1936-1978

3.9.3.3.6.4 **MONTIE, Emma Eliza** b & bp 7 & 10 Jun 1888, Ecorse, MI; d there 23 Oct 1910. She married 30 May 1907, Detroit, MI, **Godfrey George Droste** (Henry Droste & Mary Brinkman) b there 16 Dec 1885; m (2) 28 Sep 1918 Lillian B. Godley/Godely (George Godely & Bessie ____); d 1925, Wayne Co., MI.

Godfrey (also Gottfried, Godfred, Fred) G. Droste was a broker in Detroit, MI, at his first marriage. He soon moved to Ecorse, MI, where he was a bookkeeper in 1908 and a grocer in 1909 and 1910. He remained a resident of Ecorse even when he became a druggist in Detroit (World War I Draft Registration card, 1918) and was living there in 1920 in the household of his former mother-in-law, Mrs. Orellia (sic) Montie with his second wife Lillian and the children of both his marriages. He died a few years later and his widow remarried. She was living in Detroit in 1930 with her second husband, William McCabe, her stepson Godfrey A. Droste, and her own children by Godfrey Droste (US censuses).

Children:
   i   **Alvin Godfrey Droste** b 28 Mar 1908, Ecorse, MI; d 15 Apr 1973, Sterling Heights, MI. He married **Dorothy Ann Bliss** b 30 Dec 1907; d 3 Aug 1971, Mount Clemens, MI.
   ii   **William Frederick Droste** b 28 Oct 1909, Ecorse, MI.

3.9.3.3.7.1 **MONTIE, Elsie M./Helen Marie** b & bp 5 & 8 Jul 1888, Ecorse, MI. She married there 4 Nov 1907 **Paul John Stover** (John Madison Stover & Leila Ada Kellen) b 28 Oct 1885, Blanchard, OH; d 22 Feb 1955, Wayne Co., MI.

Paul J. Stover was a clerk in Ecorse, MI, at his marriage, a bookkeeper at the birth of a son in 1911, a clerk in a chemical plant in 1920, and a bookkeeper there again in 1930 (US censuses). On all these occasions as well as in the 1900 census when she is listed as a child with her parents, his wife, though named Helen Marie at her baptism, appears as Elsie or Elsie M. Montie or Stover.

Children:
   i   **Arthur P. Stover** b 30 Jun 1908, Ecorse, MI.
   ii   **Robert Lee Stover** b 3 Feb 1911, Ecorse, MI; d 29 Sep 1963, Lima, OH. He married 1933? **Alice Laverne Allen** (Harmon L. Allen & Nellie A. Norman) b 2 Jun 1910, Columbus Grove, OH; m (2) Stanley Russell Forte; d & bur 12 & 16 Oct 2000, Columbus Grove, OH.
   iii **Harry John Stover** b 25 Oct 1912, Ecorse, MI; d 10 Jun 1972, Trenton, MI. He married **Dolores M. Grimsley** (Frank Grimsley & Alma ____) b 24 Nov 1914, PA; d 29 Aug 1996, Kingman, AZ.

3.9.3.3.7.2 **MONTIE, John Baptist** b & bp 11 & 24 Jan 1892, Ecorse, MI; d 26 May 1969, Oscoda, MI. He married (1) 25 Oct 1916, Ecorse, MI, **Viola A. Alder** (Frederick Alder & Leah Seeman) b Feb 1893, Detroit, MI; d 23 Nov 1927, Ecorse, MI.

He married (2) 28 May 1935, River Rouge, MI, **Josephine Haener** b 1896?, MI; m (1) 1916? John Robert Kane.

John Montie Jr. was a laborer in Ecorse, MI, at the birth of a child in 1917 and a factory worker there in 1920. By 1930 he was the village assessor (US censuses).

Children of the first marriage:

3.9.3.3.7.2.1	Mildred Agnes	1917-	-
3.9.3.3.7.2.2	Ruth Alberta	1919-	-1923
3.9.3.3.7.2.3	Clayton John	1923-	-
3.9.3.3.7.2.4	Geraldine Ruth	1924-	-
3.9.3.3.7.2.5	Delphine Catherine	1927-1950-	

3.9.3.3.8.1 **MONTIE, Francis Xavier** b & bp 5 & 29 May 1887, Ecorse, MI. He married 8 Jun 1910, Wyandotte, MI, **Elizabeth K. Liddle** (John G. Liddle & Sarah J. Abbotts) b there 28 Nov 1890; d there 14 Mar 1982.

Francis X. Montie was a village clerk in Ecorse, MI, at his marriage and at the birth of a son the following year. In 1920 he was shipyard worker there (US census).

Child:
3.9.3.3.8.1.1   Kenneth Francis Liddle   1911-1935-1993

3.9.3.3.8.2   **MONTIE, Leo Anthony** b & bp 20 & 24 Mar 1889, Ecorse, MI; d 24 Sep 1933, Detroit, MI. He married 18 Apr 1911, Ecorse, MI, **Eugenia Ferguson** (Harry Francis Ferguson & Adelaide Cicotte) b 1890?, MI; d 27 Oct 1931, Detroit, MI.

Leo Montie was a clerk in Ecorse, MI, at his marriage when his bride was 21 years old. He was a salesman there in 1920 and a printer, owner of his own shop there in 1930 (US censuses). He and his wife were buried in Detroit's Holy Cross Cemetery.

Child:
3.9.3.3.8.2.1   Joseph Donald   1914-   -

3.9.3.3.8.3   **MONTIE, Louis Russell** b & bp 29 Sep & 7 Oct 1894, Ecorse, MI; d there 15 Nov 1894.

3.9.3.3.8.4   **MONTIE, Ada Suzanne** b & bp 12 & 22 Aug 1897, Ecorse, MI. She married there 3 Jun 1919 **Adray Columbus Labadie** (Columbus Alexander Labadie & Domitilla Octavia Leblanc) b & bp 8 & 15 Dec 1895, River Rouge & Ecorse, MI; d 15 Jun 1974, Wyandotte, MI.

Adray Labadie was a shipyard electrician in Ecorse, MI, in 1920 and a fireman in a steel mill there in 1930 when his household included his widowed mother-in-law Mrs. Susan Montie (US censuses). He was still a resident of Ecorse at his death.

Children:
i   **Margaret Labadie** b 1921?, Ecorse, MI.
ii   **Irwin Labadie** b 20 Aug 1923, Ecorse, MI; d 28 Oct 1998, Lincoln Park, MI. He married **Joan A. ____** b Aug 1924.

3.9.3.3.10.1   **MONTIE, Albert John** b & bp 15 Apr & 3 May 1896, Ecorse, MI; d there 1936. He married 1919 **Lillian E. Pickert** (John L. Pickert & Mary Elizabeth/Minnie McCarthy) b 30 Jul 1893, IL; d 25 Sep 1966.

Albert Montie was a foundry worker living with his wife in Ecorse, MI, on 1 Jan 1920. In 1930, when he was the proprietor of an Ice and Coal company there, his mother-in-law Mrs. Minnie Pickert was a member of his household (US censuses).

Children:
3.9.3.3.10.1.1   Joyce   1922?-   -
3.9.3.3.10.1.2   Noreene Elizabeth   1923-   -1983
3.9.3.3.10.1.3   Gordon Leo   1926-   -

3.9.3.3.10.2   **MONTIE, Earl Eugene** b & bp 14 & 30 Jul 1899, Ecorse, MI; d 30 Apr 1978, Wyandotte, MI. He married (1) there 30 Aug 1921 **Ruth Nellis** (Frank Nellis & Mary ____) b Apr 1894, Wyandotte, MI .

He married (2) 1927, Livingston Co., MI, **Claire M. White** (James White & Margaret ____) b 13 Jan 1906, PA; d 17 Feb 1983, Taylor, MI.

Earl E. Montie was a lawyer in Ecorse, MI, in 1930 (US census). He was a resident of Riverview, MI, and died in Wyandotte, MI, according to the Michigan Death Index. He may have been a resident of Valrico, FL, as indicated in the Social Security Death Index, but his name does not appear in the Florida Death Index for 1978.

I know of Earl E. Montie's first wife and children mainly through Denissen, *Genealogy of the French Families of the Detroit River Region*, II, 860, who notes that Daniel Montie was the child of his first wife, Ruth. Given the fact that Earl E. Montie and Claire M. White married in 1927 (Livingston Co., MI, Marriage Index, V, 92) it seems more probable that a son born in the second half of 1928 was a child of this second marriage. Claire White was a resident of Riverview at her death.

Children of the second marriage:

| 3.9.3.3.10.2.1 | Daniel | 1928- | - |
| 3.9.3.3.10.2.2 | Richard Earl | 1931- | - |

3.9.3.5.5.1   **MONTIE, Martha** b Oct 1889, Detroit, MI. She married there 20 Jan 1910 **Alexander/Alek W. Abraham** (James H. Abraham & Alice M. Loan) b there Jun 1889; d between 1910 and 1920.

Martha Montie and her husband, a bus driver, were living in 1910 in her father's household in Detroit, MI. She was a childless widow in 1920, living with her widowed mother and working as a chief operator for the telephone company in Detroit. She was still a telephone operator there in 1930 and was then living with her sister Lillian (3.9.3.5.5.6) and brother-in-law Eugene Emerald Bertrand (US censuses).

3.9.3.5.5.2   **MONTIE, Joseph** b Feb 1891, Detroit, MI; d & bur there 1916.

Joseph Montie was buried in Detroit's Holy Cross Cemetery.

3.9.3.5.5.3   **MONTIE, Alfred Octave** b & bp 17 & 22 May 1892, Detroit, MI; d 19 Nov 1901, Delray, MI.

The child of Noah Montie who died in November 1901 at the age of 9 years and 6 months is named Albert in the Wayne Co. Death Records. This is certainly an error: Albert Montie (3.9.3.5.5.4), who would in any event have been only 8 years old in November 1901, was still a member of his family in 1910 (US census). On the other hand Alfred Octave, who was not included in the 1910 census, would have been exactly 9 years and 6 months old in November 1901.

3.9.3.5.5.4   **MONTIE, Albert Felix** b 30 Nov 1893, Detroit, MI; d 20 May 1971, Salem, OR. He married (1) 23 Jan 1917, Detroit, MI, **Mary E. Smith** (Alfred Smith & Ella Austin) b 1894?

He married (2) **Cornelia Ruth** ____ b 27 Jun 1917; d 28 Aug 1981, Salem, OR.

Albert Felix Montie and the 22-year-old Mary E. Smith were married in St. Anne Church in Detroit, MI. A few months later, when he signed his World War I Draft Registration card on 5 Jun 1917, he was a farmer working for Walter Thompson in Bloomfield, MI. He was a private in the US Army from 24 Jul 1918 to 3 Apr 1919 and was buried in the Willamette National Cemetery in Portland, OR.

3.9.3.5.5.5   **MONTIE, Edward Charles** b 22 Apr 1895, Detroit, MI. He married 1920? **Evelyn C. Welch** b 1896?, AR.

Edward C. Montie (Charles Edward in his birth record) and his 34-year-old wife had been married for ten years on 1 Apr 1930 (US census). He was then an asbestos worker in Detroit, MI (US census).

Child:

| 3.9.3.5.5.5.1 | Mary Esther | 1930- | - |

3.9.3.5.5.6   **MONTIE, Lillian Elenor** b & bp 11 & 23 Aug 1896, Detroit, MI; d 16 Jun 1980, Clinton, MI. She married 1919? **Eugene Emerald Bertrand** (Joseph Alexander Bertrand & Isabelle Grondin) b & bp 30 Jan & 6 Feb 1898, Amherstburg, Ontario, Canada; d 29 Dec 1970, Detroit, MI.

Emerald Bertrand (Eugene Emerald at his baptism) came to the United States in 1916 and was a welder in Detroit, MI, in 1920 and a construction worker there in 1930. He and his wife (named Maria Helena Elenora at her baptism in St. Anne Church in Detroit, MI) had been married for eleven years in 1930 (US censuses). They were both residents of Macomb Co., MI, at their deaths: he of Roseville, MI, and she of New Baltimore, MI.

Children:

i   **Lillian Mary Bertrand** b 13 May 1920, Detroit, MI; d 18 May 2005, New Baltimore, MI. She married 28 Oct 1944, Detroit, MI, **Edward L. Lanehart** (____ Lanehart & Irene ____) b 15 Oct 1915, MI; d 12 Jul 1982, Grand Rapids, MI.

ii   **Dorothy E. Bertrand** b 19 Feb 1923, Detroit, MI; d 12 Aug 2004, St. Clair Shores, MI. She married **Arthur A. Thursam** (Arthur Thursam & Celina ____) b 18 Nov 1920, Detroit, MI.

iii   **Rosemary Bertrand** b Mar 1925, Detroit, MI. She married **Frederick M. Ritzer** (Russell J. Ritzer & Edith Isabella O'Neill) b 3 Apr 1923, Windsor, Ontario, Canada; d 14 Oct 1989, Madison Heights, MI.

iv   **Margaret Bertrand** b 3 Oct 1927, Detroit, MI. She married there 28 Apr 1951 **James Stanley Hunter** (James Stanley Hunter & Marie Catherine Landschoot) b 3 Oct 1926, MI; d 22 Apr 1992, Berlin, MI.

v   **Joseph E. Bertrand** b 23 Apr 1929, Detroit, MI; d & bur 9 & 14 May 1994, Algonac, MI. He married 24 Jan 1948, Centerline, MI, **Gloria Joan Bertani** b Jul 1931.

vi   **Charles E. Bertrand** b Nov 1932, Detroit, MI. He married **Corrine J. Valentine** b Nov 1935, Detroit, MI.

vii   **Lewis B. Bertrand** b 1934, Detroit, MI. He married 15 Mar 1958, Roseville, MI, **Lenore Dzinbinski** b 15 Dec 1938, Detroit, MI; d & bur 20 & 24 Feb 2006, Madison Heights & Beverly Hills, MI.

3.9.3.5.5.7   **MONTIE, John L.** b & bp 12 & 13 Mar 1898, Detroit, MI; d there 1898.

3.9.3.5.5.8   **MONTIE, Viola Mary** b & bp 2 & 12 Mar 1899, Detroit, MI; d 25 Jan 1971, San Diego, CA. She married 1924? **Robert Emmet Feys** (Paul Feys & Nellie ____) b 5 July 1897, Detroit, MI; d 20 Nov 1988, Harper Woods, MI.

Viola Montie and her husband, a county inspector in Detroit, MI, had been married for six years in 1930 (US census).

Child:

i   **Elizabeth L. Feys** b Jan 1930, Detroit, MI.

3.9.3.5.5.9   **MONTIE, Frances** b 2 Aug 1901, Springwells, MI; d 26 May 1902, Delray, MI.

3.9.3.5.5.10   **MONTIE, George Ernest** b 10 Apr 1903, Detroit, MI.

George E. Montie was a student along with his brother Walter in St. Joseph's Normal College in Pocantico Hills, NY, in 1920 and a student in St. Mary's Seminary of the West in Norwood, OH, in 1930 (US censuses). He was a chaplain in the US Armed Forces during World War II.

3.9.3.5.5.11   **MONTIE, Walter** b & bp 23 Jul & 6 Aug 1905, Detroit, MI; d 29 Apr 1991, Silver Spring, MD. He married **Irene D. Curran** b 1921?

The Wayne Co., MI, Birth Records for 1905 (p. 253) show that Walter, son of Noah Montie was born in Detroit, MI, on 23 Jul 1905. Two weeks later the son of Noah Montie and Mary Sarazin who was born on 23 Jul was given the name Wilfred Henry at his baptism in St. Anne's Church in Detroit on 6 Aug 1905 (p. 205, baptism #72). I have not again seen that name and cannot explain the discrepancy. Walter Montie was a 4-year-old child living in his father's household in Detroit, MI, in April 1910 and was a student, along with his brother George, in St. Joseph's Normal School in Pocantico Hills, NY, in 1920. He was a professor there in 1930 (US censuses).

Children:

3.9.3.5.5.11.1	Michael Edward	1941-	-
3.9.3.5.5.11.2	Thomas Joseph	-	-
3.9.3.5.5.11.3	John Charles	1944-	-2003
3.9.3.5.5.11.4	Catherine Anne /Kitty	1946-	-
3.9.3.5.5.11.5	Suzanne Mary	-	-

3.9.3.5.5.12   **MONTIE, Donald Elmer** (twin) b & bp 2 & 17 Nov 1907, Detroit, MI; d there 14 Nov 1981. He married there 28 Nov 1935 **Agnes Matilda Abele** (Aloysius/Alois Johann Abele & Agnes Thecla Buss) b there 28 Aug 1914; d 27 Nov 2003, Clinton, MI.

Donald E. Montie was a construction worker in Detroit, MI, in 1930 when he was living in the household of his sister Lillian (3.9.3.5.5.6) and brother-in-law Emerald Bertrand (US census).

Children:

3.9.3.5.5.12.1	Donald Elmer	1937-	-
3.9.3.5.5.12.2	Phillis Elizabeth	1941-	-
3.9.3.5.5.12.3	George E.	1943-	-
3.9.3.5.5.12.4	Mary Agnes	1947-	-
3.9.3.5.5.12.5	Jane Frances	1951-	-

3.9.3.5.5.13   **MONTIE, Dorothy Ellen** (twin) b & bp 2 & 17 Nov 1907, Detroit, MI; d there 1908.

I know of this child's death only through Denissen, *Genealogy of the French Families of the Detroit River Region*, II, 858).

3.9.3.5.5.14   **MONTIE, Rose Maria Agnes** b & bp 8 Dec 1909 & 2 Jan 1910, Detroit, MI.

Given the date of this child's baptism in St. Anne's Church in Detroit, MI, Christian Denissen is obviously wrong when he states that Marie Montie, daughter of Noah Montie, died in 1909 (*Genealogy of the French Families of the Detroit River Region*, II, 858). She may have died shortly after her baptism.

3.9.3.5.6.1   **MONTIE, Irene Marie** b & bp 30 May & 30 Jun 1894, Detroit, MI; d 24 Feb 1977, Riverview, MI. She married 17 Oct 1922, Detroit, MI, **Harry Tucker Clark** (John Aaron Clark & Louisa Ella Williams) b 12 Oct 1892, Williamsville, VA; d 18 Mar 1972, Lincoln Park, MI.

Harry Tucker Clark remained in Virginia until at least 1920 when he was a laborer on his father's farm in the Williamsville district of Bath, Co., VA. He was a millwright in Lincoln Park, MI, in 1930 (US census). Both he and his wife were residents of Ecorse, MI, at their deaths.

Children:

    i   **Edward A. Clark** b 1924?, Wayne Co., MI.

    ii   **Ellen M. Clark** b 1925?, Wayne Co., MI.

    iii   **John H. Clark** b Jan 1927, Wayne Co., MI.

    iv   **Raymond J. Clark** b 12 Jan 1928, Wayne Co., MI; d 1 Sep 1998, Dearborn, MI.

    v   **Francis Clark** b Feb 1929, Wayne Co., MI.

3.9.3.5.6.2   **MONTIE, Thomas Levi** b 16 Jan 1896, Detroit, MI. He married between 1920 and 1923 **Clara Seif** b 1894?; d Dec 1923, Ecorse, MI, at the age of 19.

Thomas Montie was single in January 1920 when he was a house carpenter living in his father's household in Ecorse, MI. He was again (or perhaps still) living in his father's household in 1930 as a widower with a 6-year-old son Thomas. He was then working for an automobile company (US censuses).

Clara Seif died in childbirth. I know of her only through Denissen, *Genealogy of the French Families of the Detroit River Region*, II, 860.

Child:
3.9.3.5.6.2.1   Thomas   1923-   -1944

3.9.3.5.6.3   **MONTIE, Marie Edith** b 28 Aug 1901, Springwells, MI; d 11 Dec 1986, Ecorse, MI. She married there 24 Oct 1925 **William Edward Ochs** (Ferdinand/Fred Ochs & Mary Ann Lohner) b 10 Jan 1898, Detroit, MI.

William Edward Ochs was a railroad worker in Frenchtown Twp, MI, in 1920 and a machinist in Ecorse, MI, in 1930 (US censuses).

3.9.3.5.6.4   **MONTIE, Dora E.** b 17 Jul 1904, Springwells, MI; d 31 Aug 1982, Taylor, MI. She married **Willard Gilbert Murphy** (Edwin A. Murphy & Grace Hawley) b 9 Nov 1904, Ionia, MI; d 14 Sep 1995, Allen Park, MI.

Dora Montie was living in her father's household in Ecorse, MI, in 1930 while Gilbert W. Murphy was a bookkeeper for an automobile company in Detroit, MI (US census). I know of their marriage only through Denissen, *Genealogy of the French Families of the Detroit River Region*, II, 858.

3.9.3.5.6.5   **MONTIE, Bernard Robert** b & bp 23 Sep & 2 Oct 1910, Algonac & Ecorse, MI; d 5 Jun 1973, Wyandotte, MI. He married (1) 12 Aug 1933, Ecorse, MI, **Marguerite Irene Malenfant** (John/Jean-Baptiste Malenfant & Elizabeth/Marie Elisabeth Côté) b & bp 26 & 27 Jul 1911, Bay City, MI; d 15 May 1936, Ecorse, MI.

He married (2) 29 Jun 1940, Ecorse, MI, **Catherine Goyette** (Leo Goyette & Nellie Ried) b 29 Oct 1918, Wyandotte, MI; d 23 Mar 1991, Taylor, MI.

Bernard Montie was an office clerk in Ecorse, MI, in 1930 (US census) and was still a resident there at his death. His second wife was a resident of Carlton, MI, at her death. I know of their children only through Denissen, *Genealogy of the French Families of the Detroit River Region*, II, 861.

Children of the first marriage:
3.9.3.5.6.5.1   Bernadette Margaret   1934-   -
3.9.3.5.6.5.2   Robert B.   1935-   -

Children of the second marriage:
3.9.3.5.6.5.3   Helen Marie   -   -
3.9.3.5.6.5.4   Louise Catherine   -   -
3.9.3.5.6.5.5   Ruth Ann   -   -
3.9.3.5.6.5.6   Rose Elizabeth   -   -
3.9.3.5.6.5.7   May Charlotte   -   -

3.9.3.5.6.6   **MONTIE, Virginia** b & bp 3 & 12 Apr 1914, Ecorse, MI; d 4 Nov 1980, Trenton, MI. She married 12 Aug 1933, Ecorse, MI, **Henry Yeager** (Louis Peter Yeager & Anna Mabel O'Connor) b 21 Mar 1911, Detroit, MI; d Jan 1959.

This woman appears in the Wayne Co., MI, Birth Records under the name of Laura Edwidge Montie, daughter of Anthony Montie and Edwidge Lacroix. She was named Virginia however when she was living with her parents in Ecorse, MI, in 1920 and 1930 (US censuses) as well as at her marriage. Mrs. Virginia Yeager was a resident of Taylor, MI, at her death.

Henry Yeager was a butcher in Detroit, MI, in 1930 (US census).

3.9.3.5.8.1   **MONTIE, Arthur Aloysius** b 4 Feb 1900, Wayne Co., MI; d & bur 10 & 17 Aug 1959 ? & Rock Island, IL. He married 4 Jun 1920, Ecorse, MI, **Hazel Harring** (John Harring & Jessie Hovell) b 1904?, MI.

Arthur Montie was living in his father's household in Ecorse, MI, in January 1920, a few months before his marriage. He had no stated occupation. He was divorced in 1930, again (or still) staying in his father's household, and still with no stated occupation. His ex-wife, Mrs. Hazel Montie, was then a 26-year-old beauty shop operator living in Ecorse with her children Gilbert, Marcella, and Dolores (US censuses).

Arthur Montie had served in the US Navy during World War I and was buried in the National Cemetery in Rock Island, IL.

Children:

3.9.3.5.8.1.1	Gilbert Arthur	1921-	-1982
3.9.3.5.8.1.2	Marcella	1922-	-
3.9.3.5.8.1.3	Robert Levi	1923-	-1930
3.9.3.5.8.1.4	Dolores May	1924-	-1997

3.9.3.5.8.2   **MONTIE, Wilfred** b 28 May 1903, Delray, MI; d there 18 Nov 1903.

3.9.3.5.8.3   **MONTIE, Marcella** b 10 Aug 1904, Springwells, MI; d & bur 26 & 27 Dec 1905, Delray, MI.

3.9.3.5.8.4   **MONTIE, Bernadette Gertrude** b & bp 18 & 24 Feb 1907, Ecorse, MI; d 18 Jan 1999, Livonia, MI. She married 9 Sep 1933, Ecorse, MI, **George E. Burns** (Thomas Burns & Laura Delaroli) b 1907?, MI.

Bernadette Montie (Gertrude Bernadette at her baptism) was a clerk in a department store in Ecorse, MI, in 1930, while George E. Burns was a 23-year-old automobile factory worker in Detroit, MI (US census).

3.9.3.5.8.5   **MONTIE, Levi Joseph** b 7 Jan 1909, Ecorse, MI; d there 1916.

3.9.3.6.2.1   **MONTIE, Thomas Antoine** b & bp 20 & 28 Jun 1891, Ecorse, MI. He married 1920?, Wayne Co., MI, **Ida Kenwell** b 14 Nov 1897, MI; d 10 Jun 1983, Wyandotte, MI.

Thomas Montie was Railroad switchman in River Rouge, MI, when he signed on 5 Jun 1917 his World War I Draft Registration card, a tinsmith there in 1920, and a municipal fireman there in 1930 when he and his wife had been married for ten years (US censuses). Ida Kenwell was still a resident there at her death.

3.9.3.6.2.2   **MONTIE, Ellen** b 23 Jun 1892, Ecorse, MI; d there 1896.

3.9.3.6.2.3   **MONTIE, Eli/Isaac** b 23 Jun 1895, Ecorse, MI; d there 15 May 1899.

Isaac Montie, son of Alexander Montie and Lillian Leblanc, was killed by a horse on 15 May 1899 at the age of four (Wayne Co., MI, Death Records). He must be the same child as Eli Montie who was born of the same parents on 23 Jun 1895 (Wayne Co., MI, Birth Records).

3.9.3.6.2.4   **MONTIE, George Sylvester** b & bp 23 Sep & 11 Oct 1896, Ecorse, MI; d Nov 1965, River Rouge, MI. He married 1916? **Clara A. Belanger** (Henry Belanger & Clara Reaume) b 29 May 1895, River Rouge, MI; d 7 Jul 1980, Lincoln Park, MI.

George Montie was an electrical contractor in River Rouge, MI, in 1920 and owned a bowling alley there in 1930 when he and his wife had been married for fourteen years (US censuses). His widow was still a resident there at her death.

Children:

3.9.3.6.2.4.1	Rita M.	1918-	-1989
3.9.3.6.2.4.2	Rose Mary H.	1919-	-
3.9.3.6.2.4.3	George S.	1920-	-1985
3.9.3.6.2.4.4	Vincent H.	1923-	-1985

3.9.3.6.2.5   **MONTIE, Walter E.** b 17 Feb 1898, Ecorse, MI; d there 1899.
I know of this child's death only through Denissen, *Genealogy of the French Families of the Detroit River Region*, II, 858.

3.9.3.6.2.6   **MONTIE, Charlotte Adelina** b & bp 10 & 21 May 1899, Ecorse, MI; d 20 Jan 1996, Monroe, MI.
Charlotte Montie was a teaching sister in St. Mary's College and Academy in Monroe, MI, in 1920 and a parochial school teacher in Detroit, MI, in 1930 (US census).

3.9.3.6.2.7   **MONTIE, Anna Ida** b & bp 7 & 20 Oct 1901, Ecorse, MI; d 24 Nov 1993, Monroe, MI.
Anna Montie was a teaching sister in St. Mary's College and Academy in Monroe, MI, in 1920 and a parochial school teacher in Wyandotte, MI, in 1930 (US censuses).

3.9.3.6.2.8   **MONTIE, Anonymous** (female) b 3 Nov 1904, Ecorse, MI; d there 6 Nov 1904.

3.9.3.6.3.1   **MONTIE, Beatrice** b 19 Dec 1907, Ecorse, MI; d 20 Oct 1983, Lincoln Park, MI. She married there 8 Jun 1926 **Ellis C. Quick** (Ira Alfred Quick & Mary Matilda Lawrence) b 8 Nov 1904, Maple Creek, Saskatchewan, Canada; d 22 Sep 1973, Van Buren, MI.
Ellis Quick arrived in the United States around 1918 and was an automobile plant worker in Lincoln Park, MI, in 1930 (US census). He was a resident there at his death.

Children:
i   **Melvin Ellis Quick** b Apr 1927, Lincoln Park, MI. He married 9 May 1953 **Esther Constance/Ester Konstancia Jamrog** (Frank Jamrog & Anna ___) b 19 Feb 1924, MI.
ii   **Elden Arnold Quick** b Oct 1935, Wayne Co., MI. He married **Jean Mae Reno** b 1937.
iii **Kenneth James Quick** b 20 Mar 1939, Wayne Co., MI; d 28 Jan 2003, Kalkaska, MI. He married **Lorraine May Siebert** b Sep 1944.

3.9.3.6.3.2   **MONTIE, Adele Catherine** b & bp 5 & 17 Jun 1917, Ecorse, MI. She married 5 Jul 1958, Lincoln Park, MI, **Frank J. Woch** (Joseph Anthony Woch & Agnes ___) b 28 Jan 1909, Detroit, MI; d 13 Apr 1973, Lincoln Park, MI.
Frank Woch was a machinist in an automobile plant in Detroit, MI, in 1930 while Adele Montie was living with her parents in Lincoln Park, MI (US census). She continued to reside there after her husband's death.

3.9.3.6.4.1   **MONTIE, Emma Ida** b & bp 22 & 26 May 1895, Ecorse, MI; d 3 Apr 1988, River Rouge, MI. She married 20 Jul 1915, Ecorse, MI, **Victor John LeBlanc** (Samuel Abraham LeBlanc & Delia/Delima Dugrey) b there 31 Jan 1887; d 27 Feb 1972, Detroit, MI.
Victor LeBlanc was a brother of Lillian LeBlanc, wife of Joseph Montie (3.9.3.6.3). He was a fireman in Ecorse, MI, in 1920 and in River Rouge, MI, in 1930 (US censuses). He and his wife were still residents there at their deaths.

Children:
i   **Leona Emma LeBlanc** b 24 Sep 1917, Ecorse, MI. She married 19 Jul 1941 **Edward Frank Lamb** (Frank Lamb & Mary ___) b 10 Sep 1918, Edwardsville, IL; d 7 Jan 1983, River Rouge, MI.
ii   **Melford John LeBlanc** b 21 Aug 1921, Wayne Co., MI; d & bur 31 Aug & 22 Sep 2006, Richmond & Arlington, VA. He married 19 Aug 1948, London, England, **Anita Christine Thomas** (Philip Thomas & ___ Morris) b 21 Sep 1921, Machen, South Wales, Great Britain.
iii **Leonard Joseph LeBlanc** b 4 Dec 1923, Wayne Co., MI.

iv   **Ralph Victor LeBlanc** b 25 Dec 1925, Wayne Co., MI; d 12 Feb 1969. He married 9 Sep 1950 **Anna K. Stipcak** (Martin Stipcak & Anna ____) b 25 Jul 1929, Detroit, MI; d there 18 Oct 1978.

v   **Dorothy Mae LeBlanc** b 10 Apr 1928, River Rouge, MI. She married 17 Jul 1978 **Robert Wayne Smalley** (Lamont Albert Smalley & Matilda A. Valade) b 1 Aug 1923, River Rouge, MI; d 23 Aug 2000, Oxford, MI.

3.9.3.6.4.2   **MONTIE, Eleanor** b 20 Feb 1898, Ecorse, MI; d 8 Apr 1971, Trenton, MI. She married (1) 24 Nov 1915, Ecorse, MI, **Anthony Pegouski** (Andrew Pegouski & Salina ____) b & bp there 18 Nov & 6 Dec 1891; d there 1920.

She married (2) 14 Jan 1922 **Nelson/Narcisse Sirois** (Odilon Sirois & Julie Giroux) b & bp 24 & 25 Nov 1890, St. André, QC; d Sep 1966, Lincoln Park, MI.

Anthony Pegouski was a mechanic in a casting foundry in Ecorse, MI, in January 1920 (US census), shortly before his death.

Nelson Sirois (Joseph Narcisse at his baptism) came to the United States around 1916 and was a house carpenter in River Rouge, MI, in 1920 and in Wyandotte, MI, in 1930. He may have adopted, formally or not, his wife's daughter Isabelle for she was listed in 1930 as his own 10-year-old daughter, Isabelle Sirois (US censuses). His widow was a resident of Ecorse at her death.

Children:

i   **Isabelle Pegouski/Sirois** b 1920?, Ecorse, MI.

ii   **Robert N. Sirois** b Feb 1923, Wayne Co., MI. He married **Marie Agnes ____** b May 1923.

iii   **Alice Sirois** b 1926?, Wayne Co., MI.

iv   **Donald J. Sirois** b Nov 1927, Wayne Co., MI. He married **Barbara A. ____** b Oct 1943.

v   **Mary L. Sirois** b Mar 1930, Wyandotte, MI.

3.9.3.6.4.3   **MONTIE, Albert John** b & bp 19 & 22 Jul 1900, Ecorse, MI; d 4 Jul 1979, Tawas City, MI. He married 1920?, Wayne Co., MI, **Clara May Courtney** (Thomas Courtney & Margaret A. Stark) b 26 Oct 1899, Enniskillen, Ontario, Canada; d 11 Mar 1988, Tawas City, MI.

Albert John Montie was a laborer in Wyandotte, MI, when he signed his World War I Draft Registration card in 5 Jun 1917 and a shipyard worker in Ecorse, MI, still single, on 1 Jan 1920. He married very shortly afterwards for he and his wife had been married for ten years on 1 Apr 1930. He was then a drug company salesman in Lincoln Park, MI (US censuses).

Children:

3.9.3.6.4.3.1	Faye Mary	1920-	-2002
3.9.3.6.4.3.2	Shirley Marie	1923-	-
3.9.3.6.4.3.3	Elizabeth Ann	1927-	-
3.9.3.6.4.3.4	Joan Alice	1930-	-
3.9.3.6.4.3.5	John Albert	1932-	-

3.9.3.6.4.4   **MONTIE, Walter Alexander** b & bp 11 & 13 Jul 1902, Ecorse, MI; d 21 Feb 1994, Detroit, MI. He married 20 Jun 1923, River Rouge, MI, **Julia Florence Mailloux** (Honoré/Henry Mailloux & Evelina Bellemare/Bellamore) b & bp 12 & 17 May 1903, St. Joachim, Ontario, Canada; d 14 Mar 1982, Detroit, MI.

The date of this couple's marriage is found in a marginal note to the baptismal record of Marie Florence Laurentia Mailloux in St. Joachim, Ontario, Canada (p. 185). The Birth Records of Essex Co., Ontario, however, show that the child born on 12 May 1903 in St. Joachim was named Marie Julia Florence Mailloux (p. 664). In the United States she was known as Julia.

Walter A. Montie was a plant worker in Ecorse, MI, in 1920, and a foreman in an automobile plant there in 1930 (US censuses). He was a resident of Royal Oak, MI, at his death while his wife was a resident of Taylor, MI, at her own death.

Children:

3.9.3.6.4.4.1	Laura Elenore	1924-	-
3.9.3.6.4.4.2	Mary Anne	1927-	-
3.9.3.6.4.4.3	Theresa Marie	1932-	-
3.9.3.6.4.4.4	Walter Albert	-	-

3.9.3.6.4.5   **MONTIE, Vina E./Melvina** b & bp 10 & 24 Jul 1904, Ecorse, MI; d 28 Feb 1988, Wyandotte, MI. She married 11 Sep 1923, Ecorse, MI, **Leo Louis Olshelfske/Olshelfski** (Joseph Olshelfski/Josef Olshewski & Joanna Meklinska) b 14 Jun 1899, PA; d Mar 1951, MI.

This couple married under the names of Melvina Montie and Leonard Olshewski according to Denissen's *Genealogy of the French Families of the Detroit River Region*, II, 858. Yet they were named Vina and Leo in all US censuses preceding their marriage as well as in the 1930 census in Ecorse, MI. Mrs. Vina E. Olshelfske was a resident of Lincoln Park, MI, at her death.

I have not found Leo Olshelfske/Olshelfski/Olshewski's birth record and am using the date found in his World War I Draft Registration card of 12 Sep 1918 rather than the one of 12 Oct 1898 shown in the Social Security Death Index. It corresponds more closely to what is indicated in earlier and later censuses and may be more accurate.

Leo Louis Olshelfske was a coal miner in Collinsville, IL, in 1918 and in 1920, though his and his father's surname were then inscribed as Olshelfski. He was a foundry worker living in Ecorse with his wife and two sons in 1930 (US censuses).

Children:

i   **Leonard J. Olshelfske** b 11 Jun 1925, Ecorse, MI; d 21 Sep 2005, Lincoln Park, MI.

ii   **Douglas Olshelfske** b 2 Nov 1928, Ecorse, MI; d 6 Jul 2000, Wyandotte, MI. He married **Barbara Alice Bondy** b May 1934, MI.

3.9.3.6.4.6   **MONTIE, Mabel G.** b & bp 8 & 17 Feb 1907, Ecorse, MI; d 1 Mar 1988, Trenton, MI. She married Aug 1937, Detroit, MI, **John Henry Haltiner/Haltinner** (John H. Haltiner & Paulina _____) b 1 Aug 1895, River Rouge, MI; d 26 Mar 1980, Wyandotte, MI.

John Henry Haltiner was an electrician in River Rouge, MI, when he signed on 26 Jun 1917 his World War I Draft Registration card. That is the surname used in US censuses until at least 1930 and also at his marriage. Yet he and his wife were named John H. and Mabel Haltinner at their deaths.

John H. Haltiner owned his own electrical business in River Rouge in 1930 (US censuses). He and his wife were both residents of Wyandotte, MI, at their deaths.

3.9.3.6.7.1   **MONTIE, Edward Gabriel** b & bp 29 May & 8 Jun 1913, Ecorse, MI; d 4 Jul 2008, Dearborn, MI. He married **Orpha Ann _____** b 13 Oct 1914; d & bur 6 & 8 Mar 2008, Dearborn, MI.

3.9.3.6.7.2   **MONTIE, Margaret Olive** b & bp 1 & 13 Sep 1914, Ecorse, MI. She married there 8 Sep 1934 **Command Cunningham** (Francis Cunningham & Catherine O'Shea) b 1912?, Ontario, Canada.

Command Cunningham came to the United States with his parents around 1925 and was 18 years old in 1930 when he was living with them in Detroit, MI (US census).

3.9.3.6.7.3   **MONTIE, Robert Donald** b & bp 14 & 19 Jun 1919, Ecorse, MI; d 1 Jul 1980, Detroit, MI.

3.9.3.6.7.4   **MONTIE, Mary Jane** b & bp 12 & 19 October 1924, Ecorse, MI. She married there **Joseph Edward Willing** (Frank Willing & Sadie Stone) b & bp 29 Jul & 7 Sep 1924, Detroit, MI; d 25 July 1991, Sumter Co., FL.

Joseph Edward Willing was an automotive parts analyst in Lincoln Park, MI, before moving to Lake Panasoffkee, FL, around 1983 (*Tampa Tribune*, 26 Jul 1991).

Children:
i   **Wilda J. Willing** b Jul 1953, Wayne Co., MI. She married **Edward Felix Gall** b Feb 1946.
ii   **Penny E. Willing** b Sep 1958, Wayne Co., MI. She married ____ **English**.

3.9.3.6.8.1   **MONTIE, Anonymous** b & d 6 Jun 1907, Ecorse, MI.
This female child was stillborn.

3.9.3.6.8.2   **MONTIE, Richard Herbert** b & bp 18 & 29 Aug 1909, Ecorse, MI; d & bur there 8 & 10 Feb 1910.

3.9.3.6.8.3   **MONTIE, Hazel Elizabeth** b & bp 22 & 25 Feb 1912, Ecorse, MI; d 17 Dec 1979, Frenchtown, MI. She married 3 Jul 1934, Ecorse, MI, **William Kiernan** (Philip Kiernan & Anna ____) b 9 Apr 1911, Ireland; d Jun 1966, Ecorse, MI.

William Kiernan came to the United States around 1920 and was in 1930 a laborer in a coal and coke yard in Detroit, MI (US census). He and his wife were both residents of Ecorse, MI, at their deaths.

3.9.3.6.8.4   **MONTIE, Myrtle Frances** b & bp 22 & 30 Nov 1914, Ecorse, MI. She married there 2 May 1936 **Clifton Arthur Hebert** (Henry Hebert & Delphine Pilon) b 15 Jul 1915, Wyandotte, MI; d 22 Dec 1976, Dearborn, MI.

Clifton Hebert was a resident of Ecorse, MI, at his death.

4.3.1.1.4.1   **MONTY, Henry W.** b 1873?, Chazy, NY.

Henry W. Monty was a 7-year-old child living with his parents in Chazy, NY, in 1880 (US census). He was not with them in 1892 (state census) and may have left home, or died, before then.

4.3.1.1.4.2   **MONTY, Nellie J.** b 1877?, Chazy, NY.

Nellie J. Monty was a 3-year-old child living with her parents in Chazy, NY, in 1880. She was still with them there in 1892 (US and state censuses).

4.3.1.1.4.3   **MONTY, Joseph Willis** b 23 May 1879, Chazy, NY; d & bur 27 & 30 Nov 1946, West Chazy & Chazy, NY. He married 1899?, **Kate Lapier/Lapiere** (Martin Lapier & Mary Tracy) b 15 Oct 1882, West Chazy, NY; d & bur 7 & 11 Jul 1967, St. Petersburg, FL & Chazy, NY.

Joseph W. Monty (often simply Willis Monty) was a day laborer in Chazy, NY, in 1900, when he and his wife had been married for one year, a farm laborer there in 1910, and a farmer there in 1920 and 1930 (US censuses). He was a carpenter in West Chazy, NY, at his death. He and his wife were buried in the Ingraham Cemetery in Chazy (*Plattsburgh Press Republican*, 29 Nov 1946 and 10 Jul 1967).

Child:
4.3.1.1.4.3.1   Eva May   1903-1922-1976

4.3.1.1.4.4   **MONTY, Thomas** b May 1882, Chazy, NY. He married 15 Aug 1910, West Chazy, NY, **Ruth Maxson** (George Maxson & ____ Honsinger) b 1892?, St. Albans, VT.

Thomas Monty's date of birth is taken from the 1900 US census in Chazy, NY. It corresponds fairly well to the year of birth ascribed to him in the 1892 state census in Chazy, when he was 9 years old. After that time though his age changes seemingly at whim: he was 25 years old in April 1910 as well as at his marriage a few months later, 38 years old in September 1918 (World War I Draft Registration card, with date of birth shown as 4 Apr 1880), and 37 years old in 1920. The earlier records are probably more accurate than the later ones.

Thomas Monty was a resident of West Chazy, NY, at his marriage while his 18-year-old bride was a resident of Malone, NY. He was then a laborer in Chazy, and a paper mill worker in Plattsburgh, NY, in 1920 (US censuses). I have not found him or his wife in any later census. By 1930 their two children, Harvey and Margaret Monte (sic), were working in Albany, NY, and boarding with the Oliver Myers family.

Children:

4.3.1.1.4.4.1	Harvey	1911-	-1978	
4.3.1.1.4.4.2	Marguerite/Margaret	1912?-	-	

4.3.1.1.4.5   **MONTY, Ellis** b 1885?, Chazy, NY.

Ellis Monty was a 7-year-old child living with his parents in Chazy, NY, in 1892 (state census). He was a resident of Hoboken, NJ, in 1946 according to the obituary of his brother Willis (4.3.1.1.4.3) in the *Plattsburgh Press Republican* of 29 Nov 1946. I have found no other reference to Ellis Monty and suspect that he may have been known during those fifty-four years and later under a completely different name and perhaps surname.

4.3.1.1.4.6   **MONTY, Charles H.** b 23 Aug 1886, West Chazy, NY; d & bur 18 & 21 Aug 1962, Plattsburgh & Chazy, NY. He married 18 Nov 1909, Chazy, NY, **Ina M. Bushey** (Peter Bushey & Nellie Lapiere) b 20 Jan 1892, West Chazy, NY; d 24 Dec 1961, Plattsburgh, NY.

Charles Monty was a farmer in West Chazy, NY, until at least 1930 (US censuses) and a carpenter there for many years before his death (*Plattsburgh Press Republican*, 20 Aug 1962). He and his wife were buried in the Ingraham Cemetery in Chazy, NY.

Children:

4.3.1.1.4.6.1	Irene May	1910-1925&	&	-1991	
4.3.1.1.4.6.2	Harold J.	1913-1934-1976			
4.3.1.1.4.6.3	Ralph E.	1916-	-1970		
4.3.1.1.4.6.4	Genevieve M.	1922-	-1989		

4.3.1.1.4.7   **MONTY, William** b 17 Aug 1889, West Chazy, NY; d & bur 22 & 25 Aug 1965, Burlington, VT & West Chazy, NY. He married 26 Nov 1919, Plattsburgh, NY, **Blanche Mary Donovan** (William Donovan & Julia Gonyea) b & bp 18 Nov 1901 & 1 Oct 1905, Chazy & West Chazy, NY; d 17 Mar 1985, Lacolle, QC.

William Monty was a laborer in West Chazy and Chazy, NY until at least 1930 (US and state censuses) and was buried in St. Joseph's Cemetery in West Chazy (*Plattsburgh Press Republican*, 23 Aug 1965). His widow died in a nursing home in Lacolle, QC (*Plattsburgh Press Republican*, 18 Mar 1985).

Child:

4.3.1.1.4.7.1	Carl E.	1926-	-

4.3.1.1.6.1   **MONTY, Ada** b 2 Jun 1873, Chazy, NY; d & bur 2 & 6 Mar 1956, Plattsburgh, NY. She married 1891? (Protestant ceremony) & 20 Apr 1894 (Catholic revalidation), Plattsburgh, NY, **John Wallace** b 1866?, NY; d 29 Dec 1928, Plattsburgh, NY, at the age of 62.

This woman was named Maria Ida when she was baptized in St. Peter's Church in Plattsburgh, NY, on 25 Mar 1894 and Ida when she married a few weeks later and also when her son was baptized in 1901. On all other occasions, as a child living with her parents in Chazy, NY, or as John Wallace's wife, she was named Ada (US censuses). She was buried as Mrs. Ada Wallace in St. Peter's Cemetery in Plattsburgh (*Plattsburgh Press Republican*, 7

Mar 1956).

John Wallace was a laborer in Plattsburgh in 1910 when he and his wife had been married for nineteen years. They had had only one child who was then no longer alive. He remained in Plattsburgh until his death (US censuses; *Plattsburgh Sentinel*, 4 Jan 1929).

Child:
  i   **James William Wallace** b & bp 28 Feb & 4 Mar 1901, Plattsburgh, NY; d before 1910.

4.3.1.1.6.2   **MONTY, Anna/Hannah** b 13 Aug 1875, Chazy, NY; bp 25 Mar 1894, Plattsburgh, NY; d & bur there 22 & 26 Aug 1940. She married (1) 23 Jun 1889, Grand Isle, VT, **Henry LaMott/LaMotte** (Antoine LaMotte & Adeline/Ida Tessier) b & bp 28 Aug 1866 & 14 Mar 1867, Grand Isle & South Hero, VT.

She married (2) **Frederick Rogers**.

Henry LaMott was a laborer in Grand Isle, VT, at his marriage. I have been unable to trace his movements after that time. Anna Monty, "Mrs. Anna Rogers," was buried in St. Peter's Cemetery in Plattsburgh, NY. She apparently left no direct descendants. According to the *Plattsburgh Press Republican* of 23 & 27 Aug 1940, her only survivors were her husband Frederick Rogers and her siblings Mrs. Ada Wallace (4.3.1.1.6.1) and William Monty (4.3.1.1.6.3).

4.3.1.1.6.3   **MONTY, William Alexander** b & bp 8 Nov 1883 & 31 Mar 1889, Chazy & Plattsburgh, NY; d & bur 8 & ? Aug 1947, Plattsburgh & Rochester, NY. He married 15 Apr 1910, Plattsburgh, NY, **Stella Baillargeon/Badger** (Joseph George Baillargeon & Louisa Perry/Louise Sophie Paré) b & bp 9 & 11 Nov 1882, Redford, NY; d 27 Jan 1946, Plattsburgh, NY.

William A. Monty was a chef and his bride a pastry cook in Plattsburgh, NY, at their marriage. They moved a few years later to Rochester, NY, where William Alexander Monty was a chef in 1918 (World War I Draft Registration card) and a foreman for a lithograph company in 1920. He returned to Plattsburgh with his family in 1928 and was a hotel cook there in 1930 (US censuses). He remained there until his death but was buried nevertheless in the family plot in Rochester (*Plattsburgh Press Republican*, 9 Aug 1947).

Children:

4.3.1.1.6.3.1	Marie Géraldine	1911- -1912
4.3.1.1.6.3.2	Geraldine	1914-1943-1959
4.3.1.1.6.3.3	Doris Viola	1915- &1955-1973
4.3.1.1.6.3.4	Harold E.	1916- -1944
4.3.1.1.6.3.5	Kenneth	1919- -
4.3.1.1.6.3.6	Floyd W.	1921-1953-2000
4.3.1.1.6.3.7	Isabelle C.	1923-1947&1965?-2006

4.3.1.2.1.1   **MONTY/MONTAY, Amos** b 1856?, Lewis, NY.

Amos Monty was a 4-year-old child living with his parents in Lewis, NY, in 1860 and was a teamster in Elizabethtown, NY, in 1880. He moved with his family to Wausau, WI, during the next decade and was in turn a laborer, a watchman, and a factory worker named Amos Montai, Montey, or Montay. He remained a bachelor, residing in 1900 with his father and several siblings and in 1910 and 1920 with his sister Katie (4.3.1.2.1.12) and brother-in-law Frank Bessey. Even after his sister's death he was still, as "uncle" Amos, a member of the Bessey household in 1930 (US censuses).

4.3.1.2.1.2   **MONTY, William W.** b 1858?, Lewis, NY. He married 31 Mar 1889, Eagle River, WI, **Augusta/Gusta Yager** (William Yager & Hannah Jofel) b 1870?, Wausau, WI.

William Monty was a 2-year-old child living with his parents in Lewis, NY, in 1860 and was a teamster in Elizabethtown, NY, in 1880 (US censuses). He moved shortly thereafter to Eagle River, WI, where he was a blacksmith at his marriage.

Augusta Yager's place of birth is taken from her marriage record. As a 10-year-old child in 1880, she was living with her parents in Texas, WI (US census).

4.3.1.2.1.3   **MONTY/MONTAY, Henry C.** b Jan 1861, Elizabethtown, NY. He married (1) 19 Nov 1889, Wausau, WI, **Christina Theresa Danielson** (Elias Danielson & Christina Gunderson) b 1871?, Grimstad, Norway.

He married (2) 24 Mar 1895, Outagamie Co., WI, **Anna Hoffman** (John Hoffman & Ida ____) b Feb 1873, Fredonia, WI.

Henry Monty was a laborer in Elizabethtown, NY, in 1880. He soon moved to Wausau, WI, where his surname became Montay and where he was a railroad man at his first marriage. He was a freight conductor in Kaukauna, WI, at the birth of his son Leland in 1896 and a railroad fireman in St. Paul, MN, in 1900. He was still in St. Paul in 1905 as a carpenter and in 1910 as a mortgage company employee. He was not there however in 1920 with his wife and children (US and state censuses). I have not found him in later years.

Christina Danielson was a 9-year-old child living with her widowed mother and siblings in Milwaukee, WI, in 1880 (US census).

Children of the second marriage:
4.3.1.2.1.3.1	Leland/Lee Henry	1896-	-1968
4.3.1.2.1.3.2	Leatha Helen	1900-1926?-1974	

4.3.1.2.1.4   **MONTY, Willis** b 1864?, Essex Co., NY.

Willis Monty was a 6-year-old child living with his parents in Elizabethtown, NY, in 1870 (US census). He does not appear with them in the 1875 state census and may have died before then.

4.3.1.2.1.5   **MONTY, Elizabeth** b & bp 7 Dec 1865 & 1 Jan 1866, Stanbridge & Iberville, QC; d between 1910 and 1920. She married 1883? **Joseph Drinkwine** (Joseph Drinkwine & Mary ____) b Jul 1862, QC.

Elizabeth Monty's date and place of birth are taken from her baptismal record. Her parents may have been on a temporary visit to Canada, for her father was employed in Vermont in 1865 and the family was living in Essex Co., NY, in 1868. According to the 1900 and 1910 censuses in Moriah, NY, though, she was born in Vermont. She and her husband had been married for seventeen years in 1900 and had had three children, all of whom were still alive (US census).

Joseph Drinkwine came to the United States as a child with his parents in 1866. He was a day laborer in Moriah, NY, in 1900, a stationary engineer there in 1910, and an iron mine worker there in 1920. He was then a widower (US censuses). Given his French Canadian origin it his highly probable that his surname was originally Boivin.

Children:
i   **Ida M. Drinkwine** b & bp 13 Sep 1884 & 31 May 1891, Moriah & Mineville, NY. She married 14 Nov 1910, Mineville, NY, **Richard Anthony Finnessey** (Thomas Finnessey & Helen Hennesey) b 10 Oct 1885, Moriah, NY; d & bur 14 & 17 Oct 1964, Burlington, VT & Mineville, NY.
ii   **William Edward Drinkwine** b & bp 23 May 1890 & 31 May 1891 Moriah & Mineville, NY. He married 1925?, **Ileen Ryan** b 1895?, NY.
iii   **Louis/Lewis Herman Drinkwine** b & bp 23 Sep & 5 Oct 1902, Moriah & Mineville, NY.

4.3.1.2.1.6   **MONTY/MONTAY, Mary** b 1868?, Elizabethtown, NY. She married 13 Nov 1892, Wausau, WI, **Albert Clark** (John Clark & Mary ____) b Apr 1870, Milwaukee, WI.

Mary Monty was 2 years old in 1870, 7 years old in 1875, and 11 years old in 1880 when she was living with her parents in Elizabethtown, NY (US and state censuses). When she moved to Wisconsin with her family in the early 1880s, her surname changed to Montay. She also became younger: the 1900 census in Wausau, WI, indicates that she was born in August 1870 while later censuses through 1930 imply that she was born in 1872. I would rather trust the earlier records.

Albert Clark's date of birth is equally uncertain. For lack of better information I am using here the date found in the 1900 census in Wausau, WI, where he was a mill worker/laborer until at least 1930. He and his wife had no children (US censuses).

4.3.1.2.1.7   MONTY/MONTAY, Emily/Millie b 1872?, Elizabethtown, NY.

Emily Monty was an 8-year-old child living with her parents in Elizabethtown, NY, in 1880. She came to Wisconsin with her family in the early 1880s and was named Millie when living in her father's household in Wausau, WI, in 1900 and 1905. She admitted though to only 24 years in 1900 and 30 in 1905 (US and state censuses). I am relying here for her date of birth on the earlier census.

4.3.1.2.1.8   MONTY/MONTAY, Albert J. b 1874, Elizabethtown, NY; d before 1920. He married 30 Sep 1894, Wausau, WI, **Anna Slarzenska** (John Slarzenski & Anna ____) b 1874?, Milwaukee, WI.

Albert Monty was a one-year-old child living with his parents in Elizabethtown, NY, in 1875. He came to Wisconsin with his family in the early 1880s and was henceforth known as Albert Montay. At his marriage he was a laborer in Wausau, WI, where his 45-year-old widow was still residing in 1920 (US and state censuses).

Children:

4.3.1.2.1.8.1	Albert	1897-	-1975
4.3.1.2.1.8.2	Mary	1906?-	-

4.3.1.2.1.9   MONTY/MONTAY, Bertrand/Bert b Jul 1876, Elizabethtown, NY.

Bertrand Monty was living with his parents in Elizabethtown, NY, in 1880. He moved to Wausau, WI, with his family a few years later and, as Bert Montai (sic), was a teamster there in 1900. He apparently never married. Bert Montay was still single in 1930 when he was a roomer in the Grand Army Home for Veterans in Waupaca, WI (US censuses).

4.3.1.2.1.10   MONTY/MONTAY, John T. b Nov 1879, Elizabethtown, NY. He married 10 Nov 1901, Wausau, WI, **Anna L. Wendt** (Karl Wendt & Ulrike ____) b Sep 1883, Hamburg, WI; d 30 Dec 1966, Wausau, WI.

John Monty came to Wisconsin as a child with his family in the early 1880s and was henceforth known as John Montay. He was a laborer in Wausau, WI, in 1900 as well as at his marriage and a mill hand or factory worker there until at least 1930 (US censuses).

Children:

4.3.1.2.1.10.1	Leonora/Lena	1902?-	-
4.3.1.2.1.10.2	Gilbert L.	1903-	-1996
4.3.1.2.1.10.3	Oska Lee	1906-	-
4.3.1.2.1.10.4	William H.	1911-	-1962

4.3.1.2.1.11   MONTY, Alicia b & bp 5 Oct 1881 & 16 Apr 1882, Elizabethtown & Westport, NY.

Alicia Monty's date of birth is taken from her baptismal record in the church of St. Philip Neri in Westport, NY. I have found no later trace of her in either New York or Wisconsin.

4.3.1.2.1.12   MONTY/MONTAY, Catherine b 5 Nov 1882, Elizabethtown, NY; d 14 May 1925, Wausau, WI. She married there 19 Dec 1903 **Frank James Bessey** (Joseph William Bessey & Agnes Parker) b 16 May 1882, Arcadia, WI; m (2) Anna Lemke (William Lemke & Emily ____); d & bur 1958, Wausau, WI.

Frank Bessey was a drayman in Wausau until at least 1920 and a city fireman there in 1930 (US censuses). He and both his wives were buried in the Pine Grove Cemetery in Wausau, WI.

4.3.1.2.3.1   **MONTY, Mary Jane/Jennie** b Apr 1870, Lewis, NY; d 6 May 1929, Wilmington, NY. She married there 13 Apr 1888 **Edgar W. Peck** (Adoniram Peck & Maria Raisey Kenada) b 6 Apr 1865, Jay, NY; m (2) there 8 Dec 1934 Melvina Murcray (Moses/Mose Murcray & Delia Kayea), widow of Nelson J. Bourdreau; d there 27 Feb 1949.

Edgar W. Peck was a farmer in Wilmington, NY, and vicinity until at least 1920 and a carpenter in Wilmington in 1930. His housekeeper then was the widowed Mrs. Melvina Bourdreau whom he later married (US censuses).

Children:
i   **Benjamin Harris Peck** b 8 Nov 1892, Wilmington, NY; d there Dec 1979. He married **Elizabeth B./Bessie Lewis** (William A. Lewis & Florence Hood) b 1905?, NY; d before 1960.
ii   **Frank E. Peck** b 11 Aug 1894, Wilmington, NY; d & bur 15 & 16 Dec 1918, Wilmington & Jay, NY.
iii **Melvin Peck** b 28 Aug 1896, Wilmington, NY; d 3 Jan 1985, Saranac Lake, NY. He married 1924? **Blanche Bowen** (George Bowen & Grace Wilkins) b 19 Oct 1909, Wilmington, NY; d & bur 14 & 17 Sep 1965, Lake Placid & Wilmington, NY.
iv   **Howard Peck** b 28 Jun 1898, Wilmington, NY; d 31 Aug 1985, Lake Placid, NY. He married 16 Feb 1925, Jay, NY, **Rosemary/Rose Lewis** (William A. Lewis & Florence Hood) b 26 Jan 1909, NY; d Nov 1985, Wilmington, NY.
v   **Albert Peck** b 29 Jul 1901, Wilmington, NY; d there 16 Jan 1905.
vi   **Minnie Peck** b 10 Nov 1906, Wilmington, NY; d & bur there 24 & 27 Dec 1937. She married there 30 Sep 1924 **Joshua Norman Wolfe** (John Casper Wolfe & Almeda J. Smith) b 8 Nov 1899, Essex Co., NY; d Jan 1980, Saranac Lake, NY.
vii **Anonymous Peck** (stillborn) b & d 25 Feb 1910, Wilmington, NY.

4.3.1.2.3.2   **MONTY, Sophia** b Mar 1872, Lewis, NY; d between 1880 and 1900.

Sophia Monty was 3 years and 3 months old in June 1875 when she was living with her parents in Lewis, NY. She was also with them there in 1880 but presumably died before 1900 when her mother had only one living child (US and state censuses).

4.3.1.2.3.3   **MONTY, Carrie** b Jul 1873, Lewis, NY; d between 1880 and 1900.

Carrie Monty was 1 year and 11 months old in June 1875 when she was living with her parents in Lewis, NY. She was also with them there in 1880 but presumably died before 1900 when her mother had only one living child (US and state censuses).

4.3.1.2.9.1   **MONTY, Harry B.** b 1879, Lewis, NY.

Harry B. Monty was a one-year-old child staying with his parents in the household of his uncle William Monty (4.3.1.2.4) in Lewis, NY, in 1880 (US census).

4.3.2.1.1.1   **MONTY, Herbert W.** b 4 Oct 1895, Essex, NY.

Herbert W. Monty served overseas during World War I in Battery B, 12th Field Artillery, US Army (*Bridgeport Telegram*, 27 Jul 1918). I have not found him in the United States after that date. He may have died before 1925 for he is not mentioned as a surviving sibling of his sister Ethel (4.3.2.1.1.2) in her obituary of 16 Feb 1925 in the *Bridgeport Telegram*.

4.3.2.1.1.2   **MONTY, Ethel** b 23 Aug 1897, Essex, NY; d & bur 14 & 16 Feb 1925, Bridgeport, CT. She married **Charles John McKenna** b 24 Nov 1895, Burlington, VT.

Ethel Monty lived with her parents in Essex, NY, and in Poultney, VT, before moving to Bridgeport, CT, where her child was born. She was buried in Lakeview Cemetery there (*Bridgeport Telegram*, 16 Feb 1925). Her son remained in Bridgeport in the care of his maternal grandmother while her widower was a soldier in the Presidio of San Francisco, CA, in 1930 (US censuses).

Child:
i   **Paul J. McKenna** b 9 Jan 1919, Bridgeport, CT; d there 15 Sep 1999. He married (1) 1941? **Leona Frances Whelan** (Joseph P. Whelan & Margaret Esther Kame) b 30 Jun 1918, Bridgeport, CT; d 23 Oct 1986, Miami, FL.
    He married (2) 27 Dec 1968, Bridgeport, CT, **Jean O. Nelson** b May 1922.

4.3.2.1.1.3   **MONTY, Meta Elizabeth** b 26 Dec 1904, Castleton, VT; d 10 Aug 1949, Bridgeport, CT. She married 1921? **Leslie Patterson** (John Patterson & Carrie ____) b 4 Jul 1901, Rochester, NY; d Oct 1964, Bridgeport, CT.
    Meta Monty was living with her parents in Poultney, VT, in 1910 and in Bridgeport, CT, in 1920. She and her husband, a factory foreman, had been married for nine years in 1930 and were living with their children in her widowed mother's household in Bridgeport (US censuses).

Children:
i   **Herbert L. Patterson** b Sep 1921, Bridgeport, CT.
ii   **Jean Patterson** b Aug 1926, Bridgeport, CT.

4.3.2.1.1.4   **MONTY, Helen Evelyn** b 4 Jan 1906, Fair Haven, VT; d Dec 1973, Salt Lake City, UT. She married (1) May 1925, Bridgeport, CT, **Edward Charles Boehm** (Henry Boehm & Anna ____) b there 15 May 1898; d there between 1940 and 1942.
    She married (2) 1943, Bridgeport, CT, **Norman Wilson** b 5 Dec 1902; d Dec 1971, Salt Lake City, UT.
    Edward C. Boehm was an assistant engineer in a steel mill in Bridgeport, CT, in 1930 (US census) and worked there until at least 1939. Mrs. Helen E. Boehm was a widow in 1942 (City Directories).

Children:
i   **Edward Boehm** b Feb 1926, Bridgeport, CT.
ii   **Harry J. Boehm** b 20 Sep 1927, Bridgeport, CT; d 14 Jan 2007, Stuart, FL. He married Nov 1954 **Anna F. Lynch** (John A. Lynch & Alice Reiley) b 3 Aug 1928, Scranton, PA; d 24 Dec 2006, Stuart, FL.

4.3.3.3.3.1   **MONTA, Anonymous** b & d 4 Nov 1879, Pownal, VT.

4.3.3.3.3.2   **MONTA, Maud A.** b 30 Jun 1881, Pownal, VT.

4.3.3.3.3.3   **MONTA, Blanche** b 7 Nov 1883, Pownal, VT; d there 12 Mar 1891.

4.3.3.4.3.1   **MONTEE, Mary** b 1875?, SD.
    Mary Montee was a 5-year-old child staying with her mother in her maternal uncle William Knight's household in Virginia, SD, in 1880 (US census). I have been unable to trace her further.

4.3.3.4.3.2   **MONTEE, Corta** (twin) b 1878?, SD.
    I know of this child only through Ramsey, *Monty-Montee History*, p. 157. She was not living with her mother and sisters in Virginia, SD, in 1880 (US census).

4.3.3.4.3.3   **MONTEE, Cuba** (twin) b 1878?, SD.
    Cuba Montee was a 2-year-old child living with her mother in her maternal uncle William Knight's household in Virginia, SD, in 1880 (US census). I have been unable to trace her further.

4.3.3.4.6.1   **MONTEE, Tracy D.** b 27 Feb 1892, Huron, SD; d 6 Nov 1934, Baguio, Philippines. He married around 1919 in the Philippines **Rosario Berenguer** b 18 Nov 1899, Barcelona, Spain; m (2) Robert F. Lasher (Herman Lasher & Helen Celestia Jewett); d 28 Feb 1982, San Antonio, TX.

Tracy Montee's early years were marked by constant traveling as he followed his family through the West and Midwest. He left South Dakota shortly after his birth and was in Little Sioux, IA, in 1894 and 1895, Albany, MO, in 1896, Yankee Hill, NE, in 1899 and 1900, South Dakota again in 1901 and 1903, and Haugen Twp, MN, in 1907. He was an engineer in a paper mill there in 1910 while still living with his parents (US and state censuses; births of his siblings). It is said that he was an army pilot in the Philippines at his marriage, though I have found no trace of his enlistment. According to an item from Manila, PI, dated 6 Nov 1934 and published in the *Bee Republican* of Fresno, CA, Tracy Montee, an aviator, had been living in the Philippines for twenty-one years when he died in the crash of a plane he was piloting.

Child:
4.3.3.4.6.1.1   Matthew P.   1920-1946&1953&1990-

4.3.3.4.6.2   **MONTEE, Jesse Abram** b 1 Jun 1894, Sioux Co., IA; d & bur 17 & 20 Jul 1961, New York, NY & Arlington, VA. He married (1) 30 Jul 1920, Blue Point, NY, and divorced 1929, Reno, NV, **Theodora Myrtle Booth** (Ballington Booth & Maud Elizabeth Charlesworth) b 1 Nov 1892, New York, NY.

He married (2) **Christina G. ____** b 26 Mar 1913; d 15 May 1976, New York, NY.

Jesse Montee was living with his parents in Yankee Hill, NE, in 1900 and in Aitkin Co. (Haugen Twp), MN, in 1910 when he was a laborer on his father's farm. A few years later he was a locomotive engineer for the Great Northern Railroad when he signed on 23 May 1917 in Superior, WI, his World War I Draft Registration card. He served in Germany as a 2nd Lieutenant in 1918 and 1919 and met his first wife there. The story of their "post-war romance" was related in a number of newspapers, among others the *Duluth News Tribune* of 17, 18, and 29 Aug 1920 and the *Kansas City Star* of 21 Aug 1920.

Jesse A. Montee had returned to Superior, WI, after his tour of duty and was a railroad fireman there in January 1920 and a railroad engineer when he married in July. He joined his wife in New York City in early September and intended, according to newspaper reports, to engage in business there. By 1930, when he and his wife Theodora were divorced, he was a civil engineer doing construction work in Manhattan, NY (US censuses). He and his second wife, Christina, were buried in the Arlington, VA, National Cemetery.

Theodora Booth was the daughter of the founder of the Volunteers of America and the granddaughter of William Booth, founder of the Salvation Army. She resumed her maiden name after her divorce and was living in Great Neck, NY, when her mother died in August 1948 (*Bridgeport Telegram*, 27 Aug 1948).

Children of the second marriage:
4.3.3.4.6.2.1   Marliss   1936-   -2003
4.3.3.4.6.2.2   Geraldine   1939-   -

4.3.3.4.6.3   **MONTEE, Hobart Cecil** b 5 Aug 1896, Albany, MO; d 13 Jun 1949, Los Angeles Co., CA. He married (1) 1922 **Lotta Agnes Murphy** b 19 Mar 1892, New York, NY; d 4 Jan 1990, Newburg, MD.

He was divorced when he married (2) 1939? **Joan Drake** b 24 Oct 1917, Detroit, MI.

Hobart Montee was living with his parents in Yankee Hill, NE, in 1900 and in Haugen Twp, MN, in 1910 (US censuses), and was a farm hand in Wheatland, WY, when he signed as Cecil H. Montee his World War I Draft Registration card on 5 Jun 1917. He soon became a newspaperman, working for several years in Japan before returning to the United States in the mid-1920s and settling with his wife Lotta in Mount Vernon, NY (1930 census). The family moved in the mid-1930s to Washington, DC, where Hobart C. Montee was a United Press staff correspondent until the early 1940s. Mrs. Lotta Montee remained in Washington, where she had a successful career as a commercial artist while he and his wife Joan moved to California a few years after their marriage.

Children of the first marriage:

4.3.3.4.6.3.1	Hobart Mansfield	1924-1947-1994
4.3.3.4.6.3.2	Patricia Ellen	1926- -

Children of the second marriage:

4.3.3.4.6.3.3	Cecil Drake (twin)	1943-1962&1998-
4.3.3,4.6.3.4	Tracy Drake (twin)	1943-1971-

4.3.3.4.6.4   **MONTEE, Floy** b Apr 1899, Yankee Hill, NE.
Floy Montee was living with her parents in Yankee Hill, NE, in 1900 and in Haugen Twp, MN, in 1910 (US censuses).

4.3.3.4.6.5   **MONTEE, Paige** b 1901?, SD; d 1919, Aitkin Co., MN.
Paige Montee was a 9-year-old child living with his parents in Haugen Twp, MN, on 15 Apr 1910 (US census). He was killed in a gun accident while hunting near his home in McGregor, MN.

4.3.3.4.6.6   **MONTEE, Perry** b 1903?, SD. He married 1927?, **Paula E. ____** b 1910?, Belgium.
Perry Montee was a 7-year-old child living with his parents in Haugen Twp, MN, in 1910 and a machinist living in his widowed mother's household in New London, IA, in January 1920. By 1930, when he and his 20-year-old wife had been married for three years, he was a mechanic employed in subway construction in Brooklyn, NY (US censuses). A few years later he was a seaman working on several ships of the Grace Line sailing from New York or, for a few months in 1933 and 1934, from Seattle, WA. In 1937, when he was a junior engineer on the *Santa Elena*, he had been at sea for five years.

Child:

4.3.3.4.6.6.1	Nita P.	1928- -1997

4.3.3.4.6.7   **MONTEE, Mary** b 1904?, SD.
Mary Montee was a 5-year-old child living with her parents in Haugen Twp, MN, in 1910. She left Minnesota following her father's death and was living with her widowed mother in New London, IA, in 1920 (US censuses).

4.3.3.4.6.8   **MONTEE, Ethel** b 1908?, McGregor, MN.
Ethel Montee was a 2-year-old child living with her parents in Haugen Twp, MN, in 1910. She left Minnesota following her father's death and was living with her widowed mother in New London, IA, in 1920 and 1925 (US and state censuses).

4.3.3.4.6.9   **MONTEE, Joy M.** b 14 Apr 1912, McGregor, MN; d 11 Nov 2002, Baldwin City, KS. She married (1) 1928? **Gerald C. Giese** (William P. Giese & ____) b 1908?, Spooner, WI.
She married (2) 1936 **Albert Leo Bubeck** (Karl Bubeck & Lydia Keller) b 7 Aug 1908, Cadott, WI; d 15 Oct 1997, Chippewa Falls, WI.
Joy M. Montee and Gerald C. Giese, a railroad brakeman, had been married for two years in April 1930. He was 22 years old and was living with his wife and daughter in his father's household in Spooner, WI (US census).
Albert L. Bubeck was a Lutheran clergyman in Spooner in 1930 (US census). He and his wife moved to Lake Wissota near Chippewa Falls, WI, in 1946 and remained there for the next fifty years (*Baldwin City Sentinel*, 20 Nov 2002).

Children:

i   **Sheila D. Giese** b 9 Oct 1929, Spooner, WI. She married **Richard E. Dahl** (____ Dahl & Minerva Kinberg) b Mar 1927, Eau Claire, WI.

ii   **Gary W. Bubeck** married **Beverly** ____ .

4.3.3.10.2.1   **MONTA, Infant** b 24 Aug 1885, Waukesha, WI.

This female child whose name is not indicated in the Register of Births of Waukesha Co., WI, apparently died before October 1894 when her brother Frederick was said to have only one living sibling, his sister Myrtle born in 1889.

4.3.3.10.2.2   **MONTA, Myrtle Pearl** b May 1889, Waukesha, WI.

Myrtle Monta was living in Kenosha, WI, at her mother's death in 1932 (*Waukesha Freeman*, 12 May 1932).

4.3.3.10.2.3   **MONTA, Frederick William/Fred W.** b 10 Oct 1894, Waukesha, WI; d 23 Nov 1964, Milwaukee, WI. He married 7 Apr 1917, Genesee, WI, **Clara O. Jacobson** (Claus Jacobson & Randina ____) b 2 Mar 1896, WI; d Feb 1968, Milwaukee, WI.

Frederick William Monta was a mechanic in Kenosha, WI, when he signed on 5 Jun 1917 his World War I Draft Registration card and a tool maker there in 1920. His household then included a 5-year-old son, Clyde, whose mother is unknown to me. He was a machinist in West Allis, WI, in 1930 (US censuses).

Children:

4.3.3.10.2.3.1	Clyde H.	1914-	-1999
4.3.3.10.2.3.2	Shirley	1924?-	-
4.3.3.10.2.3.3	Chad L.	1927-	-

4.3.3.10.3.1   **MONTA, Fred W.** b 14 Jul 1887, Knapp, WI. He married 1916? **Annie/Anna J.** ____ b 26 Nov 1897, IL; d 7 Dec 1972, Iron Mountain, MI.

Fred W. Monta was a factory worker living with his parents in Portland, OR, in 1910 and a machinist in Kenosha, WI, when he signed on 5 Jun 1917 his World War I Draft Registration card. He and his wife were then expecting their first child. They moved shortly afterwards. He was a stationary engineer in West Allis, WI, in 1920 and a machinist in Greenfield, WI, on 1 Apr 1930 when he and his wife had been married for thirteen years (US censuses).

Children:

4.3.3.10.3.1.1	Violet J.	1917-	-
4.3.3.10.3.1.2	Rose Mae	1919-1937&1986-2001	
4.3.3.10.3.1.3	June	1922?-	-

4.3.3.10.3.2   **MONTA/MONTE Clarence Henry** b 30 Jun 1892, Superior, WI; d 6 Feb 1960, Kenosha, WI. He married 1916? **Lillian Oquist** (Ole P. Oquist & Anna J. ____) b Jun 1896, Aitkin Co., MN; d 21 Dec 1963, Kenosha, WI.

Clarence Monta was a factory worker living with his parents in Portland, OR, in 1910 and an automobile mechanic in Kenosha, WI, when he signed on 5 Jun 1917 as Clarence Henry Monta his World War I Draft Registration card. He was a factory worker in Kenosha in 1920 and 1930 when he and his wife had been married for thirteen years (US censuses). His surname alternated between Monte and Monta though the latter predominated in later years.

Children:

4.3.3.10.3.2.1	Lillian Gladys	1918-	-2000
4.3.3.10.3.2.2	Virtue	1921?-	-
4.3.3.10.3.2.3	Joyce	1924?-	-
4.3.3.10.3.2.4	George C.	1925-	-

4.3.3.10.3.3   **MONTA/MONTE, Mabel** b Jan 1898, Superior, WI.

Mabel Monte was living with her parents in Superior, WI, in 1900 and, as Mabel Monta, in Portland, OR, in 1910 (US censuses). I have found no later trace of her in either Oregon or Wisconsin, where her parents were living in 1920.

4.3.3.10.3.4   **MONTA, Albert R.** b 1903?, WA. He married 1924?, **Vera May Stafford** b 1902?, IA.

Albert Monta was a 7-year-old child living with his parents in Portland, OR, in 1910. He was born in Washington State. Ten years later he was living with his parents in Milwaukee, WI. He probably married there but moved to Tacoma, WA, after the birth of his oldest child. He was a plasterer there in 1930 when he and his 28-year-old wife had been married for six years (US censuses).

Children:

4.3.3.10.3.4.1	Charles A.	1926-	-
4.3.3.10.3.4.2	Fay Marie	1927-	-
4.3.3.10.3.4.3	Clarence Charles	1928-	-

4.3.3.10.3.5   **MONTA, Howard R.** b 11 Apr 1905, ID; d 11 Oct 1988, Seattle, WA. He married 1920? **Ida George** b 2 Jan 1902, Milwaukee, WI; d 14 Sep 1981, Redmond, WA.

Howard R. Monta left Wisconsin after the births of his three children and was a woodworker in Seattle, WA, in 1930. He and his wife had then been married for ten years (US census). They were both residents of Bellevue, WA, at their deaths.

Children:

4.3.3.10.3.5.1	James C.	1920-	-1992
4.3.3.10.3.5.2	Shirley	1924?-	-
4.3.3.10.3.5.3	Betty	1925?-	-

4.3.3.10.5.1   **MONTA, William** b 1913?, WA.

William Monta was a 6-year-old child living with his parents in Tacoma, WA, on 1 Jan 1920 (US census). He was not with them in 1930 and may have died before then.

4.3.3.10.5.2   **MONTA, John David** b 9 Jan 1918, Tacoma, WA; d 12 Aug 1995, Bremerton, WA.

John D. Monta was a resident of Port Orchard, WA, at his death..

4.3.3.10.5.3   **MONTA, Mary E.** b 1922?, Tacoma, WA.

Mary E. Monta was an 8-year-old child living with her parents in Tacoma, WA, on 1 Apr 1930 (US census).

4.3.3.10.8.1   **MONTA, Lyla M.** b 1906?, Superior, WI.

Lyla M. Monta was a 4-year-old child living with her parents in Superior, WI, in 1910. She was also with them there in 1920 (US censuses).

4.3.3.12.3.1   **MONTY, Frank** b 5 Aug 1888, Nashua, NH.

I have not found this child in the 1900 US census with either his father or relatives and would suspect that he died before then. But neither have I found him in the New Hampshire Death Records.

4.3.3.12.3.2   **MONTY, Louis B.** b 13 Jul 1893, Gilford, NH; d Nov 1966, Laconia, NH. He married (1) 1917? **Myrtle G. Lairdieson** (James W. Lairdieson & Sarah ____) b 1891?, MA; m (1) 1908? Wesley Laurin (Carl G. Laurin & Hilda ____).

He married (2) 1927? **Mildred M. Morrill** (Leon Ernest Morrill & Carrie E. Kimball) b 13 Apr 1894, Gilford, NH; d Jun 1973, Laconia, NH.

Louis Monty was living with his maternal grandfather, Alonzo Dockham, in Gilford, NH, in 1900 and with his parents in Bedford, MA, in 1910. He was a teamster then and also in

1920 when his household in Lowell, MA, included his 28-year-old wife Myrtle and two Laurin stepchildren. This marriage apparently did not last very long. By 1930 Myrtle Lairdieson had resumed her first husband's surname and was living with her two children in Turner, ME.

Louis Monty also left Massachusetts. In 1930, when he and his second wife Mildred had been married for three years, he was a chauffeur for a private family in Laconia, NH (US censuses). He later had a variety of occupations, most consistently that of taxi driver (Laconia City Directories).

4.3.3.12.3.3   MONTY, Edith b 13 Oct 1895, Gilford, NH.

Edith Monty was living with her parents in Billerica, MA, in 1900 and in Bedford, MA, in 1910 (US censuses).

4.3.3.12.3.4   MONTY, Clara Jane b 12 Aug 1903, Billerica, MA; d 19 Jun 1985, Laconia, NH. She married 4 Jul 1931, Somersworth, NH, **Sam Levi Grant** (Frank B. Grant & Ruth M. Glidden) b 14 May 1891, Gilford, NH; m (1) 1913? Rosa M. Morrill (George Morrill & ____); d 15 Apr 1968, Laconia, NH.

Clara Jane Monty was living with her parents in Bedford, MA, in 1910, in Lowell, MA, in 1920, and in Gilford, NH, in 1930. Sam Levi Grant was a farm laborer there, a widower who had first married at the age of 22 (US censuses).

Children:

i   **Charles F. Grant** b 21 Mar 1932, Laconia, NH. He married there 1953? **Marilyn Goss** b 27 Jan 1932.

ii   **Edythe Claire Grant** b 22 Aug 1933, Laconia, NH. She married 29 Jun 1957, Tilton, NH, **Arnold A. Adams** (Howard Adams & Lucy Vigneault) b 25 Dec 1932.

iii   **Grace Grant** b 10 Jan 1935, Laconia, NH. She married there 1955? **Milton H. Endean** (Henry Herbert Endean & Alvena Christina Hanniq) b 25 Mar 1929, Detroit, MI.

4.3.3.12.3.5   MONTY, John A. b 1904?, Billerica, MA. He married 1927?, **Alice L. Rand** (Irvin H. Rand & Annie L. ____) b 13 Sep 1906, Laconia, NH; d 23 Dec 1996, Nashua, NH.

John Monty was a 5-year-old child living with his parents in Bedford, MA, in 1910 and a 15-year-old living with them in Lowell, MA, on 1 January 1920. In 1930, when he had been married for three years, he was a drug store clerk in Laconia, NH (US censuses). He later was a truck driver there (City Directories, 1941, 1964).

4.4.1.2.1.1   MONTY, Ann Eliza b around 1851, Plattsburgh, NY.

Ann Eliza Monty was Henry Monty's only surviving child, according to the 1856 affidavit of Mrs. Barbary (Monty) Morrison (Appendix I). Since she does not appear with her parents in the 1850 census in Plattsburgh, NY, and her father died in March 1852, she must have been born between July 1850 and December 1852. She is not found with her mother Catherine in any later census and may have died between 1856 and 1860. I strongly suspect however that she was the 9-year-old Ann Eliza Monty living with Oliver and Margaret Henry in Plattsburgh in 1860 (US census). I also suspect that the middle-aged Henrys were her maternal grandparents: it would be highly unusual for a young child to be left in the care of total strangers when so many of her paternal relatives were still living in the area and had on other occasions taken care of their orphaned relatives. This is only a suspicion: I have no proof.

4.4.1.2.2.1   MONTY, Harriet M. b 6 Apr 1856, Sandy Hill, NY; d & bur 1933, Glens Falls, NY. She married 12 Jan 1881, Hudson Falls, NY, **Orville C. Smith** (Richard Smith & Mariah Waters) b 16 Aug 1851, Horicon, NY; d & bur 1940, Glens Falls, NY.

Orville C. Smith was a grocery store owner in Glens Falls, NY, until at least 1920. In 1930 he was the mayor of Glens Falls (US censuses).

Children:

i   **Walter Monty Smith** b 21 Jan 1882, Glens Falls, NY. He married 1912? **Marjorie Case** b 1881?, NY.

ii **Clifford R. Smith** b 23 Aug 1883, Glens Falls, NY; d there 19 Feb 1945. He married 1904? **Anna May Price** (John Morgan Price & Margaret Matheu) b 24 Feb 1883, Youngstown, OH; d 28 Feb 1961, Glens Falls, NY.

4.4.1.2.2.2   MONTY, William Henry b Feb 1858, Sandy Hill, NY. He married 1884? **Frances Maybell Outterson** (James Thomas Outterson & Frances Jones) b Oct 1865, NY.

William Henry Monty was an accountant in Glens Falls, NY, in 1888 and 1890 (City Directories), a post office clerk there in 1892 (state census) and an accountant in Albany, NY, in 1900. He and his wife had then been married for sixteen years and had had four children of whom three, Frances, John, and Catherine, were still alive. This is the last time I have found him with his family. He was a manufacturer's salesman living on his own in Albany in 1910, while his wife and daughters were staying in the household of Frances' husband Charles S. Cobb in that same city. In 1920 he was also living apart from his family, in a small hotel he owned and where his sister Julia Anna (4.4.1.2.2.5) was housekeeper (US censuses). I have found no later trace of him or his wife.

Children:

4.4.1.2.2.2.1	Frances Elizabeth	1885-1906-
4.4.1.2.2.2.2	John C.	1887-1918-1945
4.4.1.2.2.2.3	Charles	1890?- -
4.4.1.2.2.2.4	Catherine	1898- -

4.4.1.2.2.3   MONTY, Benjamin Francis/Frank b Mar 1860, Sandy Hill, NY. He married 1898? **Sarah E./Nellie Smith** b Feb 1868, England; m (1) _____ Piper.

Benjamin F. Monty (occasionally Montey or Montee) was 3 months old in June 1860. He was named Francis in 1870 and 1875 when he was living with his parents in Glens Falls, NY, Benjamin F. in 1880 while still a member of his father's household there, and B. Frank Monty in the 1888 and 1890 Glens Falls City Directories. He was a mill superintendent there. He moved away from the area in the 1890s and was an insurance agent in Niagara Falls, NY, in 1900. Frank Monty and his wife had then been married for two years and included in their household three of her children by a previous marriage, Frank, Jessie, and Mabel Piper. Benjamin F. Monty was a Niagara Falls street inspector in 1910, a factory employee in 1920, and a City inspector again in 1930 (US and state censuses).

4.4.1.2.2.4   MONTY, Mary Elizabeth b 15 Jul 1863, Sandy Hill, NY; d 30 Nov 1938, Glens Falls, NY. She married there 15 Aug 1889 **Melanchton E. Smith** (James McEwan Smith & Catherine S. Garey) b 21 Feb 1856, Washington, NJ; d 25 Jan 1937, Marcy, NY.

Mary Elizabeth Monty (Mrs. Mary E. Smith) was living in Glens Falls, NY, in 1930 as head of a household which included her sister Julia Monty (4.4.1.2.2.5) but not her husband (US census). Both she and her husband were buried in the Union Cemetery in Fort Edward, NY.

A family Bible which was in her possession at the time of her death was passed on to her grandson, the late Robert Leland Smith of San Antonio, TX. In it was found a late 19th-century listing of births and deaths in the family of her great grandparents Johanna and Abraham Monty (4.4.1). It is reproduced, along with Robert L. Smith's own research, in Betty Ramsey's *Monty-Montee History*, pp. 631-657, and contains much information otherwise unavailable.

Children:

i   **Edgar Weller Smith** b 5 May 1892, Glens Falls, NY; d 27 Nov 1964, Binghamton, NY. He married (1) 10 Nov 1915, Glens Falls, NY, and divorced there 29 Mar 1941 **Daisy Ordway Hall** (Charles Duane Hall & Anna Jenkins Burnham) b 10 Mar 1893, Galesburg, IL; d 28 Oct 1991.

He married (2) **Niona Jane Cable** b 9 May 1905; d Nov 1976, Binghamton,

NY.

ii   **Marion Louisa Smith** b May 1895, Glens Falls, NY; d there Jun 1915.

4.4.1.2.2.5   **MONTY, Julia Anna** b 23 Apr 1866, Glens Falls, NY; d there 3 May 1938. She married 1900? **Daniel J. Finch Jr.** (Daniel J. Finch & Isabella _____) b Apr 1870, Kingsbury, NY.

This woman was named Annie when she was living with her parents in Glens Falls, NY, in 1892. I know of her marriage to Daniel Finch Jr. from the family Bible which belonged to her sister Mary Elizabeth (4.4.1.2.2.4) but have been unable to find husband and wife together. Mrs. Julia A. Finch was said to be a widow in 1920 when she was the housekeeper in the hotel owned by her brother William Henry (4.4.1.2.2.2) in Albany, NY. Yet when she was staying with her sister Mary Elizabeth in Glens Falls in 1930, she indicated that had married at the age of 34 and was still married (US and state censuses).

4.4.1.2.4.1   **MONTY, William H.** b Sep 1854, Rutland, VT; d 27 May 1901, Troy, NY. He married 26 Jun 1884, Boston, MA, **Mary G./Minnie Rourke** (John Rourke & Ann Bunfield) b 2 Feb 1865, Rutland, VT.

William H. Monty remained in Rutland, VT, with his parents until at least 1880. At his marriage a few years later as well as in 1900 he was an engineer for the Boston & Maine RR in Troy, NY. He was buried in Rutland's Evergreen Cemetery though his widow continued to reside in Troy until at least 1920 (US censuses). They had no children.

4.4.1.2.9.1   **MONTY, Joseph Parry** b 19 Nov 1866, Sandy Hill, NY; d 13 Feb 1914, Las Cruces, NM. He married 25 Dec 1895, Sandy Hill, NY, **Catherine Kellogg** (Charles D. Kellogg & Mary J. Baucus) b 24 Feb 1872, Northumberland, NY; m (2) 28 Jun 1918, Hudson Falls, NY, Arthur H. Carleton (Orville N. Carleton & Frances M. Brown), widower of Minnie Miller; d 24 Feb 1935.

Joseph Monty was a bookkeeper in Sandy Hill, NY, in 1890 (Glens Falls, NY, and area Directory) and a contractor in Glens Falls in 1900. He stayed in the area until at least 1907 when his last child was born but was a surveyor in Las Cruces, NM, in 1910. When he died a few years later he was buried in the Masonic Cemetery there. His wife and children then returned to New York State.

Catherine (also Katherine, Kate) Kellogg was living in Hudson Falls, NY, in 1920 with her children and second husband. Only Louise Monty though was still living in her stepfather's household when he was a furniture merchant in Orlando, FL, in 1930 (US censuses).

Children:

4.4.1.2.9.1.1	Daniel	1896-	-1898
4.4.1.2.9.1.2	Mary Kellogg (twin)	1898-1930-1991	
4.4.1.2.9.1.3	Louise Parry (twin)	1898-	-1962
4.4.1.2.9.1.4	Grace Elizabeth	1900-	-1946
4.4.1.2.9.1.5	Katherine Miriam	1907-1935-1954	

4.4.1.2.9.2   **MONTY, Elizabeth** b 5 Jun 1869, Sandy Hill, NY. She married there 10 Nov 1896 **George Warnick Wait** (John William Wait & Mary Antoinette Warnick) b there 12 Sep 1869.

George Wait was a machinist in Sandy Hill, NY, in 1900 when he and his wife were living with his parents. He had a garage in Albany, NY, in 1910 (US censuses).

4.4.1.2.9.3   **MONTY, Fannie Louise** b 1 Feb 1872, Sandy Hill, NY; d between 1910 and 1920. She married 1900? **Joseph Schneider** (Peter Schneider & Caroline _____) b 1873?, NY.

Joseph Schneider was a bookkeeper in Manhattan, NY, in 1910, when he and his wife had been married for nine years. They had had three children of whom only two, Daniel and Esther, were still alive. He was a widower in 1920 (US censuses).

Children:
    i   **Ruth Schneider** b 5 May 1901, NY; d before 1910.
    ii   **Daniel Schneider** b 11 Jul 1904, NY.
    iii   **Esther Schneider** b 19 May 1906, NY.

4.4.1.2.9.4   **MONTY, Clifford Daniel** b 26 Feb 1874, Sandy Hill, NY; d 3 Apr 1918, Fulton, NY. He married 1915? **Adelia Blodgett** (Monroe J. Blodgett & Mary A. ____) b Jul 1880, Oswego Co., NY; m (2) 11 Oct 1937, Fulton, NY, Walter Wain, widower of Elizabeth Keenan.

Clifford D. Monty was a shoe dealer in Sandy Hill, NY, in 1900 and an engineer in Oswego in 1910 (US censuses). According to the Fulton, NY, *Patriot* of 4 Apr 1918 he had moved to Oswego Co., NY, during the construction of the barge canal and later became a steam shovel operator on general construction work. He was a resident of Fulton, NY, at his death and was buried in the Pennellville Cemetery in the town of Schroeppel, NY.

Adelia Blodgett was 35 years old at her first marriage (1930 US census, Fulton, NY). She survived her second husband (*Palladium Times*, Oswego, NY, 24 Oct 1960).

4.4.1.2.12.1   **MONTY, Clara L./Lula** b 1867?, Sandy Hill, NY.

Clara L. Monty, a 3-year-old child living with her parents in Sandy Hill, NY, in 1870, was named simply Lula when her parents were in Grand Haven, MI, in 1880 (US censuses).

4.4.1.2.12.2   **MONTY, George H.** b Jan 1870, Sandy Hill, NY.

George H. Monty was born in January 1870 according to the US census of that year in Sandy Hill, NY. He does not appear with his family in later years and may have died before 1880.

4.4.1.2.12.3   **MONTY, Bertha A.** b 1872?, NY, Sandy Hill, NY.

Bertha A. Monty came to Michigan with her parents in the early 1870s and was an 8-year-old child living with them in Grand Haven, MI, in 1880 (US census).

4.4.1.2.12.4   **MONTY, Grace E.** b 14 Nov 1874, Grand Haven, MI.

Grace E. Monty was living with her parents in Grand Haven, MI, in 1880 (US census).

4.4.1.2.12.5   **MONTY, Jennie H.** b 23 Jan 1877, Grand Haven, MI.

Jennie H. Monty was living with her parents in Grand Haven, MI, in 1880 (US census).

4.4.1.2.12.6   **MONTY, William Harper** b 28 Mar 1880, Grand Haven, MI; d 30 Nov 1947, Clio, MI. He married 17 Jul 1900, Ellendale, ND, **Lulu Lenora Helms** (Webster Helms & Margaret Minerva Fairchild) b 1 Feb 1880, Ashley, MI; d & bur 23 & 26 Sep 1972, Flint, MI.

William H. Monty came to North Dakota with his parents before 1885 and was a farmer in Ellendale, ND, in 1900. Lulu L. Helms was then living with her parents in Kent Twp, ND. The couple lived in Fargo, ND, for a few years after their marriage before returning to Michigan where their third child was born in March 1907. William Monty was a farmer in Charlevoix, MI, in 1910, a carpenter there at the birth of a son in 1917, a carpenter in Genesee, MI, in 1920, and a farmer in Deep River Twp, MI, in 1930 (US censuses). The family moved shortly afterwards to Clio, MI, where both William Monty and his wife were residents at their deaths.

Children:

4.4.1.2.12.6.1	Ethel	1902-1922?&1971?-1983
4.4.1.2.12.6.2	Margaret Edith	1904-1922?&1935-1989
4.4.1.2.12.6.3	William	1907- -1973
4.4.1.2.12.6.4	Lulu Jennie	1909-1926-1985
4.4.1.2.12.6.5	Mary Martha	1912- & -1994
4.4.1.2.12.6.6	George Harper	1914-1937-1970

4.4.1.2.12.6.7   Earl C.   1917-   -1993

4.4.1.4.4.1   **MONTY, Frank Densmore** b 2 Apr 1879, St. Paul, MN; d 28 Oct 1950, Los Angeles, CA. He married 1904? **Louise W. Webb** (William B. Webb & Lizzie Spier) b 30 Aug 1883, La Crosse, WI; d 5 Dec 1939, Long Beach, CA.

Frank Monty was a student in St. Paul, MN, in 1900. He left for Montana a few years later and probably married there: he and his wife had been married for twenty-six years in 1930, and Louise Webb was already in Montana with her parents in 1900. He was in real estate in 1910 while living on his father-in-law's farm in Ward Twp, MT, in 1910, and a farmer in Hamilton (Ward Twp), MT, when he signed his World War I Draft Registration card in 1918. By 1920 though he was a civil engineer in Billings, MT, and in 1930 an engineer in Long Beach, CA (US censuses).

Children:

4.4.1.4.4.1.1	William Webb	1907-	-1977
4.4.1.4.4.1.2	Margaret	1917-1940-	

4.4.2.1.5.1   **MONTY, Susan E./Susie** b Aug 1869, West Plattsburgh, NY; d 1961, Port Kent & West Plattsburgh, NY. She married 1886? **Charles W. Hayes** (Elisha L. Hayes & Sarah Harriet Hayes) b Jul 1857, Plattsburgh, NY; d & bur 31 May & 1 Jun 1926, West Plattsburgh, NY.

Charles Hayes was a blacksmith in Saranac, NY, in 1880 and in Plattsburgh, NY, in 1900. He and his wife had then been married for fourteen years and had had six children of whom five, Ora, Harold, Richard, Stella, and Rosa were still alive. By 1910 they had had ten children of whom eight were still alive: the above five and also Elisha, Minerva, and Elizabeth (US censuses). The names of Basil E., Silas P., and Teresa E. Hayes are found with their parents on the HAYES tombstone in the West Plattsburgh, NY, Union Cemetery. They probably died in infancy.

Children:

i   **Ora J. Hayes** b Jul 1887, Plattsburgh, NY; d & bur 1929, Beekmantown & West Plattsburgh, NY. She married 1905? **Henry H. Bradley** (Colman S. Bradley & Nancy J. Comstalk) b 19 May 1879, Beekmantown, NY; bur 1957, West Plattsburgh, NY.

ii   **Harold Raymond Hayes** b 21 Jan 1890, Plattsburgh, NY; d & bur 15 & 18 Apr 1970, Saranac & Redford, NY. He married 17 Dec 1916, Champlain, NY, **Eva Catherine Lafountain** (Peter Lafountain & Dulcinea Robert) b there Jun 1892; d 29 Dec 1961, Saranac, NY.

iii   **Richard E. Hayes** b 18 Feb 1893, Plattsburgh, NY; d 3 Dec 1963, Tupper Lake, NY. He married **Celia Delude** who predeceased him.

iv   **Stella/Estella Violet Hayes** b 14 Nov 1895, Plattsburgh, NY; d there 21 Feb 1987. She married there 18 Mar 1913 **Harry F. Mooney** (Albert L. Mooney & Eunice Bradley) b there 12 Mar 1892; d 18 Nov 1964, Beekmantown, NY.

v   **Basil E. Hayes** d before 1900.

vi   **Rose L. Hayes** b 5 Feb 1899, Plattsburgh, NY; d Aug 1981, Schenectady, NY. She married **Leland Fries** b 23 Feb 1901; d 18 May 1987, Schenectady, NY.

vii   **Elisha Jefferson Hayes** b 18 Feb 1901, Plattsburgh, NY; d there 16 Feb 1981. He married there 15 Dec 1927 **Grace Garrow** (George Garrow & Mary Geddore) b 1908?, Beekmantown, NY; d 18 Aug 1968, Albany, NY, at the age of 60.

viii   **Minerva M. Hayes** b 25 Sep 1905, Plattsburgh, NY; d Feb 1991, Schenectady, NY. She married (1) 6 Aug 1922, Plattsburgh, NY, **Harry J. Raby** (Henry Raby & Lizzie Allard) b there 13 Jan 1893; d & bur there 10 & 14 Apr 1925, Plattsburgh, NY.

She married (2) 1926? **William W. Stephenson** (John F. Stephenson & Lorena _____) b Dec 1896, Albany, NY.

ix   **Silas P. Hayes** d 28 Jan 1905, Plattsburgh, NY.

x   **Dorothy Elizabeth Hayes** b 5 Dec 1908, Plattsburgh, NY; d 11 May 1987, Schenectady, NY.

xi   **Teresa E. Hayes** d between 1910 and 1920.

xii   **Hubert A. Hayes** b 25 Jun 1913, Plattsburgh, NY; d Dec 1976, Schenectady, NY.

4.4.2.1.5.2   **MONTY, Charlotte/Lottie J.** b 1871?, Plattsburgh, NY; d there 4 May 1890 at the age of 19.

Charlotte Monty was a 9-year-old child living with her parents in Plattsburgh, NY, in 1880 (US census). She was named Lottie J. when she died at the age of 19 (*Plattsburgh Sentinel*, 9 May 1890) and when she was buried in the Cadyville, NY, Protestant Cemetery.

4.4.2.1.5.3   **MONTY, Jonas** b 1874?, Plattsburgh, NY.

Jonas Monty was a 6-year-old child living with his parents in Plattsburgh, NY, in 1880. He was not with them there in 1892 (US and state censuses).

4.4.2.1.5.4   **MONTY, Charles** b 1876?, Plattsburgh, NY.

Charles Monty was a 4-year-old child living with his parents in Plattsburgh, NY, in 1880. He was not with them there in 1892 (US and state censuses).

4.4.2.1.5.5   **MONTY, Eleanor A.** b Aug 1878, Plattsburgh, NY. She married there 23 Sep 1901, **Charles F. Palmer** (____ Palmer & Phoebe ____) b Jan 1874, IA.

Charles F. Palmer was a salesman in Plattsburgh, NY, in 1900. He probably left for Georgia soon after the birth of his first child for on 22 Jul 1904 the *Plattsburgh Sentinel* reported that Frances H. Monty (4.4.2.1.5.9) had just returned from a nine-month-long visit to her sister in Savannah, GA. Charles Palmer owned a typewriter repair shop there in 1910 (US censuses).

Children:

i   **Pauline P. Palmer** b 1902?, Plattsburgh, NY.

ii   **Charles F. Palmer** b Oct 1909, Savannah, GA.

4.4.2.1.5.6   **MONTY, Laura** b Sep 1880, Plattsburgh, NY; d & bur 7 & 11 Jul 1942, Malone & Plattsburgh, NY. She married Aug 1895, Schuyler Falls, NY, **Silas D. Stevens/ Stephens** (Albert Stephens & Samantha ____) b there 13 Jan 1876; d 16 Dec 1941, Plattsburgh, NY.

Silas Stevens was a laborer in Cadyville, NY (US censuses). The family surname was generally Stephens before 1910 and Stevens in later years. He and his wife were buried in Riverside Cemetery in Plattsburgh, NY, as were several of their children.

Children:

i   **Maud Stevens** b Feb 1898, Cadyville, NY. She married 14 Mar 1916, Morrisonville, NY, **James Baker** (Nelson Baker & Dina Stevens) b 5 Sep 1892, Cadyville, NY.

ii   **Susan G. Stevens** b 10 Jun 1900, Cadyville, NY; d 7 Mar 1939, Plattsburgh, NY. She married **Clifford Swain**.

iii   **Bernard L. Stevens** b 16 Jun 1902, Cadyville, NY; d & bur 19 & 22 May 1972, Plattsburgh, NY.

iv   **Gilbert DeWitt Stevens** b 3 Nov 1904, Cadyville, NY; d & bur 24 & 27 Sep 1961, Plattsburgh, NY. He married **Viola Theresa Desotelle** (Joseph Benjamin Desotelle & Marie Larvia) b 14 Feb 1915, Plattsburgh, NY; m (2) 1966? a brother-in-law **Albert Henry Stevens** (vii); d & bur 14 & 17 Jun 1983, Peru & Plattsburgh, NY.

v   **Grace Stevens** b 1907?, Cadyville, NY. She married **Nevine Howard**.

vi   **Katherine Stevens** b Mar 1910, Cadyville, NY.

vii   **Albert Henry Stevens** b 7 Apr 1912, Cadyville, NY; d 9 Sep 1987, Peru, NY. He married 1966? a sister-in-law **Viola Theresa Desotelle** (Joseph Benjamin Desotelle & Marie Larvia) b 14 Feb 1915, Plattsburgh, NY; m (1) **Gilbert DeWitt Stevens** (iv); d & bur 14 & 17 Jun 1983, Peru & Plattsburgh, NY.

viii **Leona Stevens** b 5 Feb 1915, Cadyville, NY; d Dec 1983, Bronx, NY. She married 1930? **Leon Schreihofer** (Jacob Schreihofer & Louisa ____) b 15 Jun 1908, Newark, NJ; d 28 Jan 1991.

ix **Leeward Stevens** b 1917?, Cadyville, NY.

x **Doris Stevens** b 1920?, Cadyville, NY.

xi **Lula Stevens** b 1921?, Cadyville, NY. She married ____ **Mann**.

xii **Ruth Stevens** b Jul 1925, Cadyville, NY.

4.4.2.1.5.7 **MONTY, Clinton** b Jun 1882, Plattsburgh, NY; d between 1910 and 1920. He married 1905? **Emma Clara Grube** (John Grube & Diana ____) b 20 Dec 1885, Plattsburgh, NY; m (2) ____ Sturges; d 26 Mar 1986, Syracuse, NY.

Clinton Monty was an electrician in an auto factory in Plattsburgh, NY, in 1910 when he and his wife had been married for five years. In 1920 his widow was a machine operator in Frankfort, NY, where she was living with her three children. Her daughter Mildred Monty was also with her in 1930 in German Flats, NY, though she was then named Mrs. Emma Sturges, a widow (US censuses).

Children:

4.4.2.1.5.7.1	Maynard John	1905-1945-1970
4.4.2.1.5.7.2	Clara Helen	1907-1925-2008
4.4.2.1.5.7.3	Mildred	1912?- -1951

4.4.2.1.5.8 **MONTY, Bessie May** b Oct 1886, Plattsburgh, NY; d there 22 May 1894.

Bessie May Monty was 7 years and 7 months old at her death (*Plattsburgh Sentinel*, 25 May 1894).

4.4.2.1.5.9 **MONTY, Frances Hazel** b Dec 1889, Plattsburgh, NY. She married (1) 1907? **Charles Alfred Parton** (Charles Parton & Christina Higginson) b 23 Dec 1879, Hamilton, Ontario, Canada; d 23 May 1921, Plattsburgh, NY.

She married (2) 29 Nov 1923, Plattsburgh, NY, **Norman Dudley Hall** (Charles Millard Hall & Grace S. Harton) b 31 May 1899, Beacon, NY; d 15 May 1988, Hyattsville, MD.

Frances Hazel Monty and Charles A. Parton had been married for three years in 1910. He had arrived in the United States as a child in 1880 and was a machinist in Plattsburgh, NY, in 1900 and an engineer in the Plattsburgh Barracks from about 1903 until his death (US censuses; *Plattsburgh Sentinel*, 24 May 1921).

Norman D. Hall was a compositor in Plattsburgh, NY, at his marriage and worked there for the Clinton Press until 1929. The following year he was a printer in Peekskill, NY (US census). He was a compositor for the Harbor Press in New York City for a few years and, from 1939 on, a proofreader in the US Government Printing Office in Washington, DC.

Children:

i **Charles H. Parton** b 6 Feb 1908, Plattsburgh, NY; d Oct 1966.

ii **Esther/Hester E. Parton** b 4 Jan 1910, Plattsburgh, NY.

iii **Robert A. Parton** b Sep 1918, Plattsburgh, NY.

iv **Elizabeth Claire Hall** b 25 Aug 1930, Peekskill, NY; d 24 Dec 1993, Silver Spring, MD. She married (1) 11 Feb 1948 and divorced 1952 **Richard Orts** (Luther William Orts & Viola Jeannette ____) b 21 Jun 1929, Ossining, NY.

She married (2) **Samuel Grady Smith** b 10 Nov 1922; d 15 Sep 1988, Silver Spring, MD.

4.4.2.1.5.10 **MONTY, Edward Monroe** b 31 Oct 1891, Plattsburgh, NY; d Jan 1978, Schenectady, NY. He married 11 Aug 1911, Delanson, NY, **Mary Bessie Hyser** (Stephen Hyser & Elizabeth/Libbie Zeh) b Oct 1893, Duanesburg, NY.

He married (2) **Etta Mae Whitney** (Charles Whitney & Grace O'Dell) b 18 Oct 1907, Cohoes, NY; d Apr 1991, Schenectady, NY.

Edward M. Monty had a variety of occupations. He was a laborer in Plattsburgh, NY, in 1910, a cigar maker there at his first marriage, a farmer in Schoharie Co., NY, in 1918 when he signed as Edward Monroe Monty his World War I Draft Registration card, and a railroad laborer in Duanesburg, NY, on 1 Jan 1920 (US censuses).

Children of the first marriage:
4.4.2.1.5.10.1	Elizabeth E.	1911?-	-	
4.4.2.1.5.10.2	Frances H.	1920-	&	-1997

Children of the second marriage:
4.4.2.1.5.10.3	Etta Mae	-	&	-
4.4.2.1.5.10.4	Janet G.	1934-1952-2005		
4.4.2.1.5.10.5	William J.	1935-	-	
4.4.2.1.5.10.6	Edward	-	-	

4.4.2.1.8.1 **MONTY, Mary Louisa** b & bp 1879 & 4 Nov 1893, Plattsburgh & Cadyville, NY.

Mary Louisa Monty was a one-year-old child living with her parents in Plattsburgh, NY, in 1880 (US census). She was about 15 years old at her baptism.

4.4.2.1.8.2 **MONTY, Clara N.** b & bp Nov 1883 & 4 Nov 1893, Plattsburgh & Cadyville, NY; d 27 Jan 1971, Plattsburgh, NY. She married 1903? **Cleveland/Cleve Akey** (Ezra Akey & Alice White) b 1875?, Plattsburgh, NY; d & bur ? & 12 Aug 1955, Plattsburgh & West Plattsburgh, NY.

Cleveland Akey was a 5-year-old child living with his parents in Plattsburgh, NY, in 1880. As an adult he was generally named Cleve. He was a farm laborer on his widowed mother-in-law's farm in Plattsburgh in 1910, when he and his wife had been married for seven years, and was a farmer there until at least 1930 (US censuses). He and his wife were buried in West Plattsburgh's Union Cemetery (*Plattsburgh Press Republican*, 11 Aug 1955 and 1 Feb 1971).

Children:
i   **Peter Leroy Akey** b 4 Jan 1907, Plattsburgh, NY; d & bur 7 & 10 Jun 1964, Plattsburgh & West Plattsburgh, NY. He married **Avis Loveless**.
ii   **Arthur Charles Akey** (twin) b 6 Sep 1910, Plattsburgh , NY; d & bur 22 & 24 Aug 1974, Massena, NY. He married there Oct 1936 **Gretchel A. Page** (Frank Page & Anna Bylow) b there 27 Sep 1918; d & bur 8 & 11 Jul 1991, Massena & Raymondville, NY.
iii **Marion Mae Akey** (twin) b 6 Sep 1910, Plattsburgh, NY; d there 16 Feb 2006.
iv   **Fred Franklin Akey** b 28 Dec 1914, Plattsburgh, NY; d 15 Feb 1990, NY, Massena, NY. He married **Gretchen Page.**

4.4.2.1.11.1 **MONTY, Warren J.** b 16 Sep 1880, Plattsburgh, NY; d 24 Aug 1903, NY.
Warren J. Monty was a brakeman for the Châteauguay Railroad when he was killed in a train accident near Twin Ponds, NY (*Plattsburgh Sentinel*, 1 Jan 1904). He was buried in the Cadyville, NY, Protestant Cemetery.

4.4.2.1.11.2 **MONTY, Fred Lester** b 10 Aug 1887, Plattsburgh, NY; d 8 Apr 1971, Cadyville, NY. He married (1) between 1910 and 1915 **Mary Jenette Emery** (William E. Emery & Jenette Cline) b 22 Feb 1886, Plattsburgh, NY; m (1) 1906? Charles P. Arlin; d 4 Oct 1922, Cadyville, NY.
He married (2) Sep 1928, Clinton Co., NY, **Rose Roushia** (Joseph Roushia & Leona Deno) b 9 Jan 1886, Black Brook, NY; m (1) 1903? William Connors; d & bur 25 & 27 Sep 1975, Plattsburgh & Cadyville, NY.
Fred L. Monty was still single in 1910 when he was a farmer living with his parents in Plattsburgh, NY. He was a mill hand there in 1920 and a railroad worker in 1925 and 1930

(US and state censuses). He was a resident of Cadyville though at his death and was buried in the Community Cemetery there (*Plattsburgh Press Republican*, 13 Apr 1971).

Mrs. Mary J. Arlin had been married to her first husband for four years in 1910 (US census, Plattsburgh, NY). She was buried as Mary Arlin Monty in the Protestant Cemetery in Cadyville, NY, under an EMERY tombstone.

Mrs. Rose Connors had been married to her first husband for seven years in 1910 (US census, Plattsburgh, NY). She was buried in St. James' Cemetery in Cadyville, NY (*Plattsburgh Republican*, 26 Sep 1975).

Children of the first marriage:

4.4.2.1.11.2.1	Roswell L.	1916-	-1985
4.4.2.1.11.2.2	Ralph W.	1917-	-1988
4.4.2.1.11.2.3	Louanna May	1922-	-1922

4.4.2.1.11.3   MONTY, Neil James C. b 2 Jun 1891, Plattsburgh, NY; d 31 Oct 1970, Ogdensburg, NY.

Neil J. Monty was a farmer in Plattsburgh (Cadyville), NY, until at least 1930 (US censuses). He died after a long illness in the St. Lawrence State Hospital in Ogdensburg, NY (*Plattsburgh Press Republican*, 3 Nov 1970).

4.4.2.1.11.4   MONTY, Alverda b 1900, Plattsburgh, NY; d Mar 1961, Lacolle, QC, at the age of 60. She married 23 Apr 1921, Cadyville, NY, **Floyd A. Jock** (Joseph Jock & Rose Laplante) b 1 Mar 1899, Lyon Mountain, NY; d 6 Apr 1963, Morrisonville, NY.

Floyd Jock was a laborer in Plattsburgh, NY, and Cadyville, NY, in the early years of his marriage (US censuses) and a signal maintenance man in Lacolle, QC, for the Napierville Junction Railroad for thirty years before his death (*Plattsburgh Press Republican*, 8 Apr 1963). He and his wife were both buried in St. James' Cemetery in Cadyville.

Children:

i   **Viola Mae Jock** b 17 Nov 1921, Cadyville, NY. She married **Raymond S. Gagnon** (Leo Raymond Gagnon & Alvina Venne) b 17 Jun 1922, Champlain, NY; d 20 Nov 1953, Plattsburgh, NY.

ii   **Donald Joseph Jock** b & d 18 May 1925, Plattsburgh, NY.

4.4.3.6.2.1   MONTY, Ersie b 5 Nov 1888, Bridport, VT.

Ersie Monty was no longer alive in 1900 when her parents were living in Waterford, NY (US census).

4.4.3.6.2.2   MONTY, Carl K. b 1900?, Waterford, NY; d there 1950. He married 1924? **Louise R. Meyer** (Benjamin A. Meyer & Anna Haas) b 28 Oct 1902, Switzerland; d Feb 1980, Whitehall, NY.

Carl Monty was 19 years old on 1 Jan 1920 when he was a farm laborer working on his father's dairy farm in Whitehall, NY. He was still a farmer there in 1930, when he and his wife Louise had been married for six years. His father was then a member of his household (US censuses).

Children:

4.4.3.6.2.2.1	James K.	1926-	-1989
4.4.3.6.2.2.2	Edward K.	1927-1952-1975	

4.4.7.3.2.1   MONTEE, Lennie b & d 1881, IL.

I know of this child only through Betty Ramsey's *Monty-Montee History*, p. 256.

4.4.7.3.2.2   MONTEE, Theodore Edward b 4 Sep 1882, Macomb, IL; d 28 Sep 1921, Picher, OK. He married 1905? **Beatrice Belle Dever** b 16 Jul 1888, Erie, KS; m (2) ____ Howey; d & bur 1 & 3 Mar 1933, Columbus & Pittsburg, KS.

Theodore E. Montee was a farm laborer living with his parents in Sheridan Twp, KS, in 1900 and a coal miner in Pittsburg, KS, in 1910 when he and his wife had been married for five years. He was also a coal miner there in 1920. His six surviving children were living with their divorced mother, Mrs. Beatrice Howey, in Galena, KS, in 1930 (US censuses).

Children:

4.4.7.3.2.2.1	Marion	1906?-	-
4.4.7.3.2.2.2	Edward	1908?-	-
4.4.7.3.2.2.3	Sylvia C.	1911-	-1913
4.4.7.3.2.2.4	Virgil Ray	1913-1933-1985	
4.4.7.3.2.2.5	Bert Vance	1915-	-1979
4.4.7.3.2.2.6	Roy Morris	1918-	-1980
4.4.7.3.2.2.7	Theda M.	1921?-	-

4.4.7.3.2.3   **MONTEE, Lee Jacob** b 28 Dec 1885, Pittsburg, KS; d & bur 6 & 9 Mar 1963, Salina & Gypsum, KS. He married 8 Aug 1910, Abilene, KS, **Eliza Schwarz** (Frederick Schwarz & Katherine Kramer) b 5 Jan 1888, Schwieberdingen, Germany; d 12 Jun 1984, Salina, KS.

Lee J. Montee was a farm laborer living with his parents in Sheridan Twp, KS, in 1900. He moved soon after his marriage to Gypsum, KS, where his children were born and where he was a farmer in 1920 and a dealer in livestock in 1930 (US censuses). He remained there until his death and was buried, as was his wife, in the Gypsum City Cemetery (*Salina Journal*, 7 and 8 Mar 1963).

Children:

4.4.7.3.2.3.1	Fritz L.	1910-	-1947	
4.4.7.3.2.3.2	Claudine Marie	1912-1930-2000		
4.4.7.3.2.3.3	Elmer John	1914-1944-1992		
4.4.7.3.2.3.4	Bernice	1916-	&	-1978

4.4.7.3.2.4   **MONTEE, Della Mae** b 6 Feb 1887, Crawford Co., KS; d Nov 1980, Pittsburg, KS. She married 1907? **Charles Melvin Johnson** (Joseph Johnson & Melissa ____) b 23 Oct 1882, KS.

Charles M. Johnson and his wife had been married for three years in 1910. He was a farmer in McCune (Sheridan Twp), KS, then and until at least 1930 (US censuses). Mrs. Della Johnson was still a resident there when her brother Lee Jacob (4.4.7.3.2.3) died in 1963.

Child:

i   **Treva W. Johnson** b 10 May 1908, McCune, KS; d Apr 1979, Pittsburg, KS. She married (1) **Robert Cook** (Ramsey, p. 262).
She married (2) ____ **Merrick**.

4.4.7.3.2.5   **MONTEE, Nellie Maude** b 5 Nov 1889, Crawford Co., KS; d there 20 Jul 1890.
This child was buried in the Borland Cemetery in Cherokee, KS.

4.4.7.3.2.6   **MONTEE, Charles** b 20 Sep 1891, Crawford Co., KS; d there 6 Jan 1892.
This child was buried in the Borland Cemetery in Cherokee, KS.

4.4.7.3.2.7   **MONTEE, Mary Myrtle** b 21 Nov 1892, Cairo, NE; d 19 Nov 1972, Pittsburg, KS. She married 22 Dec 1909, Columbus, KS, **Clarence John Harry** (Walter Dewayne Harry & Susan Mary Bennett) b 9 Aug 1886, Parsons, KS; d 18 Sep 1954, Pittsburg, KS.

Clarence Harry was a carpenter in Pittsburg, KS, in 1910 and a telephone company worker there in 1918 when he signed his World War I Draft Registration card. He was a wire chief for a telephone company in Independence, KS, in 1920 but soon returned to Pittsburg where he was a railroad brakeman in 1930 (US censuses). Both he and his wife were buried in

Highland Park Cemetery in Pittsburg.

Children:

i   **Faye Catherine Harry** b 11 Nov 1910, Pittsburg, KS; d there 21 Feb 2001. She married there 10 Jan 1935 **George Mitchell Bogle** (Francis W. Bogle & Ina A. ____) b 12 Sep 1905, Sheridan Twp, KS; d 12 Jun 1973, Pittsburg, KS.

ii   **Clarence John Harry** b 2 Sep 1918, Independence, KS; d 29 Jun 2007, Joplin, MO. He married 10 Nov 1945, Pittsburg, KS, **Rosalin Schultze** (Ernest Schultze & Gesina Grotheer) b there 24 Mar 1918; d there 10 Jan 1999.

iii   **Anonymous Harry** (female) (Betty Ramsey, *Monty-Montee History*, p. 263).

iv   **Montee Gene Harry** b 5 Feb 1928, Pittsburg, KS; d 4 Oct 1990, Joplin, MO. He married there 28 May 1950 **Doris Darlene Bartlett** (Ray Bartlett & Thelma R. ____) b 9 Mar 1929, MO; d 24 Nov 1994, Joplin, MO.

4.4.7.3.2.8   **MONTEE, Nancy Ellen** b 17 Feb 1894, Sheridan Twp, KS; d 17 Jan 1933, Dallas, TX. She married Jun 1918 **Jess Gardiner**.

I have been unable to confirm any of the information above, taken from Betty Ramsey's *Monty-Montee History*, p. 263. I know only that Nancie Montee was a 5-year-old child living with her parents in Sheridan Twp, KS, in 1900 and a 15-year-old living with them in Cameron Twp, NE, in 1910. She was not with them in 1915 when her father was a farmer in Osage, KS (US and state censuses). Nor does her name appear in the Texas Death Index.

4.4.7.3.2.9   **MONTEE, Hazel Irene** b 28 Oct 1900, Sheridan Twp, KS; d 12 Apr 1953. She married around 1918 **Claude Killian** (William Riley Killian & Maggie E. Davis) b 17 Dec 1894, Seymour, MO; d 31 Jan 1968, El Paso, TX.

Claude Killian was a telephone worker in Independence, KS, when he signed on 5 Jun 1917 his World War I Draft Registration card and was still single. He married between then and 1 Jan 1920 when he was a refinery worker in Independence, KS, living with his wife in the household of her sister Myrtle (4.4.7.3.2.7) and brother-in-law Clarence Harry. The couple divorced before 1930 when Claud Killian was working in El Paso, TX (US censuses).

4.4.7.3.2.10   **MONTEE, John S.** b 3 Jan 1902, KS; d 1 Jan 1933. He married Dec 1922 **Beulah Thrasher**.

This couple left Kansas for Oklahoma soon after the birth of their daughter in 1924 (*Gypsum Advocate*, 16 Jul 1924). John S. Montee was divorced in 1930 and was then living in the household of his cousin Theodore Isaac Montee (4.4.7.3.11.1) in Oklahoma City, OK. He was a building contractor (US census).

Child:

4.4.7.3.2.10.1	Kathryn I.	1924-1942?-1994

4.4.7.3.7.1   **MONTEE, Robert Leslie** b 22 Feb 1895, Spring River, OK (Indian Territory); d & bur 2 & 6 May 1978, Greenville & Cherokee, KS. He married 12 Jun 1916, Columbus, KS, **Eugenia Olivia Bouret** (François Michel Bouret & Marie Clarisse Breaux) b & bp 21 Dec 1898 & 1 Jan 1899, Rayne, LA; d & bur 29 Jun & 1 Jul 1931, Pittsburg & Cherokee, KS.

Robert Leslie Montee arrived in Kansas only a few years after his birth and was living with his parents in Sheridan Twp, KS, in 1910. He was a coal miner in Baker Twp, KS, in 1920 and a laborer in South West Twp, MO, in 1930 (US censuses). He and his wife were buried in the Cherokee City Cemetery in Cherokee, KS.

Children:

4.4.7.3.7.1.1	Charles Elmer	1919-1942&1968&	&	-2004
4.4.7.3.7.1.2	Jean Isabelle	1921-	-1947	
4.4.7.3.7.1.3	Robert Leslie	1923-	-	
4.4.7.3.7.1.4	Donald Ivan	1925-1950-1978		

4.4.7.3.7.2   **MONTEE, Leila Emma** b 25 Nov 1896, OK; d & bur 9 & 13 Apr 1976, Sierra Madre & Whittier, CA. She married 1 Jun 1921, Kansas City, MO, **Harold Felix Roberts** (John Roberts & Myrtle Duckworth) b 18 Feb 1899, St. Joseph, MO; d 15 Sep 1958, Sierra Madre, CA.

Leila Montee was living with her parents in Sheridan Twp, KS, in 1910. In 1920 however she was a private nurse in Kansas City, MO, where Harold Roberts was an inspector for a credit company (US censuses). They moved to Los Angeles Co., CA, soon after their marriage and were buried in Rose Hill Cemetery in Whittier, CA.

Children:
  i   **Roberta Ann Roberts** b 12 Dec 1923, Pasadena, CA. She married (1) 4 Jan 1946 and divorced Jul 1967, Los Angeles, CA, **Lytton C. Musselman** (John Ellery Musselman & Myrtle E. Mayo) b 24 Mar 1911, WI; d 27 Apr 1968, Los Angeles, CA.
        She married (2) 19 May 1974, Clark Co, NV, **Robert W. Jones**.
  ii **Marvel Montee Roberts** b 29 Mar 1930, Los Angeles Co., CA; d 20 May 1984, Santa Barbara, CA. She married (1) ____ **Gilcrest** (Betty Ramsey, *Monty-Montee History*, p. 271).
        She married (2) 1961 and divorced 9 Feb 1978, Santa Barbara, CA, **Edwin S./Ted Phenix** b Mar 1929; m (2) 30 Sep 1979, Greenwich, CT, Martha S. Lunt.

4.4.7.3.7.3   **MONTEE, Percy Clinton** b 15 Apr 1900, Scammon, KS; d Jun 1988, Cherokee, KS. He married 28 Nov 1923 **Laura Lucinda Hughes** (William Hughes & Edith Haney) b 14 Sep 1906, MO; d 4 Aug 1962, Cherokee, KS.

Percy Montee was a railroad employee living with his parents in Cherokee, KS, in 1920 and a miner in West Mineral, KS, in 1930 (US censuses). He and his wife remained there until the mid-1930s and then moved to the Cherokee area. They were both buried in Cherokee City Cemetery.

Children:

4.4.7.3.7.3.1	Betty Jean	1924-1943&1950-1966
4.4.7.3.7.3.2	Doris Eleanor	1926-1945-2004
4.4.7.3.7.3.3	Albert Clinton	1927-1948-1983
4.4.7.3.7.3.4	Laura Lucille	1929-1969-2006
4.4.7.3.7.3.5	Kenneth Leroy	1931-1990-2004
4.4.7.3.7.3.6	Joan Lee	1934-1953-
4.4.7.3.7.3.7	Peggy Dean	1938-1960&1973-2004
4.4.7.3.7.3.8	Patricia Mae	1939-1959-
4.4.7.3.7.3.9	Barbara Ann	1941-1960-
4.4.7.3.7.3.10	Lana Charlene	1943-1963-
4.4.7.3.7.3.11	Judy Eileen	1945-1968-
4.4.7.3.7.3.12	Nancy Carol	1946-1967-

4.4.7.3.7.4   **MONTEE, Dorothy** b 1 Feb 1902, Cherokee, KS; d Mar 1982, Millstadt, IL. She married 11 Aug 1917, Carthage, MO, **Joseph Michael Rogers** (James Franklin Rogers & Caroline Louise Berkley) b 22 Fen 1895, Ellsworth, KS.

Joseph M. Rogers worked in Cherokee, KS, for several years after his marriage before moving to O'Fallon, IL, where he was a farmer in 1930 (US censuses).

Children:
  i   **Dorothy Mae Rogers** b 11 May 1919, Cherokee, KS; d 5 Jul 1993, Lamar, CO. She married (1) **Charles Edward Stewart** d 15 Feb 1943, POW camp, Germany.
        She married (2) 7 Nov 1945 **Walter Wesley King** (Fletcher L. King & Wanda Erna Holland) b 31 Dec 1919, Dawson, NM; d & bur 22 & 25 Nov 1998, Pueblo, CO.
  ii **Joseph Melvern Rogers** b 26 Oct 1921, Cherokee, KS; d 16 Feb 1989, O'Fallon,

IL. He married **Jacqueline Jung** b 24 May 1920; d 12 Dec 2001, O'Fallon, IL.

4.4.7.3.7.5   **MONTEE, Mark S.** b 21 Oct 1903, Cherokee, KS; d 29 Aug 1994, O'Fallon, IL. He married 23 Jan 1926, Columbus, KS, **Celestina Belleno** b 13 Jul 1907, KS; d 25 Dec 1992, Pueblo, CO.

Mark S. Montee and his wife left Kansas after the birth of their first child and were living in O'Fallon, IL, in 1930. He was a foundry worker there (US census). He and his wife were buried in College Hill Cemetery in Lebanon, IL.

Children:

4.4.7.3.7.5.1	Mark Stuart	1927-	-1948
4.4.7.3.7.5.2	Norman Curtis	1933-	-
4.4.7.3.7.5.3	James Melvern	1935-	-1992

4.4.7.3.7.6   **MONTEE, Thomas Omer** b 10 Apr 1906, Cherokee, KS; d Sep 1968, O'Fallon, IL. He married there 14 Mar 1928 **Ruby Beck** b 1912?, IL.

Tom Montee was a foundry worker in O'Fallon, IL, in 1930 when his wife was 18 years old (US census). He was buried in College Hill Cemetery in Lebanon, IL.

Children:

4.4.7.3.7.6.1	Lee (twin)	1931-	-1931
4.4.7.3.7.6.2	Dee (twin)	1931-	-1931
4.4.7.3.7.6.3	Robert Frank	1932-1951-	
4.4.7.3.7.6.4	Dorothy Anna	1935-	-
4.4.7.3.7.6.5	Joyce Elaine	1936-	-

4.4.7.3.11.1   **MONTEE, Theodore Isaac** b 12 Apr 1901, McCune, KS; d 1 Mar 1982, Anaheim, CA. He married 1929? **Alma May Koch** (August Koch & Cora ____) b 23 Aug 1909, Columbia, MO; d 22 Jan 2005, Orange, CA.

Theodore Montee was a laborer on his father's farm in Neosho, KS, in 1920 and a building carpenter in Oklahoma City, OK, in 1930 when he and his wife had been married for one year (US censuses). His first child however was born the following year in Missouri and the second some years later in Colorado. The family later moved to California.

Children:

4.4.7.3.11.1.1	Norman Lucas	1931-1952-2004
4.4.7.3.11.1.2	Gerald Keith	1938-1957-

4.4.7.3.11.2   **MONTEE, Robert Earl** b 14 Jan 1903, McCune, KS; d 19 Feb 1981, Moreno Valley, CA. He married 25 Dec 1927, Kansas City, MO, **Velma M. Magee** (Thomas Magee & Mabel Alexander) b 15 May 1909, Carthage, MO; d 27 Mar 1999, Roseburg, OR.

4.4.7.3.11.2.1	Bonnie Jean	1930-	-
4.4.7.3.11.2.2	Robert Edward	1937-	-

4.4.7.3.11.3   **MONTEE, Jess Frank/Jack** b 13 Nov 1905, McCune, KS; d 27 Dec 1983, Parsons, KS. He married there 28 Apr 1928 **Lorene Elizabeth Carson** (William Elisha Carson & Mary Luella Rutherford) b 23 Sep 1907, Dennis, KS; d 21 Mar 2005, Parsons, KS.

This couple lived in California from 1937 to 1969 before returning to Kansas. Their daughters remained in California (*Chanute Tribune*, 25 Mar 2005).

Children:

4.4.7.3.11.3.1	Edythe Marlene	-	&1958-
4.4.7.3.11.3.2	Carla Carson	1945-1965&1974-	

4.4.7.3.11.4   **MONTEE, Ray** b 23 Sep 1907, McCune, KS; d there 27 Mar 1909.

4.4.7.3.11.5   **MONTEE, Edythe Mary** b 22 Oct 1912, McCune, KS; d 15 Jan 2006, Angleton, TX. She married 1 Apr 1934, KS, **Charles Monte Elam** (John W. Elam & Adelia Goodman) b 17 Jan 1912, Parsons, KS; d 18 Nov 1990, San Diego, CA.

This couple moved to San Diego, CA, where their children were born, soon after their marriage. Charles Monte Elam was buried in Greenwood Memorial Park there.

Children:

   i   **Marilyn Annette Elam** b 17 Mar 1935, San Diego, CA. She married 4 Apr 1953, **Vernon Dale Duvall** b 1933, CA.

   ii   **Milton Monte Elam** b 14 Jan 1938, San Diego, CA; d there 9 Apr 2000. He married there 20 Aug 1966 **Carole Lynn McKibben** (____ McKibben & ____ Liptroth) b 22 Jul 1944, PA; d 19 Feb 1995, San Diego, CA.

4.4.7.3.11.6   **MONTEE, Bessie A.** b 7 Aug 1915, McCune, KS; d 2 Apr 2003, El Cajon, CA. She married **Fern M. Cary** (Alzie W. Cary & Fannie F. ____) b 11 Apr 1914, TX; d 26 Mar 2000, El Cajon, CA.

Children:

   i   **James Michael Cary** b 18 Mar 1941, San Diego, CA; d 2 May 2005, Marshall, MO. He married 1 Jan 1960, San Diego, CA, **Kathleen Louise Bostrom** (____ Bostrom & ____ Schnell) b 7 Oct 1942, San Diego, CA.

   ii   **Daniel David Cary** b 15 Sep 1944, San Diego, CA. He married **Jane Adele Bonesteele** (____ Bonesteele & ____ Lilliquist/Lillieqvest) b 3 Nov 1950, Holtville, CA.

4.4.7.5.2.1   **MONTEE, Margaret Ellen** b 2 Nov 1877, Little Sandusky, OH; d there 15 Sep 1967. She married there 21 Dec 1899 **Jacob A. Lumberson** (William Lumberson & Mary Jane Brewer) b there 21 Jul 1872; d & bur there 1919.

Margaret Ellen Montee had a son, Ivan V., who was 2 years old in June 1900 when his mother had been married to Jacob Lumberson for less than a year (US census). He may have been the child of a previous marriage who was adopted by his stepfather on his marriage.

Jacob A. Lumberson was a laborer in Pitt Twp, OH (US censuses). He and his wife were buried in the Little Sandusky, OH, Cemetery.

Children:

   i   **Virge Ivan Lumberson** b 19 Jan 1898, Little Sandusky, OH; d 8 Mar 1984, Upper Sandusky, OH. He married 5 Aug 1922 **Vivian E. Rasey** (Jacob A. Rasey & Jennie A. Kerr) b 2 Jun 1905, Pitt Twp, OH; d 12 Dec 1988, Upper Sandusky, OH.

   ii   **Monta Eckart Lumberson** b 5 Aug 1900, Little Sandusky, OH; d 12 Jun 1993, Upper Sandusky, OH.

   iii **Mary Ellen Lumberson** b 23 Aug 1906, Columbus, OH; d 3 Sep 1987, Upper Sandusky, OH. She married 21 Dec 1925, Columbus, OH, **Robert Ray Murray** (Abraham Van Murray & Minnie Evelyn Reece) b 27 Feb 1903, Plain City, OH; d 15 Jan 1973, Sycamore, OH.

4.4.7.5.2.2   **MONTEE, Myrta Edna** b 1 Feb 1880, Little Sandusky, OH; d there 4 Mar 1967. She married 13 Nov 1897, Upper Sandusky, OH, **Frank/Franklin Noah Swinehart** (Benjamin Swinehart & Mary ____) b Oct 1874, Pitt Twp, OH; bur 1957, Little Sandusky, OH.

Frank Swinehart was a farm laborer in Crane Twp, OH, in 1900 and in Pitt Twp, OH, in 1920 and 1930 (US censuses). He and his wife were buried in the Little Sandusky, OH, Cemetery, as was their daughter Helen (i).

Children:

   i   **Helen M. Swinehart** b Jul 1898, Crane Twp, OH; d & bur 20 & ? Jul 1920, Little Sandusky, OH.

ii   **James Franklin Swinehart** b 5 Nov 1899, Crane Twp, OH; d 24 Nov 1990, Cortland, NY. He married 1926?, OH, **Bertha B. Brunk** (Gustav W. Brunk & Bertha ____) b 12 Aug 1902, Mansfield, OH; d Jan 1987, Cortland, NY.

iii   **Benjamin Frank Swinehart** b 5 Apr 1902, Wyandot Co., OH; d 4 Dec 1983, Delaware, OH. He married 1926?, **Mildred** ____ b 1905?, OH.

iv   **Thomas Swinehart** b 1905?, Wyandot Co. OH.

v   **Dorothy C. Swinehart** b 29 Nov 1906, Wyandot Co., OH; d 13 Mar 1998, Atascadero, CA. She married 1926? **Calvin R. Hunter** (John H. Hunter & Laura R. ____) b 7 Sep 1906, Toledo, OH; d there 24 Jan 1962.

vi   **Ruth Anna Swinehart** b 1910?, Little Sandusky, OH; d 3 Mar 1958, Bowling Green, OH, at the age of 47. She married ____ **Neiderhouse**.

vii   **Martha M. Swinehart** b 2 Dec 1912, Upper Sandusky, OH; d & bur there 4 & 8 Dec 2000. She married 8 Jul 1939 **Cyril S. Miller** (William Miller & Mary ____) b 4 Aug 1910, OH; d 17 Mar 1988, Upper Sandusky, OH.

4.4.7.5.2.3   **MONTEE, Emma B.** b 13 Jun 1882, Little Sandusky, OH; d 25 Mar 1973, Sylvania, OH. She married 24 Sep 1904, Little Sandusky, OH, **Carless Edward Park** (James Park & Lillie Walton) b 7 Jun 1884, Richwood, OH; d 1 Jul 1964, Toledo, OH.

Emma Montee's husband was named Carl Park at his marriage (Wyandot Co., OH, Marriage Records, IX, 12). On all other occasions he was named Carless or Carless Edward Park. He was a laborer in Richwood, OH, at his marriage, in Pitt Twp, OH, in 1910, in Upper Sandusky, OH, in 1918 (World War I Draft Registration card), and a railroad worker there in 1920 (US censuses). He and his wife later moved to Toledo, OH, where they were living when her brother Grover Cleveland Montee (4.4.7.5.2.5) died in 1956 (*Upper Sandusky Daily Chief*, 6 Oct 1956). They were both residents of Toledo at their deaths.

Child:

i   **Madaline Belle Park** b 12 Feb 1902, OH; d 17 Dec 1986, Toledo, OH. She married 1925? **Clarence William Vergiels** (Frederick William Vergiels & Anna Margerite Hincklemann) b 8 Dec 1897, Toledo, OH; d there 27 Jun 1972.

4.4.7.5.2.4   **MONTEE, Frances Belle** b 18 Mar 1883/15 Sep 1884, Little Sandusky, OH; d 20 Nov 1977, Upper Sandusky, OH. She married 5 Mar 1903, Little Sandusky, OH, **Ralph Nick Fowler** (Hiram R. Fowler & Alice Hornby) b there 22 Feb 1879; d there 12 Jul 1955.

There is some uncertainty concerning Frances Montee's date of birth. I have found no birth record and secondary sources differ significantly. The 1900 US census in Little Sandusky, OH, says that Frances B. Montee, then 15 years old, was born in September 1884. That date is confirmed by the inscription on her tombstone in the Little Sandusky Cemetery which shows that Frances B. Fowler, wife of Ralph Fowler, was born on 15 Sept 1884. Yet her 1903 marriage license application states that she was born on 18 Mar 1883, a date also found in the Social Security Death Index. She would then have been born just nine months after her sister Emma (4.4.7.5.2.3). It is possible, of course, but perhaps not too probable.

Ralph N. Fowler was a farmer in Little Sandusky until at least 1920 and a laborer there in 1930 (US censuses). According to his marriage license application of 1903, he had previously been married and was divorced. I have been unable to find this first marriage. He was buried in the Little Sandusky Cemetery alongside his wife Frances and their son Max (iii).

Children:

i   **Nova G. Fowler** b 12 Oct 1904, Little Sandusky, OH; d 1 Feb 1975, Toledo, OH. She married 12 Aug 1922, Monroe, MI, **Robert Lewis Handy** (Robert F. Handy & Bernice B. Cross) b 27 Oct 1902, Seneca, OH; d 27 Apr 2000, Toledo, OH.

ii   **Hiram R. Fowler** b 13 Oct 1906, Little Sandusky, OH; d 12 Jul 1978, Maumee, OH. He married **Juanita Mae Carter** b 25 Oct 1918, Orrville, OH; d 22 Mar 1998, Lucas Co., OH.

iii   **Max N. Fowler** b 29 Oct 1908, Little Sandusky, OH; d there 27 Apr 1937.

4.4.7.5.2.5   **MONTEE, Grover Cleveland** b 25 Aug 1887, Little Sandusky, OH; d & bur 6 & 9 Oct 1956, Cleveland & Little Sandusky, OH. He married **Caroline D./Carrie Walter** (John William Walter & Lena L. Wirth) b 3 Nov 1893, Oshkosh, WI; m (1) 1919? Elmer Paul Ross; d 26 Feb 1982, Akron, OH.

Grover C. Montee was a day laborer in Little Sandusky, OH, in 1910, and a railroad fireman there in 1920. He was still single (US censuses). According to his obituary in the *Upper Sandusky Daily Chief* of 6 Oct 1956, he and his wife had moved to Cuyahoga Falls some ten years before his death.

4.4.7.5.2.6   **MONTEE, Fowler C.** b 1 May 1890, Little Sandusky, OH; d 28 Jul 1972, Upper Sandusky, OH. He married (1) 22 Aug 1917, Wyandot Co., OH, and divorced there 18 Jun 1924 **Nina May Welty** (Marion Francis Welty & Verdia Emma Pool) b 8 Dec 1889, Eden Twp, OH; m (2) 1926? Wyandot Co., OH, William Harrison Grove; d 18 Dec 1968, Marion, OH.

He married (2) 1927? Wyandot Co., OH, **Myrtle M.** ____ b 1891?, OH.

He married (3) 7 Feb 1938, Upper Sandusky, OH, **Annette Couts** (Newton O. Couts & Rosa Graham) b 28 Dec 1900, Bucyrus, OH; m (1) 1927? Frank Musser; m (3) ____ Smith; d 25 Jan 1977, Marion, OH.

Fowler C. Montee was a laborer in Little Sandusky, OH, in 1910 and a laborer/soldier there at his first marriage. He had in fact enlisted in the US Army on 3 Jun 1917 and served abroad from 25 Feb 1918 to 4 July 1919. He then returned to his father's farm. His wife Nina though was not with him in 1920. She was living in 1930 with her second husband and her son Donald Montee in Eden Twp, OH (US censuses; *Marion Daily Star*, 19 Jun 1924).

Fowler C. Montee was a railroad brakeman in Bucyrus, OH, in 1930 and had then been married for three years to his 39-year-old wife Myrtle (US census). I know nothing else about her.

Annette Couts had been married to Frank Musser for three years in 1930 (US census). Yet the announcement of her marriage to Fowler Montee in the Mansfield, OH, *News Journal* of 9 Feb 1938 refers to her as "Miss Annette Couts." She was Mrs. Annette Montee of Bucyrus when her parents celebrated their 50th wedding anniversary in 1942 but Mrs. Annette Smith when her mother died in 1952 (*Mansfield News Journal*, 30 Jun 1942 and 18 Oct 1952).

Child of the first marriage:
4.4.7.5.2.6.1   Donald Lee   1920-   -1987

4.4.7.5.2.7 **MONTEE, Lorin Edward** b 18 Dec 1892, Little Sandusky, OH; d & bur 1 & 5 Aug 1961, Fairfield, CA. He married 9 Jan 1915, Waukegan, IL, **Lillian Emily Schooley** (Louis K. Schooley & Rose Ann Beck) b there 21 Jun 1896; d & bur 25 & 27 Nov 1975, Fairfield, CA.

Lorin E. Montee was a salesman for an oil company in Waukegan, IL, in 1920 and a Vice-President for auto sales there in 1930 (US censuses). He moved to Richmond, CA, before 1942 when he signed his World War II Draft Registration card and then to Fairfield, CA, where he was the owner/operator of a Real Estate company. He was buried in Suisun-Fairfield Cemetery (*Oakland Tribune*, 3 Aug 1961).

Children:
4.4.7.5.2.7.1   Jane B.   1917-1939-1975
4.4.7.5.2.7.2   Alice Marie   1920-1943?&1951?-2000
4.4.7.5.2.7.3   James Edward   1923-1947&1968-1989

4.4.7.5.2.8   **MONTEE, Iva M.** b 15 Mar 1896, Little Sandusky, OH; d 26 Nov 1977, Jacksonville, FL. She married 1920 **Harry Howard Oborn** (Howard Ellsworth Oborn & Helen Amanda Virden) b 20 Mar 1895, Marion, OH; d 18 Jan 1965, Ashland, OH.

Harry Howard Oborn was a machinist in Bucyrus, OH, when he signed on 5 Jun 1917 his World War I Draft Registration card. He served in the 288th Air Squadron from 19 Mar 1918 to 27 Mar 1919, and then returned to Bucyrus where he was a machinist living with his parents in 1920 (US census). He soon married and lived there with his wife and children until 1927 when the family moved to Ashland, OH. He was a grocery store owner there (*Mansfield News Journal*, 19 Jan 1965).

Children:
- i **Helen Jane Oborn** b 1 Dec 1920, Bucyrus, OH; d 16 Sep 1977, Los Angeles, CA. She married 1947 **William Albert Manfrass** (William A. Manfrass & Emma Poulton) b 20 May 1921, Portage Co., OH; d 19 Sep 1989, Ventura Co., CA.
- ii **Donald Oborn** b Oct 1922 Bucyrus, OH. He married **Arlene G. ____** b Oct 1923.

4.4.7.5.2.9   MONTEE, Robert L. b 21 Nov 1898, Little Sandusky, OH; d 10 Sep 1983, Marion, OH. He married there 22 Jan 1921 **Ruth B. Sworts** (John B. Sworts & Ida M. Snyder) b 14 Aug 1900, Harpster, OH; d 27 Oct 1998, Upper Sandusky, OH.

Robert L. Montee enlisted in the US Army in Sycamore, OH, on 28 May 1917 and served as a private and, after 13 Nov 1918, a corporal in Co. A, 146th Infantry Regiment until his discharge on 13 Apr 1919. He returned to his father's farm in Little Sandusky, OH, and was a farm laborer there in 1920 and in Harpster, OH, in 1930 (US censuses).

Child:

4.4.7.5.2.9.1	Betty Louise	1923-	-

4.4.7.5.2.10   MONTEE, Villa Faye b 1 Mar 1901, Little Sandusky, OH; d 20 Jan 1971, Allen Park, MI. She married (1) 30 Jul 1917, Wyandot Co., OH, **Ray C. Watts** (Landon/Landy Watts & Diria [?] Johnson) b 18 Mar 1896, Wyandot, OH; d 17 Oct 1918, France.

She married (2) 1921? **Ray Daniel Shoop** (Nathan C. Shoop & Zilla Beckett) b 19 Feb 1895, Upper Sandusky, OH.

Villa Faye Montee's first marriage was very short-lived. Ray C. Watts, who was a farmer in Nevada, OH, at his marriage, had enlisted in the US Army on 4 Jun 1917 as a private in Co. L, 166th Infantry Regiment and was sent to France as a member of the American Expeditionary Force on 31 Oct 1917. He was killed in action less than a year later and was buried in the Meuse-Argonne American Cemetery. His widow was living in her father's household in Little Sandusky, OH, in 1920 (US censuses).

Roy Daniel Shoop was a resident of Chicago, IL, on 5 Jun 1917 (World War I Draft Registration card) but was a salesman in Upper Sandusky, OH, in 1920, when he and his wife had been married for nine years, and in Detroit, MI, in 1930 (US censuses).

Child :
- i **Richard C. Shoop** b 1921?, OH.

4.4.7.5.2.11   MONTEE, Mary B. b 1 Apr 1903, Little Sandusky, OH; d 16 Jul 1983, Crestline, OH. She married 22 May 1920 **Foster G. Beattie** (Robert Beattie & Emma Harmon) b 1 Dec 1898, Crawford Co., OH; d & bur 29 & 31 Mar 1971, Bucyrus, OH.

Foster Beattie was a salesman in Bucyrus, OH, in 1930 (US census) and a truck driver there for thirty-five years according to his obituary in the *Marion Star* of 29 Mar 1971. He and his wife were buried in Oakwood Cemetery in Bucyrus.

Children:
- i. **Mary Elizabeth Beattie** b Nov 1920, Bucyrus, OH. She married ____ **Cady**.
- ii **Janice E. Beattie** 1923?, Bucyrus, OH. She married **William McCombs**.
- iii. **Joyce M. Beattie** b 18 Jan 1925, Bucyrus, OH. She married 5 Feb 1955, Columbus, OH, **M. Lee Stuckman** (A. A. Stuckman & Emma Schaeffer) b 1 May 1916, Bucyrus, OH; d there 16 Dec 1998.

4.4.7.5.3.1   MONTEE, Stella Mae/Estella b 6 Nov 1878, Harpster, OH; d & bur 2 & 4

Feb 1922, Pitt Twp & Little Sandusky, OH. She married 12 Aug 1895, Little Sandusky, OH, **Thomas Frank Manhart** (Lewis Manhart & Frances Beltz) b 21 Apr 1873, Vigo Co., IN; m (2) Mary H. ____; d 20 Dec 1960, Columbus, OH.

This woman was named Estella Montee when she was living with her parents in Pitt Twp, OH, in 1880 as well as at her marriage. In later years her name was invariably Stella, Stella M., or Stella Mae. She and her husband moved to Illinois, where their first four children were born, soon after their marriage. They returned to Ohio before the birth of Robert (v) in 1907 though another son, Ralph (vii), was born in Illinois in 1914. Thomas F. Manhart was a farm laborer in Darwin Twp, IL, in 1900, a farmer in Marseilles, OH, in 1910, and a farmer in Pitt Twp, OH, in 1920. He left the farm after his first wife's death. In 1930, when he was a store keeper in Marion, OH, only his daughter Opal (vi) and son Charles (viii) were still living with him and his second wife Mary (US censuses). He was buried alongside his wife Stella in the Little Sandusky, OH, Cemetery.

Children:
i **Lewis Franklin Manhart** b 16 Jun 1897, Marshall, IL; d Sep 1983, Bowling Green, OH. He married 25 Feb 1922, Marseilles, OH, **Villa Edna Kramer** (George W. Kramer & Dollie M. Keller) b 29 May 1904, Mifflin Twp, OH; d 5 Apr 1970, Manatee Co., FL.

ii **Anna Marie Manhart** b 11 Feb 1899, West Union, IL; d 20 Feb 1988, Marion, OH. She married (1) 4 Dec 1920, Harpster, OH, **Marion Joseph Stansbery** (Harvey B. Stansbery & Mary Catherine Palmer) b 27 Jan 1895, Mifflin Twp, OH; d 28 Aug 1969, Upper Sandusky, OH.

She married (2) 2 May 1947, Marseilles, OH, **Delbert Hartle Sanford** (Harry Dale Sanford & Mary Etta Hartle) b there 13 Mar 1913; d 6 Mar 1996, Upper Sandusky, OH.

iii **Russell A. Manhart** b 19 Jan 1901, West Union, IL; d 24 Apr 1994, Upper Sandusky, OH. He married 1925?, **Minnie M. Dickey** (Wherry Dickey & Margaret Roszman) b 21 Jan 1902, Mifflin, OH; d 5 Jan 1978, Upper Sandusky, OH.

iv **Harry E. Manhart** b 20 Jun 1904, West Union, IL; d 16 May 1993, Norwalk, OH. He married 1927? **Florence A. Carter** (Ira H. Carter & Avadna P. Harmon) b 21 Apr 1906, Wyandot Co., OH; d 31 Aug 1985, Norwalk, OH.

v **Robert C. Manhart** b 27 Jun 1907, Marseilles, OH; d 9 Jun 1991, Columbia, MO. He married 22 Feb 1935, Marion, OH, **Madeleine Rose Cutarelli** (Carmen Cutarelli & Rosa Meo) b 13 Feb 1909, Indianapolis, IN; d 22 Oct 2003, Columbia, MO.

vi **Opal M. Manhart** b 21 Dec 1910, Marseilles, OH; d 12 Jun 1983, Upper Sandusky, OH. She married (1) 1930 **Earl H. Gamble** (Richard Gamble & Berdella O. Clutter) b 5 Jun 1910, OH; m (2) and divorced 1954, Marion, OH, Marlene ____; m (3) 6 Mar 1954, Marion. OH, Jean Lucille Gruver (James Gruver & Hallie Scofield); d there 26 Oct 1976.

She married (2) 1940 **Lloyd Lundy** (Seldon Pettit Lundy & Sarah Ann Pontius) b 7 Apr 1905, Wyandot Co., OH; m (1) 1925? Juanita ____ ; d 20 Mar 1969, Columbus, OH.

vii **Ralph R. Manhart** b 14 May 1914, IL.

viii **Charles Henry Manhart** b 1 Dec 1916, Pitt Twp, OH; d 14 Oct 2001, Hardin Co., OH. He married **Laura Stuber** (Alvin Stuber & Mary K. Wuethrich) b 22 Jul 1921, Columbus, OH; d 21 Oct 1993, Kenton, OH.

4.4.7.5.3.2   MONTEE, Charles Edward b 12 Aug 1880, Little Sandusky, OH; d there 27 Jun 1965. He married there 28 Feb 1905 **Ida May Barth** (Benjamin Eli Barth & Rebecca Belle Creger) b 4 Feb 1887, Pitt Twp, OH; d 26 Aug 1979, Upper Sandusky, OH.

Charles E. Montee was a farmer in Little Sandusky, OH. He, his wife, and their son Dale Franklin were buried in the Little Sandusky Cemetery.

Children:

4.4.7.5.3.2.1	Bernice Opal	1905-1925-1993
4.4.7.5.3.2.2	Dale Franklin	1908- -1908

4.4.7.5.3.3   MONTEE, Ralph Francis/Franklin b 6 Mar 1883, Pitt Twp, OH; d & bur 1 & 4 May 1935, Pitt Twp & Upper Sandusky, OH. He married 6 Jan 1909, Little Sandusky, OH, **Nora Amber Swihart** (Peter M. Swihart & Winifred Fitzgerald) b 23 Dec 1885, Pitt Twp, OH; d & bur 2 & 5 Sep 1973, Upper Sandusky, OH.

Ralph F. Montee was a farmer in Pitt Twp, OH. The name Ralph Francis appears on his tombstone in Oak Hill Cemetery in Upper Sandusky, OH, where he and his wife were buried. Yet he signed on 12 Sep 1918 his World War I Draft Registration card as Ralph Franklin Montee, husband of Mrs. Nora Amber Montee. They had no children.

4.4.7.5.3.4   MONTEE, Alice Lodema b 26 Oct 1886, West Union, IL; d & bur 31 Dec 1965 & 4 Jan 1966, Upper Sandusky & Marion, OH. She married 12 Oct 1904, Harpster, OH, **John Herring** (Henry Herring & Mary M. Snyder) b 24 Feb 1866, Pitt Twp, OH; d 24 Feb 1945, Upper Sandusky, OH.

John Herring was a farmer in Pitt Twp, OH, at his marriage and until at least 1920. He was still a farmer in 1930 but in Upper Sandusky, OH (US censuses). He and his wife were still residents there when they died but were buried in Chapel Heights Cemetery in Marion, OH.

Child:

  i   **Clarence Herring** b 20 Aug 1905, Pitt Twp, OH; d & bur 3 & 6 Mar 1985, Harpster & Upper Sandusky, OH. He married (1) 16 Jul 1929, Columbus, OH, **Florence Wilkinson** (Clarence Emmet Wilkinson & Emma Elizabeth Mueller) b 28 Jan 1910, Hilliard, OH; d & bur 4 & 6 Mar 1976, Harpster & Upper Sandusky, OH.
          He married (2) 28 Nov 1979, **Mrs. Ruth W. Rickenbacher** b 1904?, OH; d 1 Mar 1984, Upper Sandusky, OH, at the age of 80.

4.4.7.6.2.1   MONTEE, Hattie May b & d 12 May 1885, Pittsburg, KS.
      This child was stillborn.

4.4.7.6.2.2   MONTEE, Charles Sylvester b 16 Apr 1886, Pittsburg, KS; d 6 Apr 1954, Spokane, WA. He married 29 Aug 1909, Genesee, ID, **Mae Margaret Gehrke** b 1885?, MN.

Charles (also Charlie) S. Montee and his wife lived for a few years after their marriage in Idaho before moving to Spokane, WA, where their second child was born. Charles Montee was a railroad worker, a fireman on 1 Jan 1920, when his wife was 34 years old, and a locomotive engineer in 1930 (US censuses).

Children:

4.4.7.6.2.2.1	Clifford Sylvester	1910?-1933-1946
4.4.7.6.2.2.2	Earl Edward	1916-1938-1979

4.4.7.6.2.3   MONTEE, Nora Lee b 6 Nov 1887, Pittsburg, KS; d & bur 7 & 12 Dec 1927, Soda Springs, ID & Salt Lake City, UT. She married 9 Jan 1915, Pocatello, ID, **Stanley Abraham Hill** (Abraham Mormon Hill & Caroline/Carrie Harman) b 16 Mar 1892, Granger, UT; m (2) 14 Jul 1931, Logan, UT, Gladys Phoebe Berrey (John Alfonso Berrey & Mary Elizabeth Humphreys); d & bur 6 & 10 May 1965, Blackfoot, ID & Salt Lake City, UT.

Nora Montee was a bookkeeper/stenographer in Sheridan, KS, in 1910 before moving to Idaho. Her husband was a farmer in Pegram, ID, in 1917 when he signed his World War I Draft Registration card and a sheep man in Montpelier, ID, in 1930 (US censuses). He and his second wife lived on the ranch near Pegram until they moved to Mackay, ID, in 1942 and to Blackfoot, ID, in 1952 (*Idaho State Journal*, 7 May 1965).

Children:

  i   **Stanley Merle Hill** b 7 Jul 1919, Soda Springs, ID. He married 22 Feb 1952,

Blackfoot, ID, **Doris L. Dupont** (Raymond Earl Dupont & Clara Bell Littrel) b 7 Dec 1924, Roswell, NM; d 22 Jan 2001, Blackfoot, ID.

ii   **Maxine Marie Hill** b 31 Mar 1921, Montpelier, ID; d & bur 24 & 26 Nov 2003, St. George, UT. She married 12 Jul 1941, Pinedale, WY, **Joseph H. Olsen** (Orson H. Olsen & Zelnora Van Noy) b 3 Dec 1915, Ovid, ID; d & bur 27 Oct & 1 Nov 1977, Montpelier & Ovid, ID.

iii   **Esther Lee Hill** b 29 Sep 1923, Pegram, ID. She married 30 Jul 1943, Ogden, UT, **William Dewey Townson** (Gevernis Dewey Townson & Gladys Marie Casey) b 21 Aug 1923, Leroy, TX; d & bur 6 & 13 Jun 1996, Salt Lake City, UT & Forth Worth, TX.

4.4.7.6.2.4   **MONTEE, Iva Ruth** b 10 May 1891, Pittsburg, KS; d 23 Feb 1985, Montpelier, ID. She married 18 Aug 1916, Pocatello, ID, **William Levi Aland** (James Orchard Aland & Sarah Ann Holmes) b 6 Apr 1885, Bloomington, ID; d & bur 28 & 30 Mar 1954, Montpelier, ID.

William Levi Aland was a merchant, owner of a general store in Pegram, ID, in 1920 and 1930 (US censuses). He and his wife were residents of Montpelier, ID, when her mother died in May 1945 (*Pittsburg Headlight*, 7 May 1945) and remained there until their deaths.

Children:

i   **Montee Levi Aland** b 15 Feb 1918, Pegram, ID; d 29 Aug 1944, Pocatello, ID. He married there 18 Jul 1938 **Phyllis Helen Egli** (Ernest Niklaus Egli & Margaretha Rosen) b 9 Oct 1921, Lanark, ID; m (2) Ross M. Clark (Royal D. Clark & Mary Mumford); m (3) Calvin Riggs; m (4) 6 Dec 1961, Reno, NV, Ernest Frank Zoppi (Emilio Luigi Zoppi & Mary Baralis); d there 27 Apr 2001.

ii   **Dean Holmes Aland** b 13 Aug 1920, Pegram, ID; d & bur 18 & 21 Jul 1973, Montpelier, ID. He married 24 Mar 1942, Randolph, UT, **Mada Genevieve Sorenson** (Andrew Gregor Sorenson & Sarah Jane Weaver) b 10 Aug 1922, Dingle, ID; d 7 May 2001, Salt Lake City, UT.

iii   **Blake Neale Aland** b 5 Aug 1922, Pegram, ID. He married 28 Nov 1945, Montpelier, ID, **Fern Marie Loveday** (Kem Loveday & Delilah Eliza Welker) b there 25 Sep 1921.

iv   **Gale Aland** b 28 Nov 1923, Pegram, ID; d & bur 27 & 30 Oct 2004, Danville, VA. She married 12 Sep 1940, Pocatello, ID, **Douglas Leonard Beckwith** (Edward Jay Beckwith & Christina Rohner) b 17 Nov 1921, Montpelier, ID; d there 12 Apr 1995.

v   **Dala Ruth Aland** b 14 Mar 1929, Montpelier, ID; d there 18 Oct 1988. She married 3 Jul 1947, Logan, UT, **Noel Dean Stewart** (Glenn Floyd Stewart & Beulah Louise Stevens) b 5 July 1927, Montpelier, ID; d there 15 Sep 1978.

4.4.7.6.2.5   **MONTEE, Harry Earl** b 9 Sep 1896, Pittsburg, KS; d 15 Jun 1960, St. Louis, MO. He married 17 Aug 1923 **Vera Lorena Huston** (Hugh Findley Huston & Emma Sarah Bogle) b 24 Dec 1891, Crawford Co., KS.

Harry Earl Montee was a railroad worker in Springfield, MO, in 1930 (US census). He was a resident of St. Louis, MO, when his mother died in 1945 (*Pittsburg Headlight*, 7 May 1945).

Child:

4.4.7.6.2.5.1   Sara Jo   1926-1951-

4.4.7.6.2.6   **MONTEE, Clair Edward** b 16 Feb 1902, Pittsburg, KS; d 25 Jun 1980, Kansas City, MO. He married 15 Apr 1939, Des Moines, IA, **Dorothy Virginia Coxe** (Howard Edgar Coxe & Lottie L. _____) b 21 Jul 1909, Kansas City, MO; d there 19 Aug 1980.

This man was known under a variety of names. He was Edward C., Edward, and C. E. Montee in the 1910, 1920, and 1930 censuses in Sheridan and Pittsburg, KS, Clair Edward Montee in his father's obituary, Ted Montee in his mother's obituary (*Pittsburg Headlight,* 31

May 1929 and 7 May 1945), and Clair Montee in the Social Security Death Index. He was an electrician in Pittsburg, KS, in 1930 (US census) and in Kansas City, MO, after his marriage.

Children:

4.4.7.6.2.6.1	Richard Clair	1942-1963-
4.4.7.6.2.6.2	Stephen Howard	1947- -

4.4.7.6.2.7   **MONTEE, Ruby Nadine** b 4 May 1911, Pittsburg, KS; d 8 Oct 2008, Grove, OK. She married (1) 2 Jan 1927, Carthage, MO, **Roland Frank Cornelson** (Frank Cornelson & Anna Marie Barlow) b 25 Jul 1904, Dodge City, KS; d 6 Sep 1970, Earlton, KS.

She married (2) 1974 **Fred Gerardy** (Fred L. Gerardy & Mattie Arnold) b 10 Jan 1911, Emporia, KS; d Feb 1977, Chanute, KS.

Roland F. Cornelson was a linotype operator in Chanute, KS, in 1930 (US census). Ruby Montee lived there through her two marriages and was still a resident there when her son Frank (iii) died in 1993 (*Wichita Eagle*, 8 Oct 1993). She spent her last years in Grove, OK, near her son Roland (ii) (*Wichita Eagle*, 9 Oct 2008).

Children:
i   **Patti Ann Cornelson** b 25 Feb 1931, Chanute, KS. She married there 9 May 1953 **Dave A. Richardson** (Betty Ramsey, *Monty-Montee History*, p. 319).
ii   **Roland Frank Cornelson** (twin) b 18 Dec 1936, Chanute, KS. He married 28 Sep 1956 **Juanita P. Elliott** b 5 Apr 1938.
iii **Frank John Cornelson** (twin) b 18 Dec 1936, Chanute, KS; d & bur 6 & 9 Oct 1993, Wichita, KS. He married 24 Nov 1962 **Doris J. Buckles** (Paul Buckles & Ellen ____) b 31 Oct 1930, Red Cloud, NE; m (1) ____ Day; d 6 Apr 1995, Wichita, KS.

4.4.7.6.3.1   **MONTEE, Kenneth White** b 23 Mai 1897, Crafton, CA; d 15 Dec 1926, El Centro, CA. He married 10 Feb 1920, Santa Anna, CA, **Clemorissa Alice Hancock** (Roy Hancock & Mary Hillman) b 11 Mar 1901, Council Bluffs, IA; d 23 Jun 1955, Hollywood, CA.

Kenneth W. Montee was a 1st Lieutenant in the Army Air Corps during World War I. He became a commercial aviator after the war and founded with his father and brothers the K. W. Montee Aircraft Co. at Clover Field in Los Angeles, CA. He specialized in aerial photography and had just returned from an aerial survey of the projected Boulder Dam area in Colorado when he fell ill and died.

He and his wife had an unusual wedding, which was reported in several West Coast newspapers including the *San Jose Mercury News* of 11 Feb 1920.

Child:

4.4.7.6.3.1.1	Clemorissa	1925-1941&1972-

4.4.7.6.3.2   **MONTEE, Ralph Bunn** b 23 Jun 1899, Redlands, CA; d 16 Dec 1932, Amarillo, TX. He married (1) 1919?, Los Angeles, CA, **Ruby Jeanette Holcomb** (Thomas A. Holcomb & Anna A. Monds) b 5 Dec 1902, O'Fallon, IL; m (2) ____ Starry; d 27 Dec 1959, Los Angeles, CA.

He was divorced when he married (2) 1929? **Dessa Mae Hesse** (Andrew J. Hesse & Alice Allinda Greenwood) b 1907?, TX.

Ralph B. Montee was a machinist living with his wife Ruby in Belvedere, CA, in 1920. He was a pilot for Western Airlines in 1930, residing in Kansas City, MO, with his 23-year-old wife Dessa to whom he had been married for less than a year (US censuses). He died from injuries suffered when the mail plane he was piloting crashed in a snow storm in Amarillo, TX (*Chillicothe Constitution Tribune*, 15 & 16 Dec 1932).

Child of the first marriage:

4.4.7.6.3.2.1	Lucille Ruby	1920-1946-

Child of the second marriage:
4.4.7.6.3.2.2   Ralph Bruce   1932-1952-2007

4.4.7.6.3.3   **MONTEE, Harold Jack** b 12 Mar 1902, Redlands, CA; d & bur 26 Jan &
5 Feb 1965, Silver Springs, MD & Whittier, CA. He married (1) 6 Jun 1922, Glendale, CA,
Joyce D. Dominy (Henry Dominy & Julia Foley) b 11 Oct 1898, CA; d 25 Feb 1962, Sanger,
CA.

He married (2) **Imogene Patricia Kruidenier** (Roswell P. Kruidenier & Ruth Edwards) b 12 Feb 1916, Aberdeen, SD; m (1) Harold William Wright; d 10 Jan 2001, Palm
Springs, CA.

Harold J. Montee was an aviation mechanic in Los Angeles, CA, in 1920 and 1930 (US
censuses) and an inspector for the predecessors of the FAA in Nebraska and Missouri in the
1930s and 1940s. He was an official of the FAA in Washington, DC, at his death.

Children:
4.4.7.6.3.3.1   Margery Jean   1924-   -1969
4.4.7.6.3.3.2   Jacquelyn   1925-1948?&1960-

4.4.7.6.3.4   **MONTEE, Pauline Mildred** b 30 Oct 1911, Los Angeles, CA; d 19 Mar
1989, Yucaipa, CA. She married 16 Sep 1939, Santa Ana, CA, **James Jackson Copass**
(Alonzo Jasper Copass & Maude Tweedy) b 27 Mar 1909, Hico, TX; d & bur 16 & 21 May
1980, Yucaipa & Whittier, CA.

Children:
  i   **Diane Pauline Copass** b 2 Sep 1942, Los Angeles, CA. She married 14 Apr 1973,
     Seattle, WA, **Max Edwin Zbinden** (Max Zbinden & Elizabeth Ruprecht) b 3 Nov
     1927, Portland, OR.
  ii   **James Jackson Copass** b 12 Aug 1946, Long Beach, CA. He married 20 Jun 1969,
     Palm Springs, CA, **Ratanaporn Tamthong** (Namthae Tamthong & Pacharee Yuta-
     tat) b 7 Aug 1946, Kanchanaburi, Thailand.

4.4.7.6.6.1   **MONTEE, Donald R.** b Apr 1893, Pittsburg, KS; d there 27 Jul 1893 at
the age of 3 months.

4.4.7.6.6.2   **MONTEE, Grace Elizabeth** b 12 Jul 1894, Pittsburg, KS; d Aug 1989.
She married 29 Mar 1914, Rocky Ford, CO, **Lee Albert Rogers** (George Franklin Rogers &
Nancy Ellen Stow) b 10 Mar 1894, Jefferson City, MO; d & bur 2 & 5 Dec 1957, Oakdale,
CA.

Lee Rogers was a machinist in Rocky Ford, CO, in 1920 and a crane operator there in
1930 (US censuses). He was buried in the Odd Fellows Cemetery in Oakdale, CA. His widow
was a resident of Modesto, CA, at her death (Social Security Death Index). Yet her name is
not found in the California Death Index for the years 1940-1997.

Children:
  i   **Loene Daphne Rogers** b 9 Jan 1915, Rocky Ford, CO; d & bur 2 & 7 May 1998,
     Southworth & Port Orchard, WA. She married 8 Oct 1934, Raton, NM, **Horace**
     Seldon McAbee (Seldon Horace McAbee & Rebecca Braddock) b 4 Oct 1911,
     Roxton, TX; d 6 Apr 2004, Silverdale, WA.
  ii   **Leona Faustina Rogers** b 18 Nov 1917, Rocky Ford, CO; d & bur 30 Sep & 3 Oct
     1980, Santa Paula & Ventura, CA. She married 22 Aug 1936, Rocky Ford, CO,
     Foster Woodrow Stamps (Samuel Peale Stamps & Sarah Thomas) b 17 Aug 1912,
     Osage, AR; d & bur 19 & 22 Mar 1980, Oxnard & Ventura, CA.
  iii   **Leroy Albert Rogers** b 24 Apr 1920, Ft. Collins, CO; d 29 Jan 1992, Fresno Co.,
     CA. He married 6 Jun 1946, Modesto, CA, **Dorothy Adella Deutsch** (Everett E.
     Deutsch & Dora F. ____) b 12 Feb 1926, Paonia, CO; m (1) Edward L. McCarty

who died in the Pacific, 11 May 1945.

iv   **Loreeta Elizabeth Rogers** b 24 Oct 1923, Ft. Collins, CO. She married (1) 1941? **Leon Cidney Newberry** (George Hugh Newberry & Hattie Malinda Harris) b 1920, Parker Co., TX; d 1 Jan 1945, Lorraine, France; bur Lorraine American Cemetery, St. Avold, France.

      She married (2) 12 Jan 1946, Reno, NV, **Dewey Denver Stackhouse** (Virgil Lee Stackhouse & Mintie Beal) b 16 Aug 1919, AR; d 19 Aug 1981, Santa Cruz Co., CA.

v   **Loren William Rogers** b 27 Feb 1931, Rocky Ford, CO. He married (1) **Betty Jean Dupraun Friendly**.

      He was divorced when he married (2) 1 Apr 1954 **Donna Sedonia Davis** (Betty Ramsey, *Monty-Montee History*, p. 420).

4.4.7.6.6.3   **MONTEE, Clarence Arthur** b 23 Aug 1896, Pittsburg, KS; d 22 Jul 1908, Rocky Ford, CO.

4.4.7.6.6.4   **MONTEE, Lucy Harriet** b Sep 1899, Pittsburg, KS; d before 1 Jun 1900.

      I know of this child's birth only though Betty Ramsey's *Monty-Montee History*, p. 421. Her mother had only two living children in June 1900, Grace and Clarence (US census).

4.4.7.6.6.5   **MONTEE, Goldie Juanita** b 26 Mar 1902, Cherokee, KS; d & bur 5 & ? Sep 1976, Manteca & French Camp, CA. She married 20 Apr 1924 **Lovell Frederick Maddex** (Lewis Maddex & Nellie L. Roe) b 10 Mar 1900, Pilot Grove, MO; d & bur 19 & 24 Jun 1961, Seattle & Monroe, WA.

      Lovell F. Maddex was a recruit at the Great Lakes Naval Training Station in Illinois in 1920. He was single. Ten years later L. Fred Maddex, a packer in Phoenix, AZ, and his wife Goldie J. had been married for six years (US censuses).

Children:

i   **Lovell Frederick Maddex** b 13 Aug 1925, Stockton, CA. He married (1) 1947? **Marie Johnson Heaston** (unconfirmed).

      He was divorced when he married (2) around 1951 **Eleanor Joan Schaapman** (Johannes Schaapman & Alice Maggie Zweep) b 4 Nov 1932, Ripon, CA; m (2) John Board; d 15 May 1992, Lindsay, CA.

      He was divorced when he married (3) 14 Jul 1956, Stockton, CA, and divorced 6 Aug 1982, San Joaquin Co., CA, **Ramona Rita Eichoff** (George E. Eichoff & Clementina/Tina Heuer) b 22 Jan 1935, San Joaquin Co., CA.

ii   **Jack Edward Maddex** b 6 Nov 1928, Tolleson, AZ; d & bur 18 Apr & 4 May 1971, Mt. Pleasant, UT & French Camp, CA. He married (1) 19 Dec 1952, Seattle, WA, and divorced Oct 1968, Stanislaus Co., CA, **Lillian Litschewski** (Edward Litschewski & Mary Hahne) b 1933?, SD; m (2) Gene Stark; m (3) ____ James.

      He married (2) **Lois Young** (Betty Ramsey, *Monty-Montee History*, pp. 424-425).

4.4.7.6.6.6   **MONTEE, Sylvia Ruth** b 29 Dec 1904, Cherokee, KS; d & bur 15 & ? Sep 1984, Fairview, UT & French Camp, CA. She married 21 Feb 1925, Lawrence, KS, **Charles Robert Miller** (James Preston Miller & Mary Elizabeth Hunsucher) b 21 Mar 1906, Easton, KS; d & bur 14 & 17 Oct 1955, Tracy & French Camp, CA.

      Charles Miller was a farmer in Rocky Ford, CO, in 1930 (US census). His daughter Betty Louise (i) is the compiler of the *Monty-Montee History* from which is taken much of the information concerning her and her siblings' families (pp. 431-445).

Children:

i   **Betty Louise Miller** b 11 Jan 1926, Topeka, KS. She married 13 Dec 1945, Manteca, CA, **Earl Clayton Ramsey** (Robert Earl Ramsey & Ethel Rose Freeman) b 4 Feb 1923, Balkan, KY; d Oct 1992, Mt. Pleasant, UT.

ii **James Robert Miller** b 2 Aug 1928, Rocky Ford, CO; d 14 Jul 1986, Fairview, UT. He married (1) 18 Apr 1949, Reno, NV, **Saphronia Pearl Myatt** (James Washington Myatt & Mattie Jewel Kemp) b 5 May 1930, Canadian, TX; m (2) 12 Feb 1972, San Joaquin Co., CA, Jack Wayne Williams (_____ Williams & _____ Rice).

He was divorced when he married (2) 7 Feb 1972, Elko, NV, **Genevieve Nielson Marshall**.

iii **Juanita Ruth Miller** b 22 Jan 1931, Rocky Ford, CO. She married (1) 1 Jan 1950, **Clarence A. Edwards**.

She was divorced when she married (2) 29 Jun 1957, Carson City, NV, **Thomas Everett Bruton** (George Bruton & Maggie L. _____) b 2 Apr 1921, Bagby, CA; d 6 Apr 1984, Salt Lake City, UT.

4.4.7.6.6.7 **MONTEE, William Albert** b 7 Jul 1908, Rocky Ford, CO; d 18 Mar 1982, Rialto, CA. He married (1) 18 Jan 1931, La Cygne, KS, **Ruby Faye Cline** (Reuben Alfred Cline & Bertha Alice Rogers) b there 5 Aug 1909; m (2) 20 Jul 1953, Red Lodge, MT, and divorced 1954 DeVyr Bigham; m (3) 17 Aug 1960, Canon City, CO, Meldon Edgar Battin (Robert Wood Battin & Eliza Jane Hall); d & bur 27 Sep & 1 Oct 1994, Olathe & LaCygne, KS.

He married (2) 18 Oct 1958, San Bernardino, CA, **Dolores Faye Ingram** (Robert E. Ingram & F. Brannon) b 10 Aug 1907, Winfrey, AR; m (1) Paul Roof (Elias R. Roof & Claudia Melton); d 26 Mar 1997, Riverside, CA.

Albert Montee was a laborer on the farm of his aunt and uncle Hattie Montee (4.4.7.6.4) and Stephen Millard near LaCygne, KS, in 1930 (US census). He was a farmer there at his marriage and his children were born there. I do not know when he moved to California. He and his second wife lived in Rialto and Riverside, CA.

Children of the first marriage:
4.4.7.6.6.7.1	Betty/Bettie Eileen	1932-1947&1951-
4.4.7.6.6.7.2	Bobby Dean	1935-1956&1990-2002

4.4.7.9.4.1 **MONTEE, Jesse Howard** b 24 Dec 1888, Girard, KS; d 18 Apr 1925, Brooklyn, IL.

Jesse Montee left Kansas for Illinois as a child and was living with his mother in his maternal grandfather's household in Chalmers, IL, in 1900. He was a farmer there in 1910 and in Emmet Twp, IL, in 1920 (US censuses). He died in a farming accident and was buried on 21 Apr 1925 in Camp Creek Cemetery in McDonough Co., IL (*Rushville Times*, Apr 1925).

4.4.7.9.4.2 **MONTEE, Estella Gertrude/Stella G.** b 26 Aug 1890, KS; d 21 Feb 1935, Bardolph, IL. She married 27 Nov 1907, McDonough Co., IL, **Ernest Walter Eddington** (George Eddington & Alice Birdsell) b 3 Mar 1886, Primghar, IA; m (2) Nov 1948 Leither May Royer (Henry Benninger Royer & Sarah Catherine Engle), widow of Leslie Ambrose Eddington; d 29 Sep 1962, Colchester, IL.

Estella Gertrude Montee and her sister Grace (4.4.7.9.4.3) married two brothers. Ernest W. Eddington was a farmer in Bardolph, IL, in 1920, and a laborer there in 1930 (US censuses)

Children:
i **Dorothy Marie Eddington** b 13 Sep 1908, Good Hope, IL; d 10 Jun 1995, Brookfield, MO. She married 5 Apr 1930, Macomb, IL, **Ralph Raymond Foltz** (Edward Winfred Foltz & Ina Fremont Edgar) b 12 Aug 1909, Bucklin, MO.

ii **Naomi Lucille Eddington** b 12 Dec 1910, Good Hope, IL; d 21 Apr 2001, Kansas City, MO. She married 1 Oct 1937, Dubuque, IA, **Floyd Edison Mullinix/Mullnix** (William Rufus Mullinix & Cecelia Charlotte McQuiston) b 3 Dec 1904, New Cambria, MO; d 9 Aug 1969.

iii   **Francis Edward Eddington** b 16 Jun 1912, Bushnell, IL; d 31 Aug 1995, Chapel Hill, NC. He married 9 Aug 1937, Bardolph, IL, **Ruth Audre Harris** (Charles Lester Harris & Audre Elsie Smick) b 26 May 1919, Macomb, IL.

iv   **Dale Leroy Eddington** b 27 Jun 1916, Bushnell, IL. He married (1) 25 Nov 1939, Hartington, NE, **Maxine V. Clements** (John Clements & Blanche ____) b 6 Feb 1920, Wisner, NE; d 10 Mar 1992, Pinellas Co., FL.

He married (2) 10 Sep 1993, Pinellas Co., FL, **Juanita Jo Robertson** b 5 Nov 1927; m (1) ____ Daniel.

v   **Carl Robert Eddington** b 31 Mar 1919, Bardolph, IL; d there 25 Feb 1927.

vi   **Ross Montee Eddington** b 14 Sep 1920, Bardolph, IL; d 2 Apr 1997, St. Joseph, MO. He married **Dixie Lee Wheeler** (Richard Willis Wheeler & Alma Ward) b 1 May 1926, Osborn, MO.

vii   **Mayme Alice Eddington** b 1923?, Bardolph, IL. She married (1) ____ **McHendry**.
She married (2) ____ **Thomas**.
She married (3) ____ **Watson**.

viii   **Marvin Dean Eddington** b 26 Oct 1926, Bardolph, IL; d 12 Jul 1996, St. Petersburg, FL. He married 16 Apr 1949, Macomb, IL, **Juanita Gustavson** b 4 Feb 1931; d 17 May 1981, St. Petersburg, FL.

ix   **Elva Mae Eddington** b 20 Jan 1929, Bardolph, IL. She married 19 Jul 1946, Monmouth, IL, **Earl Lee Fitch** (Floyd Fitch & Mildred Richter) b 1927, Bushnell, IL.

4.4.7.9.4.3   MONTEE, Grace Fern b 29 Feb 1893, KS; d 2 Dec 1956, Macomb, IL. She married there 31 Dec 1912 **Ralph Alfred Eddington** (George Walter Eddington & Alice Birdsell) b 28 Nov 1890, Chalmers, IL.

Grace Fern Montee and her sister Estella Gertrude (4.4.7.9.4.2) married two brothers. Ralph Eddington was a farmer in Chalmers, IL, until at least 1930 (US censuses). His date of birth is uncertain. Various censuses place it in 1890, 1891, or 1892. I have adopted the date of birth found in his World War I Draft Registration card of 6 Jun 1917.

Children:

i   **Kenneth Alfred Eddington** b 29 Jan 1917, Chalmers, IL; d 17 Nov 1979, Colchester, IL. He married 23 Aug 1941, Lawton, OK, **Martha Mae Whisler** (Melvon Rufus Whisler & Nora Bell Hatch) b 5 Nov 1920, Avon, IL.

ii   **Bernetta Allene Eddington** b 16 Jun 1919, Chalmers, IL; d 28 Dec 1991. She married 11 Dec 1935 **Edward Woodrow Kruse** (George Hugh Kruse & Mary Frances Sullivan) b 11 Dec 1912, Macomb, IL; d 27 Oct 2002, Newport, MN.

4.4.7.9.4.4   MONTEE, Francis Edward b 8 Jan 1907, Neosho, MO; d & bur 29 Nov & 3 Dec 1968, Long Beach & Brea, CA. He married (1) 1928? **Diana W. Sinclair** b 1903?, NY.

He married (2) **Alma C.** ____ b 17 Dec 1902, IN; d 6 Mar 1960, Orange Co., CA.

He married (3) 23 Oct 1961, Los Angeles, CA, **Ruth H. Sterling** (Alfred E. Sterling & Florence Hanaford) b 1909?, MO; m (1) Herbert M. Easley (Henry D. Easly & Lelia Alice ____).

Francis E. Montee was a clerk for a Title Company in Los Angeles, CA, in 1930 when he and his 27-year-old wife Diana had been married for two years (US census). Her maiden name was Sinclair according to the birth records of her children Lucille and Francis.

Mrs. Ruth Montee survived her husband (*Independent Press Telegram*, Long Beach, CA, 1 Dec 1968).

Children:

4.4.7.9.4.4.1	Lucille Marion	1929- -
4.4.7.9.4.4.2	Francis Edward	1932-1961&1971&1980&1985-

4.4.7.9.4.5   MONTEE, Stanton Quinby b 18 Jan 1917, Lewiston, ID; d 21 Aug 1990,

Orange Co., CA. He married 24 Nov 1944, Riverside, CA, **Virginia Mitchell** (Benjamin Mitchell & Minnie ____) b 29 Oct 1916, Salt Lake City, UT; d 8 Nov 2001, Orange Co., CA.

Stanton Montee was living with his parents in Tulsa, OK, in 1920 and with his mother and stepfather in Los Angeles, CA, in 1930 (US censuses).

Child:

4.4.7.9.4.5.1	Renee	-	-

4.4.7.9.5.1   **MONTEE, Paul Leo** b 25 Mar 1905, Girard, KS; d there 2 Sep 1906.

4.4.7.9.5.2   **MONTEE, Gerald Fremont** b 29 Jan 1907, Girard, KS; d 8 Aug 1999, Pendleton, OR. He married (1) 29 Jan 1930, Erie, KS, **Bertha Elmira Bruner** (William H. Bruner & Dora B. Neighbors) b 30 Jul 1901, KS; d 18 Sep 1974, Walla Walla, WA.

He married (2) 6 May 1979, Athena, OR, **Violet May Davenport** (Earl Roy Davenport & Flora ____) b 24 Jun 1918, Ravalli Co., MT; d 22 Jun 1998, Pendleton, OR.

Gerald Montee was a laborer in Fort Scott, KS, in 1930 (US census). He moved to Oregon in the late 1930s or early 1940s and was buried alongside both his wives in the Athena, OR, Cemetery.

Children of the first marriage:

4.4.7.9.5.2.1	Lela Darlene	1931-1955-1993
4.4.7.9.5.2.2	Gerald Leon	1933-1956-1996
4.4.7.9.5.2.3	Albert Leroy	1936- -
4.4.7.9.5.2.4	Shirley	1938- -
4.4.7.9.5.2.5	Audrey	1941- -

4.4.7.9.5.3   **MONTEE, Mary Kathryn** b 10 Apr 1909, Girard, KS; d & bur 8 & 11 Jan 1993, Joplin, MO & Fulton, KS. She married 17 Dec 1928, Mound City, KS, **Raymond Franklin Cochran** (Samuel D. Cochran & Susan King) b there 17 Sep 1907; d there 12 Dec 1979.

Raymond Cochran was a farmer and stockman in Mound City, KS.

Children:

i   **Ruth Jean Cochran** b 8 Apr 1934, Mound City, KS. She married 14 Nov 1954 **Robert Earl Daylong** (Sile R. Daylong & Violet Lillian Hayes) b 19 May 1928, Moran, KS.

ii   **Dale Raymond Cochran** b 24 May 1944, Mound City, KS.

iii   **Jerry Lynn Cochran** b 9 Dec 1950, Mound City, KS. He married 7 Sep 1972, **Jodie Gail Howell** (Betty Ramsey, *Monty-Montee History*, p. 481).

4.4.7.9.5.4   **MONTEE, Albert A.** b 7 Jun 1911, Girard, KS; d 3 Jul 1987, Pendleton, OR. He married 5 Oct 1945, Girard, KS, **Elsie Eileen Ausemus** (Carl F. Ausemus & Emma Armstrong) b 14 Sep 1924, Hiattville, KS; d 12 Dec 1992, Pendleton, OR.

Albert Montee was a laborer on his father's farm in Sheridan Twp, KS, in 1930 (US census). He was a resident of Umatilla Co., OR, however when he enlisted as a private in the US Army in Portland, OR, on 13 Apr 1942. He and his bride moved to Athena, OR, soon after their marriage and made their life there. They were both were buried in the Athena Cemetery.

Children:

4.4.7.9.5.4.1	David Roger	1948-1973&1979-
4.4.7.9.5.4.2	Carl Michael	1951- -1972
4.4.7.9.5.4.3	Shawn	1958- -

4.4.7.9.5.5   **MONTEE, Frederick Dale** b 2 Aug 1913, Girard, KS; d & bur 4 & 10 Dec 2003, Exeter, CA. He married 9 Oct 1979, Reno, NV, **Fay Dock Brown** (Albert Burleson

Brown & Maude Elizabeth White) b 5 May 1912, Comanche, OK; m (1) 18 Apr 1932, Phoenix, AZ, Ralph Williams; d 5 Aug 1999, Exeter, CA.

Dale F. Montee was living on his father's farm in Sheridan, KS, in 1930 (US census). I do not know when he moved to California. Frederick Dale Montee was a resident of that state at his marriage and had been a heavy equipment operator in Exeter, CA, for a number of years before his death (*Visalia Times-Delta*, 7 Dec 2003). He was buried in the Exeter, CA, Cemetery.

4.4.7.9.5.6   **MONTEE, Clarence Edward** b 1 Oct 1915, Girard, KS; d & bur 22 & 29 May 1973, Portland, OR. He married (1) Riverside, CA, **Ollie Ann Clark** (Charles H. Clark & Lilly Ann Hesley) b 14 Apr 1916, Greenville, MO; m (1) _____ Teague; d & bur 25 & 26 Sep 2005, Ash Grove & Birch Tree, MO.

He married (2) **Betty Nicholson** b 1 Apr 1910; d & bur 20 Jan & 10 Feb 1998, Los Angeles & Portland, OR.

Clarence E. Montee was living on his father's farm in Sheridan, KS, in 1930 (US census). He was an "oil and gas man" in Umatilla Co., OR, though, when he enlisted in the US Army on 21 Jan 1941 in Portland, OR. He was still single. He and his second wife were buried in the Willamette National Cemetery in Portland.

Ollie Ann Clark was buried in Oak Forest Cemetery in Birch Tree, MO (*The Current Wave*, Eminence, MO, 25 Oct 2005).

Children of the first marriage:

4.4.7.9.5.6.1	Taundelaya Ann	1944- -1999
4.4.7.9.5.6.2	Arletta/Arlette Kay	1946-1963& -
4.4.7.9.5.6.3	Clarence Edward	1948-1972-2008

4.4.7.9.5.7   **MONTEE, Charlotte Louise** b 26 Jul 1920, Sheridan, KS; d 24 Sep 1997, Big Spring, TX. She married **Robert Glen Box** b 26 Nov 1923, Erath Co., TX; d 20 Dec 1999, Big Spring, TX.

Charlotte Montee and her husband were living in Los Angeles, CA, at the death of a newborn son in 1962. When her sister Mary Kathryn (4.4.7.9.5.3) died some thirty years later, Mrs. Charlotte Box was said to be a resident of Athena, OR (*Kansas City Star*, 8 Jan 1993). She and her husband were both residents of Big Spring, TX, at their deaths.

Child:
i   **Anonymous Box** b & d 7 Aug 1962, Los Angeles, CA.

4.4.7.9.6.1   **MONTEE, Dolly Isabelle** b 8 Feb 1907, Colchester, IL; d there 3 Sep 1907.

4.4.7.9.6.2   **MONTEE, Jewell Kenneth** b 14 Jul 1908, Colchester, IL; d & bur 15 & 18 Nov 1991, Kansas City, MO & Pittsburg, KS. He married 9 Jun 1930, Joplin, MO, **Clara Velma Davis** (Charles H. Davis & Ella Griffith) b 21 Mar 1911, MO; d & bur 28 & 30 Aug 1975, Springfield, MO & Pittsburg, KS.

Kenneth Montee was a surveyor for a mining company in Pittsburg, KS, in 1930 (US census). He moved to Appleton, MO, in 1949 and was a heavy-equipment operator there until his retirement (*Kansas City Star*, 17 Nov 1991). He and his wife were buried in Mount Olive Cemetery in Pittsburg.

4.4.7.9.7.1   **MONTEE, Sarah Frances** b 18 Jan 1907, Girard, KS; d & bur 5 & 7 Dec 1978, Eminence, MO. She married 20 Dec 1930, Arcadia, KS, **George Henry Carroll** (Alfred Edward Carroll & Amanda Ellen York) b 10 Apr 1906, Maple City, KS; d & bur 4 & 6 Sep 1994, Augusta, GA.

George H. Carroll was a real estate and insurance agent. He had moved to Augusta, GA, only four months before his death (*Augusta Chronicle*, 5 Sep 1994).

Child:
i   **James Edwin Carroll** b 15 May 1945, Joplin, MO. He married 1 Jul 1967, Louisville, KY, **Shirley Rohlander** (Fred Rohlander & Lydia Tucker) b there 6 Jul 1943.

4.4.7.9.8.1   **MONTEE, Ruth Duene** b 19 Nov 1901, Pittsburg, KS; d there 22 Mar 1995. She married there 24 Aug 1921 **Edgar Marion Conrad** (Edgar Marion Conrad & Nellie E. Riordan) b there Jan 1899; d there 26 Oct 1943.
Edgar M. Conrad was a civil engineer in Girard, KS, in 1930 (US census).

Children:
i   **Ralph William Conrad** b 17 Sep 1929, Girard, KS. He married 5 Oct 1951 **Kathleen Bradrick** b 20 Aug 1930.
ii   **Edgar Marion Conrad** b 20 Aug 1940, Pittsburg, KS; d there 11 Nov 1989. He married 11 Oct 1961, **Maxine Ray** (Abraham Ray [Abraheem Diabes] & Josephine Thomas) b 1943?; m (2) ____ Emerson.

4.4.7.9.8.2   **MONTEE, Ralph Cyril** b 28 Sep 1903, Pittsburg, KS; d Mar 1975, Tulsa, OK. He married (1) 1926? **Elizabeth Lillian Arndt** (E. Y. Arndt & Margaret Krebs) b 1907?, NE.
He married (2) 16 Nov 1956, Tulsa, OK, **Anna Bernice Dickard** (____ Dickard & Maud B. ____) b 16 Feb 1914, OK; d 12 Apr 1989, Tulsa, OK.
Ralph Cyril Montee was a clerk for an oil and gas company in Independence, KS, on 1 Apr 1930 when he and his 23-year-old wife Elizabeth had been married for four years (US censuses).

Children of the first marriage:
4.4.7.9.8.2.1	Joan Elizabeth	1928-1946-2006
4.4.7.9.8.2.2	Ralph Edward	1932-1953-

4.4.7.9.8.3   **MONTEE, Nadine Theodora** b 6 Dec 1905, Girard, KS; d 31 Mar 1999, St. Petersburg, FL. She married 29 Dec 1933 **F. Dale McClanahan** b 18 Jun 1908, Beatrice, NE; d & bur 26 & 31 May 1973, Albuquerque, NM & Dunedin, FL.
Dale McClanahan was a tobacco salesman in York, NE, in 1930 (US census).

4.4.7.9.8.4   **MONTEE, Theodore Vance** b 17 Jul 1914, Pittsburg, KS. He married 12 Oct 1946, Columbus, KS, **Martha Jeanne Ray** (James R. Ray & Vivian Blair) b 3 Jan 1923, Edna, KS.

4.4.7.9.8.5   **MONTEE, Norris Hadley** b 10 Dec 1919, Pittsburg, KS; d 18 Nov 1943.
Norris H. Montee, US Navy, died in the Pacific during World War II. He was officially declared Missing in Action and was memorialized on 11 Jan 1946 in the ABMC Memorial Cemetery in Honolulu, HI.

4.4.7.9.9.1   **MONTEE, Hazel Marie** b 30 Sep 1900, Pittsburg, KS; d 13 Oct 1990, Laurel, MT. She married (1) 1922?, KS, **Burton Lee Earl Wallace** (Lee Wallace & Etta M. ____) b 6 Sep 1899, KS; d 22 Jun 1935, Billings, MT.
She married (2) 12 May 1950 **Ethelbert Waldo Coombs** (John W. Coombs & Thirza/Thurza E. ____) b 23 Sep 1889, Billings, MT; m (1) 1914? Edna Funk (____ Funk & Ella ____); d 16 Jun 1961, Cascade Co., MT
Hazel Marie Montee was a school teacher in Sheridan Twp, KS, in 1920 while her future husband, Burton Wallace, was a laborer in Arma, KS. In 1930, when they had been married for seven years, he was an electrical engineer in an oil refinery in Laurel, MT (US censuses). The spelling of his name varies. It is Berton in 1910 and 1930 but Burton in 1920 and, perhaps more significantly, in the Montana Death Records. His half-sister Juanita May married William Valentine Montee (4.4.7.9.9.4).
Ethelbert Coombs was a farmer in Hawthorne, MT, in 1920 and 1930 when he and his

first wife, Edna, had been married for sixteen years (US census).

Children:

i **Jacque Earlene Wallace** b 15 Mar 1925, Arma, KS; d 26 Feb 1997, Billings, MT. She married 17 Nov 1945 **Louis Michael Yovetich** (Mike/Michael Yovetich & Angelina ____) b 13 Sep 1922 Butte, MT; d 4 Sep 2002, Laurel, MT.

ii **Montee Earl Wallace** b 8 Apr 1926, Arma, KS; d 17 Nov 1999, Laurel, MT. He married (1) 1946? **Joan Green**.

He married (2) 21 Mar 1954, Laurel, MT, **Donna Jean Sheets** (Glenn A. Sheets & Lena Cook) b 16 May 1932, MT.

4.4.7.9.9.2 **MONTEE, Florence Ætna** b 7 Jun 1902, Chicopee, KS; d & bur 6 & 10 Nov 1975, Fort Scott, KS. She married 8 Apr 1920, KS, **Harry E. Davis** (Bert Wallace Davis & Anna ____) b 1 Feb 1898, IL; d & bur 23 & 25 Jan 1978, Fort Scott, KS.

Harry Davis was a railroad brakeman in Cherokee, KS, in 1930 (US census). He was a World War I Army veteran and was buried with his wife in the Fort Scott, KS, National Cemetery.

Children:

i **Harry Earl Davis** b 2 Jan 1921, Cherokee, KS; d & bur 10 & 12 Oct 1988, ? & Fort Scott, KS. He married 13 Jan 1940, **Irene M. Yaeger** (Betty Ramsey, *Monty-Montee History*, p. 490).

ii **Eldonna Lenore Davis** b 15 Sep 1923, Cherokee, KS; d 25 Aug 2005, Menlo Park, CA. She married **John Nammamoku Napoleon** (____ Napoleon & ____ Keouli) b 14 Jul 1912, HI; d 8 Feb 1982, Santa Clara Co., CA.

iii **Jack Warren Davis** b 7 Oct 1925, Cherokee, KS; d & bur 24 Mar 2003 & 26 Apr 2004, Frontenac & Fort Scott, KS. He married 1946? **Marie Bonnie Dowbenko** b 29 Oct 1921; d & bur 20 & 26 Apr 2004, Frontenac & Fort Scott, KS.

iv **Merle Davis** b Mar 1928, Cherokee, KS.

v **Harold Merle Davis** b 15 Nov 1931, Cherokee, KS. He married 1953? **Emma Lou Ball** b 7 Nov 1931; m (1) Harry George Leslie (Harry M. Leslie & Georgia Ann Flood); d 4 Aug 1993, Clearwater, FL.

4.4.7.9.9.3 **MONTEE, Thelma Faye** b 10 Jun 1904, Pittsburg, KS; d 2 Nov 1962, Billings, MT. She married 25 Aug 1924, Carthage, MO, **James Milton Patterson** (Robert Winfield Patterson & Della Delora Dunlap) b 28 Oct 1902, Trinidad, CO; d 1 Dec 1995, Billings, MT.

James M. Patterson was a mine worker in Sheridan, KS, in 1930 (US census).

Children:

i **Norman D. Patterson** b 16 Jan 1926, Sheridan, KS; d 30 Mar 1984, Billings, MT. He married 10 Jun 1950 **Betty Phillips** (L. Phillips & Gertrude ____) b 15 Jul 1927, Billings, MT; d 27 Apr 2006, Denver, CO.

ii **William R. Patterson** b 29 Dec 1926, Sheridan, KS; d 28 Dec 1987, Billings, MT. He married there 19 Mar 1946 **Marie L. Novasio** (John Novasio & Viola Alexander) b there 10 Nov 1923; d there 3 Aug 1988.

iii **Helen Jeanine Patterson** b 8 Dec 1928, Sheridan, KS; d 5 Apr 1998, Billings, MT. She married there 14 Sep 1963 **Elmer Edwin Weil** (John Weil & Lydia Eckhardt) b 1920?, Billings, MT.

iv **Alice M. Patterson** b 4 Mar 1934; d 27 Dec 1997, Billings, MT. She married there 24 Sep 1957 **Cyril J. Matthias Jr.** b 1931?

4.4.7.9.9.4 **MONTEE, William Valentine** b 27 Sep 1906, Pittsburg, KS; d & bur 25 & 29 Apr 1994, Billings, MT. He married 27 Dec 1925, Neosho, MO, **Juanita Agnes May** (Edward J. May & Etta M. ____) b 1907?, Crawford Co., KS; d & bur 10 & 14 Aug 1971, Havre & Billings, MT, at the age of 64.

William Valentine "Volney" Montee moved from Kansas to Montana shortly after the birth of his first child and was a service attendant in Billings, MT, in 1930 (US census). The family later lived in Havre, MT, though both William V. Montee and his wife were buried in Mountview Cemetery in Billings.

Juanita A. May was a half-sister of Burton Wallace, first husband of Hazel Marie Montee (4.4.7.9.9.1).

Children:

4.4.7.9.9.4.1	Eulalia May	1928-1969-1982
4.4.7.9.9.4.2	Edward	1934- -1934
4.4.7.9.9.4.3	Jean Marie	1935-1954&1967-

4.4.7.9.9.5 **MONTEE, Harold Clifton** b 24 Jun 1908, Pittsburg, KS; d & bur 23 & 26 Nov 1974, Billings, MT. He married (1) there 27 Jul 1931 and divorced there 19 Jul 1949 **Iva Edith Sartin** (Ulysses Grant Sartin & Cynthia Elizabeth Green) b 2 Dec 1912, McCune, KS; d 17 Oct 1991, Girard, KS.

He married (2) 23 Sep 1950, Billings, MT, **Frieda** ____ b 20 Aug 1910; m (1) John Benner; d 12 Dec 1979, Billings, MT.

Harold Montee came to Billings, MT, around 1930 and remained there until the end of his life. He was buried there in Sunset Memorial Gardens (*Billings Gazette*, 25 Nov 1974).

Child of the first marriage:

4.4.7.9.9.5.1	Jo D'Anne	1936- -

4.4.7.9.9.6 **MONTEE, Helen Veneta** b 21 May 1911, Pittsburg, KS; d 8 Jun 2002, Troutdale, OR. She married 29 Mar 1932, Billings, MT, **Wayne Lester Satterlee** (George Z. Satterlee & Nora Stiles) b 23 Dec 1908, NE; d 28 Dec 1989, Portland, OR.

Wayne Satterlee was a resident of Laurel, MT, at his marriage. He and his wife moved to Athena, OR, at some time before 1945 and were still living there when her brother Clyde Montee (4.4.7.9.9.7) died in 1973 (*Billings Gazette*, 19 Sep 1973).

Children:

i   **Norma Joan Satterlee** b 4 Sep 1933. She married 18 Jan 1953, Athena, OR, **John William Greenlee** (W. R. Greenlee & ____ Wilkerson) b 7 May 1931, Alameda Co., CA.

ii   **Belva June Satterlee** b 1 May 1935. She married 15 Aug 1955, Athena, OR, **Arthur P. Haverland** (Verlin A. Haverland & Mary A. ____) b 5 Aug 1930, Milton, OR.

4.4.7.9.9.7 **MONTEE, Clyde Merle** b 10 Dec 1912, Pittsburg, KS; d 18 Sep 1973, Joliet, MT. He married 23 Oct 1933, Hardin, MT, **Effie Ethel Hutchins** (Eddie Lester Hutchins & Hazel Snyder) b 1915?, Wibaux, MT.

Clyde Montee came to Montana from Kansas in 1929. He was a Billings, MT, policeman for 21½ years and a Yellowstone Co., MT, probation officer for 3½ years before retiring and moving to Joliet, MT, in 1967 (*Billings Gazette*, 19 Sep 1973). His widow remained in that town after his death and was still living there when her sister, Mrs. Cecile H. DuBeau, died in early 2005 (*Billings Outpost*, 21 Jan 2005).

Children:

4.4.7.9.9.7.1	Donna Joan	1934-1952-1992
4.4.7.9.9.7.2	Richard Allen	1938-1960-

4.4.7.9.9.8 **MONTEE, Elizabeth Norma** b 6 Dec 1914, Pittsburg, KS; d 16 Feb 2004, Glendale, AZ. She married 10 Oct 1935, Custer, MT, **Leroy Joseph Bromenshenk** (Joseph John Bromenshenk & Margaret Klem) b 11 Aug 1911, Sauk Centre, MN; d & bur 25 & 30 Aug 1999, Billings, MT.

Elizabeth Montee came to Montana with her parents in the late 1920s. She and her husband lived in Billings, MT.

Children:

i   **Gary Allen Bromenshenk** b 20 Dec 1936, Billings, MT; d there 17 Apr 1937.
ii   **Larry Leroy Bromenshenk** b 5 Jan 1939, Billings, MT. He married (1) around 1958 **Nancy Louise Nicholson** (Betty Ramsey, *Monty-Montee History*, p. 493).
     He married (2) 10 Aug 1972, Contra Costa Co., CA, **Sharon Ann Denully** b 1940?

4.4.7.9.9.9   MONTEE, Marguerite Cecile b 7 Jan 1918, Pittsburg, KS; d 1 May 2001, Silverdale, WA. She married 8 Jan 1938 Joliet, MT, **John Iver Garinger** (John Herschel Garinger & Mabel Semb) b 29 Dec 1916, Pigeon Falls, WI; d 13 Aug 1976, Bremerton, WA.
     Marguerite Montee came to Montana with her parents in the late 1920s. She and her husband moved a few years after their marriage to Bremerton, WA, where they raised their family.

Children:

i   **Beverly Kay Garinger** b 11 Sep 1939, Billings, MT. She married 20 Sep 1957, **William M. Prigger** (William M. Prigger & Gladys Mable Bevens) b 18 Jun 1936, WA.
ii   **Sharon Lee Garinger** b 10 Jan 1943, Bremerton, WA. She married (1) 10 Jun 1961 **Richard Fred Voorhees** b 1940; m (2) Marcia J. ____.
     She married (2) **Toby J. Faber** (Roy Faber & Helen I. Stands) b 18 Jun 1947, Rittman, OH.
iii **Linda Lewayne Garinger** b 13 Nov 1947, Bremerton, WA. She married 8 Mar 1968 **James O. Berman** b 12 Sep 1943.

4.4.7.9.9.10   MONTEE, Charles Finley b 17 Jul 1920, Pittsburg, KS; d 30 Dec 1999, Walla Walla, WA. He married (1) 27 Mar 1938, Buffalo, MT, **Ruth Anna Corey** (Floyd Fay Corey & Luella A. Manning) b 7 Apr 1917, Lewiston, MT; m (2) 1979? William James Isaac (William Hiatt Isaac & Pearl Irene Welch); d 26 Oct 2003, Pendleton, OR.
     He married (2) 24 Oct 1962, La Vegas, NV, **Donna Jean Thomas** (Leroy Thomas & Thelma ____) b Sep 1931; m (1) ____ Peterson; m (3) 5 Sep 1981, Reno, NV, William E. Rothrock (Sam Rothrock & Denice ____).
     He married (3) **Louise E. Guenther** b Jun 1932; m (2) 31 Aug 1992, Reno, NV, William Donald Thompson.
     Charles Finley Montee came to Montana as a child with his parents in the late 1920s and lived there with his first wife until they moved to Pendleton, OR, in 1946. He was a realtor there.

Children of the first marriage:

4.4.7.9.9.10.1	Dianna Lee	1939-1958?&	-
4.4.7.9.9.10.2	Charles Roger	1940-1960?-	
4.4.7.9.9.10.3	Michal Faye	1943-1960?-	
4.4.7.9.9.10.4	Jeffrey Wayne	1947-	-
4.4.7.9.9.10.5	Kathleen Lavon	1951-	-

Child of the second marriage:

| 4.4.7.9.9.10.6 | Mark Scott | 1963- | &2001- |

Child of the third marriage:

| 4.4.7.9.9.10.7 | William Robert | 1969- | - |

4.4.7.9.9.11   MONTEE, Bernice Lavon b 2 Feb 1922, Pittsburg, KS; d & bur 23 & 26 Mar 1984, Laurel & Billings, MT. She married 14 Nov 1942, Bremerton, WA, and divorced

29 Mar 1945, Billings, MT, **Kenneth Charles Peters.**

Bernice Lavon (also LaVon) Montee resumed her maiden name after her divorce (*Billings Gazette*, 30 Mar 1945) and was even said to be "Single — Never married" at her death. She was buried in Mountview Cemetery in Billings, MT.

4.4.7.9.9.12   **MONTEE, Richard Wallace** b & d 16 May 1926, Pittsburg, KS.

4.4.7.9.13.1   **MONTEE, Mary Elizabeth** b 7 Aug 1909, Arcadia, KS; d 22 Jan 1999, Sandusky, OH. She married 29 May 1931, Pittsburg, KS, **Albert Lee Opie** (John Howard Opie & Emma Gertrude Horn) b there 16 Jan 1910; d 22 Apr 1984, Sandusky, OH.

Albert L. Opie was a decorator in Sandusky, OH, in 1930 (US census).

Children:

i   **Bill Montee Opie** b 10 Apr 1932, Sandusky, OH. He married (1) 13 Jul 1957, Seneca Falls, NY, and divorced 28 Jul 1978, San Diego, CA, **Mary Louise Knight** b 1 Nov 1935, Seneca Falls, NY; m (2) 7 Jan 1984, San Diego, CA, Sidney Lee Valentine (____ Valentine & ____ Wright).

       He married (2) 12 Aug 1978, San Diego, CA, and divorced there 15 May 1979 **Georgean Smith**, divorced wife of Raymond G. Grammer.

       He married (3) 7 Oct 1983, Las Vegas, NV, **Selma D. Utan** b Apr 1932; m (1) Stanley J. Zarakov (Bernard Zarakov & Sara ____).

ii   **John Mart Opie** b 10 Dec 1936, Sandusky, OH. He married 10 Feb 1962, Pittsburgh, PA, **Susan Aitkenhead** b there 30 May 1935.

iii   **James Frank Opie** b 14 Apr 1939, Sandusky, OH. He married as his second wife, 15 Nov 1970, Oakland, CA, **Patricia Ann Cusic** b 24 Nov 1932, Topeka, KS; m (1) ____ McReynolds; m (3) 1993 Philip Heid (Edward E. Heid & Libbie ____); d 3 Oct 2003, Portland, OR.

       He married (3) 30 Mar 1991, Woodstock, VT, **Mrs. Catherine E. Shuring** b 1935, MI.

4.4.7.9.13.2   **MONTEE, Benjamin Mohon** b 11 Jan 1911, Arcadia, KS; d 15 Jun 1992, Jacksonville, IL. He married (1) 15 Jun 1931, Pittsburg, KS, **Elinor Grace Gibb** (Robert B. Gibb & Ray N. Kirkwood) b there 7 Mar 1911; d 9 Apr 1965, Jacksonville, IL.

He married (2) 19 Nov 1965, Houston, TX, **Eunice May Hammit** b 18 Dec 1907; m (1) ____ Furneau; d Dec 1992, Jacksonville, IL.

Mohon B. Montee was living with his parents in Pittsburg, KS, in 1920 and 1930 (US censuses). He moved to Jacksonville, IL, after his first marriage and became a businessman there, generally known as Benjamin M. Montee.

4.4.7.9.13.3   **MONTEE, Dennis Lee** b 25 Aug 1915, Pittsburg, KS; d 13 Mar 1984, Poway, CA. He married (1) 12 May 1937, Newton, KS, **Mary Catherine Brown** (Louie Emerson Brown & Ida May Amlin) b 22 Jan 1912, Newton, KS; d there Feb 1980.

He married (2) 2 Nov 1968, Liberal, KS, **Wylda Wave Lacy** (Charles W. Lacy & Avis King) b 4 Jul 1918, Concord, KY; m (1) ____ Hall; d 8 May 1992, Hutchinson, KS.

Dennis Lee Montee was a theater owner living near San Diego, CA, at his death. He was buried in Memorial Park Cemetery in Hutchinson, KS (*Hutchinson News*, 15 Mar 1984).

Children of the first marriage:

4.4.7.9.9.13.3.1	Montee Lee	1938-	-
4.4.7.9.9.13.3.2	Patricia Kay	1939-	-

4.4.7.12.1.1   **MONTEE, Nona Myrtle** b 17 Sep 1894, NE; d 28 Dec 1981, Denver, CO. She married 22 May 1917, Liberty, NE, **Roy Gregg Sellon** (Charles Orlando Sellon & Margaret Ellen McNeil) b 8 Mar 1892, Randolph, NE; d 20 Aug 1976, Hugo, CO.

Nona M. Montee was living with her mother in her maternal grandmother's household in Liberty, NE, in 1900 and was still a resident there at her marriage. She then moved to

Hugo, CO, where Roy G. Sellon was a farmer (US censuses). They were both buried, as was their daughter Hazel Irene, in Evergreen Cemetery there.

Children:

i   **Margaret Lucille Sellon** b 16 Jan 1921, Hugo, CO. She married **Ora I. Stogsdill** (Alexander Harden Stogsdill & Sarah Viola Cross) b 20 Mar 1916, Dodge City, KS; d 17 Feb 1997, Longmont, CO.

ii   **Norma Gladys Sellon** b 1924?, Hugo, CO. She married 18 Jul 1945, Denver, CO, **Richard Henry Snell** (Hart Snell & Anna J. Knutson) b 2 Oct 1920, Detroit, MI; d 21 Jun 2000, Machesney Park, IL.

iii   **Hazel Irene Sellon** b 1928, Hugo, CO; d & bur there 1939.

4.4.7.12.1.2   **MONTEE, Earl Lester** b 4 Jul 1896, Gage Co., NE; d & bur 7 & 9 Nov 1960, Portland, OR. He married 22 Apr 1918 **Flo Lovell Crotchett** (John Owen Crotchett & Louisa Jane Zebley) b 23 Nov 1898, Crawford Co., KS; d & bur 19 & 23 Apr 1953, Portland, OR.

Earl Montee was living with his mother in his maternal grandmother's household in Liberty, NE, in 1900. Ten years later he was a member of his father's household in Sheridan Twp, KS. He was a coal mine worker in Pittsburg, KS, in 1920 and an office clerk there in 1930, when he and his wife had been married for twelve years (US censuses). The family later moved to Oregon.

Earl Lester Montee was an Army veteran of World War I and was buried, as were his wife and his adopted son Robert Earl, in Willamette National Cemetery in Portland, OR.

4.4.7.12.1.3   **MONTEE, Wilma Irene** b 30 Jun 1900, Liberty, NE; d there 6 Apr 1901.

This child was buried alongside her mother in the Liberty, NE, Cemetery.

4.4.7.12.1.4   **MONTEE, Francis Evelyn** b 18 Jul 1910, Sheridan, KS; d there Aug 1910.

4.4.7.12.1.5   **MONTEE, Lavaye Amelia** b 6 Sep 1911, Pittsburg, KS; d there 24 Feb 1998. She married (1) 14 Jun 1937, Cook Co., IL, **Ted Hansen**.

She married (2) 23 Jan 1945, Cook Co., IL, **Ottneal/Ottneel Adelman**.

Mrs. Lavaye Adelman lived in Pittsburg, KS, for several years in the 1990s when her daughter Mrs. Sharon Sigmon was in Arma, KS.

Child:

i   **Sharon B. Hansen** b 1 Sep 1938, Chicago, IL. She married around 1957 **Larry Ottfred Sigmon** b 23 Jan 1938, WY.

4.4.7.12.1.6   **MONTEE, Mary E.** b Jun 1915, Crawford Co., KS.

Mary E. Montee was 4 years and 6 months old on 1 Jan 1920 when she was living with her parents in Washington Twp, KS. She was not with them in 1930 (US censuses).

4.4.7.12.1.7   **MONTEE, Lillian Belle** b 11 Aug 1917, Mulberry, KS; d 5 Oct 1991, San Diego Co., CA. She married 13 Feb 1934 **Gordon Keller Sterling** (Arthur L. Sterling & Hattie Pearl Mitcham) b 20 Feb 1912, Freeman, MO; d 13 Mar 1987, El Cajon, CA.

Children:

i   **William Gordon Sterling** b 13 Feb 1937, Pittsburg, KS; d 27 Dec 2000, Yucaipa, CA. He married (1) 3 Jun 1956 and divorced Mar 1973, San Diego, CA, **Nancy Carolyn Anderson** (____ Anderson & ____ Westerfield) b 11 Nov 1938, La Mesa, CA.

He married (2) 20 Oct 1973, National City, CA, **Janice Ann Brown** (____ Brown & ____ Robinson) b 19 Dec 1935, Whittier, CA; m (1) and divorced Aug 1971, San Diego, CA, Jere B. Horsley.

ii   **Nona Mae Sterling** b 23 Dec 1938, Pittsburg, KS. She married 7 Apr 1957, San Diego, CA and divorced there 1 May 1983 **James Albert Oxe** (Carl Oxe & Mabel Nienke) b there 28 Dec 1933; m (2) there 18 Jun 1983 Victoria Baum, divorced wife of Gary Duane Heflin.

iii   **Lillian M. Sterling** b 3 Oct 1940, Pittsburg, KS. She married (1) 23 Jan 1960, San Diego, CA, and divorced there 30 Oct 1984 **Melvin Leroy Dove** b 2 May 1939, Powell, WY.

She married (2) 5 Jan 1985, San Diego, CA, **Donald Gauck** b 1945; m (1) 7 Dec 1968, Los Angeles CA, and divorced there 20 Dec 1979 Linda A. Brown.

iv   **Charles Lloyd Sterling** b 4 Dec 1943, Pittsburg, KS; d 1 Oct 2006, Waynesville, MO. He married (1) 23 Oct 1964, San Diego, CA, and divorced there May 1973 **Sandra Lee Krebs** b 1 May 1946, Pittsburg, KS.

He married (2) 25 Aug 1991, Las Vegas, NV, **Mrs. Grace Ann Smith**.

4.4.7.12.1.8   MONTEE, Angeline Irene b 13 Apr 1926, Breezy Hill, KS. She married (1) 2 May 1944, Pittsburg, KS, **Francis Joseph Meiers** b 23 Nov 1910; d 15 Jun 1998, Mulberry, KS.

She was divorced when she married (2) **Joseph Brown**.

She married (3) 19 Dec 1998, Lakemont, OK, **Clifton Carl Fletcher** (Claude Carl Fletcher & Josephine Pulatie) b 4 July 1925, Sapulpa, OK; m (1) there 15 Dec 1942 Delores Fern Long; d & bur 28 & 31 Mar 2004, Arma, KS & Sapulpa, OK.

Angeline Montee survived her third husband and was living in Arma, KS, at the death of a great-grandchild in 2008 (*Pittsburg Morning Sun*, 30 Mar 2004 and 29 Apr 2008). My information about her family is based mainly on these obituaries as well as on Betty Ramsey's *Monty-Montee History*, p. 519.

Children:
i   **Ethella Meiers** b 1946? She married (1) **James Munger**.
She was divorced when she married (2) ____ **Lloyd**.
She married (3) **Ron Ryburn**.
ii   **Francis Meiers** b 1948?, Pittsburg, KS.
iii   **Edward Meiers** b 1954?, Pittsburg, KS.
iv   **Angelina/Angela Meiers** b 1956? She married (1) **Douglas Scholes**.
She married (2) ____ **Weir**.

4.4.7.12.2.1   MONTEE, Dorothy Lucille b 6 Sep 1911, Pittsburg, KS; d 22 May 1981, Riverside, CA. She married **Daniel Bruce Pease** (Samuel James Pease & Ione K. Griggs) b 21 Aug 1910, Grand Forks, ND; m (2) 2 Oct 1982, Riverside, CA, Dorothy Mae Ruble, widow of Collin William Lovesee; d & bur 6 & 10 Aug 1995, Laguna Hills & Riverside, CA.

Daniel B. Pease had been a resident of Riverside, CA, for thirty-five years before his death. He was buried in Olivewood Cemetery there (*Riverside Press-Enterprise*, 13 Oct 2001).

Child:
i   **Daniel Montee Pease** b 25 Jul 1949, San Diego, CA; d there 1 Aug 1949.

4.4.7.12.3.1   MONTEE, Myrtle b 31 Dec 1894, Chicopee, KS; d 8 Nov 1982, Racine, WI. She married 1918, Adair Co., OK, **John Bell McLemore** (French McLemore & Julia Scott) b 29 Dec 1891, Flint district, Indian Territory (Sand Springs, OK); d 6 Apr 1969, Milwaukee, WI.

John McLemore was a Deputy County Clerk for Adair Co., OK, in 1920 when he was living with his wife Myrtle in Stilwell, OK (US census). I do not know when they left Oklahoma or moved to Wisconsin. Since both their Social Security cards were issued in Kansas before 1951, they probably lived there for a time before moving on to Wisconsin. They were both buried in Graceland Cemetery in Racine, WI.

Children:

i   **John Lewis McLemore** b 18 Mar 1926, OK; d & bur 14 & 15 Jun 1994, Concord, MN. He married (1) **Dorothy Hamilton**.

    He married (2) 7 Feb 1959 **Beatrice Betty Kniefel** (Ben Kniefel & Ella Bredlow) b 20 Oct 1925, Medford, MN; m (1) Howard Baker; d & bur 9 & 11 Nov 1997, Concord, MN.

ii   **Carl French McLemore** b 1934. He married **Ruth E. Ricker** b 23 Oct 1936 Allentown, PA; d & bur 18 & 21 Sep 2007, Fort Wayne, IN.

4.4.7.12.3.2   **MONTEE, Blanche** b 1 Jan 1896, Crawford Co., KS; d there 21 Jun 1898.

4.4.7.12.3.3   **MONTEE, Earl Merle** b 21 Feb 1899, Chicopee, KS; d & bur 16 & 18 Apr 1969, Pittsburg, KS. He married there 4 Oct 1919 **Goldie Mae Palmer** (Arthur E. Palmer & Lilly Maude Alderson) b 4 May 1900, Girard, KS.

Earl Montee was a mine worker in Sheridan Twp, KS, in 1920 and in Pittsburg, KS, in 1930 (US censuses).

Child:

4.4.7.12.3.3.1	Eugene Earl	1924-1948-

4.4.7.12.3.4   **MONTEE, Archie** b 21 Apr 1901, Crawford Co., KS; d 21 May 1965, Pittsburg, KS. He married 1922? **Anna Hiller** (John Hiller & Genevieve ____) b 8 Sep 1898, Crawford Co., KS; d 10 May 1986, Shawnee Mission, KS.

Archie Montee was a coal miner in Cherokee, KS, in 1920 and a farmer in Sheridan Twp, KS, in 1930 when he and his wife had been married for eight years (US censuses). They were of Pittsburg, KS, when their son married in 1954 (*Joplin Globe*, 12 Sep 1954).

Child:

4.4.7.12.3.4.1	Archie Dean	1929-1954-

4.4.7.12.3.5   **MONTEE, Riley Finley** b 29 Jun 1903, Pittsburg, KS; d & bur 27 & 30 Oct 1958, Parsons, KS. He married (1) 1923? **Kathryn Alexine/Katie A. Sparks** (John Wesley Sparks & Freda Raisor) b 29 Oct 1902, Fleming, KS; d 2 Jan 1989.

He was divorced when he married (2) 5 May 1945, Oswego, KS, **Margaret E. Addis** (Jesse D. Addis & Faye Margaret Ullery) b 19 Jun 1914, Parsons, KS; m (1) and divorced Joseph Pierce ; m (3) 9 Jul 1975 Argus L. Baker (William Marshall Baker & Cora Ring); d & bur 10 & 13 May 2005, Parsons, KS.

Riley Montee was a laborer on his father's farm in Cherokee, KS, in 1920 and a farmer in Ross Twp, KS, in 1930 when he and his wife Kathryn had been married for seven years (US censuses). I have not found her death record. She was a resident of Parsons, KS, at her death according to the Social Security Death Index. Louise Monty states however that she died in Cheyenne, Wyoming (*Généalogie de la famille Monty*, III, 157).

Children of the first marriage:

4.4.7.12.3.5.1	Cathern/Kathryn/Catherine	1924-	&	-1971	
4.4.7.12.3.5.2	Meril Finley	1926-1947-			
4.4.7.12.3.5.3	Mildred N.	1929-	&	&	-2001
4.4.7.12.3.5.4	Marvin Wesley	1935-1963-2001			

Children of the second marriage:

4.4.7.12.3.5.5	Margaret Gay	1947-	-
4.4.7.12.3.5.6	Robert	1948-1967-	

4.4.7.12.3.6   **MONTEE, Rolla Ray** b 17 Aug 1905, Pittsburg, KS; d 11 Oct 1994, Sterling, IL. He married 23 Aug 1924, Girard, KS, **Maurine Alta Hoffman** (Rolla Samuel Hoffman & Alice Elizabeth Norris) b 26 Jul 1907, Cherokee, KS; d Feb 1996, Whiteside Co., IL.

Children:

4.4.7.12.3.6.1	Cleda Marjorie	1928-1946-2003
4.4.7.12.3.6.2	Rolla Melvin	1932-1955-
4.4.7.12.3.6.3	Lawrence Ray	1936- -1946

4.4.7.12.3.7   **MONTEE, Carl Robert** b 22 Aug 1907, Pittsburg, KS; d there Feb 1982. He married 15 Feb 1930 **Lova Jessie Sneed** (William H. Sneed & Addie Lucinda McKinney) b 8 Aug 1907, Clay Twp, MO; d 17 Feb 2000, Afton, OK.

Carl Montee and his first cousin Montee Clinton Everitt, son of Charles Everitt and Rosa May Montee (4.4.7.12.6), married twin sisters.

Child:

4.4.7.12.3.7.1	Carolyn J.	1937- & -

4.4.7.12.3.8   **MONTEE, Fern R.** b 10 Jun 1910, Crawford Co., KS; d 6 Jun 2001, Sturtevant, WI. She married 1929?, Girard, KS, **John Joseph Parr** (Albert Parr & Josephine Schirmer) b 6 Feb 1908, Crawford Co., KS.

John Parr and his wife had been married for less than a year in April 1930, when he was a coal miner in Washington Twp, KS (US census). He moved to Racine, WI, before the birth of the twins (iii) and (iv) in 1946.

Children:

i   **Robert J. Parr** b 2 Dec 1931, Arma, KS; d 28 Dec 2007, Racine, WI. He married 1951? **Joyce M. Anderson** b 12 Nov 1931.

ii   **Shirley June Parr** b 13 Oct 1935, Arma, KS; d & bur 10 & 13 Nov 1998, Racine, WI. She married there 6 Jun 1952 (?) **Fred H. Larsen** b there 25 Mar 1931; d there 2 Aug 2006.

iii **John Allen Parr** (twin) b 28 Mar 1946, Racine, WI. He married there 18 Jun 1966 **Bernadette C. Degrand** (Herbert Degrand & Agnes ____) b 18 Oct 1947, Racine, WI.

iv   **Joanne A. Parr** (twin) b 28 Mar 1946, Racine, WI. She married 25 Jun 1966, Augusta, GA, **Bernard N. Klinkhammer** (Bernard J. Klinkhammer & Helen Mae Delray) b 13 Dec 1945, Racine, WI.

v   **Kathryn M. Parr** b 23 Dec 1947, Racine, WI. She married **Harry E. Boxler** b 23 Aug 1945; d 16 Nov 2003, Sturtevant, WI.

4.4.7.12.3.9   **MONTEE, Louis Glen** b 26 Sep 1912, Pittsburg, KS; d 18 Jun 1973, Racine, WI. He married 12 Apr 1935, Girard, KS, **Climena Greer** (Frank Greer & Bessie ____) b 11 Oct 1915, Monmouth, KS.

Louis Glen Montee and his family moved in the 1940s to Racine, WI, where his widow continued to reside after his death. He was buried in Graceland Cemetery there.

Children:

4.4.7.12.3.9.1	Jack L.	1936-1957-
4.4.7.12.3.9.2	Danny Lee	1945-1964& -

4.4.7.12.3.10   **MONTEE, Alice** b 2 Mar 1916, Pittsburg, KS. She married **Leroy Taylor**.

I know of this woman's marriage and children only through Betty Ramsey, *Monty-Montee History*, pp. 531-532.

Children:

i   **William Taylor** b 1938?; d 1978. He married (1) **Marcia ____**.
     He was divorced when he married (2) **Mrs. Eleanor Miller**.

ii   **Patricia Taylor** married **John Lizotte**.

4.4.7.12.3.11   **MONTEE, Woodrow Wilson** b 13 Jun 1918, Fleming, KS; d & bur 7 & 13 Jul 2002, Parsons & McCune, KS. He married (1) 19 Nov 1939, Uniontown, KS, **Dorothy Marie Kirk** (Charles E. Kirk & Katie A. ____) b 19 Dec 1917, Cherokee, KS; d 1967.

    He married (2) 1970 **Mrs. Bessie Miller** b 5 Jan 1910; d Aug 1981, Cherryvale, KS.

    Woodrow Montee was buried in the family plot in the McCune, KS, Cemetery (*Parsons Sun*, 18 Jul 2002).

Children of the first marriage:

4.4.7.12.3.11.1	Kathleen Marie	1940-1962-
4.4.7.12.3.11.2	Jacqueline	1942-1964-
4.4.7.12.3.11.3	Connie Jo	1944-1964-
4.4.7.12.3.11.4	Larry Dean	1949- -

4.4.7.12.7.1   **MONTEE, William Clois** b 22 May 1903, Pittsburg, KS; d 31 Dec 1984, Arcadia, KS. He married 30 Jun 1923 **Myrtle M. Gilbert** (Charles E. Gilbert & Frances G. Schrag) b 25 Jul 1905, Pittsburg, KS; d 23 Apr 1996, Arcadia, KS.

    William Montee was a coal miner in Washington Twp, KS, in 1930 (US census). Both he and his wife were buried in the Old Arcadia/Forrest Hill Cemetery in Crawford Co., KS.

Children:

4.4.7.12.7.1.1	William Gerald	1924-1946-1998
4.4.7.12.7.1.2	Delbert Dean	1926-1947?& -2002
4.4.7.12.7.1.3	Eldon Lee	1929-1948-1995
4.4.7.12.7.1.4	Marilyn J.	1933-1948?&1971?-

4.4.7.12.7.2   **MONTEE, Anna Mae** b 5 Sep 1905, Pittsburg, KS. She married 19 Jun 1939, Alta Vista, KS, **Harold Lyman Walters** (Delbert Joshua Walters & Belle O'Neal) b 13 Aug 1908, Rosalia, KS; d 9 Apr 2008, Harrisonville, MO.

    Harold L. Walters was only a few months old when his parents moved to Nebraska. He was a farm laborer in Lake, KS, though, in 1930 (US censuses) and bought a farm in Drexel, MO, a few years after his marriage. He was a grain and cattle farmer there until he retired and moved with his wife in 1981 to nearby Harrisonville, MO. He was buried in the Freeman, MO, Cemetery. Anna Mae Montee survived her husband (*Democrat Missourian*, Harrisonville, MO, 18 Apr 2008).

Child:

i   **Beverly Jean Walters** b 27 Aug 1943, Drexel, MO. She married 1961? **John O. Mabary** b 31 Dec 1939.

4.4.7.12.7.3   **MONTEE, Ora George** b 18 Jul 1907, Pittsburg, KS; d 18 Mar 2003, Meridian, ID. He married 31 Dec 1926 **Marcella Erwin** (William David Erwin & Arma Laura ____) b 30 Mar 1909, ID; d 3 Jul 1994, Meridian, ID.

    Ora Montee was a farmer in Mulberry, KS, in 1930 (US census). He moved to Idaho in the late 1930s and was a carpenter there. He and his wife were buried in Greenwood Cemetery in Kellogg, ID.

Children:

4.4.7.12.7.3.1	Marcella Lee	1927- & -
4.4.7.12.7.3.2	Lois Earlene	1929-1948?-
4.4.7.12.7.3.3	Shirley	1931- & & & -
4.4.7.12.7.3.4	Glenda	1933-1951?& -
4.4.7.12.7.3.5	Roberta Jane/Jean (twin)	1936- -1942
4.4.7.12.7.3.6	Robert Dean (twin)	1936- -
4.4.7.12.7.3.7	Anetta	1940-1975-
4.4.7.12.7.3.8	Kenneth Dale	1943-1964-
4.4.7.12.7.3.9	Merlene L.	1948-1970&1975-2003

4.4.7.12.7.4   MONTEE, James Stephen b 24 Feb 1910, Pittsburg, KS; d 2 May 1997, Joplin, MO. He married 31 Oct 1928, KS, **Mary Sikule** (Michael Sikule & Mary/Marie Lenassi) b 11 Nov 1910, Crawford Co., KS; d 24 Sep 1985, Albany, NY.

James S. Montee worked for most of his life in New York State, in Brooklyn, and later in Albany, NY. He had been living with his brother Edward (4.4.7.12.7.7) in Granby, MO, for a while prior to his death but was buried in the Medusa, NY, Cemetery, near his former residence (*Albany Times-Union*, 6 May 1997).

Children:

4.4.7.12.7.4.1	James William	1930-1957-1999
4.4.7.12.7.4.2	George Steven	1931-1955-
4.4.7.12.7.4.3	Charles Cloyse	1933- -1934
4.4.7.12.7.4.4	John Stephen	1949-1968-

4.4.7.12.7.5   MONTEE, George Henry b 5 Aug 1917, Mulberry, KS; d 7 Sep 1986, Post Falls, ID. He married 5 Apr 1938, Girard, KS, **Elizabeth Myrtle Sanders** (William Thomas Sanders & Lillian Rickey) b 22 Oct 1920, Pittsburg, KS; m (2) 1991? Rolland S. Beeson (Marion L. Beeson & Eloise H. Fueller); d & bur 15 & 25 Jan 2008, Yuma, AZ & Post Falls, ID.

George Montee and his wife moved to Shoshone Co., ID, soon after the birth of their first child and then to a farm in Kootenai Co., ID, in 1950. Elizabeth (also Betty) Sanders remained there after his death and had been married to her second husband for sixteen years when she died. All seven of her children survived her (*Coeur d'Alene Press*, 20 Jan 2008).

Children:

4.4.7.12.7.5.1	Sandra Louise	1938-1957-
4.4.7.12.7.5.2	David Henry	1941-1963& -
4.4.7.12.7.5.3	Evelyn Irene	1943-1963-
4.4.7.12.7.5.4	Raymond Cloyse	1944-1964-
4.4.7.12.7.5.5	John Thomas	1946- -
4.4.7.12.7.5.6	Dorothy Ann	1948-1967&1974-
4.4.7.12.7.5.7	Carolyn Sue	1950-1967-

4.4.7.12.7.6   MONTEE, Emilene Marie b & d 1921, Mulberry, KS.
I know of this child only through Betty Ramsey, *Monty-Montee History*, p. 570.

4.4.7.12.7.7   MONTEE, Edward Glen b 23 Dec 1922, Mulberry, KS; d & bur 4 & 8 Aug 2001, Arcadia & Pittsburg, KS. He married (1) 27 Nov 1943, Kansas City, KS, **Anna Martha Kincaid** (Preston K. Kincaid & Katherine/Katie M. Hawkins) b 19 Dec 1924, Weston, MO; d & bur 17 & 21 Sep 1999, Granby, MO & Pittsburg, KS.

He married (2) 2 Jan 2000, Liberal, MO, **Lois Lucille Warden** (Charles Clayton Warden & Ida Belle Sallee) b 3 Aug 1928, Fort Knox, KS; m (1) 5 Oct 1946, William Gerald Montee (4.4.7.12.7.1.1), Edward G. Montee's nephew.

Edward G. Montee and his first wife lived in Kansas City, KS, before his retirement in 1979. They were both buried in Mount Olive Cemetery in Pittsburg, KS (*Kansas City Star*, 20 Sep 1999 and 5 Aug 2001).

Children of the first marriage:

4.4.7.12.7.7.1	Janet S.	1948-1968-
4.4.7.12.7.7.2	Elaine	1956-1976-

4.4.7.12.10.1   MONTEE, Reba A. b 10 Aug 1909, Chicopee, KS; d & bur 18 & 21 Dec 1984, Worth, IL & Girard, KS. She married **Joseph A. Zordani** (Joseph [Yosef] Zordani & Josie ____) b 22 Mar 1908, Crawford Co., KS; d & bur 18 & 21 Feb 1977, Algonquin & Dundee, IL.

Reba Montee was buried in the Girard, KS, Cemetery while her husband was buried in River Valley Memorial Gardens in Dundee, IL. I know little about this couple and their children beyond what is found in Joseph and Reba Zordani's obituaries in the *Chicago Tribune* of 20 Feb 1977 and 12 Dec 1984.

Children:

i   **Betty Jean Zordani** married **Gary Francis** b 3 Feb 1943; d Nov 1977, IL.
ii **Carolyn Zordani** married **John P. Gilmore, Jr.**
iii **David Zordani** married (1) **Janet** ____.
    He married (2) **Karen** ____.
iv **Joseph Albert Zordani** b 2 Dec 1942, Chicago, IL; d 10 Nov 1962, NJ.

4.4.7.12.10.2   MONTEE, Ruth Evelyn b 4 Jul 1910, Chicopee, KS; d Nov 1974, Merrionette Park, IL. She married Nov 1930, Chicago, IL, **George Basile** b 7 Jun 1904, Newcastle, PA; d Sep 1971, Merrionette Park, IL.

George Basile was an engineer for International Harvester in Chicago, IL, when he and his wife celebrated their twenty-fifth wedding anniversary in November 1955. Their two children were also living in that city (*Suburban Economist*, Chicago, IL, 30 Nov 1955).

Children:

i   **Georgia May Basile** b 2 Jul 1936, Chicago, IL; d 22 May 2000, Hickory Hills, IL. She married ____ **Winkler**.
ii **David Carl Basile**.

4.4.7.12.10.3   MONTEE, David A. b 29 Jan 1922, Breezy Hill, KS; d & bur 28 & 31 Aug 1961, Chicago & Evergreen Park, IL. He married 3 Jun 1943, Cook Co., IL, **Catherine V. Fahey** (Michael Fahey & Nora ____) b 4 Sep 1918; d & bur 8 & 10 Oct 2002, Orland Park & Evergreen Park, IL.

David Montee and his wife were buried in St. Mary's Cemetery in Evergreen Park, IL (*Chicago Tribune*, 29 Aug 1961 and 9 Oct 2002).

Child:
4.4.7.12.10.3.1   David Byron   1945-1966-

4.8.5.2.1.1   MONTY, Joyce Shirley b 5 Jul 1919, Plattsburgh, NY; d 3 Apr 2006, Towson, MD. She married 26 Apr 1944, Boston, MA, **James Thomas Smith** b Apr 1917.

James Thomas Smith was of Laramie, WY, at his marriage (*Plattsburgh Press Republican*, 2 May 1944). Joyce Monty was for many years a teacher in the Baltimore, MD, City and County School Districts. She was buried however in Plattsburgh, NY (*Baltimore Sun*, 21 May 2006).

4.8.5.2.1.2   MONTY, Doris Muriel b 16 May 1921, Beekmantown, NY; d 21 Oct 2006, Burlington, VT. She married 23 Oct 1948, North Caldwell, NJ, **Robert Ambrose Lyon** (Charles A. Lyon & Alice Slimm) b 16 Apr 1924, Nyack, NY; d 28 Jan 1982, Plattsburgh, NY.

Robert A. Lyon was an attorney in Plattsburgh, NY. He was buried in the city's Riverside Cemetery (*Plattsburgh Press Republican*, 29 Jan 1982).

Children:

i   **Sandra Joyce Lyon** b 7 Mar 1951, Glen Ridge, NJ. She married 19 Jun 1971, Plattsburgh, NY, **Charles Henry Moore** (Charles Henry Moore & Veronica Deloria) b there 27 May 1951.
ii **Mark Robert Lyon** b 3 Sep 1953, Nyack, NY.
iii **Paul Stephen Lyon** b 29 Oct 1955, Plattsburgh, NY.
iv **Darlene Lynn Lyon** b 19 May 1958, Plattsburgh, NY.

4.8.5.2.1.3   **MONTY, Edward Oreon** b 11 Apr 1927, Beekmantown, NY; d & bur 30 Mar & 2 Apr 1975, Plattsburgh, NY. He married 23 Apr 1947 **Betty Jean Levitt** (Cecil Patrick Levitt & Cecelia Charland) b 23 Jun 1927, Saranac Lake, NY; d & bur 22 & 27 Oct 2006, Plattsburgh, NY.

Edward O. Monty and his wife were buried in Riverside Cemetery in Plattsburgh, NY (*Plattsburgh Press Republican*, 31 Mar 1975 and 24 Oct 2006).

Children:

4.8.5.2.1.3.1	Denice Ann	1952-1976-
4.8.5.2.1.3.2	Edward Cecil	1954- -
4.8.5.2.1.3.3	James Carl	1957-1981-
4.8.5.2.1.3.4	Michael	- -

4.10.6.2.2.1   **MONTY, Cecil Joseph** b & bp 14 & 20 Mar 1904, Altona, NY; d & bur there 26 & 29 Nov 1950. He married 13 Oct 1928 **Katherine Judd** (George Morton Judd & Cornelia Martin) b 6 Nov 1897, Wallingford, CT; d 26 Mar 1969, Mooers Forks, NY.

Cecil Monty and his wife were buried in Holy Angels Cemetery in Altona, NY (*Plattsburgh Press Republican*, 27 Nov 1950; *Adirondack Enterprise*, Saranac Lake, NY, 26 Mar 1969).

Children:

4.10.6.2.2.1.1	Mary Lou	1929?-1967-
4.10.6.2.2.1.2	Morton Joseph	1931-1953-1994
4.10.6.2.2.1.3	Julie Ann	1934-1954-

4.10.6.2.2.2   **MONTY, John Frederick** b & bp 22 Mar & 1 Apr 1907, Altona, NY; d & bur there 14 & 17 Jun 1977. He married there 20 Feb 1927 **Alice D. Goodman** (Adolph Goodman & Anna Goodrow) b 25 Feb 1903, Malone, NY; d & bur 11 & 14 Jun 1988, Plattsburgh & Altona, NY.

John Monty (Frederick John at his baptism) was a garage mechanic in Altona NY, in 1930 (US census). He was also a construction engineer there for over thirty years as well as the town's first fire chief. He and his wife were buried there in Holy Angels Cemetery (*Plattsburgh Press Republican*, 15 Jun 1977 and 12 & 15 Jun 1988).

Children:

4.10.6.2.2.2.1	Ramona	1928-1953-1997
4.10.6.2.2.2.2	John F.	1933-1954-

4.10.6.2.6.1   **MONTY, James Willard** b & bp 6 & 18 Jul 1915, Altona, NY; d 19 Dec 1989, Saranac Lake, NY. He married 1946? **Gladys E. Wood** (James Wood & Louise Brown) b 17 Oct 1908, Harrietstown, NY; d & bur 10 & 14 May 1990, Saranac Lake & Plattsburgh, NY.

James W. Monty enlisted in the US Army in Fairfield, CT, in 1942 and stayed in the Army for several years after World War II while his wife lived, after 1945, in his mother's household in Danbury, CT. He and his wife moved to Saranac Lake, NY, in 1951 (Danbury City Directories) and were residents there when they died. They were both buried in the Whispering Maples Memorial Gardens Mausoleum in Plattsburgh, NY (*Plattsburgh Press Republican*, 21 Dec 1989 and 14 May 1990).

4.10.6.2.6.2   **MONTY, Mildred Lona** 1916?, Altona, NY.

Mildred Monty was a 3-year-old child living with her parents in Altona, NY, on 1 Jan 1920 and with her widowed mother in Saranac Lake, NY, in 1930 (US censuses). She moved with her family to Danbury, CT, in the early 1940s and was henceforth known as Lona M. Monty. She was a member of her mother's household there until 1950 and of her brother Thomas' through at least 1953 (City Directories).

4.10.6.2.6.3   MONTY, Thomas Gaylord b 25 Oct 1917, Altona, NY; d 3 Sep 1973, East Hartford, CT.

Thomas G. Monty was living with his widowed mother in Saranac Lake, NY, in 1930 (US census). He moved with his family in the early 1940s to Danbury, CT, where he was a trucker (City Directories). He did not marry.

4.10.6.2.6.4   MONTY, Melvin E. b 28 Mar 1920, Altona, NY; d & bur 3 & 5 Sep 1980, Albany & Altona, NY.

Melvin Monty was living with his widowed mother in Saranac Lake, NY, in 1930 (US census). He enlisted in the Coast Artillery Corps in Albany, NY, on 13 Aug 1940 and was still in the Army in 1945 when he was listed as a member of his mother's household in Danbury, CT. He continued to live there until at least 1951 (City Directories). He died in the Veteran's Hospital in Albany, NY, and was buried in Holy Angels Cemetery in Altona, NY (*Plattsburgh Press Republican*, 4 Sep 1980).

4.10.6.2.7.1   MONTY, Orville James b 9 Mar 1921, Altona, NY; d & bur 17 & 19 Jan 1987, Burlington & Colchester, VT. He married 1 Aug 1943, Plattsburgh, NY, **Gertrude Ducharme** (George Ducharme & Daisy Wood) b 22 Apr 1919, Springfield, MA; m (2) 1 Aug 1992, Morrisonville, NY, Myron E. Lowe (Myron Lowe & Martha Krebs); d 18 May 1997, Margate, FL.

Orville Monty was a teacher in Altona, NY, the manager of several stores, and an agent of the Metropolitan Life Insurance Company in Plattsburgh, NY, after 1951. He had retired and was a resident of Coral Springs when he died on a visit to his son Robert in Colchester, VT. He was buried in the Colchester Village Cemetery (*Plattsburgh Press Republican*, 19 Jan 1987).

Gertrude Ducharme was a teacher in Altona, Long Island, and Plattsburgh, NY, until 1976 when she retired. Her second husband was also a retired educator (*Plattsburgh Press Republican*, 13 Sep 1992). She apparently did not change her surname after second marriage: both the Florida Death Index and the Social Security Death Index refer to her as Gertrude Monty. She was buried with her first husband in the Colchester Village Cemetery.

Children:

4.10.6.2.7.1.1	Robert James	1944-1965-
4.10.6.2.7.1.2	Michael George	1950-1971-

4.10.6.2.7.2   MONTY, Dorothy b Oct 1926, Altona, NY. She married **Robert P. Horne** (Lucien C. Horne & Euphemia Purcell) b 17 Jun 1915, Skaneateles, NY; d there Oct 1975.

Dorothy Monty was 3 years and 6 months old on 1 Apr 1930 (US census, Altona, NY). She lived with her husband Dr. Robert Horne in Skaneateles, NY, and was still residing there when a half-brother, Bennet W. Dame, died in 2005 (*Plattsburgh Press Republican*, 17 Oct 2005).

Children:

i   **Margaret Horne**
ii   **Bennet R. Horne** b 1963, NY.

4.10.6.2.7.3   MONTY, Elizabeth Ann b Oct 1931, Altona, NY. She married **Anthony Julio Gugliotta** (Salvatore Gugliotta & Dorothea/Carmela Lopresti) b May 1929, Whitehall, NY.

Anthony Gugliotta was 11 months old on 1 Apr 1930 when he was living with his parents in Whitehall, NY. He and his wife were in College Park, MD, at the birth of their first child in 1952, in Texas at the birth of their second in 1955, and in California when the two youngest children were born in 1963 and 1967. He and his wife were residents of Tucson, AZ, when his brother-in-law Orville Monty died in 1987 and were still living there when their son Andrew died in 2007 (*Plattsburgh Press Republican*, 19 Jan 1987; *Arizona Daily Star*, Tucson, AZ, 21 Nov 2007).

Children:
i   **Anthony Phillip Gugliotta** b 17 Feb 1952, Cheverly, MD; d Jul 1987.
ii   **Timothy Joseph Gugliotta** b 28 Nov 1955, Grayson Co., TX. He married **Wendy** ___ b 1960.
iii   **Andrew Michael Gugliotta** b 9 Jan 1961; d 14 Nov 2007, Tucson, AZ. He married **Robin Jean Pugh** (James Lane Pugh & Shelba J. Wirt) b 1958.
iv   **Ann Marie Gugliotta**
v   **Catherine E. Gugliotta** b 3 Oct 1963, Los Angeles Co., CA.
vi   **Jeannette Gugliotta** b & d 1 Dec 1967, Los Angeles Co., CA.

4.10.6.12.1.1   **MONTY, Edward** b Jul 1918, NY.
     Edward Monty was living on 1 Jan 1920 in his paternal grandmother's household in Plattsburgh, NY (US. census).

4.10.6.12.1.2   **MONTY, Francis Leroy** (twin) b Oct 1919, Plattsburgh, NY; d there 13 Jan 1920.
     Francis Leroy Monty was buried in St. Peter's Cemetery in Plattsburgh, NY (*Plattsburgh Sentinel*, 16 Jan 1920).

4.10.6.12.1.3   **MONTY, Arthur L.** (twin) b Oct 1919, Plattsburgh, NY.
     Arthur L. Monty was living on 1 Jan 1920 in his paternal grandmother's household in Plattsburgh, NY (US. census).

4.10.6.9.2.1   **MONTY, Robert W.** b 25 Aug 1913, Hartford, CT; d there 23 Jan 1994. He married **Mary Brechin** (Charles Brechin & Margaret R. ____) b 1 Feb 1914, Pittsfield, MA; d 31 Jul 1992, Hartford, CT.

Children:
4.10.6.9.2.1.1	Robert Ross	1941-	-2004
4.10.6.9.2.1.2	Diane		-1966-

4.10.6.9.2.2   **MONTY, Dorothy** b 1915?, Hartford, CT.
     Dorothy Monty was a 4-year-old child living with her parents in Hartford, CT, on 1 Jan 1920. She was also living there with her mother in 1930 (US censuses).

4.11.1.1.1.1   **MONTY, Lulu/Lulla** b Sep 1888, MN; d 22 Sep 1953, Council Bluffs, IA. She married 1911? **Charles Alexander Rockwitz** (Albert C. Rockwitz & Mary O'Connor) b 24 Sep 1887, Council Bluffs, IA; d there 1941.
     Lulla Monty was living with her parents in Austin, MN, in 1900 and moved with them to Council Bluffs, IA, in 1907. As a married woman her name was commonly Lulu. She and her husband, a candy maker in Council Bluffs, had been married for nineteen years in 1930 (US censuses). He predeceased her by twelve years according to her obituary in the *Wright County Monitor* (Clarion, IA) of 1 Oct 1953.

Child:
i   **Una Lucille Rockwitz** b Oct 1915, Council Bluffs, IA.

4.11.1.1.1.2   **MONTY, Francis/Frank D.** b 5 Jun 1898, MN; d 18 Apr 1923, Council Bluffs, IA.
     Francis D. Monty was a salesman for an insurance company in Council Bluffs, IA, in 1920 (US census). He was buried there alongside his father and mother in St. Joseph's Cemetery.

4.11.1.1.3.1   **MONTY, Mabel** b 23 Feb 1890, IA; d 11 Aug 1977, Hayward, WI. She married 23 Feb 1909, Postville, IA, **Henry Frye** (William Frye & Mary Frances Segrest) b 28

Sep 1883, Clayton Co., IA; d Sep 1971, Hayward, WI.

Mabel Monty came to Wisconsin as a child and was living with her mother and stepfather in Hayward, WI, in 1900. She and her husband were in Postville, IA, in 1910, in Franklin, IA, in 1920 and 1925, and in Hayward, WI, in 1930 (US and state censuses).

Henry Frye was a farmer. He was born in Clayton Co., IA according to the 1885 and 1895 state censuses, and probably in Monona, IA, where his father was a farmer in 1885.

Children:

i   **Margarite Frye** b 17 Jul 1910, Postville, IA; d & bur there 26 & 28 Oct 1910.

ii   **Harold Henry Frye** b 9 Jan 1912, Postville, IA; d 12 Sep 2005, Hayward, WI. He married **Vivian I. Wood** (Byron C. Wood & Maud McGuiness) b 2 Feb 1912, Vail, OR; m (2) 23 Jul 1958, Pine Co., MN, Edwin M. Johnson; d 3 May 1991.

iii   **Mildred S. Frye** b 30 Aug 1913, IA; d 23 Jan 2003, Springfield, MO. She married **B. H. Marsh** b 3 Jan 1910; d 13 Mar 2003, Springfield, MO.

iv   **Clara Frye** b 1915?, IA; d 10 Mar 1955, Hayward, WI. She married **Emil Salzman** b 1913?; d 10 Mar 1955, Hayward, WI.

v   **Darrell E. Frye** b 1920, Franklin, IA; d World War II.

vi   **Wayne W. Frye** b 14 Dec 1923, IA; d 12 May 1999, Mesa, AZ. He married **Mary L. ____**.

vii   **Norma Jean Frye** b 20 May 1927, Hayward, WI; d Jan 1987, Springfield, MO. She married ____ **Ray**.

viii   **Everett Lee Frye** b 29 Dec 1928, Hayward, WI; d there Dec 1978.

ix   **Clifford D. Frye** b 12 Jan 1934, Hayward, WI. He married **Donna M. ____** b 29 Mar 1936.

x   **Roger Leon Frye** b 21 Jun 1936, Hayward, WI; d there 15 Dec 2005. He married 18 Apr 1957 **Shirley J. Lauterbach** b 1 Sep 1938.

4.11.1.1.3.2   MONTY, Orpha b 8 Dec 1894, IA; d 19 Dec 1968, Minneapolis, MN. She married 21 Jan 1911, Hayward, WI, **Adolph Barnhard Williams** (Ben Williams & Hannah ____) b there 29 Mar 1885; d 3 Jul 1950, St. Louis Co., MN.

Adolph B. Williams was an electrician in Hayward, WI, in 1910, an automobile dealer there when he signed on 12 Sep 1918 his World War I Draft Registration card, a garage owner there in 1920, and an oil dealer there in 1930 (US censuses). He and his wife were married there in the First Congregational Church and several of their children were baptized there. Unfortunately the baptismal records seldom indicate the child's date of birth.

Children:

i   **Eleana Lorraine Williams** b 1911? (bp 24 Sep 1911), Hayward, WI.

ii   **Helen Mildred Williams** b 1913? (bp 10 May 1914), Hayward, WI.

iii   **Benford Wilcher Williams** b 12 Apr 1915 (bp 30 Jun 1916), Hayward, WI; d May 1975, Mandan, ND.

iv   **Marion Rebecca Williams** b 1917? (bp 3 Oct 1920), Hayward, WI.

v   **Robert Louis Williams** b 10 Aug 1919, Hayward, WI; d 24 Jan 1960, Minneapolis, MN.

vi   **Shirley Mae Williams** b 1920 (bp 3 Oct 1920), Hayward, WI.

vii   **Donald Edgar Williams** b 12 May 1921, Hayward, WI; d 12 Nov 1996, Durand, WI.

viii   **Lester L. Williams** b 1923?, Hayward, WI.

4.11.1.1.3.3   MONTY, Leon Dudley b 17 Jul 1896, Minneapolis, MN; d 16 Dec 1975, Tucson, AZ. He married 17 Jul 1920, MA, **Josephine Isabelle Moulison** (Freeman Moulison & Eliza/Marie Doucette) b 7 Nov 1901, Nova Scotia, Canada; d 28 Jul 1995, Phoenix, AZ.

Leon Monty was living with his mother and stepfather in Hayward, WI, in 1900 and in Lenroot, MN, in 1910. In 1920 however he was a sailor stationed at the Charlestown Navy Yard in Boston MA. He remained in the East after his marriage and although he was a chauffeur in Swampscott, MA, in 1930 (US censuses), several ship manifests of 1936 and 1937 show that he was a merchant seaman on trans-Atlantic and South American routes while his wife and children were living in Lynn, MA.

Children:

4.11.1.1.3.3.1	Marie	1921- -1921
4.11.1.1.3.3.2	Madelyn Josephine	1922-1941?&1947-2004
4.11.1.1.3.3.3	Mildred Irene	1924- -2008
4.11.1.1.3.3.4	Marion Shirley	1926-1948&1956-2003
4.11.1.1.3.3.5	Robert Lee	1928- -1957
4.11.1.1.3.3.6	Kenneth Leon	1930-1967-

4.11.1.1.5.1   **MONTY, Robert J.** b 14 Oct 1904, Austin, MN; d 4 Apr 1977, Eau Claire, WI.

Robert J. Monty lived with his parents in Austin, MN, until at least 1920 before moving with them to La Crosse, WI. He was an auditor for the electric power company there in 1930 and was still single (US censuses).

4.11.1.1.5.2   **MONTY, Lucille Margaret** b 18 Feb 1906, Austin, MN; d 21 Jun 1985, Olmsted Co., MN. She married (1) 1925? **Jack M. Nicholson** b 1900?, MN.

She married (2) **Anthony Wayne Larson** (Christian Larson & Theresa E. ____) b 10 Oct 1894, Spring Valley, MN; m (1) 1916? Ida Johnson (____ Johnson & Inga ____).

Jack M. Nicholson was a 30-year-old livestock dealer in Great Meadow, MN, in 1930 when he and his wife had been married for five years (US census).

Anthony W. Larson was a painter in Spring Valley, MN, in 1930 when he and his first wife had been married for fourteen years (US censuses).

Children:
- i   **Shirley Jean Nicholson** b May 1926, Mower Co., MN. She married **John Edward Riley** b Mar 1925.
- ii   **Jacqueline Colette Nicholson** b 6 Mar 1936, Olmsted Co., MN; d 20 Dec 2000, Rochester, MN. She married 14 Jun 1958, Olmsted Co., MN, and divorced there 30 Dec 1986 **Neal R. Olson** b Aug 1936; m (2) 4 Feb 1989, Winona Co., MN, Marianne E. Gannon, divorced wife of Francis Siebenaler.
- iii   **Robert Wayne Larson** b 4 May 1941, Fillmore Co., MN. He married 10 Aug 1963, Olmsted Co., MN, **Paula Ann Silker** (Merlin Wayne Silker & Virginia Elizabeth Weatherly) b 7 Nov 1943, Nicollet Co., MN.
- iv   **Kathleen Ann Larson** b 1 Aug 1943, Fillmore Co., MN.

4.11.1.3.1.1   **MONTY, Harry Claudius** b 3 Dec 1883, North McGregor, IA; d there 11 Jan 1884.

4.11.1.3.1.2   **MONTY, Winifred Etta** b 26 May 1885, North McGregor, IA; d & bur 4 & 8 Nov 1944, Des Moines, IA. She married 7 Apr 1904, Farley, IA, **Henry Vincent Klinkner** (John Henry Klinkner & Margaret F. Knippling) b 5 Apr 1878, Dubuque Co., IA; d & bur 4 & 6 May 1946, Des Moines, IA.

Henry V. Klinkner was a printer who owned his own shop in Farley, IA, in 1910 and a newspaper editor in Bellevue, IA, in 1920. By 1925 the family was in Des Moines, IA, where Henry V. Klinkner was manager of a men's clothing store in 1930 (US & state censuses). He, his wife, and his son were buried in St. Ambrose Cemetery in Des Moines, IA.

Child:
- i   **Henry Louis Klinkner** b Mar 1911, IA; d & bur 19 & 21 Oct 1969, Des Moines, IA.

4.11.1.3.1.3   **MONTY, Flora Almeda** b 8 Feb 1887, North McGregor, IA. She married 1927? **John Marion Baber** (John Marion Baber & Ida ____) b 16 Mar 1895, Farrell, MS.

Flora Monty was a government clerk in Washington, D.C., in 1920 and also in 1930 when she and her husband, a lawyer in private practice, had been married for three years (US censuses).

4.11.1.3.1.4   **MONTY, Lulu Jessie** b 25 Feb 1889, North McGregor, IA. She married there 24 May 1914 **Edward James Palmer** (John Palmer & Mary Govenz) b 6 May 1887, Dubuque, IA; d Jun 1970, Des Moines, IA.

Edward Palmer was an railroad engineer in Dubuque, IA, at his marriage, in Marquette, IA, in 1920, and in Dubuque Co., IA, in 1930 when his widowed mother-in-law was living in his household (US censuses).

Children:
- i   **Dorothy Gladys Palmer** b 23 Dec 1915, Marquette, IA; d & bur 4 & 9 May 1998, Cincinnati, OH & Cedar Rapids, IA. She married **Ambrose Dennis Malloy** (James P. Malloy & Josie Fitzgibbons) b 25 May 1914, Iowa City, IA; d & bur 30 Apr & 7 May 2001, Cincinnati & Cedar Rapids, IA.
- ii   **Lawrence Edward Palmer** b 22 May 1920, Marquette, IA; d 2 May 2008, Los Angeles Co., CA.

4.11.3.1.1.1   **MONTY, Francis J.** b 30 Jun 1884, Lowell, MA; d before 1900.
This child was no longer alive in 1900 (US census).

4.11.3.1.1.2   **MONTY, William Alphonse** b 9 Dec 1886, Lowell, MA. He married 27 Aug 1913, Billerica, MA, **Marie Laura Poirier** (Abondius Poirier & Rose D. ____) b May 1892, Lowell, MA; m (2) ____ Junevicius.

William Monty was a laborer in Lowell, MA, in 1910 and a woolen mill worker in Billerica, MA, in 1920 and 1930 (US censuses). He and his wife celebrated their twenty-fifth wedding anniversary there in 1938 (*Lowell Sun*, 26 Aug 1938).

I know of Marie L. Poirier's second marriage only from the obituary of her son Vincent (4.11.3.1.1.2.4) in the *Lowell Sun* of 10 Dec 1962. She was then living in Billerica.

Child:

4.11.3.1.1.2.1	Virginia	1919-	-
4.11.3.1.1.2.2	Herbert Russell	1920-	-
4.11.3.1.1.2.3	Charlotte R.	1922-	&1982-2003
4.11.3.1.1.2.4	Vincent A.	1924?-1945&	-1962
4.11.3.1.1.2.5	Everett L.	1926-	-1981
4.11.3.1.1.2.3	Teresa P.	1927-	-

4.11.3.1.1.3   **MONTY, Clifford** b 16 Jul 1888, Lowell, MA; d there 1 Sep 1888.

4.11.3.1.1.4   **MONTY, Theresa V.** b 17 Mar 1891, Lowell, MA. She married 1911? **Herbert Albert Patterson** (Charles F. Patterson & Mary ____) b 9 Sep 1887, Coopersville, NY.

Herbert Patterson was a streetcar motorman in Lowell, MA, in 1920 when his household included, in addition to his wife and son, his mother-in-law Delphine Brunelle and his wife's maternal grandfather Joseph Brunelle. He was a factory worker in Milford, MA, in 1930 when he and his wife had been married for nineteen years (US censuses). They were living in North Billerica, MA, in 1942 (World War II Draft Registration card).

Child:
- i   **Charles Patterson** b 1915?, Lowell, MA.

4.11.3.1.2.1   **MONTY, George D.** b & bp 29 May & 15 Jul 1894, Chazy & West Chazy, NY; d & bur 9 & 11 May 1974, Plattsburgh & West Chazy, NY. He married 2 Oct 1916, West Chazy, NY, **Margaret Powers** (John Powers & Maude Starks) b 7 Nov 1897, Altona,

NY; d & bur 5 & 8 Aug 1969, Plattsburgh & West Chazy, NY.

George D. Monty (George Adelbert at his baptism) was a farmer in West Chazy, NY, at his marriage and in 1920. He soon moved to Altona, NY, where he was a farm worker in 1925 and an electrician for the power company in 1930 (US and state censuses). He later operated a service station in the Chazy, NY, area. He and his wife were buried in St. Joseph's Cemetery in West Chazy (*Plattsburgh Press Republican*, 7 Aug 1969 and 13 May 1974).

Margaret Powers' brother Leon married her husband's sister Helen Gertrude Monty (4.11.3.1.2.3).

Children:

4.11.3.1.2.1.1	Russel	1917?-	-
4.11.3.1.2.1.2	Hubert	1920-1946-1996	
4.11.3.1.2.1.3	Doris Patricia	1924-1942-1994	
4.11.3.1.2.1.4	Gerald W.	1928-1953-	
4.11.3.1.2.1.5	James C.	1931-	-
4.11.3.1.2.1.6	Janet	-1951-	
4.11.3.1.2.1.7	Gordon E.	1936-	-

4.11.3.1.2.2 **MONTY, Joseph Elias** b & bp 14 Feb & 6 Jun 1897, Chazy & West Chazy, NY; d & bur Jul & 1 Aug 1912, Chazy & West Chazy, NY.

4.11.3.1.2.3 **MONTY, Helen Gertrude** b & bp 27 Dec 1898 & 5 Feb 1899, Chazy & Champlain, NY; d & bur 3 & 6 Jul 1990, Rouses Point & West Chazy, NY. She married 28 Aug 1919, West Chazy, NY, **Leon Powers** (John Powers & Maude Starks) b there 7 May 1895; d 20 Dec 1964, Plattsburgh, NY.

Helen Gertrude Monty died in a nursing home in Rouses Point and was buried in St. Joseph's Cemetery in West Chazy, NY (*Plattsburgh Press Republican*, 4 Jul 1990). She and her brother George (4.11.3.1.2.1) had married a brother and sister.

Leon Powers was a farmer in West Chazy, NY, at his marriage, a road worker in Chazy, NY, in 1925, and a telegraph lineman there in 1930 (US and state censuses). When he retired in 1960, he was a paper company employee in Plattsburgh, NY (*Plattsburgh Press Republican*, 21 Dec 1964).

Children:

i   **Norman Elias Powers** b 30 Jan 1920, West Chazy, NY; d & bur 25 & 27 Dec 1982, Lake Charles, LA. He married **Shirley Louise McCauley** (Harry Edward McCauley & Beulah May McConley) b 20 Jul 1928, Essex Co., NY.

ii   **Shirley Powers** b 4 Feb 1926, West Chazy, NY; d 25 May 1997, Plattsburgh, NY. She married 26 Nov 1949 **Charles A. Bochart** b 20 Jun 1927, Brooklyn, NY; d 22 Feb 1999, Plattsburgh, NY.

iii   **Elizabeth Powers** b Nov 1929, Chazy, NY. She married **Austin Carlton Frenyea** (Lewis T. Frenyea & Geneva Garrow or Garren) b 12 Apr 1929, Plattsburgh, NY; d there 29 Nov 2005.

iv   **Leon Powers** b Dec 1934, Clinton Co., NY. He married 7 Feb 1957, West Chazy, NY, **Phyllis Ann Peryer** (Norman Emery Peryer & Evelyn Chamberlain).

v   **Virginia Powers** b 25 Sep 1936, Plattsburgh, NY. She married 1 Sep 1958, West Chazy, NY, **Gerald Virgil Luck** (Virgil Luck & Elizabeth Parker) b 1 Sep 1937, Plattsburgh, NY.

4.11.3.1.2.4 **MONTY, Charles** b & bp 25 Apr & 25 Aug 1901, Chazy & West Chazy, NY; d & bur 4 & 6 Apr 1902, Chazy & West Chazy, NY.

4.11.3.1.2.5 **MONTY, Roy/Royal Kenneth** b & bp 8 Aug & 8 Sep 1906, Chazy & Coopersville, NY.

This man was named Roy Kenneth at his baptism, Kenneth when he was living with his parents in Beekmantown, NY, in 1910, Royal when he was with them in Chazy, NY, in

1920 (US censuses), and Roy at his mother's death four years later (*Plattsburgh Sentinel*, 3 Jun 1924). He was Royal Monty in 1930 when he was a shipping clerk in Queens, NY (US census) and Roy Monty, a New York City resident, when he visited his relatives in West Chazy, NY, in 1941 (*Plattsburgh Daily Press*, 2 Aug 1941). In 1951, though, Royal Kenneth Monty was a resident of West Chazy (*Plattsburgh Press Republican*, 14 & 15 Nov 1951).

4.11.4.4.6.1   MONTY, Frank Henry b 23 Oct 1918, Everett, WA; d 29 Jan 1990, RI. He married **Zelma ____** b 1916?; d 8 Sep 1969, New London, CT, at the age of 53.

Frank H. Monty was a career serviceman in the United States Coast Guard. He and his wife were living in Jupiter Point near Groton, CT, in 1959 (City Directory) and were both residents of North Stonington, CT, at their deaths.

4.11.4.6.5.1   MONTY/TRIPP, Lester D. b 25 Mar 1905, Snohomish Co., WA; d 2 Sep 1994, Kirkland, WA. He married 27 Aug 1927, Yakima Co., WA, **Ethel Dorothy Caroline Holzgraf** (Henry Louis Holzgraf & Sarah Fredericka Kohlmeyer) b 28 Sep 1906, Faribault, MN; d & bur 16 &19 Sep 1991, Kirkland, WA.

There are two records of this man's birth in the Washington State Vital Records. One shows that Lester D. Monty, son of George B. Monty and Evelyn E. Richardson, was born in Snohomish Co., WA, on 25 Mar 1906 while the other notes that Lester D. (Monty) Tripp, son of Geo B. Monty Tripp and Evelyn E. Richardson, was born there on 25 Mar 1905. His date of birth, according to the Social Security Death Index, was 26 (sic) Mar 1905. I have used the day found in the Washington Birth Records and the year 1905 which corresponds to his age in later censuses. So far as I know Lester Monty was known as Lester Tripp from the time of his mother's marriage to George Tripp in 1906. He was a shipping clerk in Seattle in 1930 (US censuses).

His wife's surname appears as Holsgraph in her marriage record though Holzgraf at her birth and in the 1910 and 1920 censuses when she was living with her parents in Faribault, MN, and Riverside, WA.

4.11.4.6.5.2   MONTY, Geraldine L. b 31 May 1912, Mineral, WA. She married 29 May 1931, Everett, WA, **Lawrence Widmark** (Owen Widmark & Lydia Swanson) b 23 Mar 1909, Seattle, WA; d 28 Nov 1993, Arlington, WA.

Lawrence Widmark was a merchant in Arlington, WA.

Children:
i   **Roberta Marie Widmark** b 27 Apr 1932, Cicero, WA. She married (1) 8 Oct 1950, Arlington, WA, **Stuart L. Marshlain** (John Marshlain & Iris Lewis) b 27 Feb 1930, Granite Falls, WA; m (2) 13 Aug 1954, Arlington, WA, Jean Lorene Hansen (Clarence Hansen & Leona Marie Veilleux); d 24 Mar 1991, Longview, WA.

  She was divorced when she married (2) 10 Jul 1954, Coeur D'Alene, ID, **Donald R. LaVelle** (Peter LaVelle & Elise ____) b 3 Nov 1928, Everett, WA.
ii   **Lyle Russell Widmark** b 25 Jan 1936, Arlington, WA. He married 17 Sep 1955, Coeur D'Alene, ID, **Janelle Ratekin** (Norman Wesley Ratekin & Thelma Jane Certain) b 17 Mar 1937, Spokane, WA.

4.11.4.6.5.3   MONTY, Ralph Clayton b 6 Jun 1914, Tacoma, WA; d 3 May 1974, Mt. Vernon, WA. He married 4 Jan 1940, Arlington, WA, **Bernice Tiedeman** (Edward Henry Tiedeman & Elizabeth Christine Schmidt) b 31 Oct 1919, Marysville, WA; m (2) Morris R. Molstad; d 28 Jul 2007, Marysville, WA.

Ralph Clayton Monty was a logger in Snohomish Co., WA.

Children:
| 4.11.4.6.5.3.1 | Ralph George | 1945-1963&1973- |
| 4.11.4.6.5.3.2 | Marvin D. | 1948-1968- |

4.11.4.6.5.4   **MONTY, Delores Mae** b 5 May 1922, Arlington, WA; d & bur there 13 & 18 Aug 2003. She married there 15 Apr 1942 **Howard Arnold Christianson** (Arnt Christianson & Hannah Strom) b 14 Oct 1921, Everett, WA.

Howard Christianson was a petroleum merchant in Arlington, WA. He became involved in politics and was at various times city councilman, mayor, and city manager there. He survived his wife.

Children:

i   **Christie Montyne Christianson** b 25 Dec 1948, Arlington, WA. She married (1) there 21 Sep 1968 **Wendell Adair Giebel** (Maurice A. Giebel & Christine ____) b there 10 Feb 1945; m (2) there 18 Jun 1977 Judith I. Wharton.

   She married (2) 24 Nov 1978, Arlington, WA, **Tommy Raymond Derosier** (Tommy J. Derosier & Shirley R. Mansfield) b 27 Jul 1955, Yreka, CA; m (2) Deborah L. ____.

   She married (3) 7 Dec 1991, Marysville, WA, **Gale Alfred Vanderpool** b 5 Feb 1941, IA.

ii   **Craig Howard Christianson** b 1 Apr 1957, Arlington, WA. He married there 21 Apr 1979 **Karen Gayle Espedal** (Erling W. Espedal & ____) b there 30 Aug 1957.

iii   **Cynthia Ann Christianson** b 20 Feb 1958, Arlington, WA. She married (1) there 17 Mar 1979 **Garry M. Galde** b 15 Apr 1955.

   She married (2) 27 Jun 1987, Coeur D'Alene, ID, **Lee E. Baird** b 5 Oct 1955, Lovell, WY.

4.11.4.6.9.1   **MONTY, Bertram Edgar** b 6 Dec 1920, Arlington, WA. He married there 1 Sep 1944 **Margaret Rogene Lockwood** (Charles Walter Lockwood & Mertie Conger) b 17 Dec 1922, Ericson, NE; d 4 Feb 2006, Marysville, WA.

Bertram E. Monty was a quality assurance specialist in government service before retiring to Marysville, WA, and recently to Seattle, WA. His work on the descendants of Hiram Monty (4.11.4.6) opened to me the world of the "Washington Montys," for which I am deeply grateful. Much of the information I have on Hiram Monty's family is derived from his grandson's research.

Child:

4.11.4.6.9.1.1.	Deborah Kay	1953-	&1999-

4.11.4.6.9.2   **MONTY, Melvin Morris** b 13 May 1922, Arlington, WA; d 6 Aug 1989, Mt. Vernon, WA. He married 19 Feb 1943, Arlington, WA, **Signa May Walker** (James Walker & Anna Osterland) b there 1 Apr 1921; d there 7 Aug 1996.

Melvin Monty was a farmer and trucker in Snohomish Co., WA.

Children:

4.11.4.6.9.2.1	Dale Richard	1945-1963&1982-1989
4.11.4.6.9.2.2	Dean Morris	1946- -1946
4.11.4.6.9.2.3	Nadene Marie	1947-1965-
4.11.4.6.9.2.4	Mavis	1949- -1963

4.11.4.8.1.1   **MONTY, Betty June** b 20 Jan 1924, Tacoma, WA; d 2 Aug 2002, El Segundo, CA. She married 1940?, WA, **Paul Edward Harrison** (William Edward Harrison & Anna V. Green) b 24 Apr 1920, Hurst, IL; d 24 Nov 2000, El Segundo, CA.

Children:

i   **Sandra Lee Harrison** b 6 Feb 1943, Tacoma, WA. She married 3 Oct 1964, Alameda Co., CA, **Nicholas/Nick Roland Morganelli** b Sep 1942?

ii   **Paul Edward Harrison** b 22 Jul 1946, Inglewood, CA. He married 10 Sep 1966, Los Angeles, CA, **Karen Sue Warner** (Ronnie Denzil Warner & Marvelyn Louise Wold) b 1 Feb 1947, Huntington Park, CA.

iii   **Deborah Ann Harrison** b 2 Apr 1954, Inglewood, CA. She married 14 Jul 1979, San Mateo Co., CA, **Donald Scott Ernest** (____ Ernest & ____ Moran) b 31 Mar 1949, Kern Co., CA; m (1) 29 May 1971, Los Angeles, CA, and divorced there Dec 1974 Christine Adele Salazar.

4.11.4.8.1.2   **MONTY, Janice Carol** b 30 Jan 1926, Tacoma, WA.

4.11.4.8.1.3   **MONTY, George Rank Jr.** b 22 Apr 1927, Tacoma, WA. He married (1) there Jan 1947 **Frances Farrell**.
    He married (2) 24 Jun 1950, Bremerton, WA, **Barbara Mae Hanson** (Franz Hanson & Sarah McNeil) b 29 Apr 1930, Coeur d'Alene, ID.

Child of the first marriage:

4.11.4.8.1.3.1	George Paul	1948-1970-

Children of the second marriage:

4.11.4.8.1.3.2	Pamela Jean	1951-1969-	
4.11.4.8.1.3.2	Cameron A.	1957-	&1994-

4.11.7.3.1.1   **MONTY, Earl F.** b Oct 1925, Lawrence, MA; died in World War II.
    Private Earl F. Monty was killed in action during World War II (National Archives, Massachusetts Casualties). He had enlisted in Boston, MA, on 15 Oct 1943 (World War II Enlistment Records).

5.7.1.1.6.1   **MONTY, Honoré Solyme** b & bp 4 Sep 1865, Marieville, QC; d & bur there 10 & 12 May 1867.

5.7.1.1.6.2   **MONTY, Louis Alphonse** b & bp 3 & 4 Apr 1867, Marieville, QC. He married 28 Apr 1890, Holyoke, MA, **Valida/Marie Valérie Mayer** (Joseph Mayer & Denise Barette) b & bp 7 & 8 Jul 1872, St. Didace, QC; d 1900, Easthampton, MA.
    Louis Monty came to the United States as a toddler and was living with his parents in Holyoke, MA, in 1870 and 1880. He was a house painter in Holyoke in 1890, in South Hadley, MA, at the birth of a child in 1895, and in Easthampton, MA, in 1900 (US censuses). The family fell apart following Valida Mayer's death. The 1902 Easthampton City Directory notes that Louis Monty had moved to Vermont. I have been unable to trace him there but suspect that he was the 43-year-old Louis Monty, a house painter by profession, who was an inmate in the Penobscot County Jail in Bangor, ME, in 1910. His older daughter was then living independently in Waterbury, CT, while the younger one was with her maternal grandparents in Easthampton (US census).
    Valida Mayer was baptized under the name of Marie Valérie. After her parents moved to Massachusetts in 1881 however she became known as Valida and was married and died under that name.

Children:

5.7.1.1.6.2.1	Rhea Valerie	1891-1912-1962
5.7.1.1.6.2.2	Flora	1895- -

5.7.1.1.6.3   **MONTY, Joséphat Arthur** b & bp 4 & 5 Jul 1868, Marieville, QC; d & bur 3 & 4 Sep 1869, Richelieu, QC.

5.7.1.1.6.4   **MONTY, Flora** b May 1876, Holyoke, MA.
    Flora Monty was living with her parents in Holyoke, MA, in 1880 and in Waterbury, CT, in 1900 and 1910. She was then still single (US censuses).

5.7.1.1.11.1   **MONTY, Louis Armin** b & bp 16 & 18 Mar 1883, Richelieu QC; d & bur there 9 & 10 May 1884.

5.7.1.1.11.2   MONTY, Ernestine Agnes b 27 Sep 1886, Woonsocket, RI; d Jan 1969, West Palm Beach, FL. She married 1909? **Philias Joseph Viau** (Damien/ Damase Viau & Julie E. Benoit) b & bp 24 Feb 1885, St. Sébastien, QC; d 17 May 1950, Waterbury, CT.

Philias J. Viau (Joseph Philias at his baptism) came to the United States with his parents around 1890 and was a construction worker, a lather, in Pawtucket, RI, in 1910 when he and his wife had been married for less than a year. He moved to Waterbury, CT, after the birth of his daughter in 1915 and was a lather there in 1920 and later years (US censuses; Waterbury City Directories). His name varies. Censuses refer to Felip, Phillias, Philippe, or Philip J. Viau, though he was listed as Philias or Philias J. Viau in the City Directories. He also signed his Draft Registration cards of 1918 and 1942 as Philias Joseph Viau and Philias J. Viau respectively.

Child:
i   **Clarice Ernestine Viau** b 6 Jan 1915, Pawtucket, RI; d 27 Aug 1992, West Palm Beach, FL.

5.7.1.1.11.3   MONTY, Anonymous (female) b 22 Jan 1888, Holyoke, MA.
This child is identified only as "female Monty" in the Massachusetts Birth Index. She died before 1900 when her parents had only one living child, Ernestine (5.7.1.1.11.2).

5.7.1.2.1.1   MONTY, Joseph Louis/Lewis b & bp 17 & 20 Feb 1860, Mont St. Grégoire, QC; d between 1889 and 1897. He married 6 Sep 1881, St. Jean, QC, **Marie Françoise Rebecca Marchand** (Henri Marchand & Henriette Drolet) b & bp there 4 & 5 Aug 1857; d & bur there 2 & 6 Feb 1897.

Joseph Louis Monty (Louis Joseph at his baptism) was a pharmacist in St. Johnsbury, VT, at his marriage and at the birth of his first child. He was in Clinton Co., NY, when the next two children were born, and in Providence, RI, when his son died in 1889. He predeceased his wife.

Children:

5.7.1.2.1.1.1	Marie Azilda	1882-	-
5.7.1.2.1.1.2	Marie Lucille Georgiana	1884-	-
5.7.1.2.1.1.3	Louis Joseph Henri	1887-	-1889

5.7.1.5.3.1   MONTY, Evangéline/Marie Adélaïde b & bp 12 & 14 Jan 1883, St. Jean-Baptiste, QC. She married there 18 Feb 1901 **Polydore Benoit** (Louis Benoit & Malvina Massé) b & bp 28 & 29 Aug 1873, St. Césaire, QC.

Polydore Benoit (Joseph Louis Napoléon at his baptism) was a farmer in Rougemont, QC. His wife, named Marie Adélaïde at her baptism, was known as Evangéline at her marriage and later. I cannot explain the name change.

5.7.1.5.3.2   MONTY, Alberta/Celia Albertine b & bp 12 & 13 Jan 1884, St. Jean-Baptiste, QC. She married 9 Apr 1907, Norwich, CT, **Henri/Henry Laliberté** (Albert Laliberté & Addie Sauvé) b Mar 1886, QC.

Henry Laliberté was a jeweler in North Attleboro, MA, at his marriage to Alberta Monty (Celia Albertine at her baptism). They soon returned to Canada for their oldest child was born in Sherbrooke, QC, in April 1908 (1911 Canadian Census). They later moved to St. Jean, QC, and were still living there when her mother died in 1952.

Children:
i   **Jean-Baptiste Marc Honorius Laliberté** b & bp 22 & 25 Apr 1908, Sherbrooke, QC.
ii   **Louis Albert Rosario Laliberté** b & bp 4 & 5 Oct 1910, Sherbrooke, QC. He married 10 Oct 1931, Iberville, QC, **Fabiola Irene Seney** (Frédéric Charles/Alfred Seney & Alma Goyette) b & bp there 21 Feb 1911.

iii   **Marguerite Lucile Laliberté** b & bp 30 Dec 1912 & 1 Jan 1913, Sherbrooke, QC; d & bur 19 & 21 Feb 1914, St. Jean, QC.

iv   **Roger Yvan Laliberté** b & bp 18 & 20 Jun 1914, St. Jean, QC. He married there 16 Sep 1939 **Georgette Tougas** (Hercule Tougas & Azilda Samson) b & bp 19 Feb 1916, Henryville, QC.

v   **Bernard Christian Laliberté** b & bp 15 & 17 Sep 1916, St. Jean, QC; d 21 Sep 1997, QC.

vi   **Charles Auguste Laliberté** b & bp 6 & 8 Aug 1920, St. Jean, QC; d there 21 Mar 1988. He married there 10 Jan 1942, **Rita Dussault** (Armand Dussault & Lina Chabot) b 21 Aug 1921, QC; d 19 Nov 1988, St. Jean, QC.

5.7.1.5.3.3   **MONTY, Marie Anne Flore/Mary A.** b & bp 24 & 26 Jan 1885, St. Jean-Baptiste, QC; d 20 Aug 1968, Lisbon, CT. She married 3 Jun 1907, Taftville, CT, **Peter Xavier/François Xavier Tremblay** (Arthur Tremblay & Marie Emérentienne Dallaire) b & bp 21 & 22 Feb 1884, Ste Luce, QC; d 11 Nov 1965, Lisbon, CT.

Marie Anne Flore Monty married as Marie Anne Monty but was generally known in the United States as Mary A. and even Maryann Monty or Tremblay. Her husband's name also varied. He was baptized as François Xavier Tremblay but married as Peter Tremblay. He was also known as Peter Xavier Tremblay in 1942 (World War II Draft Registration card) and as Peter X. Tremblay at his death (Connecticut Death Index).

Peter Tremblay was a weaver in Taftville, CT, at his marriage and until at least 1918. He soon moved to Northfield, VT, for he was a farmer there in 1920 and 1930 (US censuses). He and his wife later returned to Connecticut and were both residents of Lisbon, CT, at their deaths.

Children:

i   **Yvonne/Rose Alma Yvonne Tremblay** b 27 Jul 1909, Taftville, CT; d 2 Nov 1998, Griswold, CT. She married 1929? **Lorenzo Stanislas Delorme** (Armand Delorme & Edouardina Filiault) b & bp 6 & 7 May 1907, St. Adrien, QC; d 22 Feb 1977, Norwich, CT.

ii   **Louis Philip Tremblay** b 15 Apr 1911, QC; d 25 Oct 2000, Norwich, CT. He married there 18 Apr 1959 **Marie A. Gaumond** (Hormisdas Gaumond & Elizabeth ____) b Aug 1921, Lisbon, CT.

iii   **Beatrice/Marie Emma Beatrice Tremblay** b 12 Jul 1913, Taftville, CT; d 8 Dec 1985, Lisbon, CT. She married **Richard H. Cate** (Henry William Cate & Azubah ____) b 10 Oct 1909, East Montpelier, VT; d 20 May 1985, Norwich, CT.

iv   **Roger P./Pierre Roger Tremblay** b 16 Jul 1917, Norwich, CT; d & bur 16 & 20 Sep 2006, Norwich, CT. He married there 30 Nov 1946 **Shirley M. Santo** (Frank Santo & Evelyn Stott) b there 19 Sep 1927; d & bur 23 & 27 Feb 2006, Groton & Norwich, CT.

v   **Anita E. Tremblay** b Mar 1920, Northfield, VT. She married **Wilfred I. Godere** (Wilfred Godere & Barbara Winifred Phalen) b 27 Jul 1922, Norwich, CT; d there 18 Aug 1996.

5.7.1.5.3.4   **MONTY, Charles Emile** b & bp 10 & 11 Feb 1886, St. Jean-Baptiste, QC; d Nov 1973, Barre, VT. He married 27 Feb 1924, St. Jean-Baptiste, QC, a second cousin, **Valéda Bédard** (Louis Pierre Bédard [5.7.1.7.x] & Marie Louise Carrière) b & bp there 7 & 8 Aug 1896; d 17 Mar 1989, Barre, VT.

Charles Emile Monty came to the United States in 1920 and became a farmer in Northfield, VT, where his brother-in-law Peter Tremblay had settled earlier (US censuses).

Children:

5.7.1.5.3.4.1	Michel J.	1925?-	-
5.7.1.5.3.4.2	Jacqueline T.	1926-	-
5.7.1.5.3.4.3	Charles L.	1927-	-2005
5.7.1.5.3.4.4	Paul	1929-	-1969

5.7.1.5.3.4.5	Jeanne	1931-1954?-2006
5.7.1.5.3.4.6	Alfred R./Al	1934?- -
5.7.1.5.3.4.7	Lise A.	1937?-1969?-

5.7.1.5.3.5   **MONTY, Donalda** b & bp 10 & 12 Feb 1887, St. Jean-Baptiste, QC; d 11 Feb 1951, Norwich, CT. She married 19 Jan 1914, Taftville, CT, **Joseph Victor Milton Marc-Aurèle/Marcaurele** (Victor Marc-Aurèle & Marie Depot) b & bp 19 & 24 Aug 1880, St. Valérien, QC; d 22 May 1953, Norwich, CT.

Both Joseph Marc-Aurèle (Marcaurele in the United States) and his wife (named Cédulie Donalda at her baptism) came to the United States as children with their parents. He was a baker in Norwich, CT.

5.7.1.5.3.6   **MONTY, Michel Auguste** b & bp 30 & 31 Jul 1888, St. Jean-Baptiste, QC; d & bur there 5 & 8 Jul 1910.

5.7.1.5.3.7   **MONTY, Marie** b & bp 27 & 28 Jun 1892, St. Jean-Baptiste, QC; d & bur there 12 & 13 Sep 1892.

5.7.1.5.3.8   **MONTY, François Xavier Antoine** b & bp 16 & 17 Sep 1894, St. Jean-Baptiste, QC; d & bur there 3 & 6 Mar 1896.

5.7.1.5.3.9   **MONTY, Rosario Louis Philippe** b & bp 29 & 31 Jan 1897, St. Jean-Baptiste, QC; d & bur there 10 Apr 1901.

5.7.1.5.3.10   **MONTY, Alphonse** b & bp 26 Sep 1898, St. Jean-Baptiste, QC; d & bur there 24 & 27 Sep 1971. He married there 17 Sep 1927 **Estelle Chabot** (Ozias Chabot & Rose Chicoine) b & bp there 10 Jun 1904; d there 28 Mar 1973.

Alphonse Monty was a laborer in St. Jean, QC, at his marriage. His wife was a sister of Bernadette Chabot, wife of Jean-Baptiste Monty (5.7.1.5.3.11).

Children:
| 5.7.1.5.3.10.1 | Gilles | 1928-1950-2000 |
| 5.7.1.5.3.10.2 | Germain | 1929-1950-1974 |

5.7.1.5.3.11   **MONTY, Jean-Baptiste Polydore** b & bp 7 May 1901, St. Jean-Baptiste, QC. He married there 25 Jun 1924 **Bernadette Chabot** (Ozias Chabot & Rose Chicoine) b & bp there 13 Aug 1902; d & bur there 25 & 28 Oct 1961.

Jean-Baptiste Monty was a farmer in St. Jean-Baptiste, QC, at his marriage. His wife was a sister of Estelle Chabot, wife of Alphonse Monty (5.7.1.5.3.10).

5.7.1.9.1.1   **MONTY, Emma M.** b 24 Apr 1870, Holyoke, MA; d & bur 1956, Burlington, VT. She married there 24 Nov 1891 **Edward Lavallee** (Théophile Lavallée & Adélaïde/Delia Gauthier) b there Mar 1872; d & bur there 1960.

Edward Lavallee was a tailor in Burlington, VT. The years of his and his wife's death are taken from the inscription on their tombstone in Mount Calvary Cemetery there.

Children:
i   **Ella E. Lavallee** b 28 Aug 1893, Burlington, VT; d there 16 Jan 1981.
ii   **Gertrude Lavallee** b Jul 1895, Burlington, VT.
iii **Alexander J. Lavallee** b 3 Oct 1897, Burlington, VT; d there 20 Mar 1981. He married **Helen M. ____**.
iv   **Ellen/Helen S. Lavallee** b May 1900, Burlington, VT.
v   **Raymond E. Lavallee** b 7 Oct 1903, Burlington, VT; d there 19 Jan 1984. He married **Mary B. ____** b Jul 1907; d 19 Apr 1988, Burlington, VT.
vi   **Albert O. Lavallee** b 17 Apr 1906, Burlington, VT; d there 16 Apr 1971. He married **Elsie F. LaPointe** (William J. LaPointe & Elsie F. Willette) b 23 Sep 1916,

Burlington, VT; d there 7 Dec 2002.

5.7.1.9.1.2 MONTY, Henry Joseph b 11 Aug 1872, Colchester, VT. He married 23 Sep 1895, Lawrence, MA, **Rose Anna Boucher** (Eusèbe Boucher & Adeline ____) b there Aug 1876; d & bur 21 & 23 Dec 1945, Lowell, MA.

Henry J. Monty (Joseph Henry at his birth) came to Massachusetts with his father and stepmother in the early 1890s. He was a cotton mill worker in Lawrence, MA, at his marriage and until at least 1907, in Amesbury, MA, in 1910 and until at least 1917, and in Lowell, MA, in 1920 and 1930 (US censuses). He was still in Lowell in 1956, providing a home for several family members (City Directories).

Rose Anna Boucher was buried in St. Patrick's Cemetery in Lowell (*Lowell Sun*, 22 Dec 1945).

Children:

5.7.1.9.1.2.1	Anonymous	1896-	-1896
5.7.1.9.1.2.2	Arthur Henry	1897-1922-1969	
5.7.1.9.1.2.3	Priscilla B.	1898-	-
5.7.1.9.1.2.4	Leo J.	1903-1927-1992	
5.7.1.9.1.2.5	Albert F.	1905-1927?-1982	
5.7.1.9.1.2.6	Viola	1907?-	-
5.7.1.9.1.2.7	Irene	1912-	-1972

5.7.1.9.1.3 MONTY, Alexander b Apr 1875, Holyoke, MA; d there 16 May 1875, at the age of one month.

5.7.1.9.1.4 MONTY, Ella Elizabeth b 10 Apr 1878, Colchester, VT; d Jan 1923, Lawrence, MA.

Ella Monty came to Lawrence, MA, with her father and stepmother in the early 1890s. She was a shoe worker there until her death (US censuses; City Directories).

5.7.1.9.1.5 MONTY, Clara b 21 Nov 1880, Colchester, VT; d 18 Nov 1971, Lawrence, MA. She married 1901? **William Desruisseau** (Eleusippe Desruisseau & Rosalie Croteau) b & bp 24 Nov 1874, St. Flavien, QC; d between 1953 and 1956, probably in Lawrence, MA.

Clara Monty and her husband both came to Lawrence, MA, with their parents in the early 1890s and had been married for nine years in 1910. William Desruisseau (Joseph William at his baptism) was then an inspector in a shoe factory, as also in 1920 and 1930 (US censuses). According to the Lawrence City Directories, he was still alive in 1953 though deceased in 1956. At least two of his sons adopted the surname Brooks.

Children:

i **Viola Desruisseau** b 14 Jul 1903, Lawrence, MA; d there 21 Apr 1986. She married 1927? **George F. Giles** (Joseph Francis Giles & Mary Agnes Conroy) b 27 Jul 1904, Lawrence, MA; d there 15 Jan 1945.

ii **Gertrude D. Desruisseau** b 27 Dec 1905, Lawrence, MA; d 4 May 1995, Delray Beach, FL. She married **John T./Joseph Jean Télesphore Verner** (Jean Verner & Eléonore/Nora Bessette) b & bp 10 & 11 May 1903, Valleyfield, QC; d Aug 1948, Lawrence, MA.

iii **Irene Desruisseau** b 25 May 1908, Lawrence, MA; d there 31 Jan 1999. She married there 28 Nov 1929 **Wilfred Eugene Bernard** (Rudolph Eugene Bernard & Alice Mary Blanche Gagnon) b 18 Apr 1906, MA; d 4 Sep 1967, MA.

iv **Della L. Desruisseau** b Dec 1909, Lawrence, MA; d before 1920.

v **Maurice J. Desruisseau** b 1 May 1913, Lawrence, MA. He married **Yvonne F.** ____ b 1 Feb 1921; d 27 Aug 2001, Methuen, MA.

vi **Doris P. Desruisseau** b 3 Dec 1915, Lawrence, MA. She married **Robert Roland Morache** (Arthur Morache & Martha ____) b 19 Jun 1916, Lawrence, MA; d there

26 Apr 1999.

vii   **Harold J. Brooks** b 1 Aug 1918, Lawrence, MA; d 4 Oct 1999, Boston, MA. He married **Catherine Donahue** (Nicholas Donahue & Mary R. ____) b 9 Sep 1924, MA; d 29 Dec 2005, North Andover, MA.

viii   **Leo W. Brooks** b Nov 1921, Lawrence, MA. He married **Ruth A.** ____ b 6 Oct 1928; d 15 Mar 2005, Salem, NH.

5.7.1.9.1.6   **MONTY, Dora** b 12 Apr 1882, Colchester, VT. She married 1909? **Frank Thomas Flagg** (____ Flagg & ____ Kallery) b 23 Apr 1885, MA; d between 1939 and 1942.

Dora Monty came to Massachusetts with her father and stepmother in the early 1890s and was an operative in a shoe factory in Lawrence, MA, before and after her marriage. Frank Flagg was a shoe worker there in 1910 when he and his wife had been married for one year, a shipping clerk in 1920, and a salesman in 1930 and until at least 1939. Mrs. Dora Flagg was a widow however in 1942 (US censuses; Lawrence City Directories).

Child:

i   **Irene A. Flagg** b Feb 1910, Lawrence, MA.

5.7.1.9.1.7   **MONTY, Célina** b 3 Apr 1888, Colchester, VT; d there 30 Jul 1888.

5.7.1.9.1.8   **MONTY, Mary** b 30 Jan 1889, Colchester, VT.

Mary Monty was not with her father and stepmother in Lawrence, MA, in 1900 (US census) and may have died before then.

5.7.1.9.1.9   **MONTY, Joseph** b & d 18 Nov 1890, Colchester, VT.

5.7.1.9.1.10   **MONTY, Joseph** b & d 9 Sep 1891, Lawrence, MA.

5.7.1.9.1.11   **MONTY, Anonymous** b & d 22 Jul 1893, Lawrence, MA.
This child was stillborn.

5.7.1 12.5.1   **MONTY, Elmeria/Marie Sylvia** b & bp 11 & 15 Feb 1880, Holyoke, MA; d there 5 Mar 1880.

The Holyoke, MA, Birth and Death Records name this child Elmeria, though she was baptized in the church of the Precious Blood there as Marie Sylvia.

5.7.1.12.5.2   **MONTY, Rosario Armand** b & bp 14 Mar 1881, Holyoke, MA; d there 8 Dec 1910.

Rosario Monty was ordained a Catholic priest in Montreal, QC, on 22 Dec 1906 and was a curate in Indian Orchard, MA, before his death. He was buried in Notre Dame Cemetery in South Hadley, MA.

5.7.1.12.5.3   **MONTY, Adelbert Honoré** b & bp 19 Aug 1883, Holyoke, MA; d 9 Feb 1934, Providence, RI. He married 13 Aug 1906, Woonsocket, RI, **Espéralda Gaulin** (Alphonse Gaulin & Elmire Marcoux) b there 3 Dec 1883; d there 15 May 1951.

Adelbert Monty was a physician/surgeon first in Attleboro and Holyoke, MA, and after 1915 in Woonsocket, RI. He was buried in Notre Dame Cemetery in South Hadley, MA. His widow Espéralda (sometimes Esméralda) was buried in Woonsocket's Precious Blood Cemetery.

Children:

5.7.1.12.5.3.1	Germaine	1907-	-1995
5.7.1.12.5.3.2	Louis Alphonse	1908-	-1908
5.7.1.12.5.3.3	Gertrude Una	1910-1940&1973-2007	
5.7.1.12.5.3.4	Rosario Adelbert	1911-	-1912
5.7.1.12.5.3.5	Genevieve Emma Estella	1913-	-1913

| 5.7.1.12.5.3.6 | Anonymous | 1915- | -1915 |
| 5.7.1.12.5.3.7 | Joseph | 1916- | -1916 |

5.7.1.12.5.4   MONTY, Blanche Dolora b & bp 26 Jul 1885, Holyoke, MA; d & bur 13 & 16 Nov 1968, Holyoke & South Hadley, MA. She married 23 May 1911, Holyoke, MA, **Ulric Montcalm** (Chéri Payant dit Montcalm & Marie Brossard) b & bp 23 Oct 1877, Laprairie, QC; d 6 Sep 1956, Holyoke, MA.

Ulric Montcalm (Joseph Alaric Payant at his baptism) arrived in the United States as a child around 1880. He was a barber in Worcester, MA, for a few years after his marriage and later in Holyoke, MA (US censuses; City Directories; World War I and World War II Draft Registration cards). He and his wife were buried in Notre Dame Cemetery in South Hadley, MA, as were several of their children.

Children:

i   **Rosario Louis Ulric Montcalm** b 16 Feb 1912, Worcester, MA; d & bur 4 & 9 Feb 2002, Holyoke & South Hadley, MA.

ii   **Léonie Blanche Montcalm** b 16 Jan 1914, Holyoke, MA; d & bur 17 & 21 Aug 1999, Holyoke & South Hadley, MA. She married 24 Aug 1937, Holyoke, MA, **John Patrick Sullivan** (John Lawrence Sullivan & Margaret O'Connor) b there 27 Aug 1908; d & bur 10 & 15 Jul 1995, Holyoke & South Hadley, MA.

iii   **Ulric Richard Montcalm** b 5 Nov 1915, Holyoke, MA; d 29 Jul 2003, Springfield, MA. He married 1 May 1943, Monroe, LA, **Althea Edna Morin** (Conrad J. Morin & Lillian E. ____) b 10 Sep 1918, Springfield, MA; d 5 Jan 1983, Holyoke, MA.

iv   **Claire Beatrice Montcalm** b 21 Oct 1917, Holyoke, MA; d there 6 Nov 1997.

v   **Aline Lorenza Montcalm** b 5 Mar 1921, Holyoke, MA; d there 1988.

5.7.1.12.5.5   MONTY, Léonie Rosaria b & bp 11 & 12 Feb 1888, Holyoke, MA; d 11 Jan 1892, New Haven, CT.

This child was named Léonie in the Holyoke, MA, Birth Records, Marie Léonie Rosaria at her baptism, and Rosaria at her death.

5.7.1.12.5.6   MONTY, Una Azarise b & bp 11 & 16 Jun 1889, South Hadley & Holyoke, MA; d & bur 3 & ? Feb 1965, Boston & South Hadley, MA. She married 26 Dec 1913, Holyoke, MA, **René Alphonse Richard** (Alphonse R. Richard & Corinne Evanturel) b 26 Sep 1887, Holyoke, MA; d & bur 18 & 22 Apr 1947, Boston & South Hadley, MA.

René A. Richard was a civil engineer and draftsman in Holyoke, Andover, and Lawrence, MA, until at least 1930 and in North Andover, MA, in 1942 (US censuses; City Directories; World War I and World War II Draft Registration cards). He and his wife were buried in Notre Dame Cemetery in South Hadley, MA.

Children:

i   **René A. Richard** b 18 Oct 1914, Holyoke, MA; d 23 Jul 1990. He married 18 Jan 1937, Salem, NH, **Juliette Caron.**

ii   **Ernest Monty Richard** b 14 Sep 1916, Holyoke, MA; d 4 Dec 1981, Boston, MA. He married 29 Dec 1944, North Andover, MA, **Eleanor Grace Parker** (William E. Parker & Emily ____) b there 21 Jul 1920; d 27 Jan 1998, Salisbury, MA.

iii   **Oscar Evanturel Richard** b 7 May 1918, Holyoke, MA. He married 25 Jun 1948 **Mary Lynch** b 11 Feb 1923.

iv   **Helen/Hélène Marguerite Richard** b 15 Apr 1921, Lawrence, MA. She married Aug 1948 **Robert Flanagan.**

v   **Robert Charles Richard** b 16 Dec 1922, Andover, MA; d 17 Nov 1992, Winston-Salem, NC. He married 6 Apr 1991, Surry Co., NC, **Lalah Opal Sexton** (Arthur Sexton & Irene Christian) b 4 Jan 1914, Pike Co., KY; m (1) ____ Bragg; d 7 Feb 2003, Mount Airy, NC.

vi   **Una Edwilda Richard** b 22 Oct 1924, Lawrence, MA. She married 1954, MA, **Emmett J. Cullen** (John A. Cullen & Esther P. ____) b 9 Jul 1926, MA.

vii   **Marie Richard** b 19 Jan 1927, Lawrence, MA; d there 20 Jan 1927.

viii   **Paul Theodore Richard** b 3 Feb 1932, Lawrence, MA. He married **Marguerite** _____ b 12 Mar 1932.

5.7.1.12.5.7   MONTY, Ernest Louis b & bp 17 Jun 1897, Holyoke, MA; d & bur 1 & 3 Apr 1985, Jefferson Parish & New Orleans, LA. He married (1) 26 Aug 1930, Montreal, QC, **Alice Eglantine Larocque** (Joseph Larocque & Emma Robillard) b & bp 9 & 14 Jun 1902, St. Lazare, QC; d & bur 26 & 29 Dec 1972, Burlington & Shelburne, VT.

He married (2) 21 Jun 1978, New Orleans, LA, **Claire St. Germain** (George St. Germain & Valerie Morales) b 11 Apr 1907, New Orleans, LA; m (1) 1932 Leo Esdorn; d 6 Mar 2007, Smyrna, GA.

Ernest L. Monty (Louis Charles Ernest at his baptism) was an attorney in Holyoke, MA. He retired in the late 1940s and moved to Burlington, VT, and, after his wife's death, to New Orleans, LA. He was buried in the Mausoleum of Lake Lawn Metairie Cemetery in New Orleans.

Alice Larocque was buried in the Catholic Cemetery in Shelburne, VT.

Ernest L. Monty began researching his family history in the early 1940s and published many articles on individual members of the Monty and related families. His research on the early descendants of Gaspard Monty (5) has been especially valuable in the present work.

Children of the first marriage:

5.7.1.12.5.7.1	Louis	1932- -1932
5.7.1.12.5.7.2	Alice Emma	1934-1954-
5.7.1.12.5.7.3	Jeanne Ruth	1935- -
5.7.1.12.5.7.4	Monique Thérèse	1941-1962&1984-1997

5.7.1.12.5.8   MONTY, Vincent Honoré b & bp 21 & 22 Jul 1906, Holyoke, MA; d & bur 31 Oct & 3 Nov 1998, St. Jérôme, QC.

Vincent Monty was a Jesuit priest who served in Canada, Ethiopia, and the United States.

5.7.1.12.11.1   MONTY, Beatrice b 31 Mar 1898, Woonsocket, RI. She married there 12 Feb 1922 **Arthur Harrison MacPherson** (James MacPherson & Jessie Crofts) b 1 Oct 1891, Worcester, MA.

Arthur McPherson was a policeman in Woonsocket, RI, in 1930 (US census) and until 1938 when he moved to Bellingham, MA (Woonsocket City Directories).

5.7.1.12.11.2   MONTY, Antoinette b & bp 21 & 24 May 1900, Woonsocket, RI; d Aug 1975, Pawtucket, RI. She married (1) 12 May 1919, Woonsocket, RI, **Emile Fortier** (Cléophas Fortier & Anna Cadoret) b & bp 12 & 13 May 1898, Manville, RI; d 4 Apr 1934, Bristol, CT.

She married (2) 8 Apr 1958, Greenville, RI, **Frederick Tellier** b 9 Jun 1911, RI; d May 1966, RI.

Emile Fortier was a clerk in Manville, RI, when he signed on 12 Sep 1918 his World War I Draft Registration card. He was a tea store manager there in 1920 (US census).

Children:

i   **Jeannette Lianne Fortier** b & bp 28 Aug & 12 Sep 1920, Manville, RI; d 10 Dec 2001, Port Orange, FL. She married 16 Aug 1941, Woonsocket, RI, **Joseph François Boucher** (Alfred Boucher & Irene Gregory) b 9 Mar 1912, Woonsocket, RI; d 15 Aug 2003, Port Orange, FL.

ii   **Marguerite/Margaret Fortier** b & bp 30 Aug 1925, Manville, RI. She married 8 May 1948, Woonsocket, RI, **Roy/Rocco S. Bafaro** (Salvatore Bafaro & Anna Morelli) b 14 Jan 1929, Providence, RI; d 26 Apr 2006, Manchester, CT.

5.7.2.6.2.1   MONTY, Médérise b & bp 7 & 8 Nov 1875, St. Alphonse, QC.

5.7.2.6.2.2   MONTY, Delia Rosanna b & bp 18 & 19 Oct 1877, St. Alphonse, QC; d 7 Sep 1937, Chicopee, MA. She married 1899?, Dudley, MA, **Ulric Bessette** (Magloire Bessette & Rose de Lima Dextrase) b & bp 23 May 1876, St. Alexandre, QC; m (2) 1 Sep 1941, St. Jean, QC, Lina/Lena Jackson, widow of Pierre Allard.

Ulric Bessette and his wife Delia had been married for less than a year in June 1900. He was a house carpenter/builder in Dudley and Webster, MA, until about 1912 and in Chicopee, MA, until at least 1948 (US censuses; Webster and Chicopee City Directories).

Children:

i   **Maida Bessette** b 1901?, Worcester Co., MA.

ii   **Cecile Bessette** b 1904?, Worcester Co., MA.

iii   **Raoul U. Bessette** b 1906?, Webster, MA. He married 1929? **Marguerite/Margaret Tessier** (A. Tessier & Cordelia ____) b 1908?, South Hadley, MA; m (2) Wilfred Cardinal; d 25 Dec 2004, Bethlehem, PA, at the age of 96.

iv   **Claire Bessette** b 19 Oct 1908, Webster, MA; d 1 Jan 1994, Holyoke, MA. She married 1939? **Roland A. Manseau** (Antonio Manseau & Octavie Turcotte) b 24 May 1901, Holyoke, MA; d there 23 Jan 1992.

v   **Gerard A. Bessette** b 7 Oct 1910, Webster, MA; d Dec 1969. He married **Reta V. ____.**

vi   **Rosario A. Bessette** b 1 Jan 1913, Hampden Co., MA; d Nov 1966, Chicopee, MA. He married **Catherine F. Mahoney** (Peter D. Mahoney & Catherine F. ____) b 26 Jan 1916, Chicopee, MA; d 7 Jun 2004, Springfield, MA.

vii   **Antoinette L. Bessette** b 1914?, Hampden Co., MA; d 1972. She married 1938? **Robert A. Demers** (Guy A. Demers & Stella ____) b 9 Mar 1913, Chicopee, MA; m (2) Juliette Thomas; d & bur 28 Jan & 2 Feb 2001, Canton, ME & Chicopee, MA.

viii   **Lucille M. Bessette** b 15 Aug 1917, Chicopee, MA; d & bur 7 & 10 Feb 2007, Springfield & Chicopee, MA. She married 1942? **Raymond G. Benoit** b 1 May 1915, Holyoke, MA; d & bur 24 & 27 Oct 1993, Springfield & Chicopee, MA.

ix   **Jeannette A. Bessette** b 1919, MA.

5.7.2.6.2.3   MONTY, Marie Louise Rosanna b & bp 29 & 31 Aug 1879, St. Alphonse, QC; d & bur there 16 & 17 Feb 1881.

5.7.2.6.2.4   MONTY, Arthur Joseph b & bp 20 & 21 May 1881, St. Alphonse, QC. He married there 14 Jul 1908 **Marie Caroline Geneviève Ruel** (François Xavier Ruel & Malinda Couture) b & bp there 12 & 13 Jan 1880.

Arthur Monty first came to the United States around 1891 and was a house carpenter living with his sister Delia and brother-in-law Ulric Bessette (5.7.2.6.2.1) in Dudley, MA, in 1900 (US census). Though he was naturalized on 18 Oct 1902 in the First District Court in Webster, MA, he soon returned to Canada. He married there and remained in the Granby area until 1929 when he and his family settled in Franklin Co., VT. He was a dairy farm worker in Sheldon, VT, in 1930 (US census), a resident of Enosburg Falls, VT, at the marriage of his son Léopold in 1936, and a resident of Sheldon again in 1942 (World War II Draft Registration card).

Children:

5.7.2.6.2.4.1	George Henri.	1909-1955-
5.7.2.6.2.4.2	Emile Louis	1912- -1996
5.7.2.6.2.4.3	Leo Paul/Léopold	1914-1936-2002
5.7.2.6.2.4.4	Maurice Lucien	1916-1943-2006
5.7.2.6.2.4.5	Claude	1918- -1975
5.7.2.6.2.4.6	Helen/Elaine	1921- -

5.7.2.6.2.5   MONTY, Louis Joseph Henri b & bp 12 Sep 1883, St. Alphonse, QC; d &

bur 22 & 25 Jul 1958, Marieville & Ange Gardien, QC. He married 7 Oct 1912, Ange Gardien, QC, **Laura Couture** (Napoléon Couture & Joséphine Poissant) b & bp there 23 & 27 Jun 1891; d 26 Mar 1973, Marieville, QC.

Louis Joseph Henri Monty was baptized and married under that name. On most other occasions however he was simply known as Joseph Monty. He lived with his parents in Dudley, MA, for a few years in the early and mid-1890s but was back in St. Alphonse, QC, in 1901 and 1911 (Canadian censuses). He was a blacksmith there in 1911 and at his marriage and was generally described as such at his children's baptisms. In a few instances, though, he was said to be a farmer.

Children:

5.7.2.6.2.5.1	Yvon	1913-1938-1970
5.7.2.6.2.5.2	Yvonne	1915-1947-1985
5.7.2.6.2.5.3	Normand	1918-1945-
5.7.2.6.2.5.4	Lucille Marguerite	1921-1943-1955
5.7.2.6.2.5.5	Grégoire	1923-1949-
5.7.2.6.2.5.6	Laurette Jeannette	1928- -1928
5.7.2.6.2.5.7	Réjeanne Mercédès Rita	1929-1953-
5.7.2.6.2.5.8	Blaise	1932-1954-1962
5.7.2.6.2.5.9	Jacques André	1934-1956-

5.7.2.6.2.6   **MONTY, Laura** b & bp 6 & 13 Sep 1885, St. Alphonse, QC. She married there 22 Jan 1907 **Albéric Pinsonneault** (Alexandre Pinsonneault & Mary Sheridan) b 1879?, QC; d & bur 4 & 6 Jun 1917, Ange Gardien, QC, at the age of 38.

Albéric Pinsonneault (also Pinsonnault) was a farmer in Ange Gardien, QC.

Children:

i   **Anonymous Pinsonneault** (male) b 27 Dec 1908, Ange Gardien, QC; d & bur there 27 & 28 Dec 1908.

ii   **Anonymous Pinsonneault** (male) b 17 May 1910, Ange Gardien, QC; d & bur there 17 & 18 May 1910.

iii   **Béatrice Pinsonneault** b & bp 28 & 29 Jul 1911, Ange Gardien, QC. She married there 15 Sep 1931 **Joseph Arthur Mercure** (Adolphe Mercure & Ozarine Bérard) b & bp there 27 & 28 Jan 1903.

iv   **Raoul Pinsonneault** b & bp 14 & 15 Sep 1912, Ange Gardien, QC. He married there 2 Aug 1948 **Marie Jeanne Lajoie** (Hector Lajoie & Florina Laliberté) b & bp there 20 & 21 Jul 1912.

v   **Georges Aimé Pinsonneault** b & bp 27 & 29 Mar 1914, Ange Gardien, QC. He married there 14 Sep 1938 **Elisabeth Germaine Arès** (Adrien Arès & Yvonne Robert) b & bp 24 Apr 1917, Rougemont, QC.

vi   **Maurice Gaston Pinsonneault** b & bp 24 & 26 Feb 1916, Ange Gardien, QC.

vii   **Yvon Pinsonneault** b & bp 16 & 20 May 1917, Ange Gardien, QC.

5.7.2.6.2.7   **MONTY, Aldéa Angélina** b & bp 25 Dec 1887, St. Alphonse, QC. She married there 10 Jan 1911 **Uldège Fortin** (David Fortin & Emélie Lapointe) b & bp there 29 Sep & 6 Oct 1889.

Uldège Fortin was a merchant in St. Alphonse, QC, until the mid-1920s when the family moved to Farnham, QC.

Children:

i   **Marie Desanges Fortin** b & bp 31 Jan & 4 Feb 1912, St. Alphonse, QC. She married 7 Sep 1940, Farnham, QC, **Louis Philippe L'Homme** (Georges L'Homme & Rose Anna Boucher) b & bp there 10 & 11 Mar 1912.

ii   **Gaston Aimé Fortin** b & bp 30 Apr 1913, St. Alphonse, QC.

iii   **David Robert Bernard Fortin** b & bp 24 & 26 May 1915, St. Alphonse, QC. He married 21 Jun 1941, Drummondville, QC, **Laurette Pelletier** (Zabulon Pelletier &

Maria Bérubé).

iv **Jeanne d'Arc Estelle Fortin** b & bp 1 & 5 Nov 1916, St. Alphonse, QC; d & bur there 8 & 9 Apr 1919.

v **Laure Madeleine Marguerite Fortin** b & bp 3 & 4 Sep 1918, St. Alphonse, QC.

vi **Marguerite Jeanne d'Arc Fortin** b & bp 1 & 3 Mar 1921, St. Alphonse, QC. She married 13 Jun 1950, Farnham, QC, **Léopold Rocheleau** (Louis Napoléon Rocheleau & Edwina Vachon).

vii **Marthe Bernadette Fortin** b & bp 9 & 10 Apr 1923, St. Alphonse, QC. She married 1 Jul 1949, Farnham, QC, **Gérard Ally** (Omer Ally & Estelle Denault).

viii **Jean Luc Paul Fortin** b & bp 1 Sep 1926, Farnham, QC. He married there 10 Jun 1953 **Jacqueline Lacoste** (Philippe Lacoste & Yvette Mercure).

ix **Pierre Fortin** b & bp 25 & 26 May 1928, Farnham, QC. He married 7 Aug 1958, Bedford, QC, **Suzanne Langevin** (Hector Langevin & Béatrice Racine) b & bp there 1 & 2 Oct 1929.

5.7.2.6.2.8   **MONTY, Oliva** b & bp 4 Jan 1890, St. Alphonse, QC. He married 12 Jun 1916, Granby, QC, **Alma Brodeur** (Louis Brodeur & Célina Alix) b 11 Jun 1890, QC.

Oliva Monty lived with his parents in Dudley, MA, for a few years in the early and mid-1890s but returned to St. Alphonse, QC, with them before 1901 (Canadian census). He became a farmer there.

Children:

5.7.2.6.2.8.1	Béatrice	1918-1937-
5.7.2.6.2.8.2	Aline Célina Edouardina	1919-1948-
5.7.2.6.2.8.3	Georgette Jeanne d'Arc	1921-1945-
5.7.2.6.2.8.4	Joseph Conrad	1923- -1923
5.7.2.6.2.8.5	Rosaire André Roger	1925-1951-
5.7.2.6.2.8.6	Laurette	1928-1959-
5.7.2.6.2.8.7	Marie Jeanne Françoise	1933-1960-

5.7.2.6.2.9   **MONTY, Léa** b 4 Sep 1892, Webster, MA. She married 18 Nov 1913, St. Alphonse, QC, **Rosial Desnoyers** (Séraphin Desmarais dit Desnoyers & Philomène Messier) b & bp 30 Jun & 2 Jul 1889, St. Césaire, QC.

Léa Monty's parents stayed in Dudley, MA, for only a few years after her birth. In 1901, she was living on her father's farm in St. Alphonse, QC (Canadian census). Her husband, named Osée Rosialde Desmarais at his baptism, was nevertheless known as Rosial Desnoyers as an adult. He was a farmer in Granby, QC, at his marriage and until at least 1923 and then in Ange Gardien, St. Alphonse, and Stanbridge, QC, at the births of his youngest children.

Children:

i **Claire Lucille Desnoyers** b & bp 18 Sep 1914, Granby, QC; d 28 Feb 1973, Cowansville, QC. She married 18 Jun 1938, Stanbridge, QC, **Philippe/George Henri Philip Galipeau** (Levi/Elisée Galipeau & Ernestine Brodeur) b & bp there 18 & 22 Jun 1912; d 12 Nov 1986, Sherbrooke, QC.

ii **Marcel O'Leary Desnoyers** b & bp 24 & 25 Jan 1916, Granby, QC. He married there 22 Jun 1940 **Thérèse Hélène Champigny** (Rodolphe Champigny & Alice Brodeur) b & bp 16 May 1918, St. Alphonse, QC.

iii **Henri Fernand Desnoyers** b & bp 22 & 24 Sep 1919, Granby, QC. He married 5 Feb 1947, Dunham, QC, **Jeanne d'Arc Rocheleau** (Firmin Rocheleau & Yvonne Lefebvre) b & bp 1 & 2 Nov 1926, Frelighsburg, QC.

iv **Jeanne d'Arc Gabrielle Desnoyers** b & bp 22 & 23 Oct 1921, Granby, QC. She married 28 Aug 1943, Stanbridge, QC, **Léo/Emile Léon Landry** (Ulléric Landry & Emélie Lebel) b & bp 30 & 31 Mar 1910, St. Alexandre de Kamouraska, QC.

v **Anne Marie Thérèse Desnoyers** b & bp 31 Jul 1923, Granby, QC. She married 16 May 1942, Stanbridge, QC, **Oscar Thériault** (William Thériault & Louise Paradis) b & bp 29 & 30 Jul 1910, St. Jean, QC.

vi   **Louis Ulysse Desnoyers** b & bp 6 & 8 Nov 1925, Ange Gardien, QC. He married 7 May 1949, Brigham, QC, **Pauline Chalin** (Emile Chalin & Alexina Leduc) b & bp 12 & 16 Jun 1929, Huntingdon, QC.

vii   **Bernadette Desnoyers** b & bp 4 & 5 Apr 1928, Anne Gardien, QC. She married 2 Sep 1950, Stanbridge, QC, **Germain Allard** (Eusèbe Allard & Ida Rancourt).

viii   **Gérard Desnoyers** married 15 Aug 1953, Farnham, QC, **Nicole Poulin** (Rouville Poulin & Marie Jeanne Boulais) b & bp 10 & 15 Apr 1934, Ste Sabine, QC.

ix   **Marguerite Jeannine Desnoyers** b & bp 6 & 7 Mar 1930, St. Alphonse, QC. She married 23 May 1953, Stanbridge, QC, **Gilles Déragon** (Léo Déragon & Antoinette Bessette) b & bp 6 & 7 Nov 1931, Trois Rivières, QC.

x   **Viola Monique Desnoyers** b & bp 31 Aug & 2 Sep 1932, St. Alphonse, QC. She married 16 Jul 1955, Stanbridge, QC, **Guy Guertin** (Ovila Guertin & Alexina Cardinal) b & bp 15 & 20 Sep 1931, Roxton Pond, QC.

xi   **André Jean-Paul Desnoyers** b & bp 27 & 28 Oct 1936, Stanbridge, QC. He married there 2 Sep 1963 **Louise Fontaine** (Lucien Fontaine & Laura Bouchard).

5.7.2.6.2.10   **MONTY, Joseph Louis** b 3 Feb 1895, Dudley, MA.

This child does not appear with his parents in the 1901 Canadian census in St. Alphonse, QC, and may have died before then.

5.7.2.6.2.11   **MONTY, George** b 13 Dec 1897, QC. He married 17 Jul 1923, Ange Gardien, QC, **Yvonne Balthazard** (Fortunat Balthazard & Victoria Gazaille) b & bp 21 & 22 May 1906, Adamsville, QC.

George Monty's date of birth is taken from the 1901 Canadian census in St. Alphonse, QC. He was a resident there at his marriage.

5.7.2.6.2.12   **MONTY, Anonymous** b 30 Nov 1899, St. Alphonse, QC; d & bur there 30 Nov & 2 Dec 1899.

5.7.2.6.4.1   **MONTY, Marie Alphonsine** b & bp 22 & 23 Aug 1874, Bromont, QC; d & bur there 5 & 7 Nov 1874.

5.7.2.6.4.2   **MONTY, Rose/Rosa** b & bp 19 & 25 Dec 1875, Bromont, QC; d & bur 17 & 19 Dec 1917, Sherbrooke & Granby, QC. She married 20 Jan 1913, Granby, QC, **Alcide Laplante** (Ignace Laplante & Clémentine Deschênes) b & bp 22 & 23 Apr 1872, Sillery, QC; m (2) 19 Aug 1918, Richmond, QC, Caroline Girard (Cléophas Girard & Delima Dulude).

This woman was named Marie Rose Exina at her baptism, Rosa at her burial, and Ana in the text of her marriage record. She signed it though as M. Rosa Monty.

Alcide Laplante was a resident of Sherbrooke, QC, at his first marriage.

Child:

i   **Anonymous Laplante** (female) b 7 Dec 1917, Sherbrooke, QC; d & bur there 7 Dec 1917.

5.7.2.6.4.3   **MONTY, Alphonsine** b & bp 26 & 31 Mar 1878, Bromont, QC; d & bur 26 & 28 Dec 1936, Verdun & Granby, QC. She married 17 Aug 1903, Bromont, QC, **Nazaire Larivière** (Louis Larivière & Marie Louise Giard) b & Bp 22 & 24 Feb 1969, St. David, QC.

Nazaire Larivière was a tailor in Granby, QC, at his marriage and at the births of his children. He was a resident of Montreal, QC, when his wife died in 1936.

Children:

i   **Anonymous Larivière** (male) b 17 Feb 1904, Granby, QC; d & bur there 17 Feb 1904.

ii   **Marie Berthe Larivière** b & bp 25 & 28 Feb 1907, Granby, QC; d 23 Sep 1995, Cowansville, QC. She married 28 Jun 1932 **Henri Dussault** (Napoléon Dussault &

Marie Joséphine Têtu) b & bp 9 & 10 Sep 1907, L'Islet sur Mer, QC; d 23 Apr 1966, Bedford, QC.

iii **Paul Emile Larivière** b & bp 3 & 8 Nov 1908, Granby, QC. He married 9 Apr 1940, Montreal, QC, **Marie Lucille Laure Bourbeau** (Napoléon Bourbeau & Albina Fortin) b & bp 19 & 22 Mar 1908, St. Alphonse, QC.

iv **Rachel Valentine Marguerite Larivière** b & bp 4 Feb 1911, Granby, QC.

v **Lucille Thérèse Larivière** b & bp 9 & 10 Mar 1912, Granby, QC.

5.7.2.6.4.4   **MONTY, Arthur** b & bp 27 Jul & 1 Aug 1880, Bromont, QC; d & bur there 9 & 10 May 1904. He married there 22 Sep 1903 **Delphine Almina Bergeron** (Louis Bergeron & Elmire Daniel) b & bp 18 & 20 Aug 1879, Bromont & Granby, QC; m (2) 10 Jan 1910, Bromont, QC, Michel Xavier Phenix (Jean-Baptiste Phenix & Adélia Beauregard).

Child:
5.7.2.6.4.4.1   Arthur Léonide Robert   1904-   -

5.7.2.6.4.5   **MONTY, Alphonse** b & bp 26 May & 3 Jun 1883, Bromont, QC; d & bur 21 & 24 Mar 1939, Rock Island & Granby, QC. He married (1) 9 Oct 1911, Granby, QC, **Mathilde Messier** (Grégoire Messier & Octavie Dépaty) b & bp 11 & 14 Aug 1881, Ste Brigide, QC; d & bur 25 & 27 Aug 1912, Granby, QC.

He married (2) 20 Jun 1916, Granby, QC, **Lucinda Bernice Cahill** (Patrick Cahill & Margaret Carey) b & bp there 30 Sep & 2 Oct 1892; d 15 Nov 1979, Sherbrooke, QC.

Alphonse Monty was a clerk in Granby, QC, in 1911 (Canadian census). He became an innkeeper in Rock Island, QC, in the mid-1920s.

Children of the second marriage:
5.7.2.6.4.5.1	André/Andrew René	1918-1941-2005
5.7.2.6.4.5.2	Marguerite Lorraine	1920- -1920
5.7.2.6.4.5.3	George Louis	1923-1950-1991
5.7.2.6.4.5.4	Elizabeth/Betty Jeanne	1926-1954-1991
5.7.2.6.4.5.5	Helen Patricia	1927-1952-

5.7.2.6.4.6   **MONTY, Clara Eva** b & bp 25 & 29 Jun 1886, Bromont, QC. She married there 8 Feb 1909 **Joseph Narcisse Ovelus Lasnier** (Alphonse Lasnier & Amanda Gemme) b & bp 5 & 7 Jun 1885, Abbotsford, QC.

Children:
i   **Bernard Omer Lasnier** (twin) b & bp 24 & 29 Aug 1915, Granby, QC.
ii   **Marie Claire Estelle Lasnier** (twin) b & bp 24 & 29 Aug 1915, Granby, QC; d & bur there 11 & 12 Sep 1915.

5.7.2.6.4.7   **MONTY, Ernest** b & bp 2 & 9 Sep 1888, Bromont, QC; d 22 Jul 1959, Edmonton, Alberta, Canada. He married 11 Sep 1911, St. Alphonse, QC, **Valéda Martin** (Siméon Martin & Delima Charron) b & bp there 18 & 20 Apr 1893; d 1968, Granby, QC.

Ernest Monty was a farmer in Bromont, QC, at the births of his first two children. He moved to Granby, QC, shortly before the death of his son Ernest in 1916.

Children:
5.7.2.6.4.7.1	Ernest Siméon	1912- -1916
5.7.2.6.4.7.2	Blanche Anne Thérèse	1915-1953-
5.7.2.6.4.7.3	Albert Ernest	1916-1945-
5.7.2.6.4.7.4	Gaston	1923-1946-

5.7.2.6.4.8   **MONTY, Oscar Roméo André** b & bp 22 & 24 Mar 1895, Bromont, QC. He married 14 Sep 1920, Grenville, QC, **Aimée Laurin** (Honoré Laurin & Augustine Leclerc) b & bp there 20 & 29 Jan 1893.

This man was named Oscar Roméo André at his baptism and Oscar Roméo at his marriage. On other occasions he was known as simply Roméo Monty.

Children:

5.7.2.6.4.8.1	André Bernard	1922-	-
5.7.2.6.4.8.2	Gisèle Carmel	1925-	-
5.7.2.5.4.8.3	Lise Micheline Louise	1932-	-

5.7.2.6.4.9 **MONTY, Albert Rosario** b & bp 9 & 10 Jul 1898, Bromont, QC; d & bur 29 May & 1 Jun 1955, Montreal & Granby, QC. He married 14 Jun 1922, Granby, QC, **Laurette Tétrault/Tétreau** (Zébée Tétrault & Laura Bienvenu) b & bp 1 Sep 1901, Ange Gardien, QC; d 11 Sep 1962, Montreal, QC.

Albert Monty (Joseph Albert Rosario at his baptism) was a resident of Granby, QC, at his marriage and at the births of his children. He was an insurance agent there in 1929. His wife, named Laurette Tétrault at her marriage, had been baptized as Marie Laure Laureta Tétreau.

Children:

5.7.2.6.4.9.1	Clément Dollard André	1923-1950-1990
5.7.2.6.4.9.2	Andrée Thérèse	1926-1958-
5.7.2.6.4.9.3	Denyse Francine J. G.	1929- -1987

5.7.2.6.4.10 **MONTY, Marie Ange Arsena** b & bp 13 & 17 Nov 1901, Bromont, QC.
Marie Ange Montey (sic) was living with her parents in Bromont, QC, in 1911 (Canadian census).

5.7.2.6.6.1 **MONTY, Georgiana Eleonora** b & bp 21 & 28 Oct 1877, Waterloo, QC; d & bur there 20 & 21 Jan 1881.

5.7.2.6.6.2 **MONTY, Ida** b & bp 9 & 16 Feb 1879, Waterloo, QC; d & bur 8 & 10 Jul 1965, New Bedford, MA. She married 1902? **William Greenwood (Boisvert?)** b 28 May 1880, Canada.

Ida Monty (Marie Louise Ida at her baptism) came to the United States with her family in 1896 and was a cotton mill worker in New Bedford, MA, in 1900. She and her husband, a building contractor in Dartmouth, MA, had been married for twenty-eight years in 1930 (US censuses). She survived him and was buried in New Bedford's Sacred Heart Cemetery.

5.7.2.6.6.3 **MONTY, Victoria Louise** b & bp 27 Nov & 12 Dec 1880, Waterloo, QC. She married 21 Nov 1910, New Bedford, MA, **Alphonse Bourbeau** (Joseph Bourbeau & Adeline Beaumont) b & bp 8 & 18 May 1884, Waterloo, QC.

Victoria Monty came to the United States with her family in 1896 and was a cotton mill worker in New Bedford, MA, in 1900 and 1910. Alphonse Bourbeau was originally a plumber in New Bedford before moving to North Dartmouth, MA, in the mid-1920s (US censuses; City Directories).

Children:
  i   **Reina Bourbeau** b 21 Jan 1912, New Bedford, MA; d there 29 Jun 2000. She married **John F. Reilly** b 27 Jun 1915; d 25 Mar 1998, New Bedford, MA.
  ii   **Alphonse L. Bourbeau** b 4 Mar 1913, New Bedford, MA; d there 3 Sep 1987. He married **Annette ____** b 3 Feb 1914.

5.7.2.6.6.4 **MONTY, Rose Anna/Marie Dorila** b & bp 25 Aug & 3 Sep 1882, Bromont, QC; d & bur there 16 & 18 Aug 1883.

This child was baptized as Rose Anna but was named Marie Dorila at her death at the age of one. Unless there is an error in the parents' names, both records must refer to the same child.

5.7.2.6.6.5   MONTY, Honora b & bp 22 & 27 Apr 1884, Bromont, QC.
Honora Monty was not living in her father's household in New Bedford, MA, in 1900 (US census) and may have died before then.

5.7.2.6.6.6   MONTY, Emma L. b 18 Sep 1885, Waterloo, QC; d & bur 6 & 9 Feb 1956, New Bedford, MA. She married 1910? **Louis Coutu** (Hormisdas Coutu & Caroline Hénault) b & bp 25 & 27 Aug 1887, St. Félix de Valois, QC.
Louis Coutu was a laborer in Providence, RI, before moving to Massachusetts around 1919. He was a stamper in a jewelry factory in Attleboro, MA, in 1920 and a painter in New Bedford, MA, in 1930, when he and his wife had been married for twenty years (US censuses). His widow was buried in St. Mary's Cemetery in New Bedford.

Children:
i   **Louis H. Coutu** b 11 Jun 1911, Providence, RI; d 7 Feb 2008, Nantucket, MA.
ii   **Beatrice E. Coutu** b 30 Dec 1912, Providence, RI. She married **Gilbert Leger** b 7 Nov 1913, MA; d 2 Apr 1979, Nantucket, MA.
iii   **Eva J. Coutu** b 2 Mar 1917, Providence, RI; d 23 Apr 2001, South Dartmouth, MA. She married **Joseph Arruda** b 6 Jun 1914; d 26 Oct 2002, New Bedford, MA.
iv   **Irene B. Coutu** b 1921?, Bristol Co., MA. She married ____ **Kelly**.
v   **Omer E. Coutu** b 1923?, Bristol Co., MA.
vi   **Jeannette Theresa Coutu** b 29 Jan 1929, New Bedford, MA; d & bur 25 & 29 Aug 2000, Nantucket, MA. She married there 19 Oct 1957 **Maurice J. Dee** (Maurice Dee & Mabel ____) b 30 Aug 1926, MA.

5.7.2.6.6.7   MONTY, Thomas b & bp 27 Mar & 3 Apr 1887, Waterloo, QC. He married 2 Sep 1908, Providence, RI, **Amelia/Emelia D. Nolin** (Joseph Nolin & Onésime Dion) b 25 Feb 1885, MA; d 26 Mar 1982, Anaheim, CA.
Thomas Monty came to New Bedford, MA, with his family in 1896 and was naturalized in 1919. With the exception of a few years in the late 1920s when he was described as a farmer (New Bedford City Directories of 1926 and 1928), he was a cotton mill worker there until at least 1949 (US censuses; City Directories).

Children:

5.7.2.6.6.7.1	Rhea A.	1909-	-2005
5.7.2.6.6.7.2	Homer/Omer	1913?-	-1922
5.7.2.6.6.7.3	George A.	1915-1941?-	1996
5.7.2.6.6.7.4	Leo W.	1918-	-1999
5.7.2.6.6.7.5	Irene	1919-	-
5.7.2.6.6.7.6	Doris Victoria	1923-	-2005

5.7.2.6.6.8   MONTY, Anselme Ulric b & bp 14 & 19 May 1889, Waterloo, QC; d 8 Oct 1918, New Bedford, MA. He married there 21 Jun 1909 **Marie Anne/Mary A. Roy** (Joseph Roy & Constance Côté) b & bp 13 & 15 Jun 1892, Ste Angèle de Mérici, QC; m (2) 5 Apr 1920, New Bedford, MA, Samuel Joseph Bergeron (Stanislas Bergeron & Georgiana Lauzé); d & bur there 12 & 15 Jul 1970.
Anselme Monty came to New Bedford, MA, with his family in 1896. He was a weaver there and was buried in the city's New Sacred Heart Cemetery, as were his wife and her second husband.
Marie Anne Roy had arrived in the United States in 1905 and was naturalized in 1917. After her first husband's death she lived for a time with her sister Lucy and brother-in-law Leo Massé in New Bedford while her sons were in St. Joseph's Orphanage in Fall River, MA. In 1930, though, her children Philip, Ovila, and Loretta Monty were members of Samuel Bergeron's household (US censuses).

Children:

5.7.2.6.6.8.1	Omer Albert	1909-	-1990	
5.7.2.6.6.8.2	Raymond/René	1911?-	-	
5.7.2.6.6.8.3	Joseph Philip	1913-	-1988	
5.7.2.6.6.8.4	Ovila A.	1915-	-2001	
5.7.2.6.6.8.5	Loretta C.	1918-1937?&		-2007

5.7.2.6.6.9 **MONTY, Ovila** b 23 May 1891, Granby, QC; d & bur 16 & 19 Jan 1976, Middleborough & New Bedford, MA. He married 8 Sep 1913, New Bedford, MA, **Lydia Hébert** (Calixte Hébert & Marie Anne/Annie Prince) b & bp 10 Apr 1888, St. Léonard d'Aston, QC; d 9 Jun 1982, New Bedford, MA.

Ovila Monty came to the United States with his family in 1896, was naturalized in 1919, and was a cotton mill worker in New Bedford, MA, in 1920 and 1930 (US censuses). He was still there in 1945 (City Directories) and was buried there in Sacred Heart Cemetery.

Child:
5.7.2.6.6.9.1	Omer Leo	1918-	-1990

5.7.2.8.1.1 **MONTY, Minnie/Melvine** b 1876? CT. She married 21 Jan 1896, New Bedford, MA, **Robert Livesey** (Jacob Livesey & Mary Fritton) b 1875?

Melvine Monty was a 4-year-old child living with her parents in Manville, RI, in 1880 (US census). She was 20 years old and named Minnie at her marriage. Robert Livesey was then a 21-year-old weaver in New Bedford, MA.

5.7.2.8.1.2 **MONTY, Florant** b 1878?, CT.

Florant Monty was a 2-year-old child living with his parents in Manville, RI, in 1880 (US census). He does not appear with his family in later censuses.

5.7.2.8.1.3 **MONTY, Theodore Frederick** b 18 Jul 1879, Sutton, MA. He married 14 Oct 1901, Fall River, MA, **Rose Chrétien** (Stanislas Chrétien & Mary Stevenson) b & bp 13 & 14 Jul 1882, Matane, QC; d 10 Nov 1915, Fall River, MA.

Theodore Monty (at times Frederick or Fred Monty) was a weaver in Fall River, MA, in 1900 and until at least 1915, in Plainfield, CT, in 1920, and again in Fall River in 1930 (US censuses). He was still in Fall River when he signed his World War II Draft Registration card in 1942.

Children:
5.7.2.8.1.3.1	Florilda	1901-	-1904
5.7.2.8.1.3.2	Louise	1902-1921-1993	
5.7.2.8.1.3.3	Eva	1906-	-1906
5.7.2.8.1.3.4	Alice	1907-	-1907
5.7.2.8.1.3.5	Lucy	1909-	-
5.7.2.8.1.3.6	Claire	1910-	-
5.7.2.8.1.3.7	Leo Theodore	1913-1947?-1991	
5.7.2.8.1.3.8	Letria (?)	1915-	-1915

5.7.2.8.1.4 **MONTY, Rosanna** b 26 May 1881, Woonsocket, RI; d 9 Oct 1954, Plainfield, CT. She married 1898? **James Dessert** b 21 Apr 1879, Canada.

James Dessert came to the United States around 1892 and had been married for two years in 1900. He was a weaver in a cotton mill in Fall River, MA, in 1900 and 1910 and a loom fixer in Plainfield, CT, in 1920 and 1930 (US censuses).

Children:
    i   **Amedee Dessert** b 5 Jun 1900, Fall River, MA; d 20 Jun 1963, Plainfield, CT. He married 1918? **Clara Leroux** (Ernest Leroux & Marie Louise Desrosiers) b & bp 30 Nov & 1 Dec 1896, Wotton, QC; d 21 Dec 1982, Putnam, CT.

    ii   **Irene Dessert** b 15 Oct 1902, Fall River, MA; d 23 Jun 1979, Windham Co., CT.

She married **Joseph George Laflamme** b 28 Jan 1903, CT; d 13 Jul 1979, Putnam, CT.

iii   **Anna Dessert** b 1905?, Fall River, MA.

iv   **Claudia Dessert** b Dec 1908, Fall River, MA.

5.7.2.8.1.5   **MONTY, Octavie Clara Eglantine** b 14 May 1885, Woonsocket, RI.

5.7.2.8.1.6   **MONTY, Florilda/Flora** b 31 May 1888, Woonsocket, RI. She married (1) 7 May 1906, Woonsocket, RI, **Edgar Boisvert** (Edward Boisvert & Mathilda Renaud) b there 31 Aug 1882.

She married (2) around 1911 **George Edward Thompson** b 30 Jul 1892, NY.

Edgar Boisvert was an insurance agent in Woonsocket, RI, in 1910 (US census). He and his wife had apparently already separated, each staying with their respective parents, and the children staying with their father.

George E. Thompson and his wife lived in the early 1910s in Massachusetts where their children were born. In 1920, though, when his mother-in-law Mrs. Adeline Monty was a member of his household, he was a mechanic in a cotton mill in Plainfield, CT (US census). I have been unable to follow the family any further.

Children:

i   **Oscar Boisvert** b 1907?, Woonsocket, RI.

ii   **Emile L. Boisvert** b 1908?, Woonsocket, RI.

iii   **Homer Boisvert** b 28 Jan 1909, Providence, RI; d there 18 Nov 1909 at the age of 9 months and 21 days.

iv   **Hazel Thompson** b 1911?, MA.

v   **Thomas Thompson** b 1912?, MA.

vi   **George Thompson** b 1914?, MA.

5.7.2.8.1.7   **MONTY, Eva Marie** b 20 Dec 1890, Woonsocket, RI; d 14 May 1895, New Bedford, MA.

5.7.2.8.1.8   **MONTY, Oscar** b 18 Sep 1892, Woonsocket, RI; d 4 Apr 1903, Fall River, MA.

Oscar Monty was buried in Notre Dame Cemetery in Fall River, MA.

5.7.2.8.2.1   **MONTY/MONTIE, Leonard Felix** b 13 Jan 1885, MA; bur Nov 1943, Woonsocket, RI.

Leonard Monty came to Woonsocket, RI, with his parents in the 1890s and was a teamster/trucker/chauffeur there well into the 1930s (US censuses; Woonsocket City Directories). He still used the surname Monty occasionally but his surname in the City Directories from at least 1922 on was always Montie. He was also buried as Leonard Montie in Woonsocket's Precious Blood Cemetery.

5.7.2.8.2.2   **MONTY/MONTIE, Leo Louis** b & bp 22 Jun & 4 Jul 1897, Woonsocket, RI; bur there 1958. He married (1) there 23 Oct 1917 **Marie Leda Chevalier** (Napoléon Chevalier & Herminie Crépeau) b & bp there 1 & 2 Mar 1898; bur there 1943.

He married (2) 30 Sep 1944, Central Falls, RI, **Bertha Sylvia Giroux** (Leo Giroux & Eveline ____) b 1905?, RI; m (1) there 27 Jun 1927 Jean-Baptiste Joseph Légaré.

Leo Montie was a construction worker in Woonsocket, RI, when he signed on 12 Sep 1918 his World War I Draft Registration card and, more specifically, a house carpenter there in 1920 and 1930 (US censuses). He was a teamster in Pawtucket, RI, in 1932 and 1934, and a superintendent there until at least 1945 (City Directories). He and his wife Leda were buried in Woonsocket's Precious Blood Cemetery.

The 25-year-old Sylvia Giroux was living with her first husband in Pawtucket, RI, in 1930 (US censuses).

Children of the first marriage:

5.7.2.8.2.2.1	Dorothea Doris	1918-1940-1997
5.7.2.8.2.2.2	Leona Hermine	1919-1937-2000

5.7.2.8.4.1   **MONTY, Rosalie** b 23 Sep 1884, Webster, MA; d 3 Apr 1886, New Bedford, MA.

5.7.2.8.4.2   **MONTY, Louis Trefflé** b 25 May 1886, New Bedford, MA; d there Dec 1968. He married (1) there 6 Sep 1910 **Helene Goeway** (Charles Goeway & Mary Russell) b 1891?, VT.

He married (2) 30 May 1918, New Bedford, MA, **Hélène/Helen Gagnon** (Magloire Gagnon & Adèle Michaud) b & bp 1 Aug 1876, Trois Pistoles, QC.

Louis Monty was a roofer in New Bedford, MA (US censuses; City Directories). His first wife, Helene Goeway, was 19 years old at her marriage.

His second wife was named Hélène Gagnon at her marriage. She was commonly known in later records though as Mrs. Helen Monty

5.7.2.8.4.3   **MONTY, Louis** b 17 Jul 1893, Pascoag, RI; d 7 Aug 1894, Webster, MA.

5.7.2.8.4.4   **MONTY, Joseph Louis** b 7 Jun 1894, Dudley, MA; d 17 Oct 1914, Fall River, MA.

5.7.2.10.2.1   **MONTY, Anonymous** (male) b 15 Jan 1908, Milton, QC; d & bur there 15 Jan 1908.

This child was stillborn.

5.7.2.10.2.2   **MONTY, Anonymous** (male) b 28 Mar 1909, Upton, QC; d & bur there 28 Mar 1909.

5.7.2.10.2.3   **MONTY, Marie Jeanne** b Jan 1913; d & bur 16 & 17 Aug 1914, St. Jean-Baptiste, QC, at the age of 19 months.

5.7.2.10.2.4   **MONTY, Anonymous** (male) b 12 Apr 1914, St. Bruno, QC; d & bur there 12 Apr 1914.

This child was stillborn.

5.7.2.10.2.5   **MONTY, Gilberta** b & bp 20 Jul 1915, St. Basile, QC.

Gilberta Monty (Cécile Gilberte Marguerite at her baptism) came to the United States soon after her birth and was living with her parents in Newport, VT, in 1920 and 1930 (US censuses).

5.7.2.10.2.6   **MONTY, Leonard G.** b Feb 1928, Newport, VT. He married **Wilma I. ____** b 15 Nov 1928; d 27 Jul 1997, Newport, VT.

5.7.2.15.11.1   **MONTY, Anonymous** (male) b 9 Sep 1927, Drummondville, QC; d & bur there 9 & 10 Sep 1927.

5.7.2.15.11.2   **MONTY, Mariette Jeannine Aurore** b & bp 27 Dec 1928, Drummondville, QC; d 9 Apr 1993. She married 15 Jun 1957, Drummondville, QC, **Albert Caya** (André Wenceslas Caya & Georgiana Roy) b & bp 4 & 5 Apr 1927, St Germain de Grantham, QC; d May 2001, Terrebonne, QC.

5.7.2.15.11.3   **MONTY, Gilles Eddy** b & bp 21 & 22 Jul 1933, Drummondville, QC.

5.7.2.15.11.4   **MONTY, Yvon**

5.7.2.15.11.5   MONTY, Jean Guy Normand b & bp 7 & 8 Mar 1935, Drummondville, QC; d there Jan 2000. He married 29 Jun 1957, St. Germain de Grantham, QC, **Lucille Doris St. Martin** (Charles Edouard St. Martin & Simone Vanasse) b & bp there 20 Jun 1940.

5.7.2.15.11.6   MONTY, Anonymous (female) b 8 Feb 1938, Drummondville, QC; d & bur there 8 Feb 1938.

5.7.5.5.2.1   MONTY, Joseph E. b Mar 1909, Jewett City, CT.
      Joseph E. Monty was 13 months old in April 1910 when he was living with his parents in Jewett City, CT. He was a mill worker in Sterling, CT, in 1930 and a resident of Glastonbury, CT, when his brother Harold died in 1994 (US censuses; *Hartford Courant*, 12 Dec 1994).

5.7.5.5.2.2   MONTY, Harold J. b 16 Apr 1912, Jewett City, CT; d & bur 10 & 14 Dec 1994, Hartford & East Hartford, CT. He married 1942, Hartford, CT, **Anne Joan Surus** (Frank Surus & Petronella ____) b there 20 Jun 1920; d & bur 3 & 6 Mar 1997, Albuquerque, NM & East Hartford, CT.
      Harold J. Monty and his wife were owners of The Yankee Trader gift shop in East Hartford, CT. They were buried in Hillside Cemetery there (*Hartford Courant*, 12 Dec 1994 and 5 Mar 1997).

Children:
5.7.5.5.2.2.1	Harold J.	1943-	-2000
5.7.5.5.2.2.2	Ronald	-	-

5.7.5.5.2.3   MONTY, Lillian b Jun 1916, Windham Co., CT. She married **Everett J. Mader** (Joseph Mader & Antonia Ronskavitz) b 23 Jul 1921, Glastonbury, CT; d 21 May 1981, Hartford, CT.
      Everett Mader was a carpenter in Glastonbury, CT. His widow was still residing there when their son Paul died in 2002 (*Hartford Courant*, 19 Oct 2002).

Children:
i   **Paul Joseph Mader** b 4 Jan 1951, Glastonbury, CT; d & bur 17 & 21 Oct 2002, South Windsor, CT. He married (1) there 15 Mar 1974 **Cheryl A. Janco** b Dec 1952.
      He married (2) 29 Apr 1995, South Windsor, CT, **April N. Foster** (Walter G. Foster & Evelyn Little) b there 1959.
ii   **Lenore A. Mader** b Jul 1955, Glastonbury, CT. She married there 27 Oct 1978 **Bruce S. Gilnack** b May 1953.

5.7.5.5.6.1   MONTY, Lionel Fulgence b & bp 2 & 3 Jan 1912, Ste Brigide, QC; d 3 Nov 1980, Norwich, CT. He married **Ruth M. Dawley** (Albert Henry Dawley & Lydia Alice ____) b 17 Dec 1912, CT; d 18 Oct 2002, New London Co., CT.
      This man was named Joseph Fulgence Lionel Monty at his baptism and Lionel Monty when he came to the United States with his parents in April 1917 but Leon Monte when he was living with them in Jewett City, CT, in 1920 (US census). He was named Lionel F. Monty as an adult in Norwich, CT.

Child:
5.7.5.5.6.1.1	Lionel H.	1941-	-

5.7.5.5.6.2   MONTY, Wilfred Louis Alphonse b & bp 30 Apr & 1 May 1916, Ste Brigide, QC.
      Wilfred Monty (Louis Alphonse Wilfrid at his baptism) arrived in the United States with his parents in April 1917 and was living with them in Jewett City, CT, in 1920 under the name of Wilfred Monte (US census). I have not found him in later years.

5.7.5.7.4.1 **MONTY, Mathilde Joséphine Irène** b & bp 26 & 27 Dec 1904, St. Jean, QC. She married 31 Aug 1935, Montreal, QC, **Henri Anthime Limoges** (Wilfrid Limoges & Amanda Cyr) b & bp there 24 Mar 1901.

Child:
i   **Marie Huguette Limoges** b & bp 23 & 26 Oct 1940, Montreal, QC.

5.7.5.7.4.2 **MONTY, Joseph Conrad** b & bp 7 & 8 Dec 1906, Montreal, QC. He married there 14 Feb 1935 **Cécile Janson** (Arthur Janson & Joséphine Chantilly).

Children:
5.7.5.7.4.2.1	Arthur Robert	1939-	-
5.7.5.7.4.2.2	Wilfrid Arthur Armand Conrad 1940-		-

5.7.7.1.4.1 **MONTY, Julia** b 9 Sep 1874, Holyoke, MA. She married there 31 Mar 1902 **William Joseph Fleming** (Richard W. Fleming & Charlotte Winchester) b 11 Dec 1873, Brattleboro, VT.

William Fleming was a papermaker in Holyoke, MA, in 1900. He and his wife moved after their marriage to South Hadley, MA, where he was a paper mill superintendent from at least 1908 to at least 1930 (US censuses; City Directories).

Children:
i   **Charlotte Fleming** b 1903?, Hampden Co., MA.
ii   **Mary Hilda Fleming** b 8 Jun 1904, Hampden Co., MA; d 22 Jun 1982, South Hadley, MA. She married **James Allan Welsh** b 17 Nov 1906, PA; d 12 Jun 1983, Chicopee, MA.
iii   **Florence Fleming** b 11 Feb 1906, Hampden Co., MA; d 12 Nov 1986, South Hadley, MA.
iv   **Kathleen P. Fleming** b 15 Jul 1907, Hampden Co., MA; d 9 Feb 1992, Holyoke, MA.
v   **Muriel R. Fleming** b 1908?, South Hadley, MA.
vi   **Pearl T. Fleming** b Mar 1910, South Hadley, MA.

5.7.7.1.4.2 **MONTY, Anonymous** b 11 Jun 1879, Holyoke, MA; d there 12 Jun 1879.

5.7.7.1.4.3 **MONTY, Emanuel/Manuel** b & bp 15 & 16 Jun 1880, Holyoke, MA; d 21 Dec 1915, Pawtucket, RI. He married 11 Sep 1902, Holyoke, MA, **Mary Flynn** (Patrick Flynn & Bridget Stack) b 1881?, Ireland; m (2) Frank Stevens (Joseph Stevens & Elizabeth ____).

Emanuel Monty (Louis Emanuel at his baptism) was a cotton mill worker in Holyoke, MA, in 1900 and a weaver in a silk factory in Pawtucket, RI, in 1910. He and his wife had had four children of whom the two listed below were still alive. He was known then, as well as at his death, as Manuel Monty (US censuses).

Mary Flynn was 21 years old at her first marriage. She remained in Pawtucket after Manuel Monty's death and was living there in 1930 with her second husband and her daughters Irene and Mabel Monty (US census).

Children:
5.7.7.1.4.3.1	Irene	1904- -1988
5.7.7.1.4.3.2	Mabel	1908-1931?-1987

5.7.7.1.4.4 **MONTY, Adella** b 13 Oct 1881, Holyoke, MA.

5.7.7.1.4.5 **MONTY, John B.** b 15 Apr 1883, Holyoke, MA. He married there 1911 **Sadie/Sarah Annis** b there 16 Sep 1894; d there 16 Oct 1993.

John B. Monty and his wife had been married for nineteen years in 1930. He had been a paper mill worker in Holyoke, MA, since at least 1910 (US censuses).

Children:

5.7.7.1.4.5.1	Marion	1912-	-1988
5.7.7.1.4.5.2	John Roland	1914-	-1991
5.7.7.1.4.5.3	Adrian E.	1916-1945?-2005	

5.7.7.1.4.6   **MONTY, Albert Edward** b & bp 18 & 21 Jun 1885, Holyoke, MA; d there 1924. He married (1) 1907? **Exilda Renaud** (James Renaud & Exilda ____) b Jul 1888, OH; d 1916, Holyoke, MA.

He married (2) 16 Sep 1918, Pawtucket, RI, **Freda Noffke** (Henry Noffke & Mary Cadiker) b 3 Nov 1896, Holyoke, MA.

Albert Monty was a weaver in Holyoke, MA, in 1910, when he and his wife Exilda had been married for less than three years, and a loom fixer there in 1920. His second wife may have died before 1930 for by then Albert Monty's two surviving children were staying with their aunt and uncle Julia (5.7.7.1.4.1) and William J. Fleming in South Hadley, MA (US censuses).

Children of the first marriage:

5.7.7.1.4.6.1	Hazel E.	1907-	-1988
5.7.7.1.4.6.2	Albert	1909-	-1909
5.7.7.1.4.6.3	Albert F.	1914?-	-

5.7.7.1.4.7   **MONTY, Sarah** b 19 Apr 1888, Holyoke, MA; d there 20 Apr 1888.

5.7.7.1.4.8   **MONTY, Michael** b 10 Mar 1890, Holyoke, MA; d there 11 Mar 1890.

5.7.7.1.7.1   **MONTY, Alfred** b 20 Dec 1884, Holyoke, MA.

5.7.7.1.7.2   **MONTY, Lena** b 1884?, Holyoke, MA; d there 21 Dec 1888 at the age of four.

I have not found this child's birth record and have some doubts about the entry in the Massachusetts Death Records. It is quite possible that the child's age, name, or even sex are wrong.

5.7.7.1.7.3   **MONTY, Mary Agnes** b 1 Nov 1886, Holyoke, MA; d between 1921 and 1930. She married 1911? **Walter Craven** (____ Craven & Nora ____) b 24 Dec 1888, Halifax, Yorkshire, England; d Jun 1966, Holyoke, MA.

Walter Craven was a mill hand from Halifax, England, when he arrived in Boston, MA, aboard the SS *Cymric* on 17 Feb 1907. He was in Holyoke, MA, with his mother and several siblings in 1910 and remained there as a buffer and polisher until at least 1930. He was then a widower making a home for all eight of his children (US censuses).

Children:

i   **Mary A. Craven** b 1911?, Holyoke, MA.

ii   **Ellen Rose Craven** b 16 Jul 1913, Holyoke, MA; d & bur there 10 & 12 Apr 1995. She married **Wilson Arthur Latourelle** (Arthur Joseph Latourelle & Louise Lunzman) b 25 Nov 1918, Springfield, MA; d there 3 Nov 1974.

iii   **Walter L. Craven** b 19 Sep 1914, Holyoke, MA; d there 28 Nov 1982. He married there 24 Jun 1939 **Adrienne Neveu** (Eugene Neveu & Lydia ___) b 24 Feb 1914, Hampden Co., MA; d 16 Nov 1985, Pinellas Co., FL.

iv   **Constance Craven** b May 1916, Holyoke, MA. She married ____ **Reilly**.

v   **Nelson Craven** b Oct 1917, Holyoke, MA.

vi   **John E. Craven** b 15 Dec 1918, Holyoke, MA; d 22 Sep 1983, Springfield, MA.

vii   **Arnold R. Craven** b 18 Apr 1920, Holyoke, MA.

viii   **Gloria Craven** b 15 Sep 1921, Holyoke, MA; d 26 Apr 2004, Springfield, MA. She married (1) **Charles James Herlihy** (Charles James Herlihy & Emily Ruby Carroll) b Apr 1918, Brooklyn, NY; d Apr 1966, MA.

She married (2) **Warren D. Horne** b Oct 1929.

5.7.7.1.7.4   **MONTY, Leon F.** b Mar 1888, Holyoke, MA; d there 14 Aug 1889 at the age of 1 year and 5 months.

5.7.7.1.7.5   **MONTY, Mathilde** b 23 Jul 1889, Holyoke, MA.

5.7.7.1.7.6   **MONTY, Nellie** b 30 Oct 1890, Holyoke, MA.

5.7.7.1.8.1   **MONTY, Blanche I.** b 19 Dec 1886, Lawrence, MA; d 23 Feb 1888, Holyoke, MA.

5.7.7.1.8.2   **MONTY, Aurora/Ora L.** b 9 Dec 1888, Holyoke, MA.

Ora L. Monty was living with her mother in Holyoke, MA, in 1910 (US census).

5.7.7.1.8.3   **MONTY, Ella Eva** b 29 Jun 1893, Holyoke, MA.

Ella E. Monty was living with her mother in Holyoke, MA, in 1910 (US census).

5.7.7.15.1.1   **MONTY, Eugénie Antoinette Hélène** b & bp 21 & 22 Mar 1900, Montreal, QC; d & bur there 23 & 26 Oct 1901.

5.7.7.15.1.2   **MONTY, Paul** b & bp 2 & 3 Feb 1902, Montreal, QC; d there 12 Jun 1972. He married 24 Jun 1929, Warwick, QC, **Marielle Baril** (Lucien Baril & Léontine Vézina) b & bp there 26 May 1908; d & bur 15 & 19 Jun 1995, Montreal, QC.

Paul Monty (Jacques Rodolphe Paul at his baptism and marriage) was a lawyer and judge in Montreal, QC. His wife was named Marie Berthe Marielle Baril at her baptism and marriage though simply Marielle on other occasions such as the births of her children.

Children:

5.7.7.15.1.2.1	Hélène	1930-1952-
5.7.7.15.1.2.2	Pierre	1935-1958-1967

5.7.7.15.1.3   **MONTY, Dorval** b & bp 8 & 9 Apr 1904, Montreal, QC; d there 6 Mar 1958.

Dorval Monty (Joseph Arthur Dorval at his baptism) was a Jesuit priest.

5.7.7.15.1.4   **MONTY, Henri** b & bp 31 Dec 1906, Montreal, QC; d 7 May 1976, Ville Mont-Royal, QC. He married 18 Oct 1933, Montreal, QC, **Thérèse Desbois** (Désiré L. Desbois & Irène Martin) b & bp there 31 Oct & 1 Nov 1907.

Henri Monty (Joseph Jean Lucien Henri at his baptism) was a lawyer and judge in Montreal, QC. His wife had been named Marie Thérèse Irène Gilberte at her baptism.

Children:

5.7.7.15.1.4.1	Denise	1935-1959-
5.7.7.15.1.4.2	Huguette	1940-1962-

5.7.7.15.1.5   **MONTY, Marguerite** b & bp 10 & 12 Oct 1908, Montreal, QC; d there 5 May 1992. She married there 25 May 1939 **Gaston Brodeur** (Marc-Aurèle Brodeur & Cordelia Martineau) b & bp there 7 & 8 Oct 1902.

Baptismal names: Marie Laure Marguerite Monty and Joseph Adélard Gaston Brodeur.

5.7.7.15.1.6   **MONTY, Maurice** b 4 Aug 1910, Montreal, QC; d there 6 Jan 1968.

Maurice Monty was a Jesuit priest.

5.7.7.15.1.7   **MONTY, Estelle** b 27 Sep 1911, Montreal, QC; d there Sep 1995. She married there 26 Jun 1943 **Aimé Perreault** (Athanase Perreault & Azilda Laverdière) b & bp there 12 & 13 Sep 1908.

Aimé Perreault (Joseph Alphonse Aimé at his baptism) was an accountant in Montreal, QC.

Children:
   i   **Michelle Perreault** b 23 Sep 1944, Montreal, QC. She married there 9 Sep 1967 **Nino/Nicodemo Jeraci** (Antonio Jeraci & Francesca Lanzetta) b 18 Jan 1941, Italy.
   ii   **Jacques Perreault** b 23 Mar 1946, Montreal, QC. He married 22 Jun 1974, Pointe-aux-Trembles, QC, **Gilberte Paquin** (Euclide Paquin & Merelise Bordeleau) b 29 May 1947, La Sarre, QC.
   iii **Nicole Perreault** b 1 Jun 1949, Montreal, QC. She married there 12 Jan 1982 **Tom Vyboh** (Joseph Vyboh & Elizabeth Guerny) b there 25 Apr 1946.

5.7.7.15.1.8   **MONTY, Jean Aimé Rodrigue** b 11 Feb 1913, Montreal, QC; d there 22 Sep 1987. He married (1) there 3 May 1941 **Marie Cécile Madeleine Duhamel** (Gaspard Duhamel & Hélène Champoux) b & bp 20 & 21 Jul 1913, Disraëli, QC; d & bur 26 & 29 Mar 1952, Montreal, QC.

He married (2) 12 Feb 1955, Shawinigan, QC, **Mariette Boulanger**.

Jean Monty was a businessman in Montreal, QC.

Children of the first marriage:
5.7.7.15.1.8.1	Louise	1942-1969-	
5.7.7.15.1.8.2	Rodolphe	1946-1969&	-
5.7.7.15.1.8.3	Jean C.	1947-1969-	

5.7.7.15.1.9   **MONTY, Jules** b 6 May 1914, Montreal, QC; d & bur there 1 & 2 Oct 1919, at the age of 5 years, 4 months, and 25 days.

5.7.7.15.1.10   **MONTY, Andrée** b & bp 11 Feb 1917, Montreal, QC; d there 17 Apr 1992. She married there 19 Oct 1963 **Alfred Dalphond** (Arthur Dalphond & Marie Anne Levesque) b & bp 12 Apr 1915, Joliette, QC; d 22 Jul 1987, Montreal, QC.

Baptismal names: Marie Thérèse Germaine Andrée Monty and Joseph Alfred Conrad Dalphond.

5.7.7.15.1.11   **MONTY, Guy** b & bp 17 & 18 Mar 1920, Montreal, QC. He married there 27 Dec 1947 **Béatrice Larose** (Georges Larose & Délia Morin) b & bp there 4 & 6 Aug 1919.

Baptismal names: Joseph Jules Armand Guy Monty and Marie Béatrice Léola Larose.

Child:
5.7.7.15.1.11.1	Marie Claude	1950-1973-

5.7.10.2.1.1   **MONTY, Moïse Henri** b & bp 14 & 15 Oct 1888, Suncook, NH; d & bur there 28 & 29 Oct 1888.

5.7.10.2.1.2   **MONTY, Eddy Edouard** b & bp 17 & 19 Mar 1895, St. Césaire, QC. He married there 19 Feb 1917 **Donalda Jacques** (Alfred Jacques & Malvina Bourbeau) b & bp there 16 & 17 Aug 1899.

This man was named Moïse Edouard at his baptism but was most often called Eddy as an adult. His marriage record is in the name of Eddy Edouard Monty.

Children:
5.7.10.2.1.2.1	Edouard/Eddy	1918-1938-2003

5.7.10.2.1.3   MONTY, Bertha b & bp 7 & 9 Dec 1899, St. Césaire, QC; d & bur 26 & 28 Jul 1930, Abbotsford, QC. She married 5 Feb 1919 St Césaire, QC, **Joseph Lévis/Lévi Lapalme** (Hector Lapalme & Alexine Dufresne) b & bp 11 & 12 Aug 1895, St. Pie, QC; d & bur 22 & 24 Apr 1924, Abbotsford, QC.

This man's name varies: Joseph Lévis Aimé at his baptism, Joseph Lévi at his marriage, and Lévis at the births of his children and at his burial.

Children:
- i   **Anonymous Lapalme** b 22 Feb 1920, Abbotsford, QC; d & bur there 22 & 23 Feb 1920.
- ii   **Fernande Lisette Gisèle Lapalme** b & bp 29 & 30 Dec 1921, Abbotsford, QC. She married 5 Jul 1947, Drummondville, QC, **Georges Paradis** (Alphonse Paradis & Rose Alba Hénault).
- iii   **Joseph Aimé Lévis Lapalme** b & bp 19 & 20 Sep 1924, Abbotsford, QC.

5.7.10.2.1.4   MONTY, Laurier b & bp 3 & 4 Jan 1902, Suncook, NH. He married 19 Sep 1936, St. Césaire, QC, **Carmel Brault** (Ferdinand Brault & Yvonne Viens) b & bp there 28 May & 2 Jun 1912.

Laurier Monty (Joseph Deslauriers Alfred at his baptism) was a resident of Ange Gardien, QC, at his marriage and was a butter maker there when his children were born in the late 1930s. His wife Carmel Brault had been named Marie Reine Fleur de Mai Carmel at her baptism.

Children:
5.7.10.2.1.4.1	Jacques	1938-1961-
5.7.10.2.1.4.2	Yvonne France Violette	1939- -

5.7.10.2.1.5   MONTY, Rosario b & bp 4 & 5 Dec 1904, St. Césaire, QC; bur 19 Oct 1931, Abbotsford, QC. He married there 31 May 1930 **Marie Jeanne Yvette Handfield** (Hubert Handfield & Odena Dionne) b & bp 5 & 6 Mar 1910, Iberville, QC.

Rosario Monty (named Pierre Willis Rosaire at his baptism) was a butter maker in Stanbridge, QC, at his death. The burial record does not indicate the date or place of death.

5.7.10.2.1.6   MONTY, Laurence b & bp 22 May 1910, St. Césaire, QC; d & bur 18 & 20 Feb 1931, St. Jean & Abbotsford, QC. She married 23 Apr 1930, Granby, QC, **Rouville Girard** (Louis Georges Girard & Marie Louise Rainville) b & bp 9 & 10 Jan 1906, St. Barnabé Sud, QC; m (2) 21 Jul 1934, Granby, QC, Denise Bazinet (Henri Bazinet & Paméla Labrie).

5.7.10.2.3.1   MONTY, Arthur b & bp 4 & 5 Aug 1891, Pembroke (Suncook), NH; d & bur there 9 & 10 Aug 1891.

5.7.10.2.3.2   MONTY, Napoléon b & bp 30 Jul 1892, Pembroke (Suncook), NH. He married 2 Sep 1913, Abbotsford, QC, **Rose Bella/Robella Paquet** (Stanislas Paquet & Alphonsine Messier) b & bp 24 & 25 Jul 1897, Ange Gardien, QC.

Napoléon Monty was a young child when he went to Canada with his parents. He was living with them in Abbotsford, QC, in 1901 and 1911 (Canadian censuses) and was a farmer there until at least 1927 when his son Arthur was born. The family moved in the next few years for at the birth of his youngest child in 1932 Hyacinthe Monty was a day laborer in St. Hyacinthe, QC. He was still residing there when his son Adrien died in 1983.

Children:
5.7.10.2.3.2.1	Simon Adrien	1914-1938-1983
5.7.10.2.3.2.2	Thérèse	1915-1934-

5.7.10.2.3.2.3	Simonne	1921-1953-
5.7.10.2.3.2.4	Laurette	1925-1944-
5.7.10.2.3.2.5	Arthur	1927-1950-
5.7.10.2.3.2.6	Paul Emile Raymond	1932-1952-

5.7.10.2.4.1   **MONTY, Albert Joseph** b & bp 11 & 16 Apr 1892, Pembroke (Suncook), NH. He married 1918? **Genevieve/Jennie E. ____** b 1900?, QC; d 7 Jun 1955, Lawrence, MA.

Albert Monty was a mill worker in Pembroke, NH, in 1910 and in Lawrence, MA, in 1920 and until at least 1956 (US censuses; City Directories). He and his 29-year-old wife had been married for eleven years on 1 Apr 1930 (US census).

Children:

5.7.10.2.4.1.1	Elizabeth	1919-	-1998
5.7.10.2.4.1.2	Albert P.	1921-	-1985
5.7.10.2.4.1.3	Eleanor A.	1923?-	-
5.7.10.2.4.1.4	Marion	1928-	-

5.7.10.2.4.2   **MONTY, Joseph Moïse** b & bp 19 & 20 1893, Pembroke (Suncook), NH; d & bur there 28 & 29 Nov 1896.

Joseph Monty was buried in St. John the Baptist Cemetery in Suncook, NH.

5.7.10.2.4.3   **MONTY, Mary Anna L.** b & bp 17 & 19 Nov 1894, Pembroke (Suncook), NH. She married 28 Mar 1920, Manchester, NH, **Alfred Patrick/Fred P. Largy** (Peter Largy & Margaret Penny) b 11 Mar 1886, Canada.

There is a question about the date of this couple's marriage. The date shown above is taken from the records of St. Joseph's Cathedral in Manchester, NH. Yet when Alfred Patrick Largy signed on 12 Sep 1918 his World War I Draft Registration card he named as his next of kin his wife Mrs. Anna Largy. Although I have not found any earlier record, it is quite possible that the couple married in a civil or Protestant ceremony before September 1918 and then had their marriage validated in the Catholic Church in March 1920.

Alfred Frederick Largy's date and place of birth are taken from his World War I Draft Registration card of 1918. He was then a cook in Manchester. I have not found him and his wife Anna beyond 1920. Since their daughter was living in 1930 with a paternal aunt, Alice Largy, and continued to live with her until adulthood (City Directories), I tend to believe that her mother, or perhaps both her parents, died soon after her birth.

Child:
i   **Edith Mary Largy** b 24 Apr 1920, NH; d 30 May 2002, Hartford, CT. She married 11 Feb 1950, Manchester, NH, **Stephen Casimir Kapela** (Walter/Wladislaw Kapela & Christine/Kristin Debaki) b there 21 Jun 1918; d 7 Oct 1982, Stamford, CT.

5.7.10.2.4.4   **MONTY, George Arthur** b & bp 17 & 21 Oct 1896, Pembroke & Suncook, NH; d May 1974, Manchester, NH. He married (1) 1928? **Alice ____** b 1888?, MA.

He was a widower when he married (2) 14 Oct 1961, Auburn, NH, **Alice Crisham** (John Crisham & Bella McGilvery) b 17 Nov 1903, Amesbury, MA; d there 9 Jul 1976.

George Monty was a shoe worker in Manchester, NH, from at least 1918 on (US censuses; World War I and II Draft Registration cards; City Directories). He and his 42-year-old wife first wife Alice had been married for two years in 1930 (US census).

5.7.10.2.4.5   **MONTY, Agnes** b & bp 17 & 21 May 1898, Allenstown & Suncook, NH. She married 25 Oct 1930, Lawrence, MA, **Rudolph Ducharme** (Oscar Ducharme & Elodie/ Melodie Goudreau) b there Jun 1899.

Rudolph Ducharme was a blacksmith in Lawrence, MA, in 1930 (US census). He died not very long after his marriage for by 1934 Mrs. Agnes Ducharme, widow of Rudolph, was living alone in Manchester, NH (City Directory).

5.7.10.2.8.1   **MONTY, Eva Marguerite** b & bp 30 & 31 Jul 1898, Pembroke & Suncook, NH; d & bur 31 Dec 1984 & 4 Jan 1985, Concord & Suncook, NH. She married 19 May 1919, Suncook, NH, **Henry Chaput** (Napoleon Chaput & Ellen Cavanaugh) b & bp there 23 & 24 Apr 1898; d & bur 11 & 14 Jun 1979, Concord & Suncook, NH.

Henry Chaput was a cotton mill worker in Pembroke (Suncook), NH, for most of his life (US censuses). He and his wife had moved to Concord, NH, before their deaths but were buried in St. John the Baptist Cemetery in Suncook.

Children:
i   **Florence Chaput** b & bp 24 & 25 Mar 1920, Suncook, NH; d there 18 Feb 1997. She married there 23 May 1938 **William Dandurand** (Napoleon Dandurand & Rose Anna Daneault) b & bp there 22 & 23 May 1917; d 23 Oct 2007, Concord, NH.

ii   **Arthur René Chaput** b & bp 14 & 15 Jan 1924, Suncook, NH; d & bur 30 Oct & 3 Nov 2004, Allenstown & Suncook, NH. He married 7 Jul 1947, Suncook, NH, **Anita Thérèse Durant/Ladurantaye** (Arthur Durant/Ladurantaye & Anna Martel) b & bp there 8 Feb 1928.

iii   **Harvey/Hervé Chaput** b & bp 15 & 16 Sep 1926, Suncook, NH; d & bur 10 & 15 Mar 1993, Rye & Suncook, NH. He married 22 Jul 1950, Suncook, NH, **Pauline Pearl Duhaime** (Alfred Duhaime & Ida Guimond) b & bp 16 & 19 May 1931, Manchester & Suncook, NH; d & bur 24 & 29 Jun 1992, Rye & Suncook, NH.

iv   **Mary Ellen/Marie Hélène Chaput** b & bp 5 Dec 1932, Suncook, NH. She married there 4 Oct 1952 **Henry A. Laramie** (Henry Amos Laramie & Josephine Bill) b 1 Mar 1926, Enfield, NH; d 6 Jun 2002, Suncook, NH.

5.7.10.2.8.2   **MONTY, Arthur Henry** b 24 Oct 1899, Pembroke (Suncook), NH; d & bur 30 Aug & 1 Sep 1941, Allenstown & Suncook, NH. He married 1 Mar 1927, Suncook, NH, **Eva Oliva Poisson** (David Poisson & Emma Tétrault) b & bp there 31 Oct & 1 Nov 1895; d & bur 18 & 21 Feb 1981, Allenstown & Suncook, NH.

Arthur Monty was a mill worker in Pembroke (Suncook), NH, in 1920 and a musician there in 1930 (US censuses). He was later a retailer in Allenstown, NH. He and his wife were buried in St. John the Baptist Cemetery in Suncook.

Child:

5.7.10.2.8.2.1	Arthur David	1938-1965&1978-

5.7.10.2.8.3   **MONTY, Albert H.** b 27 Apr 1908, Manchester, NH; d & bur 18 & 21 Jan 1974, Suncook, NH. He married there 15 Jun 1931 **Florence Santerre** (Adelard/Dolor Santerre & Parmelia Taillefer) b & bp there 4 & 5 Mar 1912; d & bur 15 & 18 Jul 1963, Pembroke & Suncook, NH.

Albert Monty was a truck driver in Pembroke, NH, in 1930 (US census). By 1943 he was a clothier in Suncook, NH, and in 1950 the proprietor of a clothing store there (City Directories). He and his wife were buried there in St. John the Baptist Cemetery.

Children:

5.7.10.2.8.3.1	Jacqueline	1932-1969-
5.7.10.2.8.3.2	Janet Elaine	1946-1967-

5.7.10.2.8.4   **MONTY, Lillian Flora** b & bp 2 Nov 1910, Suncook, NH; d 20 Jan 1986, New Britain, CT. She married 15 Jun 1931, Suncook, NH, **Exear R./Elzéar Champagne** (Antoine/Anthony Champagne & Dorilla/Dora Racicot) b 30 Aug 1906, North Adams, MA; d 6 May 1978, New Britain, CT.

Exear Champagne (Elzéar in his marriage record) was a laborer in Hooksett, NH, in 1930 (US census) and a hospital attendant in Suncook, NH, in 1937 and 1938 (City Directories). He moved to Hartford, CT, at some time before 1950 and remained there until at least

1967 (City Directories).

Children:
i   **Arthur Elzéar Champagne** b & bp 30 Mar & 28 Apr 1933, Suncook, NH; d 6 Feb 1983, Indian River Co., FL. He married (1) 20 Aug 1955, Hartford, CT, **Lorraine J. Bolduc** b 19 Aug 1936, CT; d 19 Dec 1986, Hartford, CT.

     He was divorced when he married (2) 7 Feb 1981, Hartford, CT, **Sandra L. Peterson** b 1952?

ii   **Monty Robert Henri Champagne** b & bp 8 & 19 May 1935, Manchester & Suncook, NH. He married (1) Oct 1958, Monroe Co., FL, and divorced there Feb 1959 **Mary Roberta Jensen**.

     He married (2) 23 Aug 1986, West Hartford, CT, **Karin F. Keefer** b Jan 1942.

iii **Ray Albert Norman Champagne** b & bp 6 & 22 May 1938, Concord & Suncook, NH. He married 2 Aug 1958, Hartford, CT, **Betty Kay Merrill** (Ralph O. Merrill & Margaret ____).

     He married (2) 4 Sep 1965, New Britain, CT, **Michele Russo** (Michael E. Russo & Elizabeth W. ____) b 1943?

5.7.10.2.8.5   **MONTY, Henri Leo** b & bp 2 Mar 1915, Suncook, NH; d & bur there 7 & 9 Sep 1916.

5.7.10.2.8.6   **MONTY, Percy Alphee** b & bp 3 & 4 Dec 1917, Suncook, NH; d & bur 24 & 27 Feb 1976, Mansfield, CT & Arlington, VA. He married 3 Sep 1942, Anniston, AL, **Natalie Marion Wells** (Arthur Austin Wells & Lena Skinner) b 1 Jun 1921, Epsom, NH; d & bur 9 May & 23 Aug 2004, Mansfield, CT & Arlington, VA.

     Percy A. Monty enlisted in the US Army on 8 Feb 1941 and became a career Army officer. He retired on 1 Sep 1965 as Lt. Col. Percy A. Monty and was buried, as was his wife, in the Arlington, VA, National Cemetery.

Children:

5.7.10.2.8.6.1	Lois Mary	1943- -1943
5.7.10.2.8.6.2	Percalie	1947-1969&1989-
5.7.10.2.8.6.3	Philip A.	1949-1970-
5.7.10.2.8.6.4	Karl A.	1950- -
5.7.10.2.8.6.5	Jo D.	1955-1973-

5.7.10.3.1.1   **MONTE, Israel Joseph** b 30 Sep 1888, Putnam, CT; d Mar 1971, Coventry, RI. He married 1916? **Sophia C. Mikeuszeuska** b 10 Jul 1893, Polish Austria; d Oct 1973, Coventry, RI.

     Israel Monte was a cotton mill worker in Warwick, RI, in 1910 and in Jewett City, CT, in 1920. Ten years later, when he and his wife had been married for fourteen years, he was a cotton mill worker in Coventry, RI (US censuses). He remained in Kent Co., RI, and continued to work in Coventry though he was a resident of Anthony (West Warwick), RI, in 1942 when he signed his World War II Draft Registration card.

Children:

| 5.7.10.3.1.1.1 | Anna Mae | 1918-   -1973 |
| 5.7.10.3.1.1.2 | Ilene Virginia | 1919-   -1986 |

5.7.10.3.1.2   **MONTY/MONTE, Rose Eda/Ada** b & bp 6 & 8 May 1892, West Warwick, RI.

     This child was named Rose Eda Monty at her baptism but Ada Monte in 1910 when she was living with her father in Warwick, CT (US census).

5.7.10.3.1.3   **MONTY, Michel** b & bp 6 & 7 Jun 1896, Arkwright & West Warwick, RI; d 16 Jun 1896, Arkwright, RI.

This child was baptized and later buried in St. Joseph's Cemetery in Arctic (West Warwick), RI, under the surname Monty.

5.7.10.3.1.4　　　**MONTE, William A.** b 1899?, RI. He married 1925? **Mary F. ____** b 1904?, RI.

William Monte was 20 years old on 1 Jan 1920, when he was staying with his father in his brother Israel's household in Jewett City, CT. He was then a laborer in a cotton mill. He was a hospital technician in Pawtucket, RI, on 1 Apr 1930 when he and his 26-year-old wife had been married for five years (US censuses).

5.7.10.3.1.5　　　**MONTE, Irene** b 1901?, RI.

Irene Monte was a 9-year-old child living with her father in Warwick, RI, in 1910. She was a cotton mill worker in Jewett City, CT, in 1920 (US censuses).

5.7.10.3.3.1　　　**MONTEE, Rosanna** b & bp 18 & 19 Jun 1892, West Warwick, RI; d 3 Jul 1976, Killingly, CT. She married 1912? **Everett M. Cutler** (Daniel Cutler & Louise Covel) b 6 May 1892, Killingly, CT; d 18 Jan 1974, Putnam, CT.

Everett Cutler was a grocery store merchant in Glocester, RI, in 1920 and a dairy farmer there in 1930 when he and his wife had been married for eighteen years (US censuses). They were both buried in St. Mary's Cemetery in Putnam., CT.

Children:
- i　**Charles Ira Cutler** b 4 May 1913, RI; d 20 Dec 1981, Pomfret, CT. He married **Mary L. Doonan** b 1 Mar 1911, CT; d 26 Oct 1982, Putnam, CT.
- ii　**Doris E. Cutler** b Jan 1915, RI. She married **Arthur E. Cady** (Eugene Cady & Regina ____) b 16 June 1916, Putnam, CT; d Jan 1979, Pomfret, CT.
- iii　**Kenneth E. Cutler** b 30 Dec 1915, RI; d & bur 27 & 30 Jun 2000, Webster, MA & Danielson, CT. He married (1) 1942 **Irene E. Dayle** b 26 Nov 1915, CT; d 1 Dec 1988, Pomfret, CT.
  He married (2) 29 Dec 1990, Killingly, CT, **Thelma E. Geer** b 13 Aug 1923.
- iv　**Raymond E. Cutler** b 13 Jul 1918, Glocester, RI.
- v　**Edward M. Cutler** b 29 May 1924, Glocester, RI; d 6 May 1990, Pomfret, CT. He married 7 Apr 1947 **Geraldine B. Martineau** (Wilfred Martineau & Antoinette Baril) b 7 Nov 1927, Pomfret, CT; d there Oct 1998.

5.7.10.3.3.2　　　**MONTE/MONTEE, Edward** b 15 Nov 1893, Glocester, RI; d there 22 Jan 1909.

This child was named Edward Monte at his birth but Edward Montee at his death. His surname was also Montee in the 1900 US census in Coventry, RI, where he was living with his parents.

5.7.10.3.3.3　　　**MONTIE, Joseph H.** b 4 Apr 1896, Coventry, RI; d 26 Sep 1918.

Joseph H. Montie was a resident of Putnam, CT, when he signed on 5 Jun 1917 his World War I Draft Registration card. He was a private in the 82nd Co., 151st Brigade when he died and was buried in St. Mary's Cemetery in Putnam.

5.7.10.3.3.4　　　**MONTY, Henry A.** b 20 Sep 1901, Coventry, RI; d there 28 Sep 1901 at the age of seven days.

Although his parents' surname was Montee in the 1900 US census in Coventry, RI, this child was buried in St. Joseph's Cemetery in Arctic (West Warwick), RI, as Henry A. Monty.

5.7.10.3.3.5　　　**MONTIE, Conrad T.** b 6 Feb 1904, Coventry, RI; d Apr 1961. He married 1928? **Rose Desautels** (Napoleon Desautels & Delia Côté) b 26 May 1910, Putnam, CT; d & bur 28 Oct & 3 Nov 1997, East Hartford & Harrisville, CT.

Conrad Montie was a carder in Glocester, RI, in 1920 and a truck driver in Putnam, CT, in 1930 when he and his wife had been married for two years (US census). They moved to West Glocester, RI, in the early 1930s. Rose Desautels returned to Connecticut to live with her daughter in 1987 and was buried in St. Patrick Cemetery in Harrisville, CT (*Hartford Courant*, 31 Oct 1997).

Children:

5.7.10.3.3.5.1	Robert C.	1929-	&1997?-2005
5.7.10.3.3.5.2	Norman Kenneth	1931-	-1998
5.7.10.3.3.5.3	Theresa	1933-	-2001

5.7.10.3.9.1   MONTY, Eva b 11 Jan 1900, West Warwick, RI. She married there 11 Jan 1923 **Henry Bacon** (Joseph Bacon & Mathilda Leclerc) b there 2 Apr 1899; d Jul 1974, Coventry, RI.

Henry Bacon was a cotton mill worker in West Warwick, RI, in 1920 and 1930 (US censuses). His sister Lauretta Bacon married his wife's cousin, Ernest Salois, son of Michel Salois and Adelaide Monty (5.7.10.3.4).

Children
i   **Norman Bacon** b 1923?, West Warwick, RI.
ii   **Leonard A. Bacon** b Nov 1924, West Warwick, RI; d there 28 Jan 1925.
iii   **Donald Bacon** b Feb 1926, West Warwick, RI.
iv   **Lorraine Bacon** b Oct 1927, West Warwick, RI.
v   **Rita Bacon** b Jan 1929, West Warwick, RI.

5.7.10.3.9.2   MONTY, Marie Rose Blanche, b 5 May 1901, Natick, RI; d 20 Apr 1949, RI. She married 24 Nov 1921, Natick, RI, **Joseph Cyrille Belanger** (Gédéon Belanger & Mélina Théroux) b & bp 19 May 1899, Phenix, RI; d 7 Oct 1965, RI.

Joseph C. Belanger was a truck driver in West Warwick, RI, in 1930 (US census). Both he and his wife were buried there in Notre Dame Cemetery.

Children:
i   **Beatrice Belanger** b Mar 1926, West Warwick, RI.
ii   **Joseph Belanger**
iii   **Donald Belanger**

5.7.10.3.11.1   MONTY, Dora b 21 Feb 1897, West Warwick, RI. She married there 15 May 1916 **Alphonse Fernando Gadoury** (Alfred Gadoury & Clara Leonard) b 4 Jul 1894, Shannock, RI; d Jan 1973, Warwick, RI.

Alphonse F. Gadoury was a weaver in Centreville, RI, in 1917 and in Arctic, RI, in 1920 (World War I Draft Registration card; US census). He was living in Narragansett, RI, while working in a woolen mill in Belleville, RI, in 1942 (World War II Draft Registration card). Since he listed as the person who would always be aware of his address an Alexander Gadoury of Allenton, RI, possibly his older brother, it is likely that his wife was already deceased.

5.7.10.3.13.1   MONTE, Yvonne Blanche b 29 Jul 1906, Phenix, RI; d & bur 1 & 5 May 1975, Warwick & West Warwick, RI. She married **Rosario Joseph Russi** (Ovila Russi & Médérise Blanchette) b 9 Sep 1909, Voluntown, CT; d & bur 6 & 10 Jan 1980, Warwick & West Warwick, RI.

Rosario Russi was a building contractor in Jewett City, CT, in 1930 and was still single (US census). He later was a general contractor and builder in Phenix, RI, where he and his wife were living in 1940 (West Warwick, RI, City Directory). They were both buried in Notre Dame Cemetery in West Warwick.

5.7.10.3.13.2   MONTE, Irene A. b 30 Oct 1907, Kent Co., RI; d 10 Aug 1998, Coventry, RI. She married **Joseph G. Couture** b 23 Mar 1902; d Mar 1986, West Warwick, RI.

Irene Monte and her husband were buried in St. Joseph's Cemetery in West Warwick,

RI.

5.7.10.3.13.3 MONTE, Alma D. b 31 Dec 1908, Coventry, RI; d & bur 25 & 28 Sep 1993, Warwick & West Greenwich, RI. She married **Adrian A. Gendron** (Peter Gendron & Marie Louise Laplume) b & bp 13 Oct 1895, Montreal, QC; d & bur 30 Apr & 2 May 1987, North Kingston & West Greenwich, RI.

Alma Monte was still single on 1 Apr 1930 when she was living with her parents in West Warwick, RI. She married before 1936 when her husband Adrian Gendron (Joseph Armand Adrien at his baptism) was a plumber in West Warwick (City Directory). They were both buried in St. Joseph's Cemetery in West Greenwich, RI.

5.7.10.3.13.4 MONTE, Marie D. L. b 16 Jun 1910, Coventry, RI; d there 22 Jul 1910.

5.7.10.3.13.5 MONTE, Jeannette B. b 1913?, Coventry, RI.

Jeannette Monte was a 6-year-old child living with her parents in Coventry, RI, on 1 Jan 1920 and was still with them there in 1930 (US censuses).

5.7.10.3.13.6 MONTE, Cécile J. b Oct 1915, Coventry, RI.

Cécile Monte was 4 years and 2 months old on 1 Jan 1920 when she was living with her parents in Coventry, RI. She was also living with them there in 1930 (US censuses).

5.7.10.3.13.7 MONTE, William J. b & bp 19 & 21 May 1916, Phenix, RI; d 19 Apr 1982, Hillsborough Co., FL. He married 24 Nov 1938, West Warwick, RI, **Jeanne Gervais** (Achille Gervais & Bernadette Picard) b & bp 28 Feb & 2 Mar 1919, Arctic (West Warwick), RI.

William J. Monte was buried in St. Joseph Cemetery in West Warwick, RI. He predeceased his wife.

5.7.10.3.13.8 MONTE, Ann/Anne Mary b Jun 1918, Phenix, RI.

Ann Mary Monte was an 18-month-old child living with her parents in Coventry, RI, on 1 Jan 1920. She was still with them there in 1930, though named Anne M. Monte (US censuses).

5.7.10.3.13.9 MONTE, Gerard Joseph b & bp 31 Jul & 1 Aug 1921, Phenix, RI; d & bur 13 & 18 Oct 1982, Wareham & Bourne, MA. He married 18 Aug 1945, West Warwick, RI, **Theresa/Thérèse Marie Desrochers** (David Desrochers & Stéphanie Ducharme) b & bp 24 & 30 Nov 1924, Arctic, RI; d & bur 26 & 31 May 1995, Falmouth & Bourne, MA.

Gerard J. Monte was a Master Sergeant in the US Air Force when he left the service on 31 Dec 1968. He and his wife were residents of Buzzards Bay, MA, at their deaths and were buried in the Massachusetts National Cemetery in Bourne, MA.

Children:

5.7.10.3.13.9.1	Richard Gerard	1947-	-1990
5.7.10.3.13.9.2	Daniel Alexander	1948-	-2001
5.7.10.3.13.9.3	Bruce	-	-
5.7.10.3.13.9.4	Pamela A.	1957-	-
5.7.10.3.13.9.5	Carol Ann	1960-	-

5.7.10.5.1.1 MONTY, Louise Yvonne b & bp 17 Apr 1897, Valcourt, QC. She married 5 Jul 1920, Detroit, MI, **Oscar J. Séguin** (Moïse Séguin & Delima Clément) b & bp 3 & 9 Sep 1894, Beebe & Stanstead, QC.

Oscar Séguin had arrived in the United States in 1919 and was a factory mechanic in Detroit, MI, in January 1920 (US census). I have been unable to find him or his wife in the United States after their marriage. It is possible that they soon returned to Canada.

5.7.10.5.1.2 **MONTY, Alice Estelle** b & bp 12 & 13 Dec 1904, Valcourt, QC; d & bur 27 & 30 Nov 1933 Manchester, NH & Valcourt, QC. She married 8 Jan 1924, Valcourt, QC, **Thuribe Petit** (Joseph Petit & Zénaïde Girard) b & bp there 12 & 13 Mar 1899; m (2) there 3 Aug 1935, Antoinette Boissé (Ulysse Boissé & Vitaline Fortier).

Thuribe Petit was an auto mechanic in Manchester, NH, at his first marriage and a garage owner there in 1930 (US census) and until well into the 1940s (City Directories).

Children:
  i **Jennie Petit** b Feb 1930, Manchester, NH.
  ii **Jean Paul Petit** b Nov 1931, Manchester, NH; d & bur 20 & 22 Apr 1935, Grantham & Valcourt, QC, at the age of 3 years and 5 months.

5.7.10.5.1.3 **MONTY, Justina Aldéa** b & bp 12 & 13 Oct 1906, Valcourt, QC. She married there 26 Dec 1923 **François Eugène Albini Riel** (Eugène Riel & Elize Tranchemontagne) b & bp 5 Aug 1900, Roxton Falls, QC.

Albini (also Albani, Albain) Riel was named François Eugène Albini at his baptism. He was a laborer in Sherbrooke, QC, at his marriage and at the birth of a son in 1926. According to his daughters' birth records, he was a laborer in Valcourt, QC, in 1924 and 1931.

Children:
  i   **Laure Georgette Riel** b & bp 14 & 15 Sep 1924, Valcourt, QC.
  ii **Paul Jean Louis Riel** b & bp 13 & 14 Mar 1926, Sherbrooke, QC.
  iii **Gérard Maurice Riel** b & bp 13 & 20 Jul 1928, Sherbrooke, QC.
  iv **Rolande Gisèle Riel** b & bp 3 & 6 Sep 1931, Valcourt, QC.

5.7.10.5.1.4 **MONTY, Jeannette Irène** b & bp 13 & 14 Jun 1908, Valcourt, QC. She married 8 Sep 1925, Roxton Falls, QC, **Georges/George Brin** (Damase Brin & Joséphine Miclette) b & bp there 29 Aug 1904.

Georges Brin left Canada in 1928 and was a brass worker in Detroit, MI, in 1930 (US census).

Children:
  i   **Joseph Germain Brin** b & bp 9 Jan 1927, Valcourt, QC.
  ii **Marie Flore Alita Brin** b & bp 11 Sep 1928, Valcourt, QC.
  iii **Madeleine Brin** b Feb 1930, Detroit, MI.

5.7.10.5.1.5 **MONTY, Urgèle Maurice** b & bp 15 May 1910, Valcourt, QC; d & bur there 4 & 6 Feb 1924.

5.7.10.5.1.6 **MONTY, Flore Gertrude/Fleurette** b & bp 6 & 7 Jul 1912, Valcourt, QC. She married 29 Mar 1932, Granby, QC, **Hervé Boudreau** (Delphis Boudreau & Malvina Rémillard) b & bp 12 & 14 Aug 1904, Ste Sabine, QC.

This woman was named Flore Gertrude at her baptism but married as Fleurette Monty. Her husband, named Arthur Hervé Boudreau at his baptism, married as Hervé Boudreault. His signature, on the other hand, is invariably Boudreau, which I take to be the proper form of his surname.

Children:
  i   **Luce Paulette Boudreau** b & bp 11 & 12 Jun 1933, Granby, QC.
  ii **Yolande Monique Boudreau** b & bp 24 & 25 Apr 1937, Granby, QC. She married there 7 Aug 1956 **Alfred Larochelle** (Louis Philippe Larochelle & Emérentienne Arsenault) b & bp 1 Mar 1920, Black Lake, QC.
  iii **Anonymous Boudreau** (female) b 14 Nov 1938, Granby, QC; d & bur there 14 Nov 1938.
  iv **Lisa Micheline Boudreau** b & bp 14 Nov 1938, Granby, QC.
  v   **Marcel Boudreau** married 15 Aug 1961, Granby, QC, **Suzanne Gibeault** (Armand

Gibeault & Bellora Parent).

5.7.10.5.1.7 MONTY, George Emile b & bp 7 Apr 1914, Valcourt, QC. He married 22 Oct 1938, Drummondville, QC, **Julienne Ouellet** (André Ouellet & Ludivine Bernard) b & bp 19 Jan 1916, Thetford Mines, QC.

George Emile Monty's bride was named Julienne Ouellet at their marriage. She had been baptized as Marie Anna Elizabeth Julienne Ouellet.

Children:

5.7.10.5.1.7.1	Hélène	1939-1965-
5.7.10.5.1.7.2	Claude	-1965-

5.7.10.5.1.8 MONTY, Eugène Jean-Louis b & bp 5 & 6 Feb 1916, Valcourt, QC. He married (1) 20 Aug 1938, Drummondville, QC, **Alice Lafrenière** (Joseph Lafrenière & Marie Blanchette) b & bp 22 & 23 Oct 1909, St. Majorique de Grantham, QC.

He was a widower when he married (2) 25 Aug 1945, Granby, QC, **Juliette Légaré** (Théophile Légaré & Arzélia Sansoucy) b & bp there 7 & 9 Sep 1917.

Juliette Légaré (Marie Fernande Juliette Légaré at her baptism) was a sister of Roland Légaré, husband of Cécile Yvette Monty (5.7.10.5.1.9).

Child of the first marriage:

5.7.10.5.1.8.1	Gislaine	1939-1958-

Child of the second marriage:

5.7.10.5.1.8.2	Serge	-1965-

5.7.10.5.1.9 MONTY, Cécile Yvette b & bp 11 & 16 Sep 1917, Valcourt, QC. She married 5 Jul 1941, Granby, QC, **Roland Léo Stanislas Légaré** (Théophile Légaré & Arzélia Sansoucy) b & bp there 31 Oct & 1 Nov 1918.

Roland Légaré was a brother of Juliette Légaré, second wife of Eugène Monty (5.7.10.5.1.8).

Child:

i **Nicole Légaré** married 30 Sep 1967, Granby, QC, **Jacques Payette** (Paul Emile Payette & Anita Wilcott).

5.7.10.5.1.10 MONTY, Marguerite Bertha b & bp 30 Sep & 5 Oct 1919, Valcourt, QC. She married 26 Aug 1939, Drummondville, QC, **Joseph Louis Boucher** (Napoléon Boucher & Célanise Bolduc) b & bp there 12 & 14 Nov 1915.

5.7.10.5.1.11 MONTY, Gilberte Hélène b & bp 5 & 6 Sep 1921, Valcourt, QC. She married 3 Jun 1944, Drummondville, QC, **Lionel Languedoc** (Joseph Languedoc & Lydia Côté) b & bp 1 & 2 Sep 1916, Sherbrooke, QC.

5.7.10.5.1.12 MONTY, Paul Omer Roland b & bp 29 Nov & 2 Dec 1922, Valcourt, QC; d Apr 1998, London, Ontario. He married 25 Nov 1944, Montreal, QC, **Katherine Madge/Kay Samworth** (Nelson Samworth & Madge Ann Waugh).

5.7.10.5.2.1 MONTY, Rose Alma b & bp 7 & 9 Jul 1896, Valcourt, QC. She married there 23 Jun 1913 **Omer Beauregard** (Antoine Beauregard & Tharsile Boucher) b & bp 30 Apr 1893, Roxton Falls, QC.

5.7.10.5.2.2 MONTY, Louis Oliva b & bp 3 & 5 Sep 1897, Valcourt, QC; d there 1 & 2 Sep 1912.

5.7.10.5.2.3 MONTY, Clara Orespha b & bp 27 & 28 May 1899, Valcourt, QC; d &

bur 13 & 16 Jun 1916, Montreal & Valcourt, QC. She married 11 Jan 1915, Valcourt, QC, **Alphonse Gélineau** (Ludger Gélineau & Délia Beauregard) b & bp 3 & 4 Oct 1891, Roxton Falls, QC.

5.7.10.5.2.4   **MONTY, Marie Flore/Florise** b & bp 21 & 23 Oct 1901, Valcourt, QC; d & bur there 19 & 21 Aug 1923.
This woman was named Marie Flore at her baptism but Florise in the 1911 census in Valcourt, QC, and at her death at the age of 22.

5.7.10.5.2.5   **MONTY, Henri** b & bp 28 Oct 1903, Valcourt, QC; d & bur there 30 Jul & 2 Aug 1965. He married 9 Jan 1923, Roxton Falls, QC, **Yvonne Coderre** (Joseph Coderre & Alphonsine Dubeau) b & bp 31 Oct 1905, Ste Christine, QC.

Children:

5.7.10.5.2.5.1	Germain Gaston	1926-	-1926
5.7.10.5.2.5.2	Lucien Rolland	1928-	-1928

5.7.10.5.2.6   **MONTY, Juliette Dorila** (twin) b & bp 18 & 19 Sep 1905, Valcourt, QC. She married 19 May 1925, Roxton Falls, QC, **Léona Peck** (Georges Peck & Flore Dufault) b & bp there 11 May 1898; m (1) there 11 Sep 1916 Cora St. Martin (Rémi St. Martin & Philomène Bouchard).
Léona Peck was a laborer in Roxton Falls, QC, at the births of his first two children and in Valcourt, QC, in 1928 and later years.

Children:
i   **Orespha Joséphine Peck** b & bp 12 & 13 Mar 1926, Roxton Pond, QC. She married 14 Aug 1948, Valcourt, QC, **Paul Emile Chagnon** (Joseph Chagnon & Dorilla Lafrance) b & bp 3 & 8 Apr 1923, Frelighsburg, QC.
ii   **Georges Josaphat Peck** b & bp 19 & 22 Sep 1927, Roxton Falls, QC; d & bur 10 Jan 1929, Valcourt, QC.
iii   **Cladice Peck** b & bp 16 & 18 Nov 1928, Valcourt, QC. She married there 22 Jun 1946 **Marcel St. Georges** (William St. Georges & Rosina Boulerice).
iv   **Normand Omer Peck** b & bp 19 & 20 Jul 1930, Valcourt, QC.
v   **Dorigne/Dorenne (?) Yvonne Peck** b & bp 22 May 1932, Valcourt, QC. She married 17 Jun 1950, Stukely, QC, **Bertrand Côté** (Napoléon Côté & Clara Archambault) b & bp there 29 & 30 Apr 1929.
vi   **Henri André Peck** b & bp 21 & 23 Jul 1933, Valcourt, QC. He married 8 Jun 1963, Waterloo, QC, **Micheline Daigle** (René Daigle & Noëlla Jobin).
vii   **Florian Hubert Peck** b & bp 29 & 30 Jul 1935, Valcourt, QC. He married 4 Jul 1959, Stoke, QC, **Claudette Rodrigue** (Aimé Rodrigue & Albertine Bédard) b & bp 18 & 19 Sep 1937, Coaticook, QC.
viii **Paulette Mirella Peck** b & bp 8 & 9 Aug 1936, Valcourt, QC. She married 31 Aug 1957, Stukely, QC, **Raymond Robidoux** (Henri Robidoux et Jeannette Melançon) b & bp there 27 & 28 Jun 1929.
ix   **Marie Paule Peck** b & bp 19 & 21 Aug 1938, Valcourt, QC.
x   **Jean Claude Peck** married 25 Jun 1960, Waterloo, QC, **Claire Royer** (Adélard Royer & Emilienne Robert).
xi   **Huguette Peck** married 16 Jun 1962, Stukely, QC, **Lucien Duff** (Hormidas Duff & Carmen Therrien).

5.7.10.5.2.7   **MONTY, Georgiana Julienne** (twin) b & bp 18 & 19 Sep 1905, Valcourt, QC.

5.7.10.5.2.8   **MONTY, Germaine** b & bp 29 Aug & 1 Sep 1907, Valcourt, QC. She married 10 Jun 1930, Roxton Falls, QC, **Emile Messier** (Ménésippe Messier & Régina Beaudry) b & bp 30 Oct & 1 Nov 1894, Ange Gardien, QC.

Child:
i   **Gisèle Messier** married 8 Oct 1950, Granby, QC, **Charles Marchand** (Hervé Marchand & Rita Lamontagne).

5.7.10.5.5.1   **MONTY, Adolphe Trefflé** b & bp 11 & 12 Jul 1903, Valcourt, QC; d May 1968, Lawrence, MA. He married 24 Sep 1928, Manchester, NH, **Bertha Ursule Laventure** (George Laventure & Lumina/Lena Lemay) b & bp 20 & 21 Feb 1907, Sherbrooke, QC; d 27 Jun 1999, North Andover, MA.

Adolphe Monty (Joseph Trefflé Adolphe at his baptism) came to Manchester, NH, in April 1923 and was a weaver, laundryman, and roofer there before moving to Lawrence, MA, around 1935. He was a musician there in the late 1930s and early 1940s and an operative or helper in a machine shop in later years. His wife, named Marie Ursule Bertha at her baptism, had come to Manchester with her parents in 1909 (US censuses; City Directories).

Children:
5.7.10.5.5.1.1	Rita Lucille	1930-1948-
5.7.10.5.5.1.2	Joseph Robert Yvon	1931-1952-
5.7.10.5.5.1.3	Rose Florence	1932-1962-
5.7.10.5.5.1.4	Raymond F.	1933- -
5.7.10.5.5.1.5	Jeanne Doris	1934-1960-
5.7.10.5.5.1.6	Pauline Patricia	1936-1955-

5.7.10.5.5.2   **MONTY, Yvonne** b & bp 10 & 11 Sep 1904, Shefford, QC.
Yvonne Monty (Marie Corinne Yvonne at her baptism) arrived in the United States with her family in April 1923 and was living in Manchester, NH, in 1930 (US census).

5.7.10.5.5.3   **MONTY, Ernest Ovila** b & bp 18 & 19 Feb 1908, Valcourt, QC; d 18 Jul 1986, Springfield, MA.

5.7.10.5.5.4   **MONTY, Maurice** b & bp 23 & 24 May 1911, Valcourt, QC; d 13 Mar 1975, Miami, FL. He married 23 Sep 1933, Manchester, NH, **Lillian Bélanger** (Arthur Bélanger & Modeste Lévesque) b there 21 May 1915.

5.7.10.5.5.5   **MONTY, Céleste Léa** b & bp 19 & 23 Mar 1913, Valcourt, QC.
Céleste Monty arrived in the United States with her parents in April 1923 and was living in Nashua, NH, in 1930 (US census).

5.7.10.5.5.6   **MONTY, Alice Aline Florence** b & bp 19 & 20 Sep 1914, Valcourt, QC; d & bur there 25 & 27 Feb 1917.

5.7.10.5.6.1   **MONTY, Joseph Edward** b & bp 12 & 13 Jun 1906, Valcourt, QC; d Oct 1979, Pascoag, RI. He married 1927? **Helen Bridget Scanlon** b 1903?, Ireland.
Joseph Edward Monty (Joseph Edouard at his baptism) arrived in the United States on 15 Sep 1906 and was living in Fitchburg, MA, with his parents in 1910. By 1930, when he and his 27-year-old wife had been married for three years, he was an attendant in the State Sanatorium in Burrillville, RI (US censuses).

Children:
5.7.10.5.6.1.1	Joseph Edward	1928-1954-1991
5.7.10.5.6.1.2	Helen Margaret	1937-1958-2005

5.7.10.5.6.2   **MONTY, Yvonne** b 1908?, Fitchburg, MA.
Yvonne Monty was a 2-year-old child living with her parents in her maternal grandfather's household in Fitchburg, MA, in 1910 (US census).

5.7.10.5.6.3   **MONTY, Irene** b 1 Jul 1911, Fitchburg, MA; d Apr 1981, Mapleville, RI. She married 1928? **Theophile A. Racine** (Andrew Christopher Racine & Olive Vanasse) b 21 Nov 1910, Norwich, CT; d 27 Jul 1996, Slatersville, RI.

5.7.10.5.8.1   **MONTY, Horace** b & bp 1 & 2 May 1909, Valcourt, QC; d 4 Aug 2000, QC. He married 12 Jul 1934, Scotstown, QC, **Germaine Duval** (Joseph Duval & Aurore Laroche) b & bp 30 Jun 1917, Val Racine, QC.

Horace Monty (Louis Horace at his baptism) worked for some time in Maine, where his Social Security card was issued, but was domiciled in Canada at his death. He and his brother Louis Lionel (5.7.10.5.8.9) married two sisters.

Children:

5.7.10.5.8.1.1	Jacqueline Françoise	1936-	-
5.7.10.5.8.1.2	Réjeanne Anna	1938-	-
5.7.10.5.8.1.3	Claire Jeanne d'Arc	1939-	-
5.7.10.5.8.1.4	Anonymous (female)	1940-	-1940

5.7.10.5.8.2   **MONTY, Simone Clémentine** b & bp 31 Oct & 1 Nov 1910, Valcourt, QC. She married 14 Aug 1944, Milan, QC, **Wilfrid Roland Maheu** (Joseph Maheu & Elise Boutin).

5.7.10.5.8.3   **MONTY, Olida Agnès** b & bp 13 & 18 Aug 1912, Valcourt, QC. She married 3 Jul 1937, Outremont, QC, **Jean-Baptiste Baillargeon** (Alfred Baillargeon & Albertine Barbeau) b & bp 28 & 31 May 1911, St. Luc, QC.

Jean-Baptiste Baillargeon was a laborer in Montreal, QC, at the births of his children there.

Children:
i   **Cécile Simonne Micheline Baillargeon** b & bp 9 Feb 1938, Montreal, QC.
ii   **Jean Pierre Baillargeon** b & bp 10 & 12 Mar 1939, Montreal, QC.
iii   **Alfred Luc Baillargeon** b & bp 24 & 30 Mar 1941, Montreal, QC.

5.7.10.5.8.4   **MONTY, Cécile Liliose** b & bp 20 Feb 1914, Valcourt, QC. She married 14 Jun 1938, Piopolis, QC, **Wilfrid Vachon** (Norbert Vachon & Démérise Bizier).

5.7.10.5.8.5   **MONTY, Blanche Aimée** b & bp 5 & 6 Oct 1915, Valcourt, QC.

5.7.10.5.8.6   **MONTY, Marie Alice Aurélie** b & bp 13 & 14 Apr 1918, Piopolis, QC. She married 27 Aug 1939, Jonquières, QC, **Albert Bean** (Joseph Bean & Alexina Tremblay) b & bp there 8 & 9 Jun 1914.

5.7.10.5.8.7   **MONTY, Jean Ludovic** b & bp 13 & 15 May 1921, Piopolis, QC.

5.7.10.5.8.8   **MONTY, René Wilfrid** b & bp 29 & 30 Nov 1924, Piopolis, QC.

5.7.10.5.8.9   **MONTY, Louis Lionel Edmond** b & bp 17 & 18 Apr 1926, Piopolis, QC. He married 22 Oct 1949, Scotstown, QC, **Fleurette Duval** (Joseph Duval & Aurore Laroche) b & bp there 30 Jul & 2 Aug 1931.

Louis Lionel Monty's wife was named Marie Janine Florette at her baptism. She was a sister of Germaine Duval, wife of Horace Monty (5.7.10.5.8.1).

5.7.10.5.8.10   **MONTY, Victor Edouard** b & bp 11 & 12 Sep 1928, Piopolis, QC.

5.10.6.2.3.1   **MONTY, Joseph Louis Rémy** b & bp 3 & 4 Apr 1887, St. Césaire, QC. He married there 1 Oct 1907 **Délia Donalda Dutilly** (Joseph Dutilly & Délia Massé) b & bp there 4 & 5 Jun 1891.

Joseph Monty was a farmer in St. Césaire, QC, in 1911 (Canadian census).

5.10.6.2.3.2   **MONTY, Marie Louise Aldéa** b & bp 27 & 28 Mar 1889, St. Césaire, QC; d & bur there 2 & 3 Aug 1890.

5.10.6.2.3.3   **MONTY, Alcide** b & bp 22 May 1891, St. Césaire, QC; d & bur there 5 & 6 Apr 1892.

5.10.6.2.3.4   **MONTY, Albina** b & bp 1 & 2 Mar 1893, St. Césaire, QC; d & bur there 19 & 22 Nov 1926. She married there 22 Sep 1913 **Eldège Dieudonné Normandin** (Jean-Baptiste Normandin & Marie Herminie Leroux) b & bp there 6 & 7 Nov 1891; m (2) 7 Jan 1930, Abbotsford, QC, Eva Mailloux (Charles Mailloux & Elise Fontaine).

Eldège (also Uldège) Normandin was a farmer in St. Césaire, QC. He was a brother of Joseph Normandin, husband of Laura Monty (5.10.6.2.5.1), Albina Monty's first cousin.

Children:
- i   **Jean Armand Normandin** b & bp 22 Apr 1915, St. Césaire, QC; d & bur there 13 May 1915.
- ii   **Amande Cécile Normandin** b & bp 11 Mar 1916, St. Césaire, QC; d & bur there 7 & 8 May 1917.
- iii   **Rosaire Georges Henri Normandin** b & bp 29 Jul 1917, St. Césaire, QC. He married 27 Jul 1940, Granby, QC, **Eva Robert** (Alfred Robert & Laura Beauregard) b & bp 27 Feb 1916, Stukely, QC.
- iv   **Bernadette Louise Normandin** b & bp 19 Nov 1918, St. Césaire, QC. She married there 26 Sep 1946 **Roland Fortier** (Sylva Fortier & Aurore Juaire) b & bp 1 & 2 May 1911, Farnham, QC.
- v   **Rose Delia Normandin** b & bp 2 May 1920, St. Césaire, QC. She married there 15 Aug 1940 **Henri Julien Lacoste** (Egnus Lacoste & Eva Gaulin) b & bp there 11 Jan 1912; m (1) there 9 May 1936 Antonia Paquette (Joseph Paquette & Antoinette Demers).
- vi   **Arthur Gérard Normandin** b & bp 22 & 24 Jul 1921, St. Césaire, QC. He married 22 Jul 1943, Milton, QC, **Marie Boileau** (Ernest Boileau & Rosanna Lussier) b & bp there 27 Jan 1924.
- vii   **Marguerite Lucille Normandin** b & bp 3 Jun 1923, St. Césaire, QC. She married there 22 Jul 1943 **Gérard Normandin** (Joseph Normandin & Eva Levasseur) b & bp there 18 & 20 Apr 1921.
- viii **Marcel Antonio Normandin** b & bp 15 & 16 Nov 1924, St. Césaire, QC. He married 12 Jun 1947, Ange Gardien, QC, **Florence Gisèle Barsalou** (Albert Barsalou & Bella Barré) b & bp there 22 & 26 Jul 1925.
- ix   **Lucrèce Noëlla Normandin** b & bp 20 & 21 Feb 1926, St. Césaire, QC; d & bur there 12 & 13 Aug 1926.

5.10.6.2.3.5   **MONTY, Rose Alma** b & bp 23 & 24 May 1895, St. Césaire, QC; d & bur there 6 & 8 Sep 1910.

5.10.6.2.3.6   **MONTY, Anonymous** b 19 Mar 1897, St. Césaire, QC; d & bur there 19 & 20 Mar 1897.

5.10.6.2.3.7   **MONTY, Sergius** b & bp 30 & 31 Mar 1899, St. Césaire, QC; d Dec 1969, Burlington, VT. He married 21 Jan 1925, Chambly, QC, **Noëlla Duclos** (Solime Edéas Duclos & Arsélia Bessette) b & bp 31 Dec 1908, St. Grégoire, QC; d 2 Dec 1999, Williston, VT.

This man was named Joseph George Sergius at his baptism. He nevertheless married as Sergius Adolphe Monty. As Sergius Monty, he was a resident of Burlington, VT, from at least 1930 on (City Directories). Most of his children were born there and remained in the area.

Children:

5.10.6.2.3.7.1	Margaret H.	1926-	-1993
5.10.6.2.3.7.2	Theresa	1927-	-2002
5.10.6.2.3.7.3	Gilberta Betty	-	-
5.10.6.2.3.7.4	Jeannine M.	1931-	-2000
5.10.6.2.3.7.5	Cecile	1933-	-1989
5.10.6.2.3.7.6	Sylvia	1935-	-
5.10.6.2.3.7.7	Lillian	1937-	-1977
5.10.6.2.3.7.8	Yvette Marie	1940-1959?-2002	
5.10.6.2.3.7.9	Peter A.	1943-	-
5.10.6.2.3.7.10	Gloria	-	-
5.10.6.2.3.7.11	Veronica	1951-	-1982

5.10.6.2.3.8   **MONTY, Joseph Georges** b & bp 22 & 23 Apr 1901, St. Césaire, QC.

5.10.6.2.3.9   **MONTY, Emmela Sylvia** b & bp 15 May 1904, St. Césaire, QC; d & bur there 20 & 21 May 1904.

5.10.6.2.3.10   **MONTY, Anonymous** (male) bur 2 Oct 1907, St. Césaire, QC.

5.10.6.2.5.1   **MONTY, Laura Yvonne** b & bp 31 Aug & 1 Sep 1894, St. Césaire, QC. She married there 28 Sep 1914 **Joseph Jean-Baptiste Normandin** (Jean-Baptiste Normandin & Marie Herminie Leroux) b & bp there 4 & 5 Dec 1885.

Laura Monty lived in South Hadley, MA, with her parents from about 1897 to the early 1910s when she returned with them to Canada (1900 and 1910 US censuses; 1911 Canadian census).

Joseph Normandin was a blacksmith in St. Césaire, QC, at his marriage and at the births of his children. He was a brother of Eldège Normandin, husband of Albina Monty (5.10.6.2.3.4), his wife's first cousin.

Children:
i   **Rosaire Roland Normandin** b & bp 28 Nov 1915, St. Césaire, QC.
ii **George Armand Normandin** b & bp 15 Dec 1916, St. Césaire, QC.

5.10.6.2.5.2   **MONTY, Joseph Amédée** b & bp 23 Feb 1896, St. Césaire, QC; d 24 Jun 1982, Springfield, MA. He married 5 Feb 1917, St. Césaire, QC, **Rose Alma Larose** (Paul/ Napoléon Larose dit Saurette & Emma Goddu) b & bp there 12 & 13 Dec 1900; d 31 Dec 1984, Springfield, MA.

Joseph Amédée Monty (Joseph Sergius Amédée at his baptism) first came to the United States with his parents around 1897 and lived with them in South Hadley, MA, for several years as Amédée Monty (1900 and 1910 US censuses). He returned to Canada in the early 1910s and married there under the name of Amédée. When he came back to the United States with his wife and children in May 1924, though, he did so as Joseph A. Monty. He was an inspector in Springfield, MA, in 1930 (US census) and remained in that city and its suburbs until his death (City Directories).

His wife was named Emma Rose Alma Larose at her baptism, Rose Alma Larose at her marriage (though she signed Rose Alma Saurette), and Rose Anna Monty at her death. On other occasions she was known as Mrs. Rose A. Monty.

Children:
5.10.6.2.5.2.1	Marie Rose Amande	1918-1940-1957	
5.10.6.2.5.2.2	Marie Marthe Adeline	1919-1943?-1998	
5.10.6.2.5.2.3	Louis Philip	1920-1942?-1983	
5.10.6.2.5.2.4	John J./Jean Jacques	1923-	-1995
5.10.6.2.5.2.5	Amédée F.	1932-	-1992

5.10.6.2.5.3   **MONTY, Rose Emma** b Oct 1898, South Hadley, MA. She married 27 Jun

1916, St. Césaire, QC, **Joseph Ambroise Arès** (Emile Arès & Arsélia Théberge) b & bp there 4 & 8 Sep 1896; d 21 Oct 1974, Aresville (Laval), QC.

Rose Emma Monty lived with her parents in South Hadley, MA, until 1910 when she moved with them to St. Césaire, QC (1900 and 1910 US censuses; 1911 Canadian census). Joseph Arès was a farmer there at his marriage and at the birth of his first child and in Rougemont, QC, when the next two children were born. The family later moved to Montreal, QC, where the children married.

Children:

i   **Clovis Arès** b & bp 19 & 20 Jul 1917, St. Césaire, QC. He married (1) 12 Sep 1939, Montreal, QC, **Rosaria Trottier** (Emile Trottier & Eva Beaudet) b & bp 11 & 12 Oct 1915, Ste Sophie de Levrard, QC.

     He married (2) **Gisèle Rivet**.

ii   **Roger Arès** b & b 4 Aug 1919, Rougemont, QC. He married 17 May 1941, Montreal, QC, **Alice M. Trottier** (Emile Trottier & Eva Beaudet) b & bp 14 & 15 Nov 1914, Ste Sophie de Levrard, QC.

iii   **Florence Yvette Arès** b & bp 29 Aug & 4 Sep 1921, Rougemont, QC. She married **J. W. Truax**.

5.10.6.2.5.4   **MONTY, Rémi Louis** b 29 Sep 1899, South Hadley, MA.

Rémi Monty (Joseph Louis Rémi in his birth record) lived with his parents in South Hadley, MA, until 1910 when he moved with them to St. Césaire, QC (1900 and 1910 US censuses; 1911 Canadian census). He was a farm hand in Drinkwater, Saskatchewan, Canada, when he signed in 1918 his World War I Draft Registration card before the American consul in Regina, Saskatchewan. I have been unable to follow him further.

5.10.6.2.5.5   **MONTY, Sylvia** b Apr 1909, South Hadley, MA. She married 30 Sep 1930, Ste Angèle de Monnoir, QC, **Lucien Mailloux** (Alcibiade Mailloux & Rose Emma Bussières) b & bp there 27 Mar 1907.

Sylvia Monty left South Hadley, MA, in 1910 when her parents moved to St. Césaire, QC (1911 Canadian census). Lucien Mailloux (named Timothée Lucien Léonard at his baptism) was a farmer in Ste Angèle de Monnoir, QC, at his marriage and at the births of his children there.

Children:

i   **Monique Mailloux** b & bp 3 & 4 May 1933, St. Césaire, QC. She married 15 Aug 1953, Ste Angèle de Monnoir, QC, **Jean-Paul Laforest** (Anthime Laforest & Laura Ponton) b & bp 26 & 27 May 1926, Marieville, QC.

ii   **Jean Claude Mailloux** b & bp 18 & 19 Jun 1934, St. Césaire, QC. He married 5 Sep 1959, Montreal, QC, **Jacqueline Boucher** (Oscar Boucher & Alexina Pelletier) b & bp 13 Dec 1933, St. Vincent de Paul (Laval), QC.

iii   **Pierrette Mailloux** b & bp 27 & 28 Feb 1937, Ste Brigide, QC. She married 1 Sep 1958, Montreal, QC, **Irénée Marcoux** (Adélard Marcoux & Laura Gagné) b & bp 30 & 31 May 1928, Frampton, QC.

iv   **Louis Philippe Mailloux** b & bp 8 & 12 Mar 1939, Ste Angèle de Monnoir, QC. He married 20 Sep 1958, Montreal, QC, **Florence Archambault** (Aquila Archambault & Florence Galarneau) b & bp 14 Mar 1935, St. Vincent de Paul (Laval), QC.

v   **Réjeanne Adrienne Mailloux** b & bp 7 & 8 Dec 1940, Ste Angèle de Monnoir, QC. She married 23 Sep 1961, Montreal, QC, **Réal Boucher** (Oscar Boucher & Alexina Pelletier).

5.10.6.2.5.6   **MONTY, Médard** b & bp 20 & 23 Nov 1911, St. Césaire, QC. He married 25 Oct 1958, Ste Angèle de Monnoir, QC, **Olivine Mailloux** (Alexandre Mailloux & Angelina Choquette) b & bp there 22 & 23 Apr 1919.

Baptismal names: Joseph Emery Lucien Médard Monty and Marie Olivine Emelda Mailloux.

Child:
5.10.6.2.5.5.1   Claude   1959-1980-

5.10.6.8.1.1   **MONTY, Alice Agnès Thérèse** b & bp 21 & 22 May 1922, St. Hyacinthe, QC. She married 18 Dec 1937, Montreal, QC, **Francesco Giuseppe/François Sabino** (Antonio Sabino & Arcangela Marra) b & bp there 15 Dec 1909 & 4 Jan 1910.
    This couple's marriage record names the groom Francesco Giuseppe Sabino (Francesco Giuseppe Luigi at his baptism). He nevertheless signed François Sabino. He was a tailor in Montreal, QC.

5.10.6.8.1.2   **MONTY, Lucien Ernest** b & bp 13 & 15 Jul 1903, Montreal, QC. He married there 8 Oct 1929, **Valéda Lussier** (Albert Lussier & Alma Gauthier) b & bp there 23 & 26 Sep 1903.
    Lucien Monty (Joseph Louis Lucien Ernest at his baptism) was a printer in Montreal, QC. His wife had been named Marie Emma Valida at her baptism but was known as an adult as Valéda Lussier.

Children:
5.10.6.8.1.2.1   Jacques Emile Lucien   1930-   -
5.10.6.8.1.2.2   Emile George André   1932-   -

5.10.6.8.1.3   **MONTY, Anna Lucienne** b & bp 22 & 23 Jul 1905, Montreal, QC.

5.10.6.8.1.4   **MONTY, Gérard Paul Emile** b & bp 12 & 13 Nov 1907, Montreal, QC.

5.10.6.8.5.1   **MONTY, Louis Emile Arthur** b & bp 7 Aug 1904, Montreal, QC.
    Arthur Monty was living with his parents in Montreal, QC, in 1911 (Canadian census).

5.10.6.8.5.2   **MONTY, Emma Florence Agnès** b & bp 12 & 13 Oct 1905, Montreal, QC.
    Florence Monty was living with her parents in Montreal, QC, in 1911 (Canadian census).

5.10.6.8.5.3   **MONTY, Hervé** b & bp 27 Dec 1906, Montreal, QC. He married there 29 Dec 1941 **Jeannette Racine** (Wilfrid Racine & Rosa Grisé).
    Hervé Monty (Joseph Emile Ernest Hervé at his baptism) was a hotel manager in Montreal, QC, at his marriage.

5.10.6.8.5.4   **MONTY, Lucienne Bernadette** b & bp 11 & 13 Dec 1907, Montreal, QC; d & bur there 10 & 11 Feb 1908.

5.10.6.8.5.5   **MONTY, Blanche Simone Elisabeth** b & bp 12 & 13 Jan 1909, Montreal, QC.
    Simone Monty was living with her parents in Montreal, QC, in 1911 (Canadian census).

5.10.6.8.5.6   **MONTY, Gabrielle Gertrude Emma** b & bp 22 Mar 1910, Montreal, QC; d & bur there 28 & 29 Sep 1910.

5.10.6.8.5.7   **MONTY, Pierre Emile Ernest** b & bp 10 & 11 Jun 1911, Montreal, QC.

5.10.6.8.5.8   **MONTY, Jeanne Berthe** married 14 Jun 1938, Montreal, QC, **Pierre Lucien Girard** (Léonidas Girard & Emélie Champagne).
    Jeanne Berthe Monty and Pierre Lucien Girard, a painter in Montreal, QC, were both of age at their marriage.

5.10.6.9.1.1   **MONTY, Albert Aloysius** b & bp 21 & 22 Feb 1900, Montreal, QC; d & bur 23 & 27 Sep 1924, St. Jean-Baptiste & Montreal, QC.

5.10.6.9.1.2   **MONTY, Marguerite Mathilde** b & bp 6 & 7 Apr 1901, Montreal, QC; d & bur there 23 & 26 Sep 1921.

5.10.6.9.1.3   **MONTY, Théodore** b 3 Apr 1902, Joliette, ND; d 21 Oct 1988, Hull, QC. He married 25 Feb 1935, Singapore, **Ruth De Jongh** b 6 Nov 1905, Athens, Greece; d 21 Oct 1985.
Théodore Monty was a Canadian Trade Commissioner in Singapore at his marriage.

Children:
| 5.10.6.9.1.3.1 | Marguerite | 1936-1962?- |
| 5.10.6.9.1.3.2 | Peter B. | 1937-   - |

5.10.6.9.1.4   **MONTY, Thérèse** b 28 Sep 1903; d 3 Dec 1903 (Louise Monty, *Généalogie de la famille Monty*, II, 289).

5.10.6.9.1.5   **MONTY, Reginald** b 14 Mar 1905; d Aug 1905 (Louise Monty, *Généalogie de la famille Monty*, II, 289).

5.10.6.9.1.6   **MONTY, Gérard Arthur** b & bp 14 & 15 Jun 1906, Yamamiche, QC; d 14 Sep 1977, Dorval, QC. He married 9 Sep 1939, Ottawa, Ontario, Canada, **Mary Isabel/Marybel Quinn** (William James Quinn & Isabel McCallum) b & bp there 9 & 22 Apr 1910; d 8 Dec 1988, Dorval, QC.
Gérard Monty (Joseph Arthur Hubert Gérard at his baptism) was a businessman in Montreal, QC.

Children:
5.10.6.9.1.6.1	Mary Isabel Estelle	1940- -1940
5.10.6.9.1.6.2	Michael Richard	1941-1972&1986-2005
5.10.6.9.1.6.3	Louise Elizabeth	1945- &1982-
5.10.6.9.1.6.4	Donald John Gerard	1954-1979-

5.10.6.9.1.7   **MONTY, Gertrude Lilliane** b & bp 20 & 22 Sep 1907, Trois-Rivières, QC. She married 12 Sep 1930, Westmount, QC, **Arden Edward Hill** (Wilford/Wilfred Goodwin Hill & Jane Ann McCracken) b 22 Jun 1902, Muskoka Co., Ontario, Canada.
This woman was named Marie Emma Gertrude Lilliane at her baptism and Gertrude Lillian at her marriage. Her husband was an insurance agent in Montreal, QC, at the birth of their first child in 1932. I know of the other children mainly through Louise Monty, *Généalogie de la famille Monty*, II, 298-304.

Children:
i   **Joan Carol Hill** b & bp 30 Oct & 1 Nov 1932, Montreal, QC. She married 3 Nov 1954, Clinton, Ontario, Canada, **Norman Crawford** b 25 Oct 1925, Wiarton, Ontario, Canada; d Apr 2005, Alberta, Canada.

ii   **Joseph Bruce Hill** b 7 Jul 1937, Montreal, QC. He married there 17 Sep 1966 **Françoise Dupont** (Réal Dupont & Alice Daly) b & bp there 1 & 16 Apr 1938.

iii   **Diane Hill** b 29 Dec 1941, Montreal, QC. She married 21 Dec 1979, Charles Town, WV, **James Samuel Dwyer** b 24 May 1924, Birmingham, AL; d 3 Feb 1984, Charles Town, WV.

iv   **Gary Hill** b 15 Jul 1945, Montreal, QC.

v   **Fern Hill** b 23 Jul 1948, Montreal, QC. She married 13 Oct 1984, Nobleton, Ontario, Canada, **Gordon Carless** b 5 Mar 1947, Cooksville, Ontario, Canada.

5.10.6.9.1.8   MONTY, François Napoléon b & bp 3 & 7 Feb 1909, Trois-Rivières, QC; d 10 Jan 1984, St. Benoit Abbey, QC.

François Monty was a Benedictine monk.

5.10.6.9.1.9   MONTY, Estelle Hélène b & bp 9 & 12 Feb 1911, Trois-Rivières, QC; d 25 Apr 1981, Dorval, QC. She married 14 Apr 1939, Westmount, QC, **Maurice Louis Lavoie** (Louis Etienne Lavoie & Mary Perry/Poirier) b 1 Dec 1909, Moncton, New Brunswick, Canada; d 29 Jan 1988.

Child:
i   **Neil Lavoie** b 4 May 1942. He married 8 Aug 1970 **Pilar Montero** b 8 Aug 1950.

5.10.6.9.1.10   MONTY, Jean Pierre b & bp 18 & 20 Nov 1912, Trois-Rivières, QC; d 24 Sep 1977, Montreal, QC. He married 26 Apr 1943, Westmount, QC, **Cécile Laporte** (Eugène Laporte & Louise Fullum) b 7 Mar 1916, Montreal, QC.

Jean Pierre Monty was an insurance agent in Montreal, QC.

Children:
5.10.6.9.1.10.1	Paul	1948-1974-
5.10.6.9.1.10.2	Claire	1950-1979-1993

5.10.6.9.1.11   MONTY, Charles E. Neil b & bp 2 & 3 Jun 1914, Trois-Rivières, QC. He married 8 Nov 1947 **Helen Clark** b 9 Jun 1921.

I know of Charles Monty's wife and children only through Louise Monty, *Généalogie de la famille Monty*, II, 311-313.

Children:
5.10.6.9.1.11.1	Louis	1948- -1993
5.10.6.9.1.11.2	Mary Jane	1950- -
5.10.6.9.1.11.3	Susan	1952-1973-

5.10.6.9.1.12   MONTY, Lucille b & bp 19 & 21 Oct 1915, Trois-Rivières, QC; d 10 Jan 1958, Montreal, QC. She married there 11 Sep 1943 **Thomas John Brady** (John Brady & Mabel Gertrude Munro) b & bp 19 Dec 1910 & 10 Sep 1911, Westmount, QC; d 25 Sep 1982.

Thomas John Brady was baptized in St. Andrew Presbyterian Church in Westmount, QC. I know of his children mainly through Louise Monty, *Généalogie de la famille Monty*, II, 314-316.

Children:
i   **Stephen Brady** b 9 Nov 1946.
ii   **Ruth Brady** b 21 Apr 1954. She married 15 Jun 1974, Montreal, QC, **Robert Desautels** (Roland Desautels & Lorraine Dargis).
iii **Shelagh Brady** b 28 Mar 1956.
iv   **Teresa Brady** b 15 Aug 1957. She married 23 Sep 1989 **Lenny Thomas** b 4 Nov 1944.

5.10.6.9.1.13   MONTY, Louis b 1917, QC; d & bur 4 & 6 Nov 1918, Montreal, QC, at the age of 1 year and no months.

5.10.6.9.1.14   MONTY, Zita (twin) b & bp 13 & 15 Dec 1918, Montreal, QC. She married there 31 May 1947 **David Schwartz** b 16 May 1913; d 10 Oct 1978.

This woman was named Marie Laura Zita at her baptism but simply Zita at her marriage. I know of her children only through Louise Monty, *Généalogie de la famille Monty*, II, 318-322.

Children:
i   **Lisa Schwartz** b 9 Mar 1948. She married 20 Dec 1969 **Michael Merovitz** b 25 Mar 1947.
ii   **Philip Schwartz** b 14 Oct 1949. He married 25 Jun 1971, **Chantal Dalaudière** b 29 Sep 1943.
iii   **Paola Schwartz** (twin) b 21 Feb 1952. She married 25 Feb 1976 **David Landles** b 2 Dec 1952.
iv   **Julie Schwartz** (twin) b 21 Feb 1952. She married 15 Jul 1978 **Donato Lafera** b 15 May 1939.
v   **Eric Schwartz** b 28 Nov 1954; d 22 Jan 1989. He married 28 Jan 1981 **Ann Daeman**.

5.10.6.9.1.15   **MONTY, Françoise Claire** (twin) b & bp 13 & 15 Dec 1918, Montreal, QC; d & bur there 17 & 19 Nov 1919.

5.10.6.9.2.1   **MONTY, Paul Stanislas** b & bp 14 & 15 May 1905, Montreal, QC; d & bur 22 & 24 May 1990, QC.
Paul Monty became a Brother of the Sacred Heart known as Brother Cyprien.

5.10.6.9.2.2   **MONTY, Jeanne Aloysia** b & bp 2 & 6 Oct 1906, Montreal, QC; d & bur there 12 & 14 Mar 1907.

5.10.6.9.2.3   **MONTY, Blanche** b & bp 22 & 24 May 1908, Montreal, QC; d & bur there 29 & 31 Dec 1908.

5.10.6.9.2.4   **MONTY, Philibert Henri** b & bp 22 & 24 Aug 1911, Verdun, QC; d 26 Dec 1986, Montreal, QC. He married 8 Aug 1944, Pointe-aux-Trembles, QC, **Eveline Audren** (Adrien Julien Audren & Alice Desparois dit Champagne) b 2 Mar 1913, Montreal, QC; d there 15 Jul 1981.
Henri Monty was a funeral director in Montreal, QC.

Children:

5.10.6.9.2.4.1	Paul	1945-1972-
5.10.6.9.2.4.2	Alice	1946- -

5.10.6.9.6.1   **MONTY, Gilberte** b & bp 10 & 12 Jan 1908, Montreal, QC; d & bur there 25 & 27 Jan 1934.
This woman was known as Gilberte Monti in 1911 when she was staying with her parents in Montreal, QC (Canadian census) and as Gilberte Monty at her death. She had been named Marie Marguerite Gilberte Monty at her baptism.

5.10.6.9.6.2   **MONTY, Roland Alfred** b & bp 5 & 6 Dec 1908, Montreal, QC; d & bur there 7 & 10 Feb 1909.

5.10.6.9.6.3   **MONTY, Juliette Madeleine** b & bp 30 Nov & 2 Dec 1909, Montreal, QC; d before 1972. She married 30 Apr 1932, Montreal, QC, **Damase Eugène Roland Desjardins** (Hormisdas Desjardins & Henédine Chevalier) b & bp 25 & 26 Mar 1908, St. Jacques l'Achigan, QC; d before 1972.
Damase Desjardins was a bank teller in Montreal, QC, at his marriage. Both he and his wife were deceased when their son Jean-Guy married in 1972.

Children:
i   **Louise Marie Rita Desjardins** b & bp 24 & 25 Aug 1934, Montreal, QC.
ii   **Jean-Guy Desjardins** b & bp 5 & 6 Aug 1937, Montreal, QC. He married 5 Aug 1972, Val des Lacs, QC, **Danielle Gauthier** (Lionel Gauthier & Fernande Germain).

5.10.6.9.6.4 **MONTY, Marcel Paul Achille** b & bp 10 & 11 Jan 1912, Montreal, QC; d & bur there 27 & 29 Apr 1913.

5.10.6.9.6.5 **MONTY, Gérard Paul Emile** b & bp 29 & 30 Oct 1914, Montreal, QC; d & bur there 4 & 6 Nov 1914.

8.1.7.2.1.1 **MONTY, Louis** b 3 Jan 1878, Manchester, NH; d there 17 Jan 1883.

8.1.7.2.1.2 **MONTY, William** b 23 Jul 1879, Manchester, NH; d there 16 Jan 1883.

8.1.7.2.1.3 **MONTY, Philip** b 24 Nov 1881, Manchester, NH; d & bur there 19 & 20 Sep 1882.

8.1.7.2.1.4 **MONTY, Joseph** b 9 Jun 1883, Manchester, NH; d 24 Jan 1885, Weare, NH.

8.1.7.2.1.5 **MONTY, Mary Ann V.** b 23 Apr 1885, Bedford, NH. She married 1904?, **Guy Allison Firn** (John G. Firn & Sarah Lucinda Schoff) b 27 Apr 1877, Huntington, QC.
This woman's exact name is uncertain. The New Hampshire Birth Records identify her simply as a female daughter of Louis Montey and Victoria Baker. Her baptismal record in St. Mary's church in Manchester, NH, name her Marie Victorine Monty, daughter of Louis Monty and Victorine Bélanger. Later documents and censuses name her Mary V., Mary, Mary Ann, Mary A.
Guy Allison Firn was born in the Province of Quebec (1881 Canadian census in Huntington, QC), in Ontario (1910 US census in Bedford, NH), or in Brasher, NY (World War II Draft Registration card). The earlier census is probably more trustworthy. He had arrived in the United States in 1895 and was a cotton mill worker in Manchester, NH, in 1900. He and his wife had been married for six years in 1910. He was then a building contractor in Bedford, NH, and a house painter there in later years (US censuses; City Directories; World War I and II Draft Registration cards).

Children:
i   **Leon A. Firn** b 21 Sep 1904, Hillsborough Co., NH; d Aug 1974, Manchester, NH.
ii   **Eva M. Firn** b 1906?, Hillsborough Co., NH.
iii **Francis B. Firn** b 11 Feb 1907, Hillsborough Co., NH; d Mar 1964. He married (1) 1930?, **Frances Kerr** b 1901?, NH.
     He married (2) **Marion ___** b 28 Nov 1915; d 7 Jan 2000, Manchester, NH.
iv **Viola Cecelia Firn** b 1 Apr 1909, Bedford, NH; d 28 Feb 1994, Beaverton, OR. She married 1927? **Michael Joseph O'Connor** (Patrick J. O'Connor & Mary ___) b 19 Aug 1900, Manchester, NH; d 14 Jun 1978, Beaverton, OR.

8.1.7.2.4.1 **MONTY, William** b Nov 1882, Manchester, NH; d there 25 Aug 1883, at the age of 9 months.

8.1.7.2.4.2 **MONTE, William J.** b 10 Jul 1888, Bedford, NH; d between 1935 and 1945, MA. He married 16 Aug 1909, Manchester, NH, **Rose M. Pinaud** (Joseph Pinaud & Marie Hébert) b 1890?, Exeter, NH.
William J. Monte was a resident of Merrimack, NH, when his first two children were born. He moved to Massachusetts after the birth of his daughter Irene and was a laborer in Bridgewater, MA, in 1917 and 1920, and a machinist in Peabody, MA, in 1930 (World War I Draft Registration card; US censuses). He died between 1935, when he was a driver in Peabody, and 1945, when Mrs. Rose Monte was a widow (City Directories).
Rose Pinaud was 29 years old on 1 Jan 1920 (US census). She lived in Peabody until at least 1953 (City Directories).

Children:

8.1.7.2.4.2.1	George	1911-	-
8.1.7.2.4.2.2	William J.	1913-	-1986
8.1.7.2.4.2.3	Irene	1914?-	-
8.1.7.2.4.2.4	Dorothy	1920-	-

8.1.7.2.4.3   **MONTE, Edward Joseph Odilon** b 3 Apr 1890, Merrimack, NH; d between 1930 and 1940, MA. He married 1920? **Mary H. ____** b 1 Nov 1901, MA; d 8 Feb 1973, Lynn, MA.

Edward O. Monte was a worker in Salem, MA, shoe factory in 1930, when he and his wife had been married for ten years (US census). She was a widow living with her children in Lynn, MA, in 1940 (City Directory).

Children:

8.1.7.2.4.3.1	George W.	1922-	-1971
8.1.7.2.4.3.2	Edward E.	1923-	-1973

8.1.7.2.4.4   **MONTE, Emily** b 24 Jan 1895, Bedford, NH. She married 1917? **John Joseph LaFreniere** (Moïse/Moses LaFrenière & Catherine Grasette) b 12 Oct 1896, Peabody, MA; m (2) 1927? Celia Agnes Spain (Louis F. Spain & Clara ____); d 13 Jul 1980, Danvers, MA.

John Lafreniere was a leather worker in Peabody, MA. He and his second wife had been married for three years in 1930 (US census).

Children:

i   **Ruth LaFrenière** b 13 Sep 1919, Peabody, MA; d 21 Feb 1993, Central Point, OR.
ii   **Louise LaFrenière** b 1921?, Peabody, MA.

8.1.7.2.4.5   **MONTE, Charles Wilfred** b 7 Mar 1897, Merrimack, NH; d Sep 1966, Middleboro, MA. He married 1919? **Christine ____** b 1901?, MA.

Charles Wilfred Monte was a leather worker in Peabody, MA, in 1920 when his bride Christine was 18 years old (US census). He moved a few years later to Brockton, MA, where, according to the 1929 and 1932 City Directories, he and his wife made a home for his widowed mother. He was a resident of Lakeville, MA, at his death.

8.1.7.2.4.6   **MONTE, Henry Ernest** b 8 Oct 1898, Bedford, NH; d Jul 1977.

Henry Monte was a leather worker in Peabody, MA, in 1920 and in Brockton, MA, in 1930 (US censuses). He was a resident of Clearwater, FL, at his death.

8.1.7.4.3.1   **MONTY, John F.** b 4 Sep 1893, Savanna, IL.

John Monty was a railroad laborer in Savanna, IL, in 1910, a driver there in 1920, and a worker in an electric plant there in 1930. He was still living at home when his father died in 1944 (*Savanna Daily Journal*, 18 Aug 1944).

8.1.7.4.3.2   **MONTY, Jerome** b 30 Oct 1895, Savanna, IL; d before 1900.

Jerome Monty does not appear with his parents in the 1900 US census in Savanna, IL, and must be the deceased child noted there.

8.1.7.4.3.3   **MONTY, Raymond E.** b 13 Sep 1899, Savanna, IL; d between 1900 and 1910.

Raymond E. Monty was living with his parents in Savanna, IL, in 1900 but was not included among their three surviving children in 1910 (US censuses).

8.1.7.4.3.4   **MONTY, Lucille M.** b 9 Sep 1901, Savanna, IL; d there Oct 1985. She married 1922? **Robert Harry Spencer** (Elmer Elsworth Spencer & Eliza Ensley) b 8 Mar 1900, Elkhorn Grove, IL; d Jan 1983, Thomson, IL.

Robert Spencer was a farmer in Elkhorn Grove, IL, in 1930 when he and his wife had been married for eight years (US census).

Children:
i   **Merle Harry Spencer** b 7 Mar 1923, Milledgeville, IL; d 8 May 1998, Sterling, IL. He married 31 Jan 1954, Savanna, IL, **Nellie E. Reisinger** (Benjamin Reisinger & Anna Washburn) b 23 Jul 1917, Camanche, IA; d 22 Nov 1988, Sterling, IL.

ii   **Robert Spencer** b 4 Jun 1924, Milledgeville, IL; d there 24 Feb 1925.

iii   **Irene M. Spencer** b Feb 1926, Carroll Co., IL. She married **Leonard E. Hebeler** (Henry Hebeler & Anna ____) b 10 Jan 1923, IA; d 14 Jan 1981, Thomson, IL.

iv   **Joseph J. Spencer** b 11 Oct 1927, Carroll Co., IL. He married **Lois M. Groezinger** (Judson W. Groezinger & Mary L. Price) b Feb 1927, Lena, IL.

v   **Marguerite/Margaret Spencer** b 1936?, Carroll Co., IL. She married ____ **Beyers**.

vi   **Wilbert Cecil Spencer** b 21 Jul 1937, Carroll Co., IL. He married **Betty Lou Chapman** (Tally Dewey Chapman & Vera E. Conklin) b 7 Mar 1933, Keota, IA; d 14 Feb 1984, Clinton, IA.

8.1.7.4.3.5   **MONTY, Mary Kathleen** b 15 Dec 1905, Savanna, IL.

Mary Monty was living with her parents in Savanna, IL, in 1920 (US census) but was deceased at her father's death in 1944 (*Savanna Daily Journal*, 18 Aug 1944).

8.1.7.4.8.1   **MONTY, Donald William** b 16 Jan 1913, Savanna, IL; d 14 Feb 1991, Los Angeles, CA.

William D. Monty was living with his mother in his maternal grandfather's household in Savanna, IL, in 1920 and with both his parents in Rockford, IL, in 1930 (US censuses). He was known as Donald or Donald W. as an adult.

8.1.7.4.8.2   **MONTY, Robert Louis/Lewis** b 7 May 1920, Savanna, IL.

Robert Monty was living in Savanna, IL, in 1930 with his maternal relatives (US census). He was a resident of Rockford, IL, when his father died in 1958 (*Savanna Daily Journal*, 4 Nov 1958) and continued to live there into the 21st century.

8.1.7.6.1.1   **MONTY, Milton John** b Aug 1904, Clintonville, WI; d there 18 Jan 1906.

Milton J. Monty was 10 months old in June 1905 when he was living with his parents in Clintonville, WI (state census). He was buried in Graceland Cemetery there.

8.1.7.6.1.2   **MONTY, Marshall G.** b 24 Oct 1906, Clintonville, WI; d 1 Apr 1978, Pinellas Co., FL. He married 9 Mar 1932, Waukegan, IL, **Evelyn Kitzman** (Gustave/Gust Kitzman & Anna ____) b 1910?, WI.

Marshall Monty was working in an automobile factory in Clintonville, WI, in 1930 when Evelyn Kitzman was a 20-year-old telephone operator in Marion, WI (US censuses).

8.1.7.6.1.3   **MONTY, Margaret** b Jun 1909, Clintonville, WI. She married 13 Feb 1937, Bear Creek, WI, **Sylvester Moriarity** (James M. Moriarity & Anna McLaughlin) b 26 Apr 1904, Deer Creek, WI.

Margaret Monty was a 10-month-old infant living with her parents in Clintonville, WI, on 15 Apr 1910. She and her husband were residents of Milwaukee, WI, at the birth of a son in September 1937 (*Appleton Post Crescent*, 13 Feb 1937 and 21 Sep 1937).

Child:
i   **Unnamed Moriarity** (male) b 17 Sept 1937, Milwaukee, WI.

8.1.7.6.1.4   **MONTY, John Henry** b 9 Nov 1913, Clintonville, WI; d there 17 Feb 1985.

John H. Monty was living with his parents in Clintonville, WI, in 1920 and 1930 (US

8.1.7.6.1.5   **MONTY, Ruth E.** b 1915, Clintonville, WI; d there 1916.
I know of this child's birth and death only through the inscription on the tombstone she shares with her parents in Graceland Cemetery in Clintonville, WI.

8.1.7.6.5.1   **MONTY, Violet Bernice** b 24 Apr 1902, Crandon, WI; d 19 Aug 1970, Marinette, WI. She married 5 Jul 1920 **Arthur Olson** (Charles John Olson & Mathilda Jorgenson) b 17 May 1895, New Denmark, WI; d 10 Feb 1963, Marinette, WI.

Children:
    i   **Cleo Olson**
    ii   **Robert Olson**

8.1.7.6.5.2   **MONTY/MONTE, Claude G.** b 28 Mar 1904, Crandon, WI; d 23 May 1961. He married 1923? **Jean I. Travis** b 26 Mar 1903, Lincoln Co., WI; d 28 Oct 1979, Menomonee Falls, WI.
Claude Monte was an automobile worker in Kingsford, MI, in 1930, when he and his wife had been married for seven years (US census). He was buried though as Claude Monty alongside his parents and two siblings in Graceland Cemetery in Clintonville, WI.

Children:
8.1.7.6.5.2.1	Donald W.	1924-	-2005
8.1.7.6.5.2.2	Douglas Keith	1926-	-1960
8.1.7.6.5.2.3	Kenneth R.	1929-1965-2004	

8.1.7.6.5.3   **MONTY, Milton E.** b 24 Sep 1905, Crandon, WI; d 27 Oct 1921, Vilas Co., WI.
This child was buried with his parents in Graceland Cemetery in Clintonville, WI.

8.1.7.6.5.4   **MONTY, Howard Gladwyn** b 25 Apr 1907, Crandon, WI; d & bur 26 & 29 Apr 1994, Ontonagon, MI. He married 12 Apr 1930, Ironwood, MI, **Doris Amy Nagley** (William Henry Nagley & Amy Gertrude Naylor) b 31 Dec 1906, Ashland, WI; d 26 May 1995, Ontonagon, MI.
The date of Howard G. Monty's birth is taken from the Forest Co., WI, Birth Records (#2901). Social Security records show a birth date of 25 May 1907.

Children:
8.1.7.6.5.4.1	Jack	1931-	-1936
8.1.7.6.5.4.2	Jo Ann	1932-	-1932
8.1.7.6.5.4.3	William	1938-	-

8.1.7.6.5.5   **MONTY/MONTE, George H.** b 10 Apr 1910, Crandon, WI; d 24 Aug 1994, Shawano Co., WI. He married 26 Dec 1938, Embarrass, WI, **Rose Agnes List** (George Mathias Walter List & Rosa Behrs) b 17 Nov 1918, Frankenmuth, MI; d 14 Jul 1996, Shawano Co., WI.
This man was known as George Monty until at least 1920 when he was living with his parents in Presque Isle, WI (US census) and later as George H. Monte. He and his wife were residents of Clintonville, WI, at their deaths and were buried there in Graceland Cemetery.

Children:
8.1.7.6.5.5.1	Karen	-	-
8.1.7.6.5.5.2	Phillip	1945-	-

8.1.7.6.5.6   **MONTY/MONTE, Berdean** b 24 Mar 1915, WI; d 26 Sep 1975, Clintonville, WI. She married 7 Aug 1937, Ironwood, MI, **John A. Johnson** (Alex P. Johnson &

Veda ____) b 10 Feb 1910, WI; d 2 Sep 1973, Clintonville, WI.

Berdean Monty was a public school teacher in Embarrass, WI, at her marriage while John A. Johnson was a salesman in Ashland, WI (*Appleton Post Crescent*, 11 Aug 1937).

Children:

   i   **Marie Rose Johnson**
  ii   **Jerry Johnson**

8.1.7.6.5.7   **MONTY, Keith Jack** b 19 May 1917, WI; d 27 Mar 1987, Clintonville, WI. He married **Ione M. Welch** (Harry Roger Welch & Marie M. ____) b 24 Apr 1920, Waupaca, WI; d 11 Feb 1981, Clintonville, WI..

Keith Monty was living with his parents in Presque Isle, WI, in 1920 and in Kingsford, MI, in 1930 (US censuses).

Children:

8.1.7.6.5.7.1	Keith Jack	1942-	&1982-
8.1.7.6.5.7.2	Dennis	-	-

8.1.7.6.5.8   **MONTY, Cleo Mae** b 23 Dec 1918, WI; d 30 May 1920, Presque Isle, WI. This child was buried in Graceland Cemetery in Clintonville, WI.

8.1.7.6.5.9   **MONTY/MONTE, Warren J.** b 4 Jan 1922, Winchester, WI; d 30 Dec 2005, Green Bay, WI. He married 25 Dec 1945 **LaVerne B. Sass** (Reinhold Sass & Lydia N. Minikel) b 8 Dec 1920, WI.

Warren J. Monte lived and worked in Milwaukee, WI, La Crosse, WI, Chicago, IL, and St. Louis, MO, before moving to Green Bay, WI, in 2003. His wife and two daughters survived him (*Green Bay Press Gazette*, 1 Jan 2006).

Children:

8.1.7.6.5.9.1	Janelle J.	1947-	-
8.1.7.6.5.9.2	Adrianne L.	1949-	-

8.1.7.6.6.1   **MONTE, Everett Delford** b 15 May 1905, Everett, WA; d 4 Apr 1986, San Mateo, CA. He married 7 May 1932, Benton Co. or Franklin Co., WA, **Lucille D. Owen** (Elmer Charles Owen & Effie Jane Works) b 13 Jan 1905, Sprague, WA; d 2 Jul 1991, Simsbury, CT.

Family history has it that this couple married in Portland, OR, on 1 Jul 1933. This must be wrong. There are two references in the Washington State Digital Archives of their marriage on 7 May 1932 when marriage certificates were issued to Everett Delferd (sic) Monte and Lucille D. Owen in Benton Co., WA, and also to E. D. Monte and Lucille D. Owen in Franklin Co., WA. This last was recorded in Franklin Co. on 10 Jun 1932. The marriage may have taken place in either of the two adjoining counties.

Child:

8.1.7.6.6.1.1	Gail Gene	1936-1962-

8.1.7.6.8.1   **MONTE, Wayne N.** b 26 Jun 1914, Custer Co., MT; d 24 Sep 1987, Missoula, MT. He married 1934, Miles City, MT, **Charleen L. Stumpf** (Charles Stumpf & Elizabeth Ray) b 11 Oct 1916, Red Lodge, MT; m (2) 11 Oct 1955 John Geiger; d & bur 22 & 27 May 2006, Ronan & Glendive, MT.

Wayne N. Monte was a land surveyor in Miles City, MT, until 1948 when he moved to Glendive, MT. He and his wife later divorced (*Miles City Star*, 2 Jun 2006).

Children:

8.1.7.6.8.1.1	Gary W.	1936- -
8.1.7.6.8.1.2	Virginia Anne	1937-1960-1992-

8.1.7.6.8.1.3   Alan Ray   1945?-1971&   -

8.1.7.6.8.2   **MONTE, Amos/Rex A.** b Dec 1916, Custer Co., MT. He married **Virginia** ____ b Sep 1919.
    Amos Monte was 3 years and 1 month old on 1 Jan 1920 when he was living with his parents in Custer Co., MT. He was still there with them in 1930 but was then named Rex A. Monte (US censuses). Rex A. Monte and his wife were residents of San Diego Co., CA, at the beginning of the 21st century.

8.1.7.6.8.3   **MONTE, Glenn W.** b 1917, Custer Co., MT; d 27 May 1975, Yellowstone Co., MT, at the age of 58. He married **Athalie Light** (Edwin F. Light & Lucy Mariah Pering) b 17 Aug 1915, Lewiston, MT; d 28 Nov 1990, Yellowstone Co., MT.
    Glen W. Monte was a resident of Carbon Co., MT, at his death. His widow was a resident of Yellowstone Co., MT, at her death.

8.1.7.6.9.1   **MONTY, Harold Charles** b 11 Mar 1914, Minneapolis, MN; d & bur 25 & 31 Oct 1983, Guadalupe & Riverside, CA. He married 10 Jan 1942, Minneapolis, MN, **Arlene May Barnhart** (Arvin Nelson Barnhart & Emma Smith) b 3 Feb 1912, OH; d & bur 13 & 16 Dec 1994, Orange Co. & Riverside, CA.
    Harold Monty was a Staff Sergeant in the US Army during World War II and was buried, as was his wife, in the Riverside, CA, National Cemetery.

Child:
8.1.7.6.9.1.1   Shirley   -   -

8.1.7.6.9.2   **MONTY/MONTE, Claude Louis** b 15 Sep 1915, Hanley Falls, MN; d 13 Oct 1977, Clearwater Co., MN. He married 6 Mar 1949, Junction City, KS, **Ryeta Nan Lemon** (Guy A. Lemon & Lulu ____) b 14 Oct 1913, Chapman, KS; d 9 Aug 1976.
    Claude Monty was a farm hand on his uncle Olaf Trovatten's farm in Norman Twp, MN, in 1930 (US census). His surname later became Monte. Claude Louis Monte and his wife were buried in Junction City, KS.

Children:
8.1.7.6.9.2.1   Miss Monte   -1972&   -
8.1.7.6.9.2.2   Betty   -1970-

8.1.7.6.9.3   **MONTY/MONTE, Corinne Harriet** b 24 Mar 1921, Winchester, WI. She married 9 Sep 1946, Minneapolis, MN, **John Robert Jones** (Matthew Jones & Margaret Elizabeth Meagher) b there 5 Jun 1921; d there 12 Jan 1993.

Children:
i   **Elizabeth Ann Jones** b 22 Mar 1947, Minneapolis, MN. She married 20 Jul 1974, Bloomington, MN, **John Anderson Fundingsland** (Arnold Engvold Fundingsland & Alice Jeannette Anderson) b 9 Oct 1946, Hennepin Co., MN.
ii   **Jean Marie Jones** b 8 Sep 1948, Minneapolis, MN.
iii   **Michael Robert Jones** b 8 Sep 1949, Minneapolis, MN. He married **Catherine Henderson.**
iv   **Patrick Lawrence Jones** b 1 Apr 1952, Minneapolis, MN. He married **Sigrid Reinhardt** b 1956.
v   **Mary Katherine Jones** b 26 Jan 1956, Minneapolis, MN
vi   **Andrea Louise Jones** b 29 Jan 1960, Minneapolis, MN. She married **Brian J. Carrillo** b Sep 1962.

8.1.7.6.9.4   **MONTY/MONTE, Lauraine Anna** b 2 Dec 1922, Iron Mountain, MI; d 24 Dec 2005, Gonvick, MN. She married 19 Jan 1951, Perley, MN, **Harold R. Bruhjell** (Ole Bruhjell & Inga Malmo) b 23 Jun 1924, Gonvick, MN; d & bur 4 & 7 Jun 1988, Fargo, ND &

Gonvick, MN.

Harold R. Bruhjell was a farmer in Gonvick, MN. He was buried there, as was his wife, in Samhold Lutheran Cemetery (*Grand Forks Herald*, 5 Jun 1988).

8.1.7.6.9.5   **MONTY, Charles Ralph** b 27 Jul 1924, Iron Mountain, MI; d 6 Jun 1982, Fillmore Co., MN. He married 4 Dec 1948, Red Lake Falls, MN, **Joyce Irene Melbo** (Sigurd T. Melbo & Ella Handy) b 20 Jan 1929, Polk Co., MN.

Charles R. Monty was a resident of Grand Meadow, MN, at his death. He was buried there in Bear Creek Lutheran Cemetery. His wife survived him.

Children:

8.1.7.6.9.5.1	Marcia Renee	1949-1972-
8.1.7.6.9.5.2	Allan Clark	1951-1974&2006-
8.1.7.6.9.5.3	Karen Joy	1953-1978-

8.1.7.6.9.6   **MONTY, Hugh Otis** b 25 Apr 1929, Cicero Twp, WI; d there 15 Sep 1929.

8.1.7.6.9.7   **MONTY, Keith Harland** b 25 Apr 1931, Hanley Falls, MN; d 26 Nov 1995, Sanger, CA. He married (1) ____ **Rogge**.

He married (2) 14 Feb 1994, Clark Co., NV, **Beverly Ann Stewart** b Jan 1937.

Children of the first marriage:

8.1.7.6.9.7.1	Keith A.	1964-	-
8.1.7.6.9.7.2	Teresa L. Monty	1968-	-

8.1.7.12.2.1   **MONTY, Floyd Francis** b 10 Mar 1895, Bear Creek, WI; d 20 Jun 1921, Dickinson, ND. He married 27 Nov 1920 **Laura Eliza Bendtsen** (Lars Peter Bendtsen & Marie Anderson) b 13 Jan 1899, Prairieville Twp, MN; m (2) 30 Jan 1923 **Roy Alexander Monty** (8.1.7.12.2.3); d 17 Jun 1963, Kanabec Co., MN.

Floyd Monty came with his family to North Dakota in the early 1900s and was a farmer in Belfield, ND, when he enlisted in the US Army on 28 Mar 1918. He was wounded in action and discharged on 5 Mar 1919 with 30% disability. He returned to farming but soon died in a Dickenson, ND, hospital as a result of a farming accident in Belfield (*Roster of the Men and Women who Served in the World War, 1917-1918, from North Dakota*, III, 2208; *Scope County News*, ND, 8 Jul 1921).

Laura Bendtsen married her deceased husband's brother, Roy Alexander Monty (8.1.7. 12.2.3).

Child:

8.1.7.12.2.1.1	Frances Mary	1921-1947-

8.1.7.12.2.2   **MONTY, Rachel M.** b 14 Jun 1896, Bear Creek, WI; d 23 Dec 1984, Sherburne Co., MN. She married 1916? **Maxim Joseph/Mike Henry** b 24 Feb 1892 or 1893, MN; d 17 Apr 1975, Scott Co., MN.

Rachel Monty came with her family to North Dakota in the early 1900s and was living in her father's household in Belfield (Fryburg Twp), ND, in 1910. Maxim Joseph Henry was a farmer there in 1917 and 1920 and a house painter there on 1 Apr 1930 when he and his wife had been married for thirteen years (World War I Draft Registration card; US censuses). The family later moved to Minnesota.

I have not found Maxim or Mike Henry's birth record. Three dates of birth are given in three seemingly authoritative documents: 24 Feb 1892 (World War I Draft Registration), 24 Feb 1893 (Minnesota Death Index), and 14 Feb 1893 (Social Security Death Index). I tend to trust the earliest record.

Children:

i   **Alexander Joseph Henry** b 25 May 1917, Belfield, ND; d 3 Dec 1974, Minneapolis, MN. He married **Elsie Laverne Niemela** (Andrew Niemela & Selma Olgren) b 1925?, MN.

ii   **James Maxim Henry** b 6 Oct 1919, Belfield, ND; d 16 Feb 1975, Scott Co., MN. He married **Phyllis LaVonne Hoehne**.

iii   **Mary Ann Henry** b 1923?, Belfield, ND. She married **Robert Harrison Schmidt** (Joseph Schmidt & Lydia B. ____) b Feb 1923, Minneapolis, MN.

iv   **Raymond John Henry** b 24 May 1925, Belfield, ND; d 10 Aug 2002, Cloquet, MN. He married (1) **Bernice Florence Hietala** (Walter Elmer Hietala & Sophia ____) b 25 Mar 1930, Blueberry, MN; m (2) 22 Nov 1965, Duluth, MN, Eino/Mike Autio (Samuel Autio & Louise Jalasjarvi [?]); d there 30 Oct 2005.

He married (2) 15 Aug 1970, Duluth, MN, **Lola Marie Murphy** (Stanley Murphy & Clara Nelson) b there 6 Dec 1929; m (1) Wallace Bloyd Anderson; d 21 May 2007, Duluth, MN.

v   **Louise Emma Henry** b 18 Feb 1930, Belfield, ND; d 4 Dec 1999, Wadena, MN. She married (1) **Martin Frederick/Fredrick Nordquist** (Ben F. Nordquist & Ellen M. Bengston) b 1 Mar 1917, Otter Tail Co., MN; d there 23 Sep 1964.

She married (2) 3 Jul 1971, Wadena Co., MN, **David Ralph Tullis** (Howard Alexander Tullis & Orall Marian Glass) b May 1928, New Germany, MN; m (1) Gloria Gwendolyn Johnson.

vi   **Robert Lee Henry** b Feb 1933. He married **Vivian Alice Johnson** (Arthur Johnson & Alice Peterson) b 27 Jul 1937, Cottonwood Co., MN.

vii   **Earl David Henry** b 1935. He married **Elizabeth Ann Wangerin** (Herman Wangerin & Madelina Melle) b 5 Nov 1938, Otter Trail Co., MN.

viii   **Patrick Henry**

8.1.7.12.2.3   **MONTY, Roy Alexander** b 12 Dec 1897, Elderon, WI; d 24 Mar 1982, Mille Lacs Co., MN. He married (1) 30 Jan 1923 **Laura Eliza Bendtsen** (Lars Peter Bendtsen & Marie Anderson) b 13 Jan 1899, Prairieville Twp, MN; m (1) 27 Nov 1920 **Floyd Francis Monty** (8.1.7.12.2.1); d 17 Jun 1963, Kanabec Co., MN.

He married (2) 14 Aug 1965, Mora, MN, **Susanna Marion Illerbrun** (Henry Illerbrun & Mary Kartes) b 19 Apr 1899, Langdon, ND; m (1) 17 Feb 1917, Mount Carmel, ND, Ambrose Hell (John Hell & Regina Montag); d 22 Oct 1976, St. Cloud, MN.

Roy Monty had come to North Dakota with his parents in the early 1900s and was a farmer in Belfield (Fryburg Twp), ND, until the late 1930s (US censuses) when he moved to Minnesota with his family. He and his second wife Susanna were both residents of Ogilvie, MN, at their deaths.

Children:

8.1.7.12.2.3.1	Ralph S.	1924-1967?-2004
8.1.7.12.2.3.2	Marian Dorothy	1925-1946-2003
8.1.7.12.2.3.3	Floyd F.	1926- -

8.1.7.12.2.4   **MONTY, Florence Mary** b 23 Nov 1899, Wittenberg, WI; d 7 Jan 1975, Toppenish, WA. She married (1) 8 Nov 1920, Billings, MT, **Jacob Hausken** (Lars Johann Hausken & Amalie ____) b 29 Sep 1896, Haugesund, Norway; d 14 Dec 1934.

She married (2) 1937 **Robert Alexander McDonald** (D. A. McDonald & ____) b 8 Sep 1894, Donald, WA; d 30 Sep 1972, Toppenish, WA.

Florence Monty came to North Dakota with her family in the early 1900s and was living in her father's household in Belfield, ND, on 1 Jan 1920. Jacob Hausken was a railroad foreman there (US census). He was also a resident of Belfield when he was naturalized in Billings, ND, on 23 May 1921.

Robert Alexander McDonald was a farm laborer in the employ of his father D. A. McDonald in Wapato, WA, when he signed his World War I Draft Registration card. He and his wife were residents of Yakima, WA, at their deaths.

Children:
i   **Norman Francis Hausken** b 11 Sep 1921, Simms, ND; d 18 Jun 1994, Boise, ID. He married 25 Nov 1943 **Myrtle Jeanette Gilbert** (Ralph Stanley Gilbert & Ona Mary Jones) b 5 Jan 1925, New Meadows, ID; d 21 Dec 1993, Yakima, WA.

ii   **Floyd V. Hausken** b 24 Jul 1925; d 18 Mar 1978, Toppenish, WA. He married **Ruth F. Sodeman** (Harry A. Sodeman & Mary ____) b 25 Jul 1927, Yakima, WA; d 29 Nov 1992, Toppenish, WA.

iii   **Barbara McDonald** married ____ **Martin**.

8.1.7.12.5.1   **MONTY, Lloyd Solomon** b 16 Jan 1907, Elderon, WI; d 4 Apr 1996, Elroy, WI. He married 17 May 1937, Phelps, WI, **Alvera E. Sann** (Charles Sann & Alma Volkman) b 6 Apr 1915, Brokow, WI; d 17 Oct 1987, Eagle River, WI.

Lloyd Monty and his wife were long-term residents of Phelps, WI, and were buried in the Phelps Cemetery.

Children:

8.1.7.12.5.1.1	James	-	-	
8.1.7.12.5.1.2	Joann Carole	1941-	&	&1985-1993
8.1.7.12.5.1.3	John C.	1943 -	-	
8.1.7.12.5.1.4	Judith Ann	1946-	-1946	

8.1.7.12.5.2   **MONTY/MONTE, Abraham Joseph** b 30 Apr 1908, Elderon, WI; d 20 Feb 1989, Mesa, AZ. He married 8 Oct 1934 **Helen Martin**.

Abraham J. Monty lived with his parents in Elderon, WI, and in Phelps, WI, before moving to Milwaukee, WI, where he was a foundry worker in 1930 (US censuses). He was named Abraham Monte at his death.

Children:

8.1.7.12.5.2.1	Larry	-	-
8.1.7.12.5.2.2	Kenneth	-	-
8.1.7.12.5.2.3	Dennis	-	-

8.1.7.12.5.3   **MONTY, Carol Sophie** b 12 Nov 1909, Elderon, WI. She married (1) 1928? **Ray Hughes** b 1906?, WI.

She married (2) 4 Nov 1933 **Milton O. Dunham** (Edwin B. Dunham & Lottie E. Martin) b 25 Jun 1911, Delton, WI; d 27 Apr 1995, Waukesha, WI.

Ray Hughes was a 24-year-old foundry worker in Milwaukee, WI, on 1 Apr 1930 when he and his wife had been married for two years (US census). His household then also included his brother-in-law Abraham J. Monty (8.1.7.12.5.2).

Mrs. Carol Dunham was living in Milwaukee when her sister Ruth Mary (8.1.7.12.5.8) died in 2006 (*Milwaukee Journal Sentinel*, 27 Aug 2006).

Child:
i   **Milton Dunham** married **Laurie** ____ .

8.1.7.12.5.4   **MONTY, Verne Vincent** b 24 Jul 1911, Elderon, WI; d 13 Oct 1989, Neenah, WI. He married 3 Aug 1941 **Dorothy Blanche Weiss**.

Children

8.1.7.12.5.4.1	Kenneth Charles	1941-1983-
8.1.7.12.5.4.2	Barbara A.	1943- -

8.1.7.12.5.5   **MONTY, Algern/Algernon Lawrence** b 22 Sep 1913, Elderon, WI; d & bur 10 & 13 Aug 1981, Milwaukee & Phelps, WI. He married (1) 21 Sep 1936 **Helmi Honkala** b 1913; d 1947.

He married (2) 26 Nov 1952, Cook Co., IL, **Gertrude Rudd** (Charles Rudd & Hattie

Witt) b 1910?, IL; m (1) Russell R. Johnson; d & bur 24 & 26 May 1971, Arlington Heights & Skokie, IL, at the age of 61.

This man was named Algernon when living with his parents in Phelps, WI, in 1920 and 1930 (US censuses) though he was known in later years solely as Algern Monty. The years of his first wife's birth and death are taken from the inscription on her tombstone in the Phelps Cemetery, where he was also buried. He was a resident of Arlington Heights, IL, when his second wife died. She was buried in Memorial Park Cemetery in Skokie, IL (*Chicago Daily Herald*, 26 May 1971; *Chicago Tribune*, 12 Aug 1981).

Children:

8.1.7.12.5.5.1	Loretta	-	-
8.1.7.12.5.5.2	Betty	-	-
8.1.7.12.5.5.3	Ronald A.	1939-1973-	

8.1.7.12.5.6 **MONTY, Edward Sylvester** b 15 Jan 1915, Elderon, WI; d 15 Aug 1954, near Lomax, IL. He married around 1944, Honolulu, HI, **Esther Lily Lydia Ritari** (Herman Ritari & Matilda Saari) b 20 Apr 1919, Toledo, WA; m (2) 5 Dec 1981, Seattle, WA, John Buchholz; d 21 May 2004, Camas, WA.

Edward S. Monty was living with his parents in Phelps, WI, in 1920 and 1930 (US censuses). He moved to Washington State in the 1930s and then to Hawaii before 1941. He remained in Hawaii during and after World War II and was returning there after a visit to his relatives in Wisconsin when he was killed in a train accident near Lomax, IL. His widow returned to Washington State with her children after his death.

Children:

8.1.7.12.5.6.1	Marian Leilani	1945-	-
8.1.7.12.5.6.2	Carol Moana	1947-	-

8.1.7.12.5.7 **MONTY, Milton Benjamin** b 20 Aug 1916, Elderon, WI; d 8 Aug 1988, Milwaukee, WI. He married 21 Feb 1948 **Adeline Bartol** (Peter Bartol & Constance Kinba) b 12 Aug 1913, Ashland, WI; d Jun 1993, Milwaukee, WI.

Milton B. Monty was living with his parents in Phelps, WI, in 1920 and 1930 (US censuses). Some say that he married Edith Goodwill as his first or second wife. I know nothing about her.

Children:

8.1.7.12.5.7.1	Donna J.	1953-1981-
8.1.7.12.5.7.2	Dean Jeffrey	1959-1986-
8.1.7.12.5.7.3	John Maurice	1960-1994-
8.1.7.12.5.7.4	Lisa Renee	1961-1982-
8.1.7.12.5.7.5	Daren Steven	1964-1987-

8.1.7.12.5.8 **MONTY, Ruth Mary** b 3 Jul 1918, Eland, WI; d 18 Aug 2006, Eagle River, WI.

Ruth Mary Monty was buried in the Phelps, WI, Cemetery. She had remained single and lived in both Phelps and Milwaukee, WI (*Milwaukee Journal Sentinel*, 27 Aug 2006).

8.1.7.12.5.9 **MONTY, Vivian Shirley** b 16 Oct 1919, Phelps, WI. She married 16 Dec 1939 **Lee E. Byington** (Eugene Byington & Ethel Sheets) b 2 May 1916, MO; d 2 Apr 2000, Milwaukee, WI.

Lee Byington was buried in the Phelps, WI, Cemetery. The names of his children and their spouses are taken from his obituary in the *Milwaukee Journal Sentinel* of 5 Apr 2000. Mrs. Vivian Byington was a resident of Greenfield, WI, when her sister Ruth Monty (8.1.7.12.5.8) died in 2006 (*Milwaukee Journal Sentinel*, 27 Aug 2006).

Children:

i	**Robert Byington** married **Karen** ___ .	
ii	**Ronald E. Byington** b Apr 1943. He married **Susan** ___ .	
iii	**Susan Byington** b Sep 1949. She married **Lee W. Mein** b Feb 1950.	
iv	**David R. Byington** b 1954. He married **Karen** ___ .	
v	**Jeanne M. Byington** b Feb 1957. She married **Larry** ___ .	

8.1.7.12.5.10   **MONTY, Eleanor Jennie** b 12 Apr 1921, Phelps, WI. She married 27 Jun 1941 **Raymond D. Ushold** (John Ushold & Margaret Schmidt) b 21 Sep 1916, Milwaukee, WI; d there 28 Aug 1993.

Mrs. Eleanor Ushold was a resident of Milwaukee, WI, when her sister Ruth Monty (8.1.7.12.5.8) died in 2006 (*Milwaukee Journal Sentinel*, 27 Aug 2006).

Children:

i	**Barbara Ushold** b 1944, WI. She married **Tom Boersma**.	
ii	**Beverly Jean Ushold** b 9 Apr 1948, WI; d 10 May 1995, Los Angeles, CA. She married **Ronald Dolen**.	
iii	**John Ushold** died at the age of 7.	
iv	**Donna M. Ushold** b 5 Jul 1955, WI. She married 28 Oct 1978, Milwaukee, WI, **William R. Jansen** b 24 Nov 1953.	

8.1.7.12.5.11   **MONTY, Kenneth Charles** b 22 Oct 1922, Phelps, WI. He married 14 Jun 1948 **Rose Zak**.

Kenneth C. Monty was a resident of Norridge, IL, when his sister Ruth (8.1.7.12.5.8) died in 2006 (*Milwaukee Journal Sentinel*, 27 Aug 2006).

8.1.7.12.5.11.1	Kenneth	- -
8.1.7.12.5.11.2	Susan Mary	1964-1984&1992-
8.1.7.12.5.11.3	Sandra Ann	1966-1994-

8.1.7.12.5.12   **MONTY, Beverly Alice** b 27 Feb 1924, Phelps, WI. She married 29 Apr 1950 **Joseph George Steuer** (Joseph George Steuer & Nora Bergerson) b 24 Sep 1920, Milwaukee, WI; d there 25 May 1964.

Mrs. Beverly Steuer was a resident of Kaukauna, WI, when her sister Ruth Monty (8.1.7.12.5.8) died in 2006 (*Milwaukee Journal Sentinel*, 27 Aug 2006).

Children:

i	**Jacalyn M. Steuer** b 27 Jan 1951, WI. She married **Scott R. Vandalen** (Raymond Vandalen & Dorothy Mae Hoffman) b 30 Mar 1953, Kaukauna, WI.	
ii	**William Joseph Steuer** b 12 Feb 1954, WI. He married 23 May 1981, Manitowoc, WI, **Susan Ann Gersek** (Dale F. Gersek & Carole A. Chadek) b there 8 Jul 1959.	

8.1.7.12.5.13   **MONTY, Russell John** b 9 Jun 1926, Eagle River, WI.

Russell John Monty did not marry. He remained in the family home in Phelps, WI, and was living in Conover, WI, when his sister Ruth (8.1.7.12.5.8) died in 2006 (*Milwaukee Journal Sentinel*, 27 Aug 2006).

8.1.7.12.6.1   **MONTY, Earl Joseph** b 3 Apr 1907, Elderon, WI; d 10 Oct 1989, Bear Creek, WI. He married there 27 Dec 1932 **Irene Young** (Louis Young & Virginia Roberts) b 22 Oct 1914, Maple Creek, WI; d 17 Nov 1996, Bear Creek, WI.

Earl Joseph Monty was a farmer in Bear Creek, WI.

Children:

8.1.7.12.6.1.1	Genevieve Joann	1934-1952-
8.1.7.12.6.1.2	Shirley	1936-1960-
8.1.7.12.6.1.3	Karen L.	1939-1958-
8.1.7.12.6.1.4	Gary Joseph	1942-1963-

8.1.7.12.6.1.5	Gail	1944-	-
8.1.7.12.6.1.6	Paula Jean	1948-1966-	
8.1.7.12.6.1.7	Kevin R.	1950-1970-	
8.1.7.12.6.1.8	Jill Mary	1953-1973&2001-2007	

8.1.7.12.6.2   **MONTY, Mary** b & d 3 May 1908, Elderon, WI.
This child was stillborn.

8.1.7.12.6.3   **MONTY, Raymond Lester** b 27 Jul 1909, Elderon, WI; d 19 Jun 1997, Appleton, WI. He married 30 Aug 1947 **Jane L. Piszczatowski** (Anton Piszczatowski & Frances ____) b 4 Dec 1911, Racine, WI; d & bur 3 & 5 Dec 2001, Milwaukee & Racine, WI.

Raymond Monty was a railroad worker in Deer Creek Twp, WI, in 1930 (US census) and a resident of Milwaukee, WI, when his parents celebrated their sixtieth wedding anniversary in 1966 (*Appleton Post Crescent*, 18 May 1966). He was buried alongside his parents in St. Mary's Cemetery in Bear Creek, WI, while his wife was buried in Holy Cross Cemetery in Racine, WI.

Children:
8.1.7.12.6.3.1	John Raymond	1948-1975&	-
8.1.7.12.6.3.2	James A.	1950-1974-	
8.1.7.12.6.3.3	Rosanne F.	1951-	-
8.1.7.12.6.3.4	Charles J.	1953-	-

8.1.7.12.6.4   **MONTY, Lester Leon** b 25 Sep 1911, Elderon, WI; d 31 May 1979, Bear Creek, WI. He married 21 Sep 1940 **Elizabeth J./Betty Sabo** (Louis C. Sabo/Szabo & Esther A. ____) b 24 Oct 1915, Racine, WI; d 23 Dec 2002, Bear Creek, WI.

Lester Monty was a farmer in Bear Creek, WI. He and his wife were buried in St. Mary's Cemetery there.

Children:
8.1.7.12.6.4.1	Betty A/Elizabeth	1941-1962&	-
8.1.7.12.6.4.2	Janice	1945-	-
8.1.7.12.6.4.3	Beverly	1948-	-
8.1.7.12.6.4.4	Lester M.	1951-1976-2008	

8.1.7.12.6.5   **MONTY, Adeline Mae** b 14 May 1913, Elderon, WI; d & bur 1 & 6 Sep 2005, Appleton & Black Creek, WI. She married (1) **Gordon G. Welson** (Fred Welson & Frances ____) b 29 Jul 1913, WI; d 14 Apr 1981, Edmonds, WA.

She was divorced when she married (2) 14 May 1947 **Harold R. Habeck** (Otto Habeck & Ida ____) b 10 Dec 1921, Richmond, WI.

Adeline Monty came to Outagamie Co., WI, as a young girl with her parents and became a long-term resident there. She predeceased her second husband and was buried in St. Mary's Cemetery in Black Creek, WI. I know of her daughters mainly through her obituary in the *Appleton Post Crescent* of 5 Sep 2005.

Children:
i   **Ruby Welson** d before 2005.
ii   **Carol Welson** b 1935? She married **Marvin E. Moritz** b Mar 1933.
iii   **Joanna Welson** married ____ **Hermann.**
iv   **Leona A. Welson** b 26 Nov 1938, Appleton, WI. She married ____ **Vander-Wielen.**
v   **Alvin R. Habeck** b 15 Sep 1951, WI. He married 15 Jul 1972, New London, WI, **Carolyn Rieck** (Russell R. Rieck & Joyce McFaul) b 26 Oct 1951, Milwaukee, WI.

8.1.7.12.6.6   **MONTY, Edna Anna** b 24 Feb 1915, Elderon, WI; d & bur 4 & 8 Nov

2004, Clintonville & Bear Creek, WI. She married (1) 28 Jun 1932, Bear Creek, WI, **Arthur J. Pelky** (Charles Pelky & Eva Leanna) b May 1909, Deer Creek, WI; d 1 Dec 1963, New London, WI.

She married (2) 1972 **Raymond Leroy Terrian** (John B. Terrian & Ellen Sawyer) b 5 Feb 1907, Egg Harbor, WI; m (1) 9 Mar 1926, Menasha, WI, Geneva Crober (Charles Crober & Mary ____); m (2) 1955? Emma ____; m (3) before 1968, Menasha, WI, Minnie ____; d 12 Dec 1993, Menasha, WI.

Arthur J. Pelky was a farmer in Deer Creek, WI. He, his wife, and their children Carol A. and Leroy share a tombstone in St. Mary's Cemetery in Bear Creek, WI. I know of his widow's second marriage only through her obituary in the *Appleton Post Crescent* of 7 Nov 2004.

Children of the first marriage:
i   **Norma Pelky** b Aug 1934, Deer Creek, WI. She married **Floyd E. Grode** (Willard J. Grode & Aurelia O. Schmalz) b 13 Aug 1934, WI.
ii   **Milton Arthur Pelky** b 13 Aug 1936, Deer Creek, WI. He married 14 Sep 1960, Bear Creek, WI, **Judith Ann Schmidt** (Arthur Schmidt & Hilda Tiedt) b 29 Apr 1939.
iii   **Barbara Ann Pelky** b Aug 1938, Deer Creek, WI. She married 31 Jan 1956, Bear Creek, WI, **Carl H. Van Straten** (Aloysius Van Straten & Cecilia Dietzler) b Oct 1937, Outagamie Co., WI.
iv   **Harold J. Pelky** b 17 Dec 1939, Deer Creek, WI. He married **Shirley ____** b 20 Aug 1940.
v   **Duaine V. Pelky** b 11 Dec 1942, Deer Creek, WI. He married 1964, Outagamie Co., WI, **Patricia M. Wheeler** b 5 Jul 1946; d & bur 6 & ? Apr 2000, Shiocton & Bear Creek, WI.
vi   **Carol A. Pelky** bur Bear Creek, WI.
vii   **Leroy Pelky** bur Bear Creek, WI.

8.1.7.12.6.7   **MONTY, Orville** b & d 3 Jun 1916, Elderon, WI.

8.1.7.12.6.8   **MONTY, Reynold Nathan** b 27 Apr 1917, Elderon, WI; d 5 Dec 1999, Milwaukee, WI. He married 18 Feb 1950 **Elizabeth J. Bube** (William Bube & Emma Schalk) b 14 Dec 1927, Marathon Co., WI.

Reynold Monty was a long-term resident of Milwaukee, WI. He was a veteran of World War II and was buried in Highland Memorial Park in New Berlin, WI. His widow was still living in Milwaukee when her brother Thomas W. Bube died in 2005 (*Oshkosh Northwestern*, 7 Sep 2005).

Children:

8.1.7.12.6.8.1	Mary Jane	1950-1973?-	
8.1.7.12.6.8.2	Barbara J.	1951-	-
8.1.7.12.6.8.3	Joseph Reynold	1952-1983-	
8.1.7.12.6.8.4	Sandra E.	1955-	-
8.1.7.12.6.8.5	Cindy	-	-
8.1.7.12.6.8.6	Timothy Thomas	1959-1993-	
8.1.7.12.6.8.7	Todd E.	1966-	-
8.1.7.12.6.8.8	Troy Nathan	1973-1994-	

8.1.7.12.6.9   **MONTY, Lorraine Elizabeth** b 10 Oct 1918, Elderon, WI. She married 27 Sep 1941, Bear Creek, WI, **Vernon Royston Spence** (Roy Spence & Winifred Bergstresser) b 29 Jun 1915, Maple Creek, WI; d & bur 15 & 18 Jun 2004, Hollandale, WI.

Vernon Spence and his wife lived in Appleton, Black Creek, and West Allis, WI, before retiring in Hollandale, WI. He was buried there in Calvary Cemetery (*Appleton Post Crescent*, 16 Jun 2004).

Children:

i   **Judith Ann Spence** b 1942?, WI; d & bur 28 Mar & 2 Apr 1982, Lake Havasu City, AZ. She married **David L. High** (Leighton N. High & Luon Joy Pfaff).

ii   **Jeanne C. Spence** b 10 Nov 1947, WI. She married **Bryan R. Lisser** (Herman J. Lisser & Myrtle E. Berget) b 10 Jan 1944, Gratiot, WI.

iii **Jerold John Spence** b 6 Apr 1951, WI. He married 25 Apr 1986, Milwaukee, WI, **Barbara Reinelt** b 9 Jan 1952.

8.1.7.12.6.10   **MONTY, Delores Mary** b 25 Jan 1920, Larrabee, WI; d 21 Dec 2002, Darboy, WI. She married 29 Jun 1938, Bear Creek, WI, **William O. Ahrens** (John Ahrens & Frances Schwab) b 30 Jun 1917, Center, WI; d 16 Apr 1999, Appleton, WI.

Delores Monty and her husband were buried in Highland Memorial Park in Appleton, WI.

Children:

i   **James W. Ahrens** b 1 Mar 1939, Appleton, WI. He married 1 Jun 1963, Kimberly, WI, **Alice Marie Van Grinsven** (John Van Grinsven & Leocadia Stuckart) b 1938?, Outagamie Co., WI.

ii   **Richard L. Ahrens** b 28 Mar 1944, Appleton, WI. He married 26 Sep 1980, Outagamie Co., WI, **Priscilla Marie Oudenhoven** b 28 Oct 1952; m (2) 4 Oct 1986, Outagamie Co., WI, Lawrence Scott Leverance.

iii **John Ahrens** b 9 Mar 1949, WI; d 20 May 1977, Menasha, WI. He married **Dianne ____** b Apr 1949; m (2) 16 Jun 1979, Outagamie Co., WI, Wesley G. Stronach.

iv **William/Bill P. Ahrens** b 26 Jun 1958, Appleton, WI. He married 14 Jul 1978, Outagamie Co., WI, **Tina M. Linzmeyer** b 8 Aug 1958.

8.1.7.12.6.11   **MONTY, Llewellyn Vincent** b 28 May 1921, Bear Creek, WI; d & bur 10 & 14 Aug 2002, West Bend & Clintonville, WI. He married 11 Sep 1943, Clintonville, WI, **Joanne C. Halla** (Clarence Halla & Catherine Ahles) b 17 Jul 1926, WI; d 29 Aug 1992, Wautoma, WI.

Llewellyn V. Monty and his family lived in Clintonville, WI, until 1956 and after that time in Milwaukee, WI, where he was a machinist and construction worker. He and his wife moved to Wautoma, WI, after his retirement. He was buried in Clintonville's Graceland Cemetery (*Milwaukee Journal Sentinel*, 12 Aug 2002).

Children:

8.1.7.12.6.11.1	Daniel Robert	1944- &1984-1996
8.1.7.12.6.11.2	Daryl Lee	1947-1970-
8.1.7.12.6.11.3	Larry James	1949-1973-2000
8.1.7.12.6.11.4	Mark Rene	1953-1982-
8.1.7.12.6.11.5	Jacqueline/Jackie	1955?-1973&1981-
8.1.7.12.6.11.6	Judy	1959?-1976-

8.1.7.12.6.12   **MONTY, Marvin Norbert** b 4 Mar 1932, Deer Creek, WI; d & bur 13 & 14 Mar 1932, Deer Creek & Bear Creek, WI.

This child was buried in St. Mary's Cemetery in Bear Creek, WI.

8.1.7.12.9.1   **MONTE, Jeanette** b 27 Mar 1916, Deer Creek, WI. She married (1) 30 Jun 1934, Crystal Falls, MI, **Harold Roy Shorey** (Roy Shorey & Flossie Bertha Fenner) b 13 Jun 1912, Lincoln, WI; d 24 Aug 1974, Crandon, WI.

She married (2) **George Allen McMillion** (Lewis McMillion & Minta Parker) b 31 Dec 1909, IL; d 17 Nov 1996, Crandon, WI.

Children:

i   **Janice M. Shorey** b Jun 1935. She married 7 May 1955 **David R. Spencer** b Mar 1935.

ii   **Patricia A. Shorey** b May 1939. She married 5 Sep 1957 **Jack Palubicki** b May 1937.

8.1.7.12.9.2   MONTE, Audrey Viola b 11 Feb 1919, Currie, MN; d 24 Aug 1969, Milwaukee, WI. She married Aug 1939 **William F. Oestreich** b 13 May 1913, Underhill, WI.

Audrey Monte and her husband were of Sauk City, WI, when her brother Roland (8.1.7.12.9.6) married in 1956 (*Sheboygan Press*, 16 Oct 1956).

8.1.7.12.9.3   MONTE, Richard Vincent b 28 Jan 1921, Starks, WI; d & bur 28 May & 1 Jun 1999, Rhinelander & Argonne, WI. He married 1943? **Violet E. DeHart** (Daniel C. DeHart & Lavila ____) b Jun 1924, WI.

Richard Monte was a resident of Crandon, WI, at his death and was buried in St. Mary's Cemetery in Argonne, WI. He was survived by his wife and two sons (*Green Bay Press Gazette*, 30 May 1999).

Children:

8.1.7.12.9.3.1	Michael Richard	1947-1969-
8.1.7.12.9.3.2	Timothy Hugh	1953-1975&1986-

8.1.7.12.9.4   MONTE, Joyce Patricia b 17 Sep 1923, Starks, WI; d & bur 6 & 9 Jun 1999, Argonne, WI. She married 18 Jul 1942 **Donald B. LeMaster** (Asa Prentiss LeMaster & Ada F. Hall) b 19 Oct 1919, Nashville, WI; d 6 May 1982, Oneida Co., WI.

Donald B. LeMaster was buried in Crandon Lakeside Cemetery in Lincoln Twp, WI, while Joyce Patricia Monte was buried in St. Mary's Cemetery in Argonne, WI.

8.1.7.12.9.5   MONTE, Hugh Joseph b 6 Nov 1925, Starks, WI; d & bur 8 & 12 Nov 2003, La Porte, IN. He married there 18 Jun 1947 **Dorothy E. Kempley** (Kenneth Kempley & Evelyn A. ____) b 30 Apr 1928, Montello, WI; d 29 Apr 1971, La Porte, IN.

Hugh Joseph Monte and his wife were long-term residents of La Porte, IN, and were buried in St. Joseph Catholic Cemetery there.

Children:

8.1.7.12.9.5.1	Kenneth J.	1950-	-1999
8.1.7.12.9.5.2	James	-	-
8.1.7.12.9.5.3	Stephen H.	1957-	-

8.1.7.12.9.6   MONTE, Roland Russell b 5 Nov 1927, Argonne, WI; d 5 Jun 1998, Laona, WI. He married 6 Oct 1956, Goodman, WI, **Judith Anne Hendricks** (Joseph Hendricks & Emma ____) b there Jun 1938.

Roland Russell, a US Army veteran, was buried in the Laona, WI, Cemetery.

Child:

8.1.7.12.9.6.1	Kent V.	1971-	-

8.1.7.12.9.7   MONTE, Gordon Eugene b 18 Mar 1929, Argonne, WI. He married 1950? **Ida May Brown** b 17 May 1928; d Apr 1985, La Porte, IN.

Gordon E. Monte was a resident of La Porte, IN, when his brother Hugh Joseph (8.1.7.12.9.5) died in 2003 (*Michigan City News Dispatch*, 10 Nov 2003).

8.1.7.12.11.1   MONTE, Ellis Joseph b 1 Jan 1918, Bear Creek, WI; d 10 Aug 2005, Texarkana, TX. He married (1) 4 Sep 1937 **Dorothy Helen Gallman** (Prentiss Mathis Gallman & Jessie Lee Glover) b 5 Mar 1921, OK; d 19 Apr 2002, Branson, MO.

He married (2) **Joyce Warren** (Clint B. Warren & Lela Mitchell) b 8 Dec 1926, Texarkana, TX.

Ellis Monte came to Texas as a child around 1926, a year before his mother's death, and lived there for the rest of his life.

Child of the first marriage:

8.1.7.12.11.1.1   Carrilee   1940-   -

Children of the second marriage:

8.1.7.12.11.1.2   Alec Virgil   1947-1967&1992-
8.1.7.12.11.1.3   Ellis Joseph   1950-   -

8.3.1.3.7.1   **MONTY, Mary** b 1912?, CT. She married ____ **Spellman**.

Mary Monty was a 7-year-old child living with her mother and siblings in her maternal grandmother's household in Pawcatuck, CT, in 1920 (US census). Mrs. Mary Spellman was a resident of Pennington, NJ, when her brother Stanley Monty (8.3.1.3.7.3) died in 2002 (*Westerly Sun*, 15 Jan 2002).

8.3.1.3.7.2   **MONTY, Mildred** b 1914?, CT. She married ____ **Cirillo**.

Mildred Monty was a 5-year-old child living with her mother and siblings in her maternal grandmother's household in Pawcatuck, CT, in 1920. In 1930, she was in Westerly, RI, with her mother and stepfather William Loughborough (US censuses). Mrs. Mildred Cirillo predeceased her brother Stanley Monty (8.3.1.3.7.3) (*Westerly Sun*, 15 Jan 2002).

8.3.1.3.7.3   **MONTY, Stanley Edward** b 12 Nov 1918, Pawcatuck, CT; d & bur 13 & 16 Jan 2002, Wilmington, OH. He married 31 Jan 1941 **Geloca "Jeanette" Limanni** (Orazio Limanni & Catherine Alberti) b 23 Jul 1916, Pawcatuck, CT; d & bur 19 & 24 Jun 2006, Wilmington, OH.

Stanley E. Monty served with the US armed forces from 1935 to 1972 and retired as a Master Sergeant in the US Air Force. He and his wife moved to Ohio after his retirement and were buried in Sugar Grove Cemetery in Wilmington, OH (*Westerly Sun*, 15 Jan 2002 and 21 Jun 2006).

Child:

8.3.1.3.7.3.1   Sandra   1942-   &   -

8.3.1.3.7.4   **MONTY, Ernestine** b 25 Sep 1922, Providence, RI. She married ____ **Church**.

Ernestine Monty was living with her mother and stepfather William Loughborough in Westerly, RI, in 1930 (US census). Mrs. Ernestine Church was still a resident of that city when her brother Stanley Monty (8.3.1.3.7.3) died in 2002 (*Westerly Sun*, 15 Jan 2002).

8.3.8.1.1.1   **MONTY, Clayton Eugene** b & bp 29 Jan & 7 Feb 1905, Mansonville, QC; d & bur 9 & 11 Feb 1905, Troy, VT & Mansonville, QC.

Clayton Eugene Monty was baptized in the Methodist Church in Mansonville, QC, and was buried there by the Methodist minister.

8.3.8.1.1.2   **MONTY, Bertha Amelia** b & bp 28 Apr & 20 Nov 1906, Mansonville, QC; d 26 Dec 1980, Norwich, CT. She married 1929? **John M. Wohlleben** (Frederick Wohlleben & Catherine ____) b 28 Jun 1904, CT; d 7 Sep 1967, Windham, CT.

Bertha Amelia Montey (sic) was baptized in the Methodist Church in Mansonville, QC. She arrived in the United States with her family in August 1920 and had been married to John Wohlleben, a grocery salesman in Norwich, CT, for less than a year in April 1930 (US census). They were both residents of Lisbon, CT, at their deaths.

8.3.8.1.1.3   **MONTY, Melba Christina** b & bp 25 Dec 1909 & 14 Feb 1914, Mansonville, QC.

Melba Christina Monty was baptized in the Methodist Church in Mansonville, QC, on the same day as her brother Reginald (8.3.8.1.1.4). The church records state that she was born on 25 Dec 1910 and her brother on 3 Jun 1911. One of these dates must be wrong. Since

Reginald Monty was 16 days old and his sister 1 year old on 19 Jun 1911 (Canadian census, Potton Twp, QC), the error must be in Melba Christina's year of birth: she was most probably born in 1909 rather than in 1910.

She arrived in the United States with her parents on 6 Aug 1920 but was not with them in Norwich, CT, in 1930. She may have married, or died, before then.

8.3.8.1.1.4   MONTY, Reginald Eugene b & bp 3 Jun 1911 & 14 Feb 1914, Mansonville, QC; d 1 Mar 1994, Plainfield, CT. He married between 1930 and 1936 **Helen M. ____** b Jan 1911.

Reginald Monty Eugene was baptized in the Methodist Church in Mansonville, QC, on the same day as his sister Melba Christina (8.3.8.1.1.3). He arrived in the United States with his parents on 6 Aug 1920 and was a carpenter in Norwich, CT, in 1930 (US census). He was a salesman living with his wife Helen in New London, CT, in 1936 (City Directory), and a resident of Lisbon, CT, at his death. He predeceased his wife.

8.3.8.1.3.1   MONTY, Ruth M. b 22 Sep 1916, Sprague, CT; d 13 May 1982, Norwich, CT. She married **William J. Sheridan** (Joseph H. Sheridan & Elizabeth Monahan) b 26 Sep 1915, Norwich, CT; d there 3 Apr 1962.

William J. Sheridan was a Captain in the Norwich, CT, Fire Department.

Child:
i   **Dorothea E. Sheridan**

8.3.8.1.3.2   MONTY, Louis Eugene b Nov 1919, Sprague, CT.

Louis E. Monty was a carpenter in Norwich, CT, until at least 1953 (City Directories).

8.3.8.1.3.3   MONTY, Dorothea b Mar 1927, CT.

Dorothea Monty was 3 years and 1 month old on 1 Apr 1930 when she was living with her parents in Norwich, CT (US census).

8.3.8.1.3.4   MONTY, Barbara E. b Jan 1930, Norwich, CT. She married 1951 **John F. Cherenza** b 1 Apr 1920, Washington Co., RI; d 29 Nov 1995, Westerly, RI.

8.3.8.1.6.1   MONTY, John W. b 24 Sep 1914, Uncasville, CT; d 4 Jan 1999, Manchester, CT. He married **Ingeborg ____** b Jul 1925.

John W. Monty enlisted in the US Army Air Force during World War II and retired as a Master Sergeant in 1965. He then worked as an electronics technician in Groton, CT, until his retirement in 1980 and subsequent move to Glastonbury, CT. He predeceased his wife and was buried in Glastonbury in the Veterans section of Neipsic Cemetery (*Hartford Courant*, 7 Jan 1999).

Children:
| 8.3.8.1.6.1.1 | Douglas W. | 1949-1977- |
| 8.3.8.1.6.1.2 | Wayne S. | 1954-1975&1978&1987- |

8.3.8.1.6.2   MONTY, Douglas A. b 15 Jul 1917, Versailles, CT; d there 31 Aug 1917.

Douglas A. Monty was buried in St. Mary's Cemetery in Versailles, CT.

8.3.8.1.6.3   MONTY, Marian Elizabeth b 20 Mar 1920, Sprague, CT; d 31 Jul 1995, Santa Rosa Co., FL. She married 1942 **August Etsch Jr.** (August Etsch & Alice L. ____) b 15 Mar 1920, Mount Vernon, NY; d 22 Mar 1997, Pearl River, NY.

August Etsch Jr. was a Lt. Colonel in the US Army and was buried in the Frederick Loescher Veterans Memorial Cemetery in New City, NY.

8.3.8.5.2.1   MONTY, Blanche b 28 Oct 1915, Wethersfield, CT; d 9 Jun 1974, Griswold, CT. She married **Victor Chartier** b 1898?, CT; d 29 Aug 1958, Griswold, CT, at the age of 60.

8.3.8.5.2.2   **MONTY, Joseph Armand** b 28 Jun 1918, Plainfield, CT; d & bur 11 & 15 Nov 2006, Worcester, MA & Woodstock, CT. He married (1) 22 Sep 1945, Longmeadow, MA, **Bianca A. Pasini** b 5 Jan 1917, Italy; d 17 Jan 1976, Killingly, CT.

He married (2) 23 Apr 1977, Danielson, CT, **Bessie Weeks/Jacques** b 9 Jan 1920, CT; d 8 Mar 1993, Killingly, CT.

Joseph A. Monty lived most of his life, save for his years of service in the US Army between 1940 and 1945, in Killingly, CT, and the surrounding area. He and his first wife Bianca were buried in Elmvale Cemetery in Woodstock, CT.

He married his second wife, Bessie Weeks, on 23 Apr 1977 in St. James Church in Danielson, CT, according to his obituary of 14 Nov 2006 in the *Norwich Bulletin*. The Connecticut Marriage Index however shows that on 23 Apr 1977 Joseph A. Monty married Bessie M. Jacques in Killingly. Either Weeks or Jacques could be her maiden name, the other a first husband's surname.

Child of the first marriage:
8.3.8.5.2.2.1   Cynthia A.   1946-   -

8.3.8.5.2.3   **MONTY, Albert Charles** b 3 Apr 1921, Plainfield, CT; d & bur 23 & 28 Dec 2005, Central Village & Moosup, CT. He married 1944?, **Dorothy Rakuza** (Anthony Rakuza & Mary J. Fryc) b Feb 1926, Plainfield, CT.

Albert Charles Monty predeceased his wife of sixty-one years. He was buried in All Hallows Cemetery in Moosup, CT (*Norwich Bulletin*, 25 Dec 2005).

Children:
8.3.8.5.2.3.1	Carol A.	1945-	-
8.3.8.5.2.3.2	Albert C.	1949-1973-	
8.3.8.5.2.3.3	William J.	1951-	-
8.3.8.5.2.3.4	Deborah J.	1957-1980-	

8.3.8.5.2.4   **MONTY, Jeannette I.** b Aug 1927, Plainfield, CT. She married **Alexander J. Thibault** (Israël Thibault & Marie Louise Therrien) b & bp 23 & 25 May 1924, Ste Euphémie, QC; d 2 Jul 1984, Putnam, CT.

Mrs. Jeannette Thibault was a resident of Plainfield, CT, when her brother Joseph Monty (8.3.8.5.2.2) died in 2006 (*Norwich Bulletin*, 14 Nov 2006).

8.3.8.5.3.1   **MONTY, Roland** b 1913?, QC.
Roland Monty was a 6-year-old child living with his parents in Willimantic, CT, in 1920 (US census).

8.3.8.5.3.2   **MONTY, Beulah A.** b 31 Aug 1914, North Troy, VT; d & bur 25 & 28 Apr 1995, Holyoke & Aldenville, MA. She married 1930? **Doriea G. Capistrant** (Doriea Capistrant & Belzemire Berube) b 1 Feb 1908, South Hadley, MA; d 7 Apr 1982, Chicopee, MA.

Beulah Monty came to Connecticut as a child and was living with her parents in Willimantic, CT, in 1920. She had been married only a few months in April 1930 when Doriea Capistrant was a laborer in Hartford, CT (US censuses). The couple soon left for Hampden Co., MA, where their children were born and where they remained until their deaths. They were both buried in St. Mary's Cemetery in Aldenville, MA.

Children:
i   **Beulah Capistrant** b Jan 1931, MA. She married (1) 1953, Holyoke, MA, **Charles Joseph Denesha** (Charles Joseph Denesha & Olive K. ____) b 26 May 1929, Barre, VT; m (2) Victoria/Vickie ____; d 1 Jul 2000, Venice, FL.

    She married (2) 1968?, Brattleboro, VT, **Walter P. Makuch** (Walter Makuch &

Pearl Cecilia Vance) b 5 Jun 1929, Springfield, MA; m (1) ____; d & bur 4 & 7 May 1998, Chicopee & Ludlow, MA.

ii   **Shirley M. Capistrant** b 1 Jan 1932, Holyoke, MA; d & bur 6 & 12 May 2008, Chicopee & Aldenville, MA. She married **Michael Moroschok** b 24 Feb 1931, PA; d & bur 8 & 11 Dec 1999, Holyoke & Aldenville, MA.

iii   **Roland E. Capistrant** b Dec 1934, MA. He married 1956? Chicopee, MA, **Jeanne E. Couture** b Nov 1934.

iv   **Donald Raymond Capistrant** b 12 Mar 1936, South Hadley, MA; d 11 Jun 1999, Altoona, PA. He married (1) **Helen Jean Hipps** (Clifford Hipps & Jane Williams).

        He married (2) 16 Sep 1976, Hinesville, GA, **Judith A. Howes** b Sep 1938; m (1) ____ Van Valkenburg; m (2) ____ Sicard.

v   **David Edward Capistrant** b 30 Aug 1942, MA; d 21 Jun 1989, Holyoke, MA.

vi   **Robert Leo Capistrant** b 10 Jan 1945, Holyoke, MA; d 4 Sep 1984, Springfield, MA. He married **Carol A. Fontaine** b Dec 1947, Holyoke, MA.

8.3.8.5.3.3   **MONTY, David E.** b 29 Mar 1921, Windham, CT; d 19 Aug 1996, Holyoke, MA. He married **Laura R. Stucklen** (Harvey L. Stucklen & Mary Rose Desmanche) b 16 Mar 1926, South Hadley, MA; d there 20 Dec 2002.

David E. Monty was a car salesman in Holyoke, MA (*Springfield Union-News*, 21 Aug 1996).

Children:

8.3.8.5.3.3.1	Donna	1946-	-
8.3.8.5.3.3.2	Mary	-	-
8.3.8.5.3.3.3	David E.	1949-	-

8.3.8.8.5.1   **MONTY, Eugene H.** b Jul 1951. He married 13 Nov 1971, East Hartford, CT, **Michele Marino** b Nov 1951.

Eugene H. Monty and his wife and daughters were living in Bolton, CT, when his mother died in 2001 (*Harford Courant*, 9 Jan 2001).

Children:

8.3.8.8.5.1.1	Jamie L.	1975-	-
8.3.8.8.5.1.2	Jessica M.	1978-	-
8.3.8.8.5.1.3	Jennifer	-	-

8.3.8.8.5.2   **MONTY, George M.** b Mar 1955, Manchester, CT. He married **Pamela** ____ b 1956.

George M. Monty and his wife and children were living in Manchester, CT, when his mother died in 2001 (*Hartford Courant*, 9 Jan 2001).

Children:

8.3.8.8.5.2.1	Michael	-	-
8.3.8.8.5.2.2	Trisha	-	-
8.3.8.8.5.2.3	Jonathan	-	-

8.3.11.6.3.1   **MONTY, Elzéar Wilfred** b 7 Jun 1904, New Bedford, MA; d there 8 Aug 1955. He married there 24 Nov 1927 **Obeline Mathilda Breton** (Cyrille Breton & Eva ____) b there 14 Nov 1908.

Elzear Monty was a silk worker in New Bedford, MA (US censuses; City Directories).

Children:

8.3.11.6.3.1.1	Norman C.	1928-	-1980
8.3.11.6.3.1.2	Alfred Lorand	1930-1951-1973	

8.3.11.6.3.2   **MONTY, Lauretta/Blanche Laurette** b 7 Oct 1906, New Bedford, MA; d

11 Jan 1996, Westbrook, ME. She married **Christian Jacobus Van Eybergen** b 8 May 1883, Rotterdam, Holland; d early 1940s, Bronx, NY.

Christian J. Van Eybergen was a fireman on the *SS Ryndam* of the Holland-America Line when he apparently deserted in New York, NY, in August 1920 (Statement of the master, New York, 18 Aug 1920). He was a cafeteria worker in New York, NY, when he signed in 1942 his World War II Draft Registration card. He and his wife had probably separated before then: she is not mentioned. Neither do her siblings' obituaries ever refer to him.

Child:
i   **Christian Eybergen** b 3 Sep 1932. He married 1 Mar 1964, ME, **Esther A. Delong** b 12 Aug 1941.

8.3.11.6.3.3   **MONTY, Jeannette** b 16 Jan 1910, New Bedford, MA; d there 17 Jul 1999. She married there 1928 **Alfred J. Charpentier** (William Charpentier & Emma ____) b 14 Sep 1908, MA; d Jun 1963, MA.

Freddy Charpentier was a mill worker in Acushnet, MA, in 1930 (US census). His widow was survived by her son Arthur (iii) and her daughter Eileen (iv) (*South Coast Today*, 22 Jul 1999).

Children:
i   **William A. Charpentier** b 13 Jan 1930, Acushnet, MA; d 2 Jul 1999, Cleveland Heights, OH. He married 1951? **Doris C. Guimond** (Ferdinand Guimond & Blanche Jussaume) b 27 Apr 1932, New Bedford, MA.
ii   **Richard W. Charpentier** b 10 Mar 1932, New Bedford, MA; d there 6 Mar 1983. He married **Norma A.** ____ b 3 Jun 1936.
iii   **Arthur A. Charpentier** b 9 Dec 1933, New Bedford, MA. He married **Evelyn J.** ____ b 18 Sep 1935.
iv   **Eileen J. Charpentier** b 12 Apr 1939, New Bedford, MA. She married **Joseph J. Francis** b 2 May 1933.

8.3.11.6.3.4   **MONTY, Georgette** b 6 Apr 1913, New Bedford, MA; d there 27 Oct 1994. She married **James Joao** (Francisco Joao & Maria A. Josepha) b 11 Oct 1916, MA; d Jun 1979, New York, NY.

James Joao was a weaver in New Bedford, MA, until at least 1955 (City Directories).

8.3.11.6.3.5   **MONTY, Agnes Marie** b 18 Dec 1916, New Bedford, MA; d 26 Feb 2001, Fairhaven, MA. She married 1935, New Bedford, MA, **Wilfred Sevigny** b 27 Oct 1913, MA; d 15 Apr 1991, Boston, MA.

Agnes Monty and her husband lived in Wareham, MA, for most of their married lives. She was survived by her four children (*South Coast Today*, 27 Feb 2001).

Children:
i   **Douglas J. Sevigny** b 30 Mar 1939, MA; d 8 Jul 2008, Las Vegas, NV. He married **Eileen** ____ b 1942.
ii   **Madeline M. Sevigny** b 12 Nov 1941, MA. She married **Ole A. Larsen** b 1 Aug 1937.
iii   **Wilfred J. Sevigny** b 20 Mar 1943, MA.
iv   **Janice L. Sevigny** b 19 Nov 1945, MA. She married ____ **Mahon.**

8.3.11.6.3.6   **MONTY, Joseph Adrien/Adrian** b 5 Feb 1919, New Bedford, MA; d 1 Feb 2004, Lady Lake, FL. He married **Lucille J. Bissette** b 17 Oct 1923.

Joseph Adrien Monty (also Adrian, Adrian J., Joseph A.) was a worker in New Bedford, MA, before moving to Florida upon his retirement (US censuses, City Directories, death notice in the Lady Lake, FL, *Daily Commercial* of 4 Feb 2004).

Children:

| 8.3.11.6.3.6.1 | Denise Lucille | 1944- | &1969&1994-2001 |
| 8.3.11.6.3.6.2 | Carolyn Marie | 1946- | &1992- |

8.3.11.6.3.7   **MONTY, Cora** b 29 Apr 1921, New Bedford, MA; d & bur 2 & 5 Nov 1994, Milford & Uxbridge, MA. She married 1941? **Wilfred J. Benoit** (William Benoit & Virginia Bruneau) b 10 Sep 1918, Canada; d & bur 4 & 8 May 2006, Milford & Uxbridge, MA.

Wilfred Benoit was born in Canada of American parents who returned to the United States around 1922 and settled in Uxbridge, MA. He was a truck driver there save for a few years during World War II when he was in the US Army. He and his wife were buried there in St. Mary's Cemetery (*Worcester Telegram & Gazette*, 4 Nov 1994 and 6 May 2006).

Children:
i   **Kenneth W. Benoit** b 23 Apr 1942, MA; d 19 Jun 1988, Leominster, MA.
ii   **Florence A. Benoit** b 21 Apr 1946, MA. She married **Paul C. Phillips** b 8 Aug 1953.

8.3.11.6.3.8   **MONTY, Ernest W.** b 21 Apr 1923, New Bedford, MA; d there 11 Jul 1998. He married 1942?, **Bella M. LaPointe** (Emery Lapointe & Ludivine ____) b 9 Aug 1924, New Bedford, MA; d 10 Jun 2007, Marion, MA.

Ernest W. Monty was a welder in New Bedford, MA. He and his wife had been married for fifty-six years when he died and had had nine children who survived him (*South Coast Today*, 14 Jul 1998).

Children:
8.3.11.6.3.8.1	Cora G.	1943-	-
8.3.11.6.3.8.2	Linda J.	1948-	-
8.3.11.6.3.8.3	Joyce	1949-	-
8.3.11.6.3.8.4	Jeffrey Adrian	1951-1984&1992-	
8.3.11.6.3.8.5	Donna J.	1954-	-
8.3.11.6.3.8.6	Pamela V.	1956-	-
8.3.11.6.3.8.7	Ernest R.	1961-	-
8.3.11.6.3.8.8	Bridget	1964-	-
8.3.11.6.3.8.9	Lana D.	1967-	-

8.3.11.6.3.9   **MONTY, Linette I.** b 19 Jul 1928, New Bedford, MA; d 6 Apr 1983, Boston, MA. She married **Anthony F. Raffa** (Nunzio Raffa & Nunziatta ____) b Feb 1930, New Bedford, MA.

8.3.11.6.3.10   **MONTY, Maurice A.** b 11 Jan 1932, New Bedford, MA; d there 22 Jan 1980. He married **Jeanette V. Paquette** b 16 May 1930; m (2) Robert E. Lockwood (Francis E. Lockwood & Elizabeth ____).

Children:
8.3.11.6.3.10.1	Maurice	1952-	-
8.3.11.6.3.10.2	Linette Marguerite	1953-	-2002
8.3.11.6.3.10.3	William P.	1955-	-
8.3.11.6.3.10.4	Michelle J.	1956-	-
8.3.11.6.3.10.5	Phillip J.	1957-	-
8.3.11.6.3.10.6	Michael A.	1961-	-
8.3.11.6.3.10.7	Leon P.	1963-	-
8.3.11.6.3.10.8	Jacqueline	1964-	-
8.3.11.6.3.10.9	Christopher J.	1966-	-

8.3.11.6.3.11   **MONTY, Lionel/Leonel A.** b 7 Nov 1933, New Bedford, MA. He married **Grace M. Cunha** (Joseph Cunha & Rose Pina) b 27 Mar 1937, New Bedford, MA.

Lionel Monty and his wife were living on Cape Cod when his sister Agnes Marie (8.3.11.6.3.5) died in 2001 (*South Coast Today*, 27 Feb 2001).

8.3.11.7.8.1   **MONTY, Arthur P.** b 28 Jun 1927, Cortland, NY. He married 1947? **Roberta H. Hudson** (George Hudson & Helen J. ____) b 23 Feb 1927, Syracuse, NY; d & bur 30 Jul & 3 Aug 2006, Liverpool & Syracuse, NY.

Arthur P. Monty and his wife had been married for fifty-nine years when she died. She was buried in the Onondaga County Veterans Memorial Cemetery (*Syracuse Post-Standard*, 1 Aug 2006).

Children:

| 8.3.11.7.8.1.1 | William A. | 1949- | -2001 |
| 8.3.11.7.8.1.2 | Larry D. | 1954- | -2005 |

8.3.11.7.8.2   **MONTY, Rose Gladys** b Feb 1929, Cortland, NY. She married **Paul W. Tallman** (Moses Tallman & Lillian ____) b 24 Dec 1932, Preble, NY; d 25 Oct 2003, Moravia, NY.

8.3.11.7.8.3   **MONTY, Alfred J.** b 15 Oct 1930, Cortland, NY; d & bur 24 & 27 Jan 1979, Syracuse & Cortland, NY. He married **Lillian Storey** (Charles Earl Storey & Bernice Bonilyn Bush).

Alfred J. Monty was a resident of La Fayette, NY, at his death. He was buried in St. Mary's Cemetery in Cortland, NY.

8.3.11.7.8.4   **MONTY, Marie** married ____ **Saunders**.

Mrs. Marie Saunders was a resident of Syracuse, NY, when her father died in 1987 (*Syracuse Post-Standard*, 29 Jun 1987).

8.3.11.7.8.5   **MONTY, Elizabeth** married 1951? **John H. Leonard** (John H. Leonard & Mona M. Delberta) b 22 Jun 1934, Middlefield, NY; d & bur 25 & 27 May 2002, Clay, NY.

John H. Leonard and his wife had been married for forty-nine years at his death and had had four children of whom three, Deborah (i), Tina (iii), and Mark (iv) were still alive. He was buried in Pine Plains Cemetery in Clay, NY (*Syracuse Post-Standard*, 26 May 2002).

Children:

i   **Deborah Ann Leonard** b 28 Jan 1954, Cortland, NY; d & bur 13 & 16 Apr 2005, McLean & Groton, NY. She married 1973? **David W. Dann**.

ii   **Donna Leonard** b 1957?, Sandusky, OH; d & bur 18 & 22 May 1991, Syracuse & Clay, NY. She married ____ **Willey**.

iii   **Tina Leonard** married (1) ____ **Gagnon**.
      She married (2) **James W. Lowe**.

iv   **Mark Leonard**

8.3.11.7.8.6   **MONTY, Angela** b 11 Jul 1937, Cortland Co., NY. She married **Richard Casterline** (Dana Casterline & ____) b Sep 1935.

Mrs. Angela Casterline was a resident of Scott, NY, when her father died in 1987 (*Syracuse Post-Standard*, 29 Jun 1987).

Children:

i   **Richard Casterline** b 11 Mar 1958, Homer, NY; d Nov 1987.

ii   **Theresa Lynn Casterline** b 1959, Cortland Co., NY; d & bur 11 & 13 Jan 1976, Truxton & Cortland, NY, at the age of 16.

iii   **Mary Lou Casterline** b Mar 1960, Cortland, NY; d & bur there 13 & 15 Apr 1960 at the age of 3 weeks.

8.3.11.7.8.7   **MONTY, Edward T.** b 1943. He married **Deborah** ____ .

Edward Monty was living in Cortland, NY, when his father died in 1987 (*Syracuse Post-Standard*, 29 Jun 1987).

8.3.11.8.4.1   **MONTY, Gertrude Anita Albina** b & bp 2 & 5 Jun 1910, New Bedford & Fall River, MA.
Gertrude Monty was not listed with either of her parents in the 1920 US census and may have died before then.

8.3.11.8.4.2   **MONTY, Irene Imelda** b & bp 15 & 25 Jun 1911, New Bedford & Fall River, MA.
Irene Monty was staying with her mother in her maternal grandfather's household in Fall River, MA, in 1920 (US census). I have not found her in later years.

8.3.11.8.6.1   **MONTY, Octave Pierre Hubert** b & bp 21 & 25 Mar 1911, Bromont, QC.

8.3.11.8.6.2   **MONTY, Graziella** b & bp 22 & 23 Jul 1913, Bromont, QC. She married 20 Nov 1952, Waterloo, QC, **Louis Philippe Daniel** (Héliodore Daniel & Délia Leduc) b & bp 6 Jun 1915, Bromont, QC.
This woman was named Marie Joséphine Graziella at her baptism.

8.3.11.8.6.3   **MONTY, Jean Louis Joséphat** b & bp 22 & 24 Mar 1915, Bromont, QC. He married 4 Sep 1944, Bedford, QC, **Marguerite Gosselin** (Euclide Gosselin & Eva Moreau) b & bp there 22 & 28 Oct 1917; m (2) 15 Apr 1950, St. Jean, QC, Henri Forget (Léandre Forget & Amanda Rochette).

8.3.11.8.6.4   **MONTY, Marcel** b & bp 18 & 19 Nov 1916, Bromont, QC. He married 6 May 1942, Waterloo, QC, **Suzanne Beaulac** (Ephrem Beaulac & Germaine René) b & bp there 6 & 7 May 1922.
Marcel Monty was named Joseph Alphonse Marcel Laurent at his baptism. His wife Suzanne was named Marie Thérèse Suzanne Beaulac.

8.3.11.8.6.5   **MONTY, Marie Jeanne Juliette Victorine** b & bp 4 & 7 Mar 1919, Bromont, QC. She married 28 Jun 1948, Waterloo, QC, **Rouville Foisy** (Wilfrid Foisy & Laura Desnoyers) b & bp 23 May 1910, Abbotsford, QC.

13.3.6.4.6.1   **MONTY, Marie Reine/Irène** b & bp 9 & 10 Mar 1903, Ste Brigide, QC. She married there 24 Jan 1928 **Joseph Henri Jetté** (Henri Jetté & Victorine Daignault) b & bp 8 & 9 Jul 1897, Stanbridge, QC.
Joseph Jetté was a farmer in St. Alexandre, QC, until 1934 and in Frelighsburg, QC, in 1935 and later years. His wife, named Marie Reine Olida at her baptism and Marie Reine at her marriage, was constantly named Irène at the births and marriages of her children.

Children:
i   **Thérèse Françoise Jetté** b & bp 2 Jan 1929, St. Alexandre, QC. She married 7 Sep 1950, Bedford, QC, **Charles Auguste Berthiaume** (Vital Berthiaume & Louise Ménard) b & bp 20 & 21 Apr 1926, St. Sébastien, QC.
ii   **Laurent Edéas Jetté** b & bp 25 Apr 1930, St. Alexandre, QC; d & bur 25 & 27 Mar 2002, St. Albans & Sheldon Springs, VT. He married 26 Mar 1951, St. Armand, QC, **Gilberte Bernadette Barabé** (Joseph Barabé & Evelina Gendron) b & bp 9 & 12 Nov 1933, Farnham, QC.
iii   **Edouard André/Edward Jetté** b & bp 15 Sep 1931, St. Alexandre, QC.
iv   **Rosaire Napoléon Jetté** b & bp 19 Feb 1933, St. Alexandre, QC. He married 1 Jun 1957, Frelighsburg, QC, **Marielle Dolbec** (Dollard Dolbec & Simone Marquette) b & bp 25 & 26 Oct 1941, Sorel, QC.
v   **Wilfrid Donat Jetté** b & bp 11 & 12 Oct 1934, St. Alexandre, QC; d & bur there 6 & 7 Nov 1934.

vi   **Yvonne Cécile Jetté** b & bp 11 Nov 1935, Frelighsburg, QC. She married there 19 Jun 1954 **Denis Samson** (Joséphat Samson & Rose Anna Beauvais) b & bp 10 & 11 Oct 1934, Stanbridge, QC.

vii   **Laurette Amanda Jetté** b & bp 23 & 27 Dec 1936, Frelighsburg, QC. She married 18 Jul 1959, Bedford, QC, **Jean Guy L'Homme** (Oliva L'Homme & Cécile Phenix) b & bp 27 & 28 Nov 1935, St. Alexandre, QC.

viii   **Marie Reine Claire Jetté** b & bp 7 & 10 Sep 1938, Frelighsburg, QC. She married 7 Sep 1959, Bedford, QC, **Gérard Normand Desranleau** (Jean Desranleau & Laurette Dussault) b & bp 5 & 7 Nov 1934, Pike River, QC.

ix   **Lucille Jetté** married 16 Sep 1961, Frelighsburg, QC, **Joseph Frank/François Dew** (Ernest Dew & Béatrice Domingue) b & bp there 27 & 28 Mar 1938.

x   **Gérard Jetté** married 7 May 1966, Frelighsburg, QC, **Denise Fortin** (Wilfrid Fortin & Marie Boucher).

13.3.6.4.6.2   **MONTY, Jeanne Eva** b & bp 30 Apr & 1 May 1904, Ste Brigide, QC. She married there 21 Oct 1931 **Napoléon Lamarre** (Napoléon Lamarre & Eugénie Poirier) b & bp 6 Jul 1902, Ste Sabine, QC.

Napoléon Lamarre was a farmer in Ste Sabine, QC, at his marriage and in St. Alexandre, QC, at the births of his children.

Children:

i   **Yolande Réjane/Réjeanne Lamarre** b & bp 2 & 3 Sep 1932, St. Alexandre, QC. She married there 29 Aug 1953 **Normand Côté** (Léo Côté & Jeannette Brouillette).

ii   **Maurice Léonidas Lamarre** b & bp 9 Dec 1933, St. Alexandre, QC. He married 28 Jun 1958, Ste Sabine, QC, **Denise Harbec** (Lucien Harbec & Bernadette Tarte).

iii   **Marie Reine Jacqueline Lamarre** b & bp 19 & 20 Jan 1936, St. Alexandre, QC. She married there 1 Sep 1958 **Jules Germain Blais** (Gaston Blais & Irène Boulette) b & bp 3 & 4 Jul 1935, Abbotsford, QC.

iv   **Raoul Yvon Lamarre** b & bp 21 Aug 1938, St. Alexandre, QC. He married 7 Sep 1959, Farnham, QC, **Rita Jetté** (Philippe Jetté & Aurore Boudreau).

13.3.6.4.6.3   **MONTY, Uldéric Emilien** b & bp 20 Jul 1905, Ste Brigide, QC; d & bur there 2 & 5 May 1930.

13.3.6.4.6.4   **MONTY, Yvonne Lorenza** b & bp 12 & 16 Feb 1907, Ste Brigide, QC. She married there 18 Jun 1929 **Camille Léopold Viens** (Herménégilde Viens & Arzélia Bienvenu) b & bp there 18 & 19 Mar 1907.

Camille Viens was a farmer in Ste Brigide, QC, at his marriage. He and his brothers Alcide and Lucien married three sisters, Yvonne, Marie Jeanne (13.3.6.4.6.6), and Noëlla (13.3.6.4.6.7) Monty.

Child:

i   **Marguerite Monique Viens** b & bp 19 & 20 Jan 1932, Ste Brigide, QC. She married 16 Aug 1952, St. Hyacinthe, QC, **Gilbert Ferdinand Rondeau** (Arthur Rondeau & Alida Labarre) b & bp 7 & 8 Mar 1928, Ste Elizabeth de Warwick, QC.

13.3.6.4.6.5   **MONTY, Hervé Raphaël** b & bp 2 & 3 Aug 1909, Ste Brigide, QC. He married 18 Oct 1933, Ste Angèle, QC, **Marie Laure Loiselle** (Théodule/ Théole Loiselle & Alice Bienvenu) b & bp 3 & 4 Jun 1914, Ste Brigide, QC; d Dec 2003, Farnham, QC.

Hervé Raphaël Monty (Henri Raphaël Hervé at his baptism) was originally a farmer in Ste Brigide, QC, and after 1940 in Ste Sabine, QC.

Children:

13.3.6.4.6.5.1	Jeannine	1934-1955-1989
13.3.6.4.6.5.2	Denise Gisèle	1935-1956-
13.3.6.4.6.5.3	Fernande	1937-1957-

13.3.6.4.6.5.4	Brigitte	1938-1964-
13.3.6.4.6.5.5	Jean-Luc	1940-1964
13.3.6.4.6.5.6	Yolande	1942-1967-
13.3.6.4.6.5.7	Claudette	1944-1967-
13.3.6.4.6.5.8	Marie Ange	1947- -
13.3.6.4.6.5.9	Robert	1948-1972-
13.3.6.4.6.5.10	Lisette	1952-1977-
13.3.6.4.6.5.11	Paul Aimé	1953-1977-
13.3.6.4.6.5.12	Sylvain	1956-1977-

13.3.6.4.6.6   **MONTY, Marie Jeanne Angela** b & bp 4 & 7 Jan 1912, Ste Brigide, QC; d Feb 2000, St Césaire, QC. She married 21 Oct 1931, Ste Brigide, QC, **Alcide Viens** (Herménégilde Viens & Arzélia Bienvenu) b & bp 30 Aug 1908, St. Césaire, QC.

Alcide Viens (Joseph Godfroy Alcide at his baptism) was a farmer in Ste Brigide, QC. He and his brothers Camille and Lucien married three sisters, Marie Jeanne, Yvonne (13.3.6. 4.6.4), and Noëlla (13.3.6.4.6.7) Monty.

Children:
i   **Jeannette/Marie Rose Jeannette Viens** b & bp 17 & 18 Dec 1932, Ste Brigide, QC. She married there 9 Jun 1956 **Alain Boucher** (Florida Boucher & Anne Bessette).
ii   **Jean Noël Viens** b & bp 25 & 26 Dec 1933, Ste Brigide, QC. He married there 5 Sep 1960 **Brigitte Boulais** (Wilfrid Boulais & Béatrice Messier) b & bp there 16 & 17 Nov 1935.
iii **Gisèle Aline Viens** b & bp 29 & 30 May 1935, Ste Brigide, QC. She married there 9 Aug 1958 **Lionel Boulais** (Wilfrid Boulais & Béatrice Messier) b & bp there 30 Aug & 2 Sep 1934.
iv   **Denis Laurier Viens** b & bp 19 & 21 May 1936, Ste Brigide, QC.
v   **Laurence Françoise Viens** b & bp 18 & 19 May 1937, Ste Brigide, QC. She married there 16 Jul 1960 **Marcel Gagnon** (Joseph Paul Gagnon & Béatrice Morrisseau) b & bp there 19 Apr 1936.
vi   **Lea Rita Viens** b & bp 2 & 5 Sep 1938, Ste Brigide, QC. She married there 29 Jul 1961 **André Benoit** (Edouard Benoit & Claire Fournier).
vii **Marianne Angéline/Angelina Viens** b & bp 13 & 16 Mar 1940, Ste Brigide, QC. She married there 1 Jul 1961 **André Gagnon** (Joseph Paul Gagnon & Béatrice Morrisseau) b & bp there 22 Jun 1934.
viii **Solange Viens** married 26 Oct 1963, Ste Brigide, QC, **Léon Barrière** (Joseph A. Barrière & Béatrice Bessette) b & bp 16 & 18 Mar 1938, Mont St. Grégoire, QC.
ix   **Jeanne d'Arc Viens** married 27 Jul 1968, Ste Brigide, QC, **Serge Normandin** (Jean P. Normandin & Mariette Leroux).
x   **Huguette Viens** married 21 Dec 1968, Ste Brigide, QC, **Gilles Brouillette** (Rodrigue Brouillette & Florida Vincent) b & bp 2 Jun 1938, St. Jean-Baptiste, QC.

13.3.6.4.6.7   **MONTY, Noëlla Alva** b & bp 25 & 28 Dec 1913, Ste Brigide, QC. She married there 26 Sep 1934 **Lucien Viens** (Herménégilde Viens & Arzélia Bienvenu) b & bp there 30 Oct & 1 Nov 1919.

Lucien Viens (Joseph Edmond Lucien at his baptism) was a farmer in Ste Brigide, QC. He and his brothers Camille and Alcide married three sisters, Noëlla, Yvonne (13.3.6.4.6.4), and Marie Jeanne (13.3.6.4.6.6) Monty.

Children:
i   **André Viens** b & bp 26 Nov 1935, Ste Brigide, QC. He married 20 Jun 1959, Ange Gardien, QC, **Denise Blais** (Gaston Blais & Irène Boulet/Boulette) b & bp 8 & 12 Nov 1939, Abbotsford, QC.
ii   **Gaétan Viens** b & bp 31 Jul & 1 Aug 1937, Ste Brigide, QC. He married 3 Sep 1962, Farnham, QC, **Monique Chouinard** (Joseph Chouinard & Alice Boulet).

iii   **Lise Viens** married 16 May 1964, Ste Brigide, QC, **Charles Arthur Benoit** (Charles Emile Benoit & Paulette Tétrault) b & bp 22 Oct 1940, Rougemont, QC.

iv   **Marcel Viens** married 13 Aug 1966, Rougemont, QC, **Louise Dauphinais** (Roland Dauphinais & Jeanne Arès).

13.3.6.4.6.8   **MONTY, Thérèse** b & bp 28 & 29 Jun 1916, Ste Brigide, QC. She married 23 Jun 1938, Mont St. Grégoire, QC, **Sylvio Boucher** (Zéphir Boucher & Lucille/Lucillia Gamache) b & bp there 23 & 25 Sep 1912.

Children:
i   **Yolande Marguerite Boucher** b & bp 9 Apr 1939, Mont St. Grégoire, QC. She married 7 Apr 1958, Ste Brigide, QC, **Eugene Palin** (Richard Palin & Albertine Deneault) b & bp 22 & 24 Aug 1930, St. Jacques le Mineur, QC.

ii   **Gilles Boucher** married 30 May 1964, Mont St. Grégoire, QC, **Yolande Robitaille** (Jean Noël Robitaille & Flora Massé).

iii   **Jean Guy Boucher** married 7 Jul 1979, Sabrevois, QC, **Suzanne Brosseau** (Jacques Brosseau & Mariette Beaudin).

iv   **Ginette Boucher** married 6 Oct 1979, Ste Brigide, QC, **Jacques Laroche** (Octave Laroche & Rose Talbot).

13.3.6.4.6.9   **MONTY, Florent Emery/Laurent** b & bp 8 & 9 Mar 1919, Ste Brigide, QC; d & bur 20 & 22 Mar 1927, St Jean & Ste Brigide, QC.

13.3.6.4.8.1   **MONTY, Lucette** b & bp 8 Feb 1914, Ste Brigide, QC. She married (1) there 12 Aug 1933 **Albert Benjamin** (Hormisdas Benjamin & Délia Giroux) b & bp there 3 & 6 Sep 1903; d 21 Feb 1968, QC.
She married (2) **Armand Martel**.

Children:
i   **Jeannine Gisèle Benjamin** b & bp 16 Sep 1934, Ste Brigide, QC. She married there 3 Jun 1959 **René Tétreault** (Domina Tétreault & Antoinette Lebeau) b & bp 6 Jul 1931, Ange Gardien, QC.

ii   **Régis René Benjamin** b & bp 12 & 14 Jan 1936, Ste Brigide, QC. He married 26 May 1962, Ste Angèle, QC, **Réjeanne Jetté** (Jean-Paul Jetté & Antoinette Lambert).

iii   **René Hormisdas Benjamin** b & bp 11 & 15 Aug 1937, Ste Brigide, QC. He married 21 Jul 1962, Farnham, QC, **Pierrette Gaboriault** (Lucien Gaboriault & Marguerite Leduc).

iv   **Carmen Benjamin** married 25 Jul 1964, Marieville, QC, **Roger Guité** (Alfred Guité & Brigitte Boudreau) b & bp 19 & 20 Feb 1939, Maria, QC.

13.3.6.4.8.2   **MONTY, Gérard** b & bp 30 Mar & 2 Apr 1916, Ste Brigide, QC. He married 17 May 1939, Mont St. Grégoire, QC, **Anna/Annette Cadieux** (Stanislas Cadieux & Eva Massé) b & bp 17 & 19 Feb 1917, Ste Brigide, QC.
Gérard Monty was a farmer in Ste Brigide, QC, at his marriage.

Children:

13.3.6.4.8.2.1	Annette Suzanne Jeanne	1940-	-
13.3.6.4.8.2.2	Jean Stanislas Claude	1942-	-

13.3.6.4.9.1   **MONTY, Simone** b & bp 27 & 28 May 1908, Ste Brigide, QC; d & bur 18 & ? Aug 1973, Ste Rose & Ste Angèle, QC. She married 23 Aug 1927, Ange Gardien, QC, **Emile Wilfrid Gaudreau** (Philias Gaudreau & Alice Mandeville) b & bp 23 & 29 Sep 1901, Stanbridge, QC.
Emile Gaudreau was a mechanic in St. Hyacinthe, QC, at his marriage and at the births of his children there.

Children:
i   **Jean Charles Roger Gaudreau** b & bp 25 & 27 Oct 1928, St. Hyacinthe, QC.
ii **Paule Pierrette Gaudreau** b & bp 18 & 19 Nov 1930, St. Hyacinthe, QC.

13.3.6.4.9.2   **MONTY, Germain** b & bp 14 & 21 Apr 1909, Ste Brigide, QC; d 22 Jul 1962, Montreal, QC. He married (1) 8 Aug 1935, Timmins, Ontario, **Alice Gélineau** (Osias Gélineau & Rose Denis) b & bp 28 Feb & 5 Mar 1916, Bromont, QC.
He married (2) 3 Jun 1955, Montreal, QC, **Violet Miller**.

13.3.6.4.10.1   **MONTY, Gérard Richard** b & bp 27 & 28 Nov 1912, Bedford, QC; d & bur there 21 & 22 Mar 1913.

13.3.6.4.10.2   **MONTY, Marguerite** b & bp 3 & 4 Jan 1914, Bedford, QC. She married 7 Sep 1940, Cowansville, QC, **Charles Alton Cady** (Charles Alton Cady & Maud Alice Tracy) b & bp 19 Nov 1903 & 21 May 1905, Sweetsburg & Nelsonville, QC; d 1 Jul 1968, Cowansville, QC.
Marguerite Monty was named Angéline Marguerite Hélène at her baptism. Charles Alton Cady's date of birth is taken from the baptismal records of the Church of England parish in Nelsonville, QC.

13.3.6.4.10.3   **MONTY, Bernard** b & bp 8 & 10 Sep 1915, Bedford, QC; d 24 Mar 1993, Montreal, QC. He married there 21 Dec 1946 **Simone Cadieux** (Donat Cadieux & Rose Ida Charbonneau) b & bp 27 & 28 Jul 1921, Grenville, QC.
Bernard Monty was named Joseph Alexis Albert Bernard at his baptism.

Children:
13.3.6.4.10.3.1   Pierre   1948-1971-
13.3.6.4.10.3.2   Manon   1952-1975-

13.3.6.4.10.4   **MONTY, Rachel** b & bp 11 & 14 Oct 1917, Bedford, QC; d 13 Jan 1945, Cowansville, QC.
Rachel Monty was named Madeleine Clarissa Rachel at her baptism.

13.3.6.4.11.1   **MONTY, Anonymous** b 25 Jan 1920, Ste Brigide, QC; d & bur there 25 & 26 Jan 1920.

13.3.6.4.11.2   **MONTY, Anicet** b & bp 25 & 28 Aug 1921, Ste Brigide, QC. He married there 30 Oct 1954 **Marie Marthe Bonneville** (Stanislas Bonneville & Irène Messier) b & bp 22 & 23 May 1921, Ange Gardien, QC.
Anicet Monty was named Joseph Emery Anicet at his baptism.

Child:
13.3.6.4.11.2.1   Gino   1958-1981-

13.3.6.4.11.3   **MONTY, Jean-Paul** b & bp 25 & 28 Dec 1925, Ste Brigide, QC. He married 28 Oct 1950, Ste Sabine, QC, **Marie Jeanne Lamarche** (Polydore Lamarche & Rosina Davignon) b & bp 29 & 31 Jan 1932, Ste Sabine, QC.

Children:
13.3.6.4.11.3.1   Hélène   -1976-
13.3.6.4.11.3.2   Bertrand   -1976-

13.3.6.4.11.4   **MONTY, Anonymous** b 14 Mar 1930, Ste Brigide, QC; d & bur there 14 & 15 Mar 1930.

13.3.6.4.11.5 **MONTY, Marcelle** b & bp 12 & 14 Nov 1931, Ste Brigide, QC; d 22 May 1992, Iberville, QC. She married 16 Jul 1949 Mont St. Grégoire, QC, **Serge Allard** (Henri Allard & Thérèse Boucher) b & bp 9 & 11 Aug 1926, Mont St. Grégoire & St. Alexandre, QC.

Children:
i **Monique Allard** married 28 Apr 1973, Iberville, QC, **Jean Claude Robillard** (Jean Robillard & Rolande Chaput).
ii **Lucie Allard** married 18 Aug 1973, Iberville, QC, **Pierre Savoie** (Edgar Savoie & Rita Brosseau).
iii **Chantal Allard** married 14 Feb 1976, Iberville, QC, **Richard M. Vivier** (Arthur Vivier & Pierrette Yerland).

13.3.6.4.11.6 **MONTY, Alain** b & bp 23 & 26 Oct 1933, Ste Brigide, QC; d & bur there 8 & 10 Aug 1937.
This child was named Joseph Bruno Alain at his baptism but simply Alain at his burial.

13.3.8.2.5.1 **MONTY, Ruby Neal** b Feb 1899, Dodds Twp, IL; d Aug 1945, Bradley, IL. She married 1921? **John Edward/Jack Holland** (John Holland & Ida ____) b 30 Dec 1898, Kankakee, IL; d Jul 1974, Altona, IL.
Jack Holland was a railroad engineer in Kankakee, IL, in April 1930, when he and his wife had been married for about eight years (US census).

Children:
i **Nina Holland** b 1923?, Kankakee, IL
ii **Jack Holland** b 1927?, Kankakee, IL.

13.3.8.2.5.2 **MONTY, Nina B.** b 23 Sep 1901, Mount Vernon, IL; d & bur 16 & 18 Apr 1986, Bradley & Kankakee, IL.
Nina Monty did not marry. She was buried alongside her parents in the Mount Grove Cemetery in Kankakee, IL.

13.3.8.2.5.3 **MONTY, Walter E.** b 24 Oct 1903, Mount Vernon, IL; d 20 Jun 1971, Livonia, MI. He married there 1931 **Ruth Hunt** (Yates Frank Hunt & Mary C. ____) b Apr 1910, Deerfield, MI.
Walter Monty was a shipping clerk in Detroit, MI, in 1930 (US census). He and his wife lived there after their marriage.

Children:

13.3.8.2.5.3.1	Della R.	1933-	-2000
13.3.8.2.5.3.2	Wesley	-	-
13.3.8.2.5.3.3	Thomas P.	1948-	-
13.3.8.2.5.3.4	Peggy	-	-

13.3.8.2.5.4 **MONTY, Edgar Collins** b 11 Nov 1905, Mount Vernon, IL; d 14 Sep 1987, Wilmington, NC. He married **Hazel Dorothy Beach** (Adam Frederick Beach & Clara Dancaster) b 18 Jul 1910, Bradley, IL; d 24 Oct 1992, Wilmington, NC.

Child:

13.3.8.2.5.4.1	Edgar Lee	1934-	-

13.3.8.2.5.5 **MONTY, Everell Alonzo** b 10 Aug 1907, Mount Vernon, IL; d 4 May 1986, Bradley, IL. He married 23 Apr 1931, Watseka, IL, **Aline Edna Ray** (Leon Ray & Julia ____) b 11 Nov 1911, Kankakee Co., IL; d 1 Jul 1980, Bradley, IL.
Everell Monty was buried in the Kankakee, IL, Memorial Gardens.

Children:

13.3.8.2.5.5.1	Dale Ray	1934-	-	
13.3.8.2.5.5.2	Judith	1940?-	&	-
13.3.8.2.5.5.3	Rita	1950?-	-	

13.3.8.2.5.6 **MONTY, Richard Wayne** b 2 Oct 1915, Bradley, IL; d 10 Jun 2008, Payson, AZ. He married 11 Mar 1945, OR, **Wilma Louise Lorentz** (Newton Grant Lorentz & Cleora Bell Linder) b 2 May 1924, Trent, OR.

Richard W. Monty was a resident of Kankakee Co., IL, when he enlisted in the Army Air Corps on 30 Dec 1941 (World War II Army Enlistment Records). He lived in Arizona upon his retirement from the US Postal Service and was survived by his wife and two sons (*Payson Roundup*, 7 Jul 2008).

Children:

13.3.8.2.5.6.1	Richard L.	1947?-	-
13.3.8.2.5.6.2	Mark S.	1954?-	-

13.3.8.6.2.1 **MONTIE, Vernie W.** b 19 Dec 1896, Kankakee, IL; d 19 Oct 1994, Mountain Home, AR. He married **Dorothy** ____ b 8 Aug 1907; d May 1979, Bull Shoals, AR.

Vernie Montie was a farmer on his father's farm in St. Anne, IL, in 1917 when he signed his World War I Draft Registration card and a salesman in Chicago, IL, in 1930. He was still single (US census).

13.3.8.6.2.2 **MONTIE, Melvin C.** b 11 Oct 1900, Kankakee, IL; d 3 Jan 1921, Aroma Park, IL.

Melvin C. Montie was a laborer on his father's farm in Aroma Park, IL, in 1920 (US census). He was buried in the Aroma Park Cemetery.

13.3.8.6.2.3 **MONTIE, Elwood** b 27 Mar 1908, Aroma Park, IL; d 6 Jul 1985, Mountain Home, AR. He married **Marie A.** ____ b 25 Jun 1913; m (2) Robert W. Schmidt (John Schmidt & Ethel Grebert); d Sep 1991, Mountain Home, AR.

Elwood Montie was a timekeeper in Chicago, IL, in 1930 (US census). I do not know when he moved to Arkansas. He was buried in the Aroma Park, IL, Cemetery.

Child:

13.3.8.6.2.3.1	William Joseph	1932-	-1997

13.3.8.6.4.1 **MONTIE, Harold Jesse** b 2 Sep 1895, St. Anne, IL. He married 12 Nov 1921, Kankakee, IL, **Kathryn M. Manau** (John Manau & Kathryn M. O'Donnell) b 6 Jan 1898, Momence, IL.

Harold Montie was a machinist in Bourbonnais, IL, in 1920 (US census) and a resident of Chicago, IL, when his mother died in 1933.

13.3.8.6.4.2 **MONTIE, Claribel** b 24 Nov 1901, Kankakee, IL; d Nov 1986, Moline, IL. She married 23 Dec 1920, Kankakee, IL, **Harry Dewey Fromme** (Charles L. Fromme & Anna Jasper) b 5 May 1898, Walcott, IA.

Harry D. Fromme was a salesman in Moline, IL, at his marriage and a state highway policeman in 1930 (US census). By the late 1940s he was Chief of police in Moline.

Child:

i   **Marcella Fromme** b 1924?, Moline IL.

13.3.8.6.4.3 **MONTIE, Noah Alfred** b 22 Sep 1903, Kankakee, IL; d 7 Sep 1964, Sanger, CA. He married (1) 1928? **Florence Brennan** (Frank Brennan & Mary Florence Minnis) b 1907?, Centralia, IL.

He married (2) **Alice C. Bainbridge** (William V. Bainbridge & Adelaide/Lida Ellsworth) b 15 Apr 1914, WI; d 21 Jan 1999, Pacific Grove, CA.

Noah Montie was a railroad clerk in Chicago, IL, in 1930 when he and his 23-year-old wife Florence had been married for two years (US census). He moved to Fresno, CA, in 1945 and was buried in the Memorial Gardens there. He was survived by his second wife Alice and children Leroy and Renee (*Fresno Bee Republican*, 9 Sep 1964).

Child of the first marriage:

| 13.3.8.6.4.3.1 | Leroy Louis | 1935?- | &1975- |

Child of the second marriage:

| 13.3.8.6.4.3.2 | Renee A. | 1948-1966&1983- |

13.3.8.6.6.1   **MONTIE/MONTE, Elwyn Etheridge** b 29 Aug 1904, Waldron, IL; d 12 Aug 1967, Moline, IL. He married 1928, Rock Island, IL, **Leona Blanche Gavin** (Frederick Edward Gavin & Anna Barnes) b there 16 May 1900; d 22 Feb 1971, Moline, IL

This man was known as Elwyn Montie when living with his parents in Kankakee, IL. He was named Elwyn Monte though when he was a truck driver in Rock Island, IL, in 1930. He and his wife had then been married for two years (US censuses). The change in surname became permanent.

Children:

13.3.8.6.6.1.1	Mardelle Anne	1930-1953-
13.3.8.6.6.1.2	Don Elwyn	1933-	-
13.3.8.6.6.1.3	Gene	1935-	-

13.3.8.6.6.2   **MONTIE, Agnes Althea** b 29 Jul 1907, Waldron, IL; d & bur 1932, Kankakee Co. & Aroma Park, IL.

Althea Montie was buried alongside her mother in the Aroma Park, IL, Cemetery.

13.3.8.6.8.1   **MONTIE, Lucille Lorine** b & bp 19 & 30 Aug 1908, Kankakee, IL; d 20 Mar 1999, Las Vegas, NV. She married 20 Oct 1944, Cook Co., IL, **Charles Ross**.

Lucille Montie was a theater organist in Kankakee, IL, in 1930 (US census). She was a resident of Las Vegas, NV, as Mrs. Lucille Ross, when her father died in 1970.

13.3.8.8.2.1   **MONTY, Emma Laura** b 25 Nov 1899, Aurora, KS; d 26 Mar 2001, Edmond, OK. She married 1925? **Omer Gennette** (Stephen/Steven Gennette & Ezilda Gagnon) b 6 Sep 1892, Aurora, KS; d Feb 1980, Coffeyville, KS.

Omer Gennette was a shop owner in Concordia, KS, in 1930 when he and his wife had been married for five years (US census). The couple later resided in Coffeyville, KS.

Child:

i   **Maxine Gennette** b Apr 1927, Concordia, KS. She married 1949? **Don L. Morris** b 25 Jan 1926, Bristow, OK; d 14 Feb 2000, Edmond, OK.

13.3.8.8.2.2   **MONTY, Philip** b 11 Sep 1903, Aurora, KS; d there 15 Jul 1934.

Philip Monty was a laborer on his father's farm in Aurora, KS, in 1930 (US census). He was buried there in St. Peter's Cemetery.

13.3.8.8.2.3   **MONTY, Marcelline Leona** b 21 Feb 1908, Aurora, KS; d Sep 1973, KS. She married **Donald Vernon Appleby** (Frank Laughlin Appleby & Jennie Nellie Gabhart) b 1 Sep 1910, Ames, KS; d 12 Dec 1977, Fort Smith, AR.

Marcelline Monty was a resident of Coffeyville, KS, at her death while Donald Appleby was a resident of Stilwell, OK, at his death.

13.3.8.8.2.4   **MONTY, Irene Luella** b 16 Feb 1914, Aurora, KS; d 10 & 14 Mar 2001, Coffeyville, KS. She married 5 Oct 1937, Aurora, KS, **Leonard Joseph Leclair** (Francis Xavier/Frank Leclair & Celia Martell) b there 4 Dec 1914; d & bur 9 & 12 Feb 1983, Concordia & Coffeyville, KS.

Leonard Joseph Leclair and his wife were buried in Holy Name Catholic Cemetery in Coffeyville, KS.

Child:
i   **Sharon K. Leclair** b Aug 1945. She married (1) **Darrel D. Furnas** b 4 Nov 1944; d 29 Jan 1994.
    She married (2) **Earl Whited** b 1939.

13.3.8.8.7.1   **MONTY, Laura D.** b 19 Jul 1905, Cloud Co., KS. She married 24 Oct 1924, Concordia, KS, **Francis/Frank Joseph Bessette** (Louis Bessette & Johanna/Anna Shea) b 12 Feb 1901, Purcell, OK; d 23 Jul 1947.

Frank J. Bessette was a creamery worker in Concordia, KS, in 1930 (US census).

Children:
i   **Gloria Lee Bessette** b 11 May 1925, Concordia, KS; d & bur 25 & 28 Mar 1991, Wichita, KS. She married **Alex D. Altergott** (Henry Altergott & Amelia ____) b 2 Nov 1924, MI; d & bur 26 & 30 Nov 1991, Wichita, KS.
ii **Cornelius Patrick Bessette** b 1931?, KS; d 31 Dec 1990, Wichita, KS, at the age of 59. He married **Mrs. Shirley Lee.**
iii **Geraldine/Gerry Bessette** married ____ **Miller.**
iv **Anne Marie Bessette** married **Richard John Schock** b 4 Apr 1932; d & bur 7 & 10 Dec 1993, Wichita, KS.

13.3.8.8.7.2   **MONTY, Abner W.** b 5 Dec 1917, Cloud Co., KS; d 28 Apr 1997, Concordia, KS. He married 14 Feb 1942 **Helen Maxine Woodworth** (Cecil Paul Woodworth & Alma A. ____) b 22 Sep 1919, Miltonvale, KS.

Abner Monty was buried in St. Concordia Cemetery in Concordia, KS. The names of his three children are found in the cemetery records.

Children:
13.3.8.8.7.2.1	Paul L.	1944-	-
13.3.8.8.7.2.2	Loleda	-	-
13.3.8.8.7.2.3	Lana	-	-

13.3.8.8.8.1   **MONTY, Eldon Lee** b 16 Oct 1914, Smoky Hill, KS; d & bur 5 & 9 Aug 1995, Salina, KS. He married 19 Jul 1941 **Dorothy Whitehair** (John Leo Whitehair & Mary Agnes Morgan) b 13 Jun 1914, Abilene, KS; d & bur 29 Dec 1997 & 2 Jan 1998, Salina, KS.

Eldon Monty and his wife were buried in Mount Calvary Cemetery in Salina, KS. They were survived by all six of their children (*Wichita Eagle*, 7 Aug 1995 and 1 Jan 1998).

Children:
13.3.8.8.8.1.1	Kathleen Ann	1942-1964-	
13.3.8.8.8.1.2	John Eldon	1944-	-
13.3.8.8.8.1.3	Patricia Louise (twin)	1945-1972-	
13.3.8.8.8.1.4	Carolyn Susan (twin)	1945-1973-	
13.3.8.8.8.1.5	Mary Jane	1946-1968-	
13.3.8.8.8.1.6	Rosemary	1950-1971&	-

13.3.8.8.8.2   **MONTY, Alcid E.** b 27 Feb 1917, Smoky Hill, KS; d 15 Dec 1994, Salina, KS. He married there 20 May 1939 **Doris Mae Kindlesparger** (Delbert Ernest Kindlesparger & Anna Weaver) b 14 Mar 1917, Lincoln Co., KS; d & bur 29 & 31 Jul 2001, Salina, KS.

Child:
| 13.3.8.8.8.2.1 | William Joseph | 1941- | -1964 |

13.3.8.8.8.3   **MONTY, George Désiré** b 2 Jul 1923, Salina, KS; d 29 May 2008, Davenport, IA. He married 30 Apr 1949, Salina, KS, **Marie Margaret/Mary Karber** (Charles Karber & Catherine Ney) b 5 Oct 1927, KS.

George D. Monty was a High School coach and principal in Kansas before joining the faculty of St. Ambrose College in Davenport, IA, in 1962. He was for many years the chairman of the Education Department there. He predeceased his wife (*Salina Journal*, 4 Jun 2008).

Children:

13.3.8.8.8.3.1	Mark Louis	1950-	-
13.3.8.8.8.3.2	Diane Marie	1951-	-
13.3.8.8.8.3.3	George Charles	1953-	-
13.3.8.8.8.3.4	David Allen	1967-	-

13.3.8.8.8.4   **MONTY, Richard Eugene** b 23 Jun 1928, Salina, KS; d & bur 4 & 10 Mar 2007, Russell & Salina, KS.

Richard Eugene Monty was a sales representative in Russell, KS, before his retirement. He was buried in Mount Calvary Cemetery in Salina, KS (*Hays Daily News*, 6 Mar 2007).

13.3.8.8.8.5   **MONTY, Joan** b 29 Jan 1932, Salina, KS. She married **Donald Eugene Weis** (Clarence Arthur Weis & Mabel M. Duryee) b 5 May 1931, Salina, KS.

Joan Monty and her husband lived in Salina, KS, in the early years of their marriage. They were in Westminster, CO, however when their daughter Lynn Ann married in 1971 and also when her brother George (13.3.8.8.8.3) died in 2008 (*Salina Journal*, 31 Oct 1971 and 4 Jun 2008).

Children:

i   **Lynn Ann Weis** b 24 Dec 1952, Salina, KS. She married 23 Oct 1971, Westminster, CO, **Robert Wayne Underwood** (Robert Underwood & ____).
ii   **Gregory R. Weis** b 5 Aug 1955, Salina, KS.
iii   **Lori Weis** b 5 Jan 1959, Salina, KS.

13.3.8.8.9.1   **MONTY, Wilfred W.** b 3 Apr 1910, Aurora, KS; d & bur 9 & 13 Sep 1982, Wheat Ridge & Denver, CO. He married **Cecelia Wahlmeier** (Anton Wahlmeier & Anna Maria Buser) b 1 Jun 1907, KS; d & bur 20 Jun & 3 Jul 2000, ? & Denver, CO.

Wilfred Monty was working for a daily newspaper in Wichita, KS, in 1930 (US census). I do not know when he moved to Colorado. He was an Army Staff Sergeant in World War II and was buried, as was his wife, in Fort Logan National Cemetery in Denver, CO.

13.3.8.8.9.2   **MONTY, Mildred Victorine** b 28 Jul 1920, Newton, KS; d & bur 6 & 11 Jun 2008, Wichita, KS. She married 28 Apr 1942 **Thomas Edward Clark** (Vance Clark & Hermina Konecny) b 7 Jul 1921, Conway, KS; d 25 Nov 1969, Wichita, KS.

Mildred V. Monty's three children survived her (*Wichita Eagle*, 8 Jun 2008). She and Thomas E. Clark were buried in Calvary Cemetery in Wichita, KS.

Children:

i   **Susan Kay Clark** b Mar 1946. She married (1) 20 Aug 1966 and divorced 14 Feb 1978, Bexar Co., TX, **Michael J. Ryan** b 1942?
She married (2) 31 Mar 1978, Bexar Co., TX, **Maurice P. Bois** (Maurice P. Bois & Yeteve Vezina) b Sep 1944; m (1) 3 May 1968 and divorced 10 Feb 1978 Mary E. ____.
ii   **Michael D. Clark** b Jun 1950. He married (1) **Mary Frances/Francine Grantham**.
He married (2) **Janet Sue Burgard** (David Burgard & Eugenia Wilds) b Apr 1950.

iii   **Shirley Ann Clark** b Dec 1956. She married **Randy Moon** (Vincent Woodard Moon & Louise Ada Anderson).

13.3.8.8.9.3   **MONTY, Armeline C.** b 31 Jan 1922, KS; d 28 May 2002, Wichita, KS.

Armeline C. Monty did not marry. She was buried in Calvary Cemetery in Wichita, KS.

13.3.8.8.9.4   **MONTY, Melvin E.** b 8 Dec 1923, KS; d & bur 4 & 7 Dec 1994, Wichita, KS. He married **Margaret Evelyn Flanigan** (Martin F. Flanigan & Mary K. ____) b Jun 1929, Wichita, KS.

Melvin E. Monty and his family lived in Wichita, KS. He predeceased his wife and four children (*Wichita Eagle*, 5 Feb 1994) and was buried in Wichita's Calvary Cemetery.

Children:

13.3.8.8.9.4.1	Mary Catherine	1949- -
13.3.8.8.9.4.2	Nancy Ann	1952-1970&1974-
13.3.8.8.9.4.3	David Edward	1956-1986-
13.3.8.8.9.4.4	Douglas	- -

13.3.8.8.9.5   **MONTY, Robert Eugene** b 9 Apr 1926, KS; d & bur 5 & 11 Mar 2002, Wichita, KS. He married **Mary Jane Ervin** (Wesley Erwin & Mary Shields) b 13 Dec 1926, Wichita, KS; d & bur 10 Mar 1952, Marion Co., TX & Wichita, KS.

Robert E. Monty and his wife were buried in Calvary Cemetery in Wichita, KS.

Child:

13.3.8.8.9.5.1	Garry Joseph	1952-1978-

13.3.8.8.11.1   **MONTY, Leonard A.** b 23 Jan 1922, Aurora, KS; d & bur 8 & 11 Aug 1989, Concordia & Clyde, KS. He married 10 Jun 1944, Aurora, KS, **Wilma A. Starr** (Ulysses Earl Starr & Nellie Leta Kennedy) b 23 Sep 1925, MO.

Leonard A. Monty was buried in Mount Carmel Cemetery in Clyde, KS. He predeceased his wife.

Children:

13.3.8.8.11.1.1	Raymond Gale	1946- -1946
13.3.8.8.11.1.2	Loleta Ann	-1976-

13.3.8.8.11.2   **MONTY, Eldemore** b 9 Feb 1925, Aurora, KS; d & bur 18 & 21 Sep 2005, Beloit, KS. He married **Mrs. Norma L. Senters** b 18 Feb 1928; m (1) Charles Mead Senters (Orville Senters & Nellie Mead); d 9 Jan 2001, Beloit, KS.

Eldemore Monty was a long-term resident of Beloit, KS, and was buried there in St. John's Catholic Cemetery. He was survived by his son and four stepchildren (*Salina Journal*, 20 Sep 2005).

Child:

13.3.8.8.11.2.1	Eldemore Jr.	- -

13.3.8.8.11.3   **MONTY, LaVerne C.** b 11 Mar 1926, KS; d 23 Oct 2003, Beloit, KS. He married 30 Jan 1952, Concordia, KS, **Anna Mae Motes** (Asa Worthley Motes & Maude M. ____) b 21 Apr 1926, Scottsville, KS; m (1) ____ Williams; d 17 Jul 1994, Beloit, KS.

LaVerne Monty and his wife were long-term residents of Beloit, KS.

Children:

13.3.8.8.11.3.1	Calvin Leroy	-1973-
13.3.8.8.11.3.2	Katherine Marie	-1972?-
13.3.8.8.11.3.3	Douglas	- -

13.3.8.8.12.1   **MONTY, Maxine** d 1918, Aurora, KS, at the age of five months.

13.3.8.8.12.2   **MONTY, Della Mae** b 28 Dec 1924, Aurora, KS; d & bur 4 & 8 Apr 2008, Concordia, KS. She married there 6 Nov 1945 **Alfred Joseph David Metro** (Peter Metro & Lena Bessette) b 1 Dec 1918, Aurora, KS.

Della Mae Monty predeceased her husband. She was buried in St. Concordia Cemetery in Concordia, KS (*Salina Journal*, 6 Apr 2008).

Children:
    i   **Sandra Joyce Metro** b 22 Aug 1946, Concordia, KS. She married (1) Mar 1964 **Larry Starr** (Earl Starr & ____) b 1 Aug 1943.
        She married (2) 1973, Salina, KS, **Charles William Hittle** (Harry Lyle Hittle & Beulah Marie Potts) b 1938.
    ii   **Michael Henry Metro** b 9 Aug 1947, Concordia, KS. He married (1) 20 Aug 1966 and divorced 1974 **Leanna Marie Richard** (Leo Richard & Corinne Breen) b 1948?; m (2) 9 Oct 1995, Las Vegas, NV, Dennis Ray Nobert.
        He married (2) **Carol** ____.
    iii   **Jolene Marie Metro** b 4 Jun 1948, Concordia, KS. She married (1) 7 Sep 1967 **Lyle Paul Bonebrake** b 1948?
        She married (2) **Dave W. Clark** b Sep 1951.
    iv   **Steven Joseph Metro** b 19 Jul 1949, Concordia, KS. He married 11 May 1974, Belleville, KS, **Deborah Lee Williams** (Curtis E. Williams & Barbara J. ____) b 1950?
    v   **Monte Richard Metro** b 29 Jul 1951, Concordia, KS; d & bur there 28 Apr & 2 May 2000. He married (1) **Theresa P. Hesting** b 31 Jan 1958.
        He married (2) **Lorna Dochow** (Loren Dochow & ____).
    vi   **Larry Girard Metro** b 12 Apr 1955, Concordia, KS. He married there 23 Jul 1977 **Deanna Lynn McCall** (Dean McCall & Tootie ____).
    vii   **Geralyn Mae Metro** b 6 May 1956, Concordia, KS. She married **Robert J. Strait** b 9 Sep 1955.
    viii   **Joyce Elaine Metro** b 11 Dec 1957, Concordia, KS. She married **Charles Owen Dutton** b Nov 1948.
    ix   **James Alfred Metro** b 9 Dec 1959, Concordia, KS. He married **Michelle Renee Largent** b 28 Feb 1962.
    x   **Julie Kristine Metro** b 2 Jan 1963, Concordia, KS. She married **Kenneth/Kenny M. O'Donnell** b Aug 1967.

13.3.8.8.12.3   **MONTY, Annabel T.** b Apr 1926, Aurora, KS. She married 19 Nov 1946 **Curtis/Curt Woodworth** (Cecil Paul Woodworth & Alma A. ____) b 13 Dec 1922, KS; d Nov 1980, Concordia, KS.

Child:
    i   **Miss Woodworth** b 8 Jun 1947; d 19 Jun 1957.

13.3.8.8.12.4   **MONTY, Donald Dean** b 10 May 1928, Aurora, KS; d & bur 19 & 23 Jan 2006, Hope, KS. He married (1) 22 Jul 1949 **Emma Jean Henthorne** (John Calvin Henthorne & Ethel Leona Showalter) b 4 Dec 1932, Stockton, KS; m (2) 24 Dec 1975, Las Vegas, NV, Orville L./Jack Darrow (Orville Leon Darrow & Opal ____); d & bur 13 & 17 Jul 2004, Concordia, KS.

He married (2) 24 Apr 1975, Council Grove, KS, **Isabelle K. Morgan** (Philip Joseph Morgan & Freda Anna Schuetz) b May 1926, KS; m (1) Leo Alexander Haire (Johnston William Haire & Anna Catherine Langmin); m (2) John Holland.

Donald D. Monty was a long-time resident of Hope, KS, and was buried there in St. Philip's Cemetery. His second wife and the four children named below survived him (*Salina Journal*, 21 Jan 2006).

Emma Jean Henthorne was buried in Pleasant Hill Cemetery in Concordia, KS.

Children pf the first marriage:

13.3.8.8.12.4.1	Daniel	1950-	-
13.3.8.8.12.4.2	Robert	1951-	-
13.3.8.8.12.4.3	Janet	1954-	-
13.3.8.8.12.4.4	Dee Ann	1959-1977-	

13.3.10.8.2.1 **MONTY, Albert Solime** b & bp 22 Aug 1917, Chambly, QC.

13.3.10.8.2.2 **MONTY, Arsène Maurice** b & bp 10 & 11 May 1920, Chambly, QC; d there 11 Oct 1949.

13.3.10.8.2.3 **MONTY, Laurent** b & bp 23 & 24 May 1921, Chambly, QC. He married there 3 Jun 1950 **Louise Marcille** (Paul Marcille & Lucille Daignault) b & bp there 29 Sep 1927.
    Laurent Monty was named Joseph Arthur Laurent at his baptism. His wife was baptized as Marie Aline Louise Marcille.

Children:

13.3.10.8.2.3.1	Claudette	1951-1984-
13.3.10.8.2.3.2	Jacques	1952-1984-
13.3.10.8.2.3.3	Luc	1958- -

13.3.10.8.2.4 **MONTY, Alphonse Rodolphe** b & bp 5 & 7 Oct 1923, Chambly, QC; d & bur there 22 & 23 Nov 1923.

13.3.10.8.2.5 **MONTY, Georgette Julienne** b & bp 31 Dec 1924, Chambly, QC. She married there 8 May 1948 **Marcel Trudeau** (Théophile Trudeau & Alexandra Lévesque) b & bp 14 Aug 1922, Sherbrooke, QC.
    Marcel Trudeau was named Joseph Louis Théophile Marcel Gérard at his baptism.

Children:
    i   **Robert Trudeau** b 21 Apr 1951, Chambly, QC. He married 16 Aug 1986, Richelieu, QC, **Maryse Audy**.
    ii   **Daniel Trudeau** b 4 Oct 1955, Chambly, QC.
    iii **François Trudeau** b 9 Mar 1961, Chambly, QC. He married 11 Jul 1987, Richelieu, QC, **Hélène Darche**.

13.3.10.16.1.1 **MONTY, Jeanne d'Arc Anna** b & bp 19 & 20 Apr 1919, Roxton Pond, QC. She married there 10 Oct 1944 **Maurice Emile Maheu** (Joseph Maheu & Alma Dion) b & bp there 15 & 17 Apr 1921.

Child:
    i   **Monique Maheu** married 29 Jun 1968, Granby, QC, **André Ferland** (Daniel Ferland & Lucette Thuot).

13.3.10.16.1.2 **MONTY, Thérèse Simone Agathe** b & bp 26 & 29 Jun 1921, Roxton Pond, QC.

13.3.10.16.1.3 **MONTY, Yvonne Exeline** b & bp 11 & 16 Dec 1922, Roxton Pond, QC.

13.3.10.16.11.1 **MONTY, Lise** b & bp 10 & 11 Oct 1932, Roxton Pond, QC. She married 12 Oct 1953, Granby, QC, **Pierre Bertrand** (Henri Aimé Bertrand & Aldéa Bonneau) b & bp 28 & 31 Aug 1929, Sherbrooke, QC.
    This woman was named Marie Anne Blanche Anna Lise at her baptism. Pierre Ber-

trand was named Joseph Noël Pierre Aimé at his baptism.

Children:
- i **Alain Bertrand** b 23 Jun 1956, Montreal, QC. He married 14 Aug 1982, St. Gabriel de Brandon, QC, **Edith Corriveau**.
- ii **Johanne Bertrand** b 28 Jun 1959, St. Jérôme, QC. She married 12 Sep 1987, Rosemère, QC, **Christian Couture**.

13.3.10.19.3.1   MONTY, Robert
I know of this child only through Louise Monty, *Généalogie de la famille Monty*, IV, 139.

13.3.17.10.1.1   MONTY, Antoinette Corinne Jeannette b & bp 3 & 4 Mar 1917, Nashua, NH; d & bur there 9 & 10 Apr 1919.

13.3.17.10.1.2   MONTY, Claire Louise b & bp 13 & 14 Jun 1918, Nashua, NH.
Claire L. Monty (Marie Louise Clara at her baptism) was a travel and insurance agent in Nashua, NH.

13.3.17.10.3.1   MONTY, Infant (male) b 24 Jul 1951, Nashua, NH; d & bur there 24 & 25 Jul 1951.
This child was buried in the family plot in St. Louis de Gonzague Cemetery in Nashua, NH.

13.9.2.4.1.1   MONTY, Ardis Aileen b 31 Sep 1900, St. Croix Falls, WI; d 24 Aug 1954, Minneapolis, MN.
Ardys (sic) Monty was a stenographer in Minneapolis, MN, in 1930. She was divorced though still using her maiden name (US census).

13.9.2.4.1.2   MONTY, Kenneth b 20 Oct 1904, St. Croix Falls, WI; d 18 Apr 1938, Snohomish Co., WA.
Kenneth Monty was living with his mother in St. Croix Falls, WI, in 1930 (US census). I do not know when he left for Washington State. He was buried in Woodlawn Cemetery in Snohomish, WA.

13.9.2.4.4.1   MONTY, Ethel Mona b 13 Oct 1895, Osceola Mills, WI.
Ethel Monty was living with her parents in Sterling, WI, in 1900 and in St. Croix Falls, WI, in 1910 but does not appear with them in 1920 (US censuses).

3.1.3.3.4.1.1   **MONTA, Roy Emery** b 8 Oct 1937, Burlington, VT. He married **Patricia G. LaCasse** (Leroy LaCasse & Elizabeth Fortin) b 2 Mar 1940, Burlington, VT.

3.1.3.3.4.1.2   **MONTA, Nancy Elaine**

3.1.3.3.4.1.3   **MONTA, Emily**

3.3.2.3.4.2.1   **MONTEE, Walter Richard** b 10 Jan 1924, Detroit, MI. He married 26 Jan 1945 **Jean Patricia Millikin** (John Parton Millikin & Leafa Kathryn Mills) b 17 Mar 1925, Bay City, MI.

3.3.2.3.4.2.2   **MONTEE, Margaret M.** b 24 Oct 1926, Detroit, MI; d 11 Mar 1988, Center Line, MI. She married **Clarence Jackson** (Noah Shannon Jackson & Geneva/Genevieve/Jennie Hollifield) b 24 Apr 1914, Laurel, KY; d 20 Dec 1984, Center Line, MI.

3.3.2.3.4.4.1   **MONTEE, Josephine Florence** b 12 Mar 1917, Detroit, MI; d 28 Oct 1993, Seattle, WA. She married 6 Aug 1938, Detroit, MI, **Donald Kenmore Anderson** (Herbert H. Anderson & Nellie Bly Bingham) b 19 Jan 1915, Sebring, OH; d 28 Feb 1988, Edmonds, WA.

3.3.2.3.4.5.1   **MONTEE, June** or **Jane** (twin) b 31 Mar 1922, Detroit, MI; d there 28 Dec 1928.

3.3.2.3.4.5.2   **MONTEE, Jean** (twin) b 31 Mar 1922, Detroit, MI; d there 1928/1929.

3.3.2.3.4.5.3   **MONTEE, Jacqueline** married **John Wright.**

3.3.5.1.2.7.1   **MONTY, Nora Malvina** b & bp 21 Aug 1899 & 1 Jul 1900, Glens Falls & Ticonderoga, NY; d 23 Jan 1988, NY. She married 1922?, **Frank Willard Curtis** (____ Curtis & Emma ____) b 22 Oct 1895, East Chatham, NY; d Nov 1976, NY.
     Nora Monty and her husband had been married for eight years in 1930 (US census, Glens Falls, NY). They were both buried in Elmwood Cemetery in Schaghticoke, NY.

3.3.5.1.2.7.2   **MONTY, Edith Mary** b 18 Sep 1900, Glens Falls, NY; d & bur ? & 13 Feb 1996, Queensbury & Glens Falls, NY. She married 1922? (Catholic revalidation on 1 May 1928, St. Alphonsus Church, Glens Falls, NY) **Frank/Francis Henry Johnson** (Fred/Frederick Johnson & Julia Carter) b 17 Apr 1901, Altona, NY; d & bur 20 & 29 Apr 1982, Glens Falls, NY.
     Edith Mary Monty and her husband had been married for eight years in 1930 (US census, Glens Falls, NY). She was buried in Glens Falls' Bay Street Cemetery while Frank Johnson was buried in St. Alphonsus Cemetery there.

3.3.5.1.2.7.3   **MONTY, Ellen Mary** b Apr 1905, Glens Falls, NY; d there 25 Jul 1905 at the age of 3 months.
     Ellen Mary Monty was buried in Pineview Cemetery in Queensbury, NY.

3.3.5.1.2.7.4   **MONTY, John Henry** b 29 Dec 1906, Glens Falls, NY; d & bur 18 & 21 Oct 1983, South Glens Falls & Queensbury, NY. He married 1928?, Warren Co., NY, **Pauline R. Allen** (____ Allen & Bessie Coon) b 29 Apr 1907, Bolton, NY; d 7 Dec 1979, Glens Falls, NY.
     John H. Monty and his wife had been married for two years in 1930 (US census). He was buried in Pineview Cemetery in Queensbury, NY.

3.3.5.1.6.1.1.   **MONTY, Claude Orlin** b 28 Mar 1909, Benson, VT; d 12 Apr 1983, Rutland, VT. He married **Vera Blackburn** (Ernest Blackburn & Mildred Hatch) b 14 Sep 1918, Whitehall, NY; d 24 Sep 2002, Granville, NY.

Claude Orlin Monty and his wife were long-term residents of Whitehall, NY, and were buried in Greenmount Cemetery there (*Plattsburgh Press Republican*, 16 Apr 1983; *Rutland Herald*, 26 Sep 2002).

3.3.5.1.6.1.2   **MONTY, Marguerite** b 31 May 1915, Orwell, VT; d & bur 20 & 25 Apr 2002, Elizabethtown & Port Henry, NY. She married 1 Sep 1953, Port Henry, NY, **Henry Dean McLaughlin** (Samuel Henry McLaughlin & Fannie Ann McKee) b 30 Oct 1902, Moriah, NY; m (1) 1931, Tupper Lake, NY, Anna Margaret LaBarge (Edward LaBarge & Catherine Ann McCabe); d & bur 28 Feb & 3 Mar 1973, Ticonderoga & Port Henry, NY.

Henry Dean McLaughlin owned and operated a grocery store in Port Henry, NY, when he married Marguerite Monty. They were both buried in the Union Cemetery there (*Plattsburgh Press Republican*, 18 Sep 1953, 2 Mar 1973, and 24 Apr 2002).

3.3.5.1.6.4.1   **MONTY, Altha Genevieve** b 9 Sep 1913, Port Henry, NY; d 16 Jan 1993, Middlebury, VT. She married 11 Oct 1932, Port Henry, NY, **Martin Henry Broughton** (Henry Loren Broughton & Julia Agnes Shea) b 23 Sep 1911, Bridport, VT; d 3 Aug 1988, Middlebury, VT.

Althea Monty and Martin Broughton were buried in St. Mary's Cemetery in Middlebury, VT.

3.3.5.1.6.4.2   **MONTY, Cleo** b 22 Oct 1915, Port Henry, NY; d & bur 13 & 18 Aug 2006, Plattsburgh, NY. She married **William Eugene Goff** (Eugene W. Goff & Sarah Martin) b 25 Sep 1913, Schenectady, NY; d & bur 23 & 26 Jul 1989, Plattsburgh, NY.

William Goff was an officer in the US Customs Service. He and his wife were buried in Riverside Cemetery in Plattsburgh, NY (*Plattsburgh Press Republican*, 24 Jul 1989 and 15 Aug 2006).

3.3.5.1.6.4.3   **MONTY, Gladys L.** b 8 Oct 1919, Port Henry, NY; d 25 Nov 1975, Napa, CA. She married 15 Mar 1947, Livermore, CA, **Clarence Kelley Haney** b 12 Sep 1921, AL; d 16 Aug 1998, Napa, CA.

Gladys Monty was a surgical nurse in the US Veterans Hospital in Livermore, CA, when she married. Her husband, who had served overseas in the Medical Corps during World War II, was also on the staff there (*Ticonderoga Sentinel*, 20 Mar 1947; *Plattsburgh Press Republican*, 28 Nov 1975).

3.3.5.1.6.4.4   **MONTY, Ray R.** b 8 Oct 1922, Port Henry, NY; d & bur there 19 & 23 Sep 1964. He married there 6 Nov 1946 **Virginia Elmore** (Albert G. Elmore & Loretta Gates) b 1 Apr 1927, Westport, NY; m (2) Richard Coonrod; d 6 Feb 1980, Plattsburgh, NY.

Ray Monty was a car mechanic in Port Henry, NY, and was buried in St. Patrick's Cemetery there. Virginia Elmore was a resident of Westport, NY, at her death and was buried in the Lewis Center Cemetery in Lewis, NY (*Plattsburgh Press Republican*, 8 Feb 1980).

3.3.5.1.6.8.1   **MONTY, Walter J.** b 21 May 1920, Port Henry, NY; d & bur 8 & 12 May 1975, Albany & Troy, NY. He married **Charlotte Brazee**.

Walter J. Monty had been a resident of Rensselaer, NY, until a few months before his death. He was buried in St. Mary's Cemetery in Troy, NY (*Times Record*, 9 May 1975).

3.3.5.1.6.8.2   **MONTY, Mary** b 1925?, Essex Co., NY. She married ____ **Potter**.

Mary Monty was a 5-year-old child living with her parents in Moriah, NY, on 1 Apr 1930 (US census). Mrs. Mary Potter was a resident of Pottersville, NY, when her brother Walter J. Monty (3.3.5.1.6.8.1) died in 1975 (*Times Record*, Troy, NY, 9 May 1975).

3.3.5.1.6.8.3   **MONTY, David** b Jan 1929, Essex Co., NY.

David Monty was 1 year and 2 months old on 1 Apr 1930 when he was living with his parents in Moriah, NY (US census). He was a resident of Syracuse, NY, when his brother Walter (3.3.5.1.6.8.1) died in 1975 (*Times Record*, Troy, NY, 9 May 1975).

3.3.5.1.6.8.4 MONTY, Nancy married ____ **Thomas**.

Mrs. Nancy Thomas survived her brother Walter J. Monty (3.3.5.1.6.8.1) (*Times Record*, Troy, NY, 9 May 1975).

3.3.6.1.3.4.1 MONTY, Leon W. b 2 Apr 1908, Taunton, MA; d 10 Aug 1999, Hartford, CT. He married **Anne Andrews** b Aug 1915.

Leon W. Monty predeceased his wife. He had lived in Suffield, CT, since 1945 and was buried there in Woodlawn Cemetery (*Hartford Courant*, 11 Aug 1999).

3.3.6.1.3.4.2 MONTY, Alvin William b 7 Nov 1909, Taunton, MA; d 2 Oct 1978, Attleboro, MA. He married **Dorothea Penesis** (Theodore Penesis & Ethel L. Keating) b 6 Jan 1923, Mansfield, MA; d 9 Apr 1999, Fort Pierce, FL.

Alvin William Monty was a Sergeant in the US Army during World War II. He and his wife were buried in the Massachusetts National Cemetery in Bourne, MA.

3.3.6.1.3.4.3 MONTY, Donald Ralph b 22 May 1911, Taunton, MA; d 28 Apr 1988, St. Petersburg, FL. He married 1939?, **Alice D.** ____ b 1 Oct 1917, Boston, MA; d 18 Mar 1992, St. Petersburg, FL.

Donald R. Monty and his wife had been married for forty-nine years when he died. They had moved from Norton, MA, to St. Petersburg, FL, in 1977 (*St. Petersburg Times*, 1 May 1988 and 24 Mar 1992).

3.3.6.1.3.4.4 MONTY, Austin H. b 12 Feb 1913, Taunton, MA; d 16 Jan 1993, Attleboro, MA. He married 29 Oct 1938, MA, **Nellie L. Whitton** (George D. Whitton & Ellen/Nellie Goodrich) b 31 Jan 1908, Foxboro, MA; d 4 Mar 2000, Boston, MA.

3.3.6.1.3.4.5 MONTY, Louise E. b 28 Jun 1914, Taunton, MA; d Jun 1969, Mansfield, MA.

3.3.6.1.3.4.6 MONTY, Ursula b Oct 1920, Taunton, MA. She married **John Cinelli** (Attilio Cinelli & Livia Begini) b 24 Oct 1919, Mansfield, MA; d 11 Nov 2007, Buzzards Bay, MA.

3.3.6.1.3.6.1 MONTY, Mary L. b Nov 1916, MA. She married 1937, Springfield, MA, **Patrick S. Garvey**.

Mary L. Monty was 3 years and 1 month old on 1 Jan 1920 (US census). She and her husband, a truck driver, lived in Springfield, MA, until at least 1961 (City Directories).

3.9.2.2.15.5.1 MONTY, Bruce b Sep 1951, Woonsocket, RI. He married **Bonnie Coder** (Ronald George Coder & Frances Harter).

Bruce Monty and his wife were living in Level Green, PA, when her mother died in 2006 (*South Hills Record*, Monroeville, PA, 1 May 2006).

3.9.3.3.4.1.1 MONTIE, Charles Elijah b & bp 28 Oct & 7 Nov 1909, Ecorse, MI; bur Bellaire, MI. He married **Mary Sears** b 1912?

I know of Charles Montie's marriage and burial only through Denissen's *Genealogy of the French Families of the Detroit River Region*, II, 859.

3.9.3.3.4.1.2 MONTIE, Gerald Joseph b & bp 22 & 30 Apr 1911, Ecorse, MI. He married (1) around 1932 **Margaret Smith** b 1915?

He married (2) **Lauretta/Rita Martineau** (Leon Martineau & Lillian Grondin) b 7 Mar 1922, St. Ignace, MI; d 18 May 1992, Petosky, MI.

I know of Gerald Montie's wives mainly through Denissen's *Genealogy of the French*

3.9.3.3.4.1.3   **MONTIE, Charlotte Anita** b & bp 3 & 14 Sep 1913, Ecorse, MI. She married **Warren George Selz** (William Selz & Myrtle Sarns) b 1912, Sandusky, OH.

This couple married on 22 Sep 1929 in Fort Wayne, IN, according to Denissen (*Genealogy of the French Families of the Detroit River Region*, II, 861). He is generally well informed, yet I am doubtful. Both Charlotte Montie and the 18-year-old Warren Selz were still single and living with their parents in Wyandotte, MI, in April 1930 (US census).

3.9.3.3.4.1.4   **MONTIE, Elijah John** b & bp 6 & 17 Dec 1916, Ecorse, MI; d 3 Feb 1990, Erie, MI. He married around 1935 **Stella H. Simon** (Charles S. Simon & Mary E. ___) b 5 Aug 1919, OH; d 18 May 1991, Toledo, OH.

3.9.3.3.4.1.5   **MONTIE, Leonard Richard** b 4 Apr 1920, Ecorse, MI; d 12 Apr 2002, Belleville, MI. He married 15 Nov 1941 **Louise Catherine Mantel** (Lewis Charles Mantel & Annie Catherine Gott) b 22 Aug 1923, Detroit, MI.

3.9.3.3.4.1.6   **MONTIE, Lionel Edmund** b 3 Nov 1921, Ecorse, MI; d 4 Sep 1978, Ypsilanti, MI. He married **Louise E. Montabana** (Tony Montabana & Annie ____) b 28 Apr 1917, AL; d 27 Nov 2004, Ann Arbor, MI.

3.9.3.3.4.1.7   **MONTIE, Richard Vernon** b & bp 1 & 24 Mar 1935, Ecorse, MI; d 29 May 1936, New Boston, MI.

This child was buried in St. Stephen's Catholic Cemetery (Mallet Cemetery) in New Boston, MI.

3.9.3.3.4.1.8   **MONTIE, Richard C.** b 29 May 1939, MI; d 14 Sep 1941, MI.

This child was buried in St. Stephen's Catholic Cemetery (Mallet Cemetery) in New Boston, MI.

3.9.3.3.5.2.1   **MONTIE, Helen Isabelle** b & bp 23 Jun & 2 July 1916, Ecorse, MI; d there 4 Feb 1934.

3.9.3.3.5.4.1   **MONTIE, Raymond Edward** b & bp 9 & 30 Jun 1912, Ecorse, MI; d 19 Feb 1991, FL. He married (1) 12 Nov 1936, Ecorse, MI, **Beatrice Davidson** (Emory W. Davidson & Emma Catherine Williams) b 9 Feb 1914; d 25 Mar 1964, Ecorse, MI.

He married (2) **Edna Allener** b 26 Aug 1916; d 3 Jul 1997, Southfield, MI.

3.9.3.3.5.4.2   **MONTIE, Marian** b & d 1922 (Denissen, *Genealogy of the French Families of the Detroit River Region*, II, 859).

3.9.3.3.5.5.1   **MONTIE, Milton Benjamin** b & bp 3 & 9 Sep 1917, Ecorse, MI; d 28 Dec 1986, South Branch, MI.

3.9.3.3.6.3.1   **MONTIE, Cyril Ellsworth** b & bp 9 & 11 Dec 1910, Ecorse, MI; d 7 Dec 1971, Wyandotte, MI. He married **Helen Elizabeth Lamonde** (Earl Lamonde & Ivy Roche) b 28 Feb 1911, Detroit, MI; d 2 Jun 1982, Wyandotte, MI.

3.9.3.3.6.3.2   **MONTIE, Anonymous** (male) b & d 9 Dec 1911, Ecorse, MI.
This child was stillborn.

3.9.3.3.6.3.3   **MONTIE, Emma Josephine** b & bp 29 Oct & 3 Nov 1912, Ecorse, MI; d Oct 1978. She married 14 Jan 1936, Ecorse, MI, **Francis Ouimet** (Joseph Rodrigue Ouimet & Albertina Desmarais) b & bp 11 & 12 May 1907, Montreal, QC; d Aug 1970.

Francis Ouimet (Joseph Francis Albert Rodrigue at his baptism) was named Roderick in the 1930 US census in River Rouge, MI, but Francis at his marriage and at his death.

3.9.3.3.7.2.1 **MONTIE, Mildred Agnes** b & bp 21 & 26 Aug 1917, Ecorse, MI; d 19 Nov 2008, Canton, MI. She married 1940?, Ecorse, MI, **Arthur F. Blank** (Frank Blank & Anna Lalkowski) b 22 Aug 1915, Detroit, MI; d 27 Aug 2003, Canton, MI.

Mildred Agnes Montie and Arthur F. Blank lived in Redford, MI, before retiring in 1997 to a senior residence in Canton, MI. They had been married for sixty-three years when he died in 2003 (*Detroit Free Press*, 21 Nov 2008).

3.9.3.3.7.2.2 **MONTIE, Ruth Alberta** b Feb 1919, Ecorse, MI; d there 2 Jul 1923.
Ruth Montie was 11 months old on 1 Jan 1920 (US census, Ecorse, MI).

3.9.3.3.7.2.3 **MONTIE, Clayton John** b & bp 28 Jan & 11 Feb 1923, Ecorse, MI. He married **Marie Gertrude** _____ b 7 Mar 1923.
Clayton Montie and his wife Marie survived his sister Mildred (3.9.3.3.7.2.1) (*Detroit Free Press*, 21 Nov 2008).

3.9.3.3.7.2.4 **MONTIE, Geraldine Ruth** b & bp 24 Oct & 2 Nov 1924, Ecorse, MI. She married there **Robert Gordon Blair** (Lavelle Blair & Zelma Poindexter) b 1924, Wayne Co., MI.
Mrs. Gerri Blair and her husband Bob survived her sister Mildred A. Montie (3.9.3.3. 7.2.1) (*Detroit Free Press*, 21 Nov 2008).

3.9.3.3.7.2.5 **MONTIE, Delphine Catherine** b & bp 13 & 28 Nov 1927, Ecorse, MI. She married there 5 Sep 1950 **Ralph Bess** (Harry Alexander Bess & Cecelia Drouillard) b 26 Mar 1928, River Rouge, MI.
Mrs. Delphine Bess survived her sister Mildred A. Montie (3.9.3.3.7.2.1) (*Detroit Free Press*, 21 Nov 2008).

3.9.3.3.8.1.1 **MONTIE, Kenneth Francis Liddle** b & bp 5 & 14 May 1911; d 22 Nov 1993, Detroit, MI. He married 1935, Wayne Co., MI, **Marion Carol Blaine** (Joseph Francis Blaine & Estelle _____) b 23 Sep 1913, MI; d 5 Oct 2001, Wyandotte., MI.

3.9.3.3.8.2.1 **MONTIE, Joseph Donald** b & bp 4 & 15 Feb 1914, Ecorse, MI. He married Detroit, MI, **Violet Jeffreys** b 7 Nov 1914; d 20 Jul 1979, Wyandotte, MI.

3.9.3.3.10.1.1 **MONTIE, Joyce** b 1922?, Ecorse, MI.
Joyce Montie was a 7-year-old child living with her parents in Ecorse, MI, on 1 Apr 1930 (US census).

3.9.3.3.10.1.2 **MONTIE, Noreene Elizabeth** b 17 Oct 1923, Ecorse, MI; d & bur 12 Apr & 4 May 1983, Los Angeles & Riverside, CA.
Noreene E. Montie served in the Women's Army Corps during World War II and was buried in the Riverside, CA, National Cemetery.

3.9.3.3.10.1.3 **MONTIE, Gordon Leo** b & bp 7 Dec 1926 & 9 Jan 1927, Ecorse, MI. He married **Lois Ruth Ruediger** (Gerhardt Ruediger & Ida Emilie Krenske) b 28 Jul 1932, Marion, MI; d 3 Jan 2008, Scotia, NY.
Gordon Montie survived his wife (*Albany Times Union*, 5 Jan 2008).

3.9.3.3.10.2.1 **MONTIE, Daniel** b Aug 1928, Ecorse, MI.
Daniel Montie was a 1 year and 7 months old on 1 Apr 1930 when he was living with his parents in Ecorse, MI (US census).

3.9.3.3.10.2.2 **MONTIE, Richard Earl** b & bp 30 Dec 1931 & 24 Jan 1932, Ecorse, MI.

3.9.3.5.5.5.1 **MONTIE, Mary Esther** b 20 Jun 1930, Detroit, MI. She married **Douglas**

Wayne Fournier b 17 Jun 1933.

3.9.3.5.5.11.1   **MONTIE, Michael Edward** b 27 Dec 1941, MI.
Michael Edward Montie survived his brother John (3.9.3.5.5.11.3) (*Washington Post*, 15 Dec 2003).

3.9.3.5.5.11.2   **MONTIE, Thomas Joseph**
Thomas Joseph Montie survived his brother John (3.9.3.5.5.11.3) (*Washington Post*, 15 Dec 2003).

3.9.3.5.5.11.3   **MONTIE, John Charles** b 15 Aug 1944, MI; d 13 Dec 2003, Bowie, MD. He married **Suzanne D. ____** b Feb 1946.
John Charles Montie predeceased his wife (*Washington Post*, 15 Dec 2003).

3.9.3.5.5.11.4   **MONTIE, Catherine Anne/Kitty** b Sep 1946, MI. She married ____ **Martin.**
Mrs. Kitty Montie Martin survived her brother John C. Montie (*Washington Post*, 15 Dec 2003).

3.9.3.5.5.11.5   **MONTIE, Suzanne Mary** married ____ **Simpson.**
Mrs. Suzanne Mary Simpson survived her brother John C. Montie (*Washington Post*, 15 Dec 2003).

3.9.3.5.5.12.1   **MONTIE, Donald Elmer** b 15 Jun 1937, Detroit, MI. He married **Mary Ann Hagney** b 2 Jul 1941.
Mrs. Donald E. Montie's maiden name was Hagney according to Denissen's *Genealogy of the French Families of the Detroit River Region*, II, 860. Other reports say Heaney.

3.9.3.5.5.12.2   **MONTIE, Phyllis Elizabeth** b 8 Jun 1941, Detroit, MI. She married **Stephen Francis Gillich** (Stephen Paul Gillich & ____) b 27 May 1939, MI.

3.9.3.5.5.12.3   **MONTIE, George E.** b 22 Jul 1943, Detroit, MI.

3.9.3.5.5.12.4   **MONTIE, Mary Agnes** b 1947, Detroit, MI. She married **Nickolaus Charles Cole** b 1944.

3.9.3.5.5.12.5   **MONTIE, Jane Frances** b 15 Jun 1951, MI. She married **Thomas Allan Prisby** b Apr 1947.

3.9.3.5.6.2.1   **MONTIE, Thomas** b & bp 26 Dec 1923 & 3 Feb 1924, Ecorse, MI; d 5 Feb 1944, Sicily.
Private Thomas Montie of the 15th Infantry Regiment, 3rd Division, US Army, died in Sicily and was buried in the Sicily-Rome American Cemetery in Nettuno, Lazio, Italy.

3.9.3.5.6.5.1   **MONTIE, Bernadette Margaret** b & bp 9 & 19 Aug 1934, Ecorse, MI.

3.9.3.5.6.5.2   **MONTIE, Robert B.** b 1 Dec 1935, Ecorse, MI. He married **Nancy M. ____** b 9 Mar 1937.

3.9.3.5.6.5.3   **MONTIE, Helen Marie** (Denissen, II, 861).

3.9.3.5.6.5.4   **MONTIE, Louise Catherine** (Denissen, II, 861).

3.9.3.5.6.5.5   **MONTIE, Ruth Ann** (Denissen, II, 861).

3.9.3.5.6.5.6   **MONTIE, Rose Elizabeth** (Denissen, II, 861).

3.9.3.5.6.5.7   **MONTIE, May Charlotte** (Denissen, II, 861).

3.9.3.5.8.1.1   **MONTIE, Gilbert Arthur** b 9 Apr 1921, Ecorse, MI; d 25 Jun 1982, Fayetteville, NC. He married **Dorothy Marguerite Egan** (William Crawford Egan & Beatrice Mary Quick) b 22 Nov 1924, MI; m (1) Robert Gram; d 27 May 1980, Wyandotte, MI.

3.9.3.5.8.1.2   **MONTIE, Marcella Montie** b 1922?, Ecorse, MI.
          Marcella Montie was a 7-year-old child living with her mother in Ecorse, MI, on 1 Apr 1930 (US census).

3.9.3.5.8.1.3   **MONTIE, Robert Levi** b & bp 8 & 14 Sep 1923, Ecorse, MI; d there 1930.
          The year of Robert Levi Monty's death is taken from Denissen's *Genealogy of the French Families of the Detroit River Region*, II, 861. Since the child does not appear with either of his divorced parents in the 1 Apr 1930 US census in Ecorse, MI, he probably died in the first months of that year.

3.9.3.5.8.1.4   **MONTIE, Dolores May** b & bp 3 Jul & 10 Aug 1924, Ecorse, MI; d 28 Aug 1997, Pinellas Co., FL.

3.9.3.6.2.4.1   **MONTIE, Rita M.** b 7 Oct 1918, River Rouge, MI; d there 23 May 1989.

3.9.3.6.2.4.2   **MONTIE, Rose Mary H.** b Oct 1919, River Rouge, MI.
          Rose Mary Montie was a 2-month-old infant living with her parents in River Rouge, MI, on 1 Jan 1920. She was named Rosemary H. in 1930 (US censuses).

3.9.3.6.2.4.3   **MONTIE, George S.** b 16 Nov 1920, River Rouge, MI; d 15 May 1985, Ann Arbor, MI. He married **Dorothy Poisson** (William George Poisson & Alvina Clara Cloutier) b 6 Apr 1927, River Rouge, MI; d 1 Oct 2004, Dearborn, MI.
          George S. Montie was a resident of Dearborn, MI, at his death.

3.9.3.6.2.4.4   **MONTIE, Vincent H.** b 15 Feb 1923, River Rouge, MI; d 1 Jul 1985, Hernando Co., FL.

3.9.3.6.4.3.1   **MONTIE, Faye Mary** b 28 Oct 1920, Ecorse, MI; d 5 Nov 2002, Lincoln Park, MI. She married **Joseph W. Kelly** b 2 Feb 1920; d 7 May 1988, Trenton, MI.

3.9.3.6.4.3.2   **MONTIE, Shirley Marie** b & bp 23 Nov 1923 & 4 Feb 1924, Wayne Co. & Ecorse, MI.
          Shirley Montie was living with her parents in Lincoln Park, MI, in 1930 (US census).

3.9.3.6.4.3.3   **MONTIE, Elizabeth Ann** b & bp 12 Feb & 8 May 1927, Wayne Co. & Ecorse, MI.
          Betty A. Montie was living with her parents in Lincoln Park, IL, in 1930 (US census).

3.9.3.6.4.3.4   **MONTIE, Joan Alice** b 1930, Lincoln Park, MI.
          The year of this child's birth is found in Denissen's *Genealogy of the French Families of the Detroit River Region*, II, 861. She does not appear with her family in the census of 1 Apr 1930 in Lincoln Park, IL, and was probably born after that date.

3.9.3.6.4.3.5   **MONTIE, John Albert** b & bp 24 Nov 1932 & 26 Feb 1933, Lincoln Park & Ecorse, MI.

3.9.3.6.4.4.1   **MONTIE, Laura Elenore** b & bp 28 Sep 1924 & 11 May 1925, Ecorse, MI. She married **Nat/Nathan Van Wye** (Nathan Van Wye & Veda Doty) b 22 Jun 1919, MO; d 14 Dec 1995, Clawson, MI.

Nathan Van Wye was living with his parents in Detroit, MI, in 1930 (US census). As an adult he was known most commonly as Nat VanWye or Vanwye.

3.9.3.6.4.4.2   **MONTIE, Mary Anne** b & bp 1 & 11 Sep 1927, Ecorse, MI.

3.9.3.6.4.4.3   **MONTIE, Theresa Marie** b & bp 6 & 17 Apr 1932, Ecorse, MI.

3.9.3.6.4.4.4   **MONTIE, Walter Albert** (Denissen, *Genealogy of the French Families of the Detroit River Region*, II, 861).

4.3.1.1.4.3.1   **MONTY, Eva May** b 17 Jan 1903, Chazy, NY; d & bur 12 & 16 Aug 1976, Pinellas Park, FL. She married 29 Aug 1922, West Chazy, NY, **Albert David Brown** (George Brown & Rose Abare/Rosanne Hebert) b 6 May 1901, Chazy, NY; d & bur 16 & 19 Mar 1977, St. Petersburg & Pinellas Park, FL.

Albert David Brown was an electrician in Chazy and Plattsburgh, NY, before moving to Pinellas Park, FL, in 1962. He and his wife were buried in Calvary Catholic Cemetery there (1930 US census; *Plattsburgh Press Republican*, 14 Aug 1976 and 17 Mar 1977).

4.3.1.1.4.4.1   **MONTY/MONTE, Harvey** b 5 Jun 1911, Plattsburgh, NY; d Nov 1978, East Greenbush, NY. He married **Edith Malone** (Frank J. Malone & Emma Goyer) b 4 Mar 1914, Troy, NY; d Jul 1986, East Greenbush, NY.

Harvey Monty was living with his parents in Plattsburgh, NY, in 1920. Ten years later, when he was an elevator man in Albany, NY, his surname had become Monte (US censuses). That change became permanent. Harvey Monte and his wife were long-term residents of East Greenbush, NY.

4.3.1.1.4.4.2   **MONTY/MONTE, Marguerite/Margaret** b 1912?, Plattsburgh, NY.

Marguerite Monty was a 7-year-old child living with her parents in Plattsburgh, NY, on 1 Jan 1920. Ten years later, as Margaret Monte, she was in rooms with her brother Harvey in Albany, NY (US censuses).

4.3.1.1.4.6.1   **MONTY, Irene May** b 23 Apr 1910, West Chazy, NY; d & bur 11 & 14 Sep 1991, Plattsburgh, NY. She married (1) 3 Nov 1925, West Chazy, NY, **Joseph Adolph Lucia** (Fred Lucia & Margaret Jarvis) b & bp 19 Sep & 14 Oct 1906, Beekmantown & West Chazy, NY; d 24 Dec 1996, Morrisonville, NY.

She married (2) between 1930 and 1934 **Charles Paul Maloy** (Charles P. Maloy & Fanny _____) b 10 Feb 1874, ME; m (1) Mabel Ina Buker (Thomas M. Buker & Adeline Estes); d & bur 13 & 15 Jun 1943, Plattsburgh & Rouses Point, NY.

She married (3) between 1947 and 1955 **Ernest Bouvia** (Fred Bouvia & Elisa Trudeau/Trudo) b 8 Jun 1901, Altona, NY; m (1) 17 Mar 1925, Plattsburgh, NY, Ida Ducharme (Louis Ducharme & Lena Walker); d there Feb 1968.

The names of Joseph Adolph Lucia and of his parents are taken from his marriage record. At his baptism however he was named Joseph Adolphe Lucier, son of Alfred Lucier and Marguerite Gervais. He was a farmer in Beekmantown, NY, at his marriage and a laborer on his father's farm there in 1930. His wife was not with him (US census).

Charles P. Maloy was a widower in 1930 when he was a Railroad agent in Rouses Point, NY (US census). He soon remarried (a daughter was born in 1934) and lived in Plattsburgh, NY, until his death (*Plattsburgh Press Republican*, 14 Jun 1943). He was buried alongside his first wife in Maple Hill Cemetery in Rouses Point, NY.

Irene Monty was known as Mrs. Irene Maloy/Mrs. Charles Maloy in the pages of the *Plattsburgh Press Republican* until at least 1947. She was Mrs. Ernest Bouvia when her parents observed their 46th wedding anniversary in 1955 (*Plattsburgh Press Republican*, 18 Nov 1955) and until her death. She survived her third husband and was buried in Whispering Maples Mausoleum in Plattsburgh (*Plattsburgh Press Republican*, 13 Sep 1991).

4.3.1.1.4.6.2   **MONTY, Harold J.** b 10 Apr 1913, West Chazy, NY; d & bur 11 & 15

Nov 1976, Plattsburgh & West Chazy, NY. He married 1934, Clinton Co., NY, **Ermina Deno** (Joseph Leon Deno & Prudence Ormsby) b 4 Sep 1914, Chazy, NY; d 8 Feb 1999, Dutchess Co., NY.

Harold J. Monty was buried in St. Joseph's Cemetery in West Chazy, NY (*Plattsburgh Press Republican*, 12 Nov 1976).

4.3.1.1.4.6.3 MONTY, Ralph E. b 1 Apr 1916, West Chazy, NY; d 5 Mar 1970, Plattsburgh, NY.

Ralph E. Monty was buried in St. Joseph's Cemetery in West Chazy, NY (*Plattsburgh Press Republican*, 6 Mar 1970).

4.3.1.1.4.6.4 MONTY, Genevieve M. b 13 May 1922, West Chazy, NY; d 21 Jan 1989, Plattsburgh, NY.

Genevieve M. Monty was buried in St. Peter's Cemetery in Plattsburgh, NY (*Plattsburgh Press Republican*, 23 & 25 Jan 1989).

4.3.1.1.4.7.1 MONTY, Carl E. b 12 Jul 1926, Chazy, NY. He married **Marguerite O'Hara** (John J. O'Hara & Ruth E. Allard) b 7 Aug 1925.

4.3.1.1.6.3.1 MONTY, Marie Geraldine b & bp 11 & 19 Nov 1911, Redford, NY; bur there 26 Aug 1912.

This child was buried in Assumption of Mary Cemetery in Redford, NY.

4.3.1.1.6.3.2 MONTY, Geraldine b 1914, Plattsburgh, NY; d 1959, Morrisonville, NY. She married 21 Jun 1943, Plattsburgh, NY, **Clarence P. Darrah** (Robert Darrah & Lucy Brown) b 1907, NY; d 29 Jul 1963, Plattsburgh, NY.

The dates of Geraldine Monty and Clarence Darrah's births and the date of her death are taken from the inscription on their tombstone in St. Alexander's Cemetery in Morrisonville, NY.

4.3.1.1.6.3.3 MONTY, Doris Viola b & bp 27 Mar & 4 Apr 1915, Plattsburgh, NY; d 6 Sep 1973, Syracuse, NY. She married (1) before 1944 _____ **Price**.

She married (2) 6 Jul 1955 **Phillip E. Fletcher** (Eli C. Fletcher & Josephine H. ____) b 13 Sep 1921, Franklin Co., NY; d 25 Jul 1996, Syracuse, NY.

This woman was named Viola Dorothea at her baptism but was later known as simply Doris or Doris V. Monty, Price, or Fletcher. Mrs. Doris Price was a resident of Ray Brook, NY, when her brother Harold Monty (4.3.1.1.6.3.4) was killed in 1944 and a resident of Saranac Lake, NY, when her father died in 1947. She moved to Syracuse, NY the following year and lived there with her second husband (*Plattsburgh Press Republican*, 16 Dec 1944 and 9 Aug 1947; *Adirondack Daily Enterprise*, 7 Sep 1973). She and Phillip Fletcher were buried near his parents in St. Paul's Cemetery in Franklin, NY.

4.3.1.1.6.3.4 MONTY, Harold E. b 13 Dec 1916, Rochester, NY; d 18 Oct 1944, France.

Sergeant Harold E. Monty was killed in action during World War II and was buried in the Vosges-Lorraine American Cemetery in Epinal, France.

4.3.1.1.6.3.5 MONTY, Kenneth b Aug 1919, Rochester, NY.

Kenneth Monty was a 4-month-old infant living with his parents in Rochester, NY, on 1 Jan 1920. He was not with them in Plattsburgh, NY, in 1930 (US censuses) and may have died before then.

4.3.1.1.6.3.6 MONTY, Floyd W. b 26 Jul 1921, Rochester, NY; d & bur 12 & 14 Aug 2000, Plattsburgh & Keeseville, NY. He married 8 Aug 1953, Keeseville, NY, **Christina A. LaBounty** (George Alexander LaBounty & Merilda Lamountain) b 1923, Ausable, NY.

Floyd Monty was buried in St. John's Cemetery in Keeseville, NY. He predeceased his wife (*Plattsburgh Press Republican*, 20 Aug 2000).

4.3.1.1.6.3.7   MONTY, Isabelle C. b 18 Jul 1923, Rochester, NY; d & bur 22 & 28 Jan 2006, Plattsburgh, NY. She married (1) there 16 Aug 1947 **James C. Quincey/Quincy** (James William Quincey & Rose Agnes Levina Russell) b 10 Oct 1926, Montreal, QC; d Mar 1983, Westlake, LA.

She married (2) 1965? **Kenneth J. Maxwell** (Wyman J. Maxwell & Dorothy Monette) b 26 Jul 1931.

James C. Quincey, arrived in the United States around 1941 to live with his mother and stepfather Edgar Duchesne in Plattsburgh, NY. He enlisted in the US Navy when he was 17 years old and was an Airman First Class in the US Air Force during the Korean War while his wife remained in Plattsburgh (*Plattsburgh Press Republican*, 17 Jun 1944, 25 Jul 1953, and 12 Jul 1954).

Isabelle Monty and Kenneth J. Maxwell had been married for forty years when she died. She predeceased him and was buried in Whispering Maples Mausoleum in Plattsburgh (*Plattsburgh Press Republican*, 27 Jan 2006).

4.3.1.2.1.3.1   MONTAY, Leland/Lee Henry b 2 Feb 1896, South Kaukauna, WI; d 26 Nov 1968, St. Paul, MN.

4.3.1.2.1.3.2   MONTAY, Leatha Helen b 28 Sep 1900, St. Paul, MN; d 29 Apr 1974, Faribault Co., MN. She married 1926? **Eldren L. Kauffmann** (John B. Kauffman & Louisa Beahm) b 24 Sep 1897, Minnesota Lake, MN; d 29 Jan 1966, Faribault Co., MN.

Eldren Kauffman was a bank cashier in Minnesota Lake, MN, in 1930 when he and his wife had been married for about four years (US census).

4.3.1.2.1.8.1   MONTAY, Albert b 16 Feb 1897, Wausau, WI; d 6 Oct 1975, Black River Falls, WI.

Albert Montay was a factory worker in Wausau, WI, in 1920 (US census).

4.3.1.2.1.8.2   MONTAY, Mary b 1906?, Wausau, WI.

Mary Montay was a 13-year-old child living with her widowed mother in Wausau, WI, on 1 Jan 1920 (US census).

4.3.1.1.1.10.1   MONTAY, Leonora, b 1902?, Wausau, WI.

Leonora Montay was an 8-year-old child living with her parents in Wausau, WI, in 1910. She was still a member of her father's household there in 1930 (US censuses).

4.3.1.2.1.10.2   MONTAY, Gilbert L. b 16 Jun 1903, Wausau, WI; d 26 Sep 1996, Battle Creek, MI. He married **Eleanor C. Dressel** (Ernest Dressel & Ulrika Jaeger) b 9 Apr 1911, Wausau, WI; d 30 Apr 1992, Battle Creek, MI,

Gilbert Montay was a watchmaker in Wausau, WI, in 1930 (US census).

4.3.1.2.1.10.3   MONTAY, Oska Lee b 6 Jun 1906, Wausau, WI.

This child presumably died before 1910 since only two of his siblings, Leonora and Gilbert, were still alive in April of that year (US census, Wausau, WI).

4.3.1.2.1.10.4   MONTAY, William H. b 15 Jul 1911, Wausau, WI; d there 4 Jun 1962.

4.3.3.4.6.1.1   MONTEE, Matthew P. b 18 Jul 1920, Iloilo, Panay Island, Philippines. He married (1) 15 Feb 1946, Alamogordo, NM, **Angie Maurine Tremaine** (Arthur B. Tremaine & Angie Lois Lewis) b 21 Jun 1929, Enid, OK; m (2) 31 Nov 1953, Columbus, GA, James Oliver Schiller (Peter John Schiller & Maybel Katherine Anderson); d & bur 13 & 16 Jan 1987, Sauk Rapids, MN.

He married (2) 28 Jul 1953 and divorced 13 Mar 1987, Guadalupe Co, TX, **Charlene Brown** (Harry Charles Brown & Kimmie Myers) b 25 Oct 1932, Liberty Co., KS.

He married (3) 7 Jan 1990, Guadalupe Co., TX, and divorced there 22 Feb 1999 **Mrs. Alice H. Shue** b 1950?

Alice H. Shue was 40 years old when she married Matthew Montee.

4.3.3.4.6.2.1   **MONTEE, Marliss** b 1 Jul 1936, New York, NY; d 31 May 2003, Dover, NJ. She married **Anthony N. Ortiz.**

Anthony Ortiz survived his wife (*Star Ledger*, Newark, NJ, 3 Jun 2003).

4.3.3.4.6.2.2   **MONTEE, Geraldine** b 1939, New York, NY.

4.3.3.4.6.3.1   **MONTEE, Hobart Mansfield** b 27 Jul 1924, Mount Vernon, NY; d & bur 2 & 6 Oct 1994, Newburg & Issue, MD. He married 16 Apr 1947, Forest Glen, MD, **Katharine Marie Duvall** (Edwin Byng Duvall & Katharine Russell) b 21 Jan 1928, MD; d & bur 2 & 6 Feb 2001, Marlton, NJ & Issue, MD.

Hobart Montee founded the Wings Agency in Cherry Hill, NJ, in 1967 and operated it until 1986. He and his wife moved to Newburg, MD, the following year and were buried in Holy Ghost Cemetery in Issue, MD (*Philadelphia Inquirer*, 6 Oct 1994; *Courier Post*, Cherry Hill, NJ, 4 Feb 2001).

4.3.3.4.6.3.2   **MONTEE, Patricia Ellen** b 21 Mar 1926, Mount Vernon, NY. She married **Wilbur Menefee Sartwell** (Edward Richmond Sartwell & Jean Menefee) b 19 Dec 1921, Washington, DC.

4.3.3.4.6.3.3   **MONTEE, Cecil Drake** (twin) b 27 Jan 1943, Palo Alto, CA. She married (1) 8 Apr 1962, Clark Co., NV, **Malcolm Leroy Beaty** (Wendell Leroy Beaty & Elizabeth Marie Childs) b 23 Dec 1940, Los Angeles, CA; d & bur 29 Aug & 1 Sep 1966, Los Angeles & Burbank, CA.

She married (2) 10 Jun 1998, Clark Co., NV, **John Edward/Jack E. Girdlestone** (Jack Girdlestone & Alma Staver) b 19 Oct 1935, Los Angeles, NY; m (1) and divorced 6 May 1980, Los Angeles, CA, Jacquely L. Myers; d 4 Jan 2002, Ramona, CA.

Malcolm L. Beaty, a police officer who died in the line of duty, was buried in Valhalla Cemetery in Burbank, CA (*Los Angeles Times*, 31 Aug 1966).

4.3.3.4.6.3.4   **MONTEE, Tracy Drake** (twin) b 27 Jan 1943, Palo Alto, CA. He married (1) 2 Dec 1967, Santa Barbara Co., CA, and divorced there Jun 1970 **Lynn O. Peffley** b 1947?; m (2) 3 Jan 1981, Los Angeles, CA, Ronald R. Guillen.

He married (2) 9 May 1971, Santa Barbara Co., CA, **Tove E. Knudsen** b 1949?

Lynn O. Peffley was 20 years old and Tove E. Knudsen 22 years old when they married Tracy D. Montee.

4.3.3.4.6.6.1   **MONTEE, Nita P.** b 14 Aug 1928, NY; d 15 Aug 1997, Orem, UT. She married and divorced 15 Sep 1978, Santa Clara Co., CA, **Henry F. Sacra** b Aug 1935; m (2) 7 Oct 1978, Contra Costa Co., CA, Carolyn Sue Parker.

4.3.3.10.2.3.1   **MONTA, Clyde H.** b 13 Aug 1914, Kenosha, WI; d 28 May 1999, King, WI.

4.3.3.10.2.3.2   **MONTA, Shirley** b 1924?, WI.

Shirley Monta was a 6-year-old child living with her parents in West Allis, WI, in 1930 (US census).

4.3.3.10.2.3.3   **MONTA, Chad L.** b Mar 1927, WI.

Chad L. Monta was 3 years and 1 month old on 1 Apr 1930 when he was living with his parents in West Allis, WI (US census).

4.3.3.10.3.1.1   **MONTA, Violet J.** b Oct 1917, West Allis, WI. She married **Darryl/Dar-**

rel B. Nelson (Louis James Nelson & Elizabeth C. _____) b 6 Apr 1917, Caledonia, WI.

Mrs. Violet Nelson and her husband Darryl were residents of Franksville, WI, when her sister Rose (4.3.3.10.3.1.2) died in 2001 (*Milwaukee Journal Sentinel*, 10 Apr 2001).

4.3.3.10.3.1.2   **MONTA, Rose Mae** b 13 May 1919, West Allis, WI; d & bur 8 & 12 Apr 2001, Kingsford, MI & Florence, WI. She married (1) 30 Nov 1937 **Henry O. Eick** (August Frederick Eick & Alvina Rusch) b 20 Aug 1908, WI; d 4 Sep 1981, Iron Mountain, MI.

She married (2) 24 May 1986, Florence, WI, **Carl Phillip Belling** (Charles A. Belling & Katherine Rothbust) b 1 Dec 1913, Milwaukee, WI; d 17 Aug 2000, Kingsford, MI.

Rose Monta was buried in the Commonwealth Cemetery in Florence, WI (*Milwaukee Journal Sentinel*, 10 Apr 2001).

4.3.3.10.3.1.3   **MONTA, June** b 1922?, Milwaukee Co., WI. She married _____ **LeMay**.

June Monta was an 8-year-old child living with her parents in Greenfield, WI, in 1930 (US census). Mrs. June LeMay was a resident of Franklin, WI, when her sister Rose (4.3.3.10. 3.1.2) died in 2001 (*Milwaukee Journal Sentinel*, 10 Apr 2001).

4.3.3.10.3.2.1   **MONTA, Lillian Gladys** b 7 Jun 1918, Kenosha, WI; d there 18 Sep 2000. She married **Arnold Howard Woller** (John Richard Woller & Albertina Amelia Lenz) b 7 Jul 1915, Kenosha Co., WI; d 19 Jul 1983, Bristol, WI.

4.3.3.10.3.2.2   **MONTA, Virtue** (?) b 1921?, Kenosha, WI.

Virtue Monta was a 9-year-old child living with her parents in Kenosha, WI, in 1930 (US census).

4.3.3.10.3.2.3   **MONTA, Joyce** b 1924?, Kenosha, WI.

Joyce Monta was a 6-year-old child living with her parents in Kenosha, WI, in 1930 (US census).

4.3.3.10.3.2.4   **MONTA, George C.** b 13 Jul 1925, Kenosha, WI.

George Monta was living with his parents in Kenosha, WI, in 1930 (US census).

4.3.3.10.3.4.1   **MONTA, Charles A.** b May 1926, WI.

Charles A. Monta was 3 years and 11 months old when he was living with his parents in Tacoma, WA, on 1 Apr 1930 (US census).

4.3.3.10.3.4.2   **MONTA, Fay Marie** b 25 Jul 1927, Tacoma, WA.

4.3.3.10.3.4.3   **MONTA, Clarence Charles** b 12 Nov 1928, Tacoma, WA.

4.3.3.10.3.5.1   **MONTA, James C.** b 20 Aug 1920, WI; d 27 Jul 1992, Los Angeles, CA.

4.3.3.10.3.5.2   **MONTA, Shirley** b 1924?, WI.

Shirley Monta was a 6-year-old child living with her parents in Seattle, WA, in 1930 (US census).

4.3.3.10.3.5.3   **MONTA, Betty** b 1925?, WI.

Betty Monta was a 5-year-old child living with her parents in Seattle, WA, in 1930 (US census).

4.4.1.2.2.2.1   **MONTY, Frances Elizabeth** b Sep 1885, Glens Falls, NY. She married 3 Sep 1906, Sackets Harbor, NY, **Charles Sherman Cobb** (Watts Sherman Cobb & Lillie D. Holstein) b 14 Aug 1882, Albany, NY; d May 1964.

Charles S. Cobb was an architectural designer in Albany, NY, in 1910 (US census). He soon moved to Toronto, Ontario, Canada, where at least three children were born from 1911 through 1919, and only returned to the United States in March 1923 when his stated destination was Pasadena, CA. He was an architect there in 1930 (US census) and was still considered a resident of California when he died (Social Security Death Index). The State of California however has no record of his death.

4.4.1.2.2.2.2   MONTY, John C. b 2 Dec 1887, Glens Falls, NY; d 19 Oct 1945, Gatineau Mills, QC. He married 25 Jun 1918, New York City, NY, **Lulu/Lula Thivierge** (Onesime Joseph Thivierge & Julia Landry) b 23 Mar 1895, Rouses Point, NY.

John C. Monty lived with his parents in Glens Falls and Albany, NY, before moving to Millinocket, ME, in the mid-1910s. He enlisted in the US Army in 1917 and served overseas as a 1st Lieutenant in the 301st and 326th Infantry Regiments until his discharge in June 1919. He returned to Millinocket and was working in a paper mill there in 1920. Ten years later, he was a newsprint executive in Queens, NY (US censuses).

4.4.1.2.2.2.3   MONTY, Charles b 1890?, Glens Falls, NY.

Charles Montee (sic) was a 2-year-old child living with his parents in Glens Falls, NY, in 1892. He was no longer alive in 1900 (US and state censuses).

4.4.1.2.2.2.4   MONTY, Catherine b Feb 1898, Albany, NY.

Catherine Monty was living with her parents in Albany, NY, in 1900 and in the household of her sister Frances Elizabeth (4.4.1.2.2.2.1) and brother-in-law Charles S. Cobb in 1910 (US censuses).

4.4.1.2.9.1.1   MONTY, Daniel b 1896, Sandy Hill (Hudson Falls), NY; d there 1898.

4.4.1.2.9.1.2   MONTY, Mary Kellogg (twin) b 28 Apr 1898, Hudson Falls, NY; d 21 Oct 1991. She married 28 Jun 1930 **Ralph Weiser Harter** (Robert Harter & Harriet Teresta Weiser) b 19 Sep 1893, Millheim, PA; d 1 Nov 1989.

4.4.1.2.9.1.3   MONTY, Louise Parry (twin) b 28 Apr 1898, Hudson Falls, NY; d 2 Nov 1962.

Louise P. Monty was buried in the Union Cemetery in Fort Edward, NY

4.4.1.2.9.1 4   MONTY, Grace Elizabeth b 5 Aug 1900, Hudson Falls, NY; d 25 Aug 1946.

Grace Elizabeth Monty was buried in the Union Cemetery in Fort Edward, NY.

4.4.1.2.9.1.5   MONTY, Katherine Miriam b 19 Jan 1907, Hudson Falls, NY; d 19 Jan 1954. She married 1935 **John Berrigan** (_____ Berrigan & Bridget _____) b 13 Jul 1905, NY.

I know of this couple only through Betty Ramsey's *Monty-Montee History*, II, 655.

4.4.1.2.12.6.1   MONTY, Ethel b 27 Dec 1902, Fargo, ND; d 8 Mar 1983, Pentland, MI. She married (1) 1922? **John Jacob Sharick** (John W. Sharick & Julia Almira Alexander) b 15 Apr 1893, Mount Morris, MI; d Jan 1968, Flint, MI.

She married (2) before 1972 **Earl Doyle** (James Doyle & Blanche Begrow) b 3 Apr 1903, Boyne, MI; d 5 Sep 1978, Newberry, MI.

Ethel Monty and John J. Sharick had been married for eight years on 1 Apr 1930 (US census, Genesee, MI). She was still named Mrs. Ethel Sharick in the 12 Dec 1970 obituary of her brother George Monty (4.4.1.2.12.6.6) but "Mrs. Earl (Ethel) Doyle" in the 24 Sep 1972 obituary of her mother Lulu Lenora Helms, both in the Flint, MI, *Journal*.

4.4.1.2.12.6.2   MONTY, Margaret Edith b 25 Jul 1904, Fargo, ND; d & bur 23 & 26 Jul 1989, Flint, MI. She married (1) 1922? **Leon Pearl Vanatten** (Olin Stephen Vanatten & Mary Grace Loveless) b 17 Dec 1896, Vienna, MI; d 3 Sep 1932, Thetford, MI.

She married (2) July 1935, **Lester McLarty** (Robert McLarty & Anna _____) b 19 Dec 1899, Ontario, Canada; d Oct 1968, Flint, MI.

Margaret Monty and Leon P. Vanatten had been married for eight years in 1930 (US census, Flint, MI). Mrs. Lester McLarty was a resident of Clio, MI, in 1970 and 1972 when her brother George (4.4.1.2.12.6.6) and her mother died (*Flint Journal*, 12 Dec 1970 and 24 Sep 1972).

4.4.1.2.12.6.3   MONTY, William b 18 Mar 1907, Charlevoix, MI; d 27 Apr 1973, Sandusky, MI.

William Monty was a resident of Sanilac, MI, at his death.

4.4.1.2.12.6.4   MONTY, Lulu Jennie b 15 Dec 1909, Marion Twp, MI; d & bur 17 & 22 Jan 1985, Manatee Co., FL. She married 1 Jun 1926, Grand Blanc, MI, **Clement William McGrath** (William Patrick McGrath & Lois Grace Van Alstine) b 30 Aug 1901, Monitor Twp, MI; d 2 Sep 1972, Manatee Co., FL.

Lulu Monty and Clement McGrath were buried in Mansion Memorial Park in Ellenton, FL.

4.4.1.2.12.6.5   MONTY, Mary Martha b 25 Jul 1912, Marion Twp, MI; d 26 Sep 1994, Cheboygan, MI. She married (1) **Vernon R. Renico** (William Henry Renico & Madeline ____) b 16 Sep 1907, WA; d 19 Jul 1979, Traverse City, MI.

She married (2) **Edwin J. Parker** (Dewitt Clinton Parker & Mildred May Pixley) b 30 Mar 1912, Greenville, MI; m (1) Edna Matilda Bixby (Leon Bixby & Clara Peterson); d 6 Nov 2001, Traverse City, MI.

4.4.1.2.12.6.6   MONTY, George Harper b 25 Dec 1914, Charlevoix, MI; d & bur 11 & 14 Dec 1970, Flint & Mount Morris, MI. He married 26 Jun 1937 **Margaret Soboleski** (Anthony Soboleski & Blanche Golombeski) b 14 Jul 1918, Omer, MI; d 12 Jan 2000, Linden, MI.

George H. Monty and his wife were buried in Flint Memorial Park in Mount Morris, MI (*Flint Journal*, 12 Dec 1970 and 14 Jan 2000).

4.4.1.2.12.6.7   MONTY, Earl C. b 27 Aug 1917, Charlevoix, MI; d & bur 6 & 8 May 1993, Flint & Mount Morris, MI.

Earl C. Monty lived most of his life in the Clio-Flushing area of Michigan and was buried in Flint Memorial Park in Mount Morris, MI (*Flint Journal*, 7 May 1993).

4.4.1.4.4.1.1   MONTY, William Webb b 27 Apr 1907, Hamilton, MT; d 28 Mar 1977, Tenerife, Canary Islands. He married **Mary** ____ b 8 Mar 1911; d 28 Mar 1977, Tenerife, Canary Islands.

William Monty and his wife Mary were killed at the Tenerife airport in the Canary Islands when a KLM 747 airliner collided on take-off with the Pan American 747 airliner in which they were traveling. They were residents of Aptos, CA (*Oakland Tribune*, 29 Mar 1977).

4.4.1.4.4.1.2   MONTY, Margaret b 13 Jul 1917, MT; d 8 Mar 2001, Long Beach, CA. She married Nov 1940 **Charles H. Arnold** (Jesse H. Arnold & Louise M. ____) b 1917, Burlington, IA.

Margaret Monty was a resident of Los Alamitos, CA, at her death.

4.4.2.1.5.7.1   MONTY, Maynard John b 25 Dec 1905, Plattsburgh, NY; d Aug 1970, Burlington, VT. He married 12 Jun 1945 **Beatrice Louise Dumas** (Edward V. Dumas & Sophia Adeline Vasseur) b 18 Feb 1920, Burlington, VT; d there 19 Aug 1993.

Maynard J. Monty enlisted in the US Army when he was 19 years old. He was a sergeant stationed in Florida when the World War II began and later served in South America, Egypt, India, and China where he was awarded the Legion of Merit (*Syracuse Herald Journal*, 3 Feb 1945).

4.4.2.1.5.7.2   MONTY, Clara Helen b 5 Nov 1907, Plattsburgh, NY; d 13 Apr 2008,

Minoa, NY. She married 23 Mar 1925 **John Haas** (John Haas & Katherine ____) b 12 Mar 1905, Austria-Hungary; d 2 Jan 1984, Erieville, NY.

Clara Monty and John Haas were buried in the Erieville, NY, Cemetery.

4.4.2.1.5.7.3   MONTY, Mildred b 1912?, Plattsburgh, NY; d & bur 8 & 12 Dec 1951, Syracuse & Plattsburgh, NY, at the age of 39. She married ____ **Brown**.

Mrs. Mildred Brown was living with her mother in Syracuse, NY, in 1945 (*Syracuse Herald Journal*, 3 Feb 1945). She was named "Miss Mildred Monty" though at her death. She was buried in Riverside Cemetery in Plattsburgh, NY (*Plattsburgh Press Republican*, 10 Dec 1951).

4.4.2.1.5.10.1   MONTY, Elizabeth E. b 1911?, Clinton Co., NY. She married **Louis Van Wormer** (Charles Van Wormer & Mary ____) b 15 Sep 1903, NY; m (1) 1925? Anna ____ ; d Oct 1981, Schenectady, NY.

Elizabeth E. Monty was an 8-year-old child living with her parents in Duanesburg, NY, on 1 Jan 1920 (US census).

Louis Van Wormer and his first wife Anna had been married for five years in 1930 when he was a compositor in a printing shop in Schenectady, NY (US census).

4.4.2.1.5.10.2   MONTY, Frances H. b 7 Apr 1920, Clinton Co., NY; d 19 May 1997, Joshua Tree, CA. She married (1) **Harold Johnson**.

She married (2) **Harold Herbert Ferris** (Willard Charles Ferris & Berintha Herbert) b 2 Aug 1898, Steuben Co., NY; m (1) 1918? Bessie Elizabeth ____ ; d 13 Feb 1976, Yucca Valley, CA.

Harold Herbert Ferris was a farmer employed by his father in Angelica, NY, when he signed on 12 Sep 1918 his World War I Draft Registration card. His wife Mrs. Bessie Elizabeth Ferris was his next of kin.

4.4.2.1.5.10.3   MONTY, Etta Mae married (1) **Harold Hopkins** b 2 Dec 1919, NY; d 14 Feb 1994, Schenectady, NY.

She married (2) **George C. Lofstedt** (Carl Lofsted & Elsie ____) b 9 Oct 1911, NY; d 29 Dec 2007, Schenectady, NY.

Etta Mae Monty and her husband George Lofstedt were residents of Schenectady, NY, when her sister Janet (4.4.2.1.5.10.4) died in 2005 (*Albany Times Union*, 28 Sep 2005).

4.4.2.1.5.10.4   MONTY, Janet G. b 16 Jan 1934, Schenectady, NY; d & bur 27 Sep & 1 Oct 2005, Glenville & Schenectady, NY. She married 1952? **Robert Becker** d 1984.

Janet Monty and her husband had been married for thirty-two years when he died in 1984. She was buried in Parkview Cemetery in Schenectady, NY (*Albany Times Union*, 28 Sep 2005).

4.4.2.1.5.10.5   MONTY, William J. b 30 May 1935, Schenectady, NY. He married **Beverly J.** ____ b 29 Oct 1939.

William Monty and his wife Beverly were residents of Schenectady, NY, when his sister Janet (4.4.2.1.5.10.4) died in 2005 (*Albany Times Union*, 28 Sep 2005).

4.4.2.1.5.10.6   MONTY, Edward married **Margaret** ____ .

Edward Monty and his wife Margaret were residents of Schenectady, NY, when his sister Janet (4.4.2.1.5.10.4) died in 2005 (*Albany Times Union*, 28 Sep 2005).

4.4.2.1.11.2.1   MONTY, Roswell L. b 3 Aug 1916, Cadyville, NY; d 9 Apr 1985, Plattsburgh, NY. He married **Mae E. Bomyea** (Charles Orman Bomyea & Ella Mae Cobb) b 31 Oct 1917, Saranac Lake, NY; d 17 Jul 1994, Burlington, VT.

Roswell L. Monty, an operating engineer engaged in construction work, was a lifelong resident of Clinton Co., NY(*Plattsburgh Press Republican*, 10 Apr 1985).

4.4.2.1.11.2.2   **MONTY, Ralph W.** b 13 Dec 1917, Cadyville, NY; d 3 Aug 1988, Niagara Falls, NY. He married **Doris Collins** (Edward R. Collins & Charlotte Tallman).

Ralph W. Monty, a Lieutenant Colonel (ret.) in the United States Air Force, was buried in the Arlington, VA, National Cemetery. His wife had predeceased him (*Plattsburgh Press Republican*, 5 Aug 1988).

4.4.2.1.11.2.3   **MONTY, Louanna May** b 2 Jan 1922, Cadyville, NY; d there 7 Jan 1922.

4.4.3.6.2.2.1   **MONTY, James K.** b 8 Apr 1926, Whitehall, NY; d there 1 Aug 1989.

4.4.3.6.2.2.2   **MONTY, Edward K.** b 11 Apr 1927, Whitehall, NY; d Mar 1975. He married 21 Jun 1952 **Helen Louise Juckett** (Clayton Daniel Juckett & Mildred Eleanor Willis) b Jan 1934, Whitehall, NY; m (2) Harry John Mulhall (Harry John Mulhall & Gertrude ____).

4.4.7.3.2.2.1   **MONTEE, Marion** b 1906?, Pittsburg, KS.

Marion Montee was a 4-year-old child living with his parents in Pittsburg, KS, in 1910. He was a garage mechanic in Galena, KS, in 1930 (US censuses)

4.4.7.3.2.2.2   **MONTEE, Edward** b 1908?, Pittsburg, KS.

Edward Montee was a 2-year-old child living with his parents in Pittsburg, KS, in 1910. He was a garage mechanic in Galena, KS, in 1930 (US censuses)

4.4.7.3.2.2.3   **MONTEE, Sylvia C.** b 12 Apr 1911, Pittsburg, KS; d there 15 Feb 1913.

4.4.7.3.2.2.4   **MONTEE, Virgil Ray** b 5 Aug 1913, Pittsburg, KS; d 25 Jul 1988, Joplin, MO. He married there 23 Dec 1933 and divorced Jan 1954, Columbus, MO, **Alline Genevieve Overstreet** (James William Overstreet & Mollie C. ____) b 14 Oct 1915, Galena, KS; d 24 Oct 1998, Cherokee, KS.

Virgil R. Montee was buried in Burkhart Cemetery in Racine, MO, while Mrs. Alline G. Montee was buried in Oak Hill Cemetery in Galena, KS.

4.4.7.3.2.2.5   **MONTEE, Bert Vance** b 25 Sep 1915, KS; d Feb 1979, MO.

Bert Vance Montee was buried in the Mount Vernon, MO, Cemetery.

4.4.7.3.2.2.6   **MONTEE, Roy Morris** b 11 Aug 1918, KS; d 9 Jul 1980, Galena, KS.

Roy M. Montee was buried in Hill Crest Cemetery in Galena, KS.

4.4.7.3.2.2.7   **MONTEE, Theda M.** b 1921?, KS.

Theda M. Montee was a 9-year-old child living in her mother's household in Galena, KS, in 1930 (US census).

4.4.7.3.2.3.1   **MONTEE, Fritz L.** b 9 Apr 1910, Gypsum, KS; d 9 Oct 1947.

Fritz L. Montee was a farm laborer living with his parents in Gypsum, KS, in 1930 (US census). He was a resident of Missouri and still single when he enlisted as a private in the US Army on 4 Aug 1942 (World War II Army Enlistment Records). He was buried in the Gypsum City Cemetery.

4.4.7.3.2.3.2   **MONTEE, Claudine Marie** b 3 Jul 1912, Gypsum, KS; d 7 Jun 2000, Igo, CA. She married 16 Dec 1930, Los Angeles, CA, **Walter Earl Preston** (Walter Arthur Preston & Marian Christina Schnepf) b 18 Jul 1897, Grinell, IA; d 8 Feb 1967, Huntington Park, CA.

4.4.7.3.2.3.3   **MONTEE, Elmer John** b 22 Sep 1914, Gypsum, KS; d 8 Jun 1992. He married 8 Sep 1944, Salina KS, **Alice Marjorie Leonard** (Martin Leonard & Hattie Nelson) b there 2 Sep 1922.

Elmer John Montee was buried in the Gypsum, KS, City Cemetery.

4.4.7.3.2.3.4   **MONTEE, Bernice** b 18 Feb 1916, Gypsum, KS; d 10 Jan 1978, Salina, KS. She married (1) and divorced Jul 1951, Salina, KS, **Delmar E. Cooper** (Delmar E. Cooper & Alma E. _____) b 3 Jul 1918, Winfield, KS; m (2) Ruby _____; d & bur ? & 26 Nov 1973, Kansas City, KS.

She married (2) **Howard Lettman**.

Delmar E. Cooper was a butcher in Salina KS, before moving to Kansas City, KS, in 1954. He and his second wife were residents there at his death. He was buried in Maple Hill Cemetery there (*Salina Journal*, 27 Nov 1973).

4.4.7.3.2.10.1   **MONTEE, Kathryn I.** b 23 Feb 1924, Gypsum, KS; d 2 Aug 1994, Bakersfield, CA. She married 1942? **Clarence Robert Taylor** (Earl Raymond Taylor & Elsie _____) b 6 Jul 1915, Roswell, NM; d 12 Mar 1997, Dublin, CA.

Clarence Taylor had lived in Bakersfield, CA, for twenty-seven years before moving to Dublin, CA, six months prior to his death (*Contra Costa Times*, Walnut Creek, CA, 15 Mar 1997). He and his wife were buried in Bakersfield's Greenlawn Memorial Park.

4.4.7.3.7.1.1   **MONTEE, Charles Elmer** b 2 Jul 1919, Pittsburg, KS; d & bur 11 & 14 Aug 2004, Plano, TX & Cherokee, KS. He married (1) 19 Sep 1942, Webb City, MO, **Eva Louise Richards**.

He was divorced when he married (2) 18 May 1968 **Pearl E. Black**.

He married (3) **June Delores Mullikin** (William Arthur Mullikin & Lois Marie Allison) b 21 Jun 1926, Crawford Co., KS; m (1) 16 Jan 1946, Pittsburg, KS, Doyle Stewart; m (3) there 8 Mar 1975, John D. Bennett; d there 17 Feb 2005.

He was divorced when he married (4) **Deanne Scholes**.

Charles E. Montee was buried in Cherokee Cemetery in Cherokee, KS (*Pittsburgh Morning Sun*, 13 Aug 2004). I know of his multiple marriages and divorces mainly through Betty Ramsey's *Monty-Montee History*, p. 268.

4.4.7.3.7.1.2   **MONTEE, Jean Isabelle** b 8 Feb 1921, Pittsburg, KS; d 14 Jan 1947, Osawatomie, KS.

Jean Isabelle Montee was buried in Cherokee Cemetery in Cherokee, KS.

4.4.7.3.7.1.3   **MONTEE, Robert Leslie** b 1923.

Robert Leslie Montee died in childhood according to Betty Ramsey's *Monty-Montee History* p. 269. He is not listed with his family in the 1930 US census.

4.4.7.3.7.1.4   **MONTEE, Donald Ivan** b 12 Nov 1925, Mindenmines, MO; d 14 Jul 1978, St. Paul, MN. He married 16 Sep 1950 **Theresa K. Bogner** (Joseph M. Bogner & Catherine Dengel) b 3 Sep 1930, Lefor, ND; m (2) 26 Jun 1974, St. Paul, MN, Morris Glenn Nelson (Nils B. Nelson & Gina Hage).

Donald I. Montee was buried in Cherokee Cemetery in Cherokee, KS.

4.4.7.3.7.3.1   **MONTEE, Betty Jean** b 15 Sep 1924, Midway, KS; d 22 Oct 1966, KS. She married (1) 8 Oct 1943 and divorced Oct 1946 **Robert Samuel Beggs** (James Samuel Beggs & Lola Edna Cruickshank) b 27 Apr 1923, Hallowell, KS; m (2) 15 Apr 1971, Yuma, AZ, Ruby Doris Weaver (L. A. Weaver & Beulah Smith); d 13 Apr 1999, Joplin, MO.

She married (2) 14 Mar 1950 and divorced Oct 1965 **Albert J. Tilly** b 30 Aug 1926; m (2) Mrs. Beatrice Tucker; d & bur 22 & 25 Jun 1986, Wichita, KS.

Robert S. Beggs and his second wife were buried in McKee Cemetery in Hallowell, KS.

I know of Betty Jean Montee's second marriage and subsequent divorce through Betty Ramsey's *Monty-Montee History*, p. 272. In her siblings' obituaries in the 1990s and 2000s she was named either Mrs. Betty Beggs or Mrs. Betty Tilly.

4.4.7.3.7.3.2   **MONTEE, Doris Eleanor** b 4 Jan 1926, Midway, KS; d & bur 3 & 6 Apr

2004, El Dorado, KS. She married 28 Oct 1945, Girard, KS, **George Eugene Holloway** (Eugene J. Holloway & Anna ____) b 9 Jun 1923, Pittsburg, KS.

Doris Eleanor Montee predeceased her husband. She was buried in Sunset Lawns Cemetery in El Dorado, KS (*Pittsburg Morning Sun*, 5 Apr 2004).

4.4.7.3.7.3.3   **MONTEE, Albert Clinton** b 5 Dec 1927, MO; d Nov 1983, Kansas City, MO. He married 16 May 1948 **Jimma Lee Ward** (Clyde Ward & Annis N. Osborn) b 22 Aug 1929, Cherokee, KS.

4.4.7.3.7.3.4   **MONTEE, Laura Lucille** b 16 Aug 1929, West Mineral, KS; d & bur 9 & 14 Jan 2006, Overland Park & Cherokee, KS. She married 22 Feb 1969, Kansas City, MO, **Ezra Stout Church** (Ezra Bliss Church & Lula Gertrude Stout) b 21 Apr 1922, Redmond, KS; m (1) 30 Oct 1943, Kansas City, KS, Arlene Ruth Pettit (Frederick Pettit & O'Dessie Stevens); d & bur 17 & 20 Jun 2001, Edwardsville & Shawnee Mission, KS.

Laura Montee was buried in Cherokee Cemetery in Cherokee, KS, while Ezra Church was buried in Memory Gardens Cemetery in Shawnee Mission, KS, (*Kansas City Star*, 13 Jan 2006 and 19 Jun 2001).

4.4.7.3.7.3.5   **MONTEE, Kenneth Leroy** b 30 Jul 1931, West Mineral, KS; d & bur 3 & 7 Feb 2004, Pittsburg & Cherokee, KS. He married 15 Jun 1990, Cherokee, KS, **Maxine Goodpasture** (Frank Goodpasture & Mae Bergman) b there 14 Nov 1919; d & bur 25 & 28 Oct 2005, Pittsburg & Cherokee, KS.

Kenneth L. Montee and his wife were buried in Cherokee Cemetery in Cherokee, KS (*Parsons Sun*, 6 Feb 2004 and 28 Oct 2005).

4.4.7.3.7.3.6   **MONTEE, Joan Lee** b 20 Sep 1934, West Mineral, KS. She married 5 Apr 1953, Chicopee, KS, **James Francis Haefling** (Marion Haefling & Mary ____) b 11 Apr 1930, Strong City, KS; d 27 Dec 2002, Richardson, TX.

Joan Montee survived her husband and was a resident of Richardson, TX, when her sister Laura Lucille (4.4.7.3.7.3.4) died in 2006 (*Kansas City Star*, 13 Jan 2006).

4.4.7.3.7.3.7   **MONTEE, Peggy Dean** b 27 Apr 1938, Cherokee, KS; d & bur 3 & 7 Jun 2004, Kansas City, MO & Lenexa, KS. She married (1) 5 Apr 1960, Kansas City, MO, **Norman Lee Card**.

She was divorced when she married (2) Aug 1973, **Herbert J. Kaeberle** (John A. Kaeberle & Rose G. Marks) b Aug 1924, Topeka, KS.

Peggy Montee, a resident of Olathe, KS, predeceased her second husband. She was buried in Resurrection Cemetery in Lenexa, KS (*Pittsburg Morning Sun*, 5 Jun 2004).

4.4.7.3.7.3.8   **MONTEE, Patricia Mae** b 11 Nov 1939, Pittsburg, KS. She married 15 Aug 1959, KS, **John E. Favero**.

Mrs. Pat Favero was a resident of Prairie Village, KS, when her sister Laura Lucille (4.4.7.3.7.3.4) died in 2006 (*Kansas City Star*, 13 Jan 2006).

4.4.7.3.7.3.9   **MONTEE, Barbara Ann** b 28 Jun 1941, Cherokee, KS. She married there 4 Sep 1960, **Roy Humble** b 2 Feb 1942.

Mrs. Barbara Humble was a resident of Cherokee, KS, when her sister Laura Lucille (4.4.7.3.7.3.4) died in 2006 (*Kansas City Star*, 13 Jan 2006).

4.4.7.3.7.3.10   **MONTEE, Lana Charlene** b 27 Jan 1943, Cherokee, KS. She married 9 Nov 1963, Kansas City, MO, **John Loftus**.

Mrs. Lana Loftus was a resident of Overland Park, KS, when her sister Laura Lucille (4.4.7.3.7.3.4) died in 2006 (*Kansas City Star*, 13 Jan 2006).

4.4.7.3.7.3.11   **MONTEE, Judy Eileen** b 27 Jun 1945, Cherokee, KS. She married 22 Jun 1968, Pittsburg, KS, **John Leo Klodt** (____ Klodt & ____ Long) b 18 Jan 1945, Los Angeles, CA; d 6 Mar 2007, Brinkley, AR.

Mrs. Judy Klodt was a resident of Pittsburg, KS, when her sister Laura Lucille (4.4.7.3.7.3.4) died in 2006 (*Kansas City Star*, 13 Jan 2006).

4.4.7.3.7.3.12 **MONTEE, Nancy Carol** b 31 Dec 1946, Pittsburg, KS. She married 2 Sep 1967, **Larry Joseph Simpson** b 15 Mar 1944.

Mrs. Nancy Simpson was a resident of Olathe, KS, when her sister Laura Lucille (4.4.7.3.7.3.4) died in 2006 (*Kansas City Star*, 13 Jan 2006).

4.4.7.3.7.5.1 **MONTEE, Mark Stuart** b 2 Jan 1927, KS; d 4 May 1948, O'Fallon, IL.

Mark S. Montee, Jr. was buried in College Hill Cemetery in Lebanon, IL.

4.4.7.3.7.5.2 **MONTEE, Norman Curtis** b 11 Aug 1933, O'Fallon, IL. He married **Karen L. Boydstun** (Frederick Howell Boydstun & Lucille Bruns) b 1 Apr 1941.

4.4.7.3.7.5.3 **MONTEE, James Malvern** b 21 Nov 1935, O'Fallon, IL; d there 28 Dec 1992.

James M. Montee was buried in College Hill Cemetery in Lebanon., IL.

4.4.7.3.7.6.1 **MONTEE, Lee** (twin) b & d 18 May 1931, O'Fallon, IL.

This infant was buried in College Hill Cemetery in Lebanon, IL.

4.4.7.3.7.6.2 **MONTEE, Dee** (twin) b & d 18 May 1931, O'Fallon, IL.

This infant was buried in College Hill Cemetery in Lebanon, IL.

4.4.7.3.7.6.3 **MONTEE, Robert Frank** b 21 Apr 1932, O'Fallon, IL. He married 18 Nov 1951, Pittsburg, KS, **Barbara J. Phillips** (Maurice Phillips & Audrey Butler) b there 14 Nov 1934; d there 25 Oct 2005.

Robert Frank Montee survived his wife (*Parsons Sun*, Parsons, KS, 26 Oct 2005).

4.4.7.3.7.6.4 **MONTEE, Dorothy Anna** b 1 Jan 1935, O'Fallon, IL.

4.4.7.3.7.6.5 **MONTEE, Joyce Elaine** b 10 Nov 1936, O'Fallon, IL.

4.4.7.3.11.1.1 **MONTEE, Norman Lucas** b 28 May 1931, Kansas City, MO; d 8 Nov 2004, Aurora, CO. He married 1952 **Barbara Ann Houtz** b 24 Sep 1933, Odin, IL; d 7 Nov 2004, Aurora, CO.

Norman Montee and his wife lived most of their lives in La Puente and Capistrano Beach, CA, and were buried together in the Pacific View Memorial Park in Corona Del Mar, CA. They had moved to Aurora, CO, just a few months before they died following a car accident. They had been married for fifty-two years (*Rocky Mountain News*, Denver, CO, 21 Nov 2004).

4.4.7.3.11.1.2 **MONTEE, Gerald Keith** b 9 Oct 1938, Denver, CO. He married 17 Aug 1957, Garden Grove, CA, **Maxine Heintz** (R. H. Heintz & Florence L. Schugard) b 3 Jan 1938, Los Angeles Co., CA.

4.4.7.3.11.2.1 **MONTEE, Bonnie Jean** b 12 Nov 1930.

I know of this woman only through Betty Ramsey's *Monty-Montee History*, p. 279.

4.4.7.3.11.2.2 **MONTEE, Robert Edward** b 9 Jan 1937. He married ____ **Fulton**.

This couple's children were born in Riverside Co., CA.

4.4.7.3.11.3.1 **MONTEE, Edythe Marlene** married (1) ____ **O'Brien**.

She married (2) 11 Jul 1958, Clark Co., NV, **Ernest Nathaniel Campbell**.

I know nothing about Edythe Montee's first marriage save that she married Ernest

Campbell in 1958 under the name of Edythe Marlene O'Brien. A later record shows that Edythe M. Campbell and Ernest N. Campbell, both California residents, were married on 11 Jul 1995 in Clark Co., NV. A divorce may have separated the two marriages, which would explain the reference to a third husband, Mr. Peterson, in Betty Ramsey's *Monty-Montee History*, p. 279. I know nothing about this person. In any event, Mrs. Edythe Campbell was living in National City, CA, when her mother died in 2005 (*Chanute Tribune*, 25 Mar 2005).

4.4.7.3.11.3.2   **MONTEE, Carla Carson** b 5 Nov 1945, San Diego, CA. She married (1) there 30 Jan 1965 and divorced there Oct 1973 **Robert L. Fritsch** b Feb 1943; m (2) 12 Feb 1983, San Diego, CA, Nancy M. Henrique, divorced wife of Richard R. Motta.

She married 14 Dec 1974, San Diego, CA, **Carl F. Bock** b 1942?; m (1) 1965 and divorced Jun 1974, San Diego, CA, Eleanor J. MacSorley.

Carl F. Bock was 32 years old when he married Carla Montee in 1974. She was living in La Mesa, CA, when her mother died in 2005 (*Chanute Tribune*, 25 Mar 2005).

4.4.7.5.2.6.1   **MONTEE, Donald Lee** b 5 May 1921, Wyandot Co., OH; d 4 Sep 1987, Marion, OH. He married **Betty Bonebrake** b 8 Sep 1918, Bucyrus, OH; m (2) Peter Yost; d 24 Dec 2008, Marion, OH.

4.4.7.5.2.7.1   **MONTEE, Jane B.** b 8 Jan 1917, Waukegan, IL; d 9 Apr 1975, San Bernardino Co., CA. She married 4 Feb 1939, Waukegan, IL, **Ralph E. Fox** b 15 Mar 1910, WI; d 25 Mar 1975, Riverside Co., CA.

Jane B. Montee and her husband were both residents of Calimesa, CA, at their deaths.

4.4.7.5.2.7.2   **MONTEE, Alice Marie** b 23 Dec 1920, Waukegan, IL; d 14 Dec 2000, Pinole, CA. She married 1943? (1) **Edward P. Finneran** (Thomas J. Finneran & Edna D. ____) b 4 Nov 1922, UT; d 18 Jul 1977, Ventura Co., CA.

She married (2) 14 Dec 1951, CA, **Orrin Tillman Dahl** (Lewis K. Dahl & Stella Christopherson) b 27 Mar 1923, Elk Mound, WI; d 20 Sep 1996, Pinole, CA.

4.4.7.5.2.7.3   **MONTEE, James Edward** b 15 Nov 1923, Waukegan, IL; d 8 Oct 1989, Sacramento Co., CA. He married (1) 6 Aug 1947, Oakland, CA, **Estelle Lenore Gaskill** (Stanley Raymond Gaskill & Relina K. Friend) b 27 Nov 1925, Humboldt Co., CA; m (2) 14 Feb 1982, Solano Co., CA, James E. Wallace.

He married (2) 31 Dec 1968, Solano Co., CA, and divorced Oct 1974, Sacramento Co., CA, **Lucienne E. Husted** b Jun 1929; m (2) 11 Oct 1975, Reno, NV, Louis M. Siems (Louis Martin Siems & Helen Tietke).

4.4.7.5.2.9.1   **MONTEE, Betty Louise** b 6 Mar 1923, Harpster, OH. She married **Keith E. Gelbaugh** (Clyde Gelbaugh & Desda Neff) b 25 Aug 1919, Wyandot Co., OH; d 24 Dec 1991, Marion, OH.

4.4.7.5.3.2.1   **MONTEE, Bernice Opal** b 28 Nov 1905, Little Sandusky, OH; d & bur 30 Jul & 2 Aug 1993, Upper Sandusky & Little Sandusky, OH. She married 19 Aug 1925, Upper Sandusky, OH, **Henry Swihart** (Peter M. Swihart & Ina Garvin) b 26 Sep 1903, Pitt Twp, OH; d 26 Feb 1998, Upper Sandusky, OH.

4.4.7.5.3.2.2   **MONTEE, Dale Franklin** b & d 1908, Little Sandusky, OH.

The year of Dale F. Montee's birth and death is taken from the inscription on his tombstone in the Little Sandusky, OH, Cemetery.

4.4.7.6.2.2.1   **MONTEE, Clifford Sylvester** b 1910?, Kootenai, ID; d 16 Jul 1946, Vancouver, British Columbia, Canada. He married 11 Mar 1933, Newport, WA, **Marion C. Moliter** (Frank A. Moliter & Freda Gustafson) b 1914?, Spokane, WA; m (2) there 29 Oct 1949 Gerald E. Thomas; d there 22 Aug 1954 at the age of 40.

Clifford Montee came to Spokane, WA, with his parents soon after his birth and was a

23-year old manufacturing jeweler there at his marriage. His bride was then 19 years old.

4.4.7.6.2.2.2   **MONTEE, Earl Edward** b June 1916, Spokane, WA. He married 16 Apr 1938, Spokane, WA, **Catherine Lou/Katie L. Tranquill** (Henry Tranquill & Myrtle Culp) b Jan 1919, Wayne, NE.

Earl E. Montee was 3 years and 6 months old on 1 Jan 1920 when he was living with his parents in Spokane, WA. Katherine (sic) Tranquill was then 11 months old (US census). She was named Catherine in the 1930 census in Spokane, and Katie L. Tranquill when she married. I have not found her or her husband in later years and have been unable to confirm even the vague dates of death, 1979 and 1970, which several family historians have adopted.

4.4.7.6.2.5.1   **MONTEE, Sara Jo** b 20 Nov 1926, Springfield, MO. She married 3 Mar 1951, Richmond Heights, MO, **Kenneth D. Roettger** (William Roettger & Matilda ____) b there 24 Sep 1925; d & bur 14 & 19 Oct 1995, Fairfield, IA & St. Louis, MO.

Kenneth D. Roettger, a World War II veteran, was buried in the Jefferson Barracks National Cemetery in St. Louis, MO.

4.4.7.6.2.6.1   **MONTEE, Richard Clair** b 4 Jan 1942, Kansas City, MO. He married 1 Jun 1963, **Deloris Ann Lynch** (Leroy Lynch & Loris ____) b 23 Jan 1944, MO.

4.4.7.6.2.6.2   **MONTEE, Stephen Howard** b 8 Jul 1947, Kansas City, MO.

4.4.7.6.3.1.1   **MONTEE, Clemorissa** b 6 Mar 1925, Santa Monica, CA. She married (1) 11 Jan 1941, Las Vegas, NV, **Allan Thew Huylar** (Jason Huylar & Pearl Thew) b 28 Apr 1922, Los Angeles, CA; m (2) 26 Jun 1965, Las Vegas, NV, Mrs. Phyllis M. Norwood; m (3) 20 Sep 1971, Carson City, NV, Mrs. Louise A. Josalle; d 21 Feb 2006, Woodland Hills, CA.

She married (2) 30 May 1972, Yuma, AZ, **William Kilgore** (William Kilgore & Virginia Spreck) b 15 Mar 1935, El Centro, CA.

Clemorissa Montee and her first husband were in Los Angeles, CA, at the birth of a child in 1942, and in Bee Co., TX, at the birth of another in 1944. I can trace her no further and know of her second marriage only through Betty Ramsey's *Monty-Montee History*, p. 326.

4.4.7.6.3.2.1   **MONTEE, Lucille Ruby** b 14 Jul 1920, Los Angeles, CA. She married 11 Feb 1946, Santa Barbara, CA, **Floyd Merrill Benton** (Harold Emmet Benton & Vesta Estella Smith) b 8 Nov 1914, Los Angeles, CA; d there 1 Dec 2003.

4.4.7.6.3.2.2   **MONTEE, Ralph Bruce** b 21 Dec 1932, Kansas City, MO; d 1 Feb 2007, San Francisco, CA. He married Jul 1952, Reno, NV, **Patricia Morton** b 1934?, Salem, OR.

Ralph Bruce Montee was a resident of Sylva, NC, at his death (*Ashville Citizen-Times*, 13 Feb 2007).

4.4.7.6.3.3.1   **MONTEE, Margery Jean** b 6 Apr 1924, Los Angeles, CA; d 6 Apr 1969, Fresno, CA. She married there **Leo Simmons** (Carl Simmons & Katherine Warner) b there 16 Mar 1923; m (2) 14 Feb 1979, Carson City, NV, Nancy Jane Becker; d 6 Nov 1992, Fresno, CA.

4.4.7.6.3.3.2   **MONTEE, Jacquelyn** b 27 May 1925, Los Angeles, CA. She married (1) around 1948 **Theodore Wesley Andrew** (Vernon Jasper Andrew & Agnes S. Black) b 27 Apr 1916, Churdan, IA; d 19 Sep 1958, Orange Co., CA.

She married (2) 3 Jan 1960, Las Vegas, NV, and divorced Aug 1969, Fresno Co., CA, **Jon Martin Evanoff** (Demeter Evanoff & Wanda ____) b 10 Feb 1930, St. Louis Park, MN; m (2) 28 Jan 1971, Las Vegas, NV, and divorced Jan 1974, Orange Co., CA, Mrs. Therese L. (Racine) Gravelle; d 29 Jul 2004, Caliente, NV.

4.4.7.6.6.7.1   **MONTEE, Betty/Bettie Eileen** b 8 Jun 1932, La Cygne, KS. She married

(1) 21 Aug 1947, Clinton, MO, **William Ralph Bradley** (William Reed Elliott Bradley & Sarah Rosalyn Leuty) b 25 Nov 1928, Foster, MO; m (2) around 1951 Lillie F. ____; d 18 Jan 2003, Foster, MO.

She married (2) 10 Feb 1950, Paola, KS, and divorced 1978 **Joe Paul Jimenez** (Juan Luis Jimenez & Lorenza Nunez Yvarra) b 15 Jan 1930, Williamstown, KS; m (2) Joyce L. Pruett.

4.4.7.6.6.7.2   **MONTEE, Bobby Dean** b 11 Oct 1935, La Cygne, KS; d 30 Aug 2002, Olathe, KS. He married (1) 6 Jul 1956 Smokey Hill Air Force Base, Salina, KS, **Barbara Joyce Thatcher** (George J. Thatcher & Catherine ____) b 17 Apr 1937, Newark, NJ.

He married (2) 17 Aug 1990, Butler, MO, **Patricia Ann Miller** (Arvil Miller & Sophia Maria Wentzell) b 13 May 1937, Evansville, IN.

Bobby Dean Montee was a resident of Osawatomie, KS, at his death and was buried there in the Oaklawn Cemetery.

4.4.7.9.4.4.1   **MONTEE, Lucille Marion** b 25 Jul 1929, Los Angeles, CA.

4.4.7.9.4.4.2   **MONTEE, Francis Edward** b 17 Jan 1932, Los Angeles, CA. He married (1) 1961 and divorced Feb 1970, Los Angeles, CA, **Kathleen J. Sheffield** b Sep 1943; m (2) 5 Aug 1972, Los Angeles, CA, Adney Danley Gass (Adney D. Gass & Jean Elizabeth Swift).

He married (2) 11 Apr 1971, Las Vegas, NV, and divorced Jun 1976, Orange Co., CA, **Brenda G. Cope** b 1944; m (1) 1965 and divorced May 1970, Los Angeles, CA, Quentin Hale Ward (____ Ward & ____ Young).

He married (3) 7 Jun 1980, Los Angeles, CA, and divorced there 12 Nov 1982 **Diane L. Powell** b 1960?

He married (4) 3 Oct 1985, Stateline, NV, **Donae Jean Griggs**.

4.4.7.9.4.5.1   **MONTEE, Renee** married ____ **Chamberlain**.

Mrs. Renee Chamberlain was a resident of Pasadena, CA, when her father died in 1990 (*Orange County Register*, Santa Ana, CA, 24 Aug 1990).

4.4.7.9.5.2.1   **MONTEE, Lela Darlene** b 24 Dec 1931, Hepler, KS; d 5 Sep 1993, Washington Co., OR. She married 15 Feb 1955, Walla Walla, WA, **Eddie Joseph Miguez** (Vernice Miguez & Eve Ortamond) b 2 Nov 1930, Vermillion Parish, LA; d 17 Jan 1994, Athena, OR.

Lela Darlene Montee and her husband were buried in the Athena, OR, Cemetery.

4.4.7.9.5.2.2   **MONTEE, Gerald Leon** b 16 Nov 1933, Hepler, KS; d 12 Nov 1996, Athena, OR. He married there 10 Nov 1956 **Karen E. Moore** (Roy Moore & ____) b 14 Dec 1936, Pendleton, OR.

Gerald Leon Montee was buried in the Athena, OR, Cemetery. His widow was still living in Athena when their son Brian died in 2007 (*Amarillo Globe News*, 5 Aug 2007).

4.4.7.9.5.2.3   **MONTEE, Albert Leroy** b 21 Feb 1936, Hepler, KS.

4.4.7.9.5.2.4   **MONTEE, Shirley** b 13 Jan 1938, Hepler, KS.

4.4.7.9.5.2.5   **MONTEE, Audrey** b 22 May 1941.

4.4.7.9.5.4.1   **MONTEE, David Roger** b 7 May 1948, Pendleton, OR. He married (1) there 21 Jul 1973 and divorced Jul 1976 **Cheryl Lynn Wyrick** b 22 Mar 1953, Pendleton, OR.

He married (2) May 1979, Pendleton, OR, **Debra Kay Reynolds** b 9 May 1955.

4.4.7.9.5.4.2   **MONTEE, Carl Michael** b 17 May 1951, Pendleton, OR; d there 14 May 1972.

Carl Michael Montee was buried in the Athena, OR, Cemetery.

4.4.7.9.5.4.3   **MONTEE, Shawn** b 29 Aug 1958, Pendleton, OR.

4.4.7.9.5.6.1   **MONTEE, Taundelaya Ann** b 14 Oct 1944, Birch Tree, MO; d there 1 Feb 1999.
Taundelaya Ann Montee was buried in Oak Grove Cemetery in Birch Tree, MO.

4.4.7.9.5.6.2   **MONTEE, Arletta/Arlette Kay** b 23 Jul 1946, Birch Tree, MO. She married (1) 2 Sep 1963, Eminence, MO, **Shannon William Kelly**.
She married (2) **Richard M. Mielke** b Aug 1932.
Mrs. Arlette K. Mielke was a resident of Springfield, MO, when her mother died in 2005 (*The Current Wave*, Eminence, MO, 25 Oct 2005).

4.4.7.9.5.6.3   **MONTEE, Clarence Edward** b 12 Aug 1948, Birch Tree, MO; d & bur 20 & 23 Jul 2008, Bois D'Arc & Ash Grove, MO. He married 30 Jun 1972, Ash Grove, MO, **Doris Roberta Dyal** b 31 May 1952.
Clarence E. Montee was buried in Johns Chapel Cemetery in Ash Grove, MO (*Springfield News Leader*, 22 Jul 2008).

4.4.7.9.8.2.1   **MONTEE, Joan Elizabeth** b 13 Feb 1928, Independence, KS; d 15 Nov 2006, Bartlesville, OK. She married 11 Oct 1946, **Donald D. Norwood** (Herrell Fleming Norwood & Maurine ____) b 31 Jul 1926, Lamar, MO.

4.4.7.9.8.2.2   **MONTEE, Ralph Edward** b 23 Apr 1932, Independence, KS. He married 27 Jun 1953 **Nancy Sue Grove** b 30 Mar 1932, Tulsa, OK.

4.4.7.9.9.4.1   **MONTEE, Eulalia May** b 2 Mar 1928, Arma, KS; d & bur 30 Jul & 2 Aug 1982, Havre, MT. She married 7 May 1947 **Claude Hamilton** (William E. Hamilton & Etta May ____) b 1923?, Havre, MT.
Eulalia Montee was buried in Highland Cemetery in Havre, MT.

4.4.7.9.9.4.2   **MONTEE, Edward** b 22 Jun 1934, Billings, MT; d there 23 Jun 1934.

4.4.7.9.9.4.3   **MONTEE, Jean Marie** b 26 May 1935, Billings, MT. She married (1) 31 Dec 1954 **Earl J. Landry**.
She married (2) 18 Mar 1967 **Richard Dean Shay** b 1930.

4.4.7.9.9.5.1   **MONTEE, Jo D'Anne** b 25 Oct 1936, Billings, MT. She married (1) 1955 **Bernard James Magelky** b 24 May 1932; m (2) Betty ____.
She married (2) **John William Bell** b 1936.

4.4.7.9.9.7.1   **MONTEE, Donna Joan** b 29 Sep 1934, Billings, MT; d there 24 Oct 1992. She married there 26 Apr 1952 **Armen Henry Weiss** (Jacob Weiss & Rosa ____) b Sep 1929, Beulah, ND.

4.4.7.9.9.7.2   **MONTEE, Richard Allen** b 20 Sep 1938, Billings, MT. He married 9 Sep 1960, **Eva Mae Bird** (Albert R. Bird & Edna Mae Johnson) b 8 Jul 1938, Billings, MT.

4.4.7.9.9.10.1   **MONTEE, Dianna Lee** b 5 Apr 1939, Billings, MT. She married (1) around 1958 ____ **Baker**.
She married (2) **Rollie L. Hewitt** (Jack Otis Hewitt & Echo Eva Goodman) b 29 Oct 1938, OR.

4.4.7.9.9.10.2   **MONTEE, Charles Roger** b 23 Mar 1940, Billings, MT. He married around 1960 **Christina Stover** (Harvey Allen Stover & Elizabeth Ann Ackerman).

4.4.7.9.9.10.3   **MONTEE, Michal Faye** b 16 Jan 1943, Great Falls, MT. She married around 1960 **Thomas Edward Doepke** (James LeRoy Doepke & Julia Margaret LeSarge) b 13 Jan 1942, Crow Wing Co., MN.

4.4.7.9.9.10.4   **MONTEE, Jeffrey Wayne** b 14 Oct 1947, Pendleton, OR. He married **Donna Lou Tally** (Robert Wallace Tally & Alberta Jean Newman) b 30 Jan 1949, La Grande, OR.

4.4.7.9.9.10.5   **MONTEE, Kathleen Lavon** b 17 Mar 1951, Pendleton, OR. She married **David Gallaher** (Ernest E. Gallaher & Jean Hodgen) b Apr 1949; m (2) Cynthia/Cindy ____.

4.4.7.9.9.10.6   **MONTEE, Mark Scott** b 25 Apr 1963, Pendleton, OR. He married **Alison Marie Hopf** (____ Hopf & Charlotte A. Schneider) b 14 Jan 1965, Fayette Co., KY.
      He married (2) 28 Dec 2001, Las Vegas, NV, **Cherilyn Diane Kelly** b 8 Dec 1972; m (1) ____ Hughes.

4.4.7.9.9.10.7   **MONTEE, William Robert** b 28 May 1969, Portland, OR.

4.4.7.9.13.3.1   **MONTEE, Montee Lee** b 3 Mar 1938, Newton, KS.

4.4.7.9.13.3.2   **MONTEE, Patricia Kay** b 30 Mar 1939, Newton, KS.

4.4.7.12.3.3.1   **MONTEE, Eugene Earl** b 9 Sep 1924, Pittsburg, KS. He married there 9 Sep 1948, **Marjorie Irene Talley** (Harley R. Talley & Erma I. O'Dell) b there 9 Sep 1929; d & bur 13 & 17 Oct 2005, Olathe & Lenexa, KS.
      Eugene (also Gene) Montee survived his wife. She was buried in Resurrection Cemetery in Lenexa, KS (*Kansas City Star*, 14 Oct 2005).

4.4.7.12.3.4.1   **MONTEE, Archie Dean** b 17 Jul 1929, KS. He married 5 Sep 1954, Joplin, MO, **Marian Daniels** (John Daniels & ____) b 1931, KS.

4.4.7.12.3.5.1   **MONTEE, Cathern/Kathryn/Catherine** b 23 Sep 1924, Pittsburg, KS; d 1971. She married (1) **Calvin G. Kernell**.
      She married (2) **Mac McDaniel**.
      I know about this woman mainly through Betty Ramsey's *Monty-Montee History*, p. 526. I am uncertain about her name. She was named Kathryn in 1930 when she was living in Ross, KS, with her parents (US census), Catherine when her brother Marvin Montee (4.4.7.12.3.5.4) died in 2001 (*Wyoming Tribune Eagle*, Cheyenne, WY, 12 May 2001), and Cathern when her son Larry Kernell died in 2006 (*Macon Telegraph*, 7 Jun 2006).

4.4.7.12.3.5.2   **MONTEE, Meril Finley** b 1 Dec 1926, Fleming, KS. He married 31 Dec 1947, Bartlesville, OK, **Maxine Delores Inman** (Floyd Inman & Gladys Marie Tate) b 27 Jan 1927, Nowata, OK.
      Meril F. Montee and his wife were residents of Bartlesville, OK, when his brother Marvin (4.4.7.12.3.5.4) and sister Mildred (4.4.7.12.3.5.3) died in 2001 (*Wyoming Tribune Eagle*, 12 May 2001; *Las Vegas Review Journal*, 22 Jun 2001).

4.4.7.12.3.5.3   **MONTEE, Mildred N.** b 19 Apr 1929, Pittsburg, KS; d 17 Jun 2001, Las Vegas, NV. She married (1) **Kenneth Flannigan**.
      She married (2) **Glen McConnell**.
      She married (3) **Jim Taylor**.
      Mildred Montee had been a resident of Las Vegas, NV, for thirty-two years when she died (*Las Vegas Review Journal*, 22 Jun 2001). I know of her marriages only through Betty Ramsey's *Monty-Montee History*, p. 527.

4.4.7.12.3.5.4   **MONTEE, Marvin Wesley** b 10 Aug 1935, Pittsburg, KS; d 8 May 2001,

Burns, WY. He married 8 Feb 1963, Fort Leavenworth, KS, **Mary C. Vaughan**.
Mary C. Vaughn survived her husband (*Wyoming Tribune Eagle*, 12 May 2001).

4.4.7.12.3.5.5   **MONTEE, Margaret Gay** b 23 Mar 1947, Parsons, KS. She married **Larry Scott** (John Lowell Scott & Irene Lucille Wright) b 8 Nov 1945, Labette Co., KS.
Margaret Montee and Larry Scott were residents of Dennis, KS, when her mother died in 2005 (*Parsons Sun*, 12 May 2005).

4.4.7.12.3.5.6   **MONTEE, Robert** b 24 Oct 1948, Parsons, KS. He married there 2 Sep 1967 **Elvera/Ellie M. Lewis** b 3 Dec 1948, Wichita, KS.
Robert Montee and his wife Ellie were residents of Parsons, KS, when his mother died in 2005 (*Parsons Sun*, 12 May 2005).

4.4.7.12.3.6.1   **MONTEE, Cleda Marjorie** b 10 May 1928, Arma, KS; d & bur 14 & 18 Nov 2003, Minot & Goodrich, ND. She married 29 Jun 1946, Racine, WI, **Emanuel R. Adam** (Fred Adam & Lena ____) b 27 Dec 1923, Goodrich, ND.
Marjorie Montee predeceased her husband. She was buried in the Goodrich, ND, City Cemetery (*Bismarck Tribune*, 17 Nov 2003).

4.4.7.12.3.6.2   **MONTEE, Rolla Melvin** b 15 Oct 1932, Arma, KS. He married 17 Sep 1955, Milwaukee, WI, **Janice Koch** (Walter Koch & Estelle Stanislava) b there 27 Feb 1937.
Melvin Montee and his wife Janice were residents of Prophetstown, IL, when his sister Marjorie died in 2003 (*Bismarck Tribune*, 17 Nov 2003).

4.4.7.12.3.6.3   **MONTEE, Lawrence Ray** b 6 Jun 1936, Cherokee, KS; d 2 Jun 1946, Racine, WI.
Lawrence R. Montee was buried in Graceland Cemetery in Racine, WI.

4.4.7.12.3.7.1   **MONTEE, Carolyn J.** b 4 May 1937, Girard, KS. She married (1) **Mike Tally Noscroy** (Mike Noscroy & Wilma H. Wymer) b 1934, KS.
She married (2) Mar 1970 **Clyde Wesley Fink** (Everett Fink & Eva Black) b 23 Apr 1931, Fredonia, KS; m (1) 1951, Pittsburg, KS, Darlene Lyden; d 30 Oct 2004, Joplin, MO.
Carolyn Montee survived her second husband. She and Clyde Fink, who was in the music business all his life, lived in Colorado after their marriage and in Grove, OK, in 1998 and later years (*Pittsburg Morning Sun*, 3 Nov 2004).

4.4.7.12.3.9.1   **MONTEE, Jack L.** b 22 Sep 1936, Monmouth, KS. He married 22 Jun 1957, Racine, WI, **Carol L. Ripley** (Lewis A. Ripley & Ida A. Slade) b 28 Jun 1936, Wauwatosa, WI; d 6 Feb 2008, Racine, WI.

4.4.7.12.3.9.2   **MONTEE, Danny Lee** b 13 Apr 1945, Racine, WI. He married (1) 22 Aug 1964 **Barbara Johnson** b 29 Sep 1947.
He married (2) **Linda** ____ b 1955.

4.4.7.12.3.11.1   **MONTEE, Kathleen Marie** b 8 Sep 1940, McCune, KS. She married 29 Dec 1962, Greenbush, KS, **Lorn Raymond Lahey** (Lorn Raymond Lahey & Cecelia Alice Webb) b 22 Oct 1940, Gallup, NM.
Mrs. Kathy Lahey was a resident of Bonner Springs, KS, when her father died in 2002 (*Parsons Sun*, 18 Jul 2002).

4.4.7.12.3.11.2   **MONTEE, Jacqueline** b 21 Nov 1942, Racine, WI. She married 15 Aug 1964, McCune, KS, **James Eugene McGuire** b 10 Dec 1942, Conway, AR.
Mrs. Jackie McGuire was a resident of McCune, KS, when her father died in 2002 (*Parsons Sun*, 18 Jul 2002).

4.4.7.12.3.11.3   **MONTEE, Connie Jo** b 9 Jul 1944, Pittsburg, KS. She married 18 Jul

1964, McCune, KS, **Robert L. Depue** b 22 Jul 1945, Pittsburg, KS.

Connie Depue was a resident of Greenwood, MO, when her father died in 2002 (*Parsons Sun*, 18 Jul 2002).

4.4.7.12.3.11.4   **MONTEE, Larry Dean** b 5 Oct 1949, Pittsburg, KS.

Larry Montee was a resident of Atlanta, GA, when his father died in 2002 (*Parsons Sun*, 18 Jul 2002).

4.4.7.12.7.1.1   **MONTEE, William Gerald** b 15 Jun 1924, Mulberry, KS; d 19 Apr 1998, Arcadia, KS. He married 5 Oct 1946 **Lois Lucille Warden** (Charles Clayton Warden & Ida Belle Sallee) b 3 Aug 1928, Ft. Scott, KS; m (2) 2 Jan 2000, Liberal, MO, Edward Glen Montee (4.4.7.12.7.7), her first husband's uncle.

William Gerald Montee was buried in Forest Hill Cemetery in Arcadia, KS.

4.4.7.12.7.1.2   **MONTEE, Delbert Dean** b 9 Apr 1926, Mulberry, KS; d 2 Feb 2002, Avondale, MO. He married (1) around 1947 **Marjory Warden** (Charles Clayton Warden & Ida Belle Sallee).

He married (2) **Mrs. Alta L. Utt** b 18 Dec 1926; d 12 Oct 2003, Kansas City, MO.

Delbert Montee predeceased his wife Alta and was buried in White Chapel Memorial Gardens in Gladstone, MO (*Kansas City Star*, 4 Feb 2002). I know of his first wife, a sister of Lois Warden, wife of William Gerald Montee (4.4.7.12.7.1.1) only through Betty Ramsey's *Monty-Montee History*, p. 555.

4.4.7.12.7.1.3   **MONTEE, Eldon Lee** b 5 May 1929, Mulberry, KS; d 7 Jan 1995, Arcadia, KS. He married 18 Jul 1948, Pittsburg, KS, **Freda Lavonne Elliott** (Charles Edward Elliott & Sadie Elvira Black) b 12 May 1932, Tonkawa, OK.

4.4.7.12.7.1.4   **MONTEE, Marilyn J.** b 15 Feb 1933, Cato, KS. She married (1) around 1948 **Gene/Eugene Swafford** (Claude Swafford & Opal Viva/Arvilla Crites).

She was divorced when she married (2) around 1971 **James W. Henderson**.

4.4.7.12.7.3.1   **MONTEE, Marcella Lee** b 5 Aug 1927, Mulberry, KS. She married (1) **Herman Kelly**.

She married (2) **Dewaine D. Zumbaum** b 11 May 1931; d 25 Jan 2004, Ogden, UT.

4.4.7.12.7.3.2   **MONTEE, Lois Earlene** b 6 Jun 1929, Mulberry, KS. She married around 1948 **Walter Leroy Gilman** (Harry Gillman & Margaret ____) b 19 Feb 1929, Kellogg, ID.

4.4.7.12.7.3.3   **MONTEE, Shirley** b 1 Feb 1931, Mulberry, KS. She married (1) ____ who died in an automobile accident.

She married (2) **Jack ____**.

She was divorced when she married (3) **Dick Stear**.

She married (4) **Darrell Gray**.

I know of this woman and her husbands only through Betty Ramsey's *Monty-Montee History*, p. 560.

4.4.7.12.7.3.4   **MONTEE, Glenda** b 16 May 1933, Mulberry, KS. She married (1) 1951? **Claude Claflin** (Oscar Dewitt Claflin & Hazel Verna Jeffers b 29 Feb 1932, Sand Creek Twp, ND; m (2) Mary ____ b 1943.

She was divorced when she married (2) **Lee Lambert Benjamin** b 3 Jan 1942; d 24 Aug 2000, Boise, ID.

Lee L. Benjamin, a Vietnam War Army veteran, was buried in the Idaho State Veterans Cemetery in Boise, ID.

4.4.7.12.7.3.5   **MONTEE, Roberta Jane/Jean** (twin) b 14 Dec 1936; d 22 Jan 1942, Wallace, ID.

According to the Idaho Death Index, Roberta Jane Montee was born on 14 Dec 1936. The tombstone of Roberta Jean (sic) Montee in Greenwood Cemetery in Kellogg, ID, indicates however that she was born on 14 Dec 1937.

4.4.7.12.7.3.6   **MONTEE, Robert Dean** (twin) b 14 Dec 1936. He married **Donna Marie Henderson** (Tyrus L. Henderson & Mary Gertrude Harris) b 1942, Boise, ID.

Robert Montee and his wife Donna were residents of Coeur d'Alene, ID, when her mother died in 2007 (*Blackfoot Morning News*, 21 Sep 2007).

4.4.7.12.7.3.7   **MONTEE, Annetta** b 20 Mar 1940, Osburn, ID. She married June 1975 **James R. Bullard** b 7 Apr 1943.

4.4.7.12.7.3.8   **MONTEE, Kenneth Dale** b 3 Mar 1943, Elk Creek, ID. He married 30 Jul 1964, Amsterdam, Netherlands, **Christina Siebel** b 11 Jan 1944.

I know of Kenneth Montee's marriage only through Betty Ramsey's *Monty-Montee History*, p. 562.·

4.4.7.12.7.3.9   **MONTEE, Merlene L.** b 26 Sep 1948; d 14 Sep 2003, Phoenix, AZ. She married (1) 17 Apr 1970, Duvall, WA, **Jerry Harris**.

She was divorced when she married (2) 4 Jun 1975 Coeur d'Alene, ID, **Douglas Pederson** b Dec 1949.

4.4.7.12.7.4.1   **MONTEE, James William** b 30 Nov 1930, Milwaukee, WI; d & bur 15 & 19 Oct 1999, Latham & Medusa, NY. He married 1957 **Patricia Anne Sheehan** b 8 Jul 1934.

James W. Montee was a resident of Albany, NY, when his father died in 1997. He was buried near him in the Medusa, NY, Cemetery (*Albany Times Union*, 6 May 1997 and 16 Oct 1999).

4.4.7.12.7.4.2   **MONTEE, George Steven** b 15 Nov 1931. He married 17 Sep 1955 **Lillian Helen Gill** (Charles Gill & Lillian _____) b 28 Nov 1932, Brooklyn, NY; d & bur 4 & 6 Apr 2007, Mantua & Mullica Hill, NJ.

George S. Montee was a resident of Mantua, NJ, when his father died in 1997 (*Albany Times Union*, 6 May 1997). He survived his wife who was buried in Holy Name of Jesus Cemetery in Mullica Hill, NJ (*Courier Post*, Cherry Hill, NJ, 10 Apr 2007).

4.4.7.12.7.4.3   **MONTEE, Charles Cloyse** b 7 Dec 1933; d 1 May 1934.

4.4.7.12.7.4.4   **MONTEE, John Stephen** b 30 Jul 1949. He married 6 Apr 1968 **Maureen Florence McGee** b 15 Sep 1949.

John Montee was a resident of Yonkers, NY, when his father died in 1997. He also survived his brother James (4.4.7.12.7.4.1) (*Albany Times Union*, 6 May 1997 and 16 Oct 1999).

4.4.7.12.7.5.1   **MONTEE, Sandra Louise** b 3 Dec 1938, Mulberry, KS. She married 1957 and divorced 1968 **James R. Jenicek** (Charles Jenicek & Reba M. Cunningham) b 12 Apr 1933, Harrison, ID; m (2) 1975, Mrs. Ellen Loveseth; d 14 Jan 2004, St. Maries, ID.

Sandra Montee and James Jenicek lived in Osburn, ID, before their divorce (*Idaho Spokesman Review*, Coeur d'Alene, ID, 22 Jan 2004). She resumed her maiden name and was listed in 2008 among her mother's surviving children as Sandra Montee (*Coeur d'Alene Press*, 20 Jan 2008).

4.4.7.12.7.5.2   **MONTEE, David Henry** b 3 Apr 1941, Wallace, ID. He married (1) 22 Feb 1963, Osburn, ID, **Sandra Mae Fagg** (Aldridge Fagg & Peggy _____) b 23 Apr 1944, Alderwood Manor, WA.

He married (2) **Kathleen _____** b 2 Feb 1947.

Dave Montee and his wife Kathleen survived his mother (*Coeur d'Alene Press*, 20 Jan

2008).

4.4.7.12.7.5.3 **MONTEE, Evelyn Irene** b 3 Oct 1943, Wallace, ID. She married 31 Dec 1963, Kellogg, ID, **Barry Lee Breazeal** (Vernile Breazeal & Louise ____) b there 21 May 1940.

4.4.7.12.7.5.4 **MONTEE, Raymond Cloyse** b 18 Sep 1944, Wallace, ID. He married Aug 1964, Harrison, ID, **Sharon Lee Hill** (John Hill & Mary ____) b 21 Oct 1946.

4.4.7.12.7.5.5 **MONTEE, John Thomas** b 6 Nov 1946, Wallace, ID. He married **Virginia Fagg** (Aldridge Fagg & Peggy ____) b 25 Jun 1945, Alderwood Manor, WA.

4.4.7.12.7.5.6 **MONTEE, Dorothy Ann** b 19 Mar 1948, Wallace, ID. She married (1) 1967, Kellogg, ID, **Jeff High**.
She was divorced when she married (2) 26 Oct 1974, Coeur d'Alene, ID, **Jack H. Wilson**.

4.4.7.12.7.5.7 **MONTEE, Carolyn Sue** b 20 Jul 1950, Wallace, ID. She married 1967, Osburn, ID, **Dale E. Simpson** b 12 Nov 1950.

4.4.7.12.7.7.1 **MONTEE, Janet S.** b 24 May 1948, Kansas City, KS. She married 7 Sep 1968, Kansas City, MO, **Jerry L. Bailey** b 22 Dec 1944, MO.
Mrs. Jan Bailey was a resident of Kansas City, MO, when her father died in 2001 (*Kansas City Star*, 5 Aug 2001).

4.4.7.12.7.7.2 **MONTEE, Elaine** b 23 Oct 1956, Kansas City, KS. She married 17 Jul 1976 **Michael Thomas Perkins** b Dec 1957.
Mrs. Elaine Perkins was a resident of Shawnee, KS, when her father died in 2001 (*Kansas City Star*, 5 Aug 2001).

4.4.7.12.10.3.1 **MONTEE, David Byron** b 12 Sep 1945. He married 1966, Chicago, IL, **Patricia Ann/Patsy McElligott** (Raymond McElligott & Josephine Grace Schmehl) b 1945.

4.8.5.2.1.3.1 **MONTY, Denice Ann** b 19 Apr 1952, Saranac Lake, NY. She married 9 Oct 1976, Johnstown, NY, **Brian O. Rowback** (Robert Rowback & Ramona ____) b there 6 Sep 1952.
Mrs. Denice Rowback was a resident of New York Mills, NY, when her mother died in 2006 (*Plattsburgh Press Republican*, 24 Oct 2006).

4.8.5.2.1.3.2 **MONTY, Edward Cecil** b 18 Jun 1954, Plattsburgh, NY.
Edward Monty was a resident of Saratoga, NY, when his mother died in 2006 (*Plattsburgh Press Republican*, 24 Oct 2006).

4.8.5.2.1.3.3 **MONTY, James Carl** b 17 Mar 1957, Plattsburgh, NY. He married Jun 1981 **Colleen Ann Southerton** (Joseph Southerton & ____) b 12 Aug 1959, Levittown, NY.
James Monty and his wife Colleen were residents of Plattsburgh, NY, when his mother died in 2006 (*Plattsburgh Press Republican*, 24 Oct 2006).

4.8.5.2.1.3.4 **MONTY, Michael**
Michael Monty predeceased both his parents and may well have died in infancy or early childhood (*Plattsburgh Press Republican*, 31 Mar 1975 and 24 Oct 2006).

4.10.6.2.2.1.1 **MONTY, Mary Lou** b 1929?, NY. She married 29 Jul 1967, Tupper Lake, NY, **Wesley J. Manchester** (William Manchester & Jennie Sundt) b 4 Nov 1931, Staten Island, NY; d 27 Jan 1990, Saranac Lake, NY.
Mary Lou Monty graduated from Altona, NY, High School in 1946 and was for several

years before her marriage a Catholic nun known as Sister Mary Esther (*Plattsburgh Press Republican*, 18 May 1946, 5 Feb and 6 Oct 1953, 9 Sep 1955, 8 Jun 1956, etc.). Mrs. Mary Manchester survived her husband (*Plattsburgh Press Republican*, 1 Feb 1990).

4.10.6.2.2.1.2   **MONTY, Morton Joseph** b 15 Dec 1931, NY; d 3 Feb 1994, Mooers, NY. He married 29 Aug 1953 **Anna Marie Schoepl** (Leopold Schoepl & Fannie _____) b 24 Aug 1932, Staten Island, NY.

4.10.6.2.2.1.3   **MONTY, Julie Ann** b 10 May 1934, NY. She married 20 Oct 1954, Altona, NY, **Lloyd J. Forkey** (Arthur Forkey & Isabelle Favreau) b 12 Jun 1935, Mooers Forks, NY; d & bur 19 & 23 Jun 2003, Mooers, NY.
       Lloyd J. Forkey predeceased his wife and was buried in St. Joseph's Roman Catholic Cemetery in Mooers, NY (*Plattsburgh Press Republican*, 21 Jun 2003).

4.10.6.2.2.2.1   **MONTY, Ramona** b 22 Oct 1928, Altona, NY; d there 2 Jul 1997. She married there 6 Jun 1953 **John Louis Emmett Wood** (John Ludger Wood & Eva Elizabeth Peryer) b there 11 Oct 1927.
       Ramona Monty and her husband were residents of Altona, NY, when her mother died in 1988 (*Plattsburgh Press Republican*, 12 Jun 1988).

4.10.6.2.2.2.2   **MONTY, John F.** b 24 Mar 1933, Altona, NY. He married 17 Jul 1954 **Janice Mae Averill** (Frank Leonard Averill & Genevieve Beaubriand/Bobria) b 17 May 1942, Altona, NY.
       John F. Monty Jr. and his wife were residents of Schenectady, NY, when her stepfather Douglas G. Frenya died in 2002 (*Plattsburgh Press Republican*, 16 Aug 2002).

4.10.6.2.7.1.1   **MONTY, Robert James** b 12 Oct 1944, Rouses Point, NY. He married 10 Apr 1965, Cadyville, NY, **Joanne Ducatte** (Ross Ducatte & Edith Mousseau) b 12 Aug 1945, Plattsburgh, NY.
       Robert Monty was a resident of Colchester, VT, when his father died in 1987 and when his mother remarried in 1992. He and his wife were in Grand Isle, VT, when her mother died in 2002 (*Plattsburgh Press Republican*, 19 Jan 1987, 13 Sep 1992, and 14 Oct 2002).

4.10.6.2.7.1.2   **MONTY, Michael George** b 20 Apr 1950, Rouses Point, NY. He married 21 Aug 1971, Glenville, NY, **Rebecca Ann Newman** (Charles John Newman & _____) b 13 Jul 1949, NY.
       Michael Monty was a resident of Burnt Hills, NY, when his father died in 1987 (*Plattsburgh Press Republican*, 19 Jan 1987).

4.10.6.9.2.1.1   **MONTY, Robert Ross** b 25 Dec 1940, Hartford, CT; d & bur 4 & 10 Mar 2004, Windsor & Middletown, CT.
       Robert Ross Monty was a Vietnam War veteran and was buried in the Connecticut State Veterans Cemetery in Middletown, CT (*Hartford Courant*, 7 Mar 2004).

4.10.6.9.2.1.2   **MONTY, Diane** married 30 Apr 1966, Hartford, CT, **Ronald E. Hale** (George Alfred Hale & Beatrice A. Bunnell) b there 31 Oct 1939.
       Mrs. Diane Hale and her husband Ronald were residents of Suffield, CT, when her brother Robert died in 2004 (*Hartford Courant*, 7 Mar 2004).

4.11.1.1.3.3.1   **MONTY, Marie** b & d 1921 Lynn, MA.

4.11.1.1.3.3.2   **MONTY, Madelyn Josephine** b 30 Mar 1922, Lynn, MA; d 24 Nov 2004, Phoenix, AZ. She married (1) around 1941 **George Garland**.
       She married (2) 23 Jun 1947, Cleveland, OH, **William Louis Rendessy** (Theodore Rendessy & Anna Poremba) b 14 Oct 1912, Johnstown, PA; d Feb 1995, Phoenix, AZ.

4.11.1.1.3.3.3   **MONTY, Mildred Irene** b 8 Aug 1924, Swampscott, MA; d 27 Oct 2008, Phoenix, AZ.

4.11.1.1.3.3.4   **MONTY, Marion Shirley** b 22 Nov 1926, Swampscott, MA; d 4 Sep 2003, Mentor, OH. She married (1) OH, **Donald Toth** (John Toth & Helen ___) b 20 May 1924, Cuyahoga Co., OH; d 11 Oct 1984, Kirkland, OH.
She married (2) May 1956, Mayfield, OH, **Joseph Biely** (Paul Biely & Anna ____) b 4 Feb 1921, Cleveland, OH; d there 6 Nov 1981.

4.11.1.1.3.3.5   **MONTY, Robert Lee** b 2 Dec 1928, Swampscott, MA; d 31 Aug 1957, Tucson, AZ.

4.11.1.1.3.3.6   **MONTY, Kenneth Leon** b 6 Apr 1930, Swampscott, MA. He married 17 Mar 1967, Houston, TX, **Virginia Dowell** (Joseph Tilford Dowell & Agnes Virginia Newman) b there 10 Dec 1941.
Ken Monty and his wife Ginny survived his sister Marion (4.11.1.1.3.4) who died in 2003 (*Cleveland Plain Dealer*, 15 Dec 2003).

4.11.3.1.1.2.1   **MONTY, Virginia** b 10 Feb 1919, Billerica, MA; d 16 Aug 1986, Bexar Co., TX. She married 1942, Lowell, MA, **Harold S. Sanford** b 8 Aug 1915; d 1 Dec 1992, Webb Co., TX.
Harold S. Sanford was a tender and Virginia Monty an RN in Lowell, MA, when their "marriage intentions" were published in the *Lowell Sun* of 28 Mar 1942.

4.11.3.1.1.2.2   **MONTY, Herbert Russell** b 1920, Billerica, MA.
Herbert R. Monty was a 9-year-old child living with his parents in Billerica, MA, on 1 Apr 1930 (US census). He also enlisted in the US Army in 1942 under that name. He was named Russell Monty however when his parents celebrated their 25th wedding anniversary in 1938 and when his brother Vincent (4.11.3.1.1.2.4) died in 1962. Russell Monty was then a resident of Baltimore, MD (*Lowell Sun*, 26 Aug 1938; 10 Dec 1962).

4.11.3.1.1.2.3   **MONTY, Charlotte R.** b 3 Mar 1922, Billerica, MA; d 13 Oct 2003, Summerfield, FL. She married (1) and divorced 22 Mar 1982, Pinellas Co., FL, **Albert Capuano** (Antonio Capuano & Theresa Moreno) b 16 Mar 1910, Westford, MA; d 30 May 2000, Tewksbury, MA.
She married (2) 28 May 1982, Pinellas Co., FL, **Joseph James Coughlin** (Patrick J. Coughlin & Maria ____) b 28 Mar 1916, Lowell, MA; m (1) and divorced 14 Jan 1982, Pinellas Co., FL, Claire ____; d 25 Dec 1987, Largo, FL.

4.11.3.1.1.2.4   **MONTY, Vincent A.** b 1924?, Billerica, MA; d & bur 10 & 13 Dec 1962, Boston & Lowell, MA. He married (1) Jul 1945, North Billerica, MA, **Jewell Mae Maxfield** (Rufus A. Maxfield & Louise B. Dupuis) b 8 Oct 1926, Lowell, MA; m (2) John A. Hurley (John A. Hurley & Susan E. Myshrall).
He married (2) **Vivian Gagnon** b 12 Aug 1926.
Vincent A. Monty was 6 years old on 1 Apr 1930 (US census, Billerica, MA). He was a weaver in Lowell, MA, and was buried there in St. Patrick's Cemetery (*Lowell Sun*, 10 Dec 1962). His widow Vivian remained there for several years before moving to New Hampshire with several of her children (City Directories). She was a resident of Hudson, NH, when her son William died in 2006 (*Hampton Union*, 11 Aug 2006).

4.11.3.1.1.2.5   **MONTY, Everett L.** b 5 Mar 1926, Billerica, MA; d 26 Feb 1981, Lowell, MA.

4.11.3.1.1.2.6   **MONTY, Teresa P.** b 22 Jun 1927, Billerica, MA. She married **George R. Cummings** b 25 Dec 1923.
Mrs. Teresa Cummings was a resident of North Chelmsford, MA, when her brother

Vincent (4.11.3.1.1.2.4) died in 1962 (*Lowell Sun*, 10 Dec 1962). She and her husband later moved to Summerfield, FL.

4.11.3.1.2.1.1   MONTY, Russell b 1917?, West Chazy, NY.

Russell Monty was 2 years old when he was living with his parents in West Chazy, NY, on 1 Jan 1920 (US census). He does not appear with them in the 1925 State census and may have died before then.

4.11.3.1.2.1.2   MONTY, Hubert b 19 Feb 1920, West Chazy, NY; d & bur 23 & 27 Dec 1996, Plattsburgh & West Chazy, NY. He married 22 Aug 1946, Plattsburgh, NY, **Marion E. Goslow** (Frank Goslow & Agnes Giguere) b there 8 Aug 1919; d there 24 Dec 2001.

4.11.3.1.2.1.3   MONTY, Doris Patricia b 17 Mar 1924, Altona, NY; d 19 Jan 1994, Baton Rouge, LA. She married 14 Oct 1942, West Chazy, NY, **Wilfred J. Barcomb** (Edward Barcomb & Louise ____) b Jul 1922, NY.

Doris Monty and her husband were residents of Prairieville, LA, when she died. She was buried in Greenoaks Memorial Park in Baton Rouge, LA (*Baton Rouge Advocate*, 21 Jan 1994).

4.11.3.1.2.1.4   MONTY, Gerald W. b Oct 1928, Altona, NY. He married 7 Jan 1953, Plattsburgh, NY, **Rose Mary Latour** (Oral J. Latour & Helene Lucia).

Gerald Monty was a resident of Plattsburgh, NY, when his sister Doris (4.11.3.1.2.1.3) died in 1994 (*Baton Rouge Advocate*, 21 Jan 1994).

4.11.3.1.2.1.5   MONTY, James C. b 27 Jul 1931, Clinton Co., NY. He married **Joy Lashway** (Ellsworth Lashway & ____).

James Monty was a resident of Plattsburgh, NY, when his sister Doris (4.11.3.1.2.1.3) died in 1994 (*Baton Rouge Advocate*, 21 Jan 1994).

4.11.3.1.2.1.6   MONTY, Janet married 27 Oct 1951, Plattsburgh, NY, **Gerald D. Reid** (Willis S. Reid & Leah Rockwell) b there 25 Aug 1929; d there 21 Jun 2006.

Janet Monty survived her husband (*Plattsburgh Press Republican*, 23 Jun 2006).

4.11.3.1.2.1.7   MONTY, Gordon E. b Nov 1936, Clinton Co., NY. He married **Norma A. Terry** (Mitchell Terry & Aline Bechard) b 1946.

Gordon Monty was a resident of Plattsburgh, NY, when his sister Doris (4.11.3.1.2.1.3) died in 1994 (*Baton Rouge Advocate*, 21 Jan 1994).

4.11.4.6.5.3.1   MONTY, Ralph George b 16 May 1945, Everett, WA. He married (1) 5 Jul 1963, Arlington, WA, **Karin Roal** (Bill Roal & Louise Krauskoff) b 16 Oct 1942, Everett, WA; m (2) 30 Nov 1973, Snohomish Co., WA, Douglas J. Peterson; d 17 Feb 2006, Goldendale, WA.

He married (2) 14 Nov 1973, Reno, NV, **Mary Ann Liming** (David Liming & Doris Noonan) b 23 Mar 1943, Seattle, WA; m (1) ____ Sherrill.

4.11.4.6.5.3.2   MONTY, Marvin D. b 13 Sep 1948, Everett, WA. He married 15 Jun 1968, Arlington, WA, **Verna Lee Teague** (Lavern J. Teague & Esther Wangsmo) b there 24 Dec 1947.

4.11.4.6.9.1.1   MONTY, Deborah Kay b 8 Feb 1953, Grand Island, NE. She married as her second husband, 16 Dec 1999, Tacoma, WA, **Richard Allan Sims** b 5 Jan 1944, Clinton, IN.

4.11.4.6.9.2.1   MONTY, Dale Richard b 14 Feb 1945, Everett, WA; d 6 Aug 1989, Skagit Co., WA. He married (1) 3 Jun 1963, Everett, WA, **Dawn Rita Miller** (Bruce W. Miller & Marion Peck) b there 13 Aug 1945.

He married (2) 20 Mar 1982, Reno, NV, **Lorie McCaulley** b 2 Oct 1953, Chicago, IL.

4.11.4.6.9.2.2   **MONTY, Dean Morris** b 7 Apr 1946, Everett, WA; d there 30 Oct 1946.

4.11.4.6.9.2.3   **MONTY, Nadene Marie** b 30 Aug 1947, Everett, WA. She married 23 Jul 1965, Coeur D'Alene, ID, **Larry R. Jantz** b 1 Oct 1946, Ringwood, OK.

4.11.4.6.9.2.4   **MONTY, Mavis** b 29 Jul 1949, Juneau, AK; d 2 Jul 1963, Arlington, WA.

4.11.4.8.1.3.1   **MONTY, George Paul** b 20 Aug 1948, Camp Pendleton, CA. He married 19 Sep 1970, Vista, CA, **Jennifer Louise Brown** (____ Brown & ____ Moffitt) b 23 Mar 1950, Oceanside, CA.

4.11.4.8.1.3.2   **MONTY, Pamela Jean** b 2 Aug 1951, Visalia, CA. She married 26 Aug 1969, San Diego, CA, and divorced there May 1971 **Frederick Eugene Bass**.

4.11.4.8.1.3.3   **MONTY, Cameron A.** b 7 Jan 1957, Camp Pendleton, CA. He married (1) **Joann Baker**.
He married (2) 9 Jul 1994, Marquette, MI, **Linda Belanger** (Arthur John Belanger & Elizabeth Swenor) b 14 Jan 1963, Milwaukee, WI.

5.7.1.1.6.2.1   **MONTY, Rhea Valerie** b 29 Jan 1891, Waterbury, CT; d Aug 1962, MA. She married 19 Sep 1912, Portland, ME, **Willard Hiram Googins** (Fred A. Googins & Jennie Brazier) b 9 May 1893, Scarborough, ME; m (2) 1919? Harriet Laverty (Erastus Allen Laverty & Mary Abbie Welch); d 3 May 1931, Augusta, ME.
Willard Googins and his second wife had been married for 11 years in 1930 (US census, Westbrook, ME). They were still residents of Westbrook when he died (*Portland Press Herald*, 6 May 1931).

5.7.1.1.6.2.2   **MONTY, Flora** b Feb 1895, MA.
Flora Monty was living in her maternal grandfather's household in Easthampton, MA, in 1910 (US census).

5.7.1.2.1.1.1   **MONTY, Marie Azilda** b 18 Jun 1882, St. Johnsbury, VT.

5.7.1.2.1.1.2   **MONTY, Marie Lucille Georgiana** b & bp 26 & 31 Jan 1884, Rouses Point, NY.
Lucille Monty was living with her maternal aunt Marie Henriette Marchand and her second husband Henry Desnoyers in Clark, SD, in 1900 (US census).

5.7.1.2.1.1.3   **MONTY, Louis Joseph Henri** b & bp 4 & 5 Sep 1887, Plattsburgh, NY; d & bur 30 & 31 Jul 1889, St. Jean, QC.

5.7.1.5.3.4.1   **MONTY, Michel J.** b 1925?, Northfield, VT. He married **Thérèse Messier** (Richard Messier & Anna Blain) b Jul 1927, Barre, VT.
Michel Monty was a 5-year-old child living with his parents in Northfield, VT, in 1930 (US census). He and his wife were residents of Barre, VT, when his brother Charles (5.7.1.5. 3.4.3) died in 2005 (*Caledonian Record*, St. Johnsbury, VT, 15 Sep 2005).

5.7.1.5.3.4.2   **MONTY, Jacqueline T.** b 23 Jul 1926, Northfield, VT. She married **Marcel F. Vozzella** (Joseph Vozzella & Jennie ____) b 11 Nov 1928, Boston, MA.
Jacqueline Monty and her husband were residents of Westwood, MA, when her brother Charles (5.7.1.5.3.4.3) died in 2005 (*Caledonian Record*, St. Johnsbury, VT, 15 Sep 2005).

5.7.1.5.3.4.3   **MONTY, Charles L.** b 15 Sep 1927, Northfield, VT; d 7 Sep 2005, Littleton, NH. He married **JoAnn Percy** (Willie Percy & Alice ____).

Charles Monty was buried in Glenwood Cemetery in Littleton, NH (*Caledonian Record*, St. Johnsbury, VT, 15 Sep 2005).

5.7.1.5.3.4.4   **MONTY, Paul** b 4 Aug 1929, Northfield, VT; d & bur 18 & 20 Apr 1969, Barre, VT. He married **Janet Teresa Larocque** (André/Andrew B. Larocque & Eva Marie Therrien).

Paul Monty was buried in St. Monica Cemetery in Barre, VT.

5.7.1.5.3.4.5   **MONTY, Jeanne** b 30 Sep 1931, Northfield, VT; d & bur 10 & 14 Nov 2006, Bristol, CT. She married 1954? **Peter DellaBianca** (Pietro/Peter DellaBianca & Maria Columbo) b 13 Sep 1931, Bristol, CT; d & bur there 9 & 13 May 2003.

Peter DellaBianca and his wife had been married for forty-nine years when he died in 2003. They were both buried in St. Joseph Cemetery in Bristol, CT (*Hartford Courant*, 10 May 2003 and 12 Nov 2006).

5.7.1.5.3.4.6   **MONTY, Alfred R./Al** b 1934?, VT. He married **Anita H. Cano** (Manuel Cano & Amparo Puente) b 1929, Barre, VT.

Alfred Monty and his wife Anita were residents of Barre, VT, when his brother Charles (5.7.1.5.3.4.3) died in 2005 (*Caledonian Record*, St. Johnsbury, VT, 15 Sep 2005).

5.7.1.5.3.4.7   **MONTY, Lise A.** b 1937?, VT. She married 1969? **Robert V. Leary** (James E. Leary & Margaret _____) b 7 Feb 1932, Watertown, MA; d 23 Jul 1997, Newark, DE.

Robert V. Leary was a journalist who had been married for twenty-eight years at his death (*Tokyo Weekender*, 1 Aug 1997). Mrs. Lise Leary was a resident of Wilmington, DE, when her sister Jeanne Monty (5.7.1.5.3.4.5) died in 2006 (*Hartford Courant*, 12 Nov 2006).

5.7.1.5.3.10.1   **MONTY, Gilles** b & bp 16 Jun 1928, St. Jean, QC; d Dec 2000, Ste Foy, QC. He married 7 Apr 1950, St. Jean, QC, **Constance Provost** (Aurèle Provost & Floride Châteauneuf) b & bp there 27 Apr 1934.

Baptismal names: Louis Gilles Yvan Monty and Marie Alma Giseline Constance Provost.

5.7.1.5.3.10.2   **MONTY, Germain** b & bp 30 Jun 1929, St. Jean, QC; d there 12 Apr 1974. He married there 29 Jul 1950 **Cécile Boutin** (Wilfrid Boutin & Irène Therrien) b & bp there 22 & 23 Nov 1919.

Baptismal names: Joseph Osias Germain Monty and Marie Cécile Lucienne Gislaine Boutin.

5.7.1.9.1.2.1   **MONTY, Anonymous** b & d 8 Feb 1896, Lawrence, MA.

This child was stillborn.

5.7.1.9.1.2.2   **MONTY, Arthur Henry** b 29 Jan 1897, Lawrence, MA; d Aug 1969, Lowell, MA. He married there 9 Sep 1922, **Antoinette Chaput** (Philip Noah Chaput & Albina Larose) b there Oct 1896.

Antoinette Chaput may have died between 1938, when her name appears besides her husband's in the Lowell, MA, City Directory, and 1942, when Arthur Henry Monty's World War II Draft Registration card ignores her and refers to a daughter as the person most aware of his current address.

5.7.1.9.1.2.3   **MONTY, Priscilla B.** b Sep 1898, Lawrence, MA.

Priscilla Monty remained single and lived in her father's home in Lowell, MA, until at least 1956 (Lowell City Directories).

5.7.1.9.1.2.4   **MONTY, Leo J.** b 17 Aug 1903, Lawrence, MA; d 15 Jan 1992, Winchester, MA. He married 1927, Lowell, MA, **Evelyn J. Delahunt** (John Delahunt & Belle ____) b 9 Oct 1905, Salem, MA; d 7 Feb 1995, Winchester, MA.

The "marriage intentions" of Leo J. Monty and Evelyn Delahunt were published in the *Lowell Sunday Telegram* of 29 Oct 1927. He was a mill engineer in Stanford, ME, in 1930 (US census) and a chemical engineer in Reading, MA, in 1938 (City Directory). He and his wife were both still residents of Reading at their deaths. He was buried in Green Lawn Cemetery in Salem, MA (*Boston Herald*, 18 Jan 1992).

5.7.1.9.1.2.5   **MONTY, Albert F.** b 17 Nov 1905, Essex Co., MA; d 30 Aug 1982, Lowell, MA. He married 1927? **Theresa L.** ____ b 1907?, MA.

Albert F. Monty was a cotton mill worker in Lowell, MA, in 1930 when he and his 23-year-old wife Theresa L. had been married for three years (US census).

5.7.1.9.1.2.6   **MONTY, Viola** b 1907?, Essex Co., MA.

Viola Monty was 3 years old on 15 Apr 1910 (US census, Amesbury, MA). She remained single and was still living in her family home in Lowell, MA, in 1964 (US censuses; Lowell City Directories).

5.7.1.9.1.2.7   **MONTY, Irene** b 8 Jan 1912, Amesbury, MA; d 14 Apr 1972, Lowell, MA. She married **Alfred A. Bevins** (Arthur Bevins & Mary____) b 26 Feb 1909, Milton, VT; d 27 Aug 1991, Lowell, MA.

5.7.1.12.5.3.1   **MONTY, Germaine** b 11 Jun 1907, Attleboro, MA; d Mar 1993, Providence, RI.

5.7.1.12.5.3.2   **MONTY, Louis Alphonse** b & d 1908, Attleboro, MA.

5.7.1.12.5.3.3   **MONTY, Gertrude Una** b 27 Aug 1910, Attleboro, MA; d 27 May 2007, Pahrump, NV. She married (1) 24 Jan 1940, Woonsocket RI, **Paul Clément Dupré** (Siméon Clément Dupré & Marie Louise Guyon) b 1908; bur 1960 St. James Cemetery, Lincoln, RI.

She married (2) 25 Nov 1973, Woonsocket, RI, **Joseph Raymond McKitchen** b 9 Mar 1922; d & bur 22 Feb & 11 Mar 1993 Fort Myers, FL & Bourne, MA.

Joseph R. McKitchen was a Navy Veteran of World War II and was buried in the Massachusetts National Cemetery in Bourne, MA.

5.7.1.12.5.3.4   **MONTY, Rosario Adelbert** b 21 Nov 1911, Attleboro, MA; d there 25 Jul 1912.

This child was buried in Precious Blood Cemetery in Woonsocket, RI.

5.7.1.12.5.3.5   **MONTY, Genevieve Emma Estella** b 14 Jul 1913, Attleboro, MA; d there 4 Sep 1913.

This child was buried in Precious Blood Cemetery in Woonsocket, RI.

5.7.1.12.5.3.6   **MONTY, Anonymous** (male) b & d 1915, North Attleboro, MA.

5.7.1.12.5.3.7   **MONTY, Joseph** b & d 10 Mar 1916, Holyoke, MA.

5.7.1.12.5.7.1   **MONTY, Louis** b 23 Dec 1932, Holyoke, MA; d there 26 Dec 1932.

This child was buried in Notre Dame Cemetery in South Hadley Falls, MA.

5.7.1.12.5.7.2   **MONTY, Alice Emma** b 1 Apr 1934, Holyoke, MA. She married 28 Dec 1954, Burlington, VT, **Jean-Paul Diry** (Maurice Diry & Marie Louise Berthier) b 28 Feb 1931, Le Creuzot, France.

5.7.1.12.5.7.3   **MONTY, Jeanne Ruth** b 19 Jul 1935, Holyoke, MA.

5.7.1.12.5.7.4 **MONTY, Monique Thérèse** b 20 May 1941, Holyoke, MA; d 16 Mar 1997, Cheektowaga, NY. She married (1) 16 Jun 1962, Burlington, VT, **Charles F. O'Brien** (Francis J. O'Brien & Edith Rose McLaughlin) b 21 Mar 1939, Bronx, NY; m (2) Mrs. Emily French; d 10 Feb 2007, Ormond Beach, FL.

She was divorced when she married (2) Jan 1984, Fredonia, NY, and later divorced **Michael Valvo** (Joseph Valvo & Petrina Borzilleri) b 29 Aug 1931, NY.

Mrs. Monique O'Brien was the elementary principal at Cassadaga Valley Central School when she died (*Buffalo News*, 18 Mar 1997).

Charles O'Brien was a professor of American History at Clarkson University in Potsdam, NY, until he retired in 1999 and moved to Florida (*Burlington Free Press*, 18 Feb 2007).

5.7.2.6.2.4.1 **MONTY, George Henri** b & bp 22 Apr 1909, St. Alphonse, QC. He married there 3 Dec 1955, **Antoinette Robert** (Siméon Robert & Méranda Paquette) b & bp 13 & 14 Jun 1907, Ange Gardien, QC.

George H. Monty (Joseph François George Henri at his baptism) came to the United States with his parents in 1929 and was a dairy farm laborer in Sheldon, VT, in 1930 (US census). He predeceased his brother Leo Paul (5.7.2.6.2.4.3) (*Burlington Free Press*, 18 Dec 2002).

5.7.2.6.2.4.2 **MONTY, Emile Louis** b & bp 31 Dec 1912, St. Alphonse, QC; d 11 Jan 1996, Waterbury, CT. He married **Theresa L. Couture** (Elphège Couture & Delia Thibodeau) b 10 Feb 1920, Richford, VT; d 29 May 1998, Plymouth, CT.

Emile L. Monty (Joseph Louis Emile at his baptism) came to the United States with his parents in 1929 and was a dairy farm laborer in Swanton, VT, in 1930 (US census). He and his wife were in St. Albans, VT, until at least 1947 and then moved to Naugatuck, CT, in the 1950s (City Directories). They were still residents of Connecticut at their deaths but were both buried in St. George's Cemetery in Bakersfield, VT.

5.7.2.6.2.4.3 **MONTY, Leo Paul/Léopold** b & bp 5 & 7 May 1914, St. Alphonse, QC; d & bur 16 & 21 Dec 2002, Middlebury & Swanton, VT. He married 2 Jun 1936, St. Alphonse, QC, **Marie Reine Blanchard** (Alcide Blanchard & Evélina Martin) b & bp there 13 May 1912; d 19 Dec 1976, Swanton, VT.

This man was named Léopold Antonio at his baptism and Léopold in the text of his marriage record. Yet he signed that record as Leo Paul Monty, a name he had used since his arrival in Vermont (1930 US census, Sheldon, VT). He owned and operated farms in Franklin County, VT, and was buried in St. Mary's Cemetery in Swanton, VT (*Burlington Free Press*, 18 Dec 2002).

5.7.2.6.2.4.4 **MONTY, Maurice Lucien** b & bp 8 & 12 Mar 1916, St. Alphonse Granby, QC; d 8 & 11 Oct 2006, Enosburgh & Bakersfield, VT. He married 1943 **Lora Perry** (____ Perry & Hazel ____).

Maurice L. Monty (Joseph Lucien Maurice at his baptism) came to Enosburg, VT, with his family in 1929 and became a farmer and owner of a thrashing business there. He was buried in St. George's Cemetery in Bakersfield, VT. He and his wife Lora, who survived him, had been married for sixty-three years at his death (*St. Albans Messenger*, 10 Oct 2006).

5.7.2.6.2.4.5 **MONTY, Claude** b & bp 29 & 31 Oct 1918, St. Alphonse, QC; d Jun 1975.

Claude Monty (named Joseph Arthur Claude at his baptism) came to the United States with his parents in 1929 and was with them in Sheldon, VT, in 1930 (US census).

5.7.2.6.2.4.6 **MONTY, Helen/Elaine** b & bp 3 & 5 Feb 1921, St. Alphonse, QC. She married ____ **Trudell**.

This woman was named Marie Jeanne d'Arc Hélène at her baptism, Elaine in the 1930 US census in Sheldon, VT, where she was living with her parents, and Mrs. Helen Trudell when her brother Maurice (5.7.2.6.2.4.4) died in 2006. She had predeceased him (*St. Albans*

5.7.2.6.2.5.1   **MONTY, Yvon** b & bp 30 Sep & 4 Oct 1913, St. Alphonse, QC; d 18 Sep 1970, Marieville, QC. He married 26 Dec 1938, Sutton, QC, **Marie Rose Angèle Pollender** (Alfred Pollender & Marie Rose Côté) b & bp 19 & 20 Nov 1917, Farnham, QC.

5.7.2.6.2.5.2   **MONTY, Yvonne** b & bp 14 & 15 Jun 1915, St. Pie, QC; d 4 Mar 1985, St. Jean, QC. She married 6 Oct 1947, Ange Gardien, QC, **Eugène Roy** (Amédée Roy & Evangéline Roy) b & bp 16 & 17 Dec 1914, Abbotsford, QC.

   This woman was named Bertha Yvonne at her baptism. Her husband, named Adélard Eugène at his baptism, was a resident of St. Jean, QC, at their marriage.

5.7.2.6.2.5.3   **MONTY, Normand** b 24 Feb 1918, Indian Orchard, ME. He married 8 Nov 1945, Ghent, Belgium, **Marie Joseph DeWeer** (Odilon DeWeer & Mathilde Marie DeBarre) b 24 Sep 1917, Berchem, Belgium.

5.7.2.6.2.5.4   **MONTY, Lucille Marguerite** b & bp 28 & 29 Mar 1921, Ange Gardien, QC; d 8 Jan 1955, St. Jean, QC. She married 22 May 1943, Ange Gardien, QC, **Léo Marcel Allard** (Eusèbe Allard & Ida Rancourt) b & bp 3 & 12 Sep 1920, Lacolle, QC; d 9 Nov 1987, St. Jean, QC.

5.7.2.6.2.5.5   **MONTY, Grégoire** b & bp 4 Jul 1923, Ange Gardien, QC. He married there 5 Jan 1949 **Françoise Ménard** (Meseus Ménard & Rosanna Brodeur) b & bp 6 & 7 May 1927, Abbotsford, QC.

   Baptismal names: Joseph Arthur Grégoire Monty and Marie Jeanne Françoise Ménard.

5.7.2.6.2.5.6   **MONTY, Laurette Jeannette** b & bp 20 & 21 Feb 1928, Ange Gardien, QC; d & bur there 22 & 23 Feb 1928.

5.7.2.6.2.5.7   **MONTY, Réjeanne Mercédès Rita** b & bp 29 Sep & 1 Oct 1929, Ange Gardien, QC. She married 7 Sep 1953, Marieville, QC, **Gaston B. Charbonneau** (Bruno Charbonneau & Thérèse Dumas).

5.7.2.6.2.5.8   **MONTY, Blaise** b & bp 14 & 15 Jun 1932, Ange Gardien, QC; d & bur 18 & 21 Nov 1962, St. Jean & Marieville, QC. He married 23 Oct 1954, Marieville, QC, **Gisèle Bienvenue** (Lucien Bienvenue & Irène Ledoux) b & bur there 5 & 7 Feb 1933.

   This man was named Joseph Louis Blaise Monty at his baptism. His wife, named "Gisèle alias Isèle Bienvenue" in her marriage record, was in fact baptized under the name of Marie Yselle Jeannine Bienvenue.

5.7.2.6.2.5.9   **MONTY, Jacques André** b & bp 4 Feb 1934, Ange Gardien, QC. He married 7 Feb 1956, Marieville, QC, **Cécile Séguin** (Ovila Séguin & Cécile Monast) b & bp 12 & 18 Jul 1937, Richelieu, QC.

5.7.2.6.2.8.1   **MONTY, Béatrice** b & bp 15 & 17 Jul 1918, St. Alphonse, QC. She married there 1 Feb 1937 **Léopold Mercure** (Edouard Mercure & Rosanna Jobin) b & bp there 20 & 22 Nov 1914.

   This woman was named Marie Anne Béatrice at her baptism.

5.7.2.6.2.8.2   **MONTY, Aline Célina Edouardina** b & bp 16 & 18 Sep 1919, St. Alphonse, QC. She married 25 Sep 1948, Ange Gardien, QC, **Lucien Mailloux** (Edmond Mailloux & Rose Anna Paquette).

5.7.2.6.2.8.3   **MONTY, Georgette Jeanne d'Arc** b & bp 16 & 17 Apr 1921, St. Alphonse, QC. She married there 1 Dec 1945 **Marcel Racicot** (Maxime Racicot & Laura Belval) b & bp 2 & 5 Aug 1921, Granby, QC.

Marcel Racicot was named Joseph Roger Marcel at his baptism.

5.7.2.6.2.8.4 **MONTY, Joseph Conrad** b & bp 1 & 2 Mar 1923, St. Alphonse, QC; d & bur there 28 & 29 Mar 1923.

5.7.2.6.2.8.5 **MONTY, Rosaire André Roger** b & bp 30 Nov 1925, St. Alphonse, QC. He married 18 Oct 1951, Ange Gardien, QC, **Mariette Noëla Maynard** (Marius Maynard & Virginia Brien) b & bp there 25 & 27 Dec 1925.

5.7.2.6.2.8.6 **MONTY, Laurette** b & bp 18 Aug 1928, St. Alphonse, QC. She married 26 Sep 1959, Granby, QC, **Réjean Tétreault** (Rodolphe Tétreault & Bertha Levreault) b & bp there 27 & 28 May 1932.
Baptismal names: Marie Thérèse Lorette Monty and Joseph Léo Réjean Tétreault.

5.7.2.6.2.8.7 **MONTY, Marie Jeanne Françoise** b & bp 2 May 1933, St. Alphonse, QC. She married 16 Jul 1960, Cowansville, QC, **Marcel Rodrigue Véronneau** (Télesphore Véronneau & Marie Madeleine St. Jean) b & bp 15 Mar & 21 Apr 1940, Clarenceville, QC.

5.7.2.6.4.4.1 **MONTY, Arthur Léonide Robert** b & bp 19 & 24 Jul 1904, Bromont, QC.

5.7.2.6.4.5.1 **MONTY, André/Andrew René** b & bp 29 Apr & 5 May 1918, Sweetsburg, QC; d 10 Oct 2005, Ottawa, Ontario, Canada. He married there 11 Oct 1941 **Agnes Teresa/Theresa George** (John George & Gertrude O'Brien) b & bp 3 & 7 Dec 1919, Toronto, Ontario, Canada; d Sep 2000, Ottawa, Ontario, Canada.
This man was named André René at his baptism, Andrew René at his marriage, and A. René Monty in his obituary in the *Montreal Gazette* of 14 Oct 2005.

5.7.2.6.4.5.2 **MONTY, Marguerite Lorraine** b & bp 13 & 15 Aug 1920, Granby, QC; d & bur there 6 & 7 Nov 1920.

5.7.2.6.4.5.3 **MONTY, George Louis** b & bp 24 Apr & 6 May 1923, Montreal, QC; d 13 Jan 1991, Lennoxville, QC. He married 23 Sep 1950, Sherbrooke, QC, **Jean Abigail Farwell** (Judson Gledden Farwell & Eliza Gertrude Sykes) b & bp 26 Feb 22 Sep 1927, Compton, QC.
George Louis Monty (Marie Georges Louis at his baptism and Louis at his marriage) was buried in the small Ives Hill Cemetery near Compton, QC, along with a large number of his wife's relatives. Jean Abigail Farwell was baptized in the United Church of Canada in Compton. She survived her brother-in-law A. René Monty (5.7.2.6.4.5.1) who died in 2005 (*Montreal Gazette*, 14 Oct 2005).

5.7.2.6.4.5.4 **MONTY, Elizabeth/Betty Jeanne** b & bp 5 & 7 Jul 1926, Rock Island, QC; d 29 Oct 1991, Rochester, NY. She married 5 Jul 1954, Rock Island, QC, **John Cunningham**.

5.7.2.6.4.5.5 **MONTY, Helen Patricia** b & bp 18 & 24 Sep 1927, Rock Island, QC. She married there 29 Dec 1952 **Paul Berthiaume** (Lelmond Berthiaume & Alice Dumoulin) b & bp 10 & 16 May 1926, Pointe Gatineau, QC.
Baptismal names: Marie Hélène Patricia Monty and Joseph Léo André Paul Guy Berthiaume.

5.7.2.6.4.7.1 **MONTY, Ernest Siméon** b & bp 31 Oct & 1 Nov 1912, Bromont, QC; d & bur 7 & 9 Jul 1916, Granby & Bromont, QC.

5.7.2.6.4.7.2 **MONTY, Blanche Anne Thérèse** b & bp 16 & 18 Apr 1915, Bromont, QC. She married 12 Sep 1953, St. Alphonse, QC, **Georges Aimé Choquette** (Georges Choquette & Aldéa Viens) b & bp 3 Oct 1918, Milton, QC.

5.7.2.6.4.7.3   MONTY, Albert Ernest b & bp 13 & 17 Sep 1916, Granby, QC. He married 30 Jun 1945, Montreal, QC, **Rolande Rousseau** (Raoul Rousseau & Georgiana Parent) b & bp 21 Apr 1921, Valleyfield, QC.

5.7.2.6.4.7.4   MONTY, Gaston b & bp 21 & 22 Jan 1923, Montreal, QC. He married there 27 Apr 1946 **Marie Marthe Fernande Rousseau** (Raoul Rousseau & Georgiana Parent) b & bp 30 & 31 May 1922, Valleyfield, QC.
    Baptismal name: Joseph André Gaston Monty.

5.7.2.6.4.8.1   MONTY, André Bernard b & bp 20 & 21 May 1922, Grenville, QC.

5.7.2.6.4.8.2   MONTY, Gisèle Carmel b & bp 27 Apr & 2 May 1925, Grenville, QC.

5.7.2.6.4.8.3   MONTY, Lise Marceline Louise b & bp 11 & 18 Nov 1932, Grenville, QC.

5.7.2.6.4.9.1   MONTY, Clément Dollard André b & bp 24 & 27 May 1923, Granby, QC; d 7 Oct 1990, Montreal, QC. He married there 30 Sep 1950 **Madeleine Pauline Claire Laverdure** (Odilon Laverdure & Marie Louise Venne) b & bp there 9 Nov 1924; d May 1999, QC.

5.7.2.6.4.9.2   MONTY, Andrée Thérèse b & bp 6 & 8 Dec 1926, Granby, QC. She married 8 Dec 1958, Montreal, QC, **Jacques Chambon** (Louis Chambon & Adrienne Poulet).

5.7.2.6.4.9.3   MONTY, Denyse Francine Josette Gisèle b & bp 16 & 19 Jan 1929, Granby, QC; d 15 Aug 1987.

5.7.2.6.6.7.1   MONTY, Rhea A. b 7 Jul 1909, New Bedford, MA; d 24 Dec 2005, Sacramento, CA. She married 1936, New Bedford, MA, **Guilherme M. Luiz** (Joseph G. Luiz & Philomena ____) b there 8 Apr 1916; d 7 Apr 2000, Boston, MA.

5.7.2.6.6.7.2   MONTY, Homer/Omer b 1913?, New Bedford, MA; d there 1922.
    Homer Monty was 6 years old on 1 Jan 1920 (US census, New Bedford, MA). He was named Omer at his death.

5.7.2.6.6.7.3   MONTY, George A. b 12 Jun 1915, New Bedford, MA; d 29 May 1996, Multnomah Co., OR. He married 1941? **Mildred Souza** (Antone Souza & Ellen ____) b 6 Nov 1921, New Bedford, MA.
    George Monty and his wife lived most of their married life in Southern California where at least three of their children were born. He predeceased his wife (*Orange County Register*, 24 Jun 1996).

5.7.2.6.6.7.4   MONTY, Leo W. b 7 Feb 1918, New Bedford, MA; d there 8 Aug 1999. He married **Helena J. Desposito** (Angelo R. D'Esposito/Desposito & Marianna Faragomo) b 23 May 1925, Chelsea, MA.
    Leo W. Monty was a resident of Fairhaven, MA, at his death. He predeceased his wife (*South Coast Today*, 10 Aug 1999).

5.7.2.6.6.7.5   MONTY, Irene b 27 Oct 1919, New Bedford, MA. She married ____ **Gonsalves**.
    Mrs. Irene Gonsalves was a resident of New Bedford when her brother Leo (5.7.2.6.6.7.4) died in 1999 (*South Coast Today*, 10 Aug 1999).

5.7.2.6.6.7.6   MONTY, Doris Victoria b 9 Jun 1923, New Bedford, MA; d 1 Jul 2005,

Fullerton, CA. She married (1) **John Joseph Bousquet** (John Bousquet & Rose Boucher) b 12 Jun 1924, New Bedford, MA; d 26 Oct 1968, Fullerton, CA.

She married (2) 6 Aug 1976, Orange Co., CA, **Louis Edgar Sanford** b 20 Jan 1931; d 11 Nov 2003, CA.

Doris Victoria Monty and Louis Edgar Sanford were both residents of Chino Hills, CA, at their deaths. They were buried in the Riverside National Cemetery in Riverside, CA.

5.7.2.6.6.8.1   **MONTY, Omer Albert** b 29 Oct 1909, New Bedford, MA; d there 18 Dec 1990.

5.7.2.6.6.8.2   **MONTY, Raymond/René** b 1911?, New Bedford, MA.

René Monty was an 8-year-old student staying with his three brothers in St. Joseph's Orphanage in Fall River, MA, on 1 Jan 1920 (US census). I have been unable to find him in later years though he was most probably the deceased "Joseph Raymond Monty" referred to in his brother Ovila A. Monty's obituary (*South Coast Today*, 22 Oct 2001).

5.7.2.6.6.8.3   **MONTY, Joseph Philip** b 11 May 1913, New Bedford, MA; d there 5 Jan 1988. He married **Mary Zembik** (Jacob Zembik & Katarzyna Kot) b 2 Dec 1912, New Bedford, MA; d & bur there 30 Nov & 3 Dec 2004.

Mary Zembik was buried in Sacred Heart Cemetery in New Bedford, MA (*South Coast Today*, 1 Dec 2004),

5.7.2.6.6.8.4   **MONTY, Ovila A.** b 5 Apr 1915, New Bedford, MA; d & bur 20 & 23 Oct 2001, New Bedford & Fairhaven, MA. He married **Mildred E. Durocher** (Napoleon Durocher & Albertine E. ___) b 18 May 1917, New Bedford, MA; d there 6 Dec 1982.

Ovila Monty and his wife spent most of their married life in Fairhaven, MA (City Directories). He was buried in Riverside Cemetery there (*South Coast Today*, 22 Oct 2001).

5.7.2.6.6.8.5   **MONTY, Loretta C.** b 3 Oct 1918, New Bedford, MA; d & bur 30 Aug & 5 Sep 2007, New Bedford & Bourne, MA. She married (1) 1937?, New Bedford, MA, **James Reedy**.

She married (2) **Kenneth W. Chapman** (Clarence L. Chapman & Marie A. Lehoux) b 4 Dec 1918, New Bedford, MA; d & bur 25 & 27 Nov 2002, North Dartmouth & Bourne, MA.

Kenneth Chapman was a US Army Veteran of World War II. He and his wife were buried in the Massachusetts National Cemetery in Bourne, MA (*South Coast Today*, 26 Nov 2002 and 2 Sep 2007).

5.7.2.6.6.9.1   **MONTY, Omer Leo/Homer** b 5 Oct 1918, New Bedford, MA; d 4 Dec 1990, Carver, MA. He married **Jeannine A. Carrier** (Willie Carrier & Annette Saucier) b 9 Nov 1919, Van Buren, ME; d 27 Apr 2005, Carver, MA.

This man was known as Homer Monty in the 1920 and 1930 censuses in New Bedford, MA, where he was living with his parents. As an adult, when he enlisted in the US Army in Boston, MA, on 19 Nov 1942, and at his death, his name was Omer L. or Omer Leo Monty.

5.7.2.8.1.3.1   **MONTY, Florilda** b 1901, Fall River, MA; d there 22 Jul 1904, at the age of 3.

Florilda Monty was buried in Notre Dame Cemetery in Fall River, MA.

5.7.2.8.1.3.2   **MONTY, Louise** b 15 Oct 1902, Fall River, MA; d there 25 Feb 1993. She married there 15 Aug 1921 **Alfred Emard** (Vital Emard & Georgiana Croteau) b there 10 Dec 1897; d there 12 Sep 1981.

5.7.2.8.1.3.3   **MONTY, Eva** b 10 Jan 1906, Fall River, MA; d there 12 Jun 1906 at the age of 5 months and 2 days.

Eva Monty was buried in Notre Dame Cemetery in Fall River, MA.

5.7.2.8.1.3.4   **MONTY, Alice** b Mar 1907, Fall River, MA; d there 5 Sep 1907, at the age of 6 months.
Alice Monty was buried in Notre Dame Cemetery in Fall River, MA.

5.7.2.8.1.3.5   **MONTY, Lucy** b Jan 1909, Fall River, MA.
Lucy Monty was 15 months old on 15 Apr 1910 when she was living with her parents in Fall River, MA. She was with her father in Plainfield, CT, in 1920 (US censuses).

5.7.2.8.1.3.6   **MONTY, Claire** b Jan 1910, Fall River, MA.
Claire Monty was 3 months old on 15 Apr 1910 when she was living with her parents in Fall River, MA. She was with her father in Plainfield, CT, in 1920 (US censuses).

5.7.2.8.1.3.7   **MONTY, Leo Theodore** b 27 Oct 1913, Fall River, MA; d 23 Jan 1991, Clearwater, FL. He married around 1947 **Rachel** ____ b 12 Jun 1920.
Leo Monty was living with his father in Plainfield, CT, in 1920 and in Fall River, MA, in 1930 (US censuses). He and his wife lived in Seekonk, MA, while he worked in Providence, RI, first as a clerk and then a chauffeur for Railway Express (City Directories). He predeceased his wife.

5.7.2.8.1.3.8   **MONTY, Letria** (?) b 17 Feb 1915, Fall River, MA; d there 13 Mar 1915, at the age of 26 days.
This child was buried in Notre Dame Cemetery in Fall River, MA.

5.7.2.8.2.2.1   **MONTY/MONTIE, Dorothea Doris** b & bp 8 & 18 Feb 1918, Woonsocket & Providence, RI; d 23 Jun 1997, Pawtucket, RI. She married 2 Sep 1940, Central Falls, RI, **Réal Frédéric Blais** (Napoléon Blais & Blandine Ducharme) b & bp 1 Jul 1915, Berthierville, QC; d 20 May 1998, Pawtucket, RI.

5.7.2.8.2.2.2   **MONTY, Leona Hermine** b & bp 12 & 14 Apr 1919, Woonsocket, RI; d 10 Feb 2002, Cumberland, RI. She married 8 May 1937, Central Falls, RI, **James Kelly**.

5.7.5.5.2.2.1   **MONTY, Harold J.** b 20 Jul 1943, CT; d & bur 26 & 31 May 2000, East Hartford, CT.
Harold J. Monty did not marry. He was buried in Hillside Cemetery in East Hartford, CT (*Hartford Courant*, 30 May 2000).

5.7.5.5.2.2.2   **MONTY, Ronald** married **Maria** ____.
Ronald Monty and his wife Maria were residents of Albuquerque, NM, when his brother Harold (5.7.5.5.2.2.1) died in 2000 (*Hartford Courant*, 30 May 2000).

5.7.5.5.6.1.1   **MONTY, Lionel H.** b Aug 1941, CT.

5.7.5.7.4.2.1   **MONTY, Arthur Robert** b & bp 17 Jul & 1 Aug 1939, Montreal, QC.

5.7.5.7.4.2.2   **MONTY, Wilfrid Arthur Armand Conrad** b & bp 18 & 24 Nov 1940, Montreal, QC.

5.7.7.1.4.3.1   **MONTY, Irene** b 14 Dec 1904, Holyoke, MA; d Apr 1988, Pawtucket, RI. She married **Edward F. Handrigan** (John J. Handrigan & Mary Ellen Burton) b 1903?, Pawtucket, RI.
Edward F. Handrigan was 7 years old in 1910 when he was living with his parents in Pawtucket, RI (US census).

5.7.7.1.4.3.2   **MONTY, Mabel** b 6 Nov 1908, Pawtucket, RI; d there Mar 1987. She married 1931? **Patrick J. Beirne** (Michael Beirne & Margaret ____) b 1 Aug 1901, England; d

Jul 1976, Pawtucket, RI.

5.7.7.1.4.5.1   MONTY, Marian H. b 22 Dec 1912, Holyoke, MA; d there 27 Feb 1988. She married **William F. Kusek** b 6 Apr 1908, MA; d 1 Oct 1973, Holyoke, MA.

5.7.7.1.4.5.2   MONTY, John Roland b 17 Aug 1914, Holyoke, MA; d there 27 Nov 1991. He married there **Helena/Helen Ruell** (Jeremiah/Jerry Ruell & Mary Griffin) b there 9 Jul 1919; d there 12 Nov 1987.

5.7.7.1.4.5.3   MONTY, Adrian E. b 19 Dec 1916, Holyoke, MA; d there 18 Feb 2005. He married 1945? **Olga Klemyk** (Stefan/Stephen Klemyk & Mary ____) b 6 Nov 1921, Holyoke, MA.

Adrian Monty and his wife had been married for fifty-nine years at his death (*Springfield Republican*, 19 Feb 2005).

5.7.7.1.4.6.1   MONTY, Hazel E. b 23 Nov 1907, Holyoke, MA; d 19 Dec 1988, Springfield, MA. She married **Leonard J. Murphy** (Jeremiah Murphy & Agnes ____) b 6 Nov 1903, Chicopee, MA; d & bur 2 & 5 Jan 1994, Springfield & Chicopee, MA.

Leonard J. Murphy was a 40-year police officer in Chicopee, MA, when he retired in 1968. He was buried in St. Patrick's Cemetery there (*Springfield Union News*, 3 Jan 1994).

5.7.7.1.4.6.2   MONTY, Albert b Jan 1909, Holyoke, MA; d there 18 Feb 1909, at the age of 6 weeks.

5.7.7.1.4.6.3   MONTY, Albert F. b 1914?, Holyoke, MA.

Albert Monty was a 5-year-old child living with his parents in Holyoke, MA, on 1 Jan 1920. He was staying with his aunt Julia Monty (5.7.7.1.4.1) and her husband in South Hadley, MA, in 1930 (US censuses).

5.7.7.15.1.2.1   MONTY, Hélène b & bp 17 & 19 Apr 1930, Montreal, QC. She married there 6 Dec 1952 **Jean Guertin** (Fernand Guertin & Jeanne Poupart) b & bp there 24 & 26 Aug 1928.

Baptismal names: Marie Eugénie Léontine Hélène Monty and Joseph Albert Maurice Jean Guertin.

5.7.7.15.1.2.2   MONTY, Pierre b & bp 18 & 22 Jan 1935, Montreal, QC; d there 14 Nov 1967. He married 14 Jun 1958, Westmount, QC, **Marie Josée Roche** (Redmond Roche & Alice Brunelle) b & bp 5 Dec 1936 & 5 Jan 1937, Montreal & Chambly, QC.

Baptismal names: Joseph Henri Paul Pierre Monty and Marie Nicole Josée Jeanne Roche.

5.7.7.15.1.4.1   MONTY, Denise b & bp 5 & 13 Oct 1935, Montreal, QC. She married there 3 Oct 1959 **Jacques Levesque** (Joseph Oscar Levesque & Lucienne Bombardier) b & bp there 17 & 21 Jul 1934.

Baptismal names: Marie Albina Eugénie Denise Ginette Monty and Joseph Gaston Jacques Elzéar Levesque.

5.7.7.15.1.4.2   MONTY, Huguette b & bp 1 & 10 Aug 1940, Montreal, QC. She married there 25 Aug 1962 **Jean Valiquette** (Maurice Valiquette & Claire Brunet) b & bp 5 & 16 Oct 1938, Quebec, QC.

Baptismal names: Marie Albina Eugénie Gisèle Huguette Monty and Joseph Albert Gilles Guy Jean Valiquette.

5.7.7.15.1.8.1   MONTY, Louise b & bp 11 & 13 Aug 1942, Montreal, QC. She married there 15 Mar 1969 **Jean Demers** (Georges Demers & Lucille Besner) b 16 Mar 1942, Quebec, QC.

5.7.7.15.1.8.2   **MONTY, Rodolphe** b 16 May 1946, Montreal, QC. He married (1) there 21 Jun 1969 **Lise Crevier** (Charles Crevier & Armande Quesnel).

He married (2) **Francine Lebeau** (Jean Lebeau & Aline Poirier) b 24 Jun 1948, Baie Comeau, QC.

5.7.7.15.1.8.3   **MONTY, Jean C.** b 26 Jun 1947, Montreal, QC. He married there 17 May 1969 **Jocelyne Bélanger** (Paul Bélanger & Yvonne Quesnel).

5.7.7.15.1.11.1   **MONTY, Marie Claude** b 28 Sep 1950, Montreal, QC. She married there 28 Sep 1973 **Thomas Carter**.

5.7.10.2.1.2.1   **MONTY, Edouard/Eddy** b & bp 1 Jul 1918, St. Césaire, QC; d Sep 2003, Granby, QC. He married 29 Oct 1938, St. Césaire, QC, **Florence Gilberte Massé** (Euclide Massé & Délima Boucher) b & bp there 31 Dec 1916 & 2 Jan 1917.

5.7.10.2.1.2.2   **MONTY, Guy** married 26 Oct 1963, Acton Vale, QC, **Réjane Jutras** (Henri Jutras & Yvonne Denis) b & bp there 10 & 11 Sep 1937.

5.7.10.2.1.4.1   **MONTY, Jacques** b & bp 22 & 23 Nov 1938, Ange Gardien, QC. He married 30 Sep 1961, Ste Sabine, QC, **Simone Campbell** (Leopold Campbell & Louisa Paquette) b & bp there 5 & 6 Feb 1940.

Baptismal names: Joseph Moïse Jacques Monty and Marie Anne Irène Simone Campbell.

5.7.10.2.1.4.2   **MONTY, Yvonne France Violette** b & bp 16 & 17 Nov 1939, Ange Gardien, QC.

5.7.10.2.3.2.1   **MONTY, Simon Adrien** b & bp 1 Oct 1914, Abbotsford, QC; d 26 Jun 1963, St. Hyacinthe, QC. He married there 1 Oct 1938, **Florianne Gilberte Côté** (Elphège Côté & Antonine Beaulac) b & bp 13 May 1917, St. Cyrille, QC.

5.7.10.2.3.2.2   **MONTY, Thérèse Jeanne** b & bp 20 & 21 Aug 1915, Granby, QC. She married 29 Sep 1934, St. Hyacinthe, QC, **Félix Boisvert** (Elie Boisvert & Marie Louise Noël) b & bp 19 & 20 Nov 1909, Durham, QC.

Baptismal name: Joseph Donat Félix Boisvert.

5.7.10.2.3.2.3   **MONTY, Simonne** b & bp 6 & 7 May 1921, Abbotsford, QC. She married 1 Aug 1953, St. Hyacinthe, QC, **Charles Delisle** (Réal Delisle & Florence Casavant).

5.7.10.2.3.2.4   **MONTY, Laurette** b & bp 6 Sep 1925, Abbotsford, QC. She married 22 Jan 1944, St. Hyacinthe, QC, **Emile Gosselin** (Wilfrid Gosselin & Joséphine Beauregard).

5.7.10.2.3.2.5   **MONTY, Arthur** b & bp 8 & 10 Jul 1927, Abbotsford, QC. He married 1 Jul 1950, St. Hyacinthe, QC, **Thérèse Caouette** (Rémi Caouette & Alphonsine Provencher) b & bp there 28 Aug 1931.

Baptismal names: Jean-Baptiste Arthur Monty and Marie Thérèse Marguerite Caouette.

5.7.10.2.3.2.6   **MONTY, Paul Emile Raymond** b & bp 21 & 24 Sep 1932, St. Hyacinthe, QC. He married there 6 Sep 1952 **Clémence Gaudette** (Omer Gaudette & Imelda Bourque) b & bp there 8 Apr 1930.

Baptismal name: Marie Delphine Clémence Gaudette.

5.7.10.2.4.1.1   **MONTY, Elizabeth** b 15 Apr 1919, Lawrence, MA; d & bur 23 & 26 Jan 1998, Tewksbury & Lawrence, MA. She married **Alexander J. Stanulonis** b 20 Nov 1917,

MA; d 15 Jan 1987, Methuen, MA.

Elizabeth Monty was buried in Immaculate Conception Cemetery in Lawrence, MA (*Lawrence Eagle Tribune*, 24 Jan 1998).

5.7.10.2.4.1.2 MONTY, Albert P. b 24 Mar 1921, Lawrence, MA; d there 30 Dec 1985.

5.7.10.2.4.1.3 MONTY, Eleanor A. b 1923?, Lawrence, MA.

Eleanor Monty was 7 years old in April 1930 when she was living with her parents in Lawrence, MA (US census). She was still a member of her father's household there in 1945 (City Directories).

5.7.10.2.4.1.4 MONTY, Marion b Jun/Jul 1928, Lawrence, MA.

Marion Monty was 1 year and 9 months old on 1 Apr 1930 when she was living with her parents in Lawrence, MA (US census). She was still a member of her father's household there in 1951 (City Directories).

5.7.10.2.8.2.1 MONTY, Arthur David b & bp 28 Mar & 10 Apr 1938, Manchester & Suncook, NH. He married (1) 6 Nov 1965, Monterey, CA, **Pamela B. Ackerman** b 1944?

He married (2) 26 Nov 1978, Loudon, NH, **Mary Evelyn Goers** (James McKenzie B. Goers & Doris Childs) b 29 Mar 1947, Baltimore, MD.

Pamela B. Ackerman was 21 years old when she married in 1965.

5.7.10.2.8.3.1 MONTY, Jacqueline b & bp 27 Jan & 7 Feb 1932, Manchester & Suncook, NH. She married 8 Nov 1969, Auburn, NH, **Marcel C. Rivard** (Robert Rivard & Anna/Marie Anne Lamontagne) b 8 Sep 1921, Manchester, NH; m (1) there 3 Jul 1948 Blanche Agnes Moynihan (David L. Moynihan & Alma ____); d 19 Jan 1974.

Baptismal name: Marie Charlotte Jacqueline Liliane Monty.

5.7.10.2.8.3.2 MONTY, Janet Elaine b & bp 12 & 27 Jan 1946, Suncook, NH. She married there 4 Jul 1967 **Kenneth Grant Follansbee** (James G. Follansbee & Vilah Poor) b 1 Feb 1945, NH.

5.7.10.2.8.6.1 MONTY, Lois Mary b & bp 11 Oct 1943, Concord, NH; d 1943.

Lois Monty died in infancy according to her mother's obituary in the *Hartford Courant* of 11 May 2004.

5.7.10.2.8.6.2 MONTY, Percalie b 16 Jan 1947, Manchester, NC. She married (1) 13 Dec 1969, Mansfield, CT, **Richard A. Boucher** (Joseph A. Boucher & Elizabeth Fournier) b 29 Feb 1944, Portland, ME; d 29 Nov 1985, Manchester, CT.

She married (2) 1 Apr 1989, Hartford, CT, **Bruce A. Williamson** b 1948?; m (1) 28 Jul 1979, Wethersfield, CT, Doree C. Bascom.

Bruce A. Williamson was 41 years old at his second marriage. He and his wife Percalie were residents of Manchester, CT, when her mother died in 2004 (*Hartford Courant*, 11 May 2004).

5.7.10.2.8.6.3 MONTY, Philip A. b Apr 1949. He married 15 Aug 1970, Mansfield, CT, **Jeanne M. Alassi** b Jan 1949.

Philip Monty and his wife were residents of Willington, CT, when his mother died in 2004 (*Hartford Courant*, 11 May 2004).

5.7.10.2.8.6.4 MONTY, Karl A. b Jul 1950. He married **Michele ____** b Mar 1960.

Karl Monty was a resident of Preston, CT, when his mother died in 2004 (*Concord Monitor*, 12 May 2004).

5.7.10.2.8.6.5 MONTY, Jo D. b Apr 1955. She married 14 Apr 1973, Windham, CT, **John Paul Ouellette** b Apr 1954.

Jo Monty and her husband were residents of Mansfield, CT, when her mother died in 2004 (*Hartford Courant*, 11 May 2004).

5.7.10.3.1.1.1 **MONTE, Anna Mae** b 10 Mar 1918, Jewett City, CT; d 12 May 1973, RI. She married **Elmer Alfred Whitman** (Frederick Emerson Whitman & Susie A. Turner) b 12 Jun 1916, Scituate, RI, d there 29 Jan 1962.

Anna Mae Monte and her husband were buried in the Whitman burial lot in Scituate, RI.

5.7.10.3.1.1.2 **MONTE, Ilene Virginia** b 23 Nov 1919, Jewett City, CT; d & bur 15 & 20 Mar 1986, San Diego, CA & Honolulu, HI. She married **George Alden Schaedler** (John Schaedler & Myrtle Hollern) b Feb 1919, St. Cloud, MN.

Ilene V. Monte was buried in the National Cemetery of the Pacific in Honolulu, HI. She predeceased her husband who was living in Hawaii when his sister Mrs. Phyllis E. Prem died in 2005 (*St. Cloud Times*, 9 Jun 2005).

5.7.10.3.3.5.1 **MONTIE, Robert C.** b 23 Oct 1929, Putnam, CT; d 17 Apr 2005, Fall River, MA. He married as his second wife, 1997? **Doris Valley** b 31 May 1927.

Robert C. Montie had been married to his wife Doris for eight years at his death (*Herald News*, Fall River, MA, 20 Apr 2005). He was a World War II Army veteran and was buried in the Massachusetts National Cemetery in Bourne, MA.

5.7.10.3.3.5.2 **MONTIE, Norman Kenneth** b 12 May 1931, Putnam, CT; d 2 Dec 1998, Johnston, RI.

Norman Kenneth Montie was a US Navy veteran (Korea). He was buried in St. Anne's Cemetery in Cranston, RI.

5.7.10.3.3.5.3 **MONTIE, Theresa** b 23 Jun 1933, Putnam, CT; d & bur 19 & 23 Mar 2001, Hartford, CT & Harrisville, RI. She married **Donat A. Martel** b May 1932; m (2) 7 Sep 1996, Bolton, CT, Bette E. Turcotte (Mrs. John Arigno).

Theresa Montie was buried in St. Patrick's Cemetery in Harrisville, RI (*Hartford Courant*, 21 Mar 2001).

5.7.10.3.13.9.1 **MONTE, Richard Gerard** b 5 Feb 1947, NY; d 14 Oct 1990 & 1 Feb 1991, Wareham & Bourne, MA.

Richard Gerard Monte was a US Navy veteran (Vietnam) and was buried in the Massachusetts National Cemetery in Bourne, MA.

5.7.10.3.13.9.2 **MONTE, Daniel Alexander** b 15 Jul 1948, NY; d 4 Oct 2001, Wareham, MA.

Daniel Alexander Monte was an Air Force veteran (Vietnam) and was buried in the Massachusetts National Cemetery in Bourne, MA (*Cape Cod Times*, Hyannis, MA, 6 Oct 2001).

5.7.10.3.13.9.3 **MONTE, Bruce**

Bruce Monte was a resident of Georgia when his brother Daniel (5.7.10.3.13.9.2) died in 2001 (*Cape Cod Times*, Hyannis, MA, 6 Oct 2001).

5.7.10.3.13.9.4 **MONTE, Pamela A.** b 25 Jan 1957.

Pamela Monte was a resident of Monument Beach, MA, when her brother Daniel (5.7.10.3.13.9.2) died in 2001 (*Cape Cod Times*, Hyannis, MA, 6 Oct 2001).

5.7.10.3.13.9.5 **MONTE, Carol Ann** b 25 Apr 1960. She married **Joseph M. Johnson** (John A. Johnson & Mary L. ____) b 15 Aug 1957.

Mrs. Carol Ann Johnson was a resident of Pocasset, MA, when her brother Daniel Monty (5.7.10.3.13.9.2) died in 2001 (*Cape Cod Times*, Hyannis, MA, 6 Oct 2001).

5.7.10.5.1.7.1 **MONTY, Hélène** b & bp 21 & 23 Jul 1939, Drummondville, QC. She married there 27 Dec 1965 **Fernand Leblanc** (Théodore Leblanc & Amanda Fortier) b & bp 29 & 30 Sep 1934, Ste-Hélène-de-Chester, QC.

Baptismal names: Marie Yolande Hélène Monty and Fernand Ronald Rolland Leblanc.

5.7.10.5.1.7.2 **MONTY, Claude** married 7 Aug 1965, Drummondville, QC, **Hélène Allard** (Laval Allard & Claire Lefebvre) b 1943?; d Apr 1999, QC, at the age of 56.

5.7.10.5.1.8.1 **MONTY, Gislaine** b & bp 22 & 23 Nov 1939, Drummondville, QC. She married 25 Oct 1958, Granby, QC, **Jean-Paul Rosaire Matton** (Eudore Matton & Irène Paquette) b & bp there 26 & 27 Sep 1927.

This woman was named Marie Monique Ghyslaine at her baptism.

5.7.10.5.1.8.2 **MONTY, Serge** married 2 Oct 1965, Granby, QC, **Isabelle Coulombe** (Adélard Coulombe & Juliana Gagnon) b & bp there 2 Jan 1938; m (1) there 28 Jun 1958 Claude Rodrigue (Louis Philippe Rodrigue & Amélia Pomerleau).

5.7.10.5.2.5.1 **MONTY, Germain Gaston** b & bp 11 Feb 1926, Valcourt, QC; d & bur there 11 & 12 Feb 1926.

5.7.10.5.2.5.2 **MONTY, Lucien Rolland** b & bp 6 Dec 1928, Roxton Falls, QC; d & bur there 6 & 7 Dec 1928.

5.7.10.5.5.1.1 **MONTY, Rita Lucille** b 23 Feb 1930, Manchester, NH. She married there 19 Jun 1948 **Lionel C. Benoit**.

5.7.10.5.5.1.2 **MONTY, Joseph Robert Yvon** b 23 May 1931, Manchester, NH. He married there 16 Aug 1952 **Jeanne Morency** (Gédéon Morency & Rhea Dussault) b there 17 Oct 1929.

5.7.10.5.5.1.3 **MONTY, Rose Florence** b 8 Jun 1932, Manchester, NH. She married 19 Jul 1962, Hartford, CT, **Walter Mabe**.

5.7.10.5.5.1.4 **MONTY, Raymond F.** b 18 Aug 1933, Manchester, NH.

Raymond F. Monty was a resident of Lawrence, MA, in 1953 and 1956 while serving in the US Army (Lawrence City Directories).

5.7.10.5.5.1.5 **MONTY, Jeanne Doris** b 24 Nov 1934, Manchester, NH. She married 4 Jul 1960, Lawrence, MA, **Edward J. Anderson**.

5.7.10.5.5.1.6 **MONTY, Pauline Patricia** b 16 Jun 1936, Manchester, NH. She married 9 Apr 1955, Lawrence, MA, **James F. Blackington** (Herbert Sebastian Blackington & Gladys Anderton) b there 28 Dec 1936; d there 17 Sep 2001.

5.7.10.5.6.1.1 **MONTY, Joseph Edward** b & bp 6 & 22 Jan 1928, Pascoag, RI; d 9 Jan 1991, Milford, MA. He married 21 Aug 1954, Providence, RI, **Marie Rose Theresa Guerette**.

5.7.10.5.6.1.2 **MONTY, Helen Margaret** b & bp 19 Dec 1937 & 2 Jan 1938, Pascoag, RI; d & bur 14 & 19 Jan 2005, Plainsboro, NJ & Bellingham, MA. She married 12 Apr 1958, Pascoag, RI, **Ernest Baillargeon** (Walter Baillargeon & Rita ____) b 2 Jan 1938, Woonsocket, RI.

Helen Margaret Monty predeceased her husband. She was buried in St. John the Baptist Cemetery in Bellingham, MA (*Trenton Times*, 18 Jan 2005).

5.7.10.5.8.1.1   MONTY, Jacqueline Françoise b & bp 21 Jun 1936, Scotstown, QC.

5.7.10.5.8.1.2   MONTY, Réjeanne Anna b & bp 19 & 27 Feb 1938, Scotstown, QC.

5.7.10.5.8.1.3   MONTY, Claire Jeanne d'Arc b & bp 13 & 19 Mar 1939, Scotstown, QC.

5.7.10.5.8.1.4   MONTY, Anonymous (female) b 8 May 1940, Scotstown, QC; d & bur there 8 & 10 May 1940.

5.10.6.2.3.7.1   MONTY, Margaret H. b 5 May 1926, VT; d 22 Sep 1993, Burlington, VT. She married and divorced Charles A. Hawley.

5.10.6.2.3.7.2   MONTY, Theresa b 11 Oct 1927; d 12 Nov 2002, Scotia, NY. She married Lawrence B. Leach b 31 Jul 1921, VT; d 26 Nov 1988, Scotia, NY.

5.10.6.2.3.7.3   MONTY, Gilberta Betty
    Gilberta Monty was a resident of Burlington, VT, when her sister Yvette (5.10.6.2.3.7.8) died in 2002 (*Burlington Free Press*, 25 Nov 2002).

5.10.6.2.3.7.4   MONTY, Jeannine M. b 3 Nov 1931, VT; d 14 Oct 2000, Burlington, VT.

5.10.6.2.3.7.5   MONTY, Cecile b 22 Jul 1933, Glastonbury, CT; d 2 Sep 1989, Hartford, CT. She married Robert D. Viens (Frank Viens & Antoinette ____) b 28 Aug 1923, Burlington, VT.

5.10.6.2.3.7.6   MONTY, Sylvia b 1935. She married ____ Lapointe.
    Mrs. Sylvia Lapointe was a resident of South Burlington, VT, when her sister Yvette (5.10.6.2.3.7.8) died in 2002 (*Burlington Free Press*, 25 Nov 2002).

5.10.6.2.3.7.7   MONTY, Lillian b 19 May 1937; d Jul 1977. She married John B. Mullin b 17 May 1934, VT; d 7 Dec 1972, Lowell, MA.

5.10.6.2.3.7.8   MONTY, Yvette Marie b 21 Nov 1940, Burlington, VT; d there 24 Nov 2002. She married 1959? Andrew Joseph Luchini (Andrew Joseph Luchini & Ellen A. Casey).

5.10.6.2.3.7.9   MONTY, Peter A. b Sep 1943, Burlington, VT. He married Mary Lou Provost (Albert Provost & Irene M. Langlois) b Jan 1957.
    Peter Monty and his wife Mary Lou were residents of Colchester, VT, when her mother died in 2004 (*Burlington Free Press*, 8 May 2004).

5.10.6.2.3.7.10   MONTY, Gloria
    Gloria Monty was a resident of Burlington, VT, when her sister Yvette (5.10.6.2.3.7.8) died in 2002 (*Burlington Free Press*, 25 Nov 2002).

5.10.6.2.3.7.11   MONTY, Veronica b 16 Mar 1951, VT; d 30 Jan 1982, Burlington, VT.

5.10.6.2.5.2.1   MONTY, Marie Rose Amande b & bp 1 & 2 Jun 1918, St. Césaire, QC; d 31 Oct 1957, Stamford, CT. She married 1940, Springfield, MA, Vito J. Savickas (Charles Savickas & Mary ____) b 20 Aug 1918, Barre, MA; d 18 Aug 2001, Norwalk, CT.
    This woman was named Marie Emma Rose Amande at her baptism. She was generally known as Rose A. in the United States, and also Rosamond (1939 City Directory, Springfield, MA) and Marie R. (Connecticut Death Index).

5.10.6.2.5.2.2   MONTY, Marie Marthe Adeline b & bp 3 Aug 1919, St. Césaire, QC; d & bur 24 & 29 May 1998, Springfield, MA. She married 1943? Albino Victor Dalla Pe-

gorara (Giulio Della Pegorara & Teresa Savoia) b 15 Nov 1912, Ponton, Verona, Italy; d 14 Feb 2007, Agawam, MA,

Albino Marie M. Monty and her husband had been married for fifty-five years when she died. She was buried in St. Michael's Cemetery in Springfield, MA (*Springfield Union News*, 27 May 1998).

5.10.6.2.5.2.3　**MONTY, Louis Philip** b & bp 29 Aug 1920, St. Césaire, QC; d 17 Jan 1983, Springfield, MA. He married around 1942 **Shirley A.** ____ b 10 Dec 1925; d 31 Dec 1979, Springfield, MA.

This man was named Joseph Arthur Louis Philippe at his baptism.

5.10.6.2.5.2.4　**MONTY, John J./Jean Jacques** b & bp 30 & 31 Oct 1923, St. Césaire, QC; d 26 Aug 1995, San Diego, CA. He married **Estelle M. Benoit.**

This man was named Joseph Jean Jacques Monty at his baptism. When he came to the United States with his parents the following year, though, he came known as John J. Monty. He served in the US Navy during World War II and was buried in Fort Rosecrans National Cemetery in Point Loma, CA. His wife survived him (*Springfield Union News*, 23 Sep 1995).

5.10.6.2.5.2.5　**MONTY, Amedee F.** b 30 Nov 1932, Springfield, MA; d 7 Aug 1992, Boston, MA. He married **Helen** ____ b Nov 1931.

Amedee F. Monty was a resident of Longmeadow, MA, at his death.

5.10.6.2.5.6.1　**MONTY, Claude** b 9 Aug 1959, Laval, QC. He married 25 Oct 1980, Iberville, QC, **Suzanne Hélène Racine** (Donald Racine & Suzanne Meunier).

5.10.6.8.1.2.1　**MONTY, Jacques Emile Lucien** b & bp 19 & 20 Jul 1930, Montreal, QC.

5.10.6.8.1.2.2　**MONTY, Emile Georges André** b & bp 26 & 27 Jul 1932, Montreal, QC.

5.10.6.9.1.3.1　**MONTY, Marguerite** b 12 Feb 1936. She married **Thomas Spaulding.**

I know of Marguerite Monty's marriage only through Louise Monty's *Généalogie de la famille Monty*, II, 291.

5.10.6.9.1.3.2　**MONTY, Peter B.** b 24 Jun 1937.

5.10.6.9.1.6.1　**MONTY, Mary Isabel Estelle** b & bp 24 & 29 Oct 1940, Quebec, QC; d & bur there 4 & 5 Nov 1940.

5.10.6.9.1.6.2　**MONTY, Michael Richard** b 11 Oct 1941, Montreal, QC; d & bur 23 & 26 Feb 2005, Ajax, Ontario, Canada. He married (1) 10 Jun 1972, Montreal, QC, **Marta Irving** (Mark Irving & Ann Puritz).

He married (2) 3 May 1986, King City, Ontario, Canada, **Charlotte Ann Curtis** (Winston Curtis & Jean ____) b 20 Nov 1946, Glasgow, Scotland; married (1) ____ Rue.

5.10.6.9.1.6.3　**MONTY, Louise Elizabeth** b 20 Dec 1945, Montreal, QC. She married (1) ____ **Reynolds.**

She married (2) 23 Oct 1982, Miami, FL, **Donald Thomas Meagher** b 29 Jun 1931, NY; d 8 May 2002, Miami, FL.

Louise Monty survived her second husband *(Miami Herald*, 10 May 2002).

5.10.6.9.1.6.4　**MONTY, Donald John Gerard** b 9 Jan 1964, Montreal, QC. He married 6 Oct 1979, Calgary, Alberta, Canada, **Carol Findlay** (Victor George Findlay & Irène Gertrude Hamel) b 23 Aug 1954, Montreal, QC.

5.10.6.9.1.10.1　**MONTY, Paul** b 19 Feb 1948, Montreal, QC. He married 1 Oct 1974, Aylmer, QC, **Claire Legault** (René Legault & Lucie Lavoie) b 12 Jul 1948, Montreal, QC.

5.10.6.9.1.10.2 **MONTY, Claire** b 7 Oct 1950, Montreal, QC; d 14 Jun 1993. She married 26 May 1979, North Troy, VT, **Gary G. Viens** b 23 Aug 1954; m (2) 4 Jul 1995, Lyndon, VT, Carol S. Laclair.

5.10.6.9.1.11.1 **MONTY, Louis** b 23 Aug 1948; d 21 Mar 1993.

5.10.6.9.1.11.2 **MONTY, Mary Jane** b 11 Sep 1950.

5.10.6.9.1.11.3 **MONTY, Susan** b 17 Jan 1952. She married 24 Jun 1973 **Ronald McClements** b 21 Oct 1948.

5.10.6.9.2.4.1 **MONTY, Paul** b 15 May 1945, Montreal, QC. He married 9 May 1972, Quebec, QC, **Louise Brochu** (Roger Brochu & Célina Larochelle) b Feb 1956, Lévis, QC.

5.10.6.9.2.4.2 **MONTY, Alice** b 8 Jul 1946, Montreal, QC.

8.1.7.2.4.2.1 **MONTE, George** b & bp 28 Aug & 10 Sep 1911, Merrimack & Nashua, NH.

8.1.7.2.4.2.2 **MONTE, William** b & bp 24 Jan & 16 Feb 1913, Merrimack & Nashua, NH; d 9 Dec 1986, Salem, MA.
William Monte was a resident of Peabody, MA, at his death.

8.1.7.2.4.2.3 **MONTE, Irene** b 1914?, NH.
Irene Monte was a 5-year-old child living with her parents in Bridgewater, MA, on 1 Jan 1920. She was with them in Peabody, MA, in 1930 (US censuses).

8.1.7.2.4.2.4 **MONTE, Dorothy** b 1920, Bridgewater, MA.
Dorothy Monte was a 10-year-old child living with her parents in Peabody, MA, on 1 Apr 1930. Since she was not listed in the 1 Jan 1920 census, when her parents were in Bridgewater, MA, she must have been born in the first months of that year.

8.1.7.2.4.3.1 **MONTE, George W.** b 17 Mar 1922, Peabody, MA; d 27 Dec 1971, Lynn, MA.

8.1.7.2.4.3.2 **MONTE, Edward E.** b 6 Jul 1923, Peabody, MA; d 18 Jan 1973, Lynn, MA.

8.1.7.6.5.2.1 **MONTE, Donald W.** b 22 Dec 1924, WI; d & bur 10 & 13 Nov 2005, Menomonee Falls, WI. He married **Delma Thelen** (Arthur Thelen & Cecelia Miller) b 22 Aug 1923, IL; d & bur 27 Feb & 3 Mar 2007, Menomonee Falls, WI.
Donald Monte and his wife were long-term residents of Menomonee Falls, WI (*Milwaukee Journal Sentinel*, 7 Dec 2005 and 1 Mar 2007). Don and Del Monte share a tombstone there in St. Anthony's Cemetery.

8.1.7.6.5.2.2 **MONTE, Douglas Keith** b 14 Nov 1926, MI; d 16 Feb 1960, San Bernardino Co., CA. He married **Alice ____** b 1929?; d 16 Feb 1960, Clark Co., NV, at the age of 31.
Douglas Monte and his wife Alice were killed in a car accident on the California/Nevada border. He died instantly while she died en route to a hospital in Las Vegas, NV (*Nevada State Journal*, Reno, NV, 18 Feb 1960).

8.1.7.6.5.2.3 **MONTE, Kenneth R.** b 16 Jun 1929, WI; d 24 Jun 2004, Alameda, CA. He married 1965 and divorced Jul 1973, Alameda Co., CA, **Pearl Anna Azevedo** b there 21 Jan 1930.

8.1.7.6.5.4.1   MONTY, Jack b 1931, Winchester, WI; bur 1936 Clintonville, WI.
The years of Jack Monty's birth and death are taken from the inscription on his tombstone in Graceland Cemetery in Clintonville, WI.

8.1.7.6.5.4.2   MONTY, Jo Ann b 1932, Winchester, WI; bur 1932 Clintonville, WI.
The year of Jo Ann Monty's birth and death is taken from the inscription on her tombstone in Graceland Cemetery in Clintonville, WI.

8.1.7.6.5.4.3   MONTY, William b 18 Aug 1938, Winchester, WI.

8.1.7.6.5.5.1   MONTY, Karen

8.1.7.6.5.5.2   MONTE, Philip G. b 27 Dec 1945. He married **Linda ____** b 21 Sept 1959.

8.1.7.6.5.7.1   MONTY, Keith Jack b Oct 1942. He married (1) and divorced 2 Jun 1982, Walworth Co., WI, **Joan Louise Kramer**.
He married (2) 4 Dec 1982, Walworth Co., WI, **Sherry Lynn Freund** b Feb 1951.

8.1.7.6.5.7.2   MONTY, Dennis

8.1.7.6.5.9.1   MONTE, Janelle J. b Mar 1947, Milwaukee, WI. She married **Cole O. Geyser** b Feb 1950.
Janelle Monte and her husband Cole Geyser were residents of Waukesha, WI, when her father died in 2005 (*Green Bay Press Gazette*, 1 Jan 2006).

8.1.7.6.5.9.2   MONTE, Adrianne L. b May 1949, Milwaukee, WI. She married **Douglas John Peterson** b Jul 1949.
Adrianne Monte and her husband Douglas Peterson were residents of Suamico, WI, when her father died in 2005 (*Green Bay Press Gazette*, 1 Jan 2006).

8.1.7.6.6.1.1   MONTE, Gail Gene b 12 Dec 1936, Seattle, WA. She married 30 Jun 1962, Washington, DC, **James A. Nettles** (William Carl Nettles & Ruby Stevenson) b 20 Oct 1938, Anderson, SC.

8.1.7.6.8.1.1   MONTE, Gary W. b Feb 1936, Miles City, MT. He married (1) **Jean Agnes Messner** (Eferham Messner & Caroline Gunsch) b 22 Jun 1941; d 17 Jun 1997, Miles City, MT.
He married (2) **Eva ____**.
Gary Monte and his second wife Eva were residents of Miles City, MT, when his mother died in 2006 (*Miles City Star*, 2 Jun 2006).

8.1.7.6.8.1.2   MONTE, Virginia Anne b 30 Dec 1937, Miles City, MT; d 24 May 1992, Portland, OR. She married 16 Apr 1960, Rockaway Beach, OR, **Benjamin L. Middleton**.
Virginia Anne Monty was buried in Skyline Memorial Gardens in Portland, OR (*Portland Oregonian*, 29 May 1992).

8.1.7.6.8.1.3   MONTE, Alan Ray b 1945?, MT. He married (1) Aug 1971, Glendive, MT, **Patricia Gail Moffitt** (Norris W. Moffitt & Lola ____) b 1950?
He married (2) **Carol A. ____**.
Alan R. Monte and Patricia G. Moffitt were 26 and 21 years old respectively when they married (*Billings Gazette*, 22 Jul & 10 Aug 1971). Alan and his wife Carol were residents of Pablo, MT, when his mother died in 2006 (*Miles City Star*, 2 Jun 2006).

8.1.7.6.9.1.1   MONTY, Shirley married **Michael Eugene Kelly** (Patrick Kelly & Nora

Dixon).

Mrs. Shirley Kelly was a resident of Anaheim, CA, when her mother died in 1994 (*Orange County Register*, Santa Ana, CA, 15 Dec 1994.

8.1.7.6.9.2.1   **MONTE, Miss ___** married (1) 26 Jun 1972, Layton, UT, **Lee M. Holmer**.

She married (2) **Arthur McMurray Jr.**

8.1.7.6.9.2.2   **MONTE, Betty** married 23 Jul 1970, Hill AFB, Layton, UT, **Richard W. Sullivan** (Sherman Sullivan & Marguerite Shepard) b 12 Mar 1942, Manhattan, KS; d & bur 16 & 20 Nov 2003, Lawton & Elgin, OK.

Richard Sullivan was a resident of Fletcher, OK, at his death. He had served in the US Army for twenty years before retiring in 1983 and was buried in Fort Sill National Cemetery in Elgin, OK. His wife survived him (*Lawton Constitution*, 19 Nov 2003).

8.1.7.6.9.5.1   **MONTY, Marcia Renee** b 11 Jul 1949, Polk Co., MN. She married 30 Sep 1972, Mower Co., MN, **Clair Frederick Krebsbach** (Raymond L. Krebsbach & Ardella Ida Smith) b 10 Nov 1947.

8.1.7.6.9.5.2   **MONTY, Allan Clark** b 17 Apr 1951, Clearwater Co., MN. He married (1) 23 Jul 1974, Hennepin Co., MN, **Diana Lynn Swanson** (Merle Swanson & Elaine Marie Quirin) b 11 May 1951, Grand Meadow, MN.

He married (2) 9 Jun 2006, Grand Meadow, MN, **Mary Palmby**.

8.1.7.6.9.5.3   **MONTY, Karen Joy** b 20 Feb 1953, Clearwater Co., MN. She married 24 Jun 1978, Olmsted Co., MN, **Roger William Pritchard** b 16 Dec 1946; m (1) and divorced 4 Feb 1972, Olmsted Co., MN, Lonna K. ___.

8.1.7.6.9.7.1   **MONTY, Keith A.** b 23 Jan 1964, Marin Co., CA.

8.1.7.6.9.7.2   **MONTY, Teresa L.** b 21 Sep 1968, Marin Co., CA.

8.1.7.12.2.1.1.1   **MONTY, Frances Mary** b Jul 1921, Billings Co., ND. She married 9 Jun 1947 Roberts Co., SD, **William W. Pribbenow** (Otto J. Pribbenow & Wilhelmina/Minnie Bristlin) b 16 Feb 1920, Staples, MN; d 8 May 2005, Watkins, MN.

Mrs. Frances Pribbenow was living in Motley, MN, when her half-brother Ralph Monty (8.1.7.12.2.3.1) died in 2004 (*Argus Leader*, Sioux Falls, SD, 28 Nov 2004).

8.1.7.12.2.3.1   **MONTY, Ralph S.** b Feb 1924, Fryburg, ND; d & bur 26 & 30 Nov 2004, Huron, SD. He married 1967? **Cleota Marie Estes** (Edward Estes & Susan Usterback) b 1914, Rosebud Sioux Reservation, SD; m (1) 3 Feb 1934, Huron, SD, Samuel Stanley Serbick (Tom Serbick & Katie ___).

Ralph Monty arrived in Huron, SD, from St. Paul, MN, in 1961. He owned and operated a steak house there which his wife had inherited from her first husband and was buried there in Riverside Cemetery (*Daily Plainsman*, Huron, SD, 7 Jul 1961, 22 Jul 1964, 12 Nov 1967, and 17 May 1971; *Argus Leader*, Sioux Falls, SD, 28 Nov 2004).

8.1.7.12.2.3.2   **MONTY, Marian Dorothy** b 6 Feb 1925, Fryburg, ND; d 28 Dec 2003, St. Paul, MN. She married 15 Jun 1946, Marin Co., CA, **John Jerome Mangen** (Theodore John Mangen & Clara H. Thorsen) b 9 Sep 1922, WI; d 20 Sep 1989, St. Paul, MN.

Marian D. Monty and her husband were buried in Fort Snelling National Cemetery in Minneapolis, MN.

8.1.7.12.2.3.3   **MONTY, Floyd F.** b 10 May 1926, Fryburg, ND.

Floyd Monty was living in Pahrump, NV, when his brother Ralph (8.1.7.12.2. 3.1) died in 2004 (*Argus Leader*, Sioux Falls, SD, 28 Nov 2004).

8.1.7.12.5.1.1   **MONTY, James**

8.1.7.12.5.1.2   **MONTY, Joann Carole** b 29 Mar 1941; d Aug 1993, Vilas Co., WI. She married (1) **Clarence R. Setzer** b 22 Mar 1933; d 9 Aug 1990, Vilas Co., WI.
She married (2) and divorced 8 Sep 1983, Vilas Co., WI, **Ronald Burton Fesler**.
She married (3) 20 Dec 1985, Vilas Co., WI, **Walter Raymond Becker** b 6 Aug 1946; m (2) 25 May 1996, Vilas Co., Deborah Ann Errington.

8.1.7.12.5.1.3   **MONTY, John C.** b Mar 1943. He married **Roberta Jean ____** b Mar 1947.

8.1.7.12.5.1.4   **MONTY, Judith Ann** b 15 Apr 1946, Phelps, WI; d there 28 Apr 1946.
Judith Ann Monty was buried in the Phelps, WI, Cemetery.

8.1.7.12.5.2.1   **MONTY, Larry**

8.1.7.12.5.2.2   **MONTY, Kenneth**

8.1.7.12.5.2.3   **MONTY, Dennis**

8.1.7.12.5.4.1   **MONTY, Kenneth Charles** b 31 Dec 1941, WI. He married 27 Sep 1983, Winnebago Co., WI, **Bonnie Lee Aplin** (Raymond Aplin & Ruth Bettner) b 10 Jan 1945, WI.

8.1.7.12.5.4.2   **MONTY, Barbara A.** b 17 Jun 1943. She married **Dean M. Rosinsky** b 17 Jun 1943.

8.1.7.12.5.5.1   **MONTY, Loretta**

8.1.7.12.5.5.2   **MONTY, Betty** married **Richard Quinette**.

8.1.7.12.5.5.3   **MONTY, Ronald A.** b 30 Mar 1939. He married 3 Mar 1973, Ozaukee Co., WI, **Sandra Smith** (Elmer Smith & Jean Mereness) b 1944?
Sandra Smith was 29 years old at her marriage.

8.1.7.12.5.6.1   **MONTY, Marian Leilani** b 1945, Honolulu, HI. She married **Kenneth Goddard**.
Mrs. Marion Goddard was a resident of Palos Verdes Estates, CA, when her mother died in 2004 (*The Columbian*, Vancouver, WA, 24 May 2004).

8.1.7.12.5.6.2   **MONTY, Carol Moana** b 1947, Honolulu, HI. She married ____ **Oppie**.
Mrs. Carol Oppie was a resident of Seattle, WA, when her mother died in 2004 (*The Columbian*, Vancouver, WA, 24 May 2004).

8.1.7.12.5.7.1   **MONTY, Donna Jean** b 30 Apr 1953, WI. She married 11 Mar 1981, Milwaukee, WI, **John Michael Guetzlaff** b 1944?
John Michael Guetzlaff was 37 years old at his marriage.

8.1.7.12.5.7.2   **MONTY, Dean Jeffrey** b 1959, WI. He married 3 May 1986, Milwaukee, WI, **Jacqueline Kay Walters** b 27 Apr 1962.

8.1.7.12.5.7.3   **MONTY, John Maurice** b 4 Nov 1960, WI. He married 8 Oct 1994, Milwaukee, WI, **Jean Marie Trednic** (Robert F. Trednic & Sylvia ____) b 12 Sep 1964.

8.1.7.12.5.7.4   **MONTY, Lisa Renee** b 2 Dec 1961, WI. She married 10 Jul 1982, Milwaukee, WI, **Francis Scott Reale** b 27 Jan 1959.

8.1.7.12.5.7.5   **MONTY, Daren Steven** b 25 Oct 1964, WI. He married 2 May 1987, Milwaukee, WI, **Christine Ellen Wieland** b 1 Jun 1965; m (2) 12 May 1995, Milwaukee, WI, Randy James Pecha.

8.1.7.12.5.11.1   **MONTY, Kenneth**

8.1.7.12.5.11.2   **MONTY, Susan Mary** b 3 Aug 1964. She married (1) 4 Aug 1984, Waupaca Co., WI, **Robert John Euhardy** b May 1964; m (2) 2 Mar 1991, Faye Ann Dreier.
   She married (2) 30 Oct 1992, Outagamie Co., WI, **Robert Allen Roberts** b 24 Aug 1963.

8.1.7.12.5.11.3   **MONTY, Sandra Ann** b 8 Sep 1966. She married 28 Oct 1994, WI, **Barry Matthew Martin** b 3 Mar 1965.

8.1.7.12.6.1.1   **MONTY, Genevieve Joann** b Sep 1934, WI. She married 29 Dec 1952, Dubuque, IA, divorced 10 Aug 1981, Waupaca Co., WI, and remarried 28 Feb 1987, Outagamie Co., WI, **John Louis Moder** b 21 Feb 1935.
   Genevieve Monty and her husband were residents of Clintonville, WI, when her sister Jill (8.1.7.12.6.1.8) died in 2007 (*Appleton Post Crescent*, 6 May 2007).

8.1.7.12.6.1.2   **MONTY, Shirley** b 26 Jun 1936, Bear Creek, WI. She married there 30 Apr 1960, **Donald G. Southard** (Ward Southard & Lula Worm) b 4 Oct 1937, New London, WI.
   Shirley Monty and her husband were residents of Appleton, WI, when her sister Jill (8.1.7.12.6.1.8) died in 2007 (*Appleton Post Crescent*, 6 May 2007).

8.1.7.12.6.1.3   **MONTY, Karen L.** b 11 Jun 1939, Bear Creek, WI. She married 25 Jan 1958, Appleton, WI, **John I. Young** (George P. Young & Violet Cavner) b 12 Jul 1936, Shiocton, WI; d 7 Sep 1991.
   Mrs. Karen Young was living in Shawano, WI, when her sister Jill Monty (8.1.7.12.6.1.8) died in 2007 (*Appleton Post Crescent*, 6 May 2007).

8.1.7.12.6.1.4   **MONTY, Gary Joseph** b 13 Mar 1942, Bear Creek, WI. He married there 14 Sep 1963 **Rose Marie Lehman** (Raymond Solomon Lehman [8.1.7.12.4.iv] & Gladys H. Ramsdell) b there 5 Nov 1944.
   Gary Monty and Rose Marie Lehman were first cousins once removed. They were residents of New London, WI, when his sister Jill (8.1.7.12.6.1.8) died in 2007 (*Appleton Post Crescent*, 6 May 2007).

8.1.7.12.6.1.5   **MONTY, Gail** b Jun 1944, Bear Creek, WI. She married **Mark Griffin**.
   Mrs. Gail Griffin was living in Bear Creek, WI, when her sister Jill Monty (8.1.7.12.6.1.8) died in 2007 (*Appleton Post Crescent*, 6 May 2007).

8.1.7.12.6.1.6   **MONTY, Paula Jean** b 1948, Bear Creek, WI. She married there 3 Sep 1966 **Keith F. Postel** (Carl Postel & Lillian Shelly) b 15 Jan 1945, WI.
   Mrs. Paula Postel was living in Clintonville, WI, when her sister Jill Monty (8.1.7.12.6.1.8) died in 2007 (*Appleton Post Crescent*, 6 May 2007).

8.1.7.12.6.1.7   **MONTY, Kevin R.** b 1950, Bear Creek, WI. He married 1970, WI, **Kathy L. Sennett** (Merlin Sennett & Margaret Lucas) b Nov 1950.
   Kevin Monty and his wife were living in Bear Creek, WI, when his sister Jill (8.1.7.12.6.1.8) died in 2007 (*Appleton Post Crescent*, 6 May 2007).

8.1.7.12.6.1.8   **MONTY, Jill Mary** b 20 Dec 1953, New London, WI; d 4 May 2007, Waupaca, WI. She married (1) 18 Aug 1973, Waupaca Co., WI, **John Albert Torborg** b Nov

1950; m (2) 25 Jun 1991 (and also 21 Jun 1995), Waupaca Co., WI, Beverly E. Bate.
She married (2) 14 Nov 2001, Waupaca, WI, **John Paul Lockwood** b Apr 1959; m (1) 6 Jun 1992, Waupaca Co., WI, Barbara Ann Schultz.

8.1.7.12.6.3.1   MONTY, John Raymond b Apr 1948, Milwaukee, WI. He married (1) there 11 Apr 1975 and divorced there 27 Jun 1983 **Patti Lynn Dale** b Jul 1957.
He married (2) **Doreen** ____.
I know of John Raymond Monty's second wife only through his mother's obituary in the *Milwaukee Journal Sentinel* of 4 Dec 2001.

8.1.7.12.6.3.2   MONTY, James A. b 11 Feb 1950, Milwaukee, WI. He married there 7 Sep 1974 ____ **Pete** b 1956?
Miss Pete was 18 years old at her marriage.

8.1.7.12.6.3.3   MONTY, Rosanne F. b Mar 1951, Milwaukee, WI. She married **Bruce C. Young** b Jan 1950.

8.1.7.12.6.3.4   MONTY, Charles J. b Jun 1953, Milwaukee, WI.

8.1.7.12.6.4.1   MONTY, Betty A./Elizabeth b Aug 1941, WI. She married (1) 19 May 1962, Bear Creek, WI, **Peter J. Hagens** (Lawrence Hagens & Helen Martineau) b 11 Mar 1935, WI; m (2) 29 Sep 1973, Calumet Co., WI, Darlene Barany (Joseph Barany & ____).
She married (2) **Gerald C./Jerry Schumann** (Charles Schumann & Edwina A. Olive) b Sep 1940, WI; m (1) 30 Dec 1959 Rita Ann Kilgas (Norbert Kilgas & Agnes Gillen).
Mrs. Betty Schumann and her husband were residents of Kimberly, WI, when her mother died in 2002. She survived her brother Lester Monty (8.1.7.12.6.4.4) who died in 2008 (*Appleton Post Crescent*, 25 Dec 2002 and 21 Jan 2008).

8.1.7.12.6.4.2   MONTY, Janice b 23 May 1945, WI.
Jan Monty was a resident of Little Chute, WI, when her mother died in 2002. She survived her brother Lester (8.1.7.12.6.4.4) who died in 2008 (*Appleton Post Crescent*, 25 Dec 2002 and 21 Jan 2008).

8.1.7.12.6.4.3   MONTY, Beverly b 1948, WI. She married **Gordon E. Buschke** b May 1945.
Mrs. Beverly Buschke and her husband were residents of Wautoma, WI, when her mother died in 2002. She survived her brother Lester Monty (8.1.7.12.6.4.4) who died in 2008 (*Appleton Post Crescent*, 25 Dec 2002 and 21 Jan 2008).

8.1.7.12.6.4.4   MONTY, Lester M. b 26 Jun 1951, New London, WI; d 19 Jan 2008, Appleton, WI. He married 10 Dec 1976, Waupaca Co., WI, and divorced there 14 Apr 1980 **Pamela Jean Klatt** b 1955?; m (2) 3 May 1985, Waupaca Co., WI, Wayne Bruce Grove; m (3) there 8 Feb 1991 Ray Arnold Smith.
Pamela Jean Klatt was 21 years old at her first marriage.

8.1.7.12.6.8.1   MONTY, Mary Jane b 1 Jun 1950, WI. She married 1973? **James Howard Salmon** (James Howard Salmon & Donna Larrabee) b 24 Feb 1948, WI; d 18 Jan 1999, Milwaukee, WI.
James H. Salmon and his wife had been married for twenty-five years when he died. He was buried in Highland Memorial Park in New Berlin, WI (*Milwaukee Journal Sentinel*, 20 Jan 1999).

8.1.7.12.6.8.2   MONTY, Barbara J. b 1 Jul 1951, WI.
Barbara Monty survived her brother-in-law James H. Salmon (8.1.7.12.6.8.1) who died in 1999 (*Milwaukee Journal Sentinel*, 20 Jan 1999).

8.1.7.12.6.8.3   **MONTY, Joseph Reynold** b 2 Jun 1952, WI. He married 5 Nov 1983, Milwaukee, WI, **Barbara Lynn Ballas** b 1 May 1955.
Joe and Barb Monty survived their brother-in-law James H. Salmon (8.1.7.12.6.8.1) who died in 1999 (*Milwaukee Journal Sentinel*, 20 Jan 1999).

8.1.7.12.6.8.4   **MONTY, Sandra E.** b 7 Feb 1955, WI.
Sandra Monty survived her brother-in-law James H. Salmon (8.1.7.12.6.8.1) who died in 1999 (*Milwaukee Journal Sentinel*, 20 Jan 1999).

8.1.7.12.6.8.5   **MONTY, Cindy**
Cindy Monty survived her brother-in-law James H. Salmon (8.1.7.12.6.8.1) who died in 1999 (*Milwaukee Journal Sentinel*, 20 Jan 1999).

8.1.7.12.6.8.6   **MONTY, Timothy Thomas** b Nov 1959, WI. He married 14 Aug 1993, Door Co., WI, **Starr Annette Vincent** b 1962?
Tim and Starr Monty survived their brother-in-law James H. Salmon (8.1.7.12.6.8.1) who died in 1999 (*Milwaukee Journal Sentinel*, 20 Jan 1999). Starr Vincent was thirty-one years old at her marriage.

8.1.7.12.6.8.7   **MONTY, Todd** b 14 Mar 1966, WI. He married **Mary Jo Westphal** b 15 Feb 1968.
Todd and Mary Jo Monty survived their brother-in-law James H. Salmon (8.1.7.12.6.8.1) who died in 1999 (*Milwaukee Journal Sentinel*, 20 Jan 1999).

8.1.7.12.6.8.8   **MONTY, Troy Nathan** b 18 May 1973. He married 21 Jul 1994, Milwaukee, WI, **Christina Labro Lamias** b 5 Sep 1972.
Troy and Tina Monty survived their brother-in-law James H. Salmon (8.1.7.12.6.8.1) who died in 1999 (*Milwaukee Journal Sentinel*, 20 Jan 1999).

8.1.7.12.6.11.1   **MONTY, Daniel Robert** b 2 Aug 1944, Clintonville, WI; d & bur 2 & 6 Dec 1996, Oak Creek & Union Grove, WI. He married (1) and divorced 10 Jun 1983, Milwaukee, WI, **Judith Ann Morgan** b Nov 1946.
He married (2) 8 Sep 1984, Milwaukee, WI, **Elaine Marie Berg** b 26 Sep 1937.
Daniel Robert Monty was a US Navy veteran (Vietnam) and was buried in the Southern Wisconsin Veterans Memorial Cemetery in Union Grove, WI. His widow Elaine was still residing in Oak Creek, WI, when her father-in-law Llewellyn Monty died in 2002 (*Milwaukee Journal Sentinel*, 12 Aug 2002).

8.1.7.12.6.11.2   **MONTY, Daryl Lee** b 6 Jan 1947, Clintonville, WI. He married 1970, Milwaukee, WI, **Judy A. Sutton** (Clarence Sutton & Lena Beber) b there 29 Apr 1949.
Daryl Monty and his wife Judy were residents of Milwaukee, WI, when his father died in 2002 (*Milwaukee Journal Sentinel*, 12 Aug 2002).

8.1.7.12.6.11.3   **MONTY, Larry James** b 14 Aug 1949, Clintonville, WI; d 9 Sep 2000, Milwaukee, WI. He married 31 Dec 1973, Milwaukee, WI, **Donna Pohl** b 1953?
Donna Pohl was 20 years old at her marriage.

8.1.7.12.6.11.4   **MONTY, Mark Rene** b 10 Feb 1953, Clintonville, WI. He married 29 Apr 1982, Milwaukee, WI, **Troy Marie Deuel** (Duane Deuel & Laurel Lybbert) b 3 Mar 1956; d 29 Mar 2006, Milwaukee, WI.
Mark Monty survived his wife Troy (*Milwaukee Journal Sentinel*, 1 Apr 2006).

8.1.7.12.6.11.5   **MONTY, Jacqueline/Jackie** b 1955?, Clintonville, WI. She married (1) 26 May 1973, Milwaukee, WI, and divorced there 4 Jun 1981 **Gregory Paul Hilbert** b Jul 1949; m (2) 25 Jan 1990, Milwaukee, WI, Debra Ann Reinert.
She married (2) 12 Dec 1981, Milwaukee, WI, **Jeffrey Otto Schramm** b 19 Mar 1954.

Jacqueline Monty was 17 years old at her first marriage and 26 years old at her second. She and her husband Jeff Schramm were living in West Bend, WI, when her father died in 2002 (*Milwaukee Journal Sentinel*, 12 Aug 2002).

8.1.7.12.6.11.6   MONTY, Judy b 12 June 1958, WI. She married 23 Apr 1976, Milwaukee, WI, **Dwight Eric Daniels** b 24 Mar 1953; m (2) 31 Dec 1993, Door Co., WI, Kathleen Ann Sawicki.

Mrs. Judy Daniels was living in Milwaukee, WI, when her father died in 2002 (*Milwaukee Journal Sentinel*, 12 Aug 2002).

8.1.7.12.9.3.1   MONTE, Michael Richard b 7 Mar 1947, WI. He married 24 Jan 1969, Menasha, WI, **Linda Ann Haase** (Randolph Arnold Haase & Eileen Mary Kenny) b there 2 Jan 1947.

Mike Monte and his wife Linda were residents of Crandon, WI, when his father died in 1999 and also when her mother died in 2008 (*Green Bay Press Gazette*, 30 May 1999; *Appleton Post Crescent*, 11 Jul 2008).

8.1.7.12.9.3.2   MONTE, Timothy Hugh b 1953, Crandon, WI. He married (1) 6 Dec 1975, Forest Co., WI, and divorced there 7 Mar 1980 **Linda J. Clark** b 1959?

He married (2) 29 Nov 1986, Forest Co., WI, **Vanessa Rae Tuckwab** b 1961?

Timothy Monte was 22 and his first wife 16 years old at their marriage. His second wife was 25 years old when they married.

Tim Monte was a resident of Crandon, WI, when his father died in 1999 (*Green Bay Press Gazette*, 30 May 1999).

8.1.7.12.9.5.1   MONTE, Kenneth J. b 31 Aug 1950, LaPorte, IN; d 21 May 1999, San Antonio, TX.

8.1.7.12.9.5.2   MONTE, James

James Monte predeceased his father (*News Dispatch*, Michigan City, IN, 10 Nov 2003).

8.1.7.12.9.5.3   MONTE, Stephen H. b 15 Dec 1957, La Porte, IN.

Stephen Monte was a resident of Bradenton FL, when his father died in 2003 (*News Dispatch*, Michigan City, IN, 10 Nov 2003).

8.1.7.12.9.6.1   MONTE, Kent V. b 19 Apr 1971, WI. He married **Stacey** ____ b Apr 1971.

8.1.7.12.11.1.1   MONTE, Carrilee b 6 Mar 1940, Gregg Co., TX. She married **Carroll Duane Laramore** (William Moss Laramore & Hazel Embree) b 13 Jul 1938, Bowie Co., TX.

8.1.7.12.11.1.2   MONTE, Alec Virgil b 28 Jul 1947, Texarkana, TX. He married (1) 15 Jul 1967 and divorced 20 Oct 1989, Bowie Co., TX, **Michelle D.** ____ b 1947?

He married (2) 27 Jun 1992, Bowie Co., TX, and divorced there 16 Aug 1996, **Vicki D. Brammer** b 12 Oct 1954.

Mrs. Michelle D. Monte was 42 years old when she and her husband divorced in 1989.

8.1.7.12.11.1.3   MONTE, Ellis Joseph b 27 Feb 1950, Texarkana, TX.

8.3.1.3.7.3.1   MONTY, Sandra b Jan 1942. She married (1) ____ **Bashore**.

She married (2) **Fred R. Nadolsky** b Dec 1931.

Mrs. Sandra Nadolsky and her husband Fred Nadolsky were residents of Centerville, OH, when her mother died in 2006 (*Westerly Sun*, 21 Jun 2006).

8.3.8.1.6.1.1   MONTY, Douglas W. b Oct 1949. He married 21 Jan 1977. Woodbridge,

CT, **Claudia M. Carbonari** b Aug 1952.

Douglas Monty and his wife Dr. Claudia M. Carbonari were residents of Glastonbury, CT, when his father died in 1999 (*Hartford Courant*, 7 Jan 1999).

8.3.8.1.6.1.2   **MONTY, Wayne S.** b Dec 1954. He married (1) 11 Oct 1975, Lebanon, CT, **Paula E. Brennan** b 1958?; m (2) 14 Nov 1987, Norwich, CT, John A. Schute.

He married (2) 1 Apr 1978, New London, CT, **Kim M. Crane** b 1958?

He married (3) 15 Aug 1987, New London, CT, **Janice E. Caster** b 1946?

Paula Brennan was 17 years old in 1975, Kim Crane was 20 years old in 1978, and Janice Caster was 41 years old in 1987 (Connecticut Marriage Index).

Wayne S. and Janice Monty were residents of New London, CT, when his father died in 1999 (*Hartford Courant*, 7 Jan 1999).

8.3.8.5.2.2.1   **MONTY, Cynthia A.** b 11 Sep 1946, CT. She married **Robert Tenerowicz** b 27 Sep 1946.

Mrs. Cynthia Tenerowicz was a resident of Woodstock, CT, when her father died in 2006 (*Norwich Bulletin*, 14 Nov 2006).

8.3.8.5.2.3.1   **MONTY, Carol A.** b 21 Oct 1945, CT. She married **Robert Richard Simonds** b 22 Dec 1937; d 25 Mar 1978, Volusia Co., FL.

Mrs. Carol Simonds was a resident of Ormond Beach, FL, when her father died in 2005 (*Norwich Bulletin*, 25 Dec 2005).

8.3.8.5.2.3.2   **MONTY, Albert C.** b 3 Mar 1949, CT. He married 10 Mar 1973, Plainfield, CT, **Susan Elizabeth Perkins** b 1 Sep 1955.

Albert Monty was a resident of Moosup, CT, when his father died in 2005 (*Norwich Bulletin*, 25 Dec 2005).

8.3.8.5.2.3.3   **MONTY, William J.** b Sep 1951, CT.

William J. Monty was a resident of Woodstock, CT, when his father died in 2005 (*Norwich Bulletin*, 25 Dec 2005).

8.3.8.5.2.3.4   **MONTY, Deborah J.** b Mar 1957, CT. She married 1 Aug 1980, Killingly, CT, **Stephen J. Brine** b Jan 1954.

Mrs. Deborah Brine was a resident of Plainfield, CT, when her father died in 2005 (*Norwich Bulletin*, 25 Dec 2005).

8.3.8.5.3.3.1   **MONTY, Donna** b Jul 1946, Holyoke, MA. She married **Angelo A. Spirito** b Jan 1935.

Mrs. Donna Spirito was a resident of South Hadley, MA, when her father died in 1996 (*Springfield Union News*, 21 Aug 1996).

8.3.8.5.3.3.2   **MONTY, Mary** married **Stewart Wentz** (Herbert Wentz & Elva Stambaugh) b May 1938, York, PA.

Mrs. Mary Wentz was a resident of Athol, MA, when her father died in 1996 (*Springfield Union News*, 21 Aug 1996).

8.3.8.5.3.3.3   **MONTY, David E.** b Aug 1949, Holyoke, MA.

David Monty was a resident of Granby, MA, when his father died in 1996 (*Springfield Union News*, 21 Aug 1996).

8.3.8.8.5.1.1   **MONTY, Jamie L.** b 27 Aug 1975, CT.

Jamie Monty was living in Bolton, CT, when his paternal grandmother died in 2001 (*Hartford Courant*, 7 Jan 2001).

8.3.8.8.5.1.2   **MONTY, Jessica M.** b Mar 1978, CT.

Jessica Monty was living in Bolton, CT, when her paternal grandmother died in 2001 (*Hartford Courant,* 7 Jan 2001).

8.3.8.8.5.1.3   MONTY, Jennifer
Jennifer Monty was living in Bolton, CT, when her paternal grandmother died in 2001 (*Hartford Courant,* 7 Jan 2001).

8.3.8.8.5.2.1   MONTY, Michael
Michael Monty was living in Manchester, CT, when his paternal grandmother died in 2001 (*Hartford Courant,* 7 Jan 2001).

8.3.8.8.5.2.2   MONTY, Trisha
Trisha Monty was living in Manchester, CT, when her paternal grandmother died in 2001 (*Hartford Courant,* 7 Jan 2001).

8.3.8.8.5.2.3   MONTY, Jonathan
Jonathan Monty was living in Manchester, CT, when his paternal grandmother died in 2001 (*Hartford Courant,* 7 Jan 2001).

8.3.11.6.3.1.1   MONTY, Norman C. b 2 Oct 1928, New Bedford, MA; d there 9 May 1980. He married **Dorothy A. ____** b 16 Sep 1932, MA; d 28 Jun 1986, New Bedford, MA.

8.3.11.6.3.1.2   MONTY, Alfred Lorand b 26 Apr 1930, New Bedford, MA; d & bur 6 & 10 Oct 1973, Virginia Beach, VA. He married 13 Oct 1951, **Arline Antoinette Dube** (Antoine John Dube & Rose Delima Blanche Lapre) b 5 Oct 1933, New Bedford, MA.
I know of this marriage only through Louise Monty, *Généalogie de la famille Monty,* III, 250.

8.3.11.6.3.6.1   MONTY, Denise Lucille b 13 May 1944, New Bedford, MA; d 25 Oct 2001, Ashford, CT. She married (1) ____ **Fecteau**.
She married (2) 21 Dec 1969, Hampton, CT, **Charles F. Chesters** (Charles F. Chesters & Grace Kimball) b there 28 Oct 1942; d there 23 Oct 1981.
She married (3) 13 May 1994, Charlotte Co., FL, **Frank E. Wiley** b Jul 1927.
Frank E. Wiley survived his wife (*Hartford Courant,* 26 Oct 2001).

8.3.11.6.3.6.2   MONTY, Carolyn Marie b May 1946, New Bedford, MA. She married (1) ____ **Berube**.
She married (2) 28 Mar 1992, St. Augustine, FL, **William Gustav Jaeckel** b May 1939.
Carolyn Monty and her husband were residents of St. Augustine, FL, when her sister Denise died in 2001 (*Hartford Courant,* 26 Oct 2001).

8.3.11.6.3.8.1   MONTY, Cora G. b 4 Jul 1943, New Bedford, MA. She married **Allen D. Baker** b 12 Mar 1943.
Mrs. Cora G. Baker was a resident of Acushnet, MA, when her father died in 1998 (*South Coast Today,* New Bedford, MA, 14 Jul 1998).

8.3.11.6.3.8.2   MONTY, Linda J. M. b 4 Feb 1948, New Bedford, MA. She married **Robert R. Lavoie** b 20 Sep 1945.
Mrs. Linda J. M. Lavoie was a resident of West Palm Beach, FL, when her father died in 1998 (*South Coast Today,* New Bedford, MA, 14 Jul 1998).

8.3.11.6.3.8.3   MONTY, Joyce b 26 Jun 1949, New Bedford, MA. She married **David S. Bennett** b 25 Oct 1934, MA; d 4 Oct 2001, Westport, MA.
Mrs. Joyce L. Bennett was a resident of Mattapoisett, MA, when her father died in 1998 (*South Coast Today,* New Bedford, MA, 14 Jul 1998). She survived her husband.

8.3.11.6.3.8.4   **MONTY, Jeffrey Adrian** b 13 Jan 1951, New Bedford, MA. He married (1) 29 Apr 1984, Las Vegas, NV, and divorced there 16 Feb 1989 **Sheryl Lyn** ____ m (2) 16 Feb 1992, Las Vegas, NV, Larry Gene Doremus.

He married (2) 9 May 1992, Las Vegas, NV, **Carolyn Lynett Robinson** b 1 Oct 1957.

Jeffrey A. Monty was a resident of Las Vegas, NV, when his father died in 1998 (*South Coast Today*, New Bedford, MA, 14 Jul 1998).

8.3.11.6.3.8.5   **MONTY, Donna J.** b 22 Jan 1954, New Bedford, MA. She married ____ **Ramos**.

Mrs. Donna J. Ramos was a resident of New Bedford, MA, when her father died in 1998 (*South Coast Today*, New Bedford, MA, 14 Jul 1998).

8.3.11.6.3.8.6   **MONTY, Pamela V.** b 17 Apr 1956, New Bedford, MA. She married **George W. Arnold** b 11 Dec 1940.

Mrs. Pamela V. Arnold was a resident of Fairhaven, MA, when her father died in 1998 (*South Coast Today*, New Bedford, MA, 14 Jul 1998).

8.3.11.6.3.8.7   **MONTY, Ernest R.** b Jan 1961, New Bedford, MA. He married **Pamela Louise** ____ b 15 Aug 1951; d 14 Oct 2002, Boston, MA.

Ernest R. Monty was a resident of New Bedford, MA, when his father died in 1998 (*South Coast Today*, New Bedford, MA, 14 Jul 1998).

8.3.11.6.3.8.8   **MONTY, Bridget** b Apr 1964, New Bedford, MA. She married **Keven Docekal** b Jun 1957.

Mrs. Bridget M. Docekal was a resident of East Sandwich, MA, when her father died in 1998 (*South Coast Today*, New Bedford, MA, 14 Jul 1998).

8.3.11.6.3.8.9   **MONTY, Lana D.** b 14 Jan 1967, New Bedford, MA. She married **James C. Collis** b 26 Sep 1965.

Mrs. Lana D. Collis was a resident of Dartmouth, MA, when her father died in 1998 (*South Coast Today*, New Bedford, MA, 14 Jul 1998).

8.3.11.6.3.10.1   **MONTY, Maurice L.** b Jun 1952, New Bedford, MA. He married **Denine** ____ b Jan 1960.

Maurice Monty was living in Rhode Island when his sister Linette (8.3.11.6.3.10.2) died in 2002 (*South Coast Today*, New Bedford, MA, 21 Jun 2002).

8.3.11.6.3.10.2   **MONTY, Linette Marguerite** b 10 Jun 1953, New Bedford, MA; d & bur there 19 & 21 Jun 2002.

Linette Marguerite Monty was buried in the Sacred Heart Cemetery in New Bedford, MA (*South Coast Today*, New Bedford, MA, 21 Jun 2002).

8.3.11.6.3.10.3   **MONTY, William P.** b 19 Feb 1955, New Bedford, MA. He married **Rose A.** ____ b 4 Nov 1955.

William P. Monty was a resident of West Wareham, MA, when his sister Linette (8.3.11.6.3.10.2) died in 2002 (*South Coast Today*, New Bedford, MA, 21 Jun 2002).

8.3.11.6.3.10.4   **MONTY, Michelle J.** b 4 Apr 1956, New Bedford, MA. She married **Kenneth H. Margeson** b 18 Feb 1954.

Mrs. Michelle Margeson was a resident of Dartmouth, MA, when her sister Linette (8.3.11.6.3.10.2) died in 2002 (*South Coast Today*, New Bedford, MA, 21 Jun 2002).

8.3.11.6.3.10.5   **MONTY, Phillip J.** b 12 Aug 1957, New Bedford, MA. He married **Patricia A.** ____ b 17 Aug 1957.

Philip Monty was a resident of Sandwich, MA, when his sister Linette (8.3.11.6.3.10.2) died in 2002 (*South Coast Today*, 2 New Bedford, MA, 1 Jun 2002).

8.3.11.6.3.10.6 MONTY, Michael A. b 10 May 1961, New Bedford, MA. He married **Ruth ____** b 23 Oct 1961.

Michael Monty was a resident of Wareham, MA, when his sister Linette (8.3.11.6.3. 10.2) died in 2002 (*South Coast Today*, New Bedford, MA, 21 Jun 2002).

8.3.11.6.3.10.7 MONTY, Leon P. b Mar 1963, New Bedford, MA. He married **Maryellen ____** b Aug 1970.

Leon Monty was a resident of Wareham, MA, when his sister Linette (8.3.11.6.3.10.2) died in 2002 (*South Coast Today*, New Bedford, MA, 21 Jun 2002).

8.3.11.6.3.10.8 MONTY, Jacqueline b 8 Jul 1964, New Bedford, MA. She married **Gerald J. Sylvia** b 15 Dec 1963.

Mrs. Jacqueline Sylvia was a resident of Marion, MA, when her sister Linette (8.3.11. 6.3.10.2) died in 2002 (*South Coast Today*, New Bedford, MA, 21 Jun 2002).

8.3.11.6.3.10.9 MONTY, Christopher J. b 7 Jan 1966, New Bedford, MA. He married **Joan ____** b 3 Feb 1960.

Christopher Monty was a resident of Wareham, MA, when his sister Linette (8.3.11.6. 3.10.2) died in 2002 (*South Coast Today*, New Bedford, MA, 21 Jun 2002).

8.3.11.7.8.1.1 MONTY, William A. b 27 Sep 1949, Syracuse, NY; d & bur there 6 & 10 Aug 2001. He married **M. Catherine Unz** (Frederick Joseph Unz & Mary Jane Lawton) b 1949, Syracuse, NY.

William A. Monty was buried in Onondaga Valley Cemetery in Syracuse, NY. His wife survived him (*Syracuse Post Standard*, 9 Aug 2001).

8.3.11.7.8.1.2 MONTY, Larry D. b 10 May 1954, NY; d 17 Dec 2005, Weedsport, NY. He married **Joan Elizabeth Vorba** (Edward James Vorba & Ruth Ellen Peters) b 27 Jul 1956, Orange, CT.

Joan Vorba survived her husband (*Syracuse Post Standard*, 19 Dec 2005).

13.3.6.4.6.5.1 MONTY, Jeannine b & bp 14 & 15 May 1934, Ste Brigide, QC; d 4 Jun 1989, Ste Sabine, QC. She married there 17 Sep 1955 **Antoine Godin** (Hormisdas Godin & Denise Galipeau).

Baptismal name: Marie Claire Jeannine Monty.

13.3.6.4.6.5.2 MONTY, Denise Gisèle b & bp 20 & 22 May 1935, Ste Brigide, QC. She married 3 Sep 1956, Ste Sabine, QC, **Jean Louis Bourdon** (Adolphe Bourdon & Cécile Godin) b & bp 5 Jul 1931, Pike River, QC.

13.3.6.4.6.5.3 MONTY, Fernande b & bp 16 & 18 Oct 1937, Ste Brigide, QC. She married 7 Oct 1957, Ste Sabine, QC, **Jacques Charpentier** (Léo Charpentier & Eva Lacroix) b & bp there 5 & 6 Sep 1934.

Baptismal name: Marie Marguerite Fernande Monty.

13.3.6.4.6.5.4 MONTY, Brigitte b & bp 8 & 9 Oct 1938, Ste Brigide, QC. She married 6 Sep 1964, Ste Sabine, QC, **Ulysse Albert Delphis Charpentier** (Doria Charpentier & Maria Rolland) b & bp 13 Mar 1936, St. Alexandre, QC.

Baptismal name: Marie Marthe Brigitte Monty.

13.3.6.4.6.5.5 MONTY, Jean-Luc b & bp 12 & 14 Jul 1940, Ste Brigide, QC. He married 13 Jun 1964, Ste Sabine, QC, **Micheline Caron** (Oscar Caron & Bibiane Hamel) b 21 Sep 1943, Grantham, QC.

Baptismal name: Pierre Eméri Jean-Luc Monty.

13.3.6.4.6.5.6 **MONTY, Yolande** b 1 Nov 1942, Ste Sabine, QC. She married there 6 May 1967 **Normand Bonneau** (Eugène Bonneau & Rose Delima Fontaine) b & bp there 27 Feb 1935.
Baptismal name: Joseph François Normand Bonneau.

13.3.6.4.6.5.7 **MONTY, Claudette** b 2 Aug 1944, Ste Sabine, QC. She married 8 Sep 1967, Farnham, QC, **Jacques Luc Phénix** (Gérard Phénix & Annette Bilodeau) b & bp 29 & 30 May 1940, Ste Sabine, QC.

13.3.6.4.6.5.8 **MONTY, Marie Ange** b 7 Aug 1947, Ste Sabine, QC.
This woman became known as Sister Marie Ange Monty, a nun in the Order of St. Joseph in St. Hyacinthe, QC. She took her vows on 19 Mar 1969.

13.3.6.4.6.5.9 **MONTY, Robert** b 31 Mar 1948, Ste Sabine, QC. He married 30 Apr 1972, Acton Vale, QC, **Thérèse Ménard**.

13.3.6.4.6.5.10 **MONTY, Lisette** b 17 Mar 1952, Ste Sabine, QC. She married 15 Oct 1977, Farnham, QC, **Jean Guy Paquette**.

13.3.6.4.6.5.11 **MONTY, Paul Aimé** b 20 Sep 1953, Bedford, QC. He married 27 Aug 1977, Stanbridge, QC, **Suzanne Galipeau**.

13.3.6.4.6.5.12 **MONTY, Sylvain** b 9 Mar 1956, Bedford, QC. He married 2 Jul 1977, St. Ignace, QC, **Nicole Falcon**.

13.3.6.4.8.2.1 **MONTY, Annette Suzanne Jeanne** b & bp 5 & 10 Mar 1940, Ste Brigide, QC.

13.3.6.4.8.2.2 **MONTY, Jean Stanislas Claude** b 29 Aug 1942, St. Jean, QC.

13.3.6.4.10.3.1 **MONTY, Pierre** b 10 Mar 1948, Montreal, QC. He married there 24 Jul 1971 **Claudette Lalonde** (Yvon Lalonde & Marie Marthe Vandal) b there 9 Feb 1951.

13.3.6.4.10.3.2 **MONTY, Manon** b 9 Jan 1952, Montreal, QC. She married there 16 Aug 1975 **Claude Yves Dupont** (Jean-Claude Dupont & Gloria Bélanger) b there 27 Nov 1950.

13.3.6.4.11.2.1 **MONTY, Gino** b 21 Aug 1958, Iberville, QC. He married there 26 Dec 1981 **France Ouimette** (Charles Ouimette & Laura Laplante).

13.3.6.4.11.3.1 **MONTY, Hélène** married 18 Sep 1976, Iberville, QC, **Emile Sirois** (Léon Sirois & Yolande Doucet).

13.3.6.4.11.3.2 **MONTY, Bertrand** married 31 Jul 1976, Iberville, QC, **Lucie Turcotte** (Benoit Turcotte & Yvette Croteau).

13.3.8.2.5.3.1 **MONTY, Della R.** b 19 Mar 1933, MI; d 22 May 2000, Detroit, MI. She married **Lyle Edwin Duke** (Ralph Duke & Zella Ingland) b 19 Apr 1929, Grand Rapids, MI.

13.3.8.2.5.3.2 **MONTY, Wesley** married **Eleanore** ____ b 29 Apr 1947.

13.3.8.2.5.3.3 **MONTY, Thomas P.** b 3 Apr 1948. He married **Mary Jane** ____ b 15 Jun 1948.

13.3.8.2.5.3.4 **MONTY, Peggy**

13.3.8.2.5.4.1   **MONTY, Edgar Lee** b 22 Dec 1934. He married **Barbara Kuhn** b 1 Oct 1937.

13.3.8.2.5.5.1   **MONTY, Dale Ray** b 1 Sep 1934, IL. He married **Sharon Ann Lenfert** (Louis A. Lenfert & Genevieve L. Cyrier) b 6 Apr 1936.

13.3.8.2.5.5.2   **MONTY, Judith/Judy** b 1940? She married (1) **Brian A. Mercer** b 15 Aug 1940; d 12 Mar 1984.
She married (2) **Dwayne Pfeffinger** b 3 Mar 1944.

13.3.8.2.5.5.3   **MONTY, Rita** b 1950? She married **Michael Papineau.**

13.3.8.2.5.6.1   **MONTY, Richard L.** b 1947?
Dick Monty and his wife survived his father (*Payson Roundup*, 7 Jul 2008).

13.3.8.2.5.6.2   **MONTY, Mark S.** b 1954? He married **Diane ____** b 1954?
Marc S. Monty and his wife survived his father (*Payson Roundup*, 7 Jul 2008).

13.3.8.6.2.3.1   **MONTIE, William Joseph** b 25 Dec 1932; d 1 Feb 1997, Mountain Home, AR. He married **Eileen ____** b 3 Jul 1949.
Mrs. Eileen Montie was still living in Mountain Home, AR, when William Montie's stepfather, Robert W. Schmidt, died in 2005 (*Baxter Bulletin*, 9 Mar 2005),

13.3.8.6.4.3.1   **MONTIE, Leroy Louis** b 1935?, IL. He married (1) 1956 and divorced Feb 1974, Fresno, CA, **Donna L. Bayrich** (Pierre Bayrich & Lenora Duckworth) b 20 Jul 1938, San Bernardino, CA.
He married (2) 28 Feb 1975, Fresno, CA, and divorced there Aug 1975 **Joan Josephine Agee** b 1931?; m (1) 14 May 1968, Fresno, CA, and divorced there Nov 1971 Howard L. Sanders.
Leroy L. Montie was 39 years old when he married the 43-year-old Joan J. Agee.

13.3.8.6.4.3.2   **MONTIE, Renee Alain** b 13 Nov 1948, Fresno, CA. She married (1) there 11 Jun 1966 and divorced 4 Jun 1982, Monterey Co., CA, **Theodore Ralph Sanford** (____ Sanford & ____ Thompson) b 12 Sep 1946, Fresno Co., CA; m (2) 16 Oct 1985, Monterey Co., CA, Matilda R. Anastasia, widow of Gary Robert Jones.
She married (2) 29 Oct 1983, Monterey Co., CA, **Frederic J. Crocker** b 1950.

13.3.8.6.6.1.1   **MONTE, Mardelle Anne** b 20 Jun 1930, Rock Island, IL. She married 19 Jun 1953, WI, **Paul Richard Barber** (Pearl Barber & Mabel Cole) b 13 May 1930, Numa, IA; m (2) 30 Jun 1984, Lake Geneva, WI, Arlene Grant (Lyle E. Grant & Freda V. Johnson), widow of Virgil Molinarolo; d & bur 20 & 25 Mar 1997, Antioch & Donavan, IL.

13.3.8.6.6.1.2   **MONTE, Don Elwyn** b 27 May 1933, Rock Island, IL. He married **Glenda Faye Long** (Sam Long & Stella Pennington) b 13 Nov 1936.

13.3.8.6.6.1.3   **MONTE, Gene** b 23 Mar 1935, Rock Island, IL. He married **Nancy Lee Tompkins** b 6 Mar 1938, Davenport, IA.

13.3.8.8.7.2.1   **MONTY, Paul L.** b 30 Jan 1944, Cloud Co., KS. He married **Gayle ____** b 1 Jun 1952.

13.3.8.8.7.2.2   **MONTY, Loleda**

13.3.8.8.7.2.3   **MONTY, Lana**

13.3.8.8.8.1.1   **MONTY, Kathleen Ann** b 17 Apr 1942, Salina, KS. She married there 1

Aug 1964 **John David Hlavacek** (Joseph J. Hlavacek & Leocadia/Lottie Petkowski) b 22 Jun 1942, KS.

John Hlavacek was a CPA in Manhattan, KS, and in Topeka, KS, before moving to Overland Park, KS, where he and his wife resided for many years (*Salina Journal*, 10 Feb 1971; *Wichita Eagle*, 25 Oct 1986, 7 Aug 1995, and 1 Jan 1998; *Kansas City Star*, 8 Jan 2007).

13.3.8.8.8.1.2   **MONTY, John Eldon** b 25 Feb 1944, Salina, KS.

John Monty was a resident of Independence, MO, when his parents died in 1995 and 1997 (*Wichita Eagle*, 7 Aug 1995 and 1 Jan 1998).

13.3.8.8.8.1.3   **MONTY, Patricia Louise** (twin) b 18 Mar 1945, Salina, KS. She married there 8 Jul 1972 **Thomas J. Butler** (Thomas J. Butler & Mary Rose ____) b Dec 1942.

Thomas J. Butler III worked in Abilene, KS, before his marriage (*Salina Journal*, 23 Jan 1972). He and his wife later lived in West Linn, OR (*Wichita Eagle*, 22 May 1985, 7 Aug 1995, and 1 Jan 1998).

13.3.8.8.8.1.4   **MONTY, Carolyn Susan** (twin) b 18 Mar 1945, Salina, KS. She married there 11 Aug 1973 **Leonard Joseph Nowak** (John Paul Nowak & Angelia D. Karniski) b 1 Sep 1937, St. Louis, MO.

Carolyn Susan Monty and Leonard Joseph Nowak both worked in St. Louis, MO, before their marriage (*Salina Journal*, 10 Jun 1973). They were residents of St. Peters, MO, when her parents died in 1995 and 1997 (*Wichita Eagle*, 7 Aug 1995 and 1 Jan 1998).

13.3.8.8.8.1.5   **MONTY, Mary Jane** b 10 Aug 1946, Salina, KS. She married there 3 Aug 1968, **John Richard Wise** (Alvin Wise & ____) b 30 Sep 1946.

John Richard Wise was a student of Architecture at Kansas State University in Manhattan, KS, when he married and an architect in Atlanta, GA, after his June 1970 graduation (*Salina Journal*, 7 Apr 1968 and 6 Sep 1970). He and his wife were residents of Tucker, GA, when her parents died in 1995 and 1997 (*Wichita Eagle*, 7 Aug 1995 and 1 Jan 1998).

13.3.8.8.8.1.6   **MONTY, Rosemary** b 19 Jun 1950, Salina, KS. She married (1) there 10 Jun 1972, **Rodney Earl Jacobs** (M. E. Jacobs & ____) b 17 Dec 1949.

She married (2) **James Kauffman**.

Rodney E. Jacobs was an accountant in Atlanta, GA at his marriage (*Salina Journal*, 11 Jun 1972).

Mrs. Rosemary Kauffman was a resident of Newton, KS, when her parents died in 1995 and 1997 (*Wichita Eagle*, 7 Aug 1995 and 1 Jan 1998).

13.3.8.8.8.2.1   **MONTY, William Joseph** b 10 Oct 1941, Salina, KS; d 17 May 1964.

13.3.8.8.8.3.1   **MONTY, Mark Louis** b 11 Apr 1950, Salina, KS. He married **Terry** ____ .

Mark Monty and his wife Terry were residents of Hamilton, NY, when his father died in 2008 (*Salina Journal*, 4 Jun 2008).

13.3.8.8.8.3.2   **MONTY, Diane Marie** b 2 Apr 1951, Salina, KS. She married **Edward R. Quartell.**

Diane Monty was living in Davenport, IA, when her father died in 2008 (*Salina Journal*, 4 Jun 2008).

13.3.8.8.8.3.3   **MONTY, George Charles** b 2 Oct 1953, Salina, KS.

George C. Monty was a resident of Davenport, IA, when his father died in 2008 (*Salina Journal*, 4 Jun 2008).

13.3.8.8.8.3.4   **MONTY, David Allen** b 11 Jan 1967, Davenport, IA. He married **Kimber** ____ b 15 Oct 1970.

David Monty and his wife Kimber were residents of Davenport, IA, when his father died in 2008 (*Salina Journal*, 4 Jun 2008).

13.3.8.8.9.4.1   MONTY, Mary Catherine b Jun 1949. She married **Anthony M. Strunk** (Harold J. Strunk & Virginia LaRock).

Mrs. Anthony Strunk was a resident of Wichita, KS in 1974, when she was her sister Nancy's matron of honor (*Salina Journal*, 9 Jun 1974). She was a resident of Goddard, KS, though in 2002 as was her husband Tony Strunk in 2007 (*Wichita Eagle*, Obituaries of Armeline Monty and of Harold J. Strunk, 1 Jun 2002 and 8 May 2007).

13.3.8.8.9.4.2   MONTY, Nancy Ann b Jan 1952. She married (1) 28 Apr 1970, Wichita, KS, **Lynn Adair Miller** b 31 Aug 1949, Great Bend, KS; d & bur 1 & 3 May 1972, Wichita & Great Bend, KS.

She married (2) 8 Jun 1974, Wichita, KS, **John W. Wessling** (Edwin Henry Wessling & Mary Jane Shanahan) b Sep 1951, KS; m (2) Leora Cowsill.

Dr. John W. Wessling was a chiropractor in Modesto, CA, at his first marriage (*Salina Journal*, 9 Jun 1974) though he later practiced in Wichita, KS. Mrs. Nancy Wessling was a resident there when her father and her aunt Armeline Monty (13.3.8.8.9.3) died in 1994 and 2002 (*Wichita Eagle*, 5 Feb 1994 and 1 Jun 2002).

13.3.8.8.9.4.3   MONTY, David Edward b 1956. He married 29 Nov 1986, Rockwall Co., TX, **Stacey Stembridge** (William Ellis Stembridge & Nancy Anne Thevenet) b 2 Sep 1953, Upshur Co., TX; m (1) 10 Sep 1977, Rockwall Co., TX, and divorced 27 Apr 1983, Dallas Co., TX, Charles Bradley Hendrex (Charles Ray Hendrex & Eleanor Winfred Glass).

David E. Monty was 30 years old when he married. He was a resident of Garland, TX, in 1994, and of Grand Saline, TX, in 2002 (*Wichita Eagle*, Obituaries of Melvin E. Monty and Armeline Monty, 5 Feb 1994 and 1 Jun 2002).

13.3.8.8.9.4.4   MONTY, Douglas

Doug Monty was a resident of Forth Worth, TX, in 1994 and of Wichita, KS, in 2002 (*Wichita Eagle*, Obituaries of Melvin E. Monty and Armeline Monty, 5 Feb 1994 and 1 Jun 2002).

13.3.8.8.9.5.1   MONTY, Garry Joseph b 3 Mar 1952, McLennan Co., TX. He married 10 Jun 1978, Dallas Co., TX, **Vickie Marie Yetts** (Theodore William Yetts & Gwynne Adele Prudhomme) b there 1 Feb 1954.

Garry Monty and his wife lived in Dallas Co., TX, when their children were born. They were in Mesquite, TX, when his father died in 2002 (*Wichita Eagle*, 10 Mar 2002).

13.3.8.8.11.1.1   MONTY, Raymond Gale b & d 15 Jun 1946, Clyde, KS.
This child was buried in Mount Calvary Cemetery in Clyde, KS.

13.3.8.8.11.1.2   MONTY, Loleta Ann married 13 Aug 1976, Cloud Co., KS, **Leon F. Deaver** (Leo Deaver & Theresa Hamel) b 25 Oct 1953.

Sgt Leon Deaver was serving with the US Air Force in the Philippines when the date of his forthcoming marriage was announced in the *Salina Journal* of 8 Feb 1976.

13.3.8.8.11.2.1   MONTY, Eldemore Jr.
Eldemore Monty Jr. was a resident of Beloit, KS, when his father died in 2005 (*Salina Journal*, 20 Sep 2005).

13.3.8.8.11.3.1   MONTY, Calvin Leroy married 19 Dec 1973, Jewell, KS, **Charla Marie Holdren** (Charles Holdren & ____) b 25 Oct 1955.

Calvin Monty was with the US Army in Fort Bliss in El Paso, TX, at his marriage (*Salina Journal*, 23 Dec 1973).

13.3.8.8.11.3.2 **MONTY, Katherine Marie** married 1972? **Rodney A. White** (Chester White & _____).

Rodney A. White was with the US Army in Germany when his engagement to Katherine Marie Monty was announced in the *Salina Journal* of 2 Jan 1972.

13.3.8.8.11.3.3 **MONTY, Douglas** married _____ Colby.

13.3.8.8.12.4.1 **MONTY, Daniel** b 2 Jan 1950, Saline Co., KS. He married **Patricia** _____.

Dan Monty and his wife Pat were residents of Nickerson, KS, when his father died in 2006 (*Salina Journal*, 19 Jan 2006).

13.3.8.8.12.4.2 **MONTY, Robert** b 13 Dec 1951, Saline Co., KS.

Bob Monty was a resident of Oak Grove, MO, when his father died in 2006 (*Salina Journal*, 19 Jan 2006).

13.3.8.8.12.4.3 **MONTY, Janet** b 2 Sep 1954, Saline Co., KS. She married **Charles T. Weston** b 1954?

Mrs. Charlie Weston and her husband were from Wichita, KS, when her sister Dee Ann Monty (13.3.8.8.12.4.4) married in 1977. They were residents of Emporia, KS, when her father died in 2006 (*Salina Journal*, 24 May 1977 and 19 Jan 2006).

13.3.8.8.12.4.4 **MONTY, Dee Ann** b 20 May 1959, Saline Co., KS. She married 14 May 1977, Beloit, KS, **Carl Ray Hobbs** (Dan Hobbs & _____).

Carl Ray Hobbs was originally from Beloit, KS, but was a farmer in Arkansas at his marriage (*Salina Journal*, 17 Apr & 24 May 1977). Mrs. Dee Ann Hobbs was of Springdale, AR, when her father died in 2006 (*Salina Journal*, 19 Jan 2006).

13.3.10.8.2.3.1 **MONTY, Claudette** b 19 May 1951, Montreal, QC. She married 21 Jul 1984, Chambly, QC, **Henri Tremblay** (Roger Tremblay & Solange _____).

13.3.10.8.2.3.2 **MONTY, Jacques** b 16 Jun 1952, Montreal, QC. He married there 5 May 1984 **Jocelyne Lecavalier** (Pierre Lecavalier & Béatrice Guénette).

13.3.10.8.2.3.3 **MONTY, Luc** b 23 Nov 1958, Jacques-Cartier, QC. He married **Annie Lacombe** (William Lacombe & Lise _____) b 27 Oct 1966, Quebec, QC.

APPENDIX I

In tracing the early descendants of Francis Monty (4) in New York State I have been greatly helped by two depositions made before the Clinton Co. Court of Common Pleas in Plattsburgh, NY, by his grandchildren Mrs. Barbary Morrison (4.4.5) and John Monty (4.11.1) on 9 Oct 1856 and 3 Nov 1856 respectively. There are a few minor inaccuracies, some names could not be recalled or are misspelled, nicknames are used in lieu of a person's usual, more formal name, afterthoughts are inserted in the text seemingly haphazardly, as they occurred, while the somewhat erratic punctuation may lend itself to ambiguity. Almost all of the statements have been verified and only two found to be in error: the date of Francis Monty's death in Barbary Morrison's affidavit (see p. 12) and the name of George Trombly's wife in John Monty's deposition (see p. 79). For the rest, their recollections appear to be remarkably accurate.

This is my own transcription. I have not attempted to regularize either spelling or punctuation, which in many cases is beyond me. The only change I have made is to insert paragraphs (as I understand them to be) for ease of reading. The original runs in a single unit. The names in the margins are in the same hand as in the text itself and are due to the 1856 scribe.

A. Barbary (Monty) Morrison's Affidavit

State of New York

County of Clinton   Barbary Morrison of the town of Plattsburgh in the County of Clinton aforesaid being duly sworn doth depose & say that she is the granddaughter of Lieut. Francis Monty of Hazens Regiment of the Revolutionary war; that he died in this County the 15th day of February A.D. 1812; that his widow died on the day of [last two words crossed out] about 1822 and they left the following named children to wit: John Monty now living & a United States pensioner of the Revolutionary War;

Francis   Francis Monty, deponents father, now dead, leaving the following children viz. Johanah [inserted above the line: who married Abraham Monty], now dead, leaving the following children viz. Betsey Monty who married Eli Prindle, living; Margaret Monty who married Benjamin Monty; he is dead and she again married Nehemiah Marvin; Abraham Monty who is now dead but left the following children, viz. John Monty living, Henry Monty dead & left one child Ann Eliza; Charles Monty, Mary Monty, George Monty, Abraham, Laura, Daniel, Harriet, Benjamin. Francis Monty son of Johanna; Lucina Monty who married Peleg Stafford;

James   James Monty son of Lᵗ Monty, is dead & left children whose names she don't recollect –

Abraham   Abraham Monty son of Lᵗ Monty, who is dead & left children viz. John Monty, Phebe who married Joseph Latray; Julia who married Peter Thouville; Barbary who married Joseph Baker, Ann who married Levi Prindle, living; Benjamin Monty the 1st husband of Mrs. Marvin –

Joseph   Joseph Monty son of Lᵗ Monty, who is dead & left children, but don't remember their names.

Placid   Placid
Christopher Monty, son of Francis Monty who is the son of Lᵗ Monty, now dead & left the following children viz. Mary Monty who married [inserted above the line: James] Griffin; Julia Monty who married Paul Montville, Frederick Monty, Jane Monty married to Joseph Meso who is dead & left one child Joseph Meso –
Ann Monty, Andrew Monty;
Mary Miller, who married Andrew Bird (her mother was Jane Ann Monty)

John Miller, Benjamin Miller, Joseph Miller, Abraham Miller, Anthony Miller, Robert Miller, Elizabeth Miller, Maria Miller, all the last are married [last four words crossed out] – Catherine Miller, Matilda Miller, –

Betsey Monty daughter of Francis Monty, son of Lt Monty, who married John Ward,

Mary Monty (the daughter of Francis Monty son of Lt Monty) who married Joseph Houd

Abraham Monty son of Francis Monty son of Lt Monty,

Margaret Monty (daughter of Francis Monty who was the son of Lt Monty) married Joseph Frederick she is dead & left the following children; viz. Joseph Frederick, Francis Frederick, Angeline Frederick, Margaret Frederick, Mary Ann Frederick, Samuel M. Frederick, John Frederick, Charlotte Maria Frederick, Charles Edward Frederick, Jane Ann Frederick.

Joseph Monty brother of Johanna, the son of Francis Monty, the son of Lt Monty, who is dead & left the following children viz. John Monty, Joseph, Andrew –

Sworn before me this 9th day of Oct. 1856

her

Barbary   X   Morrison

mark

(signed) P. G. Ellsworth
           Judge of Clinton County

****

State of New York

County of Clinton   On this third day of October [last word crossed out, superscripted: November]. A.D. 1856 personally appeared before me the undersigned Justice of the Peace in the said County, John Monty Jr aged 48 years a resident of Chazy in said County, to me known to be a person of credibility, who being duly sworn did depose and say that he is well acquainted with the following children & grandchildren of Lieut. Francis Monty of Hazens Regt. Revolutionary war, & not named in the annexed affidavit of Barbary Morrison & not by her recollected so as to give their names –

That he knew Joseph Monty a son of Lt Monty who is dead & left the following named children to wit: Joseph Monty, Julia Monty who married Samuel Lock, Edward Monty, Fayette Monty, Mary Monty who married Lewis Savage, Lucy Monty who married George Trombly, Rosilla Monty who married Claudius Monty, Louisa Monty who married Charles Savage, Lucy Ann Monty who married Charles Clough, William Monty, Wellington Monty, DeWitt Monty.

And he further saith that Placid Monty son of Lt Monty who is dead & left the following children; viz. 1. Placid Monty 2. Susan Monty married to (not recollected) who is dead & she left the following [last two words crossed out and superscripted: two] children viz. [last word crossed out] names unknown 3. Parmelia Monty who married Joseph Latra, 4. Betsey Monty married to one Francis Loshway 5. Francis Monty, 6. Dominique Monty 7. Mary Monty who married one Francis Hulgate.

And he further saith that James Monty son of Lt Monty who is dead, left the following children his heirs at law viz. Christopher Monty (living), James Monty living, Matthew Monty who is dead & left the following children his heirs at law viz. Ginnie Monty who married   Payne, Katy Monty who married Joseph W. Clark; she is dead & left the following children her heirs at law viz: Matthew Clark, Cornelius Clark, Eliza Clark, Edward Clark, Saphrone Clark, Joseph Clark, Leonard Clark.

Mary Monty daughter of L$^{t\ Francis}$ Monty who married Louis Lizotte, she is dead & left the following children viz. Joseph Lizotte, Louis Lizotte & Mary who married Christopher Monty (viz [one word illegible])

Matthew [inserted above the line: (son of James)] Monty, [inserted above the line: grand] son of Lt Monty, heirs viz. Abraham Monty, Jane Ann Monty, Eunice Monty, Matilda Monty, Henry Monty, David Monty, Hepsa Monty, Allen Monty, Melvin Monty, Polly Monty, Milly Monty, Lizzy Monty dead daughter of Lt Monty; Katy Gosselin [inserted above the line: married Clement Gosselin Major] daughter of Lt Monty dead & left one child Gennie who married Louis Monty

And further deponent saith not.

(signed) John Monty Jr.

Sworn before me on the day & year first above written

(signed) M. Van Dervort Justice Peace

A list of the surviving children of Francis Monty Jr. (4.4) was drawn up by the Clinton Co. Circuit Court in Plattsburgh, NY, on 4 Jul 1846. The declaration's phrasing however makes it somewhat ambiguous. Since the text passes in the same sentence from the past (1818) to the present (1846), it is not immediately clear whether the six children named were the only ones who survived their father or the only ones who were alive in 1846. Certainly the statement that "all *are* (my italics*)* over the age of twenty one," while true in 1846, would be false in 1818: we know that at least two of the children named by the court, Abraham (4.4.7) and Margaret (4.4.8), were under the age of 21 in 1818. The court's decision must then refer to the six children who were still alive in 1846 and does not preclude the existence of others who may have been alive when their father died but were deceased in 1846.

My Transcription:

At a Circuit Court at the Court house in the village of Plattsburgh in and for the County of Clinton on the 4th day of July 1846 the Same being a Court of Record.
Present Hon John Willard Circuit Judge, William Hedding, J. Douglass Woodward and Isaac H. Putchen, Judges of Said County – It was proven to the Satisfaction of Said Court that Francis Monty was a Revolutionary Soldier of the United States, and that he died at the Town of Plattsburgh in the Said County of Clinton on the 10th day of August 1818; that he left no widow, that he left Six children who are all over the age of twenty one years and that they are his only Surviving children whose names are as follows, Christopher Monty, Abram Monty, Betsey Ward, Fanny Miller, Barbara Monty, and Margaret Frederic.

> In testimony whereof I have hereunto Subscribed my name and affixed the Seal of Said County this 4th day of July 1846

> (signed) Charles H. Jones
> Clerk

BIBLIOGRAPHY

I. PRIMARY SOURCES

With the exception of a few documents obtained from the National Archives, most of the records I have used are available on microfilm through the LDS Family History Library in Salt Lake City, UT, as well as on the Internet. A few others such as Tombstone Transcriptions and Newspapers and Obituary Archives can be found only on the Internet on several constantly evolving Web sites. All have been of constant use:

1. In the United States:
   Cemetery and Funeral Homes Records
   Censuses, 1790-1930
   City Directories
   Immigration and Naturalization Records
   Newspaper Archives
   Papers of the Continental Congress
   Social Security Death Index
   State Censuses to 1925
   Tombstone Transcriptions and Photographs
   Vital Records (births, marriages, deaths, divorces)
   War Department Records: Revolutionary War, War of 1812, Civil War, World War I, and
      World War II.
2. In Canada:
   Censuses, 1851-1911
   Notarial Archives, Province of Quebec
   Vital Records, Alberta, British Columbia, Ontario, Quebec Provinces
   Newspaper Archives

II. WORKS CITED

Only those works which are cited or referred to in my notes or which have provided information not easily found elsewhere are included here. For that reason I have omitted the numerous compilations of Vital Records in specific localities in the United States and Canada: while useful as indexes, they can not replace the actual records of a person's birth/baptism, marriage(s), or death/ burial.

The Balloting Book and Other Documents Relating to Military Bounty Lands in the State of New York. Albany, NY, 1825.

BARBER, John W. & Henry Howe. *Historical Collections of the State of New York*. New York, 1842.

BATEMAN, Newton, Paul Selby, and Charles L. Hostetter, eds. *Historical Encyclopedia of Illinois and History of Carroll County*. Chicago, IL: Munsell Publishing Co., 1913.

BILOW, John Andrew. "Census of Canadian Refugees in New York State in 1784, 1785, 1787" and "Appendix: Movements of Hazen's Regiment," *French Canadian and Acadian Genealogical Review*, IX (1981), 241-259.

Biographical Memoirs of Wyandot County, Ohio. Logansport, IN: B. F. Bowen, 1902.

BOWMAN, Fred Q. *10,000 Vital Records of Eastern New York, 1777-1834*. Baltimore, MD: Genealogical Publishing Co., 1987.

DE MARCE, Virginia Easley. "Canadian Participants in the American Revolution, an Index." Typescript, 1980.

DENISSEN, Christian. *Genealogy of the French Families of the Detroit River Region, 1701-1936*. Revised edition. Detroit, MI: Detroit Society for Genealogical Research, 1987.

Echoing Trails: Billings County History. Fargo, ND: Knight Pr. Company for Billings County Historical Society, 1979.

EVEREST, Allan S. *Moses Hazen and the Canadian Refugees in the American Revolution*. Syracuse, NY: Syracuse University Press, 1976.

GALLUP, Andrew & Donald F. Shaffer. *La Marine: The French Colonial Soldier in Canada, 1745-1761*. Bowie, MD: Heritage Books, 1992.

HANCOCK, Ellery M. *Past and Present of Allamakee County, Iowa*. 2 vols. Chicago, IL: S. J. Clarke Publishing Co., 1913.

HURD, D. Hamilton. *History of Clinton and Franklin Counties, New York*. Philadelphia, PA: J. W. Lewis & Co., 1880.

The History of Wyandot County, Ohio. Chicago, IL: Leggett, Conaway & Co., 1884.

LAREAU, Paul J. *Lareau Genealogy: Descendants of a Carpenter*. Baltimore, MD: Gateway Press, 1986.

LEONARD, Joseph A. *History of Olmsted County, Minnesota*. Chicago, IL: Goodspeed Historical Association, 1910.

MALLOY, Dorothy Palmer. "Saga of the Taney Rainbow Trails." Typescript, 1976.

MARCOTTE, Michael, transcriber and translator. "Journal of Sophie Richard, 1874-1878 and 1878-1880." (Marcotte Genealogy Web Page)

MASSICOTTE, E.-Z. "Les Disparus. Louis-Eustache Monty," *Bulletin des Recherches Historiques*, IV (1935), 755.

MONTY, Ernest L. "Major Clément Gosselin," *French Canadian and Acadian Genealogical Review*, I (1968), 27-44.

MONTY, Louise. *Généalogie de la famille Monty*. Montreal, PQ, 1993.

O'KEEFE, Barbara B. "List of Baptisms Registered in St. Joseph's Church, Philadelphia, from January 1, 1776 to October 21, 1781," , II (1886-1888), 225-275.

RAMSEY, Betty Miller. *Monty-Montee History*. Fairview, UT, 1981.

REYNOLDS, Cuyler, ed. *Hudson-Mohawk Genealogical and Family Memoirs*. New York: Lewis Historical Publishing Co., 1911.

SCHATZ, Mary Ann. *Civil War Veterans of Kankakee County, Illinois*. Kankakee, IL: Kankakee Valley Genealogical Society, 1976.

SULLIVAN, Nell Jane Barnett & David Kendall Martin. *A History of the Town of Chazy,*

Clinton County, NY. Burlington, VT: G. Little Press, 1970.

A Twentieth-Century History and Biographical Record of Crawford County, Kansas. Chicago, IL, & New York, NY: The Lewis Publishing Co., 1905.

WOODRUFF, George H., William H. Perrier, and H. H. Hill. *The History of Will County, Illinois.* Chicago, IL: Wm LeBaron Jr. & Co., 1878.

WHITFIELD, William, ed. *History of Snohomish County, Washington.* 2 vols. Chicago, IL: Pioneer Historical Publishing Co., 1926.

INDEX
DESCENDANTS AND THEIR SPOUSES

Pamela Louise (Monty) 616
Patricia (Monty) 622
Patricia A. (Monty) 616
Paula E. (Montee) 429
Philomene (Decelle) 93
Rachel (Monty) 598
Rebecca (Besset) 174
Reta V. (Bessette) 488
Roberta Jean (Monty) 609
Rosa E. (Osborn) 278
Rose/Rosanna (Brodeur) 193
Rose (Letendre) 357
Rose A. (Monty) 616
Rose Ellen (Gendron) 321
Ruby (Bennett) 285
Ruth (Bradford) 377
Ruth (Frederick) 75
Ruth (Monty) 617
Ruth (Paul) 217
Ruth A. (Brooks) 485
Sarah E. (Cross) 132
Sheryl Lyn (Monty) 616
Shirley (Pelky) 534
Shirley A. (Monty) 605
Stacey (Monty) 613
Susan (Byington) 531
Suzanne D. (Montie) 564
Teresa (?) (Montee) 229
Theresa (Montie) 244
Theresa C. (Metthe) 367
Theresa L. (Monty) 592
Tressa (?) (Montee) 229
Vern (Bennett) 285
Viola M. (Nadeau) 398
Virginia (Monte) 526-527
Wendy (Gugliotta) 473
Wilma I. (Monty) 497
Yvonne F. (Desruisseau) 484

ABARE
Edward 250
George William 400
Gertrude H. 158
Julius 158
ABELE
Agnes Matilda 415
ABERCROMBIE
Allen 261
ABRAHAM
Alexander/Aleck W. 413
ACKERMAN
Pamela 601
ADAM dit LARAMEE
Alexis/Alphonse 176
Alexis Jérémie 175

Arthur Edmond 176
Emanuel R. 583
François 171
Joseph Arthur 176
Marie/Mary 176
Marie Azilda 176
Noël 176
Philomène 176
Rosalie 176
Virginie 176
ADAMS
Arnold A. 432
Herbert G. 332
Lewis W. 345
Marguerite Catherine 408
ADDIS
Margaret E. 466
ADELMAN
Ottneal/Ottneel 464
AGEE
Joan Josephine 619
AHRENS
James W. 535
John 535
Richard L. 535
William/Bill P. 535
William O. 535
AIL
Jacob 28
AILLOT (see **AYOT**)
AINSE/HAINS/HINS
Antoine 111
Marguerite/Margaret 111
AITKENHEAD
Susan 463
AKEY
Arthur Charles 439
Cleveland/Cleve 439
Fred Franklin 439
Marian Mae 439
Peter Leroy 439
AKINS
LeRoy/Roy B. 231
ALAND
Blake Neale 451
Dala Ruth 451
Dean Holmes 451
Gale 451
Montee Levi 451
William Levi 451
ALASSI
Jeanne M. 601
ALDER
Viola A. 411
ALEXANDRE
Jean-Baptiste 22

ALLARD
Antoine/Anthony 319
Chantal 549
Germain 491
Hélène 603
Joseph 310
Lucie 549
Léo Marcel 594
Monique 549
Philomene 109
Serge 548
ALLEN
Alice Laverne 411
Ethel M. 309-310
Leroy W. 394
Monty LeRoy 395
Pauline R. 559
ALLENER
Edna 562
ALLY
Gérard 490
ALTERGOTT
Alex D. 552
AMELOTTE/AMELOT
Marguerite Elisabeth 27
ANDERSON
Donald Kenmore 559
Edward J. 603
Emmet Eldridge 285
Joyce M. 467
Minnie O. 259
Nancy Carolyn 464
Nora Rolfine 258
ANDREW
Riley Elmer 279
Theodore Wesley 579
ANDREWS
Anne 561
Annette 280-281
ANNIS
Sadie/Sarah 499
ANTAYA
Bernadette 193
APLIN
Bonnie Lee 609
APPLEBY
Donald Vernon 551
ARCHAMBAULT
Anna L./Marie Lucie 219
Florence 517
Joseph 201
Joseph Benoni 201
Louis 223
Marie Louise 212
Sophie Azilda 201
ARELE/ARELLE

Elizabeth/Eliza 235
John 235
Joseph Didier Paul 235
Joseph Napoleon 235
Luc 55
ARES
Clovis 517
Elisabeth Germaine 489
Florence Yvette 517
Joseph Ambroise 516-517
Roger 517
ARIEL/RIEL
Mary 251
ARMSTRONG
Mr. 143
Alta L. 258
Carl Just 258
Charles/Charlie Ross 258
Elsie L. 258
Guy Raymond 258
Isaac 257-258
ARNDT
Elizabeth Lillian 459
ARNOLD
Charles H. 472
George W. 616
ARRUDA
Joseph 494
ARSENAULT/ACEINO
Thomas Henry 198
ASHBY
Alberta 173
ASHWORTH
James 145
ATWOOD
Charlotte 247-248
AUBE
Marie 186
AUBRE
Jeanne d'Arc 341
Joseph Albert 341
AUCLAIR
Julie 62
Séraphine 92
Sophia 130
AUDET dit LAPOINTE/
AUDETTE
Angèle 67
Daniel 126
Edouard 126
Emilie 126
Jean-Baptiste 125
Joseph 126
Louis 126
Marguerite 125
Marie 125

Michel 125 (2)
Rosalie 93
Suzanne/Susan 125
Thankful Victoria 358-359
AUDREN
Eveline 521
AUDY
Marise 556
AUPRAY/AUPRE
Marie M. 268
AURES
Bette Helen 354
AUSEMUS
Elsie Eileen 457
AUSTEN
John William 296
AUTHIER
Marie Louise Héla 339
AVARD
Walter Remi 218
AVERILL
Janice Mae 587
Mary Lyla Laud 386
AYOT/AILLOT
Joseph
Joseph René 214
Lionel 216
Lucien 242
Madeleine 242
Napoleon 242
Pierre 17-18
Simone G. 242
AYRES
Annis 124
John 124
AZEVEDO
Pearl Anna 606
BABER
John Marion 476
BACHAND
Hector 337
Marie Bernadette Béatrix 337
Thérèse Marthe 337
BACON
Donald 508
Henry 508
Lauretta 330
Leonard A. 508
Lorraine 508
Norman 508
Rita 508
BAFARO
Roy/Rocco S. 487
BAILEY
Howard 161

Jerry L. 586
BAILLARGEON (see also
BEASHAU)
Alfred Luc 514
Cécile Simonne M. 514
Ernest 603
Flavie 105
Jean-Baptiste 514
Jean Pierre 514
Stella 423
BAINBRIDGE
Alice C. 550
BAIRD
Lee E. 479
BAKER
Mr. 581
Allen D. 615
Caroline/Carrie 271
George 271
James 437
Joann 590
Joseph 77
Joseph H. 233
June N. 320
Victoria/Victorine 344
BAKKEN
Bernard Ingvard 301
BALCH
Eli 234
BALL
Emma Lou 460
BALLARD
Henry Thomas 117
BALLAS
Barbara Lynn 612
BALTHAZAR(D)
Céleste 98
Joseph 29
Martine 50
Yvonne 491
BANKS
Frederick Dewey 286
BARABE
Gilberte Bernadette 544
BARBEAU
Mary Louisa 307-308
BARBER
Nelson John 233-234
Paul Richard 619
BARCOMB
Wilfred J. 589
BARE/BARRE
Alexine/Alexandrine 179
Augustin 44
Charles 44
Charlotte 44

David 44 (2)
David Joseph 45
Elisabeth 44 (2), 45
Jean-Baptiste 43 44 (2)
Jean Pascal 44
Joseph 44
Louis 43(2)
Louise 43
Marguerite 44
Marie 15, 44
Marie Adélaïde 44
Marie Amable 43
Marie Desanges 44 (2)
Pierre 44 (2)
BARIL
Marie Louise 102-103
Marielle 501
BARKER
Delia 233
BARKLEY
Carrie M./Mary Caroline 265
BARLOW
Winifred 269
BARNHART
Arlene May 527
George 276-277
BARON
Bertha Cynthia 159
Joseph François/Frank Jos. 329
BARR
George E. 360
BARRIERE
Anonymous 338
Arsélie/Arzelia 338
Césaire 338
Léon 546
Louis 43
Marguerite Josette 44
Pierre 44
BARRON
Benjamin 246
BARSALOU
Florence Gisèle 515
Françoise 326
BARTH
Ida May 449
BARTLETT
Doris Darlene 442
BARTLEY
Agnes Louise 153
Charles Henry 153
Chester A. 153
Daniel Harry 153
James 153

Jeremiah James 153
John F. 153
Mary E. 153
Thomas Howard 153
William Joseph 153
BARTOL
Adeline 531
BARTON
Lloyd Randall 349
BARUP
George 197
Henry R. 197
BASHORE
Mr. 613
BASILE
David Carl 470
Georgia May 470
George 470
BASS
Frederick Eugene 590
BASSETT (see **BESSETTE**)
BAXTER
Anna Maria 311
BAYRICH
Donna 619
BAZINET
Célina 96
BEACH
Hazel Dorothy 549
BEAN
Albert 514
BEANY
Mary 289
BEASHAU
Thomas 154-155
BEATTIE
Forest G. 448
Janice E. 448
Joyce M. 448
Mary Elizabeth 448
BEATY
Malcolm Leroy 569
BEAUCHAMP
Amanda 323
BEAUCHEMIN
Rose Adèle 181
BEAUCHENE
Ida 185
BEAUDET
Arthur Joseph 394
Joseph Théophile 226, 394
Julian Frederic 394
BEAUDIN
Agnes Cecile/Cecilia 231
Aurelia/Marie Aurélie 230
Beatrice P. 230

Caroline Marie 230
Florence Alice 231
Genevieve Josephine 231
Jean Narcisse 230
Leo Louis Etienne 230
Paul Edward 231
Peter/Pierre 230
Robert Peter 231
Viola F. 231
BEAUDREAU
Malvina 311
BEAUDRIAU
Marguerite 50-51
BEAUDRY
Alfred 201-202
Mathilde 66-67
Phidias 320
Pierre 165
BEAULAC
Suzanne 544
BEAULIEU
Amelia/Emilie 88-89
Leonora 105
BEAULIEU dit BER-TRAND
Mathilde/Matilda 188
BEAUMONT
Julienne 171-172
BEAUREGARD
Dorila 335
Frank 209
Marie 166
Mathilde 336-337
Omer 511
BEAUSENS (see **BEAU-CHAMP**)
BEAUSOLEIL
Louise Elizabeth 225
BEAUTRON (see **MAJOR**)
BEAUVAIS
Marguerite 56
Médérise 338
BECK
Ruby 444
BECKER
Robert 573
Walter Raymond 609
BECKMARK/BACK-MARK
Evelyn 390
Harry Frank 390
BECKWITH
Douglas Leonard 451
BEDARD
Adélaïde/Adèle 167
Angèle 167

Archibald Edmond Justin 316
Auguste Antoine 316
Aurélie Cordélie 167
Azilda 167
Bernadette 316
Célestin 167
Elias 167
Euphrosine 50
Flavie 167
Grégoire Edmond 316
Jacques 167 (2)
Joseph 167
Joseph Marie Henry 167
Louis Pierre 167
Marie 167
Marie Anne 316
Marie Aurore Lumina Bella 316
Marie Célina Rosalba 167
Philias Edmond Hervé 316
Philomène 167
Rodolphe Roméo 316
Valéda 482
BEDOR
Lila 352
BEEDY
Agnes 209
Albert Vincent 209
Charles Wesley 208-209
Izora Phoebe 209
Lillian Aurelia 209
Mattie/Martha 209
Minnie 209
Oscar Nathan 209
Walter D. 209
BEELER
William T. 278-279
BEGGS
Robert Samuel 575
BEGIN
Paul Antoine 370
BEIRNE
Patrick J. 598-599
BELANGER (see also
BLONGY)
Beatrice 508
Belzemire 331
Clara A. 417
Donald 508
Jocelyne 600
Joseph 508
Joseph Cyrille 508
Lillian 513
Linda 590
Marie 334

Sophia 36
BELHUMEUR
Célanie/Celina 315
BELISLE
Rose Alba 102
BELL
John William 581
BELLENO
Celestina 444
BELLING
Carl Phillip 570
BENAC
Alma 322
Jean-Baptiste 49
BENDER
Honora Leona/Nora 295
BENDTSEN
Laura Eliza 528, 529
BENEDICT
William Cole 124
BENJAMIN
Albert 547
Arzelia 206
Carmen 547
Jeannine Gisèle 547
Lee Lambert 547
René Hormisdas 547
Régis René 547
BENNETT (see also
BENOIT)
Alfred Raymond 241
Alice E. 285
Archie Lee 285
David S. 615
Frances 285
Freelove Amy 134
George 285
Howard 396
Howard Crawford 396
John Edward 285
Joyce 396
Lottie 285
Mary 285
Nellie Mae/Mary N. 285
Norma 396
Parmelia 133-134
Robert Lorenzo 289
William 284-285
William Byron 285
BENOIT
André 546
Antoine 44
Catherine 89
Céleste 46
Charles Arthur 546
Edouard Fr./Edward 197

Estelle 605
Florence A. 542
George J. 198
Guillaume/William 47
Honoré 47
Ida 198
Ignace 47 (2)
Joseph 197
Joseph Pascal 197
Julie 367
Kenneth W. 542
Lena 198
Lionel C. 603
Marie J. 198
Mary Emma/Marie E. 198
Onésime 47
Philip/Pascal Philippe 197
Polydore 481
Raymond G. 488
Regina E. 198
Véronique Eugénie Malvina 197
Wilfred J. 197, 541-542
BENSON
Dewey 235
Edward 235
Edward V. 235
Lisa Maria 235
BENTON
Floyd Merrill 579
BENWAY
Henry C. 136
Eli James 136
Eli Willard 136
John 136
Margaret 132
William Joseph 132
BERARD
Helen/Hélène 207
Michel 51
BERENGUER
Rosario 428
BERG
Elaine Marie 612
BERGER
Joseph 100
BERGERON
Alice 320
Delphine Almina 492
Irene Ann 320
Joseph Ovila 319-320, 320
Marguerite 386
Marie 69
Theodore L. 320
BERGEVIN dit LANGE-VIN

Josette/Marie Joseph 9-13
BERKLEY
Fred H. 267
BERMAN
James O. 462
BERNARD
Albert 318
François Xavier 107
Roderick Joseph 192
Wilfred Eugene 484
BERNIER
Marguerite 50
BERQUIST
Charles Amel/Emil 390
Geneva Evangeline 390
Irid 390
Rowe 390
BERRIGAN
John 571
BERRY
Mrs. Grace 300
Minerva Jane 138
BERTANI
Gloria Joan 414
BERTHIAUME
Charles Auguste 544
Paul 595
BERTRAND
Alain 556
Alexis 52
Charles E. 414
Dorothy E. 414
Eugene Emerald 413-414
Jean-Baptiste 95
Johanne 557
Joseph E. 414
Lillian Mary 414
Lewis B. 414
Margaret 414
Mathilde/Matilda 188
Pierre 556
Rosemary 414
BERUBE
Mr. 615
Jeanne L. 220
BESS
Ralph 563
BESSET/BESSETTE
Adée Louise 175
Adeline 50, 303
Aglaé/Agnès 210-211
Agnès 305
Alcide 372-373
Alfred 174
Alphonse 174
Anne Marie 552

Antoinette L. 488
Armande Diana/Amande 373
Athanase 175
Athanase Delphis 175
Catherine/Katherine Céleste 391
Cecile 488
Charles 174
Claire 488
Cornelius Patrick 552
Delphine 174
Domitilde/Mathilde 50
Edouard 174 (3)
Edward 391
Emery/Irénée/René 373
Eudoxie 175 (2)
Eugène Théophile 391
Euphrosine 174
Francis/Frank Joseph 552
François Xavier 108
Geraldine/Gerry 552
Gerard A. 488
Gloria Lee 552
Henri Edouard 391
Henry Ira/Henri 391
Hercule 175
Honoré 174, 175
Jeanette D.
Joseph 174
Joseph Alexandre 175
Joseph Ulric 373
Julie 206
Léontine 169
Lucille M. 488
Mabel 391
Maida 488
Marie 175
Marie Amable 391
Marie Aglaé 205
Marie Germaine 373
Marie Louise 15
Marie Louise A. 175
Marie Médérise 174
Marie Mélinda 175
Marie Virginie 165
Marie Virginie Osanna 175
Mary L. 175
Moïse 175
Ovide 96
Philomène 119
Pierre 174
Pierre/Peter 174
Raoul U. 488
Rosalie 165
Rosario A. 488

Stanislas 175
Ulric 488
BESSEY
Frank James 425-426
BETOURNE/BETOUR-NAY
M. Honorée/Honorine 55
BEVINS
Alfred A. 592
BEYERS
Mr. 524
BIBEAU
Calixte 324
Justin 324
Lea 324
Louis 175
BIDWELL
Gary Terrell 369
BIELY
Joseph 588
BIENVENU/BIENVENUE
Elise 374
Gisèle 594
Roméo 326
BIGONESSE
Albina/Albena 110
Arthur 110
Catherine 304
Charles 110
Cordelia 110
Dora/Dorey 110
Dorothy/Hattie 110
Ida 110
Jean-Baptiste 110
Josephte 51-52
Louisa 110
Napoléon 110
Octave 110
Philomène 110
BILES
Dessie Elsie 280
Edith Montee 280
Ferne Marion 280
Flora Belle/Floy B. 280
Francis Martin 280
James Edward Monroe 279
Juanita Letitia 280
Lloyd Montee 280
Mary Emily/Mamie 280
Maude Anna 280
Rufus A. 280
BILLS
Florian A. 139
BINET (see **VINET**)
BIRCHER
Marian 350

Martine 96
Michel 96
Monique 96
Olive 126
Pierre 119
Réal 517
Richard A. 601
Rose Anna 484
Sylvio 547
Yolande Marguerite 547
BOUDREAU/BOU-
DREAULT
Anonymous 510
Hervé 510
Lisa Micheline 510
Lucadia 189
Luce Paulette 510
Marcel 510
Yolande Monique 510
BOULAIS/BOULAY
Alexis 67-68
Brigitte 546
Esther 164
Lionel 546
Sadie 218
BOULANGER
Mariette 502
BOULEY/BULLEY
Ida 246
Philip 246
BOURASSA
Alberta 371
Armande/Armandine 370
Herbert Thomas/Hubert 370
Lillian 370
Mary Ann 370
Octavie Lauretta/Loretta 370
Philomene/Phyllis Ida 249
BOURBEAU
Alphonse 493
Alphonse L. 493
Marie Anne/Anna 214-215
Reina 493
BOURDON
Jean Louis 617
Marie Rose 111
Odile 67
BOURET
Eugenia Olivia 442
BOURGEOIS
Aurélie 101
Beatrice 377
BOURGERIE/BUSHERIE
Eva 233
George 234

Lillian Mary/M. Eulalie 233
Marie Elmina/Mina 233
Peter/Pierre 233
William A. 233
BOURQUE
Adeline 313-314
BOURRET
Fernand 341
BOUSQUET/BOSCA
Adeline 157
John Joseph 597
BOUTEILLE (see also
BONNEVILLE)
Adélaïde 103-104
Adolphe 104
Alexandre 104
Antoine 103 (2)
Denise 104
Edmond 104
Flavie 104
Flavien 104
Henriette 104
Marie Césarie 104
Napoléon 104
Nazaire 104
Noël 104
Vital 104
BOUTHEILLER
Marie Louise 214
BOUTIN
Cécile 591
BOUVIA
Ernest 566
BOUVIER
Arthur Adélard 240
Delia Antonia 241
Elie 240
Emelia 240
Emile Isola 241
Ernest 240
Flavie Aurore 241
Hermine 241
Joseph Elie Ulric 240
Louise Olympe 240
Maximilienne 240-241
Raoul Isola 241
Regina 240
Rose Anna Sophie 240
Victoria/Rose Alba 240
BOVAIR
Alexander 123
Angelina Azilda 123
Charles 123
Elizabeth 124
Emma 123
Fred/Alfred Alexander 123

George Edward 123
Gertrude Pauline 124
Jerome Arthur 124
Marie Anna Eliza 124
Marie Valida 123-124
William Alexander 123
BOWEN
Blanche 426
BOWERS
Mary 400-401
BOX
Anonymous 458
Robert Glen 458
BOXLER
Harry E. 467
BOYD
Stephen Lovejoy 125
Susan E. 334
BOYDSTUN
Karen L. 577
BOYER
Clara 207
Félicité 54
Marie Anne 9
BOYLE
Earl
BOYNTON
Myrtle 209
BRABANT
Joseph 56
BRACKETT
Robert A. 403
BRACONNIER
Antoine 125
BRADFORD
Euna Valeria 262
Herman 377
John Emery 377
Royal Herman 377
Stella 377
Vern Lyle 377
Wilma Lucille 377
BRADLEY
Henry H. 436
William Ralph 580
BRADRICK
Kathleen 459
BRADSHAW
Edna M. 381
BRADY
Margaret L. 241
Ruth 520
Shelagh 520
Stephen 520
Teresa 520
Thomas John 520

BRAMMER
Vicki D. 613
BRANCHAUD
Jean-Baptiste 29
BRANDT
Hazel 285
BRAULT
Alexandre 168
Carmel 503
Justina Marie 222
BRAUSS
Joseph 280
BRAY dit LABONTE
Aglaé 25
Césarie 25
Françoise 24
Honorée 25
Michel 24
Rosalie 25
BRAZEE
Charlotte 560
BREARD/BREILLARD
Joseph 8
BREAULT
Alice 389
BREAZEAL
Barry Lee 586
BRECHIN
Mary 473
BRENNAN
Florence 550
Paula E. 614
BRESS
Robert 231
BRESSE
Pierre 15
BRETON
Obeline Mathilda 540
BRICCO/BRICAULT
Mary Jane/M. Genevieve 190
BRIERE
François Xavier 98
BRIGGS
Arthur Eugene 145
BRIGHAM
Grace A. 302
BRILEYA
Andrew 403
BRIN
Georges/George 510
Joseph Germain 510
Madeleine 510
Marie Flore Alida 510
BRINE
Stephen J. 614

BRITTAIN
Roy/Leroy 301
Virginia 301
BROCHU
Louise 606
BRODEUR
Adrian 320
Alma 490
Alméda 340
Angela Clarinda 340
Anna Marie 339
Anonymous 320, 321
Arthur 339, 340
Blanche Antoinette Gertrude 321
Camille Yves Marc 388
Cécile 340
Clément Augustin 193
Denis 388
Elida 193
Emery 339-340
Emma 340
Emma Rose/Alma 193
Euclide 181
Fidélia 320
Florina 320
Francine 388
Gaston 501
George Alfred 193
Georges 339
Georgiana 193
Hector Agénar 340
Henri Louis 339
Herménégilde Philippe 193
Honoré 340
Jean 388
Joseph 193
Léona 340
Louis Adélard 340
Louis Polydore/Paul 193
Louis Rémi 340
Louise Monique Gisèle 388
Maria 193
Marie Anne 339
Marie Elmire Amelda 193
Marie Louise Alma 340
Marie Marthe 388
Marie Rose Anna 321
Mathilde 375
Napoléon Armand 340
Omer 320
Omer Adrien 320
Paul Oscar Uldéric 193
Philias David 339
Philip H. 193
Rachel 321

Raymond 388
Rémi Louis 339
Roméo 388
Rose Anna 340
Rose Delima 339
Roseline 338-339
Silvère Louis 193
Simone E. 406
Sylvia Yvonne 339
Télesphore 193
Uldège 339
BROMENSCHENK
Gary Allen 462
Larry Leroy 462
Leroy Joseph 461-462
BROMLEY
Mary Appa 80
Susan Augusta 80
BROOKS (see also **DESRUISSEAU**)
Harold J. 485
Leo W. 485
BROSSARD
Esther 106
BROSSEAU
Léo Ernest 316
Marie Anne 174
Suzanne 547
Victoria Margaret 381
BROUGHTON
Martin Henry 560
BROUILLET/BROUILLETTE
Célina 312
Gilles 546
Marie Anne 111
Philomene 108-109
BROWN
Mr. 143, 573
Albert David 566
Charlene 568
Fay Dock 458
Francis/Frank 369
Ida May 536
Janice Ann 464-465
Jennifer Louise 590
John 256
Joseph 465
Leah Caroline 279
Mary Catherine 463
BRUJHELL
Harold R. 527
BRULE
Edward Antonio 291
Florence 291
BRUN

Angèle 205
BRUNDAGE
Nancy 146
BRUNELLE
Alphonse 311
Delphine 297
Napoléon 202
Rose Anna /Rosanna 206
Sophia 81
BRUNER
Bertha Elmira 457
BRUNK
Bertha 446
BRUTON
Thomas Everett 455
BRYANT
Herman L. 163
BUBE
Elizabeth J. 534
BUBECK
Albert Leo 429
Gary W. 430
BUCHENAU
Mr. 382
BUCHHOLZ
Gus W. Jr. 381
BUCK
Florence Estelle 145
BUCKLES
Doris J. 452
BUGAUD
Edouard Auguste 186
BULLARD
George Leslie 236
James R. 585
BUREL/BURELLE
Marcelline 172
Philomène 167
BURGARD
Janet Sue 553
BURGESS
Robert Franklin 155
Thomas 154-155
BURGOYNE
Benjamin F. 228
BURNS
George 417
BURROUGHS
Anna Carolina 254
Horace James 254
Mary E./Nellie 254
Thomas F. 253-254
BURY
Freeman Green 163
BUSCHKE
Gordon E. 611

BUSHEY/BUSHY
Alton W. 403
Ina M. 422
Joseph 105
BUSHNELL
David Edward 254
BUSSELL
Josephine Alice 266
BUTCHER
Peter 119
BUTLER
Elama Mara 390
Thomas 620
BUTTENHOFF
Lillian 390
BYINGTON
David R. 531
Jeanne M. 531
Lee E. 531
Robert 531
Ronald E. 531
Susan 531
CABANA/CHARRON dit
CABANA
Abraham, 97 (2)
Alfred 98
Alphonse 98
Ambroise 98
Azilda/Ezilda 98
Janvier 98
Joseph Eudore 97-98
Joseph Jacob 98
Marie Alodie/Mélanie/
Mélodie 98
CABLE
Niona Jane 433-434
CADIEUX
Anna/Annette 547
Simone 548
CADORET
Angèle 93
David 100
CADY
Mr. 448
Arthur E. 507
Charles Alton 548
CAHILL
Lucinda Bernice 492
CALCAGNO
Napoléon 96
CALLAHAN
Adelphia/Della 211
Charles Dennis 226
CALLANT
Anonymous 296
Claudia Genevieve 296

Ellen Margaretta 295-296
Ida May 296
John Albert 296
Mary Lillian 295
Thomas Liversage 295
Zoe Blanche 296
CAMERON
David D. 400
Duncan D. 400
Earl D. 400
Esther 23
Marion 400
CAMPBELL
Ernest Nathaniel 577-578
Simone 600
CANNAN
Miretta Abigail 404
CANO
Anita H. 591
CAOUETTE
Thérèse 600
CAPISTRANT
Beulah 539
David Edward 540
Donald Raymond 540
Doriea G. 539
Robert Leo 540
Roland E. 540
Shirley M. 539
CAPUANO
Albert 588
CARBONARI
Claudia M. 614
CARD
Norman Lee 576
CAREAU
Emérentienne 45
CARLESS
Gordon 519
CARLI
Blanche/Bianca Olga A.
385
CARON
Juliette 486
Micheline 617
CARPENTER
Charles 403-404
David 82
Laura 231
Lowell 404
Marilyn 404
Ralph L. 404
CARPENTIER
Marie 93
CARRIER
Jeannine A. 597

CARRIERE
Marie Louise 167
CARRILLO
Brian J. 527
CARROLL
George Henry 458-459
James Edwin 459
CARSON
Lorene Elizabeth 444
CARTER
Florence A. 449
Juanita Mae 446
Thomas 600
CARY
Daniel David 445
Fern M. 445
James Michael 445
CASAVANT
Eugène 317-318
Joseph Wilfrid 317
Kathleen Ann 393
Leslie Lynne 393
Leslie T. 393
Philippe 317
CASE
Albert 143
Marjorie 433
CASGRAIN
Andrée 327
CASTER
Janice E. 614
CASTERLINE
Mary Lou 543
Richard 543 (2)
Theresa Lynn 543
CATE
Richard H. 482
CATER
Anna 143
CATUDAL (see also ST. JEAN)
Adeline 183
Edmond 183
Emery 182
Ephrem 182
Joseph 182 (2)
Médérise 183
Moïse 183
Rose Anna 183
CAVALLARO
Carmen 407
CAYA
Albert 497
CHABOT
Bernadette 483
Estelle 483

Joseph Charles Edouard 167-168
Joséphine 123
Marguerite M. Evelyn 309
CHAGNON
Delphis/Dolphis 167
Paul Emile 512
CHAILLE/CHAILLY
Eva/Oliva 240
CHALIFOUX
Jean-Baptiste 125
CHALIN
Pauline 491
CHAMBERLAIN
Mr. 580
CHAMBERLAND
Françoise 60
CHAMBON
Jacques 596
CHAMPAGNE
Alcide J. 370
Anna 250
Antonia 329
Arthur Elzéar 506
Exear R./Elzéar 505
Monty Robert Henri 506
Ray Albert Norman 506
CHAMPIGNY
Thérèse Hélène 490
CHAPMAN
Betty Lou 524
Kenneth W. 597
CHAPUT
Alfred 328
Antoinette 591
Arthur René 505
Florence 505
Harvey/Hervé 505
Henry 505
Mary Helen/Marie Hélène 505
CHARBONNEAU
Gaston B. 594
CHARLAND
Clerina 206
CHARLTON
Mabel Kate 279
CHAROUX/CHARROUX
Abraham 98
Adolphe 98
Alphonse 98
Hermine 98
Joseph 98 (2)
Joséphine 98
Justin 98
Marcelline 99

Marie Adeline/Célina 98
Marie Françoise 98
Philomène 98
Rosalie 98
CHARPENTIER
Alfred J. 541
Arthur A. 541
Eileen J. 541
Jacques 617
Richard W. 541
Ulysse Albert Delphis 617
William A. 541
CHARRON
Arzélie 183
Israël 178
Joséphine 181
CHARTIER
Alcide 324
Victor 538
CHASE
Eugenia Laura/Jennie 243
CHASE-CASGRAIN
Andrée 327
CHAUSSE
Philomène 127
CHENIER
Pauline 385
CHERENZA
John F. 538
CHESLEY
Frank P. 184
CHESTERS
Charles F. 615
CHEVAL (see ST. JAC-QUES dit CHEVAL)
CHEVALIER
Marie Leda 496
CHICOINE
Jean-Baptiste 93
Aurélie 68
CHILSON
Laurita C. 224
CHOINIERE/CHOI-GNIERE
Adélaïde 60
Joseph 100
Isaac 372
CHOQUET/CHOQUETTE
Achille Philias 304
Adélaïde 166-167
Adélard 173
Adèle 166
Adeline 166
Alfred 183
Ambroise 166
Edéas Alfred 203-204

Ida Agnes 205
Mary Ann 330
CORDEAU
Gertrude 384
CORENTTO
Daniel Joseph 401
COREY
Ruth Anna 462
CORNELSON
Frank John 452
Patti Ann 452
Roland Frank 452 (2)
CORNO
Louisa 223
CORRIVEAU
Edith 556
Félicité 101
COSTA
Alice 369
Anthony 369
Florence 369
Gladys 369
Marie 369
Nicola/Nicholas M. 369
COTE
Bertrand 512
Delia 339
Florianne Gilberte 600
Henri Paul 340
Marie Louise Corinne 204
Marie Olive 23
Normand 545
Wenceslas 200
COUGHLIN
Joseph James 588
COULOMBE
Isabelle 603
COUNTER
Mary 82
COURTEMANCHE
Camille 92
Marie Jeanne Emilia 386-387
Olivier 61
Sophronie 125-126
COURTIN
Catherine 16-17
Charles 17
Jean-Baptiste 17
Louis 16
Marie 17
Marie Angélique 16
Marie Madeleine 17
Marie Marthe 16, 17
Pierre 16
COURTNEY

Clara May 419
COUTS
Annette 447
COUTU
Beatrice E. 494
Eva J. 494
Irene B. 494
Jeannette Theresa 494
Louis 494
Louis H. 494
Omer E. 494
COUTURE
Anastasie 54
Christian 557
Jeanne E. 540
Joseph G. 508
Laura 489
Louise 54
Theresa L. 593
COVER
George Alford 145
Infant 145
Theodore Mortimer 145
William Oscar
COX
Amanda 88
George 88
Orlando 154-155
COXE
Dorothy Virginia 451-452
CRAFT
Emma Linda 150
CRAIG
Neil F. 368
CRANE
Iva Lillian 262
Kim M. 614
CRANNAGE
Robert P. 396
CRAVEN
Arnold R. 500
Constance 500
Ellen Rose 500
Gloria 500
John E. 500
Mary A. 500
Nelson 500
Walter 500
Walter L. 500
CRAWFORD
Bradford John 325
Henry D. 209
Norman 519
CREVIER
Lise 600
CRISHAM

Alice 504
CROCKER
Frederic J. 619
CRONIN
Ellen/Nelly 227
Julia Agnes 399
Thomas A. 227
CROSS
Alexander 132
Clarence Henry 378
Clifford Edward 377-378
Deland 377
Elizabeth 132
Gilbert A. 132
Henry W. 132
James Burton 133
John 132, 377
John Fred 377
Lottie/Charlotte 132
Paul A. 378
Rollin 378
Warren Oliver 132
CROTCHETT
Flo Lovell 464
CROTO
Mary 124
CRUM
Ernest Orville 273
Freddie 273
Stephen B. 273
Vernie Frank 273
William Bryan 273
CULBERTSON
Everett A. 283
CULLEN
Emmet J. 487
CULVER
Frances Isabel 275
CUMMINGS
Benjamin F. 276
Emma Irene 228
George R. 588-589
Hattie E. 276
Jessie 276
Lillian 136
CUNHA
Grace M. 542
CUNNINGHAM
Command 420
John 595
William 231
CURRAN
Irene D. 414
CURTIS
Charlotte Ann 605
Frank Willard 559

Louis/Lewis Herman 424
William Edward 424
DROLLET/DROLLETTE
David 227
Harvey Edmund 227
Joseph Howard 227
Marion V. 227
DROSTE
Alvin Godfrey 411
Godfrey George 411
William Frederick 411
DROUILLARD
Anonymous 246
Arthur 246
Elizabeth 128
Elizabeth M. 246
Frances L. 246
Francis Columbus 243
Gertrude S. 246
Josephine V. 246
Simon Peter 246
DUBE
Alfred W. 366
Arline Antoinette 615
DUBEAU
Ellen 245
DUBOIS
Alphonse 304
DUBREUIL
Louis Napoléon 179
DUBUC
Pascal 21
Yvette 326
DUCATTE
Joanne 587
DUCHARME
Gertrude 472
Rudolph 504
DUCLOS
Adélaïde, Mrs. 314-315
Louis 59
Noëlla 515
DUFAULT
Marguerite 64-65
DUFF
Lucien 512
DUFFUS
Guy Earl 269
DUFORT
Marie 342
DUFOUR
Marie Louise 121-122
DUFRESNE
Azilda 198
DUHAIME
Pauline Pearl 505

DUHAMEL
Marie Cécile Madeleine 502
DUKE
Lyle Edwin 618
DULUDE
Loretta Yvonne 315
DUMAS
Anastasie 106
Beatrice Louise 572
DUNHAM
Barbara Holly 393
Bruce Matthew 393
Milton 530
Milton O. 530
Paul C. 393
DUNSWORTH
Catherine Mildred 273
DUPONT
Amanda 345
Doris L. 451
Claude Yves 618
Françoise 519
DUPRE
Jules 326
Paul Clément 592
DUQUET/DUQUETTE
Anastasie 68
Berthe 388
Grace M. 363
Joseph 68 (2)
DURAND
Marthe 376
DURANLEAU
Adrien 326
Alfred 326
Claire 326
Clarinda Jeanne R. 326
Emile Lucien Aimé 326
Lucienne 326
Napoléon A. Armand 326
Paul 326
Philomène A. Cécile 326
René 326
DURANT
Anita Therese 505
DURLEY
Sarah A. 304
DUROCHER
Francis J. 409 (2)
Margaret 409
Mildred E. 597
DUSHAM/DUCHARME
Andrew 250
Anna L. 250
Elsie/Elsa 250

Martha 250
DUSSAULT
Charlotte 44
Henri 492
Rita 482
DUTILLY
Délia Donalda 514
Emma 218
DUTTON
Charles Owen 555
DUVAL
Fleurette 514
Germaine 514
DUVALL
Katharine Marie 569
Vernon Dale 445
DWYER
James Samuel 519
DYAL
Doris Roberta 581
DYER
Francis Wilson 403
DZINBINSKI
Lenore 414
EAGLE
Edna Hazel 258
EDDINGTON
Bernetta Allene 456
Carl Robert 456
Dale Leroy 456
Dorothy Marie 455
Elva Mae 456
Ernest Walter 455
Francis Edward 456
Kenneth Alfred 456
Marvin Dean 456
Mayme Alice 456
Naomi Lucille 455
Ralph Alfred 456
Ross Montee 456
EDDY
Julia A. 145
EDE
John Athol 388
John Arthur 387
EDGERLY
Mr. 132
EDWARDS
Clarence A. 455
EFFERT
Margaret 356
EGAN
Dorothy Marguerite 565
EGLI
Phyllis Helen 451
EICHMAN

Myrtle J. 153

FLYNN
Elizabeth A. 157
Mary 499

FOISY
Antoine 44
Joséphine 336
Josephte 94, 164
Louise 335
Marie Rose 335-336
Rouville 544

FOLLANSBEE
Mr. 314
Kenneth Grant 601

FOLTZ
Ralph Raymond 455

FONTAINE
Carol A. 540
Félix 306
Louise 491
M. Josette/Josephte 25-27
Marie Virginie 306

FOOTE
Margaret Sadie 329

FORAND
Virginie 175

FORCIER
Juliette 320
Marie Louise 207

FORGET dit DESPATY
Alphonse 113
Arthur 113
Azilda Marguerite 113
Henri 113
Hubert 113
Hubert Dosithée 113
Hugo/Hugues Joseph 113
Marguerite Georgina 113
Marie Rose 113
Marie Rose de Lima 113
Rose Anna 113

FORKEY
Lloyd J. 587

FORREST
William George 333

FORTIER
Adèle/Adelle 337
Antoine Dolphis 112
Emelie 98
Emile 487
Jeannette Lianne 487
Joseph 46
Marguerite/Margaret 487
Modeste Herménégilde 205
Philippe 212
Roland 515

FORTIN
Antoine 110
David Robert Bernard 490
Denise 545
Eugène A. 110
Gaston Aimé 489
Hermina 213
Jean Luc Paul 490
Jeanne d'Arc Estelle 490
Laure Madeleine Marg. 490
Marguerite Jeanne d'Arc 490
Marie Desanges 489
Marthe Bernadette 490
Pierre 490
Uldège 489

FOSTER
April N. 498
Henry William 162

FOURNIER
Alfred 94
David 53
Douglas Wayne 563-564
Olivine/Joséphine 112
Véronique 29

FOWLER
Clarence Lougee 364-365
Henry Lyman 365
Hiram R. 446
Iola 365
Lillian Belle 379
Max N. 446
Melvin C. 365
Nova G. 446
Pearl 365
Ralph Nick 446

FOX
Ralph E. 578
Simon Frederick 299-300

FRANCIS
Gary 470
James 125
Joseph J. 541
Mary 125

FRAPPIER
Antoine Elzéar 336

FRASER
Abram/Abraham Malcolm 144-145
Anetta 145
Edwina Virginia 145
Elnora Gertrude 145
Emily Irene 145
Estella N. 145
Eugene E. 145
Francis F. 145

Joseph A.,145
Minnie/Minnesota Orella 145
Sidney Ralph 145

FRECHETTE
Eusèbe 96
Malvina 94
Onésime 95

FREDERICK
Angeline 75
Betsey 75
Charles Edward 75
Charlotte Maria 75
Francis/Frank 75
Jane Ann 75
John 75
Joseph 75 (2)
Malvina 174
Margaret 75
Mary Ann 75
Samuel 75

FREDETTE
Adolphus 131

FREGEAU
Armidée 328
Domitilde/Matilda 307-308
Louis 44

FRENYEA
Austin Carlton 477

FREUND
Sherry Lynn 607

FRIENDLY
Betty Jane Dupraun 454

FRIES
Leland 436

FRIGAULT
Alfred David 368
Marie Rose Simone 368
Normand Alfred 368
Roger George 368
Therese Bertha 368

FRITSCH
Robert L. 578

FROK/FROKE
Edward Olsen 269

FROMME
Harry Dewey 550
Marcella 550

FRYE
Clara 474
Clifford D. 474
Darrell E. 474
Everett Lee 474
Harold Henry 474
Henry 474
Margarite 474

Mildred S. 474
Norma Jean 474
Roger Leon 474
Wayne W. 474
FULTON
Miss 577
Matilda 143
FULTZ
Gladys Ellen 354
FUNDINGSLAND
John Anderson 527
FURNAS
Darrell D. 552
GABORIAU dit LAPALME
Antoine 61 (2)
Joséphine 100
Marie-Anne 61
Marie Catherine 61
GABORIAULT
Pierrette 547
GADOURY
Alphonse Fernando 508
GADUE (see also **GODDU**)
Charles Henry 363
Edward F. 363
Edward T. 363
George 358
Joseph Auguste 358
Rose Marie 363
GAGNE/GAGNIER
Alfred 206
Anna Bella 339
Donat 321
Eugenia 366
Georgiana 173
Orida 340
GAGNON
Mr. 543
André 546
Hélène/Helen 497
Madeleine 326
Marcel 546
Raymond S. 440
Rose Delima 220
Vivian 588
GALDE
Garry M.
GALE
Nathan A. 253
Nettie B. 224
William Austin 234
GALIPEAU
Marie Arzélie 168
Philippe/George H. P. 490
Suzanne 618
GALL

Edward Felix 421
GALLAHER
David 582
GALLMAN
Dorothy Helen 536
GAMACHE
Adélaïde 97
Alphonse 206 (2)
Clément 94-95, 206 (2)
Didace/Didas 206
Domitilde 95
Edouard 95
Henri Victor 206
Isaïe 207
Joseph Otiochus 206
Marcel 205
Marie 95
Marie Clorinda 206
Marie Louise/Délima 206
Michel 95
Noël 95, 96 (2)
Octave 95
Odéna/Audéna 206
Osithe 97
Pierre 94 (2)
Pierre Bénoni 97
Polidore 206
Rose 97
Rose Alba 206
Salomé 95
Théodore 206
Théodore Achille 206
Theophitus 206
GAMBLE
Earl H. 449
GANNON
Emeline/Eliza Emilie 215
GARDINER
Jess 442
GAREAU dit VADEBON-COEUR
François 56
GARIEPY
François Xavier 339
GARINGER
Beverly Kay 462
John Iver 462
Linda Lewayne 462
Sharon Lee 462
GARLAND
George 587
GARNIE/GARNY
Michel 60
Rosalie 60
GARNIER
Mr. 382

GARROW
Grace 436
GARVEY
Patrick S. 561
GASKILL
Estelle Lenore 578
GATELY
Julia Ann 328
GAUCHER
Azarise 310
GAUCK
Donald 465
GAUDET
Ernest 185
GAUDETTE
Clémence 600
GAUDREAU/GAU-DREAULT (see also **GOODROW**)
Aimé 192
Arcélia 179
Blanche A. 360
Dorothy Jeanette 360
Emile Wilfrid 547
Eugène 192
George 192
George Clément 360
George Ovila 360
Helen 360
Jean Charles Roger 547
Joseph 360
Louise M. 360
Marie 182, 360
Michel 192
Napoléon 397
Paule Pierrette 547
Philip 361
Philippe 192
Pierre 180, 181
Pierre Louis
Rose A. 360
Wilfred A. 360-361
GAULIN
Espéralda 485
William 311
GAUMOND
Marie A. 482
GAUTHIER
Danielle 521
Hilda May Laure 357
Joseph Fabien 166
Noah D. 357
Stephanie L. 357
GAUVIN
Joseph Jean-Baptiste 192
Victor 107

GAVIN
Leona Blanche 551
GEE
Lorenzo Louis 246
Justina/Justine 409
GEER
Thelma E. 507
GEHRKE
Mae Margaret 450
GELBAUGH
Keith E. 578
GELINEAU/GELINOT
Alexis 21, 22
Alice 548
Alphonse 511-512
Angélique 21
François 21 (3)
Jean-Baptiste 21
Joseph 22 (2), 57-58, 58
Marie Desanges 21
Marie Louise 21 (2)
Marie Marguerite 22
Osia E. 178
Rosalie 22
GENAW
David G. 246
Nelson M. 246
GENDRON
Adrian A. 509
Aldea E. 321
Alma R. 322
Annette 322
Anonymous 322
Arthur
Arthur Joseph 321 (2)
Berthe/Bertha Eulalie 322
Fulgence Gérard 321
Joseph Athanase 207
Joseph P. 217
Rose Delima Marie 321
GENNETTE
Maxine 551
Omer 551
GEOFFRION
Arthémise 198
GEORGE
Agnes Teresa/Theresa 595
Ida 431
GEORGES
Bertha 325
GERARDY
Fred 452
GERBRUCK
Jennie 135
GERNON
John H. 112

GERRISH
Florence V. 365
GERSEK
Susan Ann 532
GERVAIS
Abraham 46
Adélaïde 169
Alfred Omer 387
Alphonse Frédéric 169
Amable 46
Barthelemy 46
Charles 169
Charles Olivier 169
Christine 169
Edouard 46
Eléonore 46
Elisée Horace 170
Elizabeth 201
Emma 313
Frédéric 169
Georgette Thérèse 387
Honoré Achille 169
Jean Gilles 387
Jean-Baptiste 46 (2)
Jeanne 509
Jerôme Arthur Louis 387
Joseph 46
Josephte 46 (2)
Louis 46 (2)
Louis Arthur 169
Louise Rachel 387
Luc Emile Lloyd 387
Marguerite 313
Marie Adrienne 169-170
Marie Eliza 201
Marie Louise 46
Marie Sophie 46
Mathias 46
Maximilien 170
Moïse 169
Philomène 169
Pierre 45, 45-46
Polydore Nestor 387
Prudent 169
Roch 387
Romuald Adrien L. 170
GEYSER
Cole O. 607
GIBB
Elinor Grace 463
GIBBS
Lena B. 153
Sidney 153
GIBEAU
Eusébie/Eusebia 51
GIBEAULT

Suzanne 510
GIBSON
Edgerton E. 255
GIEBEL
Wendell Adair 479
GIESE
Gerald C. 429
Sheila D. 430
GILBERT
Myrtle Jeanette 529
Myrtle M. 468
GILBODY
William Stephen 262
GILCREST
Mr. 443
GILES
George F. 484
GILL
Edward 224
Kathryn/Catherine E. 286
Lillian Helen 585
GILLICH
Stephen Francis 564
GILLIGAN
Mary E. 292
GILLMOR
Marshall 408
GILMAN
Ada 235
George 259
George N. 405
Leon Everett 405
Vernon Sears 259
Walter Leroy 584
GILMORE
John P. 470
GILMOUR
James 338
GILNACK
Bruce S. 498
GINCHEREAU
Marc Antoine 387
GINDER
Elizabeth V. 296
Frances Grace 296
Frank James 296
GINGRAS
Amédée 178
Olivine E. 193
GIRARD
Esther 91
Hattie A./Adeline 225
Joseph Edouard 213
Pierre Lucien 518
Rouville 503
GIRDLESTONE

John Edward/Jack E. 569

GIROUX
  Bertha Sylvia 496
  Euchariste 340
  Marie 57
GLADU
  Léo 372
GLEASON
  Mary 110
GLIDDEN
  Merton Walter 262
GLOVER
  Irene 355
GODA
  Stephen John 325
GODDARD
  Kenneth 609
GODDU
  Adonalda/Donalda 196
  Emilie 179
  Marie Onésime 179
  Pierre 179 (2)
GODERE
  Wilfred I. 482
GODIN
  Angèle 127
  Antoine 617
  Delima Alma 127
  Marie 127
GOERS
  Mary Evelyn 601
GOEWAY
  Helene 497
GOFF
  William Eugene 560
GOGUET (see also
    GOYET/GOYETTE)
  Abraham 51
  Amable 50-51
  Angèle 50
  Augustin 29, 29-30, 51
  Clément, 51
  Edouard 50, 51
  Etienne 51
  François 29, 50 (3)
  Geneviève 29
  Jacques 29 (2), 50
  Jean-Baptiste 29
  Joseph 29, 49 (2), 51
  Josephte 29
  Julie 51
  Louis 29
  Louise 48
  Lucie 51
  Madeleine 49
  Marguerite 49

Marie 29 (2)
Marie-Anne 29
Marie Louise 27, 29, 51
Maurice 51
Michel 50
Moïse 50
Paul 30
Philippe 50
GOINEAU
  Henri Oliva 372
  Joseph Albert 372
  Marie Rose Lorenza/
    Laurence 372
  Médéric Edgar 372
  Philias 372
GOLDEN
  Robert J. 303
GONSALVES
  Mr. 596
GONYA
  Avis Helen 289
  Carl Darwin 289
  Evelyn Emma 289
  Ruby Inez 288
  Willis Oreon 289
GONYEA/GAGNIER
  Anna Bertha 410
GONYOU
  Jane 116
GOOD
  Joseph Warren 254
GOODELL
  Elmer Richard 410
  Emily/Axie Amelia 127-
    128
  Russell R. 410
GOODFELLOW
  Jessie Weir 360
GOODMAN
  Alice D. 470
  Anna 285
GOODNESS
  Arthur 393
  Frank H. 393
  Marie 393
GOODPASTURE
  Maxine 576
GOODROW (see also
    GAUDREAU)
  George Leslie 398
  Helen 87
  John Louis 398
  Laura 398
  Leonard 398
  Margaret 398
  William 398

GOODSON
  Louise Elizabeth 225
GOOGINS
  Willard Hiram 590
GOOLEY
  Frank W. 268
GORDON
  Myrtle C. 274
GOSLOW
  Marion E. 589
GOSS
  Marilyn 432
GOSSELIN
  Catherine Apolline 39 (2)
  Clément 37-39, 39
  Emile 600
  Eusèbe 242
  Ferdinand 39
  Georgine/Georgiana 113
  Jane 39, 129-130
  Jean-Baptiste 39 (2)
  Joseph I. 242
  Laura 242
  Marguerite 544
  Marguerite Apolline 39
  Marie 39
  Marie Genevieve 39, 129-
    130
  Michel 39
  Pierre Jacques 39
GOULET
  Alexandre 310
GOULEY
  Jesse 356
GOYET/GOYETTE (see
    also **GOGUET**)
  Catherine 416
  Marie Geneviève/Mary 67
  Mathilde/Martine 96
GRAHAM
  Thomas Edwin 352
GRAMMER
  Archie Sinclair 377
GRANGER
  Roger G. 368
GRANT
  Charles F. 432
  Edythe Claire 432
  Grace 432
  Sam Levi 432
  William J. 289
GRANTHAM
  Mary Frances/Francine 553
GRAPPOTTE
  Frances 57
  Mary 57

HESSE
Dessa Mae 452
HESTING
Theresa 555
HEWITT
Rollie L. 581
Spurgeon 325
HIBBARD
Daniel Ide 163
Edward Leroy 163
Halo 163
HICKEY
Alice J. 300
HIETALA
Bernice Florence 529
HIGGINS
Mary L. 191
HIGH
David L. 534
Jeff 586
HILBERT
Gregory Paul 612
HILDRETH
Maude Eleanor 262
HILL
Arden Edward 519
Diane 519
Esther Lee 451
Fern 519
Gary 519
Joan Carol 519
Joseph Bruce 519
Julia Nancy 259
Maxine Marie 451
Sharon Lee 586
Stanley Abraham 450
Stanley Merle 450-451
HILLER
Anna 466
HILLMAN
Albert Donald 389
HINDS
Catherine 184
HINS/HINSE/HAINS (See
also AINSE)
François 8
HIPPS
Helen Jean 540
HITT/HIITT
Otto Edward 325
HITTLE
Charles William 555
HLAVACEK
John David 620
HOAG
Joseph 237

HOBACK
Gladys 300
HOBBS
Carl Ray 622
HODELL
Lillian Elvina 400-401
HODSKINS
Austin W. 397
Frederick/Fred 397
Rose/Rosa 397
Wesley C. 397
Willard H. 397
HOEHNE
Phyllis Lavonne 528
HOFFMAN
Anna 424
Bertha Julia 261
Maurine Alta 467
HOKE
Addie May 279
Charles Edward 279
George Albert 279
Harry Grover 279
James T. 279
Jesse Walter 279
John Francis 279
John Partee 279
Mac 279
Mary Matilda 279
Rhoda Charlotte 279
Roy Theodore 279
HOLCOMB
Ernest Perry 258
Harley James 258
James A. 258
Jennie May 258
Lettie 258
Lottie 258
Marion Elizabeth 259
Myra Austie 258
Robert 258
Ruby Florence 258
Ruby Jeanette 452
Walter Montee 259
Wendell Earl 259
HOLDMANN
Andrew Frank 349
HOLDREN
Charla Marie 621
HOLGATE (see also
HULGATE)
Cora May 138
Frances Myrtle 138
George William 138
James Franklin 137-138
HOLLAND

Jack 549
John Edward/Jack 549
Nina 549
HOLLINGWORTH
Beatrice 362
Blanche 362
John Samuel 361
Samuel 362
Yvonne 362
HOLLOWAY
George Eugene 576
HOLMER
Lee M. 608
HOLMES
Rudolf Ludwig 379
HOLZGRAF
Ethel Dorothy 478
HONKALA
Helmi 530-531
HOOKER
Beatrice A. 378
HOPF
Alison Marie 582
HOPKINS
Harold 573
HORN
May Theresa 287
HORNE
Bennet R. 472
Margaret 472
Robert P. 472
Warren D. 501
HOSKINS
James C. 110
HOUD/HOUDE
Joseph 75-76
Mary Louise 378
HOUSTON
Catherine 75
HOUTZ
Barbara Ann 577
HOWARD
Duane Allen 392
Nevine 437
William Arthur 377
HOWELL
Jodie Gail 457
HOWES
Judith A. 540
HOWLAND
Charles 142
HUBBARD
Mr. 76
HUBERT
Malvina 199
HUDON

Pierre Démétrius 306
HUDSON
Roberta H. 542-543
HUESTIS
Ervie Olive/Eva 272
Sally Ann 144
HUET
Alice 342
Antoine 54
HUGHES
Alice, Mrs. 269
Laura Lucinda 443
Ray 530
HULGATE/HOLGATE
Francis 84-85
HULL
George R. 163
HUMBLE
Roy 576
HUMPHREY
Mr. 137
Charles H. 138
George 356
Ida 138
**HUNGVILLER/HING-
   VILLER**
Joseph 112
HUNT
Ruth 549
HUNTAMER
Lawrence Cleveland 296
HUNTER
Calvin R. 446
James Stanley 414
Regiald 325
Robert R. 325
HUOT
Alphonsine 371
Charles 24
HURD
Warren L. 365
HURLBERT
Allen 261-262
Francis Allen 262
Harriet Marguerite 262
Helen Louise 262
Madeline 262
Mildred 262
HUSTED
Lucienne E. 578
HUSTON
Vera Lorena 451
HUTCHINS
Effie Ethel 461
HUYLAR
Allan Thew 579

HYSER
Mary Bessie 438-439
ILES
William Albert 255
ILLERBRUN
Susanna Marion 529
INGLEDEW
Charles 185
Elizabeth Matilda 185
George 185
George Louis 185
Margaret 185
Mary Anne Josephine 185
Matthew 185
INGRAM
Dolores Faye 455
INMAN
Maxine Delores 582
IRICK
Harold William 352
IRVING
Marta 605
JACKSON
Alva Elmer 285
Clarence 559
Claude Franklin 285
Ethel Maude 283-284
Marie 285
Martha E. 254-255
William 88, 285
William Clyde 285
JACOB
Della 333-334
JACOBS
Rodney Earl 620
JACOBSON
Clara O. 430
JACQUES
Azilda 100
Bessie 539
Donalda 502
JAECKEL
William Gustav 615
JAMES
Ida Elizabeth 286
JAMROG
Esther C./Ester K. 418
JANCO
Cheryl A. 498
JANIN
Claire 326
JANSEN
William R. 532
JANSON
Cecile 499
JANTZ

Larry R. 590
JARRY
Louis 15
JARVIS
Sarah E. 321
JEANNOTTE
Pierre, 107
JEFFREYS
Violet 563
JENICEK
James R. 585
JENNINGS
Albert 88
David 88
JENSEN/JENSON
Elmer Ernest 296
Mary Roberta 506
JEPSON
Evan Raymond 353
JERACI
Nino/Nicodemo 502
JERDO
Lulu Mary 133
JETTE
Adélard 372
Aldéric Arthur 372
Alexis 95
Bernadette Antoinette 372
Edouard André/Edward 544
Eliana 372
Eva 206
Eva Geniva Reseda 372
Gérard 545
Joseph Henri 544
Laurent Edéas 544
Laurette Amanda 544-545
Léopold 372
Lucille 545
Marie Anne 372
Marie Reine Claire 545
Réjeanne 547
Rita 545
Rosaire Napoléon 544
Rose Amanda Aurore 372
Thérèse Françoise 544
Wilfrid Donat 544
Yvonne Cécile 544
JETTO
William 288
JEWETT
Walter S. 87
JIMENEZ
Joe Paul 580
JOAO
James 541
JOCK

Henry Vincent 475
KLODT
John Leo 576-577
KNIBBS
Donald M. 291
KNIEFEL
Beatrice Betty 466
KNIGHT
Archer/Archie 257
Fern 257
Mary 257
Mary Louise 463
Mary Sanders 256
William 256
KNUDSEN
Tove E. 569
KOACELLA
Nick 285
KOCH
Alma May 444
Janice 583
KOPALA
Stephen Casimir 504
KOTTERMAN
Caroline 146-147
KRAMER
Joan Louise 607
Villa Edna 449
KREBS
Sandra Lee 465
KREBSBACH
Clair Frederick 608
KRUIDENIER
Imogene Patricia 453
KRUSE
Edward Woodrow 456
KUHN
Barbara 619
KUSEK
William F. 599
**KYMINEUR dit LA-
FLAMME**
Eulalie 176
LABADIE
Adray Columbus 412
Bernadette E. 408
Elmer J. 408
Elmer Robert 408
Everett Raymond 408
Irwin 412
John Richard 408
Margaret 412
Marie E. 408
Mary Josephine 249
Norbert F. 408
Richard Benedict 408-409

Viola G. 408
LABARE (see **LEBERT**)
LABARGE
Caroline 133
Clara 383
Della 383
Delmer Clifford 383
Dula 383
Hubert Oscar 383
Joseph 383
Lena 383
Leonard 383
Philip E. 383
Raymond 383
Vernon Lawrence 383
LABELLE
Israël 175
Rosanna 403
LABERGE
Emma 123
Léon Arthur 311
LABONTE (see also
LABOUNTY)
Helena/Ellen 314
Marie/Mary 66
LABOUNTY
Adele Velina/Lena 225
Alfred Andrew 402
Child 225
Christina A. 567-568
Clayton C. 403
Edgar 225
Frances Marion 403
Gladys R. 403
Isabelle/Isabella 403
Joseph 225
Joseph E. 225
Joyce A. 403
Lawrence Theodore 225
Louis E. 225
Marc/Michael 225
Marie 225
Milla Elizabeth 225
Narcisse Alexis/Alexandre
225
Narcisse Alfred 225
Pascal/Paschal 403
Victoria 403
LABRAM
Helen E. 235
LACASSE
Patricia G. 559
LACHANCE
Marie Louise 242-243
Siméon 333
LACOMBE

Annie 622
Marie 94
LACOSTE
Henri Julien 515
Jacqueline 490
LACROIX (see also
CROSS)
Edwidge/Addie 247
Ida 378
Virginia 128
Wylda Wave 463
LADD
Mr. 392
LADUKE
Lewis 397
LADURANTAYE
Anita Thérèse 505
LAFAY
Anna Ruth 394
Joseph A. 394
Lena Monty 394
Loren Edmond 394
Loren Fred 393-394
LAFERA
Donato 521
LAFLAMME
Joseph George 495
Maude 377
LAFLEUR
Edward George 315
Marie Paule 327
LAFOREST
Jean-Paul 517
LAFOUNTAIN
Alexander 234
Angelina Elmire 123
Azilda/Ozilda 122
Cora 234
Cordelia 123
Edward Napoleon 123
Eva Catherine 436
Ida/Adela 234
John 122
John/Jean-Baptiste 122
Louise 122
Lucy 122
Mélie Onézime 122
Philomene Domitille 122-
123
LAFRANCE
Armoza 242
LAFRENIERE
Alice 511
Anne 203
John Joseph 523
Louise 523

660

Ruth 523
LAGARDE
  Eugénie 51
LAGUE
  Alphonsine 309
  Marie Louise 111
LAHEY
  Lorn Raymond 583
LAIRDIESON
  Myrtle 431-432
LAJOIE
  Cecile 366
  Marie Jeanne 489
LALANNE
  Marie Odéna 317
LALEMAND
  Célanie 107
LALIBERTE
  Bertrand Christian 482
  Charles Auguste 482
  Henri/Henry 481
  J.-Bapt. M. Honorius 481
  Louis Alb. Rosario 481-482
  Marguerite Lucile 482
  Roger Yvan 482
LALONDE
  Claudette 618
LALUMIERE
  Rose Adeline 176
LAMARCHE
  Marie Jeanne 548
LAMARRE/LAMORE
  Adèle/Adélaïde 108
  Aglaé 109
  Camille 109
  Célina 109
  Emma 109
  François 54
  Louis 56
  Marie Reine Jacqueline 545
  Martine 108
  Maurice Léonidas 545
  Napoléon 545
  Octave 108-109
  Pierre 108
  Praxède/Sadie 109
  Raoul Yvon 545
  Théophile Trefflé 109
  Yolande Réjane/Réjeanne 545
LAMB
  Edward Frank 418
LAMBERT
  Audrey Mae 355
  Francis Leo 395
  Henry 331

John William 320
  Leo Joseph 395
  Mary Elizabeth 117
LAMIAS
  Christine Labro 612
LAMONDE
  Helen Elizabeth 562
LAMOTT/LAMOTTE
  Henry 423
LAMOUREUX
  Julie/Sophie 62
  Léonide 241
  Toussaint 55
LAMPREY
  Frank 357
LANCASTER
  Obediah 209
LANDLES
  David 521
LANDRY
  Earl J. 581
  Emilie/Emily 61-62
  Léo/Emile Léon 490
  Louis 92
  Marguerite/Margaret 60-61
  Peter Joseph 336
  Pierre 92, 336
LANEHART
  Edward L. 414
LANGEVIN
  Suzanne 490
LANGLOIS
  Aline Anne Marguerite 341
  Arthur 341
  Benoit Edouard L. C. 341
  Célina Irène Victoire 341
  Emilien 341
  Jeanne Hélène Emma 341
  René Jean Jos. Armand 341
  Samuel Arthur 341
  Simone 341
LANGUEDOC
  Lionel 511
LANOUE
  Mr. 322
  Alphonsine 169
  Eusèbe 170
LANSING
  Elizabeth 120-121
  Grace 401
LAPALME (see also **GA-BORIAU dit LAPALME**)
  Anonymous 503
  Fernande Lisette Gisèle 503
  Joseph Aimé Lévis 503
  Joseph Lévis/Lévi 503

LAPELL
  Jeanette 105
LAPIER/LAPIERE
  Kate 421
LAPLANTE (see also **LERI-GER**)
  Alcide 491
  Anonymous 491
LAPOINT/LAPOINTE (see also **AUDET dit LA-POINTE**)
  Mr. 604
  Alfred Daniel 229-230
  Bella M. 542
  Daniel 229
  Elsie L. 484
  Joseph 230
  Mary Amelia 229
LAPORTE
  Cécile 520
  Louisa 143
  Sarah 397
LAQUERRE
  Leda 216
LARAMIE
  Henry A. 505
LARAMORE
  Carroll Duane 613
LAREAU
  Achille 207
  Aglaé 204
  Alfred 189-190, 190
  Alida 207
  Azilda/Elisa 208
  Brigitte 52
  Catherine 51
  Charles 190
  Clarisse 190
  Dorile Guillaume 207
  Edmund 190
  Edouard/Edward 100
  Elisabeth 52
  Elise/Marie Louise 175
  Elzéar 100
  Emilie 51
  Emma 190
  Eugène Avila 207
  Guillaume 207 (2)
  Henri Alphonse 207
  Hervé Joseph 207
  Jean-Baptiste 48, 99, 100
  John B. 190
  Joseph 51 (2), 52, 190
  Julienne 52
  Louis 95
  M. Claire 190

661

Maggie 190
Marguerite 52, 95
Marguerite Adèle 100
Marie 52, 100
Marie Anne Armandine 207
Marie Josephte 52
Mary 190
Mathilda 190
Mathilde 99
Noël 95, 113
Odena Anna 207
Philomene 190
Ruth 190
LARGENT
Michelle Renee 555
LARGY/LARGEY
Alfred Patrick/Fred P. 504
Edith Mary 504
LARIVEE
Agathe 59
André 59
Angélique 59
Aurélie 60
Céleste 59
Fabien 60
François Xavier 59
Isaac 60
Joseph 60
Louis Abraham 60
Marie Catherine 59
Pierre 59 (2)
LARIVIERE
Anonymous 491
Jean-Baptiste 48
Joseph 48 (2)
Louis 48
Lucile Thérèse 492
Marguerite 48
Marie Berthe 492
Michel 48
Nazaire 491
Ovide 181
Paul Emile 492
Philibert/Philippe 48
Rachel V. Marguerite 492
LAROCHE
Edouard 308-309
Frédéric A. 309
George H. 309
Henry E. 309
Jacques 547
Joseph 68
Lucie 44
Victoria 204
LAROCHELLE
Alfred 510

LAROCK
Mildred 401-402
LAROCQUE
Adèle L. 94
Alice Eglantine 457
Alfred 93
Charles Philias/Phelix 304
David 24
Delore (Adelard?) 304
Edmond 93
Hélène 93
Henry 304
Janet Teresa 591
Jérémie 303
Joseph 304
Joseph Louis Alfred 304
Lena 304
Louise Joséphine 93
Marie Henriette 93
Marie Philomène 93
Mary L. 304
Michel 93
Michel Joseph 93
Odrick/Medrick 304
Olympe Anastasie 93
Pierre Richard 304
Simon 93
Virginie 93
LAROE (see **LAREAU**)
LAROSE
Ada/Addie 228
Arthur Francis/Frank 228
Béatrice 502
Elizabeth Delvina 228
Emily C./Clara Amelia 228
Frank/François Xavier 228
Frederick Albert/Fred A. 228
Henry George 228
Jean-Marie 340
Jerome 228
Leroy Edward 228
Marie Geneviève 228
Marie Josephine/Josie 228
Mary Rachel 155
Mattie 228
Rosanna 228
Rose Alma 516
LARSEN
Fred H. 467
Ole A. 541
LARSON
Anthony Wayne 475
Kathleen Ann 475
Robert Wayne 475
LARY

Mary 135-136
LASHWAY/LASHUA
Elizabeth 83
Francis 83 (2)
James 83
Joy 589
Mary 84
Sarah 83
Susan 83
LASNIER
Angèle 44
Bernard Omer 492
Hector 112
Jacques Thomas 112
Joseph Hector 112
Joseph Narcisse Ovelus 492
Marie Aglaé Ezilda 112
Marie Claire Estelle 492
Rosa/Rose Delima 168
Yvonne 316
LATOUR
Rosemary 589
LATOURNELLE
Wilson Arthur 500
LATRAY
Joseph 76, 82-83, 83
Phoebe 83
Roxena/Rosina 83
Susan 83
LAUDERMAN
Nancy Jane 147
LAUGHLIN
Winifred 210
LAURIN
Aimée 493
LAUTERBACH
Shirley J. 474
LAVALLEE
Albert O. 484
Alexander J. 483
Edward 483
Ella E. 483
Ellen/Helen S. 483
Gertrude 483
Raymond E. 483
Zoël 213
LAVELLE
Donald R. 478
LAVENTURE
Bertha Ursule 513
LAVERDURE
Madeleine Pauline C. 596
LAVINE
Elizabeth 143
LAVOIE
Alice 220

LUCIA
Joseph Adolph 566
LUCK
Gerald Virgil 477
Julia Calista 78
Samuel 77-78
LUEBKE
Clarence William 352
LUIZ
Guilherme 596
LUMBERSON
Jacob A. 445
Mary Ellen 445
Monta Eckart 445
Virge Ivan 445
LUNDY
Lloyd 449
LUSIGNAN
Amédée Joseph 365
Eunice M. 365
LUSSIER/LUCIER
Alexina 170
Blanche 311
Delphine 179
Diamond 310
Emeline Monty 310
Etienne 94
Hermina 310
Joseph 310
Joseph Antoine 310
Joseph Henri 310
Léon 311
Marie 310
Marie Desanges 48
Marie Rose Annette 384
Oscar Eugene 311
Valéda 518
William 310-311
LYNCH
Anna F. 427
Deloris Ann 579
Mary 486
LYON
Darlene Lynn 471
Frank Eugene 403-404
Leonard E. 404
Mark Robert 470
Paul Steven 470
Robert Ambrose 470
Sandra Joyce 470
LYTTLE
Doris I. 285
MA...
Frederick K. 266
MABARY
John O. 468

MABE
Walter 603
MACK
William 408
MADDEX
Jack Edward 454
Lovell Frederick 454 (2)
MADELL
Frank Josephus 379
MADER
Everett J. 498
Lenore A. 498
Paul Joseph 498
MAGEAU
Augustin M. Hormisdas
309
MAGEE
Velma M. 444
MAGELKY
Bernard James 581
MAGNERON dit LAJEU-
NESSE
Joseph 176
MAGOON
Julie 392
MAGRUDER
Eugene O. 376
Irvin C. 210
Oswald Harley 376
Virgil Lionel 376
MAGUIRE
Agnes Anna 367
MAHALAK
Clarence 408
MAHEU
Howard 254
Maurice Emile 556
Monique 556
Wilfrid Roland 514
MAHON
Mr. 541
MAHONEY
Catherine F. 488
Francis E. 368
MAILHOT (see also
MAYOTTE)
Edouard 125
MAILLE
Wilfred 311
MAILLOUX (see also
MAYO)
Jean Claude 517
Julia Florence 419-420
Louis Philippe 517
Lucien 517, 594
Monique 517

Olivine 517
Pierrette 517
Réjeanne Adrienne 517
Rose Amande 173
MAINARD (see MENARD)
MAISONNEUVE
Rose Alba 211
MAJESKI
Joseph J. 352
MAJOR
Alida 192
Ambroise 56
Clara 192
Clément 192
Clément Stanislas 192
Marie Flora 192
Matilda 192
Rose Hermine Flora/Laura
192
Stanislas 192
MAKUCH
Walter P. 539
MALENFANT
Marguerite Irene 416
MALLOY
Ambrose Dennis 476
MALO
Alphonsine 327
MALONE
Edith 566
MALOY
Charles Paul 566
MANAU
Kathryn M. 550
MANCHESTER
Wesley J. 586-587
MANFRASS
William Albert 448
MANGEN
John Jerome 608
MANHART
Anna Marie 449
Charles Henry 449
Harry E. 449
Lewis Franklin 449
Opal M. 449
Ralph R. 449
Robert C. 449
Russell A. 449
Thomas Frank 449
MANN
Mr. 438
MANNY
Cyrille 383
Dorilda Irene 383
MANOR

John S. 287
Joseph 124
Joseph John 237-238
Joyce 570
June 570
Lillian Gladys 570
Louisa 239
Lyla M. 431
Mabel 430-431
Margaret Adele 238-239
Margaret Eileen 393
Mary Anne/Nettie 238
Mary E. 431
Mary Jane 124
Maud A. 427
Myrtle Pearl 430
Nancy Elaine 559
Robert Morrow 392
Rose Mae 570
Roy Emery 559
Samuel B. 254
Sarah P. 287-288
Shirley 569, 570
Shirley Elizabeth 392
Sophia 237
Sylvia Ann 254
Violet J. 569-570
Virtue 570
Wesley Clarence 393
William 431
MONTABANA
Louise E. 562
MONTAY (see also
   MONTY)
Albert 568
Albert J. 425
Amos 423
Bertrand/Bert 425
Catherine 425-426
Emily/Millie 425
Gilbert L. 568
Henry C. 424
John T. 425
Leatha Helen 568
Leland/Lee Henry 568
Leonora 568
Mary 424-425, 568
Oska Lee 568
William H. 568
MONTCALM
Aline Lorenza 486
Claire Beatrice 486
Leonie Blanche 486
Rosario Louis Ulric 486
Ulric 486
Ulric Richard 486

MONTE (see also **MONTY**)
Miss 608
Abraham Arthur 355
Abraham Joseph 530
Achille 306
Ada 506
Adelaide 331
Adrianne L. 607
Alan Ray 607
Alec Virgil 613
Alexander 334
Alma D. 509
Amos/Rex A. 526-527
Ann/Anne Marie 509
Anna Mae 602
Annie 332
Audrey Viola 535-536
Benjamin Bernard 355
Berdean 525
Betty 608
Bruce 602
Carol Ann 602
Carrilee 613
Cecile J. 509
Celine/Celina 331-332
Charles J. 350
Charles Wilfred 523
Clarence Henry 430
Claude G. 525
Claude Louis 527
Daniel Alexander 602
Delima 335
Don Elwyn 619
Donald W. 606
Dorothy 606
Douglas Keith 606
Edward 345, 507
Edward E. 606
Edward Jos. Odilon 523
Elizabeth/Lizzie 332
Ellis Joseph 536, 613
Elwyn Etheridge 551
Emily 522
Emma 331
Everett Delford 526
Felix 334
Fred 349-350
Frederick E. 306-307
Frederick John 349-350
Gail Gene 607
Gary W. 607
Gene 619
George 606
George H. 525
George Omer 360
George W. 606

George William 349
Gerard Joseph 509
Glenn W. 527
Gordon Eugene 536
Harvey 566
Henry Ernest 523
Hugh Joseph 536
Ilene Virginia 602
Irene 507, 606
Irene A. 508
Israel 330
Israel Joseph 506
James 613
Janelle J. 607
Jean-Baptiste 333-334
Jeanette 535
Jeannette B. 509
John 333-334
Joyce Patricia 536
Kenneth J. 613
Kenneth R. 606
Kent V. 613
Lauraine Anna 527
Lewis 333
Louis 333
Mabel 430-431
Mardelle Anne 619
Marguerite/Margaret 566
Marie D. L. 509
Marie Louise 334-335
Mary Jane 241
Michael Richard 613
Mitchell 334
Nicholas W./Nicola 350
Pamela A. 602
Philip G. 607
Richard Gerard 602
Richard Vincent 536
Roland Russell 536
Stephen H. 613
Susan 260
Timothy Hugh 613
Vincent 355
Virginia Anne 607
Warren J. 526
Wayne N. 526
William 126, 241, 345, 406,
606
William A. 507
William J. 509, 522
Yvonne Blanche 508
Zénaïde 332
MONTEE (see also
   MONTY)
Addie 229-230
Adelaide 237

MONTEE (cont.)

Adeline 227, 237
Albert 228
Albert A. 457
Albert Clinton 576
Albert Leroy 580
Alberta 281
Alice 467
Alice Lodema 275-276, 450
Alice Margaret 394
Alice Marie 578
Amanda Florence 286
Amelia 119
Angeline Irene 465
Anna 273-274
Anna Alice 278-279
Anna E. 275
Anna Mae 468
Anna Pearl 393
Annetta 585
Anonymous 230
Archie 466
Archie Dean 582
Arletta/Arlette Kay 581
Audrey 580
Austie Emma 258
Barbara Ann 576
Benjamin Mohon 463
Benoni 227
Bernice 575
Bernice Lavon 463
Bernice Opal 578
Bert Vance 574
Bertha A. 393
Bessie A. 445
Betty/Bettie Eileen 579-580
Betty Jean 575
Betty Louise 578
Blanche 466
Bobby Dean 580
Bonnie Jean 577
Carl Michael 580
Carl Robert 467
Carla Carson 578
Carolyn J. 583
Carolyn Sue 586
Carrie M. 405
Catherine 148, 582
Catherine Mary Ann 395
Cathern 582
Cecil Drake 469
Charles 147, 441
Charles B. 237
Charles Clifford 277
Charles Cloyse 585
Charles Edward 283-284,

449
Charles Elmer 575
Charles Finley 281, 462
Charles Roger 581
Charles Sylvester 450
Charlotte Louise 458
Clair Edward 451-452
Clara/Clarissa 255
Clarence Arthur 454
Clarence Edward 458, 581
Clarence Martin 283
Claudine Marie 574
Cleda Marjorie 583
Clemorissa 579
Clifford Sylvester 578-579
Clois Finley 148-149
Clyde Merle 461
Connie Jo 583-584
Corta 427
Cuba 427
Dale Franklin 578
Danny Lee 583
David A. 287, 470
David Byron 586
David Henry 585-586
David Leroy 276
David Roger 580
Dee 577
Delbert Dean 584
Della 274
Della Mae 441
Delmer 274
Dennis Lee 463
Dianna Lee 581
Dolly Isabelle 458
Dolly May 283
Donald Ivan 575
Donald Lee 578
Donald R. 453
Donna Joan 581
Dora A. 274
Doris Eleanor 575-576
Dorothy 443
Dorothy Ann 586
Dorothy Anna 577
Dorothy Lucille 465
Earl Edward 579
Earl Lester 464
Earl Merle 466
Edgar M. 227
Edmond 225
Edward 146-147, 230, 507,
574, 581
Edward Glen 469
Edythe Marlene 577-578
Edythe Mary 445

Elaine 586
Eldon Lee 584
Elizabeth Norma 461-462
Ella May 257-258
Elmer John 574
Emilene Marie 469
Emilie 119
Emiline 144
Emma 235
Emma B. 446
Emma Elizabeth 287
Emma Harriet 279
Emma L. 405
Estella 448-449
Estella Gertrude 455
Ethel 429
Eugene Earl 582
Eulalia May 581
Eunice Clarinda 256
Evelyn Irene 586
Evelyn Rose 395
Fern R. 467
Florence Ætna 282-283,
460
Florence Jeanette 259
Florence M. 405
Floy 429
Fowler C. 447
Frances Belle 446
Francis Abraham 277-278
Francis Edward 276, 280-
281, 456, 580
Francis Evelyn 464
Francis Marion 147-148
Frank 274
Frank E. 276
Frederick Dale 458
Fritz L. 574
George Clois 286
George E. 231
George Edward 228-229,
272-273
George Henry 469
George Steven 585
Gerald Fremont 457
Gerald Keith 577
Gerald Leon 580
Geraldine 569
Glenda 584
Goldie Juanita 454
Grace Elizabeth 453
Grace Fern 456
Grover Cleveland 447
Harold 395
Harold Clifton 461
Harold Jack 453

MONTY (cont.)

Denice Ann 586
Denise 202, 203, 217, 599
Denise Gisèle 617
Denise Lucille 615
Dennis 607, 609
Denyse Francine J. G. 596
Desanges 104
Désiré Isaïe 211-212
DeWitt Clinton 80
Diane 587
Diane Marie 620
Didace 173
Dominique 84
Domitilde/Domitille 110, 125, 171
Dona/Donat 362
Donald Dean 555
Donald John Gerard 605
Donald Ralph 561
Donald William 524
Donalda 483
Donna 614
Donna J. 616
Donna Jean 609
Dora 485, 508
Dora Adeline 376
Dorie Mathilde 323
Dorilla 318, 319
Doris Muriel 470
Doris Patricia 589
Doris Victoria 596
Doris Viola 567
Dorothea 538
Dorothea Doris 598
Dorothy 472, 473
Dorval 501
Douglas 621, 622
Douglas A. 538
Douglas W. 613-614
Doward 297-298
Earl C. 572
Earl F. 480
Earl Frank 302
Earl Joseph 532
Eddy Edouard 502
Edéas 373
Edesse 102
Edesse Virginie 191
Edgar 386
Edgar Collins 549
Edgar Lee 619
Edgar Wesley 376
Edith 302, 432
Edith Mary 559
Edmond 122, 233, 330-331

Edna 321
Edna Anna 533-534
Edouard/Eddy 600
Edouard Flavien F. G. 308
Edward 79, 119, 198-199, 270, 311, 345, 351, 354, 473, 573
Edward A. 297-298
Edward Cecil 586
Edward D. 399
Edward Glen 471
Edward K. 574
Edward Monroe 438-439
Edward Stephen 288
Edward Sylvester 531
Edward T. 543
Eileen 388-389
Eldemore 554, 621
Eldon E. 163-164
Eldon Lee 552
Eleanor 149, 158, 392
Eleanor A. 437, 601
Eleanor Jennie 532
Electa 391
Eli Joseph 324
Elisabeth 53
Elise 173, 179
Eliza 153, 267
Elizabeth 83, 139-140, 272, 332, 357, 424, 434, 543, 600-601, 611
Elizabeth Ann 153, 472-473
Elizabeth C. 289
Elizabeth E. 573
Elizabeth Jane 354
Elizabeth Jeanne 595
Elizabeth Julia 404
Ella 151, 271
Ella Elizabeth 484
Ella Eva 501
Ellen 234
Ellen Mary 559
Ellen Nora/Elnora 223
Ellen Ruth 296
Ellis 422
Elmire 203, 303
Elmeria 485
Eloi 163
Elrick W. 152
Elzéar Wilfred 540
Emerette 391-392
Emérite 304-305
Emery 204, 208, 380
Emery Alonzo 376
Emile 374
Emile D. 407

Emile Geo. André 605
Emile Herménégilde 342
Emile Louis 593
Emilie 119, 120, 154
Emily 425
Emma 319, 321, 331
Emma Bernice 223-224
Emma Florence Agnes 518
Emma L. 494
Emma Laura 551
Emma Louise 357
Emma M. 483
Emmanuel 499
Emmela Sylvia 516
Ephrem 322
Eric 107
Ernest 492
Ernest Louis 487
Ernest Ovila 513
Ernest R. 616
Ernest Siméon 595
Ernest W. 542
Ernestine 537
Ernestine Agnes 481
Ersie 440
Estelle 501-502
Estelle Hélène 520
Esther 167, 183, 303, 365
Ethel 426-427, 571
Ethel Mona 557
Ethel Parmelee 402
Etienne Lucien Adélard 386
Etta 151, 391-392
Etta/Emetta 300-301
Etta Estella 295
Etta Mae 573
Ettie R. 152
Eudoxie 174-175, 308-309
Eugène 110-111
Eugene H. 540
Eugène Jean-Louis 511
Eugene Napoleon 358-359
Eugénie Antoinette H. 501
Eunice 136
Euphemia 222
Euphémie 207, 210
Euphrasie 316
Euphrosine 57
Eusèbe 101, 110-111
Eustache 187
Eva 372, 508, 597
Eva Anastasia 358
Eva Marguerite 504-505
Eva Marie 496
Eva May 566
Evangéline 481

MONTY (cont.)

Harriet E. 266
Harriet M. 432
Harrine 348
Harry B. 426
Harry Claudius 475
Harvey 566
Hazel 351
Hazel E. 599
Hector 371
Hector Louis 366
Helen/Elaine 593-594
Helen Evelyn 427
Helen Gertrude 477
Helen Margaret 603
Helen Patricia 595
Hélène 599, 603, 618
Henri 501, 512
Henri David 323
Henri Leo 506
Henri William 359
Henriette, 107, 202, 212
Henriette Hélène 400
Henry 136-137, 196, 235-236, 252, 264, 269-270, 303
Henry A. 384, 507
Henry C. 424
Henry George 365
Henry John B. 362
Henry Joseph 484
Henry Louis 347
Henry M. 364
Henry W. 421
Hepsabeth 137-138
Herbert Russell 588
Herbert W. 426
Hermina 318
Hermine 203, 311
Hervé 518
Hervé Raphaël 545
Hilaire 374
Hildred Alex. Octavia 387
Hiram, 161, 302
Homer 359, 360, 596, 597
Honora 493-494
Honoré 22, 168-169, 303
Honoré Bercéus 307-308
Honoré Solyme 480
Horace 384, 514
Hormisdas 215-216
Hormisdas Achille 319
Howard Gladwyn 525
Hubert 117-118, 589
Hugh Otis 528
Huguette 599
Hyacinthe 106, 212

Hyacinthe Isidore 214
Hyacinthe Zéphirin 214
Ida 493
Ida B. 151
Ida May 378
Ida Olive 376
Ignace 180
Infant 116, 223, 557
Irene 513, 544, 592, 596-597, 598
Irene Imelda 544
Irene Luella 551
Irene May 566
Isaac 91
Isabelle 44, 53, 100, 173
Isabelle C. 568
Isaïe 189
Isaïe Louis 324
Israel Oswald 382
Ivan Bert. Lloyd 386-387
Jack 607
Jackie 612
Jacob 120-121, 152, 195
Jacqueline 601, 612-613, 617
Jacqueline Françoise 604
Jacqueline T. 590
Jacques 30-31, 64-65, 90, 120-121, 177, 181, 405, 600, 622
Jacques André 594
Jacques Emile Lucien 605
Jacques Fr. X. A. 308
Jacques Frédéric 121
Jacques Philippe 195
James (see also Jacques)
James 30-31, 70, 132, 609
James A. 611
James Andrew 272
James C. 589
James Carl 586
James Jacob 253
James K. 574
James R. 152, 289
James Willard 471
Jamie L. 614
Jane 144, 154, 250, 252
Jane Ann 73, 134-135
Janet 589, 622
Janet Elaine 601
Janet G. 573
Janice 611
Janice Carol 480
Jean (see also John)
Jean 1-5, 121-122
Jean Aimé Rodrigue 502

Jean-Baptiste 30, 60-61, 65 (2), 66, 67, 92, 101, 120, 121, 127-128, 164-165, 189, 193-194, 199, 240, 323, 333-334
Jean-Baptiste Léonidas 309-310
Jean-Baptiste Polydore 483
Jean-Baptiste Trefflé 221
Jean C. 600
Jean Guy Normand 497
Jean Jacques 605
Jean-Louis Joséphat 544
Jean Luc 617
Jean Ludovic 514
Jean Marie (female) 581
Jean-Marie Claude 186
Jean-Paul 548
Jean Pierre 520
Jean Stanislas Claude 618
Jeanne 591
Jeanne Aloysia 521
Jeanne Berthe 518
Jeanne d'Arc Anna 556
Jeanne Doris 603
Jeanne Eva 545
Jeanne Ruth 592
Jeannette 541
Jeannette I. 539
Jeannette Irene 510
Jeannine 617
Jeannine M. 604
Jeffrey Adrian 616
Jennie 426
Jennie H. 435
Jennifer 615
Jerome 253, 523
Jessica M. 614-615
Jill Mary 610-611
Jo Ann 607
Jo D. 601-602
Joan 553
Joann Carole 609
Johanna 71-72
Johanna/Cordelia 376
John 40-42, 66, 76, 85, 115, 121-122, 131-132, 141-142, 272, 323, 333-334, 345, 347
John A. 360, 432
John Achille 382
John B. 193-194, 499
John B. L. 309-310
John C. 264, 571, 609
John E. 150
John Eldon 620
John F. 523, 587

John Frederick 471
John Henry 399, 524, 559
John J. 605
John Julius 348
John Maurice 609
John Raymond 611
John Roland 599
John S. 149
John T. 425
John W. 538
Jonas 141-142, 437
Jonathan 615
Joseph 23, 27, 30, 36-37,
45, 46, 56, 61-62, 63, 72,
78, 85, 90, 92, 106, 109,
117, 142, 152, 172, 174,
177, 179, 189, 192, 197,
207-208, 217, 220, 232,
240, 250-251, 269, 320,
323, 329-330, 350, 485 (2),
522, 592
Joseph Abraham 190, 353
Joseph Adrien 541
Joseph Albert 384
Joseph Alfred 405
Joseph Ambroise 199
Joseph Amédée 360, 516
Joseph Antoine 218
Joseph Armand 538-539
Joseph Conrad 499, 595
Joseph Dewey 402
Joseph E. 498
Joseph Edward 513, 603
Joseph Elias 477
Joseph Eusèbe 362
Joseph François 369
Joseph Georges 516
Joseph Hormidas 321
Joseph Howard 297
Joseph Ismaël 344
Joseph Louis 185, 342, 481,
491, 497
Joseph Louis Rémi 341
Joseph Louis Rémy 514
Joseph Moïse 504
Joseph Parry 434
Joseph Philip 597
Joseph Pierre 322
Joseph Reynold 612
Joseph Robert Yvon 603
Joseph T. 369
Joseph Trefflé 102
Joseph Willis 421
Joséphat Arthur 480
Joséphine 126, 177, 185,
197, 200, 349, 361, 364

Josephine A. 371
Josephine Bridget 364-365
Josephine Cath. Eliz. 341
Josephine R. 364
Josephte 100
Josie 349
Josie L. 197
Joyce 615
Judith 119, 619
Judith Ann 609
Judy 613, 619
Jules 502
Julia 76, 77-78, 78, 142-
143, 157-158, 191, 348, 499
Julia A. 268
Julia Anna 434
Julia B. 234
Julia C. 363
Julia Mary 351
Julie 103, 119, 174, 176,
191, 242
Julie Amable 28
Julie Ann 587
Julienne 28, 174
Juliette Dorilla 512
Juliette Madeleine 521
Julius D. 299
Justina Aldea 510
Karen 607
Karen Joy 608
Karen L. 610
Karl A. 601
Katherine Marie 622
Katherine Miriam 571
Kathleen Ann 619-620
Katy 133
Keith A. 608
Keith Harland 528
Keith Jack 526, 607
Kenneth 557, 567, 609, 610
Kenneth Charles 532, 609
Kenneth Leon 588
Kevin R. 610
Kiese/Calixte 210
Kittie 152
Lafayette 79
Lana 619
Lana D. 616
Laona Mae 302
Lara 319
Larry 609
Larry D. 617
Larry James 612
Laura 79, 383, 437, 489
Laura A. 266
Laura Ann 397

Laura D. 552
Laura Valarie 325
Laura Yvonne 516
Lauraine Anna 527
Laure 326
Laurence 388, 503
Laurent 117, 547, 556
Lauretta 540-541
Laurette 595, 600
Laurette Jeannette 594
Laurier 503
LaVerne C. 554
Léa 490
Leandra Léopoldine 319
Lena 500
Leo F. 389
Leo J. 591-592
Leo Louis 496
Leo Paul 593
Leo Theodore 598
Leo W. 596
Léon 177
Leon Dudley 474-475
Leon F. 501
Leon P. 617
Leon W. 561
Leona Hermine 598
Leonard A. 554
Leonard Felix 496
Leonard G. 497
Léonie Rosaria 486
Léopold 593
Leroy 159
Lester D. 478
Lester Leon 533
Lester M. 611
Letria 598
Lewis 129-130, 328
Lewis Albert 295
Lewis Leroy 300
Libby 163
Lilia Cordelia 326
Lilice A. 159
Lillia/Martha 162
Lillian 498, 604
Lillian E. 297
Lillian Flora 505
Lillian Josephine 368
Lillie 297
Lillie M. 299
Lilly Sarah 296
Linda J. M. 615
Linette I. 542
Linette Marguerite 616
Lionel/Leonel A. 542
Lionel Fulgence 498

MONTY (cont.)

Norman C. 615
Normand 594
Octave 202, 215
Octave Pierre Hubert 544
Octavie Clara E. 496
Odile 206, 214
Olida Agnès 514
Olier 389
Oliva 490
Olive 209, 239
Olive N. 272
Oliver 252, 389
Omer 596
Omer Albert 597
Omer Leo 597
Onésime 179
Ora L. 501
Oreon 150
Orpha 474
Orville 534
Orville James 290, 472
Oscar 496
Oscar Roméo A. 492-493
Osithe 187
Ovila 374, 495
Ovila A. 597
Paine 348
Pamela Jean 590
Pamela V. 616
Patricia Louise 620
Paul 501, 605, 606
Paul Aimé 618
Paul Emile 386
Paul Emile Raymond 600
Paul L. 619
Paul Omer Roland 511
Paul Stanislas 521
Paula Jean 610
Pauline Patricia 603
Peggy 618
Percalie 601
Percy Alphee 506
Perley B. 300
Peter 345-346
Peter A. 604
Peter B. 605
Peter Edward 382
Peter H. 321
Phebe 76
Philias 375
Philibert 48-49, 100-101
Philibert Henri 521
Philip 191, 198, 367, 384, 522, 551
Philip A. 601

Philip Adélard 358
Philippe 48-49, 100-101, 191, 198, 362
Phillip J. 616-617
Phillip Joseph 383
Philomène 180, 189-190, 203, 208-209, 216, 303
Philomène T. Eulalie 306
Phoebe 210, 346
Phyllis 363
Pierre 27, 42, 65 (2), 66 (2), 118, 599, 618
Pierre Alfred 113
Pierre Emile 344
Pierre Emile Ernest 518
Pierre Honoré 45
Placide 39-40, 82
Polly/Mary 136
Polly C. 294
Polydore 320
Priscilla B. 591
Prudent 170, 311
Rachel 107, 528, 548
Rachel M. 528
Ralph Clayton 478
Ralph E. 567
Ralph George 589
Ralph S. 608
Ralph W. 574
Ramona 587
Raoul 314
Raphaël François 385
Ray R. 560
Raymond 118, 597
Raymond E. 523
Raymond Euclide 316
Raymond F. 603
Raymond Gale 621
Raymond Leo Henri 389
Raymond Lester 533
Regina 406
Reginald 519
Reginald Eugene 538
Réjeanne Anna 604
Réjeanne M. Rita 594
Rémi 205-206, 338-339, 341
Remi Louis 517
Rena 319-320
René 597
René Wilfrid 514
Reynold Nathan 534
Rhea A. 596
Rhea Valerie 590
Richard Eugene 553
Richard L. 619

Richard Wayne 550
Riley 400-401
Rita 619
Rita Lucille 603
Robert 291, 362, 557, 618, 622
Robert Eugene 554
Robert F. 154
Robert J. 475
Robert James 587
Robert Lee 588
Robert Louis/Lewis 524
Robert Ross 587
Robert W. 473
Rodolphe 325, 600
Roland 539
Roland Alfred 521
Rollin 400-401
Romuald 119
Ronald 598
Ronald A. 609
Rosa 336, 375, 397, 491
Rosaire André Roger 595
Rosalba 318
Rosalie 69, 79, 98, 115, 218, 232, 344, 497
Rosanna 320, 495
Rosanne F. 611
Rosario 503
Rosario Adelbert 592
Rosario Armand 485
Rosario Louis Philippe 483
Rose 218, 344, 363, 369-370, 491
Rose Adeline 358
Rose Alba Priscilla 358
Rose Alma 511, 515
Rose Ameline 306
Rose Anna 320, 336, 341, 365, 493
Rose Anne 184
Rose Eda 506
Rose Emma 375, 516-517
Rose F. 397
Rose Florence 603
Rose Gladys 543
Rose Maria Agnes 415
Rosella 79, 115
Rosemary 620
Rosilda 372-373
Rosine 318
Roswell L. 573
Roy Alexander 528, 529
Roy/Royal Kenneth 477-478
Ruby Neal 549

William F. 263
MOOREHEAD
Mr. 325
MOOSO
Simeon 75
MOQUIN
Agathe/Anastasie 55
Alfred Joseph 202
Almaïs Emma 202
Amédée 202, 203
Bibiane/Caroline 55
Catherine 55
Edesse 54
Emérence/Emérentienne 55
Ernestine 202
Evariste 202 (2)
Flavie 55
Flavien Hormisdas 202
François 52, 54 (2)
Geneviève 54
Georges Aimé 202
Hippolyte 54
Jean-Baptiste 55 (2)
Joseph 55
Joseph Urgel 202
Julienne 55
Malvina Denyse 202
Marcelle/Marceline 178
Marie Georgina 202
Paul 54
Pierre 54
MORACHE
Robert Roland 485
MORACK
Victor Elmer 353
MOREAU
Delphis 375
Eva 178
Gilles Yvon Alain 375-376
Louis Azarie 167
Yolande 376
MOREHEAD
Burton Leroy 258
MORENCY
Jeanne 603
MORGAN
Charles 139
Isabelle K. 555
Judith Ann 612
MORGANELLI
Nicholas Roland 479
MORIARITY
Sylvester 524
Unnamed 524
MORIER
Alfred 112

Edouard 309
Eudore/Horace 309
Eva 309
Louis Israël 309
Rose Anna 111
William 309
MORIN
Althea Edna 486
Catherine 67
Elizabeth 51
Evelina Louise 217
Léopold 388
Marion V. 383
Trefflé 168
Yvette 385
MORISSET/MORISSETTE
Alphonse Eugene 216
David 53
MORITZ
Marvin E. 533
MOROSCHOK
Michael 539
MORRILL
Giles 142
John 142
Mildred M. 431-432
MORRIS
Don L. 551
MORRISON
Mr. 73-74
Anna Mary 274
MORROW
Ada N. 224
MORTON
Patricia 579
MOSHER
Celia 228
MOTES
Anna Mae 554
MOULISON
Josephine Isabelle 474-475
MOULTON
Bradford George 123
MOUND
Ruth Louise 289
MOUSSEAU
James 78
MULLIKIN
June Delores 575
MULLIN
John B. 604
MULLINIX/MULLNIX
Floyd Edison 455-456
MUNGER
James 465
MURPHY

Jicey/Joyce 79
Leonard J. 599
Lola Marie 529
Lotta Agnes 428-429
Willard Gilbert 416
MURRAY
Blanche Theresa 354
Edwin Joseph 354
Francis Thomas/Frank 354
Francis Vernon 354
George F. 227
Georgina E. 408
Gertrude Adeline 354
James Bernard 354
John Aloysius 355
Kenneth Ludwig 354
Leland William 354-355
Lola Marie 529
Muriel Frances 354
Robert Ray 445
Vera Elizabeth 354
Veronica Marian 354
MUSE
Edith Maxine 283
Emma 147
Fred 283
John 147 (2)
LeRoy Francis/Roy 283
William E. 147
MUSSELMAN
Lytton C. 443
MYATT
Saphronia Pearl 455
MYERS
Bonaparte M. 143
NADEAU
Adèle 185
Cyril Andrew 398
Joseph A. 398
Joseph/Octave Hubert 122
Joseph Roland 398
Louis 253
Louis J. 253
Silas William 398
NADOLSKY
Fred R. 613
NAGENGAST
Joseph 396
NAGLEY
Doris Amy 525
NANKIVELL
Laura Irene 286
NAPOLEON
John Nammamoku 460
NAYLOR
Edward 276

Milton 275-276
NEDDO (see also **NADEAU**)
Joseph 235
Joseph A. 398
NEIDERHOUSE
Mr. 446
NELLIS
Ruth 412-413
NELSON
Darryl/Darrel B. 569-570
Jean O. 427
Ruth Winifred 350
NETTLES
James A. 607
NEVEU
Adrienne 500
Josephte 48-49
NEWBERRY
Leon Cidney 454
NEWELL
Caroline C. 383
Evangeline 383
Irene Marie 383
NEWMAN
Chloris 264
Edward C. 263
Ivan F. 264
Rebecca Ann 587
NEWNAN
Emma M. 209
NICHOLSON
Betty 458
Jack M. 475
Jacqueline Colette 475
Nancy Louise 462
Shirley Jean 475
NIEMELA
Elsie Laverne 528
NIXON
Leonard Leo 354
NOFFKE
Freda 500
NOISEUX
Josephte 21
NOLIN
Amelia/Emelia D. 494
NORDQUIST
Martin Frederick 529
NOREAU/NORAULT
Joseph Pierre 176
NORMAN
Elizabeth 282
NORMANDIN
Amande Cécile 515
Arthur Gérard 515
Bernadette Louise 515

Eldège Dieudonné 515
George Armand 516
Gérard 515
Jean Armand 515
Joseph Jean-Baptiste 516
Lucrèce Noëlla 515
Marcel Antonio 515
Marguerite Lucille 515
Rosaire Georges Henri 515
Rosaire Roland 516
Rose Delia 515
Serge 546
NORWOOD
Donald D. 581
NOSCROY
Mike Tally 583
NOTTESTAD
Andreas 292
NOVASIO
Marie 460
NOWAK
Leonard Joseph 620
NULTY
Mary Elizabeth 264
NUTTER
Agnes Irene 259
OBORN
Donald 448
Harry Howard 447-448
Helen Jane 448
O'BRIEN
Mr. 577-578
Charles F. 593
Daniel 100
Edna Pauline 258
Philippe/Philibert 100
William Frederick 287
OCHS
William Edward 416
OCLAIRE
Julie 62
O'CONNELL
Frances E. 231
O'CONNOR
Michael Joseph 522
O'DONNELL
Katie/Katherine 278
Kenneth/Kenny M. 555
OESTREICH
William 535-536
O'HARA
Josephine 207
Marguerite 567
O'HARRIN
Margaret 135
O'HEARN

Hannah 226
O'HERN
Rita Irene 395
O'LEARY
Raymond F. 379
OLIVER
Alfred M. 88
Anne Eliza 88
Anonymous 404
Anthony 404
Lavina Corlista 88
Lucy F. 88
Nancy Jane 88
Robert Leslie 88
Robert Weslie 87-88
Sarah A. 88
OLSEN
Albert 392
Joseph H. 451
Olen 391
Olive 392
Paulina 392
OLSHELFSKE/
 OLSHELFSKI
Douglas 420
Leo Louis 420
Leonard J. 420
OLSON
Neil R. 475
OPIE
Albert Lee 463
Bill Montee 463
James Frank 463
John Mart 463
OPPIE
Mr. 609
OPRAY
Marie M. 268
OQUIST
Lillian 430
O'REGAN
Adeline 113
ORKINS
James A. 234
ORTIZ
Anthony N. 569
ORTS
Richard 438
OSBORN
George Ransom 278
Hattie R. 278
William B. 278
William Montee 278
OSBORNE
Lawrence Edgar 271
OSTIGUY

Anna 366
Arthur 366
Delia 112
Lucy Blanche 366
Marie Françoise 43-44
Norman 366
Raymond 366
Rita F. 366
Wilfred L. 366

OUDENHOVEN
Priscilla Marie 535

OUELLETTE/OUELETTE
Charles Louis 243
Charlotte Susan 244
Edward Albert 243
Emma 243
John Elijah 244
John Paul 601-602
Julienne 511
Russell Frank 245

OUIMET
Adolphe 178
Francis 562
Isaac 54-55

OUIMETTE
France 618

OUTTERSON
Frances Maybell 433

OVERBECK
August Henry 233

OVERSTREET
Alline Genevieve 574

OWEN
Lucille D. 256

OWENS
Albert A. 154-155
Robert 155

OXE
James Albert 465

PACENTINI/PIACENTENI
Angelina 370
Edward 370
Mary/Marie 370
Pio 369-370

PAFFORD
Robert L. 403

PAGE
Florence S. 262
Gretchel 439
Gretchen 439

PAILLAND (see **PEL-LAND**)

PAIR (see also **POIRIER**)
Mary D. 405

PALIN
Eugene 547

PALMBY
Mary 608

PALMER
Charles F. 437 (2)
Dorothy Gladys 476
Edward James 476
Goldie Mae 466
Lawrence Edward 476
Pauline P. 437
Rufus 150

PALOMBO
Anthony 357

PALUBICKI
Jack 535

PANOS
John D. 285

PAPINEAU
Adélaïde 56
Anastasie 56
Anatalie 56
Antoine 55-56, 56
Elisabeth 56
Flavie 56
Florence 56
Joseph 56
Marie Amable 56
Mathilde 177
Michael 619
Sophie Célina 186
Zoé 56 (2)

PAQUET/PAQUETTE
Adélaïde 46
Eudoxie 179
Exilia Mathilda 193
Jean Guy 618
Jeanette V. 542
Joseph Albert Adrien 340
Matilda 208
Rose Bella/Robella 503

PAQUIN
Gilberte 502
Marie Emma 343

PARADIS
Georges 503
Jacques 386
Marie Melina 123

PARADISE
Stephen R. 393

PARE
Anna 215

PARENTEAU
Anita 407

PARK
Carless Edward 446
Charles Newel 268
Cora 269

Elmina 269
Jeannette/Janet A. 269
Lillie Ann 269
Madaline Belle 446
Pearl S. 268

PARKER
Edwin J. 552
Eleanor Grace 486

PARR
Joanne A. 467
John Allen 467
John Joseph 467
Kathryn M. 467
Robert J. 467
Shirley June 467

PARRISH
Emma 155

PARRY
Louise/Sarah Louisa 265

PARSONS
William 397

PARTON
Charles Alfred 438
Charles H. 438
Esther/Hester E. 438
Robert A. 438

PASINI
Bianca A. 538-539

PASKEL
Myrtle 163

PATENAUDE
Abel Cyrille 322
Adeline 108
Alexandre/Alexander 105
Alexis 22 (2), 23
Alfred 203 (2)
Amable 104 (2)
Angélique 23
Calixte 104
Charles 93
Cyrille 105
David 23
Emery 105
Evariste Basile 203
François 23
Gédéon 105
Hyacinthe 105
Léon 23
Louis 52
Louis Ernest 203
Marguerite 23 (3)
Marguerite Blanche 203
Marie Anne 203
Marie Célina 105
Marie Desanges 22
Mathilde/Matilda 105

Mederise 105
Michel 24-25
Michel Ernest 203
Narcisse/Nelson 105
Noël 105
Octave 105
Scholastique 105
PATTERSON
Alice M. 460
Charles 476
Harry William 297
Helen Jeanine 460
Herbert Albert 476
Herbert L. 427
James Milton 460
Jean 427
Leslie 427
Norman D. 460
William R. 460
PAUL
Alma 217
Amédée 217
Edouard/Pinee (?) 216
Joseph Pierre 216
Joseph Siméon 216
Marie Louise 216
Moïse 216
Olina 216-217
Pierre 216
Rose Anna/Rosanna 330-331
Rose Delima 216
PAYETTE
Jacques 511
PAYNE
Mr. 133
PEASE
Daniel Bruce 465
Daniel Montee 465
PECK
Albert 426
Anonymous 426
Benjamin Harris 426
Cladice 512
Dorigne 512
Edgar W. 426
Florence Yvonne 512
Florian Hubert 512
Frank E. 426
Georges Josaphat 512
Henri André 512
Howard 426
Huguette 512
Jean Claude 512
Léona 512
Marie Paule 512

Melvin 426
Minnie 426
Normand Omer 512
Orespha Joséphine 512
Paulette Mirella 512
PECKHAM
Blanche Alice 254
PEDERSON
Douglas 585
PEER (see **POIRIER**)
PEFFLEY
Lynn O. 569
PEGUSKI
Anthony 419
Isabelle 419
PEILA
Lucy 364
PELKY
Arthur J. 533-534
Barbara Ann 534
Carol A. 534
Duaine V. 534
Harold J. 534
Leroy 534
Milton Arthur 534
Norma 534
PELL
Nathan T. 363
PELLAND
Hermaline/Armelia 178
PELLETIER
Laurette 490
Lydia 314
Marianne 199
PELOQUIN
Anita 315
Gerald 315
Marie V. C. 316
Oscar Peter 315
Pierre 315
Regina 315
PENESIS
Dorothea 561
PENNANT
Elizabeth Emma 260
PEPIN
Albert 200
Rosa 329
Rose Delima 98
PERCY
JoAnn 590
PERKINS
Michael Thomas 586
Susan Elizabeth 614
PERRAS
Marie-Anne 103

PERRAULT/PERREAULT
Aimé 502
Auguste 185
Corinne 185
Jacques 502
Michelle 502
Nicole 502
Prosper 93
Victoire/Victoria 63
PERRENOD
Albert Alexander 195
PERROTTE
Treva M. 404
PERRY
Mr. 287-288
Alma/Carrie Alma 259
Alva L. 347
Carl H. 347
Darrell R. 347
Eugene/Gene 259
Eugene M. 347
Frank/Francis 288
Gertrude 260
Harry L. 259-260
James D. 346-347
Lora 593
Orville 347
PERYER
Phyllis Ann 477
PETE
Miss 611
PETERS
Kenneth Charles 463
PETERSON
Douglas John 607
James C. 381
Sandra L. 506
PETIT
Della Virginia 355
Jean Paul 510
Jennie 510
Thuribe 510
PETTY
William Alonzo 398
PFEFFINGER
Dwayne 619
PHANEUF
Esther 57
PHENIX
Edwin S./Ted 443
Jacques Luc 618
PHILBRICK
Orvis P. 135
PHILLIPS
Barbara J. 577
Betty 460

Laure Georgette 510
Paul Jean Louis 510
Rolande Gisèle 510
RIENDEAU
Alfred 107
Berthe Antonie 309
Callixte 107
Edward H. 366
Jean-Baptiste 107 (2)
Joseph 107
Marie Delima 107
Marie Euphémie 107
Mathilde/Matilda 107
Médérise 107
Narcisse 107
RILEY
John Edward 475
RIPLEY
Carol L. 583
RIQUIER
Albert 360
RITARI
Esther Lily Lydia 531
RITTER
Mary Catherine 148
RITZER
Frederick M. 414
RIVARD
Marcel C. 601
RIVET
Gisèle 517
ROAL
Karin 589
ROBARE
Roger H. 403
ROBARGE
Mary Genevieve/Mary J. 79
ROBBINS
Lucien Noyes 241
ROBERT
Albina 169
Antoinette 593
Célina 232
Eva 515
Hervé 340
Joseph Adélard 200
Nathalie/Anathalie/Athalie 95
Prospère 95
ROBERTS
Estelle 279
Harold Felix 443
Henry 201
Laura 396
Marvel Montee 443
Robert Allan 610

Roberta Ann 443
ROBERTSON
Juanita Jo 456
ROBICHAUD
Georges 183
ROBIDOUX
Alfred 102
Anonymous 102
Calixte 102
Charles 102
Félix 102
François Xavier 102
Marie Louise 103
Marie Rebecca 102
Raymond 512
ROBILLARD
Ernest Francis 391
Jean-Claude 549
ROBINSON
Carolyn Lynett 616
George Washington 145
Harriet Lucinda 147
ROBITAILLE
Yolande 547
ROCH/ROCQUE
Louis 22
ROCHE
Marie Josée 599
ROCHELEAU
Jeanne d'Arc 490
Laura Emma 185
Léopold 490
Louise 44
ROCKWELL
Burton Grant 268
ROCKWITZ
Charles Alexander 473
Una Lucille 473
RODIER
Aurélie 183
RODRIGUE
Claudette 512
RODRIGUEZ
Douglas William 396
George E. 396
John A. 396
John Roosevelt 396
Robert Benedict 396
ROETTGER
Kenneth D. 579
ROGERS
Achthah/Asthah 245
Albert Lewis 245
Blanche 245
Dorothy Mae 443
Frederick 423

Gustavus A. 245 (2)
John B. 245
Joseph Malvern 443-444
Joseph Michael 443
Lee Albert 453
Leona Faustina 453
Leroy Albert 453-454
Loene Daphne 453
Loreeta Elizabeth 454
Loren William 454
ROGGE
Miss 528
ROHLANDER
Shirley 459
ROHRER
Beatrice 349
Dola 349
Gladys H. 349
Grace B. 349
Helen 349
Henry W. 348-349
Leo 349
Mildred 349
RONDEAU
Agnula Albina 329
Alcide 329
Anonymous 329
George 329
Gilbert Ferdinand 545
Glanda O. 329
Ignace 329
Joseph Alcide 329
Oswald J. 329
Siméon 329
Walter J. 329
Yvonne Agnula 329
ROOD
Leonard 250
ROSINSKY
Dean M. 609
ROSS
Charles 551
ROSSEY
Eugene Edward/Gene E. 356
John 356
John Constantine 356
John James 356
Joseph Gustav 356
LaVerne Mary 356
Shirley 356
ROTHER
Wendy S. 392
ROTHERMEL
Gertrude Rita 155
ROUGIER

Matilda 84
ROULEAU
Asilda/Exilda 69
ROURKE
Mary G./Minnie 434
ROUSHIA
Rose 439-440
ROUSSEAU
Marie 175
Marie Caroline 201
Marie Marthe Fernande 596
Rolande 596
ROWBACK
Brian O. 586
ROWE
Ellen 221
ROY
Abraham 62
Alexina 339
Eugène 594
Laura 367
Louis 17
Marguerite 62
Marie Anne/Mary A. 494
Pierre 66 (2)
ROYER
Claire 512
ROZA
Diane Margaret 393
RUDD
Gertrude 530-531
RUEDIGER
Lois Ruth 563
RUEL
Marie Caroline G. 488
RUELL
Helena/Helen 599
RUSH
Earline 356
RUSSELL
Arthur James 403
Thomas F. 82
RUSSI
Rosario Joseph 508
RUSSO
Michele 506
RYAN
Ileen 424
Michael J. 553
RYBURN
Ron 465
SAAVEDRA
Evelyn 246
SABINO
Francesco Giuseppe 518
SABO

Elizabeth J./Betty 533
SABRE
John B. 158
SACRA
Henry F. 569
SALES
Clarence J. 162
SALMON
James Howard 611
SALOIS
Adelaide 331
Blanche 331
Delia 332
Donat Pierre 331
Ernest 331
Florence 332
George Hormisdas 332 (2)
Joseph 331
Marie Adée 332
Michel/Mitchell 331
Philorome/Phillip 331
William 331
SALVAIL/SALVAILLE
Cyrille 217-218
Henry 218
Joseph Noé 218
Marie Amelie 218
Sophie 107
SALZMAN
Emil 484
SAMOISETTE
Armand Albert 341
SAMSON
Aurélie 94
Denis 544
Florence 94
Joseph 93, 94
SAMWORTH
Katherine Madge/Kay 511
SANCH/SANCHE
Edith 243
Ellen E. 243
Gideon/Gédéon 243
John Baptist Augustus 243
Melvena 243
William Albert 243
SANDERS
Elizabeth Myrtle 469
SANFORD
Delbert Hartle 449
Harold S. 588
Jeannette A./Jennie 263
Louis Edgar 597
Theodore Ralph 619
SANN
Alvera E. 530

SANSOUCI/SANSOUCY
Ida May 225
Malvina Adèle 121
SANTERRE
Florence 505
SANTO
Shirley M. 482
SANTY
Clet/Clay 210
SARAZIN
Mary Elizabeth 246-247
SARRASIN
Julie 17
SARTIN
Iva Edith 461
SARTWELL
Emma 398
Wilbur Menefee 569
SASS
LaVerne B. 526
SATTERLEE
Delva June 461
Norma Joan 461
Wayne Lester 461
SAUNDERS
Mr. 543
SAURETTE dit LAROSE
Rose Alma 180
SAURIOL
William Lionel 387
SAUVAGEAU
Eugene A. 315
SAVAGE
Antoine/Anthony 77-78
Asa Joseph 158
Austin Anthony 158
Charles 80
George 78
Henrietta Louisa 80-81
Henriette L. 79
Honoré 78
Ida May 158
Ira M. 158
Joel 78
Laura/Lauretta 81
Laura Ann 78
Lewis Courtland 80
Louis/Lewis 78
Mary Arvilla 78
Mary Frances 78
Rosalie/Rosella 78
Thomas Madison 78, 157-158
William DeWitt 78-79
SAVARIA
Jean-Baptiste 158

Casimir 55
Célina 97
Christine 55
Eusèbe 55
Joseph 55 (2)
Marie 55
Marie Domitilde 55
Pierre 51
SURUS
Anne Joan 498
SUTTON
Judy A. 612
SWAFFORD
Gene/Eugene 584
SWAIN
Alfred R. 274
Clifford 437
Robert 273-274
SWANSON
Diana Lynn 608
SWEENEY
Minnie B. 223
SWIHART
Henry 578
Nora Amber 450
SWINEHART
Benjamin Frank 446
Dorothy C. 446
Frank/Franklin Noah 445
Helen M. 445
James Franklin 446
Martha M. 446
Ruth Anna 446
Thomas 446
SWORTS
Ruth B. 448
SYLVESTRE
Marie 96, 107
SYLVIA
Gerald J. 617
TAFT
Bertha Monte 241
Emory Wood 241
Ernest Jewett 241
Frances E. 241
Frank Weston 241
Sarah Louise 241
TALBOT
Thomas F. 145
TALLEY
Marjorie Irene 582
TALLMAN
Joseph 290
Paul W. 543
TALLY
Donna Lou 582

TAMTHONG
Ratanaporn 453
TANK
Charles 410
Charles J. 410
Lewis 410
Orellia Genevieve 410
Vernon John 410
William 410
TARBOX
Lucy/Lucelia 358
TARTE
Alma Victoria 373
Bernadette Laurenza 373
Eugène Adhémar 373
Fortunat François 373
François Etienne 373
Hormisdas 373
Jeanne Annette 374
Odile Anna 373
TARTRE
Louise Hélène 216
TATE
Edna Llewella 355
TAYLOR
Mr. 319
Annie 30-31, 366
Charles E. 221
Clarence Robert 575
Jim 582
Leroy 467
Patricia 468
William 467
William A. 124
TEAGUE
Verna Lee 589
TELLIER
Frederick 487
TEMME
LeRoy Henry 280
TENEROWICZ
Robert 614
TERRIAN
Raymond Leroy 533-534
TERRIEN
Adélaïde 126
TERRILL
Esther Leora 273
TERRY
Norma A. 589
TESSIER
Césarie 99
Marguerite/Margaret 488
Scholastique 90
**TETRAULT/TETREAU/
TETREAULT**

Aloysia 187
Alphée 96
Charlotte 90
Donalda Hortense 205
Dorothée 177
Laurette 493
Réjean 595
René 547
Rosalie 96
TETRO
Esther A. 152
THARP
Charles H. 404
Herbert Charles 403-404
THATCHER
Barbara Joyce 580
THAYER
Addie A. 82
THELEN
Delma 606
**THERIAULT/THER-
RIAULT**
Joseph 217
Oscar 491
Ovila 341
THERIEN/THERRIEN
Adelaide 126
Lucienne 341
THEROUX
Léonard 331-332
THIBAULT
Alexander J. 539
Cora 409
THIBODEAU
Sophronie 105
THILL
Frank Byron 294
Harold G. 294
Joseph 294
Joseph B. 294
Robert George 294
Roy Gilbert 295
THIVIERGE
Lulu/Lula 571
THOMAS
Mr. 456, 561
Anna Christine 418
Donna Jean 462
Lenny 520
THOMPSON
Clayton L. 254
George 496
George Baker 266
George Edward 496
Hazel 496
John H. 266

Marie Louise 14, 15
Pierre 14, 15 (2)
VIPOND
Lillian M. 255
VIVIER
Richard M. 549
VOORHEES
Richard Fred 462
VORBA
Joan Elizabeth 617
VOZZELLA
Marcel F. 590
VYBOH
Tom 502
WADE
Anna M. 266-267
WAHLLEITHNER
Anna Josephine 352
WAHLMEIER
Cecelia 553
WAIT
George Warnick 434
Harriet 140
James Reuben 24
WAKEFIELD
Albert Edward 223
WALKER
Clarence J. 239
Edward J. 238 (2)
Francis Theodore 381
Harvey L. 238
Leona 238
Lucille Abigail 238
Raymond J. 238
Rose 270
Signa May 479
WALL
Henry Kirk 151-152
WALLACE
Burton Lee Earl 459-460
Hurst 228
Jacque Earlene 460
James William 423
John 422-423
Montee Earl 460
WALTER
Caroline D./Carrie 447
WALTERHOUSE
Floy E. 275
WALTERS
Beverley Jean 468
Harold Lyman 468
Jacqueline Kay 609
WANGERIN
Elizabeth Ann 529
WARD

Earl Michael 387
Jimma Lee 576
John 74
Theresa Marvela/Marvel 387
WARDEN
Lois Lucille 469, 584
Marjory 584
WARNER
Arni J. 122
Karen Sue 480
WARREN
Joyce 536
Lillie/Lillian Rebecca 273
WARY
Anthony Aloysius 381
WATERSON
William H. 78
WATKINS
Mary Dell 302
WATSON
Mr. 456
Edward 394
WATTS
Ray C. 448
WEAVER (see **TISSE-RAND**)
WEBB
Louise W. 436
WEEKS
Bessie 539
Etta C./Esta 267
WEIL
Elmer Edwin 460
WEIR
Mr. 465
WEIS
Donald Eugene 553
Gregory R. 553
Lori Ann 553
Lynn Ann 553
WEISS
Armen Henry 581
Dorothy Blanche 530
WEIST
Magdalene/Lena 276
WELCH
Charles William 275
Evelyn C. 413
Ione M. 526
Ralph E. 275
William M. 275
WELSH
James Allan 499
WELLS
Bessie V. 161

Cary E. 161
Cora E. 161
Elmer 161
John E. 161
Natalie Marion 506
Richard M. 161
William A. 161
Zia Mae
WELSON
Carol 533
Joanna 533
Gordon G. 533
Leona A. 533
Ruby 533
WELTY
Nina May 447
WENDT
Anna L. 425
WENTZ
Stewart 614
WESNER
Albert 408
WESSLING
John W. 621
WESTERMAN
Beverly Mae 355
WESTON
Charles T. 622
WESTPHAL
Mary Jo 612
WHALEN
William F. 263
WHALLEY
Joseph 193
WHEEL
Louis Herman 239
WHEELER
Dixie Lee 456
Patricia M. 534
WHELAN
Leona Frances 427
WHISLER
Martha Mae 456
WHITE
Claire M. 412-413
Irving S. 299
Jane Pauline 269
Margaret Julia 277
Rodney A. 622
WHITED
Earl L. 552
WHITEHAIR
Dorothy 552
WHITMAN
Elmer Alfred 602
WHITNEY

Etta Mae 438
WHITTON
Nellie L. 561
WIDMARK
Lawrence 478
Lyle Russell 478
Roberta Marie 478
WIELAND
Christine Ellen 610
WILEY
Frank E. 615
WILKINSON
Florence 450
WILL
Foster Rolland 327
WILLARD
Edward 226
Elizabeth 226-227
Francis Edgar/Frank 226
Frederick Edward 226
Nellie L./Helen Louise 226,
394
Josephine Eveline 226
Mary Isabelle 226
WILLEBY
Lavinia 302
WILLEY
Mr. 543
Eva 281
Herbert Alfred 405
WILLIAMS
Adolph Bernhard 474
Benford Wilcher 474
Charles Horace 298
Deborah Lee 555
Donald Edgar 474
Eleana Lorraine 474
Helen Mildred 474
Lester L. 474
Marion Rebecca 474
Robert Louis 474
Shirley Mae 474
WILLIAMSON
Bruce A. 601
Carrie 279
WILLING
Joseph Edward 421
Penny E. 421
Wilda J. 421
WILSON
Hester Ann 74-75
Jack H. 586
Norman 427
WINANS
Ethel 381
WINKLER

Mr. 470
WINTER
Lucy E. 240
WINTERS
William N. 393
WISE
John Richard 620
WOCH
Frank J. 418
WOHLLEBEN
John M. 537
WOLF
Arthur J. 351 (2)
WOLFE
Joshua Norman 426
WOLFF
Lyle Edward 357
WOLLER
Howard Arnold 570
WOOD
Gertrude E. 290
Gladys E. 471
John Louis Emmett 587
Lillian 271
Vivian I. 474
WOODHEAD
William 285
WOODLING
Nora Julia 278
WOODWARD
Carrie Gertrude 404
Luella B. 405
WOODWORTH
Miss 555
Curtis/Curt 555
Helen Maxine 552
WRIGHT
Douglas Norman 392
John 559
Lois Elaine 392
Martha Susan 392
Norma Louise 392
Seth Andrew 392
WYMETTE/OUIMETTE
Fred 131
WYRICK
Cheryl Lynn 580
YAGER
Augusta 423-424
YANDO
Agnes P. 210
Dora 210
Edgar John 210
Ezra Peter 210
Mary Regina 210
Noah 209

Noah Jerry 210
Ophelia A. 209
Rosa 210
YANULAVICH
Genevieve/Geneva 403
YARTER
Edward Delor 224
Monty Herbert 224
YEAGER
Henry 416
Irene M. 460
YETTS
Vickie Marie 621
YOUNG
Bruce C. 611
Harry Percy 185
Irene 532
Jeanne 404
John I. 610
Lois 454
YOVETICH
Louis Michael 460
ZAK   587
Rose 532
ZBINDEN
Max Edwin 453
ZELL
Gustav A. 280
ZEMBIK
Mary 597
ZIEGELBAUER
Arthur J. 356
Arthur John 357
Lila Mary Jane 357
ZOOK
Beatrice Kathryn 151
Earl A. 152
Irene M. 152
Jack L. 152
John Alexander 151
Marguerite Elizabeth 151
Robert Monty 152
ZORDANI
Betty Jean 470
Carolyn 470
David 470
Joseph A. 469-470
Joseph Albert 470
ZUMBAUM
Dewaine D. 584